VALUATION TABLES,

ON THE

"COMBINED EXPERIENCE,"

OR

"ACTUARIES'"

RATE OF MORTALITY.

Second Edition, Revised and Enlarged.

BY ELIZUR WRIGHT.

BOSTON:
WRIGHT & POTTER, PRINTERS, 79 MILK STREET.
(CORNER OF FEDERAL STREET.)
1871.

PREFACE.

THESE tables, so far as they give the net values of ordinary policies, with annual premiums payable during life (ending with page 102), were printed for the use of a few subscribing companies in 1853. Very few other than whole life or short term policies were then issued. At the present moment it will excite some surprise that some of the companies for which these tables were prepared insisted on maintaining a three per cent reserve, on which account they were cast at both three and four per cent. The tendency now is to diminish reserve by assuming a higher rate of interest in calculating it, as if this cheapened the cost of insurance to all, whereas it only does so for the half who are to die first. With an equitable method of distributing surplus in a mutual company, if the reserve be calculated at a higher rate of interest, those who die early enough will be benefited by receiving a little more surplus while they live, but for the same reason those who live too long will receive less. The interest of the latter is, in fact, to have the reserve calculated on the lowest interest, even down to 0 per cent. What the assumed rate is, provided it be certain to fall below what will always be realized on the whole aggregate of invested and uninvested funds, is plainly not a matter of great importance to any individual policy-holder whose future lifetime is unknown to him — and no other should hold a policy. It can hardly be doubted that the easy working and durable credit of a company will be better provided for by not assuming a rate of interest higher than *four* per cent, whatever may be the facility at present of obtaining a higher rate — and no matter how much higher — on actual investments.

Since 1853, and especially since 1858, different forms of policy or modes of paying premium have been greatly multiplied, requiring not only many new tables for convenience in valuing for reserve, but for settling other important questions of equity necessarily arising out of the great diversities in the conditions of the policies.

To this reprint of the old valuation tables a good many new ones, that seemed most needed, have been added, and a number of others the purpose of which will be presently explained.

All the valuation tables for the first year of the policy begin with the *net* premium, and those and subsequent values are in some of the tables pointed for a policy of $100 and in others for one of $1000. The reader will be at no loss to discover which, though it is not stated in the caption of the table; or to discover the proper arguments, though some of the tables, to economize space, are turned bottom up.

The Life Policy Tables give the net value for each successive month of the policy-year after the payment of premium, on the assumption that *equal losses occur in equal times* throughout any policy-year. In case of annual premiums during life, the value at the end of the twelfth month, when another premium becomes due, is contained in a separate table, No. III., page 95.

The Endowment Policy Valuation Tables give only the net value at the beginning of each policy-year and the monthly or yearly decrement or increment, marked + or — as the case may be, which is of course to be applied according to the sign, on the assumption above stated.

The method of calculating the net premiums assumes that the money accumulates by interest compounded at annual rests coincident with the anniversaries of the issue of the policy, and that the claim is to be settled at the end of that policy-year in which the death occurs.

The "Combined Experience," or "Actuaries'" rate of mortality (see page 186), assumes that of 100,000 persons living at the age of 10, the last will die in his 99th year. Consequently it is assumed, in calculating the premium, that the claim on any policy must be paid at the end of that year if not before, notwithstanding that by the terms of the policy it is not payable till death, and there is no impossibility of a party living some years beyond the age of 100, and paying premium in each of those years. Hence it will be seen that in the tables every whole life-policy, both as to premium and reserve, is treated precisely as if it were an endowment policy payable at 100 or previous death. Though an endowment insurance policy is in reality a combination of two contracts, — one of insurance for a fixed term and another of simple endowment for the same term, — related to each other like two bets, one of which partially hedges the other, it is more convenient for practical purposes to consider it as a simple insurance for life calculated on a scale differing only from the ordinary one by assuming that all living to reach it will die in the last year of the term. Thus regarding it, all calculations for premium and reserve of endowment insurance policies may be made with formulas identical with those for ordinary life policies, by having a series of curtate summations of the $v^x l_x = D_x$ column, thus producing N_x columns terminating at every age in which we may assume the last death will take place. These curtate summations may be distinguished in the formulas from the ordinary N_x column by using a left hand suffix, writing ${}_{\omega}N_x$ or ${}_{100}N_x$ for the ordinary N_x, and, for example, ${}_{60}N_x$ for the summation when we assume $l_{60} = 0$. Or, in general, we write ${}_{x+n}$ as the argument of the summation, when we assume $l_{x+n} = 0$.

These summations are contained in Table XVIII., page 187. If n be the term of the endowment insurance, the expressions for the net single and annual premiums of any endowment policy, including as such the ordinary whole life policy, when $n = \omega - x$, will be, with the usual symbols,

Single Premium,

$$ {}_{x+n}\Pi_x = 1 - (1 - v)\,\frac{{}_{x+n}\mathrm{N}_x}{\mathrm{D}_x} \qquad (1.) $$

Annual Premium,

$$ {}_{x+n}\varpi_x = \frac{\mathrm{D}_x}{{}_{x+n}\mathrm{N}_x} - (1 - v) \qquad (2.) $$

And the expressions for the net single and annual premiums for a temporary insurance, or insurance during the term n, will be,

Single Premium,

$$ {}_{x+n}\Pi_x = \frac{v_{x+n}\mathrm{N}_x - {}_{x+n+1}\mathrm{N}_{x+1}}{\mathrm{D}_x} $$

Annual Premium,

$$ \frac{{}_{x+n}\Gamma_x}{{}_{x+n}\mathrm{A}_x} = v - \frac{{}_{x+n+1}\mathrm{N}_{x+1}}{{}_{x+n}\mathrm{N}_x} $$

As $\frac{{}_{x+n}\mathrm{N}_x}{\mathrm{D}_x}$ in (1.) is the present value of an annuity of \$1 at the age x, to consist of n payments, the first in advance, it is of course equal to \$1 added to an annuity of $n - 1$ payments at the same age, the first payable at the end of a year, and hence it may be found in table VI., page 112, by using $n - 1$ for the argument at the top or bottom of the tables, and adding a unit to the value under or over it against the lateral argument x.

As $\frac{\mathrm{D}_x}{{}_{x+n}\mathrm{N}_x}$ is one of the factors for insurance value, in table XX., page 191, presently to be explained, the net annual premium of any endowment policy, within the range of the table, may be found by subtracting one year's discount of a dollar from this factor for the age of entry.

Reserve.

Before the utility of valuation tables can be appreciated by any mind, it must have a distinct idea of what reserve is, and why and in what cases fidelity to the fundamental assumptions requires it. The subject may be simplified by leaving wholly out of account any other expenses than the payment of the claims on the policies. The premium and reserve to meet other expenses are by no means necessarily calculated upon or regulated by the same principles. They cannot be mingled without danger of confusion. Bearing this in mind, and referring only to claims on the policy, it may be well first to view a particular case.

If out of one hundred persons of the age of the insured we assume that one will die within a year, and also assume that money will earn four per cent per annum, the least he can pay to make the company good for the insurance of one dollar is the present value of one cent payable at the end of the year, or $9\frac{61538}{1000000}$ mills. Having paid this, and no more, if he dies during the year his heirs will receive at the end of it one dollar, including of course the one cent to which his payment amounts at the time of settlement. If he lives, whether his policy continues or not, there is nothing left of his one cent, for it goes as one of the ninety-nine which the living company loses on the individual who, by the assumption, does die. But if, in reference to a contract extending beyond one year, the insured paid more than enough to amount to one cent, say enough to amount to five cents, on the same policy, then the company can only lose ninety-five cents instead of ninety-nine in case of death within the year, and, if that does not occur, inasmuch as the cost of the insurance (normally) has been only $\frac{95}{99}$ as great as when it cost but one cent, there should be on hand, applicable to the future of the contract, whatever it may be, $5 - \frac{95}{99} = 4\frac{4}{99}$ cents. This is the reserve required, provided the $v \times .05$ was the exact payment necessary to carry the contract through as to future mortality and interest.

Those who are not already familiar with the subject may get a more general view of it by referring to Table XVII, page 186, and following, with a little patience, the following elementary explanation — not of the whole table, the construction and various uses of which are explained elsewhere, but of the relations of the ratios of the living and dying, and of interest to reserve.

Against any age in the first column we find in the third the number expected to die within one year out of the number living at the beginning of it in the second. $\frac{d_x}{l_x}$ is the ratio of the dying to the living at any age x and if we take any value of x between 10 and 99 inclusive, as 40, we have, by the table, $\frac{d_{40}}{l_{40}} = \frac{815}{78653} = .0103619$, which is the probability of dying in a year at the age of 40, as $\frac{l_{41}}{l_{40}} = \frac{77838}{78653} = .9896381$. the complement of the probability of dying, is the probability of living through the year. If the premium for a year's insurance were not payable till the end of it, at any age, l_x persons would have to pay the $\frac{d_x}{l_x}$ part of a dollar each to have each of the d_x persons receive one dollar, but if it is paid in advance, only the $v\frac{d_x}{l_x}$ part of a dollar will be needed. As each of the d_x persons receives back, included in the one dollar, that part of a dollar with its interest which he himself paid, the other $l_x - 1$ persons lose by his death only $1 - \frac{d_x}{l_x} = \frac{l_{x+1}}{l_x}$th part of a dollar. This is the company's *risk* in insuring one dollar for one year on the individual aged x. The mortality assumption holding good, or, in other words, the cost of insurance being *normal*, it will have cost, principal and interest, the $\frac{d_x}{l_x}$th part of a dollar for his chance of getting the other $\frac{l_{x+1}}{l_x}$th part. If only the principal of the $\frac{d_x}{l_x}$ is paid by each, whatever the contract for the future may be, the losses will exactly use it up, and there can be no reserve. If any survivor would insure a dollar the next year he must pay in advance $v\frac{d_{x+1}}{l_{x+1}}$, and there will be no reserve. And the year after $v\frac{d_{x+2}}{l_{x+2}}$, and so on, *pro anno novo*, a series of premiums increasing more and more rapidly through life, till, if death should not occur before the 99th year, the premium at the beginning of that year would be $v\frac{d_{\omega-1}}{l_{\omega-1}} = v$. By this, for more than one reason, impracticable method, there would be normally no reserve at the end of any year. But if a policy binding for more than one year is paid for, either by a constant annual premium during its term, or any limited number of years that may be less, then there must be a reserve at the end of each year.

No matter what the kind of policy, let this premium, greater than the risk of the next succeeding year, be called φ_x. If sufficient to make the company whole, on the assumptions, though in sum not equal to the sum of the series of yearly risks,

$$\left(v\frac{d_x}{l_x} + v\frac{d_{x+1}}{l_{x+1}} + v\frac{d_{x+2}}{l_{x+2}} \ldots\ldots + v\right.$$

in case of a whole life policy), it is, considering both the greater interest and the diminution of the company's risk effected by it, equivalent. Putting r for the ratio of interest, or amount of a dollar in a year, let us notice the two effects on the first year. If the premium $v\frac{d_x}{l_x}$, to insure one dollar, exposes the company to pay the $\frac{l_{x+1}}{l_x}$th part of a dollar in case of death, the payment of φ_x will expose it to pay only $1 - r\,\varphi_x$, and hence, to get the advance cost of carrying the company's risk a year in the latter case we have,

$$\frac{l_{x+1}}{l_x} : v\frac{d_x}{l_x} :: 1 - r\,\varphi_x : \frac{d_x}{l_{x+1}}(v - \varphi_x). \qquad (3.)$$

Now if out of the φ_x we deduct this advance cost of carrying the risk a year, and accumulate the remainder at the assumed rate of interest, we shall plainly have the normal reserve at the end of the year. Putting H_{x+1} for the reserve at the end of the first year we have,

$$H_{x+1} = r\left\{\varphi_x - \frac{d_x}{l_{x+1}}(v - \varphi_x)\right\},$$

which reduces to

$$H_{x+1} = r\frac{l_x}{l_{x+1}}\varphi_x - \frac{d_x}{l_{x+1}} \qquad (4.)$$

or to

$$H_{x+1} = r\frac{l_x}{l_{x+1}}\left(\varphi_x - v\frac{d_x}{l_x}\right) \qquad (5.)$$

Obviously the proportion (3.) will hold good for the advance cost of carrying the risk through any year, if we substitute for the φ_x the fund to the credit of the policy at the beginning of the year, any premium then payable being included therein. Hence, for the reserve at the end of the second year, we have

$$H_{x+2} = r\frac{l_{x+1}}{l_{x+2}}(H_{x+1} + \varphi_x) - \frac{d_{x+1}}{l_{x+2}}$$

or,

$$H_{x+2} = r\frac{l_{x+1}}{l_{x+2}}\left(H_{x+1} + \varphi_x - v\frac{d_{x+1}}{l_{x+1}}\right)$$

and generally,

$$H_{x+t} = r\frac{l_{x+t-1}}{l_{x+t}}(H_{x+t-1} + \varphi_x) - \frac{d_{x+t-1}}{l_{x+t}} \qquad (4.)$$

or,

$$H_{x+t} = r\frac{l_{x+t-1}}{l_{x+t}}\left(H_{x+t-1} + \varphi_x - v\frac{d_{x+t-1}}{l_{x+t-1}}\right) \qquad (5.)$$

The series of quantities, $r\frac{l_x}{l_{x+1}}$, $r\frac{l_{x+1}}{l_{x+2}}$, &c., may be called *coefficients of accumulation*, and if we tabulate them, and also either the series

$$\frac{d_x}{l_{x+1}}, \frac{d_{x+1}}{l_{x+2}}, \text{\&c., or } v\frac{d_x}{l_x}, v\frac{d_{x+1}}{l_{x+1}}, \text{\&c.},$$

we may readily obtain the reserve at the end of any year, knowing what is on hand to the credit of the policy at the beginning of it. Tables on the formula (5.) were first published in the Appendix to the Reprint of the Massachusetts Life Reports in 1865. This formula, which places the subtraction before the multiplication, has the advantage of always applying the coefficient to a smaller factor, making the results more exact in some cases, and especially when an arithmeter is used. Tables on formula (4.) were published by D. Parks Fackler, Esq., in 1868, in his useful work for Life Agents, and as the subtractive quantity involves no interest factor, a single column serves for coefficients at any rate of interest, and thus abridges the tables. Table XXII, page 200, contains Coefficients of Accumulation at various rates of interest, with a $v\frac{d_x}{l_x}$ column at 4 per cent, and a $\frac{d_x}{l_{x+1}}$ column which answers for any column of coefficients.

A variation of this formula, likely to be useful in some cases, has been suggested by Emory McClintock, Esq., the ingenious Actuary of the Asbury Life Insurance Company. It requires no table but that of the coefficients. If in the second member of (4.) you add and subtract unity, it reduces to

$$H_{x+1} = 1 - r\frac{l_x}{l_{x+1}}(v - \varphi_x),$$

or, generally to

$$H_{x+t} = 1 - r\frac{l_{x+t-1}}{l_{x+t}}(v - H_{x+t-1} - \varphi_x).$$

These formulas are not suggested as the best for calculating reserve, but as the best for illustrating the law of its generation. As to the necessity of reserve, it is obvious that if at any time in the progress of a policy the present value of the premiums to be paid is not equal to the single premium that would be required at the present age, the difference should be on hand as a reserve from the past premiums. That is, the reserve at the end of t years should be

$${}_{x+n}H_{x+t} = {}_{x+n}\Pi_{x+t} - {}_{x+n}\pi_x \times \frac{{}_{x+n}N_{x+t}}{D_{x+t}},$$

and substituting for ${}_{x+n}\Pi_{x+t}$ and ${}_{x+n}\pi_x$ their values in (1.) and (2.), we have,

$${}_{x+n}H_{x+t} = 1 - \frac{D_x}{{}_{x+n}N_x} \times \frac{{}_{x+n}N_{x+t}}{D_{x+t}} \qquad (6.)$$

Self-Insurance.

Since the normal reserve which will exist on a policy at the end of any year is just so much more in the hands of the company towards the payment of the claim that might have occurred in that year, than if the insured had each year paid only its risk, it may properly be called a *Self-insurance.* Hence H_{x+t} may be called the self-insurance value of the policy. It may be regarded as a Savings Bank deposit, with only this difference, that it cannot be withdrawn till the expiration of the policy by death, or what, in case of an endowment policy, we have assumed to be death. If $x + n$ is the limiting age, up to which some may live, but none beyond, by the assumption we should have $H_{x+n} = 1$. And if S is the sum insured, the self-insurance will begin with S H_{x+1} the first year, and increase from year to year until it is S in the last year. Consequently the insurance done by the company, per dollar of the policy, is a series of complementary risks, $1 - H_{x+1}$, $1 - H_{x+2}$, $1 - H_{x+3}$, ... o. The normal cost, or contribution to claims, of each of these risks at the end of the year in which it takes effect is

$$\frac{d_x}{l_x}(1-H_{x+1}),\ \frac{d_{x+1}}{l_{x+1}}(1-H_{x+2}),\ \&c.$$

This is what becomes of the net premiums and assumed interest thereon, so far as they do not go to form the self-insurance deposits aforesaid, that is, H_{x+1}, H_{x+2}, &c. Hence the present value of all the normal contributions which a policy is liable to make for the settlement of claims other than its own, may be called the

Insurance Value.

To conduct a company either with reference to permanent profit as a stock company, or equity and stability as a mutual one, *with the present great variety of policies*, it is almost as important to know this value as the self-insurance or reserve. The new tables, which will assist in calculating this value for all single life policies, are constructed on the following principles, and their use will be presently illustrated:—

If $x+n$ be the age at which a policy becomes certainly payable, a constant annual premium being payable till that age, referring to the D and N columns, Tables XVII and XVIII, we shall have the successive self-insurance values in terms of these tables, thus,—

1st. $${}_{x+n}H_{x+1} = 1 - \frac{D_x}{{}_{x+n}N_x} \times \frac{{}_{x+n}N_{x+1}}{D_{x+1}}.$$

2d. $${}_{x+n}H_{x+2} = 1 - \frac{D_x}{{}_{x+n}N_x} \times \frac{{}_{x+n}N_{x+2}}{D_{x+2}},$$

&c., &c.

Consequently we have the insurance done by the company each year,—

1st. $$1 - {}_{x+n}H_{x+1} = \frac{D_x}{{}_{x+n}N_x} \times \frac{{}_{x+n}N_{x+1}}{D_{x+1}}.$$

2d. $$1 - {}_{x+n}H_{x+2} = \frac{D_x}{{}_{x+n}N_x} \times \frac{{}_{x+n}N_{x+2}}{D_{x+2}},$$

&c., &c.

The values of these risks will be,

1st. $$\frac{d_x}{l_x}(1 - {}_{x+n}H_{x+1}) = \frac{D_x}{{}_{x+n}N_x} \times \frac{{}_{x+n}N_{x+1}}{D_{x+1}} \times \frac{d_x}{l_x}.$$

2d. $$\frac{d_{x+1}}{l_{x+1}}(1 - {}_{x+n}H_{x+2}) = \frac{D_x}{{}_{x+n}N_x} \times \frac{{}_{x+n}N_{x+2}}{D_{x+2}} \times \frac{d_{x+1}}{l_{x+1}},$$

&c., &c.

The first of these is certain because the premium is paid in advance, but must be discounted by the factor v to refer it to the beginning of the year. The second must not only be discounted two years, but must be multiplied by the fraction $\frac{l_{x+1}}{l_x}$, expressing the probability of the party being alive to pay the second premium. Hence, the discount factor will be $v^2\frac{l_{x+1}}{l_x}$. In like manner, the discount factor for the third year will be $v^3\frac{l_{x+2}}{l_x}$, and so on. Observing that $\frac{D_x}{{}_{x+n}N_x}$ is a factor common to every term of the series to be discounted, and substituting for D_{x+1}, D_{x+2}, etc., their values, $v^{x+1}l_{x+1}$, $v^{x+2}l_{x+2}$, etc., and applying the discount factors above explained, we have the Insurance Value, which we will designate by the Symbol I.

$${}_{x+n}I_x = \frac{D_x}{{}_{x+n}N_x}\left(\frac{{}_{x+n}N_{x+1}}{v^{x+1}l_{x+1}} \times \frac{vd_x}{l_x} + \frac{{}_{x+n}N_{x+2}}{v^{x+2}l_{x+2}} \times \frac{v^2d_{x+1} \times l_{x+1}}{l_{x+1} \times l_x} + \&c.\right)$$

Multiplying numerators and denominators by v^x, we have,

$${}_{x+n}I_x = \frac{D_x}{{}_{x+n}N_x}\left(\frac{{}_{x+n}N_{x+1}}{v^{x+1}l_{x+1}} \times \frac{v^{x+1}d_x}{v^xl_x} + \frac{{}_{x+n}N_{x+2}}{v^{x+2}l_{x+2}} \times \frac{v^{x+2}d_{x+1} \times l_{x+1}}{v^xl_x \times l_{x+1}} + \&c.\right)$$

Cancelling like factors in numerator and denominator, and substituting D_x for v^xl_x, we have,

$${}_{x+n}I_x = \frac{D_x}{{}_{x+n}N_x} \times \frac{{}_{x+n}N_{x+1} \times \frac{d_x}{l_{x+1}} + {}_{x+n}N_{x+2} \times \frac{d_{x+1}}{l_{x+2}} + \&c.}{D_x} \quad (7.)$$

Obviously, if we assume $x = 10$, and perform all the multiplications of $\frac{d_{10}}{l_{11}}$ into N_{11}, $\frac{d_{11}}{l_{12}}$ into N_{12}, &c., as indicated in the numerator of the last factor of (7.), the summation of the products, (after the manner in which the N column is produced from the D,) will produce a column of *numerators* which we will call Δ, (*lucus a non*) and this will give us, instead of (7.),

$${}_{x+n}I_x = \frac{D_x}{{}_{x+n}N_x} \times \frac{{}_{x+n}\Delta_x}{D_x}, \text{ and (8.) } {}_{x+n}I_{x+t} = \frac{D_x}{{}_{x+n}N_x} \times \frac{{}_{x+n}\Delta_{x+t}}{D_{x+t}},$$

when the policy has completed t years, and the $(t+1)$th premium is just paid.

Similarly, to find the insurance value of a paid up policy, expressing the self-insurance values in terms of the D and N columns, we shall find the aggregate of the discounted future costs of insurance reduce itself to ${}_{x+n}I_{x+t} = (1-v)\frac{{}_{x+n}\Delta_{x+t}}{D_{x+t}}$.

To get the insurance values of limited premium life or endowment policies, let φ_x be the premium to be paid q times, and $v - \varphi_x = c_1$, $c_1 - H_{x+1} = c_2$, $c_1 - H_{x+2} = c_3 \ldots\ldots c_1 - H_{x+q-1} = c_q$. Then referring to Table XXII, page 200, column δ_x, and denoting the insurance value when the first premium is just paid by ${}_{x+n}I_{x|q}$, we shall have,

$${}_{x+n}I_{x|q} = \frac{\delta_xc_1 + \delta_{x+1}c_2 \ldots + \delta_{x+q-1}c_q}{D_x} + \frac{D_{x+q}}{D_x} \times \frac{{}_{x+n}\Delta_{x+q}}{D_{x+q}}$$

After having thus found the initial insurance value, we may find that of the succeeding years by applying the coefficient of accumulation, thus:—

$${}_{x+n}I_{x+1|q} = \frac{rl_x}{l_{x+1}}\left({}_{x+n}I_{x|q} - \frac{d_x}{l_{x+1}}c_1\right)$$

$${}_{x+n}I_{x+2|q} = r\frac{l_{x+1}}{l_{x+2}}\left({}_{x+n}I_{x+1|q} - \frac{d_{x+1}}{l_{x+2}}c_2\right)$$

&c., &c., &c.

For the following briefer process, applicable to any policy payable at the age $x+n$ or previous death, including of course the ordinary whole life policy, the public are indebted to the keen analysis of Mr. McClintock abovenamed. His notation is slightly modified to adapt it to the tables. Let φ_x be the annual premium to be paid q times, and when the first premium is just paid, we have,

$${}_{x+n}I_{x|q} = d\frac{{}_{x+n}\mathcal{A}_x}{D_x} + \varphi_x \frac{{}_{x+q}\mathcal{A}_x}{D_x},$$

and when the $(t+1)$th premium has just been paid,

$${}_{x+n}I_{x+t|q} = d\frac{{}_{x+n}\mathcal{A}_{x+t}}{D_{x+t}} + \varphi_x \frac{{}_{x+q}\mathcal{A}_{x+t}}{D_{x+t}}.$$

Though the insurance value of an annual premium term policy is greater than that of an endowment policy for the same term and amount, there is, except for a very long term, too little reserve on it to secure a proper surrender charge. Therefore, unless the premium is extravagantly loaded, the company is not sufficiently secured against loss by lapse, after having paid the usual commission. For this reason, and because this sort of policy is little sought by the public, which fails to see value except in the indemnity or endowment, it is hardly necessary to insert any formulas for the insurance values of term policies. But as these policies are really valuable, and when paid for by single or a limited number of annual premiums, the reserves afford sufficient security to the company paying a moderate commission, it may be well to provide for business which may arise. Putting K for the insurance value of policies of this class, we have for the ordinary term policy of n years, when the $(t+1)$th premium is just paid,

$${}_{x+n}K_{x+t} = \frac{{}_{x+n+1}\mathcal{A}_{x+t}}{D_{x+t}} - (v - {}_{x+n}\gamma_x)\frac{{}_{x+n}\mathcal{A}_{x+t}}{D_{x+t}}. \quad (9.)$$

If the premium is limited to q payments, in which case it is

$${}_{x+n}\gamma_x \frac{{}_{x+n}N_x}{{}_{x+q}N_x} = p_x,$$

the value is,

$${}_{x+n}K_{x+t|q} = \frac{{}_{x+n+1}\mathcal{A}_{x+t}}{D_{x+t}} - v\frac{{}_{x+n}\mathcal{A}_{x+t}}{D_{x+t}} + p_x\frac{{}_{x+q}\mathcal{A}_{x+t}}{D_{x+t}},$$

and a single premium term policy is,

$${}_{x+n}K_{x+t} = \frac{{}_{x+n+1}\mathcal{A}_{x+t}}{D_{x+t}} - v\frac{{}_{x+n}\mathcal{A}_{x+t}}{D_{x+t}}.$$

The insurance value of a pure endowment, or tontine policy, is of course negative, the operation being wholly the exact reverse of insurance, to wit, of term-insurance. Foi example: if T be the insurance value of a tontine or pure endowment policy, at annual premium, we have, by substituting in (8.) for $\frac{D_x}{{}_{x+n}N_x}$ its value $= d + {}_{x+n}\pi_x = d + {}_{x+n}\gamma_x + {}_{x+n}e_x$, and subtracting (9.),

$${}_{x+n}T_{x+t} = (1 + {}_{x+n}e_x)\frac{{}_{x+n}\mathcal{A}_{x+t}}{D_{x+t}} - \frac{{}_{x+n+1}\mathcal{A}_{x+t}}{D_{x+t}},$$

which is always negative, and, if paid up, it becomes,

$${}_{x+n}T_{x+t} = -\frac{{}_{x+n+1}\mathcal{A}_{x+t}}{D_{x+t}}.$$

It must not be inferred from the negativeness of the insurance value of endowment that the company loses or is weakened by it. The mortality being normal, it neither gains nor loses. It gains if the mortality is greater and loses if it is less. But the insurance of pure endowment being inverted, its negativeness indicates that the interest of the policy-holder, as a probable survivor, is to have the vitality of the company diminished. *He* can afford to pay less than nothing to increase it. Hence, *a fortiori*, he cannot be satisfied if he is charged for expenses more than his ${}_{x+n}H_{x+t}$ would cost him in a savings bank, unless there should have occurred in the company that extraordinary mortality which is the only source of prosperity to pure tontine companies. This is not to be hoped or wished for when endowment is coupled with insurance in the same policy.

Table XIX gives the insurance values, per $1000, of paid up, five premium and ten premium whole life policies, — calculated on the principles above, — and the factors for the insurance value, per dollar, of whole life annual premium policies.

Table XX gives the factors per dollar for all annual premium endowment insurance policies, payable during the term, when it does not extend beyond the age of 80.

Table XXIII will aid to apply the foregoing formulas for the insurance values of term policies.

Assessment of Expenses.

The provision for expenses, other than claims, is made by an addition to the net premium, usually called the *loading*. As the probable redundancy of the net premiums as well as the loading may prove available for expenses, the principle which may govern the loading is not necessarily applicable to the annual or periodical assessment of expenses.

The following table A contains the insurance values of fourteen policies entered at 40, for $1000 each, at the beginning of the years specified, and the contemporaneous self-insurance values, or $v\, H_{x+t}$. The first policy is one for a single year. The second is purely theoretical, a policy for the whole life to be paid for by an increasing annual premium only sufficient to cover the whole risk of $1000 in each successive year. Of course its insurance value at the start is the net single premium, or $I_x = II_x$.

The object of this table is to illustrate three of the possible methods of assessing the working expenses of a mutual company on the members holding various policies. Provision for expenses is usually made by adding to the net premium a certain percentage of itself. And if no surplus is returned, this addition is an assessment of the expenses. But whenever surplus is to be returned, the question of assessment arises anew, and is susceptible of a great number of different solutions, only one of which can well be equitable.

Suppose these fourteen policies constitute a company, of which the working expenses of the year are $96.36, and that the net premiums were all alike loaded 11½ per cent., so that it actually received in the year $936.62 on account of premiums. If at the end of the year it finds its assets only equal to the normal reserve of $2177.08, so that it has no surplus to return, and makes no dividend, it really assesses expenses in proportion to the loading, and, in this case, uses nearly the whole loading; so that the "paid up" policy in its first year, pays $43.70 for expenses, all it will ever pay, and the ordinary life policy, which enjoys about a third more insurance, pays only $2.69. This absurdity is so obvious that the paid up, and, to some extent, other largely self-insuring

TABLE A.

	Net Premium.	Insurance Value. I_{x+t-1}	Self-Insurance Value. $v\,H_{x+t}$	Normal Cost of Risk. $\frac{d_{x+t-1}}{l_{x+t-1}}(1-H_{x+t})$	½ % on $v\,H_{x+t}$	\$85.90. on I_{x+t-1}	\$85.90 on Normal Cost.	\$96.36 on Net Annual Premium.
Term, One Year, ...	\$9.96	\$9.96	\$0.00	\$10.36	\$0.000	\$0.36	\$6.56	\$2.84
Life (by risk of each year), . . . 1st Year,	9.96	381.04	0.00	10.36	0.000	13.68	6.56	2.84
Life, Annual Premium, ... 1st "	23.68	237.29	13.86	10.21	0.069	8.52	6.47	6.74
Life, Annual Premium, ... 10th "	23.68	254.48	156.70	12.60	0.783	9.14	7.98	6.74
Endowment, Annual, D, or 80, . . 1st "	24.30	214.14	14.49	10.20	0.072	7.69	6.46	6.92
Endowment, Annual, D. or 80, . . 10th "	24.30	216.40	165.13	12.47	0.825	7.77	7.90	6.92
Life, 10 Annual Premiums, . . . 1st "	47.34	164.58	37.76	9.75	0.188	5.91	6.33	6.74
Life, 10 Annual Premiums, . . . 5th "	47.34	158.84	206.50	9.18	1.032	5.70	5.82	6.74
Life, 5 Annual Premiums, . . . 1st "	84.00	154.65	74.81	9.55	0.374	5.55	6.05	6.74
Life, 5 Annual Premiums, . . . 3d "	84.00	151.67	235.43	8.23	1.177	5.44	5.21	6.74
Life, Paid Up, ... 1st "	381.04	146 87	374.96	6.32	1.874	5.27	4.00	6.74
Life, Paid Up, ... 5th "		152.58	412.06	6.85	2.060	5.48	4.34	6.74
Endowment, An. Prem., D, or 60, . 1st "	40.21	103.15	30.55	10.03	0.153	3.70	6.36	11.46
Endowment, An. Prem., D, or 60, . 10th "	40.21	47.07	371.10	9.25	1.855	1.69	5.86	11.46
Total, ...	\$840.02	\$2392.72	\$2093.35	\$135.56	\$10.462	\$85.90	\$85.90	\$96.36

policies are not loaded by so high a per centage to avoid it.

In this way some nearer approach to equity may be obtained in the case where dividend is passed. But however the premiums may be loaded, when a dividend is actually made, a share cannot be assigned to any policy without a previous actual or virtual assignment of its share of expenses. The best, obviously, that can be done, if the share of expenses is to be regulated by the premium at all, is to assess not on the actual premium, but on the net annual premium for the whole term of the policy. This would work well if the policies were all life-policies, or endowments having forty or fifty years to run. But, manifestly, it cannot be applied to endowment insurances as short as twenty years, without the most violent overthrow of equity, as will be seen by the last column of the above table, where a twenty year endowment policy pays \$4.72 more than an ordinary life policy, though the company insures much less under it. The shorter the term of the endowment the worse it grows, the party being obliged to pay the more for expenses the less the company does for him and the more he does for himself, in regard to the risk on the policy.

There seems, in fact, to be no possible way of establishing equity in the charge for expenses between the less and more self-insuring policies in the same office, other than by distinguishing, in regard to every policy, between its interest in the company, at the time, considered as a savings bank, and considered as an insurance company.

The first two policies are introduced into the above table to show the relation to each other and to the company of two widely different policies, in both of which the savings bank element is reduced to zero; and to show how, if they did exist, they would have to contribute towards expenses on three different methods of assessment. It is, of course, necessary to assume in regard to the whole life policy with premiums payable according to the risk of the year plus a loading in the same proportion, that the contract so to pay during life is as reliable on the part of the insured as it would be to pay the usual annual premium, though this cannot be so in point of fact,— as every "co-operative association" will demonstrate in due time. We only assume it for the sake of the argument. The question is, Should the party whom the company has engaged to insure for his whole life, without any self-insurance at all, pay no more than one whom it has engaged to insure only one year, other things being equal? All the working expenses of the company, except for handling the reserve, which in the case of these two policies is nothing, are for maintaining and enlarging the company as an insurance company. Plainly the interest of these two parties in the company as such, though the same for the current year, is very different. If \$9.96 represents the interest of the first policy, the second has the same interest in the first year, plus the present value of the insurance on \$1000 for all the future years covered by the policy, or \$381.04 in all. Otherwise what is the sense of introducing future values into any life-insurance calculation whatever? Supposing the pledge of the future premiums as secure to the company as the assumptions admit, the 60 possible premiums of the second policy are not worth 60 times the first, although they foot up to the formidable aggregate of \$9135.97, which is a charming prospect for the victims of the "co-operatives," but they are worth thirty-eight times as much and a little more. Plainly the second policy has a much larger *present* interest in the company than the first, and any plan which assesses the two equally for the expenses of the year, must be defective or incorrect in principle.

If the two numbers, 9.96 and 381.04, do not express relatively the interests or stock possessed by the two policies in the company, what other numbers do? The magnitude and strength of the company, as an insurance company, depends upon the future as well as the present insurance business it has secured, and as there is an equilibrium between the company, as such, and the aggregate of the individual interests concerned in it, so there must be an equilibrium between the interest of the company in each individual, and his interest in the company. If a policy is worth to the company the present value of what it will normally contribute to claims, the company is worth just that sum to the policy-holder, and why should not his share of the expenses be a function of this value?

But as there cannot be sufficient cohesion in a company consisting of long policies without reserve, these two policies destitute of reserve, having served their purpose of illustration, may be dismissed, and the table reconstructed without them, in order to be free from their disturbing effect on the assessment. Whatever principle of assessment would be applicable to these two policies, must be applicable to the others, just so far as and no farther than the insurance on them is done by the company, and not by the policy-holder himself. Any argument that may be derived from this new table in favor of assessing the excess of expenses over one half of one per cent. on the reserve, upon the insurance value, would only be strengthened by introducing a larger variety in the policies as to the age of entry and the age of the policy itself, as well as in the terms.

Let us suppose that the expenses of these twelve policies amount to $82.32. If the assessment is on net premiums the violation of equity, already noticed, is still apparent. The only direction of escape from this is in assessing separately on the insurance and self-insurance values.

TABLE B.

		Net Premium.	Insurance Value. I_{x+t-1}	Self-Insurance Value. $v\,H_{x+t}$	Normal Cost of Risk. $\frac{d_{x+t-1}}{l_{x+t-1}}(1-H_{x+t})$	½ % on $v\,H_{x+t}$	$71.86 on I_{x+t-1}	$71.86 on Normal Cost.	$82.32 on Net Annual Premium.
Life, Annual Premium, ...	1st Year.	$23.68	$237.29	$13.86	$10.21	$0.069	$8.52	$6.39	$6.12
Life, Annual Premium, ...	10th "	23.68	254.48	156.70	12.60	0.783	9 14	7.88	6.12
Endowment, Annual, D, or 80, . .	1st "	24.30	214.14	14.49	10 20	0.072	7.69	6.38	6.28
Endowment, Annual, D, or 80, . .	10th "	24.30	216.40	165.13	12.47	0.825	7.77	7.80	6.28
Life, 10 Annual Premiums, . . .	1st "	47 34	164.58	37.76	9.95	0.188	5.91	6.23	6.12
Life, 10 Annual Premiums, . . .	5th "	47.34	158.84	206.50	9.18	1.032	5.70	5.74	6.12
Life, 5 Annual Premiums, . . .	1st "	84 00	154.65	74.81	9.55	0.374	5.55	5.98	6.12
Life, 5 Annual Premiums, . . .	3d "	84 00	151.67	235.43	8.23	1.177	5.44	5.15	6.12
Life, Paid Up, ...	1st "	381.04	146.87	374.96	6.32	1.874	5.27	3 95	6.12
Life, Paid Up, ...	5th "		152.58	412.06	6.85	2.060	5.48	4.29	6.12
Endowment, An. Prem., D, or 60, .	1st "	40.21	103.15	30.55	10.03	0.153	3.70	6.28	10.40
Endowment, An. Prem., D, or 60, .	10th "	40.21	47.07	371.10	9.25	1.855	1.69	5.79	10.40
Total, ...		$820.10	$2001.72	$2093.35	$114.84	$10.462	$71.86	$71.86	$82.32

The expenses of the five largest savings banks in Boston, in 1869, did not exceed four tenths of one per cent. on $28,000,000 deposited in them. They certainly had twice as many transactions in proportion to the deposits, as any life-insurance company would have with the same amount of reserve. The only reason why it should cost the latter more to manage its funds, lies in the greater difficulty of the calculations. But one tenth of one per cent. on $28,000,000 would support a perfectly efficient actuarial department, so that one half of one per cent. on the reserve seems to be ample for all the working expenses save those of sustaining the agencies and collecting the premiums, or, in other words, those which are necessary to maintain and enlarge the basis of insurance. If we deduct from $82.32 one half of one per cent. on the self-insurance value, we have $71.86 to be assessed on the insurance value, or on the cost of insurance for the year. The latter has certainly the advantage of greater facility, but the objection of ignoring the greater part of the interests involved in the company still remains. It is obviously, as compared with the plan at present practised, an approach towards equity, but it does not go the length of justifying a short endowment insurance on an average life, in preference to an ordinary life policy. The former policy, though not overcharged on its reserve, is overcharged on its stock in the company as an insurance company relatively to the latter. It is only when you pay equitably in both departments, that there is fair-play between the more and less accumulative policies.

It is obvious that this difference exists between a Savings Bank proper and a Life Insurance Company regarded as one. The Life Insurance Company by collecting its premiums saves the depositor the trouble of visiting the bank; consequently he can afford to pay something for the trouble the company takes in collecting. He is materially aided thereby in carrying out his good resolutions to provide for the future of his family. If the collection fee is not too large, it may undoubtedly exist, and still allow the Life Insurance Company to be a desirable receptacle for all the savings any policy-holder may have to invest beyond the lowest present premium to maintain his policy. To illustrate this, Table C supposes the net annual premiums of Table B to be loaded twenty-five per cent., and the single premium five per cent., and that two and a half per cent. is assessed on every actual premium for collection, which accounts for $23.70 of the expenses. The other 58.60 is assessed one half per cent. on the self-insurance, and the balance on the insurance value.

By comparing the last two columns of this table we see how slightly a small collection fee disturbs the above defined equities, provided all other commissions and expenses over one half per cent. of the self-insurance fund are assessed on the insurance value. We still have, as we ought to, the more accumulative policies contributing less, on the whole, to expenses,

TABLE C.

	Actual Premium.	Insurance Value. I_{x+t-1}	Self-Insurance Value. $v\,H_{x+t}$	Expenses, $82.32.				
				2½ % on Premium.	½ % on $v\,H_{x+t}$	$48.14 on I_{x+t-1}	Total with collection Fee.	Total without collection Fee.
Life, Annual Premium, ... 1st Year.	$29.60	$237.29	$13.86	$0.74	$0.07	$5.71	$6.52	$8.59
Life, Annual Premium, ... 10th "	29.60	254.48	156.70	0.74	0.78	6.12	7.64	9.92
Endowment, Annual, D, or 80, . . 1st "	30.37	214.14	14.49	0.76	0.07	5.15	5.98	7.76
Endowment, Annual, D, or 80, . . 10th "	30.37	216.40	165.13	0.76	0.83	5.20	6.79	8.60
Life, 10 Annual Premiums, . . . 1st "	59.17	164.58	37.76	1.47	0.19	3.96	5.62	6.10
Life, 10 Annual Premiums, . . . 5th "	59.17	158.84	206.50	1.47	1.03	3.82	6.32	6.73
Life, 5 Annual Premiums, . . . 1st "	105.00	154.65	74.81	2.63	0.37	3.72	6.72	5.92
Life, 5 Annual Premiums, . . . 3d "	105.00	151.67	235.43	2.63	1.18	3.65	7.46	6.62
Life, Paid Up, ... 1st "	400.09	146.87	374.96	10.00	1.87	3.53	5.40	7.14
Life, Paid Up, ... 5th "		152.58	412.06		2.06	3.67	5.73	7.54
Endowment, An. Prem., D, or 60, . 1st "	50.26	103.15	30.55	1.26	0.15	2.48	3.89	3.85
Endowment, An. Prem., D, or 60, . 10th "	50.26	47.07	371.10	1.26	1.86	1.13	4.25	3.55
Total, ...	$948.89	$2001.72	$2093.35	$23.72	$10.46	$48.14	$82.32	$82.32

than the less accumulative. But if the collection fee on the premium collected is enhanced beyond two and a half per cent., it will be very hard to find any reason to justify any but the ordinary life policy.

As expenses now range, it is plain enough that they cannot be equitably assessed, if either of the last mentioned plans is to be considered equitable, without exhausting or more than exhausting the loading of many of the life policies. The expenses, however, would not be so large, but for the false practice of allowing the same percentage to agents on the premiums of the more accumulative policies and those that are less so. Should the business be procured and sustained by a percentage on its insurance value, if the expenses were not, as they probably would be, less in proportion to the premiums, they would be far less in proportion to the real value to the company of the business obtained. Hence the change of system could not fail to be satisfactory to all the parties concerned.

If the principles above explained ought to govern the assessment of expenses, it is plain that the loading on some of the premiums is excessive, or much larger than ought ever to be called for, while on some others it must be deficient, unless the prevailing habits of expense shall be reduced. With moderate expense, the ordinary whole life annual premiums will ordinarily yield a slight surplus from the first on either of the plans of assessment illustrated in Table C. But the short endowment policies will yield a very large one. They might pay their fair share of expenses with less loading. Though it is by no means necessary to make any change in the actual premiums in order to make an equitable assessment of expenses, a logical provision for expenses rests on the same base as the assessment. The loading should be a percentage of the maximum insurance value of the policy.

Surrender Value.

The strength of a company depends upon the breadth of the basis, or aggregate of insurance value, the individual risk being the same. Hence no member in good health can retire or withdraw from his contract for future insurance without weakening the company. He cannot justly be allowed to retire without leaving enough to pay for replacing the insurance value he takes away. Unless the retiring life is worse than the average, or uninsurable, the proper surrender charge seems to be what it will cost to procure a new one with an equal insurance value, sufficiently secured by self-insurance; in other words, one that cannot retire without paying an equal surrender charge. Hence, in strict equity, a company should not take a premium note beyond the surrender value of the policy, or self-insurance value less the surrender charge. As expenses generally run, this would prevent any premium note being taken the first year on an ordinary life policy. On any other it is absurd for the policy-holder to give one, as a general thing, however safe it may be for the company to take it.

Life Insurance policies always used to be, and to some extent now are, drawn with a clause by which in case of failure to pay any premium when due, *all* of those previously paid are forfeited to the company. This implies that the company has a right, in case of good health, to exact as a surrender charge the whole of the self-insurance value. Self-preservation is well said to be the first law of nature; and a mutual life insurance company from which any member might when he pleased take away his whole self-insurance deposit without paying any surrender charge, would be as much an impossibility as a solid without cohesion. But cohesion should not be excessive, otherwise shrewd people will avoid life insurance as the fox did the cave from which he noticed that no tracks led outward. The surrender charge cannot be less than the cost of replacing the insurance value withdrawn without subjecting the company to more loss by the retirement of good lives than it can realize gain by the retirement of bad ones. The reason why a company cannot consist of, or admit into it, policies like the second in Table A above is, that it has no security for the payment of a surrender charge in case the party should choose to discontinue. The third or ordinary life policy has a normal reserve at the end of the first year of $14.41, and if it does not cost more than that to procure a policy with as much insurance value, the payment of a proper surrender charge is sufficiently secured. If four per cent of the insurance value will procure such a policy, the surrender charge would be $9.49, and deducting this from the self-insurance value leaves $4.92 as the surrender value. On the same principle of charging four per cent. of the insurance value, the surrender charge on the last policy in the table would be $1.88, leaving the surrender value $384.06. The terrible want of equity in making the surrender charge a percentage of the self-insurance, instead of the insurance value, will be seen by comparing the last policy in Table A with the fourth. If, as is sometimes done, when such policies are surrendered, one fourth of the reserve is retained by the company, the ten year old life policy will pay a surrender charge of $40.74, a sum probably sufficient to procure four times the insurance value withdrawn, while the ten year old twenty year endowment policy will pay $96.48, or sufficient to procure more than fifty-one times as much as is withdrawn. If the former charge is the right thing, the latter is nearly thirteen times too large. The truth is, that both of them are excessive. If we take the life-policies alone, it has certainly cost the companies not more than four per cent. of their insurance value to obtain them, although taking the endowment policies by themselves, it has as clearly cost more than ten per cent. of their insurance value to obtain them. But when we come to the question of surrender charge, we are to consider not what the individual policy actually cost, but what it is worth to keep, or what it would cost to get another equally valuable to keep. The tariff of commissions can only be settled correctly, when we have a correct appreciation of the value to the company of the business to be obtained by the payment of commissions, and distinguish between insurance premium and self-insurance deposit.

i=yearly interest of a unit.

$r=1+i$=the amount of a unit in a year, or the ratio of interest.

$v=\frac{1}{r}$=the present value of the unit due at the end of a year.

$1-v=d$=discount of a unit for a year.

x=age of entry.

ω=the limit of age by the table of mortality.

l_x=number living by the table at age x.

d_x=number dying between the ages x and $x+1$.

$u_x=r\frac{l_x}{l_{x+1}}$ $\quad c_x=v\frac{d_x}{l_x}$ $\quad k_x=\frac{d_x}{l_{x+1}}=\frac{C_x}{D_{x+1}}$

$u_{xz}=(1+k_z)u_x$ $\quad c_{xz}=v-u_{xz}^{-1}$ $\quad k_{xz}=k_x+k_z+k_xk_z$

φ_x=any net annual premium, per unit, on a policy entered at x.

$D_x=v^xl_x$ $\quad D_{xz}=v^{\frac{z-x}{2}}l_z\times D_x$

${}_\omega N_x=D_x+D_{x+1}+D_{x+2}\ldots+D_{\omega-1}$

${}_\omega S_x={}_\omega N_x+{}_\omega N_{x+1}+{}_\omega N_{x+2}\ldots+{}_\omega N_{\omega-1}$

${}_{x+n}N_x=D_x+D_{x+1}+D_{x+2}\ldots+D_{x+n-1}$

$C_x=v^{x+1}d_x=vD_x-D_{x+1}$

${}_\omega M_x=C_x+C_{x+1}+C_{x+2}\ldots+C_{\omega-1}=v{}_\omega N_x-{}_\omega N_{x+1}$

${}_\omega R_x={}_\omega M_x+{}_\omega M_{x+1}+{}_\omega M_{x+2}\ldots+{}_\omega M_{\omega-1}=v{}_\omega S_x-{}_\omega S_{x+1}$

${}_\omega\Delta_x=\frac{d_x}{l_{x+1}}{}_\omega N_{x+1}+\frac{d_{x+1}}{l_{x+2}}{}_\omega N_{x+2}\ldots+\frac{d_{\omega-2}}{l_{\omega-1}}{}_\omega N_{\omega-1}$

${}_{x+n}\Delta_x=\frac{d_x}{l_{x+1}}{}_{x+n}N_{x+1}+\frac{d_{x+1}}{l_{x+2}}{}_{x+n}N_{x+2}\ldots+\frac{d_{x+n-2}}{l_{x+n-1}}{}_{x+n}N_{x+n-1}$

${}_{x+n}A_x=\frac{{}_{x+n}N_x}{D_x}$=Present value of an annuity of a unit, first payment immediate, last at age $x+n-1$.

${}_{x+n}\Pi_x=1-d\frac{{}_{x+n}N_x}{D_x}$=Single premium to insure a unit payable at age $x+n$ or previous death.

${}_{x+n}\pi_x=\frac{D_x}{{}_{x+n}N_x}-d$=Annual premium for the same.

${}_{x+n}E_x=\frac{D_{x+n}}{D_x}$=Single premium for the endowment of a unit, payable if the party is alive at age $x+n$.

${}_{x+n}e_x=\frac{D_{x+n}}{{}_{x+n}N_x}$=Annual premium for the same.

${}_{x+n}\Gamma_x=\frac{D_x-D_{x+n}-d_{x+n}N_x}{D_x}$=Single premium to insure a unit payable if death occurs within the term n.

${}_{x+n}\gamma_x=\frac{D_x-D_{x+n}}{{}_{x+n}N_x}-d$=Annual premium for the same.

$\frac{{}_{x+n}\Pi_x}{{}_{x+t}A_x}=\frac{D_x-d_{x+n}N_x}{{}_{x+t}N_x}$=Annual premium limited to t payments to insure a unit payable at $x+n$ or previous death.

${}_{x+n}H_{x+t}=1-\frac{D_x}{{}_{x+n}N_x}\times\frac{{}_{x+n}N_{x+t}}{D_{x+t}}$=Net self-insurance value of an ordinary policy when the $(t+1)$th payment is due.

${}_{x+n}H_{x+t}=u_{x+t-1}({}_{x+n}H_{x+t-1}+\varphi_x-c_{x+t-1})$=Net self-insurance value of any policy when the $(t+1)$th payment is due.

or ${}_{x+n}H_{x+t}=u_{x+t-1}({}_{x+n}H_{x+t-1}+\varphi_x)-k_{x+t-1}$

${}_{x+n}I_{x+t}=\frac{D_x}{{}_{x+n}N_x}\times\frac{{}_{x+n}\Delta_{x+t}}{D_{x+t}}$=Insurance value of an annual premium policy payable at age $x+n$ or previous death when the $(t+1)$th premium is just paid.

${}_{x+n}I_{x+t}=d\frac{{}_{x+n}\Delta_{x+t}}{D_{x+t}}$=Insurance value at the age $x+t$ of the same policy paid up.

${}_{x+n}I_{x+t\,|\,q}=d\frac{{}_{x+n}\Delta_{x+t}}{D_{x+t}}+\varphi_x\frac{{}_{x+q}\Delta_{x+t}}{D_{x+t}}$

=Insurance value of the same at age $x+t$ when limited to q premiums, of which the $(t+1)$th is just paid.

CONTENTS.

Age.	0	1	2	3	4	5	6	7	8	9	10	11	Day.
10	1.1932	1.1402	1.0871	1.0341	.9811	.9281	.8750	.8220	.7690	.7160	.6630	.6099	.001767
11	1.2162	1.1628	1.1095	1.0561	1.0028	.9494	.8960	.8427	.7893	.7360	.6826	.6293	.001778
12	1.2401	1.1869	1.1337	1.0806	1.0274	.9742	.9210	.8679	.8147	.7615	.7083	.6552	.001772
13	1.2652	1.2122	1.1592	1.1062	1.0533	1.0003	.9473	.8943	.8413	.7883	.7354	.6824	.001766
14	1.2914	1.2375	1.1837	1.1298	1.0759	1.0221	.9682	.9143	.8605	.8066	.7527	.6989	.001795
15	1.3187	1.2645	1.2103	1.1562	1.1020	1.0478	.9936	.9395	.8853	.8311	.7769	.7228	.001806
16	1.3472	1.2926	1.2380	1.1834	1.1289	1.0743	1.0197	.9651	.9105	.8560	.8014	.7468	.001819
17	1.3769	1.3219	1.2669	1.2119	1.1569	1.1019	1.0470	.9920	.9370	.8820	.8270	.7720	.001833
18	1.4078	1.3523	1.2968	1.2413	1.1859	1.1304	1.0749	1.0194	.9639	.9084	.8530	.7975	.001849
19	1.4401	1.3841	1.3281	1.2721	1.2161	1.1601	1.1041	1.0481	.9921	.9361	.8801	.8241	.001867
20	1.4738	1.4172	1.3606	1.3041	1.2475	1.1909	1.1343	1.0778	1.0212	.9646	.9080	.8515	.001886
21	1.5090	1.4518	1.3946	1.3374	1.2802	1.2230	1.1657	1.1085	1.0513	.9941	.9369	.8797	.001907
22	1.5457	1.4879	1.4301	1.3723	1.3145	1.2567	1.1989	1.1411	1.0833	1.0255	.9677	.9099	.001927
23	1.5840	1.5255	1.4669	1.4084	1.3499	1.2913	1.2328	1.1743	1.1157	1.0572	.9987	.9401	.001951
24	1.6240	1.5648	1.5055	1.4463	1.3871	1.3278	1.2686	1.2094	1.1501	1.0909	1.0317	.9724	.001974
25	1.6658	1.6058	1.5458	1.4858	1.4259	1.3659	1.3059	1.2459	1.1859	1.1260	1.0660	1.0060	.001999
26	1.7095	1.6487	1.5879	1.5271	1.4663	1.4055	1.3446	1.2838	1.2230	1.1622	1.1014	1.0406	.002027
27	1.7552	1.6935	1.6319	1.5702	1.5086	1.4470	1.3853	1.3236	1.2620	1.2003	1.1387	1.0770	.002055
28	1.8031	1.7405	1.6779	1.6153	1.5527	1.4901	1.4275	1.3649	1.3023	1.2397	1.1771	1.1145	.002087
29	1.8533	1.7895	1.7258	1.6620	1.5983	1.5345	1.4708	1.4070	1.3433	1.2795	1.2158	1.1520	.002125
30	1.9057	1.8412	1.7768	1.7123	1.6479	1.5834	1.5190	1.4545	1.3901	1.3256	1.2612	1.1967	.002148
31	1.9609	1.8951	1.8294	1.7636	1.6979	1.6321	1.5663	1.5006	1.4348	1.3691	1.3033	1.2376	.002192
32	2.0187	1.9518	1.8848	1.8179	1.7510	1.6840	1.6171	1.5502	1.4832	1.4163	1.3494	1.2824	.002231
33	2.0793	2.0111	1.9429	1.8747	1.8065	1.7383	1.6700	1.6018	1.5336	1.4654	1.3972	1.3290	.002273
34	2.1431	2.0735	2.0040	1.9344	1.8649	1.7953	1.6258	1.6562	1.5867	1.5171	1.4476	1.3780	.002318
35	2.2101	2.1394	2.0687	1.9980	1.9273	1.8566	1.7858	1.7151	1.6444	1.5737	1.5030	1.4323	.002357
36	2.2808	2.2086	2.1364	2.0641	1.9919	1.9197	1.8475	1.7753	1.7031	1.6308	1.5586	1.4864	.002407
37	2.3553	2.2817	2.2080	2.1344	2.0607	1.9871	1.9134	1.8398	1.7662	1.6925	1.6189	1.5452	.002455
38	2.4340	2.3588	2.2836	2.2084	2.1332	2.0580	1.9828	1.9076	1.8324	1.7572	1.6820	1.6068	.002507
39	2.5172	2.4404	2.3636	2.2868	2.2100	2.1332	2.0564	1.9797	1.9029	1.8261	1.7493	1.6725	.002560
40	2.6052	2.5268	2.4484	2.3700	2.2916	2.2132	2.1348	2.0564	1.9780	1.8996	1.8212	1.7428	.002613
41	2.6986	2.6184	2.5383	2.4581	2.3780	2.2978	2.2177	2.1375	2.0574	1.9772	1.8971	1.8169	.002672
42	2.7978	2.7155	2.6332	2.5510	2.4687	2.3864	2.3041	2.2218	2.1395	2.0572	1.9750	1.8927	.002743
43	2.9031	2.8185	2.7339	2.6493	2.5647	2.4801	2.3955	2.3110	2.2264	2.1418	2.0572	1.9726	.002820
44	3.0150	2.9270	2.8389	2.7509	2.6629	2.5748	2.4868	2.3988	2.3107	2.2227	2.1347	2.0466	.002934
45	3.1334	3.0415	2.9497	2.8578	2.7659	2.6741	2.5822	2.4903	2.3985	2.3066	2.2147	2.1229	.003062
46	3.2587	3.1621	3.0655	2.9689	2.8723	2.7757	2.6791	2.5826	2.4860	2.3894	2.2928	2.1962	.003220
47	3.3911	3.2896	3.1880	3.0865	2.9850	2.8834	2.7819	2.6804	2.5788	2.4773	2.3758	2.2742	.003384
48	3.5311	3.4236	3.3161	3.2085	3.1010	2.9935	2.8860	2.7785	2.6710	2.5634	2.4559	2.3484	.003584
49	3.6788	3.5654	3.4520	3.3386	3.2252	3.1118	2.9983	2.8849	2.7715	2.6581	2.5447	2.4313	.003780
50	3.8352	3.7152	3.5951	3.4751	3.3551	3.2351	3.1150	2.9950	2.8750	2.7550	2.6350	2.5149	.004001
51	4.0008	3.8734	3.7461	3.6187	3.4914	3.3640	3.2366	3.1093	2.9819	2.8546	2.7272	2.5999	.004245
52	4.1760	4.0409	3.9058	3.7706	3.6355	3.5004	3.3653	3.2302	3.0951	2.9600	2.8248	2.6897	.004504
53	4.3619	4.2177	4.0735	3.9293	3.7851	3.6409	3.4967	3.3525	3.2083	3.0641	2.9199	2.7757	.004807
54	4.5585	4.4052	4.2520	4.0987	3.9454	3.7921	3.6388	3.4856	3.3323	3.1790	3.0257	2.8725	.005109
55	4.7673	4.6037	4.4402	4.2766	4.1131	3.9495	3.7860	3.6224	3.4588	3.2953	3.1317	2.9682	.005452
56	4.9889	4.8143	4.6396	4.4649	4.2903	4.1156	3.9409	3.7663	3.5916	3.4169	3.2423	3.0676	.005820
57	5.2243	5.0378	4.8514	4.6649	4.4785	4.2920	4.1055	3.9191	3.7326	3.5462	3.3597	3.1733	.006215
58	5.4748	5.2754	5.0759	4.8765	4.6771	4.4776	4.2782	4.0788	3.8793	3.6799	3.4805	3.2810	.006647
59	5.7415	5.5280	5.3144	5.1009	4.8874	4.6739	4.4603	4.2468	4.0333	3.8198	3.6062	3.3927	.007117
60	6.0256	5.7961	5.5667	5.3372	5.1077	4.8783	4.6488	4.4193	4.1899	3.9604	3.7309	3.5015	.007649
61	6.3280	6.0812	5.8344	5.5876	5.3408	5.0940	4.8472	4.6005	4.3537	4.1069	3.8601	3.6133	.008226
62	6.6499	6.3840	6.1181	5.8521	5.5862	5.3203	5.0544	4.7885	4.5226	4.2566	3.9907	3.7248	.008864
63	6.9925	6.7059	6.4192	6.1326	5.8459	5.5593	5.2726	4.9860	4.6994	4.4127	4.1261	3.8394	.009555
64	7.3574	7.0480	6.7385	6.4290	6.1196	5.8101	5.5007	5.1912	4.8818	4.5723	4.2629	3.9534	.010315
65	7.7458	7.4116	7.0773	6.7431	6.4088	6.0746	5.7403	5.4061	5.0719	4.7376	4.4034	4.0691	.011141
66	8.1593	7.7981	7.4369	7.0757	6.7145	6.3533	5.9920	5.6308	5.2696	4.9084	4.5472	4.1861	.012040
67	8.5996	8.2089	7.8183	7.4276	7.0369	6.6463	6.2556	5.8649	5.4743	5.0836	4.6929	4.3023	.013020
68	9.0683	8.6459	8.2235	7.8012	7.3788	6.9564	6.5340	6.1117	5.6893	5.2669	4.8445	4.4222	.014079
69	9.5675	9.1112	8.6549	8.1985	7.7422	7.2859	6.8296	6.3733	5.9170	5.4606	5.0043	4.5480	.015210
70	10.0999	9.6067	9.1134	8.6202	8.1269	7.6337	7.1404	6.6472	6.1540	5.6607	5.1675	4.6742	.016441
71	10.6677	10.1347	9.6017	9.0687	8.5357	8.0027	7.4696	6.9366	6.4036	5.8706	5.3376	4.8046	.017767
72	11.2737	10.6977	10.1218	9.5458	8.9698	8.3939	7.8179	7.2419	6.6660	6.0900	5.5140	4.9381	.019199
73	11.9207	11.2985	10.6764	10.0542	9.4321	8.8099	8.1877	7.5656	6.9434	6.3213	5.6991	5.0770	.020738
74	12.6123	11.9401	11.2680	10.5958	9.9236	9.2514	8.5792	7.9071	7.2349	6.5627	5.8905	5.2184	.022406
75	13.3517	12.6257	11.8997	11.1737	10.4477	9.7217	8.9957	8.2698	7.5438	6.8178	6.0918	5.3658	.024200
76	14.1431	13.3593	12.5756	11.7918	11.0081	10.2243	9.4406	8.6568	7.8731	7.0893	6.3056	5.5218	.026125
77	14.9914	14.1449	13.2983	12.4518	11.6052	10.7587	9.9121	9.0656	8.2191	7.3725	6.5260	5.6794	.028218
78	15.9006	14.9861	14.0716	13.1571	12.2426	11.3281	10.4136	9.4991	8.5846	7.6701	6.7556	5.8411	.030483
79	16.8755	15.8883	14.9012	13.9140	12.9269	11.9397	10.9525	9.9654	8.9782	7.9911	7.0039	6.0168	.032902
80	17.9235	16.8584	15.7933	14.7283	13.6632	12.5981	11.5330	10.4680	9.4029	8.3378	7.2727	6.2077	.035502
81	19.0531	17.9054	16.7577	15.6100	14.4624	13.3147	12.1670	11.0193	9.8716	8.7240	7.5763	6.4286	.038256
82	20.2778	19.0428	17.8077	16.5727	15.3376	14.1026	12.8675	11.6325	10.3975	9.1624	7.9274	6.6923	.041168
83	21.6164	20.2876	18.9589	17.6301	16.3014	14.9726	13.6438	12.3151	10.9863	9.6576	8.3288	7.0001	.044292
84	23.0911	21.6621	20.2331	18.8042	17.3752	15.9462	14.5172	13.0883	11.6593	10.2303	8.8013	7.3724	.047632
85	24.7343	23.1930	21.6518	20.1105	18.5692	17.0280	15.4867	13.9454	12.4042	10.8629	9.3216	7.7804	.051375
86	26.5740	24.9097	23.2453	21.5810	19.9167	18.2524	16.5880	14.9237	13.2594	11.5951	9.9307	8.2664	.055477
87	28.6583	26.8524	25.0465	23.2405	21.4346	19.6287	17.8228	16.0169	14.2110	12.4050	10.5991	8.7932	.060197
88	31.0300	29.0605	27.0909	25.1214	23.1519	21.1823	19.2128	17.2433	15.2737	13.3042	11.3347	9.3651	.065651
89	33.7412	31.5788	29.4165	27.2541	25.0917	22.9294	20.7670	18.6046	16.4423	14.2799	12.1175	9.9552	.072079
90	36.8385	34.4540	32.0695	29.6850	27.3005	24.9160	22.5315	20.1471	17.7626	15.3781	12.9936	10.6091	.079483
91	40.4008	37.7541	35.1075	32.4608	29.8142	27.1675	24.5209	21.8742	19.2276	16.5809	13.9343	11.2876	.088222
92	44.4975	47.5338	38.5700	35.6063	32.6425	29.6788	26.7150	23.7513	20.7876	17.8238	14.8601	11.8963	.098791
93	49.1479	45.8029	42.4579	39.1130	35.7680	32.4230	29.0780	25.7330	22.3880	19.0430	15.6981	12.3531	.111499
94	54.3018	50.5175	46.7333	42.9490	39.1648	35.3805	31.5962	27.8120	24.0277	20.2435	16.4592	12.6750	.126142
95	59.8850	55.5470	51.2089	46.8709	42.5328	38.1948	33.8567	29.5187	25.1807	20.8426	16.5046	12.1665	.144601
96	65.2187	60.3317	55.4447	50.5578	45.6708	40.7838	35.8968	31.0099	26.1229	21.2359	16.3489	11.4620	.162899
97	70.0142	64.9607	59.9072	54.8538	49.8003	44.7468	39.6933	34.6399	29.5864	24.5329	19.4794	14.4260	.168449
98	77.5562	72.7208	67.8854	63.0500	58.2145	53.3791	48.5437	43.7083	38.8729	34.0374	29.2020	24.3666	.161180
99 or 10	**97.0874**	**97.3301**	**97.5728**	**97.8155**	**98.0583**	**98.3010**	**98.5437**	**98.7864**	**99.0291**	**99.2718**	**99.5146**	**99.7573**	**.008090**
Age.	0	1	2	3	4	5	6	7	8	9	10	11	Day.

Age.	0	1	2	3	4	5	6	7	8	9	10	11	Day.
10	1.7501	1.6984	1.6467	1.5950	1.5433	1.4916	1.4399	1.3882	1.3365	1.2848	1.2331	1.1814	.001723
11	1.7921	1.7406	1.6892	1.6377	1.5862	1.5348	1.4833	1.4318	1.3804	1.3289	1.2774	1.2260	.001715
12	1.8421	1.7903	1.7386	1.6868	1.6350	1.5833	1.5315	1.4797	1.4280	1.3762	1.3244	1.2727	.001725
13	1.8947	1.8421	1.7895	1.7369	1.6843	1.6317	1.5791	1.5265	1.4739	1.4213	1.3687	1.3161	.001753
14	1.9364	1.8841	1.8319	1.7796	1.7273	1.6751	1.6228	1.5705	1.5183	1.4660	1.4137	1.3615	.001742
15	1.9873	1.9347	1.8821	1.8295	1.7769	1.7243	1.6717	1.6192	1.5666	1.5140	1.4614	1.4088	.001753
16	2.0393	1.9864	1.9335	1.8805	1.8276	1.7747	1.7218	1.6688	1.6159	1.5630	1.5101	1.4571	.001764
17	2.0939	2.0407	1.9873	1.9339	1.8805	1.8272	1.7738	1.7205	1.6671	1.6138	1.5604	1.5071	.001778
18	2.1499	2.0961	2.0423	1.9885	1.9347	1.8809	1.8272	1.7734	1.7196	1.6658	1.6120	1.5582	.001793
19	2.2083	2.1540	2.0997	2.0454	1.9911	1.9369	1.8826	1.8283	1.7740	1.7197	1.6655	1.6112	.001809
20	2.2687	2.2139	2.1591	2.1043	2.0495	1.9946	1.9398	1.8850	1.8302	1.7754	1.7206	1.6657	.001827
21	2.3315	2.2762	2.2209	2.1655	2.1102	2.0549	1.9996	1.9443	1.8889	1.8336	1.7783	1.7230	.001844
22	2.3978	2.3418	2.2859	2.2299	2.1739	2.1180	2.0620	2.0060	1.9501	1.8941	1.8381	1.7822	.001865
23	2.4655	2.4090	2.3524	2.2958	2.2392	2.1827	2.1261	2.0695	2.0129	1.9564	1.8998	1.8432	.001885
24	2.5371	2.4799	2.4227	2.3655	2.3083	2.2511	2.1939	2.1367	2.0794	2.0222	1.9650	1.9078	.001907
25	2.6118	2.5539	2.4960	2.4380	2.3801	2.3222	2.2642	2.2063	2.1484	2.0904	2.0325	1.9746	.001931
26	2.6893	2.6307	2.5720	2.5133	2.4547	2.3960	2.3373	2.2786	2.2200	2.1613	2.1026	2.0440	.001955
27	2.7707	2.7111	2.6516	2.5921	2.5326	2.4731	2.4136	2.3541	2.2946	2.2351	2.1756	2.1161	.001983
28	2.8550	2.7945	2.7340	2.6734	2.6129	2.5524	2.4919	2.4313	2.3708	2.3103	2.2498	2.1892	.002017
29	2.9415	2.8804	2.8193	2.7582	2.6971	2.6360	2.5749	2.5138	2.4527	2.3916	2.3305	2.2694	.002037
30	3.0380	2.9757	2.9134	2.8512	2.7889	2.7266	2.6644	2.6021	2.5399	2.4776	2.4153	2.3531	.002075
31	3.1327	3.0694	3.0061	2.9428	2.8795	2.8161	2.7528	2.6895	2.6262	2.5629	2.4996	2.4363	.002110
32	3.2341	3.1697	3.1053	3.0408	2.9764	2.9120	2.8475	2.7831	2.7187	2.6542	2.5898	2.5254	.002147
33	3.3401	3.2745	3.2089	3.1433	3.0777	3.0121	2.9465	2.8808	2.8152	2.7496	2.6840	2.6184	.002187
34	3.4516	3.3849	3.3183	3.2517	3.1851	3.1185	3.0519	2.9853	2.9187	2.8521	2.7854	2.7188	.002220
35	3.5717	3.5037	3.4358	3.3679	3.3000	3.2320	3.1641	3.0962	3.0282	2.9603	2.8924	2.8244	.002264
36	3.6950	3.6258	3.5567	3.4875	3.4183	3.3492	3.2800	3.2108	3.1417	3.0725	3.0033	2.9341	.002305
37	3.8269	3.7564	3.6 59	3.6153	3.5448	3.4743	3.4038	3.3332	3.2627	3.1922	3.1217	3.0511	.002351
38	3.9656	3.8937	3.8218	3.7499	3.6780	3.6061	3.5342	3.4623	3.3904	3.3185	3.2466	3.1747	.002397
39	4.1129	4.0396	3.9663	3.8930	3.8198	3.7465	3.6732	3.6000	3.5267	3.4534	3.3801	3.3069	.002442
40	4.2696	4.1949	4.1201	4.0453	3.9705	3.8958	3.8210	3.7462	3.6714	3.5967	3.5219	3.4471	.002492
41	4.4354	4.3587	4.2821	4.2055	4.1288	4.0522	3.9756	3.8989	3.8223	3.7456	3.6690	3.5924	.002555
42	4.6082	4.5296	4.4509	4.3722	4.2936	4.2149	4.1362	4.0576	3.9789	3.9003	3.8216	3.7429	.002622
43	4.7911	4.7193	4.6275	4.5457	4.4639	4.3821	4.3003	4.2186	4.1368	4.0550	3.9732	3.8914	.002726
44	4.9736	4.8883	4.8030	4.7177	4 63 4	4.5470	4.4617	4.3764	4.2911	4.2058	4.1205	4.0352	.002844
45	5.1644	5.0747	4.9850	4.8953	4.8056	4.7158	4.6261	4.5364	4.4467	4.3570	4.2673	4.1776	.002990
46	5.3583	5.2640	5.1697	5.0754	4.9811	4.8868	4.7925	4.6982	4.6039	4.5096	4.4153	4.3210	.003143
47	5.5638	5.4639	5.3640	5.2641	5.1642	5.0642	4.9643	4.8644	4.7645	4.6646	4.5647	4.4648	.003330
48	5.7719	5.6665	5.5611	5.4557	5.3502	5.2448	5.1394	5.0340	4.9285	4.8231	4.7177	4.6122	.003514
49	5.9967	5.8851	5.7734	5.6618	5.5502	5.4386	5.3269	5.2153	5.1037	4.9921	4.8804	4.7688	.003720
50	6.2301	6.1116	5.9931	5.8746	5.7561	5.6376	5.5191	5.4006	5.2821	5.1636	5.0451	4.9266	.003950
51	6.4732	6.3475	6.2217	6.0959	5.9701	5.8443	5.7185	5.5928	5.4670	5.3412	5.2154	5.0896	.004192
52	6.7306	6.5963	6.4620	6.3277	6.1934	6.0591	5.9247	5.7904	5.6561	5.5218	5.3875	5.2532	.004477
53	6.9934	6.8505	6.7077	6.5648	6.4219	6.2791	6.1362	5.9934	5.8505	5.7077	5.5648	5.4220	.004762
54	7.2776	7.1251	6.9726	6.8201	6.6676	6.5151	6.3626	6.2100	6.0575	5.9050	5.7525	5.6000	.005083
55	7.5719	7.4089	7.2459	7.0830	6.9200	6.7571	6.5941	6.4312	6.2682	6.1052	5.9423	5.7793	.005432
56	7.8818	7.7077	7.5337	7.3597	7.1856	7.0116	6.8375	6.6635	6.4895	6.3154	6.1414	5.9673	.005801
57	8.2111	8.0249	7.8386	7.6524	7.4662	7.2799	7.0937	6.9075	6.7212	6.5350	6.3488	6.1625	.006207
58	8.5564	8.3569	8.1574	7.9580	7.7585	7.5590	7.3596	7.1601	6.9606	6.7612	6.5617	6.3622	.006649
59	8.9207	8.7062	8.4918	8.2773	8.0629	7.8484	7.6339	7.4195	7.2050	6.9906	6.7761	6.5617	.007148
60	9.2977	9.0669	8.8361	8.6053	8.3746	8.1438	7.9130	7.6822	7.4514	7.2206	6.9899	6.7591	.007693
61	9.6945	9.4457	9.1969	8.9481	8.6993	8.4505	8.2017	7.9529	7.7041	7.4553	7.2065	6.9577	.008293
62	10.1088	9.8405	9.5721	9.3038	9.0355	8.7671	8.4988	8.2305	7.9621	7.6938	7.4254	7.1571	.008944
63	10.5453	10.2555	9.9656	9.6758	9.3860	9.0961	8.8063	8.5165	8.2267	7.9368	7.6470	7.3572	.009661
64	11.0014	10.6882	10.3750	10.0618	9.7485	9.4353	9.1221	8.8089	8.4957	8.1825	7.8693	7.5560	.010440
65	11.4807	11.1421	10.8034	10.4640	10.1261	9.7874	9.4488	9.1101	8.7715	8.4328	8.0942	7.7555	.011288
66	11.9841	11.6177	11.2512	10.8848	10.5184	10.1519	9.7855	9.4190	9.0526	8.6862	8.3197	7.9533	.012214
67	12.5113	12.1149	11.7186	11.3222	10.9259	10.5295	10.1331	9.7368	9.3404	8.9441	8.5477	8.1514	.013212
68	13.0681	12.6398	12.2114	11.7831	11.3547	10.9264	10.4980	10.0697	9.6413	9.2130	8.7846	8.3563	.014278
69	13.6592	13.1960	12.7329	12.2698	11.8067	11.3435	10.8804	10.4173	9.9542	9.4911	9.0279	8.5648	.015437
70	14.2810	13.7804	13.2798	12.7792	12.2787	11.7781	11.2775	10.7769	10.2763	9.7757	9.2752	8.7746	.016686
71	14.9393	14.3983	13.8573	13.3163	12.7753	12.2343	11.6933	11.1524	10.6114	10.0704	9.5294	8.9884	.018033
72	15.6358	15.0514	14.4669	13.8825	13.2981	12.7136	12.1292	11.5448	10.9603	10.3759	9.7915	9.2070	.019481
73	16.3755	15.7441	15.1126	14.4812	13.8498	13.2184	12.5870	11.9555	11.3241	10.6927	10.0612	9.4298	.021047
74	17.1585	16.4764	15.7945	15.1125	14.4306	13.7487	13.0668	12.3848	11.7029	11.0210	10.3390	9.6570	.022732
75	17.9916	17.2550	16.5195	15.7835	15.0474	14.3114	13.5753	12.8393	12.1033	11.5672	10.6312	9.8951	.024535
76	18.8012	18.0863	17.2913	16.4964	15.7015	14.9065	14.1116	13.3167	12.5217	11.7268	10.9319	10.1369	.026498
77	19.8243	18.9657	18.1071	17.2486	16.3900	15.5314	14.6728	13.8143	12.9557	12.0971	11.2385	10.3800	.028619
78	20.8273	19.9007	18.9741	18.0476	17.1210	16.1944	15.2678	14.3413	13.4157	12.4881	11.5615	10.6350	.030886
79	21.9051	20.9058	19.9065	18.9072	17.9079	16.9086	15.9093	14.9100	13.9107	12.9114	11.9121	10.9128	.033310
80	23.0661	21.9899	20.9137	19.8375	18.7614	17.6852	16.6090	15.5328	14.4566	13.3804	12.3043	11.2281	.035873
81	24.3340	23.1770	22.9200	20.8630	19.7060	18.5490	17.3920	16.2350	15.0780	13.9210	12.7640	11.6070	.038567
82	25.7351	24.4921	23.2491	22.0061	20.7631	19.5201	18.2771	17.0341	15.7911	14.5481	13.3051	12.0621	.041433
83	27.2878	25.9535	24.6194	23.2852	21.9511	20.6169	19.2827	17.9485	16.6143	15.2801	13.9460	12.6118	.044473
84	29.0345	27.5993	26.1640	24.7288	23.2935	21.8583	20.4230	18.9878	17.5526	16.1173	14.6821	13.2468	.047841
85	30.9734	29.4201	27.8827	26.3374	24.7920	23.2467	21.7013	20.1560	18.6107	17.0653	15.5200	13.9746	.051511
86	33.1761	31.5054	29.8347	28.1641	26.4934	24.8227	23.1520	21.4814	19.8107	18.1400	16.4693	14.7987	.055689
87	35.6456	33.8306	32.0157	30.2007	28.3858	26.5708	24.7558	22.9409	21.1259	19.3110	17.4960	15.6811	.060496
88	38.4256	36.4411	34.4567	32.4722	30.4878	28.5033	26.5188	24.5344	22.5499	20.5655	18.5810	16.5966	.066148
89	41.5341	39.3543	37.1745	34.9947	32.8149	30.6351	28.4553	26.2755	24.0957	21.9159	19.7361	17.5563	.072660
90	45.0631	42.6541	40.2451	37.8360	35.4270	33.0180	30.6090	28.2000	25.7910	23.3820	20.9729	18.5639	.080300
91	49.0418	46.3551	43.6684	40.9818	38.2951	35.6084	32.9217	30.2351	27.5484	24.8617	22.1750	19.4884	.089556
92	53.4301	50.4056	47.3812	44.3566	41.3321	38.3076	35.2831	32.2586	29.2341	26.2096	23.1851	20.1606	.100817
93	58.1560	54.7345	51.3130	47.8915	44.4700	41.0485	37.6270	34.2055	30.7840	27.3625	23.9410	20.5195	.114050
94	63.1926	59.2618	55.3310	51.4002	47.4695	43.5387	39.6079	35.6771	31.7463	27.8155	23.8848	19.9540	.131026
95	67.7135	63.2282	58.7428	54.2575	49.7722	45.2869	40.8015	36.3162	31.8309	27.3456	22.8602	18.3749	.149511
96	71.7945	67.0893	62.3841	57.6789	52.9737	43.2685	43.5632	38.8580	34.1528	29.4476	24.7424	20.0372	.156840
97	79.3867	75.0272	70.6678	66.3083	61.9488	57.5894	53.2299	48.8704	44.5110	40.1515	35.7920	31.4326	.145315
98 or 11	**97.0374**	**97.3301**	**97.5728**	**97.8155**	**98.0583**	**98.3010**	**98.5437**	**98.7834**	**99.0291**	**99.2718**	**99.5146**	**99.7573**	**.008090**
10	96.0908	96.0744	96.0580	96.0416	96.0253	96.0089	95.9925	95.9761	95.9597	95.9433	95.9270	95.9106	.000546
Age.	0	1	2	3	4	5	6	7	8	9	10	11	Day.

Age.	0	1	2	3	4	5	6	7	8	9	10	11	Day.
10	2.3228	2.2730	2.2232	2.1733	2.1235	2.0737	2.0239	1.9741	1.9243	1.8744	1.8246	1.7748	.001660
11	2.3907	2.3406	2.2905	2.2405	2.1904	2.1403	2.0902	2.0402	1.9901	1.9400	1.8900	1.8399	.001669
12	2.4610	2.4107	2.3605	2.3102	2.2600	2.2097	2.1595	2.1092	2.0590	2.0087	1.9585	1.9082	.001675
13	2.5287	2.4783	2.4279	2.3774	2.3270	2.2766	2.2262	2.1758	2.1254	2.0750	2.0245	1.9741	.001680
14	2.6006	2.5499	2.4992	2.4485	2.3978	2.3471	2.2964	2.2458	2.1951	2.1444	2.0937	2.0430	.001690
15	2.6749	2.6239	2.5730	2.5220	2.4711	2.4201	2.3691	2.3182	2.2672	2.2163	2.1653	2.1144	.001698
16	2.7514	2.7001	2.6488	2.5975	2.5462	2.4949	2.4436	2.3923	2.3410	2.2897	2.2384	2.1871	.001710
17	2.8305	2.7788	2.7272	2.6755	2.6239	2.5722	2.5206	2.4690	2.4173	2.3656	2.3140	2.2623	.001722
18	2.9123	2.8602	2.8081	2.7561	2.7040	2.6519	2.5998	2.5478	2.4957	2.4436	2.3915	2.3395	.001736
19	2.9970	2.9445	2.8919	2.8394	2.7869	2.7343	2.6818	2.6293	2.5767	2.5242	2.4717	2.4191	.001751
20	3.0848	3.0318	2.9789	2.9260	2.8730	2.8200	2.7671	2.7141	2.6612	2.6082	2.5553	2.5023	.001765
21	3.1766	3.1231	3.0696	3.0161	2.9626	2.9091	2.8555	2.8020	2.7485	2.6950	2.6415	2.5880	.001783
22	3.2719	3.2179	3.1638	3.1098	3.0558	3.0018	2.9477	2.8937	2.8397	2.7857	2.7316	2.6776	.001801
23	3.3706	3.3160	3.2615	3.2069	3.1523	3.0978	3.0432	2.9886	2.9341	2.8795	2.8249	2.7704	.001819
24	3.4746	3.4194	3.3642	3.3090	3.2539	3.1987	3.1435	3.0883	3.0331	2.9780	2.9228	2.8676	.001839
25	3.5824	3.5266	3.4708	3.4150	3.3591	3.3033	3.2475	3.1917	3.1359	3.0800	3.0242	2.9684	.001860
26	3.6948	3.6383	3.5817	3.5252	3.4686	3.4121	3.3555	3.2990	3.2425	3.1859	3.1294	3.0728	.001885
27	3.8118	3.7544	3.6969	3.6395	3.5820	3.5246	3.4671	3.4097	3.3523	3.2948	3.2374	3.1799	.001915
28	3.9318	3.8739	3.8160	3.7581	3.7002	3.6423	3.5843	3.5264	3.4685	3.4106	3.3527	3.2948	.001930
29	4.0615	4.0026	3.9436	3.8847	3.8257	3.7668	3.7078	3.6489	3.5900	3.5310	3.4721	3.4131	.001965
30	4.1965	4.1367	4.0768	4.0170	3.9571	3.8973	3.8374	3.7776	3.7178	3.6579	3.5981	3.5382	.001995
31	4.3338	4.2730	4.2121	4.1513	4.0905	4.0297	3.9688	3.9080	3.8472	3.7864	3.7255	3.6647	.002027
32	4.4796	4.4177	4.3559	4.2940	4.2322	4.1703	4.1084	4.0466	3.9847	3.9229	3.8610	3.7992	.002062
33	4.6321	4.5694	4.5067	4.4440	4.3813	4.3186	4.2558	4.1931	4.1304	4.0677	4.0050	3.9423	.002090
34	4.7958	4.7319	4.6680	4.6041	4.5402	4.4763	4.4123	4.3484	4.2845	4.2206	4.1567	4.0928	.002130
35	4.9666	4.9017	4.8367	4.7718	4.7069	4.6420	4.5770	4.5121	4.4472	4.3823	4.3173	4.2524	.002164
36	5.1458	5.0797	5.0136	4.9475	4.8814	4.8153	4.7492	4.6832	4.6171	4.5510	4.4849	4.4188	.002203
37	5.3359	5.2686	5.2014	5.1341	5.0668	4.9996	4.9323	4.8650	4.7978	4.7305	4.6632	4.5960	.002242
38	5.5368	5.4684	5.3999	5.3315	5.2631	5.1946	5.1262	5.0578	4.9893	4.9209	4.8525	4.7840	.002281
39	5.7508	5.6811	5.6114	5.5417	5.4720	5.4023	5.3325	5.2628	5.1931	5.1234	5.0537	4.9840	.002323
40	5.9776	5.9063	5.8350	5.7636	5.6923	5.6210	5.5496	5.4783	5.4070	5.3357	5.2643	5.1930	.002377
41	6.2144	6.1413	6.0682	5.9951	5.9221	5.8490	5.7759	5.7028	5.6297	5.5566	5.4836	5.4105	.002436
42	6.4620	6.3861	6.3102	6.2343	6.1584	6.0825	6.0065	5.9306	5.8547	5.7788	5.7029	5.6270	.002530
43	6.7127	6.6336	6.5544	6.4753	6.3962	6.3171	6.2380	6.1588	6.0797	6.0006	5.9214	5.8423	.002637
44	6.9648	6.8816	6.7984	6.7152	6.6320	6.5488	6.4656	6.3825	6.2993	6.2161	6.1329	6.0497	.002773
45	7.2213	7.1338	7.0464	6.9589	6.8715	6.7840	6.6965	6.6091	6.5216	6.4342	6.3467	6.2593	.002915
46	7.4854	7.3927	7.3000	7.2072	7.1145	7.0218	6.9291	6.8364	6.7437	6.6510	6.5582	6.4655	.003090
47	7.7559	7.6580	7.5602	7.4623	7.3645	7.2666	7.1687	7.0709	6.9730	6.8752	6.7773	6.6795	.003262
48	8.0379	7.9342	7.8305	7.7268	7.6232	7.5195	7.4158	7.3121	7.2084	7.1047	7.0011	6.8974	.003456
49	8.3360	8.2259	8.1157	8.0056	7.8955	7.7854	7.6752	7.5651	7.4550	7.3449	7.2347	7.1246	.003671
50	8.6433	8.5263	8.4094	8.2924	8.1755	8.0585	7.9415	7.8246	7.7076	7.5907	7.4737	7.3568	.003898
51	8.9646	8.8396	8.7146	8.5896	8.4646	8.3396	8.2146	8.0897	7.9647	7.8397	7.7147	7.5897	.004166
52	9.2949	9.1619	9.0289	8.8959	8.7629	8.6299	8.4968	8.3638	8.2308	8.0978	7.9648	7.8318	.004433
53	9.6410	9.4989	9.3568	9.2146	9.0725	8.9304	8.7883	8.6462	8.5041	8.3620	8.2198	8.0777	.004737
54	10.0059	9.8540	9.7020	9.5501	9.3982	9.2463	9.0943	8.9424	8.7905	8.6386	8.4866	8.3347	.005064
55	10.3836	10.2212	10.0589	9.8965	9.7342	9.5718	9.4095	9.2471	9.0848	8.9224	8.7601	8.5977	.005412
56	10.7822	10.6084	10.4345	10.2607	10.0869	9.9131	9.7392	9.5654	9.3916	9.2178	9.0440	8.8701	.005794
57	11.2006	11.0143	10.8281	10.6418	10.4556	10.2693	10.0830	9.8968	9.7105	9.5243	9.3380	9.1518	.006208
58	11.6376	11.4372	11.2369	11.0365	10.8361	10.6358	10.4354	10.2350	10.0347	9.8343	9.6339	9.4336	.006679
59	12.0887	11.8730	11.6572	11.4415	11.2258	11.0101	10.7943	10.5786	10.3629	10.1472	9.9314	9.7157	.007191
60	12.5540	12.3213	12.0886	11.8558	11.6231	11.3904	11.1577	10.9250	10.6923	10.4595	10.2268	9.9941	.007757
61	13.0369	12.7858	12.5346	12.2835	12.0324	11.7812	11.5301	11.2790	11.0278	10.7767	10.5256	10.2744	.008371
62	13.5387	13.2673	12.9959	12.7245	12.4531	12.1817	11.9102	11.6388	11.3674	11.0960	10.8246	10.5532	.009047
63	14.0599	13.7664	13.4730	13.1795	12.8860	12.5926	12.2991	12.0056	11.7122	11.4187	11.1252	10.8318	.009782
64	14.6002	14.2827	13.9653	13.6478	13.3303	13.0129	12.6954	12.3779	12.0605	11.7430	11.4255	11.1081	.010582
65	15.1627	14.8190	14.4753	14.1316	13.7879	13.4442	13.1005	12.7569	12.4132	12.0695	11.7258	11.3821	.011456
66	15.7462	15.3743	15.0024	14.6304	14.2585	13.8866	13.5147	13.1428	12.7709	12.3990	12.0270	11.6551	.012397
67	16.3546	15.9525	15.5504	15.1483	14.7462	14.3441	13.9420	13.5399	13.1378	12.7357	12.3336	11.9315	.013403
68	16.9962	16.5613	16.1264	15.6915	15.2566	14.8217	14.3868	13.9520	13.5171	13.0822	12.6473	12.2124	.014496
69	17.6692	17.1990	16.7289	16.2587	15.7885	15.3184	14.8482	14.3780	13.9079	13.4377	12.9675	12.4974	.015672
70	18.3739	17.8657	17.3574	16.8492	16.3410	15.8328	15.3245	14.8163	14.3081	13.7999	13.2916	12.7834	.016941
71	19.1151	18.5660	18.0169	17.4678	16.9187	16.3696	15.8204	15.2713	14.7222	14.1731	13.6240	13.0749	.018303
72	19.8963	19.3030	18.7097	18.1164	17.5231	16.9298	16.3365	15.7433	15.1500	14.5567	13.9634	13.3701	.019776
73	20.7191	20.0783	19.4376	18.7968	18.1561	17.5153	16.8745	16.2338	15.5930	14.9523	14.3115	13.6708	.021358
74	21.5874	20.8958	20.2042	19.5125	18.8209	18.1293	17.4377	16.7461	16.0545	15.3628	14.6712	13.9796	.023054
75	22.5109	21.7640	21.0171	20.2703	19.5234	18.7765	18.0296	17.2828	16.5359	15.7890	15.0421	14.2953	.024896
76	23.4851	22.6787	21.8723	21.0659	20.2595	19.4531	18.6467	17.8404	17.0340	16.2276	15.4212	14.6148	.026880
77	24.5128	23.6427	22.7727	21.9026	21.0326	20.1625	19.2924	18.4224	17.5523	16.6823	15.8122	14.9422	.029002
78	25.6090	24.6709	23.7328	22.7947	21.8566	20.9185	19.9803	19.0422	18.1041	17.1660	16.2279	15.2898	.031270
79	26.7890	25.7792	24.7693	23.7595	22.7496	21.7398	20.7300	19.7201	18.7103	17.7004	16.6906	15.6807	.033661
80	28.0754	26.9904	25.9054	24.8203	23.7353	22.6503	21.5653	20.4803	19.3953	18.3102	17.2252	16.1402	.036167
81	29.5031	28.3386	27.1740	26.0095	24.8449	23.6804	22.5158	21.3513	20.1868	19.0222	17.8577	16.6931	.038818
82	31.0969	29.8488	28.6007	27.3525	26.1044	24.8563	23.6082	22.3601	21.1120	19.8638	18.6157	17.3676	.041604
83	32.8940	31.5539	30.2138	28.8738	27.5337	26.1936	24.8535	23.5135	22.1734	20.8333	19.4932	18.1532	.044669
84	34.9028	33.4637	32.0246	30.5856	29.1465	27.7074	26.2683	24.8293	23.3902	21.9511	20.5120	19.0730	.047969
85	37.1635	35.6122	34.0609	32.5096	30.9584	29.4071	27.8558	26.3045	24.7532	23.2020	21.6507	20.0994	.051709
86	39.7020	38.0229	36.3438	34.6647	32.9856	31.3065	29.6274	27.9483	26.2692	24.5901	22.9110	21.2319	.055970
87	42.5245	40.6957	38.8668	37.0380	35.2091	33.3803	31.5514	29.7226	27.8938	26.0649	24.2361	22.4072	.060961
88	45.6421	43.6415	41.6409	39.6403	37.6397	35.6391	33.6385	31.6379	29.6373	27.6367	25.6361	23.6355	.066687
89	49.1177	46.9153	44.7129	42.5105	40.3081	38.1057	35.9032	33.7008	31.4984	29.2960	27.0936	24.8912	.073413
90	52.9933	50.5476	48.1018	45.6561	43.2103	40.7646	38.3188	35.8731	33.4274	30.9816	28.5359	26.0901	.081525
91	57.2025	54.4603	51.7181	48.9760	46.2338	43.4916	40.7494	38.0072	35.2650	32.5228	29.7807	27.0385	.091406
92	61.6336	58.5394	55.4452	52.3510	49.2568	46.1626	43.0684	39.9743	36.8801	33.7859	30.6917	27.5975	.103140
93	66.2458	62.6910	59.1362	55.5813	52.0265	48.4717	44.9169	41.3621	37.8073	34.2524	30.6976	27.1428	.118494
94	70.3251	66.2601	62.1951	58.1302	54.0652	50.0002	45.9352	41.8703	37.8053	33.7403	29.6753	25.6104	.135499
95	73.7746	69.4567	65.1389	60.8210	56.5032	52.1853	47.8674	43.5496	39.2317	34.9139	30.5960	26.2782	.143928
96	80.5507	76.4939	72.4370	68.3802	64.3234	60.2665	56.2097	52.1529	48.0960	44.0392	39.9824	35.9255	.135228
97 or 12	**97.0874**	**97.3301**	**97.5728**	**97.8155**	**98.0583**	**98.3010**	**98.5437**	**98.7864**	**99.0291**	**99.2718**	**99.5146**	**99.7573**	**.008090**
11	96.0852	96.0674	96.0495	96.0317	96.0139	95.9960	95.9782	95.9604	95.9425	95.9247	95.9069	95.8890	.000594
10	95.5632	95.5077	95.4523	95.3968	95.3414	95.2859	95.2304	95.1750	95.1195	95.0641	95.0086	94.9532	.001848
Age.	0	1	2	3	4	5	6	7	8	9	10	11	Day.

Age.	0	1	2	3	4	5	6	7	8	9	10	11	Day.
10	2.9181	2.8697	2.8212	2.7728	2.7243	2.6759	2.6274	2.5790	2.5306	2.4821	2.4337	2.3852	.001615
11	3.0060	2.9574	2.9089	2.8603	2.8117	2.7632	2.7146	2.6660	2.6175	2.5689	2.5203	2.4718	.001619
12	3.0981	3.0494	3.0008	2.9521	2.9035	2.8548	2.8061	2.7575	2.7088	2.6602	2.6115	2.5629	.001622
13	3.1889	3.1400	3.0912	3.0423	2.9934	2.9446	2.8957	2.8468	2.7980	2.7491	2.7002	2.6514	.001629
14	3.2837	3.2346	3.1856	3.1365	3.0875	3.0384	2.9894	2.9403	2.8913	2.8422	2.7932	2.7441	.001635
15	3.3821	3.3328	3.2834	3.2341	3.1848	3.1354	3.0861	3.0368	2.9874	2.9381	2.8888	2.8394	.001644
16	3.4829	3.4333	3.3837	3.3341	3.2845	3.2349	3.1852	3.1356	3.0860	3.0364	2.9868	2.9372	.001653
17	3.5875	3.5375	3.4876	3.4376	3.3877	3.3377	3.2877	3.2378	3.1878	3.1379	3.0879	3.0380	.001665
18	3.6952	3.6449	3.5945	3.5442	3.4938	3.4435	3.3931	3.3428	3.2925	3.2421	3.1918	3.1414	.001678
19	3.8067	3.7560	3.7053	3.6546	3.6040	3.5533	3.5026	3.4519	3.4012	3.3505	3.2999	3.2492	.001689
20	3.9231	3.8720	3.8208	3.7696	3.7185	3.6673	3.6162	3.5650	3.5139	3.4627	3.4116	3.3604	.001705
21	4.0434	3.9918	3.9403	3.8887	3.8371	3.7856	3.7340	3.6824	3.6309	3.5793	3.5277	3.4762	.001719
22	4.1692	4.1172	4.0651	4.0131	3.9611	3.9090	3.8570	3.8050	3.7529	3.7009	3.6489	3.5968	.001734
23	4.2997	4.2472	4.1946	4.1421	4.0895	4.0370	3.9844	3.9319	3.8794	3.8268	3.7743	3.7217	.001751
24	4.4362	4.3831	4.3300	4.2770	4.2239	4.1708	4.1177	4.0646	4.0115	3.9584	3.9054	3.8523	.001769
25	4.5783	4.5246	4.4709	4.4172	4.3635	4.3098	4.2561	4.2024	4.1487	4.0950	4.0413	3.9876	.001790
26	4.7258	4.6713	4.6168	4.5623	4.5078	4.4533	4.3988	4.3443	4.2898	4.2353	4.1808	4.1263	.001817
27	4.8777	4.8228	4.7680	4.7131	4.6583	4.6034	4.5486	4.4937	4.4389	4.3840	4.3292	4.2743	.001828
28	5.0400	4.9842	4.9285	4.8727	4.8169	4.7612	4.7054	4.6496	4.5939	4.5381	4.4823	4.4266	.001859
29	5.2074	5.1508	5.0943	5.0377	4.9812	4.9246	4.8684	4.8115	4.7550	4.6984	4.6419	4.5853	.001885
30	5.3841	5.3267	5.2693	5.2119	5.1545	5.0971	5.0397	4.9824	4.9250	4.8676	4.8102	4.7528	.001913
31	5.5647	5.5064	5.4481	5.3898	5.3315	5.2732	5.2150	5.1567	5.0984	5.0401	4.9818	4.9235	.001943
32	5.7558	5.6968	5.6378	5.5788	5.5198	5.4608	5.4018	5.3428	5.2838	5.2248	5.1658	5.1068	.001967
33	5.9589	5.8989	5.8389	5.7789	5.7189	5.6589	5.5989	5.5389	5.4789	5.4189	5.3589	5.2989	.002000
34	6.1719	6.1110	6.0501	5.9892	5.9283	5.8674	5.8065	5.7457	5.6848	5.6239	5.5630	5.5021	.002030
35	6.3976	6.3357	6.2738	6.2119	6.1500	6.0881	6.0262	5.9644	5.9025	5.8406	5.7787	5.7168	.002063
36	6.6334	6.5705	6.5076	6.4447	6.3819	6.3190	6.2561	6.1932	6.1303	6.0674	6.0046	5.9417	.002096
37	6.8840	6.8201	6.7563	6.6924	6.6286	6.5647	6.5009	6.4370	6.3732	6.3093	6.2455	6.1816	.002128
38	7.1496	7.0847	7.0197	6.9548	6.8899	6.8250	6.7600	6.6951	6.6302	6.5653	6.5003	6.4354	.002164
39	7.4313	7.3650	7.2987	7.2324	7.1661	7.0998	7.0335	6.9672	6.9009	6.8346	6.7683	6.7020	.002210
40	7.7269	7.6591	7.5912	7.5234	7.4556	7.3878	7.3200	7.2521	7.1843	7.1165	7.0486	6.9808	.002261
41	8.0360	7.9656	7.8952	7.8249	7 7545	7.6841	7.6137	7.5434	7.4730	7.4026	7.3322	7.2619	.002346
42	8.3488	8.2755	8.2022	8.1289	8.0556	7.9823	7.9090	7.8358	7.7625	7.6892	7.6159	7.5426	.002443
43	8.6662	8.5892	8.5121	8.4351	8.3581	8.2810	8.2040	8.1270	8.0499	7.9729	7.8959	7.8188	.002568
44	8.9813	8.9003	8.8193	8.7383	8.6574	8.5764	8.4954	8.4144	8.3334	8.2524	8.1715	8.0905	.002699
45	9.3052	9.2193	9.1334	9.0475	8.9616	8.8757	8.7897	8.7038	8.6179	8.5320	8.4461	8.3602	.002863
46	9.6314	9.5407	9.4500	9.3593	9.2686	9.1779	9.0872	8.9965	8.9058	8.8151	8.7244	8.6337	.003023
47	9.9726	9.8764	9.7803	9.6841	9.5880	9.4918	9.3957	9.2995	9.2034	9.1072	9.0111	8.9150	.003205
48	10.3247	10.2225	10.1203	10.0181	9.9159	9.8137	9.7114	9.6092	9.5070	9.4048	9.3026	9.2004	.003407
49	10.6933	10.5847	10.4761	10.3674	10.2588	10.1502	10.0416	9.9330	9.8244	9.7157	9.6071	9.4985	.003629
50	11.0750	10.9588	10.8426	10.7264	10.6103	10.4941	10.3779	10.2617	10.1455	10.0293	9.9132	9.7970	.003873
51	11.4654	11.3417	11.2180	11.0943	10.9706	10.8469	10.7231	10.5994	10.4757	10.3520	10.2283	10.1046	.004123
52	11.8748	11.7425	11.6102	11.4780	11.3457	11.2134	11.0811	10.9488	10.8165	10.6842	10.5520	10.4197	.004409
53	12.2974	12.1559	12.0143	11.8728	11.7312	11.5897	11.4481	11.3066	11.1651	11.0235	10.8820	10.7404	.004718
54	12.7412	12.5899	12.4385	12.2872	12.1359	11.9846	11.8332	11.6819	11.5306	11.3793	11.2280	11.0766	.005044
55	13.2026	13.0405	12.8783	12.7162	12.5541	12.3919	12.2298	12.0677	11.9055	11.7434	11.5813	11.4191	.005404
56	13.6852	13.5113	13.3375	13.1636	12.9898	12.8160	12.6421	12.4682	12.2944	12.1205	11.9467	11.7728	.005795
57	14.1897	14.0026	13.8154	13.6283	13.4412	13.2541	13.0670	12.8798	12.6927	12.5056	12.3184	12.1313	.006237
58	14.7080	14.5064	14.3048	14.1032	13.9016	13.7000	13.4984	13.2968	13.0952	12.8936	12.6920	12.4904	.006720
59	15.2414	15.0238	14.8062	14.5886	14.3710	14.1534	13.9358	13.7183	13.5007	13.2831	13.0655	12.8479	.007253
60	15.7870	15.5520	15.3171	15.0821	14.8471	14.6122	14.3772	14.1422	13.9073	13.6723	13.4373	13.2024	.007832
61	16.3513	16.0972	15.8431	15.5890	15.3349	15.0808	14.8267	14.5726	14.3185	14.0644	13.8103	13.5562	.008470
62	16.9317	16.6568	16.3819	16.1070	15.8320	15.5571	15.2822	15.0073	14.7324	14.4574	14.1825	13.9076	.009164
63	17.5458	17.2470	16.9482	16.6493	16.3505	16.0517	15.7529	15.4541	15.1553	14.8564	14.5576	14.2588	.009960
64	18.1480	17.8257	17.5034	17.1810	16.8587	16.5364	16.2141	15.8918	15.5695	15.2471	14.9248	14.6025	.010744
65	18.7841	18.4351	18.0862	17.7372	17.3883	17.0393	16.6904	16.3414	15.9925	15.6435	15.2946	14.9456	.011632
66	19.4425	19.0651	18.6876	18.3102	17.9327	17.5553	17.1778	16.8004	16.4230	16.0455	15.6681	15.2906	.012581
67	20.1290	19.7206	19.3122	18.9038	18.4955	18.0871	17.6787	17.2703	16.8619	16.4535	16.0452	15.6368	.013613
68	20.8457	20.4040	19.9624	19.5207	19.0791	18.6374	18.1958	17.7541	17.3125	16.8708	16.4292	15.9875	.014722
69	21.5946	21.1171	20.6396	20.1621	19.6846	19.2071	18.7296	18.2522	17.7747	17.2972	16.8197	16.3422	.015916
70	22.3751	21.8591	21.3431	20.8271	20.3111	19.7951	19.2791	18.7631	18.2471	17.7311	17.2151	16.6991	.017200
71	23.1935	22.6359	22.0783	21.5208	20.9632	20.4056	19.8480	19.2905	18.7329	18.1753	17.6177	17.0602	.018586
72	24.0504	23.4482	22.8460	22.2437	21.6415	21.0393	20.4371	19.8349	19.2327	18.6304	18.0282	17.4260	.020074
73	24.9508	24.3008	23.6508	23.0008	22.3508	21.7008	21.0508	20.4008	19.7508	19.1008	18.4508	17.8008	.021667
74	25.9003	25.1985	24.4967	23.7949	23.0931	22.3913	21.6895	20.9877	20.2859	19.5841	18.8823	18.1805	.023393
75	26.9002	26.1425	25.3847	24.6270	23.8693	23.1116	22.3538	21.5961	20.8384	20.0807	19.3230	18.5652	.025257
76	27.9515	27.1342	26.3168	25.4995	24.6822	23.8648	23.0475	22.2302	21.4128	20.5955	19.7782	18.9608	.027244
77	29.0635	28.1825	27.3014	26.4204	25.5393	24.6583	23.7772	22.8962	22.0152	21.1341	20.2531	19.3720	.029368
78	30.2523	29.3042	28.3560	27.4079	26.4598	25.5116	24.5635	23.6154	22.6672	21.7191	20.7710	19.8228	.031604
79	31.5464	30.5282	29.5099	28.4917	27.4734	26.4552	25.4370	24.4187	23.4005	22.3822	21.3640	20.3457	.033941
80	32.9787	31.8865	30.7943	29.7022	28.6100	27.5178	26.4256	25.3335	24.2413	23.1491	22.0570	20.9648	.036406
81	34.5817	33.4123	32.2429	31.0735	29.9042	28.7348	27.5654	26.3960	25.2266	24.0572	22.8879	21.7185	.038979
82	36.3972	35.1435	33.8898	32.6361	31.3824	30.1287	28.8750	27.6214	26.3677	25.1140	23.8603	22.6066	.041790
83	38.4294	37.0857	35.7420	34.3983	33.0546	31.7109	30.3672	29.0236	27.6799	26.3362	24.9925	23.6488	.044790
84	40.7250	39.2803	37.8357	36.3910	34.9463	33.5017	32.0570	30.6123	29.1677	27.7230	26.2783	24.8337	.048155
85	43.2823	41.7231	40.1639	38.6047	37.0455	35.4863	33.9271	32.3680	30.8088	29.2496	27.6904	26.1312	.051973
86	46.1268	44.4347	42.7426	41.0506	39.3585	37.6664	35.9743	34.2823	32.5902	30.8981	29.2060	27.5140	.056402
87	49.2368	47.3929	45.5491	43.7052	41.8614	40.0175	38.1736	36.3298	34.4859	32.6421	30.7982	28.9544	.061462
88	52.6649	50.6434	48.6218	46.6003	44.5787	42.5572	40.5356	38.5141	36.4926	34.4710	3[illegible].4495	30.4279	.067385
89	56.4300	54.1937	51.9574	49.7212	47.4849	45.2486	43.0123	40.7761	38.5398	36.3035	34.0672	31.8310	.074542
90	60.4829	57.9862	55.4895	52.9928	50.4961	47.9994	45.5027	43.0061	40.5094	38.0127	35.5160	33.0193	.083223
91	64.6971	61.8912	59.0854	56.2795	53.4737	50.6678	47.8620	45.0561	42.2503	39.4444	36.6386	33.8327	.093528
92	69.0008	65.7852	62.5696	59.3540	56.1384	52.9228	49.7072	46.4916	43.2760	40.0604	36.8448	33.6292	.107187
93	72.7359	69.0590	65.3820	61.7051	58.0281	54.3512	50.6742	46.9973	43.3204	39.6434	35.9665	32.2895	.122565
94	75.8473	71.9349	68.0225	64.1101	60.1977	56.2853	52.3730	48.4606	44.5482	40.6358	36.7234	32.8110	.130413
95	81.8453	78.1251	74.4048	70.6846	66.9643	63.2441	59.5238	55.8036	52.0834	48.3631	44.6429	40.9226	.124008
96 or 13	**97.0874**	**97.3301**	**97.5728**	**97.8155**	**98.0583**	**98.3010**	**98.5437**	**98.7864**	**99.0291**	**99.2718**	**99.5146**	**99.7573**	**.008090**
12	96.0794	96.0601	96.0407	96.0214	96.0020	95.9827	95.9633	95.9440	95.9247	95.9053	95.8860	95.8666	.000645
11	95.5546	95.4975	95.4403	95.3832	95.3261	95.2690	95.2118	95.1547	95.0976	95.0405	94.9833	94.9262	.001904
10	95 1669	95.1005	95.0341	94.9677	94.9013	94.8349	94.7684	94.7020	94.6356	94.5692	94.5028	94.4364	.002213
Age.	0	1	2	3	4	5	6	7	8	9	10	11	Day.

Age.	0	1	2	3	4	5	6	7	8	9	10	11	Day.
10	3.5300	3.4831	3.4361	3.3892	3.3422	3.2953	3.2483	3.2014	3.1545	3.1075	3.0606	3.0136	.001565
11	3.6394	3.5924	3.5454	3.4984	3.4515	3.4045	3.3575	3.3105	3.2635	3.2165	3.1696	3.1226	.001566
12	3.7543	3.7072	3.6601	3.6130	3.5659	3.5188	3.4716	3.4245	3.3774	3.3303	3.2832	3.2361	.001570
13	3.8678	3.8206	3.7733	3.7261	3.6788	3.6316	3.5843	3.5371	3.4899	3.4426	3.3954	3.3481	.001575
14	3.9865	3.9390	3.8916	3.8441	3.7967	3.7492	3.7018	3.6543	3.6069	3.5594	3.5120	3.4645	.001582
15	4.1088	4.0611	4.0135	3.9658	3.9182	3.8705	3.8228	3.7752	3.7275	3.6799	3.6322	3.5846	.001588
16	4.2348	4.1869	4.1389	4.0910	4.0430	3.9951	3.9471	3.8992	3.8513	3.8033	3.7554	3.7074	.001598
17	4.3649	4.3167	4.2684	4.2202	4.1719	4.1237	4.0754	4.0272	3.9790	3.9307	3.8825	3.8342	.001608
18	4.4980	4.4496	4.4011	4.3527	4.3043	4.2558	4.2074	4.1590	4.1105	4.0621	4.0137	3.9652	.001614
19	4.6387	4.5898	4.5409	4.4920	4.4431	4.3942	4.3453	4.2965	4.2476	4.1987	4.1498	4.1009	.001630
20	4.7831	4.7339	4.6846	4.6354	4.5861	4.5369	4.4876	4.4384	4.3892	4.3399	4.2907	4.2414	.001641
21	4.9336	4.8840	4.8344	4.7847	4.7351	4.6855	4.6359	4.5863	4.5367	4.4870	4.4374	4.3878	.001654
22	5.0905	5.0405	4.9904	4.9404	4.8903	4.8403	4.7902	4.7402	4.6902	4.6401	4.5901	4.5400	.001666
23	5.2532	5.2027	5.1522	5.1017	5.0513	5.0008	4.9503	4.8998	4.8493	4.7988	4.7484	4.6979	.001683
24	5.4232	5.3722	5.3212	5.2702	5.2192	5.1682	5.1171	5.0661	5.0151	4.9641	4.9131	4.8621	.001700
25	5.5997	5.5480	5.4963	5.4446	5.3929	5.3412	5.2895	5.2378	5.1861	5.1344	5.0827	5.0310	.001723
26	5.7813	5.7294	5.6774	5.6255	5.5735	[illegible]	5.4696	5.4177	5.3658	5.3138	5.2619	5.2099	.001731
27	5.9747	5.9220	5.8692	5.8165	5.7637	5.7110	5.6582	5.6055	5.5528	5.5000	5.4473	5.3945	.001758
28	6.1739	6.1205	6.0671	6.0137	5.9603	5.9069	5.8534	5.8000	5.7466	5.6932	5.6398	5.5864	.001780
29	6.3820	6.3279	6.2737	6.2196	6.1655	6.1114	6.0572	6.0031	5.9490	5.8949	5.8407	5.7866	.001804
30	6.6010	6.5461	6.4912	6.4363	6.3815	6.3266	6.2717	6.2168	6.1619	6.1070	6.0522	5.9973	.001829
31	6.8261	6.7706	6.7152	6.6597	6.6042	6.5488	6.4933	6.4378	6.3824	6.3269	6.2714	6.2160	.001849
32	7.0665	7.0102	6.9538	6.8975	6.8412	6.7849	6.7285	6.6722	6.6159	6.5596	6.5032	6.4469	.001877
33	7.3182	7.2611	7.2041	7.1470	7.0899	7.0329	6.9758	6.9187	6.8617	6.8046	6.7475	6.6905	.001902
34	7.5843	7.5264	7.4685	7.4106	7.3527	7.2948	7.2368	7.1789	7.1210	7.0631	7.0052	6.9473	.001930
35	7.8650	7.8063	7.7476	7.6888	7.6301	7.5714	7.5127	7.4540	7.3953	7.3365	7.2778	7.2191	.001957
36	8.1597	8.1002	8.0407	7.9811	7.9216	7.8621	7.8026	7.7431	7.6836	7.6240	7.5645	7.5050	.001984
37	8.4731	8.4127	8.3523	8.2919	8.2315	8.1711	8.1107	8.0504	7.9900	7.9296	7.8692	7.8088	.002013
38	8.8045	8.7429	8.6813	8.6198	8.5582	8.4966	8.4350	8.3735	8.3119	8.2503	8.1887	8.1272	.002052
39	9.1528	9.0899	9.0271	8.9642	8.9013	8.8385	8.7756	8.7127	8.6499	8.5870	8.5241	8.4613	.002095
40	9.5182	9.4530	9.3879	9.3227	9.2575	9.1924	9.1272	9.0620	8.9969	8.9317	8.8665	8.8014	.002172
41	9.8901	9.8223	9.7545	9.6867	9.6189	9.5511	9.4832	9.4154	9.3476	9.2798	9.2120	9.1442	.002260
42	10.2671	10.1958	10.1246	10.0533	9.9821	9.9108	9.8396	9.7683	9.6971	9.6258	9.5546	9.4833	.002375
43	10.6448	10.5699	10.4950	10.4202	10.3453	10.2704	10.1955	10.1207	10.0458	9.9709	9.8960	9.8212	.002496
44	11.0245	10.9450	10.8655	10.7861	10.7066	10.6271	10.5476	10.4682	10.3887	10.3092	10.2297	10.1503	.002649
45	11.4077	11.3238	11.2398	11.1559	11.0719	10.9880	10.9040	10.8201	10.7362	10.6522	10.5683	10.4843	.002798
46	11.8017	11.7127	11.6236	11.5346	11.4455	11.3565	11.2674	11.1784	11.0894	11.0003	10.9113	10.8222	.002968
47	12.2099	12.1152	12.0204	11.9257	11.8310	11.7363	11.6415	11.5468	11.4521	11.3574	11.2626	11.1679	.003157
48	12.6293	12.5285	12.4278	12.3270	12.2263	12.1255	12.0248	11.9240	11.8233	11.7225	11.6218	11.5210	.003358
49	13.0687	12.9608	12.8530	12.7451	12.6372	12.5294	12.4215	12.3136	12.2058	12.0979	11.9900	11.8822	.003595
50	13.5160	13.4011	13.2861	13.1712	13.0562	12.9413	12.8263	12.7114	12.5965	12.4815	12.3666	12.2516	.003831
51	13.9817	13.8587	13.7357	13.6126	13.4896	13.3666	13.2436	13.1206	12.9976	12.8745	12.7515	12.6285	.004100
52	14.4634	14.3317	14.2000	14.0682	13.9365	13.8048	13.6730	13.5413	13.4096	13.2779	13.1461	13.0144	.004391
53	14.9608	14.8198	14.6789	14.5379	14.3969	14.2560	14.1150	13.9740	13.8331	13.6921	13.5511	13.4102	.004699
54	15.4836	15.3325	15.1814	15.0304	14.8793	14.7282	14.5771	14.4261	14.2750	14.1239	13.9728	13.8216	.005036
55	16.0243	15.8621	15.7000	15.5378	15.3756	15.2135	15.0513	14.8891	14.7270	14.5648	14.4026	14.2405	.005405
56	16.5879	16.4132	16.2385	16.0638	15.8891	15.7144	15.5397	15.3650	15.1903	15.0156	14.8409	14.6662	.005823
57	17.1684	16.9801	16.7917	16.6034	16.4151	16.2268	16.0384	15.8501	15.6618	15.4735	15.2851	15.0968	.006277
58	17.7636	17.5602	17.3568	17.1533	16.9499	16.7465	16.5431	16.3397	16.1363	15.9328	15.7294	15.5260	.006780
59	18.3717	18.1519	17.9321	17.7123	17.4926	17.2728	17.0530	16.8332	16.6134	16.3936	16.1739	15.9541	.007326
60	18.9930	18.7551	18.5173	18.2794	18.0416	17.8037	17.5659	17.3280	17.0902	16.8523	16.6145	16.3766	.007913
61	19.6301	19.3726	19.1151	18.8576	18.6001	18.3426	18.0851	17.8277	17.5702	17.3127	17.0552	16.7977	.008583
62	20.2826	20.0037	19.7248	19.4460	19.1671	18.8882	18.6093	18.3304	18.0515	17.7726	17.4938	17.2149	.009206
63	20.9525	20.6503	20.3480	20.0458	19.7435	19.4413	19.1390	18.8368	18.5346	18.2323	17.9301	17.6278	.010075
64	21.6376	21.3102	20.9828	20.6554	20.3280	20.0006	19.6732	19.3458	19.0184	18.6910	18.3636	18.0362	.010913
65	22.3425	21.9882	21.6339	21.2796	20.9254	20.5711	20.2168	19.8625	19.5082	19.1540	18.7997	18.4454	.011809
66	23.0726	22.6891	22.3056	21.9221	21.5386	21.1551	20.7716	20.3882	20.0047	19.6212	19.2377	18.8542	.012783
67	23.8280	23.4131	22.9982	22.5834	22.1685	21.7536	21.3387	20.9239	20.5090	20.0941	19.6792	19.2644	.013829
68	24.6142	24.1655	23.7168	23.2681	22.8195	22.3708	21.9221	21.4734	21.0247	20.5760	20.1274	19.6787	.014956
69	25.4322	24.9472	24.4623	23.9773	23.4924	23.0074	22.5224	22.0375	21.5525	21.0676	20.5826	20.0977	.016165
70	26.2831	25.7590	25.2348	24.7107	24.1866	23.6625	23.1383	22.6142	22.0901	21.5660	21.0418	20.5177	.017471
71	27.1703	26.6042	26.0380	25.4719	24.9058	24.3396	23.7735	23.2074	22.6412	22.0751	21.5090	20.9428	.018871
72	28.0974	27.4863	26.8753	26.2642	25.6532	25.0421	24.4311	23.8200	23.2090	22.5980	21.9869	21.3758	.020368
73	29.0715	28.4118	27.7520	27.0923	26.4326	25.7729	25.1131	24.4534	23.7937	23.1340	22.4742	21.8145	.021991
74	30.0910	29.3788	28.6665	27.9543	27.2421	26.5298	25.8176	25.1054	24.3931	23.6809	22.9687	22.2564	.023741
75	31.1593	30.3911	29.6230	28.8548	28.0867	27.3185	26.5504	25.7822	25.0141	24.2460	23.4778	22.7096	.025605
76	32.2866	31.4588	30.6310	29.8032	28.9754	28.1476	27.3198	26.4920	25.6642	24.8364	24.0086	23.1808	.027593
77	33.4824	32.5918	31.7012	30.8106	29.9201	29.0295	28.1389	27.2483	26.3577	25.4671	24.5766	23.6860	.029686
78	34.7753	33.8192	32.8631	31.9070	30.9509	29.9948	29.0386	28.0825	27.1264	26.1703	25.2142	24.2581	.031870
79	36.2031	35.1781	34.1530	33.1280	32.1030	31.0779	30.0529	29.0279	28.0028	26.9778	25.9528	24.9277	.034168
80	37.7961	36.6993	35.6026	34.5058	33.4090	32.3123	31.2155	30.1187	29.0220	27.9252	26.8284	25.7317	.036559
81	39.6022	38.4275	37.2528	36.0782	34.9035	33.7288	32.5541	31.3795	30.2048	29.0301	27.8554	26.6808	.039156
82	41.6306	40.3735	39.1164	37.8592	36.6021	35.3450	34.0879	32.8308	31.5737	30.3165	29.0594	27.8023	.041904
83	43.9215	42.5725	41.2236	39.8746	38.5256	37.1767	35.8277	34.4787	33.1298	31.7808	30.4318	29.0829	.044965
84	46.4802	45.0281	43.5760	42.1239	40.6718	39.2197	37.7675	36.3154	34.8633	33.4112	31.9591	30.5070	.048403
85	49.3062	47.7348	46.1635	44.5921	43.0208	41.4494	39.8780	38.3067	36.7353	35.1640	33.5926	32.0213	.052378
86	52.3959	50.6898	48.9837	47.2776	45.5715	43.8654	42.1593	40.4532	38.7471	37.0410	35.3349	33.6288	.056870
87	55.7688	53.9055	52.0421	50.1788	48.3155	46.4522	44.5888	42.7255	40.8622	38.9989	37.1355	35.2722	.062111
88	59.4364	57.3835	55.3306	53.2777	51.2248	49.1719	47.1190	45.0661	43.0132	40.9603	38.9074	36.8545	.068430
89	63.3359	61.0526	58.7694	56.4861	54.2029	51.9196	49.6364	47.3531	45.0699	42.7866	40.5034	38.2201	.076108
90	67.3611	64.8060	62.2509	59.6957	57.1406	54.5855	52.0304	49.4753	46.9202	44.3650	41.8099	39.2548	.085170
91	71.4277	68.5109	65.5942	62.6774	59.7606	56.8439	53.9271	51.0103	48.0936	45.1768	42.2600	39.3433	.097225
92	74.9111	71.5843	68.2575	64.9307	61.6039	58.2771	54.9503	51.6235	48.2967	44.9699	41.6431	38.3163	.110893
93	77.7605	74.2224	70.6843	67.1462	63.6082	60.0701	56.5320	52.9939	49.4558	45.9177	42.3797	38.8416	.117936
94	83.2004	79.8325	76.4646	73.0967	69.7288	66.3609	62.9930	59.6250	56.2571	52.8892	49.5213	46.1534	.112263
95 or 14	**97.0874**	**97.3301**	**97.5728**	**97.8155**	**98.0583**	**98.3010**	**98.5437**	**98.7864**	**99.0291**	**99.2718**	**99.5146**	**99.7573**	**.008090**
13	96.0733	96.0524	96.0314	96.0105	95.9896	95.9686	95.9477	95.9268	95.9058	95.8849	95.8640	95.8430	.000698
12	95.5457	95.4868	95.4280	95.3691	95.3103	95.2514	95.1925	95.1337	95.0748	95.0160	94.9571	94.8983	.001962
11	95.1561	95.0880	95.0198	94.9517	94.8836	94.8154	94.7473	94.6792	94.6110	94.5429	94.4748	94.4066	.002271
10	94.6560	94.5991	94.5423	94.4854	94.4286	94.3717	94.3148	94.2580	94.2011	94.1443	94.0874	94.0306	.001895
Age.	0	1	2	3	4	5	6	7	8	9	10	11	Day.

Age.	0	1	2	3	4	5	6	7	8	9	10	11	Day.
10	4.1599	4.1145	4.0692	4.0238	3.9784	3.9331	3.8877	3.8423	3.7970	3.7516	3.7062	3.6609	.001512
11	4.2918	4.2464	4.2009	4.1555	4.1100	4.0646	4.0191	3.9737	3.9283	3.8828	3.8374	3.7919	.001515
12	4.4290	4.3835	4.3380	4.2925	4.2470	4.2015	4.1560	4.1106	4.0651	4.0196	3.9741	3.9286	.001518
13	4.5661	4.5204	4.4748	4.4291	4.3835	4.3378	4.2922	4.2465	4.2009	4.1552	4.1096	4.0640	.001522
14	4.7085	4.6627	4.6169	4.5711	4.5253	4.4795	4.4337	4.3880	4.3422	4.2964	4.2506	4.2048	.001528
15	4.8556	4.8096	4.7636	4.7176	4.6716	4.6256	4.5796	4.5336	4.4876	4.4416	4.3956	4.3496	.001533
16	5.0066	4.9604	4.9141	4.8679	4.8217	4.7755	4.7292	4.6830	4.6368	4.5906	4.5443	4.4981	.001541
17	5.1628	5.1164	5.0700	5.0235	4.9771	4.9307	4.8842	4.8378	4.7914	4.7450	4.6985	4.6521	.001547
18	5.3247	5.2780	5.2312	5.1845	5.1378	5.0911	5.0443	4.9976	4.9509	4.9042	4.8574	4.8107	.001557
19	5.4922	5.4452	5.3982	5.3512	5.3042	5.2572	5.2102	5.1632	5.1162	5.0692	5.0222	4.9752	.001567
20	5.6660	5.6187	5.5714	5.5241	5.4769	5.4296	5.3823	5.3350	5.2877	5.2404	5.1932	5.1459	.001576
21	5.8472	5.7996	5.7519	5.7043	5.6567	5.6090	5.5614	5.5138	5.4661	5.4185	5.3709	5.3232	.001588
22	6.0356	5.9876	5.9396	5.8916	5.8437	5.7957	5.7477	5.6997	5.6517	5.6037	5.5558	5.5078	.001599
23	6.2314	6.1830	6.1346	6.0861	6.0377	5.9893	5.9409	5.8925	5.8441	5.7956	5.7472	5.6988	.001614
24	6.4351	6.3861	6.3371	6.2881	6.2391	6.1901	6.1410	6.0920	6.0430	5.9940	5.9450	5.8960	.001633
25	6.6451	6.5960	6.5468	6.4976	6.4485	6.3993	6.3502	6.3010	6.2519	6.2027	6.1536	6.1044	.001638
26	6.8675	6.8176	6.7678	6.7180	6.6681	6.6182	6.5684	6.5185	6.4687	6.4188	6.3690	6.3191	.001662
27	7.0971	7.0467	6.9963	6.9459	6.8955	6.8451	6.7947	6.7443	6.6939	6.6435	6.5931	6.5427	.001680
28	7.3362	7.2852	7.2342	7.1832	7.1322	7.0812	7.0301	6.9791	6.9281	6.8771	6.8261	6.7751	.001700
29	7.5858	7.5341	7.4825	7.4308	7.3792	7.3275	7.2759	7.2242	7.1726	7.1210	7.0693	7.0176	.001722
30	7.8481	7.7960	7.7439	7.6918	7.6397	7.5876	7.5355	7.4835	7.4314	7.3793	7.3272	7.2751	.001736
31	8.1214	8.0686	8.0157	7.9629	7.9101	7.8573	7.8044	7.7516	7.6988	7.6460	7.5931	7.5403	.001761
32	8.4093	8.3559	8.3024	8.2490	8.1956	8.1422	8.0887	8.0353	7.9819	7.9285	7.8750	7.8216	.001781
33	8.7128	8.6587	8.6046	8.5504	8.4963	8.4422	8.3881	8.3340	8.2799	8.2257	8.1716	8.1175	.001804
34	9.0325	8.9777	8.9230	8.8682	8.8134	8.7586	8.7038	8.6491	8.5943	8.5395	8.4847	8.4300	.001826
35	9.3705	9.3151	9.2597	9.2043	9.1489	9.0935	9.0381	8.9827	8.9273	8.8719	8.8165	8.7611	.001847
36	9.7263	9.6702	9.6141	9.5580	9.5019	9.4458	9.3896	9.3335	9.2774	9.2213	9.1652	9.1091	.001870
37	10.1037	10.0466	9.9895	9.9324	9.8753	9.8182	9.7611	9.7040	9.6469	9.5898	9.5327	9.4756	.001903
38	10.4996	10.4414	10.3832	10.3250	10.2668	10.2086	10.1504	10.0923	10.0341	9.9759	9.9177	9.8595	.001940
39	10.9156	10.8553	10.7951	10.7348	10.6746	10.6143	10.5540	10.4938	10.4335	10.3733	10.3130	10.2528	.002008
40	11.3414	11.2788	11.2161	11.1535	11.0909	11.0282	10.9656	10.9030	10.8403	10.7777	10.7151	10.6524	.002088
41	11.7750	11.7092	11.6434	11.5776	11.5118	11.4460	11.3802	11.3144	11.2486	11.1828	11.1170	11.0512	.002193
42	12.2098	12.1407	12.0715	12.0024	11.9333	11.8641	11.7950	11.7259	11.6567	11.5876	11.5185	11.4493	.002304
43	12.6494	12.5760	12.5026	12.4292	12.3558	12.2824	12.2090	12.1357	12.0623	11.9889	11.9155	11.8421	.002446
44	13.0858	13.0083	12.9307	12.8532	12.7756	12.6981	12.6205	12.5430	12.4655	12.3879	12.3104	12.2328	.002585
45	13.5338	13.4515	13.3692	13.2869	13.2046	13.1223	13.0400	12.9577	12.8754	12.7931	12.7108	12.6285	.002743
46	13.9919	13.9043	13.8166	13.7290	13.6413	13.5537	13.4660	13.3784	13.2908	13.2031	13.1155	13.0278	.002921
47	14.4643	14.3710	14.2777	14.1844	14.0912	13.9979	13.9046	13.8113	13.7180	13.6247	13.5315	13.4382	.003109
48	14.9514	14.8514	14.7514	14.6514	14.5514	14.4514	14.3513	14.2513	14.1513	14.0513	13.9513	13.8513	.003333
49	15.4531	15.3464	15.2398	15.1331	15.0265	14.9198	14.8132	14.7065	14.5999	14.4932	14.3866	14.2800	.003555
50	15.9719	15.8576	15.7434	15.6291	15.5149	15.4006	15.2864	15.1721	15.0579	14.9436	14.8294	14.7151	.003808
51	16.5063	16.3838	16.2614	16.1389	16.0164	15.8940	15.7715	15.6490	15.5266	15.4041	15.2816	15.1592	.004082
52	17.0588	16.9276	16.7965	16.6653	16.5341	16.4030	16.2718	16.1406	16.0095	15.8783	15.7471	15.6160	.004372
53	17.6310	17.4902	17.3495	17.2087	17.0679	16.9272	16.7864	16.6456	16.5049	16.3641	16.2233	16.0826	.004692
54	18.2285	18.0773	17.9262	17.7750	17.6239	17.4727	17.3215	17.1704	17.0192	16.8681	16.7169	16.5658	.005038
55	18.8456	18.6826	18.5196	18.3566	18.1936	18.0306	17.8676	17.7047	17.5417	17.3787	17.2157	17.0527	.005433
56	19.4804	19.3045	19.1287	18.9528	18.7770	18.6011	18.4252	18.2494	18.0735	17.8977	17.7218	17.5460	.005862
57	20.1328	19.9427	19.7526	19.5625	19.3724	19.1823	18.9922	18.8022	18.6121	18.4220	18.2319	18.0418	.006336
58	20.7974	20.5919	20.3863	20.1808	19.9753	19.7697	19.5642	19.3587	19.1531	18.9476	18.7421	18.5365	.006851
59	21.4758	21.2532	21.0306	20.8081	20.5855	20.3629	20.1403	19.9178	19.6952	19.4726	19.2500	19.0275	.007419
60	22.1645	21.9234	21.6822	21.4411	21.2000	20.9589	20.7177	20.4766	20.2355	19.9944	19.7532	19.5121	.008037
61	22.8682	22.6069	22.3455	22.0842	21.8229	21.5616	21.3002	21.0389	20.7776	20.5163	20.2550	19.9936	.008711
62	23.5859	23.3025	23.0191	22.7357	22.4523	22.1689	21.8855	21.6022	21.3188	21.0354	20.7520	20.4686	.009446
63	24.3181	24.0110	23.7038	23.3967	23.0895	22.7824	22.4752	22.1681	21.8610	21.5538	21.2467	20.9395	.010238
64	25.0662	24.7337	24.4011	24.0686	23.7361	23.4036	23.0710	22.7385	22.4060	22.0735	21.7410	21.4084	.011084
65	25.8369	25.4768	25.1167	24.7566	24.3965	24.0364	23.6763	23.3163	22.9562	22.5961	22.2360	21.8759	.012003
66	26.6301	26.2404	25.8506	25.4609	25.0712	24.6814	24.2917	23.9020	23.5122	23.1225	22.7328	22.3430	.012991
67	27.4491	27.0275	26.6058	26.1842	25.7625	25.3409	24.9192	24.4976	24.0760	23.6543	23.2327	22.8110	.014055
68	28.2982	27.8424	27.3865	26.9307	26.4748	26.0190	25.5631	25.1073	24.6515	24.1956	23.7398	23.2839	.015195
69	29.1802	28.6875	28.1947	27.7020	27.2092	26.7165	26.2237	25.7310	25.2383	24.7455	24.2528	23.7600	.016425
70	30.0935	29.5612	29.0289	28.4966	27.9643	27.4320	26.8996	26.3673	25.8350	25.3027	24.7704	24.2381	.017743
71	31.0444	30.4698	29.8952	29.3206	28.7461	28.1715	27.5969	27.0223	26.4477	25.8731	25.2986	24.7240	.019153
72	32.0385	31.4181	30.7978	30.1774	29.5570	28.9367	28.3163	27.6959	27.0756	26.4552	25.8348	25.2145	.020679
73	33.0755	32.4058	31.7361	31.0664	30.3967	29.7270	29.0573	28.3877	27.7180	27.0483	26.3786	25.7089	.022323
74	34.1565	33.4343	32.7121	31.9899	31.2677	30.5455	29.8233	29.1012	28.3790	27.6568	26.9346	26.2124	.024073
75	35.2932	34.5151	33.7370	32.9588	32.1807	31.4026	30.6244	29.8463	29.0682	28.2901	27.5120	26.7338	.025937
76	36.4961	35.6592	34.8223	33.9854	33.1486	32.3117	31.4748	30.6379	29.8010	28.9641	28.1273	27.2904	.027896
77	37.7868	36.8886	35.9904	35.0923	34.1941	33.2959	32.3977	31.4996	30.6014	29.7032	28.8050	27.9069	.029939
78	39.2026	38.2400	37.2774	36.3149	35.3523	34.3897	33.4271	32.4646	31.5020	30.5394	29.5768	28.6143	.032086
79	40.7782	39.7488	38.7194	37.6900	36.6606	35.6312	34.6018	33.5725	32.5431	31.5137	30.4843	29.4549	.034313
80	42.5584	41.4566	40.3548	39.2530	38.1513	37.0495	35.9477	34.8459	33.7441	32.6423	31.5406	30.4388	.036726
81	44.5592	43.3813	42.2034	41.0254	39.8475	38.6696	37.4917	36.3138	35.1359	33.9580	32.7800	31.6021	.039264
82	46.8230	45.5609	44.2988	43.0367	41.7746	40.5125	39.2503	37.9882	36.7261	35.4640	34.2019	32.9398	.042070
83	49.3503	47.9943	46.6383	45.2823	43.9263	42.5703	41.2143	39.8584	38.5024	37.1464	35.7904	34.4344	.045200
84	52.1461	50.6826	49.2190	47.7555	46.2919	44.8284	43.3648	41.9013	40.4378	38.9742	37.5107	36.0471	.048785
85	55.1842	53.5997	52.0152	50.4307	48.8462	47.2617	45.6771	44.0926	42.5081	40.9236	39.3391	37.7546	.052817
86	58.4967	56.7724	55.0481	53.3238	51.5996	49.8753	48.1510	46.4267	44.7024	42.9781	41.2539	39.5296	.057476
87	62.0672	60.1747	58.2822	56.3897	54.4972	52.6047	50.7122	48.8197	46.9272	45.0347	43.1422	41.2497	.063083
88	65.8316	63.7352	61.6388	59.5424	57.4460	55.3496	53.2532	51.1568	49.0604	46.9640	44.8676	42.7712	.069880
89	69.6781	67.3410	65.0038	62.6667	60.3296	57.9925	55.6553	53.3182	50.9811	48.6440	46.3068	43.9697	.077904
90	73.5381	70.8812	68.2243	65.5674	62.9105	60.2536	57.5966	54.9397	52.2828	49.6259	46.9690	44.3121	.088563
91	76.8273	73.8089	70.7906	67.7722	64.7539	61.7355	58.7171	55.6988	52.6804	49.6621	46.6437	43.6254	.100612
92	79.4870	76.2866	73.0863	69.8859	66.6855	63.4852	60.2848	57.0844	53.8841	50.6837	47.4833	44.2830	.106679
93	84.4513	81.4086	78.3660	75.3233	72.2807	69.2380	66.1954	63.1527	60.1101	57.0674	54.0248	50.9821	.101422
94 or 15	**97.0874**	**97.3301**	**97.5728**	**97.8155**	**98.0583**	**98.3010**	**98.5437**	**98.7864**	**99.0291**	**99.2718**	**99.5146**	**99.7573**	**.008090**
14	96.0670	96.0444	96.0218	95.9992	95.9767	95.9541	95.9315	95.9089	95.8863	95.8637	95.8412	95.8186	.000753
13	95.5364	95.4757	95.4150	95.3543	95.2936	95.2329	95.1722	95.1116	95.0509	94.9902	94.9295	94.8688	.002023
12	95.1449	95.0750	95.0050	94.9351	94.8652	94.7952	94.7253	94.6554	94.5854	94.5155	94.4456	94.3756	.002331
11	94.6414	94.5830	94.5245	94.4660	94.4076	94.3491	94.2907	94.2322	94.1738	94.1153	94.0569	93.9984	.001948
10	94.0170	93.9707	93.9245	93.8782	93.8320	93.7857	93.7394	93.6932	93.6469	93.6007	93.5544	93.5082	.001542
Age.	0	1	2	3	4	5	6	7	8	9	10	11	Day.

Age.	0	1	2	3	4	5	6	7	8	9	10	11	Day.
10	4.8086	4.7648	4.7209	4.6771	4.6333	4.5894	4.5456	4.5018	4.4579	4.4141	4.3703	4.3264	.001461
11	4.9627	4.9189	4.8750	4.8312	4.7874	4.7435	4.6997	4.6559	4.6120	4.5682	4.5244	4.4805	.001461
12	5.1232	5.0793	5.0355	4.9916	4.9477	4.9039	4.8600	4.8161	4.7723	4.7284	4.6845	4.6407	.001462
13	5.2835	5.2395	5.1955	5.1515	5.1076	5.0636	5.0196	4.9756	4.9316	4.8876	4.8437	4.7997	.001466
14	5.4504	5.4063	5.3621	5.3180	5.2739	5.2297	5.1856	5.1415	5.0973	5.0532	5.0091	4.9649	.001471
15	5.6223	5.5780	5.5337	5.4894	5.4451	5.4008	5.3565	5.3123	5.2680	5.2237	5.1794	5.1351	.001476
16	5.7991	5.7547	5.7102	5.6658	5.6214	5.5770	5.5325	5.4881	5.4437	5.3993	5.3548	5.3104	.001481
17	5.9826	5.9380	5.8933	5.8486	5.8040	5.7593	5 7147	5.6700	5.6254	5.5807	5.5361	5.4914	.001488
18	6.1718	6.1270	6.0821	6.0372	5.9924	5.9475	5.9027	5.8578	5.8130	5.7681	5.7233	5.6784	.001495
19	6.3683	6.3232	6.2782	6.2331	6.1881	6.1430	6.0980	6.0529	6.0078	5.9628	5.9177	5.8727	.001502
20	6.5724	6.5271	6.4817	6.4364	6.3911	6.3458	6.3004	6.2551	6.2098	6.1645	6.1191	6.0738	.001511
21	6.7846	6.7390	6.6934	6.6478	6.6022	6.5566	6.5110	6.4655	6.4199	6.3743	6.3287	6.2831	.001520
22	7.0055	6.9596	6.9136	6.8677	6.8218	6.7758	6.7299	6.6840	6.6380	6.5921	6.5462	6.5002	.001531
23	7.2344	7.1880	7.1415	7.0951	7.0487	7.0022	6.9558	6.9094	6.8629	6.8165	6.7701	6.7236	.001548
24	7.4710	7.4245	7.3780	7.3315	7.2850	7.2385	7.1920	7.1456	7.0991	7.0526	7.0061	6.9596	.001550
25	7.7210	7.6739	7.6268	7.5798	7.5327	7.4856	7.4385	7.3915	7.3444	7.2973	7.2502	7.2032	.001569
26	7.9788	7.9313	7.8837	7.8362	7.7887	7.7412	7.6936	7.6461	7.5986	7.5511	7.5035	7.4560	.001584
27	8.2475	8.1995	8.1515	8.1034	8.0554	8.0074	7.9594	7.9114	7.8634	7.8153	7.7673	7.7193	.001600
28	8.5272	8.4786	8.4301	8.3815	8.3330	8.2844	8.2359	8.1873	8.1388	8.0902	8.0417	7.9931	.001618
29	8.8192	8.7703	8.7214	8.6726	8.6237	8.5748	8.5260	8.4771	8.4282	8.3793	8.3304	8.2816	.001629
30	9.1287	9.0792	9.0298	8.9803	8.9308	8.8814	8.8319	8.7824	8.7330	8.6835	8.6340	8.5846	.001648
31	9.4484	9.3984	9.3485	9.2985	9.2486	9.1986	9.1486	9.0987	9.0487	8.9988	8.9488	8.8989	.001665
32	9.7868	9.7363	9.6858	9.6353	9.5848	9.5343	9.4837	9.4332	9.3827	9.3322	9.2817	9.2312	.001683
33	10.1427	10.0917	10.0406	9.9896	9.9386	9.8876	9.8365	9.7855	9.7345	9.6835	9.6324	9.5814	.001701
34	10.5182	10.4667	10.4152	10.3637	10.3122	10.2607	10.2092	10.1577	10.1062	10.0547	10.0032	9.9517	.001717
35	10.9158	10.8638	10.8117	10.7597	10.7076	10.6556	10.6035	10.5515	10.4995	10.4474	10.3954	10.3433	.001735
36	11.3338	11.2809	11.2281	11.1752	11.1224	11.0695	11.0166	10.9638	10.9109	10.8581	10.8052	10.7524	.001762
37	11.7738	11.7200	11.6663	11.6125	11.5588	11.5050	11.4512	11.3975	11.3437	11.2900	11.2362	11.1825	.001792
38	12.2353	12.1797	12.1241	12.0685	12.0129	11.9573	11.9016	11.8460	11.7904	11.7348	11.6792	11.6236	.001853
39	12.7097	12.6519	12.5942	12.5364	12.4786	12.4209	12.3631	12.3053	12.2476	12.1898	12.1320	12.0743	.001925
40	13.1950	13.1343	13.0737	13.0130	12.9523	12.8917	12.8310	12.7703	12.7097	12.6490	12.5883	12.5277	.002020
41	13.6840	13.6203	13.5566	13.4928	13.4291	13.3654	13.3017	13.2380	13.1743	13.1105	13.0468	12.9831	.002124
42	14.1780	14.1103	14.0427	13.9750	13.9074	13.8397	13.7720	13.7044	13.6367	13.5691	13.5014	13.4338	.002255
43	14.6718	14.6003	14.5288	14.4573	14.3858	14.3143	14.2428	14.1713	14.0998	14.0283	13.9568	13.8853	.002383
44	15.1703	15.0944	15.0184	14.9425	14.8665	14.7906	14.7146	14.6387	14.5628	14.4868	14.4109	14.3349	.002531
45	15.6796	15.5987	15.5177	15.4368	15.3559	15.2749	15.1940	15.1131	15.0321	14.9512	14.8703	14.7893	.002698
46	16.1981	16.1136	16.0290	15.9445	15.8600	15.7755	15.6910	15.6064	15.5219	15.4374	15.3528	15.2683	.002817
47	16.7360	16.6434	16.5509	16.4583	16.3657	16.2732	16.1806	16.0880	15.9955	15.9029	15.8103	15.7178	.003085
48	17.2824	17.1836	17.0847	16.9859	16.8871	16.7883	16.6894	16.5906	16.4918	16.3930	16.2941	16.1953	.003294
49	17.8521	17.7461	17.6401	17.5342	17.4282	17.3222	17.2162	17.1103	17.0043	16.8983	16.7923	16.6864	.003532
50	18.4361	18.3224	18.2086	18.0949	17.9812	17.8675	17.7537	17.6400	17.5263	17.4126	17.2988	17.1851	.003791
51	19.0374	18.9155	18.7936	18.6716	18.5497	18.4278	18.3059	18.1840	18.0621	17.9401	17.8182	17.6963	.004064
52	19.6608	19.5298	19.3988	19.2679	19.0369	19.0059	18.8750	18.7440	18.6130	18.4820	18.3510	18.2201	.004366
53	20.3037	20.1629	20.0221	19.8813	19.7405	19.5997	19.4590	19.3182	19.1774	19.0366	18.8958	18.7550	.004693
54	20.9731	20.8211	20.6692	20.5172	20.3653	20.2133	20.0613	19.9094	19.7574	19.6055	19.4535	19.3016	.005065
55	21.6570	21.4929	21.3287	21.1646	21.0005	20.8364	20.6722	20.5081	20.3440	20.1799	20.0157	19.8516	.005471
56	22.3590	22.1814	22.0039	21.8263	21.6487	21.4712	21.2936	21.1160	20.9385	20.7609	20.5833	20.4058	.005919
57	23.0760	22.8839	22.6917	22.4996	22.3074	22.1153	21.9231	21.7310	21.5389	21.3467	21.1546	20.9624	.006405
58	23.8058	23.5976	23.3893	23.1811	22.9729	22.7646	22.5564	22.3482	22.1399	21.9317	21.7235	21.5152	.006941
59	24.5464	24.3236	24.1009	23.8781	23.6554	23.4326	23.2098	22.9871	22.7643	22.5416	22.3188	22.0961	.007425
60	25.2966	25.0518	24.8070	24.5621	24.3173	24.0725	23.8276	23.5828	23.3380	23.0932	22.8483	22.6035	.008161
61	26.0603	25.7946	25.5289	25.2632	24.9976	24.7319	24.4662	24.2005	23.9348	23.6691	23.4035	23.1378	.008856
62	26.8351	26.5470	26.2588	25.9707	25.6826	25.3945	25.1063	24.8182	24.5301	24.2420	23.9538	23.6657	.009604
63	27.6250	27.3129	27.0008	26.6887	26.3766	26.0645	25.7524	25.4404	25.1283	24.8162	24.5041	24.1920	.010403
64	28.4333	28.0952	27.7570	27.4189	27.0808	26.7427	26.4045	26.0664	25.7283	25.3902	25.0520	24.7139	.011271
65	29.2616	28.8955	28.5294	28.1633	27.7972	27.4311	27.0650	26.6988	26.3327	25.9666	25.6005	25.2344	.012203
66	30.1126	29.7164	29.3201	28.9239	28.5277	28.1314	27.7352	27.3390	26.9427	26.5465	26.1503	25.7540	.013208
67	30.9890	30.5605	30.1320	29.7034	29.2749	28.8464	28.4178	27.9893	27.5608	27.1323	26.7037	26.2752	.014284
68	31.8964	31.4331	30.9697	30.5064	30.0431	29.5797	29.1164	28.6531	28.1897	27.7264	27.2631	26.7997	.015443
69	32.8347	32.3341	31.8335	31.3329	30.8323	30.3317	29.8311	29.3305	28.8299	28.3293	27.8287	27.3281	.016687
70	33.8057	33.2653	32.7249	32.1844	31.6440	31.1036	30.5632	30.0228	29.4824	28.9420	28.4015	27.8611	.018014
71	34.8171	34.2336	33.6501	33.0666	32.4831	31.8996	31.3161	30.7326	30.1491	29.5656	28.9821	28.3986	.019450
72	35.8678	35.2379	34.6080	33.9781	33.3482	32.7183	32.0884	31.4586	30.8287	30.1988	29.5689	28.9390	.020996
73	36.9599	36.2807	35.6015	34.9223	34.2431	33.5639	32.8846	32.2054	31.5262	30.8470	30.1678	29.4886	.022640
74	38.1025	37.3708	36.6391	35.9073	35.1756	34.4439	33.7122	32.9805	32.2488	31.5170	30.7853	30.0536	.024390
75	39.3074	38.5206	37.7338	36.9470	36.1602	35.3734	34.5866	33.7999	33.0131	32.2263	31.4395	30.6527	.026226
76	40.5966	39.7525	38.9083	38.0642	37.2201	36.3760	35.5318	34.6877	33.8436	32.9995	32.1553	31.3112	.028137
77	42.0001	41.0958	40.1915	39.2871	38.3828	37.4785	36.5742	35.6699	34.7656	33.8612	32.9569	32.0526	.030144
78	43.5524	42.5857	41.6189	40.6522	39.6855	38.7187	37.7520	36.7853	35.8185	34.8518	33.8851	32.9183	.032224
79	45.3010	44.2668	43.2327	42.1985	41.1644	40.1302	39.0960	38.0619	37.0277	35.9936	34.9594	33.9253	.034472
80	47.2605	46.1556	45.0508	43.9459	42.8411	41.7362	40.6313	39.5265	38.4216	37.3168	36.2119	35.1071	.036828
81	49.4773	48.2947	47.1120	45.9294	44.7468	43.5641	42.3815	41.1989	40.0162	38.8336	37.6510	36.4683	.039421
82	51.9554	50.6867	49.4179	48.1492	46.8804	45.6117	44.3430	43.0742	41.8055	40.5367	39.2680	37.9992	.042291
83	54.6948	53.3280	51.9612	50.5945	49.2277	47.8609	46.4941	45.1274	43.7606	42.3938	41.0270	39.6603	.045559
84	57.6747	56.1988	54.7229	53.2470	51.7711	50.2952	48.8192	47.3433	45 8674	44.3915	42.9156	41.4397	.049197
85	60.9044	59.3028	57.7013	56.0997	54.4981	52.8966	51.2950	49.6934	48 0919	46.4903	44.8887	43.2872	.053385
86	64.3793	62.6278	60.8762	59.1247	57.3732	55.6216	53.8701	52.1186	50.3670	48.6155	46.8640	45.1124	.058384
87	68.0155	66.0825	64.1496	62.2166	60.2837	58.3507	56.4177	54.4848	52.5518	50.6189	48.6859	46.7530	.064432
88	71.7048	69.5585	67.4122	65.2659	63.1196	60.9733	58.8270	56.6807	54.5344	52.3881	50.2418	48.0955	.071543
89	75.3738	72.9428	70.5118	68.0808	65.6498	63.2188	60.7878	58.3569	55.9259	53.4949	51.0639	48.6329	.081033
90	78.4936	75.7434	72.9933	70.2431	67.4930	64.7428	61.9927	59.2425	56.4924	53.7422	50.9921	48.2420	.091672
91	81.0078	78.1050	75.2021	72.2992	69.3964	66.4935	63.5907	60.6878	57.7850	54.8821	51.9793	49.0764	.096762
92	85.5801	82.8309	80.0817	77.3325	74.5834	71.8342	69.0850	66.3358	63.5866	60.8374	58.0883	55.3391	.091639
93 or 16	**97.0874**	**97.3301**	**97.5728**	**97.8155**	**98.0583**	**98.3010**	**98.5437**	**98.7864**	**99.0291**	**99.2718**	**99.5146**	**99.7573**	**.008090**
15	96.0604	96.0361	96.0118	95.9875	95.9632	95.9389	95.9145	95.8902	95.8659	95.8416	95.8173	95.7930	.000810
14	95.5267	95.4641	95.4015	95.3389	95.2763	95.2137	95.1511	95.0886	95.0260	94.9634	94.9008	94.8382	.002086
13	95.1332	95.0614	94.9895	94.9177	94.8459	94.7740	94.7022	94.6304	94.5585	94.4867	94.4149	94.3430	.002394
12	94.5112	94.4607	94.4101	94.3596	94.3091	94.2586	94.2080	94.1575	94.1070	94.0565	94.0060	93.9554	.001684
11	93.9998	93.9519	93.9040	93.8562	93.8083	93.7604	93.7125	93.6647	93.6168	93.5689	93.5210	93.4732	.001596
10	93.3066	93.2664	93.2261	93.1859	93.1457	93.1055	93.0652	93.0250	92.9848	92.9446	92.9043	92.8641	.001341
Age.	0	1	2	3	4	5	6	7	8	9	10	11	Day.

Age.	0	1	2	3	4	5	6	7	8	9	10	11	Day.
10	5.4758	5.4336	5.3913	5.3491	5.3068	5.2646	5.2223	5.1801	5.1379	5.0956	5.0534	5.0111	.001408
11	5.6528	5.6105	5.5683	5.5260	5.4838	5.4415	5.3992	5.3570	5.3147	5.2725	5.2302	5.1880	.001408
12	5.8364	5.7941	5.7519	5.7096	5.6673	5.6251	5.5828	5.5405	5.4983	5.4560	5.4137	5.3715	.001409
13	6.0210	5.9786	5.9363	5.8940	5.8516	5.8092	5.7669	5.7245	5.6822	5.6398	5.5975	5.5551	.001412
14	6.2122	6.1698	6.1273	6.0849	6.0424	6.0000	5.9575	5.9151	5.8727	5.8302	5.7878	5.7453	.001415
15	6.4095	6.3670	6.3245	6.2820	6.2395	6.1970	6.1544	6.1119	6.0694	6.0269	5.9844	5.9419	.001417
16	6.6132	6.5705	6.5279	6.4852	6.4426	6.3999	6.3572	6.3146	6.2719	6.2293	6.1866	6.1440	.001422
17	6.8237	6.7809	6.7381	6.6953	6.6525	6.6097	6.5670	6.5242	6.4814	6.4386	6.3958	6.3530	.001426
18	7.0415	6.9986	6.9556	6.9127	6.8698	6.8269	6.7840	6.7410	6.6981	6.6552	6.6122	6.5693	.001431
19	7.2678	7.2247	7.1816	7.1384	7.0953	7.0522	7.0091	6.9660	6.9229	6.8797	6.8366	6.7935	.001437
20	7.5023	7.4590	7.4157	7.3724	7.3291	7.2858	7.2425	7.1992	7.1559	7.1126	7.0693	7.0260	.001443
21	7.7465	7.7029	7.6594	7.6158	7.5722	7.5287	7.4851	7.4415	7.3980	7.3544	7.3108	7.2673	.001452
22	7.9999	7.9559	7.9120	7.8680	7.8240	7.7801	7.7361	7.6921	7.6482	7.6042	7.5602	7.5163	.001465
23	8.2611	8.2172	8.1732	8.1293	8.0854	8.0414	7.9975	7.9536	7.9096	7.8657	7.8218	7.7778	.001464
24	8.5371	8.4927	8.4482	8.4038	8.3594	8.3149	8.2705	8.2261	8.1816	8.1372	8.0928	8.0483	.001481
25	8.8219	8.7771	8.7323	8.6875	8.6428	8.5980	8.5532	8.5084	8.4636	8.4188	8.3741	8.3293	.001493
26	9.1180	9.0728	9.0276	8.9825	8.9373	8.8921	8.8470	8.8018	8.7566	8.7114	8.6662	8.6211	.001506
27	9.4265	9.3809	9.3353	9.2897	9.2441	9.1985	9.1530	9.1074	9.0618	9.0162	8.9706	8.9250	.001520
28	9.7477	9.7019	9.6561	9.6103	9.5645	9.5187	9.4728	9.4270	9.3812	9.3354	9.2896	9.2438	.001527
29	10.0860	10.0397	9.9934	9.9471	9.9008	9.8545	9.8082	9.7619	9.7156	9.6693	9.6230	9.5767	.001543
30	10.4408	10.3942	10.3475	10.3009	10.2542	10.2076	10.1610	10.1143	10.0677	10.0210	9.9744	9.9277	.001555
31	10.8098	10.7627	10.7157	10.6686	10.6215	10.5745	10.5274	10.4803	10.4333	10.3862	10.3391	10.2921	.001569
32	11.1994	11.1520	11.1045	11.0570	11.0096	10.9621	10.9147	10.8672	10.8198	10.7723	10.7249	10.6774	.001582
33	11.6097	11.5619	11.5141	11.4663	11.4185	11.3707	11.3230	11.2752	11.2274	11.1796	11.1318	11.0840	.001593
34	12.0433	11.9951	11.9469	11.8987	11.8506	11.8024	11.7542	11.7060	11.6578	11.6096	11.5615	11.5133	.001606
35	12.5014	12.4526	12.4037	12.3549	12.3061	12.2572	12.2084	12.1596	12.1107	12.0619	12.0131	11.9642	.001628
36	12.9803	12.9307	12.8812	12.8316	12.7820	12.7325	12.6829	12.6333	12.5838	12.5342	12.4846	12.4351	.001652
37	13.4840	13.4328	13.3815	13.3303	13.2791	13.2279	13.1766	13.1254	13.0742	13.0230	12.9717	12.9205	.001707
38	14.0020	13.9488	13.8957	13.8425	13.7893	13.7362	13.6830	13.6298	13.5767	13.5235	13.4703	13.4172	.001772
39	14.5336	14.4778	14.4220	14.3661	14.3103	14.2545	14.1986	14.1428	14.0870	14.0312	13.9753	13.9195	.001861
40	15.0722	15.0136	14.9550	14.8963	14.8377	14.7791	14.7205	14.6619	14.6033	14.5446	14.4860	14.4274	.001954
41	15.6180	15.5557	15.4934	15.4312	15.3689	15.3066	15.2443	15.1821	15.1198	15.0575	14.9952	14.9330	.002076
42	16.1638	16.0980	16.0322	15.9664	15.9006	15.8348	15.7690	15.7032	15.6374	15.5716	15.5058	15.4400	.002193
43	16.7169	16.6470	16.5771	16.5071	16.4372	16.3673	16.2974	16.2275	16.1576	16.0876	16.0177	15.9478	.002330
44	17.2740	17.1994	17.1248	17.0502	16.9757	16.9011	16.8265	16.7519	16.6773	16.6027	16.5282	16.4536	.002486
45	17.8418	17.7623	17.6827	17.6032	17.5236	17.4441	17.3645	17.2850	17.2055	17.1259	17.0464	16.9668	.002651
46	18.4425	18.3553	18.2682	18.1810	18.0939	18.0067	17.9196	17.8324	17.7453	17.6581	17.5710	17.4838	.002905
47	19.0163	18.9249	18.8335	18.7421	18.6507	18.5593	18.4679	18.3765	18.2851	18.1937	18.1023	18.0109	.003047
48	19.6276	19.5294	19.4313	19.3331	19.2349	19.1368	19.0386	18.9404	18.8423	18.7441	18.6459	18.5478	.003272
49	20.2592	20.1537	20.0483	19.9428	19.8373	19.7319	19.6264	19.5209	19.4155	19.3100	19.2045	19.0991	.003515
50	20.9066	20.7934	20.6802	20.5670	20.4538	20.3406	20.2274	20.1143	20.0011	19.8879	19.7747	19.6615	.003773
51	21.5751	21.4534	21.3316	21.2099	21.0882	20.9665	20.8447	20.7230	20.6013	20.4796	20.3578	20.2361	.004057
52	22.2651	22.1341	22.0031	21.8721	21.7411	21.6101	21.4791	21.3482	21.2172	21.0862	20.9552	20.8242	.004366
53	22.9760	22.8344	22.6928	22.5513	22.4097	22.2681	22.1265	21.9850	21.8434	21.7018	21.5602	21.4187	.004719
54	23.7080	23.5550	23.4019	23.2488	23.0958	22.9427	22.7897	22.6366	22.4836	22.3305	22.1775	22.0244	.005102
55	24.4548	24.2890	24.1232	23.9575	23.7917	23.6259	23.4601	23.2944	23.1286	22.9628	22.7970	22.6313	.005526
56	25.2171	25.0375	24.8580	24.6784	24.4988	24.3193	24.1397	23.9601	23.7806	23.6010	23.4214	23.2419	.005985
57	25.9946	25.7998	25.6051	25.4103	25.2155	25.0208	24.8260	24.6312	24.4365	24.2417	24.0469	23.8522	.006492
58	26.7818	26.5705	26.3592	26.1479	25.9366	25.7253	25.5140	25.3026	25.0913	24.8800	24.6687	24.4574	.007043
59	27.6148	27.3825	27.1502	26.9179	26.6856	26.4533	26.2210	25.9886	25.7563	25.5240	25.2917	25.0594	.007743
60	28.3844	28.1353	27.8863	27.6372	27.3882	27.1391	26.8901	26.6410	26.3920	26.1430	25.8939	25.6448	.008302
61	29.2001	28.9298	28.6596	28.3893	28.1191	27.8488	27.5786	27.3083	27.0381	26.7678	26.4976	26.2273	.009008
62	30.0276	29.7347	29.4418	29.1489	28.8560	28.5631	28.2702	27.9773	27.6844	27.3915	27.0986	26.8057	.009763
63	30.8725	30.5550	30.2375	29.9200	29.6025	29.2850	28.9675	28.6500	28.3325	28.0150	27.6975	27.3800	.010583
64	31.7332	31.3893	31.0453	30.7014	30.3575	30.0136	29.6696	29.3257	28.9818	28.6379	28.2940	27.9500	.011464
65	32.6141	32.2417	31.8694	31.4970	31.1246	30.7523	30.3799	30.0075	29.6352	29.2628	28.8904	28.5181	.012412
66	33.5172	33.1143	32.7115	32.3086	31.9058	31.5030	31.1001	30.6972	30.2944	29.8915	29.4887	29.0858	.013428
67	34.4464	34.0107	33.5750	33.1393	32.7036	32.2679	31.8321	31.3964	30.9607	30.5250	30.0893	29.6536	.014523
68	35.4047	34.9338	34.4630	33.9921	33.5212	33.0504	32.5795	32.1086	31.6378	31.1669	30.6960	30.2252	.015695
69	36.3950	35.8866	35.3782	34.8699	34.3615	33.8531	33.3447	32.8364	32.3280	31.8196	31.3112	30.8029	.016946
70	37.4206	36.8716	36.3227	35.7737	35.2248	34.6758	34.1269	33.5780	33.0290	32.4800	31.9311	31.3821	.018298
71	38.4828	37.8902	37.2976	36.7050	36.1123	35.5197	34.9271	34.3345	33.7419	33.1492	32.5566	31.9640	.019754
72	39.5827	38.9437	38.3047	37.6657	37.0267	36.3877	35.7487	35.1098	34.4708	33.8318	33.1928	32.5538	.021300
73	40.7301	40.0418	39.3535	38.6652	37.9769	37.2886	36.6002	35.9119	35.2236	34.5353	33.8470	33.1587	.022943
74	41.9342	41.1942	40.4542	39.7142	38.9742	38.2342	37.4942	36.7543	36.0143	35.2743	34.5343	33.7943	.024666
75	43.2176	42.4239	41.6302	40.8365	40.0428	39.2491	38.4554	37.6618	36.8681	36.0744	35.2807	34.4870	.026456
76	44.6102	43.7602	42.9102	42.0603	41.2103	40.3603	39.5103	38.6604	37.8104	36.9604	36.1104	35.2605	.028332
77	46.1397	45.2314	44.3231	43.4149	42.5066	41.5983	40.6900	39.7818	38.8735	37.9652	37.0570	36.1487	.030276
78	47.8523	46.8810	45.9098	44.9385	43.9673	42.9960	42.0248	41.0535	40.0823	39.1110	38.1398	37.1685	.032375
79	49.7666	48.7295	47.6924	46.6553	45.6183	44.5812	43.5441	42.5070	41.4699	40.4328	39.3958	38.3587	.034569
80	51.9257	50.8164	49.7070	48.5977	47.4884	46.3790	45.2697	44.1604	43.0510	41.9417	40.8324	39.7230	.036978
81	54.3388	53.1499	51.9610	50.7720	49.5831	48.3942	47.2052	46.0163	44.8274	43.6385	42.4495	41.2606	.039631
82	57.0083	55.7294	54.4504	53.1715	51.8925	50.6136	49.3346	48.0557	46.7768	45.4978	44.2189	42.9399	.042631
83	59.9099	58.5315	57.1530	55.7746	54.3961	53.0177	51.6392	50.2608	48.8824	47.5039	46.1255	44.7470	.045948
84	63.0549	61.5630	60.0710	58.5790	57.0871	55.5951	54.1032	52.6112	51.1193	49.6273	48.1354	46.6434	.049732
85	66.4199	64.7928	63.1657	61.5386	59.9115	58.2844	56.6573	55.0302	53.4031	51.7760	50.1489	48.5218	.054237
86	69.9349	68.1456	66.3562	64.5669	62.7776	60.9883	59.1990	57.4096	55.6203	53.8310	52.0416	50.2523	.059644
87	73.4783	71.4989	69.5196	67.5402	65.5608	63.5815	61.6021	59.6227	57.6434	55.6640	53.6846	51.7053	.065979
88	76.9792	74.7460	72.5128	70.2795	68.0463	65.8131	63.5799	61.3467	59.1135	56.8802	54.6470	52.4138	.074440
89	79.9431	77.4261	74.9092	72.3922	69.8753	67.3583	64.8413	62.3244	59.8074	57.2905	54.7735	52.2566	.083898
90	82.3303	79.6862	77.0420	74.3979	71.7537	69.1096	66.4654	63.8213	61.1772	58.5330	55.8889	53.2447	.088138
91	86.5744	84.0837	81.5931	79.1024	76.6118	74.1211	71.6305	69.1398	66.6492	64.1585	61.6679	59.1772	.083022
92 or 17	**97.0874**	**97.3301**	**97.5728**	**97.8155**	**98.0583**	**98.3010**	**98.5437**	**98.7864**	**99.0291**	**99.2718**	**99.5146**	**99.7573**	**.008090**
16	96.0534	96.0273	96.0012	95.9751	95.9490	95.9229	95.8968	95.8707	95.8446	95.8185	95.7924	95.7663	.000870
15	95.5166	95.4520	95.3874	95.3229	95.2583	95.1937	95.1291	95.0646	95.0000	94.9354	94.8708	94.8063	.002152
14	95.1209	95.0471	94.9733	94.8995	94.8257	94.7519	94.6781	94.6043	94.5305	94.4567	94.3829	94.3091	.002460
13	94.6124	94.5504	94.4883	94.4263	94.3642	94.3022	94.2401	94.1781	94.1161	94.0540	93.9920	93.9299	.002068
12	93.9820	93.9324	93.8829	93.8333	93.7837	93.7342	93.6846	93.6350	93.5855	93.5359	93.4863	93.4368	.001652
11	93.2854	93.2436	93.2018	93.1600	93.1182	93.0764	93.0345	92.9927	92.9509	92.9091	92.8673	92.8255	.001393
10	92.5330	92.4980	92.4631	92.4281	92.3931	92.3582	92.3232	92.2882	92.2533	92.2183	92.1833	92.1484	.001165
Age.	0	1	2	3	4	5	6	7	8	9	10	11	Day.

Age.	0	1	2	3	4	5	6	7	8	9	10	11	Day.
10	6.1621	6.1214	6.0807	6.0401	5.9994	5.9587	5.9180	5.8774	5.8367	5.7960	5.7553	5.7147	.001356
11	6.3619	6.3213	6.2806	6.2400	6.1994	6.1588	6.1181	6.0775	6.0369	5.9963	5.9556	5.9150	.001354
12	6.5693	6.5287	6.4880	6.4474	6.4068	6.3661	6.3255	6.2849	6.2442	6.2036	6.1630	6.1223	.001354
13	6.7780	6.7373	6.6967	6.6560	6.6153	6.5747	6.5340	6.4933	6.4527	6.4120	6.3713	6.3307	.001355
14	6.9943	6.9536	6.9130	6.8723	6.8316	6.7910	6.7503	6.7096	6.6690	6.6283	6.5876	6.5470	.001355
15	7.2181	7.1773	7.1366	7.0958	7.0551	7.0143	6.9736	6.9328	6.8921	6.8513	6.8106	6.7698	.001358
16	7.4485	7.4077	7.3669	7.3260	7.2852	7.2444	7.2036	7.1628	7.1220	7.0811	7.0403	6.9995	.001360
17	7.6871	7.6462	7.6053	7.5645	7.5236	7.4827	7.4418	7.4010	7.3601	7.3192	7.2783	7.2375	.001362
18	7.9342	7.8932	7.8522	7.8112	7.7702	7.7292	7.6882	7.6473	7.6063	7.5653	7.5243	7.4833	.001366
19	8.1905	8.1494	8.1083	8.0672	8.0261	7.9850	7.9439	7.9028	7.8617	7.8206	7.7795	7.7384	.001370
20	8.4566	8.4153	8.3740	8.3327	8.2915	8.2502	8.2089	8.1676	8.1263	8.0850	8.0438	8.0025	.001376
21	8.7327	8.6911	8.6495	8.6079	8.5663	8.5247	8.4830	8.4414	8.3998	8.3582	8.3166	8.2750	.001387
22	9.0180	8.9765	8.9350	8.8935	8.8520	8.8105	8.7690	8.7275	8.6860	8.6445	8.6030	8.5615	.001383
23	9.3179	9.2760	9.2341	9.1922	9.1503	9.1084	9.0664	9.0245	8.9826	8.9407	8.8988	8.8569	.001397
24	9.6279	9.5857	9.5436	9.5014	9.4593	9.4171	9.3750	9.3328	9.2906	9.2485	9.2063	9.1642	.001405
25	9.9503	9.9078	9.8654	9.8230	9.7805	9.7380	9.6956	9.6531	9.6107	9.5682	9.5258	9.4833	.001415
26	10.2855	10.2427	10.2000	10.1572	10.1144	10.0716	10.0288	9.9861	9.9433	9.9005	9.8577	9.8150	.001426
27	10.6346	10.5917	10.5488	10.5060	10.4631	10.4202	10.3773	10.3344	10.2915	10.2486	10.2058	10.1629	.001429
28	11.0011	10.9578	10.9146	10.8713	10.8281	10.7848	10.7416	10.6983	10.6551	10.6118	10.5686	10.5253	.001442
29	11.3837	11.3402	11.2967	11.2532	11.2097	11.1662	11.1227	11.0793	11.0358	10.9923	10.9488	10.9053	.001450
30	11.7868	11.7430	11.6992	11.6554	11.6116	11.5678	11.5240	11.4803	11.4365	11.3927	11.3489	11.3051	.001460
31	12.2059	12.1618	12.1178	12.0737	12.0297	11.9856	11.9415	11.8975	11.8534	11.8094	11.7653	11.7213	.001468
32	12.6486	12.6043	12.5601	12.5158	12.4716	12.4273	12.3830	12.3388	12.2945	12.2503	12.2060	12.1618	.001475
33	13.1156	13.0711	13.0266	12.9820	12.9375	12.8930	12.8485	12.8040	12.7595	12.7150	12.6704	12.6259	.001484
34	13.6082	13.5632	13.5181	13.4731	13.4281	13.3831	13.3380	13.2930	13.2480	13.2030	13.1580	13.1129	.001501
35	14.1255	14.0799	14.0343	13.9887	13.9431	13.8975	13.8520	13.8064	13.7608	13.7152	13.6696	13.6240	.001530
36	14.6663	14.6192	14.5722	14.5251	14.4780	14.4310	14.3839	14.3368	14.2898	14.2427	14.1956	14.1486	.001569
37	15.2246	15.1758	15.1270	15.0782	15.0294	14.9806	14.9317	14.8829	14.8341	14.7853	14.7365	14.6877	.001627
38	15.7980	15.7467	15.6955	15.6442	15.5930	15.5417	15.4905	15.4392	15.3880	15.3367	15.2855	15.2342	.001708
39	16.3809	16.3271	16.2733	16.2195	16.1657	16.1119	16.0580	16.0042	15.9504	15.8966	15.8428	15.7890	.001793
40	16.9740	16.9168	16.8596	16.8024	16.7452	16.6880	16.6308	16.5736	16.5164	16.4592	16.4020	16.3448	.001907
41	17.5693	17.5088	17.4484	17.3880	17.3275	17.2670	17.2066	17.1461	17.0857	17.0252	16.9648	16.9043	.002015
42	18.1719	18.1076	18.0433	17.9791	17.9149	17.8506	17.7863	17.7221	17.6578	17.5936	17.5293	17.4651	.002142
43	18.7809	18.7123	18.6437	18.5751	18.5065	18.4379	18.3693	18.3007	18.2321	18.1635	18.0949	18.0263	.002287
44	19.3940	19.3208	19.2475	19.1743	19.1010	19.0278	18.9545	18.8813	18.8081	18.7348	18.6616	18.5883	.002441
45	20.0207	19.9418	19.8630	19.7841	19.7053	19.6264	19.5475	19.4687	19.3898	19.3110	19.2321	19.1533	.002626
46	20.6554	20.5710	20.4866	20.4022	20.3179	20.2335	20.1491	20.0647	19.9803	19.8960	19.8116	19.7272	.002813
47	21.3106	21.2198	21.1291	21.0383	20.9476	20.8568	20.7660	20.6753	20.5845	20.4938	20.4030	20.3123	.003025
48	21.9807	21.8830	21.7854	21.6877	21.5901	21.4924	21.3947	21.2971	21.1994	21.1018	21.0041	20.9065	.003255
49	22.6724	22.5675	22.4625	22.3576	22.2526	22.1477	22.0427	21.9378	21.8329	21.7279	21.6230	21.5180	.003498
50	23.3835	23.2705	23.1575	23.0445	22.9315	22.8185	22.7055	22.5925	22.4795	22.3665	22.2535	22.1405	.003767
51	24.1151	23.9933	23.8716	23.7498	23.6281	23.5063	23.3846	23.2628	23.1411	23.0193	22.8976	22.7758	.004058
52	24.8692	24.7374	24.6057	24.4739	24.3422	24.2104	24.0786	23.9469	23.8151	23.6834	23.5516	23.4199	.004392
53	25.6390	25.4964	25.3537	25.2111	25.0684	24.9258	24.7831	24.6405	24.4979	24.3552	24.2126	24.0699	.004755
54	26.4298	26.2751	26.1204	25.9658	25.8111	25.6564	25.5017	25.3471	25.1924	25.0377	24.8830	24.7284	.005156
55	27.2327	27.0650	26.8973	26.7295	26.5618	26.3941	26.2264	26.0587	25.8910	25.7232	25.5555	25.3878	.005590
56	28.0512	27.8691	27.6870	27.5049	27.3228	27.1407	26.9585	26.7764	26.5943	26.4122	26.2301	26.0480	.006070
57	28.8817	28.6840	28.4862	28.2884	28.0907	27.8930	27.6952	27.4974	27.2997	27.1020	26.9042	26.7064	.006592
58	29.7209	29.5061	29.2913	29.0765	28.8618	28.6470	28.4322	28.2174	28.0026	27.7878	27.5731	27.3583	.007159
59	30.5685	30.3351	30.1017	29.8683	29.6349	29.4015	29.1680	28.9346	28.7012	28.4678	28.2344	28.0010	.007780
60	31.4214	31.1679	30.9145	30.6610	30.4075	30.1541	29.9006	29.6471	29.3937	29.1402	28.8867	28.6333	.008449
61	32.2851	32.0102	31.7354	31.4605	31.1856	30.9108	30.6359	30.3610	30.0862	29.8113	29.5364	29.2616	.009162
62	33.1627	32.8646	32.5665	32.2684	31.9703	31.6722	31.3740	31.0759	30.7778	30.4797	30.1816	29.8835	.009937
63	34.0551	33.7320	33.4089	33.0858	32.7628	32.4397	32.1166	31.7935	31.4704	31.1473	30.8243	30.5012	.010769
64	34.9635	34.6135	34.2636	33.9136	33.5637	33.2137	32.8637	32.5138	32.1638	31.8139	31.4639	31.1140	.011665
65	35.8914	35.5127	35.1339	34.7552	34.3765	33.9977	33.6190	33.2403	32.8615	32.4828	32.1041	31.7253	.012624
66	36.8423	36.4325	36.0228	35.6130	35.2033	34.7935	34.3837	33.9740	33.5642	33.1545	32.7447	32.3350	.013658
67	37.8175	37.3745	36.9316	36.4886	36.0457	35.6027	35.1598	34.7168	34.2739	33.8310	33.3880	32.9450	.014765
68	38.8226	38.3443	37.8660	37.3876	36.9093	36.4310	35.9527	35.4744	34.9961	34.5177	34.0394	33.5611	.015944
69	39.8620	39.3454	38.8289	38.3123	37.7958	37.2792	36.7626	36.2461	35.7295	35.2130	34.6964	34.1799	.017216
70	40.9331	40.3754	39.8177	39.2600	38.7023	38.1446	37.5870	37.0293	36.4716	35.9139	35.3562	34.7985	.018590
71	42.0391	41.4378	40.8364	40.2351	39.6338	39.0324	38.4311	37.8298	37.2284	36.6271	36.0258	35.4244	.020044
72	43.1885	42.5408	41.8931	41.2454	40.5977	39.9500	39.3023	38.6547	38.0070	37.3593	36.7116	36.0639	.021590
73	44.3912	43.6950	42.9988	42.3025	41.6063	40.9101	40.2139	39.5177	38.8215	38.1252	37.4290	36.7328	.023207
74	45.6666	44.9200	44.1734	43.4269	42.6803	41.9337	41.1871	40.4406	39.6940	38.9474	38.2008	37.4543	.024886
75	47.0451	46.2458	45.4465	44.6473	43.8480	43.0487	42.2494	41.4502	40.6509	39.8516	39.0523	38.2531	.026642
76	48.5536	47.6999	46.8461	45.9924	45.1387	44.2849	43.4312	42.5775	41.7237	40.8700	40.0163	39.1625	.028456
77	50.2318	49.3192	48.4066	47.4940	46.5815	45.6689	44.7563	43.8437	42.9311	42.0185	41.1060	40.1934	.030419
78	52.0979	51.1239	50.1498	49.1758	48.2018	47.2278	46.2537	45.2797	44.3057	43.3317	42.3576	41.3836	.032467
79	54.1972	53.1559	52.1145	51.0732	50.0319	48.9905	47.9492	46.9079	45.8665	44.8252	43.7839	42.7425	.034711
80	56.5372	55.4219	54.3066	53.1913	52.0760	50.9607	49.8454	48.7301	47.6148	46.4995	45.3842	44.2689	.037177
81	59.1248	57.9262	56.7276	55.5290	54.3305	53.1319	51.9333	50.7347	49.5361	48.3375	47.1390	45.9404	.039952
82	61.9388	60.6488	59.3589	58.0689	56.7789	55.4890	54.1990	52.9090	51.6191	50.3291	49.0391	47.7492	.042999
83	64.9850	63.5914	62.1978	60.8043	59.4107	58.0171	56.6235	55.2300	53.8364	52.4428	51.0492	49.6557	.046452
84	68.2426	66.7266	65.2106	63.6946	62.1787	60.6627	59.1467	57.6307	56.1147	54.5987	53.0826	51.5666	.050533
85	71.6289	69.9291	68.2293	66.5295	64.8297	63.1299	61.4301	59.7303	58.0305	56.3307	54.6309	52.9311	.056660
86	75.0370	73.2043	71.3717	69.5390	67.7063	65.8737	64.0410	62.2083	60.3757	58.5430	56.7103	54.8777	.061089
87	78.3842	76.3240	74.2638	72.2035	70.1433	68.0831	66.0229	63.9627	61.9025	59.8422	57.7820	55.7218	.068674
88	81.2106	78.8978	76.5849	74.2721	71.9593	69.6464	67.3336	65.0208	62.7079	60.3951	58.0823	55.7694	.077094
89	83.4804	81.0616	78.6424	76.2232	73.8040	71.3848	68.9655	66.5463	64.1271	61.7079	59.2887	56.8695	.080640
90	87.4391	85.1732	82.9074	80.6415	78.3757	76.1098	73.8440	71.5781	69.3123	67.0464	64.7806	62.5147	.075528
91 or 18	**97.0874**	**97.3301**	**97.5728**	**97.8155**	**98.0583**	**98.3010**	**98.5437**	**98.7864**	**99.0291**	**99.2718**	**99.5146**	**99.7573**	**.008090**
17	96.0462	96.0182	95.9902	95.9623	95.9343	95.9063	95.8783	95.8504	95.8224	95.7944	95.7664	95.7385	.000932
16	95.5060	95.4394	95.3727	95.3061	95.2394	95.1728	95.1061	95.0395	94.9729	94.9062	94.8396	94.7729	.002221
15	95.1082	95.0323	94.9565	94.8806	94.8048	94.7289	94.6530	94.5772	94.5013	94.4255	94.3496	94.2738	.002528
14	94.5968	94.5329	94.4689	94.4050	94.3410	94.2771	94.2131	94.1492	94.0853	94.0213	93.9574	93.8934	.002131
13	93.9631	93.9118	93.8604	93.8091	93.7578	93.7064	93.6551	93.6038	93.5524	93.5011	93.4498	93.3984	.001711
12	93.2634	93.2199	93.1765	93.1330	93.0896	93.0461	93.0026	92.9592	92.9157	92.8723	92.8288	92.7854	.001448
11	92.5075	92.4710	92.4345	92.3980	92.3614	92.3249	92.2884	92.2519	92.2154	92.1788	92.1423	92.1058	.001217
10	91.7139	91.6827	91.6516	91.6204	91.5892	91.5581	91.5269	91.4957	91.4646	91.4334	91.4022	91.3711	.001039
Age.	0	1	2	3	4	5	6	7	8	9	10	11	Day.

Age.	0	1	2	3	4	5	6	7	8	9	10	11	Day.
10	6.8672	6.8282	6.7891	6.7501	6.7110	6.6720	6.6330	6.5939	6.5549	6.5158	6.4768	6.4377	.001301
11	7.0906	7.0516	7.0126	6.9736	6.9346	6.8956	6.8566	6.8176	6.7786	6.7396	6.7006	6.6616	.001300
12	7.3217	7.2827	7.2438	7.2048	7.1659	7.1269	7.0880	7.0490	7.0100	6.9711	6.9321	6.8932	.001298
13	7.5552	7.5163	7.4774	7.4385	7.3996	7.3607	7.3218	7.2829	7.2440	7.2051	7.1662	7.1273	.001297
14	7.7977	7.7588	7.7199	7.6810	7.6420	7.6031	7.5642	7.5253	7.4864	7.4474	7.4085	7.3696	.001297
15	8.0478	8.0089	7.9700	7.9310	7.8921	7.8532	7.8143	7.7754	7.7365	7.6975	7.6586	7.6197	.001297
16	8.3059	8.2670	8.2281	8.1892	8.1503	8.1114	8.0724	8.0335	7.9946	7.9557	7.9168	7.8779	.001297
17	8.5735	8.5345	8.4956	8.4566	8.4177	8.3787	8.3397	8.3008	8.2618	8.2229	8.1839	8.1450	.001298
18	8.8502	8.8112	8.7722	8.7332	8.6942	8.6552	8.6162	8.5772	8.5382	8.4992	8.4602	8.4212	.001300
19	9.1375	9.0984	9.0593	9.0203	8.9812	8.9421	8.9030	8.8640	8.8249	8.7858	8.7467	8.7077	.001302
20	9.4350	9.3956	9.3563	9.3170	9.2776	9.2382	9.1989	9.1595	9.1202	9.0808	9.0415	9.0021	.001312
21	9.7424	9.7032	9.6641	9.6249	9.5858	9.5466	9.5074	9.4683	9.4291	9.3900	9.3508	9.3117	.001305
22	10.0657	10.0262	9.9867	9.9473	9.9078	9.8683	9.8288	9.7894	9.7499	9.7104	9.6710	9.6315	.001316
23	10.3990	10.3594	10.3197	10.2801	10.2404	10.2008	10.1611	10.1215	10.0819	10.0422	10.0026	9.9629	.001321
24	10.7460	10.7061	10.6663	10.6264	10.5866	10.5467	10.5069	10.4670	10.4272	10.3873	10.3475	10.3076	.001328
25	11.1066	11.0665	11.0265	10.9864	10.9463	10.9063	10.8662	10.8261	10.7861	10.7460	10.7059	10.6659	.001335
26	11.4817	11.4416	11.4015	11.3614	11.3214	11.2813	11.2412	11.2011	11.1610	11.1210	11.0809	11.0408	.001336
27	11.8753	11.8350	11.7946	11.7542	11.7139	11.6735	11.6332	11.5928	11.5525	11.5121	11.4718	11.4314	.001345
28	12.2852	12.2447	12.2042	12.1637	12.1233	12.0828	12.0423	12.0018	11.9613	11.9208	11.8804	11.8399	.001349
29	12.7149	12.6743	12.6336	12.5929	12.5523	12.5116	12.4709	12.4303	12.3896	12.3489	12.3083	12.2676	.001353
30	13.1670	13.1262	13.0854	13.0446	13.0038	12.9630	12.9221	12.8813	12.8405	12.7997	12.7589	12.7181	.001360
31	13.6381	13.5972	13.5563	13.5154	13.4745	13.4336	13.3927	13.3518	13.3109	13.2700	13.2291	13.1882	.001363
32	14.1361	14.0951	14.0540	14.0130	13.9720	13.9310	13.8900	13.8489	13.8079	13.7669	13.7258	13.6848	.001367
33	14.6607	14.6193	14.5779	14.5365	14.4951	14.4537	14.4123	14.3710	14.3296	14.2882	14.2468	14.2054	.001380
34	15.2110	15.1692	15.1274	15.0855	15.0437	15.0019	14.9601	14.9183	14.8765	14.8346	14.7928	14.7510	.001394
35	15.7885	15.7454	15.7023	15.6591	15.6160	15.5729	15.5298	15.4867	15.4436	15.4004	15.3573	15.3142	.001437
36	16.3823	16.3376	16.2929	16.2482	16.2036	16.1589	16.1142	16.0695	16.0248	15.9801	15.9355	15.8908	.001489
37	16.9942	16.9473	16.9003	16.8534	16.8065	16.7596	16.7126	16.6657	16.6188	16.5719	16.5250	16.4780	.001564
38	17.6170	17.5677	17.5185	17.4692	17.4199	17.3707	17.3214	17.2721	17.2229	17.1736	17.1243	17.0751	.001642
39	18.2524	18.2000	18.1476	18.0952	18.0428	17.9904	17.9380	17.8855	17.8331	17.7807	17.7283	17.6759	.001747
40	18.8929	18.8375	18.7821	18.7267	18.6713	18.6159	18.5604	18.5050	18.4496	18.3942	18.3388	18.2834	.001847
41	19.5425	19.4836	19.4246	19.3657	19.3068	19.2479	19.1890	19.1300	19.0711	19.0122	18.9532	18.8943	.001963
42	20.1986	20.1356	20.0727	20.0097	19.9468	19.8838	19.8208	19.7579	19.6949	19.6320	19.5690	19.5061	.002097
43	20.8608	20.7935	20.7262	20.6590	20.5917	20.5244	20.4571	20.3899	20.3226	20.2553	20.1880	20.1208	.002240
44	21.5301	21.4575	21.3850	21.3124	21.2399	21.1673	21.0947	21.0222	20.9496	20.8771	20.8045	20.7320	.002417
45	22.2078	22.1300	22.0522	21.9744	21 8966	21.8188	21.7410	21.6632	21.5854	21.5076	21.4298	21.3520	.002593
46	22.9016	22.8178	22.7341	22.6503	22.5666	22.4828	22.3990	22.3153	22.2315	22.1478	22.0640	21.9803	.002790
47	23.6126	23.5223	23.4321	23.3418	23.2515	23.1613	23.0710	22.9807	22.8905	22.8002	22.7099	22.6197	.003007
48	24.3399	24.2427	24.1456	24.0484	23.9513	23.8541	23.7570	23.6598	23.5627	23.4655	23.3684	23.2712	.003238
49	25.0919	24.9871	24.8824	24.7776	24.6729	24.5681	24.4633	24.3586	24.2538	24.1491	24.0443	23.9396	.003492
50	25.8627	25.7497	25.6366	25.5236	25.4106	25.2976	25.1845	25.0715	24.9585	24.8455	24.7324	24.6194	.003767
51	26.6548	26.5323	26.4098	26.2873	26.1648	26.0423	25.9198	25.7973	25.6748	25.5523	25.4298	25.3073	.004083
52	27.4642	27.3314	27.1986	27.0658	26.9330	26.8002	26.6674	26.5346	26.4018	26.2690	26.1362	26.0034	.004427
53	28.2892	28.1450	28.0008	27.8565	27.7123	27.5681	27.4239	27.2797	27.1355	26.9912	26.8470	26.7028	.004807
54	29.1322	28.9756	28.8191	28.6625	28.5060	28.3494	28.1928	28.0363	27.8797	27.7232	27.5666	27.4101	.005218
55	29.9874	29.8172	29.6470	29.4768	29.3066	29.1364	28.9662	28.7961	28.6259	28.4557	28.2855	28.1153	.005673
56	30.8548	30.6698	30.4848	30.2998	30.1148	29.9298	29.7448	29.5598	29.3748	29.1898	29.0048	28.8198	.006167
57	31.7330	31.5319	31.3308	31.1296	30.9285	30.7274	30.5263	30.3252	30.1241	29.9230	29.7218	29.5207	.006704
58	32.6183	32.3996	32.1808	31.9621	31.7433	31.5246	31.3058	31.0871	30.8684	30.6496	30.4309	30.2121	.007291
59	33.5090	33.2713	33.0336	32.7959	32.5582	32.3205	32.0828	31.8451	31.6075	31.3698	31.1321	30.8944	.007923
60	34.4055	34.1476	33.8896	33.6317	33.3738	33.1158	32.8579	32.6000	32.3420	32.0841	31.8262	31.5682	.008598
61	35.3147	35.0348	34.7549	34.4750	34.1951	33.9152	33.6352	33.3553	33.0754	32.7955	32.5156	32.2357	.009330
62	36.2353	35.9318	35.6283	35.3248	35.0213	34.7178	34.4142	34.1107	33.8072	33.5037	33.2002	32.8967	.010117
63	37.1706	36.8417	36.5128	36.1839	35.8550	35.5261	35.1972	34.8683	34.5394	34.2105	33.8816	33.5527	.010963
64	38.1215	37.7654	37.4093	37.0532	36.6971	36.3410	35.9849	35.6288	35.2727	34.9166	34.5605	34.2044	.011870
65	39.0924	38.7070	38.3216	37.9362	37.5508	37.1654	36.7800	36.3947	36.0093	35.6239	35.2385	34.8531	.012846
66	40.0845	39.6678	39.2510	38.8343	38.4176	38.0008	37.5841	37.1674	36.7506	36.3339	35.9172	35.5004	.013891
67	41.1017	40.6516	40.2014	39.7513	39.3012	38.8511	38.4010	37.9508	37.5007	37.0506	36.6004	36.1503	.015004
68	42.1511	41.6649	41.1787	40.6925	40.2063	39.7201	39.2339	38.7477	38.2615	37.7753	37.2891	36.8029	.016207
69	43.2308	42.7059	42.1809	41.6560	41.1310	40.6061	40.0811	39.5562	39.0313	38.5063	37.9814	37.4564	.017498
70	44.3407	43.7747	43.2086	42.6426	42.0765	41.5105	40.9444	40.3784	39.8124	39.2463	38.6803	38.1142	.018868
71	45.4908	44.8811	44.2715	43.6618	43.0522	42.4425	41.8328	41.2232	40.6135	40.0039	39.3942	38.7846	.020322
72	46.6898	46.0345	45.3793	44.7240	44.0688	43.4135	42.7583	42.1030	41.4478	40.7925	40.1373	39.4820	.021842
73	47.9573	47.2548	46.5523	45.8498	45.1473	44.4448	43.7423	43.0398	42.3373	41.6348	40.9323	40.2298	.023417
74	49.3201	48.5705	47.8209	47.0711	46.3216	45.5720	44.8224	44.0728	43.3232	42.5735	41.8239	41.0743	.024987
75	50.8055	50.0026	49.1998	48.3969	47.5940	46.7912	45.9883	45.1854	44.3826	43.5797	42.7768	41.9740	.026762
76	52.4519	51.5940	50.7362	49.8783	49.0205	48.1626	47.3048	46.4470	45.5891	44.7312	43.8734	43.0155	.028595
77	54.2722	53.3570	52.4417	51.5265	50.6113	49.6961	48.7808	47.8656	46.9504	46.0352	45.1200	44.2047	.030507
78	56.3102	55.3321	54.3540	53.3760	52.3979	51.4198	50.4417	49.4637	48.4856	47.5075	46.5294	45.5514	.032602
79	58.5767	57.5297	56.4827	55.4357	54.3887	53.3417	52.2947	51.2477	50.2007	49.1537	48.1067	47.0597	.034900
80	61.0771	59.9526	58.8282	57.7037	56.5792	55.4548	54.3303	53.2058	52.0814	50.9569	49.8324	48.7080	.037482
81	63.7950	62.5860	61.3769	60.1679	58.9589	57.7498	56.5408	55.3318	54.1227	52.9137	51.7047	50.4956	.040301
82	66.7369	65.4326	64.1283	62.8241	61.5198	60.2155	58.9112	57.6070	56.3027	54.9984	53.6941	52.3899	.043476
83	69.8785	68.4623	67.0460	65.6298	64.2135	62.7973	61.3810	59.9648	58.5486	57.1323	55.7161	54.2998	.047208
84	73.1419	71.5926	70.0433	68.4940	66.9447	65.3954	63.8461	62.2969	60.7476	59.1983	57.6490	56.0997	.051643
85	75.9656	74.2997	72.6338	70.9678	69.3019	67.6360	65.9701	64.3042	62.6383	60.9723	59.3064	57.6405	.055530
86	79.6190	77.7108	75.8026	73.8945	71.9863	70.0781	68.1700	66.2618	64.3536	62.4454	60.5372	58.6291	.063606
87	82.3199	80.1856	78.0514	75.9171	73.7828	71.6486	69.5143	67.3800	65.2458	63.1115	60.9772	58.8430	.071142
88	84.4866	82.2643	80.0420	77.8197	75.5974	73.3751	71.1527	68.9304	66.7081	64.4858	62.2635	60.0412	.074077
89	88.1915	86.1211	84.0507	81.9803	79.9099	77.8395	75.7690	73.6986	71.6282	69.5578	67.4874	65.4170	.069013
90 or 19	**97.0874**	**97.3301**	**97.5728**	**97.8155**	**98.0583**	**98.3010**	**98.5437**	**98.7864**	**99.0291**	**99.2718**	**99.5146**	**99.7573**	**.008090**
18	96.0387	96.0088	95.9788	95.9489	95.9190	95.8890	95.8591	95.8292	95.7992	95.7693	95.7394	95.7094	.000998
17	95.4950	95.4262	95.3574	95.2886	95.2198	95.1510	95.0822	95.0134	94.9446	94.8758	94.8070	94.7382	.002293
16	95.0948	95.0168	94.9388	94.8608	94.7828	94.7048	94.6268	94.5488	94.4708	94.3928	94.3148	94.2368	.002600
15	94.5807	94.5148	94.4488	94.3829	94.3170	94.2510	94.1851	94.1192	94.0532	93.9873	93.9214	93.8554	.002198
14	93.9436	93.8904	93.8372	93.7840	93.7309	93.6777	93.6245	93.5713	93 5181	93.4650	93.4118	93.3586	.017728
13	93.2402	93.1950	93.1498	93.1046	93.0594	93.0142	92.9690	92.9239	93.8787	92.8335	92.7883	92.7431	.001506
12	92.4810	92.4429	92.4047	92.3666	92.3284	92.2903	92.2521	92.2140	92.1759	92.1377	92.0996	92.0614	.001271
11	91.6838	91.6511	91.6184	91.5857	91.5530	91.5203	91.4876	91.4549	91.4222	91.3895	91.3568	91.3241	.001090
10	90.8644	90.8358	90.8071	90.7785	90.7499	90.7212	90.6926	90.6640	90.6353	90.6067	90.5781	90.5494	.000954
Age.	0	1	2	3	4	5	6	7	8	9	10	11	Day.

Age.	0	1	2	3	4	5	6	7	8	9	10	11	Day.
10	7.5918	7.5544	7.5169	7.4795	7.4421	7.4046	7.3672	7.3298	7.2923	7.2549	7.2175	7.1800	.001248
11	7.8387	7.8014	7.7641	7.7267	7.6894	7.6521	7.6147	7.5774	7.5401	7.5027	7.4654	7.4281	.001243
12	8.0943	8.0571	8.0199	7.9827	7.9455	7.9083	7.8710	7.8338	7.7966	7.7594	7.7222	7.6850	.001240
13	8.3536	8.3164	8.2793	8.2421	8.2049	8.1678	8.1306	8.0934	8.0563	8.0191	7.9819	7.9448	.001239
14	8.6221	8.5850	8.5479	8.5108	8.4737	8.4366	8.3995	8.3624	8.3253	8.2882	8.2511	8.2140	.001237
15	8.8996	8.8626	8.8255	8.7885	8.7515	8.7144	8.6774	8.6404	8.6033	8.5663	8.5293	8.4922	.001234
16	9.1862	9.1492	9.1122	9.0751	9.0381	9.0011	8.9641	8.9271	8.8901	8.8530	8.8160	8.7790	.001234
17	9.4828	9.4458	9.4088	9.3719	9.3349	9.2979	9.2610	9.2240	9.1870	9.1500	9.1130	9.0761	.001232
18	9.7900	9.7530	9.7160	9.6790	9.6419	9.6049	9.5679	9.5309	9.4939	9.4568	9.4198	9.3828	.001234
19	10.1084	10.0712	10.0340	9.9968	9.9596	9.9224	9.8852	9.8481	9.8109	9.7737	9.7365	9.6993	.001240
20	10.4366	10.3997	10.3628	10.3258	10.2889	10.2520	10.2151	10.1782	10.1413	10.1043	10.0674	10.0305	.001230
21	10.7815	10.7443	10.7072	10.6700	10.6329	10.5957	10.5585	10.5214	10.4842	10.4471	10.4099	10.3728	.001238
22	11.1376	11.1004	11.0631	11.0259	10.9887	10.9514	10.9142	10.8770	10.8397	10.8025	10.7653	10.7280	.001241
23	11.5073	11.4699	11.4326	11.3952	11.3579	11.3205	11.2831	11.2458	11.2084	11.1711	11.1337	11.0964	.001245
24	11.8918	11.8543	11.8168	11.7793	11.7418	11.7043	11.6668	11.6294	11.5919	11.5544	11.5169	11.4794	.001250
25	12.2916	12.2542	12.2168	12.1794	12.1420	12.1046	12.0671	12.0297	11.9923	11.9549	11.9175	11.8801	.001247
26	12.7102	12.6726	12.6350	12.5975	12.5599	12.5223	12.4847	12.4472	12.4096	12.3720	12.3344	12.2969	.001252
27	13.1463	13.1087	13.0711	13.0335	12.9959	12.9583	12.9207	12.8831	12.8455	12.8079	12.7703	12.7327	.001253
28	13.6025	13.5648	13.5271	13.4894	13.4517	13.4140	13.3763	13.3387	13.3010	13.2633	13.2256	13.1879	.001256
29	14.0802	14.0425	14.0048	13.9670	13.9293	13.8916	13.8539	13.8162	13.7785	13.7407	13.7030	13.6653	.001257
30	14.5830	14.5453	14.5076	14.4699	14.4322	14.3945	14.3568	14.3192	14.2815	14.2438	14.2061	14.1684	.001256
31	15.1082	15.0707	15.0331	14.9956	14.9580	14.9205	14.8830	14.8454	14.8079	14.7703	14.7328	14.6952	.001251
32	15.6625	15.6246	15.5866	15.5487	15.5107	15.4728	15.4348	15.3969	15.3590	15.3210	15.2831	15.2451	.001265
33	16.2433	16.2051	16.1668	16.1286	16.0904	16.0522	16.0140	15.9757	15.9375	15.8993	15.8610	15.8228	.001274
34	16.8523	16.8129	16.7735	16.7341	16.6948	16.6554	16.6160	16.5766	16.5372	16.4978	16.4585	16.4191	.001313
35	17.4812	17.4404	17.3996	17.3589	17.3181	17.2773	17.2365	17.1958	17.1550	17.1142	17.0734	17.0327	.001359
36	18.1269	18.0841	18.0412	17.9984	17.9556	17.9127	17.8699	17.8271	17.7842	17.7414	17.6986	17.6557	.001428
37	18.7864	18.7414	18.6965	18.6515	18.6065	18.5616	18.5166	18.4716	18.4267	18.3817	18.3367	18.2918	.001499
38	19.4598	19.4119	19.3640	19.3161	19.2682	19.2203	19.1724	19.1246	19.0767	19.0288	18.9809	18.9330	.001596
39	20.1406	20.0900	20.0393	19.9887	19.9380	19.8874	19.8367	19.7861	19.7355	19.6848	19.6342	19.5835	.001688
40	20.8333	20.7794	20.7255	20.6715	20.6176	20.5637	20.5098	20.4559	20.4020	20.3480	20.2941	20.2402	.001797
41	21.5340	21.4763	21.4187	21.3610	21.3034	21.2457	21.1881	21.1304	21.0728	21.0151	20.9575	20.8998	.001922
42	22.2408	22.1791	22.1175	22.0558	21.9942	21.9325	21.8708	21.8092	21.7475	21.6859	21.6242	21.5626	.002055
43	22.9566	22.8900	22.8234	22.7568	22.6902	22.6236	22.5570	22.4903	22.4237	22.3571	22.2905	22.2239	.002220
44	23.6743	23.6028	23.5314	23.4599	23.3885	23.3170	23.2455	23.1741	23.1026	23.0312	22.9597	22.8883	.002382
45	24.4077	24.3306	24.2535	24.1764	24.0994	24.0223	23.9452	23.8681	23.7910	23.7140	23.6369	23.5598	.002569
46	25.1552	25.0719	24.9887	24.9054	24.8221	24.7389	24.6556	24.5723	24.4891	24.4058	24.3225	24.2393	.002775
47	25.9205	25.8307	25.7410	25.6512	25.5614	25.4717	25.3819	25.2921	25.2024	25.1126	25.0228	24.9331	.002992
48	26.7052	26.6082	26.5112	26.4143	26.3173	26.2203	26.1233	26.0264	25.9294	25.8324	25.7354	25.6385	.003232
49	27.5136	27.4088	27.3040	27.1992	27.0945	26.9897	26.8849	26.7801	26.6753	26.5705	26.4658	26.3610	.003493
50	28.3416	28.2278	28.1141	28.0003	27.8866	27.7728	27.6590	27.5453	27.4315	27.3178	27.2040	27.0903	.003792
51	29.1856	29.0621	28.9386	28.8150	28.6915	28.5680	28.4445	28.3210	28.1975	28.0740	27.9504	27.8269	.004117
52	30.0466	29.9123	29.7779	29.6436	29.5093	29.3749	29.2406	29.1063	28.9719	28.8376	28.7033	28.5689	.004477
53	30.9204	30.7743	30.6283	30.4822	30.3362	30.1901	30.0441	29.8980	29.7520	29.6060	29.4599	29.3138	.004868
54	31.8119	31.6529	31.4940	31.3350	31.1761	31.0171	30.8581	30.6992	30.5402	30.3813	30.2223	30.0634	.005298
55	32.7124	32.5394	32.3664	32.1934	32.0204	31.8474	31.6743	31.5013	31.3283	31.1553	30.9823	30.8093	.005767
56	33.6237	33.4354	33.2471	33.0589	32.8706	32.6823	32.4940	32.3058	32.1175	31.9292	31.7410	31.5527	.006276
57	34.5439	34.3389	34.1340	33.9290	33.7241	33.5191	33.3141	33.1092	32.9042	32.6993	32.4943	32.2894	.006832
58	35.4682	35.2453	35.0224	34.7995	34.5767	34.3538	34.1309	33.9080	33.6851	33.4622	33.2394	33.0165	.007409
59	36.3982	36.1562	35.9142	35.6721	35.4301	35.1881	34.9461	34.7041	34.4621	34.2200	33.9780	33.7360	.008067
60	37.3360	37.0732	36.8104	36.5476	36.2848	36.0220	35.7591	35.4963	35.2335	34.9707	34.7079	34.4451	.008760
61	38.2838	37.9987	37.7136	37.4284	37.1433	36.8582	36.5731	36.2880	36.0029	35.7177	35.4326	35.1475	.009504
62	39.2431	38.9340	38.6248	38.3157	38.0066	37.6974	37.3883	37.0792	36.7700	36.4609	36.1518	35.8426	.010304
63	40.2164	39.8816	39.5468	39.2120	38.8771	38.5423	38.2075	37.8727	37.5379	37.2030	36.8682	36.5334	.011160
64	41.2057	40.8432	40.4807	40.1182	39.7557	39.3932	39.0307	38.6682	38.3057	37.9432	37.5807	37.2182	.012083
65	42.2135	41.8214	41.4293	41.0372	40.6451	40.2530	39.8609	39.4688	39.0767	38.6846	38.2925	37.9004	.013070
66	43.2430	42.8194	42.3957	41.9721	41.5485	41.1249	40.7012	40.2776	39.8540	39.4304	39.0067	38.5831	.014121
67	44.2998	43.8421	43.3844	42.9268	42.4691	42.0114	41.5537	41.0961	40.6384	40.1807	39.7230	39.2654	.015256
68	45.3850	44.8908	44.3966	43.9023	43.4081	42.9139	42.4197	41.9255	41.4313	40.9370	40.4428	39.9486	.016474
69	46.4990	45.9660	45.4331	44.9001	44.3672	43.8342	43.3013	42.7683	42.2354	41.7024	41.1695	40.6365	.017765
70	47.6481	47.0741	46.5000	45.9260	45.3520	44.7780	44.2040	43.6299	43.0559	42.4819	41.9078	41.3338	.019134
71	48.8426	48.2257	47.6088	46.9919	46.3750	45.7581	45.1412	44.5243	43.9074	43.2905	42.6736	42.0567	.020563
72	50.1004	49.4391	48.7779	48.1166	47.4553	46.7941	46.1328	45.4715	44.8103	44.1490	43.4877	42.8265	.022042
73	51.4480	50.7404	50.0328	49.3252	48.6176	47.9100	47.2024	46.4949	45.7873	45.0797	44.3721	43.6645	.023586
74	52.9371	52.1795	51.4218	50.6642	49.9066	49.1490	48.3913	47.6337	46.8761	46.1185	45.3608	44.6032	.025254
75	54.5229	53.7161	52.9093	52.1025	51.2958	50.4890	49.6822	48.8754	48.0686	47.2618	46.4551	45.6483	.026893
76	56.3008	55.4404	54.5801	53.7197	52.8594	51.9990	51.1386	50.2783	49.4179	48.5576	47.6972	46.8369	.028678
77	58.2809	57.3618	56.4427	55.5237	54.6046	53.6855	52.7664	51.8474	50.9283	50.0092	49.0901	48.1711	.030636
78	60.4740	59.4905	58.5071	57.5236	56.5401	55.5567	54.5732	53.5897	52.6063	51.6228	50.6393	49.6559	.032782
79	62.8882	61.8325	60.7768	59.7211	58.6654	57.6097	56.5540	55.4984	54.4427	53.3870	52.3313	51.2756	.035190
80	65.5070	64.3726	63.2383	62.1039	60.9695	59.8352	58.7008	57.5664	56.4321	55.2977	54.1633	53.0290	.037812
81	68.3397	67.1171	65.8945	64.6719	63.4494	62.2268	61.0042	59.7816	58.5590	57.3364	56.1139	54.8913	.040753
82	71.3634	70.0377	68.7120	67.3863	66.0606	64.7349	63.4092	62.0835	60.7578	59.4321	58.1064	56.7807	.044190
83	74.5000	73.0523	71.6047	70.1570	68.7093	67.2617	65.8140	64.3663	62.9187	61.4710	60.0233	58.5757	.048253
84	77.6415	76.0540	74.4664	72.8789	71.2914	69.7039	68.1163	66.5288	64.9413	63.3538	61.7662	60.1787	.052917
85	80.7089	78.9349	77.1609	75.3870	73.6130	71.8390	70.0650	68.2910	66.5170	64.7430	62.9691	61.1951	.059133
86	83.2949	81.3176	79.3403	77.3629	75.3856	73.4083	71.4309	69.4536	67.4763	65.4989	63.5216	61.5443	.065910
87	85.3671	83.3170	81.2670	79.2169	77.1668	75.1167	73.0666	71.0166	68.9665	66.9164	64.8663	62.8163	.068336
88	88.8489	86.9496	85.0503	83.1510	81.2517	79.3524	77.4531	75.5539	73.6546	71.7553	69.8560	67.9567	.063319
89 or 20	**97.0874**	**97.3301**	**97.5728**	**97.8155**	**98.0583**	**98.3010**	**98.5437**	**98.7864**	**99.0291**	**99.2718**	**99.5146**	**99.7573**	**.008090**
19	96.0309	95.9989	95.9670	95.9350	95.9030	95.8710	95.8390	95.8071	95.7751	95.7431	95.7111	95.6792	.001066
18	95.4835	95.4124	95.3414	95.2703	95.1993	95.1282	95.0572	94.9861	94.9151	94.8440	94.7730	94.7020	.002368
17	95.0710	94.9916	94.9122	94.8328	94.7534	94.6740	94.5945	94.5151	94.4357	94.3563	94.2769	94.1975	.002646
16	94.5638	94.4958	94.4278	94.3598	94.2918	94.2238	94.1557	94.0877	94.0197	93.9517	93.8837	93.8157	.002267
15	93.9232	93.8681	93.8130	93.7579	93.7028	93.6477	93.5926	93.5375	93.4824	93.4273	93.3722	93.3171	.001837
14	93.2161	93.1691	93.1221	93.0751	93.0281	92.9811	92.9341	92.8872	92.8402	92.7932	92.7462	92.6992	.001566
13	92.4531	92.4133	92.3734	92.3336	92.2937	92.2539	92.2140	92.1742	92.1344	92.0945	92.0547	92.0148	.001328
12	91.6525	91.6182	91.5839	91.5496	91.5153	91.4810	91.4467	91.4124	91.3781	91.3438	91.3095	91.2752	.001143
11	90.8296	90.7994	90.7693	90.7391	90.7090	90.6788	90.6486	90.6185	90.5883	90.5582	90.5280	90.4979	.001005
10	89.9915	89.9648	89.9381	89.9114	89.8848	89.8581	89.8314	89.8047	89.7780	89.7513	89.7247	89.6980	.000889
Age.	0	1	2	3	4	5	6	7	8	9	10	11	Day.

Age.	0	1	2	3	4	5	6	7	8	9	10	11	Day.
10	8.3358	8.3000	8.2642	8.2284	8.1927	8.1569	8.1211	8.0853	8.0495	8.0137	7.9780	7.9422	.001193
11	8.6068	8.5712	8.5356	8.5000	8.4644	8.4288	8.3932	8.3577	8.3221	8.2865	8.2509	8.2153	.001186
12	8.8879	8.8524	8.8169	8.7814	8.7459	8.7104	8.6750	8.6395	8.6040	8.5685	8.5330	8.4975	.001183
13	9.1728	9.1374	9.1021	9.0667	9.0314	8.9960	8.9607	8.9253	8.8900	8.8546	8.8193	8.7840	.001178
14	9.4683	9.4331	9.3978	9.3626	9.3274	9.2922	9.2570	9.2217	9.1865	9.1513	9.1160	9.0808	.001174
15	9.7739	9.7388	9.7036	9.6685	9.6333	9.5982	9.5630	9.5279	9.4928	9.4576	9.4225	9.3873	.001171
16	10.0892	10.0542	10.0191	9.9841	9.9490	9.9140	9.8790	9.8439	9.8089	9.7738	9.7388	9.7037	.001168
17	10.4160	10.3810	10.3460	10.3110	10.2760	10.2410	10.2060	10.1709	10.1359	10.1009	10.0659	10.0309	.001167
18	10.7537	10.7186	10.6835	10.6484	10.6133	10.5782	10.5430	10.5079	10.4728	10.4377	10.4026	10.3675	.001170
19	11.1023	11.0675	11.0327	10.9980	10.9632	10.9284	10.8936	10.8589	10.8241	10.7893	10.7545	10.7198	.001159
20	11.4674	11.4325	11.3975	11.3626	11.3277	11.2928	11.2578	11.2229	11.1880	11.1531	11.1181	11.0832	.001164
21	11.8446	11.8097	11.7747	11.7398	11.7049	11.6699	11.6350	11.6001	11.5651	11.5302	11.4953	11.4603	.001164
22	12.2364	12.2014	12.1665	12.1315	12.0965	12.0616	12.0266	11.9916	11.9567	11.9217	11.8867	11.8518	.001165
23	12.6430	12.6080	12.5730	12.5380	12.5029	12.4679	12.4329	12.3979	12.3629	12.3278	12.2928	12.2578	.001167
24	13.0659	13.0310	12.9962	12.9613	12.9265	12.8916	12.8568	12.8220	12.7871	12.7522	12.7174	12.6825	.001162
25	13.5085	13.4736	13.4386	13.4037	13.3688	13.3339	13.2990	13.2640	13.2291	13.1942	13.1592	13.1243	.001164
26	13.9688	13.9339	13.8991	13.8642	13.8294	13.7945	13.7596	13.7248	13.6899	13.6551	13.6202	13.5854	.001162
27	14.4504	14.4155	14.3807	14.3458	14.3110	14.2761	14.2413	14.2064	14.1716	14.1367	14.1019	14.0670	.001162
28	14.9534	14.9186	14.8838	14.8491	14.8143	14.7795	14.7447	14.7100	14.6752	14.6404	14.6056	14.5709	.001159
29	15.4808	15.4462	15.4115	15.3769	15.3423	15.3076	15.2730	15.2384	15.2037	15.1691	15.1345	15.0998	.001154
30	16.0364	16.0019	15.9673	15.9328	15.8983	15.8638	15.8292	15.7947	15.7602	15.7257	15.6911	15.6566	.001151
31	16.6186	16.5838	16.5490	16.5141	16.4793	16.4445	16.4097	16.3749	16.3401	16.3052	16.2704	16.2356	.001160
32	17.2259	17.1911	17.1563	17.1214	17.0866	17.0518	17.0170	16.9822	16.9474	16.9125	16.8777	16.8429	.001160
33	17.8639	17.8281	17.7922	17.7564	17.7206	17.6848	17.6490	17.6131	17.5773	17.5415	17.5056	17.4698	.001157
34	18.5228	18.4857	18.4487	18.4116	18.3745	18.3375	18.3004	18.2633	18.2263	18.1892	18.1521	18.1151	.001235
35	19.2020	19.1631	19.1241	19.0852	19.0462	19.0073	18.9683	18.9294	18.8905	18.8515	18.8126	18.7736	.001298
36	19.8937	19.8528	19.8119	19.7710	19.7301	19.6892	19.6483	19.6075	19.5666	19.5257	19.4848	19.4439	.001363
37	20.6021	20.5585	20.5149	20.4713	20.4277	20.3841	20.3404	20.2968	20.2532	20.2096	20.1660	20.1224	.001453
38	21.3191	21.2730	21.2268	21.1806	21.1345	21.0883	21.0422	20.9960	20.9499	20.9037	20.8576	20.8114	.001538
39	22.0500	22.0008	21.9516	21.9025	21.8533	21.8041	21.7550	21.7058	21.6566	21.6074	21.5582	21.5091	.001639
40	22.7916	22.7389	22.6863	22.6336	22.5810	22.5283	22.4756	22.4230	22.3703	22.3177	22.2650	22.2124	.001755
41	23.5408	23.4844	23.4280	23.3717	23.3153	23.2589	23.2025	23.1462	23.0898	23.0334	22.9770	22.9207	.001879
42	24.2987	24.2377	24.1767	24.1157	24.0547	23.9937	23.9326	23.8716	23.8106	23.7496	23.6886	23.6276	.002033
43	25.0604	24.9949	24.9293	24.8638	24.7983	24.7327	24.6672	24.6017	24.5361	24.4706	24.4051	24.3395	.002184
44	25.8317	25.7608	25.6900	25.6191	25.5483	25.4774	25.4065	25.3357	25.2648	25.1940	25.1231	25.0523	.002362
45	26.6161	26.5394	26.4628	26.3861	26.3095	26.2328	26.1562	26.0795	26.0029	25.9262	25.8496	25.7730	.002555
46	27.4147	27.3319	27.2491	27.1663	27.0836	27.0008	26.9180	26.8352	26.7524	26.6696	26.5869	26.5041	.002759
47	28.2344	28.1448	28.0552	27.9656	27.8760	27.7864	27.6968	27.6073	27.5177	27.4281	27.3385	27.2489	.002986
48	29.0726	28.9756	28.8786	28.7816	28.6846	28.5876	28.4906	28.3937	28.2967	28.1997	28.1027	28.0057	.003233
49	29.9350	29.8295	29.7240	29.6185	29.5130	29.4075	29.3020	29.1966	29.0911	28.9856	28.8801	28.7746	.003516
50	30.8117	30.6970	30.5822	30.4675	30.3527	30.2380	30.1232	30.0085	29.8938	29.7790	29.6643	29.5495	.003825
51	31.7042	31.5792	31.4542	31.3291	31.2041	31.0791	30.9541	30.8291	30.7041	30.5790	30.4540	30.3290	.004167
52	32.6107	32.4746	32.3384	32.2023	32.0662	31.9301	31.7940	31.6578	31.5217	31.3856	31.2494	31.1133	.004537
53	33.5296	33.3812	33.2328	33.0844	32.9360	32.7876	32.6392	32.4909	32.3425	32.1941	32.0457	31.8973	.004946
54	34.4628	34.3011	34.1394	33.9777	33.8160	33.6543	33.4926	33.3309	33.1692	33.0075	32.8458	32.6841	.005390
55	35.4035	35.2273	35.0511	34.8750	34.6988	34.5226	34.3464	34.1702	33.9940	33.8178	33.6417	33.4655	.005873
56	36.3533	36.1613	35.9693	35.7772	35.5852	35.3932	35.2012	35.0092	34.8172	34.6251	34.4331	34.2411	.006400
57	37.3087	37.0997	36.8907	36.6817	36.4728	36.2738	36.0548	35.8458	35.6368	35.4278	35.2189	35.0099	.006966
58	38.2684	38.0413	37.8142	37.5872	37.3601	37.1330	36.9060	36.6789	36.4518	36.2247	35.9976	35.7706	.007569
59	39.2355	38.9888	38.7420	38.4953	38.2486	38.0018	37.7551	37.5084	37.2616	37.0149	36.7682	36.5214	.008224
60	40.2079	39.9400	39.6722	39.4043	39.1365	38.8686	38.6008	38.3330	38.0651	37.7972	37.5294	37.2615	.008928
61	41.1904	40.8998	40.6093	40.3187	40.0282	39.7376	39.4471	39.1565	38.8660	38.5754	38.2849	37.9943	.009685
62	42.1835	41.8687	41.5538	41.2390	40.9241	40.6093	40.2944	39.9796	39.6648	39.3499	39.0351	38.7202	.010495
63	43.1911	42.8501	42.5091	42.1681	41.8271	41.4861	41.1451	40.8041	40.4631	40.1221	39.7811	39.4401	.011367
64	44.2131	43.8441	43.4752	43.1062	42.7372	42.3683	41.9993	41.6303	41.2614	40.8924	40.5234	40.1545	.012299
65	45.2541	44.8554	44.4566	44.0579	43.6591	43.2604	42.8616	42.4629	42.0642	41.6654	41.2667	40.8679	.013291
66	46.3189	45.8880	45.4571	45.0262	44.5953	44.1644	43.7335	43.3027	42.8718	42.4409	42.0100	41.5791	.014363
67	47.4074	46.9420	46.4766	46.0111	45.5457	45.0803	44.6149	44.1495	43.6841	43.2186	42.7532	42.2878	.015514
68	48.5227	48.0207	47.5188	47.0168	46.5149	46.0130	45.5110	45.0090	44.5 71	44.0051	43.5032	43.0012	.016732
69	49.6710	49.1304	48.5898	48.0492	47.5086	46.9680	46.4274	45.8868	45.3462	44.8056	44.2650	43.7244	.018020
70	50.8597	50.2787	49.6978	49.1168	48.5359	47.9549	47.3740	46.7930	46.2120	45.6311	45.0501	44.4692	.019365
71	52.1075	51.4848	50.8622	50.2395	49.6169	48.9942	48.3715	47.7489	47.1262	46.5036	45.8809	45.2583	.020755
72	53.4388	52.7727	52.1065	51.4404	50.7743	50.1082	49.4420	48.7759	48.1098	47.4437	46.7775	46.1114	.022204
73	54.8776	54.1667	53.4558	52.7450	52.0341	51.3232	50.6123	49.9015	49.1906	48.4797	47.7688	47.0580	.023696
74	56.4579	55.6988	54.9397	54.1807	53.4216	52.6625	51.9034	51.1444	50.3853	49.6262	48.8671	48.1081	.025302
75	58.1932	57.3840	56.5748	55.7657	54.9565	54.1473	53.3381	52.5290	51.7198	50.9106	50.1014	49.2923	.026972
76	60.1196	59.2556	58.3915	57.5275	56.6635	55.7995	54.9354	54.0714	53.2074	52.3434	51.4793	50.6153	.028801
77	62.2434	61.3192	60.3950	59.4708	58.5466	57.6224	56.6982	55.7740	54.8498	53.9256	53.0014	52.0772	.030807
78	64.5731	63.5814	62.5896	61.5979	60.6062	59.6144	58.6227	57.6310	56.6392	55.6475	54.6558	53.6640	.033058
79	67.0954	66.0303	64.9652	63.9001	62.8350	61.7699	60.7047	59.6396	58.5745	57.5094	56.4443	55.3792	.035503
80	69.8181	68.6709	67.5236	66.3764	65.2292	64.0819	62.9347	61.7875	60.6402	59.4930	58.3458	57.1985	.038241
81	72.7218	71.4789	70.2360	68.9932	67.7503	66.5074	65.2645	64.0217	62.7788	61.5359	60.2930	59.0502	.041429
82	75.7328	74.3774	73.0219	71.6665	70.3111	68.9556	67.6002	66.2448	64.8893	63.5339	62.1785	60.8230	.045181
83	78.7443	77.2606	75.7768	74.2931	72.8094	71.3257	69.8420	68.3582	66.8745	65.3908	63.9070	62.4233	.049457
84	81.6823	80.0282	78.3741	76.7200	75.0658	73.4117	71.7576	70.1035	68.4494	66.7952	65.1411	63.4870	.055137
85	84.1554	82.3166	80.4777	78.6389	76.8001	74.9613	73.1224	71.2836	69.4448	67.6060	65.7671	63.9283	.061294
86	86.1409	84.2422	82.3435	80.4448	78.5461	76.6474	74.7486	72.8499	70.9512	69.0525	67.1538	65.2551	.063290
87	89.4245	87.6749	85.9252	84.1756	82.4260	80.6764	78.9267	77.1771	75.4275	73.6779	71.9282	70.1786	.058321
88 or 21	**97.0874**	**97.3301**	**97.5728**	**97.8155**	**98.0583**	**98.3010**	**98.5437**	**98.7864**	**99.0291**	**99.2718**	**99.5146**	**99.7573**	**.008090**
20	96.0227	95.9886	95.9545	95.9204	95.8863	95.8522	95.8181	95.7840	95.7499	95.7158	95.6817	95.6476	.001137
19	95.4714	95.3980	95.3246	95.2512	95.1778	95.1044	95.0310	94.9577	94.8843	94.8109	94.7375	94.6641	.002446
18	95.0664	94.9838	94.9013	94.8187	94.7361	94.6536	94.5710	94.4884	94.4059	94.3233	94.2407	94.1582	.002752
17	94.5462	94.4760	94.4058	94.3357	94.2655	94.1953	94.1251	94.0550	93.9848	93.9146	93.8444	93.7743	.002339
16	93.9019	93.8448	93.7877	93.7306	93.6735	93.6164	93.5592	93.5021	93.4450	93.3879	93.3308	93.2737	.001903
15	93.1910	93.1421	93.0932	93.0444	92.9955	92.9466	92.8977	92.8489	92.8000	92.7511	92.7022	92.6534	.001629
14	92.4240	92.3824	92.3408	92.2992	92.2576	92.2160	92.1743	92.1327	92.0911	92.0495	92.0079	91.9663	.001387
13	91.6196	91.5836	91.5476	91.5116	91.4757	91.4397	91.4037	91.3677	91.3317	91.2957	91.2598	91.2238	.001199
12	90.7933	90.7616	90.7298	90.6981	90.6663	90.6346	90.6028	90.5711	90.5394	90.5076	90.4759	90.4441	.001058
11	89.9520	89.9238	89.8956	89.8673	89.8391	89.8109	89.7827	89.7545	89.7263	89.6980	89.6698	89.6416	.000940
10	89.0969	89.0720	89.0471	89.0223	88.9974	88.9725	88.9476	88.9228	88.8979	88.8730	88.8481	88.8233	.000829
Age.	0	1	2	3	4	5	6	7	8	9	10	11	Day.

Age.	0	1	2	3	4	5	6	7	8	9	10	11	Day.
10	9.0996	9.0656	9.0315	8.9975	8.9634	8.9294	8.8953	8.8613	8.8273	8.7932	8.7592	8.7251	.001135
11	9.3959	9.3620	9.3281	9.2942	9.2604	9.2265	9.1926	9.1587	9.1248	9.0910	9.0571	9.0232	.001129
12	9.7021	9.6684	9.6347	9.6011	9.5674	9.5337	9.5000	9.4664	9.4327	9.3990	9.3653	9.3317	.001122
13	10.0138	9.9803	9.9468	9.9133	9.8798	9.8463	9.8128	9.7794	9.7459	9.7124	9.6789	9.6454	.001116
14	10.3370	10.3036	10.2703	10.2370	10.2036	10.1702	10.1369	10.1035	10.0702	10.0368	10.0035	9.9701	.001112
15	10.6709	10.6377	10.6045	10.5713	10.5382	10.5050	10.4718	10.4386	10.4054	10.3722	10.3391	10.3059	.001106
16	11.0159	10.9828	10.9497	10.9166	10.8836	10.8505	10.8174	10.7843	10.7512	10.7181	10.6851	10.6520	.001103
17	11.3728	11.3397	11.3066	11.2734	11.2403	11.2072	11.1741	11.1410	11.1079	11.0747	11.0416	11.0085	.001104
18	11.7403	11.7076	11.6749	11.6422	11.6095	11.5768	11.5440	11.5113	11.4786	11.4459	11.4132	11.3805	.001090
19	12.1251	12.0923	12.0595	12.0267	11.9939	11.9611	11.9283	11.8956	11.8628	11.8300	11.7972	11.7644	.001093
20	12.5221	12.4894	12.4566	12.4239	12.3912	12.3585	12.3257	12.2930	12.2603	12.2276	12.1948	12.1621	.001091
21	12.9344	12.9017	12.8690	12.8363	12.8036	12.7709	12.7382	12.7056	12.6729	12.6402	12.6075	12.5748	.001090
22	13.3625	13.3298	13.2972	13.2645	13.2319	13.1992	13.1665	13.1339	13.1012	13.0686	13.0359	13.0033	.001088
23	13.8067	13.7743	13.7419	13.7095	13.6771	13.6447	13.6123	13.5799	13.5475	13.5151	13.4827	13.4503	.001080
24	14.2717	14.2393	14.2069	14.1745	14.1421	14.1097	14.0773	14.0450	14.0126	13.9802	13.9478	13.9154	.001080
25	14.7552	14.7230	14.6907	14.6585	14.6263	14.5940	14.5618	14.5296	14.4973	14.4651	14.4329	14.4006	.001074
26	15.2600	15.2279	15.1957	15.1636	15.1315	15.0994	15.0672	15.0351	15.0030	14.9709	14.9387	14.9066	.001071
27	15.7874	15.7554	15.7235	15.6915	15.6596	15.6276	15.5956	15.5637	15.5317	15.4998	15.4678	15.4359	.001065
28	16.3392	16.3075	16.2758	16.2440	16.2123	16.1806	16.1489	16.1172	16.0855	16.0537	16.0220	15.9903	.001057
29	16.9185	16.8870	16.8555	16.8240	16.7924	16.7609	16.7294	16.6979	16.6664	16.6348	16.6033	16.5718	.001050
30	17.5278	17.4963	17.4648	17.4333	17.4018	17.3703	17.3387	17.3072	17.2757	17.2442	17.2127	17.1812	.001050
31	18.1617	18.1301	18.0986	18.0670	18.0355	18.0039	17.9723	17.9408	17.9092	17.8777	17.8461	17.8146	.001052
32	18.8268	18.7944	18.7619	18.7295	18.6970	18.6646	18.6321	18.5997	18.5673	18.5348	18.5024	18.4699	.001081
33	19.5133	19.4797	19.4462	19.4127	19.3792	19.3456	19.3121	19.2786	19.2450	19.2115	19.1780	19.1444	.001118
34	20.2211	20.1858	20.1506	20.1153	20.0801	20.0448	20.0095	19.9743	19.9390	19.9038	19.8685	19.8333	.001175
35	20.9448	20.9078	20.8707	20.8337	20.7966	20.7596	20.7225	20.6855	20.6485	20.6114	20.5744	20.5373	.001235
36	21.6838	21.6442	21.6047	21.5651	21.5255	21.4860	21.4464	21.4068	21.3673	21.3277	21.2881	21.2486	.001319
37	22.4341	22.3922	22.3503	22.3084	22.2665	22.2246	22.1827	22.1408	22.0989	22.0570	22.0151	21.9732	.001397
38	23.1993	23.1546	23.1099	23.0652	23.0205	22.9758	22.9310	22.8863	22.8416	22.7969	22.7522	22.7075	.001490
39	23.9771	23.9292	23.8812	23.8333	23.7853	23.7374	23.6894	23.6415	23.5936	23.5456	23.4977	23.4497	.001598
40	24.7649	24.7135	24.6621	24.6107	24.5593	24.5079	24.4565	24.4052	24.3538	24.3024	24.2510	24.1996	.001713
41	25.5629	25.5072	25.4514	25.3957	25.3400	25.2842	25.2285	25.1728	25.1170	25.0613	25.0056	24.9498	.001858
42	26.3644	26.3045	26.2445	26.1846	26.1246	26.0647	26.0047	25.9448	25.8849	25.8249	25.7650	25.7050	.001998
43	27.1771	27.1122	27.0472	26.9823	26.9173	26.8524	26.7874	26.7225	26.6576	26.5926	26.5277	26.4627	.002165
44	27.9964	27.9260	27.8556	27.7852	27.7148	27.6444	27.5740	27.5036	27.4332	27.3628	27.2924	27.2220	.002347
45	28.8297	28.7535	28.6773	28.6012	28.5250	28.4488	28.3726	28.2965	28.2203	28.1441	28.0680	27.9918	.002539
46	29.6800	29.5974	29.5148	29.4321	29.3495	29.2669	29.1843	29.1017	29.0191	28.9364	28.8538	28.7712	.002754
47	30.5504	30.4608	30.3712	30.2815	30.1919	30.1023	30.0127	29.9231	29.8335	29.7438	29.6542	29.5646	.002987
48	31.4398	31.3421	31.2444	31.1467	31.0490	30.9513	30.8536	30.7560	30.6583	30.5606	30.4629	30.3652	.003256
49	32.3480	32.2415	32.1351	32.0286	31.9222	31.8157	31.7092	31.6028	31.4963	31.3899	31.2834	31.1770	.003548
50	33.2700	33.1538	33.0376	32.9214	32.8052	32.6890	32.5728	32.4566	32.3404	32.2242	32.1080	31.9918	.003873
51	34.2048	34.0780	33.9513	33.8245	33.6978	33.5710	33.4443	33.3175	33.1908	33.0640	32.9373	32.8105	.004225
52	35.1532	35.0148	34.8764	34.7380	34.5996	34.4612	34.3228	34.1844	34.0460	33.9076	33.7692	33.6308	.004613
53	36.1108	35.9597	35.8087	35.6576	35.5065	35.3555	35.2044	35.0533	34.9023	34.7512	34.6001	34.4491	.005035
54	37.0808	36.9160	36.7512	36.5864	36.4216	36.2568	36.0920	35.9272	35.7624	35.5976	35.4328	35.2680	.005493
55	38.0566	37.8768	37.6970	37.5171	37.3373	37.1575	36.9777	36.7979	36.6181	36.4382	36.2584	36.0786	.005994
56	39.0380	38.8421	38.6462	38.4503	38.2544	38.0585	37.8625	37.6666	37.4707	37.2748	37.0789	36.8830	.006530
57	40.0252	39.8122	39.5991	39.3861	39.1730	38.9600	38.7470	38.5339	38.3209	38.1078	37.8948	37.6817	.007101
58	41.0183	40.7866	40.5550	40.3233	40.0917	39.8600	39.6283	39.3967	39.1650	38.9334	38.7017	38.4701	.007722
59	42.0162	41.7646	41.5130	41.2613	41.0097	40.7581	40.5065	40.2549	40.0033	39.7516	39.5000	39.2484	.008387
60	43.0193	42.7462	42.4731	42.2000	41.9269	41.6538	41.3807	41.1076	40.8345	40.5614	40.2883	40.0152	.009103
61	44.0318	43.7357	43.4396	43.1436	42.8475	42.5514	42.2553	41.9593	41.6632	41.3671	41.0710	40.7750	.009869
62	45.0553	44.7345	44.4137	44.0929	43.7721	43.4513	43.1304	42.8096	42.4888	42.1680	41.8472	41.5264	.010693
63	46.0916	45.7444	45.3971	45.0499	44.7027	44.3554	44.0082	43.6610	43.3137	42.9665	42.6193	42.2720	.011574
64	47.1429	46.7675	46.3922	46.0168	45.6414	45.2661	44.8907	44.5153	44.1400	43.7646	43.3892	43.0139	.012512
65	48.2150	47.8093	47.4035	46.9978	46.5921	46.1864	45.7806	45.3749	44.9692	44.5635	44.1577	43.7520	.013524
66	49.3075	48.8692	48.4308	47.9925	47.5542	47.1159	46.6775	46.2392	45.8009	45.3626	44.9242	44.4859	.014611
67	50.4151	49.9429	49.4707	48.9984	48.5262	48.0540	47.5818	47.1096	46.6374	46.1651	45.6929	45.2207	.015740
68	51.5676	51.0583	50.5490	50.0398	49.5305	49.0212	48.5120	48.0027	47.4934	46.9841	46.4748	45.9656	.016976
69	52.7513	52.2040	51.6568	51.1095	50.5623	50.0150	49.4677	48.9205	48.3732	47.8260	47.2787	46.7315	.018242
70	53.9881	53.4016	52.8151	52.2287	51.6422	51.0557	50.4692	49.8828	49.2963	48.7098	48.1233	47.5369	.019549
71	55.3033	54.6760	54.0487	53.4213	52.7940	52.1667	51.5394	50.9121	50.2848	49.6574	49.0301	48.4028	.020910
72	56.9189	56.2496	55.5803	54.9110	54.2418	53.5725	52.9032	52.2339	51.5646	50.8953	50.0261	49.3568	.022309
73	58.2679	57.5535	56.8390	56.1246	55.4101	54.6957	53.9812	53.2668	52.5524	51.8379	51.1235	50.4090	.023815
74	59.9613	59.2000	58.4386	57.6773	56.9159	56.1546	55.3932	54.6319	53.8706	53.1092	52.3479	51.5865	.025378
75	61.8349	61.0222	60.2095	59.3968	58.5842	57.7715	56.9588	56.1461	55.3334	54.5207	53.7081	52.8954	.027089
76	63.8944	63.0255	62.1566	61.2877	60.4188	59.5499	58.6810	57.8120	56.9431	56.0742	55.2053	54.3364	.028963
77	66.1444	65.2123	64.2803	63.3482	62.4161	61.4841	60.5520	59.6199	58.6879	57.7558	56.8237	55.8917	.031069
78	68.5730	67.5723	66.5716	65.5710	64.5703	63.5696	62.5689	61.5682	60.5675	59.5668	58.5662	57.5655	.033356
79	71.1896	70.1123	69.0350	67.9576	66.8803	65.8030	64.7257	63.6484	62.5711	61.4937	60.4164	59.3391	.035910
80	3.9748	72.8083	71.6418	70.4754	69.3089	68.1424	66.9760	65.8095	64.6430	63.4765	62.3100	61.1436	.038882
81	76.8604	75.5894	74.3183	73.0473	71.7763	70.5053	69.2342	67.9632	66.6922	65.4212	64.1501	62.8791	.042367
82	79.7454	78.3559	76.9664	75.5768	74.1873	72.7978	71.4083	70.0188	68.6293	67.2397	65.8502	64.4607	.046320
83	82.5560	81.0094	79.4629	77.9163	76.3698	74.8232	73.2767	71.7301	70.1836	68.6370	67.0905	65.5440	.051552
84	84.9240	83.2089	81.4938	79.7787	78.0636	76.3485	74.6333	72.9182	71.2031	69.4880	67.7729	66.0578	.057170
85	86.8238	85.0587	83.2936	81.5285	79.7634	77.9983	76.2332	74.4682	72.7031	70.9380	69.1729	67.4078	.058836
86	89.9304	88.3123	86.6942	85.0761	83.4581	81.8400	80.2219	78.6038	76.9857	75.3676	73.7496	72.1315	.053935
87 or 22	**97.0874**	**97.3301**	**97.5728**	**97.8155**	**98.0583**	**98.3010**	**98.5437**	**98.7864**	**99.0291**	**99.2718**	**99.5146**	**99.7573**	**.008090**
21	96.0142	95.9779	95.9416	95.9052	95.8689	95.8326	95.7963	95.7600	95.7237	95.6873	95.6510	95.6147	.001210
20	95.4590	95.3832	95.3073	95.2315	95.1556	95.0798	95.0040	94.9281	94.8523	94.7764	94.7006	94.6247	.002528
19	95.0514	94.9663	94.8814	94.7964	94.7114	94.6264	94.5413	94.4563	94.3713	94.2863	94.2013	94.1163	.002833
18	94.5279	94.4555	94.3830	94.3106	94.2381	94.1657	94.0932	94.0208	93.9484	93.8759	93.8035	93.7310	.002415
17	93.8797	93.8205	93.7613	93.7021	93.6429	93.5837	93.5245	93.4653	93.4061	93.3469	93.2877	93.2285	.001973
16	93.1648	93.1140	93.0631	93.0123	92.9614	92.9106	92.8597	92.8089	92.7581	92.7072	92.6564	92.6055	.001695
15	92.3938	92.3503	92.3069	92.2634	92.2200	92.1765	92.1330	92.0896	92.0461	92.0027	91.9592	91.9158	.001448
14	91.5853	91.5476	91.5098	91.4721	91.4344	91.3967	91.3590	91.3212	91.2835	91.2458	91.2080	91.1703	.001257
13	90.7552	90.7218	90.6884	90.6550	90.6216	90.5882	90.5548	90.5214	90.4880	90.4546	90.4212	90.3878	.001113
12	89.9104	89.8806	89.8509	89.8211	89.7913	89.7616	89.7318	89.7020	89.6723	89.6425	89.6127	89.5830	.000992
11	89.0521	89.0257	88.9994	88.9730	88.9467	88.9203	88.8940	88.8676	88.8412	88.8149	88.7885	88.7622	.000878
10	88.1882	88.1645	88.1408	88.1171	88.0934	88.0697	88.0460	88.0222	87.9985	87.9748	87.9511	87.9274	.000790
Age	0	1	2	3	4	5	6	7	8	9	10	11	Day.

Age.	0	1	2	3	4	5	6	7	8	9	10	11	Day.
10	9.8843	9.8520	9.8196	9.7873	9.7549	9.7226	9.6902	9.6579	9.6256	9.5932	9.5609	9.5285	.001078
11	10.2054	10.1733	10.1412	10.1091	10.0770	10.0449	10.0128	9.9807	9.9487	9.9166	9.8845	9.8524	.001070
12	10.5381	10.5063	10.4744	10.4426	10.4108	10.3789	10.3471	10.3153	10.2834	10.2516	10.2198	10.1879	.001061
13	10.8771	10.8455	10.8138	10.7822	10.7506	10.7189	10.6873	10.6557	10.6240	10.5924	10.5608	10.5291	.001054
14	11.2282	11.1968	11.1654	11.1340	11.1026	11.0712	11.0398	11.0084	10.9770	10.9456	10.9142	10.8828	.001047
15	11.5914	11.5602	11.5289	11.4977	11.4664	11.4352	11.4040	11.3727	11.3415	11.3102	11.2790	11.2477	.001041
16	11.9661	11.9349	11.9037	11.8725	11.8413	11.8101	11.7788	11.7476	11.7164	11.6852	11.6540	11.6228	.001040
17	12.3522	12.3215	12.2907	12.2600	12.2293	12.1985	12.1678	12.1371	12.1063	12.0756	12.0449	12.0141	.001024
18	12.7556	12.7248	12.6941	12.6633	12.6326	12.6018	12.5711	12.5403	12.5096	12.4788	12.4481	12.4173	.001025
19	13.1718	13.1412	13.1106	13.0800	13.0493	13.0187	12.9881	12.9575	12.9269	12.8962	12.8656	12.8350	.001020
20	13.6032	13.5727	13.5422	13.5117	13.4812	13.4507	13.4202	13.3898	13.3593	13.3288	13.2983	13.2678	.001016
21	14.0511	14.0207	13.9903	13.9600	13.9296	13.8992	13.8688	13.8384	13.8080	13.7776	13.7473	13.7169	.001013
22	14.5163	14.4862	14.4562	14.4261	14.3961	14.3660	14.3360	14.3059	14.2758	14.2458	14.2157	14.1857	.001002
23	15.0019	14.9719	14.9420	14.9120	14.8820	14.8521	14.8221	14.7921	14.7622	14.7322	14.7022	14.6723	.000999
24	15.5070	15.4773	15.4475	15.4178	15.3881	15.3584	15.3286	15.2989	15.2692	15.2395	15.2097	15.1800	.000991
25	16.0341	16.0046	15.9751	15.9455	15.9160	15.8865	15.8570	15.8275	15.7980	15.7684	15.7389	15.7094	.000984
26	16.5840	16.5547	16.5255	16.4962	16.4670	16.4377	16.4084	16.3792	16.3499	16.3207	16.2914	16.2622	.000975
27	17.1592	17.1303	17.1013	17.0724	17.0435	17.0145	16.9856	16.9567	16.9277	16.8988	16.8699	16.8409	.000964
28	17.7617	17.7331	17.7044	17.6758	17.6472	17.6186	17.5900	17.5613	17.5327	17.5041	17.4754	17.4468	.000954
29	18.3936	18.3651	18.3365	18.3081	18.2795	18.2510	18.2224	18.1939	18.1654	18.1369	18.1083	18.0798	.000951
30	19.0554	19.0269	18.9985	18.9700	18.9416	18.9131	18.8846	18.8562	18.8277	18.7993	18.7708	18.7424	.000948
31	19.7438	19.7146	19.6854	19.6562	19.6270	19.5977	19.5685	19.5393	19.5101	19.4809	19.4517	19.4225	.000973
32	20.4562	20.4260	20.3958	20.3656	20.3355	20.3053	20.2751	20.2449	20.2147	20.1845	20.1544	20.1242	.001006
33	21.1903	21.1585	21.1268	21.0950	21.0633	21.0315	20.9997	20.9680	20.9362	20.9045	20.8727	20.8410	.001058
34	21.9411	21.9077	21.8743	21.8410	21.8076	21.7742	21.7408	21.7075	21.6741	21.6407	21.6073	21.5740	.001112
35	22.7105	22.6748	22.6390	22.6033	22.5676	22.5319	22.4961	22.4604	22.4247	22.3890	22.3532	22.3175	.001191
36	23.4898	23.4519	23.4140	23.3762	23.3383	23.3004	23.2625	23.2247	23.1868	23.1489	23.1110	23.0732	.001262
37	24.2866	24.2461	24.2056	24.1652	24.1247	24.0842	24.0437	24.0033	23.9628	23.9223	23.8818	23.8414	.001349
38	25.0968	25.0533	25.0098	24.9663	24.9229	24.8794	24.8359	24.7924	24.7489	24.7054	24.6620	24.6185	.001449
39	25.9190	25.8723	25.8256	25.7789	25.7322	25.6854	25.6387	25.5920	25.5453	25.4986	25.4519	25.4052	.001557
40	26.7534	26.7026	26.6519	26.6011	26.5503	26.4996	26.4488	26.3980	26.3473	26.2965	26.2457	26.1950	.001692
41	27.5927	27.5380	27.4833	27.4286	27.3739	27.3192	27.2645	27.2098	27.1551	27.1004	27.0457	26.9910	.001823
42	28.4429	28.3835	28.3241	28.2647	28.2054	28.1460	28.0866	28.0272	27.9678	27.9084	27.8491	27.7897	.001979
43	29.3008	29.2363	29.1718	29.1073	29.0429	28.9784	28.9139	28.8494	28.7849	28.7204	28.6560	28.5915	.002149
44	30.1666	30.0967	30.0267	29.9568	29.8869	29.8170	29.7470	29.6771	29.6072	29.5373	29.4673	29.3974	.002331
45	31.0490	30.9729	30.8968	30.8207	30.7446	30.6685	30.5924	30.5163	30.4403	30.3642	30.2881	30.2120	.002536
46	31.9474	31.8648	31.7821	31.6995	31.6168	31.5342	31.4515	31.3689	31.2863	31.2036	31.1210	31.0383	.002755
47	32.8661	32.7758	32.6855	32.5952	32.5049	32.4146	32.3243	32.2340	32.1438	32.0535	31.9632	31.8729	.003010
48	33.7986	33.7000	33.6013	33.5027	33.4041	33.3054	33.2068	33.1082	33.0095	32.9109	32.8123	32.7136	.003288
49	34.7493	34.6414	34.5335	34.4256	34.3177	34.2098	34.1019	33.9940	33.8862	33.7783	33.6704	33.5625	.003596
50	35.7108	35.5929	35.4750	35.3571	35.2392	35.1212	35.0033	34.8854	34.7675	34.6496	34.5317	34.4138	.003930
51	36.6845	36.5555	36.4265	36.2976	36.1686	36.0396	35.9106	35.7817	35.6527	35.5237	35.3947	35.2658	.004299
52	37.6684	37.5274	37.3864	37.2454	37.1044	36.9634	36.8224	36.6814	36.5404	36.3994	36.2584	36.1174	.004700
53	38.6599	38.5058	38.3517	38.1977	38.0436	37.8895	37.7354	37.5814	37.4273	37.2732	37.1191	36.9651	.005136
54	39.6617	39.4934	39.3250	39.1567	38.9884	38.8201	38.6517	38.4834	38.3151	38.1468	37.9784	37.8101	.005611
55	40.6660	40.4824	40.2988	40.1152	39.9316	39.7480	39.5643	39.3807	39.1971	39.0135	38.8299	38.6463	.006120
56	41.6760	41.4761	41.2763	41.0764	40.8765	40.6767	40.4768	40.2769	40.0771	39.8772	39.6773	39.4775	.006662
57	42.6930	42.4755	42.2580	42.0405	41.8230	41.6055	41.3880	41.1705	40.9531	40.7356	40.5181	40.3006	.007250
58	43.7132	43.4768	43.2404	43.0040	42.7677	42.5313	42.2949	42.0585	41.8221	41.5857	41.3494	41.1130	.007879
59	44.7382	44.4815	44.2248	43.9681	43.7114	43.4547	43.1980	42.9413	42.6846	42.4279	42.1712	41.9145	.008557
60	45.7678	45.4894	45.2109	44.9325	44.6540	44.3756	44.0971	43.8187	43.5403	43.2618	42.9834	42.7049	.009281
61	46.8069	46.5051	46.2032	45.9014	45.5996	45.2977	44.9959	44.6941	44.3922	44.0904	43.7886	43.4867	.010061
62	47.8555	47.5287	47.2018	46.8750	46.5482	46.2213	45.8945	45.5677	45.2408	44.9140	44.5872	44.2603	.010894
63	48.9173	48.5639	48.2105	47.8571	47.5037	47.1503	46.7969	46.4435	46.0901	45.7367	45.3833	45.0299	.011780
64	49.9959	49.6138	49.2317	48.8496	48.4675	48.0854	47.7033	47.3212	46.9392	46.5571	46.1750	45.7929	.012736
65	51.0921	50.6792	50.2663	49.8534	49.4405	49.0276	48.6147	48.2018	47.7890	47.3761	46.9632	46.5503	.013763
66	52.2069	51.7615	51.3160	50.8706	50.4252	49.9798	49.5343	49.0889	48.6435	48.1981	47.7526	47.3072	.014847
67	53.3482	52.8683	52.3885	51.9086	51.4288	50.9489	50.4690	49.9892	49.5093	49.0295	48.5496	48.0698	.015995
68	54.5246	54.0089	53.4933	52.9776	52.4620	51.9463	51.4306	50.9150	50.3993	49.8837	49.3680	48.8524	.017188
69	55.7516	55.1991	54.6465	54.0940	53.5414	52.9889	52.4363	51.8838	51.3313	50.7787	50.2262	49.6736	.018418
70	57.0503	56.4594	55.8684	55.2775	54.6865	54.0956	53.5046	52.9137	52.3228	51.7318	51.1409	50.5499	.019698
71	58.4432	57.8129	57.1826	56.5522	55.9219	55.2916	54.6613	54.0310	53.4007	52.7703	52.1400	51.5097	.021010
72	59.9612	59.2885	58.6158	57.9431	57.2705	56.5978	55.9251	55.2524	54.5797	53.9070	53.2344	52.5617	.022423
73	61.6153	60.8987	60.1820	59.4654	58.7488	58.0322	57.3155	56.5989	55.8823	55.1657	54.4490	53.7324	.023887
74	63.4375	62.6728	61.9081	61.1434	60.3787	59.6140	58.8493	58.0847	57.3200	56.5553	55.7906	55.0259	.025490
75	65.4345	64.6172	63.7998	62.9825	62.1652	61.3478	60.5305	59.7132	58.8958	58.0785	57.2612	56.4438	.027243
76	67.6106	66.7342	65.8578	64.9814	64.1050	63.2286	62.3521	61.4757	60.5993	59.7229	58.8465	57.9701	.029213
77	69.9511	69.0105	68.0699	67.1293	66.1887	65.2481	64.3075	63.3670	62.4264	61.4858	60.5452	59.6046	.031353
78	72.4655	71.4532	70.4409	69.4286	68.4163	67.4040	66.3917	65.3795	64.3672	63.3549	62.3426	61.3303	.033743
79	75.1373	74.0417	72.9461	71.8505	70.7549	69.6593	68.5637	67.4681	66.3725	65.2769	64.1813	63.0857	.036520
80	77.9006	76.7074	75.5142	74.3210	73.1279	71.9347	70.7415	69.5483	68.3551	67.1620	65.9688	64.7756	.039773
81	80.6612	79.3579	78.0546	76.7512	75.4479	74 1446	72.8413	71.5380	70.2347	68.9313	67.6280	66.3247	.043444
82	83.3490	81.9001	80.4512	79.0023	77.5534	76.1045	74.6556	73.2067	71.7578	70.3089	68.8600	67.4111	.048297
83	85.6138	84.0101	82.4063	80.8026	79.1988	77.5951	75.9913	74.3876	72.7839	71.1801	69.5764	67.9726	.053458
84	87.4338	85.7880	84.1423	82.4965	80.8508	79.2050	77.5592	75.9135	74.2677	72.6220	70.9762	69.3305	.054858
85	90.3770	88.8750	87.3730	85.8710	84.3690	82.8670	81.3650	79.8631	78.3611	76.8591	75.3571	73.8551	.050066
86 or 23	**97.0874**	**97.3301**	**97.5728**	**97.8155**	**98.0583**	**98.3010**	**98.5437**	**98.7864**	**39.0291**	**99.2718**	**99.5146**	**99.7573**	**.008090**
22	96.0053	95.9667	95.9280	95.8894	95.8508	95.8121	95.7735	95.7349	95.6962	95.6576	95.6190	95.5803	.001288
21	95.4459	95.3674	95.2890	95.2105	95.1320	95.0535	94.9750	94.8966	94.8181	94.7396	94.6611	94.5827	.002616
20	95.0356	94.9481	94.8605	94.7730	94.6854	94.5979	94.5103	94.4228	94.3353	94.2477	94.1602	94.0726	.002918
19	94.5087	94.4339	94.3591	94.2843	94.2095	94.1347	94.0600	93.9852	93.9104	93.8356	93.7608	93.6860	.002493
18	93.8565	93.7951	93.7337	93.6724	93.6110	93.5496	93.4882	93.4269	93.3655	93.3041	93.2427	93.1814	.002046
17	93.1374	93.0845	93.0316	92.9787	92.9259	92.8730	92.8201	92.7672	92.7143	92.6614	92.6086	92.5557	.001763
16	92.3622	92.3168	92.2714	92.2260	92.1807	92.1353	92.0899	92.0445	91.9991	91.9537	91.9084	91.8630	.001513
15	91.5496	91.5101	91.4705	91.4310	91.3914	91.3519	91.3123	91.2728	91.2333	91.1937	91.1542	91.1146	.001318
14	90.7155	90.6804	90.6452	90.6101	90.5750	90.5398	90.5047	90.4696	90.4344	90.3993	90.3642	90.3290	.001171
13	89.8669	89.8355	89.8041	89.7727	89.7413	89.7099	89.6784	89.6470	89.6156	89.5842	89.5528	89.5214	.001047
12	89.0056	88.9777	88.9497	88.9218	88.8938	88.8659	88.8380	88.8100	88.7821	88.7541	88.7262	88.6982	.000931
11	88.1384	88.1132	88.0880	88.0628	88.0376	88.0124	87.9872	87.9620	87.9368	87.9116	87.8864	87.8612	.000840
10	87.2689	87.2461	87.2232	87.2004	87.1776	87.1548	87.1320	87.1091	87.0863	87.0635	87.0406	87.0178	.000761
Age.	0	1	2	3	4	5	6	7	8	9	10	11	Day.

Age.	0	1	2	3	4	5	6	7	8	9	10	11	Day.
10	10.6893	10.6587	10.6282	10.5976	10.5671	10.5365	10.5060	10.4754	10.4448	10.4143	10.3837	10.3532	.001018
11	11.0365	11.0062	10.9760	10.9457	10.9155	10.8852	10.8550	10.8247	10.7945	10.7642	10.7340	10.7037	.001008
12	11.3962	11.3662	11.3362	11.3062	11.2763	11.2463	11.2163	11.1863	11.1563	11.1263	11.0964	11.0664	.000999
13	11.7628	11.7331	11.7034	11.6737	11.6440	11.6143	11.5846	11.5549	11.5252	11.4955	11.4658	11.4361	.000990
14	12.1428	12.1133	12.0838	12.0544	12.0249	11.9954	11.9660	11.9365	11.9070	11.8775	11.8480	11.8186	.000982
15	12.5352	12.5058	12.4764	12.4471	12.4177	12.3883	12.3590	12.3296	12.3002	12.2708	12.2414	12.2121	.000979
16	12.9387	12.9099	12.8810	12.8522	12.8233	12.7945	12.7656	12.7368	12.7080	12.6791	12.6503	12.6214	.000961
17	13.3603	13.3315	13.3027	13.2739	13.2451	13.2163	13.1875	13.1587	13.1300	13.1012	13.0724	13.0436	.000960
18	13.7944	13.7658	13.7372	13.7086	13.6801	13.6515	13.6229	13.5943	13.5757	13.5371	13.5086	13.4800	.000953
19	14.2446	14.2162	14.1878	14.1594	14.1310	14.1026	14.0742	14.0458	14.0174	13.9890	13.9606	13.9322	.000947
20	14.7111	14.6829	14.6547	14.6264	14.5982	14.5700	14.5418	14.5136	14.4854	14.4571	14.4289	14.4007	.000940
21	15.1955	15.1677	15.1399	15.1120	15.0842	15.0564	15.0286	15.0008	14.9730	14.9451	14.9173	14.8895	.000927
22	15.7013	15.6737	15.6460	15.6184	15.5907	15.5631	15.5354	15.5078	15.4802	15.4525	15.4249	15.3972	.000921
23	16.2263	16.1990	16.1716	16.1443	16.1170	16.0897	16.0623	16.0350	16.0077	15.9804	15.9530	15.9257	.000911
24	16.7743	16.7473	16.7202	16.6932	16.6661	16.6391	16.6120	16.5850	16.5580	16.5309	16.5039	16.4768	.000901
25	17.3456	17.3189	17.2922	17.2655	17.2389	17.2122	17.1855	17.1588	17.1321	17.1054	17.0788	17.0521	.000889
26	17.9424	17.9161	17.8898	17.8636	17.8373	17.8110	17.7847	17.7585	17.7322	17.7059	17.6796	17.6534	.000876
27	18.5672	18.5413	18.5155	18.4896	18.4637	18.4379	18.4120	18.3861	18.3603	18.3344	18.3085	18.2827	.000862
28	19.2213	19.1956	19.1700	19.1443	19.1186	19.0930	19.0673	19.0416	19.0160	18.9903	18.9646	18.9390	.000855
29	19.9046	19.8791	19.8536	19.8281	19.8026	19.7770	19.7515	19.7260	19 7005	19.6750	19.6495	19.6240	.000850
30	20.6196	20.5935	20.5673	20.5412	20.5151	20.4889	20.4628	20.4367	20.4105	20.3844	20.3583	20.3321	.000871
31	21.3542	21.3272	21.3002	21.2732	21.2463	21.2193	21.1923	21.1653	21.1383	21.1113	21.0844	21.0574	.000899
32	22.1127	22.0843	22.0559	22.0274	21.9990	21.9706	21.9422	21.9138	21.8854	21.8570	21.8285	21.8001	.000947
33	22.8886	22.8587	22.8288	22.7989	22.7690	22.7391	22.7092	22.6793	22.6494	22.6195	22.5896	22.5597	.000997
34	23.6837	23.6516	23.6195	23.5874	23.5554	23.5233	23.4912	23.4591	23.4270	23.3950	23.3629	23.3308	.001069
35	24.4919	24.4578	24.4238	24.3897	24.3557	24.3216	24.2875	24.2535	24.2194	24.1854	24.1513	24.1173	.001135
36	25.3161	25.2796	25.2432	25.2067	25.1702	25.1338	25.0973	25.0608	25.0244	24.9879	24.9514	24.9150	.001215
37	26.1562	26.1169	26.0776	26.0384	25.9991	25.9598	25.9205	25.8813	25.8420	25.8027	25.7634	25.7242	.001309
38	27.0089	26.9666	26.9244	26.8821	26.8398	26.7976	26.7553	26.7130	26.6708	26.6285	26.5862	26.5440	.001409
39	27.8757	27.8296	27.7835	27.7374	27.6914	27.6453	27.5992	27.5531	27.5070	27.4610	27.4149	27.3688	.001536
40	28.7494	28.6997	28.6499	28.6002	28.5504	28.5007	28.4510	28.4012	28.3515	28.3017	28.2520	28.2022	.001658
41	29.6349	29.5808	29.5267	29.4725	29.4184	29.3643	29.3102	29.2561	29.2020	29.1478	29.0937	29.0396	.001804
42	30.5280	30.4691	30.4102	30.3512	30.2923	30.2334	30.1745	30.1156	30.0567	29.9977	29.9388	29.8799	.001964
43	31.4301	31.3661	31.3020	31.2380	31.1740	31.1100	31.0460	30.9819	30.9179	30.8539	30.7898	30.7258	.002134
44	32.3425	32.2727	32.2030	32.1332	32.0634	31.9937	31.9239	31.8541	31.7844	31.7146	31.6448	31.5751	.002325
45	33.2693	33.1934	33.1174	33.0415	32.9655	32.8896	32.8136	32.7377	32.6618	32.5858	32.5099	32.4339	.002531
46	34.2145	34.1312	34.0479	33.9646	33.8813	33.7980	33.7147	33.6314	33.5481	33.4648	33.3815	33.2982	.002777
47	34.1737	34.1658	34.1579	34.1500	34.1422	34.1343	34.1264	34.1185	34.1106	34.1027	34.0949	34.0870	.002628
48	36.1461	36.0461	35.9460	35.8460	35.7460	35.6460	35.5460	35.4459	35.3459	35.2459	35.1458	35.0458	.003334
49	37.1334	37.0239	36.9143	36.8048	36.6952	36.5857	36.4761	36.3666	36.2571	36.1475	36.0380	35.9284	.003651
50	38.1311	38.0110	37.8910	37.7709	37.6508	37.5307	37.4106	37.2906	37.1705	37.0504	36.9303	36.8103	.004002
51	39.1376	39.0061	38.8746	38.7430	38.6115	38.4800	38.3485	38.2170	38.0855	37.9540	37.8224	37.6909	.004384
52	40.1524	40.0085	39.8645	39.7206	39.5767	39.4327	39.2888	39.1449	39.0009	38.8570	38.7131	38.5691	.004798
53	41.1729	41.0154	40.8579	40.7003	40.5428	40.3853	40.2278	40.0703	39.9128	39.7552	39.5977	39.4402	.005250
54	42.2002	42.0282	41.8562	41.6841	41.5121	41.3401	41.1681	40.9961	40.8241	40.6520	40.4800	40.3080	.005734
55	43.2300	43.0425	42.8551	42.6676	42.4802	42.2927	42.1053	41.9178	41.7304	41.5430	41.3555	41.1680	.006248
56	44.2665	44.0623	43.8582	43.6540	43.4498	43.2457	43.0415	42.8373	42.6332	42.4290	42.2248	42.0207	.006805
57	45.3074	45.0853	44.8632	44.6412	44.4191	44.1970	43.9750	43.7529	43.5308	43.3087	43.0866	42.8646	.007402
58	46.3514	46.1101	45.8688	45.6275	45.3862	45.1448	44.9035	44.6622	44.4209	44.1796	43.9383	43.6970	.008043
59	47.3993	47.1374	46.8755	46.6137	46.3518	46.0899	45.8280	45.5662	45.3043	45.0424	44.7805	44.5187	.008729
60	48.4521	48.1681	47.8841	47.6000	47.3160	47.0320	46.7480	46.4640	46.1800	45.8960	45.6119	45.3279	.009467
61	49.5129	49.2052	48.8976	48.5899	48.2823	47.9746	47.6670	47.3593	47.0516	46.7440	46.4363	46.1287	.010255
62	50.5834	50.2506	49.9178	49.5850	49.2523	48.9195	48.5867	48.2539	47.9211	47.5883	47.2556	46.9228	.011093
63	51.6690	51.3091	50.9492	50.5893	50.2294	49.8695	49.5096	49.1497	48.7898	48.4299	48.0700	47.7101	.011997
64	52.7682	52.3792	51.9902	51.6012	51.2122	50.8232	50.4342	50.0452	49.6562	49.2672	48.8782	48.4892	.012967
65	53.8832	53.4635	53.0437	52.6240	52.2043	51.7846	51.3648	50.9451	50.5254	50.1057	49.6860	49.2662	.013991
66	55.0211	54.5689	54.1167	53.6644	53.2122	52.7600	52.3078	51.8556	51.4034	50.9511	50.4989	50.0467	.015074
67	56.1895	55.7035	55.2175	54.7315	54.2455	53.7595	53.2735	52.7875	52.3016	51.8156	51.3296	50.8436	.016200
68	57.4050	56.8843	56.3635	55.8428	55.3220	54.8013	54.2805	53.7598	53.2391	52.7183	52.1976	51.6768	.017358
69	58.6886	58.1318	57.5749	57.0181	56.4613	55.9044	55.3476	54.7908	54.2339	53.6771	53.1203	52.5634	.018561
70	60.0589	59.4651	58.8713	58.2774	57.6836	57.0898	56.4960	55.9022	55.3084	54.7145	54.1207	53.5269	.019794
71	61.5471	60.9135	60.2799	59.6463	59.0128	58.3792	57.7456	57.1120	56.4784	55.8448	55.2113	54.5777	.021119
72	63.1627	62.4879	61.8131	61.1383	60.4636	59.7888	59.1140	58.4392	57.7644	57.0896	56.4149	55.7401	.022493
73	64.9365	64.2167	63.4969	62.7770	62.0572	61.3374	60.6176	59.8978	59.1780	58.4581	57.7383	57.0185	.023994
74	66.8735	66.1044	65.3352	64.5661	63.7969	63.0278	62.2586	61.4895	60.7204	59.9512	59.1821	58.4129	.025638
75	68.9783	68.1538	67.3293	66.5048	65.6804	64.8559	64.0314	63.2069	62.3824	61.5580	60.7335	59.9090	.027483
76	71.2368	70.3523	69.4678	68.5832	67.6987	66.8142	65.9297	65.0452	64.1607	63.2761	62.3916	61.5071	.029484
77	73.6554	72.7038	71.7521	70.8005	69.8489	68.8972	67.9456	66.9940	66.0423	65.0907	64.1391	63.1874	.031721
78	76.2187	75.1891	74.1594	73.1297	72.1001	71.0704	70.0407	69.0111	67.9814	66.9517	65.9221	64.8924	.034320
79	78.8656	77.7446	76.6237	75.5027	74.3818	73.2608	72.1398	71.0189	69.8979	68.7770	67.6560	66.5351	.037365
80	81.5059	80.2821	79.0583	77.8345	76.6107	75.3869	74.1630	72.9392	71.7154	70.4916	69.2678	68.0440	.040793
81	84.0745	82.7149	81.3554	79.9958	78.6362	77.2767	75.9171	74.5575	73.1980	71.8384	70.4788	69.1193	.045319
82	86.2400	84.7367	83.2334	81.7301	80.2268	78.7235	77.2202	75.7170	74.2137	72.7104	71.2071	69.7038	.050110
83	87.9853	86.4463	84.9073	83.3683	81.8293	80.2903	78.7513	77.2124	75.6734	74.1344	72.5954	71.0564	.051300
84	90.7758	89.3775	87.9792	86.5809	85.1826	83.7843	82.3860	80.9877	79.5894	78.1911	76.7928	75.3945	.046610
85 or 24	**97.0874**	**97.3301**	**97.5728**	**97.8155**	**98.0583**	**98.3010**	**98.5437**	**98.7864**	**99.0291**	**99.2718**	**99.5146**	**99.7573**	**.008090**
23	95.9960	95.9550	95.9139	95.8728	95.8318	95.7907	95.7497	95.7086	95.6676	95.6265	95.5855	95.5444	.001368
22	95.4323	95.3512	95.2702	95.1891	95.1081	95.0270	94.9460	94.8649	94.7838	94.7028	94.6217	94.5407	.002702
21	95.0192	94.9290	94.8388	94.7486	94.6584	94.5682	94.4780	94.3879	94.2977	94.2075	94.1173	94.0271	.003006
20	94.4888	94.4115	94.3343	94.2570	94.1798	94.1025	94.0252	93.9480	93.8707	93.7935	93.7162	93.6390	.002575
19	93.8323	93.7687	93.7050	93.6414	93.5777	93.5141	93.4504	93.3868	93.3232	93.2595	93.1959	93.1322	.002121
18	93.1089	93.0539	92.9988	92.9438	92.8888	92.8338	92.7787	92.7237	92.6687	92.6137	92.5586	92.5036	.001834
17	92.3292	92.2818	92.2344	92.1870	92.1397	92.0923	92.0449	91.9975	91.9501	91.9027	91.8554	91.8080	.001579
16	91.5124	91.4710	91.4295	91.3880	91.3466	91.3051	91.2637	91.2222	91.1808	91.1393	91.0979	91.0564	.001382
15	90.6742	90.6373	90.6003	90.5634	90.5264	90.4895	90.4525	90.4156	90.3787	90.3417	90.3048	90.2678	.001231
14	89.8217	89.7886	89.7554	89.7223	89.6892	89.6560	89.6229	89.5898	89.5566	89.5235	89.4904	89.4572	.001104
13	88.9566	88.9270	88.8974	88.8679	88.8382	88.8087	88.7791	88.7496	88.7200	88.6904	88.6608	88.6313	.000986
12	88.0865	88.0597	88.0330	88.0062	87.9795	87.9527	87.9260	87.8992	87.8725	87.8457	87.8190	87.7922	.000892
11	87.2139	87.1896	87.1653	87.1410	87.1167	87.0923	87.0680	87.0437	87.0194	86.9951	86.9708	86.9465	.000810
10	86.3424	86.3202	86.2980	86.2757	86.2535	86.2313	86.2091	86.1869	86.1647	86.1424	86.1202	86.0980	.000740
Age.	0	1	2	3	4	5	6	7	8	9	10	11	Day.

Age.	0	1	2	3	4	5	6	7	8	9	10	11	Day.
10	11.5158	11.4871	11.4583	11.4296	11.4009	11.3721	11.3434	11.3147	11.2859	11.2572	11.2285	11.1997	.000958
11	11.8897	11.8613	11.8329	11.8045	11.7761	11.7477	11.7192	11.6908	11.6624	11.6340	11.6056	11.5772	.000947
12	12.2765	12.2484	12.2204	12.1923	12.1643	12.1362	12.1081	12.0801	12.0520	12.0240	11.9959	11.9679	.000935
13	12.6716	12.6438	12.6160	12.5883	12.5605	12.5327	12.5050	12.4772	12.4494	12.4216	12.3938	12.3661	.000926
14	13.0805	13.0529	13.0253	12.9976	12.9700	12.9424	12.9148	12.8872	12.8596	12.8320	12.8043	12.7767	.000920
15	13.5014	13.4744	13.4473	13.4203	13.3933	13.3663	13.3392	13.3122	13.2852	13.2582	13.2311	13.2041	.000901
16	13.9398	13.9129	13.8860	13.8591	13.8322	13.8052	13.7783	13.7514	13.7245	13.6976	13.6707	13.6438	.000897
17	14.3916	14.3650	14.3383	14.3117	14.2851	14.2584	14.2318	14.2052	14.1785	14.1519	14.1253	14.0986	.000888
18	14.8593	14.8329	14.8065	14.7801	14.7537	14.7273	14.7009	14.6745	14.6482	14.6218	14.5954	14.5690	.000880
19	15.3440	15.3179	15.2917	15.2656	15.2394	15.2133	15.1871	15.1610	15.1349	15.1087	15.0826	15.0564	.000871
20	15.8464	15.8207	15.7951	15.7694	15.7437	15.7181	15.6924	15.6667	15.6411	15.6154	15.5897	15.5641	.000855
21	16.3707	16.3453	16.3199	16.2944	16.2690	16.2436	16.2182	16.1928	16.1674	16.1420	16.1165	16.0911	.000847
22	16.9153	16.8903	16.8652	16.8402	16.8152	16.7902	16.7651	16.7401	16.7151	16.6901	16.6650	16.6400	.000834
23	17.4824	17.4577	17.4331	17.4084	17.3838	17.3591	17.3344	17.3098	17.2851	17.2605	17.2358	17.2112	.000822
24	18.0738	18.0496	18.0253	18.0011	17.9769	17.9526	17.9284	17.9042	17.8799	17.8557	17.8315	17.8072	.000808
25	18.6917	18.6674	18.6436	18.6199	18.5962	18.5725	18.5487	18.5250	18.5013	18.4776	18.4538	18.4301	.000791
26	19.3366	19.3134	19.2901	19.2669	19.2437	19.2204	19.1972	19.1740	19.1507	19.1275	19.1043	19.0810	.000774
27	20.0121	19.9891	19.9662	19.9432	19.9203	19.8973	19.8744	19.8514	19.8285	19.8055	19.7826	19.7596	.000765
28	20.7164	20.6937	20.6710	20.6483	20.6257	20.6030	20.5803	20.5576	20.5349	20.5122	20.4896	20.4669	.000756
29	21.4518	21.4286	21.4054	21.3821	21.3589	21.3357	21.3125	21.2893	21.2661	21.2428	21.2196	21.1964	.000774
30	22.2117	22.1878	22.1638	22.1399	22.1160	22.0920	22.0681	22.0442	22.0202	21.9963	21.9724	21.9484	.000798
31	22.9912	22.9660	22.9407	22.9155	22.8903	22.8650	22.8398	22.8146	22.7893	22.7641	22.7389	22.7136	.000841
32	23.7904	23.7638	23.7372	23.7106	23.6841	23.6575	23.6309	23.6043	23.5777	23.5511	23.5246	23.4980	.000886
33	24.6092	24.5806	24.5520	24.5233	24.4947	24.4661	24.4375	24.4089	24.3803	24.3516	24.3230	24.2944	.000954
34	25.4418	25.4114	25.3809	25.3505	25.3201	25.2896	25.2592	25.2288	25.1983	25.1679	25.1375	25.1070	.001014
35	26.2933	26.2606	26.2280	26.1953	26.1626	26.1300	26.0973	26.0646	26.0320	25.9993	25.9666	25.9340	.001089
36	27.1593	27.1240	27.0887	27.0534	27.0181	26.9828	26.9475	26.9122	26.8770	26.8417	26.8064	26.7711	.001176
37	28.0402	28.0021	27.9640	27.9260	27.8879	27.8498	27.8117	27.7737	27.7356	27.6975	27.6594	27.6214	.001269
38	28.9357	28.8940	28.8524	28.8107	28.7691	28.7274	28.6857	28.6441	28.6024	28.5608	28.5191	28.4775	.001388
39	29.8399	29.7948	29.7497	29.7046	29.6596	29.6145	29.5694	29.5243	29.4792	29.4341	29.3891	29.3440	.001503
40	30.7577	30.7085	30.6593	30.6101	30.5610	30.5118	30.4626	30.4134	30.3642	30.3150	30.2659	30.2167	.001639
41	31.6841	31.6304	31.5767	31.5230	31.4694	31.4157	31.3620	31.3083	31.2546	31.2010	31.1473	31.0936	.001789
42	32.6188	32.5603	32.5018	32.4434	32.3849	32.3264	32.2680	32.2095	32.1510	32.0925	32.0340	31.9756	.001949
43	33.5648	33.5009	33.4371	33.3732	33.3094	33.2455	33.1816	33.1178	33.0539	32.9901	32.9262	32.8624	.002128
44	34.5203	34.4505	34.3807	34.3109	34.2411	34.1713	34.1015	34.0317	33.9620	33.8922	33.8224	33.7526	.002326
45	35.4914	35.4147	35.3380	35.2614	35.1847	35.1080	35.0313	34.9547	34.8780	34.8013	34.7246	34.6480	.002556
46	36.4736	36.3894	36.3052	36.2210	36.1368	36.0526	35.9684	35.8842	35.8000	35.7158	35.6316	35.5474	.002807
47	87.4702	37.3776	37.2850	37.1924	37.0999	37.0073	36.9147	36.8221	36.7295	36.6370	36.5444	36.4518	.003086
48	38.4769	38.3752	38.2736	38.1719	38.0703	37.9686	37.8670	37.7653	37.6636	37.5620	37.4603	37.3587	.003388
49	39.4977	39.3860	39.2743	39.1627	39.0510	38.9393	38.8276	38.7160	38.6043	38.4926	38.3810	38.2693	.003722
50	40.5254	40.4028	40.2803	40.1577	40.0352	39.9126	39.7900	39.6675	39.5449	39.4224	39.2998	39.1773	.004085
51	41.5601	41.4257	41.2913	41.1570	41.0226	40.8882	40.7538	40.6195	40.4851	40.3507	40.2163	40.0820	.004479
52	42.6012	42.4539	42.3066	42.1593	42.0121	41.8648	41.7175	41.5702	41.4229	41.2756	41.1284	40.9811	.005909
53	43.6446	43.4835	43.3224	43.1613	43.0002	42.8390	42.6779	42.5168	42.3557	42.1946	42.0335	41.8724	.005370
54	44.6945	44.5187	44.3430	44.1672	43.9915	43.8157	43.6400	43.4642	43.2885	43.1127	42.9370	42.7612	.005858
55	45.7479	45.5563	45.3646	45.1730	44.9814	44.7897	44.5981	44.4065	44.2148	44.0232	43.8316	43.6399	.006388
56	46.8054	46.5968	46.3881	46.1795	45.9709	45.7622	45.5536	45.3450	45.1363	44.9277	44.7191	44.5104	.006954
57	47.8668	47.6399	47.4131	47.1862	46.9594	46.7325	46.5056	46.2788	46.0519	45.8251	45.5982	45.3714	.007562
58	48.9305	48.6842	48.4378	48.1915	47.9452	47.6989	47.4525	47.2062	46.9599	46.7136	46.4672	46.2209	.008211
59	49.9983	49.7310	49.4637	49.1965	48.9292	48.6619	48.3946	48.1274	47.8601	47.5928	47.3255	47.0583	.008909
60	51.0695	50.7798	50.4902	50.2005	49.9109	49.6212	49.3316	49.0420	48.7523	48.4626	48.1730	47.8833	.009655
61	52.1490	51.8356	51.5222	51.2088	50.8954	50.5820	50.2685	49.9551	49.6417	49.3283	49.0149	48.7015	.010447
62	53.2400	52.9009	52.5619	52.2228	51.8838	51.5447	51.2056	50.8666	50.5275	50.1885	49.8494	49.5104	.011302
63	54.3427	53.9761	53.6096	53.2430	52.8765	52.5100	52.1434	51.7768	51.4103	51.0437	50.6772	50.3106	.012218
64	55.4526	55.0574	54.6622	54.2671	53.8719	53.4767	53.0815	52.6864	52.2912	51.8960	51.5008	51.1057	.013172
65	56.5922	56.1659	55.7397	55.3134	54.8872	54.4609	54.0346	53.6084	53.1821	52.7559	52.3296	51.9034	.014208
66	57.7538	57.2957	56.8375	56.3794	55.9213	55.4632	55.0050	54.5469	54.0888	53.6307	53.1725	52.7144	.015271
67	58.9572	58.4663	57.9754	57.4846	56.9937	56.5028	56.0120	55.5211	55.0302	54.5393	54.0484	53.5576	.016362
68	60.2244	59.6995	59.1747	58.6498	58.1250	57.6001	57.0753	56.5504	56.0256	55.5007	54.9759	54.4510	.017495
69	61.5740	61.0144	60.4548	59.8952	59.3357	58.7761	58.2165	57.6569	57.0973	56.5377	55.9782	55.4186	.018653
70	63.0331	62.4361	61.8392	61.2422	60.6453	60.0483	59.4514	58.8544	58.2575	57.6605	57.0636	56.4666	.019898
71	64.6118	63.9762	63.3406	62.7050	62.0694	61.4338	60.7982	60.1627	59.5271	58.8915	58.2559	57.6203	.021186
72	66.3390	65.6612	64.9833	64.3055	63.6277	62.9498	62.2720	61.5942	60.9163	60.2385	59.5607	58.8828	.022594
73	68.2194	67.4953	66.7713	66.0472	65.3232	64.5991	63.8750	63.1510	62.4269	61.7029	60.9788	60.2548	.024135
74	70.2562	69.4802	68.7043	67.9283	67.1523	66.3764	65.6004	64.8244	64.0485	63.2725	62.4965	61.7206	.025865
75	72.4362	71.6040	70.7718	69.9395	69.1073	68.2751	67.4429	66.6107	65.7785	64.9462	64.1140	63.2818	.027740
76	74.7657	73.8707	72.9756	72.0806	71.1855	70.2905	69.3954	68.5004	67.6054	66.7103	65.8153	64.9202	.029835
77	77.2273	76.2591	75.2910	74.3228	73.3546	72.3864	71.4182	70.4501	69.4819	68.5137	67.5455	66.5774	.032272
78	79.7633	78.7095	77.6557	76.6020	75.5482	74.4944	73.4406	72.3869	71.3331	70.2793	69.2255	68.1718	.035126
79	82.2896	81.1395	79.9895	78.8394	77.6894	76.5393	75.3893	74.2392	73.0892	71.9391	70.7891	69.6390	.038335
80	84.7437	83.4665	82.1894	80.9122	79.6350	78.3579	77.0807	75.8035	74.5264	73.2492	71.9720	70.6949	.042572
81	86.8128	85.4017	83.9906	82.5795	81.1685	79.7574	78.3463	76.9352	75.5241	74.1130	72.7020	71.2909	.047036
82	88.4782	87.0368	85.5953	84.1539	82.7124	81.2710	79.8295	78.3881	76.9467	75.5052	74.0638	72.6223	.048048
83	91.1337	89.8285	88.5232	87.2180	85.9128	84.6076	83.3023	81.9971	80.6919	79.3867	78.0814	76.7762	.043507
84 or 25	**97.0874**	**97.3301**	**97.5728**	**97.8155**	**98.0583**	**98.3010**	**98.5437**	**98.7864**	**39.0291**	**99.2718**	**99.5146**	**99.7573**	**.008090**
24	95.9863	95.9427	95.8991	95.8556	95.8120	95.7684	95.7248	95.6813	95.6377	95.5941	95.5505	95.5070	.001452
23	95.4181	95.3343	95.2504	95.1666	95.0827	94.9989	94.9150	94.8312	94.7474	94.6635	94.5797	94.4958	.002795
22	95.0020	94.9090	94.8161	94.7231	94.6302	94.5372	94.4443	94.3513	94.2584	94.1654	94.0725	93.9795	.003098
21	94.4679	94.3881	94.3083	94.2285	94.1487	94.0689	93.9890	93.9092	93.8294	93.7496	93.6698	93.5900	.002660
20	93.8071	93.7411	93.6751	93.6090	93.5430	93.4770	93.4110	93.3450	93.2790	93.2130	93.1469	93.0809	.002200
19	93.0792	93.0220	92.9647	92.9074	92.8502	92.7930	92.7357	92.6784	92.6212	92.5640	92.5067	92.4494	.001908
18	92.2949	92.2454	92.1959	92.1464	92.0970	92.0475	91.9980	91.9485	91.8990	91.8495	91.8001	91.7506	.001649
17	91.4735	91.4301	91.3866	91.3432	91.2998	91.2564	91.2130	91.1695	91.1261	91.0827	91.0392	90.9958	.001447
16	90.6310	90.5922	90.5534	90.5145	90.4757	90.4369	90.3981	90.3593	90.3205	90.2816	90.2428	90.2040	.001294
15	89.7745	89.7396	89.7047	89.6697	89.6348	89.5999	89.5650	89.5301	89.4952	89.4602	89.4253	89.3904	.001164
14	88.9057	88.8744	88.8431	88.8118	88.7806	88.7493	88.7180	88.6867	88.6554	88.6241	88.5929	88.5616	.001043
13	88.0320	88.0036	87.9752	87.9468	87.9185	87.8901	87.8617	87.8333	87.8049	87.7765	87.7482	87.7198	.000946
12	87.1567	87.1308	87.1050	87.0791	87.0533	87.0274	87.0015	86.9757	86.9498	86.9240	86.8981	86.8723	.000862
11	86.2822	86.2595	86.2348	86.2111	86.1874	86.1637	86.1400	86.1163	86.0926	86.0689	86.0452	86.0215	.000790
10	85.4040	85.3828	85.3615	85.3403	85.3191	85.2978	85.2766	85.2554	85.2341	85.2129	85.1917	85.1704	.000708
Age	0	1	2	3	4	5	6	7	8	9	10	11	Day.

Age.	0	1	2	3	4	5	6	7	8	9	10	11	Day.
10	12.3642	12.3373	12.3104	12.2835	12.2566	12.2297	12.2028	12.1759	12.1490	12.1221	12.0952	12.0683	.000897
11	12.7649	12.7384	12.7119	12.6854	12.6589	12.6324	12.6059	12.5794	12.5530	12.5265	12.5000	12.4735	.000883
12	13.1799	13.1537	13.1276	13.1014	13.0753	13.0491	13.0230	12.9968	12.9707	12.9445	12.9184	12.8922	.000872
13	13.6035	13.5776	13.5516	13.5257	13.4998	13.4738	13.4479	13.4220	13.3960	13.3701	13.3442	13.3182	.000864
14	14.0405	14.0152	13.9899	13.9646	13.9393	13.9140	13.8887	13.8634	13.8382	13.8129	13.7876	13.7623	.000843
15	14.4958	14.4707	14.4456	14.4204	14.3953	14.3702	14.3451	14.3200	14.2949	14.2697	14.2446	14.2195	.000837
16	14.9640	14.9392	14.9144	14.8897	14.8649	14.8401	14.8153	14.7905	14.7658	14.7410	14.7162	14.6915	.000826
17	15.4488	15.4243	15.3999	15.3754	15.3510	15.3265	15.3021	15.2776	15.2532	15.2287	15.2043	15.1798	.000815
18	15.9505	15.9264	15.9022	15.8781	15.8539	15.8298	15.8056	15.7815	15.7574	15.7332	15.7091	15.6849	.000805
19	16.4705	16.4469	16.4233	16.3997	16.3761	16.3525	16.3289	16.3053	16.2817	16.2581	16.2345	16.2109	.000787
20	17.0123	16.9890	16.9657	16.9424	16.9192	16.8959	16.8726	16.8493	16.8260	16.8027	16.7795	16.7562	.000776
21	17.5747	17.5519	17.5291	17.5062	17.4834	17.4606	17.4378	17.4150	17.3922	17.3693	17.3465	17.3237	.000760
22	18.1607	18.1383	18.1159	18.0935	18.0712	18.0488	18.0264	18.0040	17.9816	17.9592	17.9369	17.9145	.000746
23	18.7705	18.7486	18.7267	18.7049	18.6830	18.6611	18.6392	18.6174	18.5955	18.5736	18.5517	18.5299	.000729
24	19.4070	19.3857	19.3644	19.3431	19.3218	19.3005	19.2792	19.2580	19.2367	19.2154	19.1941	19.1728	.000710
25	20.0722	20.0515	20.0308	20.0100	19.9893	19.9686	19.9479	19.9272	19.9065	19.8857	19.8650	19.8443	.000690
26	20.7673	20.7470	20.7266	20.7063	20.6859	20.6656	20.6452	20.6249	20.6046	20.5842	20.5639	20.5435	.000678
27	21.4920	21.4720	21.4520	21.4320	21.4120	21.3920	21.3720	21.3520	21.3321	21.3121	21.2921	21.2721	.000666
28	22.2474	22.2270	22.2066	22.1861	22.1657	22.1453	22.1249	22.1045	22.0841	22.0636	22.0432	22.0228	.000680
29	23.0265	23.0055	22.9844	22.9634	22.9424	22.9214	22.9003	22.8793	22.8583	22.8373	22.8162	22.7952	.000701
30	23.8302	23.8080	23.7858	23.7636	23.7414	23.7192	23.6970	23.6748	23.6526	23.6304	23.6082	23.5860	.000740
31	24.6492	24.6258	24.6023	24.5789	24.5555	24.5321	24.5086	24.4852	24.4618	24.4384	24.4150	24.3915	.000781
32	25.4900	25.4647	25.4394	25.4140	25.3887	25.3634	25.3381	25.3128	25.2875	25.2621	25.2368	25.2115	.000844
33	26.3451	26.3181	26.2911	26.2641	26.2371	26.2101	26.1831	26.1561	26.1292	26.1022	26.0752	26.0482	.000900
34	27.2197	27.1906	27.1616	27.1325	27.1035	27.0744	27.0453	27.0163	26.9872	26.9582	26.9291	26.9001	.000968
35	28.1114	28.0799	28.0484	28.0169	27.9854	27.9539	27.9224	27.8909	27.8594	27.8279	27.7964	27.7649	.001050
36	29.0166	28.9825	28.9484	28.9143	28.8802	28.8461	28.8120	28.7779	28.7438	28.7097	28.6756	28.6415	.001137
37	29.9386	29.9011	29.8636	29.8262	29.7887	29.7512	29.7137	29.6763	29.6388	29.6013	29.5638	29.5264	.001249
38	30.8698	30.8291	30.7884	30.7478	30.7071	30.6664	30.6257	30.5851	30.5444	30.5037	30.4630	30.4224	.001356
39	31.8161	31.7721	31.7280	31.6840	31.6400	31.5960	31.5520	31.5079	31.4639	31.4199	31.3758	31.3318	.001467
40	32.7727	32.7240	32.6752	32.6264	32.5777	32.5290	32.4802	32.4314	32.3827	32.3340	32.2852	32.2364	.001625
41	33.7384	33.6852	33.6320	33.5787	33.5255	33.4722	33.4190	33.3657	33.3125	33.2592	33.2060	33.1527	.001775
42	34.7149	34.6567	34.5984	34.5402	34.4819	34.4237	34.3654	34.3072	34.2490	34.1907	34.1325	34.0742	.001941
43	35.7015	35.6376	35.5737	35.5098	35.4460	35.3821	35.3182	35.2543	35.1904	35.1265	35.0627	34.9988	.002129
44	36.6978	36.6274	36.5570	36.4865	36.4161	36.3457	36.2753	36.2049	36.1345	36.0640	35.9936	35.9232	.002347
45	37.7047	37.6271	37.5496	37.4720	37.3944	37.3169	37.2393	37.1617	37.0842	37.0066	36.9290	36.8515	.002585
46	38.7219	38.6364	38.5508	38.4653	38.3797	38.2942	38.2086	38.1231	38.0376	37.9520	37.8665	37.7809	.002851
47	39.7503	39.6561	39.5620	39.4678	39.3736	39.2795	39.1853	39.0911	38.9970	38.9028	38.8086	38.7145	.003139
48	40.7881	40.6844	40.5806	40.4769	40.3732	40.2695	40.1657	40.0620	39.9583	39.8546	39.7508	39.6471	.003457
49	41.8364	41.7223	41.6082	41.4941	41.3801	41.2660	41.1519	41.0378	40.9237	40.8096	40.6956	40.5815	.003803
50	42.8899	42.7646	42.6392	42.5139	42.3885	42.2632	42.1378	42.0125	41.8872	41.7618	41.6365	41.5111	.004178
51	43.9484	43.8107	43.6731	43.5354	43.3978	43.2601	43.1225	42.9848	42.8472	42.7095	42.5719	42.4342	.004588
52	45.0098	44.8590	44.7082	44.5574	44.4066	44.2558	44.1050	43.9542	43.8035	43.6527	43.5019	43.3511	.005026
53	46.0732	45.9085	45.7437	45.5790	45.4142	45.2495	45.0847	44.9200	44.7553	44.5905	44.4258	44.2610	.005491
54	47.1440	46.9641	46.7842	46.6042	46.4243	46.2444	46.0645	45.8846	45.7047	45.5247	45.3448	45.1649	.005997
55	48.2156	48.0196	47.8236	47.6277	47.4317	47.2357	47.0397	46.8438	46.6478	46.4518	46.2558	46.0599	.006532
56	49.2907	49.0774	48.8642	48.6509	48.4376	48.2244	48.0111	47.7978	47.5846	47.3713	47.1580	46.9448	.007109
57	50.3688	50.1371	49.9054	49.6736	49.4419	49.2102	48.9785	48.7468	48.5151	48.2833	48.0516	47.8199	.007724
58	51.4594	51.2070	50.9546	50.7022	50.4499	50.1975	49.9451	49.6927	49.4403	49.1880	48.9356	48.6832	.008413
59	52.5325	52.2598	51.9870	51.7143	51.4416	51.1689	50.8961	50.6234	50.3507	50.0780	49.8052	49.5325	.009091
60	53.6194	53.3242	53.0290	52.7337	52.4385	52.1433	51.8481	51.5529	51.2577	50.9624	50.6672	50.3720	.009840
61	54.7161	54.3966	54.0771	53.7577	53.4382	53.1187	52.7992	52.4798	52.1603	51.8408	51.5213	51.2019	.010649
62	55.8212	55.4757	55.1302	54.7847	54.4393	54.0938	53.7483	53.4028	53.0573	52.7118	52.3664	52.0209	.011516
63	56.9366	56.5637	56.1908	55.8178	55.4449	55.0720	54.6991	54.3262	53.9533	53.5803	53.2074	52.8345	.012430
64	58.0679	57.6660	57.2641	56.8622	56.4604	56.0585	55.6566	55.2547	54.8528	54.4510	54.0491	53.6472	.013396
65	59.2229	58.7910	58.3590	57.9270	57.4951	57.0631	56.6312	56.1992	55.7673	55.3353	54.9034	54.4714	.014398
66	60.4156	59.9528	59.4900	59.0271	58.5643	58.1015	57.6387	57.1759	56.7131	56.2502	55.7874	55.3246	.015427
67	61.6664	61.1716	60.6767	60.1819	59.6871	59.1923	58.6974	58.2026	57.7078	57.2130	56.7181	56.2233	.016494
68	62.9945	62.4670	61.9395	61.4120	60.8845	60.3570	59.8295	59.3020	58.7746	58.2471	57.7196	57.1921	.017583
69	64.4265	63.8639	63.3013	62.7387	62.1761	61.6135	61.0509	60.4883	59.9258	59.3632	58.8006	58.2380	.018753
70	65.9696	65.3707	64.7719	64.1730	63.5741	62.9753	62.3764	61.7775	61.1787	60.5798	59.9809	59.3821	.019962
71	67.6524	67.0139	66.3754	65.7369	65.0984	64.4598	63.8213	63.1828	62.5443	61.9058	61.2673	60.6288	.021283
72	69.4787	68.7968	68.1149	67.4330	66.7511	66.0692	65.3873	64.7054	64.0236	63.3417	62.6598	61.9779	.022730
73	71.4514	70.7208	69.9902	69.2596	68.5291	67.7985	67.0679	66.3373	65.6067	64.8761	64.1456	63.4150	.024353
74	73.5569	72.7735	71.9902	71.2068	70.4235	69.6401	68.8568	68.0734	67.2901	66.5067	65.7234	64.9400	.026112
75	75.8013	74.9590	74.1168	73.2745	72.4323	71.5900	70.7478	69.9055	69.0633	68.2210	67.3788	66.5365	.028075
76	78.1683	77.2575	76.3467	75.4359	74.5251	73.6142	72.7034	71.7926	70.8818	69.9710	69.0602	68.1494	.030360
77	80.6006	79.6095	78.6183	77.6272	76.6361	75.6450	74.6538	73.6627	72.6716	71.6805	70.6893	69.6982	.033037
78	83.0186	81.9372	80.8557	79.7743	78.6929	77.6114	76.5300	75.4486	74.3671	73.2857	72.2043	71.1228	.036048
79	85.3645	84.1638	82.9631	81.7623	80.5616	79.3609	78.1602	76.9595	75.7588	74.5580	73.3573	72.1566	.040024
80	87.3412	86.0152	84.6891	83.3631	82.0370	80.7110	79.3850	78.0589	76.7329	75.4068	74.0808	72.7547	.044201
81	88.9329	87.5804	86.2279	84.8754	83.5229	82.1704	80.8178	79.4653	78.1128	76.7603	75.4078	74.0553	.045083
82	91.4587	90.2379	89.0172	87.7964	86.5757	85.3549	84.1341	82.9134	81.6926	80.4719	79.2511	78.0304	.040692
83 or 26	**97.0874**	**97.3301**	**97.5728**	**97.8155**	**98.0583**	**98.3010**	**98.5437**	**98.7864**	**99.0291**	**99.2718**	**99.5146**	**99.7573**	**.008090**
25	95.9761	95.9299	95.8837	95.8375	95.7913	95.7451	95.6988	95.6526	95.6064	95.5602	95.5140	95.4678	.001540
24	95.5032	95.3165	95.2297	95.1430	95.0562	94.9695	94.8827	94.7960	94.7093	94.6225	94.5358	94.4490	.002891
23	94.9841	94.8883	94.7924	94.6966	94.6008	94.5049	94.4091	94.3133	94.2174	94.1216	94.0258	93.9299	.003194
22	94.4462	94.3637	94.2812	94.1987	94.1162	94.0337	93.9512	93.8688	93.7863	93.7038	93.6213	93.5388	.002750
21	93.7809	93.7124	93.6439	93.5754	93.5069	93.4384	93.3700	93.3015	93.2330	93.1645	93.0960	93.0275	.002283
20	93.0481	92.9885	92.9290	92.8694	92.8098	92.7503	92.6907	92.6311	92.5716	92.5120	92.4524	92.3929	.001985
19	92.2591	92.2074	92.1557	92.1041	92.0524	92.0007	91.9490	91.8974	91.8457	91.7940	91.7423	91.6907	.001722
18	91.4330	91.3875	91.3420	91.2965	91.2510	91.2055	91.1600	91.1145	91.0690	91.0235	90.9780	90.9325	.001517
17	90.5860	90.5452	90.5044	90.4636	90.4229	90.3821	90.3413	90.3005	90.2597	90.2190	90.1782	90.1374	.001359
16	89.7253	89.6885	89.6517	89.6149	89.5781	89.5413	89.5045	89.4678	89.4310	89.3942	89.3574	89.3206	.001226
15	88.8526	88.8195	88.7865	88.7534	88.7203	88.6873	88.6542	88.6211	88.5881	88.5550	88.5219	88.4889	.001102
14	87.9753	87.9452	87.9151	87.8850	87.8550	87.8249	87.7948	87.7647	87.7346	87.7045	87.6745	87.6444	.001003
13	87.0966	87.0691	87.0416	87.0141	86.9867	86.9592	86.9317	86.9042	86.8767	86.8492	86.8218	86.7943	.000916
12	86.2196	86.1944	86.1691	86.1439	86.1186	86.0934	86.0681	86.0429	86.0177	85.9924	85.9672	85.9419	.000841
11	85.3385	85.3158	85.2931	85.2704	85.2477	85.2250	85.2022	85.1795	85.1568	85.1341	85.1114	85.0887	.000757
10	84.4547	84.4344	84.4140	84.3937	84.3734	84.3531	84.3327	84.3124	84.2921	84.2718	84.2514	84.2311	.000677
Age.	0	1	2	3	4	5	6	7	8	9	10	11	Day.

Age.	0	1	2	3	4	5	6	7	8	9	10	11	Day.
10	13.2346	13.2096	13.1846	13.1596	13.1346	13.1096	13.0846	13.0596	13.0346	13.0096	12.9846	12.9596	.000833
11	13.6631	13.6385	13.6139	13.5893	13.5647	13.5401	13.5155	13.4909	13.4663	13.4417	13.4171	13.3925	.000820
12	14.1062	14.0819	14.0575	14.0332	14.0089	13.9846	13.9602	13.9359	13.9116	13.8873	13.8630	13.8386	.000811
13	14.5575	14.5339	14.5103	14.4866	14.4630	14.4394	14.4158	14.3922	14.3686	14.3450	14.3213	14.2977	.000787
14	15.0281	15.0047	14.9814	14.9580	14.9347	14.9113	14.8880	14.8646	14.8412	14.8179	14.7945	14.7712	.000778
15	15.5131	15.4901	15.4671	15.4441	15.4212	15.3982	15.3752	15.3522	15.3292	15.3062	15.2833	15.2603	.000766
16	16.0139	15.9913	15.9687	15.9461	15.9235	15.9009	15.8783	15.8557	15.8331	15.8105	15.7879	15.7653	.000753
17	16.5323	16.5101	16.4878	16.4656	16.4434	16.4211	16.3989	16.3767	16.3544	16.3322	16.3100	16.2877	.000741
18	17.0687	17.0471	17.0254	17.0038	16.9822	16.9606	16.9390	16.9173	16.8957	16.8741	16.8524	16.8308	.000721
19	17.6274	17.6062	17.5849	17.5637	17.5424	17.5212	17.5000	17.4787	17.4575	17.4362	17.4150	17.3937	.000708
20	18.2067	18.1860	18.1653	18.1446	18.1239	18.1031	18.0824	18.0617	18.0410	18.0203	17.9996	17.9789	.000690
21	18.8099	18.7897	18.7695	18.7493	18.7291	18.7089	18.6887	18.6685	18.6483	18.6281	18.6079	18.5877	.000673
22	19.4378	19.4182	19.3985	19.3789	19.3593	19.3397	19.3200	19.3004	19.2808	19.2612	19.2415	19.2219	.000654
23	20.0919	20.0729	20.0540	20.0350	20.0161	19.9971	19.9781	19.9592	19.9402	19.9213	19.9023	19.8834	.000632
24	20.7755	20.7572	20.7389	20.7205	20.7022	20.6839	20.6656	20.6473	20.6290	20.6106	20.5923	20.5740	.000610
25	21.4893	21.4714	21.4536	21.4357	21.4179	21.4000	21.3822	21.3643	21.3465	21.3286	21.3108	21.2930	.000595
26	22.2327	22.2153	22.1979	22.1804	22.1630	22.1456	22.1282	22.1108	22.0934	22.0760	22.0585	22.0411	.000580
27	23.0073	22.9896	22.9718	22.9541	22.9364	22.9186	22.9009	22.8832	22.8654	22.8477	22.8300	22.8122	.000591
28	23.8056	23.7873	23.7691	23.7508	23.7326	23.7143	23.6960	23.6778	23.6595	23.6413	23.6230	23.6048	.000608
29	24.6275	24.6077	24.5880	24.5682	24.5485	24.5287	24.5090	24.4892	24.4694	24.4497	24.4299	24.4102	.000658
30	25.4695	25.4491	25.4287	25.4082	25.3878	25.3674	25.3470	25.3266	25.3062	25.2857	25.2653	25.2449	.000680
31	26.3290	26.3068	26.2846	26.2625	26.2403	26.2181	26.1960	26.1738	26.1516	26.1294	26.1072	26.0851	.000739
32	27.2049	27.1812	27.1575	27.1338	27.1101	27.0863	27.0626	27.0389	27.0152	26.9915	26.9678	26.9441	.000790
33	28.1006	28.0750	28.0493	28.0237	27.9980	27.9724	27.9467	27.9211	27.8955	27.8698	27.8442	27.8185	.000855
34	29.0140	28.9861	28.9582	28.9302	28.9023	28.8744	28.8465	28.8186	28.7907	28.7627	28.7348	28.7069	.000930
35	29.9435	29.9132	29.8838	29.8525	29.8222	29.7928	29.7615	29.7312	29.7008	29.6705	29.6402	29.6098	.001011
36	30.8882	30.8547	30.8212	30.7877	30.7542	30.7206	30.6871	30.6536	30.6201	30.5866	30.5531	30.5196	.001117
37	31.8442	31.8077	31.7712	31.7347	31.6983	31.6618	31.6253	31.5888	31.5523	31.5158	31.4794	31.4429	.001216
38	32.8157	32.7756	32.7354	32.6953	32.6552	32.6151	32.5750	32.5348	32.4947	32.4546	32.4144	32.3743	.001337
39	33.7989	33.7548	33.7107	33.6666	33.6225	33.5784	33.5343	33.4902	33.4461	33.4020	33.3579	33.3138	.001470
40	34.7929	34.7446	34.6963	34.6480	34.5996	34.5513	34.5030	34.4547	34.4064	34.3580	34.3097	34.2614	.001610
41	35.7982	35.7451	35.6920	35.6389	35.5858	35.5327	35.4796	35.4265	35.3735	35.3204	35.2673	35.2142	.001770
42	36.8129	36.7546	36.6962	36.6379	36.5796	36.5212	36.4629	36.4046	36.3462	36.2879	36.2296	36.1712	.001944
43	37.8380	37.7735	37.7090	37.6444	37.5799	37.5154	37.4509	37.3864	37.3219	37.2573	37.1928	37.1283	.002150
44	38.8677	38.7964	38.7251	38.6538	38.5825	38.5112	38.4399	38.3686	38.2974	38.2261	38.1548	38.0835	.002376
45	39.9173	39.8376	39.7579	39.6782	39.5985	39.5187	39.4390	39.3593	39.2796	39.1999	39.1202	39.0405	.002657
46	40.9541	40.8670	40.7799	40.6928	40.6057	40.5186	40.4315	40.3444	40.2574	40.1703	40.0832	39.9961	.002903
47	42.0114	41.9152	41.8190	41.7228	41.6266	41.5304	41.4342	41.3380	41.2418	41.1456	41.0494	40.9532	.003207
48	43.0745	42.9684	42.8623	42.7562	42.6501	42.5440	42.4379	42.3318	42.2258	42.1197	42.0136	41.9075	.003536
49	44.1462	44.0294	43.9126	43.7957	43.6789	43.5621	43.4453	43.3285	43.2117	43.0948	42.9780	42.8612	.003894
50	45.2210	45.0925	44.9639	44.8354	44.7068	44.5783	44.4497	44.3212	44.1927	44.0641	43.9356	43.8070	.004285
51	46.2974	46.1563	46.0153	45.8742	45.7332	45.5921	45.4510	45.3100	45.1689	45.0279	44.8868	44.7458	.004702
52	47.3763	47.2220	47.0676	46.9133	46.7590	46.6047	46.4503	46.2960	46.1417	45.9874	45.8330	45.6787	.005144
53	48.4582	48.2895	48.1208	47.9521	47.7834	47.6146	47.4459	47.2772	47.1085	46.9398	46.7711	46.6024	.005623
54	49.5435	49.3595	49.1756	48.9916	48.8077	48.6237	48.4397	48.2558	48.0718	47.8879	47.7039	47.5200	.006132
55	50.6312	50.4307	50.2302	50.0297	49.8293	49.6288	49.4283	49.2278	49.0273	48.8268	48.6264	48.4259	.006683
56	51.7204	51.5024	51.2844	51.0664	50.8484	50.6304	50.4124	50.1944	49.9764	49.7584	49.5404	49.3224	.007267
57	52.8125	52.5757	52.3389	52.1021	51.8653	51.6285	51.3917	51.1549	50.9181	50.6813	50.4445	50.2077	.007893
58	53.9056	53.6487	53.3919	53.1350	52.8782	52.6213	52.3645	52.1076	51.8508	51.5940	51.3371	51.0802	.008562
59	55.0013	54.7232	54.4451	54.1670	53.8889	53.6107	53.3326	53.0545	52.7764	52.4983	52.2202	51.9421	.009270
60	56.1025	55.8014	55.5003	55.1992	54.8982	54.5971	54.2960	53.9949	53.6938	53.3927	53.0917	52.7906	.010036
61	57.2104	56.8847	56.5590	56.2333	55.9077	55.5820	55.2563	54.9306	54.6049	54.2792	53.9536	53.6279	.010856
62	58.3253	57.9737	57.6221	57.2704	56.9188	56.5672	56.2156	55.8640	55.5124	55.1607	54.8091	54.4575	.011720
63	59.4542	59.0752	58.6962	58.3172	57.9382	57.5592	57.1802	56.8012	56.4223	56.0433	55.6643	55.2853	.012633
64	60.6027	60.1953	59.7880	59 3806	58.9732	58.5659	58.1585	57.7511	57.3438	56.9364	56.5290	56.1217	.013579
65	61.7853	61.3488	60.9124	60.4759	60.0394	59.6030	59.1665	58.7300	58.2936	57.8571	57.4206	56.9842	.014549
66	63.0212	62.5546	62.0880	61.6213	61.1547	60.6881	60.2215	59.7549	59.2883	58.8216	58.3550	57.8884	.015554
67	64.3281	63.8307	63.3334	62.8360	62.3386	61.8413	61.3439	60.8465	60.3492	59.8518	59.3544	58.8571	.016579
68	65.7328	65.2024	64.6720	64.1417	63.6113	63.0809	62.5505	62.0202	61.4898	60.9594	60.4290	59.8987	.017679
69	67.2429	66.6785	66.1140	65.5496	64.9852	64.4207	63.8563	63.2919	62.7274	62.1630	61.5986	61.0341	.018814
70	68.8831	68.2814	67.6797	67.0781	66.4764	65.8747	65.2731	64.6714	64.0697	63.4681	62.8664	62.2647	.020053
71	70.6580	70.0156	69.3732	68.7308	68.0884	67.4460	66.8036	66.1613	65.5189	64.8765	64.2341	63.5917	.021413
72	72.5697	71.8816	71.1934	70.5053	69.8172	69.1291	68.4410	67.7528	67.0647	66.3766	65.6884	65.0003	.022937
73	74.6051	73.8675	73.1298	72.3922	71.6545	70.9169	70.1792	69.4416	68.7040	67.9663	67.2287	66.4910	.024588
74	76.7691	75.9762	75.1832	74.3903	73.5974	72.8044	72.0115	71.2186	70.4256	69.6327	68.8398	68.0468	.026431
75	79.0461	78.1888	77.3315	76.4742	75.6170	74.7597	73.9024	73.0451	72.1878	71.3305	70.4733	69.6160	.028576
76	81.3817	80.4490	79.5164	78.5837	77.6511	76.7184	75.7857	74.8531	73.9204	72.9878	72.0551	71.1225	.031089
77	83.6986	82.6812	81.6637	80.6463	79.6288	78.6114	77.5940	76.5765	75.5591	74.5416	73.5242	72.5067	.033915
78	85.9421	84.8125	83.6829	82.5532	81.4236	80.2940	79.1644	78.0348	76.9052	75.7755	74.6459	73.5163	.037654
79	87.8314	86.5843	85.3371	84.0900	82.8428	81.5957	80.3485	79.1014	77.8543	76.6071	75.3600	74.1128	.041571
80	89.3522	88.0817	86.8113	85.5408	84.2703	82.9999	81.7294	80.4589	79.1885	77.9180	76.6475	75.3771	.042349
81	91.7559	90.6124	89.4690	88.3255	87.1820	86.0386	84.8951	83.7516	82.6082	81.4647	80.3212	79.1778	.038115
82 or 27	**97.0874**	**97.3301**	**97.5728**	**97.8155**	**98.0583**	**98.3010**	**98.5437**	**98.7864**	**99.0291**	**99.2718**	**99.5146**	**99.7573**	**.008090**
26	95.9655	95.9165	95.8676	95.8186	95.7696	95.7207	95.6717	95.6227	95.5738	95.5248	95.4758	95.4269	.001632
25	95.3877	95.2979	95.2081	95.1183	95.0286	94.9388	94.8490	94.7592	94.6694	94.5796	94.4899	94.4001	.002993
24	94.9654	94.8666	94.7678	94.6689	94.5700	94.4712	94.3723	94.2735	94.1747	94.0758	93.9770	93.8781	.003295
23	94.4235	94.3382	94.2529	94.1676	94.0824	93.9971	93.9118	93.8265	93.7412	93.6560	93.5707	93.4854	.002843
22	93.7534	93.6823	93.6113	93.5402	93.4691	93.3981	93.3270	93.2559	93.1849	93.1138	93.0427	92.9717	.002369
21	93.0158	92.9538	92.8918	92.8298	92.7678	92.7058	92.6438	92.5819	92.5199	92.4579	92.3959	92.3339	.002066
20	92.2217	92.1677	92.1138	92.0598	92.0059	91.9520	91.8980	91.8440	91.7901	91.7361	91.6822	91.6282	.001798
19	91.3907	91.3430	91.2954	91.2477	91.2001	91.1524	91.1048	91.0571	91.0095	90.9618	90.9142	90.8665	.001588
18	90.5390	90.4962	90.4533	90.4105	90.3677	90.3249	90.2820	90.2392	90.1964	90.1536	90.1107	90.0679	.001427
17	89.6740	89.6353	89.5965	89.5578	89.5190	89.4803	89.4415	89.4028	89.3641	89.3253	89.2866	89.2478	.001291
16	88.7972	88.7623	88.7273	88.6924	88.6575	88.6226	88.5876	88.5527	88.5178	88.4829	88.4480	88.4130	.001164
15	87.9161	87.8842	87.8524	87.8205	87.7887	87.7568	87.7250	87.6931	87.6613	87.6294	87.5976	87.5657	.001062
14	87.0340	87.0048	86.9756	86.9465	86.9173	86.8881	86.8590	86.8298	86.8006	86.7714	86.7422	86.7131	.000972
13	86.1538	86.1269	86.1000	86.0732	86.0463	86.0194	85.9925	85.9657	85.9388	85.9119	85.8850	85.8582	.000896
12	85.2705	85.2462	85.2220	85.1977	85.1735	85.1492	85.1250	85.1007	85.0765	85.0522	85.0280	85.0037	.000808
11	84.3839	84.3621	84.3403	84.3185	84.2967	84.2749	84.2531	84.2314	84.2096	84.1878	84.1660	84.1442	.000726
10	83.4885	83.4696	83.4507	83.4317	83.4128	83.3939	83.3750	83.3561	83.3372	83.3182	83.2993	83.2804	.000630
Age.	0	1	2	3	4	5	6	7	8	9	10	11	Day.

Age.	0	1	2	3	4	5	6	7	8	9	10	11	Day.
10	14.1278	14.1047	14.0816	14.0584	14.0353	14.0122	13.9891	13.9660	13.9429	13.9197	13.8966	13.8735	.000770
11	14.5841	14.5613	14.5385	14.5157	14.4930	14.4702	14.4474	14.4246	14.4018	14.3790	14.3563	14.3335	.000759
12	15.0544	15.0324	15.0104	14.9883	14.9663	14.9443	14.9223	14.9003	14.8783	14.8562	14.8342	14.8122	.000734
13	15.5393	15.5176	15.4958	15.4741	15.4524	15.5307	15.4090	15.3872	15.3655	15.3438	15.3220	15.3003	.000724
14	16.0392	16.0179	15.9967	15.9754	15.9541	15.9329	15.9116	15.8903	15.8691	15.8478	15.8265	15.8053	.000709
15	16.5560	16.5352	16.5143	16.4935	16.4727	16.4518	16.4310	16.4102	16.3893	16.3685	16.3477	16.3268	.000694
16	17.0899	17.0695	17.0491	17.0287	17.0083	16.9879	16.9675	16.9471	16.9267	16.9063	16.8859	16.8655	.000680
17	17.6424	17.6227	17.6030	17.5832	17.5635	17.5438	17.5240	17.5043	17.4846	17.4649	17.4451	17.4254	.000657
18	18.2170	18.1977	18.1784	18.1591	18.1399	18.1206	18.1013	18.0820	18.0627	18.0434	18.0242	18.0049	.000643
19	18.8127	18.7940	18.7753	18.7566	18.7380	18.7193	18.7006	18.6819	18.6632	18.6445	18.6259	18.6072	.000623
20	19.4320	19.4139	19.3958	19.3777	19.3596	19.3414	19.3233	19.3052	19.2871	19.2690	19.2509	19.2328	.000603
21	20.0765	20.0586	20.0407	20.0228	20.0049	19.9870	19.9691	19.9512	19.9333	19.9154	19.8975	19.8796	.000597
22	20.7479	20.7312	20.7144	20.6977	20.6810	20.6642	20.6475	20.6308	20.6140	20.5973	20.5806	20.5638	.000558
23	21.4483	21.4323	21.4163	21.4003	21.3843	21.3682	21.3522	21.3362	21.3202	21.3042	21.2882	21.2722	.000533
24	22.1797	22.1642	22.1487	22.1333	22.1178	22.1023	22.0868	22.0714	22.0559	22.0404	22.0250	22.0095	.000516
25	22.9409	22.9259	22.9110	22.8960	22.8811	22.8661	22.8511	22.8362	22.8212	22.8063	22.7913	22.7764	.000498
26	23.7332	23.7180	23.7028	23.6876	23.6725	23.6573	23.6421	23.6269	23.6117	23.5965	23.5814	23.5662	.000506
27	24.5497	24.5341	24.5185	24.5029	24.4873	24.4717	24.4561	24.4405	24.4249	24.4093	24.3937	24.3781	.000520
28	25.3897	25.3731	25.3566	25.3400	25.3234	25.3069	25.2903	25.2737	25.2572	25.2406	25.2240	25.2075	.000552
29	26.2436	26.2265	26.2094	26.1923	26.1752	26.1580	26.1409	26.1238	26.1067	26.0896	26.0725	26.0554	.000570
30	27.1302	27.1100	27.0918	27.0727	27.0535	27.0343	27.0151	26.9960	26.9768	26.9576	26.9384	26.9193	.000639
31	28.0238	28.0032	27.9826	27.9620	27.9414	27.9208	27.9002	27.8796	27.8591	27.8385	27.8179	27.7973	.000686
32	28.9390	28.9166	28.8942	28.8719	28.8495	28.8271	28.8047	28.7824	28.7600	28.7376	28.7152	28.6929	.000746
33	29.8722	29.8477	29.8232	29.7987	29.7742	29.7497	29.7252	29.7007	29.6762	29.6517	29.6272	29.6027	.000817
34	30.8220	30.7952	30.7685	30.7317	30.7150	30.6882	30.6614	30.6347	30.6079	30.5812	30.5544	30.5277	.000892
35	31.7896	31.7598	31.7301	31.7003	31.6706	31.6408	31.6111	31.5813	31.5516	31.5218	31.4921	31.4623	.000992
36	32.7669	32.7343	32.7018	32.6692	32.6367	32.6041	32.5716	32.5390	32.5065	32.4740	32.4414	32.4088	.001085
37	33.7617	33.7257	33.6897	33.6538	33.6178	33.5818	33.5458	33.5099	33.4739	33.4379	33.4020	33.3660	.001199
38	34.7682	34.7285	34.6888	34.6491	34.6094	34.5697	34.5300	34.4903	34.4506	34.4109	34.3712	34.3315	.001323
39	35.7869	35.7432	35.6995	35.6559	35.6122	35.5685	35.5248	35.4812	35.4375	35.3938	35.3501	35.3065	.001456
40	36.8183	36.7701	36.7220	36.6738	36.6256	36.5775	36.5293	36.4811	36.4330	36.3848	36.3366	36.2885	.001605
41	37.8597	37.8066	37.7535	37.7004	37.6473	37.5942	37.5411	37.4880	37.4349	37.3818	37.3287	37.2756	.001770
42	38.9106	38.8517	38.7927	38.7338	38.6748	38.6159	38.5570	38.4980	38.4391	38.3801	38.3212	38.2622	.001965
43	39.9669	39.9015	39.8362	39.7708	39.7055	39.6401	39.5747	39.5094	39.4440	39.3787	39.3133	39.2480	.002178
44	41.0272	40.9546	40.8820	40.8095	40.7369	40.6643	40.5917	40.5192	40.4466	40.3740	40.3014	40.2289	.002419
45	42.0942	42.0138	41.9334	41.8530	41.7726	41.6922	41.6118	41.5314	41.4510	41.3706	41.2902	41.2098	.002680
46	43.1677	43.0786	42.9895	42.9004	42.8114	42.7223	42.6332	42.5441	42.4550	42.3660	42.2769	42.1878	.002969
47	44.2480	44.1495	44.0510	43.9525	43.8540	43.7554	43.6569	43.5584	43.4599	43.3614	43.2629	43.1644	.003283
48	45.3325	45.2237	45.1150	45.0062	44.8975	44.7887	44.6800	44.5712	44.4624	44.3537	44.2449	44.1362	.003625
49	46.4232	46.3041	46.1850	46.0659	45.9468	45.8277	45.7086	45.5895	45.4704	45.3513	45.2322	45.1131	.003970
50	47.5137	47.3818	47.2500	47.1181	46.9863	46.8544	46.7225	46.5907	46.4588	46.3270	46.1951	46.0633	.004395
51	48.6054	48.4609	48.3164	48.1719	48.0274	47.8829	47.7383	47.5938	47.4493	47.3048	47.1603	47.0158	.004817
52	49.7004	49.5422	49.3840	49.2258	49.0676	48.9094	48.7512	48.5931	48.4349	48.2767	48.1185	47.9603	.005273
53	50.7955	50.6227	50.4499	50.2771	50.1043	49.9315	49.7586	49.5858	49.4130	49.2402	49.0674	48.8946	.005760
54	51.8944	51.7060	51.5175	51.3291	51.1407	50.9522	50.7638	50.5754	50.3869	50.1985	50.0101	49.8216	.006281
55	52.9927	52.7876	52.5825	52.3775	52.1724	51.9673	51.7622	51.5572	51.3521	51.1470	50.9420	50.7369	.006836
56	54.0933	53.8704	53.6474	53.4245	53.2016	52.9787	52.7557	52.5328	52.3099	52.0870	51.8640	51.6411	.007431
57	55.1952	54.9533	54.7114	54.4694	54.2275	53.9856	53.7437	53.5018	53.2599	53.0180	52.7760	52.5341	.008064
58	56.2982	56.0361	55.7741	55.5120	55.2499	54.9879	54.7258	54.4637	54.2017	53.9396	53.6775	53.4155	.008735
59	57.4054	57.1216	56.8378	56.5540	56.2703	55.9865	55.7027	55.4189	55.1351	54.8513	54.5676	54.2838	.009459
60	58.5152	58.2081	57.9010	57.5940	57.2869	56.9798	56.6727	56.3656	56.0585	55.7514	55.4444	55.1373	.010236
61	59.6302	59.2986	58.9670	58.6354	58.3038	57.9722	57.6405	57.3089	56.9773	56.6457	56.3141	55.9825	.011053
62	60.7559	60.3984	60.0409	59.6834	59.3260	58.9685	58.6110	58.2535	57.8960	57.5385	57.1811	56.8236	.011916
63	61.8989	61.5146	61.1304	60.7461	60.3618	59.9776	59.5933	59.2090	58.8248	58.4405	58.0562	57.6720	.012809
64	63.0717	62.6600	62.2483	61.8365	61.4248	61.0131	60.6014	60.1897	59.7780	59.3662	58.9545	58.5428	.013724
65	64.2935	63.8534	63.4132	62.9731	62.5330	62.0929	61.6527	61.2126	60.7725	60.3324	59.8922	59.4521	.014671
66	65.5411	65.0754	64.6096	64.1439	63.6782	63.2124	62.7467	62.2810	61.8152	61.3495	60.8838	60.4180	.015524
67	66.9593	66.4592	65.9590	65.4589	64.9588	64.4586	63.9585	63.4584	62.9582	62.4581	61.9580	61.4578	.016671
68	68.5366	67.9961	67.4556	66.9151	66.3747	65.8342	65.2937	64.7532	64.2127	63.6722	63.1318	62.5913	.018016
69	70.0372	69.4701	68.9030	68.3358	67.7687	67.2016	66.6345	66.0674	65.5003	64.9331	64.3660	63.7989	.018904
70	71.7630	71.1576	70.5522	69.9468	69.3415	68.7361	68.1307	67.5253	66.9199	66.3145	65.7092	65.1038	.020179
71	73.6770	73.0236	72.3703	71.7169	71.0635	70.4102	69.7568	69.1034	68.4501	67.7967	67.1433	66.4900	.021779
72	75.5858	74.8909	74.1960	73.5012	72.8063	72.1114	71.4165	70.7217	70.0268	69.3319	68.6370	67.9422	.023162
73	77.6742	76.9274	76.1806	75.4338	74.6870	73.9402	73.1934	72.4467	71.6999	70.9531	70.2063	69.4595	.024893
74	79.8663	79.0590	78.2517	77.4445	76.6372	75.8299	75.0226	74.2154	73.4081	72.6008	71.7935	70.9863	.026909
75	82.1105	81.2324	80.3542	79.4761	78.5980	77.7199	76.8417	75.9636	75.0855	74.2074	73.3292	72.4511	.029271
76	84.3329	83.3752	82.4174	81.4597	80.5020	79.5443	78.5865	77.6288	76.6711	75.7134	74.7556	73.7979	.031924
77	86.5807	85.5174	84.3541	83.2908	82.2276	81.1643	80.1010	79.0377	77.9744	76.9111	75.8479	74.7846	.035443
78	88.2874	87.1137	85.9399	84.7662	83.5924	82.4187	81.2450	80.0712	78.8975	77.7237	76.5500	75.3762	.039125
79	89.7413	88.5469	87.3526	86.1582	84.9638	83.7695	82.5751	81.3807	80.1864	78.9920	77.7976	76.6033	.039812
80	92.0301	90.9579	89.8857	88.8135	87.7414	86.6692	85.5970	84.5248	83.4526	82.3804	81.3083	80.2361	.035739
81 or 28	**97.0874**	**97.3301**	**97.5728**	**97.8155**	**98.0583**	**98.3010**	**98.5437**	**98.7864**	**99.0291**	**99.2718**	**99.5146**	**99.7573**	**.008090**
27	95.9544	95.9025	95.8507	95.7988	95.7470	95.6951	95.6432	95.5914	95.5395	95.4877	95.4358	95.3840	.001728
26	95.3715	95.2785	95.1856	95.0926	94.9997	94.9067	94.8137	94.7208	94.6278	94.5349	94.4419	94.3490	.003098
25	94.9458	94.8438	94.7418	94.6398	94.5378	94.4358	94.3338	94.2319	94.1299	94.0279	93.9259	93.8239	.003400
24	94.3998	94.3116	94.2234	94.1352	94.0470	93.9588	93.8706	93.7824	93.6942	93.6060	93.5178	93.4296	.002940
23	93.7248	93.6510	93.5772	93.5035	93.4297	93.3559	93.2821	93.2084	93.1346	93.0608	92.9870	92.9133	.002459
22	92.9820	92.9175	92.8530	92.7884	92.7239	92.6594	92.5949	92.5304	92.4659	92.4013	92.3368	92.2723	.002150
21	92.1827	92.1264	92.0700	92.0137	91.9574	91.9011	91.8447	91.7884	91.7321	91.6758	91.6194	91.5631	.001877
20	91.3466	91.2967	91.2468	91.1969	91.1470	91.0971	91.0472	90.9973	90.9474	90.8975	90.8476	90.7977	.001663
19	90.4901	90.4451	90.4002	90.3552	90.3102	90.2653	90.2203	90.1753	90.1304	90.0854	90.0404	89.9955	.001499
18	89.6205	89.5797	89.5390	89.4982	89.4574	89.4166	89.3758	89.3351	89.2943	89.2535	89.2127	89.1720	.001359
17	88.7394	88.7025	88.6657	88.6288	88.5920	88.5551	88.5182	88.4814	88.4445	88.4077	88.3708	88.3340	.001228
16	87.8544	87.8207	87.7870	87.7533	87.7196	87.6859	87.6522	87.6185	87.5848	87.5511	87.5174	87.4837	.001123
15	86.9687	86.9378	86.9068	86.8759	86.8449	86.8140	86.7830	86.7521	86.7212	86.6902	86.6593	86.6283	.001031
14	86.0853	86.0567	86.0282	85.9996	85.9711	85.9425	85.9140	85.8854	85.8568	85.8283	85.7997	85.7712	.000952
13	85.1989	85.1730	85.1472	85.1213	85.0954	85.0696	85.0437	85.0178	84.9920	84.9661	84.9402	84.9144	.000862
12	84.3103	84.2870	84.2636	84.2403	84.2170	84.1937	84.1703	84.1470	84.1237	84.1004	84.0770	84.0537	.000777
11	83.4123	83.3919	83.3715	83.3511	83.3308	83.3104	83.2900	83.2696	83.2492	83.2288	83.2085	83.1881	.000679
10	82.5014	82.4842	82.4670	82.4499	82.4327	82.4155	82.3983	82.3812	82.3640	82.3468	82.3296	82.3125	.000572
Age	0	1	2	3	4	5	6	7	8	9	10	11	Day.

Age.	0	1	2	3	4	5	6	7	8	9	10	11	Day.
10	15.0436	15.0223	15.0010	14.9797	14.9584	14.9371	14.9158	14.8945	14.8732	14.8519	14.8306	14.8093	.000710
11	15.5269	15.5064	15.4859	15.4654	15.4449	15.4244	15.4040	15.3835	15.3630	15.3425	15.3220	15.3015	.000683
12	16.0303	16.0102	15.9900	15.9699	15.9498	15.9296	15.9095	15.8894	15.8692	15.8491	15.8290	15.8088	.000671
13	16.5438	16.5242	16.5045	16.4849	16.4653	16.4457	16.4260	16.4064	16.3868	16.3672	16.3475	16.3279	.000654
14	17.0754	17.0563	17.0371	17.0180	16.9989	16.9797	16.9606	16.9415	16.9223	16.9032	16.8841	16.8649	.000638
15	17.6247	17.6061	17.5874	17.5688	17.5502	17.5315	17.5129	17.4943	17.4756	17.4570	17.4384	17.4197	.000621
16	18.1923	18.1744	18.1565	18.1385	18.1206	18.1027	18.0848	18.0669	18.0490	18.0310	18.0131	17.9952	.000597
17	18.7825	18.7651	18.7477	18.7303	18.7129	18.6955	18.6781	18.6607	18.6433	18.6259	18.6085	18.5911	.000580
18	19.3935	19.3767	19.3600	19.3432	19.3265	19.3097	19.2930	19.2762	19.2595	19.2427	19.2260	19.2092	.000558
19	20.0286	20.0125	19.9964	19.9803	19.9642	19.9481	19.9320	19.9158	19.8997	19.8836	19.8675	19.8514	.000537
20	20.6885	20.6731	20.6577	20.6423	20.6269	20.6115	20.5961	20.5808	20.5654	20.5500	20.5346	20.5192	.000513
21	21.3760	21.3614	21.3468	21.3322	21.3176	21.3030	21.2883	21.2737	21.2591	21.2445	21.2299	21.2153	.000487
22	22.0928	22.0790	22.0652	22.0514	22.0376	22.0238	22.0100	21.9961	21.9823	21.9685	21.9547	21.9409	.000460
23	22.8401	22.8269	22.8137	22.8005	22.7873	22.7741	22.7609	22.7477	22.7345	22.7213	22.7081	22.6949	.000440
24	23.6179	23.6053	23.5927	23.5801	23.5675	23.5549	23.5423	23.5297	23.5171	23.5045	23.4919	23.4793	.000420
25	24.4272	24.4144	24.4017	24.3890	24.3762	24.3634	24.3507	24.3380	24.3252	24.3124	24.2997	24.2870	.000425
26	25.2605	25.2474	25.2343	25.2213	25.2082	25.1951	25.1820	25.1690	25.1559	25.1428	25.1297	25.1167	.000436
27	26.1177	26.1038	26.0898	26.0759	26.0620	26.0480	26.0341	26.0202	26.0062	25.9923	25.9784	25.9644	.000464
28	26.9940	26.9792	26.9644	26.9495	26.9347	26.9199	26.9051	26.8903	26.8755	26.8606	26.8458	26.8310	.000494
29	27.8915	27.8752	27.8588	27.8425	27.8262	27.8099	27.7935	27.7772	27.7609	27.7446	27.7282	27.7119	.000544
30	28.8058	28.7882	28.7706	28.7530	28.7354	28.7177	28.7001	28.6825	28.6649	28.6473	28.6297	28.6121	.000587
31	29.7376	29.7183	29.6990	29.6798	29.6605	29.6412	29.6220	29.6027	29.5834	29.5641	29.5448	29.5256	.000642
32	30.6892	30.6679	30.6467	30.6254	30.6042	30.5829	30.5616	30.5404	30.5191	30.4979	30.4766	30.4554	.000708
33	31.6575	31.6341	31.6108	31.5874	31.5641	31.5407	31.5173	31.4940	31.4706	31.4473	31.4239	31.4006	.000778
34	32.6440	32.6178	32.5916	32.5654	32.5392	32.5130	32.4868	32.4606	32.4345	32.4083	32.3821	32.3559	.000873
35	33.6427	33.6139	33.5851	33.5563	33.5275	33.4986	33.4698	33.4410	33.4122	33.3834	33.3546	33.3258	.000960
36	34.6571	34.6251	34.5930	34.5610	34.5290	34.4970	34.4650	34.4329	34.4009	34.3689	34.3368	34.3048	.001067
37	35.6853	35.6497	35.6142	35.5786	35.5431	35.5075	35.4720	35.4364	35.4009	35.3653	35.3298	35.2942	.001185
38	36.7258	36.6865	36.6472	36.6079	36.5686	36.5293	36.4900	36.4507	36.4115	36.3722	36.3329	36.2936	.001310
39	37.7800	37.7365	37.6930	37.6494	37.6059	37.5624	37.5188	37.4753	37.4318	37.3883	37.3447	37.3012	.001451
40	38 8455	38.7973	38.7491	38.7010	38.6528	38.6046	38.5564	38.5083	38.4601	38.4119	38.3637	38.3156	.001606
41	39.9211	39.8674	39.8137	39.7600	39.7062	39.6525	39.5988	39.5451	39.4914	39.4376	39.3839	39.3302	.001790
42	41.0010	40.9412	40.8814	40.8216	40.7619	40.7021	40.6423	40.5825	40.5227	40.4630	40.4032	40.3434	.001993
43	42.0856	42.0190	41.9524	41.8857	41.8191	41.7525	41.6859	41.6193	41.5527	41.4860	41.4194	41.3528	.002220
44	43.1713	43.0972	43.0231	42.9491	42.8750	42.8009	42.7268	42.6528	42.5787	42.5046	42.4305	42 3565	.002469
45	44.2628	44.1804	44.0981	44.0157	43.9334	43.8510	43.7687	43.6863	43.6040	43.5216	43.4393	43.3570	.002745
46	45.3574	45.2661	45.1747	45.0834	44.9920	44.9007	44.8093	44.7180	44.6267	44.5353	44.4440	44.3526	.003045
47	46.4370	46.3375	46.2381	46.1386	46.0392	45.9397	45.8402	45.7408	45.6413	45.5419	45.4424	45.3430	.003315
48	47.5585	47.4467	47.3349	47.2231	47.1113	46.9994	46.8876	46.7758	46.6640	46.5522	46.4404	46.3286	.003727
49	48.6728	48.5488	48.4248	48.3007	48.1767	48.0527	47.9287	47.8047	47.6807	47.5566	47.4326	47.3086	.004134
50	49.7666	49.6313	49.4961	49.3608	49.2256	49.0903	48.9551	48.8198	48.6846	48.5493	48.4141	48.2788	.004508
51	50.8721	50.7238	50.5755	50.4272	50.2789	50.1306	49.9823	49.8340	49.6858	49.5375	49.3892	49.2409	.004943
52	51.9781	51.8159	51.6537	51.4915	51.3293	51.1671	51.0049	50.8427	50.6805	50.5183	50.3561	50.1939	.005407
53	53.0837	52.9066	52.7295	52.5524	52.3753	52.1982	52.0211	51.8440	51.6670	51.4899	51.3128	51.1357	.005903
54	54.1917	53.9988	53.8059	53.6130	53.4201	53.2272	53.0343	52.8414	52.6486	52.4557	52.2628	52.0699	.006430
55	55.2991	55.0892	54.8794	54.6695	54.4596	54.2498	54.0399	53.8300	53.6202	53.4103	53.2004	52.9906	.006995
56	56.4071	56.1792	55.9513	55.7234	55.4955	55.26-6	55.0397	54.8118	54.5840	54.3561	54.1282	53.9003	.007596
57	57.5165	57.7695	57.0225	56.7755	56.5286	56.2816	56.0346	55.7876	55.5406	55.2936	55.0467	54.7997	.008233
58	58.6282	58.3606	58.0931	57.8255	57.5580	57.2904	57.0228	56.7553	56.4877	56.2202	55.9526	55.6851	.008918
59	59.7415	59.4519	59.1623	58.8727	58.5831	58.2934	58.0038	57.7142	57.4246	57.1350	56.8454	56.5558	.009653
60	60.8558	60.5430	60.2302	59.9173	59.6045	59.2917	58.9789	58.6661	58.3533	58.0404	57.7276	57.4148	.010427
61	61.9789	61.6416	61.3043	60.9670	60.6297	60.2924	59.9551	59.6179	59.2806	58.9433	58.6061	58.2689	.011242
62	63.1160	62.7534	62.3908	62.0282	61.6657	61.3031	60.9405	60.5779	60.2153	59.8527	59.4902	59.1276	.012086
63	64.2802	63.8917	63.5033	63.1148	62.7263	62.3379	61.9494	61.5609	61.1725	60.7840	60.3955	60.0071	.012949
64	65.4885	65.0733	64.6580	64.2428	63.8275	63.4123	62.9970	62.5818	62.1666	61.7513	61.3361	60 9208	.013841
65	66.7578	66.3153	65.8728	65.4304	64.9879	64.5454	64.1030	63.6605	63.2180	62.7755	62.3330	61.8906	.014749
66	68.1127	67.6409	67.1691	66.6973	66.2255	65.7536	65.2818	64.8100	64.3382	63.8664	63.3946	62.9228	.015727
67	69.5573	69.0555	68.5536	68.0518	67.5500	67.0481	66.5463	66.0445	65.5426	65.0408	64.5390	64.0371	.016728
68	71.1191	70.5844	70.0496	69.5149	68.9802	68.4455	67.9107	67.3760	66.8413	66.3066	65.7718	65.2371	.017824
69	72.7993	72.2286	71.6579	71.0872	70.5165	69.9458	69.3751	68.8044	68.2338	67.6631	67.0924	66.5217	.019023
70	74.5983	73.9872	73.3761	72.7650	72.1539	71.5427	70.9316	70.3205	69.7094	69.0983	68.4872	67.8761	.020370
71	76.5048	75.8495	75.1946	74.5398	73.8850	73.2302	72.5753	71.9205	71.2657	70.6109	69.9560	69.3012	.021827
72	78.5209	77.8173	77.1137	76.4100	75.7064	75.0028	74.2992	73.5956	72.8920	72.1883	71.4847	70.7811	.023454
73	80.6334	79.8729	79.1124	78.3519	77.5914	76.8309	76.0704	75.3100	74.5495	73.7890	73.0285	72.2680	.025350
74	82.7913	81.9641	81.1370	80.3098	79.4826	78.6555	77.8283	77.0011	76.1740	75.3468	74.5196	73.6925	.027572
75	84.9247	84.0227	83.1206	82.2186	81.3166	80.4145	79.5125	78.6105	77.7084	76.8064	75.9044	75.0023	.030068
76	86.9833	85.9819	84.9805	83.9791	82.9777	81.9762	80.9748	79.9734	78.9720	77.9706	76.9692	75.9678	.033380
77	88.7127	87.6074	86.5021	85.3968	84.2916	83.1863	82.0810	80.9757	79.8704	78.7651	77.6599	76.5546	.036843
78	90.1032	88.9796	87.8561	86.7325	85.6089	84.4854	83.3618	82.2382	81.1147	79.9911	78.8675	77.7440	.037452
79	92.2844	91.2783	90.2723	89.2662	88.2602	87.2541	86.2481	85.2420	84.2360	83.2300	82.2239	81.2178	.033535
80 or 29	**97.0874**	**97.3301**	**97.5728**	**97.8155**	**98.0583**	**98.3010**	**98.5437**	**98.7864**	**39.0291**	**99.2718**	**99.5146**	**99.7573**	**.008090**
28	95.9428	95.8879	95.8330	95.7781	95.7233	95.6684	95.6135	95.5586	95.5037	95.4488	95.3940	95.3391	.001829
27	95.3545	95.2582	95.1620	95.0657	94.9694	94.8731	94.7768	94.6806	94.5843	94.4880	94.3917	94.2955	.003209
26	94.9254	94.8201	94.7148	94.6095	94.5043	94.3990	94.2937	94.1884	94.0831	93.9778	93.8726	93.7673	.003509
25	94.3751	94.2838	94.1926	94.1013	94.0101	93.9188	93.8275	93.7363	93.6450	93.5538	93.4625	93.3713	.003042
24	93.6949	93.6183	93.5417	93.4651	93.3886	93.3120	93.2354	93.1588	93.0822	93.0056	92.9291	92.8525	.002553
23	92.9467	92.8795	92.8124	92.7452	92.6781	92.6109	92.5437	92.4766	92.4094	92.3423	92.2751	92.2080	.002238
22	92.1420	92.0832	92.0244	91.9656	91.9068	91.8480	91.7891	91.7303	91.6715	91.6127	91.5539	91.4951	.001960
21	91.3006	91.2484	91.1961	91.1439	91.0916	91.0394	90.9871	90.9349	90.8827	90.8304	90.7782	90.7259	.001741
20	90.4390	90.3918	90.3446	90.2974	90.2502	90.2030	90.1558	90.1087	90.0615	90.0143	89.9671	89.9199	.001573
19	89.5647	89.5218	89.4789	89.4360	89.3931	89.3502	89.3073	89.2645	89.2216	89.1787	89.1358	89.0929	.001430
18	88.6791	88.6402	88.6013	88.5625	88.5236	88.4847	88.4458	88.4070	88.3681	88.3292	88.2903	88.2515	.001296
17	87.7900	87.7544	87.7187	87.6831	87.6475	87.6119	87.5762	87.5406	87.5050	87.4694	87.4337	87.3981	.001187
16	86.9006	86.8678	86.8350	86.8022	86.7695	86.7367	86.7039	86.6711	86.6383	86.6055	86.5728	86.5400	.001093
15	86.0139	85.9836	85.9532	85.9229	85.8926	85.8623	85.8320	85.8016	85.7713	85.7410	85.7106	85.68[illegible]3	.001011
14	85.1244	85.0969	85.0693	85.0418	85.0142	84.9867	84.9591	84.9316	84.9041	84.8765	84.8490	84.8214	.000918
13	84.2329	84.2080	84.1830	84.1581	84 1331	84.1082	84.0832	84.0583	84.0334	84.0084	83.9835	83.9585	.000831
12	83.3331	83.3112	83.2893	83.2674	83.2455	83.2236	83.2016	83.1797	83.1578	83.1359	83.1140	83.0921	.000730
11	82.4197	82.4011	82.3824	82.3638	82.3452	82.3265	82.3079	82.2893	82.2706	82.2520	82.2334	82.2147	.000621
10	81.4426	81.4314	81.4202	81.4090	81.3978	81.3866	81.3754	81.3642	81.3530	81.3418	81.3306	81.3194	.000373
Age.	0	1	2	3	4	5	6	7	8	9	10	11	Day.

Age.	0	1	2	3	4	5	6	7	8	9	10	11	Day.
10	15.9811	15.9621	15.9430	15.9240	15.9050	15.8860	15.8670	15.8479	15.8289	15.8099	15.7908	15.7718	.000634
11	16.4971	16.4785	16.4599	16.4412	16.4226	16.4040	16.3854	16.3668	16.3482	16.3295	16.3109	16.2923	.000620
12	17.0288	17.0107	16.9927	16.9746	16.9566	16.9385	16.9205	16.9024	16.8844	16.8663	16.8483	16.8302	.000602
13	17.5735	17.5560	17.5385	17.5210	17.5035	17.4860	17.4685	17.4510	17.4335	17.4160	17.3985	17.3810	.000583
14	18.1372	18.1203	18.1033	18.0864	18.0695	18.0525	18.0356	18.0187	18.0017	17.9848	17.9679	17.9509	.000564
15	18.7198	18.7036	18.6875	18.6713	18.6551	18.6390	18.6228	18.6066	18.5905	18.5743	18.5581	18.5420	.000539
16	19.3245	19.3089	19.2933	19.2777	19.2621	19.2465	19.2309	19.2153	19.1997	19.1841	19.1685	19.1529	.000520
17	19.9505	19.9356	19.9207	19.9058	19.8910	19.8761	19.8612	19.8463	19.8314	19.8165	19.8017	19.7868	.000496
18	20.6004	20.5862	20.5720	20.5578	20.5437	20.5295	20.5153	20.5011	20.4869	20.4727	20.4586	20.4444	.000473
19	21.2755	21.2621	21.2487	21.2352	21.2218	21.2084	21.1950	21.1816	21.1682	21.1547	21.1413	21.1279	.000447
20	21.9777	21.9651	21.9526	21.9400	21.9275	21.9149	21.9023	21.8898	21.8772	21.8647	21.8521	21.8396	.000418
21	22.7097	22.6980	22.6863	22.6745	22.6628	22.6511	22.6394	22.6277	22.6160	22.6042	22.5925	22.5808	.000390
22	23.4727	23.4617	23.4507	23.4396	23.4286	23.4176	23.4066	23.3956	23.3846	23.3735	23.3625	23.3515	.000367
23	24.2657	24.2553	24.2450	24.2346	24.2243	24.2140	24.2036	24.1932	24.1829	24.1725	24.1622	24.1518	.000345
24	25.0907	25.0803	25.0699	25.0594	25.0490	25.0386	25.0282	25.0178	25.0074	24.9970	24.9865	24.9761	.000347
25	25.9400	25.9293	25.9187	25.9080	25.8974	25.8867	25.8761	25.8654	25.8548	25.8441	25.8335	25.8228	.000355
26	26.8131	26.8017	26.7903	26.7788	26.7674	26.7560	26.7446	26.7332	26.7218	26.7103	26.6989	26.6875	.000380
27	27.7058	27.6936	27.6814	27.6692	27.6570	27.6448	27.6326	27.6204	27.6082	27.5960	27.5838	27.5716	.000407
28	28.6194	28.6053	28.5922	28.5786	28.5650	28.5514	28.5378	28.5242	28.5106	28.4970	28.4634	28.4698	.000453
29	29.5489	29.5341	29.5193	29.5046	29.4898	29.4750	29.4602	29.4455	29.4307	29.4159	29.4011	29.3864	.000492
30	30.5002	30.4840	30.4678	30.4517	30.4355	30.4193	30.4031	30.3870	30.3708	30.3546	30.3384	30.3223	.000539
31	31.4672	31.4490	31.4309	31.4127	31.3946	31.3764	31.3582	31.3401	31.3219	31.3038	31.2856	31.2675	.000605
32	32.4528	32.4327	32.4125	32.3924	32.3723	32.3521	32.3320	32.3119	32.2917	32.2716	32.2515	32.2313	.000671
33	33.4565	33.4337	33.4109	33.3881	33.3653	33.3425	33.3197	33.2970	33.2742	33.2514	33.2286	33.2058	.000760
34	34.4728	34.4475	34.4223	34.3970	34.3718	34.3465	34.3213	34.2960	34.2708	34.2455	34.2203	34.1950	.000842
35	35.5071	35.4788	35.4505	35.4222	35.3940	35.3657	35.3374	35.3091	35.2808	35.2525	35.2243	35.1960	.000943
36	36.5536	36.5220	36.4904	36.4587	36.4271	36.3955	36.3639	36.3323	36.3007	36.2690	36.2374	36.2058	.001054
37	37.6140	37.5789	37.5437	37.5086	37.4735	37.4383	37.4032	37.3681	37.3329	37.2978	37.2627	37.2275	.001171
38	38.6883	38.6492	38.6100	38.5709	38.5318	38.4926	38.4535	38.4144	38.3752	38.3361	38.2970	38.2578	.001304
39	39.7749	39.7314	39.6878	39.6443	39.6007	39.5572	39.5136	39.4701	39.4266	39.3830	39.3395	39.2959	.001451
40	40.8726	40.8238	40.7750	40.7263	40.6775	40.6287	40.5800	40.5312	40.4824	40.4336	40.3848	40.3361	.001626
41	41.9752	41.9207	41.8661	41.8116	41.7571	41.7025	41.6480	41.5935	41.5389	41.4844	41.4299	41.3753	.001818
42	43.0814	43.0204	42.9593	42.8983	42.8373	42.7763	42.7152	42.6542	42.5932	42.5322	42.4711	42.4101	.002034
43	44.1892	44.1211	44.0530	43.9849	43.9168	43.8487	43.7806	43.7125	43.6445	43.5764	43.5083	43.4402	.002270
44	45.2974	45.2214	45.1454	45.0695	44.9935	44.9175	44.8415	44.7656	44.6896	44.6136	44.5376	44.4617	.002532
45	46.4080	46.3234	46.2389	46.1543	46.0698	45.9852	45.9006	45.8161	45.7315	45.6470	45.5624	45.4779	.002818
46	47.5200	47.4261	47.3322	47.2383	47.1444	47.0504	46.9565	46.8626	46.7687	46.6748	46.5809	46.4870	.003130
47	48.6346	48.5305	48.4264	48.3223	48.2182	48.1141	48.0100	47.9059	47.8018	47.6977	47.5936	47.4895	.003470
48	49.7479	49.6329	49.5179	49.4030	49.2880	49.1730	49.0580	48.9430	48.8280	48.7130	48.5981	48.4831	.003833
49	50.8634	50.7369	50.6104	50.4840	50.3575	50.2310	50.1045	49.9780	49.8515	49.7250	49.5986	49.4721	.004216
50	51.9788	51.8399	51.7010	51.5620	51.4231	51.2842	51.1453	51.0064	50.8675	50.7285	50.5896	50.4507	.004630
51	53.0934	52.9412	52.7890	52.6368	52.4847	52.3325	52.1803	52.0281	51.8759	51.7237	51.5716	51.4194	.005073
52	54.2077	54.0413	53.8750	53.7086	53.5423	53.3759	53.2095	53.0432	52.8768	52.7105	52.5441	52.3778	.005545
53	55.3205	55.1391	54.9576	54.7762	54.5948	54.4133	54.2319	54.0505	53.8690	53.6876	53.5062	53.3247	.006048
54	56.4354	56.2378	56.0403	55.8427	55.6452	55.4475	55.2500	55.0525	54.8549	54.6574	54.4598	54.2623	.006585
55	57.5480	57.3333	57.1186	56.9039	56.6892	56.4745	56.2598	56.0451	55.8304	55.6157	55.4010	55.1863	.007157
56	58.6613	58.4285	58.1956	57.9628	[illegible]7300	57.4972	57.2643	57.0315	56.7987	56.5659	56.3330	56.1002	.007761
57	59.7770	59.5247	59.2723	59.0200	58.7677	58.5154	58.2630	58.0107	57.7584	57.5061	57.2537	57.0014	.008411
58	60.8923	60.6191	60.3459	60.0727	59.7995	59.5263	59.2531	58.9799	58.7067	58.4335	58.1603	57.8871	.009107
59	62.0077	61.7125	61.4174	61.1222	60.8271	60.5320	60.2368	59.9416	59.6465	59.3513	59.0562	58.7610	.009838
60	63.1277	62.8094	62.4911	62.1728	61.8545	61.5362	61.2179	60.8996	60.5813	60.2630	59.9447	59.6264	.010610
61	64.2596	63.9174	63.5752	63.2330	62.8908	62.5486	62.2064	61.8642	61.5220	61.1798	60.8376	60.4954	.011407
62	65.4150	65.0484	64.6817	64.3151	63.9485	63.5818	63.2152	62.8486	62.4819	62.1153	61.7487	61.3820	.012221
63	66.6112	66.2193	65.8275	65.4356	65.0437	64.6519	64.2600	63.8681	63.4763	63.0844	62.6925	62.3007	.013062
64	67.8630	67.4455	67.0280	66.6105	66.1930	65.7755	65.3580	64.9404	64.5229	64.1054	63.6879	63.2704	.013917
65	69.1939	68.7489	68.3038	67.8588	67.4137	66.9687	66.5236	66.0786	65.6336	65.1885	64.7435	64.2984	.014835
66	70.6103	70.1369	69.6636	69.1902	68.7169	68.2435	67.7701	67.2968	66.8234	66.3501	65.8767	65.4034	.015778
67	72.1349	71.6306	71.1263	70.6220	70.1177	69.6133	69.1090	68.6047	68.1004	67.5961	67.0918	66.5875	.016810
68	73.7717	73.2335	72.6952	72.1570	71.6188	71.0805	70.5423	70.0041	69.4658	68.9276	68.3894	67.8511	.017941
69	75.5[illegible]85	74.9423	74.3661	73.7900	73.2138	72.6376	72.0614	71.4853	70.9091	70.3329	69.7567	69.1806	.019206
70	77.3649	76.7476	76.1303	75.5130	74.8957	74.2784	73.6611	73.0438	72.4265	71.8092	71.1919	70.5746	.020577
71	79.3141	78.6509	77.9877	77.3245	76.6613	75.9980	75.3348	74.6716	74.0084	73.3452	72.6820	72.0188	.022107
72	81.3512	80.6345	79.9177	79.2010	78.4842	77.7675	77.0507	76.3340	75.6173	74.9005	74.1838	73.4670	.023891
73	83.4282	82.6487	81.8692	81.0897	80.3102	79.5306	78.7511	77.9716	77.1921	76.4126	75.6331	74.8536	.025983
74	85.4777	84.6277	83.7777	82.9277	82.0777	81.2277	80.3777	79.5277	78.6778	77.8278	76.9778	76.1278	.028333
75	87.4521	86.5084	85.5647	84.6210	83.6774	82.7337	81.7900	80.8463	79.9026	78.9590	78.0153	77.0716	.031456
76	89.1095	88.0681	87.0267	85.9853	84.9439	83.9024	82.8610	81.8196	80.7782	79.7368	78.6954	77.6540	.034713
77	90.4407	89.3832	88.3256	87.2681	86.2106	85.1530	84.0955	83.0380	81.9804	80.9229	79.8654	78.8078	.035251
78	92.5210	91.5765	90.6320	89.6874	88.7429	87.7984	86.8538	85.9093	84.9648	84.0203	83.0757	82.1312	.031484
79 or 30	**97.0874**	**97.3301**	**97.5728**	**97.8155**	**98.0583**	**98.3010**	**98.5437**	**98.7864**	**99.0291**	**99.2718**	**99.5146**	**99.7573**	**.008090**
29	95.9306	95.8726	95.8145	95.7565	95.6984	95.6404	95.5823	95.5243	95.4663	95.4082	95.3502	95.2921	.001935
28	95.3367	95.2369	95.1372	95.0374	94.9377	94.8379	94.7381	94.6384	94.5386	94.4389	94.3391	94.2394	.003325
27	94.9040	94.7953	94.6865	94.5778	94.4691	94.3603	94.2516	94.1429	94.0341	93.9254	93.8167	93.7079	.003624
26	94.3492	94.2548	94.1603	94.0659	93.9714	93.8770	93.7825	93.6881	93.5937	93.4992	93.4048	93.3103	.003148
25	93.6636	93.5841	93.5045	93.4250	93.3455	93.2660	93.1864	93.1069	93.0274	92.9479	92.8683	92.7888	.002651
24	92.9099	92.8400	92.7701	92.7001	92.6302	92.5603	92.4904	92.4205	92.3506	92.2806	92.2107	92.1408	.002330
23	92.0995	92.0381	91.9767	91.9153	91.8539	91.7925	91.7311	91.6698	91.6084	91.5470	91.4856	91.4242	.002046
22	91.2566	91.1979	91.1432	91.0885	91.0339	90.9792	90.9245	90.8698	90.8151	90.7604	90.7058	90.6511	.001823
21	90.3858	90.3363	90.2868	90.2372	90.1877	90.1382	90.0887	90.0392	89.9897	89.9401	89.8906	89.8411	.001650
20	89.5064	89.4613	89.4162	89.3711	89.3260	89.2809	89.2358	89.1907	89.1456	89.1005	89.0554	89.0103	.001503
19	88.6162	88.5752	88.5342	88.4933	88.4523	88.4113	88.3703	88.3294	88.2884	88.2474	88.2064	88.1655	.001366
18	87.7230	87.6853	87.6476	87.6100	87.5724	87.5347	87.4971	87.4595	87.4218	87.3842	87.3466	87.3089	.001254
17	86.8296	86.7949	86.7602	86.7255	86.6908	86.6561	86.6214	86.5867	86.5520	86.5173	86.4826	86.4479	.001157
16	85.9393	85.9071	85.8750	85.8428	85.8107	85.7785	85.7463	85.7142	85.6820	85.6499	85.6177	85.5856	.001072
15	85.0467	85.0174	84.9881	84.9588	84.9295	84.9002	84.8710	84.8417	84.8124	84.7831	84.7538	84.7245	.000976
14	84.1524	84.1258	84.0992	84.0725	84.0459	84.0193	83.9927	83.9661	83.9395	83.9128	83.8862	83.8596	.000887
13	83.2498	83.2263	83.2028	83.1793	83.1558	83.1323	83.1087	83.0852	83.0617	83.0382	83.0147	82.9912	.000783
12	82.3347	82.3146	82.2944	82.2743	82.2541	82.2340	82.2138	82.1937	82.1736	82.1534	82.1333	82.1131	.000671
11	81.4007	81.3843	81.3678	81.3514	81.3350	81.3185	81.3021	81.2857	81.2692	81.2528	81.2364	81.2199	.000548
10	80.4445	80.4282	80.4120	80.3957	80.3795	80.3632	80.3470	80.3307	80.3144	80.2982	80.2819	80.2657	.000542

Age. 0 1 2 3 4 5 6 7 8 9 10 11 Day.

Age.	0	1	2	3	4	5	6	7	8	9	10	11	Day.
10	16.9460	16.9288	16.9117	16.8945	16.8773	16.8602	16.8430	16.8258	16.8087	16.7915	16.7743	16.7572	.000572
11	17.4898	17.4733	17.4567	17.4402	17.4236	17.4071	17.3905	17.3740	17.3575	17.3409	17.3244	17.3078	.000551
12	18.0523	18.0364	18.0204	18.0045	17.9885	17.9726	17.9566	17.9407	17.9248	17.9088	17.8929	17.8769	.000531
13	18.6287	18.6134	18.5980	18.5827	18.5674	18.5521	18.5367	18.5214	18.5061	18.4908	18.4754	18.4601	.000511
14	19.2254	19.2109	19.1964	19.1818	19.1673	19.1528	19.1383	19.1238	19.1093	19.0947	19.0802	19.0657	.000484
15	19.8445	19.8306	19.8167	19.8029	19.7890	19.7751	19.7612	19.7474	19.7335	19.7196	19.7057	19.6919	.000462
16	20.4845	20.4714	20.4583	20.4452	20.4321	20.4190	20.4058	20.3927	20.3796	20.3665	20.3534	20.3403	.000437
17	21.1488	21.1365	21.1241	21.1118	21.0994	21.0871	21.0747	21.0624	21.0501	21.0377	21.0254	21.0130	.000411
18	21.8380	21.8265	21.8150	21.8034	21.7919	21.7804	21.7689	21.7574	21.7459	21.7343	21.7228	21.7113	.000384
19	22.5546	22.5440	22.5334	22.5228	22.5122	22.5016	22.4910	22.4805	22.4699	22.4593	22.4487	22.4381	.000353
20	23.3008	23.2911	23.2814	23.2718	23.2621	23.2524	23.2427	23.2331	23.2234	23.2137	23.2040	23.1944	.000322
21	24.0781	24.0692	24.0603	24.0513	24.0424	24.0335	24.0246	24.0157	24.0068	23.9978	23.9889	23.9800	.000297
22	24.8862	24.8780	24.8698	24.8616	24.8534	24.8452	24.8370	24.8287	24.8205	24.8123	24.8041	24.7959	.000273
23	25.7255	25.7173	25.7091	25.7010	25.6928	25.6846	25.6764	25.6682	25.6600	25.6518	25.6437	25.6355	.000273
24	26.5897	26.5814	26.5730	26.5647	26.5563	26.5480	26.5396	26.5313	26.5230	26.5146	26.5063	26.4979	.000278
25	27.4780	27.4690	27.4600	27.4510	27.4419	27.4329	27.4239	27.4149	27.4059	27.3968	27.3878	27.3788	.000300
26	28.3856	28.3759	28.3662	28.3565	28.3468	28.3371	28.3274	28.3177	28.3080	28.2983	28.2886	28.2789	.000323
27	29.3146	29.3036	29.2926	29.2816	29.2706	29.2596	29.2486	29.2377	29.2267	29.2157	29.2047	29.1937	.000366
28	30.2593	30.2472	30.2352	30.2231	30.2110	30.1990	30.1869	30.1748	30.1628	30.1507	30.1386	30.1266	.000402
29	31.2248	31.2113	31.1978	31.1843	31.1709	31.1574	31.1439	31.1304	31.1169	31.1034	31.0900	31.0765	.000449
30	32.2118	32.1965	32.1811	32.1658	32.1504	32.1351	32.1197	32.1044	32.0891	32.0737	32.0584	32.0430	.000511
31	33.2101	33.1930	33.1760	33.1590	33.1419	33.1248	33.1078	33.0907	33.0737	33.0566	33.0396	33.0225	.000568
32	34.2299	34.2103	34.1907	34.1712	34.1516	34.1320	34.1124	34.0929	34.0733	34.0537	34.0341	34.0146	.000652
33	35.2623	35.2405	35.2185	35.1967	35.1748	35.1529	35.1310	35.1092	35.0873	35.0654	35.0435	35.0217	.000729
34	36.3129	36.2882	36.2634	36.2387	36.2140	36.1892	36.1645	36.1398	36.1150	36.0903	36.0656	36.0408	.000824
35	37.3779	37.3500	37.3221	37.2942	37.2664	37.2385	37.2106	37.1827	37.1548	37.1270	37.0991	37.0712	.000929
36	38.4551	38.4239	38.3927	38.3615	38.3303	38.2991	38.2678	38.2366	38.2054	38.1742	38.1430	38.1118	.001040
37	39.5487	39.5136	39.4785	39.4435	39.4084	39.3733	39.3382	39.3032	39.2681	39.2330	39.1980	39.1629	.001169
38	40.6527	40.6135	40.5744	40.5352	40.4961	40.4569	40.4177	40.3786	40.3394	40.3003	40.2611	40.2220	.001305
39	41.7696	41.7255	41.6813	41.6372	41.5931	41.5490	41.5048	41.4607	41.4166	41.3725	41.3283	41.2842	.001471
40	42.8925	42.8429	42.7933	42.7437	42.6942	42.6446	42.5950	42.5454	42.4958	42.4462	42.3967	42.3471	.001653
41	44.0194	43.9636	43.9079	43.8521	43.7964	43.7406	43.6849	43.6291	43.5734	43.5176	43.4619	43.4061	.001858
42	45.1469	45.0844	45.0220	44.9595	44.8970	44.8346	44.7721	44.7096	44.6472	44.5847	44.5222	44.4598	.002082
43	46.2752	46.2052	46.1353	46.0653	45.9954	45.9254	45.8554	45.7855	45.7155	45.6456	45.5756	45.5057	.002332
44	47.4006	47.3224	47.2443	47.1661	47.0880	47.0098	46.9317	46.8535	46.7754	46.6972	46.6191	46.5410	.002605
45	48.5267	48.4396	48.3526	48.2655	48.1784	48.0914	48.0043	47.9172	47.8302	47.7431	47.6560	47.5690	.002902
46	49.6519	49.5551	49.4582	49.3614	49.2646	49.1678	49.0710	48.9741	48.8773	48.7805	48.6836	48.5868	.003227
47	50.7765	50.6693	50.5621	50.4548	50.3476	50.2404	50.1332	50.0260	49.9188	49.8115	49.7043	49.5971	.003574
48	51.8991	51.7809	51.6627	51.5445	51.4263	51.3081	51.1899	51.0717	50.9535	50.8353	50.7171	50.5989	.003940
49	53.0244	52.8943	52.7642	52.6342	52.5041	52.3740	52.2440	52.1139	51.9838	51.8537	51.7236	51.5936	.004336
50	54.1470	54.0043	53.8615	53.7188	53.5761	53.4333	53.2906	53.1479	53.0051	52.8624	52.7197	52.5769	.004758
51	55.2679	55.1117	54.9554	54.7992	54.6429	54.4867	54.3304	54.1742	54.0180	53.8617	53.7055	53.5492	.005208
52	56.3874	56.2168	56.0462	55.8756	55.7050	55.5344	55.3638	55.1933	55.0227	54.8521	54.6815	54.5109	.005686
53	57.5052	57.3193	57.1333	56.9474	56.7614	56.5755	56.3895	56.2036	56.0177	55.8317	55.6458	55.4598	.006198
54	58.6232	58.4209	58.2187	58.0164	57.8141	57.6119	57.4096	57.2073	57.0051	56.8028	56.6005	56,3983	.006742
55	59.7389	59.5194	59.2999	59.0804	58.8610	58.6415	58.4220	58.2025	57.9830	57.7635	57.5441	57.3246	.007316
56	60.8563	60.6183	60.3803	60.1423	59.9043	59.6663	59.4283	59.1903	58.9523	58.7143	58.4763	58.2383	.007933
57	61.9734	61.7156	61.4578	61.2000	60.9422	60.6844	60.4266	60.1688	59.9111	59.6533	59.3955	59.1377	.008593
58	63.0887	62.8101	62.5315	62.2530	61.9744	61.6958	61.4172	61.1386	60.8600	60.5814	60.3029	60.0243	.009286
59	64.2074	63.9069	63.6065	63.3060	63 0056	62.7051	62.4046	62.1042	61.8037	61.5032	61.2027	60.9023	.010015
60	65.3338	65.0107	64.6877	64.3646	64.0415	63.7185	63.3954	63.0723	62.7493	62.4262	62.1031	61.7801	.010769
61	66.4812	66.1351	65.7890	65.4428	65.0967	64.7506	64.4045	64.0584	63.7123	63.3661	63.0200	62.6739	.011537
62	67.6653	67.2954	66.9255	66.5555	66.1856	65.8157	65.4458	65.0759	64.7060	64.3360	63.9661	63.5962	.012330
63	68.9013	68.5072	68.1132	67.7191	67.3251	66.9310	66.5370	66.1430	65.7489	65.3548	64.9608	64.5667	.013135
64	70,2103	69.7903	69.3703	68.9504	68.5304	68.1104	67.6904	67.2705	66.8505	66.4305	66.0105	65.5906	.013999
65	71.5992	71.1526	70.7060	70.2593	69.8127	69.3661	68.9195	68.4729	68.0263	67.5796	67.1330	66.6864	.014887
66	73.0893	72.6136	72.1378	71.6621	71.1863	70.7106	70.2348	69.7591	69.2834	68.8076	68.3319	67.8561	.015858
67	74.6828	74.1752	73.6676	73.1600	72.6524	72.1448	71.6371	71.1295	70.6219	70.1143	69.6067	69.0991	.016920
68	76.3812	75.8378	75.2944	74.7510	74.2075	73.6641	73.1207	72.5773	72.0339	71.4904	70.9470	70.4036	.018114
69	78.1919	77.6081	77.0243	76.4406	75.8568	75.2730	74.6892	74.1055	73.5217	72.9379	72.3541	71.7704	.019459
70	80.0572	79.4319	78.8065	78.1812	77.5559	76.9306	76.3052	75.6799	75.0546	74.4293	73.8040	73.1786	.020844
71	82.0233	81.3475	80.6718	79.9960	79.3203	78.6445	77.9688	77.2930	76.6173	75.9415	75.2658	74.5900	.022525
72	84.0240	83.2891	82.5542	81.8192	81.0843	80.3494	79.6145	78.8796	78.1447	77.4097	76.6748	75.9399	.024497
73	85.9948	85.1935	84.3922	83.5909	82.7896	81.9882	81.1869	80.3856	79.5843	78.7830	77.9817	77.1804	.026710
74	87.8901	87.0004	86.1106	85.2209	84.3311	83.4414	82.5516	81.6619	80.7722	79.8824	78.9927	78.1029	.029658
75	89.4796	88.4978	87.5160	86.5341	85.5523	84.5705	83.5886	82.6068	81.6250	80.6432	79.6613	78.6795	.032727
76	90.7557	89.7598	88.7638	87.7679	86.7720	85.7760	84.7801	83.7842	82.7882	81.7923	80.7964	79.8004	.033198
77	92.7417	91.8546	90.9674	90.0803	89.1931	88.3060	87.4188	86.5317	85.6446	84.7574	83.8703	82.9831	.029571
78 or 31	**97.0874**	**97.3301**	**97.5728**	**97.8155**	**98.0583**	**98.3010**	**98.5437**	**98.7864**	**99.0291**	**99.2718**	**99.5146**	**99.7573**	**.008090**
30	95.9179	95.8565	95.7952	95.7338	95.6725	95.6111	95.5498	95.4884	95.4271	95.3657	95.3044	95.2430	.002045
29	95.3181	95.2147	95.1113	95.0079	94.9045	94.8011	94.6977	94.5943	94.4909	94.3875	94.2841	94.1807	.003447
28	94.8816	94.7693	94.6569	94.5446	94.4323	94.3199	94.2076	94.0953	93.9829	93.8706	93 7583	93.6459	.003744
27	94.3221	94.2243	94.1265	94.0287	93.9310	93.8332	93.7354	93.6376	93.5398	93.4420	93.3443	93.2465	.003259
26	93.6309	93.5483	93.4657	93.3831	93.3005	93.2179	93.1353	93.0527	92.9701	92.8875	92.8049	92.7223	.002753
25	92.8714	92.7986	92.7258	92.6530	92.5802	92.5074	92.4346	92.3618	92.2890	92.2162	92.1434	92.0706	.002427
24	92.0545	91.9904	91.9264	91.8623	91.7983	91.7342	91.6702	91.6061	91.5421	91.4780	91.4140	91.3500	.002135
23	91.2025	91.1452	91.0880	91.0307	90.9735	90.9162	90.8590	90.8017	90.7445	90.6872	90.6300	90.5727	.001908
22	90.3302	90.2783	90.2263	90.1744	90.1224	90.0705	90.0185	89.9666	89.9147	89.8627	89.8108	89.7588	.001731
21	89.4457	89.3983	89.3509	89.3035	89.2561	89 2086	89.1612	89.1138	89.0664	89.0190	88.9716	88.9242	.001580
20	88.5507	88.5075	88.4643	88.4212	88.3780	88.3348	88.2916	88.2485	88.2053	88.1621	88.1190	88.0758	.001439
19	87.6529	87.6132	87.5734	87.5337	87.4940	87.4542	87.4145	87.3748	87.3350	87.2953	87.2556	87.2158	.001324
18	86.7555	86.7188	86.6821	86.6454	86.6087	86.5720	86.5353	86.4986	86.4619	86.4252	86.3885	86.3518	.001223
17	85.8616	85.8275	85.7934	85.7594	85.7253	85.6912	85.6571	85.6231	85.5890	85.5549	85.5208	85.4868	.001136
16	84.9657	84.9346	84.9034	84.8723	84.8412	84.8100	84.7789	84.7478	84.7166	84.6855	84.6544	84.6232	.001038
15	84.0685	84.0401	84.0117	83.9834	83.9550	83.9266	83.8982	83.8699	83.8415	83.8131	83.7847	83.7564	.000946
14	83.1631	83.1379	83.1127	83.0876	83.0624	83.0372	83.0120	82.9869	82.9617	82.9365	82.9113	82.8862	.000839
13	82.2453	82.2236	82.2018	82.1801	82.1584	82.1366	82.1149	82.0932	82.0714	82.0497	82.0280	82.0062	.000724
12	81.3098	81,2919	81.2739	81.2560	81.2381	81.2201	81.2022	81.1843	81.1663	81.1484	81.1305	81.1125	.000598
11	80.3512	80.3373	80.3234	80.3095	80.2956	80.2817	80.2678	80.2540	80.2401	80.2262	80.2123	80.1984	.000463
10	79.3693	79.3595	79.3496	79.3398	79.3300	79.3201	79.3103	79.3005	79.2906	79.2808	79.2710	79.2611	.000328
Age	0	1	2	3	4	5	6	7	8	9	10	11	Day.

Age.	0	1	2	3	4	5	6	7	8	9	10	11	Day.
10	17.9332	17.9181	17.9030	17.8879	17.8728	17.8577	17.8425	17.8274	17.8123	17.7972	17.7821	17.7670	.000503
11	18.5075	18.4930	18.4786	18.4641	18.4497	18.4352	18.4208	18.4063	18.3919	18.3774	18.3630	18.3485	.000482
12	19.1011	19.0873	19.0735	19.0598	19.0460	19.0322	19.0184	19.0047	18.9909	18.9771	18.9633	18.9496	.000459
13	19.7100	19.6971	19.6842	19.6713	19.6584	19.6455	19.6326	19.6197	19.6068	19.5939	19.5810	19.5681	.000430
14	20.3426	20.3304	20.3182	20.3060	20.2937	20.2815	20.2693	20.2571	20.2449	20.2326	20.2204	20.2082	.000407
15	20.9967	20.9853	20.9739	20.9625	20.9511	20.9397	20.9283	20.9170	20.9056	20.8942	20.8828	20.8714	.000380
16	21.6744	21.6638	21.6532	21.6427	21.6321	21.6215	21.6110	21.6004	21.5898	21.5792	21.5686	21.5581	.000352
17	22.3775	22.3678	22.3581	22.3484	22.3388	22.3291	22.3194	22.3097	22.3000	22.2903	22.2807	22.2710	.000323
18	23.1077	23.0990	23.0903	23.0815	23.0728	23.0641	23.0554	23.0467	23.0380	23.0292	23.0205	23.0118	.000290
19	23.8677	23.8600	23.8522	23.8445	23.8367	23.8290	23.8212	23.8135	23.8058	23.7980	23.7903	23.7825	.000258
20	24.6585	24.6516	24.6446	24.6377	24.6308	24.6239	24.6170	24.6100	24.6031	24.5962	24.5892	24.5823	.000231
21	25.4801	25.4740	25.4678	25.4617	25.4556	25.4494	25.4433	25.4372	25.4310	25.4249	25.4188	25.4126	.000204
22	26.3333	26.3273	26.3212	26.3152	26.3092	26.3032	26.2971	26.2911	26.2851	26.2791	26.2730	26.2670	.000201
23	27.2113	27.2052	27.1990	27.1929	27.1868	27.1807	27.1745	27.1684	27.1623	27.1562	27.1500	27.1439	.000204
24	28.1136	28.1069	28.1002	28.0934	28.0867	28.0800	28.0733	28.0666	28.0599	28.0531	28.0464	28.0397	.000224
25	29.0356	29.0283	29.0210	29.0136	29.0063	28.9990	28.9917	28.9844	28.9771	28.9697	28.9624	28.9551	.000244
26	29.9787	29.9702	29.9617	29.9532	29.9447	29.9362	29.9276	29.9191	29.9106	29.9021	29.8936	29.8851	.000283
27	30.9389	30.9293	30.9198	30.9102	30.9007	30.8911	30.8815	30.8720	30.8624	30.8529	30.8433	30.8338	.000318
28	31.9176	31.9068	31.8960	31.8852	31.8744	31.8636	31.8528	31.8421	31.8313	31.8205	31.8097	31.7989	.000360
29	32.9163	32.9039	32.8915	32.8791	32.8667	32.8543	32.8418	32.8294	32.8170	32.8046	32.7922	32.7798	.000413
30	33.9334	33.9193	33.9052	33.8911	33.8770	33.8629	33.8487	33.8346	33.8205	33.8064	33.7923	33.7782	.000470
31	34.9664	34.9499	34.9334	34.9169	34.9004	34.8839	34.8674	34.8510	34.8345	34.8180	34.8015	34.7850	.000550
32	36.0137	35.9950	35.9764	35.9577	35.9391	35.9204	35.9017	35.8831	35.8644	35.8458	35.8271	35.8085	.000622
33	37.0792	37.0578	37.0365	37.0151	36.9937	36.9724	36.9510	36.9296	36.9083	36.8869	36.8655	36.8442	.000712
34	38.1591	38.1347	38.1104	38.0861	38.0617	38.0374	38.0131	37.9887	37.9644	37.9401	37.9157	37.8914	.000810
35	39.2534	39.2259	39.1984	39.1710	39.1435	39.1160	39.0885	39.0611	39.0336	39.0061	38.9786	38.9512	.000916
36	40.3614	40.3303	40.2993	40.2682	40.2372	40.2061	40.1750	40.1440	40.1129	40.0819	40.0508	40.0198	.001035
37	41.4832	41.4482	41.4132	41.3782	41.3432	41.3082	41.2731	41.2381	41.2031	41.1681	41.1331	41.0981	.001167
38	42.6168	42.5771	42.5373	42.4976	42.4579	42.4181	42.3784	42.3387	42.2989	42.2592	42.2195	42.1797	.001324
39	43.7573	43.7124	43.6674	43.6225	43.5776	43.5327	43.4877	43.4428	43.3979	43.3530	43.3080	43.2631	.001497
40	44.9027	44.8519	44.8011	44.7503	44.6996	44.6488	44.5980	44.5472	44.4964	44.4456	44.3949	44.3441	.001693
41	46.0490	45.9918	45.9347	45.8775	45.8203	45.7632	45.7060	45.6488	45.5917	45.5345	45.4773	45.4202	.001905
42	47.1951	47.1308	47.0665	47.0022	46.9379	46.8736	46.8093	46.7450	46.6807	46.6164	46.5521	46.4878	.002143
43	48.3387	48.2666	48.1945	48.1224	48.0503	47.9782	47.9061	47.8340	47.7619	47.6898	47.6177	47.5456	.002403
44	49.4778	49.3972	49.3166	49.2360	49.1554	49.0748	48.9941	48.9135	48.8329	48.7523	48.6717	48.5911	.002687
45	50.6153	50.5254	50.4354	50.3455	50.2556	50.1657	50.0757	49.9858	49.8959	49.8060	49.7160	49.6261	.002997
46	51.7488	51.6489	51.5491	51.4492	51.3493	51.2495	51.1496	51.0497	50.9499	50.8500	50.7501	50.6503	.003329
47	52.8810	52.7706	52.6603	52.5499	52.4395	52.3292	52.2188	52.1084	51.9981	51.8877	51.7773	51.6670	.003679
48	54.0118	53.8901	53.7683	53.6466	53.5249	53.4032	53.2814	53.1597	53.0380	52.9163	52.7945	52.6728	.004057
49	55.1423	55.0085	54.8747	54.7409	54.6071	54.4733	54.3395	54.2058	54.0720	53.9382	53.8044	53.6706	.004460
50	56.2694	56.1227	55.9760	55.8293	55.6826	55.5359	55.3892	55.2426	55.0959	54.9492	54.8025	54.6558	.004890
51	57.3937	57.2333	57.0730	56.9126	56.7522	56.5918	56.4314	56.2711	56.1107	55.9503	55.7900	55.6296	.005346
52	58.5163	58.3413	58.1662	57.9912	57.8162	57.6412	57.4661	57.2911	57.1161	56.9411	56.7660	56.5910	.005834
53	59.6358	59.4452	59.2546	59.0640	58.8734	58.6828	58.4922	58.3017	58.1111	57.9205	57.7299	57.5393	.006353
54	60.7545	60.5476	60.3407	60.1337	59.9268	59.7199	59.5130	59.3061	59.0992	58.8922	58.6853	58.4784	.006897
55	61.8724	61.6479	61.4234	61.1988	60.9743	60.7498	60.5253	60.3008	60.0763	59.8517	59.6272	59.4027	.007484
56	62.9892	62.7459	62.5026	62.2593	62.0160	61.7727	61.5293	61.2860	61.0427	60.7994	60.5561	60.3128	.008110
57	64.1042	63.8412	63.5782	63.3152	63.0522	62.7892	62.5261	62.2631	62.0001	61.7371	61.4741	61.2111	.008767
58	65.2205	64.9368	64.6530	64.3693	64.0856	63.8019	63.5181	63.2344	62.9507	62.6670	62.3832	62.0995	.009457
59	66.3433	66.0382	65.7331	65.4280	65.1230	64.8179	64.5128	64.2077	63.9026	63.5975	63.2925	62.9874	.010169
60	67.4826	67.1557	66.8289	66.5020	66.1752	65.8483	65.5215	65.1946	64.8678	64.5410	64.2141	63.8872	.010895
61	68.6558	68.3065	67.9572	67.6079	67.2586	66.9093	66.5600	66.2108	65.8615	65.5122	65.1629	64.8136	.011643
62	69.8762	69.5042	69.1321	68.7601	68.3881	68.0161	67.6440	67.2720	66.9000	66.5280	66.1560	65.7839	.012401
63	71.1652	70.7688	70.3723	69.9759	69.5795	69.1830	68.7866	68.3902	67.9937	67.5973	67.2009	66.8044	.013214
64	72.5280	72.1065	71.6850	71.2635	70.8420	70.4205	69.9990	69.5775	69.1560	68.7345	68.3130	67.8915	.014050
65	73.9856	73.5367	73.0878	72.6389	72.1900	71.7411	71.2921	70.8432	70.3943	69.9454	69.4965	69.0476	.014963
66	75.5397	75.0608	74.5819	74.1030	73.6241	73.1452	72.6662	72.1873	71.7084	71.2295	70.7506	70.2717	.015963
67	77.1912	76.6785	76.1658	75.6532	75.1405	74.6278	74.1151	73.6025	73.0898	72.5771	72.0644	71.5518	.017089
68	78.9285	78.3794	77.8302	77.2811	76.7320	76.1829	75.6337	75.0846	74.5355	73.9864	73.4372	72.8881	.018304
69	80.7540	80.1642	79.5744	78.9846	78.3948	77.8050	77.2151	76.6253	76.0355	75.4457	74.8559	74.2661	.019660
70	82.6532	82.0158	81.3785	80.7411	80.1038	79.4664	78.8291	78.1917	77.5544	76.9170	76.2797	75.6423	.021245
71	84.5820	83.8888	83.1957	82.5025	81.8094	81.1162	80.4231	79.7300	79.0368	78.3436	77.6505	76.9573	.023105
72	86.4787	85.7229	84.9672	84.2114	83.4556	82.6999	81.9441	81 1883	80.4326	79.6768	78.9210	78.1653	.025192
73	88.3998	87.5522	86.7045	85.8569	85.0093	84.1617	83.3140	82.4664	81.6188	80.7712	79.9235	79.0759	.028254
74	89.8255	88.8993	87.9732	87.0470	86.1209	85.1947	84.2685	83.3424	82.4162	81.4901	80.5639	79.6378	.030872
75	91.0494	90.1110	89.1725	88.2340	87.2956	86.3571	85.4187	84.4802	83.5418	82.6033	81.6649	80.7264	.031282
76	92.9476	92.1140	91.2804	90.4468	89.6132	88.7796	87.9460	87.1123	86.2787	85.4451	84.6115	83.7779	.027787
77 or 32	**97.0874**	**97.3301**	**97.5728**	**97.8155**	**98.0583**	**98.3010**	**98.5437**	**98.7864**	**99.0291**	**99.2718**	**99.5146**	**99.7573**	**.008090**
31	95.9045	95.8397	95.7748	95.7100	95.6452	95.5803	95.5155	95.4507	95.3858	95.3210	95.2562	95.1913	.002161
30	95.2986	95.1914	95.0842	94.9770	94.8698	94.7626	94.6554	94.5482	94.4410	94.3338	94.2266	94.1194	.003573
29	94.8581	94.7420	94.6259	94.5098	94.3937	94.2776	94.1614	94.0453	93.9292	93.8131	93.6970	93.5809	.003870
28	94.2937	94.1924	94.0911	93.9899	93.8886	93.7873	93.6860	93.5848	93.4835	93.3822	93.2810	93.1797	.003376
27	93.5967	93.5109	93.4250	93.3392	93.2534	93.1676	93.0817	92.9959	92.9101	92.8243	92.7384	92.6526	.002861
26	92.8311	92.7553	92.6795	92.6037	92.5279	92.4521	92.3762	92.3004	92.2246	92.1488	92.0730	91.9972	.002527
25	92.0088	91.9419	91.8749	91.8080	91.7411	91.6741	91.6072	91.5403	91.4733	91.4064	91.3395	91.2725	.002231
24	91.1501	91.0901	91.0302	90.9702	90.9102	90.8503	90.7903	90.7303	90.6704	90.6104	90.5504	90.4905	.001999
23	90.2721	90.2176	90.1632	90.1087	90.0542	89.9998	89.9453	89.8908	89.8364	89.7819	89.7274	89.6730	.001815
22	89.3823	89.3325	89.2827	89.2328	89.1830	89.1332	89.0834	89.0336	88.9838	88.9340	88.8841	88.8343	.001660
21	88.4823	88.4368	88.3914	88.3459	88.3004	88.2550	88.2095	88.1640	88.1186	88.0731	88.0276	87.9822	.001515
20	87.5799	87.5380	87.4960	87.4541	87.4122	87.3703	87.3283	87.2864	87.2445	87.2026	87.1606	87.1187	.001397
19	86.6793	86.6404	86.6015	86.5627	86.5238	86.4849	86.4460	86.4072	86.3683	86.3294	86.2905	86.2517	.001296
18	85.7805	85.7444	85.7084	85.6723	85.6362	85.6002	85.5641	85.5280	85.4920	85.4559	85.4198	85.3838	.001202
17	84.8812	84.8482	84.8151	84.7821	84.7490	84.7160	84.6830	84.6499	84.6169	84.5838	84.5508	84.5177	.001101
16	83.9808	83.9506	83.9204	83.8902	83.8600	83.8298	83.7996	83.7695	81.7393	83.7091	83.6789	83.6487	.001006
15	83.0727	83.0458	83.0189	82.9920	82.9651	82.9382	82.9112	82.8843	82.8574	82.8305	82.8036	82.7767	.000897
14	82.1224	82.1015	82.0806	82.0597	82.0388	82.0179	81.9970	81.9762	81.9553	81.9344	81.9135	81.8926	.000696
13	81.2142	81.1947	81.1752	81.1557	81.1362	81.1167	81.0971	81.0776	81.0581	81.0386	81.0191	80.9996	.000650
12	80.2543	80.2389	80.2235	80.2081	80.1928	80.1774	80.1620	80.1466	80.1312	80.1158	80.1005	80.0851	.000513
11	79.2700	79.2588	79.2475	79.2363	79.2250	79.2138	79.2025	79.1913	79.1801	79.1688	79.1576	79.1463	.000375
10	78.2610	78.2539	78.2468	78.2398	78.2327	78.2256	78.2185	78.2115	78.2044	78.1973	78.1902	78.1832	.000236
Age.	0	1	2	3	4	5	6	7	8	9	10	11	Day.

Age.	0	1	2	3	4	5	6	7	8	9	10	11	Day.
10	18.9451	18.9321	18.9191	18.9061	18.8931	18.8801	18.8670	18.8540	18.8410	18.8280	18.8150	18.8020	.000433
11	19.5503	19.5380	19.5257	19.5134	19.5011	19.4888	19.4765	19.4642	19.4519	19.4396	19.4273	19.4150	.00041
12	20.1759	20.1645	20.1532	20.1418	20.1305	20.1191	20.1077	20.0964	20.0850	20.0737	20.0623	20.0510	.000378
13	20.8204	20.8098	20.7991	20.7885	20.7779	20.7672	20.7566	20.7460	20.7353	20.7247	20.7141	20.7034	.000354
14	21.4874	21.4776	21.4679	21.4581	21.4484	21.4386	21.4289	21.4191	21.4094	21.3996	21.3899	21.3801	.000325
15	22.1787	22.1698	22.1609	22.1520	22.1431	22.1342	22.1253	22.1165	22.1076	22.0987	22.0898	22.0809	.000296
16	22.8947	22.8867	22.8788	22.8708	22.8629	22.8550	22.8470	22.8390	22.8311	22.8231	22.8152	22.8072	.000265
17	23.6381	23.6312	23.6243	23.6174	23.6105	23.6036	23.5966	23.5897	23.5828	23.5759	23.5690	23.5621	.000230
18	24.4110	24.4051	24.3992	24.3933	24.3875	24.3816	24.3757	24.3698	24.3639	24.3580	24.3522	24.3463	.000196
19	25.2150	25.2100	25.2050	25.2000	25.1949	25.1899	25.1849	25.1799	25.1749	25.1698	25.1648	25.1598	.000167
20	26.0492	26.0450	26.0409	26.0367	26.0326	26.0284	26.0243	26.0201	26.0160	26.0118	26.0077	26.0035	.000138
21	26.9155	26.9115	26.9075	26.9035	26.8995	26.8955	26.8915	26.8875	26.8835	26.8795	26.8755	26.8715	.000133
22	27.8066	27.8026	27.7986	27.7946	27.7906	27.7866	27.7826	27.7786	27.7746	27.7706	27.7666	27.7626	.000133
23	28.7218	28.7173	28.7128	28.7082	28.7037	28.6992	28.6947	28.6902	28.6857	28.6811	28.6766	28.6721	.000150
24	29.6570	29.6520	29.6470	29.6419	29.6369	29.6319	29.6268	29.6218	29.6168	29.6118	29.6067	29.6017	.000167
25	30.6136	30.6075	30.6013	30.5952	30.5891	30.5829	30.5768	30.5707	30.5645	30.5584	30.5523	30.5461	.000204
26	31.5861	31.5791	31.5721	31.5651	31.5581	31.5511	31.5440	31.5370	31.5300	31.5230	31.5160	31.5090	.000233
27	32.5794	32.5712	32.5630	32.5547	32.5465	32.5383	32.5301	32.5219	32.5137	32.5054	32.4972	32.4890	.000274
28	33.5913	33.5816	33.5719	33.5621	33.5524	33.5427	33.5330	33.5233	33.5136	33.5038	33.4941	33.4844	.000324
29	34.6207	34.6094	34.5981	34.5867	34.5754	34.5641	34.5528	34.5415	34.5302	34.5188	34.5075	34.4962	.000377
30	35.6698	35.6562	35.6427	35.6291	35.6156	35.6020	35.5884	35.5749	35.5613	35.5478	35.5342	35.5207	.000452
31	36.7294	36.7138	36.6982	36.6826	36.6670	36.6514	36.6358	36.6202	36.6046	36.5890	36.5734	36.5578	.000520
32	37.8085	37.7903	37.7722	37.7540	37.7359	37.7177	37.6995	37.6814	37.6632	37.6451	37.6269	37.6088	.000605
33	38.9021	38.8811	38.8601	38.8392	38.8182	38.7972	38.7762	38.7553	38.7343	38.7133	38.6923	38.6714	.000699
34	40.0101	39.9862	39.9622	39.9383	39.9143	39.8904	39.8664	39.8425	39.8186	39.7946	39.7707	39.7467	.000798
35	41.1338	41.1065	41.0792	41.0518	41.0245	40.9972	40.9698	40.9425	40.9152	40.8878	40.8605	40.8332	.000910
36	42.2695	42.2384	42.2073	42.1762	42.1452	42.1141	42.0830	42.0519	42.0208	41.9897	41.9587	41.9276	.001036
37	43.4184	43.3828	43.3472	43.3117	43.2761	43.2405	43.2050	43.1694	43.1338	43.0982	43.0626	43.0271	.001186
38	44.5740	44.5335	44.4930	44.4525	44.4120	44.3715	44.3310	44.2904	44.2499	44.2094	44.1689	44.1284	.001350
39	45.7354	45.6893	45.6432	45.5971	45.5510	45.5049	45.4588	45.4127	45.3666	45.3205	45.2744	45.2283	.001537
40	46.8985	46.8463	46.7942	46.7420	46.6898	46.6377	46.5855	46.5333	46.4812	46.4290	46.3768	46.3247	.001739
41	48.0617	48.0027	47.9437	47.8848	47.8258	47.7668	47.7078	47.6489	47.5899	47.5309	47.4720	47.4130	.001966
42	49.2213	49.1549	49.0885	49.0221	48.9557	48.8893	48.8229	48.7565	48.6901	48.6237	48.5573	48.4909	.002213
43	50.3765	50.3020	50.2275	50.1530	50.0785	50.0040	49.9295	49.8551	49.7806	49.7061	49.6316	49.5571	.002483
44	51.5255	51.4421	51.3587	51.2753	51.1919	51.1085	51.0250	50.9416	50.8582	50.7748	50.6914	50.6080	.002780
45	52.9696	52.5767	52.4838	52.3909	52.2980	52.2051	52.1121	52.0192	51.9263	51.8334	51.7405	51.6476	.003097
46	53.8091	53.7061	53.6032	53.5002	53.3973	53.2943	53.1914	53.0884	52.9855	52.8825	52.7796	52.6766	.003432
47	54.9477	54.8339	54.7201	54.6063	54.4925	54.3787	54.2648	54.1510	54.0372	53.9234	53.8096	53.6958	.003793
48	56.0822	55.9568	55.8315	55.7061	55.5808	55.4554	55.3300	55.2047	55.0793	54.9540	54.8286	54.7033	.004178
49	57.2156	57.0779	56.9403	56.8026	56.6649	56.5273	56.3896	56.2519	56.1143	55.9766	55.8389	55.7013	.004587
50	58.3443	58.1936	58.0428	57.8921	57.7414	57.5907	57.4400	57.2892	57.1385	56.9878	56.8370	56.6863	.005024
51	59.4700	59.3053	59.1406	58.9759	58.8112	58.6465	58.4818	58.3171	58.1524	57.9877	57.8230	57.6583	.005490
52	60.5921	60.4126	60.2331	60.0536	59.8742	59.6947	59.5152	59.3357	59.1562	58.9767	58.7973	58.6178	.005983
53	61.7106	61.5155	61.3204	61.1253	60.9303	60.7352	60.5401	60.3450	60.1499	59.9548	59.7598	59.5647	.006503
54	62.8300	62.6182	62.4064	62.1945	61.9827	61.7709	61.5591	61.3473	61.1355	60.9236	60.7118	60.5000	.007060
55	63.9455	63.7158	63.4861	63.2564	63.0266	62.7971	62.5674	62.3377	62.1080	61.8783	61.6487	61.4190	.007656
56	65.0584	64.8100	64.5616	64.3132	64.0649	63.8165	63.5681	63.3197	63.0713	62.8230	62.5746	62.3262	.008279
57	66.1723	65.9043	65.6363	65.3683	65.1003	64.8323	64.5643	64.2963	64.0283	63.7603	63.4923	63.2243	.008933
58	67.2906	67.0024	66.7142	66.4260	66.1378	65.8496	65.5614	65.2733	64.9851	64.6969	64.4087	64.1205	.009606
59	68.4238	68.1151	67.8063	67.4976	67.1888	66.8801	66.5713	66.2626	65.9539	65.6451	65.3364	65.0276	.010291
60	69.5861	69.2562	68.9262	68.5963	68.2664	67.9365	67.6065	67.2766	66.9467	66.6168	66.2868	65.9569	.010997
61	70.7923	70.4409	70.0896	69.7383	69.3869	69.0356	68.6843	68.3329	67.9816	67.6303	67.2789	66.9276	.011710
62	72.0618	71.6875	71.3131	70.9388	70.5645	70.1902	69.8158	69.4415	69.0672	68.6929	68.3185	67.9442	.012477
63	73.4005	73.0086	72.6167	72.2248	71.8330	71.4411	71.0492	70.6573	70.2654	69.8735	69.4817	69.0898	.013063
64	74.8274	74.4037	73.9800	73.5563	73.1326	72.7089	72.2852	71.8615	71.4378	71.0141	70.5904	70.1667	.014123
65	76.3445	75.8925	75.4406	74.9886	74.5367	74.0847	73.6327	73.1808	72.7288	72.2769	71.8249	71.3730	.015065
66	77.9521	77.4683	76.9846	76.5008	76.0170	75.5333	75.0495	74.5657	74.0820	73.5982	73.1144	72.6307	.016125
67	79.6388	79.1206	78.6025	78.0843	77.5662	77.0480	76.5299	76.0117	75.4936	74.9754	74.4573	73.9391	.017272
68	81.4073	80.8508	80.2943	79.7378	79.1813	78.6248	78.0682	77.5117	76.9552	76.3987	75.8422	75.2857	.018550
69	83.2438	82.6425	82.0411	81.4398	80.8384	80.2371	79.6357	79.0344	78.4331	77.8317	77.2304	76.6290	.020045
70	85.1049	84.4509	83.7968	83.1428	82.4888	81.8348	81.1807	80.5267	79.8727	79.2187	78.5646	77.9106	.021801
71	86.9319	86.2188	85.5056	84.7925	84.0794	83.3663	82.6531	81.9400	81.2269	80.5138	79.8006	79.0875	.023771
72	88.6832	87.8911	87.0990	86.3069	85.5148	84.7227	83.9306	83.1385	82.3464	81.5543	80.7622	79.9701	.026403
73	90.1490	89.2749	88.4008	87.5267	86.6526	85.7785	84.9044	84.0303	83.1563	82.2822	81.4081	80.5340	.029136
74	91.3239	90.4391	89.5544	88.6696	87.7849	86.9001	86.0154	85.1306	84.2459	83.3611	82.4764	81.5916	.029492
75	93.1397	92.3560	91.5723	90.7887	90.0050	89.2213	88.4376	87.6540	86.8703	86.0866	85.3030	84.5193	.026122
76 or 33	**97.0874**	**97.3301**	**97.5728**	**97.8155**	**98.0583**	**98.3010**	**98.5437**	**98.7864**	**39.0291**	**99.2718**	**99.5146**	**99.7573**	**.008090**
32	95.8905	95.8220	95.7535	95.6850	95.6166	95.5481	95.4796	95.4111	95.3426	95.2741	95.2057	95.1372	.002283
31	95.2782	95.1670	95.0558	94.9445	94.8333	94.7221	94.6109	94.4997	94.3885	94.2772	94.1660	94.0548	.003707
30	94.8336	94.7135	94.5935	94.4734	94.3534	94.2333	94.1132	93.9932	93.8731	93.7531	93.6330	93.5130	.004002
29	94.2641	94.1592	94.0542	93.9493	93.8444	93.7394	93.6345	93.5296	93.4246	93.3197	93.2148	93.1098	.003498
28	93.5609	93.4717	93.3825	93.2933	93.2041	93.1149	93.0257	92.9365	92.8474	92.7582	92.6690	92.5798	.002973
27	92.7890	92.7100	92.6311	92.5521	92.4732	92.3942	92 3152	92.2363	92.1573	92.0784	91.9994	91.9205	.002632
26	91.9603	91.8904	91.8205	91.7506	91.6807	91.6108	91.5410	91.4711	91.4012	91.3313	91.2614	91.1915	.002330
25	91.0954	91.0327	90.9700	90.9073	90.8446	90.7819	90.7192	90.6565	90.5938	90.5311	90.4684	90.4057	.002090
24	90.2115	90.1544	90.0973	90.0401	89.9830	89.9259	89.8688	89.8117	89.7546	89.6974	89.6403	89.5832	.001904
23	89.3161	89.2638	89.2114	89.1591	89.1068	89.0544	89.0021	88.9498	88.8974	88.8451	88.7928	88.7404	.001714
22	88.4109	88.3630	88.3152	88.2673	88.2195	88.1716	88.1237	88.0759	88.0280	87.9802	87.9323	87.8845	.001595
21	87.5037	87.4595	87.4153	87.3711	87.3269	87.2827	87.2385	87.1943	87.1501	87.1059	87.0617	87.0175	.001473
20	86.5977	86.5567	86.5157	86.4748	86.4338	86.3928	86.3518	86.3109	86.2699	86.2289	86.1880	86.1470	.001366
19	85.6960	85.6578	85.6197	85.5815	85.5434	85.5052	85.4671	85.4290	85.3908	85.3526	85.3145	85.2763	.001272
18	84.7930	84.7580	84.7230	84.6879	84.6529	84.6179	84.5828	84.5478	84.5128	84.4778	84.4427	84.4077	.001167
17	83.8894	83.8573	83.8252	83.7931	83.7610	83.7289	83.6968	83.6647	83.6327	83.6006	83.5685	83.5364	.001070
16	82.9784	82.9497	82.9209	82.8922	82.8635	82.8347	82.8060	82.7773	82.7485	82.7198	82.6911	82.6623	.000958
15	82.0554	82.0303	82.0052	81.9800	81.9549	81.9298	81.9047	81.8796	81.8545	81.8293	81.8042	81.7791	.000837
14	81.1148	81.0936	81.0725	81.0513	81.0302	81.0090	80.9879	80.9667	80.9456	80.9244	80.9033	80.8821	.000705
13	80.1523	80.1354	80.1184	80.1015	80.0845	80.0676	80.0506	80.0337	80.0168	79.9998	79.9829	79.9659	.000565
12	79.1668	79.1541	79.1414	79.1286	79.1159	79.1032	79.0905	79.0778	79.0651	79.0523	79.0396	79.0269	.000424
11	78.1555	78.1470	78.1386	78.1301	78.1216	78.1132	78.1047	78.0962	78.0878	78.0793	78.0708	78.0624	.000282
10	77.1204	77.1160	77.1116	77.1072	77.1029	77.0985	77.0941	77.0897	77.0853	77.0810	77.0766	77.0722	.000146
Age.	0	1	2	3	4	5	6	7	8	9	10	11	Day.

Age.	0	1	2	3	4	5	6	7	8	9	10	11	Day.
10	19.9821	19.9712	19.9603	19.9495	19.9386	19.9277	19.9168	19.9060	19.8951	19.8842	19.8733	19.8625	.000362
11	20.6187	20.6088	20.5989	20.5890	20.5792	20.5693	20.5594	20.5495	20.5396	20.5297	20.5199	20.5100	.000329
12	21.2796	21.2705	21.2614	21.2523	21.2432	21.2341	21.2250	21.2158	21.2067	21.1976	21.1885	21.1794	.000303
13	21.9581	21.9499	21.9417	21.9335	21.9254	21.9172	21.9090	21.9008	21.8926	21.8844	21.8763	21.8681	.000273
14	22.6618	22.6545	22.6473	22.6400	22.6327	22.6255	22.6182	22.6109	22.6037	22.5964	22.5891	22.5819	.000242
15	23.3907	23.3844	23.3782	23.3719	23.3656	23.3594	23.3531	23.3468	23.3406	23.3343	23.3280	23.3218	.000209
16	24.1465	24.1413	24.1361	24.1310	24.1258	24.1206	24.1154	24.1102	24.1050	24.0998	24.0947	24.0895	.000173
17	24.9321	24.9280	24.9239	24.9198	24.9157	24.9116	24.9075	24.9034	24.8993	24.8952	24.8911	24.8870	.000137
18	25.7482	25.7450	25.7419	25.7387	25.7355	25.7324	25.7292	25.7260	25.7229	25.7197	25.7165	25.7134	.000105
19	26.5949	26.5926	26.5904	26.5881	26.5859	26.5836	26.5814	26.5791	26.5769	26.5746	26.5724	26.5701	.000075
20	27.4732	27.4712	27.4691	27.4671	27.4651	27.4630	27.4610	27.4590	27.4569	27.4549	27.4529	27.4508	.000068
21	28.3765	28.3745	28.3725	28.3706	28.3686	28.3666	28.3646	28.3627	28.3607	28.3587	28.3567	28.3548	.000066
22	29.3042	29.3018	29.2994	29.2970	29.2946	29.2922	29.2897	29.2873	29.2849	29.2825	29.2801	29.2777	.000080
23	30.2515	30.2487	30.2458	30.2430	30.2401	30.2373	30.2344	30.2316	30.2288	30.2259	30.2231	30.2202	.000095
24	31.2206	31.2167	31.2129	31.2090	31.2052	31.2013	31.1974	31.1936	31.1897	31.1859	31.1820	31.1782	.000128
25	32.2058	32.2011	32.1965	32.1918	32.1872	32.1825	32.1779	32.1732	32.1686	32.1640	32.1593	32.1546	.000155
26	33.2115	33.2057	33.2000	33.1942	33.1885	33.1827	33.1770	33.1712	33.1654	33.1597	33.1539	33.1482	.000192
27	34.2360	34.2289	34.2217	34.2146	34.2074	34.2003	34.1931	34.1860	34.1789	34.1717	34.1646	34.1574	.000238
28	35.2778	35.2692	35.2605	35.2519	35.2432	35.2346	35.2260	35.2173	35.2087	35.2000	35.1914	35.1827	.000288
29	36.3382	36.3274	36.3166	36.3059	36.2951	36.2843	36.2735	36.2628	36.2520	36.2412	36.2304	36.2197	.000359
30	37.4128	37.4002	37.3875	37.3748	37.3622	37.3495	37.3368	37.3242	37.3115	37.2988	37.2862	37.2735	.000420
31	38.5031	38.4880	38.4729	38.4578	38.4427	38.4276	38.4125	38.3974	38.3823	38.3672	38.3521	38.3370	.000503
32	39.6093	39.5915	39.5738	39.5560	39.5382	39.5205	39.5027	39.4849	39.4672	39.4494	39.4316	39.4139	.000592
33	40.7298	40.7092	40.6886	40.6680	40.6475	40.6269	40.6063	40.5857	40.5651	40.5445	40.5240	40.5034	.000686
34	41.8659	41.8421	41.8183	41.7945	41.7707	41.7469	41.7231	41.6993	41.6755	41.6517	41.6279	41.6041	.000793
35	43.0159	42.9885	42.9612	42.9338	42.9065	42.8791	42.8518	42.8244	42.7971	42.7697	42.7424	42.7150	.000912
36	44.1774	44.1458	44.1141	44.0825	44.0508	44.0192	43.9875	43.9559	43.9243	43.8926	43.8610	43.8293	.001055
37	45.3468	45.3105	45.2741	45.2378	45.2014	45.1651	45.1287	45.0924	45.0561	45.0197	44.9834	44.9470	.001211
38	46.5219	46.4802	46.4385	46.3969	46.3552	46.3135	46.2718	46.2302	46.1885	46.1468	46.1051	46.0635	.001389
39	47.6994	47.6519	47.6045	47.5570	47.5095	47.4621	47.4146	47.3671	47.3197	47.2722	47.2247	47.1773	.001582
40	48.8777	48.8237	48.7698	48.7158	48.6619	48.6080	48.5540	48.5000	48.4461	48.3921	48.3382	48.2842	.001798
41	50.0526	49.9916	49.9305	49.8695	49.8085	49.7475	49.6864	49.6254	49.5644	49.5034	49.4423	49.3813	.002034
42	51.2223	51.1535	51.0848	51.0160	50.9473	50.8785	50.8097	50.7410	50.6722	50.6035	50.5347	50.4660	.002292
43	52.3857	52.3085	52.2312	52.1540	52.0767	51.9995	51.9222	51.8450	51.7678	51.6905	51.6133	51.5360	.002575
44	53.5396	53.4533	53.3669	53.2806	53.1942	53.1079	53.0215	52.9352	52.8489	52.7625	52.6762	52.5898	.002878
45	54.6881	54.5922	54.4962	54.4003	54.3044	54.2084	54.1125	54.0166	53.9206	53.8247	53.7288	53.6328	.003198
46	55.8324	55.7261	55.6198	55.5134	55.4071	55.3008	55.1945	55.0882	54.9819	54.8755	54.7692	54.6629	.003544
47	56.9731	56.8557	56.7384	56.6210	56.5037	56.3863	56.2690	56.1516	56.0342	55.9169	55.7995	55.6822	.003912
48	58.1090	57.9799	57.8507	57.7216	57.5924	57.4633	57.3341	57.2050	57.0759	56.9467	56.8176	56.6884	.004305
49	59.2424	59.1008	58.9592	58.8176	58.6760	58.5344	58.3927	58.2511	58.1095	57.9679	57.8263	57.6847	.004720
50	60.3708	60.2159	60.0609	59.9060	59.7511	59.5961	59.4412	59.2863	59.1313	58.9764	58.8215	58.6665	.005164
51	61.4944	61.3254	61.1563	60.9873	60.8182	60.6492	60.4801	60.3111	60.1421	59.9730	59.8040	59.6349	.005635
52	62.6143	62.4304	62.2465	62.0626	61.8787	61.6948	61.5109	61.3270	61.1431	60.9592	60.7753	60.5914	.006130
53	63.7315	63.5316	63.3318	63.1319	62.9321	62.7322	62.5323	62.3325	62.1326	61.9328	61.7329	61.5331	.006662
54	64.8467	64.6299	64.4130	64.1962	63.9794	63.7625	63.5457	63.3289	63.1120	62.8952	62.6784	62.4615	.007228
55	65.9566	65.7220	65.4874	65.2528	65.0182	64.7836	64.5490	64.3143	64.0797	63.8451	63.6105	63.3759	.007820
56	67.0667	66.8135	66.5602	66.3070	66.0538	65.8006	65.5473	65.2941	65.0409	64.7877	64.5344	64.2812	.008441
57	68.1806	67.9083	67.6359	67.3636	67.0913	66.8189	66.5466	66.2743	66.0019	65.7296	65.4573	65.1849	.009077
58	69.3071	69.0153	68.7236	68.4318	68.1401	67.8483	67.5566	67.2648	66.9731	66.6813	66.3896	66.0978	.009725
59	70.4604	70.1487	69.8370	69.5252	69.2135	68.9018	68.5901	68.2784	67.9667	67.6550	67.3432	67.0315	.010390
60	71.6526	71.3207	70.9888	70.6569	70.3250	69.9931	69.6612	69.3294	68.9975	68.6656	68.3337	68.0018	.011063
61	72.9043	72.5507	72.1972	71.8436	71.4901	71.1365	70.7830	70.4294	70.0758	69.7223	69.3687	69.0152	.011785
62	74.2198	73.8441	73.4683	73.0926	72.7168	72.3411	71.9653	71.5896	71.2139	70.8381	70.4624	70.0866	.012525
63	75.6904	75.2844	74.8783	74.4723	74.0663	73.6602	73.2542	72.8482	72.4421	72.0361	71.6301	71.2240	.013534
64	77.1004	76.6738	76.2471	75.8205	75.3938	74.9672	74.5405	74.1139	73.6873	73.2606	72.8340	72.4073	.014221
65	78.6668	78.2102	77.7535	77.2969	76.8402	76.3836	75.9270	75.4703	75.0137	74.5570	74.1004	73.6437	.015221
66	80.3062	79.8171	79.3281	78.8390	78.3500	77.8610	77.3719	76.8828	76.3938	75.9047	75.4157	74.9266	.016302
67	82.0207	81.4954	80.9702	80.4450	79.9197	79.3944	78.8692	78.3440	77.8187	77.2934	76.7682	76.2430	.017508
68	83.7975	83.2299	82.6623	82.0948	81.5272	80.9596	80.3920	79.8245	79.2569	78.6893	78.1217	77.5542	.018919
69	85.5952	84.9778	84.3605	83.7432	83.1258	82.5085	81.8912	81.2738	80.6565	80.0392	79.4218	78.8045	.020577
70	87.3565	86.6833	86.0102	85.3370	84.6639	83.9907	83.3176	82.6444	81.9713	81.2981	80.6250	79.9518	.022438
71	89.0421	88.2942	87.5463	86.7984	86.0505	85.3026	84.5547	83.8069	83.0590	82.3111	81.5632	80.8153	.024930
72	90.4517	89.6263	88.8010	87.9756	87.1502	86.3248	85.4994	84.6741	83.8487	83.0233	82.1980	81.3726	.027512
73	91.5807	90.7462	89.9116	89.0771	88.2426	87.4080	86.5735	85.7390	84.9044	84.0699	83.2354	82.4008	.027818
74	93.3192	92.5822	91.8452	91.1081	90.3711	89.6341	88.8971	88.1601	87.4231	86.6860	85.9490	85.2120	.024567
75 or 34	**97.0874**	**97.3301**	**97.5728**	**97.8155**	**98.0583**	**98.3010**	**98.5437**	**98.7864**	**99.0291**	**99.2718**	**99.5146**	**99.7573**	**.008090**
33	95.8737	95.8016	95.7294	95.6573	95.5851	95.5130	95.4408	95.3687	95.2966	95.2244	95.1523	95.0801	.002405
32	95.2567	95.1413	95.0259	94.9105	94.7951	94.6797	94.5642	94.4488	94.3334	94.2180	94.1026	93.9872	.003847
31	94.8078	94.6836	94.5594	94.4352	94.3110	94.1868	94.0625	93.9383	93.8141	93.6899	93.5657	93.4415	.004140
30	94.2429	94.1333	94.0237	93.9141	93.8046	93.6950	93.5854	93.4758	93.3662	93.2566	93.1471	93.0375	.003653
29	93.5234	93.4307	93.3380	93.2452	93.1525	93.0598	92.9671	92.8744	92.7817	92.6890	92.5962	92.5035	.003090
28	92.7449	92.6626	92.5804	92.4981	92.4159	92.3336	92.2513	92.1691	92.0868	92.0046	91.9223	91.8401	.002742
27	91.9095	91.8365	91.7635	91.6906	91.6176	91.5446	91.4716	91.3987	91.3257	91.2527	91.1797	91.1068	.002432
26	91.0382	90.9726	90.9070	90.8413	90.7757	90.7101	90.6445	90.5789	90.5133	90.4476	90.3820	90.3164	.002187
25	90.1481	90.0882	90.0283	89.9685	89.9086	89.8487	89.7888	89.7290	89.6691	89.6092	89.5493	89.4895	.001996
24	89.2470	89.1920	89.1371	89.0821	89.0272	88.9722	88.9172	88.8623	88.8073	88.7524	88.6974	88.6425	.001832
23	88.3363	88.2860	88.2356	88.1852	88.1349	88.0845	88.0342	87.9838	87.9335	87.8831	87.8328	87.7824	.001678
22	87.4242	87.3776	87.3310	87.2844	87.2379	87.1913	87.1447	87.0981	87.0515	87.0050	86.9584	86.9118	.001553
21	86.5137	86.4704	86.4272	86.3840	86.3407	86.2974	86.2542	86.2110	86.1677	86.1244	86.0812	86.0380	.001442
20	85.6078	85.5675	85.5271	85.4868	85.4465	85.4062	85.3658	85.3255	85.2852	85.2449	85.2045	85.1642	.001344
19	84.7012	84.6641	84.6270	84.5898	84.5527	84.5156	84.4785	84.4414	84.4043	84.3671	84.3300	84.2929	.001237
18	83.7941	83.7600	83.7260	83.6919	83.6578	83.6237	83.5896	83.5556	83.5215	83.4874	83.4533	83.4193	.001136
17	82.8800	82.8494	82.8188	82.7881	82.7575	82.7269	82.6963	82.6657	82.6351	82.6044	82.5738	82.5432	.001020
16	81.9542	81.9273	81.9004	81.8734	81.8465	81.8196	81.7927	81.7658	81.7389	81.7120	81.6850	81.6581	.000897
15	81.0111	80.9882	80.9654	80.9425	80.9196	80.8968	80.8739	80.8510	80.8282	80.8053	80.7824	80.7596	.000762
14	80.0462	80.0276	80.0091	79.9905	79.9719	79.9534	79.9348	79.9162	79.8977	79.8791	79.8605	79.8420	.000619
13	79.0583	79.0440	79.0298	79.0155	79.0012	78.9870	78.9727	78.9584	78.9442	78.9299	78.9156	78.9014	.000475
12	78.0459	78.0360	78.0260	78.0161	78.0061	77.9962	77.9863	77.9764	77.9664	77.9565	77.9466	77.9366	.000331
11	77.0085	77.0027	76.9970	76.9912	76.9855	76.9797	76.9740	76.9682	76.9624	76.9567	76.9509	76.9452	.000192
10	75.9491	75.9473	75.9454	75.9436	75.9418	75.9400	75.9381	75.9363	75.9345	75.9327	75.9308	75.9290	.000061
Age.	0	1	2	3	4	5	6	7	8	9	10	11	Day.

Age.	0	1	2.	3	4	5	6	7	8	9	10	11	Day.
10	21.0447	21.0362	21.0277	21.0192	21.0107	21.0022	20.9937	20.9852	20.9768	20.9683	20.9598	20.9513	.000283
11	21.7162	21.7085	21.7009	21.6932	21.6856	21.6779	21.6702	21.6626	21.6549	21.6473	21.6396	21.6320	.000255
12	22.4104	22.4037	22.3971	22.3904	22.3837	22.3771	22.3704	22.3637	22.3571	22.3504	22.3437	22.3371	.000222
13	23.1251	23.1194	23.1137	23.1080	23.1023	23.0966	23.0909	23.0852	23.0795	23.0738	23.0681	23.0624	.000190
14	23.8660	23.8613	23.8567	23.8520	23.8474	23.8427	23.8380	23.8334	23.8287	23.8241	23.8194	23.8148	.000155
15	24.6342	24.6307	24.6271	24.6236	24.6201	24.6166	24.6130	24.6095	24.6060	24.6025	24.5990	24.5954	.000117
16	25.4315	25.4291	25.4267	25.4243	25.4219	25.4195	25.4171	25.4147	25.4124	25.4100	25.4076	25.4052	.000080
17	26.2597	26.2583	26.2569	26.2555	26.2541	26.2526	26.2512	26.2498	26.2484	26.2470	26.2456	26.2442	.000047
18	27.1180	27.1176	27.1171	27.1167	27.1163	27.1158	27.1154	27.1150	27.1145	27.1141	27.1137	27.1132	.000014
19	28.0080	28.0078	28.0077	28.0075	28.0074	28.0072	28.0070	28.0069	28.0067	28.0066	28.0064	28.0063	.000005
20	28.9226	28.9226	28.9225	28.9225	28.9225	28.9225	28.9224	28.9224	28.9224	28.9224	28.9223	28.9223	.000001
21	29.8618	29.8614	29.8610	29.8606	29.8602	29.8598	29.8594	29.8590	29.8587	29.8583	29.8579	29.8575	.000013
22	30.8210	30.8202	30.8195	30.8187	30.8180	30.8172	30.8165	30.8157	30.8150	30.8142	30.8135	30.8127	.000025
23	31.8014	31.7997	31.7980	31.7963	31.7946	31.7929	31.7912	31.7895	31.7879	31.7862	31.7845	31.7828	.000056
24	32.7982	32.7958	32.7934	32.7910	32.7887	32.7863	32.7839	32.7815	32.7791	32.7767	32.7744	32.7720	.000079
25	33.8158	33.8124	33.8090	33.8056	33.8022	33.7987	33.7953	33.7919	33.7885	33.7851	33.7817	33.7783	.000113
26	34.8519	34.8472	34.8425	34.8378	34.8331	34.8283	34.8236	34.8189	34.8142	34.8095	34.8048	34.8001	.000157
27	35.9056	35.8995	35.8934	35.8873	35.8812	35.8750	35.8689	35.8628	35.8567	35.8506	35.8445	35.8384	.000203
28	36.9772	36.9691	36.9610	36.9529	36.9448	36.9367	36.9286	36.9205	36.9124	36.9043	36.8962	36.8881	.000270
29	38.0622	38.0523	38.0424	38.0325	38.0226	38.0127	38.0028	37.9930	37.9831	37.9732	37.9633	37.9534	.000330
30	39.1665	39.1543	39.1421	39.1300	39.1178	39.1056	39.0934	39.0812	39.0690	39.0568	39.0447	39.0325	.000406
31	40.2828	40.2681	40.2534	40.2386	40.2239	40.2092	40.1945	40.1798	40.1651	40.1503	40.1356	40.1209	.000490
32	41.4147	41.3973	41.3800	41.3626	41.3452	41.3278	41.3104	41.2931	41.2757	41.2583	41.2410	41.2236	.000579
33	42.5622	42.5418	42.5213	42.5009	42.4804	42.4600	42.4395	42.4191	42.3987	42.3782	42.3578	42.3373	.000681
34	43.7234	43.6996	43.6758	43.6520	43.6281	43.6043	43.5805	43.5567	43.5329	43.5090	43.4852	43.4614	.000794
35	44.8978	44.8699	44.8420	44.8141	44.7862	44.7583	44.7303	44.7024	44.6745	44.6466	44.6187	44.5908	.000930
36	46.0785	46.0461	46.0137	45.9813	45.9489	45.9165	45.8841	45.8517	45.8193	45.7869	45.7545	45.7221	.001080
37	47.2660	47.2285	47.1910	47.1535	47.1160	47.0785	47.0410	47.0036	46.9661	46.9286	46.8911	46.8536	.001250
38	48.4558	48.4128	48.3697	48.3267	48.2837	48.2407	48.1976	48.1546	48.1116	48.0686	48.0255	47.9825	.001434
39	49.6469	49.5977	49.5485	49.4993	49.4501	49.4009	49.3516	49.3024	49.2532	49.2040	49.1548	49.1056	.001640
40	50.8355	50.7795	50.7236	50.6676	50.6116	50.5557	50.4997	50.4437	50.3878	50.3318	50.2758	50.2199	.001865
41	52.0189	51.9555	51.8922	51.8288	51.7655	51.7021	51.6388	51.5754	51.5121	51.4487	51.3854	51.3220	.002112
42	53.1950	53.1235	53.0521	52.9806	52.9092	52.8377	52.7662	52.6948	52.6233	52.5519	52.4804	52.4090	.002382
43	54.3619	54.2818	54.2016	54.1215	54.0414	53.9612	53.8811	53.8010	53.7208	53.6407	53.5606	53.4804	.002671
44	55.5185	55.4292	55.3399	55.2506	55.1613	55.0720	54.9827	54.8935	54.8042	54.7149	54.6256	54.5363	.002976
45	56.6703	56.5711	56.4718	56.3726	56.2734	56.1742	56.0750	55.9757	55.8765	55.7773	55.6780	55.5788	.003307
46	57.8154	57.7056	57.5958	57.4860	57.3762	57.2664	57.1566	57.0468	56.9370	56.8272	56.7174	56.6076	.003660
47	58.9559	58.8348	58.7138	58.5927	58.4717	58.3506	58.2295	58.1085	57.9874	57.8664	57.7453	57.6243	.004035
48	60.0904	59.9574	59.8244	59.6914	59.5584	59.4254	59.2924	59.1595	59.0265	58.8935	58.7605	58.6275	.004433
49	61.2219	61.0762	60.9305	60.7847	60.6390	60.4933	60.3476	60.2019	60.0562	59.9104	59.7647	59.6190	.004857
50	62.3468	62.1876	62.0284	61.8692	61.7101	61.5509	61.3917	61.2325	61.0733	60.9141	60.7550	60.5958	.005306
51	63.4666	63.2932	63.1199	62.9465	62.7732	62.5998	62.4265	62.2531	62.0798	61.9064	61.7331	61.5597	.005778
52	64.5835	64.3950	64.2064	64.0179	63.8293	63.6408	63.4522	63.2637	63.0752	62.8866	62.6981	62.5095	.006285
53	65.6951	65.4904	65.2856	65.0809	64.8761	64.6714	64.4666	64.2619	64.0572	63.8524	63.6477	63.4429	.006825
54	66.8031	66.5815	66.3598	66.1382	65.9166	65.6950	65.4733	65.2517	65.0301	64.8085	64.5868	64.3652	.007387
55	67.9086	67.6693	67.4300	67.1906	66.9513	66.7120	66.4727	66.2334	65.9941	65.7547	65.5154	65.2761	.007977
56	69.0169	68.7595	68.5020	68.2446	67.9871	67.7297	67.4722	67.2148	66.9574	66.6999	66.4425	66.1850	.008581
57	70.1368	69.8610	69.5852	69.3094	69.0337	68.7579	68.4821	68.2063	67.9305	67.6547	67.3790	67.1032	.009193
58	71.2809	70.9863	70.6916	70.3970	70.1024	69.8077	69.5131	69.2185	68.9238	68.6292	68.3346	68.0399	.009821
59	72.4613	72.1477	71.8340	71.5205	71.2068	70.8931	70.5795	70.2659	69.9522	69.6386	69.3250	69.0113	.010454
60	73.6956	73.3615	72.0275	72.6934	72.3594	72.0253	71.6913	71.3572	71.0232	70.6891	70.3551	70.0210	.011135
61	74.9896	74.6347	74.2798	73.9248	73.5699	73.2150	72.8601	72.5052	72.1503	71.7953	71.4404	71.0855	.011830
62	76.3609	75.9831	75.6053	75.2275	74.8497	74.4719	74.0941	73.7163	73.3385	72.9607	72.5829	72.2051	.012593
63	77.8105	77.4076	77.0048	76.6019	76.1990	75.7962	75.3933	74.9904	74.5876	74.1847	73.7818	73.3790	.013429
64	79.3381	78.9069	78.4758	78.0446	77.6135	77.1823	76.7511	76.3200	75.8888	75.4577	75.0265	74.5954	.014372
65	80.9329	80.4712	80.0095	79.5478	79.0861	78.6244	78.1626	77.7009	77.2392	76.7775	76.3158	75.8541	.015390
66	82.5970	82.1011	81.6052	81.1094	80.6135	80.1176	79.6217	79.1259	78.6300	78.1341	77.6382	77.1424	.016529
67	84.3174	83.7815	83.2456	82.7097	82.1739	81.6380	81.1021	80.5662	80.0303	79.4944	78.9586	78.4227	.017863
68	86.0548	85.4719	84.8889	84.3060	83.7231	83.1401	82.5572	81.9743	81.3913	80.8084	80.2255	79.6425	.019431
69	87.7546	87.1189	86.4832	85.8476	85.2119	84.5762	83.9405	83.3049	82.6692	82.0335	81.3978	80.7622	.021189
70	89.3786	88.6721	87.9656	87.2591	86.5527	85.8462	85.1397	84.4332	83.7267	83.0202	82.3138	81.6073	.023549
71	90.7351	89.9553	89.1756	88.3958	87.6161	86.8363	86.0566	85.2768	84.4971	83.7173	82.9376	82.1578	.025992
72	91.8209	91.0334	90.2458	89.4583	88.6707	87.8832	87.0956	86.3081	85.5206	84.7330	83.9455	83.1579	.026251
73	93.4870	92.7936	92.1003	91.4069	90.7135	90.0202	89.3268	88.6334	87.9401	87.2467	86.5533	85.8600	.023112
74 or 35	**97.0874**	**97.3301**	**97.5728**	**97.8155**	**98.0583**	**98.3010**	**98.5437**	**98.7864**	**39.0291**	**99.2718**	**99.5146**	**99.7573**	**.008090**
34	95.8603	95.7839	95.7076	95.6313	95.5549	95.4786	95.4023	95.3259	95.2496	95.1733	95.0969	95.0206	.002543
33	95.2342	95.1144	94.9946	94.8747	94.7549	94.6351	94.5153	94.3955	94.2757	94.1558	94.0360	93.9162	.003994
32	94.7808	94.6522	94.5237	94.3951	94.2665	94.1380	94.0094	93.8808	93.7523	93.6237	93.4951	93.3666	.004285
31	94.2002	94.0874	93.9746	93.8619	93.7491	93.6363	93.5235	93.4108	93.2980	93.1852	93.0724	92.9597	.003759
30	93.4842	93.3878	93.2914	93.1950	93.0985	93.0021	92.9057	92.8093	92.7129	92.6164	92.5200	92.4236	.003214
29	92.6987	92.6130	92.5273	92.4415	92.3558	92.2701	92.1844	92.0986	92.0130	91.9272	91.8415	91.7558	.002857
28	91.8564	91.7802	91.7040	91.6277	91.5515	91.4753	91.3991	91.3229	91.2467	91.1704	91.0942	91.0180	.002540
27	90.9783	90.9096	90.8410	90.7723	90.7036	90.6350	90.5663	90.4976	90.4290	90.3603	90.2916	90.2230	.002289
26	90.0818	90.0190	89.9563	89.8935	89.8308	89.7680	89.7052	89.6425	89.5797	89.5170	89.4542	89.3915	.002092
25	89.1747	89.1170	89.0593	89.0016	88.9439	88.8862	88.8285	88.7708	88.7131	88.6554	88.5977	88.5400	.001923
24	88.2585	88.2055	88.1526	88.0996	88.0467	87.9937	87.9407	87.8878	87.8348	87.7819	87.7289	87.6760	.001765
23	87.3412	87.2921	87.2430	87.1940	87.1449	87.0958	87.0467	86.9977	86.9486	86.8995	86.8504	86.8014	.001636
22	86.4260	86.3804	86.3347	86.2891	86.2435	86.1979	86.1522	86.1066	86.0610	86.0154	85.9697	85.9241	.001521
21	85.5159	85.4733	85.4307	85.3881	85.3455	85.3029	85.2603	85.2177	85.1751	85.1325	85.0899	85.0473	.001420
20	84.6053	84.5660	84.5267	87.4875	84.4482	84.4089	84.3696	84.3304	84.2911	84.2318	84.2125	84.1733	.001309
19	83.6948	83.6586	83.6225	83.5863	83.5502	83.5140	83.4779	83.4417	83.4056	83.3694	83.3333	83.2971	.001205
18	82.7774	82.7448	82.7122	82.6796	82.6470	82.6144	82.5818	82.5492	82.5167	82.4841	82.4515	82.4189	.001086
17	81.8488	81.8200	81.7912	81.7624	81.7336	81.7047	81.6759	81.6471	81.6183	81.5895	81.5607	81.5319	.000960
16	80.9029	80.8782	80.8536	80.8290	80.8043	80.7796	80.7550	80.7303	80.7057	80.6810	80.6564	80.6317	.000822
15	79.9356	79.9153	79.8951	79.8748	79.8545	79.8343	79.8140	79.7937	79.7735	79.7532	79.7329	79.7127	.000675
14	78.9453	78.9294	78.9135	78.8977	78.8818	78.8659	78.8500	78.8342	78.8183	78.8024	78.7865	78.7707	.000529
13	77.9305	77.9190	77.9076	77.8961	77.8847	77.8732	77.8617	77.8503	77.8388	77.8274	77.8159	77.8045	.000382
12	76.8922	76.8850	76.8778	76.8706	76.8634	76.8562	76.8490	76.8418	76.8346	76.8274	76.8202	76.8130	.000240
11	75.8307	75.8275	75.8243	75.8211	75.8179	75.8147	75.8115	75.8083	75.8052	75.8020	75.7988	75.7956	[illegible]
10	74.7468	74.7476	74.7483	74.7491	74.7498	74.7506	74.7513	74.7521	74.7529	74.7536	74.7544	74.7551	.000025
Age.	0	1	2	3	4	5	6	7	8	9	10	11	Day.

Age.	0	1	2	3	4	5	6	7	8	9	10	11	Day.
10	22.1360	22.1297	22.1235	22.1172	22.1110	22.1047	22.0984	22.0922	22.0859	22.0797	22.0734	22.0672	.000208
11	22.8405	22.8353	22.8300	22.8248	22.8196	22.8143	22.8091	22.8039	22.7986	22.7934	22.7882	22.7829	.000174
12	23.5705	23.5663	23.5621	23.5578	23.5536	23.5494	23.5452	23.5410	23.5368	23.5325	23.5283	23.5241	.000140
13	24.3219	24.3188	24.3156	24.3125	24.3094	24.3063	24.3031	24.3000	24.2969	24.2938	24.2906	24.2875	.000104
14	25.1015	25.0996	25.0976	25.0957	25.0938	25.0918	25.0899	25.0880	25.0860	25.0841	25.0822	25.0802	.000064
15	25.9106	25.9098	25.9091	25.9083	25.9076	25.9068	25.9061	25.9053	25.9046	25.9038	25.9031	25.9023	.000025
16	26.7500	26.7503	26.7506	26.7508	26.7511	26.7514	26.7517	26.7520	26.7523	26.7525	26.7528	26.7531	.000009
17	27.6197	27.6210	27.6223	27.6236	27.6249	27.6262	27.6275	27.6289	27.6302	27.6315	27.6328	27.6341	.000043
18	28.5206	28.5222	28.5239	28.5255	28.5272	28.5288	28.5304	28.5321	28.5337	28.5354	28.5370	28.5387	.000055
19	29.4463	29.4481	29.4500	29.4518	29.4536	29.4555	29.4573	29.4591	29.4610	29.4628	29.4646	29.4665	.000061
20	30.3961	30.3976	30.3992	30.4007	30.4023	30.4038	30.4053	30.4069	30.4084	30.4100	30.4115	30.4131	.000051
21	31.3660	31.3673	31.3685	31.3698	31.3710	31.3723	31.3735	31.3748	31.3761	31.3773	31.3786	31.3798	.000042
22	32.3576	32.3580	32.3584	32.3588	32.3592	32.3596	32.3600	32.3603	32.3607	32.3611	32.3615	32.3619	.000013
23	33.3651	33.3649	33.3646	33.3644	33.3642	33.3640	33.3637	33.3635	33.3633	33.3631	33.3628	33.3626	.000007
24	34.3936	34.3924	34.3913	34.3901	34.3889	34.3878	34.3866	34.3854	34.3843	34.3831	34.3819	34.3808	.000039
25	35.4407	35.4383	35.4360	35.4336	35.4312	35.4289	35.4265	35.4241	35.4218	35.4194	35.4170	35.4147	.000079
26	36.5049	36.5012	36.4976	36.4940	36.4903	36.4866	36.4830	36.4793	36.4757	36.4720	36.4684	36.4647	.000122
27	37.5876	37.5820	37.5765	37.5709	37.5654	37.5598	37.5542	37.5487	37.5431	37.5376	37.5320	37.5265	.000185
28	38.6831	38.6759	38.6686	38.6614	38.6542	38.6469	38.6397	38.6325	38.6252	38.6180	38.6108	38.6035	.000241
29	39.7968	39.7874	39.7780	39.7686	39.7592	39.7498	39.7403	39.7309	39.7215	39.7121	39.7027	39.6933	.000313
30	40.9260	40.9142	40.9024	40.8906	40.8788	40.8670	40.8552	40.8434	40.8316	40.8198	40.8080	40.7962	.000393
31	42.0671	42.0527	42.0384	42.0241	42.0097	41.9954	41.9811	41.9667	41.9524	41.9381	41.9237	41.9094	.000477
32	43.2249	43.2077	43.1904	43.1732	43.1559	43.1387	43.1214	43.1042	43.0870	43.0697	43.0525	43.0352	.000575
33	44.3962	44.3757	44.3553	44.3348	44.3144	44.2939	44.2734	44.2530	44.2325	44.2121	44.1916	44.1712	.000682
34	45.5807	45.5563	45.5320	45.5076	45.4832	45.4589	45.4345	45.4101	45.3858	45.3614	45.3370	45.3127	.000812
35	46.7730	46.7443	46.7157	46.6870	46.6584	46.6297	46.6011	46.5724	46.5438	46.5151	46.4865	46.4578	.000955
36	47.9705	47.9370	47.9034	47.8699	47.8364	47.8029	47.7693	47.7358	47.7023	47.6688	47.6352	47.6017	.001117
37	49.1714	49.1326	49.0938	49.0550	49.0161	48.9773	48.9385	48.8997	48.8609	48.8220	48.7832	48.7444	.001294
38	50.3735	50.3288	50.2840	50.2393	50.1945	50.1498	50.1050	50.0603	50.0156	49.9708	49.9261	49 8813	.001491
39	51.5735	51.5223	51.4711	51.4199	51.3687	51.3175	51.2663	51.2151	51.1639	51.1127	51.0615	51.0103	.001707
40	52.7691	52.7108	52.6526	52.5943	52.5361	52.4778	52.4195	52.3613	52.3030	52.2448	52.1865	52.1283	.001942
41	53.9573	53.8913	53.8253	53.7593	53.6933	53.6273	53.5613	53.4953	53.4293	53 3633	53.2973	53.2313	.002200
42	55.1353	55.0610	54.9867	54.9124	54.8382	54.7639	54.6896	54.6153	54.5410	54.4667	54.3925	54.3182	.002476
43	56.3033	56.2203	56.1372	56.0542	55.9712	55.8882	55.8051	55.7221	55.6391	55.5561	55.4730	55.3900	.002767
44	57.4619	57.3694	57.2768	57.1843	57.0918	56.9992	56.9067	56.8142	56.7216	56.6291	56.5366	56.4440	.003084
45	58.6130	58.5104	58.4077	58.3051	58.2024	58.0998	57.9971	57.8945	57.7919	57.6892	57.5866	57.4839	.003421
46	59.7565	59.6431	59.5296	59.4162	59.3028	59.1894	59.0760	58.9625	58.8491	58.7357	58.6222	58.5088	.003781
47	60.8942	60.7694	60.6445	60.5197	60.3949	60.2701	60.1452	60.0204	59.8956	59.7708	59.6460	59.5211	.004161
48	62.0256	61.8886	61.7516	61.6145	61.4775	61.3405	61.2035	61.0665	60.9295	60.7924	60.6554	60.5184	.004567
49	63.1521	63.0022	62.8523	62.7025	62.5526	62.4027	62.2528	62.1030	61.9531	61.8032	61.6533	61.5035	.004996
50	64.2718	64.1084	63.9450	63.7816	63.6183	63.4549	63.2915	63.1281	62.9647	62.8013	62.6380	62.4746	.005446
51	65.3872	65.2093	65.0314	64.8535	64.6757	64.4978	64.3199	64.1420	63.9641	63.7862	63.6084	63.4305	.005929
52	66.4970	66.3037	66.1104	65.9171	65.7238	65.5305	65.3371	65.1438	64.9505	64.7572	64.5639	64.3706	.006443
53	67.6000	67.3906	67.1812	66.9718	66.7624	66.5530	66.3435	66.1341	65.9247	65.7153	65.5059	65.2965	.006980
54	68.7021	68.4759	68.2497	68.0234	67.7972	67.5710	67.3448	67.1186	66.8924	66.6661	66.4399	66.2137	.007540
55	69.8041	69.5607	69.3173	69.0739	68.8305	68.5871	68.3436	68.1002	67.8568	67.6134	67.3700	67.1266	.008113
56	70.9165	70.6557	70.3949	70.1341	69.8734	69.6126	69.3518	69.0910	68.8302	68.5694	68.3087	68.0479	.008693
57	72.0517	71.7731	71.4945	71.2160	70.9374	70.6588	70.3802	70.1016	69.8230	69.5444	69.2659	68.9873	.009286
58	73.2201	72.9236	72.6271	72.3306	72.0342	71.7377	71.4412	71.1447	70.8482	70.5517	70.2553	69.9588	.009883
59	74.4392	74.1235	73.8078	73.4921	73.1764	72.8607	72.5450	72.2292	71.9135	71.5978	71.2821	70.9664	.010523
60	75.7127	75.3773	75.0420	74.7066	74.3712	74.0359	73.7005	73.3651	73.0298	72.6944	72.3590	72.0237	.011179
61	77.0586	76.7017	76.3448	75.9879	75.6310	75.2741	74.9171	74.5602	74.2033	73.8464	73.4895	73.1326	.011897
62	78.4772	78.0967	77.7161	77.3356	76.9551	76.5746	76.1940	75.8135	75.4330	75.0525	74.6720	74.2914	.012684
63	79.9687	79.5615	79.1543	78.7470	78.3398	77.9326	77.5254	77.1182	76.7110	76.3037	75.8965	75.4893	.013574
64	81.5216	81.0856	80.6495	80.2135	79.7774	79.3414	78.9053	78.4693	78.0333	77.5972	77.1612	76.7251	.014535
65	83.1382	82.6699	82.2016	81.7333	81.2650	80.7967	80.3284	79.8602	79.3919	78.9236	78.4553	77.9870	.015610
66	84.8058	84.2997	83.7936	83.2875	82.7814	82.2753	81.7691	81.2630	80.7569	80.2508	79.7447	79.2386	.016870
67	86.4864	85.9358	85.3851	84.8345	84.2838	83.7332	83.1825	82.6319	82.0813	81.5306	80.9800	80.4293	.018355
68	88.1279	87.5274	86.9268	86.3263	85.7257	85.1252	84.5246	83.9241	83.3236	82.7230	82.1225	81.5219	.020018
69	89.6940	89.0264	88.3587	87.6911	87.0234	86.3558	85.6881	85.0205	84.3529	83.6852	83.0176	82.3499	.022255
70	91.0007	90.2637	89.5267	88.7897	88 0527	87.3157	86.5787	85.8417	85.1047	84.3677	83.6307	82.8937	.024567
71	92.0458	91.3023	90.5587	89.8152	89.0717	88.3282	87.5846	86.8411	86.0976	85.3541	84.6105	83.8670	.024784
72	93.6441	92.9916	92.3390	91.6865	91.0340	90.3815	89.7289	89.0764	88.4238	87.7713	87.1188	86.4662	.021751
73 or **36**	**97.0874**	**97.3301**	**97.5728**	**97.8155**	**98.0583**	**98.3010**	**98.5437**	**98.7864**	**99.0291**	**99.2718**	**99.5146**	**99.7573**	**.008090**
35	95.8440	95.7634	95.6829	95.6023	95.5218	95.4412	95.3606	95.2801	95.1995	95.1190	95.0384	94.9579	.002685
34	95.2105	95.0861	94.9616	94.8372	94.7127	94.5883	94.4638	94.3394	94.2150	94.0905	93.9661	93.8416	.004148
33	94.7524	94.6193	94.4861	94.3530	94.2199	94.0867	93.9536	93.8205	93.6873	93.5542	93.4211	93.2879	.004438
32	94.1660	94.0490	93.9320	93.8150	93.6980	93.5810	93.4640	93.3470	93.2301	93.1131	92.9961	92.8791	.003900
31	93.4429	93.3426	93.2423	93.1420	93.0417	92.9414	92.8411	92.7408	92.6405	92.5402	92.4399	92.3396	.003343
30	92.6505	92.5612	92.4718	92.3825	92.2932	92.2038	92.1145	92.0252	91.9358	91.8465	91.7572	91.6678	.002978
29	91.8008	91.7212	91.6416	91.5620	91.4824	91.4027	91.3231	91.2435	91.1639	91.0843	91.0047	90.9251	.002653
28	90.9156	90.8437	90.7719	90.7000	90.6282	90.5563	90.4844	90.4126	90.3407	90.2689	90.1970	90.1252	.002395
27	90.0125	89.9467	89.8809	89.8151	89.7494	89.6836	89.6178	89.5520	89.4862	89.4204	89.3547	89.2889	.002193
26	89.0991	89.0385	88.9780	88.9174	88.8568	88.7963	88.7357	88.6751	88.6146	88.5540	88.4934	88.4329	.002019
25	88.1771	88.1214	88.0657	88.0100	87.9544	87.8987	87.8430	87.7873	87.7316	87.6760	87.6203	87.5646	.001856
24	87.2545	87.2028	87.1512	87.0995	87.0478	86.9962	86.9445	86.8928	86.8412	86.7895	86.7378	86.6862	.001722
23	86.3344	86.2863	86.2382	86.1901	86.1420	86.0939	86.0458	85.9977	85.9496	85.9015	85.8534	85.8053	.001603
22	85.4199	85.3749	85.3300	85.2850	85.2400	85.1951	85.1501	85.1051	85.0602	85.0152	84.9702	84.9253	.001499
21	84.5053	84.4638	84.4222	84.3807	84.3392	84.2976	84.2561	84.2146	84.1730	84.1315	84.0900	84.0484	.001384
20	83.5911	83.5528	83.5145	83.4762	83.4379	83.3995	83.3612	83.3229	83.2846	83.2463	83.2080	83.1697	.001277
19	82.6704	82.6357	82.6011	82.5664	82.5318	82.4971	82.4625	82.4278	82.3932	82.3585	82.3239	82.2892	.001155
18	81.7387	81.7079	81.6772	81.6464	81.6157	81.5849	81.5541	81.5234	81.4926	81.4619	81.4311	81.4004	.001025
17	80.7901	80.7636	80.7371	80.7105	80.6840	80.6575	80.6310	80.6045	80.5780	80.5514	80.5249	80.4984	.000884
16	79.8202	79.7982	79.7761	79.7541	79.7320	79.7100	79.6880	79.6659	79.6439	79.6218	79.5998	79.5777	.000735
15	78.8276	78.8100	78.7925	78.7749	78.7574	78.7398	78.7222	78.7047	78.6871	78.6696	78.6520	78.6345	.000585
14	77.8105	77.7974	77.7844	77.7713	77.7583	77.7452	77.7322	77.7191	77.7061	77.6930	77.6800	77.6670	.000435
13	76.7699	76.7612	76.7525	76.7437	76.7350	76.7263	76.7176	76.7089	76.7002	76.6914	76.6827	76.6740	.000290
12	75.7076	75.7030	75.6984	75.6937	75.6891	75.6845	75.6799	75.6753	75.6707	75.6660	75.6614	75.6568	.000154
11	74.6217	74.6211	74.6205	74.6199	74.6193	74.6187	74.6181	74.6175	74.6169	74.6163	74.6157	74.6151	.000020
10	73.5138	73.5171	73.5204	73.5237	73.5271	73.5304	73.5337	73.5370	73.5403	73.5436	73.5470	73.5503	.000110
Age.	0	1	2	3	4	5	6	7	8	9	10	11	Day.

Age.	0	1	2	3	4	5	6	7	8	9	10	11	Day.
10	23.2540	23.2501	23.2463	23.2424	23.2386	23.2347	23.2309	23.2270	23.2232	23.2193	23.2155	23.2116	.000128
11	23.9939	23.9911	23.9883	23.9855	23.9827	23.9799	23.9771	23.9743	23.9716	23.9688	23.9660	23.9632	.000093
12	24.7600	24.7584	24.7567	24.7551	24.7534	24.7518	24.7501	24.7485	24.7469	24.7452	24.7436	24.7419	.000055
13	25.5496	25.5492	25.5488	25.5484	25.5480	25.5475	25.5471	25.5467	25.5463	25.5459	25.5455	25.5451	.000013
14	26.3697	26 3705	26.3713	26.3721	26.3730	26.3738	26.3746	26.3754	26.3762	26.3770	26.3779	26.3787	.000027
15	27.2203	27.2222	27.2241	27.2260	27.2279	27.2298	27.2317	27.2336	27.2355	27.2374	27.2393	27.2412	.000063
16	28.1006	28.1036	28.1065	28.1095	28.1125	28.1154	28.1184	28.1214	28.1243	28.1273	28.1303	28.1332	.000099
17	29.0122	29.0156	29.0190	29.0223	29.0257	29.0291	29.0324	29.0358	29.0392	29.0426	29.0460	29.0493	.000112
18	29.9482	29.9518	29.9554	29.9591	29.9627	29.9663	29.9700	29.9736	29.9772	29.9808	29.9844	29.9881	.000121
19	30.9084	30.9118	30.9152	30.9186	30.9220	30.9254	30.9288	30.9322	30.9356	30.9390	30.9424	30.9458	.000113
20	31.8884	31.8916	31.8947	31.8979	31.9011	31.9043	31.9074	31.9106	31.9138	31.9170	31.9201	31.9233	.000106
21	32.8901	32.8925	32.8949	32.8972	32.8996	32.9020	32.9044	32.9068	32.9092	32.9115	32.9139	32.9163	.000079
22	33.9080	33.9098	33.9117	33.9135	33.9154	33.9172	33.9190	33.9209	33.9227	33.9246	33.9264	33.9283	.000061
23	34.9463	34.9473	34.9483	34.9493	34.9503	34.9512	34.9522	34.9532	34.9542	34.9552	34.9562	34.9572	.000033
24	36.0036	36.0035	36.0033	36.0032	36.0031	36.0030	36.0028	36.0027	36.0026	36.0025	36.0023	36.0022	.000004
25	37.0781	37.0768	37.0754	37.0741	37.0728	37.0715	37.0701	37.0688	37.0675	37.0662	37.0648	37.0635	.000044
26	38.1706	38.1675	38.1643	38.1612	38.1581	38.1550	38.1518	38.1487	38.1456	38.1425	38.1393	38.1362	.000104
27	39.2762	39.2715	39.2668	39.2621	39.2574	39.2527	39.2480	39.2433	39.2386	39.2339	39.2292	39.2245	.000157
28	40.3994	40.3926	40.3859	40.3791	40.3724	40.3656	40.3589	40.3521	40.3454	40.3386	40.3319	40.3251	.000225
29	41.5372	41.5282	41.5191	41.5101	41.5011	41.4920	41.4830	41.4740	41.4649	41.4559	41.4469	41.4378	.000301
30	42.6901	42.6787	42.6673	42.6558	42.6444	42.6330	42.6216	42.6102	42.5988	42.5873	42.5759	42.5645	.000380
31	43.8560	43.8418	43.8276	43.8134	43.7992	43.7850	43.7708	43.7567	43.7425	43.7283	43.7141	43.6999	.000473
32	45.0366	45.0193	45.0021	44.9848	44.9676	44.9503	44.9330	44.9158	44.8985	44.8813	44.8640	44.8468	.000575
33	46.2301	46.2091	46.1881	46.1671	46.1461	46.1251	46.1041	46.0831	46.0621	46.0411	46.0201	45.9991	.000700
34	47.4314	47.4063	47.3812	47.3561	47.3310	47.3059	47.2808	47.2557	47.2306	47.2055	47.1804	47.1553	.000837
35	48.6393	48.6095	48.5798	48 5500	48.5202	48.4905	48.4607	48.4309	48.4012	48.3714	48.3416	48.3119	.000992
36	49.8491	49.8143	49.7794	49.7446	49.7097	49.6749	49.6400	49.6052	49.5704	49.5355	49.5007	49.4658	.001161
37	51.0609	51.0204	50.9799	50.9394	50.8989	50.8584	50.8178	50.7773	50.7368	50.6963	50.6558	50.6153	.001350
38	52.2706	52.2239	52.1772	52.1305	52.0838	52.0371	51.9904	51.9437	51.8970	51.8503	51.8036	51.7569	.001557
39	53.4762	53.4227	53.3693	53.3158	53.2624	53.2090	53.1555	53.1020	53.0486	52.9951	52.9417	52.8882	.001782
40	54.6752	54.6143	54.5535	54.4926	54.4317	54.3709	54.3100	54.2491	54.1883	54.1274	54.0665	54.0057	.002029
41	55.8639	55.7951	55.7263	55.6576	55.5888	55.5200	55.4512	55.3825	55.3137	55.2449	55.1761	55.1074	.002292
42	57.0417	56.9646	56.8874	56.8103	56.7332	56.6560	56.5789	56.5018	56.4246	56.3475	56.2704	56.1932	.002571
43	58.2101	58.1239	58.0377	57.9515	57.8653	57.7790	57.6928	57.6066	57.5204	57.4342	57.3480	57.2618	.002873
44	59.3665	59.2706	59.1747	59.0789	58.9830	58.8871	58.7912	58.6954	58.5995	58.5036	58.4077	58.3119	.003196
45	60.5147	60.4085	60.3023	60.1961	60.0899	59.9837	59.8775	59.7713	59.6652	59.5590	59.4528	59.3466	.003540
46	61.6541	61.5370	61.4199	61.3028	61.1857	61.0685	60.9514	60.8343	60.7172	60.6001	60.4830	60.3659	.003903
47	62.7874	62.6586	62.5299	62.4011	62.2723	62.1436	62.0148	61.8860	61.7573	61.6285	61.4997	61.3710	.000429
48	63.9125	63.7714	63.6303	63.4893	63.3482	63.2071	63.0660	62.9250	62.7839	62.6428	62.5017	62.3607	.004702
49	65.0324	64.8784	64.7245	64.5705	64.4165	64.2626	64.1086	63.9546	63.8007	63.6467	63.4927	63.3388	.005132
50	66.1464	65.9786	65.8108	65.6430	65.4751	65.3073	65.1395	64.9717	64.8039	64.6360	64.4682	64.3004	.005594
51	67.2534	67.0709	66.8883	66.7058	66.5233	66.3407	66.1582	65.9757	65.7931	65.6106	65.4281	65.2455	.006084
52	68.3533	68.1554	67.9576	67.7597	67.5619	67.3640	67.1661	66.9683	66.7704	66.5726	66.3747	66.1769	.006595
53	69.4490	69.2351	69.0213	68.8074	68.5935	68.3797	68.1658	67.9519	67.7381	67.5242	67.3103	67.0965	.007129
54	70.5460	70.3158	70.0856	69.8554	69.6252	69.3950	69.1648	68.9346	68.7045	68.4743	68.2441	68.0139	.007673
55	71.6505	71.4038	71.1572	70.9105	70.6638	70.4172	70.1705	69.9238	69.6772	69.4305	69.1838	68.9372	.008222
56	72.7760	72.5125	72.2490	71.9855	71.7220	71.4585	71.1950	70.9314	70.6679	70.4044	70.1409	69.8774	.008783
57	73.9330	73.6526	73.3722	73.0919	72.8115	72.5311	72.2507	71.9704	71.6900	71.4096	71.1292	70.8489	.009346
58	75.1371	74.8386	74.5401	74.2416	73.9431	73.6446	73.3461	73.0476	72.7491	72.4506	72.1521	71.8536	.009950
59	76.3922	76.0752	75.7582	75.4412	75.1243	74.8073	74.4903	74.1733	73.8563	73.5393	73.2224	72.9054	.010566
60	77.7140	77.3767	77.0394	76.7021	76.3648	76.0275	75.6902	75.3530	75.0157	74.6784	74.3411	74.0038	.011243
61	79.1037	78.7441	78.3846	78.0250	77.6655	77.3060	76.9464	76.5868	76.2273	75.8677	75.5082	75.1486	.011985
62	80.5608	80.1761	79.7913	79.4066	79.0219	78.6371	78.2524	77.8677	77.4829	77.0982	76.7135	76.3287	.012824
63	82.0746	81.6627	81.2507	80.8388	80.4269	80.0150	79.6030	79.1911	78.7792	78.3673	77.9553	77.5434	.013731
64	83.6475	83.2050	82.7626	82.3201	81.8776	81.4352	80.9927	80.5502	80.1078	79.6653	79.2228	78.7804	.014749
65	85.2645	84.7864	84.3082	83.8301	83.3520	82.8738	82.3957	81.9176	81.4394	80.9613	80.4832	80.0050	.015938
66	86.8919	86.3716	85.8513	85.3310	84.8107	84.2904	83.7701	83.2498	82.7295	82.2092	81.6889	81.1686	.017343
67	88.4784	87.9108	87.3433	86.7757	86.2082	85.6406	85.0730	84.5055	83.9379	83.3704	82.8028	82.2353	.018918
68	89.9897	89.3585	88.7272	88.0960	87.4648	86.8336	86.2023	85.5711	84.9399	84.3087	83.6774	83.0462	.021041
69	91.2498	90.5529	89.8560	89.1591	88.4622	87.7652	87.0683	86.3714	85.6745	84 9776	84.2807	83.5838	.023230
70	92.2566	91.5543	90.8520	90.1497	89.4474	88.7451	88.0428	87.3405	86.6383	85.9360	85.2337	84.5314	.023410
71	93.7912	93.1769	92.5626	91.9483	91.3340	90.7197	90.1054	89.4911	88.8769	88.2626	87.6483	87.0340	.020476
72 or 37	**97.0874**	**97.3301**	**97.5728**	**97.8155**	**98.0583**	**98.3010**	**98.5437**	**98.7864**	**99.0291**	**99.2718**	**99.5146**	**99.7537**	**.008090**
36	95.8268	95.7418	95.6568	95.5717	95.4867	95.4017	95.3167	95.2317	95.1467	95.0616	94.9766	94.8916	.002834
35	95.1856	95.0563	94.9270	94.7977	94.6684	94.5391	94 4097	94.2804	94.1511	94.0218	93.8925	93.7632	.004310
34	94.7226	94.5847	94.4467	94.3088	94.1709	94.0329	93.8950	93.7571	93.6191	93.4812	93.3433	93.2053	.004598
33	94.1301	94.0087	93.8872	93.7658	93.6444	93.5230	93.4015	93.2801	93.1587	93.0373	92.9158	92.7944	.004047
32	93.3997	93.2953	93.1910	93.0866	92.9822	92.8779	92.7735	92.6691	92.5648	92.4604	92.3560	92.2517	.003479
31	92.5996	92.5065	92.4133	92.3202	92.2271	92.1339	92.0408	91.9477	91.8545	91.7614	91.6683	91.5751	.003104
30	91.7426	91.6594	91.5763	91.4931	91.4100	91.3268	91.2437	91.1605	91.0774	90.9942	90.9111	90.8280	.002772
29	90.8500	90.7748	90.6996	90.6244	90.5492	90.4740	90.3987	90.3235	90.2483	90.1731	90.0979	90.0227	.002507
28	89.9399	89.8709	89.8020	89.7330	89.6641	89.5951	89.5262	89.4572	89.3883	89.3193	89.2504	89.1814	.002298
27	89.0200	88.9564	88.8929	88.8293	88.7658	88.7022	88.6386	88.5751	88.5115	88.4480	88.3844	88.3209	.002118
26	88.0606	88.0047	87.9488	87.8928	87.8369	87.7810	87.7251	87 6692	87.6133	87.5573	87.5014	87.4455	.001864
25	87.1638	87.1094	87.0551	87.0007	86.9463	86.8920	86.8376	86.7832	86.7289	86.6745	86.6201	86.5658	.001812
24	86.2387	86.1880	86.1373	86.0866	86.0360	85.9853	85.9346	85.8839	85.8332	85.7825	85.7319	85.6812	.001689
23	85.3196	85.2722	85.2247	85.1773	85.1299	85.0824	85.0350	84.9876	84.9401	84.8927	84.8453	84.7978	.001581
22	84.4009	84.3570	84.3131	84.2692	84.2253	84.1814	84.1375	84.0936	84.0498	84.0059	83.9620	83.9181	.001463
21	83.4820	83.4415	83.4010	83.3606	83.3201	83.2796	83.2391	83.1987	83.1582	83.1177	83.0772	83.0368	.001349
20	82.5588	82.5220	82.4852	82.4484	82.4116	82.3748	82.3380	82.3012	82.2644	82.2276	82.1908	82.1540	.001227
19	81.6240	81.5912	81.5584	81.5256	81.4928	81.4600	81.4271	81.3943	81.3615	81.3287	81.2959	81.2631	.001093
18	80.6724	80.6439	80.6155	80.5870	80.5586	80.5301	80.5016	80.4732	80.4447	80.4163	80.3878	80.3594	.000948
17	79.6998	79.6759	79.6520	79.6281	79.6043	79.5804	79.5565	79.5326	79.5087	79.4848	79.4610	79.4371	.000796
16	78.7046	78.6853	78.6660	78.6467	78.6274	78.6081	78.5888	78.5695	78.5502	78.5309	78.5116	78.4923	.000643
15	77.6854	77.6707	77.6560	77.6413	77.6266	77.6119	77.5971	77.5824	77.5677	77.5530	77.5383	77.5236	.000490
14	76.6426	76.6323	76.6220	76.6117	76.6014	76.5911	76.5808	76.5706	76.5603	76.5500	76.5397	76.5294	.000343
13	75.5781	75.5720	75.5659	75.5597	75.5536	75.5475	75.5414	75.5353	75.5292	75.5230	75.5169	75.5108	.000204
12	74.4915	74.4895	74.4875	74.4855	74.4835	74.4815	74.4795	74.4775	74.4755	74.4735	74.4715	74.4695	.000067
11	73.3817	73.3837	73.3857	73.3877	73.3897	73.3917	73.3936	73.3956	73.3976	73.3996	73.4016	73.4036	.000066
10	72.2513	72.2571	72.2628	72.2686	72.2744	72.2802	72.2860	72.2917	72.2975	72.3033	72.3090	72.3148	.000192
Age.	0	1	2	3	4	5	6	7	8	9	10	11	Day.

Age.	0	1	2	3	4	5	6	7	8	9	10	11	Day.
10	24.4010	24.3996	24.3981	24.3967	24.3953	24.3939	24.3924	24.3910	24.3896	24.3882	24.3867	24.3853	.000047
11	25.1766	25.1764	25.1761	25.1759	25.1757	25.1754	25.1752	25.1750	25.1747	25.1745	25.1743	25.1740	.000008
12	25.9804	25.9814	25.9825	25.9835	25.9846	25.9856	25.9867	25.9877	25.9888	25.9898	25.9909	25.9920	.000035
13	26.8099	26.8122	26.8145	26.8169	26.8192	26.8215	26.8238	26.8262	26.8285	26.8308	26.8331	26.8355	.000077
14	27.6709	27.6743	27.6778	27.6812	27.6847	27.6881	27.6916	27.6950	27.6985	27.7020	27.7054	27.7088	.000115
15	28.5618	28.5664	28.5710	28.5755	28.5801	28.5847	28.5892	28.5938	28.5984	28.6030	28.6075	28.6121	.000152
16	29.4834	29.4884	29.4935	29.4985	29.5035	29.5086	29.5136	29.5186	29.5237	29.5287	29.5337	29.5388	.000168
17	30.4296	30.4349	30.4403	30.4456	30.4509	30.4563	30.4616	30.4669	30.4723	30.4776	30.4829	30.4883	.000178
18	31.3995	31.4047	31.4098	31.4150	31.4202	31.4253	31.4305	31.4357	31.4408	31.4460	31.4512	31.4563	.000172
19	32.3893	32.3943	32.3993	32.4043	32.4093	32.4143	32.4193	32.4243	32.4294	32.4344	32.4394	32.4444	.000167
20	33.4003	33.4046	33.4089	33.4132	33.4175	33.4218	33.4261	33.4304	33.4347	33.4390	33.4433	33.4476	.000143
21	34.4277	34.4315	34.4353	34.4392	34.4430	34.4468	34.4506	34.4545	34.4583	34.4621	34.4660	34.4698	.000127
22	35.4758	35.4788	35.4819	35.4850	35.4880	35.4910	35.4941	35.4971	35.5002	35.5032	35.5063	35.5093	.000102
23	36.5422	36.5442	36.5462	36.5482	36.5503	36.5523	36.5543	36.5563	36.5583	36.5603	36.5624	36.5644	.000067
24	37.6260	37.6269	37.6278	37.6287	37.6296	37.6305	37.6314	37.6323	37.6333	37.6342	37.6351	37.6360	.000030
25	38.7280	38.7272	38.7264	38.7256	38.7248	38.7240	38.7232	38.7224	38.7216	38.7208	38.7200	38.7192	.000027
26	39.8426	39.8403	39.8381	39.8358	39.8335	39.8313	39.8290	39.8267	39.8245	39.8222	39.8199	39.8177	.000075
27	40.9751	40.9709	40.9666	40.9624	40.9582	40.9540	40.9497	40.9455	40.9413	40.9371	40.9328	40.9286	.000141
28	42.1215	42.1151	42.1087	42.1023	42.0960	42.0896	42.0832	42.0768	42.0704	42.0640	42.0577	42.0513	.000213
29	43.2821	43.2734	43.2648	43.2561	43.2475	43.2388	43.2301	43.2215	43.2128	43.2042	43.1955	43.1869	.000288
30	44.4588	44.4475	44.4362	44.4249	44.4136	44.4023	44.3910	44.3797	44.3685	44.3572	44.3459	44.3346	.000376
31	45.6466	45.6324	45.6182	45.6040	45.5897	45.5755	45.5613	45.5471	45.5329	45.5186	45.5044	45.4902	.000474
32	46.8482	46.8304	46.8126	46.7948	46.7770	46.7592	46.7414	46.7236	46.7059	46.6881	46.6703	46.6525	.000593
33	48.0575	48.0358	48.0140	47.9923	47.9706	47.9489	47.9271	47.9054	47.8837	47.8620	47.8402	47.8185	.000724
34	49.2732	49.2470	49.2208	49.1946	49.1684	49.1422	49.1160	49.0898	49.0637	49.0375	49.0113	48.9851	.000873
35	50.4922	50.4611	50.4301	50.3990	50.3680	50.3370	50.3059	50.2748	50.2438	50.2127	50.1817	50.1506	.001035
36	51.7118	51.6753	51.6388	51.6023	51.5658	51.5293	51.4928	51.4563	51.4198	51.3833	51.3468	51.3103	.001217
37	52.9301	52.8877	52.8452	52.8028	52.7603	52.7179	52.6754	52.6330	52.5906	52.5481	52.5057	52.4632	.001415
38	54.1442	54.0953	54.0464	53.9974	53.9485	53.8996	53.8507	53.8018	53.7529	53.7040	53.6550	53.6061	.001630
39	55.3520	55.2960	55.2400	55.1839	55.1279	55.0719	55.0158	54.9598	54.9038	54.8478	54.7917	54.7357	.001867
40	56.5500	56.4864	56.4228	56.3592	56.2957	56.2321	56.1685	56.1049	56.0413	55.9777	55.9142	55.8506	.002119
41	57.7372	57.6656	57.5940	57.5225	57.4509	57.3793	57.3077	57.2362	57.1646	57.0930	57.0214	56.9499	.002386
42	58.9139	58.8336	58.7534	58.6731	58.5929	58.5126	58.4324	58.3521	58.2719	58.1916	58.1114	58.0311	.002675
43	60.0787	59.9892	59.8997	59.8102	59.7208	59.6313	59.5418	59.4523	59.3628	59.2733	59.1839	59.0944	.002983
44	61.2310	61.1316	61.0323	60.9329	60.8336	60.7342	60.6348	60.5355	60.4361	60.3368	60.2374	60.1381	.003312
45	62.3738	62.2640	62.1542	62.0444	61.9346	61.8247	61.7149	61.6051	61.4953	61.3855	61.2757	61.1659	.003660
46	63.5075	63.3865	63.2656	63.1446	63.0236	62.9027	62.7817	62.6607	62.5398	62.4188	62.2978	62.1769	.004032
47	64.6333	64.5006	64.3678	64.2351	64.1024	63.9696	63.8369	63.7042	63.5714	63.4387	63.3060	63.1732	.004424
48	65.7507	65.6056	65.4605	65.3154	65.1704	65.0253	64.8802	64.7351	64.5900	64.4450	64.2999	64.1548	.004836
49	66.8636	66.7053	66.5470	66.3887	66.2304	66.0721	65.9138	65.7555	65.5972	65.4389	65.2806	65.1223	.005277
50	68.0178	67.8413	67.6648	67.4883	67.3118	67.1353	66.9587	66.7822	66.6057	66.4292	66.2527	66.0762	.005883
51	69.0638	68.8768	68.6899	68.5029	68.3159	68.1290	67.9420	67.7550	67.5681	67.3811	67.1941	67.0072	.006232
52	70.1550	69.9528	69.7506	69.5484	69.3462	69.1440	68.9418	68.7396	68.5374	68.3352	68.1330	67.9308	.006740
53	71.2444	71.0267	70.8089	70.5912	70.3734	70.1557	69.9380	69.7202	69.5025	69.2847	69.0670	68.8492	.007258
54	72.3422	72.1088	71.8755	71.6421	71.4087	71.1754	70.9420	70.7086	70.4753	70.2419	70.0085	69.7752	.007779
55	73.4578	73.2085	72.9592	72.7099	72.4606	72.2113	71.9620	71.7126	71.4633	71.2140	70.9647	70.7154	.008310
56	74.6028	74.3376	74.0723	73.8071	73.5418	73.2766	73.0113	72.7461	72.4809	72.2156	71.9504	71.6851	.008841
57	75.7928	75.5105	75.2281	74.9458	74.6634	74.3811	74.0987	73.8164	73.5341	73.2517	72.9694	72.6870	.009411
58	77.0299	76.7302	76.4304	76.1307	75.8310	75.5312	75.2315	74.9318	74.6320	74.3323	74.0326	73.7328	.009991
59	78.3299	78.0110	77.6922	77.3733	77.0545	76.7356	76.4168	76.0980	75.7791	75.4602	75.1414	74.8225	.010628
60	79.6922	79.3524	79.0125	78.6727	78.3328	77.9930	77.6531	77.3133	76.9735	76.6336	76.2938	75.9539	.011328
61	81.1171	80.7535	80.3899	80.0263	79.6627	79.2991	78.9354	78.5718	78.2082	77.8446	77.4810	77.1174	.012120
62	82.5939	82.2046	81.8153	81.4260	81.0368	80.6475	80.2582	79.8689	79.4796	79.0903	78.7011	78.3118	.012976
63	83.1240	82.7060	82.2879	81.8699	81.4518	81.0338	80.6157	80.1977	79.7797	79.3616	79.9436	79.5255	.013935
64	85.6953	85.2434	84.7916	84.3397	83.8878	83.4360	82.9841	82.5322	82.0804	81.6285	81.1766	80.7248	.015062
65	87.2727	86.7809	86.2891	85.7973	85.3055	84.8137	84.3219	83.8301	83.3383	82.8465	82.3547	81.8629	.016393
66	88.7077	88.2711	87.7345	87.1980	86.6614	86.1248	85.5882	85.0517	84.5151	83.9785	83.4420	82.9054	.017886
67	90.2673	89.6703	89.0732	88.4762	87.8791	87.2821	86.6850	86.0880	85.4910	84.8939	84.2969	83.6998	.019901
68	91.4833	90.8240	90.1646	89.5053	88.8460	88.1866	87.5273	86.8680	86.2086	85.5493	84.8900	84.2306	.021978
69	92.4544	91.7908	91.1271	90.4635	89.7999	89.1362	88.4726	87.8090	87.1453	86.4817	85.8181	85.1544	.022121
70	93.9290	93.3505	92.7721	92.1936	91.6152	91.0367	90.4582	89.8798	89.3013	88.7229	88.1444	87.5660	.019282
71 or 38	**97.0874**	**97.3301**	**97.5728**	**97.8155**	**98.0583**	**98.3010**	**98.5437**	**98.7864**	**99.0291**	**99.2718**	**99.5146**	**99.7573**	**.008090**
37	95.8087	95.7190	95.6293	95.5395	95.4498	95.3601	95.2704	95.1807	95.0910	95.0012	94.9115	94.8218	.002990
36	95.1594	95.0250	94.8905	94.7560	94.6216	94.4871	94.3527	94.2182	94.0838	93.9493	93.8149	93.6804	.004482
35	94.6912	94.5482	94.4052	94.2623	94.1193	93.9763	93.8333	93.6904	93.5474	93.4044	93.2614	93.1185	.004766
34	94.0923	93.9662	93.8402	93.7141	93.5880	93.4620	93.3359	93.2098	93.0838	92.9577	92.8316	92.7056	.004202
33	93.3543	93.2457	93.1370	93.0284	92.9198	92.8111	92.7025	92.5939	92.4852	92.3766	92.2680	92.1593	.003621
32	92.5464	92.4493	92.3522	92.2550	92.1579	92.0608	91.9637	91.8666	91.7695	91.6723	91.5752	91.4781	.003237
31	91.6815	91.5946	91.5077	91.4208	91.3339	91.2470	91.1601	91.0732	90.9864	90.8995	90.8126	90.7257	.002896
30	90.7814	90.7027	90.6240	90.5453	90.4666	90.3879	90.3092	90.2305	90.1518	90.0731	89.9944	89.9157	.002623
29	89.8639	89.7916	89.7194	89.6471	89.5749	89.5026	89.4303	89.3581	89.2858	89.2136	89.1413	89.0691	.002408
28	88.9373	88.8706	88.8039	88.7372	88.6705	88.6037	88.5370	88.4703	88.4036	88.3369	88.2702	88.2035	.002223
27	88.0030	87.9415	87.8800	87.8184	87.7569	87.6954	87.6339	87.5724	87.5109	87.4493	87.3878	87.3263	.002050
26	87.0691	87.0093	86.9494	86.8896	86.8298	86.7699	86.7101	86.6503	86.5904	86.5306	86.4708	86.4109	.001994
25	86.1387	86.0853	86.0319	85.9785	85.9252	85.8718	85.8184	85.7650	85.7116	85.6582	85.6049	85.5515	.001779
24	85.2149	85.1649	85.1149	85.0648	85.0148	84.9648	84.9148	84.8648	84.8148	84.7647	84.7147	84.6647	.001667
23	84.2919	84.2455	84.1992	84.1528	84.1065	84.0601	84.0137	83.9674	83.9210	83.8747	83.8283	83.7820	.001545
22	83.3701	83.3272	83.2843	83.2414	83.1985	83.1555	83.1126	83.0697	83.0268	82.9839	82.9410	82.8981	.001430
21	82.4424	82.4034	82.3643	82.3253	82.2863	82.2472	82.2082	82.1692	82.1301	82.0911	82.0521	82.0130	.001301
20	81.5043	81.4694	81.4344	81.3995	81.3645	81.3296	81.2946	81.2597	81.2248	81.1898	81.1549	81.1199	.001165
19	80.5497	80.5192	80.4887	80.4582	80.4277	80.3972	80.3667	80.3362	80.3058	80.2753	80.2448	80.2143	.001016
18	79.5742	79.5484	79.5226	79.4968	79.4710	79.4451	79.4193	79.3935	79.3677	79.3419	79.3161	79.2903	.000860
17	78.5765	78.5554	78.5342	78.5131	78.4920	78.4708	78.4497	78.4286	78.4074	78.3863	78.3652	78.3440	.000704
16	77.5548	77.5384	77.5219	77.5055	77.4890	77.4726	77.4561	77.4397	77.4233	77.4068	77.3904	77.3739	.000548
15	76.5099	76.4980	76.4860	76.4741	76.4622	76.4502	76.4383	76.4264	76.4144	76.4025	76.3906	76.3786	.000398
14	75.4433	75.4356	75.4280	75.4203	75.4126	75.4049	75.3972	75.3896	75.3819	75.3742	75.3665	75.3589	.000256
13	74.3547	74.3512	74.3477	74.3442	74.3407	74.3372	74.3337	74.3303	74.3268	74.3233	74.3198	74.3163	.000116
12	73.2444	73.2450	73.2456	73.2462	73.2468	73.2474	73.2480	73.2485	73.2491	73.2497	73.2503	73.2509	.000020
11	72.1122	72.1166	72.1211	72.1255	72.1300	72.1344	72.1389	72.1433	72.1478	72.1522	72.1567	72.1611	.000148
10	70.9598	70.9680	70.9762	70.9844	70.9926	71.0007	71.0089	71.0171	71.0253	71.0335	71.0417	71.0499	.000273
Age.	0	1	2	3	4	5	6	7	8	9	10	11	Day.

Age.	0	1	2	3	4	5	6	7	8	9	10	11	Day.
10	25.5771	25.5782	25.5793	25.5805	25.5816	25.5827	25.5838	25.5850	25.5861	25.5872	25.5883	25.5895	.000037
11	26.3899	26.3923	26.3948	26.3972	26.3997	26.4021	26.4045	26.4070	26.4094	26.4119	26.4143	26.4168	.000081
12	27.2331	27.2369	27.2406	27.2444	27.2482	27.2519	27.2557	27.2595	27.2632	27.2670	27.2708	27.2745	.000125
13	28.1031	28.1080	28.1130	28.1179	28.1229	28.1278	28.1327	28.1377	28.1426	28.1476	28.1525	28.1575	.000165
14	29.0037	29.0098	29.0159	29.0220	29.0282	29.0343	29.0404	29.0465	29.0526	29.0587	29.0649	29.0710	.000204
15	29.9354	29.9420	29.9486	29.9553	29.9619	29.9685	29.9751	29.9818	29.9884	29.9950	30.0016	30.0083	.000221
16	30.8909	30.8979	30.9049	30.9118	30.9188	30.9258	30.9328	30.9398	30.9468	30.9537	30.9607	30.9677	.000233
17	31.8705	31.8774	31.8842	31.8911	31.8980	31.9048	31.9117	31.9186	31.9254	31.9323	31.9392	31.9460	.000229
18	32.8694	32.8762	32.8830	32.8897	32.8965	32.9033	32.9100	32.9168	32.9236	32.9304	32.9371	32.9439	.000226
19	33.8896	33.8957	33.9018	33.9080	33.9141	33.9202	33.9263	33.9325	33.9386	33.9447	33.9508	33.9570	.000204
20	34.9257	34.9314	34.9371	34.9429	34.9486	34.9543	34.9600	34.9658	34.9715	34.9772	34.9830	34.9887	.000191
21	35.9826	35.9876	35.9926	35.9976	36.0027	36.0077	36.0127	36.0177	36.0227	36.0277	36.0328	36.0378	.000167
22	37.0580	37.0621	37.0661	37.0702	37.0743	37.0783	37.0824	37.0865	37.0905	37.0946	37.0987	37.1027	.000135
23	38.1503	38.1533	38.1564	38.1594	38.1625	38.1655	38.1685	38.1716	38.1746	38.1777	38.1807	38.1838	.000101
24	39.2609	39.2623	39.2637	39.2652	39.2666	39.2680	39.2694	39.2709	39.2723	39.2737	39.2751	39.2766	.000047
25	40.3842	40.3842	40 3843	40.3843	40.3844	40.3844	40.3844	40.3845	40.3845	40.3846	40.3846	40.3847	.000001
26	41.5249	41.5231	41.5213	41.5195	41.5177	41.5159	41.5141	41.5123	41.5105	41.5087	41.5069	41.5051	.000060
27	42.6797	42.6758	42.6720	42.6681	42.6643	42.6604	42.6565	42.6527	42.6488	42.6450	42.6411	42.6373	.000128
28	43.8481	43.8421	43.8361	43.8300	43.8240	43.8180	43.8120	43.8060	43.8000	43.7940	43.7879	43.7819	.000200
29	45.0315	45.0230	45.0144	45.0059	44.9974	44.9889	44.9803	44.9718	44.9633	44.9548	44.9462	44.9377	.000284
30	46.2290	46.2187	46.2085	46.1982	46.1879	46.1777	46.1674	46.1571	46.1469	46.1366	46.1263	46.1161	.000342
31	47.4369	47.4222	47.4074	47.3927	47.3779	47.3632	47.3484	47.3337	47.3190	47.3042	47.2895	47.2747	.000491
32	48.6534	48.6349	48.6164	48.5978	48.5793	48.5608	48.5423	48.5238	48.5053	48.4867	48.4682	48.4497	.000617
33	49.8761	49.8533	49.8305	49.8077	49.7849	49.7621	49.7392	49.7164	49.6936	49.6708	49.6480	49.6252	.000760
34	51.1019	51.0744	51.0470	51.0195	50 9920	50.9645	50.9370	50.9096	50.8821	50.8546	50.8271	50.7997	.000916
35	52.3297	52.2970	52.2643	52.2316	52.1989	52.1661	52.1334	52.1007	52.0680	52.0353	52.0026	51.9699	.001090
36	53.5546	53.5162	53.4778	53.4394	53.4010	53.3625	53.3241	53.2857	53.2473	53.2089	53.1705	53.1321	.001280
37	54.7761	54.7320	54.6878	54.6437	54.5996	54.5555	54.5113	54.4672	54.4231	54.3790	54.3348	54.2907	.001471
38	55.9912	55.9398	55.8883	55.8369	55.7854	55.7340	55.6825	55.6311	55.5797	55.5282	55.4768	55.4253	.001715
39	57.1969	57.1382	57.0795	57.0208	56.9621	56.9034	56.8447	56.7860	56.7273	56.6686	56.6099	56.5512	.001957
40	58.3922	58.3258	58.2595	58.1931	58.1268	58.0604	57.9941	57.9277	57.8614	57.7950	57.7287	57.6623	.002212
41	59.5769	59.5023	59.4276	59.3530	59.2783	59.2037	59.1290	59.0544	58.9798	58.9051	58.8305	58.7558	.002488
42	60.7487	60.6652	60.5818	60.4983	60.4148	60.3314	60.2479	60.1644	60.0810	59.9975	59.9140	59.8306	.002782
43	61.9080	61.8151	61.7222	61.6293	61.5364	61.4435	61.3506	61.2577	61.1648	61.0719	60.9790	60.8861	.003097
44	63.0537	62.9509	62.8480	62.7452	62.6424	62.5395	62.4367	62.3339	62.2310	62.1282	62.0254	61.9225	.003428
45	64.1895	64.0759	63.9623	63.8488	63.7352	63.6216	63.5080	63.3945	63.2809	63.1673	63.0537	62.9402	.003786
46	65.3147	65.1898	65.0650	64.9401	64.8153	64.6904	64.5656	64.4407	64.3159	64.1910	64.0662	63.9413	.004162
47	66.4316	66.2949	66.1583	66.0216	65.8850	65.7483	65.6116	65.4750	65.3383	65.2017	65.0650	64.9284	.004555
48	67.5408	67.3915	67.2422	67.0929	66.9436	66.7942	66.6449	66.4956	66.3463	66.1970	66.0477	65.8984	.004977
49	68.6428	68.4801	68.3173	68.1546	67.9919	67.8292	67.6664	67.5037	67.3410	67.1783	67.0155	66.8528	.005424
50	69.7349	69.5582	69.3815	69.2049	69.0282	68.8515	68.6748	68.4982	68.3215	68.1448	67.9681	67.7915	.005889
51	70.8209	70.6297	70.4385	70.2473	70.0561	69.8649	69.6737	69.4825	69.2913	69.1001	68.9089	68.7177	.006373
52	71.9046	71.6986	71.4926	71.2866	71.0807	70.8747	70.6687	70.4627	70.2567	70.0507	69.8448	69.6388	.006866
53	72.9933	72.7725	72.5516	72.3310	72.1100	71 8891	71.6683	71.4475	71.2266	71.0058	70.7850	70.5641	.007361
54	74.1003	73.8644	73.6284	73.3925	73.1566	72.9207	72.6847	72.4488	72.2129	71.9770	71.7410	71.5051	.007864
55	75.2334	74.9824	74.7314	74.4804	74.2294	73.9784	73.7274	73.4764	73.2254	72.9744	72.7234	72.4724	.008367
56	76.4088	76.1416	75.8745	75.6073	75.3402	75.0730	74.8059	74.5387	74.2716	74.0044	73.7373	73.4701	.008905
57	77.6290	77.3455	77.0619	76.7784	76.4949	76.2113	75.9278	75.6443	75.3607	75.0772	74.7937	74.5101	.009451
58	78.9079	78.6064	78.3048	78.0033	77.7017	77.4002	77.0986	76.7971	76.4956	76.1940	75.8925	75.5909	.010051
59	80.2452	79.9239	79.6025	79.3812	78.9599	78.6386	78.3172	77.9959	77.6746	77.3533	77.0320	76.7106	.010711
60	81.6397	81.2959	80.9521	80.6084	80.2646	79.9208	79.5770	79.2333	78.8895	78.5457	78.2020	77.8582	.011459
61	83.0818	82.7138	82.3458	81.9778	81.6098	81.2417	80.8737	80.5057	80.1377	79.7697	79.4017	79.0337	.012267
62	74.5724	74.1772	73.7820	73.3868	72.9917	72.5965	72.2013	71.8061	71.4109	71.0157	70.6206	70.2254	.013173
63	86.1001	85.6729	85.2457	84.8185	84.3913	83.9641	83.5369	83.1097	82.6826	82.2554	81.8282	81.4010	.014240
64	87.6303	87.1653	86.7002	86.2352	85.7702	85.3052	84.8401	84.3751	83.9101	83.4451	82.9800	82.5150	.015501
65	89.1169	88.6094	88.1020	87.5945	87.0871	86.5796	86.0721	85.5647	85.0572	84.5498	84.0423	83.5349	.016915
66	90.5282	89.9633	89.3983	88.8334	88.2685	87.7036	87.1386	86.5737	86.0088	85.4439	84.8790	84.3140	.018831
67	91.7025	91.0785	90.4544	89.8304	89.2063	88.5823	87.9582	87.3342	86.7102	86.0861	85.4621	84.8380	.020801
68	92.6396	92.0122	91.3848	90.7575	90.1301	89.5027	88.8753	88.2480	87.6206	86.9932	86.3658	85.7385	.020912
69	94.0582	93.5133	92.9685	92.4236	91.8788	91.3339	90.7890	90.2442	89.6993	89.1545	88.6096	88.0648	.018162
70 0-39	**97.0874**	**97.3301**	**97.5728**	**97.8155**	**98.0583**	**98.3010**	**98.5437**	**98.7864**	**99.0291**	**99.2718**	**99.5146**	**99.7573**	**.008090**
38	95.7897	95.6950	95.6003	95.5056	95.4109	95.3162	95.2215	95.1268	95.0322	94.9375	94.8428	94.7481	.003156
37	95.1317	94.9918	94.8520	94.7121	94.5723	94.4324	94.2925	94.1527	94.0128	93.8730	93.7331	93.5933	.004662
36	94.6581	94.5098	94.3615	94.2132	94.0649	93.9166	93.7683	93.6200	93.4718	93.3235	93.1752	93.0269	.004843
35	94.0526	93.9216	93.7907	93.6597	93.5288	93.3978	93.2668	93.1359	93.0049	92.8740	92.7430	92.6121	.004365
34	93.3067	93.1936	93.0804	92.9673	92.8542	92.7411	92.6280	92.5148	92.4017	92.2886	92.1754	92.0623	.003771
33	92.4906	92.3893	92.2880	92.1867	92.0854	91.9841	91.8828	91.7815	91.6802	91.5789	91.4776	91.3763	.003377
32	91.6171	91.5263	91.4355	91.3448	91.2540	91.1632	91.0724	90.9817	90.8909	90.8001	90.7093	90.6186	.003026
31	90.7092	90.6268	90.5444	90.4620	90.3797	90.2973	90.2149	90.1325	90.0501	89.9677	89.8854	89.8030	.002746
30	89.7845	89.7088	89.6330	89.5573	89.4816	89.4058	89.3301	89.2544	89.1786	89.1029	89.0272	88.9514	.002524
29	88.8507	88.7807	88.7107	88.6407	88.5707	88.5007	88.4307	88.3607	88.2907	88.2207	88.1507	88.0807	.002333
28	87.9098	87.8452	87.7805	87.7159	87.6513	87.5866	87.5220	87.4574	87.3927	87.3281	87.2635	87.1988	.002154
27	86.9699	86.9097	86.8495	86.7894	86.7292	86.6690	86.6088	86.5487	86.4885	86.4283	86.3681	86.3080	.002008
26	86.0342	85.9780	85.9218	85.8655	85.8093	85.7531	85.6969	85.6407	85.5845	85.5282	85.4720	85.4158	.001874
25	85.1055	85.0528	85.0001	84.9474	84.8947	84.8420	84.7892	84.7365	84.6838	84.6311	84.5784	84.5257	.001757
24	84.1781	84.1292	84.0802	84.0313	83.9824	83.9335	83.8845	83.8356	83.7867	83.7378	83.6888	83.6399	.001631
23	83.2522	83.2068	83.1615	83.1161	83.0708	83.0254	82.9800	82.9347	82.8893	82.8440	82.7986	82.7533	.001512
22	82.3214	82.2800	82.2386	82.1972	82.1558	82.1144	82.0730	82.0315	81.9901	81.9487	81.9073	81.8659	.001380
21	81.3794	81.3422	81.3051	81.2679	81.2307	81.1936	81.1564	81.1192	81.0821	81.0449	81.0077	80.9706	.001239
20	80.4216	80.3890	80.3564	80.3238	80.2912	80.2586	80.2260	80.1934	80.1608	80.1282	80.0956	80.0630	.001087
19	79.4433	79.4155	79.3877	79.3598	79.3320	79.3042	79.2764	79.2486	79.2208	79.1930	79.1651	79.1373	.000927
18	78.4428	78.4198	78.3967	78.3737	78.3507	78.3276	78.3046	78.2816	78.2585	78.2355	78.2125	78.1894	.000768
17	77.4186	77.4003	77.3821	77.3638	77.3456	77.3273	77.3091	77.2908	77.2726	77.2543	77.2361	77.2178	.000608
16	76.3714	76.3577	76.3441	76.3304	76.3168	76.3031	76.2895	76.2758	76.2622	76.2485	76.2349	76.2212	.000455
15	75.3028	75.2935	75.2842	75.2749	75.2656	75.2563	75.2470	75.2377	75.2284	75.2191	75.2098	75.2005	.000310
14	74.2223	74.2164	74.2106	74.2247	74.1988	74.1930	74.1871	74.1812	74.1754	74.1695	74.1636	74.1578	.000195
13	73.1000	73.0991	73.0982	73.0973	73.0965	73.0956	73.0947	73.0938	73.0929	73.0920	73.0912	73.0903	.000029
12	71.9675	71.9706	71.9736	71.9767	71.9798	71.9828	71.9859	71.9890	71.9920	71.9951	71.9982	72.0012	.000102
11	70.8135	70.8204	70.8272	70.8341	70.8410	70.8479	70.8547	70.8616	70.8685	70.8754	70.8822	70.8891	.000229
10	69.6406	69.6511	69.6616	69.6721	69.6826	69.6931	69.7036	69.7142	69.7247	69.7352	69.7457	69.7562	.000350
Age.	0	1	2	3	4	5	6	7	8	9	10	11	Day.

Age.	0	1	2	3	4	5	6	7	8	9	10	11	Day.
10	26.7837	26.7875	26.7912	26.7950	26.7988	26.8026	26.8063	26.8101	26.8139	26.8177	26.8214	26.8252	.000126
11	27.6354	27.6405	27.6457	27.6508	27.6560	27.6611	27.6663	27.6714	27.6766	27.6817	27.6869	27.6920	.000172
12	28.5184	28.5248	28.5311	28.5375	28.5439	28.5503	28.5566	28.5630	28.5694	28.5758	28.5821	28.5885	.000212
13	29.4246	29.4324	29.4403	29.4481	29.4560	29.4638	29.4716	29.4795	29.4873	29.4952	29.5030	29.5109	.000261
14	30.3685	30.3766	30.3848	30.3929	30.4011	30.4092	30.4173	30.4255	30.4336	30.4418	30.4499	30.4581	.000271
15	31.3336	31.3421	31.3507	31.3592	31.3678	31.3763	31.3849	31.3934	31.4020	31.4105	31.4191	31.4276	.000285
16	32.3219	32.3304	32.3389	32.3474	32.3559	32.3644	32.3729	32.3814	32.3899	32.3984	32.4069	32.4154	.000283
17	33.3298	33.3383	33.3467	33.3552	33.3637	33.3721	33.3806	33.3891	33.3975	33.4060	33.4145	33.4229	.000282
18	34.3585	34.3664	34.3743	34.3821	34.3900	34.3979	34.4058	34.4137	34.4216	34.4294	34.4373	34.4452	.000263
19	35.4032	35.4107	35.4182	35.4257	35.4333	35.4408	35.4484	35.4560	35.4635	35.4710	35.4786	35.4861	.000252
20	36.4682	36.4751	36.4820	36.4890	36.4959	36.5028	36.5097	36.5166	36.5235	36.5304	36.5374	36.5443	.000230
21	37.5518	37.5578	37.5639	37.5699	37.5759	37.5820	37.5880	37.5940	37.6001	37.6061	37.6121	37.6182	.000201
22	38.6525	38.6576	38.6627	38.6677	38.6728	38.6779	38.6830	38.6881	38.6932	38.6982	38.7033	38.7084	.000169
23	39.7708	39.7743	39.7779	39.7814	39.7850	39.7885	39.7921	39.7956	39.7992	39.8027	39.8063	39.8098	.000118
24	40.9020	40.9043	40.9065	40.9088	40.9110	40.9133	40.9155	40.9178	40.9201	40.9223	40.9246	40.9268	.000075
25	42.0505	42.0510	42.0515	42.0520	42.0526	42.0531	42.0536	42.0541	42.0546	42.0551	42.0557	42.0562	.000017
26	43.2128	43.2114	43.2099	43.2085	43.2070	43.2056	43.2041	43.2027	43.2013	43.1998	43.1984	43.1969	.000048
27	44.3887	44.3852	44.3817	44.3782	44.3748	44.3713	44.3678	44.3643	44.3608	44.3573	44.3539	44.3504	.000116
28	45.5791	45.5732	45.5673	45.5614	45.5556	45.5497	45.5438	45.5379	45.5320	45.5261	45.5203	45.5144	.000196
29	46.7825	46.7740	46.7654	46.7569	46.7483	46.7398	46.7312	46.7227	46.7142	46.7056	46.6971	46.6885	.000285
30	48.0115	47.9986	47.9858	47.9729	47.9601	47.9472	47.9343	47.9215	47.9086	47.8958	47.8829	47.8701	.000428
31	49.2219	49.2064	49.1908	49.1753	49.1598	49.1442	49.1287	49.1132	49.0976	49.0821	49.0666	49.0510	.000518
32	50.4499	50.4303	50.4107	50.3911	50.3716	50.3520	50.3324	50.3128	50.2932	50.2736	50.2541	50.2345	.000653
33	51.6817	51.6576	51.6336	51.6095	51.5854	51.5614	51.5373	51.5132	51.4892	51.4651	51.4410	51.4170	.000802
34	52.9153	52.8862	52.8571	52.8280	52.7989	52.7698	52.7407	52.7116	52.6825	52.6534	52.6243	52.5952	.000970
35	54.1473	54.1127	54.0781	54.0435	54.0090	53.9744	53.9398	53.9052	53.8706	53.8360	53.8015	53.7669	.001153
36	55.3745	55.3339	55.2934	55.2528	55.2122	55.1717	55.1311	55.0905	55.0500	55.0094	54.9688	54.9283	.001352
37	56.6019	56.5543	56.5067	56.4591	56.4115	56.3638	56.3162	56.2686	56.2210	56.1734	56.1258	56.0782	.001587
38	57.8079	57.7538	57.6997	57.6456	57.5915	57.5374	57.4833	57.4292	57.3752	57.3211	57.2670	57.2129	.001803
39	59.0096	58.9482	58.8868	58.8254	58.7640	58.7025	58.6411	58.5797	58.5183	58.4569	58.3955	58.3341	.002047
40	60.2012	60.1318	60.0625	59.9931	59.9238	59.8544	59.7851	59.7157	59.6464	59.5770	59.5077	59.4383	.002312
41	61.3798	61.3020	61.2242	61.1464	61.0686	60.9908	60.9130	60.8352	60.7574	60.6796	60.6018	60.5240	.002593
42	62.5449	62.4581	62.3712	62.2844	62.1976	62.1108	62.0240	61.9371	61.8503	61.7635	61.6766	61.5898	.002894
43	63.6962	63.5998	63.5034	63.4071	63.3107	63.2143	63.1180	63.0216	62.9252	62.8288	62.7324	62.6361	.003212
44	64.8347	64.7280	64.6213	64.5147	64.4080	64.3013	64.1946	64.0880	63.9813	63.8746	63.7680	63.6613	.003556
45	65.9600	65.8426	65.7252	65.6078	65.4905	65.3731	65.2557	65.1383	65.0209	64.9035	64.7862	64.6688	.003913
46	67.0752	66.9465	66.8178	66.6891	66.5604	66.4317	66.3030	66.1744	66.0457	65.9170	65.7883	65.6596	.004290
47	68.1828	68.0420	67.9012	67.7604	67.6196	67.4788	67.3380	67.1973	67.0565	66.9157	66.7749	66.6341	.004693
48	69.2802	69.1266	68.9729	68.8193	68.6656	68.5120	68.3583	68.2047	68.0511	67.8974	67.7438	67.5901	.005121
49	70.3689	70.2019	70.0350	69.8680	69.7011	69.5341	69.3671	69.2002	69.0332	68.8663	68.6993	68.5324	.005565
50	71.4500	71.2692	71.0884	70.9075	70.7267	70.5459	70.3651	70.1843	70.0035	69.8226	69.6418	69.4610	.006027
51	71.5272	71.3323	71.1374	71.9425	71.7476	71.5527	71.3578	71.1630	70.9681	70.7732	70.5783	70.3834	.006496
52	73.6088	73.3998	73.1908	72.9818	72.7728	72.5638	72.3548	72.1459	71.9369	71.7279	71.5189	71.3099	.006966
53	74.7052	74.4819	74.2585	74.0352	73.8119	73.5886	73.3652	73.1419	72.9186	72.6953	72.4720	72.2486	.007444
54	75.8277	75.5901	75.3525	75.1150	74.8774	74.6398	74.4022	74.1647	73.9271	73.6895	73.4520	73.2144	.007919
55	76.9887	76.7359	76.4830	76.2302	75.9773	75.7245	75.4716	75.2188	74.9660	74.7131	74.4603	74.2074	.008428
56	78.1919	77.9236	77.6554	77.3871	77.1189	76.8506	76.5823	76.3141	76.0458	75.7776	75.5093	75.2411	.008942
57	79.4509	79.1656	78.8803	78.5950	78.3097	78.0244	77.7391	77.4539	77.1686	76.8833	76.5980	76.3127	.009510
58	80.7642	80.4603	80.1563	79.8524	79.5484	79.2445	78.9405	78.6366	78.3327	78.0287	77.7248	77.4208	.010131
59	82.1308	81.8057	81.4805	81.1554	80.8303	80.5052	80.1800	79.8549	79.5298	79.2047	78.8795	78.5544	.010837
60	83.5401	83.1921	82.8440	82.4960	82.1480	81.8000	81.4520	81.1039	80.7559	80.4079	80.0598	79.7118	.011601
61	84.9937	84.6200	84.2463	83.8726	83.4989	83.1251	82.7514	82.3777	82.0040	81.6303	81.2566	80.8829	.012457
62	86.4801	86.0761	85.6721	85.2680	84.8640	84.4600	84.0560	83.6520	83.2480	82.8440	82.4399	82.0359	.013467
63	87.9663	87.5264	87.0865	86.6466	86.2068	85.7669	85.3270	84.8871	84.4472	84.0073	83.5675	83.1276	.014663
64	89.4074	88.9273	88.4471	87.9670	87.4869	87.0067	86.5266	86.0465	85.5663	85.0862	84.6061	84.1259	.016004
65	90.7731	90.2383	89.7036	89.1688	88.6341	88.0993	87.5646	87.0298	86.4951	85.9603	85.4256	84.8908	.017825
66	91.9084	91.3175	90.7266	90.1357	89.5448	88.9539	88.3630	87.7721	87.1813	86.5904	85.9995	85.4086	.019696
67	92.8136	92.2203	91.6269	91.0336	90.4402	89.8469	89.2535	88.6602	88.0669	87.4735	86.8802	86.2868	.019778
68	94.1794	93.6660	93.1527	92.6393	92.1260	91.6126	91.0992	90.5859	90.0725	89.5592	89.0458	88.5325	.017112
69 or 40	**97.0874**	**97.3301**	**97.5728**	**97.8155**	**98.0583**	**98.3010**	**98.5437**	**98.7864**	**99.0291**	**99.2718**	**99.5146**	**99.7573**	**.008090**
39	95.7695	95.6696	95.5696	95.4697	95.3697	95.2698	95.1698	95.0699	94.9700	94.8700	94.7701	94.6701	.003331
38	95.1025	94.9569	94.8114	94.6658	94.5202	94.3747	94.2291	94.0835	93.9380	93.7924	93.6468	93.5013	.004852
37	94.6233	94.4694	94.3155	94.1616	94.0077	93.8537	93.6998	93.5459	93.3920	93.2381	93.0842	92.9303	.005130
36	94.0107	93.8746	93.7385	93.6023	93.4662	93.3301	93.1940	93.0579	92.9218	92.7856	92.6495	92.5134	.004537
35	93.2565	93.1387	93.0208	92.9030	92.7852	92.6673	92.5495	92.4317	92.3138	92.1960	92.0782	91.9603	.003928
34	92.4319	92.3262	92.2205	92.1148	92.0091	91.9034	91.7977	91.6920	91.5864	91.4807	91.3750	91.2693	.003523
33	91.5500	91.4551	91.3602	91.2653	91.1704	91.0755	90.9806	90.8857	90.7908	90.6959	90.6010	90.5061	.003163
32	90.6336	90.5473	90.4611	90.3748	90.2885	90.2023	90.1160	90.0297	89.9435	89.8572	89.7709	89.6847	.002875
31	89.7008	89.6214	89.5420	89.4627	89.3833	89.3039	89.2245	89.1452	89.0658	88.9864	88.9070	88.8277	.002646
30	88.7601	88.6867	88.6132	88.5398	88.4663	88.3929	88.3194	88.2460	88.1726	88.0991	88.0257	87.9522	.002448
29	87.8123	87.7444	87.6765	87.6086	87.5407	87.4727	87.4048	87.3369	87.2690	87.2011	87 1332	87.0653	.002263
28	86.8661	86.8028	86.7395	86.6762	86.6130	86.5497	86.4864	86.4231	86.3598	86.2965	86.2333	86.1700	.002109
27	85.9248	85.8656	85.8064	85.7473	85.6881	85.6289	85.5697	85.5106	85.4514	85.3922	85.3330	85.2739	.001972
26	84.9911	84.9356	84.8800	84.8245	84.7690	84.7134	84.6579	84.6024	84.5468	84.4913	84.4358	84.3802	.001851
25	84.0591	84.0075	83.9559	83.9042	83.8526	83.8010	83.7494	83.6978	83.6462	83.5945	83.5429	83.4913	.001720
24	83.1292	83.0813	83.0333	82.9854	82.9375	82.8896	82.8416	82.7937	82.7458	82.6979	82.6500	82.6020	.001597
23	82.1941	82.1503	82.1065	82.0626	82.0188	81.9750	81.9312	81.8874	81.8436	81.7997	81.7559	81.7121	.001460
22	81.2491	81.2096	81.1702	81.1307	81.0913	81.0518	81.0124	80.9730	80.9335	80.8940	80.8546	80.8151	.001315
21	80.2881	80.2533	80.2185	80.1837	80.1489	80.1140	80.0792	80.0444	80.0096	79.9748	79.9400	79.9052	.001160
20	79.3067	79.2768	79.2469	79.2170	79.1871	79.1571	79.1272	79.0973	79.0674	79.0375	79.0076	78.9777	.000997
19	78.3035	78.2785	78.2534	78.2284	78.2034	78.1784	78.1533	78.1283	78.1033	78.0783	78.0532	78.0282	.000834
18	77.2766	77.2565	77.2363	77.2162	77.1961	77.1759	77.1558	77.1357	77.1155	77.0954	77.0753	77.0551	.000671
17	76.2270	76.2116	76.1961	76.1807	76.1653	76.1498	76.1344	76.1190	76.1035	76.0881	76.0727	76.0572	.000514
16	75.1562	75.1452	75.1342	75.1232	75.1122	75.1012	75.0902	75.0792	75.0682	75.0572	75.0462	75.0352	.000367
15	74.0638	74.0572	74.0505	74.0439	74.0372	74.0306	74.0240	74.0173	74.0107	74.0040	73.9974	73.9907	.000221
14	72.9497	72.9481	72.9465	72.9450	72.9434	72.9418	72.9402	72.9387	72.9371	72.9355	72.9340	72.9324	.000052
13	71.8153	71.8169	71.8185	71.8201	71.8218	71.8234	71.8250	71.8266	71.8282	71.8298	71.8315	71.8331	.000054
12	70.6613	70.6668	70.6723	70.6778	70.6833	70.6888	70.6943	70.6999	70.7054	70.7109	70.7164	70.7219	.000183
11	69.4869	69.4961	69.5053	69.5145	69.5237	69.5329	69.5421	69.5513	69.5605	69.5697	69.5789	69.5881	.000307
10	68.2945	68.3072	68.3200	68.3327	68.3455	68.3582	68.3710	68.3837	68.3964	68.4092	68.4219	68.4347	.000425
Age.	0	1	2	3	4	5	6	7	8	9	10	11	Day.

Age.	0	1	2	3	4	5	6	7	8	9	10	11	Day.
10	28.0222	28.0287	28.0351	28.0416	28.0481	28 0546	28.0610	28.0675	28.0740	28.0805	28.0870	28.0934	.000216
11	28.9133	28.9210	28.9288	28.9365	28.9442	28.9520	28.9597	28.9674	28.9752	28.9829	28.9906	28.9984	.000258
12	29.8350	29.8440	29.8530	29.8620	29.8710	29.8800	29.8890	29.8980	29.9070	29.9160	29.9250	29.9340	.000300
13	30.7839	30.7935	30.8031	30.8127	30.8223	30.8319	30.8415	30.8511	30.8607	30.8703	30.8799	30.8895	.000320
14	31.7576	31.7677	31.7777	31.7878	31.7979	31.8079	31.8180	31.8281	31.8381	31.8482	31.8583	31.8683	.000335
15	32.7549	32.7650	32.7750	32.7851	32.7952	32.8053	32.8153	32.8254	32.8355	32.8456	32.8556	32.8657	.000336
16	33.7711	33.7812	33.7913	33.8014	33.8115	33.8216	33.8316	33.8417	33.8518	33.8619	33.8720	33.8821	.000336
17	34.8083	34.8179	34.8274	34.8370	34.8466	34.8561	34.8657	34.8753	34.8848	34.8944	34.9040	34.9135	.000319
18	35.8609	35.8702	35.8795	35.8888	35.8981	35.9074	35.9166	35.9259	35.9352	35.9445	35.9538	35.9631	.000310
19	36.9339	36.9424	36.9509	36.9594	36.9679	36.9764	36.9850	36.9935	37.0020	37.0105	37.0190	37.0275	.000283
20	38.0250	38.0329	38.0408	38.0487	38.0566	38.0645	38.0724	38.0804	38.0883	38.0962	38.1041	38.1120	.000263
21	39.1331	39.1401	39.1472	39.1542	39.1613	39.1683	39.1753	39.2824	39.1894	39.1965	39.2035	39.2106	.000235
22	40.2591	40.2647	40.2703	40.2759	40.2815	40.2871	40.2926	40.2982	40.3038	40.3094	40.3150	40.3206	.000186
23	41.3974	41.4018	41.4062	41.4105	41.4149	41.4193	41.4237	41.4281	41.4325	41.4368	41.4412	41.4456	.000146
24	42.5531	42.5558	42.5585	42.5613	42.5640	42.5667	42.5694	42.5722	42.5749	42.5776	42.5803	42.5831	.000091
25	43.7225	43.7234	43.7242	43.7251	43.7260	43.7269	43.7277	43.7286	43.7295	43.7304	43.7312	43.7321	.000029
26	44.9050	44.9039	44.9029	44.9018	44.9007	44.8997	44.8986	44.8975	44.8965	44.8954	44.8943	44.8933	.000353
27	46.1021	46.0987	46.0954	46.0920	46.0887	46.0853	46.0820	46.0786	46.0752	46.0719	46.0685	46.0652	.000112
28	47.3116	47.3057	47.2998	47.2939	47.2880	47.2821	47.2762	47.2704	47.2645	47.2586	47.2527	47.2468	.000196
29	48.5333	48.5242	48.5152	48.5061	48.4971	48.4880	48.4790	48.4700	48.4609	48.4518	48.4428	48.4337	.000302
30	49.7629	49.7504	49.7378	49.7253	49.7128	49.7003	49.6877	49.6752	49.6627	49.6502	49.6376	49.6251	.000417
31	50.9964	50.9799	50.9634	50.9469	50.9304	50.9139	50.8973	50.8808	50.8643	50.8478	50.8313	50.8148	.000550
32	52.2336	52.2128	52.1920	52.1711	52.1503	52.1295	52.1086	52.0878	52.0670	52.0462	52.0253	52.0045	.000694
33	53.4722	53.4465	43.4208	53.3952	53.3695	53.3438	53.3182	53.2925	53.2668	53.2412	53.2155	53.1898	.000853
34	54.7092	54.6782	54.6473	54.6163	54.5854	54.5544	54.5234	54.4925	54.4615	54.4306	54.3996	54.3687	.001032
35	55.9424	55.9057	55.8690	55.8323	55.7956	55.7589	55.7222	55.6855	55.6488	55.6121	55.5754	55.5387	.001223
36	57.1685	57.1255	57.0825	57.0395	56.9965	56.9535	56.9104	56.8674	56.8244	56.7814	56.7384	56.6954	.001433
37	58.3859	58.3362	58.2865	58.2367	58.1870	58.1373	58.0876	58.0379	57.9882	57.9384	57.8887	57.8390	.001657
38	59.5928	59.5360	59.4793	59.4225	59.3658	59.3090	59.2523	59.1955	59.1388	59.0820	59.0253	58.9685	.001892
39	60.7898	60.7254	60.6610	60.5967	60.5323	60.4679	60.4035	60.3392	60.2748	60.2104	60.1460	60.0817	.002146
40	61.9742	61.9017	61.8292	61.7568	61.6843	61.6118	61.5393	61.4669	61.3944	61.3219	61.2494	61.1770	.002416
41	63.1448	63.0637	62.9826	62.9015	62.8204	62.7393	62.6582	62.5771	62.4960	62.4149	62.3338	62.2527	.002703
42	64.3007	64.2105	64.1202	64.0300	63.9398	63.8495	63.7593	63.6691	63.5788	63.4886	63.3984	63.3081	.003008
43	65.4428	65.3428	65.2428	65.1428	65.0428	64.9428	64.8427	64.7427	64.6427	64.5427	64.4427	64.3427	.003333
44	66.5696	66.4593	66.3490	66.2386	66.1283	66.0180	65.9076	65.7973	65.6870	65.5767	65.4663	65.3560	.003677
45	67.6848	67.5636	67.4425	67.3213	67.2002	67.0790	66.9579	66.8367	66.7156	66.5944	66.4733	66.3521	.004038
46	68.7996	68.6660	68.5325	68.3989	68.2653	68.1318	67.9982	67.8646	67.7311	67.5975	67.4639	67.3304	.004452
47	69.8844	69.7394	69.5943	69.4493	69.3043	69.1592	69.0142	68.8692	68.7241	68.5791	68.4341	68.2890	.004834
48	70.9676	70.8098	70.6520	70.4943	70.3365	70.1787	70.0210	69.8632	69.7054	69.5476	69.3898	69.2321	.005259
49	72.0442	71.8732	71.7022	71.5312	71.3602	71.1892	71.0182	70.8472	70.6763	70.5053	70.3343	70.1633	.005700
50	73.1154	72.9310	72.7466	72.5622	72.3778	72.1933	72.0089	71.8245	71.6401	71.4557	71.2713	71.0869	.006147
51	74.1893	73.9915	73.7936	73.5958	73.3980	73.2002	73.0023	72.8045	72.6067	72.4089	72.2110	72.0132	.006594
52	75.2770	75.0656	74.8541	74.6427	74.4313	74.2199	74.0084	73.7970	73.5856	73.3742	73.1627	72.9513	.007047
53	76.3871	76.1622	75.9372	75.7123	75.4874	75.2624	75.0375	74.8126	74.5876	74.3627	74.1378	73.9128	.007498
54	77.5352	77.2958	77.0565	76.8171	76.5777	76.3384	76.0990	75.8596	75.6203	75.3809	75.1415	74.9022	.007979
55	78.7219	78.4679	78.2139	77.9600	77.7060	77.4520	77.1980	76.9440	76.6900	76.4360	76.1821	75.9281	.008466
56	79.9617	79.6916	79.4216	79.1515	78.8815	78.6114	78.3413	78.0713	77.8012	77.5312	77.2611	76.9911	.009002
57	81.2517	80.9641	80.6765	80.3889	80.1013	79.8136	79.5260	79.2384	78.9508	78 6632	78.3756	78.0880	.009587
58	82.5917	82.2841	81.9764	81.6688	81.3612	81.0535	80.7459	80.4383	80.1306	79.8230	79.5154	79.2077	.010254
59	83.9707	83.6415	83.3122	82.9830	82.6537	82.3245	81.9952	81.6660	81.3368	81.0075	80.6783	80.3490	.010975
60	85.3894	85.0359	84.6823	84.3288	83.9752	83.6217	83.2681	82.9146	82.5611	82.2075	81.8540	81.5004	.011785
61	86.8372	86.4550	86.0727	85.6904	85.3082	84.9260	84.5437	84.1614	83.7792	83.3970	83.0147	82.6324	.012742
62	87.2818	86.8655	86.4492	86.0330	86.6167	86.2004	85.7841	85.3679	84.9516	84.5353	84.1190	83.7028	.013876
63	89.6802	89.2258	88.7713	88.3169	87.8624	87.4080	86.9535	86.4991	86.0447	85.5902	85.1358	84.6813	.015148
64	91.0032	90.4968	89.9903	89.4839	88.9775	88.4711	87.9646	87.4582	86.9518	86.4454	85.9390	85.4325	.016881
65	92.1019	91.5421	90.9824	90.4226	89.8629	89.3031	88.7433	88.1836	87.6238	87.0641	86.5043	85.9446	.018658
66	92.9771	92.4157	91.8544	91.2930	90.7316	90.1703	89.6089	89.0475	88.4862	87.9248	87.3634	86.8021	.018712
67	94.2931	93.8093	93.3255	92.8417	92.3580	91.8742	91.3904	90.9066	90.4228	89.9390	89.4553	88.9715	.016126
68 or 41	**97.0874**	**97.3301**	**97.5728**	**97.8155**	**98.0583**	**98.3010**	**98.5437**	**98.7864**	**99.0291**	**99.2718**	**99.5146**	**99.7573**	**.008090**
40	95.7481	95.6426	95.5371	95.4316	95.3261	95.2206	95.1151	95.0096	94.9042	94.7987	94.6932	94.5877	.003516
39	95.0716	94.9200	94.7684	94.6168	94.4652	94.3135	94.1619	94.0103	93.8587	93.7071	93.5555	93.4039	.005053
38	94.5865	94.4267	94.2668	94.1070	93.9472	93.7873	93.6275	93.4677	93.3078	93.1480	92.9882	92.8283	.005328
37	93.9666	93.8250	93.6835	93.5420	93.4004	93.2588	93.1173	92.9757	92.8342	92.6926	92.5511	92.4095	.004718
36	93.2037	93.0809	92.9581	92.8352	92.7124	92.5896	92.4668	92.3440	92.2212	92.0983	91.9755	91.8527	.004094
35	92.3701	92.2598	92.1495	92.0392	91.9289	91.8185	91.7082	91.5979	91.4876	91.3773	91.2670	91.1567	.003677
34	91.4793	91.3801	91.2809	91.1817	91.0825	90.9832	90.8840	90.7848	90.6856	90.5864	90.4872	90.3880	.003307
33	90.5541	90.4638	90.3735	90.2832	90.1930	90.1027	90.0124	89.9221	89.8318	89.7415	89.6513	89.5610	.003009
32	89.6133	89.5301	89.4469	89.3637	89.2805	89.1973	89.1141	89.0309	88.9477	88.8645	88.7813	88.6981	.002773
31	88.6647	88.5876	88.5106	88.4335	88.3565	88.2794	88.2023	88.1253	88.0482	87.9712	87.8941	87.8171	.002568
30	87.7102	87.6389	87.5676	87.4962	87.4249	87.3536	87.2823	87.2110	87.1397	87.0683	86.9970	86.9257	.002377
29	86.7575	86.6910	86.6244	86.5579	86.4913	86.4248	86.3582	86.2917	86.2252	86.1586	86.0921	86.0255	.002218
28	85.8103	85.7480	85.6857	85.6235	85.5612	85.4989	85.4366	85.3744	85.3121	85.2498	85.1875	85.1253	.002076
27	84.8714	84.8129	84.7544	84.6959	84.6374	84.5789	84.5204	84.4620	84.4035	84.3450	84.2865	84.2280	.001950
26	83.9347	83.8803	83.8258	83.7714	83.7170	83.6626	83.6081	83.5537	83.4993	83.4449	83.3904	83.3360	.001814
25	83.0005	82.9499	82.8993	82.8487	82.7981	82.7475	82.6969	82.6463	82.5957	82.5451	82.4945	82.4439	.001687
24	82.0616	82.0152	81.9689	81.9225	81.8761	81.8298	81.7834	81.7370	81.6907	81.6443	81.5979	81.5516	.001545
23	81.1130	81.0711	81.0292	80.9873	80.9454	80.9035	80.8615	80.8196	80.7777	80.7358	80.6939	80.6520	.001397
22	80.1488	80.1117	80.0746	80.0375	80.0004	79.9633	79.9261	79.8890	79.8519	79.8148	79.7777	79.7406	.001237
21	79.1643	79.1322	79.1001	79.0680	79.0359	79.0038	78.9717	78.9396	78.9075	78.8754	78.8433	78.8112	.001070
20	78.1580	78.1309	78.1038	78.0767	78.0496	78.0225	77.9954	77.9684	77.9413	77.9142	77.8871	77.8600	.000903
19	77.1285	77.1064	77.0843	77.0622	77.0401	77.0180	76.9959	76.9738	76.9517	76.9296	76.9075	76.8854	.000737
18	76.0764	76.0591	76.0418	76.0245	76.0072	75.9899	75.9725	75.9552	75.9379	75.9206	75.9033	75.8860	.000577
17	75.0033	74.9905	74.9778	74.9650	74.9522	74.9395	74.9267	74.9139	74.9012	74.8884	74.8756	74.8629	.000425
16	73.9088	73.9005	73.8922	73.8838	73.8755	73.8672	73.8589	73.8506	73.8423	73.8340	73.8256	73.8173	.000277
15	72.7930	72.7890	72.7850	72.7810	72.7770	72.7730	72.7690	72.7651	72.7611	72.7571	72.7531	72.7491	.000133
14	71.6570	71.6571	71.6572	71.6573	71.6574	71.6575	71.6576	71.6578	71.6579	71.6580	71.6581	71.6582	.000003
13	70.5012	70.5053	70.5093	70.5134	70.5175	70.5216	70.5256	70.5297	70.5338	70.5379	70.5420	70.5460	.000136
12	69.3270	69.3348	69.3427	69.3505	69.3584	69.3662	69.3741	69.3820	69.3898	69.3976	69.4055	69.4133	.000262
11	68.1332	68.1447	68.1561	68.1676	68.1790	68.1905	68.2020	68.2134	68.2249	68.2363	68.2478	68.2592	.000382
10	66.9238	66.9386	66.9534	66.9682	66.9830	66.9978	67.0125	67.0273	67.0421	67.0569	67.0717	67.0865	.000493
Age.	0	1	2	3	4	5	6	7	8	9	10	11	Day.

Age.	0	1	2	3	4	5	6	7	8	9	10	11	Day.
10	29.2930	29.3020	29.3111	29.3201	29.3292	29.3382	29.3473	29.3563	29.3654	29.3744	29.3835	29.3925	.000302
11	30.2223	30.2326	30.2430	30.2533	30.2637	30.2740	30.2844	30.2947	30.3051	30.3154	30.3258	30.3361	.000345
12	31.1831	31.1941	31.2051	31.2161	31.2271	31.2381	31.2491	31.2601	31.2712	31.2822	31.2932	31.3042	.000367
13	32.1644	32.1759	32.1874	32.1989	32.2104	32.2219	32.2334	32.2450	32.2565	32.2680	32.2795	32.2910	.000383
14	33.1698	33.1814	33.1930	33.2045	33.2161	33.2277	33.2392	33.2508	33.2624	33.2740	33.2855	33.2971	.000386
15	34.1945	34.2065	34.2184	34.2304	34.2424	34.2544	34.2663	34.2783	34.2903	34.3023	34.3142	34.3262	.000399
16	35.2393	35.2505	35.2617	35.2728	35.2840	35.2952	35.3064	35.3176	35.3288	35.3400	35.3511	35.3623	.000373
17	36.2999	36.3109	36.3218	36.3328	36.3438	36.3547	36.3657	36.3767	36.3876	36.3986	36.4096	36.4205	.000365
18	37.3803	37.3908	37.4012	37.4117	37.4221	37.4326	37.4430	37.4535	37.4640	37.4744	37.4849	37.4953	.000348
19	38.4761	38.4860	38.4960	38.5059	38.5158	38.5258	38.5357	38.5456	38.5556	38.5655	38.5754	38.5854	.000331
20	39.5938	39.6027	39.6116	39.6205	39.6294	39.6383	39.6472	39.6561	39.6651	39.6740	39.6829	39.6918	.000297
21	40.7266	40.7341	40.7417	40.7492	40.7567	40.7643	40.7718	40.7793	40.7869	40.7944	40.8019	40.8095	.000251
22	41.8719	41.8783	41.8847	41.8911	41.8975	41.9039	41.9103	41.9167	41.9232	41.9296	41.9360	41.9424	.000213
23	43.0340	43.0388	43.0437	43.0485	43.0533	43.0582	43.0630	43.0678	43.0727	43.0775	43.0823	43.0872	.000161
24	44.2098	44.2129	44.2160	44.2190	44.2221	44.2252	44.2283	44.2314	44.2345	44.2375	44.2406	44.2437	.000103
25	45.3987	45.3999	45.4012	45.4024	45.4036	45.4049	45.4061	45.4073	45.4086	45.4098	45.4110	45.4123	.000041
26	46.6017	46.6007	46.5998	46.5988	46.5979	46.5970	46.5960	46.5950	46.5941	46.5931	46.5922	46.5912	.000032
27	47.8171	47.8137	47.8103	47.8070	47.8036	47.8002	47.7968	47.7935	47.7901	47.7867	47.7833	47.7800	.000112
28	49.0440	49.0376	49.0312	49.0248	49.0184	49.0120	49.0056	48.9992	48.9928	48.9864	48.9800	48.9736	.000213
29	50.2779	50.2681	50.2584	50.2486	50.2389	50.2291	50.2194	50.2096	50.1999	50.1901	50.1804	50.1706	.000325
30	51.5183	51.5047	51.4911	51.4776	51.4640	51.4504	51.4368	51.4233	51.4097	51.3961	51.3825	51.3690	.000452
31	52.7572	52.7415	52.7237	52.7060	52.6882	52.6705	52.6527	52.6350	52.6173	52.5995	52.5818	52.5640	.000591
32	54.0023	53.9799	53.9575	53.9351	53.9127	53.8902	53.8678	53.8454	53.8230	53.8006	53.7782	53.7558	.000747
33	55.2435	55.2160	55.1885	55.1610	55.1335	55.1060	55.0784	55.0509	55.0234	54.9959	54.9684	54.9409	.000917
34	56.4808	56.4477	56.4147	56.3816	56.3486	56.3155	56.2825	56.2494	56.2164	56.1833	56.1503	56.1172	.001102
35	57.7121	57.6730	57.6338	57.5947	57.5556	57.5165	57.4773	57.4382	57.3991	57.3600	57.3208	57.2817	.001304
36	58.9332	58.8876	58.8420	58.7964	58.7509	58.7053	58.6597	58.6141	58.5685	58.5230	58.4774	58.4318	.001519
37	60.1446	60.0922	60.0399	59.9875	59.9352	59.8828	59.8305	59.7781	59.7258	59.6734	59.6211	59.5687	.001745
38	61.3458	61.2861	61.2264	61.1668	61.1071	61.0474	60.9877	60.9281	60.8684	60.8087	60.7490	60.6894	.001989
39	62.5346	62.4672	62.3997	62.3322	62.2647	62.1973	62.1298	62.0624	61.9950	61.9275	61.8601	61.7926	.002248
40	63.7098	63.6341	63.5584	63.4826	63.4069	63.3312	63.2555	63.1798	63.1041	63.0283	62.9526	62.8769	.002524
41	64.8702	64.7857	64.7013	64.6168	64.5324	64.4479	64.3634	64.2790	64.1945	64.1101	64.0256	63.9412	.002815
42	66.0157	65.9219	65.8281	65.7343	65.6405	65.5467	65.4529	65.3591	65.2653	65.1715	65.0777	64.9839	.003127
43	67.1458	67.0422	66.9385	66.8348	66.7312	66.6275	66.5238	66.4202	66.3165	66.2128	66.1092	66.0055	.003453
44	68.2606	68.1466	68.0326	67.9185	67.8045	67.6905	67.5765	67.4625	67.3485	67.2344	67.1204	67.0064	.003800
45	69.3644	69.2393	69.1142	68.9890	68.8639	68.7388	68.6137	68.4886	68.3635	68.2383	68.1132	67.9881	.004170
46	70.4555	70.3186	70.1817	70.0448	69.9079	69.7710	69.6341	69.4973	69.3604	69.2235	69.0866	68.9497	.004563
47	71.5351	71.3860	71.2370	71.0879	70.9388	70.7897	70.6406	70.4916	70.3425	70.1934	70.0443	69.8953	.004969
48	72.6054	72.4437	72.2820	72.1202	71.9585	71.7968	71.6350	71.4733	71.3116	71.1499	70.9881	70.8264	.005391
49	73.6711	73.4966	73.3221	73.1475	72.9730	72.7985	72.6240	72.4495	72.2750	72.1004	71.9259	71.7514	.005817
50	74.7377	74.5504	74.3631	74.1759	73.9886	73.8013	73.6140	73.4268	73.2395	73.0522	72.8650	72.6777	.006242
51	75.8162	75.6160	75.4158	75.2156	75.0154	74.8152	74.6150	74.4149	74.2147	74.0145	73.8143	73.6141	.006673
52	76.9159	76.7029	76.4899	76.2770	76.0640	75.8510	75.6380	75.4250	75.2120	74.9990	74.7861	74.5731	.007099
53	78.0498	77.8231	77.5964	77.3697	77.1430	76.9163	76.6896	76.4630	76.2363	76.0096	75.7829	75.5562	.007556
54	79.2213	78.9808	78.7403	78.4999	78.2594	78.0189	77.7784	77.5380	77.2975	77.0570	76.8165	76.5761	.008016
55	80.4414	80.1858	79.9301	79.6745	79.4189	79.1632	78.9076	78.6520	78.3963	78.1407	77.8851	77.6294	.008521
56	81.7099	81.4376	81.1653	80.8931	80.6208	80.3485	80.0762	79.8040	79.5317	79.2594	78.9871	78.7149	.009076
57	83.0246	82.7334	82.4422	82.1510	81.8598	81.5686	81.2774	80.9863	80.6951	80.4039	80.1127	79.8215	.009706
58	84.3749	84.0633	83.7517	83.4400	83.1284	82.8168	82.5052	82.1936	81.8820	81.5703	81.2587	80.9471	.010387
59	85.7613	85.4267	85.0921	84.7575	84.4230	84.0884	83.7538	83.4192	83.0846	82.7500	82.4155	82.0809	.011153
60	87.1726	86.8108	86.4490	86.0872	85.7254	85.3636	85.0018	84.6400	84.2782	83.9164	83.5546	83.1928	.012060
61	88.5782	88.1841	87.7900	87.3959	87.0018	86.6077	86.2136	85.8196	85.4255	85.0314	84.6373	84.2432	.013136
62	89.9364	89.5061	89.0757	88.6454	88.2151	87.7847	87.3544	86.9241	86.4937	86.0634	85.6331	85.2027	.014343
63	91.2194	90.7396	90.2598	89.7800	89.3102	88.8304	88.3505	87.8707	87.3909	86.9111	86.4213	85.9415	.015993
64	92.2835	91.7530	91.2225	90.6920	90.1615	89.6310	89.1004	88.5699	88.0394	87.5089	86.9784	86.4479	.017683
65	93.1306	92.5993	92.0679	91.5366	91.0053	90.4739	89.9426	89.4113	88.8799	88.3486	87.8173	87.2859	.017710
66	94.4000	93.9440	93.4880	93.0320	92.5760	92.1200	91.6640	91.2080	90.7520	90.2960	89.8400	89.3840	.015200
67 or **42**	**97.0874**	**97.3301**	**97.5728**	**97.8155**	**98.0583**	**98.3010**	**98.5437**	**98.7864**	**99.0291**	**99.2718**	**99.5146**	**99.7573**	**.008090**
41	95.7254	95.6140	95.5026	95.3912	95.2799	95.1685	95.0571	94.9457	94.8343	94.7230	94.6116	94.5002	.003713
40	95.0390	94.8810	94.7230	94.5650	94.4070	94.2490	94.0910	93.9329	93.7749	93.6169	93.4589	93.3009	.005267
39	94.5486	94.3824	94.2162	94.0501	93.8839	93.7177	93.5515	93.3854	93.2192	93.0530	92.8868	92.7207	.005539
38	93.9199	93.7726	93.6253	93.4780	93.3308	93.1835	93.0362	92.8889	92.7416	92.5943	92.4471	92.2998	.004909
37	93.1480	93.0199	92.8919	92.7638	92.6357	92.5077	92.3796	92.2515	92.1235	91.9954	91.8673	91.7393	.004269
36	92.3050	92.1898	92.0746	91.9594	91.8443	91.7291	91.6139	91.4987	91.3835	91.2683	91.1532	91.0380	.003839
35	91.4050	91.3012	91.1975	91.0937	90.9900	90.8862	90.7825	90.6787	90.5750	90.4712	90.3675	90.2637	.003458
34	90.4707	90.3762	90.2816	90.1871	90.0925	89.9980	89.9034	89.8089	89.7144	89.6198	89.5253	89.4307	.003151
33	89.5213	89.4341	89.3469	89.2597	89.1725	89.0853	88.9980	88.9108	88.8236	88.7364	88.6492	88.5620	.002907
32	88.5648	88.4840	88.4031	88.3222	88.2414	88.1605	88.0797	87.9988	87.9180	87.8371	87.7563	87.6754	.002695
31	87.6028	87.5279	87.4530	87.3780	87.3031	87.2282	87.1533	87.0784	87.0035	86.9285	86.8536	86.7787	.002497
30	86.6438	86.5739	86.5039	86.4340	86.3640	86.2941	86.2241	86.1542	86.0843	86.0143	85.9444	85.8744	.002331
29	85.6904	85.6249	85.5594	85.4938	85.4283	85.3628	85.2973	85.2318	85.1663	85.1007	85.0352	84.9697	.002184
28	84.7461	84.6845	84.6229	84.5613	84.4998	84.4382	84.3766	84.3150	84.2534	84.1918	84.1303	84.0687	.002053
27	83.8045	83.7471	83.6898	83.6324	83.5750	83.5177	83.4603	83.4029	83.3456	83.2882	83.2308	83.1735	.001912
26	82.8660	82.8126	82.7592	82.7058	82.6524	82.5990	82.5456	82.4922	82.4388	82.3854	82.3320	82.2786	.001780
25	81.9231	81.8741	81.8250	81.7760	81.7270	81.6780	81.6290	81.5799	81.5309	81.4819	81.4328	81.3838	.001634
24	80.9709	80.9265	80.8820	80.8376	80.7931	80.7487	80.7042	80.6598	80.6154	80.5709	80.5265	80.4820	.001481
23	80.0032	79.9637	79.9242	79.8847	79.8452	79.8057	79.7661	79.7266	79.6871	79.6476	79.6081	79.5686	.001317
22	79.0156	78.9812	78.9468	78.9125	78.8781	78.8437	78.8093	78.7750	78.7406	78.7062	78.6718	78.6375	.001146
21	78.0064	77.9771	77.9479	77.9186	77.8893	77.8601	77.8308	77.8016	77.7723	77.7431	77.7138	77.6846	.000975
20	76.9740	76.9498	76.9257	76.9015	76.8774	76.8532	76.8291	76.8050	76.7808	76.7566	76.7325	76.7083	.000805
19	75.9193	75.9001	75.8808	75.8616	75.8423	75.8231	75.8038	75.7846	75.7654	75.7461	75.7269	75.7076	.000641
18	74.8438	74.8292	74.8146	74.8000	74.7854	74.7708	74.7561	74.7415	74.7269	74.7123	74.6977	74.6831	.000487
17	73.7472	73.7371	73.7271	73.7170	73.7070	73.6969	73.6868	73.6768	73.6667	73.6567	73.6466	73.6366	.000335
16	72.6295	72.6238	72.6182	72.6125	72.6069	72.6012	72.5955	72.5899	72.5842	72.5786	72.5729	72.5673	.000188
15	71.4919	71.4904	71.4890	71.4875	71.4860	71.4846	71.4831	71.4816	71.4802	71.4787	71.4772	71.4758	.000049
14	70.3347	70.3373	70.3398	70.3424	70.3450	70.3476	70.3501	70.3527	70.3553	70.3579	70.3604	70.3630	.000086
13	69.1588	69.1652	69.1717	69.1781	69.1845	69.1910	69.1974	69.2038	69.2103	69.2167	69.2231	69.2296	.000214
12	67.9655	67.9756	67.9857	67.9958	68.0060	68.0161	68.0262	68.0363	68.0464	68.0565	68.0667	68.0768	.000337
11	66.7548	66.7683	66.7818	66.7953	66.8089	66.8224	66.8359	66.8494	66.8629	66.8764	66.8900	66.9035	.000450
10	65.5287	65.5455	65.5623	65.5792	65.5960	65.6128	65.6296	65.6465	65.6633	65.6801	65.6970	65.7138	.000561
Age.	0	1	2	3	4	5	6	7	8	9	10	11	Day.

Age.	0	1	2	3	4	5	6	7	8	9	10	11	Day.
10	30.5947	30.6063	30.6180	30.6296	30.6413	30.6530	30.6646	30.6762	30.6879	30.6995	30.7112	30.7228	.000388
11	31.5627	31.5750	31.5874	31.5997	31.6121	31.6244	31.6367	31.6491	31.6614	31.6738	31.6861	31.6985	.000411
12	32.5553	32.5682	32.5811	32.5940	32.6069	32.6198	32.6327	32.6456	32.6585	32.6714	32.6843	32.6972	.000430
13	33.5677	33.5807	33.5937	33.6067	33.6198	33.6328	33.6458	33.6588	33.6718	33.6848	33.6979	33.7109	.000434
14	34.6001	34.6132	34.6264	34.6395	34.6526	34.6658	34.6789	34.6920	34.7052	34.7183	34.7314	34.7446	.000438
15	35.6569	35.6693	35.6817	35.6941	35.7065	35.7189	35.7312	35.7436	35.7560	35.7684	35.7808	35.7932	.000413
16	36.7207	36.7333	36.7458	36.7584	36.7710	36.7835	36.7961	36.8087	36.8212	36.8338	36.8464	36.8589	.000419
17	37.8084	37.8205	37.8326	37.8448	37.8569	37.8690	37.8811	37.8933	37.9054	37.9175	37.9296	37.9418	.000404
18	38.9136	38.9250	38.9365	38.9479	38.9594	38.9708	38.9822	38.9937	39.0051	39.0166	39.0280	39.0395	.000381
19	40.0355	40.0463	40.0561	40.0668	40.0776	40.0884	40.0992	40.1100	40.1208	40.1315	40.1423	40.1531	.000359
20	41.1745	41.1839	41.1933	41.2027	41.2122	41.2216	41.2310	41.2404	41.2498	41.2592	41.2687	41.2781	.000314
21	42.3260	42.3344	42.3427	42.3511	42.3594	42.3678	42.3761	42.3845	42.3929	42.4012	42.4096	42.4179	.000278
22	43.4945	43.5014	43.5082	43.5151	43.5220	43.5288	43.5357	43.5426	43.5494	43.5563	43.5632	43.5700	.000229
23	44.6760	44.6812	44.6864	44.6916	44.6968	44.7020	44.7071	44.7123	44.7175	44.7227	44.7279	44.7331	.000173
24	45.8707	45.8741	45.8776	45.8810	45.8845	45.8879	45.8913	45.8948	45.8982	45.9017	45.9051	45.9086	.000115
25	47.0793	47.0807	47.0820	47.0834	47.0847	47.0861	47.0874	47.0888	47.0902	47.0915	47.0929	47.0942	.000045
26	48.2999	48.2989	48.2980	48.2970	48.2960	48.2951	48.2941	48.2931	48.2922	48.2912	48.2902	48.2893	.000032
27	49.5319	49.5280	49.5241	49.5203	49.5164	49.5125	49.5086	49.5048	49.5009	49.4970	49.4931	49.4893	.000129
28	50.7703	50.7632	50.7561	50.7490	50.7419	50.7348	50.7277	50.7206	50.7136	50.7065	50.6994	50.6923	.000236
29	52.0142	52.0034	51.9926	51.9818	51.9711	51.9603	51.9495	51.9387	51.9279	51.9171	51.9064	51.8956	.000359
30	53.2611	53.2463	53.2315	53.2167	53.2019	53.1871	53.1723	53.1576	53.1428	53.1280	53.1132	53.0984	.000493
31	54.5072	54.4879	54.4686	54.4493	54.4300	54.4107	54.3913	54.3720	54.3527	54.3334	54.3141	54.2948	.000643
32	55.7521	55.7279	55.7036	55.6794	55.6552	55.6310	55.6067	55.5825	55.5583	55.5341	55.5098	55.4856	.000807
33	56.9928	56.9632	56.9336	56.9041	56.8745	56.8449	56.8153	56.7858	56.7562	56.7266	56.6970	56.6675	.000986
34	58.2273	58.1919	58.1564	58.1210	58.0855	58.0501	58.0146	57.9792	57.9438	57.9083	57.8729	57.8374	.001181
35	59.4527	59.4110	59.3694	59.3277	59.2861	59.2444	59.2027	59.1611	59.1194	59.0778	59.0361	58.9945	.001388
36	60.6670	60.6188	60.5706	60.5225	60.4743	60.4261	60.3780	60.3298	60.2816	60.2334	60.1852	60.1371	.001606
37	61.8717	61.8165	61.7612	61.7060	61.6508	61.5956	61.5403	61.4851	61.4299	61.3747	61.3194	61.2642	.001841
38	63.0637	63.0010	62.9383	62.8756	62.8129	62.7502	62.6875	62.6249	62.5622	62.4995	62.4368	62.3741	.002090
39	64.2424	64.1718	64.1011	64.0305	63.9599	63.8892	63.8186	63.7480	63.6773	63.6067	63.5361	63.4654	.002354
40	65.4064	65.3274	65.2484	65.1694	65.0904	65.0114	64.9323	64.8533	64.7743	64.6953	64.6163	64.5373	.002633
41	66.5554	66.4674	66.3795	66.2915	66.2036	66.1156	66.0276	65.9397	65.8517	65.7638	65.6758	65.5879	.002932
42	67.6879	67.5905	67.4931	67.3957	67.2983	67.2009	67.1035	67.0061	66.9087	66.8113	66.7139	66.6165	.003247
43	68.8049	68.6976	68.5903	68.4830	68.3757	68.2684	68.1611	68.0539	67.9466	67.8393	67.7320	67.6247	.003576
44	69.9073	69.7894	69.6715	69.5536	69.4357	69.3178	69.1998	69.0819	68.9640	68.8461	68.7282	68.6103	.003930
45	70.9964	70.8672	70.7380	70.6088	70.4797	70.3505	70.2213	70.0921	69.9629	69.8337	69.7046	69.5754	.004306
46	72.0716	71.9307	71.7899	71.6490	71.5082	71.3673	71.2265	71.0856	70.9448	70.8040	70.6631	70.5222	.004695
47	73.1373	72.9844	72.8314	72.6785	72.5256	72.3726	72.2197	72.0668	71.9138	71.7609	71.6080	71.4550	.005098
48	74.1958	74.0306	73.8655	73.7003	73.5351	73.3700	73.2048	73.0396	72.8745	72.7093	72.5441	72.3790	.005505
49	75.2557	75.0784	74.9011	74.7238	74.5465	74.3692	74.1919	74.0146	73.8373	73.6600	73.4827	73.3054	.005910
50	76.3256	76.1360	75.9464	75.7568	75.5673	75.3777	75.1881	74.9985	74.8089	74.6193	74.4298	74.2402	.006319
51	77.4147	77.2178	77.0208	76.8239	76.6270	76.4300	76.2331	76.0362	75.8392	75.6423	75.4454	75.2484	.006564
52	78.5361	78.3214	78.1067	77.8920	77.6773	77.4626	77.2480	77.0333	76.8186	76.6039	76.3892	76.1745	.007156
53	79.6914	79.4636	79.2359	79.0081	78.7804	78.5526	78.3248	78.0971	77.8693	77.6416	77.4138	77.1861	.007590
54	80.8940	80.6519	80.4098	80.1678	79.9257	79.6836	79.4415	79.1995	78.9574	78.7153	78.4732	78.2312	.008069
55	82.1411	81.8833	81.6254	81.3676	81.1098	80.8520	80.5941	80.3363	80.0785	79.8207	79.5628	79.3050	.008594
56	83.4315	83.1557	82.8800	82.6042	82.3285	82.0527	81.7770	81.5012	81.2255	80.9497	80.6740	80.3982	.009192
57	84.7546	84.4595	84.1645	83.8694	83.5744	83.2793	82.9842	82.6892	82.3941	82.0991	81.8040	81.5090	.009835
58	86.1103	85.7969	85.4835	85.1701	84.8567	84.5433	84.2299	83.9165	83.6031	83.2897	82.9763	82.6629	.010447
59	87.4878	87.1452	86.8026	86.4600	86.1175	85.7749	85.4323	85.0897	84.7471	84.4045	84.0620	83.7194	.011419
60	88.4166	88.0800	87.7434	87.4068	87.0703	86.7337	86.3971	86.0605	85.7239	85.3873	85.0508	84.7142	.011219
61	90.1771	89.7694	89.3618	88.9541	88.5464	88.1388	87.7311	87.3234	86.9158	86.5081	86.1004	85.6928	.013589
62	91.4224	90.9676	90.5127	90.0579	89.6031	89.1483	88.6934	88.2386	87.7838	87.3290	86.8741	86.4193	.015161
63	92.4542	91.9512	91.4481	90.9451	90.4420	89.9390	89.4360	88.9329	88.4299	87.9268	87.4238	86.9207	.016768
64	93.2748	92.7717	92.2685	91.7654	91.2623	90.7592	90.2560	89.7529	89.2498	88.7467	88.2435	87.7404	.016771
65	94.5004	94.0705	93.6406	93.2107	92.7808	92.3509	91.9210	91.4911	91.0612	90.6313	90.2014	89.7715	.014330
66 or 43	**97.0874**	**97.3301**	**97.5728**	**97.8155**	**98.0583**	**98.3010**	**98.5437**	**98.7864**	**99.0291**	**99.2718**	**99.5146**	**99.7573**	**.008090**
42	95.7014	95.5837	95.4661	95.3484	95.2308	95.1131	94.9955	94.8778	94.7602	94.6425	94.5249	94.4072	.003922
41	95.0043	94.8395	94.6747	94.5099	94.3451	94.1803	94.0155	93.8507	93.6860	93.5212	93.3564	93.1916	.005493
40	94.5064	94.3337	94.1610	93.9882	93.8155	93.6428	93.4700	93.2973	93.1246	92.9519	92.7791	92.6064	.005757
39	93.8707	93.7173	93.5640	93.4106	93.2573	93.1039	92.9505	92.7972	92.6438	92.4905	92.3371	92.1838	.005112
38	93.0891	92.9555	92.8219	92.6883	92.5547	92.4211	92.2875	92.1540	92.0204	91.8868	91.7532	91.6196	.004453
37	92.2363	92.1160	91.9957	91.8754	91.7551	91.6348	91.5144	91.3941	91.2738	91.1535	91.0332	90.9129	.004010
36	91.3265	91.2180	91.1094	91.0009	90.8924	90.7839	90.6753	90.5668	90.4583	90.3498	90.2412	90.1327	.003617
35	90.3830	90.2840	90.1850	90.0860	89.9870	89.8880	89.7890	89.6899	89.5909	89.4919	89.3929	89.2939	.003300
34	89.4247	89.3333	89.2418	89.1504	89.0590	88.9676	88.8761	88.7847	88.6933	88.6019	88.5104	88.4190	.003047
33	88.4600	88.3762	88.2913	88.2065	88.1217	88.0368	87.9520	87.8662	87.7813	87.6965	87.6117	87.5268	.002828
32	87.4904	87.4117	87.3330	87.2543	87.1757	87.0970	87.0183	86.9396	86.8609	86.7822	86.7036	86.6249	.002623
31	86.5242	86.4507	86.3771	86.3036	86.2301	86.1566	86.0830	86.0095	85.9360	85.8625	85.7890	85.7154	.002451
30	85.5650	85.4961	85.4272	85.3583	85.2894	85.2204	85.1515	85.0826	85.0137	84.9448	84.8759	84.8070	.002297
29	84.6149	84.5501	84.4853	84.4204	84.3556	84.2908	84.2260	84.1612	84.0964	84.0315	83.9667	83.9019	.002160
28	83.6682	83.6078	83.5473	83.4869	83.4264	83.3660	83.3055	83.2451	83.1847	83.1242	83.0638	83.0033	.002015
27	82.7252	82.6689	82.6125	82.5562	82.4999	82.4436	82.3872	82.3309	82.2746	82.2183	82.1620	82.1056	.001877
26	81.7783	81.7265	81.6747	81.6228	81.5710	81.5192	81.4674	81.4156	81.3638	81.3120	81.2601	81.2083	.001727
25	80.8224	80.7753	80.7282	80.6811	80.6340	80.5869	80.5398	80.4927	80.4457	80.3986	80.3515	80.3044	.001570
24	79.8512	79.8092	79.7672	79.7251	79.6831	79.6411	79.5991	79.5571	79.5151	79.4730	79.4310	79.3890	.001400
23	78.8603	78.8235	78.7868	78.7500	78.7133	78.6765	78.6397	78.6030	78.5662	78.5295	78.4927	78.4560	.001225
22	77.8482	77.8167	77.7852	77.7536	77.7221	77.6906	77.6591	77.6276	77.5961	77.5645	77.5330	77.5015	.001050
21	76.8128	76.7865	76.7602	76.7340	76.7077	76.6814	76.6551	76.6288	76.6025	76.5762	76.5500	76.5237	.000876
20	75.7554	75.7341	75.7128	75.6916	75.6703	75.6490	75.6277	75.6065	75.5852	75.5639	75.5426	75.5214	.000709
19	74.6776	74.6611	74.6445	74.6280	74.6114	74.5949	74.5783	74.5618	74.4453	74.5287	74.5122	74.4956	.000551
18	73.5787	73.5668	73.5549	73.5430	73.5311	73.5192	73.5073	73.4955	73.4836	73.4717	73.4598	73.4479	.000396
17	72.4590	72.4516	72.4442	72.4368	72.4295	72.4221	72.4147	72.4073	72.3999	72.3925	72.3852	72.3778	.000246
16	71.3196	71.3165	71.3134	71.3103	71.3072	71.3041	71.3010	71.2978	71.2947	71.2916	71.2885	71.2854	.000103
15	70.1610	70.1620	70.1630	70.1640	70.1651	70.1661	70.1671	70.1681	70.1691	70.1701	70.1712	70.1722	.000034
14	68.9839	68.9888	68.9938	68.9987	69.0037	69.0086	69.0136	69.0185	69.0235	69.0284	69.0334	69.0383	.000165
13	67.7891	67.7978	67.8065	67.8152	67.8239	67.8326	67.8413	67.8501	67.8588	67.8675	67.8762	67.8849	.000290
12	66.5791	66.5913	66.6035	66.6157	66.6279	66.6401	66.6522	66.6644	66.6766	66.6888	66.7010	66.7132	.000406
11	65.3519	65.3675	65.3830	65.3986	65.4142	65.4297	65.4453	65.4609	65.4764	65.4920	65.5076	65.5231	.000519
10	64.1104	64.1292	64.1479	64.1667	64.1854	64.2042	64.2230	64.2417	64.2605	64.2792	64.2980	64.3167	.000625
Age.	0	1	2	3	4	5	6	7	8	9	10	11	Day.

Age.	0	1	2	3	4	5	6	7	8	9	10	11	Day.
10	31.9276	31.9412	31.9548	31.9685	31.9821	31.9957	32.0093	32.0230	32.0366	32.0502	32.0638	32.0775	.000454
11	32.9269	32.9411	32.9554	32.9696	32.9838	32.9981	33.0123	33.0265	33.0408	33.0550	33.0692	33.0835	.000474
12	33.9502	33.9646	33.9790	33.9934	34.0078	34.0222	34.0365	34.0509	34.0653	34.0797	34.0941	34.1085	.000480
13	34.9891	35.0037	35.0182	35.0328	35.0474	35.0619	35.0765	35.0911	35.1056	35.1202	35.1348	35.1493	.000485
14	36.0491	36.0633	36.0775	36.0917	36.1059	36.1201	36.1343	36.1486	36.1628	36.1770	36.1912	36.2054	.000473
15	37.1243	37.1384	37.1525	37.1666	37.1807	37.1948	37.2090	37.2231	37.2372	37.2513	37.2654	37.2795	.000470
16	38.2187	38.2324	38.2461	38.2598	38.2736	38.2873	38.3010	38.3147	38.3284	38.3421	38.3559	38.3696	.000457
17	39.3307	39.3438	39.3569	39.3700	39.3831	39.3962	39.4093	39.4224	39.4355	39.4486	39.4617	39.4748	.000437
18	40.4588	40.4712	40.4836	40.4961	40.5085	40.5209	40.5333	40.5458	40.5582	40.5706	40.5830	40.5955	.000414
19	41.6041	41.6153	41.6265	41.6377	41.6489	41.6601	41.6713	41.6825	41.6937	41.7049	41.7161	41.7273	.000373
20	42.7613	42.7715	42.7817	42.7920	42.8022	42.8124	42.8226	42.8329	42.8431	42.8533	42.8635	42.8738	.000341
21	43.9353	43.9441	43.9529	43.9617	43.9705	43.9793	43.9881	43.9970	44.0058	44.0146	44.0234	44.0322	.000293
22	45.1226	45.1298	45.1370	45.1442	45.1515	45.1587	45.1659	45.1731	45.1803	45.1875	45.1948	45.2020	.000240
23	46.3223	46.3278	46.3334	46.3390	46.3445	46.3500	46.3556	46.3611	46.3667	46.3722	46.3778	46.3833	.000185
24	47.5360	47.5396	47.5431	47.5467	47.5502	47.5538	47.5573	47.5609	47.5645	47.5680	47.5716	47.5751	.000118
25	48.7614	48.7627	48.7641	48.7654	48.7668	48.7681	48.7695	48.7708	48.7722	48.7735	48.7749	48.7762	.000045
26	49.9978	49.9963	49.9949	49.9934	49.9920	49.9905	49.9891	49.9876	49.9862	49.9847	49.9833	49.9818	.000048
27	51.2406	51.2360	51.2315	51.2269	51.2224	51.2178	51.2132	51.2087	51.2041	51.1996	51.1950	51.1905	.000152
28	52.4883	52.4802	52.4721	52.4640	52.4558	52.4477	52.4396	52.4315	52.4234	52.4152	52.4071	52.3990	.000270
29	53.7380	53.7260	53.7140	53.7020	53.6901	53.6781	53.6661	53.6541	53.6421	53.6301	53.6182	53.6062	.000399
30	54.9893	54.9730	54.9566	54.9403	54.9240	54.9076	54.8913	54.8750	54.8586	54.8423	54.8260	54.8096	.000544
31	56.2364	56.2153	56.1942	56.1731	56.1520	56.1309	56.1098	56.0888	56.0677	56.0466	56.0255	56.0044	.000703
32	57.4801	57.4538	57.4276	57.4013	57.3750	57.3488	57.3225	57.2962	57.2700	57.2437	57.2174	57.1912	.000875
33	58.7172	58.6852	58.6533	58.6214	58.5895	58.5576	58.5256	58.4937	58.4618	58.4299	58.3980	58.3660	.001064
34	59.9451	59.9072	59.8692	59.8313	59.7934	59.7554	59.7175	59.6796	59.6416	59.6037	59.5658	59.5278	.001264
35	61.1629	61.1187	61.0745	61.0302	60.9860	60.9418	60.8976	60.8534	60.8092	60.7650	60.7207	60.6765	.001474
36	62.3697	62.3209	62.2721	62.2233	62.1745	62.1257	62.0768	62.0280	61.9792	61.9304	61.8816	61.8328	.001627
37	63.5644	63.5062	63.4480	63.3898	63.3316	63.2734	63.2152	63.1570	63.0988	63.0406	62.9824	62.9242	.001940
38	64.7454	64.6796	64.6137	64.5479	64.4821	64.4162	64.3504	64.2846	64.2187	64.1529	64.0871	64.0212	.002194
39	65.9120	65.8381	65.7642	65.6904	65.6165	65.5426	65.4687	65.3949	65.3210	65.2471	65.1732	65.0994	.002462
40	67.0635	66.9810	66.8986	66.8161	66.7337	66.6512	66.5688	66.4863	66.4039	66.3214	66.2390	66.1565	.002748
41	68.1985	68.1070	68.0155	67.9240	67.8325	67.7410	67.6495	67.5581	67.4666	67.3751	67.2836	67.1921	.003050
42	69.3169	69.2160	69.1150	69.0140	68.9131	68.8121	68.7112	68.6102	68.5093	68.4083	68.3074	68.2064	.003365
43	70.4205	70.3094	70.1983	70.0872	69.9761	69.8650	69.7539	69.6428	69.5317	69.4206	69.3095	69.1984	.003703
44	71.5074	71.3855	71.2636	71.1417	71.0198	70.8979	70.7760	70.6542	70.5323	70.4104	70.2885	70.1666	.004063
45	72.5796	72.4465	72.3135	72.1804	72.0474	71.9143	71.7813	71.6482	71.5152	71.3821	71.2491	71.1160	.004435
46	73.6402	73.4956	73.3509	73.2063	73.0617	72.9170	72.7724	72.6278	72.4831	72.3385	72.1939	72.0492	.004821
47	74.6931	74.5368	74.3805	74.2242	74.0679	73.9116	73.7553	73.5991	73.4428	73.2865	73.1302	72.9739	.005210
48	75.7449	75.5770	75.4091	75.2412	75.0733	74.9054	74.7375	74.5697	74.4018	74.2339	74.0660	73.8981	.005596
49	76.8069	76.6273	76.4478	76.2682	76.0886	75.9091	75.7295	75.5499	75.3704	75.1908	75.0112	74.8317	.005985
50	77.8858	77.6947	77.5036	77.3125	77.1215	76.9304	76.7393	76.5482	76.3571	76.1660	75.9750	75.7839	.006369
51	79.0523	78.8441	78.6359	78.4277	78.2196	78.0114	77.8032	77.5950	77.3868	77.1786	76.9705	76.7623	.006939
52	80.1358	79.9201	79.7043	79.4886	79.2728	79.0571	78.8413	78.6256	78.4099	78.1941	77.9784	77.7626	.007191
53	81.3202	81.0909	80.8615	80.6322	80.4029	80.1736	79.9442	79.7149	79.4856	79.2563	79.0270	78.7976	.007644
54	82.5475	82.3033	82.0591	81.8148	81.5706	81.3264	81.0822	80.8380	80.5938	80.3495	80.1053	79.8611	.008140
55	83.8145	83.5533	83.2921	83.0309	82.7697	82.5085	82.2472	81.9860	81.7248	81.4636	81.2024	80.9412	.008707
56	85.1114	84.8319	84.5524	84.2729	83.9934	83.7139	83.4344	83.1549	82.8754	82.5959	82.3164	82.0369	.009317
57	86.4382	86.1381	85.8380	85.5380	85.2379	84.9378	84.6377	84.3376	84.0375	83.7374	83.4374	83.1373	.010003
58	87.8243	87.4964	87.1684	86.8405	86.5126	86.1846	85.8567	85.5288	85.2008	84.8729	84.5450	84.2170	.010931
59	89.1183	88.7646	88.4110	88.0573	87.7036	87.3500	86.9963	86.6426	86.2890	85.9353	85.5816	85.2280	.011789
60	90.4032	90.0168	89.6304	89.2440	88.8576	88.4712	88.0848	87.6985	87.3121	86.9257	86.5393	86.1529	.012880
61	91.6131	91.1818	90.7504	90.3191	89.8877	89.4564	89.0250	88.5937	88.1624	87.7310	87.2997	86.8683	.014378
62	92.6145	92.1372	91.6600	91.1827	90.7055	90.2282	89.7510	89.2737	88.7965	88.3192	87.8420	87.3647	.015908
63	93.4102	92.9336	92.4570	91.9803	91.5037	91.0271	90.5504	90.0738	89.5972	89.1206	88.6440	88.1673	.015887
64	94.5947	94.1893	93.7839	93.3785	92.9731	92.5677	92.1623	91.7570	91.3516	90.9462	90.5408	90.1354	.013513
65 or 44	**97.0874**	**97.3301**	**97.5728**	**97.8155**	**98.0583**	**98.3010**	**98.5437**	**98.7864**	**99.0291**	**99.2718**	**99.5146**	**99.7573**	**.008090**
43	95.6758	95.5515	95.4272	95.3029	95.1786	95.0543	94.9300	94.8058	94.6815	94.5572	94.4329	94.3086	.004143
42	94.9675	94.7955	94.6235	94.4515	94.2795	94.1075	93.9355	93.7636	93.5916	93.4196	93.2476	93.0756	.005733
41	94.4627	94.2830	94.1032	93.9234	93.7437	93.5640	93.3842	93.2044	93.0247	92.8450	92.6652	92.4854	.005992
40	93.8185	93.6587	93.4990	93.3392	93.1794	93.0196	92.8598	92.7001	92.5403	92.3805	92.2207	92.0610	.005326
39	93.0269	92.8874	92.7480	92.6085	92.4691	92.3296	92.1902	92.0507	91.9113	91.7718	91.6324	91.4930	.004648
38	92.1640	92.0383	91.9125	91.7868	91.6610	91.5353	91.4095	91.2838	91.1581	91.0323	90.9066	90.7808	.004191
37	91.2439	91.1303	91.0167	90.9032	90.7896	90.6760	90.5624	90.4489	90.3353	90.2217	90.1081	89.9946	.003786
36	90.2904	90.1867	90.0830	89.9792	89.8755	89.7718	89.6680	89.5643	89.4606	89.3569	89.2531	89.1494	.003457
35	89.3231	89.2272	89.1314	89.0355	88.9397	88.8438	88.7480	88.6521	88.5563	88.4604	88.3646	88.2687	.003195
34	88.3495	88.2605	88.1715	88.0825	87.9935	87.9045	87.8155	87.7266	87.6376	87.5486	87.4596	87.3706	.002966
33	87.3723	87.2897	87.2070	87.1244	87.0417	86.9591	86.8764	86.7938	86.7112	86.6285	86.5459	86.4632	.002755
32	86.3990	86.3217	86.2444	86.1672	86.0899	86.0126	85.9353	85.8581	85.7808	85.7035	85.6262	85.5490	.002576
31	85.4330	85.3605	85.2880	85.2156	85.1431	85.0706	84.9981	84.9257	84.8532	84.7807	84.7082	84.6358	.002416
30	84.4776	84.4094	84.3412	84.2730	84.2048	84.1366	84.0684	84.0003	83.9321	83.8639	83.7957	83.7275	.002273
29	83.5266	83.4628	83.3991	83.3353	83.2716	83.2078	83.1441	83.0803	83.0166	82.9528	82.8891	82.8253	.002125
28	82.5779	82.5185	82.4592	82.3998	82.3405	82.2811	82.2218	82.1624	82.1031	82.0437	81.9844	81.9250	.001978
27	81.6268	81.5721	81.5173	81.4626	81.4079	81.3531	81.2984	81.2437	81.1889	81.1342	81.0795	81.0247	.001824
26	80.6671	80.6172	80.5674	80.5175	80.4677	80.4178	80.3680	80.3181	80.2682	80.2184	80.1685	80.1187	.001662
25	79.6924	79.6477	79.6031	79.5584	79.5138	79.4691	79.4245	79.3798	79.3352	79.2905	79.2459	79.2012	.001488
24	78.6982	78.6590	78.6197	78.5805	78.5412	78.5020	78.4627	78.4235	78.3843	78.3450	78.3058	78.2665	.001308
23	77.6828	77.6489	77.6150	77.5812	77.5473	77.5134	77.4795	77.4457	77.4118	77.3779	77.3440	77.3102	.001129
22	76.6447	76.6162	76.5877	76.5592	76.5307	76.5022	76.4736	76.4451	76.4166	76.3881	76.3596	76.3311	.000950
21	75.5845	75.5611	75.5377	75.5143	75.4910	75.4676	75.4442	75.4208	75.3974	75.3740	75.3507	75.3273	.000779
20	74.5041	74.4856	74.4670	74.4485	74.4299	74.4114	74.3928	74.3743	74.3558	74.3372	74.3187	74.3001	.000618
19	73.4029	73.3891	73.3753	73.3615	73.3477	73.3339	73.3201	73.3064	73.2926	73.2788	73.2650	73.2512	.000460
18	72.2812	72.2720	72.2628	72.2536	72.2444	72.2352	72.2260	72.2168	72.2076	72.1984	72.1892	72.1800	.000307
17	71.1400	71.1352	71.1303	71.1255	71.1207	71.1159	71.1110	71.1062	71.1014	71.0966	71.0917	71.0869	.000161
16	69.9798	69.9792	69.9786	69.9780	69.9774	69.9768	69.9761	69.9755	69.9749	69.9743	69.9737	69.9731	.000020
15	68.8014	68.8048	68.8082	68.8116	68.8150	68.8184	68.8218	68.8253	68.8287	68.8321	68.8355	68.8389	.000113
14	67.6055	67.6127	67.6200	67.6272	67.6345	67.6417	67.6490	67.6562	67.6635	67.6707	67.6780	67.6852	.000242
13	66.3943	66.4051	66.4159	66.4267	66.4375	66.4483	66.4591	66.4699	66.4807	66.4915	66.5023	66.5131	.000360
12	65.1681	65.1823	65.1966	65.2108	65.2251	65.2393	65.2535	65.2678	65.2820	65.2963	65.3105	65.3248	.000475
11	63.9256	63.9431	63.9606	63.9781	63.9957	64.0132	64.0307	64.0482	64.0657	64.0832	64.1008	64.1183	.000584
10	62.6716	62.6921	62.7125	62.7330	62.7535	62.7739	62.7944	62.8149	62.8353	62.8558	62.8763	62.8967	.000682
Age.	0	1	2	3	4	5	6	7	8	9	10	11	Day.

Age.	0	1	2	3	4	5	6	7	8	9	10	11	Day.
10	33.2843	33.2998	33.3153	33.3308	33.3463	33.3618	33.3773	33.3928	33.4083	33.4238	33.4393	33.4548	.000517
11	34.3139	34.3296	34.3453	34.3610	34.3767	34.3924	34.4081	34.4238	34.4395	34.4552	34.4709	34.4866	.000523
12	35.3630	35.3789	35.3949	35.4108	35.4267	35.4427	35.4586	35.4745	35.4905	35.5064	35.5223	35.5383	.000531
13	36.4291	36.4447	36.4604	36.4760	36.4916	36.5073	36.5229	36.5385	36.5542	36.5698	36.5854	36.6011	.000521
14	37.5111	37.5267	37.5422	37.5578	37.5734	37.5890	37.6045	37.6201	37.6357	37.6513	37.6668	37.6824	.000519
15	38.6123	38.6275	38.6428	38.6580	38.6733	38.6885	38.7038	38.7190	38.7343	38.7495	38.7648	38.7800	.000508
16	39.7305	39.7452	39.7599	39.7746	39.7893	39.8040	39.8186	39.8333	39.8480	39.8627	39.8774	39.8921	.000490
17	40.8648	40.8789	40.8930	40.9070	40.9211	40.9352	40.9492	40.9633	40.9774	40.9915	41.0055	41.0196	.000469
18	42.0158	42.0287	42.0416	42.0545	42.0675	42.0804	42.0933	42.1062	42.1191	42.1320	42.1450	42.1579	.000430
19	43.1786	43.1906	43.2026	43.2146	43.2266	43.2386	43.2506	43.2627	43.2747	43.2867	43.2987	43.3107	.000400
20	44.3578	44.3685	44.3792	44.3898	44.4005	44.4112	44.4218	44.4325	44.4432	44.4538	44.4645	44.4752	.000353
21	45.5500	45.5592	45.5683	45.5775	45.5866	45.5958	45.6050	45.6141	45.6233	45.6324	45.6416	45.6507	.000305
22	46.7548	46.7624	46.7700	46.7775	46.7851	46.7927	46.8002	46.8078	46.8154	46.8230	46.8305	46.8381	.000252
23	47.9729	47.9786	47.9843	47.9899	47.9956	48.0013	48.0069	48.0126	48.0183	48.0239	48.0296	48.0353	.000187
24	49.2027	49.2062	49.2098	49.2133	49.2169	49.2204	49.2240	49.2275	49.2311	49.2346	49.2382	49.2417	.000118
25	50.4433	50.4442	50.4450	50.4459	50.4467	50.4476	50.4484	50.4493	50.4502	50.4510	50.4519	50.4527	.000028
26	51.6899	51.6878	51.6856	51.6835	51.6813	51.6792	51.6770	51.6749	51.6728	51.6706	51.6685	51.6663	.000071
27	52.9412	52.9356	52.9301	52.9245	52.9189	52.9134	52.9078	52.9022	52.8967	52.8911	52.8855	52.8800	.000185
28	54.1940	54.1847	54.1754	54.1661	54.1568	54.1475	54.1382	54.1289	54.1196	54.1103	54.1010	54.0917	.000310
29	55.4475	55.4340	55.4205	55.4070	55.3934	55.3799	55.3664	55.3529	55.3394	55.3258	55.3123	55.2988	.000450
30	56.6990	56.6809	56.6628	56.6447	56.6266	56.6085	56.5903	56.5722	56.5541	56.5360	56.5179	56.4998	.000603
31	57.9442	57.9211	57.8980	57.8749	57.8518	57.8287	57.8055	57.7824	57.7593	57.7362	57.7131	57.6900	.000770
32	59.1836	59.1550	59.1264	59.0978	59.0692	59.0406	59.0120	58.9835	58.9549	58.9263	58.8977	58.8691	.000953
33	60.4134	60.3790	60.3446	60.3102	60.2758	60.2414	60.2070	60.1726	60.1382	60.1038	60.0694	60.0350	.001147
34	61.6330	61.5925	61.5521	61.5116	61.4711	61.4307	61.3902	61.3497	61.3093	61.2688	61.2283	61.1879	.001349
35	62.8424	62.7953	62.7484	62.7014	62.6544	62.6074	62.5603	62.5133	62.4663	62.4193	62.3723	62.3253	.001567
36	64.0648	64.0087	63.9525	63.8964	63.8403	63.7841	63.7280	63.6719	63.6157	63.5596	63.5035	63.4473	.001871
37	65.2213	65.1600	65.0987	65.0374	64.9762	64.9149	64.8536	64.7923	64.7310	64.6697	64.6085	64.5472	.002043
38	66.3894	66.3204	66.2513	66.1823	66.1133	66.0443	65.9752	65.9062	65.8372	65.7682	65.6991	65.6301	.002301
39	67.5426	67.4653	67.3881	67.3108	67.2336	67.1563	67.0790	67.0018	66.9245	66.8473	66.7700	66.6928	.002575
40	68.6793	68.5934	68.5074	68.4215	68.3356	68.2497	68.1637	68.0778	67.9919	67.9060	67.8200	67.7341	.002864
41	69.7992	69.7042	69.6092	69.5142	69.4193	69.3243	69.2293	69.1343	69.0393	68.9443	68.8494	68.7544	.003166
42	70.9033	70.7986	70.6939	70.5892	70.4845	70.3798	70.2751	70.1704	70.0657	69.9610	69.8563	69.7516	.003490
43	71.9904	71.8754	71.7604	71.6453	71.5303	71.4153	71.3003	71.1853	71.0703	70.9552	70.8402	70.7252	.003834
44	73.0596	72.9339	72.8082	72.6825	72.5568	72.4311	72.3054	72.1798	72.0541	71.9284	71.8027	71.6770	.004190
45	74.1164	73.9796	73.8429	73.7061	73.5693	73.4326	73.2958	73.1590	73.0223	72.8855	72.7487	72.6120	.004559
46	75.1633	75.0154	74.8675	74.7195	74.5716	74.4237	74.2758	74.1279	73.9800	73.8320	73.6841	73.5362	.004930
47	76.2086	76.0496	75.8907	75.7317	75.5727	75.4138	75.2548	75.0958	74.9369	74.7779	74.6189	74.4600	.005299
48	77.2613	77.0912	76.9211	76.7510	76.5809	76.4108	76.2407	76.0706	75.9005	75.7304	75.5603	75.3902	.005670
49	78.3309	78.1499	77.9688	77.7878	77.6068	77.4258	77.2447	77.0637	76.8827	76.7017	76.5206	76.3396	.006034
50	79.4280	79.2353	79.0426	78.8499	78.6572	78.4645	78.2718	78.0791	77.8864	77.6937	77.5010	77.3083	.006423
51	80.5549	80.3505	80.1461	79.9417	79.7373	79.5329	79.3285	79.1241	78.9197	78.7153	78.5109	78.3065	.006813
52	81.7229	81.5056	81.2884	81.0711	80.8539	80.6366	80.4193	80.2021	79.9848	79.7676	79.5503	79.3331	.007242
53	82.9301	82.6987	82.4673	82.2359	82.0045	81.7731	81.5417	81.3103	81.0789	80.8475	80.6161	80.3847	.007713
54	84.1754	83.9279	83.6804	83.4329	83.1854	82.9379	82.6903	82.4428	82.1953	81.9478	81.7003	81.4528	.008250
55	85.4473	85.1824	84.9176	84.6527	84.3879	84.1230	83.8581	83.5933	83.3284	83.0636	82.7987	82.5339	.008828
56	86.7463	86.4619	86.1775	85.8931	85.6088	85.3244	85.0400	84.7556	84.4712	84.1868	83.9025	83.6181	.009479
57	88.0615	87.7539	87.4463	87.1387	86.8311	86.5235	86.2159	85.9083	85.6007	85.2931	84.9855	84.6779	.010253
58	89.3639	89.0286	88.6933	88.3580	88.0227	87.6874	87.3521	87.0169	86.6816	86.3463	86.0110	85.6757	.011176
59	90.6157	90.2493	89.8829	89.5165	89.1501	88.7837	88.4173	88.0510	87.6846	87.3182	86.9518	86.5854	.012213
60	91.7922	91.3829	90.9736	90.5643	90.1551	89.7458	89.3365	88.9272	88.5179	88.1086	87.6994	87.2901	.013643
61	92 7650	92.3120	91.8590	91.4060	90.9530	90.5000	90.0470	89.5939	89.1409	88.6879	88.2349	87.7819	.015100
62	93.5374	93.0857	92.6339	92.1822	91.7304	91.2787	90.8270	90.3752	89.9235	89.4717	89.0200	88.5682	.015058
63	94.6832	94.3008	93.9185	93 5361	93.1537	92.7714	92.3890	92.0066	91.6243	91.2419	90.8595	90.4772	.012745
64 or 45	**97.0874**	**97.3301**	**97.5728**	**97.8155**	**98.0583**	**98.3010**	**98.5437**	**98.7864**	**99.0291**	**99.2718**	**99.5146**	**99.7573**	**.008090**
44	95.6486	95.5172	95.3859	95.2545	95.1232	94.9918	94.8605	94.7291	94.5978	94.4664	94.3351	94.2037	.004378
43	94.9284	94.7488	94.5691	94.3895	94.2098	94.0302	93.8505	93.6709	93.4913	93.3116	93.1320	92.9523	.005988
42	94.4163	94.2291	94.0419	93.8546	93.6674	93.4802	93.2930	93.1058	92.9186	92.7313	92.5441	92.3569	.006240
41	93.7632	93.5966	93.4300	93.2634	93.0968	92.9302	92.7636	92.5971	92.4305	92.2639	92.0973	91.9307	.005553
40	92.9611	92.8154	92.6698	92.5241	92.3785	92.2328	92.0872	91.9415	91.7959	91.6502	91.5046	91.3590	.004855
39	92.0874	91.9559	91.8245	91.6930	91.5615	91.4301	91.2986	91.1671	91.0357	90.9042	90.7727	90.6413	.004382
38	91.1566	91.0377	90.9188	90.8000	90.6811	90.5622	90.4433	90.3244	90.2055	90.0866	89.9678	89.8489	.003963
37	90.1930	90.0843	89.9756	89.8669	89.7582	89.6495	89.5408	89.4321	89.3234	89.2147	89.1060	88.9973	.003623
36	89.2159	89.1154	89.0148	88.9143	88.8138	88.7133	88.6127	88.5122	88.4117	88.3112	88.2106	88.1101	.003351
35	88.2356	88.1420	88.0485	87.9550	87.8614	87.7678	87.6743	87.5807	87.4872	87.3936	87.3001	87.2065	.003118
34	87.2483	87.1615	87.0746	86.9878	86.9010	86.8142	86.7273	86.6405	86.5537	86.4669	86.3800	86.2932	.002894
33	86.2675	86.1863	86.1051	86.0239	85.9427	85.8615	85.7802	85.6990	85.6178	85.5366	85.4554	85.3742	.002707
32	85.2949	85.2187	85.1425	85.0662	84.9900	84.9138	84.8376	84.7614	84.6852	84.6090	84.5327	84.4565	.002540
31	84.3332	84.2614	84.1897	84.1180	84.0462	83.9744	83.9027	83.8310	83.7592	83.6874	83.6157	83.5440	.002392
30	83.3764	83.3094	83.2423	83.1753	83.1083	83.0412	82.9742	82.9072	82.8401	82.7731	82.7061	82.6390	.002234
29	82.4237	82.3612	82.2986	82.2361	82.1736	82.1110	82.0485	81.9860	81.9234	81.8609	81.7984	81.7358	.002084
28	81.4682	81.4104	81.3526	81.2948	81.2371	81.1793	81.1215	81.0637	81.0059	80.9481	80.8904	80.8326	.001926
27	80.5046	80.4518	80.3991	80.3463	80.2936	80.2408	80.1880	80.1353	80.0825	80.0298	79.9770	79.9243	.001758
26	79.5263	79.4789	79.4315	79.3841	79.3367	79.2893	79.2419	79.1945	79.1471	79.0997	79.0523	79.0049	.001580
25	78.5287	78.4869	78.4450	78.4032	78.3613	78.3195	78.2776	78.2358	78.1940	78.1521	78.1103	78.0684	.001395
24	77.5102	77.4739	77.4375	77.4012	77.3649	77.3285	77.2922	77.2559	77.2195	77.1832	77.1469	77.1105	.001211
23	76.4690	76.4381	76.4073	76.3764	76.3456	76.3147	76.2839	76.2530	76.2222	76.1913	76.1605	76.1296	.001028
22	75.4062	75.3806	75.3550	75.3294	75.3038	75.2782	75.2526	75.2270	75.2014	75.1758	75.1502	75.1246	.000853
21	74.3231	74.3025	74.2818	74.2612	74.2406	74.2199	74.1993	74.1787	74.1580	74.1374	74.1168	74.0961	.000688
20	73.2196	73.2038	73.1880	73.1722	73.1565	73.1407	73.1249	73.1091	73.0933	73.0775	73.0618	73.0460	.000526
19	72.0957	72.0846	72.0735	72.0625	72.0514	72.0403	72.0292	72.0182	72.0071	71.9960	71.9850	71.9739	.000369
18	70.9526	70.9460	70.9395	70.9329	70.9263	70.9198	70.9132	70.9066	70.9001	70.8935	70.8869	70.8804	.000219
17	69.7908	69.7885	69.7862	69.7839	69.7816	69.7793	69.7770	69.7747	69.7724	69.7701	69.7678	69.7655	.000077
16	68.6110	68.6128	68.6146	68.6164	68.6182	68.6200	68.6218	68.6236	68.6254	68.6272	68.6290	68.6308	.000060
15	67.4142	67.4199	67.4256	67.4313	67.4370	67.4427	67.4484	67.4542	67.4599	67.4656	67.4713	67.4770	.000190
14	66.2020	66.2113	66.2207	66.2300	66.2394	66.2487	66.2580	66.2674	66.2767	66.2861	66.2954	66.3048	.000311
13	64.9748	64.9877	65.0005	65.0134	65.0262	65.0391	65.0520	65.0648	65.0777	65.0905	65.1034	65.1162	.000428
12	63.7335	63.7497	63.7659	63.7821	63.7983	63.8145	63.8307	63.8470	63.8632	63.8794	63.8956	63.9118	.000540
11	62.4788	62.4980	62.5172	62.5365	62.5557	62.5749	62.5941	62.6134	62.6326	62.6518	62.6710	62.6903	.000641
10	61.2148	61.2368	61.2587	61.2807	61.3027	61.3246	61.3466	61.3686	61.3905	61.4125	61.4345	61.4564	.000732
Age.	0	1	2	3	4	5	6	7	8	9	10	11	Day.

Age.	0	1	2	3	4	5	6	7	8	9	10	11	Day.
10	34.6635	34.6805	34.6974	34.7144	34.7314	34.7483	34.7653	34.7823	34.7992	34.8162	34.8332	34.8501	.000565
11	35.7185	35.7357	35.7530	35.7702	35.7875	35.8047	35.8220	35.8392	35.8564	35.8737	35.8909	35.9082	.000575
12	36.7943	36.8113	36.8283	36.8453	36.8623	36.8793	36.8963	36.9133	36.9303	36.9473	36.9643	36.9813	.000567
13	37.8820	37.8990	37.9160	37.9330	37.9500	37.9670	37.9840	38.0009	38.0179	38.0349	38.0519	38.0689	.000566
14	38.9894	39.0061	39.0228	39.0395	39.0563	39.0730	39.0897	39.1064	39.1231	39.1398	39.1566	39.1733	.000557
15	40.1140	40.1302	40.1464	40.1626	40.1789	40.1951	40.2113	40.2275	40.2437	40.2600	40.2762	40.2924	.000540
16	41.2540	41.2697	41.2853	41.3010	41.3166	41.3323	41.3480	41.3636	41.3793	41.3949	41.4106	41.4262	.000522
17	42.4146	42.4288	42.4431	42.4573	42.4715	42.4858	42.5000	42.5142	42.5285	42.5427	42.5569	42.5712	.000474
18	43.5786	43.5923	43.6060	43.6198	43.6335	43.6472	43.6610	43.6747	43.6884	43.7021	43.7158	43.7296	.000457
19	44.7629	44.7753	44.7878	44.8002	44.8127	44.8251	44.8376	44.8500	44.8625	44.8750	44.8874	44.8998	.000415
20	45.9596	45.9706	45.9816	45.9926	46.0037	46.0147	46.0257	46.0367	46.0477	46.0587	46.0698	46.0808	.000367
21	47.1688	47.1783	47.1878	47.1973	47.2068	47.2163	47.2258	47.2354	47.2449	47.2544	47.2639	47.2734	.000317
22	48.3913	48.3990	48.4067	48.4144	48.4221	48.4298	48.4374	48.4451	48.4528	48.4605	48.4682	48.4759	.000256
23	49.6249	49.6306	49.6362	49.6419	49.6475	49.6532	49.6588	49.6645	49.6702	49.6758	49.6815	49.6871	.000188
24	50.8693	50.8724	50.8754	50.8785	50.8815	50.8846	50.8876	50.8907	50.8938	50.8968	50.8999	50.9029	.000102
25	52.1194	52.1196	52.1197	52.1199	52.1201	52.1203	52.1204	52.1206	52.1208	52.1210	52.1211	52.1213	.000006
26	53.3737	53.3706	53.3674	53.3643	53.3612	53.3580	53.3549	53.3518	53.3486	53.3455	53.3424	53.3392	.000104
27	54.6296	54.6228	54.6161	54.6093	54.6026	54.5958	54.5891	54.5823	54.5756	54.5688	54.5621	54.5553	.000225
28	55.8855	55.8747	55.8638	55.8530	55.8422	55.8314	55.8205	55.8097	55.7989	55.7881	55.7772	55.7664	.000361
29	57.1386	57.1233	57.1080	57.0928	57.0775	57.0622	57.0470	57.0317	57.0164	57.0011	56.9858	56.9706	.000509
30	58.3874	58.3673	58.3472	58.3271	58.3070	58.2869	58.2668	58.2467	58.2266	58.2065	58.1864	58.1663	.000670
31	59.6277	59.6023	59.5769	59.5515	59.5261	59.5007	59.4752	59.4498	59.4244	59.3990	59.3736	59.3482	.000847
32	60.8591	60.8281	60.7970	60.7660	60.7350	60.7040	60.6730	60.6419	60.6109	60.5799	60.5488	60.5178	.001034
33	62.0800	62.0431	62.0062	61.9693	61.9324	61.8955	61.8586	61.8218	61.7849	61.7480	61.7111	61.6742	.001230
34	63.2905	63.2473	63.2041	63.1608	63.1176	63.0744	63.0312	62.9880	62.9448	62.9015	62.8583	62.8151	.001440
35	64.4884	64.4385	64.3886	64.3387	64.2888	64.2389	64.1890	64.1391	64.0892	64.0393	63.9894	63.9395	.001663
36	65.6720	65.6150	65.5580	65.5010	65.4440	65.3870	65.3300	65.2731	65.2161	65.1591	65.1021	65.0451	.001900
37	66.8412	66.7768	66.7123	66.6479	66.5834	66.5190	66.4545	66.3901	66.3257	66.2612	66.1968	66.1323	.002148
38	67.9951	67.9227	67.8504	67.7780	67.7057	67.6333	67.5610	67.4886	67.4162	67.3439	67.2715	67 1992	.002412
39	69.1326	69.0519	68.9712	68.8906	68.8099	68.7292	68.6485	68.5679	68.4872	68.4065	68.3258	68.2452	.002689
40	70.2534	70.1640	70.0747	69.9853	69.8960	69.8066	69.7172	69.6279	69.5385	69.4492	69.3598	69.2705	.002978
41	71.3581	71.2594	71.1607	71.0621	70.9634	70.8647	70.7661	70.6674	70.5687	70.4701	70.3714	70.2727	.003287
42	72.4447	72.3362	72.2276	72.1191	72.0106	71.9020	71.7935	71.6850	71.5764	71.4679	71.3594	71.2508	.003618
43	73.5133	73.3946	73.2758	73.1571	73.0383	72.9196	72.8008	72.6821	72.5634	72.4446	72.3259	72.2071	.003958
44	74.5663	74.4369	74.3076	74.1783	74.0489	73.9196	73.7903	73.6609	73.5316	73.4023	73.2729	73.1436	.004310
45	75.5086	75.3686	75.2286	75.0886	74.9486	74.8086	74.6686	74.6287	74.4887	74.3487	74.2087	74.0687	.004666
46	76.6470	76.4965	76.3459	76.1954	76.0449	75.8943	75.7438	75.5933	75.4427	75.2922	75.1417	74.9911	.005018
47	77.6921	77.5310	77.3698	77.2087	77.0476	76.8864	76.7253	76.5642	76.4030	76.2419	76.0808	75.9196	.005371
48	78.7512	78.5797	78.4081	78.2366	78.0651	77.8935	77.7220	77.5505	77.3789	77.2074	77.0359	76.8643	.005718
49	79.8374	79.6548	79.4722	79.2896	79.1070	78.9244	78.7417	78.5591	78.3765	78.1939	78.0113	77.8287	.006087
50	80.9508	80.7571	80.5634	80.3697	80.1760	79.9823	79.7886	79.5950	79.4013	79.2076	79.0139	78.8202	.006456
51	82.1028	81.8969	81.6910	81.4851	81.2792	81.0733	80.8674	80.6616	80.4557	80.2498	80.0439	79.8380	.006863
52	83.2918	83.0725	82.8532	82.6339	82.4146	82.1953	81.9760	81.7568	81.5375	81.3182	81.0989	80.8796	.007310
53	84.5152	84.2806	84.0460	83.8114	83.5768	83.3422	83.1075	82.8729	82.6383	82.4037	82.1691	81.9345	.007820
54	85.7638	85.5127	85.2617	85.0106	84.7596	84.5085	84.2574	84.0064	83.7553	83.5043	83.2532	83.0022	.008368
55	87.0363	86.7667	86.4971	86.2275	85.9579	85.6883	85.4187	85.1491	84.8795	84.6099	84.3403	84.0707	.008987
56	88.3226	88.0309	87.7392	87.4475	87.1559	86.8642	86.5725	86.2808	85.9891	85.6974	85.4058	85.1141	.009723
57	89.5946	89.2766	88.9585	88.6405	88.3225	88.0044	87.6864	87.3684	87.0503	86.7323	86.4143	86.0962	.010601
58	90.8152	90.4676	90.1200	89.7723	89.4247	89.0771	88.7294	88.3818	88.0342	87.6866	87.3390	86.9913	.011587
59	91.9605	91.5720	91.1834	90.7948	90.4063	90.0177	89.6292	89.2406	88.8521	88.4635	88.0750	87.6864	.012952
60	92.9065	92.4762	92.0460	91.6157	91.1855	90.7552	90.3250	89.8947	89.4645	89.0342	88.6040	88.1737	.014342
61	93.6569	93.2285	92.8002	92.3718	91.9434	91.5151	91.0867	90.6583	90.2300	89.8016	89.3732	88.9449	.014279
62	94.7664	94.4057	94.0449	93.6842	93.3234	92.9627	92.6020	92.2412	91.8805	91.5197	91.1590	90.7982	.012025
63 or 46	**97.0874**	**97.3301**	**97.5728**	**97.8155**	**98.0583**	**98.3010**	**98.5437**	**98.7864**	**99.0291**	**99.2718**	**99.5146**	**99.7573**	**.008090**
45	95.6199	95.4811	95.3422	95.2034	95.0645	94.9257	94.7868	94.6480	94.5092	94.3703	94.2315	94.0926	.004628
44	94.8868	94.6990	94.5112	94.3235	94.1358	93.9480	93.7602	93.5725	93.3847	93.1970	93.0092	92.8215	.006258
43	94.3671	94.1720	93.9768	93.7816	93.5865	93.3913	93.1962	93.0010	92.8059	92.6107	92.4156	92.2204	.006505
42	93.7044	93.5306	93.3567	93.1829	93.0091	92.8353	92.6614	92.4876	92.3138	92.1400	91.9661	91.7923	.005794
41	92.8913	92.7391	92.5868	92.4346	92.2824	92.1302	91.9780	91.8257	91.6735	91.5213	91.3690	91.2168	.005074
40	92.0066	91.8690	91.7315	91.5939	91.4564	91.3188	91.1812	91.0437	90.9061	90.7686	90.6310	90.4935	.004585
39	91.0644	90.9399	90.8154	90.6908	90.5663	90.4418	90.3173	90.1928	90.0683	89.9437	89.8192	89.6947	.004150
38	90.0898	89.9759	89.8619	89.7480	89.6341	89.5201	89.4062	89.2923	89.1783	89.0644	88.9505	88.8365	.003798
37	89.1030	88.9975	88.8921	88.7866	88.6812	88.5757	88.4703	88.3648	88.2594	88.1540	88.0485	87.9430	.003515
36	88.1117	88.0136	87.9156	87.8175	87.7195	87.6214	87.5234	87.4253	87.3273	87.2292	87.1312	87.0331	.003268
35	87.1178	87.0268	86.9357	86.8447	86.7537	86.6626	86.5716	86.4806	86.3895	86.2985	86.2075	86.1164	.003034
34	86.1293	86.0440	85.9586	85.8733	85.7879	85.7026	85.6172	85.5319	85.4466	85.3612	85.2759	85.1905	.002845
33	85.1498	85.0697	84.9895	84.9094	84.8292	84.7491	84.6690	84.5888	84.5087	84.4285	84.3484	84.2682	.002671
32	84.1820	84.1065	84.0310	83.9555	83.8801	83.8046	83.7291	83.6536	83.5781	83.5026	83.4272	83.3517	.002516
31	83.2193	83.1487	83.0781	83.0075	82.9370	82.8664	82.7958	82.7252	82.6546	82.5840	82.5135	82.4429	.002353
30	82.2623	82.1963	82.1304	82.0644	81.9984	81.9325	81.8665	81.8005	81.7346	81.6686	81.6026	81.5367	.002199
29	81.2548	81.1978	81.1407	81.0837	81.0267	80.9696	80.9126	80.8556	80.7985	80.7415	80.6845	80.6274	.001901
28	80.3345	80.2787	80.2229	80.1671	80.1113	80.0555	79.9997	79.9440	79.8882	79.8324	79.7766	79.7208	.001860
27	79.3525	79.3022	79.2520	79.2017	79.1514	79.1012	79.0509	79.0006	78.9504	78.9001	78.8498	78.7996	.001675
26	78.3515	78.3069	78.2624	78.2178	78.1733	78.1287	78.0841	78.0396	77.9950	77.9505	77.9059	77.8614	.001485
25	77.3298	77.2909	77.2520	77.2131	77.1742	77.1353	77.0963	77.0574	77.0185	76.9796	76.9407	76.9018	.001297
24	76.2856	76.2523	76.2190	76.1857	76.1525	76.1192	76.0859	76.0526	76.0193	75.9860	75.9528	75.9195	.001109
23	75.2199	75.1920	75.1641	75.1362	75.1083	75.0804	75.0524	75.0245	74.9966	74.9687	74.9408	74.9129	.000930
22	74.1343	74.1115	74.0887	74.0658	74.0430	74.0202	73.9974	73.9746	73.9518	73.9290	73.9061	73.8833	.000760
21	73.0283	73.0104	72.9926	72.9747	72.9569	72.9390	72.9212	72.9033	72.8855	72.8676	72.8498	72.8320	.000595
20	71.9022	71.8892	71.8761	71.8631	71.8500	71.8370	71.8240	71.8109	71.7979	71.7848	71.7718	71.7587	.000435
19	70.7572	70.7487	70.7403	70.7318	70.7233	70.7149	70.7064	70.6979	70.6895	70.6810	70.6725	70.6641	.000282
18	69.5937	69.5896	69.5855	69.5815	69.5774	69.5733	69.5692	69.5652	69.5611	69.5570	69.5530	69.5489	.000136
17	68.4126	68.4127	68.4128	68.4130	68.4131	68.4132	68.4133	68.4134	68.4135	68.4136	68.4138	68.4139	.000004
16	67.2144	67.2185	67.2226	67.2268	67.2309	67.2350	67.2391	67.2433	67.2474	67.2515	67.2556	67.2598	.000137
15	66.0015	66.0093	66.0172	66.0250	66.0328	66.0407	66.0485	66.0563	66.0642	66.0720	66.0798	66.0877	.000261
14	64.7736	64.7850	64.7964	64.8078	64.8193	64.8307	64.8421	64.8535	64.8649	64.8763	64.8878	64.8992	.000380
13	63.5315	63.5463	63.5612	63.5760	63.5908	63.6057	63.6205	63.6353	63.6502	63.6650	63.6798	63.6947	.000494
12	62.2784	62.2963	62.3142	62.3322	62.3501	62.3680	62.3860	62.4039	62.4218	62.4397	62.4576	62.4756	.000597
11	61.0139	61.0346	61.0554	61.0761	61.0968	61.1176	61.1383	61.1590	61.1798	61.2005	61.2212	61.2420	.000691
10	59.7421	59.7654	59.7887	59.8120	59.8353	59.8586	59.8818	59.9051	59.9284	59.9517	59.9750	59.9983	.000776
Age.	0	1	2	3	4	5	6	7	8	9	10	11	Day.

Age.	0	1	2	3	4	5	6	7	8	9	10	11	Day.
10	36.0603	36.0788	36.0973	36.1158	36.1343	36.1528	36.1713	36.1898	36.2083	36.2268	36.2453	36.2638	.000617
11	37.1416	37.1599	37.1782	37.1965	37.2148	37.2331	37.2514	37.2697	37.2880	37.3063	37.3246	37.3429	.000610
12	38.2384	38.2568	38.2751	38.2935	38.3118	38.3302	38.3485	38.3669	38.3853	38.4036	38.4220	38.4403	.000612
13	39.3511	39.3692	39.3873	39.4055	39.4236	39.4417	39.4598	39.4780	39.4961	39.5142	39.5323	39.5505	.000604
14	40.4814	40.4991	40.5168	40.5344	40.5521	40.5698	40.5875	40.6052	40.6229	40.6405	40.6582	40.6759	.000589
15	41.6273	41.6445	41.6616	41.6788	41.6960	41.7132	41.7303	41.7475	41.7647	41.7819	41.7990	41.8162	.000572
16	42.7891	42.8052	42.8214	42.8375	42.8537	42.8698	42.8860	42.9021	42.9182	42.9344	42.9505	42.9667	.000538
17	43.9628	43.9777	43.9926	44.0075	44.0224	44.0373	44.0522	44.0671	44.0820	44.0969	44.1118	44.1267	.000497
18	45.1511	45.1653	45.1794	45.1936	45.2077	45.2219	45.2360	45.2502	45.2644	45.2785	45.2927	45.3068	.000438
19	46.2524	46.3652	46.3780	46.3908	46.4036	46.4164	46.4291	46.4419	46.4547	46.4675	46.4803	46.4931	.000426
20	47.5656	47.5770	47.5883	47.5997	47.6110	47.6224	47.6337	47.6451	47.6564	47.6678	47.6792	47.6905	.000378
21	48.7919	48.8015	48.8111	48.8208	48.8304	48.8400	48.8496	48.8593	48.8689	48.8785	48.8881	48.8978	.000321
22	50.0293	50.0370	50.0446	50.0523	50.0600	50.0677	50.0753	50.0830	50.0907	50.0984	50.1060	50.1137	.000256
23	51.2768	51.2820	51.2871	51.2923	51.2975	51.3027	51.3078	51.3130	51.3182	51.3234	51.3285	51.3337	.000172
24	52.5300	52.5324	52.5348	52.5372	52.5396	52.5420	52.5443	52.5467	52.5491	52.5515	52.5539	52.5563	.000080
25	53.7873	53.7865	53.7857	53.7849	53.7841	53.7833	53.7824	53.7816	53.7808	53.7800	53.7792	53.7784	.000027
26	55.0456	55.0413	55.0370	55.0327	55.0284	55.0241	55.0198	55.0155	55.0112	55.0069	55.0026	54.9983	.000143
27	56.3039	56.2956	56.2874	56.2791	56.2709	56.2626	56.2544	56.2461	56.2379	56.2296	56.2214	56.2131	.000275
28	57.5587	57.5461	57.5336	57.5210	57.5085	57.4960	57.4834	57.4708	57.4583	57.4457	57.4332	57.4206	.000418
29	58.8086	58.7914	58.7741	58.7569	58.7396	58.7224	58.7051	58.6879	58.6707	58.6534	58.6362	58.6189	.000575
30	60.0519	60.0295	60.0071	59.9848	59.9624	59.9400	59.9176	59.8953	59.8729	59.8505	59.8281	59.8058	.000746
31	61.2837	61.2559	61.2280	61.2002	61.1724	61.1446	61.1167	61.0889	61.0611	61.0333	61.0054	60.9776	.000927
32	62.5055	62.4720	62.4385	62.4050	62.3715	62.3380	62.3045	62.2711	62.2376	62.2041	62.1706	62.1371	.001116
33	63.7166	63.6770	63.6374	63.5978	63.5582	63.5186	63.4790	63.4393	63.3997	63.3601	63.3205	63.2809	.001320
34	64.9150	64.8689	64.8228	64.7768	64.7307	64.6846	64.6385	64.5925	64.5464	64.5003	64.4542	64.4082	.001536
35	66.0997	66.0468	65.9939	65.9410	65.8881	65.8352	65.7822	65.7293	65.6764	65.6235	65.5706	65.5177	.001763
36	67.2689	67.2088	67.1487	67.0886	67.0285	66.9684	66.9083	66.8483	66.7882	66.7281	66.6680	66.6079	.002003
37	68.4232	68.3555	68.2878	68.2200	68.1523	68.0846	68.0169	67.9492	67.8815	67.8137	67.7460	67.6783	.002257
38	69.5608	69.4851	69.4093	69.3336	69.2579	69.1821	69.1064	69.0307	68.9549	68.8792	68.8035	68.7277	.002524
39	70.6816	70.5975	70.5135	70.4294	70.3454	70.2613	70.1772	70.0932	70.0091	69.9251	69.8410	69.7570	.002802
40	71.7863	71.6933	71.6003	71.5073	71.4144	71.3214	71.2284	71.1354	71.0424	70.9494	70.8565	70.7635	.003099
41	72.8727	72.7703	72.6678	72.5654	72.4630	72.3605	72.2581	72.1557	72.0532	71.9508	71.8484	71.7459	.003414
42	73.9401	73.8279	73.7157	73.6035	73.4913	73.3791	73.2669	73.1547	73.0425	72.9303	72.8181	72.7059	.003740
43	74.9915	74.8692	74.7469	74.6246	74.5023	74.3800	74.2576	74.1353	74.0130	73.8907	73.7684	73.6461	.004077
44	76.0293	75.8968	75.7643	75.6318	75.4993	75.3668	75.2343	75.1019	74.9694	74.8369	74.7044	74.5719	.004416
45	77.0621	76.9195	76.7770	76.6344	76.4919	76.3493	76.2068	76.0642	75.9217	75.7791	75.6366	75.4940	.004752
46	78.0993	77.9466	77.7940	77.6413	77.4887	77.3360	77.1833	77.0307	76.8780	76.7254	76.5727	76.4201	.005088
47	79.1496	78.9871	78.8245	78.6620	78.4995	78.3369	78.1744	78.0119	77.8493	77.6868	77.5243	77.3617	.005418
48	80.2239	80.0508	79.8777	79.7047	79.5316	79.3585	79.1854	79.0124	78.8393	78.6662	78.4931	78.3201	.005769
49	81.3249	81.1413	80.9577	80.7741	80.5906	80.4070	80.2234	80.0398	79.8562	79.6726	79.4891	79.3055	.006119
50	82.4617	82.2665	82.0714	81.8762	81.6811	81.4860	81.2908	81.0956	80.9005	80.7053	80.5102	80.3150	.006505
51	83.6329	83.4250	83.2172	83.0093	82.8014	82.5936	82.3857	82.1778	81.9700	81.7621	81.5542	81.3464	.006929
52	84.8363	84.6138	84.3915	84.1691	83.9467	83.7243	83.5018	83.2794	83.0570	82.8346	82.6122	82.3898	.007413
53	86.0618	85.8237	85.5857	85.3476	85.1095	84.8715	84.6334	84.3953	84.1573	83.9192	83.6811	83.4431	.007935
54	87.3096	87.0539	86.7983	86.5426	86.2869	86.0313	85.7756	85.5199	85.2643	85 0086	84.7529	84.4973	.008520
55	88.5684	88.2917	88.0150	87.7383	87.4616	87.1849	86.9082	86.6316	86.3549	86.0782	85.8015	85.5248	.009223
56	89.8113	89.5095	89 2077	88.9059	88.6041	88.3023	88.0005	87.6987	87.3969	87.0951	86.7933	86.4915	.010060
57	91.0025	90.6725	90.3425	90.0125	89.6825	89.3525	89.0225	88.6926	88.3626	88.0326	87.7026	87.3726	.011000
58	92.1185	91.7494	91.3803	91.0112	90.6421	90.2730	89.9039	89.5348	89.1657	88.7966	88.4275	88.0584	.012303
59	93.0394	92.6305	92.2217	91.8128	91.4040	90.9951	90.5863	90.1774	89.7686	89.3597	88.9509	88.5420	.013628
60	93.7691	93.3627	92.9563	92.5499	92.1435	91.7371	91.3306	90.9242	90.5178	90.1114	89.7050	89.2986	.013547
61	94.8445	94.5041	94.1636	93.8232	93.4828	93.1424	92.8020	92.4615	92.1211	91.7807	91.4402	91.0998	.011347
62 or 47	**97.0874**	**97.3301**	**97.5728**	**97.8155**	**98.0583**	**98.3010**	**98.5437**	**98.7864**	**99.0291**	**99.2718**	**99.5146**	**99.7573**	**.008090**
46	95.5895	95.4428	95.2960	95.1493	95.0025	94.8558	94.7090	94.5623	94.4156	94.2688	94.1221	93.9753	.004891
45	94.8489	94.6465	94.4502	94.2538	94.0574	93.8611	93.6647	93.4683	93.2720	93.0756	92.8792	92.6829	.006545
44	94.3147	94.1111	93.9075	93.7040	93.5004	93.2968	93.0932	92.8897	92.6861	92.4825	92.2790	92.0754	.006786
43	93.6421	93.4606	93.2791	93.0976	92.9161	92.7346	92.5530	92.3715	92.1900	92.0085	91.8270	91.6455	.006050
42	92.8171	92.6579	92.4987	92.3395	92.1803	92.0211	91.8618	91.7026	91.5434	91.3842	91.2250	91.0658	.005307
41	91.9203	91.7763	91.6323	91.4884	91.3444	91.2004	91.0564	90.9125	90.7685	90.6245	90.4805	90.3366	.004799
40	90.9667	90.8363	90.7058	90.5754	90.4449	90.3145	90.1840	90.0536	89.9232	89.7927	89.6623	89.5318	.004348
39	89.9811	89.8616	89.7421	89.6226	89.5031	89.3836	89.2641	89.1447	89.0252	88.9057	88.7862	88.6667	.003983
38	89.0838	88.9648	88.8458	88.7268	88.6078	88.4888	88.3698	88.2508	88.1318	88.0128	87.8938	87.7748	.003967
37	87.9830	87.8801	87.7771	87.6742	87.5712	87.4683	87.3653	87.2624	87.1595	87.0565	86.9536	86.8506	.003431
36	86.9802	86.8844	86.7886	86.6929	86.5971	86.5013	86.4055	86.3098	86.2140	86.1182	86.0224	85.9267	.003192
35	85.9840	85.8943	85.7046	85.6949	85.6052	85.5155	85.4258	85.3562	85.2665	85.1768	85.0871	84.9974	.002990
34	84.9973	84.9130	84.8288	84.7445	84.6603	84.5760	84.4917	84.4075	84.3232	84.2390	84.1547	84.0705	.002808
33	84.0232	83.9438	83.8644	83.7850	83.7056	83.6262	83.5468	83.4674	83.3880	83.3086	83.2292	83.1498	.002647
32	83.0549	82.9806	82.9063	82.8320	82.7577	82.6834	82.6091	82.5348	82.4605	82.3862	82.3119	82.2376	.002477
31	82.0936	82.0240	81.9544	81.8848	81.8152	81.7456	81.6760	81.6065	81.5369	81.4673	81.3977	81.3281	.002320
30	81.1285	81.0642	80.9998	80.9355	80.8712	80.8069	80.7425	80.6782	80.6139	80.5496	80.4852	80.4209	.002144
29	80.1564	80.0935	80.0306	79.9677	79.9048	79.8419	79.7790	79.7160	79.6531	79.5902	79.5273	79.4644	.002097
28	79.1705	79.1172	79.0640	79.0107	78.9574	78.9042	78.8509	78.7976	78.7444	78.6911	78.6378	78.5846	.001775
27	78.1660	78.1186	78.0712	78.0238	77.9764	77.9290	77.8816	77.8343	77.7869	77.7395	77.6921	77.6447	.001580
26	77.1411	77.0995	77.0579	77.0163	76.9747	76.9331	76.8915	76.8500	76.8084	76.7668	76.7252	76.6836	.001386
25	76.0939	76.0581	76.0222	75.9864	75.9506	75.9148	75.8790	75.8431	75.8073	75.7715	75.7356	75.6998	.001194
24	75.0253	74.9950	74.9647	74.9344	74.9041	74.8738	74.8434	74.8131	74.7828	74.7525	74.7222	74.6919	.001010
23	73.9371	73.9120	73.8869	73.8618	73.8367	73.8116	73.7865	73.7614	73.7363	73.7112	73.6861	73.6610	.000837
22	72.8288	72.8088	72.7888	72.7688	72.7488	72.7288	72.7087	72.6887	72.6687	72.6487	72.6287	72.6087	.000667
21	71.7004	71.6853	71.6702	71.6551	71.6401	71.6250	71.6099	71.5948	71.5797	71.5646	71.5496	71.5345	.000503
20	70.5534	70.5430	70.5326	70.5221	70.5117	70.5013	70.4909	70.4805	70.4701	70.4596	70.4492	70.4388	.000347
19	69.3881	69.3822	69.3763	69.3703	69.3644	69.3585	69.3526	69.3467	69.3408	69.3348	69.3289	69.3230	.000197
18	68.2055	68.2039	68.2022	68.2006	68.1989	68.1973	68.1956	68.1940	68.1924	68.1907	68.1891	68.1874	.000055
17	67.0062	67.0087	67.0111	67.0136	67.0160	67.0185	67.0210	67.0234	67.0259	67.0283	67.0308	67.0332	.000082
16	65.7923	65.7985	65.8048	65.8110	65.8173	65.8235	65.8297	65.8360	65.8422	65.8485	65.8547	65.8610	.000208
15	64.5638	64.5737	64.5836	64.5935	64.6035	64.6134	64.6233	64.6332	64.6431	64.6530	64.6630	64.6729	.000330
14	63.3213	63.3347	63.3481	63.3615	63.3749	63.3883	63.4017	63.4152	63.4286	63.4420	63.4554	63.4688	.000447
13	62.0675	62.0841	62.1006	62.1172	62.1338	62.1503	62.1669	62.1835	62.2000	62.2166	62.2332	62.2497	.000552
12	60.8049	60.8243	60.8438	60.8632	60.8827	60.9021	60.9216	60.9410	60.9605	60.9800	60.9994	61.0188	.000648
11	59.5330	59.5551	59.5771	59.5992	59.6212	59.6433	59.6653	59.6874	59.7095	59.7315	59.7536	59.7756	.000735
10	58.2570	58.2813	58.3057	58.3300	58.3543	58.3787	58.4030	58.4273	58.4517	58.4760	58.5003	58.5247	.000811
Age.	0	1	2	3	4	5	6	7	8	9	10	11	Day.

Age.	0	1	2	3	4	5	6	7	8	9	10	11	Day.
10	37.4754	37.4950	37.5145	37.5341	37.5536	37.5732	37.5927	37.6123	37.6319	37.6514	37.6710	37.6905	.000652
11	38.5774	38.5970	38.6167	38.6363	38.6560	38.6756	38.6952	38.7149	38.7345	38.7542	38.7738	38.7935	.000655
12	39.6988	39.7183	39.7377	39.7572	39.7767	39.7962	39.8156	39.8351	39.8546	39.8741	39.8935	39.9130	.000649
13	40.8339	40.8530	40.8720	40.8911	40.9102	40.9293	40.9483	40.9674	40.9865	41.0056	41.0246	41.0437	.000636
14	41.9850	42.0036	42.0223	42.0409	42.0595	42.0782	42.0968	42.1154	42.1341	42.1527	42.1713	42.1900	.000621
15	43.1521	43.1697	43.1874	43.2051	43.2227	43.2404	43.2581	43.2757	43.2934	43.3111	43.3287	43.3464	.000587
16	44.3300	44.3469	44.3639	44.3808	44.3977	44.4147	44.4316	44.4485	44.4655	44.4824	44.4993	44.5163	.000564
17	45.5235	45.5393	45.5551	45.5709	45.5867	45.6025	45.6183	45.6341	45.6499	45.6657	45.6815	45.6973	.000527
18	46.7288	46.7433	46.7578	46.7723	46.7868	46.8013	46.8158	46.8303	46.8448	46.8593	46.8738	46.8883	.000483
19	47.9461	47.9592	47.9724	47.9855	47.9986	48.0118	48.0249	48.0380	48.0512	48.0643	48.0774	48.0906	.000438
20	49.1758	49.1873	49.1987	49.2102	49.2217	49.2332	49.2446	49.2561	49.2676	49.2791	49.2905	49.3020	.000382
21	50.4164	50.4260	50.4356	50.4452	50.4548	50.4644	50.4740	50.4837	50.4933	50.5029	50.5125	50.5221	.000320
22	51.6671	51.6743	51.6815	51.6887	51.6959	51.7031	51.7103	51.7175	51.7247	51.7319	51.7391	51.7463	.000240
23	52.9229	52.9274	52.9319	52.9364	52.9409	52.9454	52.9500	52.9545	52.9590	52.9635	52.9680	52.9725	.000150
24	54.1827	54.1841	54.1855	54.1870	54.1884	54.1898	54.1912	54.1926	54.1940	54.1954	54.1969	54.1983	.000047
25	55.4434	55.4414	55.4395	55.4375	55.4355	55.4336	55.4316	55.4296	55.4277	55.4257	55.4237	55.4218	.000065
26	56.7035	56.6977	56.6919	56.6861	56.6803	56.6745	56.6687	56.6630	56.6572	56.6514	56.6456	56.6398	.000193
27	57.9601	57.9501	57.9402	57.9302	57.9203	57.9103	57.9003	57.8904	57.8804	57.8705	57.8605	57.8506	.000332
28	59.2112	59.1967	59.1822	59.1677	59.1532	59.1387	59.1241	59.1096	59.0951	59.0806	59.0661	59.0516	.000483
29	60.4549	60.4354	60.4159	60.3964	60.3769	60.3574	60.3380	60.3185	60.2990	60.2795	60.2600	60.2405	.000650
30	61.6891	61.6643	61.6396	61.6148	61.5901	61.5653	61.5405	61.5158	61.4910	61.4663	61.4415	61.4168	.000825
31	62.9107	62.8804	62.8502	62.8199	62.7897	62.7594	62.7291	62.6989	62.6686	62.6384	62.6081	62.5779	.001008
32	64.1222	64.0860	64.0498	64.0136	63.9775	63.9413	63.9051	63.8689	63.8327	63.7965	63.7604	63.7242	.001206
33	65.3206	65.2782	65.2357	65.1933	65.1509	65.1084	65.0660	65.0236	64.9811	64.9387	64.8963	64.8538	.001414
34	66.5052	66.4562	66.4071	66.3581	66.3090	66.2600	66.2110	66.1619	66.1129	66.0638	66.0148	65.9657	.001635
35	67.6749	67.6189	67.5630	67.5070	67.4510	67.3951	67.3391	67.2831	67.2272	67.1712	67.1152	67.0593	.001865
36	68.8286	68.7652	68.7019	68.6386	68.5752	68.5119	68.4486	68.3852	68.3219	68.2586	68.1952	68.1319	.002110
37	69.9659	69.8949	69.8238	69.7528	69.6817	69.6107	69.5396	69.4686	69.3976	69.3265	69.2555	69.1844	.002368
38	71.0860	71.0069	70.9279	70.8488	70.7698	70.6907	70.6116	70.5326	70.4535	70.3745	70.2954	70.2164	.002635
39	72.1900	72.1024	72.0148	71.9271	71.8395	71.7519	71.6643	71.5767	71.4891	71.4014	71.3138	71.2262	.002920
40	73.2758	73.1791	73.0824	72.9857	72.8890	72.7923	72.6956	72.5990	72.5023	72.4056	72.3089	72.2122	.003223
41	74.3421	74.2361	74.1300	74.0240	73.9180	73.8119	73.7059	73.5999	73.4938	73.3878	73.2818	73.1757	.003534
42	75.3915	75.2758	75.1601	75.0444	74.9287	74.8130	74.6973	74.5816	74.4659	74.3502	74.2345	74.1188	.003857
43	76.4269	76.3015	76.1761	76.0507	75.9253	75.7999	75.6744	75.5490	75.4236	75.2982	75.1728	75.0474	.004180
44	77.4544	77.3194	77.1844	77.0494	76.9144	76.7794	76.6443	76.5093	76.3743	76.2393	76.1043	75.9693	.004500
45	78.4849	78.3403	78.1956	78.0510	77.9064	77.7618	77.6171	77.4725	77.3279	77.1833	77.0386	76.8940	.004821
46	79.5262	79.3722	79.2181	79.0641	78.9101	78.7561	78.6020	78.4480	78.2940	78.1400	77.9860	77.8319	.005134
47	80.5903	80.4263	80.2622	80.0982	79.9341	79.7701	79.6060	79.4420	79.2780	79.1139	78.9499	78.7858	.005468
48	81.6781	81.5041	81.3300	81.1560	80.9820	80.8080	80.6340	80.4599	80.2859	80.1119	79.9378	79.7638	.005801
49	82.8007	82.6157	82.4307	82.2457	82.0607	81.8757	81.6907	81.5057	81.3207	81.1357	80.9507	80.7657	.006167
50	83.9551	83.7580	83.5610	83.3639	83.1668	82.9697	82.7726	82.5756	82.3785	82.1814	81.9843	81.7873	.006569
51	85 1392	84.9283	84.7174	84.5065	84.2956	84.0847	83.8737	83.6628	83.4519	83.2410	83.0301	82.8192	.007030
52	86.3434	86.1176	85.8918	85.6661	85.4403	85.2145	84.9887	84.7630	84.5372	84.3114	84.0856	83.8599	.007526
53	87.5669	87.3243	87.0818	86.8392	86.5967	86.3541	86.1116	85.8690	85.6265	85.3840	85.1414	84.8988	.008085
54	88.8001	88.5375	88.2750	88.0124	87.7498	87.5872	87.2246	86.9621	86.6995	86.4369	86.1743	85.9118	.008752
55	90.0154	89.7289	89.4423	89.1558	88.8693	88.5827	88.2962	88.0097	87.7231	87.4366	87.1501	86.8635	.009551
56	91.1786	90.8652	90.5517	90.2383	89.9249	89.6115	89.2980	88.9846	88.6712	88.3578	88.0443	87.7309	.010447
57	92.2669	91.9161	91.5652	91.2144	90.8636	90.5128	90.1620	89.8111	89.4603	89.1095	88.7586	88.4078	.011694
58	93.1641	92.7753	92.3865	91.9978	91.6090	91.2202	90.8314	90.4427	90.0539	89.6651	89.2763	88.8876	.012959
59	93.8746	93.4888	93.1031	92.7173	92.3315	91.9458	91.5600	91.1742	90.7885	90.4027	90.0169	89.6312	.012859
60	94.9179	94.5965	94.2752	93.9538	93.6325	93.3111	92.9898	92.6684	92.3471	92.0257	91.7044	91.3830	.010712
61 or 48	**97.0874**	**97.3301**	**97.5728**	**97.8155**	**98.0583**	**98.3010**	**98.5437**	**98.7864**	**99.0291**	**99.2718**	**99.5146**	**99.7573**	**.008090**
47	95.5573	95.4022	95.2471	95.0920	94.9370	94.7819	94.6268	94.4717	94.3166	94.1615	94.0065	93.8514	.005169
46	94.7963	94.5908	94.3854	94.1799	93.9744	93.7690	93.5635	93.3580	93.1526	92.9471	92.7416	92.5362	.006849
45	94.2593	94.0468	93.8343	93.6218	93.4094	93.1969	92.9844	92.7719	92.5594	92.3470	92.1345	91.9220	.007083
44	93.5758	93.3861	93.1964	93.0068	92.8171	92.6274	92.4377	92.2481	92.0584	91.8687	91.6790	91.4894	.006322
43	92.7384	92.5718	92.4052	92.2385	92.0719	91.9053	91.7387	91.5721	91.4055	91.2388	91.0722	90.9056	.005554
42	91.8290	91.6782	91.5274	91.3766	91.2258	91.0750	90.9241	90.7733	90.6225	90.4717	90.3209	90.1701	.005027
41	90.8631	90.7263	90.5895	90.4527	90.3160	90.1792	90.0424	89.9056	89.7688	89.6320	89.4953	89.3585	.004559
40	89.8659	89.7405	89.6152	89.4898	89.3644	89.2391	89.1137	88.9883	88.8630	88.7376	88.6122	88.4869	.004179
39	88.8577	88.7416	88.6254	88.5093	88.3931	88.2770	88.1608	88.0447	87.9286	87.8124	87.6963	87.5801	.003871
38	87.8470	87.7389	87.6308	87.5227	87.4146	87.3065	87.1984	87.0903	86.9822	86.8741	86.7660	86.6579	.003603
37	86.8352	86.7346	86.6340	86.5333	86.4327	86.3321	86.2314	86.1308	86.0302	85.9296	85.8290	85.7283	.003354
36	85.8307	85.7364	85.6421	85.5478	85.4536	85.3593	85.2650	85.1707	85.0764	84.9821	84.8879	84.7936	.003143
35	84.8370	84.7484	84.6598	84.5712	84.4826	84.3940	84.3054	84.2169	84.1283	84.0397	83.9511	83.8625	.002953
34	83.8564	83.7729	83.6894	83.6058	83.5223	83.4388	83.3583	83.2748	83.1983	83.1047	83.0212	82.9377	.002784
33	82.8823	82.8041	82.7259	82.6477	82.5695	82.4913	82.4131	82.3349	82.2567	82.1785	82.1003	82.0221	.002607
32	81.9148	81.8416	81.7684	81.6952	81.6220	81.5488	81.4755	81.4023	81.3291	81.2559	81.1827	81.1095	.002440
31	80.9457	80.8779	80.8100	80.7422	80.6744	80.6065	80.5387	80.4709	80.4030	80.3352	80.2674	80.1995	.002261
30	79.9701	79.9078	79.8455	79.7833	79.7210	79.6587	79.5964	79.5342	79.4719	79.4096	79.3473	79.2851	.002076
29	78.9801	78.9237	78.8673	78.8108	78.7544	78.6980	78.6416	78.5852	78.5288	78.4723	78.4159	78.3595	.001880
28	77.9719	77.9215	77.8711	77.8208	77.7704	77.7200	77.6696	77.6193	77.5689	77.5185	77.4681	77.4178	.001679
27	76.9437	76.8993	76.8549	76.8105	76.7661	76.7217	76.6772	76.6328	76.5884	76.5440	76.4996	76.4552	.001480
26	75.8934	75.8549	75.8164	75.7780	75.7395	75.7010	75.6625	75.6240	75.5855	75.5470	75.5086	75.4701	.001283
25	74.8220	74.7892	74.7563	74.7235	74.6907	74.6579	74.6250	74.5922	74.5594	74.5266	74.4937	74.4609	.001094
24	73.7311	73.7036	73.6761	73.6487	73.6212	73.5937	73.5662	73.5388	73.5113	73.4838	73.4563	73.4289	.000916
23	72.6203	72.5980	72.5758	72.5535	72.5312	72.5090	72.4867	72.4644	72.4422	72.4199	72.3976	72.3754	.000742
22	71.4899	71.4727	71.4554	71.4382	71.4210	71.4037	71.3865	71.3693	71.3520	71.3348	71.3176	71.3003	.000574
21	70.3408	70.3284	70.3159	70.3035	70.2910	70.2786	70.2661	70.2537	70.2413	70.2288	70.2164	70.2039	.000415
20	69.1737	69.1659	69.1580	69.1502	69.1423	69.1345	69.1266	69.1188	69.1110	69.1031	69.0953	69.0874	.000261
19	67.9896	67.9861	67.9827	67.9792	67.9757	67.9723	67.9688	67.9653	67.9619	67.9584	67.9549	67.9515	000115
18	66.7890	66.7897	66.7904	66.7911	66.7919	66.7926	66.7933	66.7940	66.7947	66.7954	66.7962	66.7969	.000024
17	65.5742	65.5788	65.5834	65.5880	65.5926	65.5972	65.6017	65.6063	65.6109	65.6155	65.6201	65.6247	.000153
16	64.3449	64.3532	64.3616	64.3700	64.3783	64.3866	64.3950	64.4033	64.4117	64.4200	64.4284	64.4367	.000278
15	63.1021	63.1140	63.1259	63.1378	63.1498	63.1617	63.1736	63.1855	63.1974	63.2093	63.2213	63.2332	.000397
14	61.8481	61.8632	61.8784	61.8935	61.9087	61.9238	61.9390	61.9541	61.9693	61.9844	61.9996	62.0147	.000505
13	60.5851	60.6032	60.6213	60.6394	60.6575	60.6756	60.6937	60.7118	60.7299	60.7480	60.7661	60.7842	.000603
12	59.3154	59.3362	59.3570	59.3777	59.3985	59.4193	59.4401	59.4609	59.4817	59.5024	59.5232	59.5440	.000693
11	58.0395	58.0626	58.0857	58.1088	58.1319	58.1550	58.1781	58.2013	58.2244	58.2475	58.2706	58.2937	.000770
10	56.7612	56.7864	56.8116	56.8368	56.8621	56.8873	56.9125	56.9377	56.9629	56.9881	57.0134	57.0386	.000840
Age.	0	1	2	3	4	5	6	7	8	9	10	11	Day.

Age.	0	1	2	3	4	5	6	7	8	9	10	11	Day.
10	38.9032	38.9241	38.9450	38.9659	38.9868	39.0077	39.0285	39.0494	39.0703	39.0912	39.1121	39.1330	.000696
11	40.0293	40.0501	40.0708	40.0916	40.1123	40.1331	40.1538	40.1746	40.1954	40.2161	40.2369	40.2576	.000692
12	41.1726	41.1929	41.2133	41.2336	41.2539	41.2743	41.2946	41.3149	41.3353	41.3556	41.3759	41.3963	.000677
13	42.3280	42.3480	42.3681	42.3881	42.4081	42.4282	42.4482	42.4682	42.4883	42.5083	42.5283	42.5484	.000668
14	43.5000	43.5191	43.5382	43.5573	43.5764	43.5955	43.6146	43.6338	43.6529	43.6720	43.6911	43.7102	.000637
15	44.6828	44.7012	44.7197	44.7381	44.7566	44.7750	44.7934	44.8119	44.8303	44.8488	44.8672	44.8857	.000615
16	45.8804	45.8978	45.9151	45.9325	45.9499	45.9672	45.9846	46.0020	46.0193	46.0367	46.0541	46.0714	.000579
17	47.0899	47.1060	47.1222	47.1383	47.1544	47.1706	47.1867	47.2028	47.2190	47.2351	47.2512	47.2674	.000538
18	48.3107	48.3255	48.3404	48.3552	48.3700	48.3849	48.3997	48.4145	48.4294	48.4442	48.4590	48.4739	.000494
19	49.5438	49.5571	49.5703	49.5836	49.5968	49.6101	49.6233	49.6366	49.6499	49.6631	49.6764	49.6896	.000442
20	50.7873	50.7988	50.8102	50.8217	50.8332	50.8446	50.8561	50.8676	50.8790	50.8905	50.9020	50.9134	.000382
21	52.0407	52.0498	52.0590	52.0681	52.0772	52.0864	52.0955	52.1046	52.1138	52.1229	52.1320	52.1412	.000304
22	53.2991	53.3056	53.3122	53.3187	53.3253	53.3318	53.3384	53.3450	53.3515	53.3580	53.3646	53.3711	.000218
23	54.5610	54.5645	54.5681	54.5716	54.5752	54.5787	54.5822	54.5858	54.5893	54.5929	54.5964	54.6000	.000118
24	55.8236	55.8239	55.8241	55.8244	55.8247	55.8249	55.8252	55.8255	55.8257	55.8260	55.8263	55.8265	.000009
25	57.0856	57.0822	57.0787	57.0753	57.0718	57.0684	57.0650	57.0615	57.0581	57.0546	57.0512	57.0477	.000115
26	58.3435	58.3360	58.3285	58.3210	58.3136	58.3061	58.2986	58.2911	58.2836	58.2761	58.2687	58.2612	.000249
27	59.5958	59.5839	59.5720	59.5601	59.5482	59.5363	59.5244	59.5126	59.5007	59.4888	59.4769	59.4650	.000396
28	60.8403	60.8236	60.8068	60.7901	60.7734	60.7566	60.7399	60.7232	60.7064	60.6897	60.6730	60.6562	.000558
29	62.0743	62.0524	62.0306	62.0087	61.9869	61.9650	61.9432	61.9213	61.8995	61.8776	61.8558	61.8340	.000728
30	63.2977	63.2706	63.2435	63.2164	63.1893	63.1622	63.1351	63.1081	63.0810	63.0539	63.0268	62.9997	.000903
31	64.5085	64.4756	64.4427	64.4097	64.3768	64.3439	64.3110	64.2781	64.2452	64.2122	64.1793	64.1464	.001097
32	65.7067	65.6677	65.6288	65.5898	65.5508	65.5119	65.4729	65.4339	65.3950	65.3560	65.3170	65.2781	.001299
33	66.8908	66.8454	66.8001	66.7547	66.7093	66.6640	66.6186	66.5732	66.5279	66.4825	66.4371	66.3918	.001512
34	68.0598	68.0077	67.9557	67.9036	67.8515	67.7995	67.7474	67.6953	67.6433	67.5912	67.5391	67.4871	.001735
35	69.2134	69.1542	69.0950	69.0359	68.9767	68.9175	68.8583	68.7992	68.7400	68.6808	68.6216	68.5625	.001972
36	70.3494	70.2828	70.2162	70.1496	70.0830	70.0164	69.9497	69.8831	69.8165	69.7499	69.6833	69.6167	.002220
37	71.4687	71.3944	71.3200	71.2457	71.1714	71.0971	71.0227	70.9484	70.8741	70.7998	70.7254	70.6511	.002477
38	72.5713	72.4887	72.4062	72.3236	72.2411	72.1585	72.0760	71.9934	71.9109	71.8283	71.7458	71.6632	.002752
39	73.6557	73.5644	73.4731	73.3819	73.2906	73.1993	73.1080	73.0168	72.9255	72.8342	72.7430	72.6517	.003042
40	74.7207	74.6205	74.5202	74.4200	74.3198	74.2196	74.1193	74.0191	73.9189	73.8187	73.7184	73.6182	.003341
41	75.7683	75.6588	75.5493	75.4399	75.3304	75.2209	75.1114	75.0020	74.8925	74.7830	74.6735	74.5641	.003649
42	76.8009	76.6822	76.5634	76.4447	76.3259	76.2072	76.0884	75.9697	75.8510	75.7322	75.6135	75.4947	.003958
43	77.8250	77.6973	77.5696	77.4419	77.3142	77.1865	77.0588	76.9311	76.8034	76.6757	76.5480	76.4203	.004257
44	78.8493	78.7123	78.5752	78.4382	78.3011	78.1641	78.0270	77.8900	77.7530	77.6159	77.4789	77.3418	.004568
45	79.8828	79.7368	79.5909	79.4449	79.2990	79.1530	79.0070	78.8611	78.7151	78.5692	78.4232	78.2773	.004865
46	80.9367	80.7812	80.6257	80.4702	80.3147	80.1592	80.0036	79.8481	79.6926	79.5371	79.3816	79.2261	.005183
47	82.0129	81.8479	81.6830	81.5180	81.3530	81.1880	81.0230	80.8581	80.6931	80.5281	80.3631	80.1982	.005499
48	83.1209	82.9455	82.7701	82.5946	82.4192	82.2438	82.0684	81.8930	81.7176	81.5421	81.3667	81.1913	.005847
49	84.2595	84.0726	83.8857	83.6988	83.5120	83.3251	83.1382	82.9513	82.7644	82.5775	82.3907	82.2038	.006229
50	85.4254	85.2253	85.0253	84.8252	84.6252	84.4251	84.2251	84.0250	83.8250	83.6250	83.4249	83.2248	.006668
51	86.6091	86.3949	86.1807	85.9665	85.7523	85.5381	85.3239	85.1097	84.8955	84.6813	84.4671	84.2529	.007140
52	87.8101	87.5799	87.3498	87.1196	86.8895	86.6593	86.4291	86.1990	85.9688	85.7387	85.5085	85.2784	.007672
53	89.0181	88.7688	88.5196	88.2703	88.0210	87.7718	87.5225	87.2732	87.0240	86.7747	86.5254	86.2762	.008309
54	90.2077	89.9356	89.6634	89.3913	89.1191	88.8470	88.5748	88.3027	88.0306	87.7584	87.4863	87.2141	.009071
55	91.3443	91.0465	90.7486	90.4508	90.1530	89.8552	89.5573	89.2595	88.9617	88.6639	88.3660	88.0682	.009927
56	92.4064	92.0727	91.7391	91.4054	91.0718	90.7381	90.4044	90.0708	89.7371	89.4035	89.0698	88.7362	.011122
57	93.2813	92.9114	92.5415	92.1716	91.8017	91.4318	91.0618	90.6919	90.3220	89.9521	89.5822	89.2123	.012330
58	93.9736	93.6072	93.2408	92.8744	92.5080	92.1416	91.7752	91.4088	91.0424	90.6760	90.3096	89.9432	.012213
59	94.9869	94.6835	94.3801	94.0766	93.7732	93.4698	93.1664	92.8630	92.5596	92.2561	91.9527	91.6493	.010114
60 or 49	**97.0874**	**97.3301**	**97.5728**	**97.8155**	**98.0583**	**98.3010**	**98.5437**	**98.7864**	**99.0291**	**99.2718**	**99.5146**	**99.7573**	**.008090**
48	95.5234	95.3595	95.1955	95.0316	94.8677	94.7038	94.5398	94.3759	94.2120	94.0481	93.8841	93.7202	.005464
47	94.7472	94.5321	94.3170	94.1020	93.8869	93.6718	93.4567	93.2417	93.0266	92.8115	92.5964	92.3814	.007169
46	94.1907	93.9696	93.7485	93.5274	93.3063	93.0852	92.8641	92.6431	92.4220	92.2009	91.9798	91.7587	.007370
45	93.5056	93.3073	93.1090	92.9107	92.7124	92.5141	92.3157	92.1174	91.9191	91.7208	91.5225	91.3242	.006610
44	92.6546	92.4801	92.3056	92.1311	91.9567	91.7822	91.6077	91.4332	91.2587	91.0842	90.9098	90.7353	.005816
43	91.7320	91.5739	91.4159	91.2578	91.0998	90.9417	90.7836	90.6256	90.4675	90.3095	90.1514	89.9934	.005268
42	90.7531	90.6096	90.4661	90.3226	90.1791	90.0356	89.8921	89.7487	89.6052	89.4617	89.3182	89.1747	.004783
41	89.7437	89.6121	89.4805	89.3489	89.2173	89.0857	88.9541	88.8225	88.6909	88.5593	88.4277	88.2961	.004389
40	88.7243	88.6023	88.4804	88.3584	88.2364	88.1145	87.9925	87.8705	87.7486	87.6266	87.5046	87.3827	.004065
39	87.7033	87.5897	87.4762	87.3626	87.2490	87.1355	87.0219	86.9083	86.7948	86.6812	86.5676	86.4541	.003785
38	86.6820	86.5762	86.4705	86.3647	86.2590	86.1532	86.0475	85.9417	85.8360	85.7302	85.6245	85.5187	.003525
37	85.6693	85.5702	85.4711	85.3720	85.2728	85.1737	85.0746	84.9755	84.8764	84.7772	84.6781	84.5790	.003304
36	84.6679	84.5747	84.4816	84.3884	84.2952	84.2021	84.1089	84.0157	83.9226	83.8294	83.7362	83.6431	.003105
35	83.6810	83.5932	83.5053	83.4175	83.3296	83.2418	83.1540	83.0661	82.9783	82.8904	82.8026	82.7147	.002928
34	82.7009	82.6186	82.5363	82.4540	82.3717	82.2894	82.2071	82.1248	82.0425	81.9602	81.8779	81.7956	.002743
33	81.7281	81.6510	81.5739	81.4968	81.4197	81.3426	81.2655	81.1884	81.1113	81.0342	80.9571	80.8800	.002570
32	80.7543	80.6828	80.6113	80.5397	80.4682	80.3967	80.3252	80.2537	80.1822	80.1106	80.0391	79.9676	.002384
31	79.7740	79.7082	79.6425	79.5767	79.5109	79.4452	79.3794	79.3136	79.2479	79.1821	79.1163	79.0506	.002192
30	78.7809	78.7212	78.6615	78.6018	78.5421	78.4824	78.4226	78.3629	78.3032	78.2435	78.1838	78.1241	.001990
29	77.7687	77.7152	77.6617	77.6082	7-.5547	77.5012	77.4477	77.3943	77.3408	77.2873	77.2338	77.1803	.001783
28	76.7370	76.6896	76.6423	76.5950	76.5476	76.5002	76.4529	76.4055	76.3582	76.3108	76.2635	76.2161	.001578
27	75.6837	75.6424	75.6011	75.5599	75.5186	75.4773	75.4360	75.3948	75.3535	75.3122	75.2710	75.2297	.001376
26	74.6094	74.5739	74.5385	74.5030	74.4676	74.4321	74.3966	74.3612	74.3257	74.2903	74.2548	74.2194	.001182
25	73.5169	73.4868	73.4568	73.4267	73.3967	73.3666	73.3365	73.3065	73.2764	73.2464	73.2163	73.1863	.001002
24	72.4027	72.3781	72.3534	72.3288	72.3042	72.2796	72.2550	72.2303	72.2057	72.1811	72.1564	72.1318	.000821
23	71.2699	71.2504	71.2310	71.2115	71.1921	71.1726	71.1531	71.1337	71.1142	71.0948	71.0753	71.0559	.000648
22	70.1190	70.1044	70.0899	70.0753	70.0607	70.0462	70.0316	70.0170	70.0025	69.9879	69.973	69.9588	.000485
21	68.9501	68.9402	68.9304	68.9205	68.9107	68.9008	68.8910	68.8811	68.8713	68.8614	68.851	68.8417	.000328
20	67.7643	67.7589	67.7536	67.7482	67.7428	67.7375	67.7321	67.7267	67.7214	67.7160	67.7106	67.7053	.000178
19	66.5625	66.5614	66.5603	66.5592	66.5581	66.5570	66.5560	66.5549	66.5538	66.5527	66.5516	66.5505	.000036
18	65.3466	65.3495	65.3523	65.3552	65.3581	65.3610	65.3638	65.3667	65.3696	65.3725	65.3753	65.3782	.000096
17	64.1167	64.1234	64.1301	64.1368	64.1436	64.1503	64.1570	64.1637	64.1704	64.1771	64.1839	64.1906	.000224
16	62.8733	62.8837	62.8940	62.9044	62.9148	62.9251	62.9355	62.9459	62.9562	62.9666	62.9770	62.9873	.000345
15	61.6194	61.6331	61.6467	61.6604	61.6741	61.6877	61.7014	61.7151	61.7287	61.7424	61.7561	61.7697	.000455
14	60.3565	60.3732	60.3899	60.4065	60.4232	60.4399	60.4566	60.4733	60.4900	60.5066	60.5233	60.5400	.000556
13	59.0866	59.1060	59.1255	59.1449	59.1644	59.1838	59.2032	59.2227	59.2421	59.2616	59.2810	59.3005	.000648
12	57.8133	57.8351	57.8570	57.8788	57.9006	57.9225	57.9443	57.9661	57.9880	58.0098	58.0316	58.0535	.000728
11	56.5354	56.5594	56.5834	56.6073	56.6313	56.6553	56.6793	56.7033	56.7273	56.7512	56.7752	56.7992	.000799
10	55.2582	55.2840	55.3098	55.3357	55.3615	55.3873	55.4131	55.4390	55.4648	55.4906	55.5164	55.5423	.000861
Age.	0	1	2	3	4	5	6	7	8	9	10	11	Day.

Age.	0	1	2	3	4	5	6	7	8	9	10	11	Day.
10	40.3471	40.3691	40.3911	40.4131	40.4351	40.4571	40.4791	40.5011	40.5231	40.5451	40.5671	40.5891	.000733
11	41.4946	41.5163	41.5380	41.5597	41.5814	41.6031	41.6248	41.6465	41.6682	41.6899	41.7116	41.7333	.000723
12	42.6567	42.6782	42.6996	42.7211	42.7425	42.7640	42.7854	42.8069	42.8284	42.8498	42.8713	42.8927	.000715
13	43.8336	43.8541	43.8746	43.8951	43.9156	43.9361	43.9566	43.9772	43.9977	44.0182	44.0387	44.0592	.000683
14	45.0207	45.0406	45.0605	45.0804	45.1004	45.1203	45.1402	45.1601	45.1800	45.2000	45.2199	45.2398	.000664
15	46.2228	46.2417	46.2606	46.2795	46.2985	46.3174	46.3363	46.3552	46.3741	46.3930	46.4120	46.4309	.000630
16	47.4360	47.4537	47.4714	47.4891	47.5068	47.5245	47.5422	47.5599	47.5776	47.5953	47.6130	47.6307	.000590
17	48.6604	48.6769	48.6933	48.7098	48.7263	48.7428	48.7592	48.7757	48.7922	48.8087	48.8251	48.8416	.000549
18	49.8966	49.9115	49.9263	49.9412	49.9561	49.9710	49.9858	50.0007	50.0156	50.0305	50.0453	50.0602	.000496
19	51.1430	51.1562	51.1695	51.1827	51.1960	51.2092	51.2224	51.2357	51.2489	51.2622	51.2754	51.2887	.000441
20	52.3987	52.4097	52.4207	52.4317	52.4427	52.4537	52.4647	52.4757	52.4867	52.4977	52.5087	52.5197	.000367
21	53.6593	53.6678	53.6763	53.6848	53.6933	53.7018	53.7102	53.7187	53.7272	53.7357	53.7442	53.7527	.000283
22	54.9233	54.9289	54.9345	54.9400	54.9456	54.9512	54.9568	54.9624	54.9680	54.9735	54.9791	54.9847	.000186
23	56.1875	56.1899	56.1923	56.1947	56.1971	56.1995	56.2019	56.2043	56.2067	56.2091	56.2115	56.2139	.000080
24	57.4509	57.4497	57.4485	57.4473	57.4461	57.4449	57.4437	57.4425	57.4413	57.4401	57.4389	57.4377	.000040
25	58.7101	58.7050	58.6998	58.6947	58.6896	58.6845	58.6793	58.6742	58.6691	58.6640	58.6588	58.6537	.000171
26	59.9632	59.9538	59.9444	59.9350	59.9256	59.9162	59.9068	59.8974	59.8880	59.8786	59.8692	59.8598	.000313
27	61.2083	61.1942	61.1801	61.1660	61.1520	61.1379	61.1238	61.1097	61.0956	61.0815	61.0675	61.0534	.000469
28	62.4426	62.4235	62.4045	62.3854	62.3663	62.3473	62.3282	62.3091	62.2901	62.2710	62.2519	62.2329	.000635
29	63.6654	63.6412	63.6170	63.5927	63.5685	63.5443	63.5200	63.4958	63.4716	63.4474	63.4231	63.3989	.000807
30	64.8783	64.8484	64.8186	64.7887	64.7588	64.7290	64.6991	64.6692	64.6394	64.6095	64.5796	64.5498	.000995
31	66.0744	66.0387	66.0031	65.9674	65.9317	65.8961	65.8604	65.8247	65.7891	65.7534	65.7177	65.6821	.001189
32	67.2578	67.2159	67.1741	67.1322	67.0903	67.0485	67.0066	66.9647	66.9229	66.8810	66.8391	66.7973	.001395
33	68.4257	68.3774	68.3290	68.2807	68.2323	68.1840	68.1356	68.0873	68.0390	67.9906	67.9423	67.8939	.001611
34	69.5781	69.5229	69.4677	69.4124	69.3572	69.3020	69.2468	69.1916	69.1364	69.0811	69.0259	68.9707	.001840
35	70.7135	70.6511	70.5887	70.5263	70.4639	70.4015	70.3391	70.2767	70.2143	70.1519	70.0895	70.0271	.002080
36	71.8310	71.7612	71.6913	71.6215	71.5516	71.4818	71.4120	71.3421	71.2723	71.2024	71.1326	71.0627	.002328
37	72.9321	72.8543	72.7765	72.6988	72.6210	72.5432	72.4654	72.3877	72.3099	72.2321	72.1543	72.0766	.002592
38	74.0147	73.9285	73.8424	73.7562	73.6700	73.5839	73.4977	73.4115	73.3254	73.2392	73.1530	73.0669	.002872
39	75.0776	74.9828	74.8881	74.7933	74.6986	74.6038	74.5090	74.4143	74.3195	74.2248	74.1300	74.0353	.003158
40	76.1232	76.0196	75.9160	75.8123	75.7087	75.6051	75.5015	75.3979	75.2943	75.1906	75.0870	74.9834	.003454
41	77.1532	77.0407	76.9283	76.8158	76.7033	76.5909	76.4784	76.3659	76.2535	76.1410	76.0285	75.9161	.003749
42	78.1738	78.0526	77.9315	77.8103	77.6891	77.5680	77.4468	77.3256	77.2045	77.0833	76.9621	76.8410	.004039
43	79.1956	79.0656	78.9355	78.8055	78.6755	78.5454	78.4154	78.2854	78.1553	78.0253	77.8953	77.7652	.004334
44	80.2198	80.0814	79.9431	79.8047	79.6664	79.5280	79.3897	79.2513	79.1130	78.9746	78.8363	78.6980	.004612
45	81.2647	81.1173	80.9699	80.8224	80.6750	80.5276	80.3802	80.2328	80.0854	79.9380	79.7905	79.6431	.004914
46	82.3294	82.1730	82.0166	81.8601	81.7037	81.5473	81.3909	81.2345	81.0781	80.9216	80.7652	80.6088	.005214
47	83.4243	83.2579	83.0916	82.9253	82.7589	82.5926	82.4263	82.2599	82.0936	81.9273	81.7609	81.5946	.005543
48	84.5469	84.3696	84.1924	84.0151	83.8379	83.6606	83.4833	83.3061	83.1288	82.9516	82.7743	82.5971	.005908
49	85.6957	85.5059	85.3161	85.1263	84.9366	84.7468	84.5570	84.3672	84.1774	83.9876	83.7979	83.6081	.006326
50	86.8600	86.6567	86.4535	86.2502	86.0470	85.8437	85.6405	85.4372	85.2340	85.0307	84.8275	84.6242	.006775
51	88.0395	87.8210	87.6026	87.3841	87.1656	86.9472	86.7287	86.5102	86.2918	86.0733	85.8548	85.6364	.007282
52	89.2243	88.9876	88.7509	88.5142	88.2775	88.0408	87.8040	87.5673	87.3306	87.0939	86.8572	86.6205	.007890
53	90.3887	90.1301	89.8715	89.6129	89.3543	89.0957	88.8371	88.5786	88.3200	88.0614	87.8028	87.5442	.008620
54	91.5004	91.2173	90.9341	90.6510	90.3679	90.0848	89.8016	89.5185	89.2354	88.9523	88.6691	88.3860	.009437
55	92.5377	92.2202	91.9027	91.5852	91.2677	90.9502	90.6327	90.3153	89.9978	89.6803	89.3628	89.0453	.010583
56	93.3914	93.0392	92.6870	92.3348	91.9826	91.6304	91.2782	90.9261	90.5739	90.2217	89.8695	89.5173	.011740
57	94.0667	93.7185	93.3703	93.0220	92.6738	92.3256	91.9774	91.6292	91.2810	90.9327	90 5845	90.2363	.011607
58	95.0516	94.7650	94.4784	94.1918	93.9053	93.6187	93.3321	93.0455	92.7589	92.4723	92.1858	91.8992	.009553
59 or 50	**97.0874**	**97.3301**	**97.5728**	**97.8155**	**98.0583**	**98.3010**	**98.5437**	**98.7864**	**99.0291**	**99.2718**	**99.5146**	**99.7573**	**.008090**
49	95.4875	95.3143	95.1410	94.9678	94.7945	94.6213	94.4480	94.2748	94.1016	93.9283	93.7551	93.5818	.005775
48	94.6952	94.4700	94.2447	94.0195	93.7942	93.5690	93.3437	93.1185	92.8933	92.6680	92.4428	92.2175	.007508
47	94.1388	93.9069	93.6750	93.4431	93.2112	92.9793	92.7474	92.5156	92.2837	92.0518	91.8199	91.5880	.007730
46	93.4314	93.2240	93.0165	92.8090	92.6016	92.3941	92.1867	91.9792	91.7718	91.5643	91.3569	91.1494	.006915
45	92.5661	92.3833	92.2004	92.0176	91.8348	91.6520	91.4691	91.2863	91.1035	90.9207	90.7378	90.5550	.006094
44	91.6290	91.4632	91.2974	91.1317	90.9659	90.8001	90.6343	90.4686	90.3028	90.1370	89.9712	89.8055	.005526
43	90.6363	90.4857	90.3351	90.1845	90.0339	89.8833	89.7326	89.5820	89.4314	89.2808	89.1302	88.9796	.005020
42	89.6139	89.4757	89.3375	89.1992	89.0610	88.9228	88.7846	88.6464	88.5082	88.3700	88.2317	88.0935	.004607
41	88.5827	88.4546	88.3264	88.1983	88.0702	87.9420	87.8139	87.6858	87.5576	87.4295	87.3014	87.1732	.004271
40	87.5511	87.4317	87.3124	87.1931	87.0737	86.9544	86.8351	86.7157	86.5964	86.4771	86.3577	86.2384	.003977
39	86.5202	86.4090	86.2978	86.1867	86.0755	85.9643	85.8531	85.7420	85.6308	85.5196	85.4084	85.2973	.003706
38	85.4984	85.3942	85.2900	85.1858	85.0816	84.9774	84.8732	84.7690	84.6648	84.5606	84.4564	84.3522	.003473
37	84.4898	84.3918	84.2938	84.1958	84.0979	83.9999	83.9019	83.8039	83.7059	83.6080	83.5100	83.4120	.003266
36	83.4960	83.4036	83.3112	83.2188	83.1264	83.0340	82.9415	82.8491	82.7567	82.6643	82.5719	82.4795	.003080
35	82.5102	82.4236	82.3370	82.2504	82.1638	82.0772	81.9905	81.9039	81.8173	81.7307	81.6441	81.5575	.002887
34	81.5320	81.4508	81.3696	81.2884	81.2073	81.1261	81.0449	80.9637	80.8825	80.8013	80.7202	80.6390	.002706
33	80.5533	80.4779	80.4025	80.3272	80.2518	80.1764	80.1010	80.0257	79.9503	79.8749	79.7995	79.7242	.002512
32	79.5688	79.4994	79.4299	79.3605	79.2911	79.2216	79.1522	79.0828	79.0133	78.9439	78.8745	78.8050	.002314
31	78.5712	78.5080	78.4449	78.3817	78.3185	78.2554	78.1922	78.1290	78.0659	78.0027	77.9395	77.8764	.002105
30	77.5562	77.4994	77.4427	77.3860	77.3292	77.2724	77.2157	77.1590	77.1022	77.0454	76.9887	76.9320	.001892
29	76.5207	76.4703	76.4198	76.3694	76.3190	76.2685	76.2181	76.1677	76.1172	76.0668	76.0164	75.9659	.001681
28	75.4641	75.4199	75.3757	75.3315	75.2874	75.2432	75.1990	75.1548	75.1106	75.0664	75.0223	74.9781	.001473
27	74.3869	74.3487	74.3105	74.2723	74.2341	74.1959	74.1576	74.1194	74.0812	74.0430	74.0048	73.9666	.001273
26	73.2908	73.2582	73.2256	73.1930	73.1605	73.1279	73.0953	73.0627	73.0301	72.9975	72.9650	72.9324	.001086
25	72.1752	72.1481	72.1210	72.0939	72.0668	72.0397	72.0126	71.9856	71.9585	71.9314	71.9043	71.8772	.000903
24	71.0403	71.0185	70.9967	70.9749	70.9531	70.9313	70.9095	70.8877	70.8659	70.8441	70.8223	70.8005	.000727
23	69.8873	69.8705	69.8537	69.8370	69.8202	69.8034	69.7866	69.7699	69.7531	69.7363	69.7195	69.7028	.000559
22	68.7167	68.7048	68.6928	68.6809	68.6689	68.6570	68.6450	68.6331	68.6212	68.6092	68.5973	68.5853	.000398
21	67.5294	67.5220	67.5147	67.5073	67.5000	67.4926	67.4852	67.4779	67.4705	67.4632	67.4558	67.4485	.000245
20	66.3262	66.3232	66.3202	66.3173	66.3143	66.3113	66.3083	66.3054	66.3024	66.2994	66.2964	66.2935	.000099
19	65.1093	65.1104	65.1115	65.1125	65.1136	65.1147	65.1158	65.1169	65.1180	65.1190	65.1201	65.1212	.000036
18	63.8786	63.8836	63.8886	63.8936	63.8986	63.9036	63.9086	63.9137	63.9187	63.9237	63.9287	63.9337	.000167
17	62.6349	62.6436	62.6524	62.6611	62.6699	62.6786	62.6873	62.6961	62.7048	62.7136	62 7223	62.7311	.000291
16	61.3806	61.3927	61.4049	61.4170	61.4291	61.4413	61.4534	61.4655	61.4777	61.4898	61.5019	61.5141	.000404
15	60.1180	60.1332	60.1484	60.1637	60.1789	60.1941	60.2093	60.2246	60.2398	60.2550	60.2702	60.2855	.000507
14	58.8486	58.8666	58.8847	58.9027	58.9207	58.9388	58.9568	58.9748	58.9929	59.0109	59.0289	59.0470	.000601
13	57.5754	57.5959	57.6164	57.6369	57 6574	57.6779	57.6984	57.7189	57.7394	57.7599	57.7804	57.8009	.000683
12	56.3005	56.3232	56.3460	56.3687	56.3914	56.4142	56.4369	56.4596	56.4824	56.5051	56.5278	56.5506	.000758
11	55.0240	55.0486	55.0732	55.0978	55.1224	55.1470	55.1716	55.1962	55.2208	55.2454	55.2700	55.2946	.000820
10	53.7499	53.7762	53.8024	53.8287	53.8550	53.8812	53.9075	53.9338	53.9600	53 9863	54.0126	54.0388	.000875
Age.	0	1	2	3	4	5	6	7	8	9	10	11	Day.

Age.	0	1	2	3	4	5	6	7	8	9	10	11	Day.
10	41.8042	41.8271	41.8501	41.8730	41.8959	41.9189	41.9418	41.9647	41.9877	42.0106	42.0335	42.0565	.000764
11	42.9712	42.9938	43.0165	43.0391	43.0618	43.0844	43.1070	43.1297	43.1523	43.1750	43.1976	43.2203	.000755
12	44.1542	44.1760	44.1979	44.2197	44.2416	44.2634	44.2853	44.3071	44.3290	44.3508	44.3727	44.3945	.000728
13	45.3449	45.3662	45.3874	45.4087	45.4300	45.4513	45.4725	45.4938	45.5151	45.5364	45.5576	45.5789	.000709
14	46.5511	46.5714	46.5917	46.6120	46.6323	46.6526	46.6729	46.6932	46.7135	46.7338	46.7541	46.7744	.000677
15	47.7680	47.7872	47.8064	47.8256	47.8448	47.8640	47.8832	47.9025	47.9217	47.9409	47.9601	47.9793	.000640
16	48.9956	49.0136	49.0317	49.0497	49.0678	49.0858	49.1038	49.1219	49.1399	49.1580	49.1760	49.1941	.000601
17	50.2349	50.2515	50.2681	50.2847	50.3013	50.3179	50.3344	50.3510	50.3676	50.3842	50.4008	50.4174	.000553
18	51.4829	51.4979	51.5130	51.5280	51.5430	51.5581	51.5731	51.5881	51.6032	51.6182	51.6332	51.6483	.000501
19	52.7421	52.7549	52.7676	52.7804	52.7932	52.8059	52.8187	52.8315	52.8442	52.8570	52.8698	52.8825	.000425
20	54.0045	54.0148	54.0252	54.0355	54.0459	54.0562	54.0666	54.0770	54.0873	54.0976	54.1080	54.1183	.000345
21	55.2702	55.2777	55.2852	55.2928	55.3003	55.3078	55.3153	55.3229	55.3304	55.3379	55.3454	55.3530	.000251
22	56.5359	56.5404	56.5448	56.5493	56.5537	56.5582	56.5626	56.5671	56.5716	56.5760	56.5805	56.5849	.000148
23	57.8003	57.8013	57.8022	57.8032	57.8041	57.8051	57.8060	57.8070	57.8080	57.8089	57.8099	57.8108	.000032
24	59.0605	59.0576	59.0548	59.0519	59.0491	59.0462	59.0433	59.0405	59.0376	59.0348	59.0319	59.0291	.000095
25	60.3144	60.3074	60.3004	60.2933	60.2863	60.2793	60.2723	60.2653	60.2583	60.2512	60.2442	60.2372	.000234
26	61.5599	61.5483	61.5367	61.5251	61.5136	61.5020	61.4904	61.4788	61.4672	61.4556	61.4441	61.4325	.000386
27	62.7946	62.7782	62.7617	62.7453	62.7289	62.7125	62.6960	62.6796	62.6632	62.6468	62.6303	62.6139	.000547
28	64.0169	63.9955	63.9721	63.9526	63.9312	63.9098	63.8884	63.8670	63.8456	63.8241	63.8027	63.7813	.000714
29	65.2279	65.2011	65.1742	65.1474	65.1206	65.0938	65.0670	65.0401	65.0133	64.9865	64.9596	64.9328	.000894
30	66.4256	66.3931	66.3606	66.3280	66.2955	66.2630	66.2305	66.1980	66.1655	66.1330	66.1004	66.0679	.001084
31	67.6073	67.5688	67.5302	67.4917	67.4532	67.4147	67.3761	67.3376	67.2991	67.2606	67.2220	67.1835	.001284
32	68.7741	68.7293	68.6845	68.6397	68.5949	68.5501	68.5052	68.4604	68.4156	68.3708	68.3260	68.2812	.001493
33	69.9249	69.8734	69.8220	69.7705	69.7191	69.6676	69.6161	69.5647	69.5132	69.4618	69.4103	69.3589	.001715
34	71.0585	71.0001	70.9417	70.8833	70.8249	70.7665	70.7081	70.6497	70.5913	70.5329	70.4745	70.4161	.001947
35	72.1748	72.1092	72.0436	71.9781	71.9125	71.8469	71.7813	71.7158	71.6502	71.5846	71.5190	71.4535	.002186
36	73.2737	73.2005	73.1272	73.0540	72.9807	72.9075	72.8342	72.7610	72.6878	72.6145	72.5413	72.4680	.002441
37	74.3541	74.2728	74.1915	74.1101	74.0288	73.9475	73.8662	73.7849	73.7036	73.6222	73.5409	73.4596	.002710
38	75.4147	75.3251	75.2355	75.1460	75.0564	74.9668	74.8772	74.7876	74.6980	74.6084	74.5189	74.4293	.002986
39	76.4577	76.3596	76.2615	76.1634	76.0654	75.9673	75.8692	75.7711	75.6730	75.5750	75.4769	75.3788	.003269
40	77.4850	77.3784	77.2719	77.1653	77.0588	76.9522	76.8457	76.7391	76.6326	76.5260	76.4195	76.3130	.003552
41	78.5023	78.3874	78.2726	78.1577	78.0429	77.9280	77.8132	77.6983	77.5835	77.4686	77.3538	77.2390	.003828
42	79.5176	79.3945	79.2713	79.1482	79.0251	78.9020	78.7788	78.6557	78.5326	78.4095	78.2863	78.1632	.004104
43	80.5383	80.4071	80.2760	80.1448	80.0137	79.8825	79.7513	79.6202	79.4890	79.3579	79.2267	79.0956	.004372
44	81.5746	81.4348	81.2950	81.1553	81.0155	80.8757	80.7360	80.5962	80.4564	80.3166	80.1768	80.0371	.004659
45	82.6291	82.4808	82.3325	82.1842	82.0359	81.8876	81.7392	81.5909	81.4426	81.2943	81.1460	80.9977	.004943
46	83.7111	83.5534	83.3956	83.2379	83.0801	82.9224	82.7646	82.6069	82.4492	82.2914	82.1337	81.9759	.005258
47	84.8194	84.6513	84.4831	84.3150	84.1469	83.9787	83.8106	83.6425	83.4743	83.3062	83.1381	82.9699	.005604
48	85.9509	85.7708	85.5907	85.4106	85.2305	85.0504	84.8703	84.6903	84.5102	84.3301	84.1500	83.9699	.006003
49	87.0971	86.9042	86.7113	86.5183	86.3254	86.1325	85.9396	85.7467	85.5538	85.3608	85.1679	84.9750	.006430
50	88.2561	88.0487	87.8413	87.6338	87.4264	87.2190	87.0116	86.8042	86.5968	86.3893	86.1819	85.9745	.006914
51	89.4187	89.1938	88.9690	88.7441	88.5193	88.2944	88.0696	87.8447	87.6199	87.3950	87.1702	86.9453	.007495
52	90.5598	90.3140	90.0682	89.8224	89.5767	89.3309	89.0851	88.8393	88.5935	88.3477	88.1020	87.8562	.008193
53	91.6474	91.3781	91.1088	90.8395	90.5703	90.3010	90.0317	89.7624	89.4931	89.2238	88.9546	88.6853	.008976
54	92.6614	92.3591	92.0569	91.7546	91.4524	91.1501	90.8478	90.5456	90.2433	89.9411	89.6388	89.3366	.010075
55	93.4951	93.1596	92.8241	92.4886	92.1531	91.8176	91.4820	91.1465	90.8110	90.4755	90.1400	89.8045	.011183
56	94.1540	93.8229	93.4918	93.1606	92.8295	92.4984	92.1673	91.8362	91.5051	91.1740	90.8428	90.5117	.011037
57	95.1124	94.8416	94.5708	94.3001	94.0293	93.7585	93.4877	93.2170	92.9462	92.6754	92.4046	92.1339	.009026
58 or 51	**97.0874**	**97.3301**	**97.5728**	**97.8155**	**98.0583**	**98.3010**	**98.5437**	**98.7864**	**99.0291**	**99.2718**	**99.5146**	**99.7573**	**.008090**
50	95.4496	95.2665	95.0834	94.9002	94.7171	94.5340	94.3509	94.1678	93.9847	93.8015	93.6184	93.4353	.006104
49	94.6404	94.4044	94.1684	93.9325	93.6965	93.4605	93.2245	92.9886	92.7526	92.5166	92.2806	92.0447	.007866
48	94.0733	93.8309	93.5884	93.3460	93.1036	92.8611	92.6187	92.3763	92.1338	91.8914	91.6490	91.4065	.008081
47	93.3530	93.1359	92.9188	92.7017	92.4846	92.2675	92.0503	91.8332	91.6161	91.3990	91.1819	90.9648	.007237
46	92.4726	92.2809	92.0893	91.8976	91.7059	91.5143	91.3226	91.1309	90.9393	90.7476	90.5559	90.3643	.006387
45	91.5199	91.3460	91.1720	90.9981	90.8242	90.6502	90.4763	90.3024	90.1284	89.9545	89.7806	89.6066	.005798
44	90.5122	90.3540	90.1958	90.0376	89.8795	89.7213	89.5631	89.4049	89.2467	89.0885	88.9304	88.7722	.005273
43	89.4761	89.3309	89.1856	89.0404	88.8951	88.7499	88.6046	88.4594	88.3142	88.1689	88.0237	87.8784	.004841
42	88.4324	88.2977	88.1630	88.0283	87.8936	87.7589	87.6242	87.4896	87.3549	87.2202	87.0855	86.9508	.004490
41	87.3897	87.2642	87.1388	87.0133	86.8878	86.7624	86.6369	86.5114	86.3860	86.2605	86.1350	86.0096	.004182
40	86.3489	86.2320	86.1151	85.9981	85.8812	85.7643	85.6474	85.5305	85.4136	85.2966	85.1797	85.0628	.003897
39	85.3185	85.2089	85.0992	84.9896	84.8800	84.7704	84.6607	84.5511	84.4415	84.3319	84.2222	84.1126	.003654
38	84.3016	84.1985	84.0954	83.9923	83.8892	83.7861	83.6830	83.5799	83.4768	83.3737	83.2706	83.1675	.003437
37	83.3010	83.2038	83.1066	83.0094	82.9122	82.8150	82.7177	82.6205	82.5233	82.4261	82.3289	82.2317	.003240
36	82.3089	82.2177	82.1266	82.0354	81.9443	81.8531	81.7620	81.6708	81.5797	81.4885	81.3974	81.3062	.003038
35	81.3257	81.2402	81.1548	81.0693	80.9838	80.8984	80.8129	80.7274	80.6420	80.5565	80.4710	80.3856	.002849
34	80.3422	80.2628	80.1833	80.1039	80.0244	79.9450	79.8655	79.7861	79.7067	79.6272	79.5478	79.4683	.002648
33	79.3532	79.2799	79.2067	79.1334	79.0601	78.9869	78.9136	78.8403	78.7671	78.6938	78.6205	78.5473	.002442
32	78.3517	78.2849	78.2181	78.1513	78.0845	78.0177	77.9509	77.8841	77.8173	77.7505	77.6837	77.6169	.002227
31	77.3325	77.2723	77.2121	77.1520	77.0918	77.0316	76.9714	76.9112	76.8510	76.7908	76.7307	76.6705	.002006
30	76.2944	76.2407	76.1871	76.1334	76.0798	76.0261	75.9724	75.9188	75.8651	75.8115	75.7578	75.7042	.001788
29	75.2342	75.1870	75.1397	75.0925	75.0453	74.9980	74.9508	74.9036	74.8563	74.8091	74.7619	74.7146	.001574
28	74.1540	74.1129	74.0718	74.0307	73.9897	73.9486	73.9075	73.8664	73.8253	73.7842	73.7432	73.7021	.001369
27	73.0553	73.0200	72.9847	72.9494	72.9141	72.8788	72.8435	72.8082	72.7729	72.7376	72.7023	72.6670	.001177
26	71.9373	71.9076	71.8779	71.8483	71.8186	71.7889	71.7593	71.7296	71.6999	71.6703	71.6406	71.6109	.000987
25	70.8002	70.7760	70.7517	70.7275	70.7033	70.6790	70.6548	70.6306	70.6063	70.5821	70.5579	70.5336	.000808
24	69.6453	69.6262	69.6071	69.5880	69.5690	69.5499	69.5308	69.5117	69.4926	69.4735	69.4545	69.4354	.000636
23	68.4729	68.4588	68.4446	68.4305	68.4164	68.4022	68.3881	68.3740	68.3598	68.3457	68.3316	68.3174	.000471
22	67.2842	67.2748	67.2653	67.2559	67.2465	67.2370	67.2276	67.2182	67.2087	67.1993	67.1899	67.1804	.000314
21	66.0797	66.0748	66.0698	66.0649	66.0599	66.0550	66.0500	66.0451	66.0402	66.0352	66.0303	66.0253	.000165
20	64.8617	64.8609	64.8601	64.8593	64.8586	64.8578	64.8570	64.8562	64.8554	64.8546	64.8539	64.8531	.000026
19	63.6303	63.6335	63.6368	63.6400	63.6433	63.6465	63.6497	63.6530	63.6562	63.6595	63.6627	63.6660	.000108
18	62.3861	62.3931	62.4002	62.4072	62.4143	62.4213	62.4284	62.4354	62.4425	62.4495	62.4566	62.4636	.000235
17	61.1318	61.1423	61.1528	61.1633	61.1739	61.1844	61.1949	61.2054	61.2159	61.2264	61.2370	62.2475	.000350
16	59.8692	59.8829	59.8966	59.9103	59.9240	59.9377	59.9513	59.9650	59.9787	59.9924	60.0061	60.0198	.000456
15	58.6003	58.6169	58.6335	58.6500	58.6666	58.6832	58.6998	58.7164	58.7330	58.7495	58.7661	58.7827	.000553
14	57.3279	57.3470	57.3661	57.3852	57.4043	57.4234	57.4425	57.4616	57.4807	57.4998	57.5189	57.5380	.000637
13	56.0534	56.0748	56.0962	56.1176	56.1390	56.1604	56.1818	56.2032	56.2246	56.2460	56.2674	56.2888	.000713
12	54.7803	54.8036	54.8270	54.8503	54.8737	54.8970	54.9203	54.9437	54.9670	54.9904	55.0137	55.0371	.000778
11	53.5072	53.5322	53.5573	53.5823	53.6074	53.6324	53.6575	53.6825	53.7076	53.7326	53.7577	53.7827	.000835
10	52.2415	52.2678	52.2940	52.3203	52.3466	52.3729	52.3991	52.4254	52.4517	52.4780	52.5042	52.5305	.000876
Age.	0	1	2	3	4	5	6	7	8	9	10	11	Day.

Age.	0	1	2	3	4	5	6	7	8	9	10	11	Day.
10	43.2726	43.2965	43.3203	43.3442	43.3681	43.3919	43.4158	43.4397	43.4635	43.4874	43.5113	43.5351	.000795
11	44.4591	44.4822	44.5053	44.5284	44.5516	44.5747	44.5978	44.6209	44.6440	44.6671	44.6903	44.7134	.000770
12	45.6564	45.6790	45.7016	45.7242	45.7469	45.7695	45.7921	45.8147	45.8373	45.8600	45.8826	45.9052	.000754
13	46.8655	46.8872	46.9089	46.9306	46.9523	46.9740	46.9957	47.0174	47.0391	47.0608	47.0825	47.1042	.000723
14	48.0861	48.1067	48.1274	48.1480	48.1687	48.1893	48.2100	48.2306	48.2512	48.2719	48.2925	48.3132	.000688
15	49.3172	49.3367	49.3563	49.3758	49.3954	49.4149	49.4344	49.4540	49.4735	49.4931	49.5126	49.5322	.000651
16	50.5592	50.5774	50.5955	50.6137	50.6318	50.6500	50.6681	50.6863	50.7045	50.7226	50.7408	50.7589	.000605
17	51.8109	51.8275	51.8440	51.8606	51.8772	51.8938	51.9103	51.9269	51.9435	51.9601	51.9766	51.9932	.000552
18	53.0711	53.0856	53.1000	53.1145	53.1290	53.1435	53.1580	53.1724	53.1869	53.2014	53.2158	53.2303	.000482
19	54.3355	54.3476	54.3598	54.3719	54.3840	54.3962	54.4083	54.4204	54.4326	54.4447	54.4568	54.4690	.000404
20	55.6025	55.6119	55.6213	55.6307	55.6401	55.6495	55.6589	55.6683	55.6777	55.6871	55.6965	55.7059	.000313
21	56.8695	56.8759	56.8823	56.8887	56.8952	56.9016	56.9080	56.9144	56.9208	56.9272	56.9337	56.9401	.000214
22	58.1350	58.1380	58.1410	58.1441	58.1471	58.1501	58.1531	58.1562	58.1592	58.1622	58.1652	58.1683	.000101
23	59.3958	59.3951	59.3944	59.3937	59.3930	59.3923	59.3916	59.3910	59.3903	59.3896	59.3889	59.3882	.000023
24	60.6502	60.6455	60.6407	60.6360	60.6313	60.6265	60.6218	60.6171	60.6123	60.6076	60.6029	60.5981	.000158
25	61.8960	61.8868	61.8776	61.8685	61.8593	61.8501	61.8410	61.8318	61.8226	61.8134	61.8042	61.7951	.000306
26	63.1304	63.1165	63.1027	63.0888	63.0749	63.0611	63.0472	63.0333	63.0195	63.0056	62.9917	62.9779	.000462
27	64.3527	64.3340	64.3152	64.2965	64.2778	64.2590	64.2403	64.2216	64.2028	64.1841	64.1654	64.1466	.000624
28	65.5630	65.5390	65.5150	65.4910	65.4670	65.4430	65.4190	65.3951	65.3711	65.3471	65.3231	65.2991	.000800
29	66.7593	66.7298	66.7002	66.6707	66.6412	66.6117	66.5821	66.5526	66.5231	66.4936	66.4640	66.4345	.000984
30	67.9411	67.9058	67.8704	67.8351	67.7997	67.7644	67.7290	67.6937	67.6584	67.6230	67.5877	67.5523	.001178
31	69.1059	69.0645	69.0230	68.9816	68.9401	68.8987	68.8572	68.8158	68.7744	68.7329	68.6915	68.6500	.001381
32	70.2551	70.2072	70.1593	70.1114	70.0635	70.0156	69.9677	69.9199	69.8720	69.8241	69.7762	69.7283	.001596
33	71.3867	71.3321	71.2775	71.2229	71.1683	71.1137	71.0591	71.0045	70.9499	70.8953	70.8407	70.7861	.001820
34	72.5008	72.4392	72.3777	72.3161	72.2546	72.1930	72.1315	72.0700	72.0084	71.9468	71.8853	71.8237	.002052
35	73.5980	73.5290	73.4601	73.3911	73.3222	73.2532	73.1843	73.1153	73.0464	72.9774	72.9085	72.8395	.002298
36	74.6756	74.5989	74.5221	74.4454	74.3687	74.2919	74.2152	74.1385	74.0617	73.9850	73.9083	73.8315	.002558
37	75.7336	75.6489	75.5642	75.4795	75.3948	75.3101	75.2254	75.1408	75.0561	74.9714	74.8867	74.8020	.002823
38	76.7737	76.6808	76.5880	76.4951	76.4022	76.3094	76.2165	76.1236	76.0308	75.9379	75.8450	75.7522	.003095
39	77.7978	77.6968	77.5958	77.4949	77.3939	77.2929	77.1919	77.0910	76.9900	76.8890	76.7880	76.6871	.003366
40	78.8116	78.7027	78.5938	78.4849	78.3760	78.2671	78.1582	78.0494	77.9405	77.8316	77.7227	77.6138	.003630
41	79.8227	79.7059	79.5892	79.4724	79.3556	79.2389	79.1221	79.0053	78.8886	78.7718	78.6550	78.5383	.003892
42	80.8379	80.7135	80.5891	80.4647	80.3403	80.2159	80.0915	79.9672	79.8428	79.7184	79.5940	79.4696	.004146
43	81.8675	81.7349	81.6024	81.4698	81.3373	81.2047	81.0721	80.9396	80.8070	80.6745	80.5419	80.4094	.004418
44	82.9123	82.7716	82.6310	82.4903	82.3497	82.2090	82.0684	81.9277	81.7871	81.6464	81.5058	81.3651	.004688
45	83.9828	83.8332	83.6836	83.5340	83.3844	83.2348	83.0851	82.9355	82.7859	82.6363	82.4867	82.3371	.004987
46	85.0770	84.9175	84.7580	84.5985	84.4390	84.2795	84.1200	83.9604	83.8009	83.6414	83.4819	83.3224	.005317
47	86.1929	86.0220	85.8511	85.6802	85.5093	85.3384	85.1674	84.9965	84.8256	84.6547	84.4838	84.3129	.005697
48	87.3209	87.1377	86.9546	86.7714	86.5883	86.4051	86.2220	86.0388	85.8557	85.6725	85.4894	85.3062	.006105
49	88.4609	88.2639	88.0669	87.8699	87.6729	87.4759	87.2790	87.0820	86.8850	86.6880	86.4910	86.2940	.006566
50	89.6023	89.3886	89.1750	88.9613	88.7477	88.5340	88.3204	88.1067	87.8931	87.6794	87.4658	87.2521	.007122
51	90.7212	90.4875	90.2538	90.0201	89.7864	89.5527	89.3190	89.0852	88.8515	88.6178	88.3841	88.1504	.007790
52	91.7864	91.5302	91.2740	91.0178	90.7616	90.5054	90.2491	89.9929	89.7367	89.4805	89.2243	88.9681	.008540
53	92.7778	92.4899	92.2020	91.9140	91.6261	91.3382	91.0503	90.7624	90.4745	90.1865	89.8986	89.6107	.009597
54	93.5927	93.2729	92.9531	92.6334	92.3136	91.9938	91.6740	91.3543	91.0345	90.7147	90.3950	90.0752	.010659
55	94.2363	93.9213	93.6062	93.2912	92.9762	92.6612	92.3461	92.0311	91.7161	91.4011	91.0860	90.7710	.010501
56	95.1695	94.9136	94.6577	94.4017	94.1458	93.8899	93.6340	93.3781	93.1222	92.8662	92.6103	92.3544	.008530
57 or 52	**97.0874**	**97.3301**	**97.5728**	**97.8155**	**98.0583**	**98.3010**	**98.5437**	**98.7864**	**99.0291**	**99.2718**	**99.5146**	**99.7573**	**.008090**
51	95.4094	95.2158	95.0223	94.8287	94.6351	94.4416	94.2480	94.0544	93.8609	93.6673	93.4737	93.2802	.006452
50	94.5823	94.3350	94.0876	93.8403	93.5930	93.3457	93.0983	92.8510	92.6037	92.3564	92.1090	91.8617	.008244
49	94.0042	93.7506	93.4971	93.2435	92.9900	92.7364	92.4829	92.2293	91.9758	91.7222	91.4687	91.2151	.008452
48	93.2700	93.0427	92.8154	92.5880	92.3607	92.1334	91.9061	91.6788	91.4515	91.2241	90.9968	90.7695	.007577
47	92.3734	92.1724	91.9715	91.7705	91.5696	91.3686	91.1676	90.9667	90.7657	90.5648	90.3638	90.1629	.006698
46	91.4045	91.2220	91.0394	90.8568	90.6743	90.4917	90.3092	90.1266	89.9441	89.7615	89.5790	89.3964	.006085
45	90.3808	90.2146	90.0484	89.8822	89.7160	89.5498	89.3836	89.2175	89.0513	88.8851	88.7189	88.5527	.005540
44	89.3296	89.1769	89.0242	88.8715	88.7188	88.5661	88.4134	88.2607	88.1080	87.9553	87.8026	87.6499	.005090
43	88.2728	88.1311	87.9895	87.8478	87.7062	87.5645	87.4229	87.2812	87.1396	86.9980	86.8563	86.7146	.004722
42	87.2183	87.0863	86.9543	86.8224	86.6904	86.5584	86.4264	86.2945	86.1625	86.0305	85.8985	85.7666	.004399
41	86.1671	86.0441	85.9211	85.7981	85.6751	85.5521	85.4291	85.3061	85.1831	85.0601	84.9371	84.8141	.004100
40	85.1277	85.0124	84.8970	84.7817	84.6664	84.5510	84.4357	84.3204	84.2050	84.0897	83.9744	83.8590	.003844
39	84.1028	83.9943	83.8859	83.7774	83.6690	83.5605	83.4520	83.3436	83.2351	83.1267	83.0182	82.9098	.003615
38	83.0951	82.9928	82.8905	82.7882	82.6859	82.5836	82.4813	82.3791	82.2768	82.1745	82.0722	81.9699	.003410
37	82.0969	82.0010	81.9050	81.8091	81.7131	81.6172	81.5212	81.4253	81.3294	81.2334	81.1375	81.0415	.003198
36	81.1082	81.0182	80.9282	80.8382	80.7482	80.6582	80.5681	80.4781	80.3881	80.2981	80.2081	80.1181	.003000
35	80.1202	80.0365	79.9528	79.8690	79.7853	79.7016	79.6179	79.5342	79.4505	79.3667	79.2830	79.1993	.002790
34	79.1268	79.0495	78.9722	78.8949	78.8176	78.7403	78.6630	78.5856	78.5083	78.4310	78.3537	78.2764	.002577
33	78.1211	78.0505	77.9799	77.9093	77.8387	77.7681	77.6975	77.6269	77.5563	77.4857	77.4151	77.3445	.002353
32	77.0983	77.0345	76.9707	76.9070	76.8432	76.7794	76.7156	76.6519	76.5881	76.5243	76.4605	76.3968	.002126
31	76.0563	75.9992	75.9422	75.8851	75.8281	75.7710	75.7140	75.6569	75.5998	75.5428	75.4857	75.4287	.001902
30	74.9938	74.9434	74.8930	74.8425	74.7921	74.7417	74.6912	74.6408	74.5904	74.5400	74.4895	74.4391	.001681
29	73.9102	73.8661	73.8220	73.7779	73.7338	73.6897	73.6456	73.6015	73.5574	73.5133	73.4692	73.4251	.001470
28	72.8088	72.7706	72.7325	72.6943	72.6562	72.6180	72.5798	72.5417	72.5035	72.4654	72.4272	72.3891	.001272
27	71.6884	71.6560	71.6237	71.5913	71.5589	71.5266	71.4942	71.4618	71.4295	71.3971	71.3647	71.3324	.001079
26	70.5492	70.5224	70.4956	70.4688	70.4421	70.4153	70.3885	70.3617	70.3349	70.3081	70.2814	70.2546	.000893
25	69.3924	69.3709	69.3494	69.3279	69.3064	69.2849	69.2634	69.2420	69.2205	69.1990	69.1775	69.1560	.000716
24	68.2184	68.2020	68.1855	68.1691	68.1527	68.1363	68.1198	68.1034	68.0870	68.0706	68.0541	68.0377	.000547
23	67.0281	67.0165	67.0049	66.9933	66.9817	66.9701	66.9585	66.9470	66.9354	66.9238	66.9122	66.9006	.000386
22	65.8225	65.8155	65.8085	65.8015	65.7945	65.7875	65.7805	65.7736	65.7666	65.7596	65.7526	65.7456	.000233
21	64.6036	64.6009	64.5981	64.5954	64.5926	64.5899	64.5871	64.5844	64.5817	64.5789	64.5762	64.5734	.000091
20	63.3713	63.3727	63.3741	63.3754	63.3768	63.3782	63.3796	63.3810	63.3824	63.3837	63.3851	63.3865	.000046
19	62.1267	62.1320	62.1373	62.1426	62.1479	62.1532	62.1584	62.1637	62.1690	62.1743	62.1796	62.1849	.000176
18	60.8721	60.8809	60.8898	60.8986	60.9075	60.9163	60.9251	60.9340	60.9428	60.9517	60.9605	60.9694	.000295
17	59.6098	59.6219	59.6340	59.6461	59.6582	59.6703	59.6823	59.6944	59.7065	59.7186	59.7307	59.7428	.000403
16	58.3413	58.3564	58.3714	58.3865	58.4015	58.4166	58.4316	58.4467	58.4618	58.4768	58.4919	58.5069	.000502
15	57.0698	57.0874	57.1051	57.1227	57.1404	59.1580	57.1757	57.1933	57.2110	57.2286	57.2463	57.2640	.000588
14	55.7963	55.8163	55.8363	55.8563	55.8764	55.8964	55.9164	55.9364	55.9564	55.9764	55.9965	56.0165	.000667
13	54.5240	54.5460	54.5680	54.5900	54.6121	54.6341	54.6561	54.6781	54 7001	54.7221	54.7442	54.7662	.000734
12	53.2548	53.2786	53.3024	53.3261	53.3499	53.3737	53.3975	53.4213	53.4451	53.4688	53.4926	53.5164	.000793
11	51.9903	52.0154	52.0404	52.0655	52.0905	52.1156	52.1406	52.1657	52.1908	52.2158	52.2409	52.2659	.000835
10	50.7344	50.7606	50.7867	50.8129	50.8390	50.8652	50.8913	50.9175	50.9437	50.9698	50.9960	51.0221	.000872
Age.	0	1	2	3	4	5	6	7	8	9	10	11	Day.

Age.	0	1	2	3	4	5	6	7	8	9	10	11	Day.
10	44.7522	44.7765	44.8009	44.8252	44.8496	44.8739	44.8982	44.9226	44.9469	44.9713	44.9956	45.0200	.000811
11	45.9526	45.9765	46.0004	46.0242	46.0481	46.0720	46.0959	46.1198	46.1437	46.1675	46.1914	46.2153	.000796
12	47.1678	47.1908	47.2139	47.2369	47.2599	47.2830	47.3060	47.3290	47.3521	47.3751	47.3981	47.4212	.000768
13	48.3911	48.4131	48.4352	48.4572	48.4793	48.5013	48.5233	48.5454	48.5674	48.5895	48.6115	48.6336	.000735
14	49.6253	49.6463	49.6672	49.6882	49.7092	49.7302	49.7511	49.7721	49.7931	49.8141	49.8350	49.8560	.000699
15	50.8704	50.8900	50.9097	50.9293	50.9490	50.9686	50.9883	51.0080	51.0276	51.0472	51.0669	51.0865	.000655
16	52.1243	52.1424	52.1606	52.1787	52.1969	52.2150	52.2331	52.2513	52.2694	52.2876	52.3057	52.3239	.000605
17	53.3867	53.4028	53.4189	53.4350	53.4512	53.4673	53.4834	53.4995	53.5156	53.5317	53.5479	53.5640	.000537
18	54.6527	54.6665	54.6804	54.6942	54.7081	54.7219	54.7357	54.7496	54.7634	54.7773	54.7911	54.8050	.000461
19	55.9212	55.9324	55.9436	55.9548	55.9660	55.9772	55.9883	55.9995	56.0107	56.0219	56.0331	56.0443	.000373
20	57.1892	57.1975	57.2058	57.2141	57.2224	57.2307	57.2390	57.2472	57.2555	57.2638	57.2721	57.2804	.000276
21	58.4554	58.4604	58.4654	58.4704	58.4754	58.4804	58.4853	58.4903	58.4953	58.5003	58.5053	58.5103	.000166
22	59.7169	59.7183	59.7197	59.7210	59.7224	59.7238	59.7252	59.7266	59.7280	59.7293	59.7307	59.7321	.000046
23	60.9715	60.9690	60.9664	60.9638	60.9613	60.9587	60.9562	60.9536	60.9511	60.9485	60.9460	60.9434	.000085
24	62.2174	62.2105	62.2036	62.1967	62.1899	62.1830	62.1761	62.1692	62.1623	62.1554	62.1486	62.1417	.000229
25	63.4517	63.4403	63.4288	63.4174	63.4059	63.3945	63.3830	63.3716	63.3602	63.3487	63.3373	63.3258	.000381
26	64.6735	64.6573	64.6411	64.6250	64.6088	64.5926	64.5764	64.5603	64.5441	64.5279	64.5117	64.4956	.000539
27	65.8832	65.8619	65.8406	65.8193	65.7981	65.7768	65.7555	65.7342	65.7129	65.6916	65.6704	65.6491	.000709
28	67.0783	67.0516	67.0250	66.9983	66.9717	66.9450	66.9183	66.8917	66.8650	66.8384	66.8117	66.7851	.000888
29	68.2583	68.2260	68.1937	68.1613	68.1290	68.0967	68.0644	68.0321	67.9998	67.9674	67.9351	67.9028	.001077
30	69.4227	69.3845	69.3462	69.3080	69.2698	69.2316	69.1933	69.1551	69.1169	69.0787	69.0404	69.0022	.001274
31	70.5695	70.5250	70.4805	70.4360	70.3916	70.3471	70.3026	70.2581	70.2136	70.1691	70.1247	70.0802	.001483
32	71.6991	71.6481	71.5971	71.5461	71.4951	71.4441	71.3931	71.3422	71.2912	71.2402	71.1892	71.1382	.001700
33	72.8108	72.7531	72.6954	72.6377	72.5800	72.5223	72.4645	72.4068	72.3491	72.2914	72.2337	72.1760	.001923
34	73.9053	73.8404	73.7756	73.7107	73.6458	73.5810	73.5161	73.4512	73.3864	73.3215	73.2566	73.1918	.002162
35	74.9808	74.9084	74.8360	74.7636	74.6912	74.6188	74.5464	74.4741	74.4017	74.3293	74.2569	74.1845	.002413
36	76.0356	75.9555	75.8755	75.7954	75.7153	75.6353	75.5552	75.4751	75.3951	75.3150	75.2349	75.1549	.002669
37	77.0726	76.9847	76.8967	76.8088	76.7209	76.6329	76.5450	76.4571	76.3691	76.2812	76.1933	76.1053	.002931
38	78.0933	77.9976	77.9019	77.8061	77.7104	77.6147	77.5190	77.4233	77.3276	77.2318	77.1361	77.0404	.003190
39	79.1032	78.9999	78.8966	78.7933	78.6901	78.5868	78.4835	78.3802	78.2769	78.1736	78.0704	77.9671	.003443
40	80.1101	79.9993	79.8885	79.7777	79.6669	79.5561	79.4453	79.3346	79.2238	79.1130	79.0022	78.8914	.003693
41	81.1201	81.0021	80.8841	80.7661	80.6481	80.5301	80.4120	80.2940	80.1760	80.0580	79.9400	79.8220	.003933
42	82.1430	82.0172	81.8915	81.7657	81.6400	81.5142	81.3884	81.2627	81.1369	81.0112	80.8854	80.7597	.004192
43	83.1799	83.0465	82.9131	82.7797	82.6463	82.5129	82.3794	82.2460	82.1126	81.9792	81.8458	81.7124	.004447
44	84.2395	84.0976	83.9556	83.8137	83.6718	83.5299	83.3880	83.2460	83.1041	82.9622	82.8202	82.6783	.004731
45	85.3209	85.1696	85.0183	84.8669	84.7156	84.5643	84.4129	84.2616	84.1103	83.9589	83.8076	83.6563	.005043
46	86.4216	86.2594	86.0972	85.9350	85.7727	85.6105	85.4483	85.2861	85.1239	84.9616	84.7994	84.6372	.005407
47	87.5331	87.3592	87.1853	87.0114	86.8375	86.6636	86.4897	86.3158	86.1419	85.9680	85.7941	85.6202	.005797
48	88.6541	88.4670	88.2798	88.0927	87.9056	87.7185	87.5313	87.3442	87.1571	86.9700	86.7828	86.5957	.006237
49	89.7758	89.5727	89.3696	89.1666	88.9635	88.7604	88.5573	88.3543	88.1512	87.9481	87.7450	87.5420	.006769
50	90.8737	90.6514	90.4291	90.2068	89.9845	89.7622	89.5399	89.3176	89.0953	88.8730	88.6507	88.4284	.007410
51	91.9175	91.6736	91.4297	91.1859	90.9420	90.6981	90.4542	90.2104	89.9665	89.7226	89.4787	89.2349	.008129
52	92.8879	92.6135	92.3392	92.0648	91.7905	91.5161	91.2417	90.9674	90.6930	90.4187	90.1443	89.8700	.009145
53	93.6847	93.3797	93.0747	92.7698	92.4648	92.1598	91.8548	91.5499	91.2449	90.9399	90.6350	90.3300	.010166
54	94.3138	94.0139	93.7141	93.4142	93.1144	92.8145	92.5146	92.2148	91.9149	91.6151	91.3152	91.0154	.009995
55	95.2233	94.9814	94.7394	94.4975	94.2556	94.0136	93.7717	93.5298	93.2878	93.0459	92.8040	92.5620	.008064
56 or 53	**97.0874**	**97.3301**	**97.5729**	**97.8155**	**98.0583**	**98.3010**	**98.5437**	**98.7864**	**99.9291**	**99.2718**	**99.5146**	**99.7573**	**.008090**
52	95.3678	95.1631	94.9584	94.7537	94.5490	94.3443	94.1395	93.9348	93.7301	93.5254	93.3207	93.1160	.006823
51	94.5209	94.2615	94.0022	93.7428	93.4835	93.2241	92.9647	92.7054	92.4460	92.1867	91.9273	91.6680	.008645
50	93.9310	93.6657	93.4003	93.1350	92.8797	92.6044	92.3390	92.0737	91.8084	91.5431	91.2777	91.0124	.008844
49	93.1825	92.9444	92.7063	92.4682	92.2301	91.9920	91.7540	91.5159	91.2778	91.0397	90.8016	90.5635	.007936
48	92.2687	92.0579	91.8471	91.6362	91.4254	91.2146	91.0038	90.7930	90.5822	90.3713	90.1605	89.9497	.007027
47	91.2827	91.0910	90.8993	90.7076	90.5159	90.3242	90.1325	89.9408	89.7491	89.5574	89.3657	89.1740	.006390
46	90.2418	90.0671	89.8925	89.7178	89.5431	89.3685	89.1938	89.0191	88.8445	88.6698	88.4951	88.3205	.005822
45	89.1746	89.0140	88.8534	88.6928	88.5322	88.3716	88.2110	88.0504	87.8898	87.7292	87.5686	87.4080	.005353
44	88.1032	87.9541	87.8051	87.6560	87.5070	87.3580	87.2089	87.0598	86.9108	86.7617	86.6127	86.4636	.004968
43	87.0363	86.8974	86.7585	86.6196	86.4808	86.3419	86.2030	86.0641	85.9252	85.7863	85.6475	85.5086	.004629
42	85.9741	85.8446	85.7152	85.5857	85.4562	85.3268	85.1973	85.0678	84.9384	84.8089	84.6794	84.5500	.004315
41	84.9252	84.8038	84.6824	84.5610	84.4396	84.3182	84.1968	84.0755	83.9541	83.8327	93.7113	83.5899	.004046
40	83.8922	83.7780	83.6639	83.5497	83.4356	83.3214	83.2073	83.0931	82.9790	82.8648	82.7507	82.6365	.003805
39	82.8774	82.7697	82.6621	82.5544	82.4468	82.3391	82.2315	82.1238	82.0162	81.9085	81.8009	81.6932	.003588
38	81.8730	81.7720	81.6710	81.5700	81.4690	81.3680	81.2670	81.1661	81.0651	80.9641	80.8631	80.7621	.003366
37	80.8789	80.7841	80.6893	80.5946	80.4998	80.4050	80.3102	80.2155	80.1207	80.0259	79.9311	79.8364	.003159
36	79.8860	79.7978	79.7095	79.6213	79.5331	79.4449	79.3566	79.2684	79.1802	79.0920	79.0037	78.9155	.002941
35	78.8886	78.8071	78.7255	78.6440	78.5624	78.4809	78.3993	78.3178	78.2363	78.1547	78.0732	77.9916	.002718
34	77.8790	77.8044	77.7298	77.6552	77.5806	77.5060	77.4313	77.3567	77.2821	77.2075	77.1329	77.0583	.002487
33	76.8523	76.7848	76.7172	76.6497	76.5821	76.5146	76.4470	76.3795	76.3120	76.2444	76.1769	76.1093	.002251
32	75.8069	75.7463	75.6857	75.6251	75.5645	75.5039	75.4432	75.3826	75.3220	75.2614	75.2008	75.1402	.002020
31	74.7408	74.6870	74.6332	74.5794	74.5257	74.4719	74.4181	74.3643	74.3105	74.2567	74.2030	74.1492	.001793
30	73.6553	73.6080	73.5608	73.5135	73.4662	73.4190	73.3717	73.3244	73.2772	73.2299	73.1826	73.1354	.001575
29	72.5507	72.5096	72.4684	72.4273	72.3861	72.3450	72.3038	72.2627	72.2216	72.1804	72.1393	72.0981	.001371
28	71.4278	71.3926	71.3574	71.3222	71.2871	71.2519	71.2167	71.1815	71.1463	71.1111	71.0760	71.0408	.001173
27	70.2865	70.2571	70.2276	70.1982	70.1687	70.1393	70.1098	70.0804	70.0510	70.0215	69.9921	69.9626	.000981
26	69.1279	69.1039	69.0798	69.0558	69.0318	69.0078	68.9837	68.9597	68.9357	68.9117	68.8876	68.8636	.000801
25	67.9523	67.9335	67.9147	67.8959	67.8771	67.8583	67.8394	67.8206	67.8018	67.7830	67.7642	67.7454	.000627
24	66.7607	66.7468	66.7330	66.7191	66.7053	66.6914	66.6775	66.6637	66.6498	66.6360	66.6221	66.6083	.000462
23	65.5539	65.5447	65.5356	65.5264	65.5173	65.5081	65.4990	65.4898	65.4807	65.4715	65.4624	65.4532	.000305
22	64.3341	64.3293	64.3246	64.3198	64.3150	64.3103	64.3055	64.3007	64.2960	64.2912	64.2864	64.2817	.000159
21	63.1012	63.1006	63.1001	63.0995	63.0990	63.0984	63.0979	63.0973	63.0968	63.0962	63.0957	63.0951	.000018
20	61.8359	61.8410	61.8462	61.8513	61.8564	61.8616	61.8667	61.8718	61.8770	61.8821	61.8872	61.8924	.000171
19	60.6014	60.6085	60.6156	60.6227	60.6298	60.6369	60.6440	60.6510	60.6581	60.6652	60.6723	60.6794	.000236
18	59.3391	59.3495	59.3600	59.3704	59.3808	59.3912	59.4016	59.4121	59.4225	59.4329	59.4433	59.4538	.000347
17	58.0712	58.0847	58.0981	58.1116	58.1251	58.1386	58.1520	58.1655	58.1790	58.1925	58.2060	58.2194	.000449
16	56.8004	56.8165	56.8327	56.8488	56.8650	56.8811	56.8972	56.9134	56.9295	56.9457	56.9618	56.9780	.000538
15	55.5283	55.5469	55.5654	55.5840	55.6026	55.6211	55.6397	55.6583	55.6768	55.6954	55.7140	55.7325	.000619
14	54.2574	54.2780	54.2986	54.3193	54.3399	54.3605	54.3811	54.4018	54.4224	54.4430	54.4636	54.4843	.000687
13	52.9892	53.0117	53.0341	53.0566	53.0791	53.1015	53.1240	53.1465	53.1689	53.1914	53.2139	53.2363	.000749
12	51.7291	51.7529	51.7767	51.8005	51.8243	51.8481	51.8719	51.8957	51.9195	51.9433	51.9671	51.9909	.000793
11	50.4747	50.4996	50.5246	50.5495	50.5745	50.5994	50.6244	50.6493	50.6743	50.6992	50.7242	50.7491	.000832
10	49.2311	49.2569	49.2828	49.3086	49.3345	49.3603	49.3861	49.4120	49.4378	49.4687	49.4895	49.5154	.000861
Age.	0	1	2	3	4	5	6	7	8	9	10	11	Day.

Age.	0	1	2	3	4	5	6	7	8	9	10	11	Day.
10	46.2374	46.2625	46.2876	46.3127	46.3378	46.3629	46.3880	46.4131	46.4382	46.4633	46.4884	46.5135	.000837
11	47.4554	47.4797	47.5040	47.5283	47.5526	47.5769	47.6011	47.6254	47.6497	47.6740	47.6983	47.7226	.000810
12	48.6843	48.7077	48.7310	48.7544	48.7777	48.8011	48.8244	48.8478	48.8712	48.8945	48.9179	48.9412	.000778
13	49.9208	49.9432	49.9655	49.9879	50.0102	50.0326	50.0550	50.0773	50.0997	50.1220	50.1444	50.1667	.000745
14	51.1684	51.1895	51.2106	51.2317	51.2528	51.2739	51.2950	51.3161	51.3372	51.3583	51.3794	51.4005	.000703
15	52.4249	52.4445	52.4642	52.4838	52.5035	52.5231	52.5428	52.5624	52.5821	52.6017	52.6214	52.6410	.000655
16	53.6892	53.7069	53.7246	53.7422	53.7599	53.7776	53.7953	53.8130	53.8307	53.8483	53.8660	53.8837	.000589
17	54.9569	54.9724	54.9879	55.0034	55.0189	55.0344	55.0498	55.0653	55.0808	55.0963	55.1118	55.1273	.000516
18	56.2267	56.2396	56.2525	56.2654	56.2784	56.2913	56.3042	56.3171	56.3300	56.3430	56.3559	56.3688	.000432
19	57.4957	57.5058	57.5159	57.5260	57.5361	57.5462	57.5562	57.5663	57.5764	57.5865	57.5966	57.6067	.000336
20	58.7625	58.7694	58.7763	58.7831	58.7900	58.7969	58.8038	58.8107	58.8176	58.8244	58.8313	58.8382	.000229
21	60.0243	60.0277	60.0310	60.0344	60.0378	60.0411	60.0445	60.0479	60.0512	60.0546	60.0580	60.0613	.000112
22	61.2792	61.2787	61.2783	61.2778	61.2773	61.2769	61.2764	61.2759	61.2755	61.2750	61.2745	61.2741	.000015
23	62.5248	62.5201	62.5154	62.5108	62.5061	62.5014	62.4967	62.4921	62.4874	62.4827	62.4780	62.4734	.000156
24	63.7588	63.7497	63.7406	63.7314	63.7223	63.7132	63.7041	63.6950	63.6859	63.6767	63.6676	63.6585	.000304
25	64.9802	64.9665	64.9527	64.9390	64.9253	64.9116	64.8978	64.8841	64.8704	64.8567	64.8430	64.8292	.000457
26	66.1889	66.1702	66.1514	66.1327	66.1140	66.0953	66.0765	66.0578	66.0391	66.0204	66.0016	65.9829	.000624
27	67.3830	67.3591	67.3352	67.3112	67.2873	67.2634	67.2395	67.2156	67.1917	67.1677	67.1438	67.1199	.000797
28	68.5616	68.5322	68.5027	68.4733	68.4439	68.4145	68.3850	68.3556	68.3262	68.2968	68.2673	68.2379	.000981
29	69.7238	69.6903	69.6568	69.6233	69.5898	69.5563	69.5228	69.4893	69.4558	69.4223	69.3888	69.3553	.001117
30	70.8697	70.8285	70.7872	70.7460	70.7048	70.6636	70.6223	70.5811	70.5399	70.4987	70.4574	70.4162	.001374
31	71.9966	71.9490	71.9015	71.8540	71.8064	71.7588	71.7113	71.6637	71.6162	71.5686	71.5211	71.4735	.001585
32	73.1059	73.0519	72.9979	72.9439	72.8899	72.8359	72.7818	72.7278	72.6738	72.6198	72.5658	72.5118	.001800
33	74.1976	74.1366	74.0756	74.0146	73.9537	73.8927	73.8317	73.7707	73.7097	73.6487	73.5878	73.5268	.002033
34	75.2700	75.2017	75.1335	75.0652	74.9970	74.9287	74.8604	74.7922	74.7239	74.6557	74.5874	74.5192	.002275
35	76.3222	76.2465	76.1709	76.0952	76.0195	75.9439	75.8682	75.7925	75.7169	75.6412	75.5655	75.4899	.002522
36	77.3556	77.2723	77.1891	77.1058	77.0226	76.9393	76.8561	76.7728	76.6896	76.6063	76.5231	76.4398	.002775
37	78.3728	78.2821	78.1913	78.1006	78.0098	77.9191	77.8283	77.7376	77.6469	77.5561	77.4654	77.3746	.003025
38	79.3787	79.2807	79.1827	79.0847	78.9868	78.8888	78.7908	78.6928	78.5948	78.4968	78.3989	78.3009	.003266
39	80.3810	80.2758	80.1707	80.0655	79.9604	79.8552	79.7501	79.6450	79.5398	79.4346	79.3295	79.2243	.003505
40	81.3859	81.2739	81.1619	81.0499	80.9379	80.8259	80.7138	80.6018	80.4898	80.3778	80.2658	80.1538	.003733
41	82.4026	82.2832	82.1639	82.0445	81.9252	81.8058	81.6864	81.5671	81.4477	81.3284	81.2090	81.0897	.003945
42	83.4317	83.3051	83.1785	83.0519	82.9253	82.7987	82.6721	82.5455	82.4189	82.2923	82.1657	82.0391	.004220
43	84.4820	84.3473	84.2127	84.0780	83.9434	83.8087	83.6740	83.5394	83.4047	83.2701	83.1354	83.0008	.004488
44	85.5514	85.4078	85.2641	85.1205	84.9769	84.8333	84.6896	84.5460	84.4024	84.2588	84 1151	83.9715	.004787
45	86.6383	86.4843	86.3303	86.1763	86.0223	85.8683	85.7143	85.5603	85.4063	85.2523	85.0983	84.9443	.005133
46	87.7337	87.5685	87.4034	87.2382	87.0731	86.9080	86.7428	86.5776	86.4125	86.2473	86.0822	85.9170	.005505
47	88.8374	88.6596	88.4818	88.3040	88.1262	87.9484	87.7706	87.5929	87.4151	87.2373	87.0595	86.8817	.005926
48	89.9397	89.7466	89.5535	89.3604	89.1673	88.9742	88.7811	88.5881	88.3950	88.2019	88.0088	87.8157	.006436
49	91.0177	90.8062	90.5947	90.3831	90.1716	89.9601	89.7486	89.5371	89.3256	89.1140	88.9025	88.6910	.007050
50	92.0413	91.8091	91.5768	91.3446	91.1124	90.8802	90.6480	90.4157	90.1835	89.9513	89.7190	89.4868	.007741
51	92.9918	92.7302	92.4686	92.2070	91.9455	91.6839	91.4223	91.1607	90.8991	90.6375	90.3760	90.1144	.008719
52	93.7716	93.4806	93.1896	92.8986	92.6077	92.3167	92.0257	91.7347	91.4437	91.1527	90.8618	90.5708	.009699
53	94.3868	94.1012	93.8156	93.5301	93.2445	92.9589	92.6733	92.3878	92.1022	91.8166	91.5310	91.2455	.009519
54	95.2740	95.0452	94.8165	94.5877	94.3590	94.1302	93.9014	93.6727	93.4439	93.2152	92.9864	92.7577	.007625
55 or 54	**97.0874**	**97.3301**	**97.5728**	**97.8155**	**98.0583**	**98.3010**	**98.5437**	**98.7864**	**99.0291**	**99.2718**	**99.5146**	**99.7573**	**.008090**
53	95.3217	95.1053	94.8890	94.6726	94.4563	94.2400	94.0236	93.8072	93.5909	93.3745	93.1582	92.9418	.007212
52	94.4558	94.1838	93.9118	93.6398	93.3678	93.0958	92.8238	92.5518	92.2798	92.0078	91.7358	91.4638	.009067
51	93.8536	93.5758	93.2980	93.0202	92.7424	92.4646	92.1868	91.9091	91.6313	91.3535	91.0757	90.7979	.009260
50	93.0898	92.8403	92.5908	92.3413	92.0918	91.8423	91.5928	91.3433	91.0938	90.8443	90.5948	90.3453	.008317
49	92.1583	91.9371	91.7159	91.4946	91.2734	91.0522	90.8310	90.6098	90.3886	90.1673	89.9461	89.7249	.007374
48	91.1537	90.9524	90.7510	90.5497	90.3483	90.1470	89.9456	89.7443	89.5430	89.3416	89.1403	88.9389	.006711
47	90.0950	89.9114	89.7278	89.5441	89.3605	89.1769	88.9933	88.8097	88.6261	88.4424	88.2588	88.0752	.006120
46	89.0106	88.8416	88.6727	88.5037	88.3347	88.1658	87.9968	87.8278	87.6589	87.4899	87.3209	87.1520	.005632
45	87.9237	87.7668	87.6100	87.4531	87.2962	87.1393	86.9824	86.8256	86.6687	86.5118	86.3550	86.1981	.005229
44	86.8429	86.6967	86.5504	86.4042	86.2580	86.1118	85.9655	85.8193	85.6731	85.5269	85.3806	85.2344	.004874
43	85.7692	85.6329	85.4965	85.3602	85.2239	85.0876	84.9512	84.8149	84.6786	84.5423	84.4060	84.2696	.004544
42	84.7102	84.5824	84.4545	84.3267	84.1989	84.0711	83.9432	83.8154	83.6876	83.5598	83.4320	83.3041	.004261
41	83.6689	83.5487	83.4285	83.3083	83.1881	83.0679	82.9477	82.8276	82.7074	82.5872	82.4670	82.3468	.004006
40	82.6470	82.5336	82.4203	82.3070	82.1936	82.0803	81.9670	81.8536	81.7403	81.6270	81.5136	81.4003	.003777
39	81.6364	81.5301	81.4237	81.3174	81.2110	81.1047	80.9983	80 8920	80.7857	80.6793	80.5730	80.4666	.003545
38	80.6369	80.5371	80.4372	80.3374	80.2376	80.1378	80.0380	79.9381	79.8383	79.7385	79.6386	79.5388	.003327
37	79.6393	79.5463	79.4533	79.3604	79.2674	79.1744	79.0814	78.9885	78.8955	78.8025	78.7095	78.6166	.003099
36	78.6374	78.5514	78.4654	78.3793	78.2933	78.2073	78.1213	78.0353	77.9493	77.8632	77.7772	77.6912	.002867
35	77.6243	77.5455	77.4667	77.3878	77.3090	77.2302	77.1514	77.0726	76.9938	76.9150	76.8361	76.7573	.002627
34	76.5939	76.5224	76.4509	76.3794	76.3079	76.2364	76.1649	76.0934	76.0219	75.9504	75.8789	75.8074	.002383
33	75.5451	75.4808	75.4164	75.3521	75.2877	75.2234	75.1590	75.0947	75.0304	74.9660	74.9017	74.8373	.002145
32	74.4764	74.4191	74.3617	74.3044	74.2470	74.1897	74.1323	74.0750	74.0177	73.9603	73.9030	73.8456	.001911
31	73.3869	73.3363	73.2857	73.2351	73.1846	73.1340	73.0834	73.0328	72.9822	72.9316	72.8811	72.8305	.001686
30	72.2807	72.2364	72.1922	72.1479	72.1037	72.0594	72.0151	71.9709	71.9266	71.8824	71.8381	71.7939	.001475
29	71.1751	71.1353	71.0955	71.0557	71.0159	70.9761	70.9362	70.8964	70.8566	70.8168	70.7770	70.7372	.001327
28	70.0116	69.9794	69.9471	69.9149	69.8826	69.8504	69.8181	69.7859	69.7537	69.7214	69.6892	69.6569	.001075
27	68.8512	68.8245	68.7979	68.7712	68.7446	68.7179	68.6912	68.6646	68.6379	68.6113	68.5846	68.5580	.000888
26	67.6737	67.6524	67.6311	67.6099	67.5886	67.5673	67.5460	67.5248	67.5035	67.4822	67.4610	67.4397	.000709
25	66.4812	66.4650	66.4487	66.4325	66.4163	66.4001	66.3838	66.3676	66.3514	66.3352	66.3190	66.3027	.000540
24	65.2734	65.2620	65.2506	65.2392	65.2279	65.2165	65.2051	65.1937	65.1823	65.1710	65.1596	65.1482	.000379
23	64.0527	64.0458	64.0389	64.0320	64.0251	64.0182	64.0113	64.0044	63.9975	63.9906	63.9837	63.9768	.000230
22	62.8193	62.8167	62.8142	62.8116	62.8090	62.8065	62.8039	62.8013	62.7988	62.7962	62.7936	62.7911	.000085
21	61.5737	61.5752	61.5768	61.5783	61.5799	61.5814	61.5830	61.5845	61.5860	61.5876	61.5891	61.5907	.000051
20	60.3189	60.3225	60.3261	60.3297	60.3333	60.3369	60.3405	60.3441	60.3477	60.3513	60.3549	60.3585	.000120
19	59.0569	59.0656	59.0743	59.0830	59.0917	59.1004	59.1090	59.1177	59.1264	59.1351	59.1438	59.1525	.000290
18	57.7895	57.8013	57.8131	57.8250	57.8368	57.8486	57.8604	57.8722	57.8840	57.8958	57.9077	57.9195	.000394
17	56.5196	56.5342	56.5487	56.5633	56.5778	56.5924	56.6070	56.6215	56.6361	56.6506	56.6652	56.6797	.000485
16	55.2485	55.2656	55.2826	55.2997	55.3168	55.3338	55.3509	55.3680	55.3850	55.4021	55.4192	55.4362	.000569
15	53.9794	53.9986	54.0178	54.0370	54.0561	54.0753	54.0945	54.1137	54.1329	54.1520	54.1712	54.1904	.000639
14	52.7130	52.7341	52.7552	52.7762	52.7973	52.8184	52.8395	52.8606	52.8818	52.9027	52.9238	52.9449	.000703
13	51.4543	51.4768	51.4992	51.5217	51.5442	51.5667	51.5891	51.6116	51.6341	51.6566	51.6790	51.7015	.000749
12	50.2047	50.2284	50.2521	50.2758	50.2995	50.3232	50.3468	50.3705	50.3942	50.4179	50.4416	50.4653	.000790
11	48.9631	48.9877	49.0123	49.0370	49.0616	49.0862	49.1108	49.1355	49.1601	49.1847	49.2093	49.2340	.000821
10	47.7318	47.7573	47.7828	47.8083	47.8339	47.8594	47.8849	47.9104	47.9359	47.9614	47.9870	48.0125	.000850
Age.	0	1	2	3	4	5	6	7	8	9	10	11	Day.

Age.	0	1	2	3	4	5	6	7	8	9	10	11	Day.
10	1.0429	.9903	.9377	.8850	.8324	.7798	.7272	.6746	.6220	.5693	.5167	.4641	.001754
11	1.0632	1.0104	.9577	.9044	.8521	.7994	.7466	.6938	.6411	.5883	.5355	.4828	.001759
12	1.0843	1.0314	.9785	.9256	.8727	.8198	.7670	.7141	.6612	.6083	.5554	.5025	.001763
13	1.1066	1.0535	1.0004	.9472	.8941	.8410	.7879	.7348	.6817	.6285	.5754	.5223	.001770
14	1.1300	1.0766	1.0232	.9697	.9163	.8629	.8095	.7561	.7027	.6492	.5958	.5424	.001780
15	1.1544	1.1007	1.0470	.9932	.9395	.8858	.8321	.7784	.7247	.6710	.6172	.5635	.001790
16	1.1800	1.1259	1.0718	1.0177	.9636	.9095	.8553	.8012	.7471	.6930	.6389	.5848	.001803
17	1.2068	1.1523	1.0978	1.0433	.9888	.9343	.8798	.8254	.7709	.7164	.6619	.6074	.001816
18	1.2349	1.1799	1.1249	1.0700	1.0150	.9600	.9050	.8500	.7950	.7400	.6851	.6301	.001833
19	1.2643	1.2088	1.1534	1.0979	1.0425	.9870	.9315	.8761	.8206	.7652	.7097	.6543	.001848
20	1.2948	1.2387	1.1827	1.1266	1.0706	1.0145	.9585	.9024	.8464	.7903	.7343	.6782	.001868
21	1.3273	1.2706	1.2140	1.1573	1.1007	1.0440	.9874	.9307	.8741	.8174	.7608	.7041	.001888
22	1.3610	1.3038	1.2465	1.1893	1.1320	1.0748	1.0175	.9603	.9031	.8458	.7886	.7313	.001908
23	1.3963	1.3384	1.2804	1.2225	1.1646	1.1066	1.0487	.9908	.9328	.8749	.8170	.7590	.001931
24	1.4334	1.3748	1.3161	1.2575	1.1988	1.1402	1.0815	1.0229	.9643	.9056	.8470	.7883	.001955
25	1.4722	1.4128	1.3535	1.2942	1.2348	1.1754	1.1161	1.0567	.9974	.9380	.8787	.8193	.001978
26	1.5129	1.4527	1.3926	1.3324	1.2723	1.2121	1.1520	1.0918	1.0316	.9715	.9113	.8512	.002005
27	1.5557	1.4947	1.4337	1.3727	1.3118	1.2508	1.1898	1.1288	1.0678	1.0068	.9459	.8849	.002033
28	1.6005	1.5386	1.4767	1.4148	1.3529	1.2910	1.2291	1.1672	1.1053	1.0434	.9815	.9196	.002063
29	1.6477	1.5848	1.5220	1.4591	1.3962	1.3333	1.2705	1.2076	1.1447	1.0818	1.0190	.9561	.002096
30	1.6972	1.6333	1.5694	1.5056	1.4417	1.3778	1.3140	1.2501	1.1862	1.1223	1.0584	.9946	.002129
31	1.7492	1.6842	1.6193	1.5543	1.4894	1.4244	1.3594	1.2945	1.2295	1.1646	1.0996	1.0347	.002165
32	1.8040	1.7379	1.6717	1.6056	1.5395	1.4733	1.4072	1.3411	1.2749	1.2088	1.1426	1.0765	.002204
33	1.8616	1.7943	1.7269	1.6596	1.5923	1.5249	1.4576	1.3903	1.3229	1.2556	1.1883	1.1209	.002244
34	1.9225	1.8539	1.7854	1.7168	1.6483	1.5797	1.5111	1.4426	1.3740	1.3055	1.2369	1.1684	.002285
35	1.9866	1.9167	1.8468	1.7770	1.7071	1.6372	1.5673	1.4975	1.4276	1.3577	1.2878	1.2180	.002329
36	2.0544	1.9831	1.9118	1.8405	1.7693	1.6980	1.6267	1.5554	1.4841	1.4128	1.3416	1.2703	.002376
37	2.1260	2.0534	1.9808	1.9083	1.8357	1.7631	1.6905	1.6180	1.5454	1.4728	1.4002	1.3277	.002419
38	2.2018	2.1277	2.0535	1.9794	1.9053	1.8312	1.7570	1.6829	1.6088	1.5347	1.4605	1.3864	.002471
39	2.2823	2.2066	2.1310	2.0553	1.9797	1.9040	1.8283	1.7527	1.6770	1.6014	1.5257	1.4501	.002522
40	2.3677	2.2905	2.2133	2.1361	2.0589	1.9817	1.9044	1.8272	1.7500	1.6728	1.5956	1.5184	.002573
41	2.4586	2.3797	2.3008	2.2219	2.1430	2.0641	1.9852	1.9063	1.8274	1.7485	1.6696	1.5907	.002630
42	2.5554	2.4746	2.3937	2.3129	2.2321	2.1513	2.0704	1.9896	1.9088	1.8280	1.7471	1.6663	.002694
43	2.6585	2.5752	2.4918	2.4085	2.3251	2.2418	2.1585	2.0751	1.9918	1.9084	1.8251	1.7417	.002778
44	2.7682	2.6816	2.5951	2.5085	2.4220	2.3354	2.2489	2.1623	2.0758	1.9892	1.9027	1.8161	.002885
45	2.8845	2.7942	2.7039	2.6135	2.5232	2.4329	2.3426	2.2523	2.1620	2.0716	1.9813	1.8910	.003010
46	3.0080	2.9130	2.8181	2.7231	2.6282	2.5332	2.4382	2.3433	2.2483	2.1534	2.0584	1.9635	.003165
47	3.1385	3.0385	2.9385	2.8385	2.7385	2.6385	2.5385	2.4386	2.3386	2.2386	2.1386	2.0386	.003333
48	3.2767	3.1711	3.0655	2.9600	2.8544	2.7488	2.6432	2.5377	2.4321	2.3265	2.2210	2.1154	.003519
49	3.4227	3.3113	3.1999	3.0884	2.9770	2.8656	2.7542	2.6428	2.5314	2.4200	2.3085	2.1971	.003713
50	3.5775	3.4595	3.3415	3.2235	3.1055	2.9875	2.8695	2.7516	2.6336	2.5156	2.3976	2.2796	.003933
51	3.7415	3.6163	3.4911	3.3659	3.2407	3.1155	2.9903	2.8652	2.7400	2.6148	2.4896	2.3644	.004173
52	3.9151	3.7821	3.6490	3.5160	3.3829	3.2499	3.1168	2.9838	2.8508	2.7177	2.5847	2.4516	.004435
53	4.0996	3.9580	3.8164	3.6747	3.5331	3.3915	3.2499	3.1083	2.9667	2.8250	2.6834	2.5418	.004720
54	4.2950	4.1442	3.9934	3.8426	3.6918	3.5410	3.3902	3.2394	3.0886	2.9378	2.7870	2.6362	.005026
55	4.5025	4.3417	4.1808	4.0200	3.8591	3.6983	3.5374	3.3766	3.2158	3.0549	2.8941	2.7332	.005361
56	4.7230	4.5512	4.3793	4.2075	4.0356	3.8638	3.6920	3.5201	3.3483	3.1764	3.0046	2.8327	.005728
57	4.9571	4.7736	4.5902	4.4067	4.2232	4.0398	3.8563	3.6728	3.4894	3.3059	3.1224	2.9390	.006115
58	5.2067	5.0104	4.8142	4.6179	4.4217	4.2254	4.0291	3.8329	3.6366	3.4404	3.2441	3.0479	.006542
59	5.4724	5.2622	5.0520	4.8418	4.6316	4.4214	4.2112	4.0010	3.7908	3.5806	3.3704	3.1602	.007006
60	5.7556	5.5297	5.3037	5.0778	4.8519	4.6260	4.4000	4.1741	3.9482	3.7223	3.4963	3.2704	.007531
61	6.0572	5.8142	5.5711	5.3281	5.0851	4.8420	4.5990	4.3560	4.1129	3.8699	3.6269	3.3838	.008101
62	6.3782	6.1163	5.8543	5.5924	5.3305	5.0685	4.8066	4.5447	4.2827	4.0208	3.7589	3.4969	.008731
63	6.7199	6.4375	6.1550	5.8726	5.5902	5.3078	5.0253	4.7429	4.4605	4.1781	3.8956	3.6132	.009414
64	7.0841	6.7791	6.4742	6.1692	5.8643	5.5593	5.2544	4.9494	4.6445	4.3395	4.0346	3.7296	.010165
65	7.4718	7.1424	6.8130	6.4837	6.1543	5.8249	5.4955	5.1662	4.8368	4.5074	4.1780	3.8487	.010979
66	7.8846	7.5283	7.1719	6.8156	6.4592	6.1029	5.7465	5.3902	5.0339	4.6775	4.3212	3.9648	.011878
67	8.3237	7.9384	7.5530	7.1677	6.7824	6.3971	6.0117	5.6264	5.2411	4.8558	4.4704	4.0851	.012844
68	8.7913	8.3746	7.9579	7.5412	7.1245	6.7078	6.2911	5.8744	5.4577	5.0410	4.6243	4.2076	.013890
69	9.2892	8.8389	8.3886	7.9383	7.4880	7.0377	6.5874	6.1371	5.6868	5.2365	4.7862	4.3359	.015010
70	9.8202	9.3333	8.8465	8.3596	7.8728	7.3860	6.8991	6.4122	5.9254	5.4385	4.9517	4.4648	.016228
71	10.3865	9.8603	9.3340	8.8078	8.2816	7.7554	7.2292	6.7029	6.1767	5.6505	5.1243	4.5980	.017541
72	10.9906	10.4219	9.8532	9.2844	8.7157	8.1470	7.5783	7.0096	6.4409	5.8721	5.3034	4.7347	.018957
73	11.6356	11.0210	10.4065	9.7920	9.1774	8.5628	7.9483	7.3337	6.7192	6.1046	5.4901	4.8755	.020485
74	12.3247	11.6606	10.9966	10.3325	9.6685	9.0044	8.3404	7.6763	7.0123	6.3482	5.6842	5.0201	.022135
75	13.0611	12.3438	11.6264	10.9091	10.1917	9.4744	8.7570	8.0397	7.3224	6.6050	5.8877	5.1703	.023911
76	13.8491	13.0746	12.3001	11.5256	10.7511	9.9766	9.2021	8.4276	7.6531	6.8786	6.1041	5.3296	.025817
77	14.6936	13.8569	13.0202	12.1836	11.3469	10.5102	9.6735	8.8369	8.0002	7.1635	6.3268	5.4902	.027889
78	15.5980	14.6940	13.7899	12.8859	11.9818	11.0778	10.1737	9.2697	8.3657	7.4616	6.5576	5.6535	.030135
79	16.5679	15.5919	14.6159	13.6398	12.6638	11.6878	10.7118	9.7358	8.7598	7.7837	6.8077	5.8317	.032534
80	17.6099	16.5567	15.5036	14.4504	13.3972	12.3441	11.2909	10.2377	9.1846	8.1314	7.0782	6.0251	.035105
81	18.7321	17.5971	16.4621	15.3271	14.1921	13.0571	11.9221	10.7871	9.6521	8.5171	7.3821	6.2471	.037833
82	19.9487	18.7272	17.5057	16.2842	15.0627	13.8412	12.6197	11.3983	10.1768	8.9553	7.7338	6.5123	.040716
83	21.2779	19.9636	18.6493	17.3350	16.0208	14.7065	13.3922	12.0779	10.7636	9.4493	8.1351	6.8208	.043809
84	22.7422	21.3287	19.9153	18.5018	17.0883	15.6749	14.2614	12.8479	11.4345	10.0210	8.6075	7.1941	.047115
85	24.3733	22.8494	21.3256	19.8017	18.2779	16.7540	15.2301	13.7063	12.1824	10.6586	9.1347	7.6109	.050795
86	26.2025	24.5551	22.9077	21.2604	19.6130	17.9656	16.3182	14.6709	13.0235	11.3761	9.7287	8.0814	.054912
87	28.2688	26.4823	24.6958	22.9093	21.1228	19.3363	17.5498	15.7633	13.9768	12.1903	10.4038	8.6173	.059550
88	30.6234	28.6750	26.7265	24.7781	22.8296	20.8812	18.9327	16.9843	15.0359	13.0874	11.1390	9.1905	.064948
89	33.3146	31.1754	29.0362	26.8969	24.7577	22.6185	20.4793	18.3401	16.2009	14.0616	11.9224	9.7832	.071307
90	36.3903	34.0311	31.6720	29.3128	26.9536	24.5945	22.2353	19.8761	17.5170	15.1578	12.7986	10.4395	.078639
91	39.9271	37.3084	34.6897	32.0711	29.4524	26.8337	24.2150	21.5964	18.9777	16.3590	13.7403	11.1217	.087289
92	43.9954	41.0618	38.1281	35.1945	32.2609	29.3272	26.3936	23.4600	20.5263	17.5927	14.6591	11.7254	.097788
93	48.6070	45.2978	41.9886	38.6794	35.3702	32.0610	28.7517	25.4425	22.1333	18.8241	15.5149	12.2057	.110307
94	53.7286	49.9829	46.2373	42.4915	38.7460	35.0003	31.2547	27.5090	23.7634	20.0177	16.2721	12.5264	.124855
95	59.2714	54.9766	50.6819	46.3871	42.0924	37.7976	33.5029	29.2081	24.9134	20.6186	16.3239	12.0291	.143158
96	64.5617	59.7222	54.8827	50.0432	45.2038	40.3643	35.5248	30.6853	25.8458	21.0063	16.1669	11.3274	.161316
97	69.3077	64.3038	59.2998	54.2959	49.2920	44.2881	39.2841	34.2802	29.2763	24.2724	19.2684	14.2645	.166797
98	76.7739	71.9911	67.2082	62.4254	57.6426	52.8597	48.0769	43.2941	38.5112	33.7284	28.9456	24.1627	.159427
10 or 99	**96.1538**	**96.4743**	**96.7948**	**97.1153**	**97.4359**	**97.7564**	**98.0769**	**98.3974**	**98.7179**	**99.0384**	**99.3590**	**99.6795**	**.010684**
Age.	0	1	2	3	4	5	6	7	8	9	10	11	Day.

Age.	0	1	2	3	4	5	6	7	8	9	10	11	Day.
10	1.4544	1.4032	1.3519	1.3007	1.2495	1.1983	1.1470	1.0958	1.0446	.9934	.9421	.8909	.001707
11	1.4932	1.4419	1.3906	1.3393	1.2880	1.2367	1.1854	1.1342	1.0829	1.0316	.9803	.9290	.001710
12	1.5340	1.4826	1.4311	1.3797	1.3282	1.2768	1.2253	1.1739	1.1225	1.0710	1.0196	.9681	.001715
13	1.5758	1.5241	1.4725	1.4208	1.3692	1.3175	1.2659	1.2142	1.1626	1.1109	1.0593	1.0076	.001722
14	1.6190	1.5671	1.5152	1.4633	1.4114	1.3595	1.3076	1.2558	1.2039	1.1520	1.1001	1.0482	.001729
15	1.6642	1.6120	1.5598	1.5076	1.4554	1.4032	1.3510	1.2988	1.2466	1.1944	1.1422	1.0900	.001740
16	1.7107	1.6582	1.6056	1.5531	1.5006	1.4481	1.3955	1.3430	1.2905	1.2380	1.1854	1.1329	.001751
17	1.7598	1.7069	1.6540	1.6010	1.5481	1.4952	1.4423	1.3894	1.3365	1.2835	1.2306	1.1777	.001764
18	1.8099	1.7566	1.7033	1.6500	1.5968	1.5435	1.4902	1.4369	1.3836	1.3303	1.2771	1.2238	.001776
19	1.8632	1.8094	1.7555	1.7017	1.6479	1.5941	1.5402	1.4864	1.4326	1.3788	1.3249	1.2711	.001794
20	1.9170	1.8627	1.8084	1.7541	1.6999	1.6456	1.5913	1.5370	1.4827	1.4284	1.3742	1.3199	.001809
21	1.9748	1.9200	1.8652	1.8104	1.7556	1.7008	1.6460	1.5912	1.5364	1.4816	1.4268	1.3720	.001827
22	2.0352	1.9798	1.9244	1.8690	1.8136	1.7582	1.7028	1.6475	1.5921	1.5367	1.4813	1.4259	.001846
23	2.0975	2.0415	1.9855	1.9296	1.8736	1.8176	1.7616	1.7057	1.6497	1.5937	1.5377	1.4818	.001866
24	2.1631	2.1065	2.0499	1.9934	1.9368	1.8802	1.8236	1.7671	1.7105	1.6539	1.5973	1.5408	.001886
25	2.2322	2.1749	2.1177	2.0604	2.0031	1.9459	1.8886	1.8313	1.7741	1.7168	1.6595	1.6023	.001909
26	2.3040	2.2460	2.1881	2.1301	2.0721	2.0142	1.9562	1.8982	1.8403	1.7823	1.7243	1.6664	.001932
27	2.3796	2.3208	2.2621	2.2033	2.1446	2.0858	2.0271	1.9683	1.9096	1.8508	1.7921	1.7333	.001958
28	2.4582	2.3986	2.3390	2.2795	2.2199	2.1603	2.1007	2.0412	1.9816	1.9220	1.8624	1.8029	.001986
29	2.5409	2.4805	2.4200	2.3596	2.2992	2.2388	2.1783	2.1179	2.0575	1.9971	1.9366	1.8762	.002014
30	2.6279	2.5665	2.5051	2.4438	2.3824	2.3210	2.2596	2.1983	2.1369	2.0755	2.0141	1.9528	.002046
31	2.7189	2.6565	2.5941	2.5318	2.4694	2.4070	2.3446	2.2823	2.2199	2.1575	2.0951	2.0328	.002079
32	2.8145	2.7511	2.6877	2.6242	2.5608	2.4974	2.4340	2.3706	2.3072	2.2437	2.1803	2.1169	.002113
33	2.9153	2.8508	2.7864	2.7219	2.6575	2.5930	2.5286	2.4641	2.3997	2.3352	2.2708	2.2063	.002148
34	3.0223	2.9567	2.8911	2.8255	2.7600	2.6944	2.6288	2.5632	2.4976	2.4320	2.3665	2.3009	.002186
35	3.1347	3.0679	3.0011	2.9343	2.8676	2.8008	2.7340	2.6672	2.6004	2.5336	2.4669	2.4001	.002226
36	3.2533	3.1854	3.1176	3.0497	2.9819	2.9140	2.8461	2.7783	2.7104	2.6426	2.5747	2.5069	.002262
37	3.3811	3.3119	3.2427	3.1735	3.1044	3.0352	2.9660	2.8968	2.8276	2.7584	2.6893	2.6201	.002306
38	3.5141	3.4436	3.3732	3.3027	3.2323	3.1618	3.0914	3.0209	2.9505	2.8800	2.8096	2.7391	.002348
39	3.6567	3.5850	3.5132	3.4415	3.3698	3.2980	3.2263	3.1546	3.0828	3.0111	2.9394	2.8676	.002391
40	3.8089	3.7358	3.6626	3.5895	3.5164	3.4432	3.3701	3.2970	3.2238	3.1507	3.0776	3.0044	.002438
41	3.9704	3.8956	3.8209	3.7461	3.6714	3.5966	3.5218	3.4471	3.3723	3.2976	3.2228	3.1481	.002492
42	4.1408	4.0639	3.9869	3.9100	3.8331	3.7561	3.6792	3.6023	3.5253	3.4484	3.3715	3.2945	.002564
43	4.3170	4.2372	4.1574	4.0776	3.9978	3.9180	3.8381	3.7583	3.6785	3.5987	3.5189	3.4391	.002660
44	4.4978	4.4146	4.3313	4.2481	4.1649	4.0817	3.9984	3.9152	3.8320	3.7488	3.6655	3.5823	.002774
45	4.6852	4.5977	4.5103	4.4228	4.3353	4.2479	4.1604	4.0729	3.9855	3.8980	3.8105	3.7231	.002915
46	4.8765	4.7844	4.6922	4.6001	4.5080	4.4159	4.3237	4.2316	4.1395	4.0474	3.9552	3.8631	.003071
47	5.0771	4.9798	4.8825	4.7852	4.6879	4.5906	4.4933	4.3960	4.2987	4.2014	4.1041	4.0068	.003243
48	5.2865	5.1838	5.0810	4.9783	4.8755	4.7728	4.6700	4.5673	4.4646	4.3618	4.2591	4.1563	.003425
49	5.5084	5.3995	5.2907	5.1818	5.0730	4.9641	4.8552	4.7464	4.6375	4.5287	4.4198	4.3110	.003628
50	5.7391	5.6235	5.5080	5.3924	5.2769	5.1613	5.0457	4.9302	4.8146	4.6991	4.5835	4.4680	.003852
51	5.9807	5.8578	5.7349	5.6120	5.4891	5.3662	5.2433	5.1204	4.9975	4.8746	4.7517	4.6288	.004097
52	6.2337	6.1028	5.9719	5.8410	5.7102	5.5793	5.4484	5.3175	5.1866	5.0557	4.9249	4.7940	.004363
53	6.4997	6.3602	6.2207	6.0812	5.9418	5.8023	5.6628	5.5233	5.3838	5.2443	5.1049	4.9654	.004649
54	6.7803	6.6314	6.4826	6.3337	6.1849	6.0360	5.8871	5.7383	5.5894	5.4406	5.2917	5.1429	.004962
55	7.0748	6.9156	6.7565	6.5973	6.4382	6.2790	6.1199	5.9607	5.8016	5.6424	5.4833	5.3241	.005305
56	7.3839	7.2138	7.0437	6.8737	6.7036	6.5335	6.3634	6.1934	6.0233	5.8532	5.6831	5.5131	.005669
57	7.7126	7.5306	7.3486	7.1666	6.9846	6.8026	6.6205	6.4385	6.2565	6.0745	5.8925	5.7105	.006066
58	8.0583	7.8632	7.6682	7.4731	7.2780	7.0830	6.8879	6.6928	6.4978	6.3027	6.1076	5.9126	.006502
59	8.4224	8.2126	8.0028	7.7930	7.5832	7.3734	7.1635	6.9537	6.7439	6.5341	6.3243	6.1145	.006993
60	8.8001	8.5742	8.3483	8.1225	7.8966	7.6707	7.4448	7.2190	6.9931	6.7672	6.5413	6.3155	.007529
61	9.1979	8.9543	8.7106	8.4670	8.2233	7.9797	7.7360	7.4924	7.2488	7.0051	6.7615	6.5178	.008121
62	9.6133	9.3504	9.0874	8.8245	8.5616	8.2987	8.0357	7.7728	7.5099	7.2470	6.9840	6.7211	.008764
63	10.0507	9.7666	9.4825	9.1984	8.9143	8.6302	8.3461	8.0620	7.7779	7.4938	7.2097	6.9256	.009470
64	10.5088	10.2017	9.8946	9.5875	9.2804	8.9733	8.6661	8.3590	8.0519	7.7448	7.4377	7.1306	.010237
65	10.9910	10.6585	10.3259	9.9934	9.6609	9.3284	8.9958	8.6633	8.3308	7.9983	7.6657	7.3332	.011084
66	11.4931	11.1332	10.7734	10.4135	10.0537	9.6938	9.3339	8.9741	8.6142	8.2544	7.8945	7.5347	.011995
67	12.0235	11.6341	11.2446	10.8552	10.4658	10.0764	9.6869	9.2975	8.9081	8.5187	8.1292	7.7398	.012981
68	12.5822	12.1611	11.7400	11.3189	10.8979	10.4768	10.0557	9.6346	9.2135	8.7924	8.3714	7.9503	.014036
69	13.1748	12.7193	12.2638	11.8084	11.3529	10.8974	10.4419	9.9865	9.5310	9.0755	8.6200	8.1646	.015182
70	13.7982	13.3057	12.8131	12.3206	11.8281	11.3355	10.8430	10.3505	9.8579	9.3654	8.8729	8.3803	.016418
71	14.4583	13.9258	13.3933	12.8608	12.3283	11.7958	11.2632	10.7307	10.1982	9.6657	9.1332	8.6007	.017750
72	15.1566	14.5810	14.0054	13.4298	12.8542	12.2786	11.7030	11.1275	10.5519	9.9763	9.4007	8.8251	.019186
73	15.8966	15.2745	14.6524	14.0303	13.4082	12.7861	12.1640	11.5420	10.9199	10.2978	9.6757	9.0536	.020736
74	16.6808	16.0087	15.3365	14.6644	13.9922	13.3201	12.6479	11.9758	11.3037	10.6315	9.9594	9.2872	.022405
75	17.5141	16.7884	16.0626	15.3369	14.6112	13.8854	13.1597	12.4340	11.7082	10.9825	10.2568	9.5310	.024191
76	18.4042	17.6202	16.8363	16.0523	15.2683	14.4844	13.7004	12.9164	12.1325	11.3485	10.5645	9.7806	.026132
77	19.3470	18.4999	17.6528	16.8057	15.9587	15.1116	14.2645	13.4174	12.5703	11.7232	10.8762	10.0291	.028236
78	20.3475	19.4331	18.5187	17.6043	16.6899	15.7755	14.8610	13.9466	13.0322	12.1178	11.2034	10.2890	.030480
79	21.4236	20.4371	19.4507	18.4642	17.4778	16.4913	15.5049	14.5184	13.5320	12.5455	11.5591	10.5726	.032882
80	22.5818	21.5191	20.4565	19.3938	18.3311	17.2685	16.2058	15.1431	14.0805	13.0178	11.9551	10.8925	.035422
81	23.8442	22.7016	21.5589	20.4163	19.2736	18.1310	16.9883	15.8457	14.7031	13.5694	12.4178	11.2751	.038088
82	25.2395	24.0117	22.7839	21.5561	20.3283	19.1005	17.8727	16.6449	15.4171	14.[illegible]893	12.9615	11.7337	.040926
83	26.7844	25.4664	24.1484	22.8305	21.5125	20.1945	18.8765	17.5586	16.2406	14.9226	13.6046	12.2867	.043932
84	28.5228	27.1056	25.6883	24.2711	22.8538	21.4366	20.0193	18.6021	17.1849	15.7676	14.3504	12.9331	.047241
85	30.4603	28.9327	27.4052	25.8776	24.3501	22.8225	21.2949	19.7674	18.2398	16.7123	15.1847	13.6572	.050918
86	32.6365	30.9856	29.3346	27.6837	26.0328	24.3819	22.7309	21.0800	19.4291	17.7782	16.1272	14.4763	.055031
87	35.0997	33.3062	31.5128	29.7193	27.9259	26.1324	24.3389	22.5455	20.7520	18.9586	17.1651	15.3717	.059782
88	37.8655	35.9044	33.9433	31.9822	30.0212	28.0601	26.0990	24.1379	22.1768	20.2157	18.2547	16.2936	.065369
89	40.9586	38.8043	36.6499	34.4956	32.3413	30.1869	28.0326	25.8783	23.7239	21.5696	19.4153	17.2609	.071811
90	44.4706	42.0894	39.7082	37.3270	34.9458	32.5646	30.1834	27.8022	25.4210	23.0398	20.6586	18.2774	.079373
91	48.4302	45.7733	43.1164	40.4594	37.8025	35.1456	32.4887	29.8318	27.1749	24.5179	21.8610	19.2041	.088564
92	52.7872	49.7971	46.8070	43.8169	40.8269	37.8368	34.8467	31.8566	28.8665	25.8764	22.8864	19.8963	.099669
93	57.5035	54.1195	50.7356	47.3516	43.9677	40.5837	37.1998	33.8158	30.4319	27.0479	23.6640	20.2800	.112798
94	62.5094	58.6200	54.7305	50.8411	46.9516	43.0622	39.1727	35.2833	31.3939	27.5044	23.6150	19.7255	.129648
95	67.0058	62.5654	58.1249	53.6845	49.2440	44.8036	40.3631	35.9227	31.4823	27.0418	22.6014	18.1609	.148014
96	71.0496	66.3911	61.7326	57.0741	52.4156	47.7571	43.0986	38.4402	33.7817	29.1232	24.4647	19.8062	.155283
97	78.5684	74.2581	69.9479	65.6376	61.3274	57.0171	52.7069	48.3966	44.0864	39.7761	35.4659	31.1556	.143675
98 or 11	**96.1538**	**96.4743**	**96.7948**	**97.1153**	**97.4359**	**97.7564**	**98.0769**	**98.3974**	**98.7179**	**99.0384**	**99.3590**	**99.6795**	**.010684**
10	94.9786	94.9896	95.0006	95.0117	95.0227	95.0337	95.0447	95.0558	95.0668	95.0778	95.0888	95.0999	.000367
Age.	0	1	2	3	4	5	6	7	8	9	10	11	Day.

Age.	0	1	2	3	4	5	6	7	8	9	10	11	Day.
10	1.8826	1.8328	1.7831	1.7333	1.6836	1.6338	1.5841	1.5343	1.4846	1.4348	1.3851	1.3353	.001658
11	1.9409	1.8911	1.8412	1.7914	1.7415	1.6917	1.6418	1.5920	1.5422	1.4923	1.4425	1.3926	.001661
12	2.0011	1.9511	1.9011	1.8511	1.8012	1.7512	1.7012	1.6512	1.6012	1.5512	1.5013	1.4513	.001666
13	2.0625	2.0124	1.9622	1.9121	1.8620	1.8118	1.7617	1.7116	1.6614	1.6113	1.5612	1.5110	.001671
14	2.1264	2.0760	2.0256	1.9752	1.9248	1.8744	1.8240	1.7737	1.7233	1.6729	1.6225	1.5721	.001679
15	2.1922	2.1416	2.0910	2.0404	1.9898	1.9392	1.8885	1.8379	1.7873	1.7367	1.6861	1.6355	.001687
16	2.2604	2.2095	2.1586	2.1077	2.0568	2.0059	1.9550	1.9040	1.8531	1.8022	1.7513	1.7004	.001696
17	2.3316	2.2804	2.2291	2.1779	2.1267	2.0755	2.0242	1.9730	1.9218	1.8706	1.8193	1.7681	.001707
18	2.4053	2.3536	2.3020	2.2503	2.1986	2.1470	2.0953	2.0436	1.9920	1.9403	1.8886	1.8370	.001722
19	2.4816	2.4295	2.3775	2.3254	2.2734	2.2213	2.1692	2.1172	2.0651	2.0131	1.9610	1.9090	.001735
20	2.5605	2.5081	2.4556	2.4032	2.3507	2.2983	2.2458	2.1934	2.1410	2.0885	2.0361	1.9836	.001748
21	2.6445	2.5915	2.5386	2.4856	2.4327	2.3797	2.3268	2.2738	2.2209	2.1679	2.1150	2.0620	.001765
22	2.7316	2.6782	2.6247	2.5713	2.5178	2.4644	2.4110	2.3575	2.3041	2.2506	2.1972	2.1437	.001781
23	2.8221	2.7682	2.7142	2.6603	2.6064	2.5524	2.4985	2.4446	2.3906	2.3367	2.2828	2.2288	.001794
24	2.9176	2.8631	2.8086	2.7541	2.6996	2.6451	2.5905	2.5360	2.4815	2.4270	2.3725	2.3180	.001817
25	3.0172	2.9621	2.9070	2.8520	2.7969	2.7418	2.6867	2.6316	2.5765	2.5214	2.4664	2.4113	.001836
26	3.1214	3.0656	3.0099	2.9541	2.8984	2.8426	2.7868	2.7311	2.6753	2.6196	2.5638	2.5081	.001858
27	3.2302	3.1737	3.1173	3.0608	3.0044	2.9479	2.8915	2.8350	2.7786	2.7221	2.6657	2.6092	.001882
28	3.3438	3.2866	3.2295	3.1723	3.1151	3.0580	3.0008	2.9436	2.8865	2.8293	2.7721	2.7150	.001905
29	3.4634	3.4054	3.3474	3.2895	3.2315	3.1735	3.1155	3.0576	2.9996	2.9416	2.8836	2.8257	.001932
30	3.5886	3.5298	3.4710	3.4122	3.3534	3.2946	3.2357	3.1769	3.1181	3.0593	3.0004	2.9416	.001960
31	3.7196	3.6599	3.6002	3.5405	3.4808	3.4211	3.3614	3.3018	3.2421	3.1824	3.1227	3.0630	.001989
32	3.8575	3.7969	3.7364	3.6758	3.6152	3.5547	3.4941	3.4335	3.3730	3.3124	3.2518	3.1913	.002019
33	4.0035	3.9420	3.8805	3.8190	3.7574	3.6959	3.6344	3.5729	3.5114	3.4498	3.3883	3.3268	.002050
34	4.1577	4.0952	4.0327	3.9701	3.9076	3.8451	3.7826	3.7201	3.6576	3.5950	3.5325	3.4700	.002084
35	4.3199	4.2565	4.1931	4.1297	4.0663	4.0029	3.9395	3.8761	3.8127	3.7493	3.6859	3.6225	.002113
36	4.4934	4.4289	4.3644	4.2999	4.2354	4.1709	4.1063	4.0418	3.9773	3.9128	3.8483	3.7838	.002150
37	4.6769	4.6113	4.5458	4.4802	4.4147	4.3491	4.2836	4.2180	4.1525	4.0870	4.0214	3.9558	.002185
38	4.8706	4.8040	4.7374	4.6708	4.6042	4.5376	4.4710	4.4045	4.3379	4.2713	4.2047	4.1381	.002220
39	5.0782	5.0105	4.9427	4.8750	4.8073	4.7395	4.6718	4.6041	4.5363	4.4686	4.4009	4.3331	.002258
40	5.2990	5.2299	5.1609	5.0918	5.0227	4.9537	4.8846	4.8155	4.7465	4.6774	4.6083	4.5393	.002302
41	5.5319	5.4610	5.3900	5.3191	5.2482	5.1773	5.1063	5.0354	4.9645	4.8936	4.8226	4.7517	.002364
42	5.7730	5.6995	5.6261	5.5526	5.4792	5.4057	5.3322	5.2588	5.1853	5.1119	5.0384	4.9650	.002448
43	6.0178	5.9413	5.8647	5.7882	5.7117	5.6352	5.5586	5.4821	5.4056	5.3291	5.2525	5.1760	.002551
44	6.2673	6.1869	6.1064	6.0260	5.9456	5.8652	5.7847	5.7043	5.6239	5.5435	5.4630	5.3826	.002681
45	6.5201	6.4354	6.3507	6.2660	6.1813	6.0966	6.0119	5.9272	5.8425	5.7578	5.6731	5.5884	.002823
46	6.7790	6.6895	6.6000	6.5105	6.4210	6.3315	6.2420	6.1525	6.0630	5.9735	5.8840	5.7945	.002983
47	7.0480	6.9535	6.8589	6.7644	6.6699	6.5753	6.4808	6.3863	6.2917	6.1972	6.1027	6.0081	.003151
48	7.3302	7.2300	7.1297	7.0295	6.9293	6.8291	6.7288	6.6286	6.5284	6.4282	6.3279	6.2277	.003341
49	7.6248	7.5183	7.4119	7.3054	7.1990	7.0925	6.9860	6.8796	6.7731	6.6667	6.5602	6.4538	.003548
50	7.9299	7.8166	7.7033	7.5900	7.4766	7.3633	7.2500	7.1367	7.0234	6.9100	6.7967	6.6834	.003777
51	8.2475	8.1267	8.0059	7.8851	7.7643	7.6435	7.5227	7.4019	7.2811	7.1603	7.0395	6.9187	.004026
52	8.5783	8.4495	8.3207	8.1919	8.0631	7.9343	7.8054	7.6766	7.5478	7.4190	7.2902	7.1614	.004293
53	8.9254	8.7878	8.6502	8.5126	8.3750	8.2374	8.0998	7.9623	7.8247	7.6871	7.5495	7.4119	.004586
54	9.2889	9.1417	8.9944	8.8472	8.6999	8.5527	8.4054	8.2582	8.1110	7.9637	7.8165	7.6692	.004908
55	9.6674	9.5100	9.3525	9.1951	9.0376	8.8802	8.7227	8.5653	8.4079	8.2504	8.0930	7.9355	.005248
56	10.0660	9.8974	9.7287	9.5601	9.3914	9.2228	9.0541	8.8855	8.7169	8.5482	8.3796	8.2109	.005621
57	10.4856	10.3047	10.1239	9.9430	9.7622	9.5813	9.4005	9.2196	9.0388	8.8580	8.6771	8.4962	.006028
58	10.9242	10.7295	10.5348	10.3401	10.1454	9.9507	9.7560	9.5614	9.3667	9.1720	8.9773	8.7826	.006490
59	11.3771	11.1673	10.9576	10.7478	10.5381	10.3283	10.1185	9.9088	9.6990	9.4893	9.2795	9.0698	.006992
60	11.8452	11.6187	11.3923	11.1658	10.9394	10.7129	10.4864	10.2600	10.0335	9.8071	9.5806	9.3542	.007548
61	12.3314	12.0868	11.8422	11.5976	11.3530	11.1084	10.8637	10.6191	10.3745	10.1299	9.8853	9.6407	.008153
62	12.8364	12.5718	12.3073	12.0427	11.7782	11.5136	11.2490	10.9845	10.7199	10.4554	10.1908	9.9263	.008818
63	13.3614	13.0752	12.7890	12.5028	12.2166	11.9304	11.6442	11.3580	11.0718	10.7856	10.4994	10.2132	.009540
64	13.9075	13.5973	13.2872	12.9770	12.6669	12.3567	12.0466	11.7364	11.4263	11.1161	10.8060	10.4958	.010338
65	14.4725	14.1366	13.8007	13.4647	13.1288	12.7929	12.4570	12.1211	11.7852	11.4492	11.1133	10.7774	.011197
66	15.0594	14.6956	14.3318	13.9680	13.6042	13.2404	12.8765	12.5127	12.1489	11.7851	11.4213	11.0575	.012127
67	15.6741	15.2805	14.8868	14.4932	14.0995	13.7059	13.3122	12.9186	12.5250	12.1313	11.7377	11.3440	.013121
68	16.3205	15.8944	15.4684	15.0423	14.6162	14.1902	13.7641	13.3380	12.9120	12.4859	12.0598	11.6338	.014202
69	16.9983	16.5373	16.0764	15.6154	15.1545	14.6935	14.2326	13.7716	13.3107	12.8497	12.3888	11.9278	.015365
70	17.7081	17.2095	16.7110	16.2124	15.7138	15.2153	14.7167	14.2181	13.7196	13.2210	12.7224	12.2239	.016619
71	18.4547	17.9156	17.3765	16.8374	16.2983	15.7592	15.2200	14.6809	14.1418	13.6027	13.0636	12.5245	.017970
72	19.2401	18.6573	18.0744	17.4916	16.9088	16.3260	15.7431	15.1603	14.5775	13.9947	13.4118	12.8290	.019427
73	20.0670	19.4372	18.8073	18.1775	17.5477	16.9179	16.2880	15.6582	15.0284	14.3986	13.7687	13.1389	.020994
74	20.9399	20.2597	19.5795	18.8994	18.2192	17.5390	16.8588	16.1787	15.4985	14.8183	14.1381	13.4580	.022672
75	21.8664	21.1316	20.3968	19.6620	18.9273	18.1925	17.4577	16.7229	15.9881	15.2533	14.5186	13.7838	.024493
76	22.8457	22.0518	21.2579	20.4640	19.6701	18.8762	18.0822	17.2883	16.4944	15.7005	14.9066	14.1127	.026463
77	23.8755	23.0185	22.1615	21.3046	20.4476	19.5906	18.7336	17.8767	17.0197	16.1627	15.3057	14.4488	.028566
78	24.9726	24.0482	23.1239	22.1995	21.2752	20.3508	19.4265	18.5021	17.5778	16.6534	15.7291	14.8047	.030812
79	26.1541	25.1586	24.1631	23.1676	22.1721	21.1766	20.1811	19.1857	18.1902	17.1947	16.1992	15.2037	.033183
80	27.4397	26.3698	25.2998	24.2299	23.1600	22.0901	21.0201	19.9502	18.8803	17.8104	16.7404	15.6705	.035664
81	28.8646	27.7160	26.5673	25.4187	24.2701	23.1214	21.9728	20.8242	19.6755	18.5269	17.3783	16.2296	.038289
82	30.4546	29.2233	27.9920	26.7607	25.5295	24.2982	23.0669	21.8356	20.6043	19.3730	18.1418	16.9105	.041043
83	32.2467	30.9252	29.6036	28.2821	26.9606	25.6390	24.3175	22.9960	21.6744	20.3529	19.0314	17.7098	.044051
84	34.2581	32.8373	31.4166	29.9958	28.5751	27.1543	25.7335	24.3128	22.8920	21.4713	20.0505	18.6298	.047358
85	36.5029	34.9720	33.4411	31.9101	30.3792	28.8483	27.3174	25.7865	24.2556	22.7246	21.1937	19.6628	.051030
86	39.0279	37.3705	35.7130	34.0556	32.3981	30.7407	29.0832	27.4258	25.7684	24.1109	22.4535	20.7960	.055248
87	41.8470	40.0418	38.2365	36.4313	34.6261	32.8209	31.0156	29.2104	27.4052	25.6000	23.7947	21.9895	.060174
88	44.9559	42.9808	41.0057	39.0306	37.0555	35.0804	33.1052	31.1301	29.1550	27.1799	25.2048	23.2297	.065837
89	48.4212	46.2465	44.0718	41.8972	39.7225	37.5478	35.3731	33.1985	31.0238	28.8491	26.6744	24.4998	.072489
90	52.2865	49.8702	47.4538	45.0375	42.6212	40.2048	37.7885	35.3722	32.9558	30.5395	28.1232	25.7068	.080543
91	56.4743	53.7657	51.0572	48.3486	45.6401	42.9315	40.2230	37.5144	34.8059	32.0973	29.3888	26.6802	.090285
92	60.9016	57.8433	54.7851	51.7268	48.6686	45.6103	42.5520	39.4938	36.4355	33.3773	30.3190	27.2608	.101942
93	65.5031	61.9881	58.4732	54.9582	51.4433	47.9283	44.4134	40.8984	37.3835	33.8685	30.3536	26.8386	.117165
94	69.5646	65.5423	61.5199	57.4976	53.4752	49.4529	45.4305	41.4082	37.3859	33.3635	29.3412	25.3188	.134078
95	72.9918	68.7184	64.4449	60.1715	55.8980	51.6246	47.3511	43.0777	38.8043	34.5308	30.2574	25.9839	.142448
96	79.7094	75.6996	71.6898	67.6800	63.6702	59.6604	55.6505	51.6407	47.6309	43.6211	39.6113	35.6015	.133660
97 or 12	**96.1538**	**96.4743**	**96.7948**	**97.1153**	**97.4359**	**97.7564**	**98.0769**	**98.3974**	**98.7179**	**99.0384**	**99.3590**	**99.6795**	**.010684**
11	94.9737	94.9834	94.9932	95.0030	95.0127	95.0224	95.0322	95.0420	95.0517	95.0614	95.0712	95.0810	.000325
10	94.3597	94.3244	94.2890	94.2537	94.2183	94.1830	94.1476	94.1123	94.0770	94.0416	94.0063	93.9709	.001178
Age.	0	1	2	3	4	5	6	7	8	9	10	11	Day.

Age.	0	1	2	3	4	5	6	7	8	9	10	11	Day.
10	2.3285	2.2802	2.2319	2.1835	2.1352	2.0869	2.0386	1.9903	1.9420	1.8936	1.8453	1.7970	.001610
11	2.4060	2.3576	2.3092	2.2608	2.2124	2.1640	2.1156	2.0673	2.0189	1.9705	1.9221	1.8737	.001613
12	2.4856	2.4371	2.3886	2.3402	2.2917	2.2432	2.1947	2.1463	2.0978	2.0493	2.0008	1.9524	.001616
13	2.5675	2.5189	2.4702	2.4216	2.3729	2.3243	2.2756	2.2270	2.1784	2.1297	2.0811	2.0324	.001621
14	2.6517	2.6029	2.5541	2.5053	2.4565	2.4077	2.3589	2.3102	2.2614	2.2126	2.1638	2.1150	.001626
15	2.7393	2.6903	2.6412	2.5922	2.5432	2.4941	2.4451	2.3961	2.3470	2.2980	2.2490	2.1999	.001634
16	2.8295	2.7802	2.7310	2.6817	2.6325	2.5832	2.5340	2.4847	2.4355	2.3862	2.3370	2.2877	.001642
17	2.9237	2.8741	2.8245	2.7749	2.7253	2.6757	2.6260	2.5764	2.5268	2.4772	2.4276	2.3780	.001653
18	2.0202	2.9703	2.9204	2.8705	2.8206	2.7707	2.7207	2.6708	2.6209	2.5710	2.5211	2.4712	.001663
19	3.1212	3.0710	3.0207	2.9705	2.9203	2.8701	2.8198	2.7696	2.7194	2.6692	2.6189	2.5687	.001674
20	3.2260	3.1754	3.1248	3.0742	3.0236	2.9730	2.9224	2.8718	2.8212	2.7706	2.7200	2.6694	.001687
21	3.3364	3.2854	3.2344	3.1833	3.1323	3.0813	3.0303	2.9793	2.9283	2.8772	2.8262	2.7752	.001700
22	3.4513	3.3999	3.3485	3.2971	3.2457	3.1943	3.1428	3.0914	3.0400	2.9886	2.9372	2.8858	.001713
23	3.5713	3.5194	3.4675	3.4157	3.3638	3.3119	3.2600	3.2082	3.1563	3.1044	3.0525	3.0007	.001729
24	3.6969	3.6446	3.5922	3.5399	3.4875	3.4352	3.3828	3.3305	3.2782	3.2258	3.1735	3.1211	.001745
25	3.8284	3.7755	3.7226	3.6697	3.6168	3.5639	3.5110	3.4582	3.4053	3.3524	3.2995	3.2466	.001763
26	3.9653	3.9118	3.8583	3.8049	3.7514	3.6979	3.6444	3.5910	3.5375	3.4840	3.4305	3.3771	.001782
27	4.1085	4.0544	4.0004	3.9463	3.8923	3.8382	3.7841	3.7301	3.6760	3.6220	3.5679	3.5139	.001802
28	4.2583	4.2036	4.1489	4.0941	4.0394	3.9847	3.9300	3.8753	3.8206	3.7658	3.7111	3.6564	.001824
29	4.4155	4.3601	4.3046	4.2492	4.1938	4.1383	4.0828	4.0274	3.9719	3.9165	3.8611	3.8056	.001848
30	4.5799	4.5237	4.4676	4.4114	4.3553	4.2991	4.2430	4.1868	4.1306	4.0745	4.0183	3.9622	.001872
31	4.7525	4.6956	4.6387	4.5819	4.5250	4.4681	4.4112	4.3544	4.2975	4.2406	4.1837	4.1269	.001896
32	4.9347	4.8770	4.8194	4.7617	4.7041	4.6464	4.5887	4.5311	4.4734	4.4158	4.3581	4.3005	.001922
33	5.1270	5.0685	5.0100	4.9515	4.8931	4.8346	4.7761	4.7176	4.6591	4.6006	4.5422	4.4837	.001949
34	5.3299	5.2707	5.2115	5.1523	5.0932	5.0340	4.9748	4.9156	4.8564	4.7972	4.7381	4.6789	.001973
35	5.5457	5.4856	5.4255	5.3654	5.3054	5.2453	5.1852	5.1251	5.0650	5.0050	4.9449	4.8848	.002002
36	5.7736	5.7127	5.6518	5.5908	5.5299	5.4690	5.4081	5.3472	5.2863	5.2253	5.1644	5.1035	.002030
37	6.0163	5.9546	5.8928	5.8311	5.7693	5.7076	5.6458	5.5841	5.5224	5.4606	5.3989	5.3371	.002058
38	6.2733	6.2107	6.1480	6.0854	6.0228	5.9601	5.8975	5.8349	5.7722	5.7096	5.6470	5.5843	.002088
39	6.5477	6.4840	6.4203	6.3566	6.2929	6.2292	6.1654	6.1017	6.0380	5.9743	5.9106	5.8469	.002123
40	6.8379	6.7726	6.7073	6.6420	6.5768	6.5115	6.4462	6.3809	6.3156	6.2503	6.1851	6.1198	.002176
41	7.1393	7.0718	7.0043	6.9368	6.8693	6.8018	6.7343	6.6668	6.5993	6.5318	6.4643	6.3968	.002250
42	7.4468	7.3766	7.3063	7.2361	7.1659	7.0957	7.0254	6.9552	6.8850	6.8148	6.7445	6.6743	.002341
43	7.7580	7.6842	7.6104	7.5367	7.4629	7.3891	7.3153	7.2416	7.1678	7.0940	7.0202	6.9465	.002459
44	8.0704	7.9927	7.9150	7.8373	7.7596	7.6819	7.6042	7.5266	7.4489	7.3712	7.2935	7.2158	.002590
45	8.3883	8.3062	8.2241	8.1420	8.0598	7.9777	7.8956	7.8135	7.7314	7.6492	7.5671	7.4850	.002737
46	8.7130	8.6262	8.5394	8.4526	8.3659	8.2791	8.1923	8.1055	8.0187	7.9320	7.8452	7.7584	.002893
47	9.0521	8.9600	8.8680	8.7759	8.6838	8.5918	8.4997	8.4076	8.3156	8.2235	8.1314	8.0394	.003069
48	9.4042	9.3063	9.2084	9.1105	9.0126	8.9147	8.8168	8.7190	8.6211	8.5232	8.4253	8.3274	.003263
49	9.7700	9.6657	9.5614	9.4572	9.3529	9.2486	9.1443	9.0401	8.9358	8.8315	8.7272	8.6230	.003476
50	10.1476	10.0363	9.9251	9.8138	9.7026	9.5913	9.4800	9.3688	9.2575	9.1463	9.0350	8.9238	.003708
51	10.5395	10.4207	10.3020	10.1832	10.0644	9.9457	9.8269	9.7081	9.5894	9.4706	9.3518	9.2331	.003959
52	10.9477	10.8207	10.6938	10.5668	10.4399	10.3129	10.1860	10.0590	9.9320	9.8051	9.6781	9.5512	.004232
53	11.3738	11.2378	11.1018	10.9657	10.8297	10.6937	10.5577	10.4217	10.2857	10.1496	10.0136	9.8776	.004534
54	11.8169	11.6713	11.5258	11.3802	11.2347	11.0891	10.9435	10.7980	10.6524	10.5069	10.3613	10.2158	.004852
55	12.2806	12.1245	11.9685	11.8124	11.6564	11.5003	11.3442	11.1882	11.0321	10.8761	10.7200	10.5640	.005202
56	12.7652	12.5977	12.4302	12.2626	12.0951	11.9276	11.7601	11.5926	11.4251	11.2575	11.0900	10.9225	.005584
57	13.2725	13.0920	12.9115	12.7311	12.5506	12.3701	12.1896	12.0092	11.8287	11.6482	11.4677	11.2873	.006016
58	13.7946	13.6000	13.4053	13.2107	13.0161	12.8214	12.6268	12.4322	12.2375	12.0429	11.8483	11.6536	.006488
59	14.3323	14.1220	13.9117	13.7014	13.4911	13.2807	13.0704	12.8601	12.6497	12.4394	12.2291	12.0187	.007010
60	14.8833	14.6559	14.4285	14.2011	13.9737	13.7463	13.5189	13.2915	13.0641	12.8367	12.6093	12.3819	.007580
61	15.4532	15.2070	14.9608	14.7146	14.4685	14.2223	13.9761	13.7299	13.4837	13.2375	12.9914	12.7452	.008206
62	16.0399	15.7733	15.5067	15.2401	14.9736	14.7070	14.4404	14.1738	13.9072	13.6406	13.3741	13.1075	.008886
63	16.6469	16.3578	16.0686	15.7795	15.4904	15.2012	14.9121	14.6230	14.3338	14.0447	13.7556	13.4664	.009638
64	17.2708	16.9573	16.6438	16.3302	16.0167	15.7032	15.3897	15.0762	14.7627	14.4491	14.1356	13.8221	.010450
65	17.9133	17.5736	17.2338	16.8941	16.5544	16.2147	15.8750	15.5352	15.1955	14.8558	14.5160	14.1763	.011324
66	18.5783	18.2104	17.8425	17.4746	17.1068	16.7389	16.3710	16.0031	15.6352	15.2673	14.8995	14.5316	.012263
67	19.2741	18.8757	18.4772	18.0788	17.6803	17.2819	16.8834	16.4850	16.0866	15.6881	15.2897	14.8912	.013281
68	19.9990	19.5670	19.1350	18.7031	18.2711	17.8391	17.4071	16.9752	16.5432	16.1112	15.6792	15.2473	.014399
69	20.7562	20.2894	19.8227	19.3560	18.8892	18.4224	17.9557	17.4890	17.0222	16.5554	16.0887	15.6220	.015558
70	21.5455	21.0406	20.5357	20.0308	19.5259	19.0210	18.5160	18.0111	17.5062	17.0013	16.4964	15.9915	.016830
71	22.3719	21.8259	21.2798	20.7338	20.1877	19.6417	19.0956	18.5496	18.0036	17.4575	16.9115	16.3654	.018201
72	23.2369	22.6466	22.0564	21.4661	20.8759	20.2856	19.6954	19.1051	18.5149	17.9246	17.3344	16.7441	.019675
73	24.1446	23.5071	22.8696	22.2320	21.5945	20.9570	20.3195	19.6820	19.0445	18.4070	17.7694	17.1319	.021250
74	25.1025	24.4137	23.7249	23.0360	22.3472	21.6584	20.9696	20.2808	19.5920	18.9031	18.2143	17.5255	.022960
75	26.1101	25.3658	24.6215	23.8773	23.1330	22.3887	21.6444	20.9002	20.1559	19.4116	18.6673	17.9231	.024809
76	27.1679	26.3646	25.5612	24.7579	23.9545	23.1512	22.3478	21.5445	20.7412	19.9378	19.1345	18.3311	.026778
77	28.2854	27.4189	26.5525	25.6860	24.8196	23.9531	23.0866	22.2202	21.3537	20.4873	19.6208	18.7544	.028882
78	29.4784	28.5454	27.6125	26.6795	25.7466	24.8136	23.8806	22.9477	22.0147	21.0818	20.1488	19.2159	.031098
79	30.7762	29.7738	28.7714	27.7690	26.7666	25.7642	24.7617	23.7593	22.7569	21.7545	20.7521	19.7497	.033413
80	32.2104	31.1348	30.0592	28.9836	27.9080	26.8324	25.7567	24.6811	23.6055	22.5299	21.4543	20.3787	.035853
81	33.8131	32.6612	31.5092	30.3573	29.2053	28.0534	26.9014	25.7495	24.5976	23.4456	22.2937	21.1417	.038398
82	35.6279	34.3932	33.1586	31.9239	30.6893	29.4546	28.2200	26.9853	25.7506	24.5160	23.2813	22.0467	.041155
83	37.6662	36.3413	35.0165	33.6916	32.3668	31.0419	29.7170	28.3922	27.0673	25.7425	24.4176	23.0928	.044162
84	39.9512	38.5273	37.1034	35.6795	34.2556	32.8317	31.4078	29.9839	28.5600	27.1361	25.7122	24.2883	.047463
85	42.5052	40.9682	39.4311	37.8941	36.3571	34.8200	33.2830	31.7460	30.2089	28.6719	27.1349	25.5978	.051234
86	45.3411	43.6726	42.0042	40.3357	38.6673	36.9988	35.3304	33.6619	31.9935	30.3250	28.6566	26.9881	.055615
87	48.4531	46.6348	44.8165	42.9982	41.1799	39.3616	37.5433	35.7251	33.9068	32.0885	30.2702	28.4519	.060609
88	51.8780	49.8840	47.8901	45.8961	43.9021	41.9082	39.9142	37.9202	35.9263	33.9323	31.9383	29.9444	.066465
89	55.6397	53.4326	51.2254	49.0183	46.8112	44.6040	42.3969	40.1898	37.9826	35.7755	33.5684	31.3612	.073571
90	59.6808	57.2170	54.7532	52.2893	49.8255	47.3617	44.8979	42.4341	39.9703	37.5064	35.0426	32.5788	.082126
91	63.8988	60.1279	58.3569	55.5860	52.8151	50.0441	47.2732	44.5023	41.7313	38.9604	36.1895	33.4185	.092364
92	68.1979	65.0202	61.8424	58.6647	55.4869	52.3092	49.1314	45.9537	42.7760	39.5982	36.4205	33.2427	.105925
93	71.9307	68.2947	64.6586	61.0226	57.3866	53.7506	50.1145	46.4785	42.8425	39.2065	35.5704	31.9344	.121201
94	75.0251	71.1551	67.2851	63.4150	59.5450	55.6750	51.8050	47.9350	44.0650	40.1950	36.3249	32.4549	.129000
95	80.9818	77.3069	73.6319	69.9570	66.2821	62.6071	58.9322	55.2573	51.5823	47.9074	44.2325	40.5575	.122498
96 or 13	**96.1538**	**96.4743**	**96.7948**	**97.1153**	**97.4359**	**97.7564**	**98.0769**	**98.3974**	**98.7179**	**99.0384**	**99.3590**	**99.6795**	**.010684**
12	94.9770	94.9854	94.9938	95.0022	95.0106	95.0190	95.0275	95.0359	95.0443	95.0527	95.0611	95.0695	.000280
11	94.3523	94.3155	94.2787	94.2419	94.2051	94.1683	94.1314	94.0946	94.0578	94.0210	93.9842	93.9474	.001227
10	93.8958	93.8475	93.7993	93.7510	93.7028	93.6545	93.6062	93.5580	93.5097	93.4615	93.4132	93.3650	.001608
Age.	0	1	2	3	4	5	6	7	8	9	10	11	Day.

Age.	0	1	2	3	4	5	6	7	8	9	10	11	Day.
10	2.7916	2.7447	2.6979	2.6510	2.6041	2.5573	2.5104	2.4635	2.4167	2.3698	2.3229	2.2761	.001562
11	2.8885	2.8416	2.7947	2.7478	2.7009	2.6540	2.6071	2.5603	2.5134	2.4665	2.4196	2.3727	.001563
12	2.9883	2.9413	2.8943	2.8473	2.8004	2.7534	2.7064	2.6594	2.6124	2.5654	2.5185	2.4715	.001566
13	3.0904	3.0433	2.9963	2.9492	2.9022	2.8551	2.8080	2.7610	2.7139	2.6669	2.6198	2.5728	.001568
14	3.1962	3.1490	3.1017	3.0545	3.0073	2.9600	2.9128	2.8656	2.8183	2.7711	2.7239	2.6766	.001574
15	3.3053	3.2579	3.2106	3.1632	3.1158	3.0684	3.0210	2.9737	2.9263	2.8789	2.8315	2.7842	.001579
16	3.4185	3.3708	3.3232	3.2755	3.2279	3.1803	3.1326	3.0850	3.0373	2.9896	2.9420	2.8944	.001588
17	3.5352	3.4873	3.4395	3.3916	3.3437	3.2959	3.2480	3.2001	3.1523	3.1044	3.0565	3.0087	.001595
18	3.6561	3.6080	3.5599	3.5118	3.4638	3.4157	3.3676	3.3195	3.2714	3.2233	3.1753	3.1272	.001602
19	3.7828	3.7344	3.6860	3.6376	3.5892	3.5408	3.4924	3.4440	3.3956	3.3472	3.2988	3.2504	.001613
20	3.9136	3.8649	3.8162	3.7676	3.7189	3.6702	3.6215	3.5729	3.5242	3.4755	3.4268	3.3782	.001622
21	4.0515	4.0025	3.9535	3.9045	3.8555	3.8065	3.7575	3.7085	3.6595	3.6105	3.5615	3.5125	.001633
22	4.1954	4.1460	4.0967	4.0473	3.9979	3.9486	3.8992	3.8498	3.8005	3.7511	3.7017	3.6524	.001645
23	4.3451	4.2954	4.2457	4.1959	4.1462	4.0965	4.0467	3.9970	3.9473	3.8976	3.8478	3.7982	.001657
24	4.5021	4.4519	4.4018	4.3516	4.3014	4.2513	4.2011	4.1509	4.1008	4.0506	4.0004	3.9503	.001672
25	4.6658	4.6152	4.5646	4.5140	4.4633	4.4127	4.3621	4.3115	4.2609	4.2102	4.1596	4.1090	.001687
26	4.8366	4.7855	4.7344	4.6833	4.6322	4.5811	4.5300	4.4789	4.4278	4.3767	4.3256	4.2745	.001703
27	5.0154	4.9638	4.9122	4.8605	4.8089	4.7573	4.7057	4.6540	4.6024	4.5508	4.4992	4.4475	.001720
28	5.2022	5.1500	5.0978	5.0456	4.9934	4.9412	4.8890	4.8367	4.7845	4.7323	4.6801	4.6279	.001740
29	5.3979	5.3451	5.2923	5.2395	5.1867	5.1339	5.0811	5.0283	4.9755	4.9227	4.8699	4.8171	.001760
30	5.6032	5.5498	5.4965	5.4431	5.3898	5.3364	5.2830	5.2297	5.1763	5.1230	5.0696	5.0163	.001778
31	5.8192	5.7652	5.7112	5.6572	5.6033	5.5493	5.4953	5.4413	5.3873	5.3333	5.2794	5.2254	.001799
32	6.0468	5.9921	5.9375	5.8828	5.8282	5.7735	5.7188	5.6642	5.6095	5.5549	5.5002	5.4456	.001822
33	6.2868	6.2316	6.1764	6.1213	6.0661	6.0109	5.9557	5.9006	5.8454	5.7902	5.7350	5.6799	.001839
34	6.5422	6.4863	6.4304	6.3745	6.3186	6.2627	6.2068	6.1509	6.0950	6.0391	5.9832	5.9273	.001863
35	6.8113	6.7548	6.6984	6.6419	6.5855	6.5290	6.4725	6.4161	6.3596	6.3032	6.2467	6.1903	.001882
36	7.0970	7.0398	6.9827	6.9255	6.8684	6.8112	6.7541	6.6970	6.6398	6.5826	6.5255	6.4684	.001905
37	7.4014	7.3436	7.2847	7.2279	7.1701	7.1123	7.0544	6.9966	6.9388	6.8810	6.8231	6.7653	.001927
38	7.7236	7.6649	7.6063	7.5476	7.4889	7.4303	7.3716	7.3129	7.2543	7.1956	7.1369	7.0783	.001955
39	8.0655	8.0055	7.9455	7.8855	7.8256	7.7656	7.7056	7.6456	7.5856	7.5256	7.4657	7.4057	.001999
40	8.4222	8.3603	8.2984	8.2365	8.1746	8.1127	8.0507	7.9888	7.9269	7.8650	7.8031	7.7412	.002063
41	8.7879	8.7236	8.6592	8.5949	8.5306	8.4663	8.4020	8.3376	8.2733	8.2090	8.1446	8.0803	.002144
42	9.1594	9.0919	9.0244	8.9568	8.8893	8.8218	8.7543	8.6868	8.6193	8.5517	8.4842	8.4167	.002250
43	9.5312	9.4601	9.3890	9.3179	9.2468	9.1757	9.1046	9.0336	8.9626	8.8914	8.8203	8.7492	.002369
44	9.9063	9.8311	9.7560	9.6808	9.6057	9.5305	9.4553	9.3802	9.3050	9.2299	9.1547	9.0796	.002505
45	10.2875	10.2081	10.1286	10.0492	9.9697	9.8903	9.8108	9.7314	9.6520	9.5725	9.4931	9.4136	.002648
46	10.6797	10.5953	10.5110	10.4266	10.3423	10.2579	10.1735	10.0892	10.0048	9.9205	9.8361	9.7518	.002812
47	11.0858	10.9960	10.9063	10.8165	10.7267	10.6370	10.5472	10.4574	10.3677	10.2779	10.1881	10.0984	.002992
48	11.5062	11.4105	11.3147	11.2190	11.1232	11.0275	10.9317	10.8360	10.7403	10.6445	10.5488	10.4530	.003191
49	11.9414	11.8391	11.7369	11.6346	11.5324	11.4301	11.3279	11.2256	11.1234	11.0211	10.9189	10.8166	.003404
50	12.3901	12.2808	12.1716	12.0623	11.9530	11.8438	11.7345	11.6252	11.5160	11.4067	11.2974	11.1882	.003642
51	12.8559	12.7389	12.6220	12.5050	12.3881	12.2711	12.1541	12.0372	11.9202	11.8033	11.6863	11.5694	.003898
52	13.3393	13.2139	13.0885	12.9630	12.8376	12.7122	12.5868	12.4614	12.3360	12.2105	12.0851	11.9597	.004180
53	13.8411	13.7067	13.5723	13.4380	13.3036	13.1692	13.0348	12.9005	12.7661	12.6317	12.4973	12.3630	.004479
54	14.3651	14.2209	14.0767	13.9325	13.7883	13.6440	13.4998	13.3556	13.2114	13.0672	12.9230	12.7788	.004806
55	14.9104	14.7554	14.6005	14.4455	14.2906	14.1356	13.9806	13.8257	13.6707	13.5158	13.3608	13.2059	.005165
56	15.4780	15.3108	15.1437	14.9765	14.8094	14.6422	14.4750	14.3079	14.1407	13.9736	13.8064	13.6393	.005572
57	16.0639	15.8835	15.7030	15.5226	15.3422	15.1617	14.9813	14.8009	14.6204	14.4400	14.2596	14.0791	.006014
58	16.6656	16.4704	16.2752	16.0800	15.8848	15.6896	15.4944	15.2993	15.1041	14.9089	14.7137	14.5185	.006506
59	17.2808	17.0696	16.8583	16.6471	16.4358	16.2246	16.0133	15.8021	15.5909	15.3796	15.1684	14.9571	.007041
60	17.9100	17.6811	17.4521	17.2232	16.9943	16.7654	16.5364	16.3075	16.0786	15.8497	15.6207	15.3918	.007630
61	18.5561	18.3080	18.0598	17.8117	17.5635	17.3154	17.0672	16.8191	16.5710	16.3228	16.0747	15.8265	.008271
62	19.2191	18.9497	18.6803	18.4108	18.1414	17.8720	17.6026	17.3332	17.0638	16.7943	16.5249	16.2555	.008980
63	19.8972	19.6048	19.3126	19.0203	18.7280	18.4357	18.1433	17.8510	17.5587	17.2664	16.9741	16.6818	.009743
64	20.5927	20.2756	19.9585	19.6414	19.3243	19.0072	18.6900	18.3729	18.0558	17.7387	17.4216	17.1045	.010570
65	21.3084	20.9647	20.6211	20.2774	19.9338	19.5901	19.2464	18.9028	18.5591	18.2155	17.8718	17.5282	.011455
66	22.0483	21.6758	21.3033	20.9308	20.5583	20.1858	19.8133	19.4408	19.0683	18.6958	18.3233	17.9508	.012416
67	22.8165	22.4130	22.0095	21.6060	21.2025	20.7990	20.3954	19.9919	19.5884	19.1849	18.7814	18.3779	.013450
68	23.6006	23.1648	22.7291	22.3933	21.8576	21.4218	20.9861	20.5503	20.1146	19.6788	19.2431	18.8073	.014525
69	24.4445	23.9717	23.4988	23.0260	22.5532	22.0803	21.6075	21.1347	20.6618	20.1890	19.7162	19.2433	.015761
70	25.3069	24.7953	24.2838	23.7722	23.2606	22.7491	22.2375	21.7259	21.2144	20.7028	20.1912	19.6797	.017052
71	26.2059	25.6527	25.0996	24.5464	23.9933	23.4401	22.8869	22.3338	21.7806	21.2275	20.6743	20.1212	.018438
72	27.1445	26.5469	25.9493	25.3517	24.7541	24.1565	23.5588	22.9612	22.3636	21.7660	21.1684	20.5708	.019920
73	28.1299	27.4841	26.8383	26.1925	25.5467	24.9009	24.2551	23.6093	22.9635	22.3177	21.6719	21.0261	.021526
74	29.1614	28.4635	27.7656	27.0677	26.3698	25.6719	24.9740	24.2760	23.5781	22.8802	22.1823	21.4844	.023263
75	30.2398	29.4865	28.7332	27.9799	27.2266	26.4733	25.7200	24.9658	24.2135	23.4602	22.7069	21.9536	.025109
76	31.3769	30.5600	29.7431	28.9262	28.1093	27.2924	26.4755	25.6586	24.8417	24.0248	23.2079	22.3910	.027230
77	32.5815	31.7068	30.8322	29.9575	29.0829	28.2082	27.3335	26.4589	25.5842	24.7096	23.8349	22.9603	.029155
78	33.8809	32.9414	32.0182	31.0633	30.1227	29.1832	28.2436	27.3041	26.3646	25.4250	24.4855	23.5459	.031318
79	35.3152	34.3074	33.2996	32.2918	31.2840	30.2762	29.2684	28.2605	27.2527	26.2449	25.2371	24.2293	.033593
80	36.9129	35.8341	34.7554	33.6766	32.5979	31.5191	30.4403	29.3616	28.2828	27.2041	26.1253	25.0465	.035625
81	38.7219	37.5668	36.4116	35.2565	34.1013	32.9462	31.7910	30.6359	29.4808	28.3256	27.1705	26.0153	.038505
82	40.7607	39.5229	38.2851	37.0473	35.8095	34.5717	33.3338	32.0960	30.8582	29.6204	28.3826	27.1448	.041260
83	43.0458	41.7180	40.3901	39.0623	37.7345	36.4066	35.0788	33.7510	32.4231	31.0953	29.7675	28.4396	.044261
84	45.6066	44.1769	42.7473	41.3176	39.8879	38.4583	37.0286	35.5989	34.1693	32.7396	31.3099	29.8803	.047653
85	48.4342	46.8868	45.3394	43.7920	42.2447	40.6973	39.1499	37.6025	36.0551	34.5077	32.9604	31.4130	.051579
86	51.5222	49.8415	48.1608	46.4801	44.7995	43.1188	41.4381	39.7574	38.0767	36.3960	34.7154	33.0347	.056023
87	54.9024	53.0665	51.2307	49.3948	47.5589	45.7231	43.8872	42.0513	40.2155	38.3796	36.5437	34.7079	.061195
88	58.5738	56.5497	54.5256	52.5015	50.4775	48.4534	46.4293	44.4052	42.3811	40.3570	38.3330	36.3089	.067169
89	62.4687	60.2148	57.9608	55.7068	53.4529	51.1990	48.9450	46.6910	44.4371	42.1831	39.9292	37.6752	.075132
90	66.5053	63.9841	61.4630	58.9418	56.4207	53.8995	51.3783	48.8572	46.3360	43.8149	41.2937	38.7726	.084038
91	70.5747	67.6944	64.8142	61.9339	59.0536	56.1734	53.2931	50.4128	47.5326	44.6523	41.7720	38.8918	.096008
92	74.0604	70.7722	67.4840	64.1959	60.9077	57.6195	54.3313	51.0432	47.7550	44.4668	41.1786	37.8905	.109605
93	76.9054	73.4082	69.9109	66.4136	62.9164	59.4191	55.9219	52.4246	48.9274	45.4301	41.9329	38.4356	.116575
94	82.3135	78.9894	75.6654	72.3413	69.0173	65.6932	62.3691	59.0451	55.7210	52.3970	49.0729	45.7489	.110802
95 or 14	**96.1538**	**96.4743**	**96.7948**	**97.1153**	**97.4359**	**97.7564**	**98.0769**	**98.3974**	**98.7179**	**99.0384**	**99.3590**	**99.6795**	**.010684**
13	94.9633	94.9703	94.9773	94.9843	94.9913	94.9983	95.0052	95.0122	95.0192	95.0262	95.0332	95.0402	.000233
12	94.3444	94.3061	94.2677	94.2294	94.1910	94.1527	94.1143	94.0760	94.0377	93.9993	93.9610	93.9226	.001278
11	93.8866	93.8368	93.7870	93.7372	93.6874	93.6376	93.5878	93.5381	93.4883	93.4385	93.3887	93.3389	.001659
10	93.2969	93.2599	93.2229	93.1859	93.1489	93.1119	93.0749	93.0379	93.0009	92.9639	92.9269	92.8899	.001233
Age.	0	1	2	3	4	5	6	7	8	9	10	11	Day.

Age.	0	1	2	3	4	5	6	7	8	9	10	11	Day.
10	3.2721	3.2267	3.1813	3.1340	3.0906	3.0452	2.9998	2.9545	2.9091	2.8637	2.8183	2.7730	.001512
11	3.3870	3.3418	3.2965	3.2513	3.2060	3.1608	3.1155	3.0703	3.0251	2.9798	2.9346	2.8893	.001508
12	3.5088	3.4634	3.4180	3.3726	3.3272	3.2818	3.2364	3.1910	3.1456	3.1002	3.0548	3.0094	.001513
13	3.6323	3.5868	3.5413	3.4958	3.4503	3.4048	3.3593	3.3138	3.2683	3.2228	3.1773	3.1318	.001516
14	3.7594	3.7138	3.6682	3.6227	3.5771	3.5315	3.4860	3.4404	3.3948	3.3492	3.3036	3.2581	.001519
15	3.8912	3.8454	3.7997	3.7539	3.7081	3.6624	3.6166	3.5708	3.5251	3.4793	3.4335	3.3878	.001528
16	4.0267	3.9808	3.9349	3.8890	3.8430	3.7971	3.7512	3.7053	3.6594	3.6134	3.5675	3.5216	.001530
17	4.1676	4.1215	4.0755	4.0294	3.9834	3.9373	3.8913	3.8452	3.7992	3.7531	3.7071	3.6610	.001535
18	4.3139	4.2676	4.2213	4.1751	4.1288	4.0825	4.0362	3.9900	3.9437	3.8974	3.8511	3.8049	.001542
19	4.4663	4.4198	4.3733	4.3268	4.2803	4.2338	4.1873	4.1408	4.0943	4.0478	4.0013	3.9548	.001550
20	4.6243	4.5776	4.5309	4.4842	4.4376	4.3909	4.3442	4.2975	4.2508	4.2041	4.1575	4.1108	.001556
21	4.7908	4.7438	4.6969	4.6499	4.6029	4.5560	4.5090	4.4620	4.4151	4.3681	4.3211	4.2742	.001565
22	4.9640	4.9168	4.8695	4.8223	4.7751	4.7278	4.6806	4.6334	4.5861	4.5389	4.4917	4.4444	.001574
23	5.1447	5.0971	5.0496	5.0020	4.9544	4.9069	4.8593	4.8117	4.7642	4.7166	4.6690	4.6215	.001585
24	5.3335	5.2856	5.2377	5.1897	5.1418	5.0939	5.0460	4.9981	4.9502	4.9022	4.8543	4.8064	.001597
25	5.5305	5.4822	5.4340	5.3857	5.3374	5.2892	5.2409	5.1926	5.1444	5.0961	5.0478	4.9996	.001605
26	5.7364	5.6877	5.6390	5.5903	5.5417	5.4930	5.4443	5.3956	5.3469	5.2982	5.2496	5.2009	.001622
27	5.9516	5.9025	5.8533	5.8042	5.7551	5.7059	5.6568	5.6077	5.5585	5.5094	5.4603	5.4111	.001637
28	6.1763	6.1267	6.0771	6.0275	5.9779	5.9283	5.8787	5.8292	5.7796	5.7300	5.6804	5.6308	.001653
29	6.4120	6.3620	6.3120	6.2620	6.2119	6.1619	6.1119	6.0619	6.0119	5.9618	5.9118	5.8618	.001667
30	6.6600	6.6095	6.5590	6.5085	6.4580	6.4075	6.3570	6.3065	6.2560	6.2055	6.1550	6.1045	.001683
31	6.9206	6.8696	6.8186	6.7675	6.7165	6.6655	6.6145	6.5635	6.5125	6.4614	6.4104	6.3594	.001700
32	7.1950	7.1436	7.0922	7.0408	6.9894	6.9380	6.8866	6.8353	6.7839	6.7325	6.6811	6.6297	.001713
33	7.4863	7.4344	7.3824	7.3305	7.2786	7.2267	7.1748	7.1228	7.0709	7.0190	6.9670	6.9151	.001730
34	7.7939	7.7415	7.6891	7.6367	7.5843	7.5319	7.4795	7.4272	7.3748	7.3224	7.2700	7.2176	.001746
35	8.1204	8.0675	8.0146	7.9617	7.9088	7.8559	7.8030	7.7501	7.6972	7.6443	7.5914	7.5385	.001763
36	8.4655	8.4122	8.3589	8.3056	8.2523	8.1990	8.1457	8.0925	8.0392	7.9859	7.9326	7.8793	.001776
37	8.8335	8.7796	8.7257	8.6718	8.6179	8.5640	8.5100	8.4561	8.4022	8.3483	8.2944	8.2405	.001796
38	9.2215	9.1665	9.1115	9.0565	9.0016	8.9466	8.8916	8.8366	8.7816	8.7266	8.6717	8.6167	.001833
39	9.6280	9.5713	9.5147	9.4580	9.4014	9.3447	9.2881	9.2314	9.1748	9.1181	9.0615	9.0048	.001888
40	10.0470	9.9882	9.9294	9.8707	9.8119	9.7531	9.6943	9.6356	9.5768	9.5180	9.4592	9.4005	.001959
41	10.4746	10.4129	10.3513	10.2896	10.2280	10.1663	10.1047	10.0430	9.9814	9.9197	9.8581	9.7964	.002055
42	10.9046	10.8397	10.7748	10.7099	10.6451	10.5802	10.5153	10.4504	10.3855	10.3206	10.2558	10.1909	.002162
43	11.3366	11.2680	11.1994	11.1308	11.0622	10.9936	10.9250	10.8565	10.7879	10.7193	10.6507	10.5821	.002286
44	11.7726	11.7001	11.6275	11.5550	11.4825	11.4100	11.3374	11.2649	11.1924	11.1199	11.0473	10.9748	.002414
45	12.2187	12.1416	12.0646	11.9875	11.9105	11.8334	11.7563	11.6793	11.6022	11.5252	11.4481	11.3711	.002568
46	12.6754	12.5933	12.5112	12.4291	12.3470	12.2649	12.1827	12.1006	12.0185	11.9364	11.8543	11.7722	.002736
47	13.1471	13.0594	12.9684	12.8791	12.7898	12.7004	12.6111	12.5218	12.4324	12.3431	12.2538	12.1644	.002977
48	13.6339	13.5402	13.4464	13.3527	13.2589	13.1652	13.0714	12.9777	12.8839	12.7902	12.6964	12.6027	.003125
49	14.1371	14.0368	13.9365	13.8362	13.7359	13.6356	13.5353	13.4350	13.3347	13.2344	13.1341	13.0338	.003343
50	14.6564	14.5489	14.4414	14.3339	14.2264	14.1189	14.0114	13.9039	13.7964	13.6889	13.5814	13.4739	.003583
51	15.1940	15.0785	14.9631	14.8476	14.7322	14.6167	14.5013	14.3858	14.2704	14.1550	14.0395	13.9240	.003848
52	15.7494	15.6256	15.5018	15.3780	15.2542	15.1304	15.0065	14.8827	14.7589	14.6351	14.5113	14.3875	.004126
53	16.3282	16.1951	16.0621	15.9290	15.7960	15.6629	15.5298	15.3968	15.2637	15.1307	14.9976	14.8646	.004435
54	16.9296	16.7865	16.6433	16.5002	16.3570	16.2139	16.0707	15.9276	15.7845	15.6413	15.4982	15.3550	.004771
55	17.5534	17.3988	17.2442	17.0896	16.9350	16.7804	16.6257	16.4711	16.3165	16.1619	16.0073	15.8527	.005153
56	18.1951	18.0280	17.8609	17.6937	17.5266	17.3595	17.1924	17.0253	16.8582	16.6910	16.5239	16.3568	.005570
57	18.8558	18.6748	18.4938	18.3129	18.1319	17.9509	17.7700	17.5890	17.4080	17.2270	17.0460	16.8651	.006032
58	19.5900	19.3889	19.1878	18.9868	18.7857	18.5846	18.3835	18.1825	17.9814	17.7803	17.5792	17.3782	.006702
59	20.2183	20.0056	19.7928	19.5801	19.3674	19.1547	18.9420	18.7292	18.5165	18.3038	18.0910	17.8783	.007090
60	20.9185	20.6877	20.4568	20.2260	19.9952	19.7644	19.5335	19.3027	19.0719	18.8411	18.6102	18.3794	.007694
61	21.6355	21.3846	21.1337	20.8828	20.6319	20.3810	20.1301	19.8792	19.6283	19.3774	19.1265	18.8756	.008363
62	22.3643	22.0918	21.8193	21.5468	21.2743	21.0018	20.7293	20.4569	20.1844	19.9119	19.6394	19.3669	.009083
63	23.1094	22.8135	22.5177	22.2218	21.9260	21.6301	21.3342	21.0384	20.7425	20.4467	20.1503	19.8550	.009862
64	23.8715	23.5506	23.2297	22.9088	22.5879	22.2670	21.9461	21.6252	21.3043	20.9834	20.6625	20.3416	.010696
65	24.6563	24.3082	23.9601	23.6120	23.2639	22.9158	22.5677	22.2195	21.8714	21.5233	21.1752	20.8271	.011603
66	25.4629	25.0855	24.7081	24.3308	23.9534	23.5760	23.1986	22.8213	22.4439	22.0665	21.6891	21.3118	.012579
67	26.2982	25.8893	25.4804	25.0715	24.6627	24.2538	23.8449	23.4360	23.0271	22.6182	22.2094	21.8005	.013629
68	27.1629	26.7201	26.2774	25.8346	25.3919	24.9491	24.5063	24.0636	23.6208	23.1781	22.7353	22.2926	.014758
69	28.0597	27.5805	27.1012	26.6220	26.1428	25.6635	25.1843	24.7051	24.2258	23.7466	23.2674	22.7881	.015974
70	28.9884	28.4700	27.9516	27.4332	26.9148	26.3964	25.8780	25.3596	24.8412	24.3228	23.8044	23.2860	.017280
71	29.9545	29.3943	28.8340	28.2738	27.7136	27.1533	26.5931	26.0329	25.4726	24.9124	24.3522	23.7919	.018674
72	30.9638	30.3583	29.7527	29.1472	28.5416	27.9360	27.3305	26.7250	26.1194	25.5138	24.9083	24.3027	.020185
73	32.0158	31.3613	30.7068	30.0523	29.3978	28.7433	28.0888	27.4343	26.7798	26.1253	25.4708	24.8163	.021816
74	33.1113	32.4048	31.6982	30.9917	30.2852	29.5786	28.8721	28.1656	27.4590	26.7525	26.0460	25.3394	.023551
75	34.2614	33.4995	32.7375	31.9756	31.2136	30.4517	29.6897	28.9278	28.1659	27.4039	26.6420	25.8800	.025398
76	35.4232	34.6075	33.7918	32.9761	32.1604	31.3447	30.5289	29.7132	28.8975	28.0818	27.2661	26.4504	.027190
77	36.7792	35.8983	35.0173	34.1364	33.2554	32.3745	31.4935	30.6126	29.7317	28.8507	27.9698	27.0888	.029364
78	38.2044	37.2597	36.3150	35.3703	34.4256	33.4809	32.5362	31.5916	30.6469	29.7022	28.7575	27.8128	.031489
79	39.7894	38.7786	37.7678	36.7570	35.7462	34.7354	33.7245	32.7137	31.7029	30.6921	29.6813	28.6705	.033693
80	41.5777	40.4959	39.4141	38.3323	37.2505	36.1687	35.0868	34.0050	32.9232	31.8414	30.7596	29.6778	.036060
81	43.5923	42.4342	41.2760	40.1179	38.9598	37.8016	36.6435	35.4854	34.3272	33.1691	32.0110	30.8528	.038604
82	45.8557	44.6151	43.3744	42.1338	40.8932	39.6526	38.4120	37.1713	35.9307	34.6901	33.4494	32.2088	.041354
83	48.3897	47.0564	45.7231	44.3899	43.0566	41.7233	40.3900	39.0568	37.7235	36.3902	35.0570	33.7237	.044442
84	51.1928	49.7534	48.3140	46.8745	45.4351	43.9957	42.5563	41.1169	39.6775	38.2380	36.7986	35.3592	.047980
85	54.2389	52.6800	51.1212	49.5624	48.0035	46.4446	44.8858	43.3269	41.7681	40.2092	38.6504	37.0915	.051962
86	57.5565	55.8594	54.1622	52.4651	50.7680	49.0709	47.3737	45.6766	43.9795	42.2824	40.5852	38.8881	.056570
87	61.1408	59.2769	57.4129	55.5490	53.6851	51.8212	49.9572	48.0933	46.2294	44.3655	42.5015	40.6376	.062131
88	64.9082	62.8434	60.7787	58.7140	56.6492	54.5844	52.5197	50.4550	48.3902	46.3254	44.2607	42.1960	.068825
89	68.7359	66.4349	64.1340	61.8330	59.5320	57.2311	54.9301	52.6291	50.3282	48.0272	45.7262	43.4203	.076698
90	72.6417	70.0201	67.3984	64.7768	62.1551	59.5335	56.9118	54.2902	51.6686	49.0469	46.4253	43.8036	.087388
91	75.9386	72.9573	69.9760	66.9947	64.0134	61.0321	58.0508	55.0695	52.0882	49.1069	46.1256	43.1443	.099376
92	78.5977	75.4361	72.2745	69.1129	65.9513	62.7897	59.6281	56.4665	53.3049	50.1433	46.9817	43.8201	.105386
93	83.5454	80.5455	77.5457	74.5458	71.5459	68.5461	65.5462	62.5463	59.5465	56.5466	53.5467	50.5469	.099995
94 or 15	**96.1538**	**96.4743**	**96.7948**	**97.1153**	**97.4359**	**97.7564**	**98.0769**	**98.3974**	**98.7179**	**99.0384**	**99.3590**	**99.6795**	**.010684**
14	94.9577	94.9632	94.9687	94.9742	94.9798	94.9853	94.9908	94.9963	95.0018	95.0073	95.0129	95.0184	.000283
13	94.3363	94.2963	94.2564	94.2164	94.1764	94.1365	94.0965	94.0565	94.0166	93.9766	93.9366	93.8967	.001332
12	93.8768	93.8254	93.7740	93.7226	93.6712	93.6198	93.5684	93.5171	93.4657	93.4143	93.3629	93.3115	.001713
11	93.2850	93.2465	93.2081	93.1696	93.1312	93.0927	93.0542	93.0158	92.9773	92.9389	92.9004	92.8620	.001282
10	92.5512	92.5264	92.5017	92.4769	92.4521	92.4273	92.4025	92.3778	92.3530	92.3282	92.3035	92.2787	.000825
Age.	0	1	2	3	4	5	6	7	8	9	10	11	Day.

Age.	0	1	2	3	4	5	6	7	8	9	10	11	Day.
10	3.7705	3.7266	3.6828	3.6389	3.5950	3.5511	3.5073	3.4634	3.4195	3.3756	3.3318	3.2879	.001462
11	3.9073	3.8635	3.8196	3.7758	3.7319	3.6881	3.6442	3.6004	3.5566	3.5127	3.4689	3.4250	.001461
12	4.0483	4.0044	3.9606	3.9167	3.8729	3.8290	3.7851	3.7413	3.6974	3.6536	3.6097	3.5659	.001462
13	4.1929	4.1490	4.1052	4.0613	4.0175	3.9736	3.9297	3.8859	3.8420	3.7982	3.7548	3.7105	.001462
14	4.3425	4.2985	4.2545	4.2105	4.1666	4.1226	4.0786	4.0346	3.9906	3.9466	3.9027	3.8587	.001466
15	4.4964	4.4524	4.4083	4.3643	4.3202	4.2762	4.2321	4.1881	4.1440	4.1000	4.0559	4.0119	.001468
16	4.6558	4.6117	4.5676	4.5235	4.4794	4.4353	4.3912	4.3472	4.3031	4.2590	4.2149	4.1708	.001469
17	4.8218	4.7775	4.7333	4.6890	4.6448	4.6005	4.5562	4.5120	4.4677	4.4235	4.3792	4.3350	.001475
18	4.9934	4.9490	4.9047	4.8603	4.8159	4.7715	4.7272	4.6828	4.6384	4.5940	4.5497	4.5053	.001479
19	5.1727	5.1282	5.0837	5.0392	4.9947	4.9502	4.9056	4.8611	4.8166	4.7721	4.7276	4.6831	.001483
20	5.3590	5.3143	5.2697	5.2250	5.1803	5.1357	5.0910	5.0463	5.0017	4.9570	4.9123	4.8677	.001488
21	5.5544	5.5096	5.4647	5.4199	5.3750	5.3302	5.2853	5.2405	5.1956	5.1508	5.1059	5.0610	.001495
22	5.7583	5.7132	5.6681	5.6230	5.5779	5.5328	5.4877	5.4427	5.3976	5.3525	5.3074	5.2623	.001503
23	5.9703	5.9249	5.8796	5.8343	5.7889	5.7436	5.6983	5.6529	5.6076	5.5623	5.5169	5.4716	.001510
24	6.1919	6.1463	6.1007	6.0551	6.0096	5.9640	5.9184	5.8728	5.8272	5.7816	5.7361	5.6905	.001519
25	6.4235	6.3776	6.3318	6.2859	6.2400	6.1941	6.1483	6.1024	6.0565	6.0106	5.9648	5.9189	.001529
26	6.6651	6.6189	6.5727	6.5265	6.4803	6.4341	6.3879	6.3416	6.2954	6.2492	6.2030	6.1568	.001540
27	6.9176	6.8711	6.8245	6.7780	6.7314	6.6849	6.6383	6.5918	6.5453	6.4987	6.4522	6.4056	.001551
28	7.1817	7.1349	7.0880	7.0412	6.9943	6.9475	6.9006	6.8538	6.8070	6.7601	6.7133	6.6664	.001561
29	7.4594	7.4122	7.3650	7.3178	7.2706	7.2234	7.1762	7.1291	7.0819	7.0347	6.9875	6.9403	.001573
30	7.7511	7.7035	7.6560	7.6084	7.5609	7.5133	7.4658	7.4182	7.3706	7.3231	7.2755	7.2280	.001585
31	8.0576	8.0098	7.9620	7.9142	7.8665	7.8187	7.7709	7.7231	7.6753	7.6275	7.5798	7.5320	.001592
32	8.3824	8.3342	8.2860	8.2379	8.1897	8.1415	8.0933	8.0452	7.9970	7.9488	7.9006	7.8525	.001605
33	8.7248	8.6763	8.6279	8.5794	8.5310	8.4825	8.4340	8.3856	8.3371	8.2887	8.2402	8.1918	.001615
34	9.0876	9.0389	8.9902	8.9415	8.8928	8.8441	8.7953	8.7466	8.6979	8.6492	8.6005	8.5518	.001623
35	9.4723	9.4233	9.3743	9.3253	9.2763	9.2273	9.1783	9.1293	9.0803	9.0313	8.9823	8.9333	.001633
36	9.8804	9.8310	9.7816	9.7321	9.6827	9.6333	9.5839	9.5345	9.4851	9.4356	9.3862	9.3368	.001647
37	10.3126	10.2623	10.2120	10.1618	10.1115	10.0612	10.0110	9.9607	9.9104	9.8601	9.8098	9.7596	.001675
38	10.7635	10.7118	10.6601	10.6084	10.5567	10.5050	10.4533	10.4016	10.3499	10.2982	10.2465	10.1948	.001723
39	11.2305	11.1769	11.1234	11.0698	11.0163	10.9627	10.9091	10.8556	10.8020	10.7485	10.6949	10.6414	.001785
40	11.7094	11.6533	11.5971	11.5410	11.4848	11.4287	11.3725	11.3164	11.2603	11.2041	11.1480	11.0918	.001871
41	12.1934	12.1343	12.0753	12.0162	11.9572	11.8981	11.8390	11.7800	11.7209	11.6619	11.6028	11.5438	.001965
42	12.6814	12.6190	12.5565	12.4941	12.4317	12.3693	12.3068	12.2444	12.1820	12.1196	12.0572	11.9947	.002080
43	13.1690	13.1032	13.0375	12.9717	12.9060	12.8402	12.7744	12.7087	12.6429	12.5772	12.5114	12.4457	.002191
44	13.6705	13.6003	13.5301	13.4599	13.3897	13.3195	13.2493	13.1792	13.1090	13.0388	12.9686	12.8984	.002339
45	14.1785	14.1037	14.0288	13.9540	13.8791	13.8043	13.7294	13.6545	13.5797	13.5048	13.4300	13.3551	.002495
46	14.6981	14.6181	14.5380	14.4580	14.3780	14.2979	14.2179	14.1379	14.0578	13.9778	13.8978	13.8177	.002667
47	15.2336	15.1479	15.0622	14.9764	14.8907	14.8050	14.7193	14.6336	14.5479	14.4621	14.3764	14.2907	.002857
48	15.7855	15.6937	15.6018	15.5100	15.4181	15.3263	15.2344	15.1426	15.0508	14.9589	14.8671	14.7752	.003061
49	16.3562	16.2576	16.1590	16.0605	15.9619	15.8633	15.7647	15.6662	15.5676	15.4690	15.3704	15.2719	.003252
50	16.9440	16.8380	16.7319	16.6259	16.5199	16.4138	16.3078	16.2018	16.0957	15.9897	15.8837	15.7776	.003534
51	17.5501	17.4362	17.3223	17.2084	17.0946	16.9807	16.8668	16.7529	16.6390	16.5251	16.4113	16.2974	.003796
52	18.1788	18.0563	17.9338	17.8112	17.6887	17.5662	17.4437	17.3212	17.1987	17.0761	16.9536	16.8311	.004083
53	18.8311	18.6991	18.5671	18.4350	18.3030	18.1710	18.0390	17.9070	17.7750	17.6430	17.5109	17.3789	.004400
54	19.5068	19.3640	19.2212	19.0784	18.9356	18.7928	18.6500	18.5073	18.3645	18.2217	18.0789	17.9361	.004759
55	20.2005	20.0459	19.8914	19.7368	19.5823	19.4277	19.2731	19.1186	18.9640	18.8095	18.6549	18.5004	.005152
56	20.9127	20.7451	20.5774	20.4098	20.2421	20.0745	19.9068	19.7392	19.5716	19.4039	19.2363	19.0686	.005588
57	21.6412	21.4594	21.2775	21.0957	20.9139	20.7320	20.5502	20.3684	20.1865	20.0047	19.8229	19.6410	.006061
58	22.3837	22.1862	21.9887	21.7911	21.5936	21.3961	21.1986	21.0011	20.8036	20.6060	20.4085	20.2110	.006583
59	23.1380	22.9234	22.7089	22.4943	22.2797	22.0652	21.8506	21.6360	21.4215	21.2069	20.9923	20.7778	.007152
60	23.9042	23.6707	23.4972	23.2037	22.9702	22.7367	22.5032	22.2697	22.0362	21.8027	21.5692	21.3357	.007783
61	24.6819	24.4280	24.1742	23.9203	23.6664	23.4125	23.1587	22.9048	22.6509	22.3970	22.1432	21.8893	.008462
62	25.4726	25.1967	24.9207	24.6448	24.3689	24.0929	23.8170	23.5411	23.2651	22.9892	22.7133	22.4373	.009197
63	26.2790	25.9795	25.6800	25.3804	25.0809	24.7814	24.4819	24.1823	23.8828	23.5833	23.2838	22.9842	.009984
64	27.1048	26.7796	26.4544	26.1292	25.8040	25.4788	25.1535	24.8283	24.5031	24.1779	23.8527	23.5275	.010840
65	27.9507	27.5979	27.2451	26.8922	26.5394	26.1866	25.8338	25.4810	25.1282	24.7753	24.4225	24.0697	.011760
66	28.8290	28.4456	28.0622	27.6788	27.2954	26.9120	26.5286	26.1452	25.7618	25.3784	24.9950	24.6116	.012780
67	29.7154	29.3009	28.8864	28.4718	28.0573	27.6428	27.2283	26.8138	26.3993	25.9847	25.5702	25.1557	.013817
68	30.6411	30.1922	29.7433	29.2943	28.8454	28.3965	27.9476	27.4987	27.0498	26.6008	26.1519	25.7030	.014630
69	31.5981	31.1123	30.6265	30.1407	29.6549	29.1691	28.6833	28.1975	27.7117	27.2259	26.7401	26.2543	.016193
70	32.5878	32.0626	31.5374	31.0122	30.4871	29.9619	29.4367	28.9115	28.3863	27.8611	27.3360	26.8108	.017506
71	33.6182	33.0504	32.4825	31.9147	31.3468	30.7790	30.2111	29.6433	29.0755	28.5076	27.9398	27.3719	.018924
72	34.6878	34.0739	33.4600	32.8461	32.2323	31.6184	31.0045	30.3906	29.7767	29.1628	28.5490	27.9351	.020462
73	35.7974	35.1352	34.4730	33.8108	33.1486	32.4864	31.8242	31.1620	30.4998	29.8376	29.1754	28.5132	.022073
74	36.9576	36.2428	35.5280	34.8132	34.0984	33.3836	32.6688	31.9541	31.2393	30.5245	29.8097	29.0949	.023826
75	38.1792	37.4098	36.6404	35.8710	35.1015	34.3321	33.5627	32.7933	32.0239	31.2544	30.4850	29.7156	.025647
76	39.4838	38.6576	37.8314	37.0051	36.1789	35.3527	34.5265	33.7003	32.8741	32.0478	31.2216	30.3954	.027540
77	40.9015	40.0156	39.1298	38.2439	37.3581	36.4722	35.5863	34.7005	33.8146	32.9288	32.0429	31.1571	.029528
78	42.4660	41.5185	40.5709	39.6234	38.6758	37.7283	36.7807	35.8332	34.8857	33.9381	32.9906	32.0430	.031584
79	44.2276	43.2139	42.2002	41.1865	40.1728	39.1591	38.1454	37.1317	36.1180	35.1043	34.0906	33.0769	.033790
80	46.2059	45.1213	44.0366	42.9520	41.8673	40.7827	39.6980	38.6134	37.5288	36.4441	35.3595	34.2748	.036154
81	48.4269	47.2661	46.1053	44.9445	43.7837	42.6229	41.4620	40.3012	39.1404	37.9796	36.8188	35.6580	.038693
82	50.9169	49.7711	48.5253	47.2795	45.9338	44.6880	43.4422	42.1964	40.9506	39.7048	38.4591	37.2133	.041526
83	53.6684	52.3259	50.9834	49.6409	48.2984	46.9559	45.6134	44.2710	42.9285	41.5860	40.2435	38.9010	.044749
84	56.6620	55.2118	53.7615	52.3113	50.8611	49.4108	47.9606	46.5104	45.0601	43.6099	42.1597	40.7094	.048341
85	59.9060	58.3317	56.7574	55.1831	53.6088	52.0345	50.4601	48.8858	47.3115	45.7372	44.1629	42.5886	.052443
86	63.3935	61.6701	59.9468	57.2234	56.5000	54.7767	53.0533	51.3299	49.6066	47.8832	46.1598	44.4365	.057442
87	67.0426	65.1408	63.2390	61.3371	59.4353	57.5335	55.6316	53.7298	51.8280	49.9262	48.0244	46.1225	.063394
88	70.7546	68.6407	66.5269	64.4130	62.2991	60.1853	58.0714	55.9575	53.8437	51.7298	49.6159	47.5021	.070462
89	74.4390	72.0422	69.6455	67.2488	64.8520	62.4553	60.0585	57.6618	55.2650	52.8683	50.4715	48.0748	.079892
90	77.5723	74.8578	72.1433	69.4287	66.7142	63.9997	61.2852	58.5706	55.8561	53.1416	50.4270	47.7125	.090484
91	80.0902	77.2247	74.3592	71.4937	68.6282	65.7627	62.8972	60.0318	57.1663	54.3008	51.4353	48.5698	.095516
92	84.6539	81.9460	79.2380	76.5301	73.8221	71.1142	68.4063	65.6983	62.9904	60.2824	57.5745	54.8665	.090264
93 or 16	**96.1538**	**96.4743**	**96.7948**	**97.1153**	**97.4359**	**97.7564**	**98.0769**	**98.3974**	**98.7179**	**99.0384**	**99.3590**	**99.6795**	**.010684**
15	94.9517	94.9557	94.9596	94.9636	94.9676	94.9716	94.9755	94.9795	94.9835	94.9875	94.9914	94.9954	.000132
14	94.3278	94.2861	94.2444	94.2028	94.1611	94.1194	94.0777	94.0361	93.9944	93.9527	93.9110	93.8694	.001389
13	93.8665	93.8134	93.7604	93.7073	93.6542	93.6012	93.5481	93.4950	93.4420	93.3889	93.3358	93.2828	.001769
12	93.2727	93.2327	93.1927	93.1526	93.1126	93.0726	93.0326	92.9926	92.9526	92.9125	92.8725	92.8325	.001333
11	92.5364	92.5102	92.4840	92.4578	92.4316	92.4054	92.3791	92.3529	92.3267	92.3005	92.2743	92.2481	.000873
10	91.7220	91.7042	91.6864	91.6686	91.6508	91.6330	91.6151	91.5973	91.5795	91.5617	91.5439	91.5261	.000594
Age.	0	1	2	3	4	5	6	7	8	9	10	11	Day.

Age.	0	1	2	3	4	5	6	7	8	9	10	11	Day.
10	4.2870	4.2447	4.2023	4.1600	4.1176	4.0753	4.0329	3.9906	3.9482	3.9059	3.8635	3.8212	.001412
11	4.4444	4.4022	4.3598	4.3175	4.2752	4.2329	4.1907	4.1484	4.1061	4.0638	4.0215	3.9792	.001409
12	4.6063	4.5641	4.5219	4.4797	4.4375	4.3953	4.3531	4.3108	4.2686	4.2264	4.1842	4.1420	.001406
13	4.7732	4.7309	4.6887	4.6464	4.6041	4.5619	4.5196	4.4773	4.4351	4.3928	4.3505	4.3083	.001408
14	4.9447	4.9024	4.8602	4.8179	4.7756	4.7333	4.6911	4.6488	4.6065	4.5642	4.5220	4.4797	.001409
15	5.1222	5.0800	5.0377	4.9955	4.9532	4.9110	4.8687	4.8265	4.7842	4.7420	4.6997	4.6575	.001408
16	5.3067	5.2644	5.2220	5.1797	5.1373	5.0950	5.0527	5.0103	4.9680	4.9256	4.8833	4.8409	.001411
17	5.4976	5.4552	5.4129	5.3705	5.3281	5.2858	5.2434	5.2010	5.1587	5.1163	5.0739	5.0316	.001412
18	5.6958	5.6534	5.6110	5.5686	5.5262	5.4838	5.4414	5.3990	5.3566	5.3142	5.2718	5.2294	.001413
19	5.9029	5.8604	5.8179	5.7754	5.7329	5.6904	5.6480	5.6055	5.5630	5.5205	5.4780	5.4355	.001416
20	6.1179	6.0753	6.0328	5.9902	5.9477	5.9051	5.8626	5.8200	5.7774	5.7349	5.6923	5.6498	.001418
21	6.3435	6.3008	6.2581	6.2154	6.1726	6.1299	6.0872	6.0445	6.0018	5.9590	5.9163	5.8736	.001423
22	6.5783	6.5354	6.4926	6.4497	6.4068	6.3639	6.3210	6.2782	6.2353	6.1924	6.1496	6.1067	.001427
23	6.8226	6.7796	6.7366	6.6936	6.6506	6.6076	6.5646	6.5215	6.4785	6 4355	6.3925	6.3495	.001433
24	7.0783	7.0351	6.9919	6.9487	6.9055	6.8623	6.8190	6.7758	6.7326	6.6894	6.6462	6.6030	.001440
25	7.3452	7.3018	7.2584	7.2149	7.1715	7.1281	7.0847	7.0412	6.9978	6.9544	6.9110	6.8675	.001447
26	7.6235	7.5798	7.5362	7.4925	7.4489	7.4052	7.3616	7.3179	7.2742	7.2306	7.1869	7.1433	.001455
27	7.9148	7.8710	7.8272	7.7834	7.7395	7.6957	7.6519	7.6080	7.5643	7.5204	7.4766	7.4328	.001460
28	8.2201	8.1761	8.1320	8.0880	8.0440	7.9999	7.9559	7.9119	7.8678	7.8238	7.7798	7.7357	.001467
29	8.5407	8.4964	8.4522	8.4079	8.3636	8.3193	8.2751	8.2308	8.1865	8.1422	8.0980	8.0537	.001476
30	8.8775	8.8332	8.7888	8.7445	8.7001	8.6558	8.6114	8.5671	8.5227	8.4784	8.4340	8.3897	.001478
31	9.2335	9.1889	9.1443	9.0997	9.0551	9.0105	8.9659	8.9213	8.8767	8.8321	8.7875	8.7429	.001486
32	9.6084	9.5637	9.5189	9.4742	9.4294	9.3847	9.3400	9.2952	9.2505	9.2057	9.1610	9.1162	.001491
33	10.0049	9.9601	9.9153	9.8705	9.8257	9.7809	9.7360	9.6912	9.6464	9.6016	9.5568	9.5120	.001493
34	10.4256	10.3807	10.3357	10.2908	10.2459	10.2009	10.1560	10.1111	10.0661	10.0212	9.9763	9.9313	.001497
35	10.8709	10.8257	10.7806	10.7354	10.6902	10.6451	10.5999	10.5547	10.5096	10.4644	10.4192	10.3741	.001505
36	11.3418	11.2960	11.2501	11.2043	11.1585	11.1126	11.0668	11.0210	10.9751	10.9293	10.8835	10.8376	.001524
37	11.8353	11.7883	11.7412	11.6942	11.6472	11.6001	11.5531	11.5061	11.4590	11.4120	11.3650	11.3179	.001567
38	12.3449	12.2963	12.2476	12.1990	12.1503	12.1017	12.0530	12.0044	11.9557	11.9070	11.8584	11.8098	.001622
39	12.8701	12.8171	12.7682	12.7172	12.6662	12.6153	12.5643	12.5133	12.4624	12.4114	12.3604	12.3095	.001698
40	13.4034	13.3498	13.2962	13.2427	13.1891	13.1355	13.0819	13.0283	12.9747	12.9212	12.8676	12.8140	.001786
41	13.9433	13.8867	13.8300	13.7734	13.7168	13.6601	13.6035	13.5469	13.4902	13.4336	13.3770	13.3203	.001887
42	14.4877	14.4278	14.3679	14.3080	14.2482	14.1783	14.1284	14.0685	14.0086	13.9487	13.8889	13.8290	.001996
43	15.0384	14.9747	14.9110	14.8473	14.7836	14.7199	14.6562	14.5924	14.5287	14.4650	14.4013	14.3376	.002123
44	15.5964	15.5284	15.4604	15.3923	15.3243	15.2563	15.1883	15.1202	15.0522	14.9842	14.9162	14.8481	.002267
45	16.1648	16.0920	16.0192	15.9463	15.8735	15.8007	15.7279	15.6561	15.5823	15.5094	15.4366	15.3638	.002427
46	16.7457	16.6676	16.5894	16.5113	16.4332	16.3550	16.2769	16.1988	16.1206	16.0425	15.9644	15.8862	.002604
47	17.3435	17.2597	17.1758	17.0920	17.0081	16.9243	16.8404	16.7566	16.6727	16.5889	16.5050	16.4212	.002795
48	17.9600	17.8699	17.7797	17.6896	17.5994	17.5093	17.4191	17.3290	17.2388	17.1487	17.0585	16.9684	.003005
49	18.5960	18.4989	18.4017	18.3046	18.2075	18.1103	18.0132	17.9161	17.8189	17.7218	17.6247	17.5275	.003237
50	19.2492	19.1447	19.0402	18.9357	18.8312	18.7267	18.6222	18.5177	18.4132	18.3087	18.2042	18.0997	.003483
51	19.9250	19.8124	19.6998	19.5871	19.4745	19.3619	19.2493	19.1367	19.0241	18.9114	18.7988	18.6862	.003753
52	20.6237	20.5022	20.3807	20.2592	20.1377	20.0162	19.8947	19.7732	19.6517	19.5302	19.4087	19.2872	.004050
53	21.3465	21.2148	21.0832	20.9515	20.8198	20.6881	20.5565	20.4248	20.2931	20.1614	20.0298	19.8981	.004389
54	22.0882	21.9455	21.8027	21.6600	21.5172	21.3745	21.2317	21.0890	20.9462	20.8035	20.6607	20.5180	.004755
55	22.8483	22.6932	22.5382	22.3831	22.2280	22.0729	21.9179	21.7628	21.6077	21.4526	21.2976	21.1425	.005169
56	23.6240	23.4555	23.2871	23.1186	22.9501	22.7816	22.6132	22.4447	22.2762	22.1077	21.9393	21.7708	.005615
57	24.4163	24.2331	24.0498	23.8666	23.6834	23.5001	23.3169	23.1337	22.9504	22.7672	22.5840	22.4007	.006107
58	25.2202	25.0209	24.8216	24.6223	24.4230	24.2237	24.0244	23.8250	23.6257	23.4264	23.2271	23.0278	.006643
59	26.0356	25.8184	25.6013	25.3841	25.1670	24.9498	24.7326	24.5155	24.2983	24.0812	23.8640	23.6469	.007238
60	26.8578	26.6214	26.3851	26.1487	25.9123	25.6759	25.4396	25.2032	24.9668	24.7304	24.4940	24.2577	.007879
61	27.6926	27.4354	27.1782	26.9210	26.6638	26.4066	26.1494	25.8921	25.6349	25.3777	25.1205	24.8633	.008573
62	28.5396	28.2601	27.9807	27.7012	27.4217	27.1422	26.8628	26.5833	26.3038	26.0243	25.7449	25.4654	.009315
63	29.4046	29.1009	28.7972	28.4935	28.1898	27.8861	27.5824	27.2788	26.9751	26.6714	26.3677	26.0640	.010123
64	30.2864	29.9567	29 6269	29.2972	28.9674	28.6377	28.3079	27.9782	27.6484	27.3187	26.9889	26.6592	.010992
65	31.1887	30.8309	30.4731	30.1152	29.7574	29.3996	29.0418	28.6840	28.3262	27.9683	27.6105	27.2527	.011927
66	32.1128	31.7248	31.3368	30.9488	30.5608	30.1728	29.7848	29.3969	29.0089	28.6209	28.2329	27.8449	.012933
67	33.0649	32.6445	32.2240	31.8036	31.3831	30.9627	30.5422	30.1218	29.7013	29.2809	28.8604	28.4400	.014015
68	34.0454	33.5962	33.1349	32.6797	32.2244	31.7692	31.3140	30.8587	30.4035	29.9482	29.4930	29.0377	.015175
69	35.0577	34.5654	34.0730	33.5807	33.0884	32.5961	32.1038	31.6114	31.1191	30.6268	30.1345	29.6421	.016410
70	36.1058	35.5733	35.0408	34.5083	33.9758	33.4433	32.9108	32.3784	31.8459	31.3134	30.7809	30.2484	.017749
71	37.1906	36.6148	36.0389	35.4631	34.8873	34.3114	33.7356	33.1598	32.5839	32.0081	31.4323	30.8564	.019194
72	38.3119	37.6901	37.0683	36.4466	35.8248	35.2030	34.5812	33.9595	33.3377	32.7159	32.0941	31.4724	.020726
73	39.4865	38.8153	38.1440	37.4728	36.8016	36.1304	35.4591	34.7879	34.1167	33.4455	32.7742	32.1030	.022374
74	40.7048	39.9828	39.2609	38.5390	37.8170	37.0950	36.3731	35.6511	34.9292	34.2072	33.4853	32.7633	.024065
75	42.0073	41.2321	40.4570	39.6818	38.9067	38.1315	37.3564	36.5812	35.8061	35.0310	34.2558	33.4806	.025838
76	43.4183	42.5874	41.7565	40.9256	40.0947	39.2638	38.4329	37.6020	36.7711	35.9402	35.1093	34.2784	.027697
77	44.9648	44.0762	43.1877	42.2991	41.4105	40.5220	39.6334	38.7448	37.8563	36.9677	36.0791	35.1906	.029619
78	46.6935	45.7432	44.7929	43.8426	42.8923	41.9420	40.9917	40.0414	39.0911	38.1408	37.1905	36.2402	.031677
79	48.6311	47.6147	46.5983	45.5819	44.5655	43.5491	42.5327	41.5163	40.4999	39.4835	38.4671	37.4507	.033880
80	50.8001	49.7129	48.6257	47.5385	46.4514	45.3642	44.2770	43.1898	42.1026	41.0154	39.9283	38.8411	.036239
81	53.2293	52.0636	50.8979	49.7322	48.5665	47.4008	46.2351	45.0694	43.9037	42.7380	41.5723	40.4066	.038857
82	55.9192	54.6617	53.4072	52.1527	50.8982	49.6437	48.3892	47.1348	45.8803	44.6258	43.3713	42.1168	.041816
83	58.8364	57.4837	56.1310	54.7783	53.4256	52.0729	50.7201	49.3674	48.0147	46.6620	45.3093	43.9566	.045090
84	62.0015	60.5367	59.0719	57.6071	56.1423	54.6775	53.2127	51.7480	50.2832	48.8184	47.3536	45.8888	.048826
85	65.3876	63.7886	62.1897	60.5907	58.9918	57.3928	55.7939	54.1950	52.5960	50.9970	49.3981	47.7991	.053298
86	68.9156	67.1568	65.3979	63.6391	61.8803	60.1214	58.3626	56.6038	54.8449	53.0861	51.3273	49.5684	.058628
87	72.4896	70.5420	68.5944	66.6468	64.6993	62.7517	60.8041	58.8565	56.9089	54.9613	53.0138	51.0662	.064919
88	76.0116	73.8116	71.6117	69.4117	67.2117	65.0118	62.8118	60.6118	58.4119	56.2119	54.0119	51.8120	.073332
89	78.9926	76.5101	74.0276	71.5450	69.0625	66.5800	64.0975	61.6150	59.1325	56.6500	54.1674	51.6849	.082750
90	81.3883	78.7806	76.1729	73.5652	70.9576	68.3499	65.7422	63.1345	60.5268	57.9191	55.3115	52.7038	.086923
91	85.6314	83.1810	80.7306	78.2802	75.8298	73.3794	70.9290	68.4786	66.0282	63.5778	61.1274	58.6770	.081680
92 or 17	**96.1538**	**96.4743**	**96.7948**	**97.1153**	**97.4359**	**97.7564**	**98.0769**	**98.3974**	**98.7179**	**99.0384**	**99.3590**	**99.6795**	**.010684**
16	94.9456	94.9480	94.9503	94.9526	94.9550	94.9573	94.9597	94.9620	94.9644	94.9667	94.9691	94.9714	.000078
15	94.3187	94.2753	94.2318	94.1884	94.1449	94.1015	94.0580	94.0146	93.9712	93.9277	93.8843	93.8408	.001448
14	93.8558	93.8010	93.7461	93.6913	93.6365	93.5816	93.5268	93.4720	93.4171	93.3623	93.3075	93.2526	.001828
13	93.2596	93.2180	93.1763	93.1347	93.0931	93.0514	93.0098	92.9682	92.9265	92.8849	92.8433	92.8016	.001388
12	92.5207	92.4930	92.4653	92.4376	92.4099	92.3822	92.3545	92.3268	92.2991	92.2714	92.2437	92.2160	.000923
11	91.7037	91.6845	91.6653	91.6461	91.6269	91.6077	91.5884	91.5692	91.5500	91.5308	91.5116	91.4924	.000640
10	90.8235	90.8115	90.7994	90.7874	90.7753	90.7633	90.7512	90.7392	90.7272	90.7151	90.7031	90.6910	.000401
Age.	0	1	2	3	4	5	6	7	8	9	10	11	Day.

Age.	0	1	2	3	4	5	6	7	8	9	10	11	Day.
10	4.8217	4.7809	4.7401	4.6993	4.6585	4.6177	4.5769	4.5361	4.4953	4.4545	4.4137	4.3729	.001360
11	5.0001	4.9594	4.9188	4.8781	4.8374	4.7968	4.7561	4.7154	4.6748	4.6341	4.5934	4.5528	.001355
12	5.1841	5.1435	5.1028	5.0622	5.0215	4.9809	4.9402	4.8996	4.8590	4.8183	4.7777	4.7370	.001355
13	5.3727	5.3321	5.2916	5.2510	5.2104	5.1698	5.1293	5.0887	5.0481	5.0075	4.9670	4.9264	.001352
14	5.5675	5.5270	5.4865	5.4460	5.4056	5.3651	5.3246	5.2841	5.2436	5.2032	5.1627	5.1222	.001349
15	5.7696	5.7291	5.6887	5.6482	5.6077	5.5673	5.5268	5.4863	5.4459	5.4054	5.3649	5.3245	.001348
16	5.9787	5.9383	5.8978	5.8574	5.8169	5.7765	5.7360	5.6956	5.6552	5.6147	5.5743	5.5338	.001348
17	6.1960	6.1556	6.1152	6.0748	6.0344	5.9940	5.9536	5.9132	5.8728	5.8324	5.7920	5.7516	.001347
18	6.4219	6.3815	6.3411	6.3007	6.2603	6.2199	6.1795	6.1390	6.0986	6.0582	6.0178	5.9774	.001347
19	6.6573	6.6169	6.5765	6.5361	6.4957	6.4553	6.4149	6.3745	6.3341	6.2937	6.2533	6.2129	.001346
20	6.9020	6.8616	6.8211	6.7807	6.7403	6.7098	6.6594	6.6190	6.5785	6.5381	6.4977	6.4572	.001348
21	7.1582	7.1177	7.0772	7.0367	6.9961	6.9556	6.9151	6.8746	6.8341	6.7936	6.7530	6.7125	.001350
22	7.4249	7.3843	7.3438	7.3032	7.2626	7.2220	7.1815	7.1409	7.1003	7.0597	7.0192	6.9786	.001352
23	7.7028	7.6622	7.6215	7.5709	7.5302	7.4996	7.4589	7.4183	7.3776	7.3370	7.2963	7.2557	.001355
24	7.9931	7.9524	7.9116	7.8709	7.8301	7.7894	7.7486	7.7079	7.6671	7.6264	7.5856	7.5449	.001358
25	8.2963	8.2554	8.2146	8.1737	8.1328	8.0920	8.0511	8.0102	7.9694	7.9275	7.8876	7.8468	.001362
26	8.6128	8.5719	8.5309	8.4900	8.4491	8.4081	8.3672	8.3263	8.2853	8.2444	8.2035	8.1625	.001364
27	8.9446	8.9036	8.8625	8.8215	8.7805	8.7394	8.6984	8.6574	8.6163	8.5753	8.5343	8.4932	.001368
28	9.2922	9.2510	9.2099	9.1688	9.1276	9.0865	9.0453	9.0042	8.9630	8.9219	8.8807	8.8396	.001372
29	9.6571	9.6160	9.5749	9.5338	9.4927	9.4516	9.4106	9.3695	9.3284	9.2873	9.2462	9.2051	.001369
30	10.0425	10.0013	9.9601	9.9189	9.8777	9.8365	9.7953	9.7541	9.7129	9.6717	9.6305	9.5893	.001373
31	10.4476	10.4064	10.3652	10.3240	10.2828	10.2416	10.2004	10.1592	10.1180	10.0768	10.0356	9.9944	.001373
32	10.8755	10.8344	10.7933	10.7521	10.7110	10.6699	10.6288	10.5876	10.5465	10.5054	10.4643	10.4231	.001371
33	11.3288	11.2877	11.2466	11.2056	11.1645	11.1234	11.0823	11.0412	11.0001	10.9590	10.9180	10.8769	.001369
34	11.8088	11.7677	11.7265	11.6854	11.6442	11.6031	11.5620	11.5208	11.4797	11.4385	11.3974	11.3562	.001371
35	12.3155	12.2739	12.2323	12.1906	12.1490	12.1074	12.0658	12.0241	11.9825	11.9409	11.8993	11.8576	.001387
36	12.8462	12.8036	12.7610	12.7183	12.6757	12.6331	12.5905	12.5478	12.5052	12.4626	12.4200	12.3773	.001421
37	13.3969	13.3529	13.3089	13.2648	13.2208	13.1768	13.1328	13.0887	13.0447	13.0007	12.9567	12.9126	.001467
38	13.9630	13.9169	13.8708	13.8247	13.7786	13.7325	13.6865	13.6404	13.5943	13.5482	13.5021	13.4560	.001536
39	14.5408	14.4924	14.4439	14.3955	14.3470	14.2986	14.2502	14.2017	14.1533	14.1048	14.0564	14.0079	.001614
40	15.1281	15.0769	15.0257	14.9745	14.9233	14.8721	14.8210	14.7698	14.7186	14.6674	14.6162	14.5650	.001708
41	15.7223	15.6682	15.6140	15.5599	15.5058	15.4516	15.3975	15.3434	15.2892	15.2351	15.1810	15.1268	.001804
42	16.3244	16.2668	16.2092	16.1516	16.0939	16.0363	15.9787	15.9211	15.8635	15.8059	15.7482	15.6906	.001920
43	16.9324	16.8708	16.8093	16.7477	16.6861	16.6245	16.5630	16.5014	16.4398	16.3782	16.3167	16.2551	.002052
44	17.5483	17.4823	17.4163	17.3503	17.2842	17.2182	17.1522	17.0862	17.0202	16.9542	16.8881	16.8221	.002200
45	18.1755	18.1046	18.0336	17.9627	17.8917	17.8208	17.7498	17.6789	17.6080	17.5370	17.4661	17.3951	.002364
46	18.8161	18.7407	18.6654	18.5900	18.5146	18.4392	18.3639	18.2885	18.2131	18.1377	18.0624	17.9870	.002512
47	19.4758	19.3936	19.3114	19.2292	19.1471	19.0649	18.9827	18.9005	18.8183	18.7361	18.6540	18.5718	.002739
48	20.1548	20.0661	19.9773	19.8886	19.7998	19.7111	19.6224	19.5336	19.4449	19.3561	19.2674	19.1786	.002958
49	20.8531	20.7575	20.6619	20.5662	20.4706	20.3750	20.2794	20.1837	20.0881	19.9925	19.8969	19.8012	.003254
50	21.5728	21.4695	21.3663	21.2630	21.1598	21.0565	20.9533	20.8500	20.7467	20.6435	20.5402	20.4370	.003442
51	22.3152	22.2036	22.0920	21.9803	21.8687	21.7571	21.6455	21.5338	21.4222	21.3106	21.1990	21.0873	.003721
52	23.0808	22.9596	22.8385	22.7173	22.5961	22.4749	22.3538	22.2326	22.1114	21.9902	21.8690	21.7479	.004039
53	23.8659	23.7343	23.6026	23.4710	23.3394	23.2077	23.0761	22.9445	22.8128	22.6812	22.5496	22.4179	.004387
54	24.6701	24.5269	24.3836	24.2404	24.0971	23.9539	23.8106	23.6674	23.5241	23.3809	23.2376	23.0944	.004775
55	25.4898	25.3339	25.1780	25.0221	24.8662	24.7103	24.5545	24.3986	24.2427	24.0868	23.9309	23.7750	.005196
56	26.3253	26.1555	25.9856	25.8158	25.6459	25.4761	25.3063	25.1364	24.9666	24.7967	24.6269	24.4570	.005661
57	27.1746	26.9896	26.8047	26.6197	26.4347	26.2497	26.0648	25.8798	25.6948	25.5098	25.3249	25.1399	.006165
58	28.0351	27.8333	27.6315	27.4296	27.2278	27.0260	26.8242	26.6223	26.4205	26.2187	26.0169	25.8150	.006727
59	28.9021	28.6827	28.4622	28.2422	28.0223	27.8023	27.5824	27.3624	27.1424	26.9225	26.7025	26.4826	.007332
60	29.7768	29.5372	29.2976	29.0580	28.8184	28.5788	28.3392	28.0995	27.8599	27.6203	27.3807	27.1411	.007986
61	30.6633	30.4027	30.1420	29.8814	29.6207	29.3601	29.0994	28.8388	28.5782	28.3175	28.0569	27.7962	.008688
62	31.5641	31.2806	30.9971	30.7136	30.4301	30.1466	29.8630	29.5795	29.2960	29.0125	28.7290	28.4455	.009450
63	32.4802	32.1721	31.8640	31.5559	31.2479	30.9398	30.6317	30.3236	30.0155	29.7074	29.3993	29.0913	.010269
64	33.4134	33.0788	32.7443	32.4097	32.0757	31.7411	31.4066	31.0720	30.7374	30.4028	30.0677	29.7330	.011155
65	34.3666	34.0035	33.6405	33.2774	32.9144	32.5513	32.1882	31.8252	31.4621	31.0991	30.7360	30.3730	.012102
66	35.3415	34.9478	34.5541	34.1604	33.7666	33.3729	32.9792	32.5855	32.1918	31.7981	31.4043	31.0106	.013123
67	36.3432	35.9167	35.4901	35.0636	34.6371	34.4105	33.7840	33.3575	32.9309	32.5044	32.0779	31.6513	.014217
68	37.3738	36.9123	36.4508	35.9893	35.5278	35.0663	34.6048	34.1432	33.6817	33.2202	32.7587	32.2972	.015383
69	38.4391	37.9397	37.4404	36.9410	36.4417	35.9428	35.4430	34.9436	34.4442	33.9449	33.4455	32.9462	.016645
70	39.5361	38.9959	38.4558	37.9156	37.3754	36.8352	36.2951	35.7549	35.2147	34.6745	34.1344	33.5942	.018005
71	40.6671	40.0837	39.5002	38.9168	38.3333	37.7499	37.1664	36.5830	35.9996	35.4161	34.8327	34.2492	.019448
72	41.8412	41.2118	40.5824	39.9530	39.3236	38.6942	38.0648	37.4354	36.8060	36.1766	35.5472	34.9178	.020980
73	43.0674	42.3899	41.7123	41.0348	40.3573	39.6798	39.0022	38.3247	37.6472	36.9697	36.2921	35.6146	.022584
74	44.3661	43.6387	42.9112	42.1838	41.4564	40.7289	40.0015	39.2741	38.5466	37.8192	37.0918	36.3643	.024248
75	45.7666	44.9870	44.2073	43.4277	42.6481	41.8685	41.0888	40.3092	39.5296	38.7500	37.9703	37.1907	.025987
76	47.2965	46.4630	45.6295	44.7960	43.9625	43.1290	42.2955	41.4621	40.6286	39.7951	38.9616	38.1281	.027783
77	48.9955	48.1043	47.2131	46.3219	45.4307	44.5395	43.6483	42.7572	41.8660	40.9748	40.0836	39.1924	.029706
78	50.8879	49.9350	48.9821	48.0293	47.0764	46.1235	45.1706	44.2178	43.2649	42.3120	41.3591	40.4063	.031762
79	53.0022	51.9834	50.9646	49.9457	48.9269	47.9081	46.8893	45.8705	44.8517	43.8328	42.8140	41.7952	.033960
80	55.3638	54.2720	53.1801	52.0883	50.9965	49.9046	48.8128	47.7210	46.6291	45.5373	44.4455	43.3536	.036394
81	57.9731	56.7991	55.6251	54.4511	53.2772	52.1032	50.9292	49.7552	48.5812	47.4072	46.2333	45.0593	.039133
82	60.8110	59.5468	58.2826	57.0184	55.7542	54.4900	53.2258	51.9616	50.6974	49.4332	48.1690	46.9048	.042140
83	63.8819	62.5154	61.1490	59.7825	58.4160	57.0496	55.6831	54.3166	52.9502	51.5837	50.2172	48.8508	.045549
84	67.1663	65.6783	64.1903	62.7023	61.2143	59.7263	58.2382	56.7502	55.2622	53.7742	52.2862	50.7982	.049600
85	70.5736	68.9413	67.3091	65.6768	64.0446	62.4123	60.7801	59.1478	57.5156	55.8833	54.2511	52.6188	.054418
86	74.0121	72.2104	70.4088	68.6071	66.8055	65.0038	63.2022	61.4005	59.5989	57.7972	55.9956	54.1940	.060055
87	77.3874	75.3596	73.3318	71.3040	69.2763	67.2485	65.2207	63.1929	61.1651	59.1373	57.1096	55.0818	.067593
88	80.2355	77.9560	75.6764	73.3969	71.1174	68.8379	66.5583	64.2788	61.9993	59.7198	57.4402	55.1607	.075984
89	82.5170	80.1328	77.7486	75.3644	72.9802	70.5960	68.2117	65.8275	63.4433	61.0591	58.6749	56.2907	.079473
90	86.4865	84.2596	82.0327	79.8057	77.5788	75.3519	73.1250	70.8981	68.6712	66.4442	64.2173	61.9904	.074230
91 or 18	**96.1538**	**96.4743**	**96.7948**	**97.1153**	**97.4359**	**97.7564**	**98.0769**	**98.3974**	**98.7179**	**99.0384**	**99.3590**	**99.6795**	**.010684**
17	94.9398	94.9404	94.9411	94.9417	94.9424	94.9430	94.9437	94.9444	94.9450	94.9457	94.9463	94.9470	.000022
16	94.3093	94.2640	94.2187	94.1734	94.1281	94.0828	94.0374	93.9921	93.9468	93.9015	93.8562	93.8109	.001510
15	93.8445	93.7878	93.7311	93.6744	93.6178	93.5611	93.5044	93.4477	93.3910	93.3343	93.2777	93.2210	.001889
14	93.2460	93.2026	93.1593	93.1160	93.0726	93.0292	92.9859	92.9425	92.8992	92.8558	92.8125	92.7691	.001445
13	92.5043	92.4750	92.4457	92.4165	92.3872	92.3579	92.3286	92.2994	92.2701	92.2408	92.2115	92.1823	.000976
12	91.6843	91.6637	91.6430	91.6223	91.6017	91.5810	91.5603	91 5397	91.5190	91.4983	91.4777	91.4571	.000689
11	90.8015	90.7881	90.7747	90.7612	90.7478	90.7344	90.7210	90.7076	90.6942	90.6807	90.6673	90.6539	.000444
10	89.8738	89.8660	89.8583	89.8505	89.8427	89.8350	89.8272	89.8194	89.8117	89.8039	89.7961	89.7884	.000259
Age.	0	1	2	3	4	5	6	7	8	9	10	11	Day.

Age.	0	1	2	3	4	5	6	7	8	9	10	11	Day.
10	5.3751	5.3359	5.2968	5.2576	5.2184	5.1792	5.1401	5.1009	5.0617	5.0225	4.9834	4.9442	.001306
11	5.5753	5.5362	5.4971	5.4580	5.4189	5.3798	5.3407	5.3016	5.2626	5.2235	5.1844	5.1453	.001303
12	5.7807	5.7418	5.7028	5.6639	5.6250	5.5860	5.5471	5.5082	5.4692	5.4303	5.3914	5.3524	.001298
13	5.9924	5.9536	5.9148	5.8760	5.8373	5.7985	5.7597	5.7209	5.6821	5.6433	5.6046	5.5658	.001292
14	6.2117	6.1730	6.1343	6.0956	6.0569	6.0182	5.9794	5.9407	5.9020	5.8633	5.8246	5.7859	.001290
15	6.4384	6.3998	6.3612	6.3226	6.2840	6.2454	6.2068	6.1682	6.1296	6.0910	6.0524	6.0138	.001287
16	6.6734	6.6349	6.5964	6.5579	6.5195	6.4810	6.4425	6.4040	6.3655	6.3270	6.2886	6.2501	.001282
17	6.9181	6.8797	6.8413	6.8028	6.7644	6.7260	6.6876	6.6492	6.6108	6.5723	6.5339	6.4955	.001280
18	7.1719	7.1336	7.0953	7.0569	7.0186	6.9803	6.9420	6.9036	6.8653	6.8270	6.7887	6.7503	.001278
19	7.4368	7.3985	7.3602	7.3219	7.2836	7.2453	7.2070	7.1687	7.1304	7.0921	7.0538	7.0155	.001276
20	7.7116	7.6734	7.6351	7.5969	7.5586	7.5204	7.4821	7.4439	7.4057	7.3674	7.3292	7.2909	.001274
21	7.9993	7.9611	7.9229	7.8846	7.8464	7.8082	7.7700	7.7318	7.6936	7.6553	7.6171	7.5789	.001273
22	8.2992	8.2608	8.2226	8.1844	8.1462	8.1080	8.0697	8.0315	7.9933	7.9551	7.9169	7.8787	.001273
23	8.6114	8.5732	8.5349	8.4967	8.4585	8.4202	8.3820	8.3438	8.3055	8.2673	8.2291	8.1908	.001274
24	8.9374	8.8991	8.8609	8.8226	8.7843	8.7461	8.7078	8.6695	8.6313	8.5930	8.5547	8.5165	.001275
25	9.2780	9.2398	9.2017	9.1635	9.1253	9.0871	9.0490	9.0108	8.9726	8.9344	8.8963	8.8581	.001273
26	9.6345	9.5963	9.5582	9.5200	9.4818	9.4436	9.4055	9.3673	9.3291	9.2909	9.2528	9.2146	.001273
27	10.0079	9.9697	9.9316	9.8934	9.8552	9.8171	9.7789	9.7407	9.7026	9.6644	9.6262	9.5881	.001272
28	10.3990	10.3610	10.3230	10.2850	10.2470	10.2090	10.1710	10.1331	10.0951	10.0571	10.0191	9.9811	.001266
29	10.8116	10.7736	10.7357	10.6977	10.6597	10.6218	10.5838	10.5458	10.5079	10.4699	10.4319	10.3940	.001265
30	11.2453	11.2075	11.1696	11.1318	11.0940	11.0561	11.0183	10.9805	10.9426	10.9048	10.8670	10.8291	.001261
31	11.7024	11.6648	11.6272	11.5895	11.5519	11.5143	11.4767	11.4391	11.4015	11.3638	11.3262	11.2886	.001253
32	12.1860	12.1486	12.1111	12.0737	12.0363	11.9988	11.9614	11.9240	11.8865	11.8491	11.8117	11.7742	.001247
33	12.6975	12.6602	12.6228	12.5855	12.5482	12.5108	12.4735	12.4362	12.3988	12.3615	12.3242	12.2868	.001244
34	13.2375	13.1999	13.1622	13.1246	13.0870	13.0493	13.0117	12.9741	12.9364	12.8988	12.8612	12.8235	.001254
35	13.8026	13.7642	13.7257	13.6873	13.6488	13.6104	13.5719	13.5335	13.4950	13.4566	13.4181	13.3797	.001281
36	14.3891	14.3495	14.3098	14.2702	14.2305	14.1909	14.1512	14.1116	14.0719	14.0323	13.9926	13.9530	.001322
37	14.9946	14.9531	14.9116	14.8701	14.8286	14.7871	14.7456	14.7042	14.6627	14.6212	14.5797	14.5382	.001383
38	15.6117	15.5681	15.5245	15.4809	15.4373	15.3947	15.3501	15.3066	15.2630	15.2194	15.1758	15.1322	.001453
39	16.2418	16.1957	16.1496	16.1035	16.0574	16.0113	15.9652	15.9192	15.8731	15.8270	15.7809	15.7448	.001536
40	16.8815	16.8328	16.7840	16.7353	16.6866	16.6378	16.5891	16.5404	16.4916	16.4429	16.3942	16.3454	.001624
41	17.5313	17.4794	17.4275	17.3756	17.3237	17.2718	17.2199	17.1680	17.1161	17.0642	17.0123	16.9604	.001730
42	18.1884	18.1329	18.0774	18.0218	17.9663	17.9108	17.8553	17.7998	17.7443	17.6887	17.6332	17.5777	.001850
43	18.8520	18.7924	18.7328	18.6731	18.6135	18.5539	18.4943	18.4347	18.3751	18.3154	18.2558	18.1962	.001987
44	19.5243	19.4601	19.3959	19.3317	19.2676	19.2034	19.1392	19.0750	19.0108	18.9466	18.8825	18.8183	.002139
45	20.2087	20.1396	20.0704	20.0013	19.9321	19.8629	19.7938	19.7247	19.6555	19.5864	19.5172	19.4480	.002305
46	20.9196	20.8440	20.7684	20.6929	20.6173	20.5417	20.4661	20.3905	20.3149	20.2393	20.1638	20.0882	.002519
47	21.6281	21.5473	21.4665	21.3857	21.3049	21.2241	21.1433	21.0625	20.9817	20.9009	20.8201	20.7393	.002693
48	22.3666	22.2793	22.1921	22.1048	22.0175	21.9303	21.8430	21.7557	21.6685	21.5812	21.4939	21.4067	.002909
49	23.1283	23.0339	22.9395	22.8450	22.7506	22.6562	22.5618	22.4674	22.3730	22.2785	22.1841	22.0897	.003147
50	23.9113	23.8090	23.7067	23.6044	23.5022	23.3999	23.2976	23.1953	23.0930	22.9907	22.8885	22.7862	.003409
51	24.7173	24.6060	24.4947	24.3834	24.2721	24.1608	24.0494	23.9381	23.8268	23.7155	23.6042	23.4929	.003710
52	25.5418	25.4207	25.2995	25.1784	25.0573	24.9361	24.8150	24.6939	24.5727	24.4516	24.3305	24.2093	.004037
53	26.3859	26.2538	26.1217	25.9895	25.8574	25.7253	25.5932	25.4610	25.3289	25.1968	25.0647	24.9325	.004404
54	27.2461	27.1020	26.9580	26.8140	26.6699	26.5259	26.3818	26.2378	26.0937	25.9497	25.8056	25.6616	.004801
55	28.1216	27.9644	27.8072	27.6499	27.4927	27 3355	27.1783	27.0210	26.8638	26.7066	26.5494	26.3921	.005240
56	29.0102	28.0387	28.6671	28.4956	28.3240	28.1525	27.9810	27.8094	27.6379	27.4663	27.2948	27.1232	.005718
57	29.9120	29.7246	29.5372	29.3497	29.1623	28.9749	28.7875	28.6000	28.4126	28.2252	28.0378	27.8503	.006247
58	30.8199	30.6154	30.4108	30.2063	30.0017	29.7972	29.5926	29.3881	29.1835	28.9790	28.7744	28.5699	.006818
59	31.7350	31.5119	31.2888	31.0657	30.8426	30.6195	30.3964	30.1734	29.9503	29.7272	29.5041	29.2810	.007436
60	32.6571	32.4142	32.1712	31.9283	31.6853	31.4424	31.1994	30.9565	30.7136	30.4706	30.2277	29.9847	.008093
61	33.5928	33.3283	33.0637	32.7992	32.5346	32.2701	32.0055	31.7410	31.4764	31.2119	30.9473	30.6828	.008818
62	34.5402	34.2524	33.9647	33.6769	33.3892	33.1014	32.8136	32.5259	32.2381	31.9504	31.6626	31.3749	.009592
63	35.5031	35.1904	34.8776	34.5649	34.2521	33.9394	33.6266	33.3139	33.0011	32.6884	32.3756	32.0629	.010425
64	36.4826	36.1430	35.8033	35.4637	35.1240	34.7844	34.4447	34.1051	33.7654	33.4258	33.0861	32.7465	.011321
65	37.4817	37.1131	36.7445	36.3759	36.0074	35.6388	35.2702	34.9016	34.5330	34.1644	33.7959	33.4273	.012286
66	38.5015	38.1019	37.7024	37.3028	36.9032	36.5036	36.1041	35.7045	35.3049	34.9053	34.5058	34.1062	.013319
67	39.5486	39.1160	38.6834	38.2508	37.8183	37.3857	36.9531	36.5205	36.0879	35.6553	35.2228	34.7902	.014419
68	40.6270	40.1587	39.6905	39.2222	38.7539	38.2856	37.8174	37.3491	36.8808	36.4125	35.9443	35.4760	.015609
69	41.7360	41.2293	40.7226	40.2158	39 7091	39.2024	38.6957	38.1889	37.6822	37.1755	36.6688	36.1620	.016890
70	42.8743	42.3268	41.7794	41.2319	40.6844	40.1370	39.5895	39.0420	38.4946	37.9471	37.3996	36.8522	.018248
71	44.0523	43.4616	42.8709	42.2802	41.6895	41.0988	40.5081	39.9174	39.3268	38.7361	38.1454	37.5547	.019689
72	45.2790	44.6430	44.0071	43.3711	42.7352	42.0992	41.4633	40.8273	40.1914	39.5554	38.9195	38.2835	.021198
73	46.5726	45.8898	45.2071	44.5243	43.8415	43.1588	42.4760	41.7932	41.1105	40.4277	39.7449	39.0622	.022759
74	47.9617	47.2300	46.4982	45.7665	45.0348	44.3031	43.5713	42.8396	42.1079	41.3762	40.6444	39.9127	.024391
75	49.4722	48.6901	47.9080	47.1259	46.3438	45.5617	44.7795	43.9974	43.2153	42.4332	41.6511	40.8690	.026070
76	51.1437	50.3077	49.4717	48.6357	47.7997	46.9637	46.1276	45.2916	44.4556	43.6196	42.7836	41.9476	.027867
77	53.9947	52.1010	51.2074	50.3137	49.4201	48.5264	47.6328	46.7391	45.8455	44.9518	44.0582	43.1645	.029788
78	55.0513	54.0961	53.1409	52.1858	51.2306	50.2754	49.3202	48.3651	47.4099	46.4547	45.4995	44.5444	.031839
79	57.3443	56.3211	55.2978	54.2746	53.2513	52.2281	51.2048	50.1816	49.1584	48.1351	47.1119	46.0886	.034108
80	59.8717	58.7720	57.6723	56.5726	55.4729	54.3732	53.2735	52.1738	51.0741	49.9744	48.8747	47.7750	.036657
81	62.6175	61.4343	60.2512	59.0680	57.8848	56.7017	55.5185	54.3353	53.1522	51.9690	50.7858	49.6027	.039439
82	65.5883	64.3112	63.0340	61.7569	60.4798	59.2027	57.9255	56.6484	55.3713	54.0942	52.8170	51.5399	.042571
83	68.7623	67.3739	65.9855	64.5971	63.2087	61.8203	60.4318	59.0434	57.6550	56.2666	54.8782	53.4898	.046280
84	72.0524	70.5330	69.0136	67.4942	65.9749	64.4555	62.9361	61.4167	59.8973	58.3780	56.8586	55.3392	.050646
85	75.3599	73.6874	72.0150	70.3425	68.6700	66.9976	65.3251	63.6526	61.9802	60.3077	58.6352	56.9628	.055745
86	78.5948	76.7181	74.8414	72.9647	71.0880	69.2113	67.3346	65.4580	63.5813	61.7046	59.8279	57.9512	.062556
87	81.3228	79.2209	77.1190	75.0170	72.9151	70.8132	68.7113	66.6094	64.5075	62.4055	60.3036	58.2017	.070064
88	83.5046	81.3163	79.1280	76.9396	74.7513	72.5630	70.3746	68.1863	65.9980	63.8097	61.6213	59.4330	.072944
89	87.2212	85.1894	83.1575	81.1257	79.0939	77.0620	75.0302	72.9984	70.9665	68.9347	66.9029	64.8710	.067728
90 or 19	**96.1538**	**96.4743**	**96.7948**	**97.1153**	**97.4359**	**97.7564**	**98.0769**	**98.3974**	**98.7179**	**99.0384**	**99.3590**	**99.6795**	**.010684**
18	94.9324	94.9313	94.9301	94.9290	94.9279	94.9268	94.9256	94.9245	94.9234	94.9223	94.9211	94.9200	.000037
17	94.2995	94.2522	94.2050	94.1577	94.1104	94.0632	94.0159	93.9686	93.9214	93.8741	93.8268	93.7796	.001575
16	93.8326	93.7740	93.7154	93.6568	93.5982	93.5396	93.4810	93.4223	93.3637	93.3051	93.2465	93.1879	.001953
15	93.2317	93.1866	93.1414	93.0963	93.0512	93.0060	92.9609	92.9158	92.8706	92.8255	92.7804	92.7352	.001504
14	92.4871	92.4562	92.4252	92.3943	92.3634	92.3325	92.3015	92.2706	92.2397	92.2088	92.1778	92.1469	.001031
13	91.6643	91.6421	91.6199	91.5976	91.5754	91.5532	91.5310	91.5088	91.4866	91.4643	91.4421	91.4199	.000774
12	90.7783	90.7634	90.7486	90.7337	90.7189	90.7040	90.6892	90.6743	90.6595	90.6446	90.6298	90.6150	.000495
11	89.8479	89.8388	89.8296	89.8205	89.8114	89.8023	89.7931	89.7840	89.7749	89.7658	89.7566	89.7475	.000304
10	88.8919	88.8868	88.8817	88.8766	88.8716	88.8665	88.8614	88.8563	88.8512	88.8461	88.8411	88.8360	.000169
Age.	0	1	2	3	4	5	6	7	8	9	10	11	Day.

Age.	0	1	2	3	4	5	6	7	8	9	10	11	Day.
10	5.9479	5.9103	5.8727	5.8351	5.7975	5.7599	5.7223	5.6847	5.6471	5.6095	5.5719	5.5343	.001253
11	6.1694	6.1320	6.0946	6.0572	6.0198	5.9824	5.9450	5.9077	5.8703	5.8329	5.7955	5.7581	.001246
12	6.3978	6.3606	6.3235	6.2863	6.2491	6.2120	6.1748	6.1376	6.1005	6.0633	6.0261	5.9890	.001239
13	6.6336	6.5966	6.5596	6.5225	6.4855	6.4485	6.4115	6.3745	6.3375	6.3004	6.2634	6.2264	.001234
14	6.8772	6.8403	6.8035	6.7666	6.7298	6.6930	6.6561	6.6192	6.5824	6.5455	6.5087	6.4718	.001228
15	7.1295	7.0928	7.0562	7.0195	6.9829	6.9462	6.9096	6.8730	6.8363	6.7996	6.7630	6.7263	.001222
16	7.3916	7.3551	7.3186	7.2821	7.2456	7.2091	7.1725	7.1360	7.0995	7.0630	7.0265	6.9900	.001217
17	7.6639	7.6276	7.5912	7.5549	7.5185	7.4822	7.4458	7.4095	7.3732	7.3368	7.3005	7.2641	.001211
18	7.9469	7.9107	7.8744	7.8382	7.8020	7.7657	7.7295	7.6933	7.6570	7.6208	7.5846	7.5483	.001208
19	8.2415	8.2054	8.1693	8.1331	8.0970	8.0609	8.0248	7.9887	7.9526	7.9164	7.8803	7.8442	.001204
20	8.5475	8.5115	8.4756	8.4396	8.4036	8.3677	8.3317	8.2957	8.2598	8.2238	8.1878	8.1519	.001199
21	8.8678	8.8319	8.7960	8.7601	8.7243	8.6884	8.6525	8.6166	8.5807	8.5448	8.5090	8.4731	.001196
22	9.2016	9.1658	9.1300	9.0941	9.0583	9.0225	8.9867	8.9509	8.9151	8.8792	8.8434	8.8076	.001194
23	9.5489	9.5132	9.4775	9.4417	9.4060	9.3703	9.3346	9.2989	9.2632	9.2274	9.1917	9.1560	.001190
24	9.9115	9.8760	9.8404	9.8049	9.7694	9.7339	9.6983	9.6628	9.6273	9.5918	9.5562	9.5207	.001184
25	10.2920	10.2565	10.2211	10.1856	10.1502	10.1147	10.0793	10.0438	10.0084	9.9730	9.9375	9.9020	.001182
26	10.6893	10.6539	10.6186	10.5833	10.5479	10.5126	10.4773	10.4419	10.4066	10.3713	10.3359	10.3006	.001177
27	11.1055	11.0705	11.0354	11.0004	10.9654	10.9303	10.8953	10.8603	10.8252	10.7902	10.7552	10.7201	.001168
28	11.5436	11.5087	11.4738	11.4389	11.4040	11.3691	11.3342	11.2994	11.2645	11.2296	11.1947	11.1598	.001163
29	12.0037	11.9691	11.9344	11.8998	11.8652	11 8305	11.7959	11.7613	11.7266	11.6920	11.6574	11.6227	.001154
30	12.4885	12.4542	12.4199	12.3856	12.3513	12.3170	12.2827	12.2485	12.2142	12.1799	12.1456	12.1113	.001143
31	13.0002	12.9662	12.9323	12.8983	12.8644	12.8304	12.7964	12.7625	12.7285	12.6946	12.6606	12.6267	.001132
32	13.5408	13.5071	13.4734	13.4396	13.4059	13.3722	13.3385	13.3048	13.2711	13.2373	13.2036	13.1699	.001124
33	14.1111	14.0772	14.0434	14.0095	13.9757	13.9418	13.9080	13.8741	13.8402	13.8064	13.7725	13.7387	.001128
34	14.7084	14.6739	14.6394	14.6049	14.5704	14.5359	14.5013	14.4668	14.4323	14.3978	14.3633	14.3288	.001150
35	15.3278	15.2923	15.2568	15.2212	15.1857	15.1502	15.1147	15.0792	15.0437	15.0081	14.9726	14.9371	.001184
36	15.9677	15.9305	15.8934	15.8562	15.8191	15.7819	15.7447	15.7076	15.6704	15.6333	15.5961	15.5590	.001238
37	16.6227	16.5837	16.5446	16.5056	16.4666	16.4275	16.3885	16.3495	16.3104	16.2714	16.2324	16.1933	.001301
38	17.2904	17.2491	17.2078	17.1666	17.1253	17.0840	17.0427	17.0015	16.9602	16.9189	16.8776	16.8364	.001376
39	17.9710	17.9273	17.8837	17.8400	17.7964	17.7527	17.7091	17.6654	17.6218	17.5781	17.5345	17.4908	.001455
40	18.6644	18.6179	18.5713	18.5248	18.4783	18.4317	18.3852	18.3387	18.2921	18.2456	18.1991	18.1525	.001551
41	19.3671	19.3173	19.2674	19.2176	19.1678	19.1179	19.0681	19.0183	18.9684	18.9186	18.8688	18.8189	.001661
42	20.0776	20.0240	19.9704	19.9168	19.8632	19.8096	19.7560	19.7025	19.6489	19.5953	19.5417	19.4881	.001786
43	20.7951	20.7373	20.6795	20.6217	20.5639	20.5061	20.4483	20.3905	20.3327	20.2749	20.2171	20.1593	.001927
44	21.5223	21.4599	21.3974	21.3350	21.2726	21.2101	21.1477	21.0853	21.0228	20.9604	20.8980	20.8355	.002081
45	22.2634	22.1959	22.1283	22.0608	21.9933	21.9257	21.8582	21.7907	21.7231	21.6556	21.5881	21.5205	.002251
46	23.0206	22.9473	22.8740	22.8007	22.7274	22.6541	22.5808	22.5075	22.4342	22.3609	22.2876	22.2143	.002443
47	23.7970	23.7176	23.6383	23.5589	23.4796	23.4002	23.3208	23.2415	23.1621	23.0828	23.0034	22.9241	.002645
48	24.5961	24.5100	24.4239	24.3378	24.2517	24.1656	24.0795	23.9935	23.9074	23.8213	23.7352	23.6491	.002870
49	25.4180	25.3245	25.2311	25.1376	25.0441	24.9507	24.8572	24.7637	24.6703	24.5768	24.4833	24.3899	.003115
50	26.2614	26.1594	26.0575	25.9555	25.8535	25.7516	25.6496	25.5476	25.4457	25.3437	25.2417	25.1398	.003399
51	27.1231	27.0118	26.9006	26.7893	26.6781	26.5668	26.4555	26.3443	26.2330	26.1218	26.0105	25.8993	.003708
52	28.0033	27.8817	27.7601	27.6385	27.5169	27.3953	27.2736	27.1520	27.0304	26.9088	26.7872	26.6656	.004053
53	28.9000	28.7671	28.6342	28.5013	28.3684	28.2355	28.1025	27.9696	27.8367	27.7038	27.5709	27.4380	.004430
54	29.8125	29.6671	29.5218	29.3764	29.2311	29.0857	28.9403	28.7950	28.6496	28.5043	28.3589	28.2136	.004845
55	30.7374	30.5785	30.4196	30.2608	30.1019	29.9430	29.7841	29.6253	29.4664	29.3075	29.1486	28.9898	.005296
56	31.6748	31.5009	31.3270	31.1530	30.9791	30.8052	30.6312	30.4573	30.2834	30.1095	29.9355	29.7616	.005797
57	32.6200	32.4299	32.2399	32.0498	31.8597	31.6697	31.4796	31.2895	31.0995	30.9094	30.7193	30.5293	.006335
58	33.5720	33.3644	33.1568	32.9492	32.7416	32.5340	32.3264	32.1189	31.9113	31.7037	31.4961	31.2885	.006920
59	34.5303	34.3040	34.0776	33.8513	33.6256	33.3987	33.1723	32.9460	32.7197	32.4934	32.2670	32.0407	.007544
60	35.4974	35.2507	35.0040	34.7572	34.5105	34.2638	34.0170	33.7703	33.5236	33.2769	33.0301	32.7834	.008224
61	36.4754	36.2067	35.9381	35.6694	35.4008	35.1321	34.8634	34.5948	34.3261	34.0575	33.7888	33.5202	.008955
62	37.4653	37.1730	36.8807	36.5885	36.2962	36.0039	35.7116	35.4194	35.1271	34.8348	34.5425	34.2503	.009742
63	38.4700	38.1523	37.8347	37.5170	37.1994	36.8817	36.5641	36.2464	35.9288	35.6111	35.2935	34.9758	.010588
64	39.4909	39.1459	38.8010	38.4560	38.1110	37.7660	37.4210	37.0761	36.7311	36.3861	36.0411	35.6962	.011499
65	40.5305	40.1563	39.7820	39.4078	39.0335	38.6593	38.2850	37.9108	37.5366	37.1623	36.7881	36.4138	.012475
66	41.5912	41.1858	40.7804	40.3750	39.9696	39.5642	39.1587	38.7533	38.3479	37.9425	37.5371	37.1317	.013513
67	42.6813	42.2422	41.8031	41.3640	40.9249	40.4858	40.0467	39.6077	39.1686	38.7295	38.2904	37.8513	.014636
68	43.7990	43.3236	42.8482	42.3729	41.8975	41.4221	40.9467	40.4714	39.9960	39.5206	39.0452	38.5699	.015846
69	44.9445	44.4308	43.9170	43.4033	42.8896	42.3758	41.8621	41.3484	40.8346	40.3209	39.8072	39.2934	.017124
70	46.1249	45.5705	45.0160	44.4616	43.9071	43.3527	42.7982	42.2438	41.6894	41.1349	40.5805	40.0260	.018482
71	47.3505	46.7535	46.1565	45.5595	44.9625	44.3655	43.7685	43.1715	42.5745	41.9775	41.3805	40.7835	.019900
72	48.6372	47.9963	47.3554	46.7145	46.0737	45.4328	44.7919	44.1510	43.5101	42.8692	42.2284	41.5875	.021363
73	50.0150	49.3281	48.6413	47.9544	47.2675	46.5807	45.8938	45.2069	44.5201	43.8332	43.1463	42.4595	.022895
74	51.5057	50.7716	50.0375	49.3034	48.5694	47.8353	47.1012	46.3671	45.6330	44.8990	44.1649	43.4308	.024469
75	53.1480	52.3635	51.5790	50.7945	50.0100	49.2255	48.4410	47.6564	46.8719	46.0874	45.3029	44.5184	.026150
76	54.9607	54.1223	53.2840	52.4456	51.6073	50.7690	49.9306	49.0922	48.2539	47.4155	46.5772	45.7388	.027945
77	56.9645	56.0686	55.1728	54.2770	53.3811	52.4852	51.5894	50.6935	49.7977	48.9018	48.0060	47.1101	.029862
78	59.1872	58.2278	57.2684	56.3090	55.3496	54.3902	53.4308	52.4715	51.5121	50.5527	49.5933	48.6339	.031980
79	61.6333	60.6026	59.5718	58.5411	57.5104	56.4797	55.4490	54.4182	53.3875	52.3568	51.3260	50.2953	.034357
80	64.2852	63.1768	62.0683	60.9599	59.8515	58.7431	57.6346	56.5262	55.4178	54.3094	53.2010	52.0925	.036947
81	67.1516	65.9561	64.7606	63.5650	62.3695	61.1740	59.9785	58.7830	57.5875	56.3920	55.1964	54.0009	.039850
82	70.2115	68.9135	67.6155	66.3175	65.0195	63.7215	62.4235	61.1256	59.8276	58.5296	57.2316	55.9336	.043266
83	73.3793	71.9612	70.5432	69.1251	67.7071	66.2890	64.8710	63.4530	62.0349	60.6168	59.1988	57.7807	.047268
84	76.5620	75.0047	73.4475	71.8902	70.3329	68.7757	67.2184	65.6611	64.1039	62.5466	60.9893	59.4321	.051908
85	79.6636	77.9207	76.1777	74.4348	72.6918	70.9489	69.2060	67.4630	65.7201	63.9771	62.2342	60.4912	.058098
86	82.2770	80.3309	78.3849	76.4388	74.4928	72.5467	70.6006	68.6546	66.7085	64.7625	62.8164	60.8704	.064868
87	84.3686	82.3516	80.3347	78.3177	76.3008	74.2838	72.2669	70.2500	68.2330	66.2160	64.1991	62.1821	.067232
88	87.8681	86.0066	84.1451	82.2837	80.4222	78.5607	76.6992	74.8378	72.9763	71.1148	69.2533	67.3919	.062049
89 or 20	**96.1538**	**96.4743**	**96.7948**	**97.1153**	**97.4359**	**97.7564**	**98.0769**	**98.3974**	**98.7179**	**99.0384**	**99.3590**	**99.6795**	**.010684**
19	94.9953	94.9865	94.9777	94.9688	94.9600	94.9512	94.9424	94.9336	94.9248	94.9160	94.9071	94.8983	.000294
18	94.9591	94.8540	94.7488	94.6437	94.5386	94.4334	94.3283	94.2232	94.1180	94.0129	93.9078	93.8026	.003504
17	93.8203	93.7597	93.6990	93.6384	93.5778	93.5171	93.4565	93.3959	93.3352	93.2746	93.2140	93.1533	.002021
16	93.2167	93.1697	93.1227	93.0757	93.0287	92.9817	92.9346	92.8876	92.8406	92.7936	92.7466	92.6996	.001567
15	92.4690	92.4364	92.4037	92.3711	92.3384	92.3058	92.2731	92.2405	92.2079	92.1752	92.1426	92.1099	.001088
14	91.6432	91.6194	91.5955	91.5717	91.5478	91.5240	91.5001	91.4763	91.4525	91.4286	91.4048	91.3809	.000795
13	90.7540	90.7376	90.7213	90.7049	90.6886	90.6722	90.6558	90.6395	90.6231	90.6068	90.5904	90.5741	.000545
12	89.8206	89.8100	89.7995	89.7890	89.7784	89.7678	89.7573	89.7467	89.7362	89.7256	89.7151	89.7045	.000352
11	88.8620	88.8556	88.8491	88.8427	88.8362	88.8298	88.8233	88.8169	88.8105	88.8040	88.7976	88.7911	.000215
10	87.8863	87.8832	87.8801	87.8770	87.8739	87.8708	87.8676	87.8645	87.8614	87.8583	87.8552	87.8521	.000103
Age.	0	1	2	3	4	5	6	7	8	9	10	11	Day.

Age.	0	1	2	3	4	5	6	7	8	9	10	11	Day.
10	6.5396	6.5037	6.4678	6.4318	6.3959	6.3600	6.3241	6.2882	6.2523	6.2163	6.1804	6.1445	.001197
11	6.7838	6.7482	6.7125	6.6769	6.6413	6.6056	6.5700	6.5344	6.4987	6.4631	6.4275	6.3918	.001188
12	7.0361	7.0007	6.9653	6.9299	6.8945	6.8591	6.8236	6.7882	6.7528	6.7174	6.6820	6.6466	.001180
13	7.2960	7.2608	7.2257	7.1905	7.1553	7.1202	7.0850	7.0498	7.0147	6.9795	6.9443	6.9092	.001172
14	7.5650	7.5301	7.4952	7.4602	7.4253	7.3904	7.3555	7.3206	7.2857	7.2507	7.2158	7.1809	.001164
15	7.8441	7.8094	7.7747	7.7400	7.7053	7.6706	7.6360	7.6013	7.5666	7.5319	7.4972	7.4625	.001156
16	8.1335	8.0990	8.0646	8.0301	7.9957	7.9612	7.9268	7.8923	7.8579	7.8234	7.7890	7.7545	.001148
17	8.4346	8.4003	8.3661	8.3318	8.2976	8.2633	8.2290	8.1948	8.1605	8.1263	8.0920	8.0578	.001142
18	8.7470	8.7129	8.6789	8.6448	8.6108	8.5767	8.5426	8.5086	8.4745	8.4405	8.4064	8.3724	.001135
19	9.0724	9.0385	9.0047	8.9708	8.9370	8.9031	8.8692	8.8354	8.8015	8.7677	8.7338	8.7000	.001128
20	9.4107	9.3770	9.3434	9.3097	9.2761	9.2424	9.2088	9.1751	9.1415	9.1078	9.0742	9.0405	.001122
21	9.7645	9.7310	9.6975	9.6640	9.6305	9.5970	9.5634	9.5299	9.4964	9.4629	9.4294	9.3959	.001117
22	10.1328	10.0995	10.0662	10.0328	9.9995	9.9662	9.9329	9.8996	9.8663	9.8330	9.7996	9.7663	.001110
23	10.5166	10.4835	10.4505	10.4174	10.3844	10.3513	10.3182	10.2852	10.2521	10.2191	10.1860	10.1530	.001102
24	10.9185	10.8857	10.8528	10.8200	10.7871	10.7543	10.7214	10.6886	10.6558	10.6229	10.5901	10.5572	.001095
25	11.3388	11.3062	11.2735	11.2409	11.2083	11.1757	11.1430	11.1104	11.0778	11.0452	11.0125	10.9799	.001087
26	11.7782	11.7460	11.7138	11.6815	11.6493	11.6171	11.5849	11.5527	11.5205	11.4882	11.4560	11.4238	.001074
27	12.2408	12.2088	12.1768	12.1449	12.1129	12.0809	12.0490	12.0170	11.9850	11.9530	11.9210	11.8891	.001066
28	12.7254	12.6938	12.6622	12.6306	12.5991	12.5675	12.5359	12.5043	12.4727	12.4411	12.4096	12.3780	.001053
29	13.2357	13.2046	13.1735	13.1423	13.1112	13.0801	13.0490	13.0179	12.9868	12.9556	12.9245	12.8934	.001037
30	13.7742	13.7435	13.7128	13.6822	13.6515	13.6208	13.5902	13.5595	13.5288	13.4982	13.4675	13.4368	.001020
31	14.3419	14.3116	14.2813	14.2510	14.2208	14.1905	14.1602	14.1299	14.0996	14.0693	14.0391	14.0088	.001009
32	14.9402	14.9099	14.8796	14.8494	14.8191	14.7888	14.7585	14.7283	14.6980	14.6677	14.6374	14.6072	.001009
33	15.5664	15.5356	15.5049	15.4741	15.4434	15.4126	15.3818	15.3511	15.3203	15.2896	15.2588	15.2281	.001025
34	16.2168	16.1852	16.1536	16.1220	16.0904	16.0588	16.0271	15.9955	15.9639	15.9323	15.9007	15.8691	.001053
35	16.8882	16.8552	16.8221	16.7891	16.7560	16.7230	16.6900	16.6569	16.6239	16.5908	16.5578	16.5247	.001101
36	17.5762	17.5415	17.5068	17.4720	17.4373	17.4026	17.3679	17.3332	17.2985	17.2637	17.2290	17.1943	.001157
37	18.2803	18.2436	18.2068	18.1701	18.1333	18.0966	18.0598	18.0231	17.9864	17.9496	17.9129	17.8761	.001225
38	18.9969	18.9597	18.9225	18.8853	18.8481	18.8109	18.7737	18.7365	18.6993	18.6621	18.6249	18.5877	.001240
39	19.7295	19.6880	19.6465	19.6050	19.5635	19.5220	19.4805	19.4391	19.3976	19.3561	19.3146	19.2731	.001383
40	20.4737	20.4292	20.3847	20.3402	20.2957	20.2512	20.2067	20.1623	20.1178	20.0733	20.0288	19.9843	.001483
41	21.2277	21.1798	21.1318	21.0839	21.0360	20.9880	20.9401	20.8922	20.8442	20.7963	20.7484	20.7004	.001598
42	21.9899	21.9381	21.8863	21.8345	21.7827	21.7309	21.6790	21.6272	21.5754	21.5236	21.4718	21.4200	.001726
43	22.7600	22.7039	22.6479	22.5918	22.5357	22.4797	22.4236	22.3675	22.3115	22.2554	22.1993	22.1433	.001869
44	23.5413	23.4805	23.4196	23.3588	23.2980	23.2372	23.1763	23.1155	23.0547	22.9939	22.9330	22.8722	.002027
45	24.3375	24.2713	24.2051	24.1389	24.0727	24.0065	23.9402	23.8740	23.8078	23.7416	23.6754	23.6092	.002207
46	25.1490	25.0771	25.0052	24.9333	24.8615	24.7896	24.7177	24.6458	24.5739	24.5020	24.4302	24.3583	.002396
47	25.9832	25.9050	25.8268	25.7486	25.6704	25.5922	25.5140	25.4359	25.3577	25.2795	25.2013	25.1231	.002606
48	26.8397	26.7545	26.6694	26.5842	26.4991	26.4140	26.3288	26.2436	26.1585	26.0733	25.9882	25.9030	.002838
49	27.7191	27.6259	27.5328	27.4396	27.3465	27.2533	27.1601	27.0670	26.9738	26.8807	26.7875	26.6944	.003105
50	28.6153	28.5134	28.4114	28.3095	28.2076	28.1056	28.0037	27.9018	27.7998	27.6979	27.5960	27.4940	.003398
51	29.5295	29.4178	29.3060	29.1943	29.0826	28.9709	28.8591	28.7474	28.6357	28.5240	28.4122	28.3005	.003724
52	30.4591	30.3367	30.2144	30.0920	29.9696	29.8473	29.7249	29.6025	29.4802	29.3578	29.2354	29.1131	.004079
53	31.4047	31.2705	31.1364	31.0022	30.8680	30.7339	30.5997	30.4655	30.3314	30.1972	30.0630	29.9289	.004472
54	32.3632	32.2162	32.0693	31.9223	31.7754	31.6284	31.4814	31.3345	31.1875	31.0406	30.8936	30.7467	.004898
55	33.3334	33.1722	33.0110	32.8498	32.6886	32.5274	32.3662	32.2051	32.0439	31.8827	31.7215	31.5603	.005373
56	34.3107	34.1342	33.9577	33.7812	33.6047	33.4282	33.2517	33.0753	32.8988	32.7223	32.5458	32.3693	.005883
57	35.2963	35.1033	34.9102	34.7172	34.5242	34.3311	34.1381	33.9451	33.7520	33.5590	33.3660	33.1729	.006434
58	36.2876	36.0769	35.8661	35.6554	35.4447	35.2339	35.0232	34.8125	34.6017	34.3910	34.1803	33.9695	.007024
59	37.2868	37.0568	36.8268	36.5968	36.3668	36.1368	35.9068	35.6768	35.4468	35.2168	34.9868	34.7568	.007667
60	38.2922	38.0415	37.7908	37.5401	37.2894	37.0387	36.7880	36.5372	36.2865	36.0358	35.7851	35.5344	.008357
61	39.3087	39.0357	38.7626	38.4896	38.2165	37.9435	37.6704	37.3974	37.1244	36.8513	36.5783	36,3052	.009101
62	40.3362	40.0392	39.7422	39.4452	39.1482	38.8512	38.5541	38.2571	37.9601	37.6631	37.3661	37.0691	.009900
63	41.3781	41.0553	40.7325	40.4097	40.0869	39.7641	39.4413	39.1186	38.7958	38.4730	38.1502	37.8274	.010760
64	42.4353	42.0849	41.7344	41.3840	41.0336	40.6831	40.3327	39.9823	39.6318	39.2814	38.9310	38.5805	.011681
65	43.5114	43.1315	42.7517	42.3718	41.9920	41.6121	41.2322	40.8524	40.4725	40.0927	39.7128	39.3330	.012662
66	44.6109	44.1992	43.7875	43.3758	42.9642	42.5525	42.1408	41.7291	41.3174	40.9057	40.4941	40.0824	.013723
67	45.7359	45.2900	44.8440	44.3981	43.9522	43.5063	43.0603	42.6144	42.1685	41.7226	41.2766	40.8307	.014864
68	46.8858	46.4037	45.9216	45.4395	44.9574	44.4753	43.9931	43.5110	43.0289	42.5468	42.0647	41.5826	.016070
69	48.0689	47.5484	47.0280	46.5075	45.9871	45.4666	44.9462	44.4257	43.9053	43.3848	42.8644	42.3440	.017348
70	49.2918	48.7313	48.1708	47.6103	47.0498	46.4893	45.9288	45.3684	44.8079	44.2474	43.6869	43.1264	.018683
71	50.5730	49.9712	49.3693	48.7675	48.1657	47.5639	46.9620	46.3602	45.7584	45.1566	44.5547	43.9529	.020061
72	51.9372	51.2923	50.6474	50.0025	49.3576	48.7127	48.0677	47.4228	46.7779	46.1330	45.4881	44.8432	.021497
73	53.4081	52.7190	52.0298	51.3407	50.6515	49.9624	49.2732	48.5841	47.8950	47.2058	46.5167	45.8275	.022971
74	55.0214	54.2850	53.5486	52.8123	52.0759	51.3395	50.6031	49.8668	49.1304	48.3940	47.6576	46.9213	.024546
75	56.7950	56.0083	55.2215	54.4348	53.6480	52.8613	52.0745	51.2878	50.5011	49.7143	48.9276	48.1408	.026225
76	58.7496	57.9092	57.0687	56.2283	55.3878	54.5474	53.7070	52.8665	52.0261	51.1856	50.3452	49.5047	.028015
77	60.9089	60.0090	59.1090	58.2090	57.3091	56.4091	55.5092	54.6092	53.7093	52.8093	51.9094	51.0094	.029998
78	63.2725	62.3060	61.3395	60.3730	59.4064	58.4399	57.4734	56.5069	55.5404	54.5738	53.6073	52.6408	.032217
79	65.8325	64.7935	63.7544	62.7154	61.6764	60.6373	59.5983	58.5593	57.5202	56.4812	55.4422	54.4031	.034634
80	68.5940	67.4738	66.3536	65.2335	64.1133	62.9931	61.8730	60.7528	59.6326	58.5124	57.3922	56.2721	.037339
81	71.5375	70.3223	69.1070	67.8918	66.6766	65.4613	64.2461	63.0309	61.8156	60.6004	59.3852	58.1699	.040508
82	74.5843	73.2582	71.9322	70.6061	69.2800	67.9540	66.6279	65.3018	63.9758	62.6497	61.3236	59.9976	.044202
83	77.6406	76.1867	74.7329	73.2790	71.8252	70.3713	68.9175	67.4636	66.0098	64.5560	63.1021	61.6482	.048462
84	80.6170	78.9933	77.3696	75.7460	74.1223	72.4986	70.8750	69.2513	67.6276	66.0039	64.3802	62.7566	.054122
85	83.1216	81.3135	79.5054	77.6974	75.8893	74.0812	72.2731	70.4651	68.6570	66.8489	65.0408	63.2328	.060269
86	85.1268	83.2602	81.3937	79.5271	77.6606	75.7940	73.9275	72.0610	70.1944	68.3278	66.4613	64.5947	.062218
87	88.4340	86.7216	85.0092	83.2967	81.5843	79.8719	78.1595	76.4471	74.7347	73.0222	71.3098	69.5974	.057080
88 or 21	**96.1538**	**96.4743**	**96.7948**	**97.1158**	**97.4359**	**97.7564**	**98.0769**	**98.3974**	**98.7179**	**99.0384**	**99.3590**	**99.6795**	**.010684**
20	94.9177	94.9128	94.9079	94.9030	94.8980	94.8931	94.8882	94.8833	94.8784	94.8734	94.8685	94.8636	.000164
19	94.2784	94.2270	94.1755	94.1240	94.0726	94.0211	93.9697	93.9182	93.8668	93.8153	93.7639	93.7124	.001715
18	93.8072	93.7445	93.6817	93.6190	93.5562	93.4935	93.4307	93.3680	93.3053	93.2425	93.1798	93.1170	.002091
17	93.2011	93.1521	93.1031	93.0542	93.0052	92.9562	92.9072	92.8583	92.8093	92.7603	92.7113	92.6624	.001632
16	92.4502	92.4157	92.3813	92.3468	92.3124	92.2779	92.2434	92.2090	92.1745	92.1401	92.1056	92.0712	.001148
15	91.6209	91.5954	91.5699	91.5443	91.5188	91.4933	91.4678	91.4423	91.4168	91.3912	91.3657	91.3402	.000850
14	90.7287	90.7107	90.6928	90.6748	90.6568	90.6389	90.6209	90.6029	90.5850	90.5670	90.5490	90.5311	.000599
13	89.7920	89.7800	89.7679	89.7559	89.7438	89.7318	89.7197	89.7077	89.6957	89.6836	89.6716	89.6595	.000401
12	88.8304	88.8226	88.8147	88.8069	88.7990	88.7912	88.7833	88.7755	88.7677	88.7598	88.7520	88.7441	.000261
11	87.8521	87.8477	87.8432	87.8388	87.8343	87.8299	87.8254	87.8210	87.8166	87.8121	87.8077	87.8032	.000148
10	86.8591	86.8578	86.8565	86.8551	86.8538	86.8525	86.8512	86.8499	86.8486	86.8472	86.8459	86.8446	.000044
Age.	0	1	2	3	4	5	6	7	8	9	10	11	Day.

Age.	0	1	2	3	4	5	6	7	8	9	10	11	Day.
10	7.1515	7.1173	7.0832	7.0490	7.0148	6.9807	6.9465	6.9123	6.8782	6.8440	6.8098	6.7757	.001139
11	7.4194	7.3855	7.3516	7.3177	7.2838	7.2499	7.2160	7.1822	7.1483	7.1144	7.0805	7.0466	.001129
12	7.6955	7.6619	7.6284	7.5948	7.5612	7.5277	7.4941	7.4605	7.4270	7.3934	7.3598	7.3263	.001119
13	7.9806	7.9474	7.9141	7.8809	7.8476	7.8144	7.7811	7.7479	7.7147	7.6814	7.6482	7.6149	.001108
14	8.2760	8.2430	8.2101	8.1771	8.1442	8.1112	8.0782	8.0453	8.0123	7.9794	7.9464	7.9135	.001098
15	8.5822	8.5496	8.5169	8.4843	8.4517	8.4190	8.3864	8.3538	8.3211	8.2885	8.2559	8.2232	.001088
16	8.9001	8.8677	8.8353	8.8030	8.7706	8.7382	8.7058	8.6735	8.6411	8.6087	8.5763	8.5440	.001079
17	9.2303	9.1982	9.1661	9.1340	9.1019	9.0698	9.0377	9.0056	8.9735	8.9414	8.9093	8.8772	.001070
18	9.5731	9.5413	9.5095	9.4777	9.4459	9.4141	9.3822	9.3504	9.3186	9.2868	9.2550	9.2232	.001060
19	9.9304	9.8988	9.8673	9.8357	9.8042	9.7726	9.7411	9.7095	9.6780	9.6464	9.6149	9.5833	.001052
20	10.3017	10.2704	10.2391	10.2078	10.1766	10.1453	10.1140	10.0827	10.0514	10.0201	9.9889	9.9576	.001043
21	10.6897	10.6587	10.6276	10.5966	10.5656	10.5346	10.5035	10.4725	10.4415	10.4105	10.3794	10.3484	.001034
22	11.0940	11.0633	11.0326	11.0020	10.9713	10.9406	10.9099	10.8792	10.8485	10.8178	10.7872	10.7565	.001023
23	11.5162	11.4858	11.4554	11.4251	11.3947	11.3643	11.3340	11.3036	11.2732	11.2428	11.2124	11.1821	.001012
24	11.9578	11.9277	11.8977	11.8676	11.8376	11.8075	11.7775	11.7474	11.7174	11.6873	11.6573	11.6272	.001002
25	12.4195	12.3900	12.3604	12.3309	12.3013	12.2718	12.2422	12.2127	12.1832	12.1536	12.1241	12.0945	.000985
26	12.9045	12.8753	12.8461	12.8170	12.7878	12.7586	12.7294	12.7003	12.6711	12.6419	12.6127	12.5836	.000972
27	13.4128	13.3841	13.3554	13.3267	13.2981	13.2694	13.2407	13.2120	13.1833	13.1546	13.1260	13.0973	.000956
28	13.9469	13.9188	13.8907	13.8626	13.8345	13.8064	13.7783	13.7502	13.7221	13.6940	13.6659	13.6378	.000937
29	14.5100	14.4825	14.4550	14.4274	14.3999	14.3724	14.3448	14.3173	14.2898	14.2623	14.2347	14.2072	.000917
30	15.1034	15.0764	15.0493	15.0223	14.9953	14.9683	14.9412	14.9142	14.8872	14.8602	14.8331	14.8061	.000901
31	15.7277	15.7008	15.6739	15.6470	15.6202	15.5933	15.5664	15.5395	15.5126	15.4857	15.4589	15.4320	.000896
32	16.3809	16.3537	16.3264	16.2992	16.2720	16.2448	16.2175	16.1903	16.1631	16.1359	16.1086	16.0814	.000907
33	17.0589	17.0310	17.0031	16.9752	16.9474	16.9195	16.8916	16.8637	16.8358	16.8080	16.7801	16.7522	.000929
34	17.7600	17.7308	17.7017	17.6725	17.6434	17.6142	17.5850	17.5559	17.5267	17.4976	17.4684	17.4393	.000972
35	18.4783	18.4477	18.4170	18.3864	18.3557	18.3251	18.2944	18.2638	18.2332	18.2025	18.1719	18.1412	.001021
36	19.2140	19.1815	19.1491	19.1166	19.0842	19.0517	19.0192	18.9868	18.9543	18.9219	18.8894	18.8570	.001082
37	19.9654	19.9310	19.8967	19.8623	19.8279	19.7936	19.7592	19.7248	19.6905	19.6561	19.6217	19.5874	.001145
38	20.7523	20.7139	20.6755	20.6371	20.5987	20.5603	20.5219	20.4835	20.4451	20.4067	20.3683	20.3299	.001280
39	21.5139	21.4744	21.4350	21.3955	21.3560	21.3165	21.2770	21.2376	21.1981	21.1586	21.1191	21.0797	.001316
40	22.3075	22.2649	22.2223	22.1796	22.1370	22.0944	22.0518	22.0092	21.9666	21.9240	21.8813	21.8387	.001420
41	23.1111	23.0649	23.0187	22.9726	22.9264	22.8802	22.8340	22.7879	22.7417	22.6955	22.6493	22.6032	.001539
42	23.9236	23.8735	23.8234	23.7733	23.7232	23.6731	23.6230	23.5730	23.5229	23.4728	23.4227	23.3726	.001670
43	24.7457	24.6912	24.6367	24.5822	24.5277	24.4732	24.4186	24.3641	24.3096	24.2551	24.2006	24.1461	.001817
44	25.5796	25.5201	25.4605	25.4010	25.3415	25.2820	25.2224	25.1629	25.1034	25.0439	24.9843	24.9248	.001984
45	26.4275	26.3627	26.2979	26.2330	26.1682	26.1034	26.0386	25.9738	25.9090	25.8441	25.7793	25.7145	.002160
46	27.2944	27.2236	27.1529	27.0821	27.0114	26.9406	26.8699	26.7991	26.7284	26.6576	26.5869	26.5161	.002358
47	28.1834	28.1061	28.0288	27.9515	27.8743	27.7970	27.7197	27.6424	27.5651	27.4878	27.4106	27.3333	.002576
48	29.0946	29.0097	28.9249	28.8400	28.7552	28.6703	28.5855	28.5006	28.4158	28.3310	28.2461	28.1612	.002828
49	30.0239	29.9308	29.8377	29.7445	29.6514	29.5583	29.4652	29.3721	29.2790	29.1858	29.0927	28.9996	.003104
50	30.9696	30.8672	30.7648	30.6625	30.5601	30.4577	30.3553	30.2530	30.1506	30.0482	29.9458	29.8435	.003412
51	31.9303	31.8178	31.7054	31.5929	31.4804	31.3680	31.2555	31.1430	31.0306	30.9181	30.8056	30.6932	.003749
52	32.9058	32.7822	32.6586	32.5350	32.4114	32.2878	32.1641	32.0405	31.9169	31.7933	31.6697	31.5461	.004120
53	33.8943	33.7586	33.6228	33.4871	33.3513	33.2156	33.0798	32.9441	32.8084	32.6726	32.5369	32.4011	.004525
54	34.8947	34.7455	34.5963	34.4470	34.2978	34.1486	33.9994	33.8502	33.7010	33.5517	33.4025	33.2533	.004974
55	35.9016	35.7379	35.5742	35.4105	35.2468	35.0831	34.9193	34.7556	34.5919	34.4282	34.2645	34.1008	.005457
56	36.9158	36.7364	36.5570	36.3777	36.1983	36.0189	35.8395	35.6602	35.4808	35.3014	35.1220	34.9427	.005979
57	37.9370	37.7409	37.5448	37.3487	37.1527	36.9566	36.7605	36.5644	36.3683	36.1722	35.9762	35.7801	.006536
58	38.9655	38 7512	38.5369	38.3226	38.1083	37.8940	37.6797	37.4654	37.2511	37.0368	36.8225	36.6082	.007143
59	39.9992	39.7653	39.5315	39.2976	39.0637	38.8299	38.5960	38.3621	38.1283	37.8944	37.6605	37.4267	.007795
60	41.0392	40.7842	40.5293	40.2743	40.0194	39.7644	39.5095	39.2545	38.9996	38.7446	38.4897	38.2347	.008498
61	42.0894	41.8118	41.5341	41.2565	40.9789	40.7013	40.4236	40.1460	39.8684	39.5908	39.3131	39.0355	.009254
62	43.1503	42.8483	42.5463	42.2443	41.9423	41.6403	41.3383	41.0364	40.7344	40.4324	40.1304	39.8284	.010066
63	44.2245	43.8964	43.5683	43.2402	42.9122	42.5841	42.2560	41.9279	41.5998	41.2717	40.9437	40.6156	.010936
64	45.3142	44.9583	44.6025	44.2466	43.8907	43.5349	43.1790	42.8231	42.4673	42.1114	41.7555	41.3997	.011862
65	46.4248	46.0389	45.6530	45.2671	44.8812	44.4953	44.1093	43.7234	43.3375	42.9516	42.5657	42.1798	.012863
66	47.5553	47.1370	46.7187	46.3005	45.8822	45.4639	45.0456	44.6274	44.2091	43.7908	43.3725	42.9543	.013942
67	48.7085	48.2561	47.8037	47.3513	46.8989	46.4465	45.9940	45.5416	45.0892	44.6368	44.1844	43.7320	.015080
68	50.8918	50.3199	49.7480	49.1761	48.6042	48.0323	47.4603	46.8884	46.3165	45.7446	45.1727	44.6008	.019063
69	51.1127	50.5864	50.0602	49.5339	49.0076	48.4814	47.9551	47.4288	46.9026	46.3763	45.8500	45.3238	.017542
70	52.3861	51.8210	51.2558	50.6907	50.1256	49.5605	48.9953	48.4302	47.8651	47.3000	46.7348	46.1697	.018837
71	53.7376	53.1320	52.5264	51.9208	51.3152	50.7096	50.1040	49.4984	48.8928	48.2872	47.6816	47.0760	.020187
72	55.1889	54.5418	53.8947	53.2477	52.6006	51.9535	51.3064	50.6594	50.0123	49.3652	48.7181	48.0711	.021569
73	56.7739	56.0826	55.3913	54.6999	54.0086	53.3173	52.6259	51.9346	51.2433	50.5519	49.8606	49.1693	.023043
74	58.5096	57.7711	57.0326	56.2940	55.5555	54.8170	54.0785	53.3400	52.6015	51.8630	51.1244	50.3859	.024617
75	60.4152	59.6265	58.8377	58.0490	57.2602	56.4715	55.6827	54.8940	54.1053	53.3165	52.5278	51.7390	.026291
76	62.5134	61.6691	60.8248	59.9805	59.1363	58.2920	57.4477	56.6034	55.7591	54.9148	54.0706	53.2263	.028143
77	64.8030	63.8963	62.9897	62.0830	61.1764	60.2697	59.3630	58.4564	57.5497	56.6431	55.7364	54.8298	.030222
78	67.2723	66.2979	65.3234	64.3490	63.3746	62.4001	61.4257	60.4513	59.4768	58.5024	57.5280	56.5535	.032481
79	69.9320	68.8818	67.8316	66.7814	65.7312	64.6810	63.6308	62.5806	61.5304	60.4802	59.4300	58.3798	.035007
80	72.7618	71.6229	70.4840	69.3451	68.2062	67.0673	65.9283	64.7894	63.6505	62.5116	61.3727	60.2338	.037963
81	75.6868	74.4449	73.2030	71.9611	70.7193	69.4774	68.2355	66.9936	65.7517	64.5098	63.2680	62.0261	.041396
82	78.6202	77.2602	75.9002	74.5402	73.1803	71.8203	70.4603	69.1003	67.7403	66.3803	65.0204	63.6604	.045333
83	81.4723	79.9557	78.4391	76.9225	75.4059	73.8893	72.3727	70.8561	69.3395	67.8229	66.3063	64.7897	.050553
84	83.8751	82.1901	80.5050	78.8200	77.1349	75.4499	73.7648	72.0798	70.3948	68.7097	67.0247	65.3396	.056168
85	85.7980	84.0646	82.3312	80.5977	78.8643	77.1309	75.3975	73.6641	71.9307	70.1972	68.4638	66.7304	.057780
86	88.9307	87.3491	85.7675	84.1858	82.6042	81.0226	79.4410	77.8594	76.2778	74.6961	73.1145	71.5329	.052720
87 or 22	**96.1538**	**96.4743**	**96.7948**	**97.1153**	**97.4359**	**97.7564**	**98.0769**	**98.3974**	**98.7179**	**99.0384**	**99.3590**	**99.6795**	**.010684**
21	94.9102	94.9032	94.8962	94.8893	94.8823	94.8753	94.8683	94.8614	94.8544	94.8474	94.8404	94.8335	.000232
20	94.2668	94.2132	94.1595	94.1058	94.0522	93.9985	93.9448	93.8912	93.8375	93.7838	93.7302	93.6765	.001787
19	93.7937	93.7287	93.6638	93.5988	93.5338	93.4689	93.4039	93.3389	93.2740	93.2090	93.1440	93.0791	.002165
18	93.1846	93.1336	93.0826	93.0315	92.9805	92.9295	92.8785	92.8275	92.7765	92.7254	92.6744	92.6234	.001700
17	92.4304	92.3940	92.3577	92.3213	92.2850	92.2486	92.2123	92.1760	92.1396	92.1032	92.0669	92.0305	.001212
16	91.5977	91.5704	91.5431	91.5158	91.4885	91.4612	91.4340	91.4067	91.3794	91.3521	91.3248	91.2975	.000910
15	90.7020	90.6824	90.6627	90.6431	90.6235	90.6039	90.5842	90.5646	90.5450	90.5254	90.5057	90.4861	.000654
14	89.7621	89.7485	89.7349	89.7212	89.7076	89.6940	89.6804	89.6668	89.6532	89.6395	89.6259	89.6123	.000454
13	88.7974	88.7881	88.7787	88.7694	88.7601	88.7507	88.7414	88.7321	88.7227	88.7134	88.7041	88.6947	.000311
12	87.8163	87.8104	87.8046	87.7987	87.7929	87.7870	87.7812	87.7753	87.7695	87.7636	87.7578	87.7520	.000195
11	86.8206	86.8180	86.8153	86.8127	86.8101	86.8074	86.8048	86.8022	86.7995	86.7969	86.7943	86.7916	.000088
10	85.8191	85.8188	85.8186	85.8183	85.8181	85.8178	85.8176	85.8173	85.8171	85.8168	85.8166	85.8163	.000008

Age. 0 1 2 3 4 5 6 7 8 9 10 11 Day.

Age.	0	1	2	3	4	5	6	7	8	9	10	11	Day
10	7.7844	7.7520	7.7196	7.6871	7.6547	7.6223	7.5899	7.5575	7.5251	7.4926	7.4602	7.4278	.001080
11	8.0759	8.0438	8.0118	7.9797	7.9477	7.9156	7.8836	7.8515	7.8195	7.7874	7.7554	7.7233	.001068
12	8.3770	8.3454	8.3137	8.2821	8.2504	8.2188	8.1871	8.1555	8.1239	8.0922	8.0606	8.0289	.001055
13	8.6883	8.6570	8.6257	8.5944	8.5631	8.5318	8.5005	8.4693	8.4380	8.4067	8.3754	8.3441	.001043
14	9.0106	8.9797	8.9487	8.9178	8.8869	8.8560	8.8250	8.7941	8.7632	8.7323	8.7013	8.6704	.001031
15	9.3450	9.3144	9.2838	9.2532	9.2227	9.1921	9.1615	9.1309	9.1003	9.0697	9.0392	9.0086	.001019
16	9.6916	9.6614	9.6311	9.6009	9.5707	9.5404	9.5102	9.4800	9.4497	9.4195	9.3893	9.3590	.001008
17	10.0519	10.0220	9.9922	9.9623	9.9324	9.9026	9.8727	9.8428	9.8130	9.7831	9.7532	9.7234	.000999
18	10.4262	10.3967	10.3671	10.3376	10.3081	10.2786	10.2490	10.2195	10.1900	10.1605	10.1310	10.1014	.000984
19	10.8161	10.7869	10.7577	10.7285	10.6993	10.6701	10.6410	10.6118	10.5826	10.5534	10.5242	10.4950	.000973
20	11.2212	11.1924	11.1636	11.1347	11.1059	11.0771	11.0483	11.0195	10.9907	10.9618	10.9330	10.9042	.000960
21	11.6447	11.6163	11.5879	11.5595	11.5311	11.5027	11.4742	11.4458	11.4174	11.3890	11.3606	11.3322	.000947
22	12.0868	12.0588	12.0308	12.0028	11.9748	11.9468	11.9187	11.8907	11.8627	11.8347	11.8067	11.7787	.000933
23	12.5481	12.5205	12.4929	12.4653	12.4377	12.4101	12.3825	12.3550	12.3274	12.2998	12.2722	12.2446	.000920
24	13.0305	13.0035	12.9765	12.9495	12.9226	12.8956	12.8686	12.8416	12.8146	12.7876	12.7607	12.7337	.000899
25	13.5372	13.5107	13.4842	13.4576	13.4311	13.4046	13.3781	13.3516	13.3251	13.2985	13.2720	13.2455	.000884
26	14.0673	14.0414	14.0155	13.9895	13.9636	13.9377	13.9118	13.8859	13.8600	13.8340	13.8081	13.7822	.000864
27	14.6243	14.5991	14.5738	14.5486	14.5234	14.4981	14.4729	14.4477	14.4224	14.3972	14.3720	14.3467	.000841
28	15.2102	15.1857	15.1611	15.1366	15.1121	15.0875	15.0630	15.0385	15.0139	14.9894	14.9649	14.9403	.000818
29	15.8273	15.8034	15.7795	15.7555	15.7316	15.7077	15.6838	15.6599	15.6360	15.6120	15.5881	15.5642	.000797
30	16.4763	16.4526	16.4290	16.4053	16.3817	16.3580	16.3344	16.3107	16.2871	16.2634	16.2398	16.2161	.000788
31	17.1543	17.1305	17.1066	17.0828	17.0589	17.0351	17.0112	16.9874	16.9636	16.9397	16.9159	16.8920	.000795
32	17.8582	17.8338	17.8095	17.7851	17.7607	17.7364	17.7120	17.6876	17.6633	17.6389	17.6145	17.5902	.000812
33	18.5859	18.5604	18.5350	18.5095	18.4840	18.4586	18.4331	18.4076	18.3822	18.3567	18.3312	18.3058	.000849
34	19.3326	19.3058	19.2790	19.2523	19.2255	19.1987	19.1720	19.1452	19.1184	19.0916	19.0648	19.0381	.000892
35	20.0973	20.0689	20.0405	20.0121	19.9837	19.9553	19.9269	19.8985	19.8701	19.8417	19.8133	19.7849	.000947
36	20.8789	20.8488	20.8187	20.7886	20.7585	20.7284	20.6982	20.6681	20.6380	20.6079	20.5778	20.5477	.001003
37	21.6790	21.6467	21.6145	21.5822	21.5500	21.5177	21.4854	21.4532	21.4209	21.3887	21.3564	21.3242	.001075
38	22.4934	22.4586	22.4239	22.3891	22.3544	22.3196	22.2849	22.2501	22.2154	22.1806	22.1459	22.1111	.001158
39	23.3225	23.2849	23.2472	23.2096	23.1720	23.1343	23.0967	23.0591	23.0214	22.9838	22.9462	22.9085	.001254
40	24.1638	24.1229	24.0820	24.0411	24.0002	23.9593	23.9184	23.8776	23.8367	23.7958	23.7549	23.7140	.001363
41	25.0156	24.9711	24.9266	24.8821	24.8376	24.7931	24.7486	24.7042	24.6597	24.6152	24.5707	24.5262	.001483
42	25.8779	25.8293	25.7807	25.7322	25.6836	25.6350	25.5864	25.5379	25.4893	25.4407	25.3921	25.3436	.001619
43	26.7501	26.6969	26.6436	26.5904	26.5372	26.4840	26.4307	26.3775	26.3243	26.2711	26.2178	26.1646	.001774
44	27.6335	27.5753	27.5172	27.4590	27.4009	27.3427	27.2845	27.2264	27.1682	27.1101	27.0519	26.9938	.001938
45	28.5343	28.4706	28.4069	28.3432	28.2795	28.2158	28.1521	28.0884	28.0247	27.9610	27.8973	27.8336	.002123
46	29.4534	29.3836	29.3137	29.2439	29.1740	29.1042	29.0343	28.9645	28.8947	28.8248	28.7550	28.6851	.002328
47	30.3945	30.3175	30.2405	30.1635	30.0866	30.0096	29.9326	29.8556	29.7786	29.7016	29.6247	29.5477	.002566
48	31.3531	31.2683	31.1835	31.0986	31.0138	30.9290	30.8442	30.7594	30.6746	30.5897	30.5049	30.4201	.002827
49	32.3292	32.2356	32.1421	32.0485	31.9549	31.8614	31.7678	31.6742	31.5807	31.4871	31.3935	31.3000	.003119
50	33.3186	33.2155	33.1124	33.0093	32.9062	32.8031	32.7000	32.5968	32.4937	32.3906	32.2875	32.1844	.003437
51	34.3223	34.2086	34.0949	33.9812	33.8676	33.7539	33.6402	33.5265	33.4128	33.2991	33.1855	33.0718	.003789
52	35.3376	35.2125	35.0873	34.9622	34.8371	34.7119	34.5868	34.4617	34.3365	34.2114	34.0863	33.9611	.004171
53	36.3650	36.2271	36.0891	35.9512	35.8132	35.6753	35.5373	35.3994	35.2615	35.1235	34.9856	34.8476	.004598
54	37.3990	37.2473	37.0957	36.9440	36.7923	36.6407	36.4890	36.3373	36.1857	36.0340	35.8823	35.7307	.005053
55	38.4396	38.2731	38.1066	37.9401	37.7736	37.6071	37.4405	37.2740	37.1075	36.9410	36.7745	36.6080	.005550
56	39.4862	39.3039	39.1215	38.9392	38.7568	38.5745	38.3921	38.2098	38.0275	37.8451	37.6628	37.4804	.006078
57	40.5412	40.3416	40.1421	39.9425	39.7430	39.5434	39.3438	39.1443	38.9447	38.7452	38.5456	38.3461	.006653
58	41.6006	41.3825	41.1645	40.9464	40.7283	40.5103	40.2922	40.0741	39.8561	39.6380	39.4199	39.2019	.007269
59	42.6652	42.4272	42.1892	41.9512	41.7132	41.4752	41.2372	40.9993	40.7613	40.5233	40.2853	40.0473	.007933
60	43.7353	43.4759	43.2165	42.9571	42.6977	42.4383	42.1788	41.9194	41.6600	41.4006	41.1412	40.8818	.008647
61	44.8151	44.5326	44.2502	43.9677	43.6853	43.4028	43.1204	42.8380	42.5555	42.2730	41.9906	41.7081	.009415
62	45.9046	45.5975	45.2904	44.9833	44.6762	44.3691	44.0620	43.7548	43.4477	43.1406	42.8335	42.5264	.010237
63	47.0074	46.6741	46.3407	46.0074	45.6741	45.3408	45.0074	44.6741	44.3408	44.0075	43.6741	43.3408	.011111
64	48.1279	47.7662	47.4045	47.0427	46.6810	46.3193	45.9576	45.5959	45.2342	44.8724	44.5107	44.1490	.012057
65	49.2657	48.8734	48.4811	48.0889	47.6966	47.3043	46.9120	46.5198	46.1275	45.7352	45.3430	44.9507	.013076
66	50.4206	49.9961	49.5715	49.1470	48.7225	48.2980	47.8734	47.4489	47.0244	46.5999	46.1753	45.7508	.014151
67	51.6033	51.1447	50.6860	50.2274	49.7688	49.3101	48.8515	48.3929	47.9342	47.4756	47.0170	46.5583	.015288
68	52.8202	52.3260	51.8319	51.3377	50.8435	50.3494	49.8552	49.3610	48.8669	48.3727	47.8785	47.3844	.016472
69	54.0867	53.5560	53.0253	52.4946	51.9639	51.4332	50.9024	50.3717	49.8410	49.3103	48.7796	48.2489	.017690
70	55.4248	54.8561	54.2873	53.7186	53.1498	52.5811	52.0123	51.4436	50.8749	50.3061	49.7374	49.1686	.018958
71	56.8569	56.2492	55.6415	55.0339	54.4262	53.8185	53.2108	52.6032	51.9955	51.3878	50.7801	50.1725	.020256
72	58.4146	57.7654	57.1162	56.4670	55.8179	55.1687	54.5195	53.8703	53.2211	52.5720	51.9228	51.2736	.021639
73	60.1135	59.4201	58.7267	58.0333	57.3400	56.6466	55.9532	55.2598	54.5664	53.8730	53.1797	52.4863	.023113
74	61.9721	61.2317	60.4912	59.7508	59.0104	58.2699	57.5295	56.7891	56.0486	55.3082	54.5678	53.8273	.024681
75	64.0114	63.2190	62.4266	61.6342	60.8418	60.0494	59.2570	58.4645	57.6721	56.8797	56.0873	55.2949	.026413
76	66.2311	65.3803	64.5296	63.6788	62.8281	61.9773	61.1265	60.2758	59.4250	58.5743	57.7235	56.8728	.028358
77	68.6167	67.7025	66.7883	65.8741	64.9599	64.0457	63.1314	62.2172	61.3030	60.3888	59.4746	58.5604	.030473
78	71.1771	70.1920	69.2070	68.2219	67.2368	66.2517	65.2666	64.2816	63.2965	62.3114	61.3263	60.3413	.032836
79	73.8975	72.8295	71.7614	70.6934	69.6254	68.5573	67.4893	66.4213	65.3532	64.2852	63.2172	62.1491	.035601
80	76.7047	75.5405	74.3762	73.2120	72.0478	70.8836	69.7193	68.5551	67.3909	66.2267	65.0624	63.8982	.038807
81	79.5164	78.2423	76.9683	75.6942	74.4202	73.1461	71.8720	70.5980	69.3239	68.0499	66.7758	65.5018	.042468
82	82.2491	80.8297	79.4103	77.9909	76.5715	75.1521	73.7327	72.3133	70.8939	69.4745	68.0551	66.6357	.047313
83	84.5510	82.9764	81.4018	79.8272	78.2526	76.6780	75.1034	73.5289	71.9543	70.3797	68.8051	67.2305	.052486
84	86.3968	84.7821	83.1674	81.5527	79.9380	78.3233	76.7086	75.0939	73.4792	71.8645	70.2498	68.6351	.053823
85	89.3703	87.9045	86.4386	84.9728	83.5070	82.0412	80.5753	79.1095	77.6437	76.1779	74.7120	73.2462	.048861
86 or 23	**96.1538**	**96.4743**	**96.7948**	**97.1153**	**97.4359**	**97.7564**	**98.0769**	**98.3974**	**98.7179**	**99.0384**	**99.3590**	**99.6795**	**.010684**
22	94.9021	94.8930	94.8839	94.8748	94.8657	94.8566	94.8474	94.8383	94.8292	94.8201	94.8110	94.8019	.000303
21	94.2553	94.1993	94.1432	94.0872	94.0312	93.9751	93.9191	93.8631	93.8070	93.7510	93.6950	93.6389	.001868
20	93.7792	93.7119	93.6447	93.5774	93.5101	93.4429	93.3756	93.3083	93.2411	93.1738	93.1065	93.0393	.002242
19	93.1675	93.1143	93.0611	93.0073	92.9548	92.9016	92.8484	92.7953	92.7421	92.6889	92.6357	92.5826	.001772
18	92.4097	92.3714	92.3331	92.2947	92.2564	92.2181	92.1797	92.1414	92.1031	92.0647	92.0264	91.9880	.001277
17	91.5734	91.5442	91.5151	91.4860	91.4568	91.4276	91.3985	91.3693	91.3402	91.3110	91.2819	91.2527	.000972
16	90.6740	90.6526	90.6313	90.6099	90.5886	90.5672	90.5458	90.5245	90.5031	90.4818	90.4604	90.4391	.000712
15	89.7306	89.7153	89.7001	89.6848	89.6696	89.6543	89.6391	89.6238	89.6086	89.5933	89.5781	89.5628	.000508
14	88.7627	88.7518	88.7409	88.7300	88.7192	88.7083	88.6974	88.6865	88.6756	88.6647	88.6539	88.6430	.000363
13	87.7786	87.7713	87.7640	87.7566	87.7493	87.7420	87.7347	87.7274	87.7201	87.7127	87.7054	87.6981	.000244
12	86.7803	86.7763	86.7722	86.7682	86.7642	86.7601	86.7561	86.7521	86.7480	86.7440	86.7400	86.7359	.000134
11	85.7764	85.7748	85.7732	85.7717	85.7701	85.7685	85.7670	85.7654	85.7638	85.7622	85.7606	85.7591	.000052
10	84.7723	84.7726	84.7730	84.7733	84.7736	84.7739	84.7742	84.7746	84.7749	84.7752	84.7755	84.7759	.000011
Age.	0	1	2	3	4	5	6	7	8	9	10	11	Day.

Age.	0	1	2	3	4	5	6	7	8	9	10	11	Day.
10	8.4383	8.4077	8.3771	8.3465	8.3159	8.2853	8.2547	8.2241	8.1935	8.1629	8.1323	8.1017	.001020
11	8.7545	8.7244	8.6942	8.6641	8.6340	8.6038	8.5737	8.5436	8.5134	8.4833	8.4532	8.4230	.001004
12	9.0816	9.0519	9.0222	8.9924	8.9627	8.9330	8.9033	8.8736	8.8439	8.8141	8.7844	8.7547	.000990
13	9.4194	9.3901	9.3609	9.3316	9.3023	9.2731	9.2438	9.2145	9.1853	9.1560	9.1267	9.0975	.000975
14	9.7696	9.7407	9.7118	9.6830	9.6541	9.6252	9.5963	9.5675	9.5386	9.5097	9.4808	9.4520	.000962
15	10.1324	10.1040	10.0755	10.0470	10.0186	9.9901	9.9617	9.9332	9.9048	9.8763	9.8479	9.8194	.000948
16	10.5088	10.4808	10.4528	10.4248	10.3968	10.3688	10.3407	10.3127	10.2847	10.2567	10.2287	10.2007	.000933
17	10.9003	10.8727	10.8451	10.8175	10.7899	10.7623	10.7347	10.7072	10.6796	10.6520	10.6244	10.5968	.000919
18	11.3068	11.2796	11.2524	11.2252	11.1981	11.1709	11.1437	11.1165	11.0893	11.0621	11.0350	11.0078	.000906
19	11.7301	11.7033	11.6766	11.6498	11.6231	11.5963	11.5696	11.5428	11.5161	11.4893	11.4626	11.4358	.000892
20	12.1703	12.1441	12.1178	12.0916	12.0654	12.0392	12.0130	11.9867	11.9605	11.9343	11.9080	11.8818	.000874
21	12.6310	12.6053	12.5795	12.5538	12.5280	12.5023	12.4765	12.4508	12.4251	12.3993	12.3736	12.3478	.000858
22	13.1117	13.0865	13.0612	13.0360	13.0107	12.9855	12.9602	12.9350	12.9098	12.8845	12.8593	12.8340	.000841
23	13.6133	13.5887	13.5642	13.5396	13.5151	13.4905	13.4660	13.4414	13.4169	13.3923	13.3678	13.3432	.000818
24	14.1401	14.1161	14.0921	14.0681	14.0442	14.0202	13.9962	13.9722	13.9482	13.9242	13.9003	13.8763	.000799
25	14.6912	14.6679	14.6446	14.6213	14.5980	14.5747	14.5514	14.5282	14.5049	14.4816	14.4583	14.4350	.000776
26	15.2692	15.2467	15.2242	15.2017	15.1792	15.1567	15.1342	15.1117	15.0892	15.0667	15.0442	15.0217	.000750
27	15.8771	15.8554	15.8337	15.8120	15.7903	15.7686	15.7470	15.7253	15.7036	15.6819	15.6602	15.6385	.000723
28	16.5163	16.4953	16.4744	16.4534	16.4324	16.4115	16.3905	16.3695	16.3486	16.3276	16.3066	16.2857	.000699
29	17.1880	17.1674	17.1468	17.1262	17.1057	17.0851	17.0645	17.0439	17.0233	17.0027	16.9822	16.9616	.000686
30	17.8896	17.8690	17.8483	17.8277	17.8070	17.7864	17.7657	17.7451	17.7245	17.7038	17.6832	17.6625	.000688
31	18.6174	18.5964	18.5753	18.5543	18.5333	18.5123	18.4912	18.4702	18.4492	18.4282	18.4071	18.3861	.000701
32	19.3698	19.3478	19.3258	19.3039	19.2819	19.2599	19.2380	19.2160	19.1940	19.1720	19.1500	19.1281	.000732
33	20.1420	20.1189	20.0958	20.0726	20.0495	20.0264	20.0033	19.9802	19.9571	19.9340	19.9108	19.8877	.000770
34	20.9337	20.9091	20.8846	20.8600	20.8355	20.8109	20.7863	20.7618	20.7372	20.7127	20.6881	20.6636	.000818
35	21.7431	21.7170	21.6909	21.6648	21.6387	21.6126	21.5865	21.5605	21.5344	21.5083	21.4822	21.4561	.000869
36	22.5719	22.5439	22.5158	22.4878	22.4598	22.4318	22.4037	22.3757	22.3477	22.3197	22.2916	22.2636	.000934
37	23.4179	23.3876	23.3573	23.3270	23.2967	23.2664	23.2361	23.2059	23.1756	23.1453	23.1150	23.0847	.001009
38	24.2782	24.2453	24.2123	24.1794	24.1465	24.1136	24.0806	24.0477	24.0148	23.9819	23.9490	23.9160	.001097
39	25.1532	25.1173	25.0814	25.0454	25.0095	24.9736	24.9377	24.9018	24.8659	24.8300	24.7940	24.7581	.001197
40	26.0408	26.0016	25.9623	25.9231	25.8839	25.8447	25.8054	25.7662	25.7270	25.6878	25.6485	25.6093	.001307
41	26.9403	26.8973	26.8543	26.8113	26.7684	26.7254	26.6824	26.6394	26.5964	26.5534	26.5105	26.4675	.001433
42	27.8504	27.8031	27.7558	27.7085	27.6612	27.6139	27.5666	27.5194	27.4721	27.4248	27.3775	27.3302	.001576
43	28.7699	28.7180	28.6661	28.6143	28.5624	28.5105	28.4586	28.4068	28.3549	28.3030	28.2511	28.1993	.001729
44	29.7038	29.6467	29.5897	29.5326	29.4756	29.4185	29.3615	29.3044	29.2474	29.1903	29.1333	29.0762	.001902
45	30.6545	30.5917	30.5289	30.4660	30.4032	30.3404	30.2776	30.2148	30.1520	30.0891	30.0263	29.9635	.002094
46	31.6233	31.5537	31.4842	31.4146	31.3451	31.2755	31.2060	31.1364	31.0668	30.9973	30.9277	30.8582	.002318
47	32.6092	32.5323	32.4553	32.3784	32.3014	32.2245	32.1475	32.0706	31.9937	31.9167	31.8398	31.7628	.002565
48	33.6120	33.5267	33.4415	33.3562	33.2710	33.1857	33.1005	33.0152	32.9300	32.8447	32.7595	32.6742	.002841
49	34.6291	34.5348	34.4405	34.3463	34.2520	34.1577	34.0634	33.9692	33.8749	33.7806	33.6863	33.5921	.003142
50	35.6588	35.5545	35.4502	35.3459	35.2416	35.1373	35.0330	34.9288	34.8245	34.7202	34.6159	34.5116	.003476
51	36.6997	36.5845	36.4693	36.3541	36.2390	36.1238	36.0086	35.8934	35.7782	35.6630	35.5479	35.4327	.003839
52	37.7511	37.6238	37.4965	37.3692	37.2419	37.1146	36.9873	36.8600	36.7327	36.6054	36.4781	36.3508	.004243
53	38.8092	38.6688	38.5285	38.3882	38.2478	38.1075	37.9672	37.8268	37.6865	37.5462	37.4058	37.2655	.004677
54	39.8740	39.7196	39.5652	39.4108	39.2564	39.1020	38.9476	38.7932	38.6388	38.4844	38.3300	38.1756	.005147
55	40.9440	40.7746	40.6052	40.4358	40.2664	40.0970	39.9275	39.7581	39.5887	39.4193	39.2499	39.0805	.005647
56	42.0211	41.8354	41.6496	41.4639	41.2782	41.0925	40.9067	40.7210	40.5353	40.3496	40.1638	39.9781	.006191
57	43.1037	42.9005	42.6973	42.4940	42.2908	42.0876	41.8844	41.6812	41.4780	41.2747	41.0715	40.8683	.006774
58	44.1905	43.9684	43.7464	43.5243	43.3023	43.0802	42.8581	42.6361	42.4140	42.1920	41.9699	41.7479	.007402
59	45.2817	45.0394	44.7971	44.5548	44.3125	44.0702	43.8279	43.5856	43.3433	43.1010	42.8587	42.6164	.008077
60	46.3780	46.1139	45.8498	45.5857	45.3217	45.0576	44.7935	44.5294	44.2653	44.0012	43.7372	43.4731	.008803
61	47.4828	47.1954	46.9080	46.6206	46.3332	46.0458	45.7584	45.4710	45.1836	44.8962	44.6088	44.3214	.009580
62	48.5985	48.2862	47.9740	47.6617	47.3494	47.0371	46.7248	46.4126	46.1003	45.7880	45.4757	45.1635	.010409
63	49.7274	49.3884	49.0494	48.7104	48.3715	48.0325	47.6935	47.3545	47.0155	46.6765	46.3376	45.9986	.011299
64	50.8713	50.5034	50.1356	49.7677	49.3999	49.0320	48.6642	48.2963	47.9285	47.5606	47.1928	46.8250	.012262
65	52.0302	51.6319	51.2336	50.8353	50.4370	50.0387	49.6403	49.2420	48.8437	48.4454	48.0471	47.6488	.013277
66	53.2110	52.7805	52.3500	51.9194	51.4889	51.0584	50.6278	50.1973	49.7668	49.3363	48.9057	48.4752	.014351
67	54.4234	53.9594	53.4953	53.0313	52.5673	52.1033	51.6393	51.1752	50.7112	50.2472	49.7831	49.3191	.015467
68	55.6815	55.1830	54.6846	54.1861	53.6877	53.1892	52.6908	52.1923	51.6939	51.1954	50.6970	50.1985	.016615
69	57.0074	56.4732	55.9390	55.4048	54.8706	54.3364	53.8022	53.2681	52.7339	52.1997	51.6655	51.1313	.017806
70	58.4201	57.8493	57.2786	56.7078	56.1371	55.5663	54.9956	54.4248	53.8541	53.2833	52.7126	52.1418	.019025
71	59.9513	59.3416	58.7319	58.1222	57.5125	56.9028	56.2931	55.6834	55.0737	54.4640	53.8543	53.2446	.020323
72	61.6150	60.9638	60.3127	59.6615	59.0104	58.3592	57.7081	57.0570	56.4058	55.7546	55.1035	54.4523	.021705
73	63.4285	62.7333	62.0381	61.3428	60.6476	59.9524	59.2572	58.5620	57.8668	57.1715	56.4763	55.7811	.023174
74	65.4116	64.6677	63.9237	63.1798	62.4359	61.6919	60.9480	60.2041	59.4601	58.7162	57.9723	57.2283	.024798
75	67.5636	66.7650	65.9664	65.1678	64.3692	63.5706	62.7720	61.9733	61.1747	60.3761	59.5775	58.7789	.026620
76	69.8710	69.0130	68.1551	67.2971	66.4392	65.5812	64.7232	63.8653	63.0073	62.1494	61.2914	60.4335	.028598
77	72.3398	71.4154	70.4911	69.5667	68.6424	67.7180	66.7937	65.8693	64.9450	64.0206	63.0963	62.1720	.030811
78	74.9542	73.9521	72.9501	71.9480	70.9460	69.9440	68.9419	67.9398	66.9378	65.9357	64.9337	63.9316	.033401
79	77.6490	76.5569	75.4647	74.3726	73.2805	72.1884	71.0962	70.0041	68.9120	67.8199	66.7277	65.6356	.036404
80	80.3439	79.1491	77.9543	76.7595	75.5647	74.3699	73.1750	71.9802	70.7854	69.5906	68.3958	67.2010	.039827
81	82.9598	81.6294	80.2989	78.9685	77.6380	76.3076	74.9771	73.6467	72.3163	70.9858	69.6554	68.3249	.044348
82	85.1649	83.6906	82.2163	80.7419	79.2676	77.7933	76.3189	74.8446	73.3703	71.8959	70.4216	68.9473	.049143
83	86.9339	85.4258	83.9176	82.4095	80.9014	79.3933	77.8851	76.3770	74.8689	73.3608	71.8526	70.3445	.050271
84	89.7626	88.4000	87.0374	85.6749	84.3123	82.9497	81.5871	80.2246	78.8620	77.4994	76.1368	74.7743	.045419
85 or 24	**96.1538**	**96.4743**	**96.7948**	**97.1153**	**97.4359**	**97.7564**	**98.0769**	**98.3974**	**98.7179**	**99.0384**	**99.3590**	**99.6795**	**.010684**
23	94.8936	94.8823	94.8709	94.8596	94.8482	94.8369	94.8255	94.8142	94.8029	94.7915	94.7802	94.7688	.000378
22	94.1802	94.1269	94.0737	94.0204	93.9672	93.9139	93.8606	93.8074	93.7541	93.7009	93.6476	93.5944	.001775
21	93.7646	93.6949	93.6252	93.5554	93.4857	93.4160	93 3463	93.2766	93.2069	93.1371	93.0674	92.9977	.002324
20	93.1492	93.0938	93.0384	92.9830	92.9276	92.8722	92.8168	92.7614	92.7060	92.6506	92.5952	92.5398	.001847
19	92.3881	92.3477	92.3073	92.2669	92.2265	92.1861	92.1456	92.1052	92.0648	92.0244	91.9840	91.9436	.001347
18	91.5478	91.5167	91.4856	91.4545	91.4235	91.3924	91.3613	91.3302	91.2991	91.2680	91.2370	91.2059	.001036
17	90.6448	90.6216	90.5984	90.5752	90.5520	90.5288	90.5056	90.4825	90.4593	90.4361	90.4129	90.3897	.000773
16	89.6977	89.6807	89.6637	89.6468	89.6298	89.6128	89.5958	89.5789	89.5619	89.5449	89.5280	89.5110	.000566
15	88.7264	88.7139	88.7014	88.6888	88.6763	88.6638	88.6513	88.6388	88.6263	88.6137	88.6012	88.5887	.000417
14	87.7392	87.7303	87.7214	87.7126	87.7037	87.6948	87.6860	87.6771	87.6682	87.6593	87.6504	87.6416	.000296
13	86.7380	86.7325	86.7270	86.7215	86.7160	86.7105	86.7050	86.6995	86.6940	86.6885	86.6830	86.6775	.000183
12	85.7316	85.7286	85.7257	85.7227	85.7197	85.7168	85.7138	85.7108	85.7079	85.7049	85.7019	85.6990	.000099
11	84.7253	84.7243	84.7233	84.7223	84.7213	84.7203	84.7193	84.7183	84.7173	84.7163	84.7153	84.7143	.000033
10	83.7176	83.7186	83.7195	83.7205	83.7215	83.7225	83.7234	83.7244	83.7254	83.7264	83.7273	83.7283	.000032
Age.	0	1	2	3	4	5	6	7	8	9	10	11	Day.

Age.	0	1	2	3	4	5	6	7	8	9	10	11	Day.
10	9.1141	9.0854	9.0567	9.0280	8.9993	8.9706	8.9420	8.9133	8.8846	8.8559	8.8272	8.7985	.000956
11	9.4560	9.4278	9.3996	9.3714	9.3432	9.3150	9.2867	9.2585	9.2303	9.2021	9.1739	9.1457	.000940
12	9.8093	9.7816	9.7539	9.7262	9.6985	9.6708	9.6431	9.6155	9.5878	9.5601	9.5324	9.5047	.000923
13	10.1748	10.1476	10.1203	10.0931	10.0659	10.0387	10.0114	9.9842	9.9570	9.9298	9.9025	9.8753	.000907
14	10.5532	10.5264	10.4997	10.4730	10.4462	10.4194	10.3927	10.3660	10.3392	10.3124	10.2857	10.2590	.000892
15	10.9454	10.9192	10.8929	10.8667	10.8405	10.8142	10.7880	10.7618	10.7355	10.7093	10.6831	10.6568	.000874
16	11.3537	11.3279	11.3020	11.2762	11.2504	11.2245	11.1987	11.1729	11.1470	11.1212	11.0954	11.0695	.000861
17	11.7760	11.7507	11.7255	11.7002	11.6749	11.6497	11.6244	11.5991	11.5739	11.5486	11.5233	11.4981	.000842
18	12.2155	12.1908	12.1660	12.1413	12.1165	12.0918	12.0670	12.0423	12.0176	11.9928	11.9681	11.9433	.000825
19	12.6734	12.6492	12.6251	12.6010	12.5768	12.5526	12.5285	12.5043	12.4802	12.4560	12.4319	12.4077	.000805
20	13.1505	13.1269	13.1033	13.0798	13.0562	13.0326	13.0090	12.9855	12.9619	12.9383	12.9147	12.8912	.000766
21	13.6493	13.6263	13.6033	13.5803	13.5573	13.5343	13.5113	13.4883	13.4653	13.4423	13.4193	13.3963	.000787
22	14.1698	14.1476	14.1254	14.1031	14.0809	14.0587	14.0365	14.0143	13.9921	13.9698	13.9476	13.9254	.000740
23	14.7151	14.6935	14.6720	14.6504	14.6288	14.6073	14.5857	14.5641	14.5426	14.5210	14.4994	14.4779	.000719
24	15.2856	15.2648	15.2440	15.2233	15.2025	15.1817	15.1610	15.1402	15.1194	15.0986	15.0778	15.0571	.000692
25	15.8839	15.8640	15.8441	15.8242	15.8043	15.7844	15.7645	15.7447	15.7248	15.7049	15.6850	15.6651	.000663
26	16.5122	16.4932	16.4742	16.4552	16.4362	16.4172	16.3982	16.3793	16.3603	16.3413	16.3223	16.3033	.000633
27	17.1724	17.1542	17.1361	17.1180	17.0998	17.0816	17.0635	17.0453	17.0272	17.0090	16.9909	16.9727	.000605
28	17.8652	17.8475	17.8299	17.8122	17.7946	17.7770	17.7593	17.7416	17.7240	17.7063	17.6887	17.6710	.000588
29	18.5886	18.5710	18.5534	18.5358	18.5183	18.5007	18.4831	18.4655	18.4479	18.4303	18.4128	18.3952	.000586
30	19.3391	19.3213	19.3034	19.2856	19.2677	19.2499	19.2320	19.2142	19.1964	19.1785	19.1607	19.1428	.000595
31	20.1144	20.0957	20.0771	20.0584	20.0398	20.0211	20.0024	19.9838	19.9651	19.9465	19.9278	19.9092	.000622
32	20.9101	20.8904	20.8708	20.8511	20.8315	20.8118	20.7922	20.7725	20.7529	20.7332	20.7136	20.6940	.000655
33	21.7262	21.7053	21.6843	21.6634	21.6425	21.6215	21.6006	21.5797	21.5587	21.5378	21.5169	21.4959	.000698
34	22.5615	22.5392	22.5170	22.4947	22.4724	22.4501	22.4278	22.4056	22.3833	22.3610	22.3387	22.3165	.000742
35	23.4166	23.3926	23.3686	23.3445	23.3205	23.2965	23.2725	23.2485	23.2245	23.2004	23.1764	23.1524	.000800
36	24.2900	24.2639	24.2378	24.2117	24.1857	24.1596	24.1335	24.1074	24.0813	24.0552	24.0292	24.0031	.000869
37	25.1804	25.1519	25.1234	25.0949	25.0664	25.0379	25.0094	24.9809	24.9524	24.9239	24.8954	24.8669	.000950
38	26.0850	26.0537	26.0225	25.9912	25.9600	25.9287	25.8975	25.8662	25.8350	25.8037	25.7725	25.7412	.001042
39	27.0045	26.9702	26.9359	26.9016	26.8674	26.8331	26.7988	26.7645	26.7302	26.6960	26.6617	26.6274	.001143
40	27.9378	27.9000	27.8623	27.8245	27.7868	27.7490	27.7113	27.6735	27.6358	27.5980	27.5603	27.5225	.001258
41	28.8830	28.8413	28.7995	28.7578	28.7161	28.6743	28.6326	28.5909	28.5491	28.5074	28.4657	28.4239	.001391
42	29.8382	29.7922	29.7463	29.7003	29.6543	29.6084	29.5624	29.5164	29.4705	29.4245	29.3785	29.3326	.001532
43	30.8059	30.7551	30.7043	30.6535	30.6027	30.5519	30.5011	30.4503	30.3995	30.3487	30.2979	30.2471	.001693
44	31.7874	31.7312	31.6750	31.6188	31.5626	31.5064	31.4502	31.3941	31.3379	31.2817	31.2255	31.1693	.001873
45	32.7852	32.7227	32.6601	32.5976	32.5351	32.4726	32.4100	32.3475	32.2850	32.2225	32.1600	32.0974	.002084
46	33.7966	33.7271	33.6576	33.5880	33.5185	33.4490	33.3795	33.3100	33.2405	33.1710	33.1014	33.0319	.002317
47	34.8244	34.7470	34.6696	34.5923	34.5149	34.4375	34.3601	34.2828	34.2054	34.1280	34.0506	33.9733	.002579
48	35.8657	35.7798	35.6938	35.6079	35.5219	35.4360	35.3500	35.2641	35.1782	35.0922	35.0063	34.9203	.002865
49	36.9205	36.8251	36.7296	36.6342	36.5388	36.4433	36.3479	36.2525	36.1570	36.0616	35.9662	35.8707	.003181
50	37.9848	37.8790	37.7733	37.6675	37.5618	37.4560	37.3502	37.2445	37.1387	37.0330	36.9272	36.8215	.003525
51	39.0590	38.9417	38.8244	38.7071	38.5899	38.4726	38.3553	38.2380	38.1207	38.0034	37.8862	37.7689	.003909
52	40.1386	40.0090	39.8793	39.7497	39.6201	39.4904	39.3608	39.2312	39.1015	38.9719	38.8423	38.7126	.004321
53	41.2248	41.0818	40.9388	40.7958	40.6528	40.5098	40.3668	40.2238	40.0808	39.9378	39.7948	39.6518	.004767
54	42.3161	42.1589	42.0016	41.8444	41.6872	41.5300	41.3727	41.2155	41.0583	40.9011	40.7438	40.5866	.005241
55	43.4136	43.2409	43.0682	42.8955	42.7228	42.5501	42.3774	42.2047	42.0320	41.8593	41.6866	41.5139	.005757
56	44.5154	44.3261	44.1368	43.9475	43.7582	43.5689	43.3796	43.1904	43.0011	42.8118	42.6225	42.4332	.006310
57	45.6222	45.4151	45.2080	45.0009	44.7938	44.5867	44.3796	44.1725	43.9654	43.7583	43.5512	43.3441	.006903
58	46.7324	46.5061	46.2799	46.0536	45.8274	45.6011	45.3749	45.1486	44.9224	44.6961	44.4699	44.2436	.007542
59	47.8465	47.5996	47.3528	47.1060	46.8591	46.6122	46.3654	46.1185	45.8717	45.6248	45.3780	45.1311	.008228
60	48.9645	48.6956	48.4267	48.1578	47.8890	47.6201	47.3512	47.0823	46.8134	46.5445	46.2757	46.0068	.008963
61	50.0912	49.7989	49.5065	49.2142	48.9219	48.6296	48.3372	48.0449	47.7526	47.4603	47.1680	46.8756	.009744
62	51.2294	50.9117	50.5941	50.2764	49.9588	49.6411	49.3235	49.0058	48.6882	48.3705	48.0529	47.7352	.010588
63	52.3795	52.0346	51.6897	51.3447	50.9998	50.6549	50.3100	49.9651	49.6202	49.2752	48.9303	48.5854	.011497
64	53.5412	53.1675	52.7938	52.4201	52.0465	51.6728	51.2991	50.9254	50.5517	50.1780	49.8044	49.4307	.012456
65	54.7222	54.3181	53.9140	53.5099	53.1058	52.7017	52.2976	51.8936	51.4895	51.0854	50.6813	50.2772	.013470
66	55.9293	55.4936	55.0579	54.6221	54.1864	53.7507	53.3150	52.8793	52.4436	52.0078	51.5721	51.1364	.014524
67	57.1789	56.7107	56.2426	55.7744	55.3063	54.8381	54.3700	53.9018	53.4337	52.9655	52.4974	52.0292	.015605
68	58.4914	57.9896	57.4878	56.9860	56.4842	55.9824	55.4806	54.9789	54.4771	53.9753	53.4735	52.9717	.016726
69	59.8863	59.3502	58.8140	58.2779	57.7418	57.2057	56.6695	56.1334	55.5973	55.0612	54.5250	53.9889	.017871
70	61.3913	60.8186	60.2459	59.6732	59.1006	58.5279	57.9552	57.3825	56.8098	56.2371	55.6645	55.0918	.019089
71	63.0214	62.4098	61.7982	61.1866	60.5751	59.9635	59.3519	58.7403	58.1287	57.5171	56.9056	56.2940	.020386
72	64.7918	64.1389	63.4860	62.8331	62.1802	61.5273	60.8744	60.2215	59.5686	58.9157	58.2628	57.6099	.021763
73	66.7214	66.0228	65.3243	64.6257	63.9271	63.2286	62.5300	61.8314	61.1329	60.4343	59.7357	59.0372	.023285
74	68.8091	68.0592	67.3094	66.5595	65.8096	65.0598	64.3099	63.5600	62.8102	62.0603	61.3104	60.5606	.024995
75	71.0414	70.2359	69.4304	68.6250	67.8195	67.0140	66.2085	65.4030	64.5975	63.7920	62.9866	62.1811	.026849
76	73.4246	72.5570	71.6893	70.8216	69.9540	69.0863	68.2187	67.3510	66.4834	65.6157	64.7481	63.8804	.028922
77	75.9411	75.0006	74.0600	73.1195	72.1789	71.2384	70.2978	69.3573	68.4168	67.4762	66.5357	65.5951	.031351
78	78.5275	77.5025	76.4775	75.4525	74.4275	73.4025	72.3775	71.3525	70.3275	69.3025	68.2775	67.2525	.034167
79	81.1114	79.9902	78.8690	77.7478	76.6266	75.5054	74.3841	73.2629	72.1417	71.0205	69.8993	68.7781	.037373
80	83.6161	82.3677	81.1193	79.8710	78.6226	77.3742	76.1258	74.8774	73.6290	72.3806	71.1323	69.8839	.041613
81	85.7266	84.3440	82.9615	81.5789	80.1963	78.8138	77.4312	76.0486	74.6661	73.2835	71.9009	70.5184	.046085
82	87.4217	86.0103	84.5990	83.1876	81.7762	80.3648	78.9534	77.5421	76.1307	74.7193	73.3080	71.8966	.047046
83	90.1143	88.8444	87.5745	86.3047	85.0348	83.7649	82.4950	81.2252	79.9553	78.6854	77.4155	76.1457	.042329
84 or 25	**96.1538**	**96.4743**	**96.7948**	**97.1153**	**97.4359**	**97.7564**	**98.0769**	**98.3974**	**98.7179**	**99.0384**	**99.3590**	**99.6795**	**.010684**
24	94.8847	94.8710	94.8573	94.8436	94.8299	94.8162	94.8025	94.7889	94.7752	94.7615	94.7478	94.7341	.000456
23	94.2299	94.1688	94.1078	94.0467	93.9857	93.9246	93.8635	93.8025	93.7414	93.6804	93.6193	93.5583	.002035
22	93.7491	93.6716	93.5941	93.5166	93.4391	93.3616	93.2842	93.2067	93.1292	93.0517	92.9742	92.8967	.002583
21	93.1307	93.0729	93.0151	92.9573	92.8996	92.8418	92.7840	92.7262	92.6684	92.6106	92.5529	92.4951	.001926
20	92.3657	92.3231	92.2805	92.2379	92.1953	92.1527	92.1100	92.0674	92.0248	91.9822	91.9396	91.8970	.001420
19	91.5213	91.4882	91.4550	91.4219	91.3888	91.3556	91.3225	91.2894	91.2562	91.2231	91.1900	91.1568	.001104
18	90.6141	90.5890	90.5639	90.5388	90.5137	90.4886	90.4635	90.4385	90.4134	90.3883	90.3632	90.3381	.000836
17	89.6632	89.6444	89.6257	89.6069	89.5881	89.5694	89.5506	89.5318	89.5131	89.4943	89.4755	89.4568	.000625
16	88.6883	88.6741	88.6598	88.6456	88.6314	88.6172	88.6030	88.5887	88.5745	88.5603	88.5460	88.5318	.000474
15	87.6978	87.6873	87.6768	87.6663	87.6559	87.6454	87.6349	87.6244	87.6139	87.6034	87.5930	87.5825	.000349
14	86.6937	86.6867	86.6796	86.6726	86.6655	86.6585	86.6514	86.6444	86.6374	86.6303	86.6233	86.6162	.000235
13	85.6845	85.6801	85.6756	85.6712	85.6668	85.6624	85.6580	85.6535	85.6491	85.6447	85.6402	85.6358	.000147
12	84.6759	84.6735	84.6711	84.6687	84.6664	84.6640	84.6616	84.6592	84.6568	84.6544	84.6521	84.6497	.000079
11	83.6663	83.6660	83.6656	83.6652	83.6649	83.6645	83.6642	83.6638	83.6635	83.6631	83.6628	83.6624	.000012
10	82.6547	82.6564	82.6580	82.6597	82.6614	82.6630	82.6647	82.6664	82.6680	82.6697	82.6714	82.6730	.000053
Age.	0	1	2	3	4	5	6	7	8	9	10	11	Day.

Age.	0	1	2	3	4	5	6	7	8	9	10	11	Day
10	9.8127	9.7859	9.7592	9.7324	9.7056	9.6789	9.6521	9.6253	9.5986	9.5718	9.5450	9.5183	.000892
11	10.1806	10.1544	10.1282	10.1020	10.0758	10.0496	10.0234	9.9973	9.9711	9.9449	9.9187	9.8925	.000873
12	10.5613	10.5356	10.5100	10.4843	10.4587	10.4330	10.4074	10.3817	10.3561	10.3304	10.3048	10.2791	.000855
13	10.9547	10.9296	10.9045	10.8794	10.8543	10.8292	10.8040	10.7789	10.7538	10.7287	10.7036	10.6785	.000837
14	11.3622	11.3377	11.3131	11.2886	11.2640	11.2395	11.2150	11.1904	11.1659	11.1413	11.1168	11.0922	.000818
15	11.7850	11.7610	11.7370	11.7130	11.6891	11.6651	11.6411	11.6171	11.5931	11.5691	11.5452	11.5212	.000799
16	12.2237	12.2003	12.1768	12.1534	12.1300	12.1066	12.0831	12.0597	12.0363	12.0129	11.9894	11.9660	.000781
17	12.6796	12.6568	12.6339	12.6111	12.5883	12.5654	12.5426	12.5198	12.4969	12.4741	12.4513	12.4284	.000761
18	13.1535	13.1313	13.1091	13.0870	13.0648	13.0426	13.0204	12.9982	12.9760	12.9538	12.9317	12.9095	.000739
19	13.6479	13.6263	13.6048	13.5832	13.5617	13.5401	13.5186	13.4970	13.4755	13.4540	13.4324	13.4108	.000718
20	14.1624	14.1416	14.1207	14.0999	14.0790	14.0582	14.0373	14.0165	13.9957	13.9748	13.9540	13.9331	.000695
21	14.7006	14.6808	14.6609	14.6411	14.6212	14.6014	14.5815	14.5617	14.5419	14.5220	14.5022	14.4823	.000661
22	15.2642	15.2449	15.2256	15.2064	15.1871	15.1678	15.1485	15.1293	15.1100	15.0907	15.0714	15.0522	.000642
23	15.8526	15.8342	15.8158	15.7974	15.7791	15.7607	15.7423	15.7239	15.7055	15.6871	15.6688	15.6504	.000613
24	16.4697	16.4523	16.4349	16.4175	16.4001	16.3827	16.3652	16.3478	16.3304	16.3130	16.2956	16.2782	.000580
25	17.1174	17.1010	17.0846	17.0682	17.0518	17.0354	17.0190	17.0025	16.9861	16.9697	16.9533	16.9369	.000547
26	17.7972	17.7817	17.7663	17.7508	17.7353	17.7199	17.7044	17.6889	17.6735	17.6580	17.6425	17.6271	.000515
27	18.5103	18.4954	18.4806	18.4657	18.4508	18.4360	18.4211	18.4062	18.3914	18.3765	18.3616	18.3468	.000495
28	19.2540	19.2393	19.2246	19.2099	19.1952	19.1805	19.1658	19.1511	19.1364	19.1217	19.1070	19.0923	.000490
29	20.0252	20.0104	19.9955	19.9807	19.9659	19.9511	19.9362	19.9214	19.9066	19.8918	19.8770	19.8621	.000494
30	20.8221	20.8066	20.7911	20.7756	20.7601	20.7446	20.7291	20.7136	20.6981	20.6826	20.6671	20.6516	.000517
31	21.6397	21.6234	21.6070	21.5907	21.5743	21.5580	21.5416	21.5253	21.5090	21.4926	21.4763	21.4599	.000545
32	22.4784	22.4609	22.4434	22.4260	22.4085	22.3910	22.3735	22.3560	22.3385	22.3210	22.3036	22.2861	.000583
33	23.3366	23.3180	23.2993	23.2807	23.2620	23.2434	23.2247	23.2061	23.1875	23.1688	23.1502	23.1315	.000621
34	24.2167	24.1965	24.1762	24.1560	24.1357	24.1155	24.0952	24.0750	24.0548	24.0345	24.0143	23.9940	.000675
35	25.1150	25.0929	25.0708	25.0487	25.0266	25.0045	24.9823	24.9602	24.9381	24.9160	24.8939	24.8718	.000737
36	26.0314	26.0071	25.9828	25.9584	25.9341	25.9098	25.8855	25.8612	25.8369	25.8125	25.7882	25.7639	.000810
37	26.9644	26.9376	26.9107	26.8839	26.8571	26.8302	26.8034	26.7766	26.7497	26.7229	26.6961	26.6692	.000894
38	27.9118	27.8822	27.8526	27.8230	27.7933	27.7637	27.7341	27.7045	27.6749	27.6452	27.6156	27.5860	.000987
39	28.8754	28.8426	28.8097	28.7769	28.7441	28.7113	28.6784	28.6456	28.6128	28.5800	28.5471	28.5143	.001094
40	29.8596	29.8225	29.7854	29.7483	29.7112	29.6741	29.6370	29.5999	29.5628	29.5257	29.4886	29.4515	.001237
41	30.8408	30.8004	30.7599	30.7195	30.6791	30.6386	30.5982	30.5578	30.5173	30.4769	30.4365	30.3960	.001348
42	31.8419	31.7970	31.7521	31.7072	31.6623	31.6174	31.5724	31.5275	31.4826	31.4377	31.3928	31.3479	.001497
43	32.8549	32.8050	32.7550	32.7050	32.6551	32.6051	32.5552	32.5052	32.4553	32.4053	32.3554	32.3054	.001665
44	33.8813	33.8254	33.7695	33.7135	33.6576	33.6017	33.5458	33.4899	33.4340	33.3780	33.3221	33.2662	.001864
45	34.9194	34.8569	34.7944	34.7319	34.6694	34.6069	34.5444	34.4820	34.4195	34.3570	34.2945	34.2320	.002083
46	35.9704	35.9005	35.8305	35.7606	35.6906	35.6207	35.5507	35.4808	35.4109	35.3409	35.2710	35.2010	.002331
47	37.0344	36.9563	36.8783	36.8002	36.7222	36.6441	36.5660	36.4880	36.4099	36.3319	36.2538	36.1758	.002602
48	38.1110	38.0239	37.9368	37.8498	37.7627	37.6756	37.5885	37.5015	37.4144	37.3273	37.2402	37.1532	.002902
49	39.1980	39.1011	39.0043	38.9074	38.8105	38.7137	38.6168	38.5199	38.4231	38.3262	38.2293	38.1325	.003228
50	40.2932	40.1854	40.0775	39.9697	39.8619	39.7541	39.6462	39.5384	39.4306	39.3228	39.2150	39.1071	.003594
51	41.3931	41.2735	41.1540	41.0344	40.9148	40.7953	40.6757	40.5561	40.4366	40.3170	40.1974	40.0779	.003985
52	42.4981	42.3659	42.2336	42.1014	41.9692	41.8369	41.7047	41.5725	41.4402	41.3080	41.1758	41.0435	.004408
53	43.6083	43.4625	43.3168	43.1710	43.0253	42.8795	42.7337	42.5880	42.4422	42.2965	42.1507	42.0050	.004858
54	44.7244	44.5640	44.4035	44.2431	44.0826	43.9222	43.7617	43.6013	43.4409	43.2804	43.1200	42.9595	.005348
55	45.8437	45.6675	45.4914	45.3152	45.1390	44.9629	44.7867	44.6105	44.4344	44.2582	44.0820	43.9059	.005872
56	46.9669	46.7738	46.5807	46.3877	46.1946	46.0015	45.8084	45.6154	45.4223	45.2292	45.0361	44.8431	.006436
57	48.0941	47.8829	47.6717	47.4605	47.2494	47.0382	46.8270	46.6158	46.4046	46.1934	45.9823	45.7711	.007039
58	49.2240	48.9933	48.7627	48.5320	48.3013	48.0707	47.8400	47.6093	47.3787	47.1480	46.9173	46.6867	.007687
59	50.3567	50.1052	49.8537	49.6022	49.3507	49.0992	48.8476	48.5961	48.3446	48.0931	47.8416	47.5901	.008383
60	51.4934	51.2197	50.9461	50.6724	50.3988	50.1251	49.8515	49.5778	49.3042	49.0305	48.7569	48.4832	.009122
61	52.6405	52.3429	52.0452	51.7476	51.4500	51.1524	50.8547	50.5571	50.2595	49.9619	49.6642	49.3666	.009921
62	53.7958	53.4724	53.1490	52.8256	52.5022	52.1788	51.8554	51.5320	51.2086	50.8852	50.5618	50.2384	.010780
63	54.9604	54.6098	54.2593	53.9087	53.5582	53.2076	52.8571	52.5065	52.1560	51.8054	51.4549	51.1043	.011685
64	56.1411	55.7618	55.3825	55.0033	54.6240	54.2447	53.8654	53.4862	53.1069	52.7276	52.3483	51.9691	.012642
65	57.3449	56.9358	56.5267	56.1176	55.7085	55.2994	54.8903	54.4812	54.0721	53.6630	53.2539	52.8448	.013637
66	58.5853	58.1456	57.7059	57.2662	56.8265	56.3868	55.9471	55.5075	55.0678	54.6281	54.1884	53.7487	.014656
67	59.8848	59.4134	58.9421	58.4707	57.9993	57.5280	57.0566	56.5852	56.1139	55.6425	55.1711	54.6998	.015712
68	61.2612	60.7575	60.2539	59.7502	59.2466	58.7430	58.2393	57.7356	57.2320	56.7283	56.2247	55.7210	.016788
69	62.7421	62.2041	61.6661	61.1281	60.5902	60.0522	59.5142	58.9762	58.4382	57.9002	57.3623	56.8243	.017933
70	64.3393	63.7648	63.1903	62.6158	62.0413	61.4668	60.8923	60.3178	59.7433	59.1688	58.5943	58.0198	.019150
71	66.0689	65.4556	64.8423	64.2291	63.6158	63.0025	62.3892	61.7760	61.1627	60.5494	59.9361	59.3229	.020442
72	67.9476	67.2915	66.6354	65.9792	65.3231	64.6670	64.0109	63.3548	62.6987	62.0425	61.3864	60.7303	.021870
73	69.9741	69.2699	68.5656	67.8614	67.1571	66.4529	65.7486	65.0444	64.3402	63.6359	62.9317	62.2274	.023475
74	72.1355	71.3790	70.6226	69.8661	69.1097	68.3532	67.5968	66.8403	66.0839	65.3274	64.5710	63.8145	.025215
75	74.4367	73.6220	72.8072	71.9925	71.1777	70.3630	69.5482	68.7335	67.9188	67.1040	66.2893	65.4745	.027158
76	76.8619	75.9788	75.0957	74.2126	73.3295	72.4464	71.5632	70.6801	69.7970	68.9139	68.0308	67.1477	.029437
77	79.3482	78.3858	77.4233	76.4609	75.4985	74.5361	73.5736	72.6112	71.6488	70.6864	69 7240	68.7615	.032081
78	81.8255	80.7728	79.7201	78.6674	77.6147	76.5620	75.5092	74.4565	73.4038	72.3511	71.2984	70.2457	.035090
79	84.2248	83.0526	81.8804	80.7082	79.5360	78.3638	77.1916	76.0194	74.8472	73.6750	72.5028	71.3306	.039073
80	86.2453	84.9474	83.6495	82.3515	81.0536	79.7557	78.4578	77.1599	75.8620	74.5640	73.2661	71.9682	.043264
81	87.8680	86.5452	85.2223	83.8995	82.5767	81.2538	79.9310	78.6082	77.2853	75.9625	74.6397	73.3168	.044094
82	90.4339	89.2482	88.0624	86.8767	85.6909	84.5052	83.3194	82.1337	80.9480	79.7622	78.5765	77.3907	.039525
83 or 26	**96.1538**	**96.4743**	**96.7948**	**97.1153**	**97.4359**	**97.7564**	**98.0769**	**98.3974**	**98.7179**	**99.0384**	**99.3590**	**99.6795**	**.010684**
25	94.8754	94.8592	94.8431	94.8270	94.8108	94.7946	94.7785	94.7623	94.7462	94.7300	94.7139	94.6977	.000538
24	94.2163	94.1525	94.0888	94.0250	93.9613	93.8975	93.8338	93.7700	93.7063	93.6425	93.5788	93.5150	.002125
23	93 7326	93.6577	93.5828	93.5078	93.4329	93.3580	93.2831	93.2082	93.1333	93.0583	92.9834	92.9085	.002497
22	93.1110	93.0507	92.9905	92.9302	92.8700	92.8097	92.7495	92.6892	92.6290	92.5687	92.5085	92.4482	.002008
21	92.3416	92.2967	92.2519	92.2070	92.1622	92.1173	92.0725	92.0276	91.9828	91.9380	91.8931	91.8482	.001495
20	91.4931	91.4579	91.4226	91.3874	91.3522	91.3169	91.2817	91.2465	91.2112	91.1760	91.1408	91.1055	.001174
19	90.5821	90.5550	90.5279	90.5008	90.4737	90.4466	90.4195	90.3925	90.3654	90.3383	90.3112	90.2841	.000903
18	89.6270	89.6063	89.5857	89.5650	89.5444	89.5237	89.5031	89.4824	89.4618	89.4411	89.4205	89.3998	.000688
17	88.6485	88.6325	88.6165	88.6005	88.5845	88.5685	88.5524	88.5364	88.5204	88.5044	88.4884	88.4724	.000533
16	87.6544	87.6422	87.6300	87.6179	87.6057	87.5935	87.5813	87.5692	87.5570	87.5448	87.5326	87.5205	.000406
15	86.6471	86.6385	86.6298	86.6212	86.6125	86.6039	86.5952	86.5866	86.5780	86.5693	86.5607	86.5520	.000288
14	85.6353	85.6293	85.6234	85.6174	85.6114	85.6055	85.5995	85.5935	85.5876	85.5816	85.5756	85.5697	.000199
13	84.6240	84.6202	84.6163	84.6125	84.6087	84.6048	84.6010	84.5972	84.5933	84.5895	84.5857	84.5818	.000128
12	83.6123	83.6106	83.6088	83.6071	83.6054	83.6037	83.6020	83.6002	83.5985	83.5968	83.5950	83.5933	.000057
11	82.5990	82.5993	82.5997	82.6000	82.6004	82.6007	82.6011	82.6014	82.6018	82.6021	82.6025	82.6028	.000012
10	81.5831	81.5855	81.5879	81.5903	81.5927	81.5951	81.5974	81.5998	81.6022	81.6046	81.6070	81.6094	.000080
Age.	0	1	2	3	4	5	6	7	8	9	10	11	Day.

Age.	0	1	2	3	4	5	6	7	8	9	10	11	Day.
10	10.5344	10.5096	10.4849	10.4601	10.4353	10.4106	10.3858	10.3610	10.3363	10.3115	10.2867	10.2620	.000825
11	10.9294	10.9052	10.8811	10.8569	10.8327	10.8086	10.7844	10.7602	10.7361	10.7119	10.6877	10.6636	.000805
12	11.3378	11.3142	11.2907	11.2671	11.2436	11.2200	11.1964	11.1729	11.1493	11.1258	11.1022	11.0787	.000785
13	11.7600	11.7371	11.7142	11.6912	11.6683	11.6454	11.6225	11.5996	11.5767	11.5537	11.5308	11.5079	.000764
14	12.1977	12.1754	12.1531	12.1308	12.1085	12.0862	12.0638	12.0415	12.0192	11.9969	11.9746	11.9523	.000743
15	12.6516	12.6299	12.6082	12.5866	12.5649	12.5432	12.5215	12.4999	12.4782	12.4565	12.4348	12.4132	.000722
16	13.1226	13.1016	13.0806	13.0595	13.0385	13.0175	12.9965	12.9755	12.9545	12.9334	12.9124	12.8914	.000700
17	13.6124	13.5921	13.5718	13.5515	13.5313	13.5110	13.4907	13.4704	13.4501	13.4298	13.4096	13.3893	.000676
18	14.1222	14.1026	14.0831	14.0635	14.0439	14.0244	14.0048	13.9852	13.9657	13.9461	13.9265	13.9070	.000652
19	14.6537	14.6349	14.6160	14.5972	14.5784	14.5596	14.5407	14.5219	14.5031	14.4843	14.4654	14.4466	.000627
20	15.2071	15.1892	15.1714	15.1535	15.1356	15.1178	15.0999	15.0820	15.0642	15.0463	15.0284	15.0106	.000595
21	15.7898	15.7726	15.7553	15.7381	15.7209	15.7037	15.6864	15.6692	15.6520	15.6348	15.6175	15.6003	.000574
22	16.3940	16.3779	16.3618	16.3457	16.3296	16.3135	16.2973	16.2812	16.2651	16.2490	16.2329	16.2168	.000537
23	17.0283	17.0133	16.9982	16.9832	16.9682	16.9531	16.9381	16.9231	16.9080	16.8930	16.8780	16.8629	.000501
24	17.6942	17.6802	17.6663	17.6523	17.6384	17.6244	17.6105	17.5965	17.5826	17.5686	17.5547	17.5407	.000465
25	18.3927	18.3798	18.3669	18.3539	18.3410	18.3281	18.3152	18.3023	18.2894	18.2764	18.2635	18.2506	.000430
26	19.1245	19.1123	19.1001	19.0878	19.0756	19.0634	19.0512	19.0390	19.0268	19.0145	19.0023	18.9901	.000407
27	19.8875	19.8756	19.8636	19.8517	19.8398	19.8279	19.8160	19.8040	19.7921	19.7802	19.7682	19.7563	.000397
28	20.6782	20.6662	20.6543	20.6423	20.6304	20.6184	20.6065	20.5945	20.5826	20.5706	20.5587	20.5467	.000398
29	21.4950	21.4825	21.4700	21.4575	21.4450	21.4325	21.4200	21.4075	21.3950	21.3825	21.3700	21.3575	.000417
30	22.3333	22.3201	22.3069	22.2936	22.2804	22.2672	22.2540	22.2408	22.2276	22.2143	22.2011	22.1879	.000440
31	23.1928	23.1786	23.1644	23.1502	23.1360	23.1218	23.1076	23.0934	23.0792	23.0650	23.0508	23.0366	.000473
32	24.0727	24.0574	24.0422	24.0270	24.0117	23.9964	23.9812	23.9660	23.9507	23.9354	23.9202	23.9050	.000508
33	24.9745	24.9579	24.9412	24.9246	24.9080	24.8913	24.8747	24.8581	24.8414	24.8248	24.8082	24.7915	.000554
34	25.8963	25.8780	25.8596	25.8413	25.8229	25.8046	25.7862	25.7679	25.7496	25.7312	25.7129	25.6945	.000611
35	26.8363	26.8160	26.7956	26.7753	26.7549	26.7346	26.7142	26.6939	26.6736	26.6532	26.6329	26.6125	.000678
36	27.7939	27.7713	27.7486	27.7259	27.7033	27.6806	27.6579	27.6353	27.6126	27.5899	27.5673	27.5446	.000753
37	28.7684	28.7432	28.7179	28.6927	28.6675	28.6422	28.6170	28.5918	28.5665	28.5413	28.5161	28.4908	.000841
38	29.7583	29.7301	29.7019	29.6737	29.6456	29.6174	29.5892	29.5610	29.5328	29.5046	29.4765	29.4483	.000939
39	30.7639	30.7323	30.7007	30.6690	30.6374	30.6058	30.5742	30.5426	30.5110	30.4793	30.4477	30.4161	.001054
40	31.7821	31.7469	31.7116	31.6764	31.6412	31.6059	31.5707	31.5355	31.5002	31.4650	31.4298	31.3945	.001174
41	32.8142	32.7748	32.7354	32.6960	32.6567	32.6173	32.5779	32.5385	32.4991	32.4597	32.4204	32.3810	.001313
42	33.8584	33.8143	33.7703	33.7262	33.6821	33.6381	33.5940	33.5499	33.5059	33.4618	33.4177	33.3737	.001469
43	34.9139	34.8643	34.8146	34.7649	34.7153	34.6656	34.6159	34.5663	34.5166	34.4669	34.4173	34.3676	.001653
44	35.9785	35.9226	35.8667	35.8109	35.7550	35.6991	35.6432	35.5874	35.5315	35.4756	35.4197	35.3639	.001862
45	37.0540	36.9911	36.9282	36.8653	36.8024	36.7395	36.6766	36.6137	36.5508	36.4879	36.4250	36.3621	.002097
46	38.1391	38.0685	37.9979	37.9272	37.8566	37.7860	37.7154	37.6448	37.5742	37.5035	37.4329	37.3623	.002354
47	39.2362	39.1570	39.0779	38.9987	38.9195	38.8404	38.7612	38.6820	38.6029	38.5237	38.4445	38.3654	.002639
48	40.3428	40.2543	40.1658	40.0773	39.9888	39.9003	39.8118	39.7234	39.6349	39.5464	39.4579	39.3694	.002950
49	41.4582	41.3593	41.2604	41 1615	41.0627	40.9638	40.8649	40.7660	40.6671	40.5682	40.4694	40.3705	.003296
50	42.5768	42.4667	42.3567	42.2466	42.1366	42.0265	41.9165	41.8064	41.6964	41.5863	41.4763	41.3662	.003668
51	43.6999	43.5777	43.4556	43.3335	43.2114	43.0893	42.9671	42.8450	42.7229	42.6008	42.4786	42.3565	.004071
52	44.8264	44.6915	44.5565	44.4216	44.2867	44.1517	44.0168	43.8819	43.7469	43.6120	43.4771	43.3421	.004498
53	45.9588	45.8099	45.6610	45.5121	45.3632	45.2143	45.0654	44.9165	44.7676	44.6187	44.4698	44.3209	.004963
54	47.0941	46.9303	46.7664	46.6026	46.4388	46.2750	46.1111	45.9473	45.7835	45.6197	45.4558	45.2920	.005461
55	48.2322	48.0523	47.8725	47.6926	47.5128	47.3329	47.1530	46.9732	46.7933	46.6135	46.4336	46.2538	.005995
56	49.3720	49.1750	48.9781	48.7811	48.5842	48.3872	48.1902	47.9933	47.7963	47.5994	47.4024	47.2055	.006565
57	50.5171	50.3016	50.0861	49.8707	49.6552	49.4397	49.2242	49.0088	48.7933	48.5778	48.3623	48.1469	.007182
58	51.6627	51.4275	51.0923	50.9571	50.7219	50.4867	50.2515	50.0163	49.7811	49.5459	49.3107	49.0755	.007840
59	52.8110	52.5549	52.2987	52.0426	51.7865	51.5303	51.2742	51.0181	50.7619	50.5058	50.2497	49.9935	.008543
60	53.9651	53.6863	53.4075	53.1287	52.8499	52.5711	52.2923	52.0136	51.7348	51.4560	51.1772	50.8984	.009293
61	55.1262	54.8230	54.5198	54.2166	53.9135	53.6103	53.3071	53.0039	52.7007	52.3975	52.0944	51.7912	.010106
62	56.2932	55.9643	55.6355	55.3066	54.9778	54.6490	54.3201	53.9912	53.6624	53.3335	53.0047	52.6758	.010962
63	57.4737	57.1177	56.7618	56.4058	56.0499	55.6940	55.3380	54.9820	54.6261	54.2701	53.9142	53.5582	.011865
64	58.6739	58.2898	57.9057	57.5216	57.1375	56.7534	56.3692	55.9851	55.6010	55.2169	54.8328	54.4487	.012803
65	59.9074	59.4945	59.0815	58.6686	58.2557	57.8427	57.4298	57.0169	56.6039	56.1910	55.7781	55.3651	.013764
66	61.1936	60.7508	60.3080	59.8652	59.4224	58.9796	58.5368	58.0940	57.6512	57.2084	56.7656	56.3228	.014760
67	62.5521	62.0789	61.6058	61.1326	60.6595	60.1863	59.7131	59.2400	58.7668	58.2937	57.8205	57.3474	.015772
68	64.0087	63.5033	62.9978	62.4924	61.9869	61.4815	60.9760	60.4706	59.9652	59.4597	58.9543	58.4488	.016848
69	65.5755	65.0358	64.4960	63.9563	63.4166	62.8769	62.3371	61.7974	61.2577	60.7180	60.1782	59.6385	.017991
70	67.2656	66.6895	66.1134	65.5372	64.9611	64.3850	63.8089	63.2328	62.6567	62.0805	61.5044	60.9283	.019204
71	69.0961	68.4797	67.8634	67.2470	66.6307	66.0143	65.3980	64.7816	64.1653	63.5490	62.9326	62.3162	.020545
72	71.0648	70.4032	69.7417	69.0801	68.4186	67.7570	67.0954	66.4339	65.7723	65.1108	64.4492	63.7877	.022052
73	73.1587	72.4482	71.7376	71.0271	70.3165	69.6060	68.8954	68.1849	67.4744	66.7638	66.0533	65.3427	.023685
74	75.3828	74.6175	73.8522	73.0869	72.3216	71.5563	70.7910	70.0258	69.2605	68.4952	67.7299	66.9646	.025510
75	77.7209	76.8914	76.0619	75.2324	74.4029	73.5734	72.7439	71.9144	71.0849	70.2554	69.4259	68.5964	.027650
76	80.1137	79.2097	78.3057	77.4017	76.4978	75.5938	74.6898	73.7858	72.8818	71.9778	71.0739	70.1699	.030133
77	82.4927	81.5039	80.5150	79.5262	78.5373	77.5485	76.5596	75.5708	74.5820	73.5931	72.6043	71.6154	.032961
78	84.7910	83.6897	82.5885	81.4872	80.3859	79.2847	78.1834	77.0821	75.9809	74.8796	73.7783	72.6771	.036709
79	86.7263	85.5070	84.2877	83.0683	81.8490	80.6297	79.4104	78.1911	76.9718	75.7524	74.5331	73.3138	.040644
80	88.2802	87.0391	85.7979	84.5568	83.3156	82.0745	80.8333	79.5922	78.3511	77.1099	75.8688	74.6276	.041371
81	90.7261	89.6174	88.5087	87.3999	86.2912	85.1825	84.0738	82.9651	81.8564	80.7476	79.6389	78.5302	.036957
82 or 27	**96.1538**	**96.4743**	**96.7948**	**97.1153**	**97.4359**	**97.7564**	**98.0769**	**98.3974**	**98.7179**	**99.0384**	**99.3590**	**99.6795**	**.010684**
26	94.8656	94.8469	94.8281	94.8094	94.7907	94.7720	94.7532	94.7345	94.7158	94.6971	94.6783	94.6596	.000624
25	94.2021	94.1355	94.0690	94.0024	93.9358	93.8692	93.8026	93.7361	93.6695	93.6029	93.5363	93.4698	.002219
24	93.7156	93.6379	93.5602	93.4824	93.4047	93.3270	93.2493	93.1716	93.0939	93.0161	92.9384	92.8607	.002590
23	93.0903	93.0275	92.9646	92.9018	92.8389	92.7761	92.7132	92.6504	92.5876	92.5247	92.4619	92.3990	.002095
22	92.3168	92.2696	92.2223	92.1751	92.1279	92.0806	92.0334	91.9862	91.9389	91.8917	91.8445	91.7972	.001574
21	91.4642	91.4267	91.3892	91.3517	91.3143	91.2768	91.2393	91.2018	91.1643	91.1268	91.0894	91.0519	.001249
20	90.5483	90.5191	90.4900	90.4608	90.4316	90.4025	90.3733	90.3441	90.3150	90.2858	90.2566	90.2275	.000972
19	89.5894	89.5668	89.5441	89.5215	89.4989	89.4762	89.4536	89.4310	89.4083	89.3857	89.3631	89.3404	.000754
18	88.6067	88.5888	88.5710	88.5531	88.5352	88.5173	88.4994	88.4816	88.4637	88.4458	88.4280	88.4101	.000596
17	87.6090	87.5950	87.5811	87.5671	87.5532	87.5392	87.5253	87.5113	87.4974	87.4834	87.4695	87.4555	.000465
16	86.5984	86.5881	86.5777	86.5674	86.5571	86.5467	86.5364	86.5261	86.5157	86.5054	86.4951	86.4847	.000343
15	85.5835	85.5759	85.5684	85.5608	85.5532	85.5457	85.5381	85.5305	85.5230	85.5154	85 5078	85.5003	.000252
14	84.5698	84.5644	84.5590	84.5536	84.5483	84.5429	84.5375	84.5321	84.5267	84.5213	84.5160	84.5106	.000179
13	83.5557	83.5525	83.5493	83.5461	83.5430	83.5398	83.5366	83.5334	83.5302	83.5270	83.5239	83.5207	.000106
12	82.5404	82.5394	82.5383	82.5373	82.5363	82.5352	82.5342	82.5332	82.5321	82.5311	82.5301	82.5290	.000034
11	81.5230	81.5241	81.5251	81.5262	81.5273	81.5283	81.5294	81.5305	81.5315	81.5326	81.5337	81.5347	.000035
10	80.4961	80.4998	80.5035	80.5071	80.5108	80.5145	80.5181	80.5218	80.5255	80.5292	80.5328	80.5365	.000122
Age.	0	1	2	3	4	5	6	7	8	9	10	11	Day.

Age.	0	1	2	3	4	5	6	7	8	9	10	11	Day.
10	11.2801	11.2573	11.2346	11.2118	11.1891	11.1663	11.1436	11.1208	11.0981	11.0753	11.0526	11.0298	.000758
11	11.7025	11.6804	11.6583	11.6363	11.6142	11.5921	11.5700	11.5480	11.5259	11.5038	11.4817	11.4597	.000736
12	12.1394	12.1180	12.0966	12.0753	12.0539	12.0325	12.0111	11.9898	11.9684	11.9470	11.9256	11.9043	.000712
13	12.5915	12.5708	12.5501	12.5294	12.5088	12.4881	12.4674	12.4467	12.4260	12.4053	12.3847	12.3640	.000689
14	13.0600	13.0400	13.0200	13.0000	12.9800	12.9600	12.9400	12.9200	12.9000	12.8800	12.8600	12.8400	.000667
15	13.5459	13.5266	13.5073	13.4881	13.4688	13.4495	13.4302	13.4110	13.3917	13.3724	13.3531	13.3339	.000642
16	14.0504	14.0319	14.0134	13.9950	13.9765	13.9580	13.9395	13.9211	13.9026	13.8841	13.8656	13.8472	.000616
17	14.5758	14.5581	14.5404	14.5227	14.5050	14.4873	14.4696	14.4520	14.4343	14.4166	14.3989	14.3812	.000590
18	15.1223	15.1054	15.0886	15.0717	15.0548	15.0380	15.0211	15.0042	14.9874	14.9705	14.9536	14.9368	.000562
19	15.6921	15.6762	15.6604	15.6445	15.6287	15.6128	15.5970	15.5811	15.5652	15.5494	15.5335	15.5177	.000528
20	16.2876	16.2727	16.2577	16.2428	16.2278	16.2129	16.1980	16.1830	16.1681	16.1531	16.1382	16.1232	.000498
21	16.9103	16.8964	16.8825	16.8685	16.8546	16.8407	16.8268	16.8129	16.7990	16.7850	16.7711	16.7572	.000464
22	17.5618	17.5490	17.5362	17.5235	17.5107	17.4979	17.4851	17.4724	17.4596	17.4468	17.4340	17.4213	.000426
23	18.2443	18.2327	18.2211	18.2095	18.1979	18.1863	18.1746	18.1630	18.1514	18.1398	18.1282	18.1166	.000387
24	18.9602	18.9497	18.9392	18.9287	18.9183	18.9078	18.8973	18.8868	18.8763	18.8658	18.8554	18.8449	.000349
25	19.7099	19.7002	19.6905	19.6808	19.6712	19.6615	19.6518	19.6421	19.6324	19.6227	19.6131	19.6034	.000322
26	20.4908	20.4815	20.4722	20.4629	20.4536	20.4443	20.4350	20.4257	20.4164	20.4071	20.3978	20.3885	.000310
27	21.3000	21.2908	21.2816	21.2724	21.2632	21.2540	21.2447	21.2355	21.2263	21.2171	21.2079	21.1987	.000307
28	22.1353	22.1257	22.1160	22.1064	22.0967	22.0871	22.0774	22.0678	22.0582	22.0485	22.0389	22.0292	.000321
29	22.9926	22.9824	22.9721	22.9619	22.9517	22.9414	22.9312	22.9210	22.9107	22.9005	22.8903	22.8800	.000341
30	23.8719	23.8608	23.8497	23.8386	23.8275	23.8164	23.8053	23.7943	23.7832	23.7721	23.7610	23.7499	.000370
31	24.7716	24.7596	24.7476	24.7357	24.7237	24.7117	24.6997	24.6878	24.6758	24.6638	24.6518	24.6399	.000399
32	25.6938	25.6806	25.6673	25.6541	25.6409	25.6276	25.6144	25.6012	25.5879	25.5747	25.5615	25.5482	.000441
33	26.6365	26.6217	26.6070	26.5922	26.5774	26.5627	26.5479	26.5331	26.5184	26.5036	26.4888	26.4741	.000492
34	27.5987	27.5821	27.5655	27.5489	27.5323	27.5157	27.4991	27.4825	27.4659	27.4493	27.4327	27.4161	.000553
35	28.5788	28.5601	28.5413	28.5226	28.5039	28.4852	28.4664	28.4477	28.4290	28.4103	28.3915	28.3728	.000624
36	29.5763	29.5552	29.5341	29.5130	29.4920	29.4709	29.4498	29.4287	29.4076	29.3865	29.3655	29.3444	.000703
37	30.5916	30.5678	30.5440	30.5202	30.4964	30.4726	30.4487	30.4249	30.4011	30.3773	30.3535	30.3297	.000793
38	31.6219	31.5949	31.5679	31.5410	31.5140	31.4870	31.4600	31.4330	31.4060	31.3790	31.3521	31.3251	.000899
39	32.6668	32.6365	32.6061	32.5758	32.5454	32.5151	32.4847	32.4544	32.4241	32.3937	32.3634	32.3330	.001011
40	33.7270	33.6928	33.6586	33.6244	33.5902	33.5560	33.5218	33.4877	33.4535	33.4193	33.3851	33.3509	.001140
41	34.8002	34.7616	34.7231	34.6845	34.6460	34.6074	34.5688	34.5303	34.4917	34.4532	34.4146	34.3761	.001285
42	35.8850	35.8412	35.7974	35.7536	35.7098	35.6660	35.6222	35.5784	35.5346	35.4908	35.4470	35.4032	.001460
43	36.9765	36.9269	36.8772	36.8276	36.7780	36.7283	36.6787	36.6291	36.5794	36.5298	36.4802	36.4305	.001654
44	38.0762	38.0199	37.9636	37.9074	37.8511	37.7948	37.7385	37.6823	37.6260	37.5697	37.5134	37.4572	.001876
45	39.1837	39.1201	39.0566	38.9930	38.9294	38.8659	38.8023	38.7387	38.6752	38.6116	38.5480	38.4845	.002119
46	40.2997	40.2280	40.1563	40.0846	40.0129	39.9412	39.8695	39.7978	39.7261	39.6544	39.5827	39.5110	.002390
47	41.4246	41.3440	41.2635	41.1830	41.1024	41.0218	40.9413	40.8607	40.7802	40.6996	40.6191	40.5385	.002685
48	42.5576	42.4671	42.3767	42.2862	42.1957	42.1053	42.0148	41.9243	41.8339	41.7434	41.6529	41.5625	.003015
49	43.6942	43.5931	43.4921	43.3910	43.2899	43.1889	43.0878	42.9867	42.8857	42.7846	42.6835	42.5825	.003369
50	44.8337	44.7211	44.6086	44.4960	44.3835	44.2710	44.1584	44.0458	43.9333	43.8207	43.7082	43.5956	.003752
51	45.9760	45.8512	45.7265	45.6017	45.4770	45.3522	45.2275	45.1027	44.9780	44.8532	44.7285	44.6037	.004158
52	47.1224	46.9844	46.8464	46.7084	46.5704	46.4324	46.2944	46.1565	46.0185	45.8805	45.7425	45.6045	.004600
53	48.2716	48.1194	47.9672	47.8150	47.6628	47.5106	47.3584	47.2062	47.0540	46.9018	46.7496	46.5974	.005073
54	49.4232	49.2591	49.0950	48.9310	48.7669	48.6028	48.4387	48.2746	48.1105	47.9464	47.7824	47.6183	.005469
55	50.5764	50.3927	50.2090	50.0252	49.8415	49.6578	49.4740	49.2903	49.1066	48.9229	48.7391	48.5554	.006124
56	51.7315	51.5303	51.3291	51.1278	50.9266	50.7254	50.5242	50.3230	50.1218	49.9205	49.7193	49.5181	.006707
57	52.8885	52.6686	52.4487	52.2289	52.0090	51.7891	51.5692	51.3494	51.1295	50.9096	50.6897	50.4699	.007329
58	54.0470	53.8073	53.5676	53.3279	53.0882	52.8485	52.6088	52.3692	52.1295	51.8898	51.6501	51.4104	.007990
59	55.2098	54.9487	54.6876	54.4264	54.1653	53.9042	53.6431	53.3820	53.1209	52.8597	52.5986	52.3375	.008704
60	56.3752	56.0910	55.8068	55.5226	55.2385	54.9543	54.6701	54.3859	54.1017	53.8175	53.5334	53.2492	.009473
61	57.5452	57.2367	56.9283	56.6198	56.3113	56.0029	55.6944	55.3859	55.0775	54.7690	54.4605	54.1521	.010282
62	58.7252	58.3911	58.0570	57.7230	57.3889	57.0548	56.7207	56.3866	56.0525	55.7184	55.3844	55.0503	.011136
63	59.9222	59.5616	59.2010	58.8403	58.4797	58.1191	57.7584	57.3978	57.0372	56.6766	56.3160	55.9553	.012021
64	61.1487	60.7609	60.3731	59.9853	59.5975	59.2097	58.8218	58.4340	58.0462	57.6584	57.2706	56.8828	.012927
65	62.4240	62.0081	61.5921	61.1762	60.7602	60.3443	59.9283	59.5124	59.0965	58.6805	58.2646	57.8486	.013865
66	63.7646	63.3201	62.8756	62.4310	61.9865	61.5420	61.0975	60.6530	60.2085	59.7640	59.3194	58.8749	.014817
67	65.1980	64.7231	64.2482	63.7733	63.2985	62.8236	62.3487	61.8738	61.3989	60.9240	60.4492	59.9743	.015829
68	66.7347	66.2276	65.7205	65.2133	64.7062	64.1991	63.6920	63.1849	62.6778	62.1706	61.6635	61.1564	.016904
69	68.3880	67.8467	67.3054	66.7642	66.2229	65.6816	65.1403	64.5991	64.0578	63.5165	62.9752	62.4340	.018042
70	70.1724	69.5933	69.0142	68.4352	67.8561	67.2770	66.6980	66.1189	65.5398	64.9607	64.3816	63.8026	.019302
71	72.0864	71.4648	70.8433	70.2217	69.6001	68.9786	68.3570	67.7354	67.1139	66.4923	65.8707	65.2492	.020719
72	74.1167	73.4491	72.7815	72.1139	71.4463	70.7787	70.1111	69.4436	68.7760	68.1084	67.4408	66.7732	.022253
73	76.2677	75.5487	74.8297	74.1106	73.3916	72.6726	71.9536	71.2346	70.5156	69.7965	69.0775	68.3585	.023967
74	78.5240	77.7446	76.9652	76.1857	75.4063	74.6269	73.8475	73.0681	72.2887	71.5092	70.7298	69.9504	.025980
75	80.8280	79.9785	79.1291	78.2796	77.4302	76.5807	75.7312	74.8818	74.0323	73.1829	72.3334	71.4840	.028315
76	83.1150	82.1858	81.2566	80.3274	79.3982	78.4690	77.5398	76.6106	75.6814	74.7522	73.8230	72.8938	.030973
77	85.3202	84.2851	83.2499	82.2148	81.1796	80.1445	79.1093	78.0742	77.0391	76.0039	74.9688	73.9336	.034505
78	87.1737	86.0275	84.8814	83.7352	82.5891	81.4430	80.2968	79.1506	78.0045	76.8583	75.7122	74.5660	.038205
79	88.6624	87.4971	86.3318	85.1665	84.0012	82.8359	81.6705	80.5052	79.3399	78.1746	77.0093	75.8440	.038843
80	90.9963	89.9586	88.9209	87.8832	86.8455	85.8078	84.7701	83.7325	82.6948	81.6571	80.6194	79.5817	.034590
81 or 28	**96.1538**	**96.4743**	**96.7948**	**97.1153**	**97.4359**	**97.7564**	**98.0769**	**98.3974**	**98.7179**	**99.0384**	**99.3590**	**99.6795**	**.010684**
27	94.8553	94.8339	94.8124	94.7910	94.7696	94.7482	94.7267	94.7053	94.6839	94.6625	94.6410	94.6196	.000714
26	94.1872	94.1177	94.0481	93.9786	93.9090	93.8395	93.7700	93.7004	93.6309	93.5613	93.4918	93.4222	.002318
25	93.6977	93.6170	93.5364	93.4557	93.3751	93.2944	93.2138	93.1331	93.0525	92.9718	92.8912	92.8105	.002688
24	93.0687	93.0032	92.9376	92.8721	92.8066	92.7410	92.6755	92.6100	92.5444	92.4789	92.4134	92.3478	.002184
23	92.2908	92.2411	92.1913	92.1416	92.0919	92.0421	91.9924	91.9427	91.8929	91.8432	91.7935	91.7437	.001658
22	91.4337	91.3939	91.3540	91.3142	91.2744	91.2346	91.1947	91.1549	91.1151	91.0753	91.0354	90.9956	.001327
21	90.5134	90.4820	90.4506	90.4193	90.3879	90.3565	90.3251	90.2938	90.2624	90.2310	90.1996	90.1683	.001046
20	89.5496	89.5249	89.5002	89.4755	89.4509	89.4262	89.4015	89.3768	89.3521	89.3274	89.3028	89.2781	.000823
19	88.5631	88.5433	88.5234	88.5036	88.4838	88.4639	88.4441	88.4243	88.4044	88.3846	88.3648	88.3449	.000661
18	87.5615	87.5457	87.5299	87.5141	87.4983	87.4825	87.4667	87.4509	87.4351	87.4193	87.4035	87.3877	.000527
17	86.5339	86.5229	86.5120	86.5010	86.4900	86.4790	86.4680	86.4571	86.4461	86.4351	86.4241	86.4132	.000366
16	85.5293	85.5201	85.5108	85.5016	85.4923	85.4831	85.4738	85.4646	85.4554	85.4461	85.4369	85.4276	.000308
15	84.5128	84.5058	84.4988	84.4919	84.4849	84.4779	84.4710	84.4640	84.4570	84.4500	84.4430	84.4361	.000232
14	83.4964	83.4917	83.4870	83.4822	83.4775	83.4728	83.4680	83.4633	83.4586	83.4539	83.4491	83.4444	.000157
13	82.4789	82.4764	82.4740	82.4714	82.4690	82.4665	82.4640	82.4615	82.4590	82.4565	82.4541	82.4516	.000083
12	81.4598	81.4595	81.4592	81.4589	81.4586	81.4583	81.4580	81.4576	81.4573	81.4570	81.4567	81.4564	.000010
11	80.4314	80.4338	80.4361	80.4385	80.4409	80.4432	80.4456	80.4480	80.4503	80.4527	80.4551	80.4574	.000079
10	79.3891	79.3944	79.3997	79.4051	79.4104	79.4157	79.4211	79.4264	79.4317	79.4371	79.4424	79.4477	.000177
Age.	0	1	2	3	4	5	6	7	8	9	10	11	Day.

Age.	0	1	2	3	4	5	6	7	8	9	10	11	Day.
10	12.0500	12.0293	12.0087	11.9880	11.9673	11.9467	11.9260	11.9053	11.8847	11.8640	11.8633	11.8227	.000689
11	12.5007	12.4808	12.4609	12.4410	12.4211	12.4012	12.3812	12.3613	12.3414	12.3215	12.3016	12.2817	.000663
12	12.9673	12.9481	12.9290	12.9098	12.8907	12.8715	12.8523	12.8332	12.8140	12.7949	12.7757	12.7566	.000638
13	13.4499	13.4315	13.4131	13.3947	13.3763	13.3579	13.3394	13.3210	13.3026	13.2842	13.2658	13.2474	.000613
14	13.9500	13.9324	13.9147	13.8971	13.8795	13.8619	13.8442	13.8266	13.8090	13.7914	13.7737	13.7561	.000587
15	14.4690	14.4522	14.4355	14.4187	14.4020	14.3852	14.3685	14.3517	14.3350	14.3182	14.3015	14.2847	.000558
16	15.0087	14.9928	14.9769	14.9610	14.9451	14.9292	14.9133	14.8975	14.8816	14.8657	14.8498	14.8339	.000530
17	15.5704	15.5554	15.5404	15.5254	15.5104	15.4954	15.4803	15.4653	15.4503	15.4353	15.4203	15.4053	.000500
18	16.1548	16.1409	16.1270	16.1130	16.0991	16.0852	16.0712	16.0573	16.0434	16.0295	16.0155	16.0016	.000464
19	16.7661	16.7531	16.7402	16.7272	16.7143	16.7013	16.6884	16.6754	16.6625	16.6495	16.6366	16.6236	.000432
20	17.4031	17.3913	17.3795	17.3676	17.3558	17.3440	17.3322	17.3204	17.3086	17.2967	17.2849	17.2731	.000394
21	18.0706	18.0600	18.0494	18.0387	18.0281	18.0175	18.0069	17.9963	17.9857	17.9750	17.9644	17.9538	.000354
22	18.7695	18.7601	18.7508	18.7414	18.7320	18.7227	18.7133	18.7039	18.6946	18.6852	18.6758	18.6665	.000312
23	19.5013	19.4932	19.4850	19.4768	19.4687	19.4605	19.4523	19.4442	19.4360	19.4279	19.4197	19.4116	.000272
24	20.2677	20.2604	20.2531	20.2459	20.2386	20.2313	20.2240	20.2168	20.2095	20.2022	20.1950	20.1877	.000242
25	21.0659	21.0591	21.0523	21.0455	21.0387	21.0319	21.0251	21.0184	21.0116	21.0048	20.9980	20.9912	.000226
26	21.8921	21.8855	21.8789	21.8723	21.8657	21.8591	21.8525	21.8459	21.8393	21.8327	21.8261	21.8195	.000220
27	22.7452	22.7383	22.7313	22.7244	22.7175	22.7106	22.7036	22.6967	22.6898	22.6829	22.6760	22.6690	.000231
28	23.6201	23.6127	23.6053	23.5979	23.5905	23.5831	23.5757	23.5684	23.5610	23.5536	23.5462	23.5388	.000246
29	24.5175	24.5094	24.5012	24.4931	24.4850	24.4769	24.4687	24.4606	24.4525	24.4444	24.4363	24.4281	.000271
30	25.4360	25.4271	25.4182	25.4093	25.4005	25.3916	25.3827	25.3738	25.3649	25.3560	25.3472	25.3383	.000296
31	26.3771	26.3671	26.3571	26.3471	26.3371	26.3271	26.3171	26.3071	26.2971	26.2871	26.2771	26.2671	.000333
32	27.3390	27.3276	27.3162	27.3048	27.2935	27.2821	27.2707	27.2593	27.2479	27.2365	27.2252	27.2138	.000379
33	28.3210	28.3080	28.2949	28.2819	28.2688	28.2558	28.2427	28.2297	28.2167	28.2036	28.1906	28.1775	.000435
34	29.3220	29.3070	29.2920	29.2770	29.2620	29.2470	29.2320	29.2170	29.2020	29.1870	29.1720	29.1570	.000500
35	30.3407	30.3235	30.3064	30.2892	30.2720	30.2549	30.2377	30.2205	30.2034	30.1862	30.1690	30.1519	.000572
36	31.3777	31.3580	31.3383	31.3186	31.2990	31.2793	31.2596	31.2399	31.2202	31.2005	31.1809	31.1612	.000656
37	32.4319	32.4093	32.3866	32.3640	32.3414	32.3188	32.2961	32.2735	32.2509	32.2283	32.2056	32.1830	.000754
38	33.4999	33.4742	33.4484	33.4227	33.3970	33.3712	33.3455	33.3198	33.2940	33.2683	33.2426	33.2168	.000858
39	34.5851	34.5558	34.5264	34.4971	34.4678	34.4385	34.4091	34.3798	34.3505	34.3212	34.2918	34.2625	.000977
40	35.6844	35.6510	35.6176	35.5843	35.5509	35.5175	35.4841	35.4508	35.4174	35.3840	35.3506	35.3173	.001112
41	36.7961	36.7578	36.7195	36.6812	36.6429	36.6046	36.5663	36.5281	36.4898	36.4515	36.4132	36.3749	.001276
42	37.9147	37.8709	37.8272	37.7834	37.7397	37.6959	37.6521	37.6084	37.5646	37.5209	37.4771	37.4334	.001458
43	39.0394	38.9894	38.9393	38.8893	38.8393	38.7892	38.7392	38.6892	38.6391	38.5891	38.5391	38.4890	.001668
44	40.1691	40.1122	40.0552	39.9983	39.9414	39.8845	39.8275	39.7706	39.7137	39.6568	39.5998	39.5429	.001897
45	41.3055	41.2409	41.1762	41.1116	41.0469	40.9823	40.9176	40.8530	40.7884	40.7237	40.6591	40.5944	.002155
46	42.4473	42.3742	42.3012	42.2281	42.1551	42.0820	42.0090	41.9359	41.8628	41.7898	41.7167	41.6437	.002435
47	43.5965	43.5140	43.4315	43.3490	43.2665	43.1840	43.1015	43.0191	42.9366	42.8541	42.7716	42.6891	.002750
48	44.7487	44.6561	44.5635	44.4709	44.3783	44.2857	44.1930	44.1004	44.0078	43.9152	43.8226	43.7300	.003087
49	45.9040	45.8005	45.6970	45.5934	45.4899	45.3864	45.2829	45.1794	45.0759	44.9723	44.8688	44.7653	.003450
50	47.0606	46.9455	46.8303	46.7152	46.6001	46.4849	46.3698	46.2547	46.1395	46.0244	45.9093	45.7941	.003838
51	48.2205	48.0928	47.9650	47.8373	47.7095	47.5818	47.4540	47.3263	47.1986	47.0708	46.9431	46.8153	.004258
52	49.3816	49.2404	49.0992	48.9580	48.8167	48.6755	48.5343	48.3931	48.2519	48.1106	47.9694	47.8282	.004707
53	50.5448	50.3891	50.2334	50.0777	49.9220	49.7663	49.6105	49.4548	49.2991	49.1434	48.9877	48.8320	.005190
54	51.7092	51.5380	51.3668	51.1956	51.0244	50.8532	50.6820	50.5109	50.3397	50.1685	49.9973	49.8261	.005706
55	52.8742	52.6864	52.4986	52.3108	52.1230	51.9352	51.7474	51.5597	51.3719	51.1841	50.9963	50.8085	.006260
56	54.0398	53.8348	53.6297	53.4247	53.2197	53.0146	52.8096	52.6046	52.3995	52.1945	51.9895	51.7844	.006834
57	55.2071	54.9829	54.7586	54.5344	54.3101	54.0859	53.8616	53.6374	53.4132	53.1889	52.9647	52.7404	.007475
58	56.3774	56.1329	55.8883	55.6438	55.3993	55.1547	54.9102	54.6657	54.4211	54.1766	53.9321	53.6875	.008151
59	57.5487	57.2823	57.0160	56.7496	56.4833	56.2170	55.9506	55.6842	55.4179	55.1515	54.8852	54.6188	.008878
60	58.7205	58.4312	58.1419	57.8526	57.5633	57.2740	56.9846	56.6953	56.4060	56.1167	55.8274	55.5381	.009643
61	59.9008	59.5873	59.2737	58.9602	58.6467	58.3332	58.0196	57.7061	57.3926	57.0791	56.7655	56.4520	.010451
62	61.0944	60.7558	60.4172	60.0786	59.7400	59.4014	59.0628	58.7242	58.3856	58.0470	57.7084	57.3698	.011287
63	62.3146	61.9504	61.5862	61.2220	60.8577	60.4935	60.1293	59.7651	59.4009	59.0366	58.6724	58.3082	.012140
64	63.5790	63.1883	62.7976	62.4069	62.0162	61.6255	61.2347	60.8440	60.4533	60.0626	59.6719	59.2812	.013023
65	64.9045	64.4869	64.0693	63.6517	63.2341	62.8165	62.3990	61.9814	61.5638	61.1462	60.7286	60.3110	.013920
66	66.3150	65.8688	65.4226	64.9765	64.5303	64.0841	63.6380	63.1918	62.7456	62.2994	61.8532	61.4071	.014872
67	67.8231	67.3466	66.8701	66.3936	65.9171	65.4406	64.9641	64.4877	64.0112	63.5347	63.0582	62.5817	.015883
68	69.4406	68.9320	68.4234	67.9148	67.4062	66.8976	66.3890	65.8803	65.3717	64.8631	64.3545	63.8459	.016953
69	71.1820	70.6379	70.0937	69.5496	69.0055	68.4614	67.9172	67.3731	66.8290	66.2849	65.7407	65.1966	.018137
70	73.0437	72.4596	71.8755	71.2914	70.7074	70.1233	69.5392	68.9551	68.3710	67.7870	67.2029	66.6188	.019469
71	75.0140	74.3866	73.7593	73.1319	72.5046	71.8772	71.2498	70.6225	69.9951	69.3678	68.7404	68.1131	.020912
72	77.0962	76.4205	75.7448	75.0691	74.3934	73.7177	73.0420	72.3662	71.6905	71.0148	70.3391	69.6634	.022523
73	79.2751	78.5426	77.8100	77.0775	76.3449	75.6124	74.8798	74.1473	73.4148	72.6822	71.9497	71.2171	.024418
74	81.4957	80.6972	79.8987	79.1002	78.3017	77.5032	76.7047	75.9062	75.1077	74.3092	73.5107	72.7122	.026617
75	83.6956	82.8220	81.9485	81.0750	80.2014	79.3278	78.4543	77.5807	76.7072	75.8336	74.9601	74.0865	.029118
76	85.8137	84.8403	83.8669	82.8935	81.9201	80.9467	79.9733	79.0000	78.0266	77.0532	76.0798	75.1064	.032446
77	87.5920	86.5141	85.4361	84.3582	83.2803	82.2023	81.1244	80.0465	78.9685	77.8906	76.8127	75.7347	.035931
78	89.0178	87.9231	86.8284	85.7337	84.6390	83.5443	82.4496	81.3549	80.2602	79.1655	78.0708	76.9761	.036490
79	91.2466	90.2749	89.3031	88.3314	87.3597	86.3880	85.4162	84.4445	83.4728	82.5011	81.5293	80.5576	.032391
80 or 29	**96.1538**	**96.4743**	**96.7948**	**97.1153**	**97.4359**	**97.7564**	**98.0769**	**98.3974**	**98.7179**	**99.0384**	**99.3590**	**99.6795**	**.010684**
28	94.8445	94.8202	94.7960	94.7717	94.7474	94.7232	94.6989	94.6746	94.6504	94.6261	94.6018	94.5776	.000809
27	94.1715	94.0988	94.0262	93.9535	93.8809	93.8082	93.7356	93.6630	93.5903	93.5176	93.4450	93.3723	.002422
26	93.6789	93.5952	93.5115	93.4277	93.3440	93.2603	93.1766	93.0929	93.0092	92.9254	92.8417	92.7580	.002790
25	93.0460	92.9776	92.9092	92.8409	92.7725	92.7041	92.6357	92.5674	92.4990	92.4306	92.3622	92.2939	.002279
24	92.2635	92.2111	92.1588	92.1064	92.0541	92.0017	91.9494	91.8970	91.8447	91.7923	91.7400	91.6876	.001745
23	91.4016	91.3593	91.3171	91.2748	91.2325	91.1903	91.1480	91.1057	91.0635	91.0212	90.9789	90.9367	.001409
22	90.4767	90.4430	90.4093	90.3757	90.3420	90.3083	90.2746	90.2410	90.2073	90.1736	90.1400	90.1063	.001122
21	89.5085	89.4816	89.4548	89.4279	89.4011	89.3742	89.3473	89.3205	89.2936	89.2668	89.2399	89.2131	.000895
20	88.5171	88.4952	88.4734	88.4515	88.4296	88.4078	88.3859	88.3640	88.3422	88.3203	88.2984	88.2766	.000729
19	87.5119	87.4941	87.4764	87.4586	87.4409	87.4231	87.4053	87.3876	87.3698	87.3521	87.3343	87.3166	.000592
18	86.4939	86.4800	86.4660	86.4521	86.4381	86.4242	86.4102	86.3963	86.3824	86.3684	86.3545	86.3405	.000465
17	85.4726	85.4605	85.4483	85.4362	85.4241	85.4120	85.3998	85.3877	85.3756	85.3635	85.3513	85.3392	.000404
16	84.4531	84.4444	84.4358	84.4271	84.4185	84.4098	84.4012	84.3925	84.3839	84.3752	84.3666	84.3580	.000288
15	83.4341	83.4278	83.4215	83.4152	83.4089	83.4026	83.3962	83.3899	83.3836	83.3773	83.3710	83.3647	.000210
14	82.4146	82.4106	82.4065	82.4025	82.3985	82.3945	82.3904	82.3864	82.3824	82.3784	82.3743	82.3703	.000134
13	81.3934	81.3916	81.3899	81.3881	81.3864	81.3846	81.3828	81.3811	81.3793	81.2776	81.3758	81.3741	.000058
12	80.3634	80.3644	80.3654	80.3664	80.3674	80.3684	80.3694	80.3704	80.3714	80.3724	80.3734	80.3744	.000033
11	79.3198	79.3238	79.3279	79.3319	79.3359	79.3400	79.3440	79.3480	79.3521	79.3561	79.3601	79.3642	.000134
10	78.2562	78.2637	78.2712	78.2787	78.2862	78.2937	78.3012	78.3087	78.3162	78.3237	78.3312	78.3387	.000250
Age.	0	1	2	3	4	5	6	7	8	9	10	11	Day.

Age.	0	1	2	3	4	5	6	7	8	9	10	11	Day
10	12.8449	12.8264	12.8079	12.7894	12.7709	12.7524	12.7338	12.7153	12.6968	12.6783	12.6598	12.6413	.000617
11	13.3250	13.3073	13.2896	13.2719	13.2542	13.2365	13.2188	13.2011	13.1834	13.1657	13.1480	13.1303	.000590
12	13.8217	13.8048	13.7880	13.7711	13.7542	13.7373	13.7204	13.7036	13.6867	13.6698	13.6530	13.6361	.000562
13	14.3356	14.3196	14.3035	14.2875	14.2715	14.2555	14.2394	14.2234	14.2074	14.1914	14.1753	14.1593	.000534
14	14.8686	14.8535	14.8384	14.8232	14.8081	14.7930	14.7779	14.7628	14.7477	14.7325	14.7174	14.7023	.000504
15	15.4224	15.4082	15.3940	15.3798	15.3657	15.3515	15.3373	15.3231	15.3089	15.2947	15.2806	15.2664	.000473
16	15.9980	15.9848	15.9715	15.9583	15.9451	15.9319	15.9186	15.9054	15.8922	15.8790	15.8657	15.8525	.000441
17	16.5971	16.5850	16.5730	16.5609	16.5488	16.5367	16.5246	16.5126	16.5005	16.4884	16.4763	16.4643	.000402
18	17.2226	17.2116	17.2005	17.1895	17.1785	17.1674	17.1564	17.1454	17.1343	17.1233	17.1123	17.1012	.000368
19	17.8750	17.8651	17.8553	17.8454	17.8356	17.8257	17.8159	17.8060	17.7962	17.7863	17.7765	17.7666	.000328
20	18.5562	18.5477	18.5391	18.5306	18.5221	18.5135	18.5050	18.4965	18.4879	18.4794	18.4709	18.4623	.000284
21	19.2705	19.2633	19.2560	19.2488	19.2416	19.2344	19.2271	19.2199	19.2127	19.2055	19.1982	19.1910	.000241
22	20.0182	20.0122	20.0063	20.0003	19.9944	19.9884	19.9825	19.9765	19.9706	19.9646	19.9587	19.9527	.000198
23	20.7998	20.7948	20.7898	20.7849	20.7799	20.7749	20.7700	20.7650	20.7600	20.7550	20.7500	20.7451	.000166
24	21.6138	21.6094	21.6050	21.6006	21.5962	21.5918	21.5874	21.5830	21.5786	21.5742	21.5698	21.5654	.000147
25	22.4566	22.4525	22.4483	22.4442	22.4401	22.4360	22.4318	22.4277	22.4236	22.4195	22.4153	22.4112	.000137
26	23.3259	23.3216	23.3173	23.3129	23.3086	23.3043	23.2999	23.2956	23.2913	23.2869	23.2826	23.2783	.000143
27	24.2178	24.2131	24.2084	24.2037	24.1990	24.1943	24.1896	24.1849	24.1802	24.1755	24.1708	24.1661	.000157
28	25.1319	25.1266	25.1213	25.1160	25.1107	25.1054	25.1001	25.0948	25.0895	25.0842	25.0789	25.0736	.000177
29	26.0676	26.0617	26.0557	26.0498	26.0438	26.0379	26.0320	26.0260	26.0201	26.0141	26.0082	26.0022	.000198
30	27.0266	27.0197	27.0127	27.0058	26.9989	26.9919	26.9850	26.9781	26.9711	26.9642	26.9573	26.9503	.000231
31	28.0063	27.9981	27.9100	27.9818	27.9737	27.9655	27.9573	27.9492	27.9410	27.9329	27.9247	27.9166	.000272
32	29.0065	28.9968	28.9871	28.9774	28.9678	28.9581	28.9484	28.9387	28.9290	28.9193	28.9097	28.9000	.000323
33	30.0261	30.0146	30.0032	29.9917	29.9803	29.9688	29.9573	29.9459	29.9344	29.9230	29.9115	29.9001	.000382
34	31.0645	31.0510	31.0376	31.0241	31.0107	30.9972	30.9838	30.9703	30.9569	30.9434	30.9300	30.9165	.000448
35	32.1214	32.1056	32.0898	32.0740	32.0583	32.0425	32.0267	32.0109	31.9951	31.9793	31.9636	31.9478	.000526
36	33.1959	33.1774	33.1589	33.1404	33.1219	33.1034	33.0848	33.0663	33.0478	33.0293	33.0108	32.9923	.000617
37	34.2864	34.2650	34.2436	34.2222	34.2008	34.1794	34.1580	34.1366	34.1152	34.0938	34.0724	34.0510	.000713
38	35.3930	35.3683	35.3435	35.3188	35.2941	35.2694	35.2446	35.2199	35.1952	35.1705	35.1457	35.1210	.000824
39	36.5155	36.4870	36.4585	36.4300	36.4014	36.3729	36.3444	36.3159	36.2874	36.2588	36.2303	36.2018	.000950
40	37.6516	37.6185	37.5853	37.5522	37.5191	37.4860	37.4528	37.4197	37.3866	37.3535	37.3203	37.2872	.001104
41	38.7952	38.7569	38.7187	38.6804	38.6422	38.6039	38.5656	38.5274	38.4891	38.4509	38.4126	38.3744	.001275
42	39.9449	39.9007	39.8566	39.8124	39.7683	39.7241	39.6800	39.6358	39.5917	39.5475	39.5034	39.4592	.001472
43	41.0975	41.0468	40.9952	40.9455	40.8948	40.8432	40.7935	40.7428	40.6921	40.6414	40.5908	40.5402	.001687
44	42.2542	42.1961	42.1381	42.0800	42.0219	41.9639	41.9058	41.8477	41.7897	41.7316	41.6735	41.6155	.001935
45	43.4143	43.3483	43.2824	43.2164	43.1504	43.0845	43.0185	42.9525	42.8866	42.8206	42.7546	42.6887	.002199
46	44.5786	44.5036	44.4287	44.3537	44.2787	44.2038	44.1288	44.0538	43.9789	43.9039	43.8289	43.7540	.002499
47	45.7451	45.6605	45.5759	45.4913	45.4067	45.3221	45.2375	45.1530	45.0684	44.9838	44.8992	44.8146	.002820
48	46.9140	46.8190	46.7240	46.6290	46.5340	46.4390	46.3440	46.2490	46.1540	46.0590	45.9640	45.8690	.003167
49	48.0845	47.9785	47.8724	47.7664	47.6603	47.5543	47.4482	47.3422	47.2362	47.1301	47.0241	46.9180	.003535
50	49.2566	49.1385	49.0205	48.9024	48.7844	48.6663	48.5483	48.4302	48.3122	48.1941	48.0761	47.9580	.003935
51	50.4291	50.2982	50.1673	50.0364	49.9055	49.7746	49.6437	49.5129	49.3820	49.2511	49.1202	48.9893	.004363
52	51.6021	51.4574	51.3128	51.1681	51.0235	50.8788	50.7342	50.5895	50.4449	50.3002	50.1556	50.0110	.004822
53	52.7759	52.6165	52.4571	52.2977	52.1383	51.9789	51.8195	51.6602	51.5008	51.3414	51.1820	51.0226	.005313
54	53.9499	53.7747	53.5996	53.4244	53.2493	53.0741	52.8990	52.7238	52.5486	52.3735	52.1983	52.0232	.005838
55	55.1232	54.9312	54.7393	54.5473	54.3553	54.1634	53.9714	53.7794	53.5875	53.3955	53.2035	53.0116	.006399
56	56.3023	56.0921	55.8819	55.6716	55.4614	55.2512	55.0410	54.8308	54.6206	54.4103	54.2001	53.9899	.007007
57	57.4733	57.2443	57.0154	56.7864	56.5575	56.3285	56.0995	55.8706	55.6416	55.4127	55.1837	54.9548	.007632
58	58.6496	58.4000	58.1504	57.9007	57.6511	57.4015	57.1519	56.9023	56.6527	56.4030	56.1534	55.9038	.008320
59	59.8249	59.5536	59.2822	59.0109	58.7396	58.4683	58.1970	57.9256	57.6543	57.3830	57.1116	56.8403	.009044
60	61.0044	60.7102	60.4160	60.1217	59.8275	59.5333	59.2391	58.9449	58.6507	58.3564	58.0622	57.7680	.009807
61	62.1956	61.8777	61.5598	61.2419	60.9240	60.6061	60.2881	59.9702	59.6523	59.3344	59.0165	58.6986	.010596
62	63.4094	63.0673	62.7253	62.3832	62.0411	61.6991	61.3570	61.0149	60.6729	60.3308	59.9887	59.6467	.011402
63	64.6639	64.2969	63.9299	63.5629	63.1959	62.8289	62.4618	62.0948	61.7278	61.3608	60.9938	60.6268	.012233
64	65.9746	65.5823	65.1900	64.7977	64.4054	64.0131	63.6207	63.2284	62.8361	62.4438	62.0515	61.6592	.013077
65	67.3652	66.9460	66.5268	66.1076	65.6884	65.2692	64.8500	64.4308	64.0116	63.5924	63.1732	62.7540	.013973
66	68.8455	68.3978	67.9500	67.5023	67.0545	66.6068	66.1590	65.7113	65.2636	64.8158	64.3681	63.9203	.014925
67	70.4290	69.9511	69.4731	68.9952	68.5173	68.0393	67.5614	67.0835	66.6055	66.1276	65.6497	65.1717	.015931
68	72.1286	71.6173	71.1059	70.5946	70.0832	69.5719	69.0605	68.5492	68.0379	67.5265	67.0152	66.5038	.017045
69	73.9417	73.3928	72.8438	72.2949	71.7459	71.1970	70.6480	70.0991	69.5502	69.0012	68.4523	67.9033	.018298
70	75.8549	75.2653	74.6756	74.0860	73.4963	72.9067	72.3170	71.7274	71.1378	70.5481	69.9585	69.3688	.019655
71	77.8722	77.2370	76.6019	75.9667	75.3316	74.6964	74.0613	73.4261	72.7910	72.1558	71.5207	70.8855	.021172
72	79.9783	79.2896	78.6010	77.9123	77.2236	76.5349	75.8462	75.1576	74.4689	73.7802	73.0915	72.4029	.022956
73	82.1201	81.3693	80.6185	79.8677	79.1169	78.3661	77.6153	76.8645	76.1137	75.3629	74.6121	73.8613	.025027
74	84.2384	83.4169	82.5953	81.7738	80.9522	80.1307	79.3091	78.4876	77.6661	76.8445	76.0230	75.2014	.027385
75	86.2742	85.3584	84.4426	83.5268	82.6111	81.6953	80.7795	79.8637	78.9479	78.0321	77.1164	76.2006	.030526
76	87.9820	86.9678	85.9535	84.9393	83.9251	82.9108	81.8966	80.8824	79.8681	78.8539	77.8397	76.8254	.033808
77	89.3503	88.3214	87.2925	86.2636	85.2348	84.2059	83.1770	82.1481	81.1192	80.0903	79.0615	78.0326	.034296
78	91.4793	90.5690	89.6586	88.7483	87.8380	86.9277	86.0173	85.1070	84.1967	83.2864	82.3760	81.4657	.030344
79 or 30	**96.1538**	**96.4743**	**96.7948**	**97.1153**	**97.4359**	**97.7564**	**98.0769**	**98.3974**	**98.7179**	**99.0384**	**99.3590**	**99.6795**	**.010684**
29	94.8331	94.8059	94.7786	94.7514	94.7241	94.6969	94.6696	94.6424	94.6152	94.5879	94.5607	94.5334	.000908
28	94.1550	94.0791	94.0032	93.9272	93.8513	93.7754	93.6995	93.6236	93.5477	93.4717	93.3958	93.3199	.002530
27	93.6592	93.5722	93.4853	93.3983	93.3114	93.2244	93.1375	93.0505	92.9636	92.8766	92.7897	92.7027	.002898
26	93.0222	92.9508	92.8795	92.8081	92.7368	92.6654	92.5941	92.5227	92.4514	92.3800	92.3087	92.2373	.002378
25	92.2349	92.1798	92.1247	92.0696	92.0145	91.9594	91.9043	91.8493	91.7942	91.7391	91.6840	91.6289	.001836
24	91.3680	91.3232	91.2783	91.2335	91.1887	91.1439	91.0990	91.0542	91.0094	90.9646	90.9197	90.8749	.001494
23	90.4381	90.4020	90.3660	90.3299	90.2938	90.2577	90.2216	90.1856	90.1495	90.1134	90.0773	90.0413	.001202
22	89.4652	89.4361	89.4070	89.3778	89.3487	89.3196	89.2904	89.2613	89.2322	89.2031	89.1740	89.1448	.000971
21	88.4695	88.4455	88.4214	88.3974	88.3734	88.3494	88.3253	88.3013	88.2773	88.2533	88.2292	88.2052	.000801
20	87.4595	87.4397	87.4200	87.4002	87.3804	87.3607	87.3409	87.3211	87.3014	87.2816	87.2618	87.2421	.000659
19	86.4382	86.4223	86.4064	86.3905	86.3746	86.3587	86.3428	86.3270	86.3111	86.2952	86.2793	86.2634	.000530
18	85.4132	85.4003	85.3875	85.3746	85.3618	85.3490	85.3361	85.3232	85.3104	85.2975	85.2847	85.2718	.000428
17	84.3907	84.3803	84.3699	84.3595	84.3491	84.3387	84.3282	84.3178	84.3074	84.2970	84.2866	84.2762	.000347
16	83.3689	83.3609	83.3529	83.3450	83.3370	83.3290	83.3210	83.3130	83.3050	83.2970	83.2891	83.2811	.000266
15	82.3469	82.3413	82.3357	82.3301	82.3245	82.3189	82.3133	82.3077	82.3021	82.2965	82.2909	82.2853	.000187
14	81.3239	81.3206	81.3173	81.3140	81.3108	81.3075	81.3042	81.3009	81.2976	81.2943	81.2911	81.2878	.000109
13	80.2921	80.2917	80.2912	80.2908	80.2903	80.2899	80.2894	80.2890	80.2886	80.2881	80.2877	80.2872	.000015
12	79.2471	79.2497	79.2524	79.2551	79.2577	79.2604	79.2631	79.2657	79.2684	79.2711	79.2737	79.2764	.000087
11	78.1822	78.1884	78.1946	78.2008	78.2070	78.2132	78.2194	78.2257	78.2319	78.2381	78.2443	78.2505	.000207
10	77.0932	77.1032	77.1132	77.1232	77.1332	77.1432	77.1532	77.1632	77.1732	77.1832	77.1932	77.2032	.000333
Age.	0	1	2	3	4	5	6	7	8	9	10	11	Day.

Age.	0	1	2	3	4	5	6	7	8	9	10	11	Day
10	13.6658	13.6495	13.6332	13.6169	13.6006	13.5843	13.5680	13.5516	13.5353	13.5190	13.5027	13.4864	.000543
11	14.1758	14.1604	14.1449	14.1295	14.1141	14.0986	14.0832	14.0678	14.0523	14.0369	14.0215	14.0060	.000514
12	14.7035	14.6890	14.6745	14.6600	14.6454	14.6309	14.6164	14.6019	14.5874	14.5728	14.5583	14.5438	.000484
13	15.2498	15.2363	15.2227	15.2092	15.1957	15.1822	15.1686	15.1551	15.1416	15.1281	15.1145	15.1010	.000451
14	15.8173	15.8047	15.7922	15.7796	15.7671	15.7545	15.7420	15.7294	15.7169	15.7043	15.6918	15.6792	.000418
15	16.4066	16.3951	16.3836	16.3720	16.3605	16.3490	16.3375	16.3260	16.3145	16.3030	16.2914	16.2799	.000384
16	17.0193	17.0090	16.9987	16.9884	16.9781	16.9678	16.9574	16.9471	16.9368	16.9265	16.9162	16.9059	.000343
17	17.6591	17.6499	17.6407	17.6315	17.6223	17.6131	17.6038	17.5946	17.5854	17.6762	17.5670	17.5578	.000307
18	18.3251	18.3171	18.3092	18.3012	18.2933	18.2853	18.2774	18.2694	18.2615	18.2535	18.2456	18.2376	.000265
19	19.0211	19.0145	19.0079	19.0013	18.9948	18.9882	18.9816	18.9750	18.9684	18.9618	18.9553	18.9487	.000219
20	19.7486	19.7434	19.7383	19.7331	19.7279	19.7228	19.7176	19.7124	19.7073	19.7021	19.6969	19.6918	.000172
21	20.5111	20.5073	20.5034	20.4996	20.4958	20.4919	20.4881	20.4843	20.4804	20.4766	20.4728	20.4689	.000128
22	21.3078	21.3050	21.3022	21.2994	21.2967	21.2939	21.2911	21.2883	21.2855	21.2827	21.2800	21.2772	.000093
23	22.1364	22.1343	22.1321	22.1300	22.1279	22.1258	22.1236	22.1215	22.1194	22.1173	22.1151	22.1130	.000071
24	22.9943	22.9926	22.9908	22.9891	22.9873	22.9856	22.9838	22.9821	22.9804	22.9786	22.9769	22.9751	.000058
25	23.8793	23.8774	23.8756	23.8737	23.8719	23.8700	23.8681	23.8663	23.8644	23.8626	23.8607	23.8589	.000062
26	24.7868	24.7847	24.7825	24.7804	24.7783	24.7762	24.7740	24.7719	24.7698	24.7677	24.7655	24.7634	.000071
27	25.7171	25.7145	25.7118	25.7092	25.7066	25.7040	25.7013	25.6987	25.6961	25.6935	25.6908	25.6882	.000087
28	26.6688	26.6656	26.6625	26.6593	26.6562	26.6530	26.6499	26.6467	26.6436	26.6404	26.6373	26.6341	.000105
29	27.6440	27.6400	27.6360	27.6320	27.6280	27.6240	27.6200	27.6160	27.6120	27.6080	27.6040	27.6000	.000133
30	28.6406	28.6355	28.6304	28.6253	28.6202	28.6151	28.6100	28.6048	28.5997	28.5946	28.5895	28.5844	.000170
31	29.6576	29.6511	29.6446	29.6382	29.6317	29.6252	29.6187	29.6123	29.6058	29.5993	29.5928	29.5864	.000216
32	30.6944	30.6863	30.6782	30.6701	30.6620	30.6539	30.6457	30.6376	30.6295	30.6214	30.6133	30.6052	.000270
33	31.7503	31.7404	31.7304	31.7205	31.7106	31.7007	31.6907	31.6808	31.6709	31.6610	31.6510	31.6411	.000331
34	32.8256	32.8135	32.8014	32.7894	32.7773	32.7652	32.7531	32.7411	32.7290	32.7169	32.7048	32.6928	.000402
35	33 9186	33.9044	33.8902	33.8760	33.8618	33.8476	33.8334	33.8193	33.8051	33.7909	33.7767	33.7625	.000473
36	35.0281	35.0108	34.9935	34.9762	34.9589	34.9416	34.9243	34.9071	34.8898	34.8725	34.8552	34.8379	.000576
37	36.1557	36.1353	36.1149	36.0945	36.0741	36.0537	36.0333	36.0129	35.9925	35.9721	35.9517	35.9313	.000680
38	37.2981	37.2742	37.2502	37.2263	37.2024	37.1784	37.1545	37.1306	37.1066	37.0827	37.0588	37.0348	.000798
39	38.4556	38.4273	38.3991	38.3708	38.3426	38.3143	38.2861	38.2578	38.2296	38.2013	38.1731	38.1448	.000942
40	39.6219	39.5888	39.5557	39.5226	39.4895	39.4564	39.4233	39.3903	39.3572	39.3241	39.2910	39.2579	.001103
41	40.7947	40.7561	40.7174	40.6788	40.6401	40.6015	40.5628	40.5242	40.4856	40.4469	40.4083	40.3696	.001288
42	41.9704	41.9256	41.8808	41.8360	41.7913	41.7465	41.7017	41.6569	41.6121	41.5673	41.5226	41.4778	.001493
43	43.1481	43.0964	43.0447	42.9930	42.9413	42.8896	42.8378	42.7861	42.7344	42.6827	42.6310	42.5793	.001723
44	44.3256	44.2664	44.2072	44.1480	44.0888	44.0296	43.9703	43.9111	43.8519	43.7927	43.7335	43.6743	.001973
45	45.5073	45.4395	45.3716	45.3038	45.2359	45.1681	45.1002	45.0324	44.9646	44.8967	44.8289	44.7610	.002261
46	46.6870	46.6100	46.5330	46.4560	46.3789	46.3019	46.2249	46.1479	46.0709	45.9938	45.9168	45.8398	.002567
47	47.8685	47.7816	47.6946	47.6077	47.5208	47.4338	47.3469	47.2600	47.1730	47.0861	46.9992	46.9122	.002898
48	49.0507	48.9532	48.8557	48.7583	48.6608	48.5633	48.4658	48.3684	48.2709	48.1734	48.0760	47.9785	.003249
49	50.2347	50.1258	50.0169	49.9080	49.7991	49.6902	49.5813	49.4724	49.3635	49.2546	49.1457	49.0368	.003630
50	51.4175	51.2964	51.1752	51.0541	50.9329	50.8118	50.6906	50.5695	50.4484	50.3272	50.2061	50.0849	.004038
51	52.5999	52.4656	52.3314	52.1971	52.0629	51.9286	51.7944	51.6601	51.5259	51.3916	51.2574	51.1231	.004475
52	53.7815	53.6332	53.4850	53.3367	53.1885	53.0402	52.8920	52.7437	52.5955	52.4472	52.2990	52.1507	.004942
53	54.9628	54.7995	54.6363	54.4730	54.3098	54.1465	53.9832	53.8200	53.6567	53.4935	53.3302	53.1670	.005442
54	56.1430	55.9638	55.7845	55.6053	55.4261	55.2468	55.0676	54.8884	54.7091	54.5299	54.3507	54.1714	.005974
55	57.3220	57.1259	56.9298	56.7337	56.5376	56.3415	56.1453	55.9492	55.7531	55.5570	55.3609	55.1648	.006537
56	58.5026	58.2883	58.0739	57.8596	57.6452	57.4309	57.2165	57.0022	56.7879	56.5735	56.3592	56.1448	.007145
57	59.6830	59.4491	59.2152	58.9813	58.7474	58.5135	58.2795	58.0456	57.8117	57.5778	57.3439	57.1100	.007797
58	60.8609	60.6064	60.3520	60.0975	59.8431	59.5886	59.3342	59.0797	58.8253	58.5708	58.3164	58.0620	.008482
59	62.0414	61.7653	61.4892	61.2131	60.9370	60.6609	60.3848	60.1088	59.8327	59.5566	59.2805	59.0044	.009203
60	63.2294	62.9309	62.6325	62.3340	62.0355	61.7371	61.4386	61.1401	60.8417	60.5432	60.2447	59.9463	.009949
61	64.4379	64.1166	63.7954	63.4741	63.1528	62.8316	62.5103	62.1890	61.8678	61.5465	61.2252	60.9040	.010709
62	65.6828	65.3380	64.9932	64.6484	64.3037	63.9589	63.6141	63.2693	62.9245	62.5797	62.2350	61.8902	.011493
63	66.9798	66.6112	66.2427	65.8741	65.5055	65.1370	64.7684	64.3998	64.0313	63.6627	63.2941	62.9256	.012285
64	68.3510	67.9571	67.5633	67.1694	66.7756	66.3817	65.9878	65.5940	65.2001	64.8063	64.4124	64.0186	.013128
65	69.8065	69.3858	68.9651	68.5444	68.1237	67.7030	67.2823	66.8617	66.4410	66.0203	65.5996	65.1789	.014023
66	71.3572	70.9081	70.4590	70.0098	69.5607	69.1116	68.6625	68.2134	67.7643	67.3151	66.8660	66.4169	.014970
67	73.0175	72.5369	72.0563	71.5758	71.0952	70.6146	70.1340	69.6535	69.1729	68.6923	68.2117	67.7312	.016019
68	74.7837	74.2677	73.7517	73.2358	72.7198	72.2038	71.6878	71.1719	70.6559	70.1399	69.6240	69.1080	.017199
69	76.6437	76.0894	75.5351	74.9808	74.4266	73.8723	73.3180	72.7637	72.2094	71.6551	71.1009	70.5466	.018476
70	78.5994	78.0023	77.4051	76.8080	76.2109	75.6138	75.0166	74.4195	73.8224	73.2253	72.6281	72.0310	.019904
71	80.6369	79.9893	79.3417	78.6942	78.0466	77.3990	76.7514	76.1039	75.4563	74.8087	74.1611	73.5136	.021586
72	82.7048	81.9986	81.2924	80.5863	79.8801	79.1739	78.4677	77.7616	77.0554	76.3492	75.6430	74.9369	.023539
73	84.7460	83.9731	83.2003	82.4274	81.6545	80.8817	80.1088	79.3359	78.5631	77.7902	77.0173	76.2445	.025762
74	86.7046	85.8427	84.9807	84.1188	83.2569	82.3950	81.5330	80.6711	79.8092	78.9473	78.0853	77.2234	.028731
75	88.3459	87.3911	86.4363	85.4815	84.5267	83.5719	82.6171	81.6623	80.7075	79.7527	78.7979	77.8431	.031827
76	89.6603	88.6929	87.7254	86.7580	85.7906	84.8232	83.8557	82.8883	81.9209	80.9535	79.9860	79.0186	.032247
77	91.6973	90.8442	89.9911	89.1380	88.2850	87.4319	86.5788	85.7257	84.8726	84.0195	83.1665	82.3134	.028436
78 or 31	**96.1538**	**96.4743**	**96.7948**	**97.1153**	**97.4359**	**97.7564**	**98.0769**	**98.3974**	**98.7179**	**99.0384**	**99.3590**	**99.6795**	**.010684**
30	94.8213	94.7909	94.7605	94.7301	94.6997	94.6693	94.6390	94.6086	94.5782	94.5478	94.5174	94.4870	.001013
29	94.1377	94.0583	93.9790	93.8996	93.8203	93.7410	93.6616	93.5822	93.5029	93.4235	93.3442	93.2648	.002645
28	93.6385	93.5482	93.4578	93.3675	93.2772	93.1868	93.0965	93.0062	92.9158	92.8255	92.7352	92.6448	.003011
27	92.9973	92.9228	92.8483	92.7738	92.6994	92.6249	92.5504	92.4759	92.4014	92.3270	92.2525	92.1780	.002483
26	92.2049	92.1469	92.0890	92.0310	91.9730	91.9151	91.8571	91.7991	91.7412	91.6832	91.6252	91.5673	.001932
25	91.3328	91.2853	91.2378	91.1903	91.1428	91.0953	91.0477	91.0002	90.9527	90.9052	90.8577	90.8102	.001583
24	90.3978	90.3592	90.3206	90.2820	90.2434	90.2048	90.1662	90.1277	90.0891	90.0505	90.0119	89.9733	.001286
23	89.4198	89.3883	89.3568	89.3253	89.2938	89.2623	89.2308	89.1993	89.1678	89.1363	89.1048	89.0733	.001050
22	88.4195	88.3932	88.3670	88.3407	88.3144	88.2881	88.2618	88.2356	88.2093	88.1830	88.1567	88.1305	.000876
21	87.4053	87.3834	87.3615	87.3395	87.3176	87.2957	87.2738	87.2519	87.2300	87.2080	87.1861	87.1642	.000730
20	86.3793	86.3614	86.3435	86.3256	86.3078	86.2899	86.2720	86.2541	86.2362	86.2183	86.2005	86.1826	.000596
19	85.3511	85.3363	85.3215	85.3068	85.2920	85.2772	85.2624	85.2477	85.2329	85.2181	85.2033	85.1886	.000492
18	84.3252	84.3130	84.3007	84.2885	84.2762	84.2640	84.2517	84.2395	84.2273	84.2150	84.2028	84.1905	.000408
17	83.3007	83.2910	83.2812	83.2715	83.2618	83.2520	83.2423	83.2326	83.2228	83.2131	83.2034	83.1936	.000324
16	82.2762	82.2689	82.2616	82.2544	82.2471	82.2398	82.2325	82.2253	82.2180	82.2107	82.2034	82.1962	.000242
15	81.2509	81.2460	81.2412	81.2363	81.2314	81.2266	81.2217	81.2168	81.2120	81.2071	81.2022	81.1974	.000162
14	80.2175	80.2155	80.2136	80.2116	80.2096	80.2077	80.2057	80.2037	80.2018	80.1998	80.1978	80.1959	.000065
13	79.1707	79.1719	79.1732	79.1744	79.1756	79.1769	79.1781	79.1793	79.1806	79.1818	79.1830	79.1843	.000041
12	78.1046	78.1094	78.1143	78.1191	78.1240	78.1288	78.1337	78.1385	78.1434	78.1482	78.1531	78.1580	.000162
11	77.0145	77.0232	77.0319	77.0406	77.0494	77.0581	77.0668	77.0755	77.0842	77.0930	77.1017	77.1104	.000290
10	75.8990	75.9116	75.9242	75.9368	75.9494	75.9620	75.9746	75.9873	75.9999	76.0125	76.0251	76.0377	.000420
Age.	0	1	2	3	4	5	6	7	8	9	10	11	Day.

Age.	0	1	2	3	4	5	6	7	8	9	10	11	Day.
10	14.5131	14.4990	14.4850	14.4710	14.4569	14.4428	14.4288	14.4147	14.4007	14.3866	14.3726	14.3585	.000468
11	15.0537	15.0406	15.0275	15.0145	15.0014	14.9883	14.9752	14.9622	14.9491	14.9360	14.9230	14.9099	.000436
12	15.6136	15.6016	15.5895	15.5775	15.5655	15.5535	15.5414	15.5294	15.5174	15.5054	15.4933	15.4813	.000401
13	16.1941	16.1831	16.1721	16.1612	16.1502	16.1392	16.1282	16.1173	16.1063	16.0953	16.0843	16.0734	.000366
14	16.7967	16.7868	16.7769	16.7670	16.7571	16.7472	16.7372	16.7273	16.7174	16.7075	16.6976	16.6877	.000330
15	17.4228	17.4142	17.4055	17.3969	17.3883	17.3796	17.3710	17.3624	17.3537	17.3451	17.3365	17.3278	.000288
16	18.0756	18.0681	18.0607	18.0532	18.0458	18.0383	18.0309	18.0234	18.0160	18.0085	18.0011	17.9936	.000248
17	18.7554	18.7493	18.7431	18.7370	18.7309	18.7248	18.7186	18.7125	18.7064	18.7003	18.6941	18.6880	.000204
18	19.4646	19.4599	19.4552	19.4505	19.4458	19.4411	19.4364	19.4317	19.4270	19.4223	19.4176	19.4129	.000157
19	20.2064	20.2032	20.1999	20.1967	20.1934	20.1902	20.1870	20.1837	20.1805	20.1772	20.1740	20.1707	.000108
20	20.9814	20.9796	20.9778	20.9760	20.9742	20.9724	20.9706	20.9689	20.9671	20.9653	20.9635	20.9617	.000060
21	21.7924	21.7917	21.7910	21.7903	21.7896	21.7889	21.7882	21.7876	21.7869	21.7862	21.7855	21.7848	.000023
22	22.6354	22.6354	22.6355	22.6355	22.6356	22.6356	22.6357	22.6357	22.6358	22.6358	22.6359	22.6360	.000002
23	23.5072	23.5077	23.5082	23.5087	23.5093	23.5098	23.5103	23.5108	23.5113	23.5118	23.5124	23.5129	.000017
24	24.4067	24.4072	24.4077	24.4082	24.4087	24.4092	24.4097	24.4102	24.4107	24.4112	24.4117	24.4122	.000017
25	25.3292	25.3295	25.3298	25.3302	25.3305	25.3308	25.3311	25.3315	25.3318	25.3321	25.3324	25.3328	.000011
26	26.2743	26.2742	26.2742	26.2741	26.2740	26.2740	26.2739	26.2738	26.2738	26.2737	26.2736	26.2736	.000002
27	27.2413	27.2408	27.2403	27.2399	27.2394	27.2389	27.2384	27.2380	27.2375	27.2370	27.2365	27.2361	.000016
28	28.2315	28.2303	28.2291	28.2279	28.2267	28.2255	28.2242	28.2230	28.2218	28.2206	28.2194	28.2182	.000040
29	29.2436	29.2414	29.2392	29.2370	29.2348	29.2326	29.2304	29.2283	29.2261	29.2239	29.2217	29.2195	.000073
30	30.2765	30.2731	30.2696	30.2662	30.2628	30.2593	30.2559	30.2525	30.2490	30.2456	30.2422	30.2387	.000114
31	31.3291	31.3242	31.3193	31.3143	31.3094	31.3045	31.2996	31.2947	31.2898	31.2848	31.2799	31.2750	.000164
32	32.4011	32.3945	32.3879	32.3813	32.3747	32.3681	32.3615	32.3550	32.3484	32.3418	32.3352	32.3286	.000220
33	33.4928	33.4842	33.4757	33.4671	33.4585	33.4500	33.4414	33.4328	33.4243	33.4157	33.4071	33.3986	.000285
34	34.6031	34.5922	34.5812	34.5703	34.5594	34.5485	34.5375	34.5266	34.5157	34.5048	34.4938	34.4829	.000364
35	35.7299	35.7165	35.7031	35.6896	35.6762	35.6628	35.6494	35.6360	35.6226	35.6091	35.5957	35.5823	.000447
36	36.8750	36.8587	36.8424	36.8261	36.8098	36.7935	36.7771	36.7608	36.7445	36.7282	36.7119	36.6956	.000543
37	38.0369	38.0173	37.9977	37.9780	37.9584	37.9388	37.9192	37.8996	37.8800	37.8603	37.8407	37.8211	.000654
38	39.2128	39.1891	39.1654	39.1417	39.1181	39.0944	39.0707	39.0470	39.0233	38.9996	38.9760	38.9523	.000789
39	40.3989	40.3707	40.3424	40.3142	40.2860	40.2577	40.2295	40.2013	40.1730	40.1448	40.1166	40.0883	.000941
40	41.5926	41.5591	41.5257	41.4922	41.4587	41.4253	41.3918	41.3583	41.3249	41.2914	41.2579	41.2245	.001115
41	42.7896	42.7503	42.7111	42.6718	42.6326	42.5933	42.5540	42.5148	42.4755	42.4363	42.3970	42.3578	.001308
42	43.9884	43.9426	43.8968	43.8510	43.8052	43.7594	43.7136	43.6678	43.6220	43.5762	43.5304	43.4846	.001527
43	45.1861	45.1331	45.0801	45.0271	44.9741	44.9211	44.8681	44.8152	44.7622	44.7092	44.6562	44.6032	.001766
44	46.3833	46.3222	46.2610	46.1999	46.1388	46.0776	46.0165	45.9554	45.8942	45.8331	45.7720	45.7108	.002038
45	47.5777	47.5078	47.4380	47.3681	47.2983	47.2284	47.1585	47.0887	47.0188	46.9490	46.8791	46.8093	.002328
46	48.7708	48.6915	48.6121	48.5328	48.4535	48.3742	48.2948	48.2155	48.1362	48.0569	47.9775	47.8982	.002644
47	49.9637	49.8743	49.7850	49.6956	49.6063	49.5169	49.4275	49.3382	49.2488	49.1595	49.0701	48.9808	.002978
48	51.1577	51.0574	50.9571	50.8568	50.7566	50.6563	50.5560	50.4557	50.3554	50.2551	50.1549	50.0546	.003343
49	52.3505	52.2386	52.1266	52.0147	51.9028	51.7909	51.6790	51.5670	51.4551	51.3432	51.2312	51.1193	.003731
50	53.5414	53.4190	53.2945	53.1701	53.0457	52.9213	52.7968	52.6724	52.5480	52.4236	52.2971	52.1727	.004147
51	54.7305	54.5927	54.4550	54.3172	54.1794	54.0417	53.9039	53.7661	53.6284	53.4906	53.3528	53.2151	.004592
52	55.9177	55.7657	55.6136	55.4616	55.3096	55.1576	55.0055	54.8535	54.7015	54.5495	54.3974	54.2454	.005067
53	57.1033	56.9361	56.7688	56.6016	56.4343	56.2671	56.0998	55.9326	55.7654	55.5981	55.4309	55.2636	.005575
54	58.2871	58.1038	57.9206	57.7373	57.5540	57.3708	57.1875	57.0042	56.8210	56.6377	56.4544	56.2712	.006109
55	59.4712	59.2706	59.0700	58.8694	58.6689	58.4683	58.2677	58.0671	57.8665	57.6660	57.4654	57.2648	.006686
56	60.6535	60.4343	60.2152	59.9960	59.7769	59.5577	59.3385	59.1194	58.9002	58.6811	58.4619	58.2428	.007305
57	61.8332	61.5946	61.3560	61.1174	60.8788	60.6402	60.4016	60.1631	59.9245	59.6859	59.4473	59.2087	.007953
58	63.0142	62.7551	62.4960	62.2370	61.9779	61.7188	61.4597	61.2007	60.9416	60.6825	60.4234	60.1644	.008636
59	64.2007	63.9205	63.6403	63.3601	63.0799	62.7997	62.5194	62.2392	61.9590	61.6788	61.3986	61.1184	.009340
60	65.4034	65.1018	64.8001	64.4985	64.1969	63.8952	63.5936	63.2920	62.9903	62.6887	62.3871	62.0854	.010054
61	66.6399	66.3160	65.9921	65.6682	65.3443	65.0204	64.6965	64.3727	64.0488	63.7249	63.4010	63.0771	.010796
62	67.9237	67.5774	67.2311	66.8848	66.5386	66.1923	65.8460	65.4997	65.1534	64.8071	64.4609	64.1146	.011543
63	69.2769	68.9068	68.5368	68.1667	67.7967	67.4266	67.0566	66.6865	66.3165	65.9464	65.5764	65.2063	.012335
64	70.7087	70.3134	69.9181	69.5228	69.1275	68.7322	68.3369	67.9416	67.5463	67.1510	66.7557	66.3604	.013177
65	72.2299	71.8079	71.3858	70.9638	70.5418	70.1197	69.6977	69.2757	68.8536	68.4316	68.0096	67.5875	.014068
66	73.8524	73.4007	72.9491	72.4974	72.0457	71.5941	71.1424	70.6907	70.2391	69.7874	69.3357	68.8841	.015053
67	75.5744	75.0894	74.6043	74.1193	73.6343	73.1492	72.6642	72.1792	71.6941	71.2091	70.7241	70.2390	.016168
68	77.3833	76.8622	76.3410	75.8199	75.2988	74.7777	74.2565	73.7354	73.2143	72.6932	72.1720	71.6509	.017371
69	79.2815	78.7200	78.1585	77.5971	77.0356	76.4741	75.9126	75.3512	74.7897	74.2282	73.6667	73.1053	.018716
70	81.2541	80.6450	80.0360	79.4269	78.8179	78.2088	77.5997	76.9907	76.3816	75.7726	75.1635	74.5545	.020302
71	83.2524	82.5880	81.9237	81.2593	80.5949	79.9306	79.2662	78.6018	77.9375	77.2731	76.6087	75.9444	.022145
72	85.2213	84.4940	83.7666	83.0393	82.3120	81.5847	80.8573	80.1300	79.4027	78.6754	77.9480	77.2207	.024244
73	87.1071	86.2956	85.4840	84.6725	83.8610	83.0494	82.2379	81.4264	80.6148	79.8033	78.9918	78.1802	.027051
74	87.6862	87.7869	86.8877	85.9884	85.0892	84.1899	83.2906	82.3914	81.4921	80.5929	79.6936	78.7944	.029975
75	89.9494	89.0393	88.1293	87.2192	86.3091	85.3991	84.4890	83.5789	82.6689	81.7588	80.8487	79.9387	.030335
76	91.9003	91.1007	90.3010	89.5014	88.7018	87.9022	87.1025	86.3029	85.5033	84.7037	83.9040	83.1044	.026654
77 or 32	**96.1538**	**96.4743**	**96.7948**	**97.1153**	**97.4359**	**97.7564**	**98.0769**	**98.3974**	**98.7179**	**99.0384**	**99.3590**	**99.6795**	**.010684**
31	94.8088	94.7751	94.7714	94.7077	94.6741	94.6404	94.6067	94.5730	94.5393	94.5056	94.4720	94.4383	.001123
30	94.1196	94.0616	94.0037	93.9457	93.8878	93.8298	93.7718	93.7139	93.6559	93.5980	93.5400	93.4821	.001932
29	93.6167	93.5228	93.4289	93.3350	93.2412	93.1473	93.0534	92.9595	92.8656	92.7717	92.6779	92.5840	.003129
28	92.9710	92.8932	92.8155	92.7377	92.6600	92.5822	92.5045	92.4267	92.3490	92.2712	92.1935	92.1157	.002592
27	92.1734	92.1124	92.0514	91.9904	91.9295	91.8685	91.8075	91.7465	91.6855	91.6245	91.5636	91.5026	.002033
26	91.2960	91.2457	91.1953	91.1450	91.0947	91.0443	90.9940	90.9437	90.8933	90.8430	90.7927	90.7423	.001677
25	90.3555	90.3143	90.2730	90.2318	90.1906	90.1493	90.1081	90.0669	90.0256	89.9844	89.9432	89.9019	.001374
24	89.3722	89.3382	89.3042	89.2703	89.2363	89.2023	89.1683	89.1344	89.1004	89.0664	89.0324	88.9985	.001132
23	88.3670	88.3384	88.3097	88.2811	88.2525	88.2239	88.1952	88.1666	88.1380	88.1094	88.0807	88.0521	.000954
22	87.3484	87.3242	87.3001	87.2759	87.2518	87.2276	87.2034	87.1793	87.1551	87.1310	87.1068	87.0827	.000805
21	86.3184	86.2984	86.2783	86.2583	86.2383	86.2183	86.1982	86.1782	86.1582	86.1382	86.1181	86.0981	.000667
20	85.2858	85.2690	85.2522	85.2355	85.2187	85.2019	85.1851	85.1684	85.1516	85.1348	85.1180	85.1013	.000559
19	84.2569	84.2427	84.2285	84.2144	84.2002	84.1860	84.1718	84.1577	84.1435	84.1293	84.1151	84.1010	.000472
18	83.2292	83.2176	83.2061	83.1945	83.1829	83.1714	83.1598	83.1482	83.1367	83.1251	83.1135	83.1020	.000385
17	82.2021	82.1931	82.1841	82.1750	82.1660	82.1570	82.1480	82.1390	82.1300	82.1210	82.1119	82.1029	.000300
16	81.1746	81.1681	81.1615	81.1550	81.1484	81.1419	81.1353	81.1288	81.1223	81.1157	81.1092	81.1026	.000218
15	80.1390	80.1355	80.1319	80.1284	80.1248	80.1213	80.1177	80.1142	80.1107	80.1071	80.1036	80.1000	.000118
14	79.0908	79.0905	79.0902	79.0900	79.0897	79.0894	79.0891	79.0888	79.0885	79.0882	79.0880	79.0877	.000009
13	78.0230	78.0264	78.0299	78.0333	70.0367	78.0402	78.0436	78.0470	78.0505	78.0539	78.0573	78.0608	.000114
12	76.9318	76.9392	76.9465	76.9539	76.9613	76.9687	76.9760	76.9834	76.9909	76.9982	77.0055	77.0129	.000246
11	75.8153	75.8266	75.8379	75.8493	75.8606	75.8719	75.8833	75.8946	75.9059	75.9173	75.9286	75.9399	.000377
10	74.6710	74.6872	74.7025	74.7179	74.7332	74.7486	74.7640	74.7793	74.7947	74.8100	74.8254	74.8407	.000512
Age.	0	1	2	3	4	5	6	7	8	9	10	11	Day.

Age.	0	1	2	3	4	5	6	7	8	9	10	11	Day.
10	15.3874	15.3757	15.3640	15.3523	15.3406	15.3289	15.3172	15.3055	15.2938	15.2821	15.2704	15.2587	.000390
11	15.9600	15.9494	15.9388	15.9282	15.9176	15.9070	15.8964	15.8858	15.8752	15.8646	15.8540	15.8434	.000353
12	16.5537	16.5442	16.5347	16.5252	16.5157	16.5062	16.4967	16.4873	16.4778	16.4683	16.4588	16.4493	.000316
13	17.1690	17.1606	17.1523	17.1440	17.1356	17.1272	17.1189	17.1105	17.1022	17.0938	17.0855	17.0771	.000278
14	17.8079	17.8009	17.7938	17.7868	17.7798	17.7728	17.7657	17.7587	17.7517	17.7447	17.7376	17.7306	.000234
15	18.4736	18.4678	18.4620	18.4563	18.4505	18.4447	18.4390	18.4332	18.4274	18.4216	18.4158	18.4101	.000192
16	19.1662	19.1618	19.1574	19.1530	19.1486	19.1442	19.1398	19.1354	19.1310	19.1266	19.1222	19.1178	.000147
17	19.8887	19.8858	19.8829	19.8800	19.8771	19.8742	19.8712	19.8683	19.8654	19.8625	19.8596	19.8567	.000097
18	20.6431	20.6417	20.6403	20.6390	20.6376	20.6362	20.6348	20.6335	20.6321	20.6307	20.6293	20.6280	.000046
19	21.4318	21.4319	21.4321	21.4322	21.4323	21.4325	21.4326	21.4327	21.4329	21.4330	21.4331	21.4333	.000004
20	22.2548	22.2562	22.2575	22.2588	22.2602	22.2615	22.2628	22.2642	22.2655	22.2668	22.2682	22.2695	.000043
21	23.1114	23.1135	23.1156	23.1178	23.1199	23.1220	23.1241	23.1263	23.1284	23.1305	23.1326	23.1348	.000071
22	23.9970	23.9996	24.0023	24.0049	24.0076	24.0103	24.0129	24.0156	24.0183	24.0209	24.0236	24.0263	.000087
23	24.9098	24.9125	24.9153	24.9180	24.9207	24.9235	24.9262	24.9289	24.9317	24.9344	24.9371	24.9399	.000091
24	25.8460	25.8486	25.8513	25.8539	25.8566	25.8593	25.8619	25.8646	25.8673	25.8689	25.8726	25.8753	.000087
25	26.8053	26.8077	26.8100	26.8124	26.8148	26.8172	26.8195	26.8219	26.8243	26.8267	26.8290	26.8314	.000079
26	27.7864	27.7885	27.7905	27.7926	27.7947	27.7967	27.7988	27.8009	27.8029	27.8050	27.8071	27.8091	.000069
27	28.7912	28.7926	28.7941	28.7955	28.7969	28.7984	28.7998	28.8012	28.8027	28.8041	28.8055	28.8070	.000048
28	29.8175	29.8181	29.8186	29.8192	29.8198	29.8204	29.8210	29.8215	29.8221	29.8227	29.8232	29.8238	.000019
29	30.8649	30.8644	30.8638	30.8633	30.8627	30.8622	30.8616	30.8611	30.8606	30.8600	30.8595	30.8589	.000018
30	31.9325	31.9306	31.9287	31.9268	31.9249	31.9230	31.9211	31.9193	31.9174	31.9155	31.9136	31.9117	.000063
31	33.0193	33.0159	33.0125	33.0090	33.0056	33.0022	32.9988	32.9954	32.9920	32.9885	32.9851	32.9817	.000114
32	34.1260	34.1207	34.1155	34.1102	34.1050	34.0997	34.0945	34.0892	34.0840	34.0787	34.0735	34.0682	.000175
33	35.2516	35.2442	35.2367	35.2293	35.2219	35.2144	35.2070	35.1996	35.1921	35.1847	35.1773	35.1698	.000248
34	36.3944	36.3847	36.3749	36.3652	36.3554	36.3457	36.3360	36.3262	36.3165	36.3067	36.2970	36.2872	.000325
35	37.5555	37.5431	37.5306	37.5182	37.5058	37.4933	37.4809	37.4685	37.4560	37.4436	37.4312	37.4187	.000414
36	38.7337	38.7182	38.7026	38.6871	38.6715	38.6560	38.6404	38.6249	38.6094	38.5938	38.5783	38.5627	.000518
37	39.9275	39.9081	39.8888	39.8694	39.8500	39.8307	39.8113	39.7919	39.7726	39.7532	39.7338	39.7145	.000645
38	41.1305	41.1068	41.0832	41.0595	41.0359	41.0122	40.9886	40.9650	40.9413	40.9176	40.8940	40.8703	.000788
39	42.3425	42.3139	42.2853	42.2567	42.2281	42.1995	42.1708	42.1422	42.1136	42.0850	42.0564	42.0278	.000953
40	43.5587	43.5246	43.4905	43.4565	43.4224	43.3883	43.3542	43.3202	43.2861	43.2520	43.2180	43.1839	.001136
41	44.7770	44.7367	44.6965	44.6562	44.6160	44.5757	44.5354	44.4952	44.4549	44.4147	44.3744	44.3342	.001342
42	45.9941	45.9470	45.9000	45.8529	45.8058	45.7588	45.7117	45.6646	45.6176	45.5705	45.5234	45.4764	.001569
43	47.2087	47.1539	47.0991	47.0443	46.9895	46.9347	46.8799	46.8251	46.7703	46.7155	46.6607	46.6059	.001827
44	48.4180	48.3549	48.2918	48.2286	48.1655	48.1024	48.0393	47.9762	47.9131	47.8500	47.7868	47.7237	.002104
45	49.6239	49.5518	49.4797	49.4075	49.3354	49.2633	49.1912	49.1191	49.0470	48.9748	48.9027	48.8306	.002404
46	50.8269	50.7452	50.6635	50.5818	50.5001	50.4184	50.3366	50.2549	50.1732	50.0915	50.0098	49.9281	.002723
47	52.0299	51.9378	51.8457	51.7535	51.6614	51.5693	51.4772	51.3851	51.2930	51.2008	51.1087	51.0166	.003070
48	53.2310	53.1278	53.0245	52.9213	52.8180	52.7148	52.6115	52.5083	52.4051	52.3018	52.1986	52.0953	.003441
49	54.4301	54.3150	54.1998	54.0847	53.9695	53.8544	53.7392	53.6241	53.5090	53.3938	53.2787	53.1635	.003838
50	55.6259	55.4980	55.3702	55.2423	55.1145	54.9866	54.8587	54.7309	54.6030	54.4752	54.3473	54.2195	.004262
51	56.8188	56.6773	56.5359	56.3944	56.2530	56.1115	55.9700	55.8286	55.6871	55.5457	55.4042	55.2628	.004715
52	58.0085	57.8526	57.6967	57.5408	57.3849	57.2290	57.0730	56.9171	56.7612	56.6053	56.4494	56.2935	.005197
53	59.1960	59.0248	58.8536	58.6824	58.5113	58.3401	58.1689	57.9977	57.8265	57.6553	57.4842	57.3130	.005706
54	60.3828	60.1952	60.0075	59.8199	59.6323	59.4447	59.2570	59.0694	58.8818	58.6942	58.5065	58.3189	.006254
55	61.5667	61.3614	61.1562	60.9509	60.7456	60.5404	60.3351	60.1298	59.9246	59.7193	59.5140	59.3088	.006842
56	62.7466	62.5229	62.2991	62.0754	61.8517	61.6279	61.4042	61.1805	60.9567	60.7330	60.5093	60.2855	.007458
57	63.9272	63.6841	63.4410	63.1979	62.9548	62.7117	62.4686	62.2255	61.9824	61.7393	61.4962	61.2531	.008103
58	65.1120	64.8489	64.5858	64.3227	64.0597	63.7966	63.5335	63.2704	63.0073	62.7442	62.4812	62.2181	.008769
59	66.3106	66.0272	65.7439	65.4605	65.1771	64.8938	64.6104	64.3270	64.0437	63.7603	63.4769	63.1936	.009445
60	67.5393	67.2350	66.9306	66.6263	66.3219	66.0176	65.7132	65.4089	65.1046	64.8002	64.4959	64.1915	.010145
61	68.8104	68.4851	68.1597	67.8344	67.5090	67.1837	66.8583	66.5330	66.2077	65.8823	65.5570	65.2316	.010845
62	70.1466	69.7989	69.4511	69.1034	68.7557	68.4079	68.0602	67.7125	67.3647	67.0170	66.6693	66.3215	.011591
63	71.5562	71.1847	70.8133	70.4418	70.0704	69.6989	69.3274	68.9560	68.5845	68.2131	67.8416	67.4702	.012382
64	73.0492	72.6526	72.2560	71.8594	71.4628	71.0662	70.6696	70.2730	69.8764	69.4798	69.0832	68.6866	.013220
65	74.6372	74.2127	73.7882	73.3637	72.9393	72.5148	72.0903	71.6658	71.2413	70.8168	70.3924	69.9679	.014149
66	76.3170	75.8610	75.4051	74.9491	74.4931	74.0372	73.5812	73.1252	72.6693	72.2133	71.7573	71.3014	.015199
67	78.0777	77.5877	77.0977	76.6078	76.1178	75.6278	75.1378	74.6479	74.1579	73.6679	73.1780	72.6880	.016332
68	79.9211	79.3931	78.8650	78.3370	77.8090	77.2809	76.7529	76.2249	75.6968	75.1688	74.6408	74.1127	.017601
69	81.8331	81.2601	80.6872	80.1142	79.5413	78.9683	78.3954	77.8224	77.2495	76.6765	76.1036	75.5306	.019098
70	83.7656	83.1408	82.5160	81.8913	81.2665	80.6417	80.0170	79.3922	78.7674	78.1426	77.5178	76.8931	.020826
71	85.6664	84.9817	84.2971	83.6124	82.9278	82.2431	81.5585	80.8738	80.1892	79.5045	78.8199	78.1352	.022822
72	87.4840	86.7196	85.9552	85.1909	84.4265	83.6621	82.8977	82.1334	81.3690	80.6046	79.8402	79.0759	.025479
73	89.0042	88.1569	87.3097	86.4624	85.6151	84.7679	83.9206	83.0733	82.2261	81.3788	80.5315	79.6843	.028242
74	90.2198	89.3633	88.5068	87.6503	86.7939	85.9374	85.0809	84.2244	83.3679	82.5114	81.6550	80.7985	.028549
75	92.0897	91.3400	90.5902	89.8405	89.0907	88.3410	87.5912	86.8415	86.0918	85.3420	84.5923	83.8425	.024991
76 or 33	**96.1538**	**96.4743**	**96.7948**	**97.1153**	**97.4359**	**97.7564**	**98.0769**	**98.3974**	**98.7179**	**99.0384**	**99.3590**	**99.6795**	**.010684**
32	94.7956	94.7584	94.7213	94.6841	94.6470	94.6098	94.5727	94.5355	94.4984	94.4612	94.4241	94.3870	.001238
31	94.1005	94.0137	93.9270	93.8402	83.7535	93.6667	93.5800	93.4932	93.4065	93.3197	93.2330	93.1462	.002892
30	93.5938	93.4962	93.3986	93.3010	93.2033	93.1057	93.0081	92.9105	92.8129	92.7152	92.6176	92.5200	.003254
29	92.9435	92.8623	92.7811	92.6999	92.6187	92.5375	92.4563	92.3751	92.2939	92.2127	92.1315	92.0503	.002707
28	92.1393	92.0752	92.0112	91.9471	91.8830	91.8190	91.7549	91.6908	91.6268	91.5627	91.4986	91.4346	.002135
27	91.2572	91.2039	91.1506	91.0973	91.0441	90.9908	90.9375	90.8842	90.8309	90.7776	90.7244	90.6711	.001776
26	90.3111	90.2671	90.2231	90.1791	90.1351	90.0911	90.0470	90.0030	89.9590	89.9150	89.8710	89.8270	.001467
25	89.3224	89.2858	89.2492	89.2126	89.1760	89.1394	89.1028	89.0663	89.0297	88.9931	88.9565	88.9199	.001220
24	88.3120	88.2809	88.2498	88.2187	88.1876	88.1565	88.1254	88.0944	88.0633	88.0322	88.0011	87.9700	.001036
23	87.2886	87.2621	87.2356	87.2091	87.1826	87.1561	87.1296	87.1031	87.0766	87.0501	87.0236	86.9971	.000883
22	86.2544	86.2321	86.2099	86.1876	86.1654	86.1431	86.1209	86.0986	86.0764	86.0541	86.0319	86.0096	.000742
21	85.2180	85.1991	85.1802	85.1613	85.1424	85.1235	85.1045	85.0856	85.0667	85.0478	85.0289	85.0100	.000630
20	84.1849	84.1687	84.1526	84.1364	84.1203	84.1041	84.0880	84.0718	84.0556	84.0395	84.0233	84.0072	.000538
19	83.1545	83.1410	83.1275	83.1140	83.1005	83.0870	83.0735	83.0601	83.0466	83.0331	83.0196	83.0061	.000450
18	82.1245	82.1136	82.1028	82.0920	82.0811	82.0702	82.0594	82.0485	82.0377	82.0268	82.0160	82.0051	.000362
17	81.0947	81.0864	81.0781	81.0698	81.0616	81.0533	81.0450	81.0367	81.0284	81.0201	81.0119	81.0036	.000276
16	80.0570	80.0518	80.0466	80.0414	80.0362	80.0310	80.0257	80.0205	80.0153	80.0101	80.0049	79.9997	.000173
15	79.0068	79.0050	79.0031	79.0013	78.9994	78.9976	78.9957	78.9939	78.9921	78.9902	78.9884	78.9865	.000061
14	77.9377	77.9396	77.9415	77.9435	77.9454	77.9473	77.9492	77.9512	77.9531	77.9550	77.9570	77.9589	.000064
13	76.8450	76.8510	76.8569	76.8629	76.8688	76.8748	76.8807	76.8867	76.8927	76.8986	76.9046	76.9105	.000298
12	75.7275	75.7375	75.7475	75.7575	75.7675	75.7775	75.7875	75.7975	75.8075	75.8175	75.8275	75.8375	.000333
11	74.5831	75.5972	74.6118	74.6254	74.6395	74.6536	74.6676	74.6817	74.6958	74.7099	74.7240	74.7381	.000470
10	73.4133	73.4313	73.4492	73.4672	73.4852	73.5031	73.5211	73.5391	73.5570	73.5750	73.5930	73.6109	.000599
Age.	0	1	2	3	4	5	6	7	8	9	10	11	Day.

Age.	0	1	2	3	4	5	6	7	8	9	10	11	Day.
10	16.2899	16.2807	16.2714	16.2622	16.2530	16.2437	16.2345	16.2253	16.2160	16.2068	16.1976	16.1883	.000308
11	16.8959	16.8878	16.8798	16.8717	16.8636	16.8556	16.8475	16.8394	16.8314	16.8233	16.8152	16.8072	.000269
12	17.5241	17.5172	17.5104	17.5035	17.4967	17.4898	17.4830	17.4761	17.4693	17.4624	17.4556	17.4487	.000228
13	18.1754	18.1699	18.1644	18.1590	18.1535	18.1480	18.1425	18.1370	18.1315	18.1260	18.1206	18.1151	.000183
14	18.8536	18.8494	18.8452	18.8410	18.8368	18.8326	18.8284	18.8243	18.8201	18.8159	18.8117	18.8075	.000140
15	19.5587	19.5560	19.5532	19.5505	19.5477	19.5450	19.5422	19.5395	19.5368	19.5340	19.5313	19.5285	.000091
16	20.2934	20.2922	20.2910	20.2898	20.2886	20.2874	20.2862	20.2851	20.2839	20.2827	20.2815	20.2803	.000040
17	21.0607	21.0611	21.0615	21.0619	21.0623	21.0627	21.0631	21.0635	21.0639	21.0643	21.0647	21.0651	.000013
18	21.8615	21.8635	21.8654	21.8674	21.8693	21.8713	21.8732	21.8752	21.8772	21.8791	21.8811	21.8830	.000065
19	22 6977	22.7009	22.7041	22.7073	22.7105	22.7137	22.7170	22.7202	22.7234	22.7266	22.7298	22.7330	.000107
20	23.5656	23.5697	23.4738	23.5780	23.5821	23.5862	23.5903	23.5945	23.5986	23.6027	23.6068	23.6110	.000137
21	24.4642	24.4689	24.4737	24.4784	24.4831	24.4879	24.4926	24.4973	24.5021	24.5068	24.5115	24.5163	.000158
22	25.3900	25.3949	25.3998	25.4046	25.4095	25.4144	25.4193	25.4242	25.4291	25.4340	25.4388	25.4437	.000163
23	26.3389	26.3438	26.3487	26.3536	26.3585	26.3634	26.3683	26.3732	26.3781	26.3830	26.3879	26.3928	.000163
24	27.3114	27.3161	27.3208	27.3255	27.3302	27.3349	27.3395	27.3442	27.3489	27.3536	27.3583	27.3630	.000156
25	28.3060	28.3105	28.3150	28.3194	28.3239	28.3284	28.3329	28.3374	28.3419	28.3463	28.3508	28.3553	.000149
26	29.3291	29.3326	29.3362	29.3397	29.3433	29.3468	29.3503	29.3539	29.3574	29.3610	29.3645	29.3681	.000118
27	30.3641	30.3673	30.3705	30.3737	30.3769	30.3801	30.3833	30.3866	30.3898	30.3930	30.3962	30.3994	.000107
28	31.4249	31.4271	31.4293	31.4315	31.4338	31.4360	31.4382	31.4404	31.4426	31.4448	31.4471	31.4493	.000074
29	32.5061	32.5071	32.5081	32.5091	32.5101	32.5111	32.5120	32.5130	32.5140	32.5150	32.5160	32.5170	.000033
30	33.6070	33.6066	33.6062	33.6058	33.6054	33.6050	33.6045	33.6041	33.6037	33.6033	33.6029	33.6025	.000013
31	34.7275	34.7254	34.7233	34.7212	34.7191	34.7170	34.7150	34.7129	34.7108	34.7087	34.7066	34.7045	.000070
32	35.8670	35.8629	35.8587	35.8546	35.8505	35.8464	35.8422	35.8381	35.8340	35.8299	35.8257	35.8216	.000137
33	37.0240	37.0177	37.0115	37.0052	36.9990	36.9927	36.9865	36.9802	36.9740	36.9677	36.9615	36.9552	.000208
34	38.2000	38.1912	38.1824	38.1737	38.1649	38.1561	38.1473	38.1386	38.1298	38.1210	38.1122	38.1035	.000292
35	39.3929	39.3812	39.3695	39.3579	39.3462	39.3345	39.3228	39.3112	39.2995	39.2878	39.2761	39.2645	.000389
36	40.6016	40.5863	40.5710	40.5557	40.5405	40.5252	40.5099	40.4946	40.4793	40.4640	40.4488	40.4335	.000509
37	41.8211	41.8018	41.7824	41.7631	41.7438	41.7245	41.7051	41.6858	41.6665	41.6472	41.6278	41.6085	.000644
38	43.0486	43.0246	43.0006	42.9765	42.9525	42.9285	42.9045	42.8805	42.8565	42.8324	42.8084	42.7844	.000800
39	44.2816	44.2524	44.2232	44.1940	44.1648	44.1356	44.1063	44.0771	44.0479	44.0187	43.9895	43.9603	.000973
40	45.5175	45.4824	45.4474	45.4123	45.3772	45.3422	45.3071	45.2720	45.2370	45.2019	45.1668	45.1318	.001169
41	46.7525	46.7110	46.6695	46.6280	46.5864	46.5449	46.5034	46.4619	46.4204	46.3788	46.3373	46.2958	.001384
42	47.9847	47.9358	47.8870	47.8381	47.7893	47.7404	47.6916	47.6427	47.5939	47.5450	47.4962	47.4473	.001628
43	49.2096	49.1528	49.0961	49.0393	48.9826	48.9258	48.8691	48.8123	48.7556	48.6988	48.6421	48.5853	.001892
44	50.4288	50.3635	50.2981	50.2328	50.1674	50.1021	50.0367	49.9714	49.9061	49.8407	49.7754	49.7100	.002178
45	51.6430	51.5685	51.4941	51.4196	51.3452	51.2707	51.1962	51.1218	51.0473	50.9729	50.8984	50.8240	.002482
46	52.8544	52.7700	52.6856	52.6012	52.5168	52.4324	52.3480	52.2635	52.1791	52.0947	52.0103	51.9259	.002813
47	54.0630	53.9680	53.8730	53.7780	53.6829	53.5879	53.4929	53.3979	53.3029	53.2078	53.1128	53.0178	.003167
48	55.2687	55.1623	55.0559	54.9495	54.8432	54.7368	54.6304	54.5240	54.4176	54.3112	54.2049	54.0985	.003546
49	56.4711	56.3526	56.2341	56.1156	55.9971	55.8786	55.7601	55.6416	55.5231	55.4046	55.2861	55.1676	.003950
50	57.6691	57.5376	57.4061	57.2747	57.1432	57.0117	56.8802	56.7488	56.6173	56.4858	56.3543	56.2229	.004382
51	58.8628	58.7175	58.5723	58.4270	58.2818	58.1365	57.9913	57.8460	57.7008	57.5555	57.4103	57.2650	.004842
52	60.0527	59.8929	59.7332	59.5734	59.4137	59.2539	59.0941	58.9344	58.7746	58.6149	58.4551	58.2954	.005325
53	61.2414	61.0660	60.8905	60.7151	60.5397	60.3642	60.1888	60.0134	59.8379	59.6625	59.4871	59.3116	.005848
54	62.4263	62.2341	62.0419	61.8497	61.6575	61.4653	61.2731	61.0809	60.8887	60.6965	60.5043	60.3121	.006407
55	63.6059	63.3962	63.1865	62.9767	62.7670	62.5573	62.3476	62.1379	61.9282	61.7184	61.5087	61.2990	.006990
56	64.7848	64.5567	64.3286	64.1005	63.8724	63.6443	63.4161	63.1880	62.9599	62.7318	62.5037	62.2756	.007603
57	65.9672	65.7202	65.4732	65.2262	64.9792	64.7322	64.4852	64.2383	63.9913	63.7443	63.4973	63.2503	.008233
58	67.1616	66.8954	66.6293	66.3631	66.0970	65.8308	65.5647	65.2985	65.0324	64.7662	64.5001	64.2340	.008872
59	68.3825	68.0967	67.8108	67.5250	67.2392	66.9533	66.6675	66.3817	66.0958	65.8100	65.5242	65.2383	.009528
60	69.6427	69.3371	69.0314	68.7257	68.4201	68.1144	67.8087	67.5031	67.1974	66.8917	66.5861	66.2804	.010187
61	70.9635	70.6367	70.3100	69.9832	69.6565	69.3297	69.0030	68.6762	68.3495	68.0227	67.6960	67.3692	.010892
62	72.3521	72.0030	71.6539	71.3048	70.9558	70.6067	70.2576	69.9085	69.5594	69.2103	68.8613	68.5122	.011636
63	73.8186	73.4459	73.0732	72.7005	72.3278	71.9551	71.5824	71.2097	70.8370	70.4643	70.0916	69.7189	.012423
64	75.3740	74.9750	74.5761	74.1771	73.7781	73.3792	72.9802	72.5812	72.1823	71.7833	71.3843	70.9854	.013299
65	77.0151	76.5865	76.1578	75.7292	75.3006	74.8719	74.4433	74.0147	73.5860	73.1574	72.7288	72.3001	.014288
66	78.7300	78.2693	77.8085	77.3478	76.8871	76.4263	75.9656	75.5049	75.0441	74.5834	74.1227	73.6619	.015358
67	80.5217	80.0251	79.5284	79.0318	78.5351	78.0385	77.5418	77.0452	76.5486	76.0519	75.5553	75.0586	.016555
68	82.3760	81.8370	81.2979	80.7589	80.2199	79.6808	79.1418	78.6028	78.0637	77.5247	76.9857	76.4466	.017968
69	84.2470	83.6585	83.0701	82.4816	81.8932	81.3047	80.7163	80.1278	79.5394	78.9510	78.3625	77.7740	.019615
70	86.0835	85.4430	84.8025	84.1620	83.5215	82.8810	82.2404	81.5999	80.9594	80.3189	79.6784	79.0379	.021350
71	87.8370	87.1168	86.3966	85.6764	84.9562	84.2360	83.5158	82.7956	82.0754	81.3552	80.6350	79.9148	.024007
72	89.3021	88.5035	87.7048	86.9062	86.1076	85.3090	84.5103	83.7117	82.9131	82.1145	81.3158	80.5172	.029621
73	90.4725	89.6662	88.8599	88.0536	87.2473	86.4410	85.6346	84.8283	84.0220	83.2157	82.4094	81.6031	.026877
74	92.2667	91.5636	90.8605	90.1573	89.4542	88.7511	88.0480	87.3449	86.6418	85.9386	85.2355	84.5324	.023437
75 or 34	**96.1538**	**96.4743**	**96.7948**	**97.1153**	**97.4359**	**97.7564**	**98.0769**	**98.3974**	**98.7179**	**99.0384**	**99.3590**	**99.6795**	**.010684**
33	94.7817	94.7409	94.7001	94.6593	94.6185	94.5777	94.5369	94.4961	94.4553	94.4145	94.3737	94.3329	.001360
32	94.0804	93.9897	93.8989	93.8082	93.7175	93.6267	93.5360	93.4453	93.3545	93.2638	93.1731	93.0823	.003024
31	93.5698	93.4682	93.3667	93.2651	93.1636	93.0620	92.9605	92.8590	92.7574	92.6558	92.5543	94.4527	.003385
30	92.9146	92.8298	92.7450	92.6601	92.5753	92.4905	92.4056	92.3208	92.2360	92.1512	92.0663	91.9815	.002827
29	92.1056	92.0381	91.9706	91.9031	91.8357	91.7682	91.7007	91.6332	91.5657	91.4982	91.4308	91.3633	.002249
28	91.2165	91.1601	91.1037	91.0473	90.9909	90.9345	90.8781	90.8218	90.7654	90.7090	90.6526	90.5962	.001880
27	90.2645	90.2176	90.1707	90.1238	90.0769	90.0300	89.9830	89.9361	89.8892	89.8423	89.7954	89.7485	.001563
26	89.2701	89.2308	89.1914	89.1521	89.1128	89.0735	89.0341	88.9948	88.9555	88.9162	88.8768	88.8375	.001311
25	88.2544	88.2207	88.1870	88.1533	88.1197	88.0860	88.0523	88.0186	87.9849	87.9512	87.9176	87.8839	.001123
24	87.2260	87.1970	87.1681	87.1391	87.1102	87.0812	87.0523	87.0233	86.9944	86.9654	86.9365	86.9075	.000965
23	86.1871	86.1625	86.1380	86.1134	86.0888	86.0642	86.0396	86.0151	85.9905	85.9659	85.9413	85.9168	.000819
22	85.1468	85.1257	85.1045	85.0834	85.0623	85.0412	85.0200	84.9989	84.9778	84.9567	84.9355	84.9144	.000704
21	84.1102	84.0919	84.0736	84.0553	84.0370	84.0187	84.0004	83.9822	83.9639	83.9456	83.9273	83.9090	.000610
20	83.0759	83.0604	83.0449	83.0294	83.0140	82.9985	82.9830	82.9675	82.9520	82.9365	82.9211	82.9056	.000516
19	82.0434	82.0306	82.0179	82.0051	81.9923	81.9796	81.9668	81.9540	81.9413	81.9285	81.9157	81.9030	.000425
18	81.0109	81.0008	80.9907	80.9806	80.9705	80.9604	80.9502	80.9401	80.9300	80.9199	80.9098	80.8997	.000337
17	79.9711	79.9642	79.9572	79.9503	79.9433	79.9364	79.9294	79.9225	79.9156	79.9086	79.9017	79.8947	.000231
16	78.9190	78.9155	78.9120	78.9085	78.9050	78.9015	78.8980	78.8945	78.8910	78.8875	78.8840	78.8805	.000117
15	77.8481	77.8485	77.8488	77.8492	77.8495	77.8499	77.8502	77.8506	77.8510	77.8513	77.8517	77.8520	.000012
14	76.7541	76.7586	76.7630	76.7675	76.7720	76.7764	76.7809	76.7854	76.7898	76.7943	76.7988	76.8032	.000149
13	75.6352	75.6438	75.6524	75.6610	75.6696	75.6782	75.6868	75.6954	75.7040	75.7126	75.7212	75.7298	.000287
12	74.4899	74.5027	74.5154	74.5282	75.5410	74.5538	74.5665	74.5793	74.5921	74.6049	74.6176	74.6304	.000426
11	73.3193	73.3360	73.3527	73.3695	73.3862	73.4029	73.4196	73.4364	73.4531	73.4698	73.4865	73.5033	.000557
10	72.1256	72.1460	72.1664	72.1868	72.2072	72.2276	72.2480	72.2684	72.2888	72.3092	72.3296	72.3500	.000680
Age.	0	1	2	3	4	5	6	7	8	9	10	11	Day.

Age.	0	1	2	3	4	5	6	7	8	9	10	11	Day.
10	17.2220	17.2153	17.2086	17.2018	17.1951	17.1884	17.1817	17.1750	17.1683	17.1615	17.1548	17.1481	.000224
11	17.8622	17.8567	17.8513	17.8458	17.8404	17.8349	17.8294	17.8240	17.8185	17.8131	17.8076	17.8022	.000182
12	18.5262	18.5222	18.5181	18.5141	18.5101	18.5060	18.5020	18.4980	18.4939	18.4899	18.4859	18.4818	.000134
13	19.2162	19.2135	19.2109	19.2082	19.2056	19.2029	19.2002	19.1976	19.1949	19.1923	19.1896	19.1870	.000088
14	19.9333	19.9321	19.9310	19.9298	19.9286	19.9275	19.9263	19.9251	19.9240	19.9228	19.9216	19.9205	.000039
15	20.6801	20.6806	20.6810	20.6815	20.6819	20.6824	20.6828	20.6833	20.6838	20.6842	20.6847	20.6851	.000015
16	21.4592	21.4613	21.4634	21.4655	21.4676	21.4697	21.4718	21.4739	21.4760	21.4781	21.4802	21.4823	.000070
17	22.2723	22.2760	22.2797	22.2835	22.2872	22.2909	22.2946	22.2984	22.3021	22.3058	22.3095	22.3133	.000124
18	23.1199	23.1250	23.1300	23.1350	23.1401	23.1451	23.1502	23.1552	23.1603	23.1653	23.1704	23.1754	.000168
19	24.0006	24.0066	24.0126	24.0186	24.0246	24.0306	24.0365	24.0425	24.0485	24.0545	24.0605	24.0665	.000200
20	24.9100	24.9167	24.9234	24.9301	24.9369	24.9436	24.9503	24.9570	24.9637	24.9704	24.9772	24.9839	.000224
21	25.8482	25.8551	25.8620	25.8690	25.8759	25.8828	25.8897	25.8967	25.9036	25.9105	25.9174	25.9244	.000231
22	26.8096	26.8166	26.8236	26.8307	26.8377	26.8447	26.8517	26.8588	26.8658	26.8728	26.8798	26.8869	.000234
23	27.7940	27.8009	27.8078	27.8147	27.8217	27.8286	27.8355	27.8424	27.8493	27.8562	27.8632	27.8701	.000230
24	28.8011	28.8079	28.8147	28.8215	28.8283	28.8351	28.8418	28.8486	28.8554	28.8622	28.8690	28.8758	.000226
25	29.8320	29.8384	29.8447	29.8511	29.8574	29.8638	29.8701	29.8765	29.8829	29.8892	29.8956	29.9019	.000212
26	30.8845	30.8902	30.8959	30.9016	30.9074	30.9131	30.9188	30.9245	30.9302	30.9360	30.9417	30.9474	.000190
27	31.9582	31.9630	31.9679	31.9727	31.9775	31.9824	31.9872	31.9920	31.9969	32.0017	32.0065	32.0114	.000161
28	33.0520	33.0557	33.0594	33.0632	33.0669	33.0706	33.0743	33.0781	33.0818	33.0855	33.0892	33.0930	.000124
29	34.1656	34.1681	34.1705	34.1730	34.1755	34.1779	34.1804	34.1829	34.1853	34.1878	34.1903	34.1927	.000082
30	35.2992	35.3001	35.3010	35.3020	35.3029	35.3038	35.3047	35.3056	35.3065	35.3074	35.3084	35.3093	.000030
31	36.4517	36.4507	36.4497	36.4487	36.4478	36.4468	36.4458	36.4448	36.4438	36.4428	36.4419	36.4409	.000033
32	37.6216	37.6186	37.6157	37.6127	37.6098	37.6068	37.6038	37.6009	37.5979	37.5950	37.5920	37.5891	.000098
33	38.8106	38.8053	38.8000	38.7947	38.7894	38.7841	38.7787	38.7734	38.7681	38.7628	38.7575	38.7522	.000177
34	40.0171	40.0091	40.0011	39.9930	39.9850	39.9770	39.9690	39.9610	39.9530	39.9450	39.9369	39.9289	.000267
35	41.2394	41.2280	41.2165	41.2051	41.1937	41.1822	41.1708	41.1594	41.1479	41.1365	41.1251	41.1136	.000381
36	42.4725	42.4572	42.4420	42.4267	42.4115	42.3962	42.3810	42.3657	42.3505	42.3352	42.3200	42.3047	.000508
37	43.7152	43.6955	43.6758	43.6561	43.6364	43.6167	43.5970	43.5773	43.5576	43.5379	43.5182	43.4985	.000657
38	44.9622	44.9376	44.9130	44.8884	44.8638	44.8392	44.8146	44.7900	44.7654	44.7408	44.7162	44.6916	.000820
39	46.2135	46.1833	46.1531	46.1230	46.0928	46.0626	46.0324	46.0022	45.9720	45.9418	45.9117	45.8815	.001006
40	47.4644	47.4281	47.3918	47.3555	47.3192	47.2829	47.2466	47.2104	47.1741	47.1378	47.1015	47.0652	.001209
41	48.7129	48.6696	48.6264	48.5831	48.5399	48.4966	48.4533	48.4101	48.3668	48.3236	48.2803	48.2371	.001442
42	49.9539	49.9031	49.8523	49.8016	49.7508	49.7000	49.6492	49.5985	49.5477	49.4969	49.4461	49.3954	.001692
43	51.1871	51.1282	51.0692	51.0103	50.9513	50.8924	50.8334	50.7745	50.7156	50.6566	50.5977	50.5387	.001965
44	52.4129	52.3453	52.2776	52.2100	52.1424	52.0747	52.0071	51.9395	51.8718	51.8042	51.7366	51.6689	.002254
45	53.6340	53.5569	53.4798	53.4027	53.3256	53.2485	53.1713	53.0942	53.0171	52.9400	52.8629	52.7858	.002570
46	54.8495	54.7622	54.6750	54.5877	54.5005	54.4132	54.3260	54.2387	54.1514	54.0642	53.9769	53.8897	.002908
47	56.0613	55.9632	55.8651	55.7670	55.6689	55.5708	55.4726	55.3745	55.2764	55.1783	55.0802	54.9821	.003270
48	57.2688	57.1591	57.0494	56.9397	56.8300	56.7203	56.6106	56.5010	56.3913	56.2816	56.1719	56.0622	.003656
49	58.4717	58.3497	58.2276	58.1056	57.9835	57.8615	57.7394	57.6174	57.4954	57.3733	57.2513	57.1292	.004068
50	59.6689	59.5337	59.3985	59.2633	59.1281	58.9929	58.8577	58.7226	58.5874	58.4522	58.3170	58.1818	.004506
51	60.8613	60.7123	60.5632	60.4142	60.2652	60.1162	59.9671	59.8181	59.6691	59.5201	59.3710	59.2220	.004967
52	62.0507	61.8868	61.7229	61.5590	61.3950	61.2311	61.0672	60.9033	60.7394	60.5754	60.4115	60.2476	.005464
53	63.2358	63.0559	63.8760	62.6961	62.5162	62.3363	62.1564	61.9766	61.7967	61.6168	61.4369	61.2570	.005996
54	64.4148	64.2183	64.0217	63.8252	63.6286	63.4321	63.2355	63.0390	62.8425	62.6459	63.4494	62.2528	.006551
55	65.5917	65.3777	65.1637	64.9497	64.7358	64.5218	64.3078	64.0938	63.8798	63.6658	63.4519	63.2379	.007133
56	66.7705	66.5386	66.3067	66.0748	65.8429	65.6110	65.3791	65.1472	64.9153	64.6834	64.4515	64.2196	.007730
57	67.9604	67.7104	67.4604	67.2105	66.9605	66.7105	66.4605	66.2106	65.9606	65.7106	65.4606	65.2107	.008332
58	69.1745	68.9060	68.6374	68.3689	68.1003	67.8318	67.5632	67.2947	67.0262	66.7576	66.4891	66.2205	.008951
59	70.4249	70.1377	69.8505	69.5633	69.2761	68.9889	68.7017	68.4145	68.1273	67.8401	67.5529	67.2657	.009573
60	71.7303	71.4233	71.1162	70.8092	70.5022	70.1951	69.8881	69.5811	69.2740	68.9670	68.6600	68.3529	.010234
61	73.0997	72.7716	72.4436	72.1155	71.7875	71.4594	71.1313	70.8033	70.4752	70.1472	69.8191	69.4911	.010935
62	74.5513	74.2010	73.8507	73.5004	73.1501	72.7998	72.4495	72.0993	71.7390	71.3887	71.0384	70.6881	.011676
63	76.0661	75.6911	75.3161	74.9411	74.5661	74.1911	73.8161	73.4411	73.0661	72.6911	72.3161	71.9411	.012500
64	77.6705	77.2675	76.8645	76.4616	76.0586	75.6556	75.2526	74.8497	74.4467	74.0437	73.6407	73.2378	.013432
65	79.3432	78.9100	78.4767	78.0435	77.6102	77.1770	76.7437	76.3105	75.8773	75.4440	75.0108	74.5775	.014441
66	81.0858	80.6186	80.1515	79.6843	79.2172	78.7500	78.2828	77.8157	77.3485	76.8814	76.4142	75.9471	.015572
67	82.8857	82.3784	81.8712	81.3639	80.8566	80.3494	79.8421	79.3348	78.8276	78.3203	77.8130	77.3058	.016909
68	84.6989	84.1449	83.5908	83.0368	82.4828	81.9287	81.3747	80.8207	80.2666	79.7126	79.1586	78.6045	.018468
69	86.4748	85.8676	85.2605	84.6533	84.0462	83.4390	82.8318	82.2247	81.6175	81.0104	80.4032	79.7961	.020238
70	88.2176	87.5347	86.8517	86.1688	85.4858	84.8029	84.1200	83.4370	82.7541	82.0711	81.3882	80.7052	.022765
71	89.5811	88.8280	88.0750	87.3219	86.5689	85.8158	85.0727	84.3097	83.5566	82.8036	82.0505	81.2975	.025102
72	90.7092	89.9498	89.1905	88.4311	87.6717	86.9124	86.1530	85.3936	84.6343	83.8749	83.1155	82.3562	.025312
73	92.4323	91.7728	91.1133	90.4538	89.7943	89.1348	88.4753	87.8158	87.1563	86.4968	85.8373	85.1778	.021983
74 or 35	**96.1538**	**96.4743**	**96.7948**	**97.1153**	**97.4359**	**97.7564**	**98.0769**	**98.3974**	**98.7179**	**99.0384**	**99.3590**	**99.6795**	**.010684**
34	94.7671	94.7224	94.6778	94.6331	94.5885	94.5438	94.4992	94.4545	94.4099	94.3652	94.3206	94.2760	.001488
33	94.0591	93.9642	93.8692	93.7743	93.6794	93.5845	93.4895	93.3946	93.2997	93.2048	93.1098	93.0149	.003164
32	93.5445	93.4388	93.3331	93.2274	93.1218	93.0161	92.9104	92.8047	92.6990	92.5933	92.4877	92.3820	.003523
31	92.8841	92.7955	92.7068	92.6182	92.5296	92.4410	92.3523	92.2637	92.1751	92.0865	91.9978	91.9092	.002954
30	92.0692	91.9982	91.9272	91.8562	91.7853	91.7143	91.6433	91.5723	91.5013	91.4303	91.3594	91.2884	.002366
29	91.1738	91.1141	91.0545	90.9948	90.9352	90.8755	90.8159	90.7562	90.6966	90.6370	90.5773	90.5176	.001988
28	90.2156	90.1656	90.1157	90.0657	90.0157	89.9658	89.9158	89.8658	89.8159	89.7659	89.7159	89.6660	.001665
27	89.2152	89.1730	89.1308	89.0886	89.0464	89.0042	88.9620	88.9199	88.8777	88.8355	88.7933	88.7511	.001406
26	88.1939	88.1575	88.1211	88.0847	88.0483	88.0119	87.9755	87.9392	87.9028	87.8664	87.8300	87.7936	.001213
25	87.1604	87.1289	87.0974	87.0658	87.0343	87.0028	86.9713	86.9398	86.9083	86.8767	86.8452	86.8137	.001050
24	86.1168	86.0898	86.0628	86.0357	86.0087	85.9817	85.9547	85.9277	85.9007	85.8736	85.8466	85.8196	.000900
23	85.0720	85.0486	85.0251	85.0017	84.9783	84.9548	84.9314	84.9080	84.8845	84.8611	84.8377	84.8142	.000781
22	84.0318	84.0113	83.9908	83.9703	83.9498	83.9293	83.9087	83.8882	83.8677	83.8472	83.8267	83.8062	.000683
21	82.9943	82.9767	82.9591	82.9415	82.9239	82.9063	82.8886	82.8710	82.8534	82.8358	82.8182	82.8006	.000587
20	81.9581	81.9433	81.9286	81.9138	81.8991	81.8843	81.8696	81.8548	81.8401	81.8253	81.8106	81.7958	.000492
19	80.9233	80.9113	80.8993	80.8872	80.8752	80.8632	80.8512	80.8392	80.8272	80.8151	80.8031	80.7911	.000400
18	79.8811	79.8723	79.8636	79.8548	79.8461	79.8373	79.8285	79.8198	79.8110	79.8023	79.7935	79.7848	.000292
17	78.8270	78.8218	78.8165	78.8113	78.8061	78.8009	78.7956	78.7904	78.7852	78.7800	78.7747	78.7695	.000174
16	77.7543	77.7530	77.7517	77.7505	77.7492	77.7479	77.7466	77.7454	77.7441	77.7428	77.7415	77.7403	.000042
15	76.6586	76.6615	76.6644	76.6674	76.6703	76.6732	76.6761	76.6791	76.6820	76.6849	76.6878	76.6908	.000097
14	75.5386	75.5457	75.5528	75.5600	75.5671	75.5742	75.5813	75.5884	75.5955	75.6026	75.6098	75.6169	.000237
13	74.3920	74.4034	74.4148	74.4261	74.4375	74.4489	74.4603	74.4717	74.4831	74.4944	74.5058	74.5172	.000379
12	73.2207	73.2361	73.2515	73.2669	73.2823	73.2977	73.3131	73.3286	73.3440	73.3594	73.3748	73.3902	.000513
11	72.0263	72.0455	72.0646	72.0838	72.1029	72.1221	72.1412	72.1604	72.1796	72.1987	72.2179	72.2370	.000638
10	70.8086	70.8314	70.8543	70.8771	70.9000	70.9228	70.9456	70.9685	70.9913	71.0142	71.0370	71.0599	.000761
Age.	0	1	2	3	4	5	6	7	8	9	10	11	Day.

Age.	0	1	2	3	4	5	6	7	8	9	10	11	Day.
10	18.1844	18.1803	18.1761	18.1720	18.1679	18.1638	18.1596	18.1555	18.1514	18.1473	18.1431	18.1390	.000137
11	18.8599	18.8573	18.8546	18.8520	18.8494	18.8468	18.8441	18.8415	18.8389	18.8363	18.8336	18.8310	.000087
12	19.5622	19.5610	19.5598	19.5585	19.5573	19.5561	19.5549	19.5537	19.5525	19.5512	19.5500	19.5488	.000040
13	20.2909	20.2912	20.2916	20.2919	20.2923	20.2926	20.2930	20.2933	20.2936	20.2940	20.2943	20.2947	.000011
14	21.0493	21.0513	21.0533	21.0553	21.0573	21.0593	21.0613	21.0634	21.0654	21.0674	21.0694	21.0714	.000067
15	21.8400	21.8437	21.8474	21.8511	21.8549	21.8586	21.8623	21.8660	21.8697	21.8734	21.8772	21.8809	.000124
16	22.6644	22.6698	22.6752	22.6806	22.6860	22.6914	22.6968	22.7022	22.7076	22.7130	22.7184	22.7238	.000180
17	23.5238	23.5306	23.5374	23.5442	23.5510	23.5578	23.5645	23.5713	23.5781	23.5849	23.5917	23.5985	.000226
18	24.4154	24.4232	24.4310	24.4388	24.4467	24.4545	24.4623	24.4701	24.4779	24.4857	24.4936	24.5014	.000260
19	25.3368	25.3454	25.3540	25.3625	25.3711	25.3797	25.3882	25.3968	25.4054	25.4140	25.4225	25.4311	.000286
20	26.2854	26.2943	26.3032	26.3121	26.3210	26.3299	26.3387	26.3476	26.3565	26.3654	26.3743	26.3832	.000296
21	27.2586	27.2677	27.2767	27.2858	27.2949	27.3039	27.3130	27.3221	27.3311	27.3402	27.3493	27.3583	.000302
22	28.2549	28.2639	28.2730	28.2820	28.2910	28.3000	28.3090	28.3181	28.3271	28.3361	28.3451	28.3542	.000301
23	29.2733	29.2823	29.2913	29.3003	29.3093	29.3183	29.3272	29.3362	29.3452	29.3542	29.3632	29.3722	.000300
24	30.3160	30.3246	30.3333	30.3420	30.3506	30.3592	30.3679	30.3765	30.3852	30.3938	30.4025	30.4111	.000288
25	31.3805	31.3886	31.3967	31.4048	31.4129	31.4210	31.4291	31.4373	31.4454	31.4535	31.4616	31.4697	.000270
26	32.4660	32.4733	32.4806	32.4879	32.4953	32.5026	32.5099	32.5173	32.5246	32.5319	32.5393	32.5466	.000243
27	33.5719	33.5782	33.5846	33.5909	33.5973	33.6036	33.6100	33.6163	33.6226	33.6290	33.6353	33.6417	.000211
28	34.6973	34.7025	34.7077	34.7128	34.7180	34.7232	34.7284	34.7336	34.7388	34.7440	34.7491	34.7543	.000173
29	35.8429	35.8467	35.8504	35.8542	35.8579	35.8617	35.8654	35.8692	35.8730	35.8767	35.8805	35.8842	.000125
30	37.0073	37.0093	37.0113	37.0133	37.0154	37.0174	37.0194	37.0214	37.0234	37.0254	37.0275	37.0295	.000067
31	38.1892	38.1894	38.1895	38.1897	38.1899	38.1901	38.1902	38.1904	38.1906	38.1908	38.1910	38.1911	.000006
32	39.3901	39.3881	39.3861	39.3840	39.3820	39.3800	39.3780	39.3760	39.3740	39.3720	39.3699	39.3679	.000067
33	40.6086	40.6040	40.5995	40.5949	40.5904	40.5858	40.5812	40.5767	40.5721	40.5676	40.5630	40.5585	.000152
34	41.8433	41.8355	41.8277	41.8200	41.8122	41.8044	41.7966	41.7889	41.7811	41.7733	41.7655	41.7578	.000259
35	43.0888	43.0784	43.0660	43.0546	43.0432	43.0318	43.0204	43.0090	42.9976	42.9862	42.9748	42.9634	.000380
36	44.3439	44.3283	44.3127	44.2970	44.2814	44.2658	44.2502	44.2346	44.2190	44.2033	44.1877	44.1721	.000520
37	45.6048	45.5845	45.5642	45.5440	45.5237	45.5034	45.4831	45.4628	45.4425	45.4222	45.4020	45.3817	.000676
38	46.8688	46.8432	46.8176	46.7921	46.7665	46.7409	46.7153	46.6898	46.6642	46.6386	46.6130	46.5875	.000852
39	48.1336	48.1022	48.0708	48.0394	48.0081	47.9767	47.9453	47.9139	47.8825	47.8511	47.8198	47.7884	.001046
40	49.3966	49.3586	49.3206	49.2825	49.2445	49.2065	49.1685	49.1305	49.0925	49.0544	49.0164	48.9784	.001267
41	50.6523	50.6071	50.5620	50.5168	50.4717	50.4265	50.3814	50.3362	50.2911	50.2460	50.2008	50.1556	.001505
42	51.9000	51.8471	51.7941	51.7412	51.6883	51.6354	51.5824	51.5295	51.4766	51.4237	51.3707	51.3178	.001764
43	53.1383	53.0771	53.0159	52.9547	52.8935	52.8323	52.7711	52.7100	52.6488	52.5876	52.5264	52.4652	.002040
44	54.3695	54.2993	54.2290	54.1588	54.0885	54.0183	53.9480	53.8778	53.8076	53.7373	53.6671	53.5968	.002341
45	55.5932	55.5142	55.4351	55.3561	55.2770	55.1980	55.1190	55.0399	54.9609	54.8818	54.8028	54.7237	.002635
46	56.8104	56.7201	56.6298	56.5395	56.4493	56.3590	56.2687	56.1784	56.0881	55.9978	55.9076	55.8173	.003009
47	58.0225	57.9212	57.8198	57.7185	57.6171	57.5158	57.4144	57.3131	57.2118	57.1104	57.0091	56.9077	.003378
48	59.2292	59.1160	59.0029	58.8897	58.7765	58.6634	58.5502	58.4370	58.3239	58.2107	58.0975	57.9844	.003772
49	60.4298	60.3041	60.1784	60.0527	59.9271	59.8014	59.6757	59.5500	59.4243	59.2986	59.1730	59.0473	.004189
50	61.6242	61.4853	61.3464	61.2076	61.0687	60.9298	60.7910	60.6521	60.5132	60.3743	60.2354	60.0966	.004629
51	62.8145	62.6614	62.5083	62.3552	62.2022	62.0491	61.8960	61.7429	61.5898	61.4367	61.2837	61.1306	.005103
52	63.9988	63.8305	63.6622	63.4940	63.3257	63.1574	62.9891	62.8209	62.6526	62.4843	62.3160	62.1478	.005609
53	65.1766	64.9925	64.8083	64.6242	64.4401	64.2559	64.0718	63.8877	63.7035	63.5194	63.3353	63.1511	.006138
54	66.3513	66.1506	65.9499	65.7492	65.5485	65.3478	65.1471	64.9464	64.7457	64.5450	64.3443	64.1436	.006690
55	67.5263	67.3086	67.0909	66.8732	66.6556	66.4379	66.2202	66.0025	65.7848	65.5671	65.3495	65.1318	.007256
56	68.7107	68.4759	68.2411	68.0063	67.7715	67.5367	67.3018	67.0670	66.8322	66.5974	66.3626	66.1278	.007827
57	69.9178	69.6655	69.4132	69.1609	68.9086	68.6563	68.4040	68.1516	67.8993	67.6470	67.3947	67.1424	.008410
58	71.1586	70.8887	70.6188	70.3490	70.0791	69.8092	69.5393	69.2695	68.9996	68.7297	68.4598	68.1900	.008996
59	72.4508	72.1623	71.8738	71.5852	71.2967	71.0082	70.7197	70.4312	70.1427	69.8541	69.5656	69.2771	.009617
60	73.7015	73.4015	73.1016	72.8016	72.5016	72.2017	71.9017	71.6017	71.3018	71.0018	70.7018	70.4019	.009999
61	75.2202	74.8910	74.5617	74.2325	73.9033	73.5741	73.2448	72.9156	72.5864	72.2572	71.9280	71.5987	.010974
62	76.7161	76.3636	76.0111	75.6586	75.3061	74.9536	74.6010	74.2485	73.8960	73.5435	73.1910	72.8385	.011750
63	78.2860	77.9113	77.5366	77.1619	76.7872	76.4125	76.0378	75.6631	75.2884	74.9137	74.5390	74.1643	.012490
64	79.9188	79.5113	79.1038	78.6963	78.2889	77.8814	77.4739	77.0664	76.6589	76.2514	75.8440	75.4365	.013583
65	81.6161	81.1767	80.7372	80.2978	79.8583	79.4189	78.9794	78.5400	78.1006	77.6611	77.2217	76.7822	.014648
66	83.3645	82.8871	82.4097	81.9323	81.4549	80.9775	80.5001	80.0227	79.5453	79.0679	78.5905	78.1131	.015913
67	85.1222	84.6006	84.0789	83.5573	83.0357	82.5140	81.9924	81.4708	80.9491	80.4275	79.9059	79.3842	.017388
68	86.8418	86.2698	85.6978	85.1258	84.5538	83.9818	83.4098	82.8378	82.2658	81.6938	81.1218	80.5498	.019067
69	88.4781	87.8381	87.1982	86.5582	85.9182	85.2783	84.6383	83.9983	83.3584	82.7184	82.0784	81.4385	.021332
70	89.8425	89.1322	88.4218	87.7115	87.0011	86.2908	85.5804	84.8701	84.1598	83.4494	82.7391	82.0287	.023678
71	90.9309	90.2155	89.5001	88.7847	88.0693	87.3539	86.6385	85.9232	85.2078	84.4924	83.7770	83.0616	.023846
72	92.5874	91.9687	91.3500	90.7314	90.1127	89.4940	88.8753	88.2567	87.6380	87.0193	86.4006	85.7820	.020622
73 or 36	**96.1538**	**96.4743**	**96.7948**	**97.1153**	**97.4359**	**97.7564**	**98.0769**	**98.3974**	**98.7179**	**99.0384**	**99.3590**	**99.6795**	**.010684**
35	94.7517	94.7030	94.6543	94.6056	94.5569	94.5082	94.4594	94.4107	94.3620	94.3133	94.2646	94.2159	.001623
34	94.0369	93.9375	93.8382	93.7388	93.6395	93.5401	93.4408	93.3414	93.2421	93.1427	93.0434	92.9440	.003312
33	93.5178	93.4078	93.2977	93.1877	93.0777	92.9677	92.8576	92.7476	92.6376	92.5276	92.4175	92.3075	.003667
32	92.8521	92.7595	92.6668	92.5742	92.4816	92.3889	92.2963	92.2037	92.1110	92.0184	91.9258	91.8331	.003088
31	92.0308	91.9561	91.8815	91.8068	91.7322	91.6575	91.5828	91.5082	91.4335	91.3589	91.2842	91.2096	.002488
30	91.1290	91.0659	91.0028	90.9397	90.8767	90.8136	90.7505	90.6874	90.6243	90.5612	90.4982	90.4351	.002103
29	90.1642	90.1110	90.0579	90.0047	89.9515	89.8984	89.8452	89.7920	89.7389	89.6857	89.6325	89.5794	.001772
28	89.1575	89.1123	89.0671	89.0219	88.9767	88.9315	88.8863	88.8411	88.7959	88.7507	88.7055	88.6603	.001507
27	88.1304	88.0912	88.0519	88.0127	87.9735	87.9342	87.8950	87.8558	87.8165	87.7773	87.7381	87.6988	.001308
26	87.0915	87.0573	87.0231	86.9889	86.9547	86.9205	86.8862	86.8520	86.8178	86.7836	86.7494	86.7152	.001140
25	86.0430	86.0134	85.9839	85.9543	85.9247	85.8952	85.8656	85.8360	85.8065	85.7769	85.7473	85.7178	.000985
24	84.9934	84.9676	84.9417	84.9159	84.8901	84.8642	84.8384	84.8126	84.7867	84.7609	84.7351	84.7092	.000861
23	83.9495	83.9267	83.9039	83.8810	83.8582	83.8354	83.8126	83.7898	83.7670	83.7441	83.7213	83.6985	.000760
22	82.9086	82.8888	82.8690	82.8491	82.8293	82.8095	82.7897	82.7699	82.7501	82.7302	82.7104	82.6906	.000660
21	81.8695	81.8526	81.8357	81.8189	81.8020	81.7851	81.7682	81.7514	81.7345	81.7176	81.7007	81.6839	.000562
20	80.8313	80.8173	80.8033	80.7893	80.7753	80.7613	80.7473	80.7333	80.7193	80.7053	80.6913	80.6773	.000467
19	79.7869	79.7763	79.7656	79.7549	79.7443	79.7336	79.7229	79.7123	79.7016	79.6909	79.6803	79.6696	.000353
18	78.7306	78.7236	78.7165	78.7095	78.7025	78.6954	78.6884	78.6814	78.6743	78.6673	78.6603	78.6532	.000234
17	77.6561	77.6531	77.6501	77.6471	77.6441	77.6411	77.6381	77.6352	77.6322	77.6292	77.6262	77.6232	.000100
16	76.5587	76.5600	76.5613	76.5626	76.5639	76.5652	76.5665	76.5678	76.5691	76.5704	76.5717	76.5730	.000043
15	75.4372	75.4428	75.4484	75.4540	75.4595	75.4651	75.4707	75.4763	75.4819	75.4874	75.4930	75.4986	.000186
14	74.2896	74.2995	74.3094	74.3193	74.3293	74.3392	74.3491	74.3590	74.3689	74.3788	74.3888	74.3987	.000330
13	73.1171	73.1311	73.1452	73.1592	73.1732	73.1873	73.2013	73.2153	73.2294	73.2434	73.2574	73.2715	.000468
12	71.9221	71.9400	71.9578	71.9757	71.9935	72.0114	72.0292	72.0471	72.0650	72.0828	72.1007	72.1185	.000595
11	70.7039	70.7255	70.7471	70.7687	70.7903	70.8119	70.8335	70.8552	70.8768	70.8984	70.9200	70.9416	.000720
10	69.4629	69.4881	69.5133	69.5386	69.5638	69.5890	69.6142	69.6395	69.6647	69.6899	69.7151	69.7404	.000841
Age.	0	1	2	3	4	5	6	7	8	9	10	11	Day.

Age.	0	1	2	3	4	5	6	7	8	9	10	11	Day.
10	19.1778	19.1765	19.1752	19.1740	19.1727	19.1714	19.1701	19.1688	19.1675	19.1662	19.1650	19.1637	.000043
11	19.8915	19.8917	19.8918	19.8920	19.8922	19.8924	19.8925	19.8927	19.8929	19.8931	19.8932	19.8934	.000006
12	20.6320	20.6338	20.6356	20.6373	20.6391	20.6409	20.6427	20.6445	20.6463	20.6480	20.6498	20.6516	.000059
13	21.4016	21.4051	21.4086	21.4121	21.4157	21.4192	21.4227	21.4262	21.4297	21.4332	21.4368	21.4403	.000117
14	22.2035	22.2088	22.2140	22.2193	22.2245	22.2298	22.2350	22.2403	22.2456	22.2508	22.2561	22.2613	.000175
15	23.0390	23.0460	23.0530	23.0600	23.0670	23.0740	23.0810	23.0881	23.0951	23.1021	23.1091	23.1161	.000233
16	23.9092	23.9177	23.9261	23.9346	23.9430	23.9515	23.9600	23.9684	23.9769	23.9853	23.9938	24.0022	.000282
17	24.8121	24.8216	24.8312	24.8407	24.8503	24.8598	24.8693	24.8789	24.8884	24.8980	24.9075	24.9171	.000318
18	25.7440	25.7544	25.7647	25.7751	25.7855	25.7959	25.8062	25.8166	25.8270	25.8374	25.8477	25.8581	.000346
19	26.7040	26.7147	26.7255	26.7362	26.7470	26.7577	26.7684	26.7792	26.7899	26.8007	26.8114	26.8222	.000358
20	27.6870	27.6980	27.7090	27.7200	27.7310	27.7420	27.7530	27.7641	27.7751	27.7861	27.7971	27.8081	.000367
21	28.6947	28.7057	28.7167	28.7278	28.7388	28.7498	28.7608	28.7719	28.7829	28.7939	28.8050	28.8160	.000367
22	29.7242	29.7353	29.7464	29.7575	29.7686	29.7797	29.7907	29.8018	29.8129	29.8240	29.8351	29.8462	.000370
23	30.7775	30.7883	30.7992	30.8100	30.8209	30.8317	30.8426	30.8534	30.8643	30.8751	30.8860	30.8968	.000362
24	31.8532	31.8636	31.8740	31.8844	31.8948	31.9052	31.9155	31.9259	31.9363	31.9467	31.9571	31.9675	.000346
25	32.9500	32.9597	32.9694	32.9791	32.9889	32.9986	33.0083	33.0180	33.0277	33.0374	33.0472	33.0569	.000324
26	34.0669	34.0757	34.0845	34.0934	34.1022	34.1110	34.1198	34.1287	34.1375	34.1463	34.1551	34.1640	.000294
27	35.2037	35.2115	35.2193	35.2270	35.2348	35.2426	35.2504	35.2582	35.2660	35.2737	35.2815	35.2893	.000259
28	36.3601	36.3666	36.3731	36.3795	36.3860	36.3925	36.3990	36.4055	36.4120	36.4184	36.4249	36.4314	.000216
29	37.5356	37.5405	37.5453	37.5502	37.5550	37.5599	37.5647	37.5696	37.5745	37.5793	37.5842	37.5890	.000162
30	38.7286	38.7318	38.7349	38.7381	38.7412	38.7444	38.7475	38.7507	38.7539	38.7570	38.7602	38.7633	.000105
31	39.9405	39.9416	39.9427	39.9438	39.9449	39.9460	39.9471	39.9483	39.9494	39.9505	39.9516	39.9527	.000037
32	41.1699	41.1686	41.1673	41.1661	41.1648	41.1635	41.1622	41.1610	41.1597	41.1584	41.1571	41.1559	.000042
33	42.4155	42.4112	42.4069	42.4025	42.3982	42.3939	42.3896	42.3853	42.3810	42.3766	42.3723	42.3680	.000144
34	43.6724	43.6647	43.6569	43.6492	43.6414	43.6337	43.6260	43.6182	43.6105	43.6027	43.5950	43.5872	.000258
35	44.9386	44.9268	44.9151	44.9033	44.8916	44.8798	44.8681	44.8563	44.8446	44.8328	44.8211	44.8093	.000392
36	46.2108	46.1946	46.1784	46.1622	46.1460	46.1298	46.1136	46.0975	46.0813	46.0651	46.0489	46.0327	.000540
37	47.4874	47.4662	47.4449	47.4237	47.4025	47.3812	47.3600	47.3388	47.3175	47.2963	47.2751	47.2538	.000708
38	48.7638	48.7370	48.7103	48.6835	48.6567	48.6300	48.6032	48.5764	48.5497	48.5229	48.4961	48.4694	.000892
39	50.0393	50.0062	49.9731	49.9400	49.9070	49.8739	49.8408	49.8077	49.7746	49.7415	49.7085	49.6754	.001103
40	51.3081	51.2682	51.2283	51.1884	51.1486	51.1087	51.0688	51.0289	50.9890	50.9491	50.9093	50.8694	.001329
41	52.5690	52.5217	52.4744	52.4272	52.3799	52.3326	52.2853	52.2381	52.1908	52.1435	52.0962	52.0490	.001576
42	53.8203	53.7652	53.7100	53.6549	53.5997	53.5446	53.4894	53.4343	53.3792	53.3240	53.2689	53.2137	.001838
43	55.0625	54.9987	54.9350	54.8712	54.8074	54.7437	54.6799	54.6161	54.5524	54.4886	54.4248	54.3611	.002125
44	56.2948	56.2218	56.1488	56.0758	56.0028	55.9298	55.8568	55.7839	55.7109	55.6379	55.5649	55.4919	.002433
45	57.5293	57.4455	57.3618	57.2780	57.1943	57.1105	57.0267	56.9430	56.8592	56.7755	56.6917	56.6080	.002792
46	58.7350	58.6415	58.5481	58.4546	58.3612	58.2677	58.1742	58.0808	57.9873	57.8939	57.8004	57.7070	.003115
47	59.9449	59.8402	59.7354	59.6307	59.5259	59.4212	59.3164	59.2117	59.1070	59.0022	58.8975	58.7927	.003491
48	61.1479	61.0312	60.9144	60.7977	60.6810	60.5643	60.4475	60.3308	60.2141	60.0974	59.9806	59.8639	.003891
49	62.3443	62.2150	62.0857	61.9564	61.8271	61.6978	61.5685	61.4393	61.3100	61.1807	61.0514	60.9221	.004310
50	63.5352	63.3923	63.2495	63.1066	62.9638	62.8210	62.6781	62.5352	62.3924	62.2495	62.1067	61.9638	.004762
51	64.7190	64.5617	64.4043	64.2470	64.0896	63.9323	63.7750	63.6176	63.4603	63.3029	63.1456	62.9882	.005245
52	65.8946	65.7223	65.5500	65.3776	65.2053	65.0330	64.8606	64.6883	64.5160	64.3437	64.1713	63.9990	.005744
53	67.0666	66.8784	66.6902	66.5020	66.3138	66.1256	65.9374	65.7493	65.5611	65.3729	65.1847	64.9965	.006273
54	68.2378	68.0335	67.8292	67.6249	67.4206	67.2163	67.0120	66.8076	66.6033	66.3990	66.1947	65.9904	.006810
55	69.4166	69.1961	68.9756	68.7551	68.5346	68.3141	68.0935	67.8730	67.6525	67.4320	67.2115	66.9910	.007350
56	70.6160	70.3789	70.1418	69.9048	69.6677	69.4306	69.1935	68.9565	68.7194	68.4823	68.2452	68.0082	.007902
57	71.8471	71.5935	71.3399	71.0863	70.8328	70.5792	70.3256	70.0720	69.8184	69.5648	69.3113	69.0577	.008453
58	73.1268	72.8556	72.5845	72.3133	72.0422	71.7710	71.4998	71.2287	70.9575	70.6864	70.4152	70.1441	.009038
59	74.4609	74.1711	73.8814	73.5916	73.3019	73.0121	72.7223	72.4326	72.1428	71.8531	71.5633	71.2736	.009658
60	75.8574	75.5480	75.2385	74.9291	74.6197	74.3102	74.0008	73.6914	73.3819	73.0725	72.7631	72.4536	.010314
61	77.3267	76.9953	76.6639	76.3325	76 0012	75.6698	75.3384	75.0070	74.6756	74.3442	74.0129	73.6815	.011046
62	78.8642	78.5080	78.1517	77.7954	77.4392	77.0830	76.7267	76.3704	76.0142	75.6580	75.3017	74.9454	.011875
63	80.4595	80.0763	79.6932	79.3100	78.9268	78.5437	78.1605	77.7773	77.3942	77.0110	76.6278	76.2447	.012772
64	82.1139	81.7005	81.2871	80.8737	80.4603	80.0469	79.6334	79.2200	78.8066	78.3932	77.9798	77.5664	.013780
65	83.8146	83.3653	82.9160	82.4666	82.0173	81.5680	81.1186	80.6693	80.2200	79.7707	79.3213	78.8720	.014977
66	85.5203	85.0290	84.5378	84.0465	83.5553	83.0640	82.5728	82.0815	81.5903	81.0990	80.6078	80.1165	.016375
67	87.1863	86.6473	86.1083	85.5692	85.0302	84.4912	83.9522	83.4132	82.8742	82.3351	81.7961	81.2571	.017967
68	88.7691	88.1655	87.5620	86.9584	86.3549	85.7513	85.1477	84.5442	83.9406	83.3371	82.7335	82.1300	.020118
69	90.0877	89.4174	88.7471	88.0768	87.4066	86.7363	86.0660	85.3957	84.7254	84.0551	83.3849	82.7146	.022343
70	91.1386	90 4644	89.7902	89.1160	88.4419	87.7677	87.0935	86.4193	85.7451	85.0710	84.3968	83.7226	.022473
71	92.7326	92.1522	91.5717	90.9913	90.4109	89.8304	89.2500	88.6696	88.0891	87.5087	86.9283	86.3478	.019348
72 or 37	**96.1538**	**96.4743**	**96.7948**	**97.1153**	**97.4359**	**97.7564**	**98.0769**	**98.3974**	**98.7179**	**99.0384**	**99.3590**	**99.6795**	**.010684**
36	94.7354	94.6824	94.6294	94.5764	94.5234	94.4704	94.4174	94.3644	94.3114	94.2584	94.2054	94.1524	.001767
35	94.0133	93.9093	93.8053	93.7012	93.5972	93.4932	93.3892	93.2852	93.1812	93.0771	92.9731	92.8691	.003467
34	93.4898	93.3752	93.2606	93.1460	93.0313	92.9167	92.8021	92.6875	92.5729	92.4582	92.3436	92.2290	.003820
33	92.8183	92.7214	92.6246	92.5277	92.4309	92.3340	92.2372	92.1403	92.0435	91.9466	91.8498	91.7530	.003228
32	91.9904	91.9119	91.8333	91.7548	91.6763	91.5978	91.5192	91.4407	91.3622	91.2837	91.2051	91.1266	.002617
31	91.0817	91.0150	90.9483	90.8816	90.8150	90.7483	90.6816	90.6149	90.5482	90.4815	90.4149	90.3482	.002223
30	90.1102	90.0537	89.9971	89.9406	89.8841	89.8275	89.7710	89.7145	89.6579	89.6014	89.5449	89.4883	.001884
29	89.0970	89.0486	89.0003	88.9519	88.9035	88.8552	88.8068	88.7584	88.7101	88.6617	88.6133	88.5650	.001612
28	88.0638	88.0216	87.9793	87.9371	87.8949	87.8526	87.8104	87.7682	87.7259	87.6837	87.6415	87.5992	.001408
27	87.0193	86.9823	86.9452	86.9082	86.8711	86.8341	86.7970	86.7600	86.7230	86.6859	86.6489	86.6118	.001235
26	85.9658	85.9335	85.9013	85.8690	85.8367	85.8045	85.7722	85.7399	85.7077	85.6754	85.6431	85.6109	.001075
25	84.9117	84.8833	84.8549	84.8265	84.7981	84.7697	84.7412	84.7128	84.6844	84.6560	84.6276	84.5992	.000947
24	83.8633	83.8380	83.8128	83.7875	83.7622	83.7370	83.7117	83.6864	83.6612	83.6359	83.6106	83.5854	.000842
23	82.8186	82.7965	82.7744	82.7522	82.7301	82.7080	82.6859	82.6638	82.6417	82.6195	82.5974	82.5753	.000737
22	81.7765	81.7574	81.7383	81.7192	81.7002	81.6811	81.6620	81.6429	81.6238	81.6047	81.5857	81.5666	.000636
21	80.7359	80.7198	80.7036	80.6875	80.6713	80.6552	80.6390	80.6229	80.6068	80.5906	80.5745	80.5583	.000538
20	79.6882	79.6756	79.6629	79.6503	79.6376	79.6250	79.6123	79.5997	79.5871	79.5744	79.5618	79.5491	.000421
19	78.6299	78.6210	78.6120	78.6031	78.5942	78.5852	78.5763	78.5674	78.5584	78.5495	78.5406	78.5316	.000298
18	77.5532	77.5484	77.5436	77.5388	77.5341	77.5293	77.5245	77.5197	77.5149	77.5101	77.5054	77.5006	.000159
17	76.4542	76.4538	76.4534	76.4530	76.4526	76.4522	76.4517	76.4513	76.4509	76.4505	76.4501	76.4497	.000013
16	75.3310	75.3350	75.3390	75.3429	75.3469	75.3509	75.3548	75.3588	75.3628	75.3668	75.3707	75.3747	.000132
15	74.1820	74.1904	74.1988	74.2072	74.2156	74.2240	74.2324	74.2408	74.2492	74.2576	74.2660	74.2744	.000280
14	73.0086	73.0212	73.0337	73.0463	73.0589	73.0715	73.0840	73.0966	73.1092	73.1218	73.1343	73.1469	.000419
13	71.8126	71.8291	71.8456	71.8621	71.8786	71.8951	71.9115	71.9280	71.9445	71.9610	71.9775	71.9940	.000550
12	70.5939	70.6142	70.6345	70.6549	70.6752	70.6955	70.7158	70.7362	70.7565	70.7768	70.7971	70.8175	.000677
11	69.3527	69.3767	69.4007	69.4247	69.4487	69.4727	69.4967	69.5207	69.5447	69.5687	69.5927	69.6167	.000800
10	68.0901	68.1176	68.1451	68.1726	68.2001	68.2276	68.2550	68.2825	68.3100	68.3375	68.3650	68.3925	.000916
Age.	0	1	2	3	4	5	6	7	8	9	10	11	Day.

Age.	0	1	2	3	4	5	6	7	8	9	10	11	Day.
10	20.2053	20.2068	20.2083	20.2098	20.2113	20.2128	20.2142	20.2157	20.2172	20.2187	20.2202	20.2217	.000050
11	20.9567	20.9599	20.9630	20.9662	20.9693	20.9725	20.9756	20.9788	20.9820	20.9851	20.9883	20.9914	.000105
12	21.7377	21.7426	21.7476	21.7525	21.7575	21.7624	21.7673	21.7723	21.7772	21.7822	21.7871	21.7921	.000165
13	22.5543	22.5607	22.5671	22.5736	22.5800	22.5864	22.5928	22.5993	22.6057	22.6121	22.6185	22.6250	.000214
14	23.3967	23.4052	23.4138	23.4223	23.4308	23.4394	23.4479	23.4564	23.4650	23.4735	23.4820	23.4906	.000284
15	24.2775	24.2875	24.2976	24.3076	24.3177	24.3277	24.3378	24.3478	24.3579	24.3680	24.3780	24.3880	.000335
16	25.1907	25.2019	25.2131	25.2243	25.2355	25.2467	25.2578	25.2690	25.2802	25.2914	25.3026	25.3138	.000373
17	26.1334	26.1455	26.1576	26.1696	26.1817	26.1938	26.2059	26.2180	26.2301	26.2421	26.2542	26.2663	.000403
18	27.1034	27.1159	27.1284	27.1410	27.1535	27.1660	27.1785	27.1911	27.2036	27.2161	27.2286	27.2412	.000417
19	28.0972	28.1100	28.1229	28.1357	28.1486	28.1614	28.1743	28.1871	28.2000	28.2128	28.2257	28.2385	.000428
20	29.1140	29.1270	29.1400	29.1530	29.1659	29.1789	29.1919	29.2049	29.2179	29.2308	29.2438	29.2568	.000433
21	30.1543	30.1674	30.1805	30.1936	30.2067	30.2198	30.2328	30.2459	30.2590	30.2721	30.2852	30.2983	.000436
22	31.2183	31.2312	31.2442	31.2571	31.2700	31.2830	31.2959	31.3088	31.3218	31.3347	31.3476	31.3606	.000431
23	32.3040	32.3166	32.3291	32.3417	32.3543	32.3668	32.3794	32.3920	32.4045	32.4171	32.4297	32.4422	.000419
24	33.4112	33.4232	33.4352	33.4472	33.4592	33.4712	33.4831	33.4951	33.5071	33.5191	33.5311	33.5431	.000400
25	34.5388	34.5500	34.5612	34.5724	34.5836	34.5948	34.6060	34.6171	34.6283	34.6395	34.6507	34.6619	.000373
26	35.6858	35.6961	35.7063	35.7166	35.7268	35.7371	35.7473	35.7576	35.7679	35.7781	35.7884	35.7986	.000342
27	36.8527	36.8618	36.8708	36.8799	36.8890	36.8981	36.9071	36.9162	36.9253	36.9344	36.9434	36.9525	.000302
28	38.0384	38.0460	38.0535	38.0611	38.0687	38.0762	38.0838	38.0914	38.0989	38.1065	38.1141	38.1216	.000252
29	39.2416	39.2476	39.2536	39.2596	39.2656	39.2716	39.2775	39.2835	39.2895	39.2955	39.3015	39.3075	.000200
30	40.4637	40.4678	40.4719	40.4760	40.4800	40.4841	40.4882	40.4923	40.4964	40.5004	40.5045	40.5086	.000136
31	41.7031	41.7049	41.7068	41.7086	41.7105	41.7123	41.7141	41.7160	41.7178	41.7197	41.7215	41.7234	.000061
32	42.9586	42.9576	42.9565	42.9555	42.9544	42.9534	42.9523	42.9513	42.9503	42.9492	42.9482	42.9471	.000035
33	44.2254	44.2211	44.2168	44.2125	44.2083	44.2040	44.1997	44.1954	44.1911	44.1868	44.1826	44.1783	.000143
34	45.5029	45.4947	45.4865	45.4783	45.4702	45.4620	45.4538	45.4456	45.4374	45.4292	45.4211	45.4129	.000273
35	46.7842	46.7719	46.7595	46.7472	46.7349	46.7226	46.7102	46.6979	46.6856	46.6733	46.6610	46.6486	.000411
36	48.0709	48.0538	48.0366	48.0195	48.0024	47.9852	47.9681	47.9510	47.9338	47.9167	47.8996	47.8824	.000571
37	49.3586	49.3362	49.3138	49.2914	49.2690	49.2466	49.2241	49.2017	49.1793	49.1569	49.1345	49.1121	.000747
38	50.6444	50.6160	50.5875	50.5590	50.5306	50.5021	50.4737	50.4452	50.4168	50.3883	50.3599	50.3314	.000948
39	51.9246	51.8897	51.8547	51.8198	51.7848	51.7499	51.7150	51.6800	51.6451	51.6101	51.5752	51.5402	.001165
40	53.1972	53.1536	53.1099	53.0663	53.0226	52.9790	52.9353	52.8917	52.8481	52.8044	52.7608	52.7171	.001455
41	54.4603	54.4108	54.3614	54.3119	54.2624	54.2130	54.1635	54.1140	54.0646	54.0151	53.9656	53.9162	.001649
42	55.7149	55.6571	55.5994	55.5416	55.4839	55.4261	55.3684	55.3106	55.2529	55.1951	55.1374	55.0796	.001925
43	56.9559	56.8894	56.8230	56.7565	56.6900	56.6236	56.5571	56.4906	56.4242	56.3577	56.2912	56.2248	.002015
44	58.1871	58.1112	58.0353	57.9594	57.8835	57.8076	57.7316	57.6557	57.5798	57.5039	57.4280	57.3521	.002530
45	59.4088	59.3228	59.2368	59.1508	59.0648	58.9788	58.8927	58.8067	58.7207	58.6347	58.5487	58.4627	.002867
46	60.6215	60.5247	60.4279	60.3311	60.2343	60.1375	60.0407	59.9439	59.8471	59.7503	59.6535	59.5567	.003227
47	61.8264	61.7182	61.6099	61.5017	61.3935	61.2852	61.1770	61.0688	60.9605	60.8523	60.7441	60.6358	.003608
48	63.0239	62.9036	62.7834	62.6631	62.5429	62.4226	62.3023	62.1821	62.0618	61.9416	61.8213	61.7011	.004008
49	64.2155	64.0823	63.9491	63.8160	63.6828	63.5496	63.4164	63.2832	63.1500	63.0168	62.8837	62.7505	.004439
50	65.3985	65.2515	65.1045	64.9574	64.8104	64.6634	64.5164	64.3694	64.2224	64.0753	63.9283	63.7813	.004900
51	66.5724	66.4110	66.2496	66.0882	65.9268	65.7654	65.6040	65.4427	65.2813	65.1199	64.9585	64.7971	.005380
52	67.7418	67.5653	67.3889	67.2124	67.0359	66.8595	66.6830	66.5065	66.3301	66.1536	65.9771	65.8007	.005882
53	68.9079	68.7162	68.5245	68.3327	68.1410	67.9493	67.7576	67.5659	67.3742	67.1824	66.9907	66.7990	.006390
54	70.0811	69.8740	69.6670	69.4599	69.2528	69.0458	68.8387	68.6316	68.4246	68.2175	68.0104	67.8034	.006902
55	71.2729	71.0502	70.8274	70.6047	70.3820	70.1593	69.9365	69.7138	69.4911	69.2684	69.0456	68.8229	.007424
56	72.4941	72.2558	72.0174	71.7791	71.5408	71.3025	71.0641	70.8258	70.5875	70.3492	70.1108	69.8725	.007944
57	73.7612	73.5063	73.2515	72.9966	72.7418	72.4870	72.2321	71.9772	71.7224	71.4675	71.2127	70.9578	.008495
58	74.0796	73.8072	73.5349	73.2625	72.9902	72.7178	72.4454	72.1731	71.9007	71.6284	71.3560	71.0837	.009078
59	76.4562	76.1653	75.8745	75.5836	75.2928	75.0019	74.7110	74.4202	74.1293	73.8385	73.5476	73.2568	.009695
60	77.8997	77.5882	77.3767	76.9651	76.6536	76.3421	76.0306	75.7191	75.4076	75.0960	74.7845	74.4730	.010384
61	79.4073	79.0723	78.7373	78.4023	78.0673	77.7323	77.3972	77.0622	76.7272	76.3922	76.0572	75.7222	.011167
62	80.9674	80.6070	80.2466	79.8862	79.5258	79.1654	78.8050	78.4445	78.0841	77.7237	77.3633	77.0029	.012014
63	82.5814	82.1924	81.8035	81.4145	81.0256	80.6366	80.2477	79.8587	79.4698	79.0808	78.6919	78.3030	.012965
64	84.2371	83.8141	83.3912	82.9682	82.5453	82.1223	81.6994	81.2764	80.8535	80.4305	80.0076	79.5846	.014098
65	85.8945	85.4318	84.9691	84.5065	84.0438	83.5811	83.1184	82.6558	82.1931	81.7304	81.2677	80.8051	.015422
66	87.5099	87.0019	86.4940	85.9860	85.4781	84.9701	84.4621	83.9542	83.4462	82.9383	82.4303	81.9224	.016932
67	89.0418	88.4724	87.9030	87.3336	86.7642	86.1948	85.6253	85.0559	84.4865	83.9171	83.3477	82.7783	.018980
68	90.3177	89.6850	89.0522	88.4195	87.7868	87.1541	86.5213	85.8886	85.2559	84.6232	83.9904	83.3577	.021091
69	91.3335	90.6980	90.0624	89.4269	88.7914	88.1558	87.5203	86.8848	86.2492	85.6137	84.9782	84.3426	.021184
70	92.8687	92.3241	91.7795	91.2349	90.6903	90.1457	89.6011	89.0566	88.5120	87.9674	87.4228	86.8782	.018153
71 or 38	**96.1538**	**96.4743**	**96.7948**	**97.1153**	**97.4359**	**97.7564**	**98.0769**	**98.3974**	**98.7179**	**99.0384**	**99.3590**	**99.6795**	**.010684**
37	94.7182	94.6607	94.6031	94.5456	94.4881	95.4305	94.3730	94.3155	94.2579	94.2004	94.1429	94.0853	.001918
36	93.9885	93.8795	93.7706	93.6616	93.5527	93.4437	93.3348	93.2258	93.1169	93.0080	92.8990	92.7900	.003632
35	93.4601	93.3406	93.2212	93.1017	92.9823	92.8628	92.7434	92.6240	92.5045	92.3850	92.2656	92.1461	.003982
34	92.7829	92.6816	92.5803	92.4790	92.3777	92.2764	92.1751	92.0738	91.9725	91.8712	91.7699	91.6686	.003377
33	91.9478	91.8652	91.7826	91.7000	91.6174	91.5348	91.4522	91.3697	91.2871	91.2045	91.1219	91.0393	.002753
32	91.0321	90.9616	90.8911	90.8207	90.7502	90.6797	90.6092	90.5388	90.4683	90.3978	90.3273	90.2569	.002349
31	90.0537	89.9936	89.9335	89.8734	89.8133	89.7532	89.6931	89.6330	89.5729	89.5128	89.4527	89.3926	.002003
30	89.0335	88.9818	88.9301	88.8784	88.8267	88.7750	88.7233	88.6716	88.6199	88.5682	88.5165	88.4648	.001723
29	87.9938	87.9484	87.9031	87.8577	87.8123	87.7670	87.7216	87.6762	87.6309	87.5855	87.5401	87.4948	.001512
28	86.9434	86.9034	86.8634	86.8233	86.7833	86.7433	86.7033	86.6633	86.6233	86.5832	86.5432	86.5032	.001334
27	85.8843	85.8492	85.8142	85.7791	85.7441	85.7090	85.6740	85.6389	85.6038	85.5688	85.5337	85.4987	.001168
26	84.8257	84.7946	84.7636	84.7325	84.7014	84.6704	84.6393	84.6082	84.5772	84.5461	84.5150	84.4840	.001035
25	83.7730	83.7452	83.7174	83.6896	83.6619	83.6341	83.6063	83.5785	83.5507	83.5230	83.4952	83.4674	.000926
24	82.7245	82.7000	82.6754	82.6509	82.6263	82.6018	82.5772	82.5527	82.5282	82.5036	82.4791	82.4545	.000818
23	81.6789	81.6575	81.6361	81.6147	81.5934	81.5720	81.5506	81.5292	81.5078	81.4864	81.4651	81.4437	.000713
22	80.6352	80.6169	80.5986	80.5802	80.5619	80.5436	80.5253	80.5070	80.4887	80.4703	80.4520	80.4337	.000610
21	79.5853	79.5706	79.5559	79.5411	79.5264	79.5117	79.4970	79.4823	79.4676	79.4528	79.4381	79.4234	.000490
20	78.5241	78.5132	78.5023	78.4914	78.4805	78.4696	78.4587	78.4478	78.4369	78.4260	78.4151	78.4042	.000363
19	77.4457	77.4390	77.4323	77.4257	77.4190	77.4123	77.4056	77.3990	77.3923	77.3856	77.3790	77.3723	.000222
18	76.3446	76.3424	76.3402	76.3380	76.3359	76.3337	76.3315	76.3293	76.3271	76.3250	76.3228	76.3206	.000073
17	75.2200	75.2223	75.2246	75.2268	75.2291	75.2314	75.2337	75.2360	75.2383	75.2405	75.2428	75.2451	.000076
16	74.0695	74.0763	74.0831	74.0899	74.0967	74.1035	74.1102	74.1170	74.1238	74.1306	74.1374	74.1442	.000226
15	72.8948	72.9059	72.9170	72.9280	72.9391	72.9502	72.9612	72.9723	72.9834	72.9945	73.0055	73.0166	.000369
14	71.6980	71.7130	71.7281	71.7431	71.7582	71.7732	71.7883	71.8033	71.8184	71.8334	71.8485	71.8635	.000502
13	70.4785	70.4975	70.5164	70.5354	70.5544	70.5733	70.5923	70.6113	70.6302	70.6492	70.6682	70.6871	.000632
12	69.2469	69.2688	69.2907	69.3126	69.3345	69.3564	69.3782	69.4001	69.4220	69.4439	69.4658	69.4877	.000730
11	67.9742	68.0005	68.0267	68.0530	68.0793	68.1056	68.1318	68.1581	68.1844	68.2107	68.2370	68.2632	.000876
10	66.6914	66.7210	66.7507	66.7803	66.8100	66.8396	66.8693	66.8990	66.9286	66.9582	66.9879	67.0175	.000988
Age.	0	1	2	3	4	5	6	7	8	9	10	11	Day.

Age.	0	1	2	3	4	5	6	7	8	9	10	11	Day.
10	21.2661	21.2706	21.2750	21.2795	21.2840	21.2884	21.2929	21.2974	21.3018	21.3063	21.3108	21.3152	.000149
11	22.0577	22.0640	22.0703	22.0766	22.0829	22.0892	22.0954	22.1017	22.1080	22.1143	22.1206	22.1269	.000210
12	22.8813	22.8895	22.8976	22.9058	22.9140	22.9221	22.9303	22.9385	22.9466	22.9548	22.9630	22.9711	.000272
13	23.7380	23.7480	23.7580	23.7680	23.7780	23.7880	23.7980	23.8080	23.8180	23.8280	23.8380	23.8480	.000333
14	24.6291	24.6407	24.6522	24.6638	24.6753	24.6869	24.6984	24.7100	24.7216	24.7331	24.7447	24.7562	.000385
15	25.5525	25.5653	25.5780	25.5908	25.6035	25.6163	25.6290	25.6418	25.6546	25.6673	25.6801	25.6928	.000425
16	26.5050	26.5187	26.5324	26.5461	26.5599	26.5736	26.5873	26.6010	26.6147	26.6284	26.6422	26.6559	.000457
17	27.4852	27.4994	27.5136	27.5279	27.5421	27.5563	27.5705	27.5848	27.5990	27.6132	27.6274	27.6417	.000474
18	28.4885	28.5031	28.5177	28.5324	28.5470	28.5616	28.5762	28.5909	28.6055	28.6201	28.6347	28.6494	.000487
19	29.5157	29.5305	29.5453	29.5601	29.5749	29.5897	29.6045	29.6194	29.6342	29.6490	29.6638	29.6786	.000493
20	30.5647	30.5797	30.5947	30.6098	30.6248	30.6398	30.6548	30.6699	30.6849	30.6999	30.7150	30.7300	.000501
21	31.6387	31.6536	31.6685	31.6835	31.6984	31.7133	31.7282	31.7432	31.7581	31.7730	31.7880	31.8029	.000497
22	32.7345	32.7491	32.7638	32.7784	32.7930	32.8077	32.8223	32.8369	32.8516	32.8662	32.8808	32.8955	.000488
23	33.8511	33.8652	33.8794	33.8935	33.9077	33.9218	33.9360	33.9501	33.9643	33.9784	33.9926	34.0067	.000472
24	34.9884	35.0018	35.0153	35.0287	35.0422	35.0556	35.0691	35.0825	35.0960	35.1094	35.1229	35.1363	.000448
25	36.1453	36.1579	36.1705	36.1831	36.1958	36.2084	36.2210	36.2336	36.2462	36.2588	36.2715	36.2841	.000420
26	37.3218	37.3333	37.3449	37.3564	37.3679	37.3795	37.3910	37.4025	37.4141	37.4256	37.4371	37.4487	.000384
27	38.5172	38.5273	38.5375	38.5476	38.5578	38.5679	38.5780	38.5882	38.5983	38.6085	38.6186	38.6288	.000338
28	39.7297	39.7384	39.7471	39.7558	39.7645	39.7732	39.7818	39.7905	39.7992	39.8079	39.8166	39.8253	.000290
29	40.9611	40.9680	40.9749	40.9818	40.9887	40.9956	41.0025	41.0095	41.0164	41.0233	41.0302	41.0371	.000230
30	42.2098	42.2146	42.2194	42.2242	42.2291	42.2339	42.2387	42.2435	42.2483	42.2531	42.2580	42.2628	.000160
31	43.4744	43.4765	43.4786	43.4806	43.4827	43.4848	43.4869	43.4890	43.4911	43.4931	43.4952	43.4973	.000069
32	44.7502	44.7492	44.7482	44.7471	44.7461	44.7451	44.7441	44.7431	44.7421	44.7410	44.7400	44.7390	.000034
33	46.0356	46.0310	46.0263	46.0217	46.0171	46.0124	46.0078	46.0032	45.9985	45.9939	45.9893	45.9846	.000154
34	47.3272	47.3185	47.3098	47.3012	47.2925	47.2838	47.2752	47.2665	47.2578	47.2492	47.2405	47.2318	.000287
35	48.6229	48.6096	48.5964	48.5831	48.5699	48.5566	48.5433	48.5301	48.5168	48.5036	48.4903	48.4771	.000442
36	49.9197	49.9014	49.8831	49.8648	49.8465	49.8282	49.8099	49.7916	49.7733	49.7550	49.7367	49.7184	.000610
37	51.2157	51.1916	51.1675	51.1435	51.1194	51.0953	51.0712	51.0472	51.0231	50.9990	50.9750	50.9509	.000802
38	52.5059	52.4755	52.4452	52.4148	52.3845	52.3541	52.3238	52.2934	52.2631	52.2327	52.2024	52.1720	.001012
39	53.7876	53.7506	53.7136	53.6766	53.6396	53.6026	53.5656	53.5287	53.4917	53.4547	53.4177	53.3807	.001233
40	55.0412	54.9987	54.9563	54.9138	54.8713	54.8289	54.7864	54.7439	54.7015	54.6590	54.6165	54.5741	.001415
41	56.3253	56.2733	56.2214	56.1694	56.1175	56.0655	56.0136	55.9616	55.9097	55.8577	55.8058	55.7538	.001732
42	57.5773	57.5170	57.4566	57.3963	57.3360	57.2757	57.2153	57.1550	57.0947	57.0344	56.9740	56.9137	.002011
43	58.8168	58.7475	58.6781	58.6088	58.5394	58.4701	58.4007	58.3314	58.2621	58.1927	58.1234	58.0540	.002311
44	60.0444	59.9654	59.8864	59.8074	59.7285	59.6495	59.5705	59.4915	59.4125	59.3335	59.2546	59.1756	.002633
45	61.2613	61.1720	61.0827	60.9934	60.9042	60.8149	60.7256	60.6363	60.5470	60.4577	60.3685	60.2792	.002976
46	62.4679	62.3677	62.2674	62.1672	62.0670	61.9668	61.8665	61.7663	61.6661	61.5659	61.4656	61.3654	.003341
47	63.6661	63.5544	63.4427	63.3310	63.2193	63.1076	62.9958	62.8841	62.7724	62.6607	62.5490	62.4373	.003723
48	64.8575	64.7334	64.6093	64.4853	64.3612	64.2371	64.1130	63.9890	63.8649	63.7408	63.6167	63.4927	.004136
49	66.0400	65.9027	65.7655	65.6282	65.4909	65.3537	65.2164	65.0791	64.9419	64.8046	64.6673	64.5301	.004575
50	67.2119	67.0609	66.9099	66.7590	66.6080	66.4570	66.3060	66.1550	66.0040	65.8530	65.7021	65.5511	.005033
51	68.3772	68.2119	68.0467	67.8814	67.7161	67.5509	67.3856	67.2203	67.0551	66.8898	66.7245	66.5593	.005509
52	69.5394	69.3596	69.1798	69.0000	68.8201	68.6403	68.4605	68.2807	68.1009	67.9210	67.7412	67.5614	.005994
53	70.7069	70.5125	70.3181	70.1237	69.9293	69.7349	69.5405	69.3461	69.1517	68.9573	68.7629	68.5685	.006480
54	71.8913	71.6821	71.4728	71.2636	71.0544	70.8452	70.6360	70.4267	70.2175	70.0083	69.7990	69.5898	.006974
55	73.1027	72.8787	72.6548	72.4308	72.2069	71.9830	71.7590	71.5350	71.3111	71.0871	70.8632	70.6392	.007465
56	74.3571	74.1176	73.8780	73.6385	73.3989	73.1594	72.9198	72.6803	72.4408	72.2012	71.9617	71.7221	.007985
57	75.6602	75.4042	75.1482	74.8921	74.6361	74.3801	74.1241	73.8681	73.6121	73.3560	73.1000	72.8440	.008534
58	77.0179	76.7445	76.4710	76.1976	75.9242	75.6508	75.3773	75.1039	74.8305	74.5571	74.2836	74.0102	.009114
59	78.4383	77.1454	77.8525	77.5596	77.2668	76.9739	76.6810	76.3881	76.0952	75.8023	75.5095	75.2166	.009763
60	79.9170	79.6024	79.2878	78.9733	78.6587	78.3441	78.0295	77.7150	77.4004	77.0858	76.7712	76.4567	.010488
61	81.4444	81.1054	80.7663	80.4273	80.0883	79.7492	79.4102	79.0712	78.7321	78.3931	78.0541	77.7150	.011301
62	83.0207	82.6547	82.2887	81.9226	81.5566	81.1906	80.8246	80.4586	80.0926	79.7265	79.3605	78.9945	.012200
63	84.6339	84.2357	83.8375	83.4394	83.0412	82.6430	82.2448	81.8467	81.4485	81.0503	80.6521	80.2540	.013272
64	86.1457	85.7182	85.2907	84.8632	84.4357	84.0082	83.5806	83.1531	82.7256	82.2981	81.8706	81.4431	.014250
65	87.8141	87.3353	86.8565	86.3777	85.8989	85.4201	84.9413	84.4625	83.9837	83.5049	83.0261	82.5473	.015960
66	89.2990	88.7617	88.2245	87.6872	87.1500	86.6127	86.0754	85.5382	85.0009	84.4637	83.9264	83.3892	.017908
67	90.5326	89.9352	89.3378	88.7405	88.1431	87.5457	86.9483	86.3510	85.7536	85.1562	84.5588	83.9615	.019912
68	91.4162	90.8252	90.2343	89.6433	89.0524	88.4614	87.8704	87.2795	86.6885	86.0976	85.5066	84.9157	.019698
69	92.9963	92.4853	91.9743	91.4634	90.9524	90.4414	89.9304	89.4195	88.9085	88.3975	87.8865	87.3756	.017032
70 or 39	**96.1538**	**96.4743**	**96.7948**	**97.1153**	**97.4359**	**97.7564**	**98.0769**	**98.3974**	**98.7179**	**99.0384**	**99.3590**	**99.6795**	**.010684**
38	94.6999	94.6376	94.5753	94.5129	94.4506	94.3883	94.3259	94.2636	94.2013	94.1389	94.0766	94.0143	.002077
37	93.9622	93.8480	93.7339	93.6197	93.5055	93.3914	93.2772	93.1630	93.0489	92.9347	92.8205	92.7064	.003805
36	93.4289	93.3043	93.1798	93.0552	92.9306	92.8061	92.6815	92.5569	92.4324	92.3078	92.1832	92.0587	.004152
35	92.7454	92.6394	92.5334	92.4274	92.3214	92.2154	92.1094	92.0035	91.8975	91.7915	91.6855	91.5795	.003533
34	91.9031	91.8162	91.7293	91.6424	91.5555	91.4686	91.3817	91.2949	91.2080	91.1211	91.0342	90.9473	.002896
33	90.9797	90.9052	90.8308	90.7563	90.6819	90.6074	90.5330	90.4585	90.3840	90.3096	90.2351	90.1607	.002482
32	89.9937	89.9299	89.8661	89.8023	89.7385	89.6747	89.6108	89.5470	89.4832	89.4194	89.3556	89.2918	.002127
31	88.9665	88.9113	88.8562	88.8010	88.7458	88.6907	88.6355	88.5803	88.5252	88.4700	88.4148	88.3597	.001839
30	87.9202	87.8715	87.8229	87.7742	87.7256	87.6769	87.6282	87.5796	87.5309	87.4823	87.4336	87.3850	.001622
29	86.8637	86.8206	86.7774	86.7343	86.6912	86.6480	86.6049	86.5618	86.5186	86.4755	86.4324	86.3892	.001438
28	85.7990	85.7610	85.7230	85.6850	85.6469	85.6089	85.5709	85.5329	85.4949	85.4568	85.4188	85.3808	.001267
27	84.7354	84.7015	84.6676	84.6337	84.5998	84.5659	84.5320	84.4982	84.4643	84.4304	84.3965	84.3626	.001130
26	83.6782	83.6477	83.6173	83.5868	83.5564	83.5260	83.4955	83.4650	83.4346	83.4041	83.3737	83.3432	.001015
25	82.6258	82.5987	82.5716	82.5445	82.5175	82.4904	82.4633	82.4362	82.4091	82.3820	82.3550	82.3279	.000903
24	81.5773	81.5534	81.5296	81.5057	81.4819	81.4580	81.4342	81.4103	81.3865	81.3626	81.3388	81.3150	.000795
23	80.5298	80.5092	80.4886	80.4680	80.4474	80.4268	80.4061	80.3855	80.3649	80.3443	80.3237	80.3031	.000687
22	79.4774	79.4605	79.4435	79.4266	79.4097	79.3927	79.3758	79.3589	79.3419	79.3250	79.3081	79.2911	.000564
21	78.4140	78.4010	78.3880	78.3750	78.3620	78.3490	78.3360	78.3230	78.3100	78.2970	78.2840	78.2710	.000433
20	77.3327	77.3241	77.3154	77.3068	77.2982	77.2896	77.2810	77.2723	77.2637	77.2551	77.2464	77.2378	.000287
19	76.2301	76.2260	76.2220	76.2179	76.2139	76.2098	76.2057	76.2017	76.1976	76.1936	76.1895	76.1855	.000135
18	75.1035	75.1040	75.1045	75.1050	75.1056	75.1061	75.1066	75.1071	75.1076	75.1081	75.1087	75.1092	.000017
17	73.9515	73.9566	73.9618	73.9669	73.9721	73.9772	73.9823	73.9875	73.9926	73.9978	74.0029	74.0081	.000171
16	72.7756	72.7851	72.7946	72.8040	72.8135	72.8230	72.8325	72.8420	72.8515	72.8610	72.8704	72.8799	.000316
15	71.5777	71.5913	71.6048	71.6184	71.6319	71.6455	71.6590	71.6726	71.6862	71.6997	71.7133	71.7268	.000452
14	70.3575	70.3750	70.3926	70.4101	70.4277	70.4452	70.4627	70.4803	70.4978	70.5154	70.5329	70.5505	.000585
13	69.1153	69.1367	69.1581	69.1794	69.2008	69.2222	69.2436	69.2650	69.2864	69.3077	69.3291	69.3505	.000713
12	67.8525	67.8775	67.9025	67.9275	67.9525	67.9775	68.0025	68.0276	68.0526	68.0776	68.1026	68.1276	.000833
11	66.5697	66.5981	66.6266	66.6550	66.6835	66.7119	66.7403	66.7688	66.7972	66.8257	66.8541	66.8826	.000948
10	65.2683	65.3000	65.3316	65.3633	65.3950	65.4267	65.4583	65.4900	65.5217	65.5534	65.5850	65.6167	.001056
Age.	0	1	2	3	4	5	6	7	8	9	10	11	Day.

Age.	0	1	2	3	4	5	6	7	8	9	10	11	Day.
10	22.3626	22.3700	22.3775	22.3849	22.3924	22.3998	22.4072	22.4147	22.4221	22.4296	22.4370	22.4445	.000248
11	23.1964	23.2059	23 2154	23.2249	23.2344	23.2439	23.2534	23.2629	23.2724	23.2819	23.2914	23.3009	.000317
12	24.0636	24.0750	24.0864	24.0978	24.1092	24.1206	24.1320	24.1434	24.1548	24.1662	24.1776	24.1890	.000380
13	24.9646	24.9776	24.9906	25.0036	25.0167	25.0297	25.0427	25.0557	25.0687	25.0817	25.0948	25.1078	1000434
14	25.8978	25.9121	25.9263	25.9406	25.9549	25.9691	25.9834	25.9977	26.0119	26.0262	26.0405	26.0547	.000475
15	26.8600	26.8753	26.8906	26.9058	26.9211	26.9364	26.9517	26.9670	26.9823	26.9975	27.0128	27.0281	.000509
16	27.8496	27.8654	27.8813	27.8971	27.9130	27.9288	27.9447	27.9605	27.9764	27.9922	28.0081	28.0240	.000528
17	28.8627	28.8790	28.8953	28.9116	28.9279	28.9442	28.9605	28.9769	28.9932	29.0095	29.0258	29.0421	.000543
18	29.8989	29.9155	29.9320	29.9486	29.9652	29.9817	29.9983	30.0149	30.0314	30.0480	30.0646	30.0811	.000552
19	30.9577	30.9745	30.9914	31.0082	31.0250	31.0419	31.0587	31.0755	31.0924	31.1092	31.1260	31.1429	.000561
20	32.0398	32.0566	32.0735	32.0903	32.1072	32.1240	32.1409	32.1577	32.1746	32.1914	32.2083	32.2251	.000562
21	33.1451	33.1617	33.1783	33.1950	33.2116	33.2282	33.2448	33.2614	33.2780	33.2946	33.3113	33.3279	.000554
22	34.2712	34.2874	34.3036	34.3198	34.3360	34.3522	34.3684	34.3847	34.4009	34.4171	34.4333	34.4495	.000540
23	35.4173	35.4329	35.4485	35.4641	35.4798	35.4954	35.5110	35.5266	35.5422	35.5578	35.5735	35.5891	.000520
24	36.5832	36.5981	36.6129	36.6278	36.6427	36.6575	36.6724	36.6873	36.7021	36.7170	36.7319	36.7467	.000495
25	37.7689	37.7828	37.7967	37.8105	37.8244	37.8383	37.8522	37.8661	37.8800	37.8938	37.9077	37.9216	.000463
26	38.9731	38.9857	38.9983	39.0109	39.0235	39.0361	39.0487	39.0613	39.0739	39.0865	39.0991	39.1117	.000420
27	40.1946	40.2059	40.2171	40.2284	40.2396	40.2509	40.2621	40.2734	40.2847	40.2959	40.3072	40.3184	.000375
28	41.4345	41.4441	41.4537	41.4633	41.4729	41.4825	41.4921	41.5017	41.5113	41.5209	41.5305	41.5401	.000320
29	42.6917	42.6993	42.7070	42.7146	42.7222	42.7298	42.7374	42.7451	42.7527	42.7603	42.7680	42.7756	.000254
30	43.9647	43.9697	43.9748	43.9798	43.9849	43.9899	43.9950	44.0000	44.0050	44.0101	44.0151	44.0202	.000168
31	45.2486	45.2507	45.2528	45.2549	45.2570	45.2591	45.2612	45.2634	45.2655	45.2676	45.2697	45.2718	.000070
32	46.5420	46.5406	46.5393	46.5380	46.5366	46.5352	46.5339	46.5325	46.5312	46.5298	46.6285	46.5271	.000045
33	47.8416	47.8364	47.8312	47.8260	47.8208	47.8156	47.8104	47.8053	47.8001	47.7949	47.7897	47.7845	.000173
34	49.1456	49.1360	49.1264	49.1168	49.1073	49.0977	49.0881	49.0785	49.0689	49.0593	49.0498	49.0402	.000319
35	50.4504	50.4360	50.4216	50.4072	50.3928	50.3784	50.3640	50.3495	50.3351	50.3207	50.3063	50.2919	.000480
36	51.7544	51.7345	51.7145	51.6946	51.6746	51.6547	51 6347	51.6148	51.5949	51.5749	51.5550	51.5350	.000665
37	53.0528	53.0269	53.0010	52.9752	52.9493	52.9234	52.8975	52.8717	52.8458	52.8199	52.7940	52.7682	.000862
38	54.3435	54.3112	54.2789	54.2466	54.2143	54.1820	54.1497	54.1175	54.0852	54.0529	54.0206	53.9883	.001076
39	55.6260	55.5869	55.5477	55.5086	55.4695	55.4304	55.3912	55.3521	55.3130	55.2739	55.2347	55.1956	.001304
40	56.8993	56.8527	56.8061	56.7595	56.7130	56.6664	56.6198	56.5732	56.5266	56.4800	56.4335	56.3869	.001553
41	58.1605	58.1059	58.0513	57.9968	57.9422	57.8876	57.8330	57.7785	57.7239	57.6693	57.6147	57.5602	.001819
42	59.4087	59.3455	59.2824	59.2192	59.1561	59.0929	59.0297	58.9666	58.9034	58.8403	58.7771	58.7140	.002105
43	60.6432	60.5708	60.4985	60.4261	60.3538	60.2814	60.2091	60.1367	60.0644	59.9920	59.9197	59.8473	.002412
44	61.8648	61.7826	61.7004	61.6182	61.5360	61.4538	61.3716	61.2894	61.2072	61.1250	61.0428	60.9606	.002740
45	63.0744	62.9817	62.8891	62.7964	62.7038	62.6111	62.5185	62.4258	62.3332	62.2405	62.1479	62.0552	.003088
46	64.2732	64.1696	64.0659	63.9623	63.8587	63.7550	63.6514	63.5478	63.4441	63.3405	63.2369	63.1332	.003454
47	65.4641	65.3487	65.2332	65.1178	65.0023	64.8869	64.7714	64.6560	64.5406	64.4251	64.3097	64.1942	.003848
48	66.6453	66.5172	66.3891	66.2611	66.1330	66.0049	65.8768	65.7488	65.6207	65.4926	65.3645	65.2365	.004269
49	67.8155	67.6744	67.5332	67.3921	67.2509	67.1098	66.9686	66.8275	66.6864	66.5452	66.4041	66.2629	.004705
50	68.9777	68.8229	68.6681	68.5134	68.3586	68.2038	68.0490	67.8943	67.7395	67.5847	67.4300	67.2752	.005159
51	70.1355	69.9669	69.7982	69.6296	69.4610	69.2924	69.1237	68.9551	68.7865	68.6179	68.4492	68.2806	.005621
52	71.2967	71.1143	70.9318	70.7494	70.5669	70.3845	70.2020	70.0196	69.8372	69.6547	79.4723	69.2898	.006081
53	72.4736	72.2771	72.0806	71.8841	71.6876	71.4911	71.2945	71.0980	70.9015	70.7050	70.5085	70.3120	.006550
54	73.6756	73.4652	73.2548	73.0443	72.8339	72.6235	72.4131	72.2027	71.9923	71.7818	71.5714	71.3610	.007014
55	74.9178	74.6927	74.4675	74.2424	74.0173	73.7921	73.5670	73.3419	73.1167	72.8916	72.6665	72.4413	.007504
56	76.2055	75.9648	75.7241	75.4835	75.2428	75.0021	74.7614	74.5208	74.2801	74.0394	73.7987	73.5581	.008022
57	77.5451	77.2880	77.0310	76.7740	76.5169	76.2598	76.0028	75.7457	75.4887	75.2316	74.9746	74.7175	.008568
58	78.9435	78.6681	78.3927	78.1173	77.8419	77.5665	77.2911	77.0158	76.7404	76.4650	76.1896	75.9142	.009180
59	80.3961	80.0998	79.8035	79.5072	79.2109	78.9146	78.6183	78.3220	78.0257	77.7294	77.4331	77.1368	.009877
60	81.8976	81.5782	81.2588	80.9394	80.6200	80.3006	79.9812	79.6618	79.3424	79.0230	78.7036	78.3842	.010647
61	83.4332	83.0887	82.7443	82.3998	82.0554	81.7109	81.3664	81.0220	80.6775	80.3331	79.9886	79.6442	.011482
62	85.0067	84.6318	84.2568	83.8819	83.5069	83.1320	82.7570	82.3821	82.0072	81.6322	81.2573	80.8823	.012498
63	86.5757	86.1650	85.7544	85.3437	84.9331	84.5224	84.1118	83.7011	83.2905	82.8798	82.4692	82.0585	.013688
64	88.0996	87.6482	87.1968	86.7453	86.2939	85.8425	85.3911	84.9397	84.4883	84.0368	83.5854	83.1340	.015047
65	89.5402	89.0331	88.5261	88.0190	87.5119	87.0049	86.4978	85.9907	85.4837	84.9766	84.4695	83.9625	.016902
66	90.7365	90.1722	89.6078	89.0435	88.4791	87.9148	87.3504	86.7861	86.2218	85.6574	85.0931	84.5287	.018811
67	91.6878	91.1225	90.5573	89.9920	89.4268	88.8615	88.2962	87.7310	87.1657	86.6005	86.0352	85.4700	.018842
68	93.1160	92.6365	92.1571	91.6776	91.1982	90.7187	90.2392	89.7598	89.2803	88.8009	88.3214	87.8420	.015982
69 or 40	**96.1538**	**96.4743**	**96.7948**	**97.1153**	**97.4359**	**97.7564**	**98.0769**	**98.3974**	**98.7179**	**99.0384**	**99.3590**	**99.6795**	**.010684**
39	94.6806	94.6132	94.5457	94.4783	94.4109	94.3435	94.2760	94.2086	94.1412	94.0738	94.0063	93.9389	.002247
38	93.9343	93.8146	93.6949	93.5752	93.4556	93.3359	93.2162	93.0965	92.9768	92.8571	92.7375	92.6178	.003989
37	93.3958	93.2658	93.1359	93.0059	92.8759	92.7460	92.6160	92.4860	92.3561	92.2261	92.0961	91.9662	.004332
36	92.7058	92.5949	92.4839	92.3730	92.2620	92.1511	92.0401	91.9292	91.8183	91.7073	91.5964	91.4854	.003698
35	91.8558	91.7644	91.6730	91.5815	91.4901	91.3987	91.3073	91.2159	91.1245	91.0330	90.9416	90.8502	.003047
34	90.9247	90.8460	90.7673	90.6887	90.6100	90.5313	90.4526	90.3740	90.2953	90.2166	90.1380	90.0593	.002622
33	89.9308	89.8631	89.7953	89.7276	89.6599	89.5922	89.5244	89.4567	89.3890	89.3213	89.2535	89.1858	.002257
32	88.8962	88.8373	88.7784	88.7196	88.6607	88.6018	88.5430	88.4841	88.4252	88.3663	88.3074	88.2486	.001962
31	87.8429	87.7908	87.7386	87.6865	87.6344	87.5822	87.5301	87.4780	87.4258	87.3737	87.3216	87.2694	.001738
30	86.7800	86.7336	86.6872	86.6408	86.5944	86.5480	86.5015	86.4551	86.4087	86.3623	86.3159	86.2695	.001547
29	85.7094	85.6683	85.6272	85.5860	85.5449	85.5038	85.4627	85.4216	85.3805	85.3393	85.2982	85.2571	.001370
28	84.6405	84.6037	84.5668	84.5300	84.4932	84.4563	84.4195	84.3827	84.3458	84.3090	84.2722	84.2353	.001228
27	83.5787	83.5454	83.5122	83.4790	83.4457	83.4124	83.3792	83.3460	83.3127	83.2794	83.2462	83.2130	.001108
26	82.5222	82.4925	82.4627	82.4330	82.4032	82.3735	82.3437	82.3140	82.2843	82.2545	82.2248	82.1950	.000991
25	81.4695	81.4432	81.4168	81.3905	81.3642	81.3379	81.3115	81.2852	81.2589	81.2326	81.2062	81.1799	.000877
24	80.4195	80.3965	80.3736	80.3506	80.3277	80.3047	80.2817	80.2588	80.2358	80.2129	80.1899	80.1670	.000765
23	79.3641	79.3449	79.3257	79.3064	79.2872	79.2680	79.2488	79.2296	79.2104	79.1911	79.1719	79.1527	.000640
22	78.2984	78.2832	78.2680	78.2529	78.2377	78.2225	78.2073	78.1922	78.1770	78.1618	78.1466	78.1315	.000506
21	77.2151	77.2044	77.1937	77.1830	77.1723	77.1616	77.1509	77.1402	77.1295	77.1188	77.1081	77.0974	.000357
20	76.1098	76.1038	76.0978	76.0918	76.0858	76.0798	76.0738	76.0679	76.0619	76.0559	76.0499	76.0439	.000200
19	74.9818	74.9805	74.9792	74.9778	74.9765	74.9752	74.9738	74.9725	74.9712	74.9698	74.9685	74.9672	.000043
18	73.8281	73.8315	73.8348	73.8382	73.8416	73.8450	73.8483	73.8517	73.8551	73.8585	73.8618	73.8652	.000112
17	72.6509	72.6587	72.6665	72.6743	72.6822	72.6900	72.6978	72.7056	72.7134	72.7212	72.7291	72.7369	.000260
16	71.4518	71.4638	71.4758	71.4877	71.4997	71.5117	71.5237	71.5357	71.5477	71.5596	71.5716	71.5836	.000399
15	70.2307	70.2467	70.2628	70.2788	70.2949	70.3110	70.3270	70.3430	70.3591	70.3751	70.3912	70.4072	.000535
14	68.9880	69.0080	69.0279	69.0479	69.0678	69.0878	69.1077	69.1277	69.1477	69.1676	69.1876	69.2075	.000665
13	67.7246	67.7483	67.7720	67.7956	67.8193	67.8430	67.8666	67.8903	67.9140	67.9377	67.9613	67.9850	.000789
12	66.4419	66.4691	66.4963	66.5234	66.5506	66.5778	66.6050	66.6322	66.6594	66.6865	66.7137	66.7409	.000906
11	65.1407	65.1712	65.2017	65.2321	65.2626	65.2931	65.3236	65.3541	65.3846	65.4150	65.4455	65.4760	.001016
10	63.8220	63.8556	63.8892	63.9228	63.9564	63.9900	64.0236	64.0573	64.0909	64.1245	64.1581	64.1917	.001120
Age.	0	1	2	3	4	5	6	7	8	9	10	11	Day.

Age.	0	1	2	3	4	5	6	7	8	9	10	11	Day.
10	23.4948	23.5057	23.5167	23.5276	23.5385	23.5495	23.5604	23.5713	23.5823	23.5932	23.6041	23.6151	.000364
11	24.3736	24.3863	24.3990	24.4118	24.4245	24.4372	24.4500	24.4627	24.4754	24.4881	24.5008	24.5136	.000424
12	25.2847	25.2991	25.3135	25.3279	25.3423	25.3567	25.3711	25.3855	25.3999	25.4143	25.4287	25.4431	.000480
13	26.2274	26.2431	26.2588	26.2745	26.2902	26.3059	26.3216	26.3374	26.3531	26.3688	26.3845	26.4002	.000523
14	27.1990	27.2158	27.2325	27.2493	27.2661	27.2828	27.2996	27.3164	27.3331	27.3499	27.3667	27.3834	.000559
15	28.1978	28.2152	28.2326	28.2500	28.2674	28.2848	28.3022	28.3197	28.3371	28.3545	28.3719	28.3893	.000580
16	29.2198	29.2377	29.2556	29.2736	29.2915	29.3094	29.3273	29.3453	29.3632	29.3811	29.3990	29.4170	.000597
17	30.2652	30.2834	30.3017	30.3200	30.3382	30.3564	30.3747	30.3930	30.4112	30.4294	30.4477	30.4660	.000608
18	31.3326	31.3512	31.3698	31.3883	31.4069	31.4255	31.4441	31.4627	31.4813	31.4998	31.5184	31.5370	.000619
19	32.4241	32.4427	32.4614	32.4800	32.4987	32.5173	32.5360	32.5546	32.5732	32.5919	32.6105	32.6292	.000621
20	33.5368	33.5553	33.5739	33.5924	33.6110	33.6295	33.6480	33.6666	33.6851	33.7037	33.7222	33.7408	.000618
21	34.6718	34.6900	34.7082	34.7263	34.7445	34.7627	34.7809	34.7991	34.8173	34.8354	34.8536	34.8718	.000606
22	35.8267	35.8444	35.8620	35.8797	35.8973	35.9150	35.9326	35.9503	35.9680	35.9856	36.0033	36.0209	.000588
23	37.0010	37.0180	37.0350	37.0520	37.0690	37.0860	37.1030	37.1200	37.1370	37.1540	37.1710	37.1880	.000567
24	38.1950	38.2111	38.2272	38.2433	38.2595	38.2756	38.2917	38.3078	38.3239	38.3400	38.3562	38.3723	.000537
25	39.4077	39.4226	39.4376	39.4525	39.4675	39.4824	39.4973	39.5123	39.5272	39.5422	39.5571	39.5721	.000498
26	40.6373	40.6510	40.6647	40.6784	40.6921	40.7058	40.7195	40.7332	40.7469	40.7606	40.7743	40.7880	.000457
27	41.8854	41.8976	41.9097	41.9219	41.9340	41.9462	41.9583	41.9705	41.9827	41.9948	42.0070	42.0191	.000405
28	43.1502	43.1605	43.1708	43.1811	43.1915	43.2018	43.2121	43.2224	43.2327	43.2430	43.2534	43.2637	.000344
29	44.4309	44.4388	44.4466	44.4545	44.4623	44.4702	44.4780	44.4859	44.4938	44.5016	44.5095	44.5173	.000262
30	45.7224	45.7275	45.7325	45.7376	45.7427	45.7478	45.7528	45.7579	45.7630	45.7681	45.7731	45.7782	.000169
31	47.0232	47.0250	47.0267	47.0285	47.0302	47.0320	47.0337	47.0355	47.0373	47.0390	47.0408	47.0425	.000058
32	48.3298	48.3279	48.3260	48.3241	48.3222	48.3203	48.3183	48.3164	48.3145	48.3126	48.3107	48.3088	.000063
33	49.6409	49.6348	49.6287	49.6226	49.6165	49.6104	49.6043	49.5982	49.5921	49.5860	49.5799	49.5738	.000203
34	50.9531	50.9424	50.9316	50.9209	50.9102	50.8995	50.8887	50.8780	50.8673	50.8566	50.8458	50.8351	.000357
35	52.2642	52.2482	52.2321	52.2161	52.2001	52.1840	52.1680	52.1520	52.1359	52.1199	52.1039	52.0878	.000534
36	53.5694	53.5477	53.5260	53.5043	53.4826	53.4609	53.4392	53.4175	53.3958	53.3741	53.3524	53.3307	.000723
37	54.8684	54.8405	54.8126	54.7847	54.7569	54.7290	54.7011	54.6732	54.6453	54.6174	54.5896	54.5617	.000929
38	56.1578	56.1234	56.0890	56.0546	56.0202	55.9858	55.9514	55.9170	55.8826	55.8482	55.8138	55.7794	.001147
39	57.4388	57.3973	57.3557	57.3142	57.2727	57.2311	57.1896	57.1481	57.1065	57.0650	57.0235	56.9819	.001384
40	58.7081	58.6589	58.6098	58.5606	58.5114	58.4623	58.4131	58.3639	58.3148	58.2656	58.2164	58.1673	.001639
41	59.9642	59.9076	59.8510	59.7945	59.7379	59.6813	59.6247	59.5682	59.5116	59.4550	59.3984	59.3419	.001886
42	61.2062	61.1401	61.0740	61.0078	60.9417	60.8756	60.8094	60.7433	60.6772	60.6111	60.5450	60.4788	.002204
43	62.4335	62.3580	62.2824	62.2069	62.1314	62.0559	61.9803	61.9048	61.8293	61.7538	61.6782	61.6027	.002517
44	63.6466	63.5611	63.4756	63.3901	63.3046	63.2191	63.1335	63.0480	62.9625	62.8770	62.7915	62.7060	.002850
45	64.8472	64.7512	64.6552	64.5592	64.4632	64.3672	64.2712	64.1753	64.0793	63.9833	63.8873	63.7913	.003200
46	66.0375	65.9302	65.8229	65.7156	65.6083	65.5010	65.3937	65.2865	65.1792	65.0719	64.9646	64.8573	.003576
47	67.2172	67.0978	66.9785	66.8591	66.7398	66.6204	66.5010	66.3817	66.2623	66.1430	66.0236	65.9043	.003978
48	68.3851	68.2532	68.1214	67.9895	67.8576	67.7258	67.5939	67.4620	67.3302	67.1983	67.0664	66.9346	.004395
49	69.5445	69.3996	69.2548	69.1099	68.9651	68.8202	68.6753	68.5305	68.3856	68.2408	68 0959	67.9511	.004828
50	70.6977	70.5397	70.3816	70.2236	70.0656	69.9075	69.7495	69.5915	69.4334	69.2754	69.1174	68.9593	.005268
51	71.8535	71.6823	71.5111	71.3399	71.1687	70.9975	70.8263	70.6551	70.4839	70.3127	70.1415	69.9703	.005707
52	73.0225	72.8380	72.6535	72.4690	72.2845	72.1000	71.9155	71.7310	71.5465	71.3620	71.1775	70.9930	.006150
53	74.2151	74.0174	73.8197	73.6221	73.4244	73.2267	73.0290	72.8314	72.6337	72.4360	72.2383	72.0407	.006589
54	75.4456	75.2340	75.0224	74.8109	74.5993	74.3877	74.1761	73.9646	73.7530	73.5414	73.3298	73.1183	.007052
55	76.7187	76.4925	76.2662	76.0400	75.8137	75.5875	75.3612	75.1350	74.9088	74.6825	74.4563	74.2300	.007541
56	78.0404	77.7987	77.5570	77.3153	77.0736	76.8319	76.5902	76.3486	76.1069	75.8652	75.6235	75.3818	.008056
57	79.4176	79.1586	78.8997	78.6407	78.3818	78.1228	77.8638	77.6049	77.3459	77.0870	76.8280	76.5691	.008632
58	80.8455	80.5668	80.2881	80.0094	79.7307	79.4520	79.1732	78.8945	78.6158	78.3371	78.0584	77.7797	.009290
59	82.3129	82.0128	81.7127	81.4126	81.1126	80.8125	80.5124	80.2123	79.9122	79.6121	79.3121	79.0120	.010003
60	83.8203	83.4961	83.1719	82.8477	82.5235	82.1993	81.8751	81.5510	81.2268	80.9026	80.5784	80.2542	.010806
61	85.3569	85.0038	84.6507	84.2976	83.9445	83.5914	83.2383	82.8852	82.5321	82.1790	81.8259	81.4728	.011770
62	86.8856	86.4986	86.1116	85.7246	85.3376	84.9506	84.5636	84.1766	83.7896	83.4026	83.0156	82.6286	.012900
63	88.3678	87.9421	87.5164	87.0907	86.6650	86.2393	85.8136	85.3879	84.9622	84.5365	84.1108	83.6851	.014190
64	89.7666	89.2879	88.8092	88.3304	87.8517	87.3730	86.8943	86.4156	85.9369	85.4581	84.9794	84.5007	.015957
65	90.9271	90.3939	89.8607	89.3275	88.7943	88.2611	87.7279	87.1947	86.6615	86.1283	85.5951	85.0619	.017773
66	91.8490	91.3157	90.7824	90.2491	89.7158	89.1825	88.6492	88.1159	87.5826	87.0493	86.5160	85.9827	.017777
67	93.2284	92.7785	92.3287	91.8788	91.4290	90.9791	90.5292	90.0794	89.6295	89.1797	88.7298	88.2800	.014995
68 or 41	**96.1538**	**96.4743**	**96.7948**	**97.1153**	**97.4359**	**97.7564**	**98.0769**	**98.3974**	**98.7179**	**99.0384**	**99.3590**	**99.6795**	**.010684**
40	94.6611	94.5882	94.5153	94.4423	94.3694	94.2965	94.2236	94.1507	94.0778	94.0048	93.9319	93.8590	.002430
39	93.9048	93.7793	93.6537	93.5282	93.4026	93.2771	93.1515	93.0260	92.9005	92.7749	94.6494	92.5238	.004185
38	93.3607	93.2250	93.0893	92.9536	92.8180	92.6823	92.5466	92.4109	92.2752	92.1395	92.0039	91.8682	.004523
37	92.6640	92.5478	92.4316	92.3154	92.1993	92.0831	91.9669	91.8507	91.7345	91.6183	91.5022	61.3860	.003870
36	91.8059	91.7097	91.6135	91.5173	91.4211	91.3249	91.2286	91.1324	91.0362	90.9400	90.8438	90.7476	.003207
35	90.8665	90.7834	90.7003	90.6172	90.5341	90.4510	90.3678	90.2847	90.2016	90.1185	90.0354	89.9523	.002770
34	89.8648	89.7929	89.7210	89.6491	89.5773	89.5054	89.4335	89.3616	89.2897	89.2178	89.1460	89.0741	.002396
33	88.8220	88.7593	88.6965	88.6338	88.5710	88.5083	88.4455	88.3828	88.3201	88.2573	88.1946	88.1318	.002091
32	87.7615	87.7057	87.6499	87.5941	87.5384	87.4826	87.4268	87.3710	87.3152	87.2594	87.2037	87.1479	.001859
31	86.6919	86.6420	86.5922	86.5423	86.4925	86.4426	86.3927	86.3429	86.2930	86.2432	86.1933	86.1435	.001662
30	85.6153	85.5709	85.5265	85.4822	85.4378	85.3934	85.3490	85.3047	85.2603	85.2159	85.1715	85.1272	.001479
29	84.5409	84.5010	84.4610	84.4211	84.3812	84.3413	84.3013	84.2614	84.2215	84.1816	84.1416	84.1017	.001331
28	83.4742	83.4380	83.4018	83.3656	83.3295	83.2933	83.2571	83.2209	83.1847	83.1485	83.1124	83.0762	.001206
27	82.4135	82.3810	82.3484	82.3159	82.2834	82.2508	82.2183	82.1858	82.1532	82.1207	82.0882	82.0556	.001084
26	81.3571	81.3281	81.2991	81.2701	81.2412	81.2122	81.1832	81.1542	81.1252	81.0962	81.0673	81.0383	.000966
25	80.3039	80.2783	80.2528	80.2272	80.2017	80.1761	80.1506	80.1250	80.0995	80.0740	80.0484	80.0228	.000852
24	79.2456	79.2240	79.2024	79.1807	79.1591	79.1375	79.1159	79.0943	79.0727	79.0510	79.0294	79.0078	.000720
23	78.1771	78.1597	78.1422	78.1248	78.1073	78.0899	78.0724	78.0550	78.0376	78.0201	78.0027	77.9852	.000581
22	77.0918	77.0789	77.0661	77.0532	77.0403	77.0275	77.0146	77.0017	76.9889	76.9760	76.9631	76.9503	.000429
21	75.9846	75.9765	75.9685	75.9604	75.9524	75.9443	75.9362	75.9282	75.9201	75.9121	75.9040	75.8960	.000268
20	74.8540	74.8507	75.8475	74.8442	74.8410	74.8377	74.8345	74.8312	74.8280	74.8247	74.8215	74.8182	.000108
19	73.6991	73.7006	73.7022	73.7037	73.7052	73.7068	73.7083	73.7098	73.7114	73.7129	73.7144	73.7160	.000051
18	72.5201	72.5262	72.5323	72.5384	72.5445	72.5506	72.5567	72.5628	72.5689	72.5750	72.5811	72.5872	.000203
17	71.3200	71.3303	71.3406	71.3509	71.3613	71.3716	71.3819	71.3923	71.4026	71.4129	71.4233	71.4336	.000343
16	70.0978	70.1123	70.1268	70.1413	70.1558	70.1703	70.1848	70.1993	70.2138	70.2283	70.2428	70.2573	.000483
15	68.8543	68.8728	68.8913	68.9098	68.9283	68.9468	68.9653	68.9838	69.0023	69.0208	69.0393	69.0578	.000617
14	67.5907	67.6130	67.6352	67.6575	67.6798	67.7020	67.7243	67.7466	67.7688	67.7911	67.8134	67.8356	.000742
13	66.3077	66.3336	66.3594	66.3853	66.4111	66.4370	66.4628	66.4887	66.5146	66.5404	66.5663	66.5921	.000862
12	65.0067	65.0358	65.0649	65.0940	65.1231	65.1522	65.1812	65.2103	65.2394	65.2685	65.2976	65.3267	.000970
11	63.6884	63.7208	63.7532	63.7857	63.8181	63.8505	63.8830	63.9154	63.9478	63.9802	64.0126	64.0451	.001081
10	62.3564	62.3916	62.4268	62.4621	62.4973	62.5325	62.5677	62.6030	62.6382	62.6734	62.7086	62.7439	.001174
Age.	0	1	2	3	4	5	6	7	8	9	10	11	Day.

Age.	0	1	2	3	4	5	6	7	8	9	10	11	Day.
10	24.6689	24.6829	24.6969	24.7109	24.7249	24.7389	24.7529	24.7669	24.7809	24.7949	24.8089	24.8229	.000467
11	25.5895	25.6052	25.6209	25.6366	25.6523	25.6680	25.6837	25.6995	25.7152	25.7309	25.7466	25.7623	.000523
12	26.5418	26.5589	26.5760	26.5930	26.6101	26.6272	26.6442	26.6613	26.6784	26.6955	26.7125	26.7296	.000569
13	27.5224	27.5406	27.5588	27.5770	27.5952	27.6134	27.6316	27.6499	27.6681	27.6863	27.7045	27.7227	.000607
14	28.5303	28.5492	28.5680	28.5869	28.6058	28.6247	28.6435	28.6624	28.6813	28.7002	28.7190	28.7379	.000629
15	29.5610	29.5805	29.5999	29.6194	29.6389	29.6583	29.6778	29.6973	29.7167	29.7362	29.7557	29.7751	.000649
16	30.6149	30.6347	30.6546	30.6744	30.6943	30.7141	30.7340	30.7538	30.7737	30.7935	30.8134	30.8332	.000662
17	31.6910	31.7112	31.7315	31.7517	31.7720	31.7922	31.8125	31.8327	31.8530	31.8732	31.8935	31.9137	.000675
18	32.7905	32.8109	32.8313	32.8516	32.8720	32.8924	32.9128	32.9332	32.9536	32.9740	32.9943	33.0147	.000679
19	33.9121	33.9324	33.9527	33.9730	33.9934	34.0137	34.0340	34.0543	34.0746	34.0950	34.1153	34.1356	.000677
20	35.0541	35.0742	35.0943	35.1143	35.1344	35.1545	35.1746	35.1947	35.2148	35.2348	35.2549	35.2750	.000669
21	36.2173	36.2369	36.2565	36.2762	36.2958	36.3154	36.3350	36.3547	36.3743	36.3939	36.4135	36.4332	.000654
22	37.3997	37.4187	37.4378	37.4568	37.4759	37.4950	37.5140	37.5330	37.5521	37.5711	37.5902	37.6092	.000635
23	38.6013	38.6196	38.6378	38.6561	38.6743	38.6926	38.7108	38.7291	38.7474	38.7656	38.7839	38.8021	.000608
24	39.8218	39 8390	39.8561	39.8733	39.8905	39.9076	39.9248	39.9420	39.9591	39.9763	39.9935	40.0106	.000572
25	41.0591	41.0751	41.0912	41.1072	41.1233	41.1393	41.1553	41.1714	41.1874	41.2035	41.2195	41.2356	.000535
26	42.3147	42.3293	42.3439	42.3585	42.3731	42.3877	42.4022	42.4168	42.4314	42.4460	42.4606	42.4752	.000486
27	43.5870	43.5999	43.6127	43.6256	43.6385	43.6513	43.6642	43.6771	43.6899	43.7028	43.7157	43.7285	.000429
28	44.8745	44.8850	44.8956	44.9061	44.9167	44.9272	44.9377	44.9483	44.9588	44.9694	44.9799	44.9905	.000351
29	46.1729	46.1808	46.1887	46.1965	46.2044	46.2123	46.2202	46.2281	46.2360	46.2438	46.2517	46.2596	.000263
30	47.4804	47.4851	47.4899	47.4946	47.4993	47.5041	47.5088	47.5135	47.5183	47.5230	47.5277	47.5325	.000158
31	48.7936	48.7948	48.7960	48.7972	48.7985	48.7997	48.8009	48.8021	48.8033	48.8045	48.8058	48.8070	.000040
32	50.1110	50.1082	50.1054	50.1026	50.0998	50.0970	50.0941	50.0913	50.0885	50.0857	50.0829	50.0801	.000093
33	51.4293	51.4221	51.4148	51.4076	51.4004	51.3931	51.3859	51.3787	51.3714	51.3642	51.3570	51.3497	.000241
34	52.7469	52.7346	52.7223	52.7099	52.6976	52.6853	52.6729	52.6606	52.6483	52.6359	52.6236	52.6113	.000410
35	54.0584	54.0406	54.0228	54.0050	53.9873	53.9695	53.9517	53.9339	53.9161	53.8983	53.8806	53.8628	.000593
36	55.3633	55.3396	55.3159	55.2922	55.2685	55.2448	55.2211	55.1975	55.1738	55.1501	55.1264	55.1027	.000790
37	56.6598	56.6298	56.5999	56.5700	56.5400	56.5100	56.4801	56.4501	56.4202	56.3902	56.3603	56.3303	.000998
38	57.9468	57.9100	57.8732	57.8365	57.7997	57.7629	57.7261	57.6894	57.6526	57.6158	57.5790	57.5423	.001226
39	59.2227	59.1786	59.1345	59.0904	59.0464	59.0023	58.9582	58.9141	58.8700	58.8260	58.7819	58.7378	.001469
40	60.4858	60.4339	60.3820	60.3301	60.2782	60.2263	60.1743	60.1224	60.0705	60.0186	59.9667	59.9148	.001730
41	61.7439	61.6828	61.6218	61.5607	61.4997	61.4386	61.3775	61.3165	61.2554	61.1944	61.1333	61.0723	.002035
42	62.9681	62.8989	62.8296	62.7604	62.6911	62.6219	62.5526	62.4834	62.4142	62.3449	62.2757	62.2064	.002308
43	64.1858	64.1070	64.0282	63.9494	63.8707	63.7919	63.7131	63.6343	63.5555	63.4767	63.3980	63.3192	.002626
44	65.3887	65.2999	65.2111	65.1223	65.0335	64.9447	64.8560	64.7672	64.6784	64.5896	64.5008	64.4120	.002960
45	66.5798	66.4802	66.3806	66.2810	66.1814	66.0818	65.9822	65.8827	65.7831	65.6835	65.5839	65.4843	.003320
46	67.7580	67.6468	67.5357	67.4245	67.3134	67.2022	67.0911	66.9800	66.8688	66.7576	66.6465	66.5353	.003705
47	68.9233	68.8002	68.6771	68.5540	68.4310	68.3079	68.1848	68.0617	67.9386	67.8155	67.6925	67.5694	.004103
48	70.0793	69.9438	69.8083	69.6728	69.5373	69.4018	69.2662	69.1307	68.9952	68.8597	68.7242	68.5887	.004517
49	71.2288	71.0807	70.9327	70.7846	70.6365	70.4885	70.3404	70.1923	70.0443	69.8962	69.7481	69.6001	.004935
50	72.3785	72.2180	72.0574	71.8968	71.7363	71.5757	71.4152	71.2546	71.0941	70.9335	70.7730	70.6124	.005352
51	73.5406	73.3674	73.1942	73.0210	72.8478	72.6746	72.5013	72.3281	72.1549	71.9817	71.8085	71.6353	.005773
52	74.7236	74.5380	74.3523	74.1667	73.9810	73.7954	73.6097	73.4241	73.2385	73.0528	72.8672	72.6815	.006188
53	75.9426	75.7438	75.5450	75.3362	75.1374	74.9386	74.7398	74.5410	74.3422	74.1434	73.9546	73.7558	.006627
54	77.2017	76.9890	76.7764	76.5637	76.3511	76.1384	75.9258	75.7131	75.5005	75.2878	75.0752	74.8625	.007088
55	78.5063	78.2791	78.0518	77.8246	77.5974	77.3702	77.1430	76.9157	76.6885	76.4613	76.2340	76.0068	.007574
56	79.8630	79.6194	79.3759	79.1323	78.8888	78.6452	78.4017	78.1581	77.9146	77.6710	77.4275	77.1840	.008118
57	81.2672	81.0050	80.7428	80.4806	80.2184	79.9562	79.6940	79.4319	79.1697	78.9075	78.6453	78.3831	.008740
58	82.7076	82.4252	82.1428	81.8604	81.5780	81.2956	81.0132	80.7309	80.4485	80.1661	79.8837	79.6013	.009413
59	84.1843	83.8791	83.5739	83.2687	82.9635	82.6583	82.3531	82.0480	81.7428	81.4376	81.1324	80.8272	.010173
60	85.6855	85.3529	85.0203	84.6877	84.3552	84.0226	83.6900	83.3574	83.0248	82.6922	82.3597	82.0271	.011086
61	87.1768	86.8120	86.4472	86.0824	85.7177	85.3529	84.9881	84.6233	84.2585	83.8937	83.5290	83.1642	.012159
62	88.6198	88.2182	87.8166	87.4151	87.0135	86.6119	86.2103	85.8088	85.4072	85.0056	84.6040	84.2025	.013386
63	89.9793	89.5272	89.0751	88.6230	88.1709	87.7188	87.2667	86.8147	86.3626	85.9105	85.4584	85.0063	.015070
64	91.1060	90.6020	90.0981	89.5941	89.0902	88.5862	88.0823	87.5783	87.0744	86.5704	86.0665	85.5625	.016798
65	92.0005	91.4972	90.9940	90.4907	89.9875	89.4842	88.9810	88.4777	87.9745	87.4712	86.9680	86.4647	.016775
66	93.3340	92.9119	92.4899	92.0678	91.6457	91.2237	90.8016	90.3795	89.9575	89.5354	89.1133	88.6913	.014069
67 or 42	**96.1538**	**96.4743**	**96.7948**	**97.1153**	**97.4359**	**97.7564**	**96.0769**	**98.3974**	**98.7179**	**99.0384**	**99.3590**	**99.6795**	**.010684**
41	94.6383	94.5597	94.4811	94.4025	94.3239	94.2453	94.1667	94.0882	94.0096	94.9310	93.8524	93.7738	.002620
40	93.8735	93.7417	93.6100	93.4782	93.3465	93.2147	93.0830	92.9512	92.8194	92.6877	92.5559	92.4242	.004392
39	94.3236	94.1818	94.0401	93.8983	93.7566	93.6148	93.4730	93.3313	93.1895	92.0478	91.9060	91.7643	.004725
38	92.6196	92.4979	92.3761	92.2544	92.1327	92.0110	91.8892	91.7675	91.6458	91.5241	91.4023	91.2806	.004057
37	91.7532	91.6519	91.5507	91.4494	91.3481	91.2469	91.1456	91.0443	90.9431	90.8418	90.7405	90.6393	.003375
36	90.8051	90.7173	90.6295	90.5417	90.4539	90.3661	90.2783	90.1905	90.1027	90.0149	89.9271	89.8393	.002927
35	89.7946	89.7184	89.6421	89.5659	89.4897	89.4135	89.3372	89.2610	89.1848	89.1086	89.0323	88.9561	.002541
34	88.7440	88.6772	88.6104	88.5436	88.4768	88.4100	88.3432	88.2764	88.2096	88.1428	88.0760	88.0092	.002227
33	87.6757	87.6161	87.5565	89.4969	87.4373	87.3777	87.3180	87.2584	87.1988	87.1392	87.0796	87.0200	.001987
32	86.5992	86.5457	86.4922	86.4388	86.3853	86.3318	86.2783	86.2249	86.1714	86.1179	86.0644	86.0110	.001782
31	85.5163	85.4685	85.4207	85.3729	85.3251	85.2773	85.2294	85.1816	85.1338	85.0860	85.0382	84.9904	.001593
30	84.4362	84.3930	84.3498	84.3067	84.2635	84.2203	84.1771	84.1340	84.0908	84.0476	84.0044	83.9613	.001439
29	83.3646	83.3253	83.2860	83.2468	83.2075	83.1682	83.1290	83.0897	83.0504	83.0111	82.9718	82.9326	.001309
28	82.2993	82.2638	82.2284	82.1929	82.1574	82.1220	82.0865	82.0510	82.0156	81.9801	81.9446	81.9092	.001182
27	81.2391	81.2073	81.1755	81.1438	81.1120	81.0802	81.0484	81.0167	80.9849	80.9531	80.9213	80.8896	.001059
26	80.1825	80.1543	80.1261	80.0979	80.0697	80.0415	80.0133	79.9851	79.9569	79.9287	79.9005	79.8723	.000940
25	79.1213	79.0972	79.0730	79.0489	79.0248	79.0006	78.9765	78.9524	78.9282	78.9041	78.8800	78.8558	.000804
24	78.0502	78.0304	78.0105	77.9907	77.9709	77.9511	77.9312	77.9114	77.8916	77.8718	77.8520	77.8321	.000661
23	76.9523	76.9380	76.9237	76.9094	76.8951	76.8808	76.8665	76.8523	76.8380	76.8237	76.8094	76.7951	.000476
22	75.8532	75.8430	75.8328	75.8226	75.8124	75.8022	75.7920	75.7817	75.7715	75.7613	75.7511	75.7409	.000340
21	74.7208	74.7155	74.7102	74.7049	74.6996	74.6943	74.6890	74.6838	74.6785	74.6732	74.6679	74.6626	.000176
20	73.5635	73.5631	73.5628	73.5624	73.5621	73.5617	73.5613	73.5610	73.5606	73.5603	73.5599	73.5596	.000012
19	72.3835	72.3878	72.3920	72.3963	72.4006	72.4048	72.4091	72.4134	72.4176	72.4219	72.4262	72.4304	.000142
18	71.1819	71.1905	71.1991	71.2077	71.2164	71.2250	71.2336	71.2422	71.2508	71.2594	71.2681	71.2767	.000287
17	69.9588	69.9717	69.9845	69.9974	70.0103	70.0231	70.0360	70.0489	70.0617	70.0746	70.0875	70.1003	.000429
16	68.7145	68.7314	68.7484	68.7653	68.7823	68.7992	68.8161	68.8331	68.8500	68.8670	68.8839	68.9009	.000565
15	67.4502	67.4710	67.4918	67.5126	67.5335	67.5543	67.5751	67.5959	67.6167	67.6375	67.6584	67.6792	.000694
14	66.1671	66.1916	66.2160	66.2405	66.2650	66.2894	66.3139	66.3384	66.3628	66.3873	66.4118	66.4362	.000815
13	64.8660	64.8939	64.9218	64.9498	64.9777	65.0056	65.0335	65.0615	65.0894	65.1173	65.1452	65.1732	.000931
12	63.5482	63.5794	63.6106	63.6417	63.6729	63.7041	63.7353	63.7665	63.7977	63.8288	63.8600	63.8912	.001039
11	62.2158	62.2499	62.2840	62.3182	62.3523	62.3864	62.4205	62.4547	62.4888	62.5229	62.5570	62.5912	.001137
10	60.8691	60.9061	60.9432	60.9802	61.0172	61.0543	61.0913	61.1283	61.1654	61.2024	61.2394	61.2765	.001234
Age.	0	1	2	3	4	5	6	7	8	9	10	11	Day.

Age.	0	1	2	3	4	5	6	7	8	9	10	11	Day.
10	25.8798	25.8968	25.9137	25.9307	25.9477	25.9646	25.9816	25.9986	26.0155	26.0325	26.0495	26.0664	.000565
11	26.8411	26.8595	26.8779	26.8962	26.9146	26.9330	26.9514	26.9698	26.9882	27.0065	27.0249	27.0433	.000613
12	27.8310	27.8506	27.8701	27.8897	27.9093	27.9288	27.9484	27.9680	27.9875	28.0071	28.0267	28.0462	.000652
13	28.8474	28.8677	28.8880	28.9083	28.9286	28.9489	28.9692	28.9895	29.0098	29.0301	29.0504	29.0707	.000677
14	29.8868	29.9077	29.9286	29.9496	29.9705	29.9914	30.0123	30.0333	30.0542	30.0751	30.0960	30.1170	.000697
15	30.9490	30.9704	30.9918	31.0131	31.0345	31.0559	31.0773	31.0987	31.1201	31.1414	31.1628	31.1842	.000713
16	32.0331	32.0549	32.0768	32.0986	32.1205	32.1423	32.1641	32.1860	32.2078	32.2297	32.2515	32.2734	.000728
17	33.1409	33.1629	33.1850	33.2070	33.2290	33.2511	33.2731	33.2951	33.3172	33.3392	33.3612	33.3833	.000734
18	34.2699	34.2920	34.3140	34.3361	34.3581	34.3802	34.4022	34.4243	34.4464	34.4684	34.4905	34.5125	.000735
19	35.4202	35.4421	35.4639	35.4858	35.5077	35.5295	35.5514	35.5733	35.5951	35.6170	35.6389	35.6607	.000729
20	36.5899	36.6114	36.6329	36.6544	36.6760	36.6975	36.7190	36.7405	36.7620	36.7835	36.8051	36.8266	.000717
21	37.7800	37.8010	37.8220	37.8430	37.8641	37.8851	37.9061	37.9271	37.9481	37.9691	37.9902	38.0112	.000700
22	38.9893	39.0096	39.0299	39.0502	39.0705	39.0908	39.1110	39.1313	39.1516	39.1719	39.1922	39.2125	.000676
23	40.2167	40.2360	40.2553	40.2746	40.2940	40.3133	40.3326	40.3519	40.3712	40.3905	40.4099	40.4292	.000644
24	41.4612	41.4795	41.4977	41.5160	41.5342	41.5525	41.5707	41.5890	41.6073	41.6255	41.6438	41.6620	.000608
25	42.7238	42.7407	42.7576	42.7746	42.7915	42.8084	42.8253	42.8423	42.8592	42.8761	42.8930	42.9100	.000564
26	44.0028	44.0181	44.0334	44.0487	44.0640	44.0793	44.0946	44.1099	44.1252	44.1405	44.1558	44.1711	.000510
27	45.2970	45.3101	45.3232	45.3363	45.3494	45.3625	45.3756	45.3887	45.4018	45.4149	45.4280	45.4411	.000437
28	46.6015	46.6121	46.6226	46.6332	46.6438	46.6544	46.6650	46.6755	46.6861	46.6967	46.7072	46.7178	.000352
29	47.9152	47.9227	47.9303	47.9378	47.9454	47.9530	47.9605	47.9680	47.9756	47.9831	47.9907	47.9982	.000252
30	49.2344	49.2384	49.2424	49.2465	49.2505	49.2545	49.2585	49.2626	49.2666	49.2706	49.2746	49.2787	.000134
31	50.5574	50.5577	50.5581	50.5584	50.5587	50.5591	50.5594	50.5597	50.5601	50.5604	50.5607	50.5611	.000010
32	51.8813	51.8774	51.8735	51.8696	51.8657	51.8618	51.8580	51.8541	51.8502	51.8463	51.8424	51.8385	.000130
33	53.2041	53.1953	53.1865	53.1776	53.1688	53.1600	53.1512	53.1424	53.1336	53.1247	53.1159	53.1071	.000294
34	54.5214	54.5073	54.4933	54.4792	54.4651	54.4511	54.4370	54.4229	54.4089	54.3948	54.3807	54.3667	.000469
35	55.8316	55.8119	55.7921	55.7724	55.7526	55.7329	55.7131	55.6934	55.6737	55.6539	55.6342	55.6144	.000658
36	57.1333	57.1076	57.0818	57.0561	57.0303	57.0046	56.9788	56.9531	56.9274	56.9016	56.8759	56.8501	.000858
37	58.4265	58.3942	58.3619	58.3296	58.2973	58.2650	58.2326	58.2003	58.1680	58.1357	58.1034	58.0711	.001077
38	59.7073	59.6680	59.6287	59.5894	59.5501	59.5108	59.4715	59.4323	59.3930	59.3537	59.3144	59.2751	.001310
39	60.9760	60.9292	60.8824	60.8356	60.7888	60.7420	60.6952	60.6485	60.6017	60.5549	60.5081	60.4613	.001560
40	62.2306	62.1758	62.1210	62.0662	62.0114	61.9566	61.9018	61.8471	61.7923	61.7375	61.6827	61.6279	.001826
41	63.4698	63.4057	63.3417	63.2776	63.2135	63.1495	63.0854	63.0213	62.9573	62.8932	62.8291	62.7651	.002135
42	64.6926	64.6201	64.5477	64.4752	64.4028	64.3303	64.2579	64.1854	64.1130	64.0405	63.9681	63.8956	.002415
43	65.8990	65.8170	65.7350	65.6530	65.5710	65.4890	65.4070	65.3249	65.2429	65.1609	65.0789	64.9969	.002733
44	67.0914	66.9991	66.9067	66.8144	66.7221	66.6297	66.5374	66.4451	66.3527	66.2604	66.1681	66.0757	.003077
45	68.2692	68.1658	58.0625	67.9591	67.8557	67.7524	67.6490	67.5456	67.4423	67.3389	67.2355	67.1322	.003445
46	69.4322	69.3174	69.2026	69.0878	68.9730	68.8582	68.7433	68.6285	68.5137	68.3989	68.2841	68.1693	.003827
47	70.5847	70.4580	70.3314	70.2047	70.0781	69.9514	69.8247	69.6981	69.5714	69.4448	69.3181	69.1915	.004222
48	71.7299	71.5913	71.4526	71.3139	71.1753	71.0366	70.8979	70.7593	70.6206	70.4819	70.3433	70.2046	.004620
49	72.8746	72.7241	72.5735	72.4230	72.2725	72.1219	71.9714	71.8209	71.6703	71.5198	71.3693	71.2187	.005018
50	74.0295	73.8670	73.7044	73.5419	73.3793	73.2168	73.0542	72.8917	72.7292	72.5666	72.4041	72.2415	.005418
51	75.2036	75.0293	74.8550	74.6806	74.5063	74.3320	74.1577	73.9834	73.8091	73.6347	73.4604	73.2861	.005810
52	76.4110	76.2243	76.0375	75.8508	75.6640	75.4773	75.2905	75.1038	74.9171	74.7303	74.5436	74.3568	.006225
53	77.6566	77.4567	77.2569	77.0570	76.8572	76.6573	76.4575	76.2576	76.0578	75.8580	75.6581	75.4582	.006662
54	78.9449	78.7313	78.5177	78.3041	78.0905	77.8769	77.6632	77.4496	77.2360	77.0224	76.8088	76.5952	.007120
55	80.2821	80.0531	79.8240	79.5950	79.3660	79.1369	78.9079	78.6789	78.4498	78.2208	77.9918	77.7627	.007634
56	81.6634	81.4167	81.1700	80.9233	80.6766	80.4299	80.1832	79.9366	79.6899	79.4432	79.1965	78.9498	.008223
57	83.0780	82.8122	82.5465	82.2807	82.0149	81.7492	81.4834	81.2176	80.9519	80.6861	80.4203	80.1546	.008859
58	84.5256	84.2383	83.9509	83.6636	83.3762	83.0889	82.8015	82.5142	82.2269	81.9395	81.6522	81.3648	.009578
59	85.9944	85.6811	85.3677	85.0544	84.7411	84.4278	84.1144	83.8011	83.4878	83.1745	82.8611	82.5478	.010444
60	87.4500	87.1061	86.7622	86.4182	86.0743	85.7304	85.3865	85.0426	84.6987	84.3547	84.0108	83.6669	.011464
61	88.8565	88.4776	88.0987	87.7198	87.3409	86.9620	86.5831	86.2042	85.8253	85.4464	85.0675	84.6886	.012630
62	90.1792	89.7521	89.3250	88.8978	88.4707	88.0436	87.6165	87.1894	86.7623	86.3351	85.9080	85.4809	.014237
63	91.2741	90.7976	90.3211	89.8446	89.3682	88.8917	88.4152	87.9387	87.4622	86.9857	86.5093	86.0328	.015883
64	92.1427	91.6677	91.1926	90.7176	90.2426	89.7675	89.2925	88.8175	88.3424	87.8674	87.3924	86.9173	.015834
65	93.4332	93.0373	92.6413	92.2454	91.8495	91.4536	91.0576	90.6617	90.2658	89.8699	89.4740	89.0780	.013197
66 or 43	**96.1538**	**96.4743**	**96.7948**	**97.1153**	**97.4359**	**97.7564**	**98.0769**	**98.3974**	**98.7179**	**99.0384**	**99.3590**	**99.6795**	**.010684**
42	94.6150	94.5303	94.4456	94.3608	94.2761	94.1914	94.1067	94.0220	93.9373	93.8525	93.7678	93.6831	.002824
41	93.8401	93.7017	93.5634	93.4250	93.2866	93.1483	93.0099	92.8715	92.7332	92.5948	92.4564	92.3181	.004612
40	93.2842	93.1360	92.9878	92.8396	92.6914	92.5432	92.3950	92.2468	92.0986	91.9504	91.8022	91.6540	.004940
39	92.5726	92.4450	92.3174	92.1898	92.0622	91.9346	91.8070	91.6793	91.5517	91.4241	91.2965	91.1689	.004253
38	91.6971	91.5905	91.4839	91.3772	91.2706	91.1640	91.0574	90.9508	90.8442	90.7375	90.6309	90.5243	.003554
37	90.7402	90.6474	90.5547	90.4620	90.3692	90.2764	90.1837	90.0910	89.9982	89.9054	89.8127	89.7200	.003092
36	89.7208	89.6400	89.5591	89.4783	89.3975	89.3166	89.2358	89.1550	89.0741	88.9933	88.9125	88.8316	.002694
35	88.6616	88.5905	88.5193	88.4482	88.3771	88.3059	88.2348	88.1637	88.0925	88.0214	87.9503	87.8791	.002371
34	87.5855	87.5218	87.4582	87.3945	87.3308	87.2672	87.2035	87.1398	87.0762	87.0125	86.9488	86.8852	.002120
33	86.5016	86.4443	86.3870	86.3297	86.2724	86.2151	86.1578	86.1006	86.0433	85.9860	85.9287	85.8714	.001910
32	85.4121	85.3607	85.3093	85.2579	85.2065	85.1551	85.1036	85.0522	85.0008	84.9494	84.8980	84.8466	.001713
31	84.3261	84.2795	84.2329	84.1863	84.1398	84.0932	84.0466	84.0000	83.9534	83.9068	83.8603	83.8137	.001553
30	83.2493	83.2068	83.1643	83.1217	83.0792	83.0367	82.9942	82.9517	82.9092	82.8666	82.8241	82.7816	.001417
29	82.1795	82.1410	82.1024	82.0638	82.0253	81.9867	81.9482	81.9096	81.8711	81.8325	81.7940	81.7554	.001285
28	81.1152	81.0805	81.0458	81.0111	80.9764	80.9417	80.9070	80.8723	80.8376	80.8029	80.7682	80.7335	.001157
27	80.0552	80.0242	79.9932	79.9622	79.9313	79.9003	79.8693	79.8383	79.8073	79.7763	79.7454	79.7144	.001033
26	78.9909	78.9641	78.9373	78.9106	78.8838	78.8570	78.8302	78.8035	78.7767	78.7499	78.7231	78.6964	.000892
25	77.9172	77.8948	77.8725	77.8502	77.8278	77.8055	77.7832	77.7608	77.7385	77.7162	77.6938	77.6715	.000743
24	76.8268	76.8093	76.7918	76.7743	76.7568	76.7393	76.7218	76.7044	76.6869	76.6694	76.6519	76.6344	.000583
23	75.7153	75.7020	75.6887	75.6755	75.6622	75.6489	75.6356	75.6224	75.6091	75.5958	75.5825	75.5693	.000442
22	74.5812	74.5738	74.5663	74.5589	74.5515	74.5441	74.5366	74.5292	74.5218	74.5144	74.5070	74.4995	.000247
21	73.4223	73.4199	73.4175	73.4151	73.4127	73.4103	73.4079	73.4055	73.4031	73.4007	73.3983	73.3959	.000080
20	72.2400	72.2424	72.2448	72.2472	72.2496	72.2520	72.2543	72.2567	72.2591	72.2615	72.2639	72.2663	.000080
19	71.0375	71.0443	71.0511	71.0579	71.0647	71.0715	71.8783	71.0852	71.0920	71.0988	71.1056	71.1124	.000227
18	69.8131	69.8243	69.8354	69.8466	69.8577	69.8689	69.8800	69 8912	69.9024	69.9135	69.9247	69.9358	.000372
17	68.5681	68.5834	68.5987	68.6141	68.6294	68.6447	68.6600	68.6754	68.6907	68.7060	68.7213	68.7367	.000511
16	67.3032	67.3225	67.3417	67.3610	67.3803	67.3995	67.4188	67.4381	67.4573	67.4766	67.4959	67.5151	.000642
15	66.0196	66.0426	66.0656	66.0886	66.1117	66.1347	66.1577	66.1807	66.2037	66.2267	66.2498	66.2728	.000767
14	64.7186	64.7451	64.7717	64.7982	64.8247	64.8513	64.8778	64.9043	64.9309	64.9574	64.9839	65.0105	.000884
13	63.4009	63.4308	63.4606	63.4905	63.5204	63.5503	63.5801	63.6100	63.6399	63.6698	63.6996	63.7295	.000996
12	62.0692	62.1021	62.1350	62.1679	62.2008	62.2337	62.2665	62.2994	62.3323	62.3652	62.3981	62.4310	.001096
11	60.7233	60.7591	60.7948	60.8306	60.8664	60.9022	60.9380	60.9737	61.0095	61.0453	61.0810	61.1168	.001192
10	59.3651	59.4035	59.4419	59.4803	59.5187	59.5571	59.5955	59.6340	59.6724	59.7108	59.7492	59.7876	.001280
Age.	0	1	2	3	4	5	6	7	8	9	10	11	Day.

Age.	0	1	2	3	4	5	6	7	8	9	10	11	Day.
10	27.1263	27.1459	27.1655	27.1852	27.2048	27.2244	27.2440	27.2637	27.2833	27.3029	27.3225	27.3422	.000654
11	28.1248	28.1457	28.1665	28.1874	28.2082	28.2291	28.2500	28.2708	28.2917	28.3125	28.3334	28.3542	.000695
12	29.1501	29.1717	29.1934	29.2150	29.2367	29.2583	29.2800	29.3016	29.3233	29.3450	29.3666	29.2882	.000722
13	30.1976	30.2199	30.2423	30.2646	30.2870	30.3093	30.3316	30.3540	30.3763	30.3987	30.4210	30.4434	.000745
14	31.2680	31.2908	31.3137	31.3365	31.3593	31.3822	31.4050	31.4278	31.4507	31.4735	31.4963	31.5192	.000761
15	32.3600	32.3834	32.4067	32.4301	32.4535	32.4768	32.5002	32.5236	32.5469	32.5703	32.5937	32.6170	.000779
16	33.4753	33.4989	33.5225	33.5461	33.5698	33.5934	33.6170	33.6406	33.6642	33.6878	33.7115	33.7351	.000787
17	34.6122	34.6359	34.6596	34.6833	34.7070	34.7307	34.7543	34.7780	34.8017	34.8254	34.8491	34.8728	.000790
18	35.7694	35.7930	35.8166	35.8402	35.8638	35.8874	35.9110	35.9345	35.9581	35.9817	36.0053	36.0289	.000786
19	36.9469	36.9702	36.9935	37.0167	37.0400	37.0633	37.0866	37.1099	37.1332	37.1564	37.1797	37.2030	.000776
20	38.1430	38.1659	38.1888	38.2117	38.2346	38.2575	38.2803	38.3032	38.3261	38.3490	38.3719	38.3948	.000763
21	39.3594	39.3816	39.4039	39.4261	39.4484	39.4706	39.4928	39.5151	39.5373	39.5596	39.5818	39.6041	.000741
22	40.5939	40.6152	40.6365	40.6579	40.6792	40.7005	40.7218	40.7432	40.7645	40.7858	40.8071	40.8285	.000711
23	41.8448	41.8652	41.8855	41.9059	41.9263	41.9466	41.9670	41.9874	42.0077	42.0281	42.0485	42.0688	.000679
24	43.1137	43.1328	43.1520	43.1711	43.1903	43.2094	43.2285	43.2477	43.2668	43.2860	43.3051	43.3243	.000638
25	44.3991	44.4167	44.4343	44.4520	44.4696	44.4872	44.5048	44.5225	44.5401	44.5577	44.5753	44.5930	.000587
26	45.6993	45.7148	45.7303	45.7459	45.7614	45.7769	45.7924	45.8080	45.8235	45.8390	45.8545	45.8701	.000517
27	47.0098	47.0229	47.0360	47.0492	47.0623	47.0754	47.0885	47.1017	47.1148	47.1279	47.1410	47.1542	.000437
28	48.3289	48.3391	48.3494	48.3596	48.3699	48.3801	48.3903	48.4006	48.4108	48.4211	48.4313	48.5416	.000341
29	49.6535	49.6605	49.6675	49.6745	49.6816	49.6886	49.6956	49.7026	49.7096	49.7166	49.7237	49.7307	.000234
30	50.9818	50.9851	50.9884	50.9917	50.9950	50.9983	51.0016	51.0050	51.0083	51.0116	51.0149	51.0182	.000110
31	52.3106	52.3098	52.3090	52.3082	52.3075	52.3067	52.3059	52.3051	52.3043	52.3035	52.3028	52.3020	.000026
32	53.6387	53.6332	53.6276	53.6221	53.6166	53.6110	53.6055	53.6000	53.5944	53.5889	53.5834	53.5778	.000184
33	54.9600	54.9495	54.9389	54.9284	54.9179	54.9073	54.8968	54.8863	54.8757	54.8652	54.8547	54.8441	.000351
34	56.2751	56.2591	56.2431	56.2271	56.2111	56.1951	56.1791	56.1631	56.1471	56.1311	56.1151	56.0991	.000533
35	57.5813	57.5595	57.5378	57.5160	57.4942	57.4725	57.4507	57.4289	57.4072	57.3854	57.3636	57.3419	.000725
36	58.8788	58.8507	58.8226	58.7946	58.7665	58.7384	58.7103	58.6823	58.6542	58.6261	58.5980	58.5700	.000936
37	60.1648	60.1300	60.0952	60.0604	60.0257	59.9909	59.9561	59.9213	59.8865	59.8517	59.8170	59.7822	.001159
38	61.4376	61.3956	61.3537	61.3117	61.2697	61.2278	61.1858	61.1438	61.1019	61.0599	61.0179	60.9760	.001399
39	62.6969	62.6473	62.5976	62.5480	62.4984	62.4487	62.3991	62.3495	62.2998	62.2502	62.2006	62.1509	.001654
40	63.9408	63.8830	63.8252	63.7673	63.7095	63.6517	63.5939	63.5361	63.4783	63.4204	63.3626	63.3048	.001927
41	65.1596	65.0972	65.0348	64.9725	64.9101	64.8477	64.7853	64.7230	64.6606	64.5982	64.5358	64.4735	.002079
42	66.3786	66.3030	66.2273	66.1517	66.0761	66.0005	65.9248	65.8492	65.7736	65.6980	65.6223	65.5467	.002521
43	67.5734	67.4879	67.4024	67.3169	67.2314	67.1459	67.0604	66.9750	66.8895	66.8040	66.7185	66.6330	.002850
44	68.7516	68.6555	68.5595	68.4634	68.3674	68.2713	68.1753	68.0792	67.9832	67.8871	67.7911	67.6950	.003202
45	69.9133	69.8063	69.6994	69.5924	69.4855	69.3785	69.2715	69.1646	69.0576	68.9507	68.8437	68.7368	.003565
46	71.0625	70.9442	70.8259	70.7076	70.5893	70.4710	70.3526	70.2343	70.1160	69.9977	69.8794	69.7611	.003943
47	72.2033	72.0735	71.9438	71.8140	71.6843	71.5545	71.4247	71.2950	71.1652	71.0355	70.9057	70.7760	.004325
48	73.3426	73.2015	73.0604	72.9194	72.7783	72.6372	72.4961	72.3551	72.2140	72.0729	71.9318	71.7908	.004702
49	74.4909	74.3384	74.1860	74.0335	73.8810	73.7286	73.5761	73.4236	73.2712	73.1187	72.9662	72.8138	.005082
50	75.6565	75.4929	75.3292	75.1656	75.0020	74.8384	74.6747	74.5111	74.3475	74.1839	74.0202	73.8566	.005454
51	76.8533	76.6779	76.5025	76.3271	76.1517	75.9763	75.8009	75.6255	75.4501	75.2747	75.0993	74.9239	.005847
52	78.0852	77.8974	77.7097	77.5219	77.3341	77.1464	76.9586	76.7708	76.5831	76.3953	76.2075	76.0198	.006259
53	79.3579	79.1571	78.9563	78.7555	78.5547	78.3539	78.1531	77.9524	77.7516	77.5508	77.3500	77.1492	.006693
54	80.6765	80.4611	80.2457	80.0304	79.8150	79.5996	79.3842	79.1689	78.9535	78.7381	78.5227	78.3074	.007179
55	82.0361	81.8040	81.5719	81.3398	81.1077	80.8756	80.6435	80.4115	80.1794	79.9473	79.7152	79.4831	.007736
56	83.4261	83.1759	82.9257	82.6756	82.4254	82.1752	81.9250	81.6749	81.4247	81.1745	80.9243	80.6742	.008339
57	84.8459	84.5753	84.3047	84.0341	83.7636	83.4930	83.2224	82.9518	82.6812	82.4106	82.1401	81.8695	.009019
58	86.2841	85.9888	85.6936	85.3983	85.1031	84.8078	84.5126	84.2173	83.9221	83.6268	83.3316	83.0363	.009842
59	87.7069	87.3826	87.0582	86.7339	86.4096	86.0853	85.7610	85.4366	85.1123	84.7880	84.4636	84.1393	.010811
60	89.0786	88.7210	88.3634	88.0058	87.6482	87.2906	86.9330	86.5754	86.2178	85.8602	85.5026	85.1450	.011920
61	90.3669	89.9633	89.5596	89.1560	88.7524	88.3487	87.9451	87.5415	87.1378	86.7342	86.3306	85.9269	.013454
62	91.4321	90.9814	90.5307	90.0800	89.6292	89.1785	88.7278	88.2771	87.8264	87.3756	86.9249	86.4742	.015024
63	92.2762	91.7860	91.2958	90.8056	90.3154	89.8252	89.3350	88.8448	88.3546	87.8644	87.3742	86.8840	.016340
64	93.5263	93.1549	92.7835	92.4121	92.0408	91.6694	91.2980	90.9266	90.5552	90.1838	89.8125	89.4411	.012379
65 or 44	**96.1538**	**96.4743**	**96.7948**	**97.1153**	**97.4359**	**97.7564**	**98.0769**	**98.3974**	**98.7179**	**99.0384**	**99.3590**	**99.6795**	**.010648**
43	94.5902	94.4990	94.4077	94.3165	94.2252	94.1340	94.0427	93.9515	93.8603	93.7690	93.6778	93.5865	.003041
42	93.8045	93.6591	93.5137	93.3683	93.2229	93.0775	92.9320	92.7866	92.6412	92.4958	92.3504	92.2050	.004847
41	93.2422	93.0871	92.9321	92.7770	92.6220	92.4670	92.3119	92.1568	92.0018	91.8467	91.6917	91.5366	.005168
40	92.5227	92.3888	92.2550	92.1211	91.9873	91.8534	91.7195	91.5857	91.4518	91.3180	91.1841	91.0503	.004462
39	91.6380	91.5257	91.4134	91.3011	91.1888	91.0765	90.9641	90.8518	90.7395	90.6272	90.5149	90.4026	.003743
38	90.6714	90.5734	90.4754	90.3774	90.2794	90.1814	90.0833	89.9853	89.8873	89.7893	89.6913	89.5933	.003267
37	89.6427	89.5570	89.4713	89.3856	89.2999	89.2142	89.1284	89.0427	88.9570	88.8713	88.7856	88.6999	.002857
36	88.5746	88.4989	88.4232	88.3475	88.2719	88.1962	88.1205	88.0448	87.9691	87.8934	87.8178	87.7421	.002523
35	87.4902	87.4223	87.3543	87.2864	87.2185	87.1505	87.0826	87.0147	86.9467	86.8788	86.8109	86.7429	.002264
34	86.3989	86.3376	86.2763	86.2150	86.1536	86.0923	86.0310	85.9697	85.9084	85.8470	85.7857	85.7244	.002044
33	85.3024	85.2472	85.1920	85.1368	85.0816	85.0264	84.9712	84.9160	84.8608	84.8056	84.7504	84.6952	.001840
32	84.2103	84.1601	84.1099	84.0597	84.0096	83.9594	83.9092	83.8590	83.8088	83.7586	83.7085	83.6583	.001673
31	83.1280	83.0821	83.0361	82.9902	82.9443	82.8984	82.8524	82.8065	82.7606	82.7147	82.6687	82.6228	.001531
30	82.0536	82.0118	81.9700	81.9282	81.8864	81.8446	81.8028	81.7611	81.7193	81.6775	81.6357	81.5939	.001393
29	80.9851	80.9473	80.9095	80.8718	80.8340	80.7962	80.7584	80.7207	80.6829	80.6451	80.6073	80.5696	.001259
28	79.9214	79.8875	79.8536	79.8197	79.7858	79.7519	79.7180	79.6841	79.6502	79.6163	79.5824	79.5485	.001130
27	78.8541	78.8245	78.7950	78.7654	78.7359	78.7063	78.6768	78.6472	78.6177	78.5881	78.5586	78.5290	.000985
26	77.7775	77.7525	77.7276	77.7026	77.6777	77.6527	77.6277	77.6028	77.5778	77.5529	77.5279	77.5030	.000832
25	76.6848	76.6648	76.6448	76.6248	76.6049	76.5849	76.5649	76.5449	76.5249	76.5050	76.4850	76.4650	.000666
24	75.5710	75.5562	75.5414	75.5266	75.5118	75.4970	75.4822	75.4675	75.4527	75.4379	75.4231	75.4083	.000493
23	74.4348	74.4251	74.4155	74.4058	74.3962	74.3865	74.3769	74.3672	74.3576	74.3480	74.3383	74.3286	.000322
22	73.2742	73.2697	73.2652	73.2607	73.2562	73.2517	73.2472	73.2427	73.2382	73.2337	73.2292	73.2247	.000150
21	72.0906	72.0910	72.0913	72.0917	72.0921	72.0925	72.0928	72.0932	72.0936	72.0940	72.0943	72.0947	.000012
20	70.8859	70.8908	70.8958	70.9007	70.9057	70.9106	70.9155	70.9205	70.9254	70.9304	70.9353	70.9403	.000165
19	69.6608	69.6702	69.6795	69.6889	69.6983	69.7076	69.7170	69.7264	69.7357	69.7451	69.7535	69.7638	.000312
18	68.4146	68.4282	68.4419	68.4555	68.4692	68.4828	68.4964	68.5101	68.5237	68.5374	68.5510	68.5647	.000455
17	67.1492	67.1668	67.1845	67.2022	67.2198	67.2375	67.2552	67.2728	67.2905	67.3082	67.3258	67.3435	.000587
16	65.8652	65.8867	65.9082	65.9297	65.9512	65.9727	65.9941	66.0156	66.0371	66.0586	66.0801	66.1016	.000716
15	64.5640	64.5891	64.6142	64.6393	64.6644	64.6895	64.7146	64.7397	64.7648	64.7899	64.8150	64.8401	.000837
14	63.2466	63.2751	63.3036	63.3321	63.3606	63.3891	63.4176	63.4461	63.4746	63.5031	63.5316	63.5601	.000950
13	61.9152	61.9468	61.9784	62.0100	62.0416	62.0732	62.1048	62.1364	62.1680	62.1996	62.2312	62.2628	.001053
12	60.5703	60.6048	60.6394	60.6739	60.7085	60.7430	60.7776	60.8121	60.8467	60.8812	60.9158	60.9503	.001152
11	59.2131	59.2504	59.2876	59.3249	59.3621	59.3994	59.4366	59.4739	59.5112	59.5484	59.5857	59.6229	.001242
10	57.8449	57.8847	57.9244	57.9642	58.0040	58.0438	58.0835	58.1233	58.1631	58.2029	58.2426	58.2824	.001326
Age.	0	1	2	3	4	5	6	7	8	9	10	11	Day.

Age.	0	1	2	3	4	5	6	7	8	9	10	11	Day.
10	28.4048	28.4269	28.4490	28.4710	28.4931	28.5152	28.5373	28.5594	28.5815	28.6035	28.6256	28.6477	.000736
11	29.4382	29.4611	29.4841	29.5070	29.5299	29.5529	29.5758	29.5987	29.6217	29.6446	29.6675	29.6905	.000764
12	30.4942	30.5179	30.5416	30.5652	30.5889	30.6126	30.6363	30.6600	30.6837	30.7073	30.7310	30.7547	.000789
13	31.5723	31.5965	31.6208	31.6450	31.6693	31.6935	31 7177	31.7420	31.7662	31.7905	31.8147	31.8390	.000808
14	32.6720	32.6968	32.7216	32.7464	32.7713	32.7961	32.8209	32.8457	32.8705	32.8953	32.9202	32.9450	.000827
15	33.7948	33.8199	33.8451	33.8702	33.8953	33.9205	33.9456	33.9707	33.9959	34.0110	34.0461	34.0713	.000838
16	34.9388	34.9641	34.9893	35.0146	35.0399	35.0651	35.0904	35.1157	35.1409	35.1662	35.1915	35.2167	.000842
17	36.1033	36.1285	36.1537	36.1790	36.2042	36.2294	36.2546	36.2799	36.3051	36.3303	36.3555	36.3808	.000841
18	37.2873	37.3123	37.3373	37.3623	37.3873	37.4123	37.4373	37.4623	37.4873	37.5123	37.5373	37.5623	.000833
19	38.4906	38.5153	38.5399	38.5646	38.5892	38.6139	38.6385	38.6632	38.6879	38.7125	38.7372	38.7618	.000822
20	39.7125	39.7366	39.7607	39.7848	39.8090	39.8331	39.8572	39.8813	39.9054	39.9295	39.9537	39.9778	.000804
21	40.9536	40.9769	41.0001	41.0234	41.0467	41.0699	41.0932	41.1165	41.1397	41.1630	41.1863	41.2095	.000775
22	42.2108	42.2332	42.2556	42.2780	42.3004	42.3228	42.3452	42.3676	42.3900	42.4124	42.4348	42.4572	.000747
23	43.4856	43.5068	43.5281	43.5493	43.5706	43.5918	43.6131	43.6343	43.6556	43.6768	43.6981	43.7193	.000708
24	44.7768	44.7966	44.8165	44.8363	44.8561	44.8760	44.8958	44.9156	44.9355	44.9553	44.9751	44.9950	.000661
25	46.0827	46.1005	46.1184	46.1362	46.1541	46.1720	46.1898	46.2076	46.2255	46.2433	46.2612	46.2790	.000595
26	47.3986	47.4141	47.4297	47.4452	47.4608	47.4763	47.4919	47.5074	47.5230	47.5385	47.5541	47.5696	.000518
27	48.7230	48.7358	48.7486	48.7614	48.7742	48.7870	48.7997	48.8126	48.8253	48.8381	48.8509	48.8637	.000426
28	50.0523	50.0620	50.0717	50.0814	50.0911	50.1008	50.1105	50.1203	50.1300	50.1397	50.1494	50.1591	.000323
29	51.3853	51.3914	51.3976	51.4037	51.4099	51.4160	51.4221	51.4283	51.4344	51.4406	51.4467	51.4529	.000205
30	52.7187	52.7209	52.7231	52.7253	52.7275	52.7297	52.7320	52.7342	52.7364	52.7386	52.7408	52.7430	.000073
31	54.0505	54.0482	54.0458	54.0435	54.0412	54.0388	54.0365	54.0342	54.0318	54.0295	54.0272	54.0248	.000078
32	55.3763	55.3691	55.3619	55.3547	55.3475	55.3403	55.3331	55.3260	55.3188	55.3116	55.3044	55.2972	.000240
33	56.6952	56.6827	56.6703	56.6578	56.6454	56.6330	56.6205	56.6080	56.5956	56.5831	56.5707	56.5582	.000415
34	58.0055	57.9875	57.9695	57.9515	57.9335	57.9155	57.8975	57.8795	57.8615	57.8435	57.8255	57.8075	.000600
35	59.3069	59.2828	59.2587	59.2346	59.2106	59.1865	59.1624	59.1383	59.1142	59.0901	59.0661	59.0420	.000803
36	60.5963	60.5658	60.5352	60.5047	60.4742	60.4437	60.4131	60.3826	60.3521	60.3216	60.2910	60.2605	.001017
37	61.8734	61.8359	61.7985	61.7611	61.7236	61.6862	61.6488	61.6114	61.5740	61.5366	61.4991	61.4617	.001247
38	63.1359	63.0911	63.0463	63.0016	62.9568	62.9120	62.8672	62.8225	62.7777	62.7329	62.6881	62.6434	.001492
39	64.3836	64.3310	64.2784	64.2257	64.1731	64.1205	64.0679	64.0153	63.9627	63.9100	63.8574	63.8048	.001754
40	65.6148	65.5539	65.4930	65.4320	65.3711	65.3102	65.2492	65.1883	65.1274	65.0665	65.0055	64.9446	.002031
41	66.8697	66.7966	66.7236	66.6505	66.5775	66.5044	66.4314	66.3583	66.2853	66.2122	66.1392	66.0661	.002435
42	68.0265	67.9474	67.8684	67.7893	67.7103	67.6312	67.5522	67.4731	67.3941	67.3150	67.2360	67.1570	.002635
43	69.2061	69.1170	69.0278	68.9387	68.8495	68.7604	68.6712	68.5821	68.4930	68.4038	68.3147	68.2255	.002971
44	70.3672	70.2676	70.1680	70.0685	69.9689	69.8693	69.7697	69.6702	69.5706	69.4710	69.3714	69.2719	.003319
45	71.5143	71.4039	71.2935	71.1831	71.0727	70.9623	70.8519	70.7415	70.6311	70.5207	70.4103	70.2999	.003680
46	72.6508	72.5295	72.4081	72.2867	72.1653	72.0440	71.9226	71.8013	71.6801	71.5587	71.4374	71.3160	.004045
47	73.7847	73.6526	73.5205	73.3883	73.2562	73.1241	72.9920	72.8599	72.7278	72.5956	72.4635	72.3314	.004404
48	74.9263	74.7833	74.6404	74.4974	74.3545	74.2115	74.0685	73.9256	73.7826	73.6397	73.4967	73.3538	.004765
49	76.0840	75.9305	75.7769	75.6234	75.4699	75.3163	75.1628	75.0093	74.8557	74.7022	74.5487	74.3951	.005118
50	77.2705	77.1058	76.9411	76.7764	76.6118	76.4471	76.2824	76.1177	75.9530	75.7883	75.6237	75.4590	.005489
51	78.4900	78.3136	78.1372	77.9608	77.7844	77.6080	77.4316	77.2552	77.0788	76.9024	76.7260	76.5496	.005880
52	79.7471	79.5584	79.3697	79.1810	78.9924	78.8037	78.6150	78.4263	78.2376	78.0490	77.8603	77.6716	.006289
53	81.0480	80.8455	80.6430	80.4404	80.2379	80.0354	79.8329	79.6304	79.4279	79.2253	79.0228	78.8203	.006750
54	82.3870	82.1686	81.9503	81.7319	81.5135	81.2952	81.0768	80.8584	80.6401	80.4217	80.2033	79.9850	.007279
55	83.7534	83.5179	83.2824	83.0469	82.8114	82.5759	82.3404	82.1050	81.8695	81.6340	81.3985	81.1630	.007850
56	85.1469	84.8920	84.6372	84.3823	84.1274	83.8726	83.6177	83.3628	83.1080	82.8531	82.5982	82.3434	.008495
57	86.5560	86.2777	85.9994	85.7212	85.4429	85.1646	84.8863	84.6081	84.3298	84.0515	83.7732	83.4950	.009276
58	87.9478	87.6419	87.3359	87.0300	86.7240	86.4181	86.1121	85.8062	85.5003	85.1943	84.8884	84.5824	.010198
59	89.2874	88.9498	88.6122	88.2746	87.9370	87.5994	87.2618	86.9242	86.5866	86.2490	85.9114	85.5738	.011253
60	90.5430	90.1614	89.7798	89.3982	89.0167	88.6351	88.2535	87.8719	87.4903	87.1087	86.7272	86.3456	.012719
61	91.5804	91.1539	90.7274	90.3009	89.8744	89.4479	89.0214	88.5950	88.1685	87.7420	87.3155	86.8890	.014216
62	92.4017	91.9780	91.5544	91.1307	90.7071	90.2834	89.8597	89.4361	89.0124	88.5888	88.1651	87.7415	.014122
63	93.6138	93.2655	92.9171	92.5688	92.2205	91.8721	91.5238	91.1755	90.8271	90.4788	90.1305	89.7821	.011611
64 or 45	**96.1538**	**96.4743**	**96.7948**	**97.1153**	**97.4359**	**97.7564**	**98.0769**	**98.3974**	**98.7179**	**99.0384**	**99.3590**	**99.6795**	**.010684**
44	94.5639	94.4657	94.3675	94.2693	94.1711	94.0729	93.9747	93.8766	93.7784	93.6802	93.5820	93.4838	.003273
43	93.7668	93.6139	93.4610	93.3080	93.1551	93.0022	92.8492	92.6963	92.5434	92.3905	92.2375	92.0846	.005097
42	93.1975	93.0351	92.8728	92.7104	92.5481	92.3857	92.2233	92.0610	91.8986	91.7363	91.5739	91.4116	.005412
41	92.4696	92.3291	92.1886	92.0481	91.9076	91.7671	91.6266	91.4861	91.3456	91.2051	91.0646	90.9241	.004683
40	91.5750	91.4567	91.3383	91.2200	91.1017	90.9833	90.8650	90.7467	90.6283	90.5100	90.3917	90.2733	.003944
39	90.5985	90.4949	90.3914	90.2878	90.1842	90.0807	89.9771	89.8735	89.7700	89.6664	69.5628	89.4593	.003452
38	89.5599	89.4690	89.3782	89.2873	89.1964	89.1056	89.0147	88.9238	88.8330	88.7421	88.6512	88.5604	.003029
37	88.4826	88.4021	88.3216	88.2411	88.1606	88.0801	87.9996	87.9192	87.8387	87.7582	87.6777	87.5972	.002683
36	87.3896	87.3172	87.2448	87.1723	87.0999	87.0274	86.9549	86.8824	86.8100	86.7375	86.6651	86.5926	.002415
35	86.2904	86.2248	86.1593	86.0937	86.0281	85.9626	85.8970	85.8314	85.7659	85.7003	85.6347	85.5692	.002185
34	85.1869	85.1277	85.0685	85.0093	84.9501	84.8909	84.8316	84.7724	84.7132	84.6540	84.5948	84.5356	.001973
33	84.0883	84.0343	83.9804	83.9264	83.8725	83.8185	83.7645	83.7106	83.6566	83.6027	83.5487	83.4948	.001798
32	83.0005	82.9510	82.9015	82.8520	82.8024	82.7529	82.7034	82.6539	82.6044	82.5548	82.5053	82.4558	.001650
31	81.9211	81.8759	81.8307	81.7855	81.7403	81.6951	81.6500	81.6048	81.5596	81.5144	81.4692	81.4240	.001506
30	80.8484	80.8074	80.7664	80.7254	80.6844	90.6434	80.6024	80.5614	80.5204	80.4794	80.4384	80.3974	.001367
29	79.7810	79.7440	79.7071	79.6701	79.6331	79.5962	79.5592	79.5222	79.4853	79.4483	79.4113	79.3744	.001232
28	78.7103	78.6778	78.6454	78.6130	78.5805	78.5480	78.5156	78.4831	78.4507	78.4182	78.3858	78.3533	.001082
27	77.6310	77.6033	77.5756	77.5478	77.5291	77.4924	77.4647	77.4370	77.4093	77.3815	77.3538	77.3261	.000924
26	76.5357	76.5131	76.4905	76.4679	76.4453	76.4227	76.4001	76.3776	76.3550	76.3324	76.3098	76.2872	.000753
25	75.4197	75.4024	75.3852	75.3679	75.3507	75.3334	75.3161	75.2989	75.2816	75.2644	75.2471	75.2299	.000575
24	74.2815	74.2695	74.2575	74.2455	74.2336	74.2216	74.2096	74.1976	74.1856	74.1736	74.1617	74.1497	.000399
23	73.1189	73.1122	73.1055	73.0988	73.0921	73.0554	73.0787	73.0720	73.0653	73.0586	73.0519	73.0452	.000223
22	71.9338	71.9321	71.9304	71.9286	71.9269	71.9252	71.9235	71.9218	71.9201	71.9183	71.9166	71.9149	.000057
21	70.7280	70.7309	70.7339	70.7368	70.7398	70.7427	70.7456	70.7486	70.7515	70.7545	70.7574	70.7604	.000098
20	69.5010	69.5085	69.5160	69.5235	69.5310	69.5385	69.5460	69.5536	69.5611	69.5686	69.5761	69.5836	.000250
19	68.2543	68.2661	68.2780	68.2898	68.3017	68.3135	68.3254	68.3372	68.3491	68.3610	68.3728	68.3846	.000395
18	66.9879	67.0039	67.0199	67.0359	67.0519	67.0679	67.0838	67.0998	67.1158	67.1318	67.1478	67.1638	.000533
17	65.7036	65.7235	65.7434	65.7633	65.7832	65.8031	65.8230	65.8429	65.8628	65.8827	65.9026	65.9225	.000663
16	64.4022	64.4258	64.4494	64.4730	64.4965	64.5201	64.5437	64.5673	64.5909	64.6144	64.6380	64.6616	.000786
15	63.0848	63.1119	63.1389	63.1660	63.1931	63.2201	63.2472	63.2743	63.3013	63.3284	63.3555	63.3825	.000902
14	61.7539	61.7841	61.8143	61.8446	61.8748	61.9050	61.9352	61.9655	61.9957	62.0259	62.0561	62.0864	.001007
13	60.4095	60.4428	60.4760	60.5093	60.5426	60.5758	60.6091	60.6424	60.6756	60.7089	60.7422	60.7754	.001109
12	59.0537	59.0897	59.1257	59.1618	59.1978	59.2338	59.2698	59.3059	59 3419	59.3779	59.4140	59.4500	.001201
11	57.6866	57.7252	57.7638	57.8024	57.8411	57.8797	57.9183	57.9569	57.9955	58.0341	58.0728	58.1114	.001287
10	56 3130	56.3537	56.3945	56.4352	56.4760	56.5167	56.5574	56.5982	56.6389	56.6797	56.7204	56.7612	.001358
Age.	0	1	2	3	4	5	6	7	8	9	10	11	Day.

Age.	0	1	2	3	4	5	6	7	8	9	10	11	Day.
10	29.7127	29.7369	29.7610	29.7852	29.8093	29.8335	29.8576	29.8818	29.9060	29.9301	29.9543	29.9784	.000805
11	30.7766	30.8015	30.8265	30.8514	30.8764	30.9013	30.9263	30.9512	30.9762	31.0011	31.0261	31.0510	.000832
12	31.8627	31.8883	31.9138	31.9394	31.9650	31.9906	32.0161	32.0417	32.0673	32.0929	32.1184	32.1440	.000852
13	32.9698	32.9960	33.0222	33.0484	33.0746	33.1008	33.1270	33.1533	33.1795	33.2057	33.2319	33.2581	.000873
14	34.0999	34.1265	34.1530	34.1796	34.2062	34.2327	34.2593	34.2859	34.3124	34.3390	34.3656	34.3921	.000885
15	35.2508	35.2776	35.3044	35.3311	35.3579	35.3847	35.4115	35.4383	35.4651	35.4918	35.5186	35.5454	.000893
16	36.4220	36.4488	36.4755	36.5024	36.5292	36.5560	36.5827	36.6095	36.6363	36.6631	36.6899	36.7167	.000893
17	37.6129	37.6395	37.6661	37.6928	37.7194	37.7460	37.7726	37.7993	37.8259	37.8525	37.8791	37.9058	.000887
18	38.8222	38.8486	38.8749	38.9013	38.9276	38.9540	38.9803	39.0067	39.0331	39.0594	39.0858	39.1121	.000878
19	40.0508	40.0767	40.1025	40.1284	40.1543	40.1801	40.2060	40.2319	40.2577	40.2836	40.3095	40.3353	.000862
20	41.2968	41.3219	41.3471	41.3722	41.3973	41.4225	41.4476	41.4727	41.4979	41.5230	41.5481	41.5733	.000838
21	42.5600	42.5843	42.6087	42.6330	42.6574	42.6817	42.7060	42.7304	42.7547	42.7791	42.8034	42.8278	.000811
22	43.8407	43.8640	43.8872	43.9105	43.9338	43.9570	43.9803	44.0036	44.0268	44.0501	44.0734	44.0966	.000775
23	45.1370	45.1589	45.1809	45.2028	45.2248	45.2467	45.2686	45.2906	45.3125	45.3345	45.3564	45.3784	.000731
24	46.4481	46.4682	46.4882	46.5083	46.5283	46.5484	46.5684	46.5885	46.6086	46.6286	46.6487	46.6687	.000668
25	47.7691	47.7870	47.8048	47.8227	47.8406	47.8585	47.8763	47.8942	47.9121	47.9300	47.9478	47.9657	.000596
26	49.0982	49.1134	49.1286	49.1439	49.1591	49.1743	49.1895	49.2048	49.2200	49.2352	49.2504	49.2657	.000507
27	50.4321	50.4444	50.4566	50.4689	50.4812	50.4934	50.5057	50.5180	50.5302	50.5425	50.5548	50.5670	.000409
28	51.7693	51.7781	51.7870	51.7958	51.8046	51.8135	51.8223	51.8311	51.8400	51.8488	51.8576	51.8665	.000294
29	53.1066	53.1117	53.1167	53.1218	53.1268	53.1319	53.1370	53.1420	53.1471	53.1521	53.1572	53.1622	.000168
30	54.4424	54.4431	54.4437	54.4444	54.4451	54.4457	54.4464	54.4471	54.4477	54.4484	54.4491	54.4497	.000020
31	55.7717	55.7677	55.7637	55.7596	55.7556	55.7516	55.7476	55.7436	55.7396	55.7355	55.7315	55.7275	.000134
32	57.0940	57.0849	57.0758	57.0667	57.0576	57.0485	57.0394	57.0304	57.0213	57.0122	57.0031	56.9940	.000303
33	58.4074	58.3930	58.3785	58.3641	58.3497	58.3352	58.3208	58.3064	58.2919	58.2775	58.2631	58.2486	.000481
34	59.7120	59.6917	59.6714	59.6511	59.6309	59.6106	59.5903	59.5700	59.5497	59.5294	59.5092	59.4889	.000676
35	61.0045	60.9780	60.9515	60.9250	60.8985	60.8720	60.8455	60.8191	60.7926	60.7661	60.7396	60.7131	.000883
36	62.2844	62.2513	62.2181	62.1850	62.1519	62.1187	62.0856	62.0525	62.0193	61.9862	61.9531	61.9199	.001104
37	63.5503	63.5101	63.4699	63.4297	63.3895	63.3493	63.3091	63.2690	63.2288	63.1886	63.1484	63.1082	.001340
38	64.8005	64.7528	64.7051	64.6573	64.6096	64.5619	64.5142	64.4665	64.4188	64.3710	64.3233	64.2756	.001590
39	66.0345	65.9788	65.9231	65.8674	65.8118	65.7561	65.7004	65.6447	65.5890	65.5333	65.4777	65.4220	.001856
40	67.2514	67.1874	67.1234	67.0593	66.9953	66.9313	66.8673	66.8033	66.7393	66.6752	66.6112	66.5472	.002134
41	68.4517	68.3787	68.3057	68.2327	68.1597	68.0867	68.0136	67.9406	67.8676	67.7946	67.7216	67.6486	.002433
42	69.6333	69.5507	69.4680	69.3854	69.3027	69.2201	69.1374	69.0548	68.9722	68.8895	68.8069	68.7242	.002755
43	70.7949	70.7023	70.6097	70.5171	70.4245	70.3319	70.2392	70.1466	70.0540	69.9614	69.8688	69.7762	.003087
44	71.9405	71.8375	71.7346	71.6316	71.5287	71.4257	71.3227	71.2198	71.1168	71.0139	70.9109	70.8080	.003432
45	73.0740	72.9606	72.8472	72.7338	72.6205	72.5071	72.3937	72.2803	72.1669	72.0535	71.9402	71.8268	.003779
46	74.2027	74.0791	73.9554	73.8317	73.7081	73.5844	73.4607	73.3371	73.2134	73.0897	72.9661	72.8424	.004120
47	75.3378	75.2038	75.0698	74.9359	74.8019	74.6679	74.5340	74.4000	74.2660	74.1320	73.9980	73.8641	.004466
48	76.4874	76.3434	76.1994	76.0554	75.9114	75.7674	75.6233	75.4793	75.3353	75.1913	75.0473	74.9033	.004800
49	77.6643	77.5097	77.3552	77.2006	77.0461	76.8915	76.7370	76.5824	76.4278	76.2733	76.1187	75.9642	.005152
50	78.8719	78.7063	78.5406	78.3749	78.2093	78.0436	77.8779	77.7123	77.5466	77.3809	77.2153	77.0496	.005520
51	80.1147	79.9374	79.7601	79.5828	79.4055	79.2282	79.0509	78.8736	78.6963	78.5190	78.3417	78.1644	.005910
52	81.3980	81.2076	81.0173	80.8269	80.6365	80.4462	80.2558	80.0654	79.8751	79.6847	79.4943	79.3040	.006345
53	82.7174	82.5120	82.3065	82.1011	81.8957	81.6903	81.4848	81.2794	81.0740	80.8686	80.6631	80.4577	.006847
54	84.0616	83.8399	83.6183	83.3966	83.1749	82.9533	82.7316	82.5099	82.2883	82.0666	81.8449	81.6233	.007387
55	85.4300	85.1899	84.9499	84.7098	84.4698	84.2297	83.9896	83.7496	83.5095	83.2695	83.0294	82.7894	.008002
56	86.8115	86.5491	86.2868	86.0244	85.7621	85.4997	85.2373	84.9750	84.7126	84.4503	84.1879	83.9256	.008745
57	88.1738	87.8852	87.5965	87.3078	87.0192	86.7305	86.4418	86.1532	85.8645	85.5758	85.2872	84.9985	.009620
58	89.4832	89.1644	88.8455	88.5267	88.2079	87.8890	87.5702	87.2514	86.9325	86.6137	86.2949	85.9760	.010628
59	90.7086	90.3477	89.9868	89.6260	89.2651	88.9042	88.5433	88.1825	87.8216	87.4607	87.0998	86.7390	.012029
60	91.7195	91.3158	90.9120	90.5083	90.1045	89.7008	89.2970	88.8933	88.4896	88.0858	87.6821	87.2783	.013458
61	92.5197	92.1194	91.7191	91.3188	90.9185	90.5182	90.1179	89.7176	89.3173	88.9170	88.5167	88.1164	.013343
62	93.6961	93.3694	93.0427	92.7160	92.3893	92.0626	91.7358	91.4091	91.0824	90.7557	90.4290	90.1023	.010890
63 or 46	**96.1538**	**96.4743**	**96.7948**	**97.1153**	**97.4359**	**97.7564**	**98.0769**	**98.3974**	**98.7179**	**99.0384**	**99.3590**	**99.6795**	**.010684**
45	94.5358	94.4302	94.3247	94.2191	94.1136	94.0080	93.9025	93.7970	93.6914	93.5858	93.4803	93.3747	.003518
44	93.7265	93.5656	93.4047	93.2438	93.0829	92.9220	92.7611	92.6002	92.4393	92.2784	92.1175	91.9566	.005363
43	93.1499	92.9798	92.8096	92.6395	92.4694	92.2992	92.1291	91.9590	91.7888	91.6187	91.4486	91.2784	.005671
42	92.4131	92.2655	92.1179	91.9703	91.8228	91.6752	91.5276	91.3800	91.2324	91.0848	90.9373	90.7897	.004919
41	91.5081	91.3833	91.2586	91.1338	91.0091	90.8843	90.7595	90.6348	90.5100	90.3853	90.2605	90.1358	.004158
40	90.5211	90.4116	90.3021	90.1926	90.0832	89.9737	89.8642	89.7547	89.6452	89.5357	89.4263	89.3168	.003649
39	89.4723	89.3760	89.2796	89.1833	89.0869	88.9906	88.8942	88.7979	88.7016	88.6052	88.5089	88.4125	.003211
38	88.3851	88.2995	88.2139	88.1283	88.0428	87.9572	87.8716	87.7860	87.7004	87.6148	87.5293	87.4437	.002853
37	87.2833	87.2061	87.1288	87.0516	86.9744	86.8972	86.8200	86.7427	86.6655	86.5883	86.5110	86.4338	.002574
36	86.1759	86.1058	86.0358	85.9657	85.8957	85.8256	85.7556	85.6855	85.6155	85.5454	85.4754	85.4053	.002335
35	85.0650	85.0016	84.9381	84.8747	84.8113	84.7478	84.6844	84.6210	84.5575	84.4941	84.4307	84.3672	.002114
34	83.9599	83.9019	83.8440	83.7860	83.7281	83.6701	83.6121	83.5542	83.4962	83.4383	83.3803	83.3224	.001932
33	82.8662	82.8129	82.7596	82.7063	82.6530	82.5997	82.5464	82.4932	82.4399	82.3866	82.3333	82.2800	.001776
32	81.7817	81.7329	81.6842	81.6354	81.5866	81.5379	81.4891	81.4403	81.3916	81.3428	81.2940	81.2453	.001625
31	80.7046	80.6602	80.6158	80.5714	80.5270	80.4826	80.4382	80.3938	80.3494	80.3050	80.2606	80.2162	.001480
30	79.6335	79.5933	79.5531	79.5129	79.4727	79.4325	79.3923	79.3522	79.3120	79.2718	79.2316	79.1914	.001340
29	78.5594	78.5239	78.4884	78.4529	78.4174	78.3819	78.3463	78.3108	78.2753	78.2398	78.2043	78.1688	.001183
28	77.4771	77.4465	77.4159	77.3853	77.3547	77.3241	77.2934	77.2628	77.2322	77.2016	77.1710	77.1404	.001020
27	76.3793	76.3540	76.3286	76.3033	76.2780	76.2527	76.2273	76.2020	76.1767	76.1514	76.1260	76.1007	.000844
26	75.2610	75.2411	75.2213	75.2014	75.1816	75.1617	75.1419	75.1220	75.1022	75.0823	75.0625	75.0426	.000662
25	74.1207	74.1063	74.0918	74.0774	74.0630	74.0486	74.0341	74.0197	74.0053	73.9909	73.9764	73.9620	.000481
24	72.9563	72.9473	72.9383	72.9292	72.9202	72.9112	72.9022	72.8932	72.8842	72.8751	72.8661	72.8571	.000300
23	71.7694	71.7655	71.7616	71.7577	71.7538	71.7499	71.7460	71.7421	71.7382	71.7343	71.7304	71.7265	.000130
22	70.5623	70.5632	70.5640	70.5649	70.5658	70.5667	70.5675	70.5684	70.5693	70.5702	70.5710	70.5719	.000029
21	69.3344	69.3399	69.3454	69.3510	69.3565	69.3620	69.3675	69.3731	69.3786	69.3841	69.3896	69.3952	.000184
20	68.0859	68.0959	68.1059	68.1160	68.1260	68.1360	68.1460	68.1560	68.1660	68.1760	68.1861	68.1961	.000334
19	66.8193	66.8335	66.8477	66.8620	66.8762	66.8904	66.9046	66.9189	66.9331	66.9473	66.9615	66.9758	.000474
18	65.5343	65.5525	65.5708	65.5890	65.6072	65.6255	65.6437	65.6619	65.6801	65.6984	65.7166	65.7349	.000608
17	64.2328	64.2548	64.2768	64.2988	64.3208	64.3428	64.3648	64.3868	64.4088	64.4308	64.4528	64.4748	.000733
16	62.9154	62.9410	62.9665	62.9921	63.0177	63.0432	63.0688	63.0944	63.1199	63.1455	63.1711	63.1966	.000852
15	61.5848	61.6136	61.6424	61.6712	61.7000	61.7288	61.7576	61.7864	61.8152	61.8440	61.8728	61.9016	.000960
14	60.2411	60.2730	60.3049	60.3368	60.3687	60.4006	60.4325	60.4644	60.4963	60.5282	60.5601	60.5920	.001063
13	58.8860	58.9207	58.9555	58.9902	59.0250	59.0597	59.0945	59.1292	59.1640	59.1987	59.2335	59.2682	.001158
12	57.5205	57.5579	57.5953	57.6327	57.6701	57.7075	57.7450	57.7824	57.8198	57.8572	57.8946	57.9320	.001247
11	56.1484	56.1880	56.2276	56.2672	56.3068	56.3464	56.3860	56.4255	56.4651	56.5047	56.5443	56.5839	.001320
10	54.7718	54.8133	54.8548	54.8965	54.9379	54.9794	55.0210	55.0625	55.1040	55.1455	55.1870	55.2286	.001384
Age.	0	1	2	3	4	5	6	7	8	9	10	11	Day.

Age.	0	1	2	3	4	5	6	7	8	9	10	11	Day.
10	31.0455	31.0717	31.0978	31.1240	31.1502	31.1764	31.2025	31.2287	31.2549	31.2811	31.3072	31.3334	.000872
11	32.1392	32.1660	32.1929	32.2197	32.2466	32.2734	32.3002	32.3271	32.3539	32.3808	32.4076	32.4345	.000895
12	33.2539	33.2814	33.3090	33.3365	33.3640	33.3916	33.4191	33.4466	33.4742	33.5017	33.5292	33.5568	.000918
13	34.3909	34.4189	34.4468	34.4748	34.5027	34.5307	34.5586	34.5866	34.6146	34.6425	34.6705	34.6984	.000932
14	35.5487	35.5769	35.6051	35.6333	35.6615	35.6897	35.7180	35.7462	35.7744	35.8026	35.8308	35.8590	.000940
15	36.7265	36.7548	36.7831	36.8114	36.8397	36.8680	36.8962	36.9245	36.9528	36.9811	37.0094	37.0377	.000943
16	37.9235	37.9517	37.9799	38.0081	38.0363	38.0645	38.0926	38.1208	38.1490	38.1772	38.2054	38.2336	.000940
17	39.1392	39.1672	39.1952	39.2231	39.2511	39.2791	39.3071	39.3351	39.3631	39.3910	39.4190	39.4470	.000933
18	40.3733	40.4009	40.4284	40.4560	40.4836	40.5112	40.5387	40.5663	40.5939	40.6215	40.6490	40.6766	.000919
19	41.6255	41.6524	41.6793	41.7061	41.7330	41.7599	41.7868	41.8137	41.8406	41.8674	41.8943	41.9212	.000896
20	42.8932	42.9194	42.9456	42.9718	42.9980	43.0242	43.0504	43.0766	43.1028	43.1290	43.1552	43.1814	.000873
21	44.1793	44.2046	44.2299	44.2552	44.2805	44.3058	44.3310	44.3563	44.3816	44.4069	44.4322	44.4575	.000843
22	45.4810	45.5050	45.5289	45.5528	45.5768	45.6007	45.6247	45.6486	45.6726	45.6965	45.7205	45.7444	.000798
23	46.7966	46.8188	46.8409	46.8631	46.8853	46.9074	46.9296	46.9518	46.9739	46.9961	47.0183	47.0404	.000739
24	48.1222	48.1423	48.1624	48.1824	48.2025	48.2226	48.2427	48.2628	48.2829	48.3030	48.3230	48.3431	.000669
25	49.4558	49.4733	49.4909	49.5084	49.5260	49.5435	49.5610	49.5786	49.5961	49.6137	49.6312	49.6488	.000585
26	50.7938	50.8085	50.8232	50.8379	50.8526	50.8673	50.8820	50.8968	50.9115	50.9262	50.9409	50.9556	.000490
27	52.1350	52.1464	52.1578	52.1692	52.1806	52.1920	52.2034	52.2148	52.2262	52.2376	52.2490	52.2604	.000380
28	53.4758	53.4836	53.4913	53.4991	53.5069	53.5146	53.5224	53.5302	53.5379	53.5457	53.5535	53.5612	.000259
29	54.8149	54.8184	54.8220	54.8255	54.8290	54.8325	54.8360	54.8396	54.8431	54.8466	54.8501	54.8537	.000117
30	56.1476	56.1467	56.1456	56.1446	56.1436	56.1426	56.1416	56.1406	56.1396	56.1386	56.1376	56.1366	.000033
31	57.4728	57.4669	57.4610	57.4551	57.4492	57.4433	57.4374	57.4315	57.4256	57.4197	57.4138	57.4079	.000197
32	58.7889	58.7778	58.7668	58.7557	58.7447	58.7336	58.7226	58.7115	58.7005	58.6894	58.6784	58.6673	.000368
33	60.0959	60.0792	60.0625	60.0458	60.0292	60.0125	59.9958	59.9791	59.9624	59.9457	59.9291	59.9124	.000556
34	61.3911	61.3684	61.2457	61.3231	61.3004	61.2777	61.2550	61.2324	61.2097	61.1870	61.1643	61.1417	.000756
35	62.6732	62.6441	62.6151	62.5860	62.5569	62.5279	62.4988	62.4697	62.4407	62.4116	62.3825	62.3535	.000969
36	63.9412	63.9053	63.8695	63.8336	63.7978	63.7619	63.7260	63.6902	63.6543	63.6185	63.5826	63.5468	.001195
37	65.1940	65.1510	65.1081	65.0651	65.0222	64.9792	64.9362	64.8933	64.8503	64.8074	64.7644	64.7215	.001432
38	66.4297	66.3790	66.3282	66.2775	66.2267	66.1760	66.1252	66.0745	66.0238	65.9730	65.9223	65.8715	.001691
39	67.6486	67.5899	67.5311	67.4724	67.4137	67.3550	67.2962	67.2375	67.1788	67.1201	67.0613	67.0026	.001957
40	68.8510	68.7837	68.7163	68.6490	68.5816	68.5143	68.4470	68.3796	68.3123	68.2449	68.1776	68.1102	.002245
41	70.0342	69.9576	69.8811	69.8045	69.7280	69.6514	69.5749	69.4983	69.4218	69.3452	69.2687	69.1921	.002552
42	71.1969	71.1108	71.0248	70.9387	70.8527	70.7666	70.6805	70.5945	70.5084	70.4224	70.3363	70.2503	.002868
43	72.3421	72.2462	72.1502	72.0543	71.9584	71.8624	71.7665	71.6706	71.5746	71.4787	71.3828	71.2868	.003198
44	73.4732	73.3673	73.2614	73.1555	73.0497	72.9438	72.8379	72.7320	72.6261	72.5202	72.4144	72.3085	.003529
45	74.5979	74.4831	74.3682	74.2534	74.1386	74.0238	73.9090	73.7941	73.6793	73.5645	73.4496	73.3348	.003827
46	75.7268	75.6013	75.4758	75.3503	75.2249	75.0994	74.9739	74.8484	74.7229	74.5974	74.4720	74.3465	.004183
47	76.8686	76.7336	76.5986	76.4636	76.3286	76.1936	76.0586	75.9237	75.7887	75.6537	75.5187	75.3837	.004500
48	78.0360	77.8910	77.7460	77.6010	77.4559	77.3109	77.1659	77.0209	76.8759	76.7308	76.5858	76.4408	.004834
49	79.2323	79.0768	78.9212	78.7657	78.6102	78.4547	78.2991	78.1436	77.9881	77.8326	77.6770	77.5215	.005184
50	80.4614	80.2949	80.1283	79.9618	79.7952	79.6287	79.4621	79.2956	79.1291	78.9625	78.7960	78.6294	.005551
51	81.7286	81.5497	81.3707	81.1918	81.0128	80.8339	80.6550	80.4760	80.2971	80.1181	79.9392	79.7602	.005965
52	83.0287	82.8355	82.6423	82.4491	82.2559	82.0627	81.8694	81.6762	81.4830	81.2898	81.0966	80.9034	.006440
53	84.3513	84.1427	83.9341	83.7255	83.5169	83.3083	83.0996	82.8910	82.6824	82.4738	82.2652	82.0566	.006953
54	85.6965	85.4704	85.2442	85.0181	84.7920	84.5659	84.3397	84.1136	83.8875	83.6614	83.4352	83.2091	.007537
55	87.0518	86.8044	86.5571	86.3097	86.0624	85.8150	85.5676	85.3203	85.0729	84.8256	84.5782	84.3309	.008245
56	88.3862	88.1137	87.8413	87.5688	87.2963	87.0239	86.7514	86.4789	86.2065	85.9340	85.6615	85.3891	.009082
57	89.6669	89.3657	89.0645	88.7633	88.4622	88.1610	87.8598	87.5586	87.2574	86.9562	86.6551	86.3539	.010039
58	90.8639	90.5224	90.1810	89.8395	89.4981	89.1566	88.8152	88.4737	88.1323	87.7908	87.4494	87.1080	.011382
59	91.8504	91.4680	91.0856	90.7032	90.3209	89.9385	89.5561	89.1737	88.7913	88.4090	88.0266	87.6442	.012746
60	92.6302	92.2519	91.8735	91.4952	91.1168	90.7385	90.3601	89.9818	89.6035	89.2251	88.8468	88.4684	.012611
61	93.7733	93.4669	93.1605	92.8541	92.5478	92.2414	91.9350	91.6286	91.3222	91.0158	90.7095	90.4031	.010213
62 or 47	**96.1538**	**96.4743**	**96.7948**	**97.1153**	**97.4359**	**97.7564**	**98.0769**	**98.3974**	**98.7179**	**99.0384**	**99.3590**	**99.6795**	**.010684**
46	94.5062	94.3928	94.2795	94.1661	94.0527	93.9394	93.8260	93.7126	93.5993	93.4859	93.3725	93.2592	.003779
45	93.6838	93.5144	93.3450	93.1757	93.0063	92.8369	92.6675	92.4982	92.3288	92.1594	91.9900	91.8207	.005646
44	93.[illegible]92	92.9208	92.7424	92.5640	92.3856	92.2072	92.0287	91.8503	91.6719	91.4935	91.3151	91.1367	.005947
43	92.3528	92.1977	92.0426	91.8874	91.7323	91.5772	91.4221	91.2670	91.1119	90.9567	90.8016	90.6465	.005170
42	91.4368	91.3052	91.1736	91.0420	90.9104	90.7788	90.6472	90.5157	90.3841	90.2525	90.1209	89.9893	.004386
41	90.4387	90.3229	90.2072	90.0914	89.9756	89.8599	89.7441	89.6283	89.5126	89.3968	89.2810	89.1653	.003859
40	89.3792	89.2770	89.1749	89.0727	88.9706	88.8684	88.7663	88.6641	88.5620	88.4598	88.3577	88.2555	.003405
39	88.2818	88.1908	88.0998	88.0088	87.9179	87.8269	87.7359	87.6449	87.5539	87.4630	87.3720	87.2810	.003033
38	87.1705	87.0882	87.0060	86.9237	86.8414	86.7591	86.6768	86.5946	86.5123	86.4300	86.3477	86.2655	.002742
37	86.0548	85.9800	85.9052	85.8304	85.7556	85.6808	85.6060	85.5313	85.4565	85.3817	85.3069	85.2321	.002493
36	84.9362	84.8683	84.8004	84.7325	84.6646	84.5967	84.5288	84.4610	84.3931	84.3252	84.2573	84.1894	.002263
35	83.8243	83.7621	83.7000	83.6378	83.5756	83.5135	83.4513	83.3891	83.3270	83.2648	83.2026	83.1405	.002072
34	82.7247	82.6674	82.6102	82.5529	82.4956	82.4384	82.3811	82.3238	82.2666	82.2093	82.1520	82.0948	.001909
33	81.6349	81.5824	81.5298	81.4773	81.4248	81.3722	81.3197	81.2672	81.2146	81.1621	81.1096	81.0570	.001751
32	80.5533	80.5053	80.4574	80.4094	80.3614	80.3135	80.2655	80.2175	80.1696	80.1216	80.0736	80.0257	.001599
31	79.4773	79.4338	79.3903	79.3468	79.3033	79.2598	79.2163	79.1728	79.1293	79.0858	79.0423	78.9988	.001450
30	78.4009	78.3622	78.3235	78.2847	78.2460	78.2073	78.1686	78.1299	78.0912	78.0524	78.0137	77.9750	.001290
29	77.3156	77.2820	77.2483	77.2146	77.1810	77.1473	77.1137	77.0800	77.0464	77.0127	76.9791	76.9454	.001122
28	76.2150	76.1868	76.1586	76.1304	76.1022	76.0740	76.0458	76.0176	75.9894	75.9612	75.9330	75.9048	.000940
27	75.0944	75.0718	75.0493	75.0267	75.0041	74.9816	74.9590	74.9364	74.9139	74.8913	74.8687	74.8462	.000752
26	73.9520	73.9350	73.9180	73.9010	73.8840	73.8670	73.8500	73.8330	73.8160	73.7990	73.7820	73.7650	.000567
25	72.7858	72.7744	72.7629	72.7515	72.7400	72.7286	72.7171	72.7057	72.6943	72.6828	72.6714	72.6599	.000381
24	71.5972	71.5910	71.5848	71.5786	71.5724	71.5662	71.5600	71.5539	71.5477	71.5415	71.5353	71.5291	.000206
23	70.3886	70.3873	70.3860	70.3847	70.3834	70.3821	70.3808	70.3795	70.3782	70.3769	70.3756	70.3743	.000043
22	69.1596	69.1631	69.1665	69.1700	69.1735	69.1770	69.1804	69.1839	69.1874	69.1909	69.1943	69.1978	.000116
21	67.9105	67.9185	67.9266	67.9346	67.9427	67.9507	67.9588	67.9668	67.9749	67.9830	67.9910	67.9990	.000268
20	66.6423	66.6547	66.6671	66.6795	66.6919	66.7043	66.7167	66.7291	66.7415	66.7539	66.7663	66.7787	.000413
19	65.3572	65.3737	65.3902	65.4066	65.4231	65.4396	65.4561	65.4726	65.4891	65.5055	65.5220	65.5385	.000549
18	64.0552	64.0755	64.0959	64.1162	64.1366	64.1570	64.1773	64.1976	64.2180	64.2383	64.2587	64.2790	.000678
17	62.7381	62.7621	62.7861	62.8101	62.8341	62.8581	62.8820	62.9060	62.9300	62.9540	62.9780	63.0020	.000800
16	61.4072	61.4345	61.4619	61.4892	61.5166	61.5440	61.5713	61.5986	61.6260	61.6533	61.6807	61.7080	.000912
15	60.0646	60.0951	60.1256	60.1560	60.1865	60.2170	60.2475	60.2780	60.3085	60.3390	60.3694	60.3999	.001016
14	58.7104	58.7438	58.7772	58.8106	58.8440	58.8774	58.9107	58.9441	58.9775	59.0109	59.0443	59.0777	.001113
13	57.3459	57.3820	57.4181	57.4543	57.4904	57.5265	57.5626	57.5988	57.6349	57.6710	57.7071	57.7433	.001204
12	55.9756	56.0140	56.0523	56.0907	56.1291	56.1675	56.2058	56.2442	56.2826	56.3210	56.3593	56.3977	.001279
11	54.6008	54.6412	54.6815	54.7219	54.7623	54.8027	54.8430	54.8834	54.9238	54.9642	55.0045	55.0449	.001346
10	53.2248	53.2668	53.3088	53.3508	53.3928	53.4348	53.4768	53.5189	53.5609	53.6029	53.6449	53.6869	.001400
Age.	0	1	2	3	4	5	6	7	8	9	10	11	Day.

Age.	0	1	2	3	4	5	6	7	8	9	10	11	Day.
10	32.4026	32.4306	32.4587	32.4867	32.5148	32.5428	32.5709	32.5990	32.6270	32.6550	32.6831	32.7111	.000935
11	33.5244	33.5532	33.5820	33.6108	33.6396	33.6684	33.6971	33.7259	33.7547	33.7835	33.8123	33.8411	.000960
12	34.6686	34.6979	34.7271	34.7564	34.7857	34.8150	34.8442	34.8735	34.9028	34.9321	34.9613	34.9906	.000976
13	35.8330	35.8626	35.8922	35.9218	35.9514	35.9810	36.0105	36.0401	36.0697	36.0993	36.1289	36.1585	.000986
14	37.0173	37.0470	37.0767	37.1064	37.1361	37.1658	37.1955	37.2252	37.2549	37.2846	37.3143	37.3440	.000990
15	38.2204	38.2501	38.2797	38.3094	38.3391	38.3688	38.3984	38.4281	38.4578	38.4875	38.5171	38.5468	.000989
16	39.4418	39.4713	39.5009	39.5304	39.5599	39.5895	39.6190	39.6485	39.6781	39.7076	39.7371	39.7667	.000984
17	40.6818	40.7110	40.7402	40.7693	40.7985	40.8277	40.8569	40.8861	40.9153	40.9444	40.9736	41.0028	.000973
18	41.9390	41.9676	41.9962	42.0247	42.0533	42.0819	42.1105	42.1391	42.1677	42.1962	42.2248	42.2534	.000953
19	43.2124	43.2403	43.2683	43.2962	43.3242	43.3521	43.3800	43.4080	43.4359	43.4639	43.4918	43.5198	.000931
20	44.5025	44.5295	44.5566	44.5836	44.6107	44.6377	44.6648	44.6918	44.7189	44.7460	44.7730	44.8000	.000902
21	45.8101	45.8359	45.8617	45.8874	45.9132	45.9390	45.9648	45.9906	46.0164	46.0421	46.0679	46.0937	.000859
22	47.1294	47.1536	47.1777	47.2019	47.2261	47.2502	47.2744	47.2986	47.3227	47.3469	47.3711	47.3952	.000805
23	48.4589	48.4811	48.5033	48.5255	48.5477	48.5699	48.5920	48.6142	48.6364	48.6586	48.6808	48.7030	.000740
24	49.7965	49.8163	49.8360	49.8558	49.8756	49.8953	49.9151	49.9349	49.9546	49.9744	49.9942	50.0139	.000659
25	51.1385	51.1555	51.1726	51.1896	51.2066	51.2237	51.2407	51.2577	51.2748	51.2918	51.3088	51.3259	.000568
26	52.4832	52.4970	52.5109	52.5247	52.5386	52.5524	52.5663	52.5801	52.5940	52.6078	52.6217	52.6355	.000462
27	53.8275	53.8378	53.8482	53.8585	53.8688	53.8792	53.8895	53.8998	53.9102	53.9205	53.9308	53.9412	.000343
28	55.1695	55.1757	55.1820	55.1882	55.1945	55.2007	55.2070	55.2132	55.2194	55.2257	55.2319	55.2382	.000208
29	56.5049	56.5068	56.5086	56.5105	56.5124	56.5143	56.5161	56.5180	56.5199	56.5218	56.5236	56.5255	.000062
30	57.8328	57.8299	57.8271	57.8242	57.8214	57.8185	57.8156	57.8128	57.8099	57.8071	57.8042	57.8014	.000095
31	59.1512	59.1434	59.1355	59.1277	59.1199	59.1120	59.1042	59.0964	59.0885	59.0807	59.0729	59.0650	.000261
32	60.4603	60.4470	60.4337	60.4204	60.4072	60.3939	60.3806	60.3673	60.3540	60.3407	60.3275	60.3142	.000443
33	61.7573	61.7382	61.7192	61.7001	61.6811	61.6620	61.6430	61.6240	61.6049	61.5858	61.5668	61.5477	.000635
34	63.0415	63.0163	62.9910	62.9658	62.9406	62.9154	62.8901	62.8649	62.8397	62.8145	62.7892	62.7640	.000841
35	64.3110	64.2792	64.2475	64.2157	64.1839	64.1522	64.1204	64.0886	64.0569	64.0251	63.9933	63.9616	.001059
36	65.5652	65.5265	65.4877	65.4490	65.4103	65.3715	65.3328	65.2941	65.2553	65.2166	65.1779	65.1391	.001291
37	66.8045	66.7583	66.7120	66.6658	66.6196	66.5734	66.5271	66.4809	66.4347	66.3885	66.3422	66.2960	.001541
38	68.0227	67.9690	67.9152	67.8614	67.8077	67.7540	67.7002	67.6464	67.5927	67.5390	67.4852	67.4314	.001792
39	69.2262	69.1642	69.1022	69.0402	68.9782	68.9162	68.8542	68.7922	68.7302	68.6682	68.6062	68.5442	.002067
40	70.4106	70.3398	70.2690	70.1981	70.1273	70.0565	69.9856	69.9148	69.8440	69.7732	69.7023	69.6315	.002361
41	71.5742	71.4943	71.4144	71.3345	71.2546	71.1747	71.0947	71.0148	70.9349	70.8550	70.7751	70.6952	.002663
42	72.7196	72.6303	72.5409	72.4516	72.3623	72.2729	72.1836	72.0943	72.0049	71.9156	71.8263	71.7369	.002977
43	73.8494	73.7506	73.6518	73.5530	73.4541	73.3553	73.2565	73.1577	73.0589	72.9600	72.8612	72.7624	.003294
44	74.9708	74.8627	74.7545	74.6464	74.5383	74.4302	74.3220	74.2139	74.1058	73.9977	73.8895	73.7814	.003604
45	76.1045	75.9862	75.8680	75.7497	75.6314	75.5131	75.3948	75.2766	75.1583	75.0400	74.9217	74.8035	.003942
46	77.2290	77.1025	76.9760	76.8495	76.7231	76.5966	76.4701	76.3436	76.2171	76.0906	75.9642	75.8377	.004216
47	78.3872	78.2512	78.1152	77.9792	77.8432	77.7072	77.5712	77.4353	77.2993	77.1633	77.0273	76.8913	.004533
48	79.5725	79.4266	79.2807	79.1348	78.9890	78.8431	78.6972	78.5513	78.4054	78.2595	78.1137	77.9678	.004863
49	80.7887	80.6323	80.4760	80.3196	80.1632	80.0068	79.8504	79.6941	79.5377	79.3813	79.2250	79.0686	.005212
50	82.0405	81.8723	81.7042	81.5360	81.3679	81.1997	81.0316	80.8634	80.6953	80.5271	80.3590	80.1908	.005605
51	83.3228	83.1444	82.9660	82.7876	82.6092	82.4308	82.2524	82.0741	81.8957	81.7173	81.5389	81.3605	.005946
52	84.6253	84.4289	84.2325	84.0362	83.8398	83.6434	83.4470	83.2507	83.0543	82.8579	82.6615	82.4652	.006546
53	85.9475	85.7345	85.5215	85.3085	85.0955	84.8825	84.6694	84.4564	84.2434	84.0304	83.8174	83.6044	.007100
54	87.2780	87.0448	86.8115	86.5783	86.3450	86.1118	85.8785	85.6453	85.4121	85.1788	84.9456	84.7123	.007775
55	88.5860	88.3288	88.0716	87.8144	87.5572	87.3000	87.0427	86.7855	86.5283	86.2711	86.0139	85.7567	.008573
56	89.8396	89.5549	89.2702	88.9856	88.7009	88.4162	88.1315	87.8469	87.5622	87.2775	86.9928	86.7082	.009489
57	91.0098	90.6866	90.3634	90.0401	89.7169	89.3937	89.0705	88.7473	88.4241	88.1008	87.7776	87.4544	.010774
58	91.9732	91.6109	91.2485	90.8862	90.5238	90.1615	89.7991	89.4368	89.0745	88.7121	88.3498	87.9874	.012078
59	92.7342	92.3765	92.0187	91.6610	91.3033	90.9456	90.5878	90.2301	89.8724	89.5147	89.1570	88.7992	.011924
60	93.8457	93.5584	93.2711	92.9838	92.6965	92.4092	92.1220	91.8347	91.5474	91.2601	90.9728	90.6855	.009576
61, or 48	**96.1538**	**96.4743**	**96.7948**	**97.1153**	**97.4359**	**97.7564**	**98.0769**	**98.3974**	**98.7179**	**99.0384**	**99.3590**	**99.6795**	**.010684**
47	94.4748	94.3532	94.2315	94.1099	93.9883	93.8666	93.7450	93.6234	93.5017	93.3801	93.2585	93.1368	.004054
46	93.6385	93.4601	93.2818	93.1034	92.9251	92.7467	92.5683	92.3900	92.2116	92.0333	91.8549	91.6766	.005945
45	93.0454	92.8582	92.6710	92.4838	92.2967	92.1095	91.9223	91.7351	91.5479	91.3607	91.1736	90.9864	.006239
44	92.2887	92.1256	91.9624	91.7993	91.6361	91.4730	91.3098	91.1467	90.9836	90.8204	90.6573	90.4941	.005438
43	91.3608	91.2219	91.0830	90.9442	90.8053	90.6664	90.5275	90.3887	90.2498	90.1109	89.9720	89.8332	.004629
42	90.3510	90.2285	90.1061	89.9836	89.8611	89.7387	89.6162	89.4937	89.3713	89.2488	89.1263	89.0039	.004082
41	89.2801	89.1718	89.0634	88.9551	88.8468	88.7384	88.6301	88.5218	88.4134	88.3051	88.1968	88.0884	.003611
40	88.1721	88.0754	87.9786	87.8819	87.7852	87.6885	87.5917	87.4950	87.3983	87.3016	87.2048	87.1081	.003224
39	87.0511	86.9635	86.8758	86.7882	86.7006	86.6129	86.5253	86.4377	86.3500	86.2624	86.1748	86.0871	.002921
38	85.9264	85.8466	85.7668	85.6870	85.6072	85.5274	85.4475	85.3677	85.2879	85.2081	85.1283	85.0485	.002660
37	84.8001	84.7275	84.6549	84.5823	84.5097	84.4371	84.3644	84.2918	84.2192	84.1466	84.0740	84.0014	.002420
36	83.6811	83.6145	83.5479	83.4813	83.4147	83.3481	83.2814	83.2148	83.1482	83.0816	83.0150	82.9484	.002220
35	82.5754	82.5139	82.4524	82.3910	82.3295	82.2680	82.2065	82.1451	82.0836	82.0221	81.9606	81.8992	.002049
34	81.4804	81.4239	81.3674	81.3109	81.2544	81.1979	81.1413	81.0848	81.0283	80.9718	80.9153	80.8588	.001883
33	80.3940	80.3423	80.2905	80.2388	80.1871	80.1354	80.0836	80.0319	79.9802	79.9285	79.8767	79.8250	.001724
32	79.3149	79.2678	79.2206	79.1735	79.1264	79.0792	79.0321	78.9850	78.9378	78.8907	78.8436	78.7964	.001571
31	78.2341	78.1919	78.1498	78.1076	78.0654	78.0233	77.9811	77.9389	77.8968	77.8546	77.8124	77.7703	.001405
30	77.1458	77.1090	77.0721	77.0353	76.9984	76.9616	76.9247	76.8879	76.8511	76.8142	76.7774	76.7405	.001228
29	76.0425	76.0113	75.9801	75.9488	75.9176	75.8864	75.8552	75.8240	75.7928	75.7615	75.7303	75.6991	.001040
28	74.9294	74.9032	74.8769	74.8507	74.8244	74.7982	74.7720	74.7457	74.7195	74.6932	74.6670	74.6407	.000875
27	73.7749	73.7552	73.7355	73.7158	73.6962	73.6765	73.6568	73.6371	73.6174	73.5977	73.5781	73.5584	.000656
26	72.6068	72.5928	72.5788	72.5648	72.5509	72.5369	72.5229	72.5089	72.4949	72.4810	72.4670	72.4530	.000466
25	71.4167	71.4081	71.3995	71.3909	71.3823	71.3737	71.3651	71.3566	71.3480	71.3394	71.3308	71.3222	.000286
24	70.2067	70.2031	70.1996	70.1960	70.1924	70.1889	70.1853	70.1817	70.1782	70.1746	70.1710	70.1675	.000119
23	68.9763	68.9776	68.9790	68.9803	68.9816	68.9830	68.9843	68.9856	68.9870	68.9883	68.9896	68.9910	.000044
22	67.7264	67.7324	67.7384	67.7444	67.7505	67.7565	67.7625	67.7685	67.7745	67.7805	67.7866	67.7926	.000200
21	66.4578	66.4682	66.4787	66.4891	66.4996	66.5100	66.5205	66.5310	66.5414	66.5518	66.5623	66.5727	.000348
20	65.1714	65.1861	65.2007	65.2154	65.2301	65.2448	65.2594	65.2741	65.2888	65.3035	65.3181	65.3328	.000489
19	63.8696	63.8882	63.9068	63.9254	63.9440	63.9626	63.9812	63.9999	64.0185	64.0371	64.0557	64.0743	.000620
18	62.5522	62.5745	62.5969	62.6192	62.6416	62.6640	62.6863	62.7086	62.7310	62.7533	62.7757	62.7980	.000745
17	61.2223	61.2480	61.2738	61.2995	61.3253	61.3510	61.3767	61.4025	61.4282	61.4540	61.4797	61.5055	.000858
16	59.8796	59.9086	59.9375	59.9665	59.9954	60.0244	60.0533	60.0823	60.1113	60.1402	60.1692	60.1981	.000965
15	58.9102	58.5583	58.5903	58.6223	58.6543	58.6863	58.7182	58.7502	58.7822	58.8142	58.8462	58.8782	.001066
14	57.1631	57.1979	57.2326	57.2674	57.3022	57.3370	57.3717	57.4065	57.4413	57.4761	57.5108	57.5456	.001159
13	55.7941	55.8312	55.8683	55.9054	55.9425	55.9796	56.0167	56.0539	56.0910	56.1281	56.1652	56.2023	.001237
12	54.4214	54.4606	54.4997	54.5389	54.5780	54.6172	54.6563	54.6955	54.7347	54.7738	54.8130	54.8521	.001305
11	53.0515	53.0920	53.1325	53.1730	53.2136	53.2541	53.2946	53.3351	53.3756	53.4161	53.4567	53.4972	.001350
10	51.6743	51.7166	51.7589	51.8012	51.8435	51.8858	51.9281	51.9704	52.0127	52.0550	52.0973	52.1396	.001410
Age.	0	1	2	3	4	5	6	7	8	9	10	11	Day.

Age.	0	1	2	3	4	5	6	7	8	9	10	11	Day.
10	33.7821	33.8121	33.8421	33.8721	33.9021	33.9321	33.9620	33.9920	34.0220	34.0520	34.0820	34.1120	.001000
11	34.9330	34.9635	34.9940	35.0246	35.0551	35.0856	35.1161	35.1467	35.1772	35.2077	35.2382	35.2688	.001017
12	36.1043	36.1352	36.1661	36.1970	36.2279	36.2588	36.2896	36.3205	36.3514	36.3823	36.4132	36.4441	.001030
13	37.2946	37.3257	37.3568	37.3878	37.4189	37.4500	37.4811	37.5122	37.5433	37.5743	37.6054	37.6365	.001036
14	38.5038	38.5349	38.5660	38.5971	38.6282	38.6593	38.6903	38.7214	38.7525	38.7836	38.8147	38.8458	.001036
15	39.7309	39.7619	39.7929	39.8240	39.8550	39.8860	39.9170	39.9480	39.8790	40.0100	40.0411	40.0721	.001034
16	40.9762	41.0069	41.0377	41.0684	41.0991	41.1299	41.1606	41.1913	41.2221	41.2528	41.2835	41.3143	.001024
17	42.2388	42.2690	42.3992	42.3294	42.3596	42.3898	42.4200	42.4502	42.4804	42.5106	42.5408	42.5710	.001007
18	43.5168	43.5464	43.5761	43.6057	43.6353	43.6650	43.6946	43.7242	43.7539	43.7835	43.8131	43.8428	.000988
19	44.8120	44.8408	44.8696	44.8984	44.9272	44.9560	44.9847	45.0135	45.0423	45.0711	45.0999	45.1287	.000960
20	46.1220	46.1497	46.1774	46.2052	46.2329	46.2606	46.2883	46.3161	46.3438	46.3715	46.3992	46.4270	.000924
21	47.4468	47.4729	47.4990	47.5251	47.5512	47.5773	47.6033	47.6294	47.6555	47.6816	47.7077	47.7338	.000870
22	48.7805	48.8047	48.8289	48.8531	48.8773	48.9015	48.9257	48.9499	48.9741	48.9983	49.0225	49.0467	.000807
23	50.1216	50.1435	50.1653	50.1872	50.2091	50.2309	50.2528	50.2747	50.2965	50.3184	50.3403	50.3621	.000729
24	51.4670	51.4862	51.5055	51.5247	51.5440	51.5632	51.5825	51.6017	51.6210	51.6402	51.6595	51.6787	.000642
25	52.8150	52.8312	52.8474	52.8635	52.8797	52.8959	52.9121	52.9283	52.9445	52.9606	52.9768	52.9930	.000539
26	54.1623	54.1751	54.1879	54.2007	54.2135	54.2263	54.2390	54.2518	54.2646	54.2774	54.2902	54.3030	.000426
27	55.5072	55.5160	55.5249	55.5337	55.5425	55.5514	55.5602	55.5690	55.5779	55.5867	55.5955	55.6044	.000294
28	56.8450	56.8496	56.8542	56.8589	56.8635	56.8681	56.8727	56.8774	56.8820	56.8866	56.8912	56.8959	.000154
29	58.1751	58.1751	58.1751	58.1752	58.1752	58.1752	58.1752	58.1753	58.1753	58.1753	58.1753	58.1754	.000001
30	59.4956	59.4908	59.4860	59.4812	59.4765	59.4717	59.4669	59.4621	59.4573	59.4525	59.4478	59.4430	.000159
31	60.8064	60.7964	60.7863	60.7763	60.7662	60.7562	60.7461	60.7361	60.7261	60.7160	60.7060	60.6959	.000335
32	62.1050	62.0894	62.0737	62.0581	62.0425	62.0268	62.0112	61.9956	61.9799	61.9643	61.9487	61.9330	.000521
33	63.3903	63.3687	63.3471	63.3256	63.3040	63.2824	63.2608	63.2393	63.2177	63.1961	63.1745	63.1530	.000719
34	64.6612	64.6333	64.6054	64.5775	64.5496	64.5217	64.4938	64.4660	64.4381	64.4102	64.3823	64.3544	.000930
35	65.9164	65.8818	65.3472	65.8125	65.7779	65.7433	65.7087	65.6741	65.6395	65.6048	65.5702	65.5356	.001154
36	67.1547	67.1130	67.0713	67.0296	66.9879	66.9462	66.9045	66.8628	66.8211	66.7794	66.7377	66.6960	.001390
37	68.3758	68.3267	68.2777	68.2286	68.1796	68.1305	68.0814	68.0324	67.9833	67.9343	67.8852	67.8362	.001635
38	69.5795	69.5225	69.4655	69.4086	69.3516	69.2946	69.2376	69.1807	69.1237	69.0667	69.0097	68.9528	.001899
39	70.7645	70.6990	70.6336	70.5681	70.5027	70.4372	70.3718	70.3063	70.2409	70.1754	70.1100	70.0445	.002182
40	71.9284	71.8543	71.7801	71.7060	71.6319	71.5577	71.4836	71.4095	71.3353	71.2612	71.1871	71.1129	.002471
41	73.0739	72.9908	72.9076	72.8245	72.7414	72.6582	72.5751	72.4920	72.4088	72.3257	72.2426	72.1594	.002771
42	74.2030	74.1108	74.0187	73.9265	73.8343	73.7422	73.6500	73.5578	73.4657	73.3735	73.2813	73.1892	.003072
43	75.3222	75.2212	75.1202	75.0191	74.9181	74.8171	74.7161	74.6151	74.5141	74.4130	74.3120	74.2110	.003367
44	76.4415	76.3316	76.2217	76.1119	76.0020	75.8921	75.7822	75.6724	75.5625	75.4526	75.3427	75.2329	.003662
45	77.5697	77.4513	77.3328	77.2144	77.0960	76.9775	76.8591	76.7407	76.6222	76.5038	76.3854	76.2669	.003948
46	78.7192	78.5917	78.4643	78.3368	78.2094	78.0819	77.9544	77.8270	77.6995	77.5721	77.4446	77.3172	.004248
47	79.8938	79.7569	79.6200	79.4831	79.3462	79.2093	79.0723	78.9354	78.7985	78.6616	78.5247	78.3878	.004563
48	81.0986	80.9517	80.8048	80.6580	80.5111	80.3642	80.2173	80.0704	79.9235	79.7766	79.6298	79.4829	.004896
49	82.3349	82.1769	82.0190	81.8610	81.7030	81.5451	81.3871	81.2291	81.0712	80.9132	80.7552	80.5973	.005265
50	83.6002	83.4293	83.2584	83.0876	82.9167	82.7458	82.5750	82.4041	82.2332	82.0623	81.8914	81.7206	.005696
51	84.9236	84.7355	84.5473	84.3592	84.1710	83.9829	83.7947	83.6066	83.4185	83.2303	83.0422	82.8540	.006271
52	86.1839	85.9833	85.7827	85.5820	85.3814	85.1808	84.9802	84.7796	84.5790	84.3783	84.1777	83.9771	.006687
53	87.4910	87.2710	87.0511	86.8311	86.6112	86.3912	86.1713	85.9513	85.7314	85.5114	85.2915	85.0715	.007332
54	88.7741	88.5313	88.2884	88.0456	87.8027	87.5599	87.3170	87.0742	86.8314	86.5885	86.3457	86.1028	.008095
55	90.0020	89.7329	89.4638	89.1947	88.9256	88.6565	88.3874	88.1183	87.8492	87.5801	87.3110	87.0419	.008970
56	91.1465	90.8404	90.5343	90.2283	89.9222	89.6161	89.3100	89.0040	88.6979	88.3918	88.0857	87.7797	.010202
57	92.0863	91.7448	91.4013	91.0577	90.7142	90.3707	90.0272	89.6837	89.3402	88.9966	88.6531	88.3096	.011450
58	92.8317	92.4933	92.1549	91.8165	91.4782	91.1398	90.8014	90.4630	90.1246	89.7862	89.4479	89.1095	.011279
59	93.9139	93.6445	93.3752	93.1058	92.8364	92.5671	92.2977	92.0283	91.7590	91.4896	91.2202	90.9509	.008979
60 or 49	**96.1538**	**96.4743**	**96.7948**	**97.1153**	**97.4359**	**97.7564**	**98.0769**	**98.3974**	**98.7179**	**99.0384**	**99.3590**	**99.6795**	**.010684**
48	94.4417	94.3113	94.1810	94.0506	93.9202	93.7898	93.6594	93.5291	93.3987	93.2683	93.1380	93.0076	.004346
47	93.5906	93.4027	93.2149	93.0270	92.8392	92.6513	92.4634	92.2756	92 0877	91.8999	91.7120	91.5242	.006262
46	92.9885	92.7920	92.5955	92.3990	92.2025	92.0060	91.8095	91.6130	91.4165	91.2200	91.0235	90.8270	.006550
45	92.2206	92.0490	91.8773	91.7057	91.5340	91,3624	91.1907	91.0191	90.8475	90.6758	90.5042	90.3325	.005721
44	91.2800	91.1334	90.9867	90.8401	90.6935	90.5469	90.4002	90.2536	90.1070	89.9604	89.8137	89.6671	.004887
43	90.2575	90.1279	89.9983	89.8687	89.7391	89.6095	89.4799	89.3503	89.2207	89.0911	88.9615	88.8319	.004320
42	89.1746	89.0597	88.9448	88.8298	88.7149	88.6000	88.4851	88.3702	88.2553	88.1403	88.0254	87.9105	.003830
41	88.0554	87.9526	87.8497	87.7469	87.6441	87.5413	87.4384	87.3356	87.2328	87.1300	87.0271	86.9243	.003427
40	86.9242	86.8309	86.7376	86.6442	86.5509	86.4576	86.3643	86.2710	86.1777	86.0843	85.9910	85.8977	.003110
39	85.7904	85.7053	85.6201	85.5350	85.4499	85.3647	85.2796	85.1945	85.1093	85.0242	84.9391	84.8539	.002838
38	84.6557	84.5781	84.5005	84.4229	84.3453	84.2677	84.1901	84.1126	84.0350	83.9574	83.8798	83.8022	.002586
37	83.5298	83.4585	83.3872	83.3159	83.2446	83.1733	83.1020	83.0306	82.9593	82.8880	82.8167	82.7454	.002377
36	82.4177	82.3518	82.2859	82.2200	82.1541	82.0882	82.0222	81.9563	81.8904	81.8245	81.7586	81.6927	.002197
35	81.3172	81.2565	81.1958	81.1351	81.0744	81.0137	80.9530	80.8923	80.8316	80.7709	80.7102	80.6495	.002023
34	80.2262	80.1705	80.1148	80.0591	80.0034	79.9477	79.8920	79.8364	79.7807	79.7250	79.6693	79.6136	.001856
33	79.1430	79.0921	79.0412	78.9903	78.9394	78.8885	78.8376	78.7868	78.7359	78.6850	78.6341	78.5832	.001696
32	78.0586	78.0130	77.9673	77.9217	77.8760	77.8304	77.7847	77.7391	77.6935	77.6478	77.6022	77.5565	.001521
31	76.9672	76.9270	76.8868	76.8466	76.8064	76.7662	76.7260	76.6858	76.6456	76.6054	76.5652	76.5250	.001340
30	75.8613	75.8269	75.7925	75.7581	75.7237	75.6893	75.6550	75.6206	75.5862	75.5518	75.5174	75.4830	.001146
29	74.7357	74.7073	74.6789	74.6505	74.6221	74.5937	74.5652	74.5368	74.5084	74.4800	74.4516	74.4232	.000947
28	73.5890	73.5665	73.5440	73.5215	73.4990	73.4765	73.4540	73.4314	73.4089	73.3864	73.3639	73.3414	.000750
27	72.4191	72.4024	72.3858	72.3691	72.3525	72.3358	72.3192	72.3025	72.2859	72.2692	72.2526	72.2360	.000555
26	71.2273	71.2162	71.2051	71.1940	71.1828	71.1717	71.1606	71.1495	71.1384	71.1272	71.1161	71.1050	.000370
25	70.0159	70.0100	70.0040	69.9980	69.9921	69.9861	69.9802	69.9742	69.9683	69.9623	69.9564	69.9504	.000198
24	68.7845	68.7836	68.7826	68.7817	68.7808	68.7798	68.7789	68.7780	68.7770	68.7761	68.7752	68.7742	.000031
23	67.5334	67.5373	67.5412	67.5450	67.5489	67.5528	67.5567	67.5606	67.5645	67.5683	67.5722	67.5761	.000129
22	66.2643	66.2727	66.2811	66.2896	66.2980	66.3064	66.3148	66.3233	66.3317	66.3401	66.3485	66.3570	.000281
21	64.9777	64.9904	65.0032	65.0159	65.0286	65.0414	65.0541	65.0668	65.0796	65.0923	65.1050	65.1178	.000424
20	63.6749	63.6917	63.7085	63.7253	63.7421	63.7589	63.7757	63.7926	63.8094	63.8262	63.8430	63.8598	.000560
19	62.3579	62.3785	62.3991	62.4197	62.4404	62.4610	62.4816	62.5022	62.5228	62.5434	62.5641	62.5847	.000687
18	61.0280	61.0521	61.0762	61.1003	61.1244	61.1485	61.1726	61.1968	61.2209	61.2450	61.2691	61.2932	.000803
17	59.6861	59.7135	59.7410	59.7684	59.7959	59.8233	59.8507	59.8782	59.9056	59.9331	59.9605	59.9880	.000915
16	58.3335	58.3640	58.3945	58.4250	58.4555	58.4860	58.5165	58.5471	58.5776	58.6081	58.6386	58.6691	.001017
15	56.9714	57.0048	57.0381	57.0715	57.1049	57.1383	57.1716	57.2050	57.2384	57.2718	57.3051	57.3385	.001112
14	55.6040	55.6398	55.6755	55.7113	55.7470	55.7828	55.8185	55.8543	55.8901	55.9258	55.9616	55.9973	.001192
13	54.2329	54.2708	54.3087	54.3466	54.3845	54.4224	54.4602	54.4981	54.5360	54.5739	54.6118	54.6497	.001263
12	52.8613	52.9009	52.9406	52.9802	53.0199	53.0595	53.0991	53.1388	53.1784	53.2181	53.2577	53.2974	.001321
11	51.4905	51.5320	51.5735	51.6150	51.6564	51.6979	51.7894	51.7809	51.8224	51.8638	51.9053	51.9468	.001383
10	50.1241	50.1664	50.2086	50.2509	50.2932	50.3355	50.3777	50.4200	50.4623	50.5046	50.5468	50.5891	.001409
Age.	0	1	2	3	4	5	6	7	8	9	10	11	Day.

Age.	0	1	2	3	4	5	6	7	8	9	10	11	Day.
10	35.1849	35.2166	35.2483	35.2800	35.3118	35.3435	35.3752	35.4069	35.4386	35.4703	35.5021	35.5338	.001057
11	36.3625	36.3946	36.4268	36.4589	36.4910	36.5232	36.5553	36.5874	36.6196	36.6517	36.6838	36.7160	.001071
12	37.5593	37.5917	37.6241	37.6564	37.6888	37.7212	37.7536	37.7860	37.8184	37.8507	37.8831	37.9155	.001079
13	38.7742	38.8067	38.8391	38.8716	38.9040	38.9365	38.9690	39.0014	39.0339	39.0663	39.0988	39.1312	.001082
14	40.0069	40.0393	40.0717	40.1042	40.1366	40.1690	40.2014	40.2339	40.2663	40.2987	40.3311	40.3636	.001081
15	41.2575	41.2897	41.3219	41.3541	41.3863	41.4185	41.4507	41.4830	41.5152	41.5474	41.5796	41.6118	.001073
16	42.5250	42.5567	42.5884	42.6202	42.6519	42.6836	42.7153	42.7471	42.7788	42.8105	42.8422	42.8740	.001057
17	43.8081	43.8393	43.8705	43.9017	43.9330	43.9642	43.9954	44.0266	44.0578	44.0890	44.1203	44.1515	.001040
18	45.1072	45.1377	45.1681	45.1986	45.2291	45.2596	45.2900	45.3205	45.3510	45.3815	45.4120	45.4424	.001016
19	46.4218	46.4513	46.4807	46.5102	46.5397	46.5691	46.5986	46.6281	46.6575	46.6870	46.7165	46.7459	.000982
20	47.7496	47.7775	47.8055	47.8334	47.8614	47.8893	47.9172	47.9452	47.9731	48.0011	48.0290	48.0570	.000931
21	49.0872	49.1133	49.1394	49.1655	49.1917	49.2178	49.2439	49.2700	49.2961	49.3222	49.3484	49.3745	.000870
22	50.4319	50.4558	50.4797	50.5035	50.5274	50.5513	50.5752	50.5991	50.6230	50.6468	50.6707	50.6946	.000796
23	51.7803	51.8017	51.8230	51.8444	51.8657	51.8871	51.9084	51.9298	51.9512	51.9725	51.9939	52.0152	.000712
24	53.1313	53.1497	53.1681	53.1865	53.2049	53.2233	53.2417	53.2601	53.2785	53.2969	53.3153	53.3337	.000613
25	54.4814	54.4965	54.5117	54.5268	54.5419	54.5571	54.5722	54.5873	54.6025	54.6176	54.6327	54.6479	.000504
26	55.8287	55.8400	55.8513	55.8626	55.8739	55.8852	55.8965	55.9078	55.9191	55.9304	55.9417	55.9530	.000377
27	57.1688	57.1760	57.1832	57.1904	57.1977	57.2049	57.2121	57.2193	57.2265	57.2337	57.2410	57.2482	.000240
28	58.5010	58.5038	58.5065	58.5093	58.5120	58.5148	58.5175	58.5203	58.5231	58.5258	58.5286	58.5313	.000092
29	59.8231	59.8212	59.8193	59.8174	59.8156	59.8137	59.8118	59.8099	59.8080	59.8061	59.8043	59.8024	.000063
30	61.1354	61.1284	61.1215	61.1145	61.1075	61.1006	61.0936	61.0866	61.0797	61.0727	61.0657	61.0588	.000232
31	62.4351	62.4227	62.4104	62.3980	62.3856	62.3733	62.3609	62.3485	62.3362	62.3238	62.3114	62.2991	.000412
32	63.7214	63.7033	63.6851	63.6670	63.6489	63.6308	63.6126	63.5945	63.5764	63.5583	63.5401	63.5220	.000604
33	64.9930	64.9688	64.9446	64.9203	64.8961	64.8719	64.8477	64.8235	64.7993	64.7750	64.7508	64.7266	.000807
34	66.2489	66.2182	66.1875	66.1568	66.1261	66.0954	66.0647	66.0340	66.0033	65.9726	65.9419	65.9112	.001023
35	67.4876	67.4501	67.4125	67.3750	67.3375	67.3000	67.2624	67.2249	67.1874	67.1499	67.1123	67.0748	.001251
36	68.7087	68.6641	68.6195	68.5749	68.5303	68.4857	68.4410	68.3964	68.3518	68.3072	68.2626	68.2180	.001487
37	69.9132	69.8610	69.8087	69.7564	69.7042	69.6520	69.5997	69.5474	69.4952	69.4430	69.3907	69.3384	.001742
38	71.0976	71.0372	70.9768	70.9165	70.8561	70.7957	70.7353	70.6750	70.6146	70.5542	70.4938	70.4335	.002012
39	72.2614	72.1927	72.1240	72.0552	71.9865	71.9178	71.8491	71.7804	71.7117	71.6430	71.5742	71.5055	.002290
40	73.4065	73.3292	73.2519	73.1745	73.0972	73.0199	72.9426	72.8653	72.7880	72.7106	72.6333	72.5560	.002577
41	74.5348	74.4489	74.3630	74.2770	74.1911	74.1052	74.0193	73.9334	73.8475	73.7615	73.6756	73.5897	.002864
42	75.6524	75.5581	75.4637	75.3694	75.2751	75.1807	75.0864	74.9921	74.8977	74.8034	74.7091	74.6147	.003143
43	76.7685	76.6658	76.5630	76.4603	76.3575	76.2548	76.1520	76.0493	75.9466	75.8438	75.7411	75.6383	.003425
44	77.8912	77.7803	77.6695	77.5586	77.4478	77.3370	77.2261	77.1152	77.0044	76.8935	76.7827	76.6718	.003695
45	79.0331	78.9137	78.7943	78.6749	78.5555	78.4361	78.3167	78.1974	78.0780	77.9586	77.8392	77.7198	.003980
46	80.1977	80.0693	79.9410	79.8126	79.6842	79.5559	79.4275	79.2991	79.1708	79.0424	78.9140	78.7857	.004279
47	81.3894	81.2478	81.1061	80.9645	80.8229	80.6812	80.5396	80.3980	80.2563	80.1147	79.9731	79.8314	.004721
48	82.6126	82.4643	82.3159	82.1676	82.0192	81.8709	81.7225	81.5742	81.4259	81.2775	81.1292	80.9808	.004945
49	83.8620	83.7014	83.5407	83.3801	83.2195	83.0589	82.8982	82.7376	82.5770	82.4164	82.2557	82.0951	.005354
50	85.1272	84.9533	84.7794	84.6055	84.4317	84.2578	84.0839	83.9100	83.7361	83.5622	83.3884	83.2145	.005796
51	86.4074	86.2184	86.0295	85.8405	85.6515	85.4626	85.2736	85.0846	84.8957	84.7067	84.5177	84.3288	.006299
52	87.6917	87.4843	87.2769	87.0695	86.8621	86.6547	86.4473	86.2399	86.0325	85.8251	85.6177	85.4103	.006913
53	88.9512	88.7219	88.4925	88.2632	88.0339	87.8046	87.5752	87.3459	87.1166	86.8873	86.6580	86.4286	.007644
54	90.1549	89.9004	89.6460	89.3915	89.1371	88.8826	88.6282	88.3737	88.1193	87.8648	87.6104	87.3559	.008482
55	91.2753	90.9853	90.6954	90.4054	90.1155	89.8255	89.5355	89.2456	88.9556	88.6657	88.3757	88.0858	.009665
56	92.1965	91.8706	91.5448	91.2190	90.8931	90.5672	90.2414	89.9155	89.5897	89.2638	88.9380	88.6121	.010862
57	92.9232	92.6030	92.2827	91.9625	91.6423	91.3221	91.0018	90.6816	90.3614	90.0412	89.7210	89.4007	.010674
58	93.9778	93.7252	93.4727	93.2201	92.9676	92.7150	92.4624	92.2099	91.9573	91.7048	91.4522	91.1997	.008418
59 or 50	**96.1538**	**96.4743**	**96.7948**	**97.1153**	**97.4359**	**97.7564**	**98.0769**	**98.3974**	**98.7179**	**99.0384**	**99.3590**	**99.6795**	**.010684**
49	94.4065	94.2669	94.1273	93.9876	93.8480	93.7084	93.5688	93.4292	93.2896	93.1500	93.0103	92.8707	.004654
48	93.5400	93.3421	93.1442	92 9462	92.7483	92.5504	92.3525	92.1546	91.9567	91.7587	91.5608	91.3629	.006597
47	92.9281	92.7217	92.5154	92.3091	92.1027	91.8964	91.6901	91.4837	91.2774	91.0711	90.8647	90.6584	.006877
46	92.1485	91.9678	91.7871	91.6065	91.4258	91.2451	91.0644	90.8838	90.7031	90.5224	90.3417	90.1611	.006022
45	91.1941	91.0393	90.8844	90 7296	90.5748	90.4199	90.2651	90.1103	89.9554	89.8006	89.6458	89.4909	.005161
44	90.1581	90.0259	89.8937	89 7615	89.6293	89.4971	89.3650	89.2328	89.1006	88.9684	88.8362	88.7040	.004406
43	89.0622	88.9403	88.8183	88.6964	88.5745	88.4525	88.3306	88.2087	88.0867	87.9648	87.8429	87.7209	.004064
42	87.9311	87.8218	87.7124	87.6031	87.4938	87.3845	87.2751	87.1658	87.0565	86.9472	86.8378	86.7285	.003644
41	86.7893	86.6899	86.5905	86 4912	86.3918	86.2924	86.1930	86.0937	85.9943	85.8949	85.7955	85.6962	.003312
40	85.6460	85.5552	85.4644	85 3736	85.2828	85.1920	85.1012	85.0105	84.9197	84.8289	84.7381	84.6473	.003026
39	84.5029	84.4200	84.3371	84.2542	84.1713	84.0884	84.0055	83.9226	83.8397	83.7568	83.6739	83.5910	.002763
38	83.3693	83.2930	83.2167	83.1404	83.0642	82.9879	82.9116	82.8353	82.7590	82.6827	82.6065	82.5302	.002543
37	82.2510	82.1804	82.1098	82.0392	81.9686	81.8980	81.8274	81.7568	81.6862	81.6156	81.5450	81.4744	.002353
36	81.1449	81.0798	81.0146	80.9495	80.8844	80.8192	80.7541	80.6890	80.6238	80.5587	80.4936	80.4284	.002171
35	80.0491	79.9892	79.9293	79.8695	79.8096	79.7497	79.6898	79.6300	79.5701	79.5102	79.4503	79.3905	.001996
34	78.9619	78.9070	78.8522	78.7973	78.7425	78.6876	78.6328	78.5780	78.5231	78.4682	78.4134	78.3585	.001828
33	77.8738	77.8244	77.7750	77.7257	77.6763	77.6269	77.5775	77.5282	77.4788	77.4294	77.3800	77.3307	.001646
32	76.7793	76.7356	76.6918	76.6481	76.5044	76.5607	76.5170	76.4732	76.4295	76.3858	76.3420	76.2983	.001460
31	75.6705	75.6328	75.5951	75.5574	75.5197	75.4820	75.4442	75.4065	75.3688	75.3311	75.2934	75.2557	.001257
30	74.5427	74.5111	74.4796	74.4480	74.4165	74.3850	74.3534	74.3218	74.2903	74.2587	74.2272	74.1956	.001052
29	73.3938	73.3683	73.3428	73.3174	73.2919	73.2664	73.2410	73.2155	73.1900	73.1645	73.1390	73.1136	.000849
28	72.2219	72.2024	72.1830	72.1635	72.1441	72.1246	72.1052	72.0857	72.0663	72.0468	72.0274	72.0080	.000648
27	71.0285	71.0147	71.0010	70.9872	70.9735	70.9597	70.9460	70.9322	70.9184	70.9047	70.8909	70.8772	.000458
26	69.8158	69.8073	69.7989	69.7904	69.7820	69.7735	69.7651	69.7566	69.7482	69.7397	69.7313	69.7228	.000282
25	68.5833	68.5800	68.5767	68.5734	68.5701	68.5668	68.5635	68.5603	68.5570	68.5537	68.5504	68.5471	.000110
24	67.3314	67.3330	67.3347	67.3363	67.3380	67.3396	67.3412	67.3429	67.3445	67.3462	67.3478	67.3495	.000055
23	66.0614	66.0677	66.0740	66.0803	66.0866	66.0929	66.0992	66.1056	66.1119	66.1182	66.1245	66.1308	.000210
22	64.7746	64.7853	64.7960	64.8068	64.8175	64.8282	64.8390	64.8497	64.8604	64.8711	64.8818	64.8926	.000357
21	63.4718	63.4867	63.5016	63.5164	63.5313	63.5462	63.5611	63.5760	63.5909	63.6057	63.6206	63.6355	.000496
20	62.1540	62.1728	62.1917	62.2105	62.2294	62.2482	62.2670	62.2859	62.3047	62.3236	62.3424	62.3613	.000628
19	60.8259	60.8482	60.8705	60.8928	60.9151	60.9374	60.9597	60.9821	61.0044	61.0267	61.0490	61.0713	.000743
18	59.4833	59.5091	59.5349	59.5607	59.5866	59.6124	59.6382	59.6640	59.6898	59.7156	59.7415	59.7673	.000860
17	58.1318	58.1608	58.1897	58.2187	58.2476	58.2766	58.3055	58.3345	58.3635	58.3924	58.4214	58.4503	.000965
16	56.7706	56.8025	56.8344	56.8663	56.8982	56.9301	56.9620	56.9940	57.0259	57.0578	57.0897	57.1216	.001063
15	55.4046	55.4390	55.4733	55.5077	55.5421	55.5764	55.6108	55.6452	55.6795	55.7139	55.7483	55.7826	.001145
14	54.0353	54.0719	54.1084	54.1450	54.1815	54.2181	54.2546	54.2912	54.3278	54.3643	54.4009	54.4374	.001218
13	52.6658	52.7042	52.7425	52.7809	52.8193	52.8577	52.8960	52.9344	52.9728	53.0112	53.0495	53.0879	.001279
12	51.2977	51.3376	51.3776	51.4175	51.4575	51.4974	51.5373	51.5773	51.6172	51.6572	51.6971	51.7371	.001331
11	49.9339	49.9750	50.0161	50.0573	50.0984	50.1395	50.1806	50.2218	50.2629	50.3040	50.3451	50.3863	.001370
10	48.5763	48.6184	48.6604	48.7025	48.7446	48.7866	48.8287	48.8708	48.9128	48.9549	48.9970	49.0390	.001402
Age.	0	1	2	3	4	5	6	7	8	9	10	11	Day.

Age.	0	1	2	3	4	5	6	7	8	9	10	11	Day.
10	36.6085	36.6418	36.6751	36.7085	36.7418	36.7751	36.8084	36.8418	36.8751	36.9084	36.9417	36.9751	.001111
11	37.8113	37.8449	37.8785	37.9121	37.9458	37.9794	38.0130	38.0466	38.0802	38.1138	38.1475	38.1811	.001120
12	39.0322	39.0660	39.0997	39.1334	39.1672	39.2010	39.2347	39.2684	39.3022	39.3360	39.3697	39.4034	.001125
13	40.2703	40.3041	40.3379	40.3716	40.4054	40.4392	40.4730	40.5068	40.5406	40.5743	40.6081	40.6419	.001126
14	41.5260	41.5596	41.5932	41.6268	41.6604	41.6940	41.7276	41.7613	41.7949	41.8285	41.8621	41.8957	.001120
15	42.7984	42.8316	42.8648	42.8980	42.9312	42.9644	42.9976	43.0308	43.0640	43.0972	43.1304	43.1636	.001107
16	44.0857	44.1185	44.1512	44.1840	44.2168	44.2495	44.2823	44.3151	44.3478	44.3806	44.4134	44.4461	.001092
17	45.3895	45.4216	45.4536	45.4857	45.5178	45.5499	45.5820	45.6140	45.6461	45.6782	45.7102	45.7423	.001069
18	46.7078	46.7389	46.7701	46.8012	46.8323	46.8635	46.8946	46.9257	46.9569	46.9880	47.0191	47.0503	.001038
19	48.0397	48.0694	48.0990	48.1287	48.1584	48.1881	48.2177	48.2474	48.2771	48.3068	48.3364	48.3661	.000989
20	49.3798	49.4078	49.4357	49.4637	49.4917	49.5196	49.5476	49.5756	49.6035	49.6315	49.6595	49.6874	.000932
21	50.7279	50.7537	50.7795	50.8053	50.8311	50.8569	50.8827	50.9085	50.9343	50.9601	50.9859	51.0117	.000860
22	52.0795	52.1029	52.1262	52.1496	52.1730	52.1964	52.2197	52.2431	52.2665	52.2899	52.3132	52.3366	.000779
23	53.4329	53.4534	53.4740	53.4945	53.5150	53.5355	53.5560	53.5766	53.5971	53.6176	53.6381	53.6587	.000684
24	54.7855	54.8029	54.8202	54.8376	54.8549	54.8723	54.8896	54.9070	54.9244	54.9417	54.9591	54.9764	.000578
25	56.1351	56.1488	56.1624	56.1761	56.1897	56.2034	56.2170	56.2307	56.2444	56.2580	56.2717	56.2853	.000455
26	57.4772	57.4869	57.4966	57.5063	57.5160	57.5257	57.5353	57.5450	57.5547	57.5644	57.5741	57.5838	.000323
27	58.8110	58.8164	58.8218	58.8272	58.8326	58.8380	58.8434	58.8488	58.8542	58.8596	58.8650	58.8704	.000180
28	60.1347	60.1356	60.1365	60.1373	60.1382	60.1391	60.1400	60.1409	60.1418	60.1426	60.1435	60.1444	.000029
29	61.4482	61.4442	61.4401	61.4361	61.4320	61.4280	61.4240	61.4199	61.4159	61.4118	61.4078	61.4037	.000135
30	62.7490	62.7397	62.7304	62.7212	62.7119	62.7026	62.6933	62.6841	62.6748	62.6655	62.6562	62.6470	.000309
31	64.0359	64.0211	64.0062	63.9914	63.9765	63.9617	63.9468	63.9320	63.9172	63.9023	63.8875	63.8726	.000495
32	65.3080	65.2872	65.2665	65.2457	65.2250	65.2042	65.1835	65.1627	65.1420	65.1212	65.1005	65.0797	.000692
33	66.5640	66.5370	66.5100	66.4830	66.4560	66.4290	66.4020	66.3750	66.3480	66.3210	66.2940	66.2670	.000900
34	67.8029	67.7693	67.7357	67.7021	67.6685	67.6349	67.6013	67.5678	67.5342	67.5006	67.4670	67.4334	.001120
35	69.0239	68.9835	68.9430	68.9026	68.8622	68.8218	68.7813	68.7409	68.7005	68.6601	68.6196	68.5792	.001347
36	70.2277	70.1799	70.1321	70.0844	70.0366	69.9888	69.9410	69.8933	69.8455	69.7977	69.7500	69.7022	.001592
37	71.4122	71.3566	71.3010	71.2454	71.1898	71.1342	71.0785	71.0229	70.9673	70.9117	70.8561	70.8005	.001853
38	72.5749	72.5113	72.4477	72.3841	72.3205	72.2569	72.1933	72.1297	72.0661	72.0025	71.9389	71.8753	.002120
39	73.7191	73.6473	73.5754	73.5036	73.4317	73.3599	73.2880	73.2162	73.1444	73.0725	73.0007	72.9288	.002395
40	74.8464	74.7663	74.6863	74.6061	74.5262	74.4461	74.3660	74.2859	74.2059	74.1258	74.0457	73.9657	.002669
41	75.9623	75.8742	75.7862	75.6981	75.6101	75.5220	75.4340	75.3460	75.2579	75.1698	75.0818	74.9937	.002935
42	77.0758	76.9798	76.8837	76.7877	76.6917	76.5956	76.4996	76.4036	76.3075	76.2115	76.1155	76.0194	.003201
43	78.1941	78.0904	77.9867	77.8830	77.7793	77.6756	77.5719	77.4683	77.3646	77.2609	77.1572	77.0535	.003456
44	79.3292	79.2174	79.1056	78.9938	78.8821	78.7703	78.6585	78.5467	78.4349	78.3231	78.2114	78.0996	.003726
45	80.4849	80.3646	80.2443	80.1241	80.0038	79.8835	79.7632	79.6430	79.5227	79.4024	79.2821	79.1619	.004009
46	81.6653	81.5361	81.4070	81.2778	81.1486	81.0194	80.8902	80.7611	80.6319	80.5027	80.3735	80.2444	.004306
47	82.8283	82.6929	82.5576	82.4222	82.2869	82.1515	82.0161	81.8808	81.7454	81.6101	81.4747	81.3394	.004512
48	84.1091	83.9581	83.8072	83.6562	83.5053	83.3543	83.2033	83.0524	82.9014	82.7505	82.5995	82.4486	.005032
49	85.3572	85.1936	85.0300	84.8665	84.7029	84.5393	84.3757	84.2122	84.0486	83.8850	83.7214	83.5579	.005452
50	86.6181	86.4401	86.2622	86.0842	85.9063	85.7283	85.5503	85.3724	85.1944	85.0165	84.8385	84.6606	.005932
51	87.8813	87.6857	87.4901	87.2945	87.0989	86.9033	86.7077	86.5122	86.3166	86.1210	85.9254	85.7298	.006520
52	89.1180	88.9014	88.6849	88.4683	88.2518	88.0352	87.8186	87.6021	87.3855	87.1690	86.9524	86.7359	.007218
53	90.2989	90.0582	89.8176	89.5770	89.3363	89.0956	88.8550	88.6143	88.3737	88.1330	87.8924	87.6517	.008022
54	91.3965	91.1217	90.8469	90.5721	90.2974	90.0226	89.7478	89.4730	89.1982	88.9234	88.6487	88.3739	.009159
55	92.2983	91.9891	91.6798	91.3706	91.0614	90.7522	90.4430	90.1337	89.8245	89.5153	89.2060	88.8968	.010307
56	93.0092	92.7060	92.4028	92.0996	91.7965	91.4933	91.1901	90.8869	90.5837	90.2805	89.9774	89.6742	.010106
57	94.0376	93.8008	93.5641	93.3273	93.0906	92.8538	92.6171	92.3803	92.1436	91.9068	91.6701	91.4333	.007892
58 or 51	**96.1538**	**96.4743**	**96.7948**	**97.1153**	**97.4359**	**97.7564**	**98.0769**	**98.3974**	**98.7179**	**99.0384**	**99.3590**	**99.6795**	**.010684**
50	94.3693	94.2199	94.0705	93.9210	93.7716	93.6222	93.4728	93.3234	93.1740	93.0245	92.8751	92.7257	.004980
49	93.4863	93.2778	93.0692	92.8607	92.6521	92.4436	92.2350	92.0265	91.8180	91.6094	91.4009	91.1923	.006951
48	92.8645	92.6477	92.4310	92.2142	91.9974	91.7807	91.5639	91.3471	91.1304	90.9136	90.6968	90.4801	.007225
47	92.0722	91.8820	91.6918	91.5016	91.3114	91.1212	90.9310	90.7407	90.5505	90.3603	90.1701	89.9799	.006340
46	91.1032	90.9396	90.7761	90.6125	90.4490	90.2854	90.1218	89.9583	89.7947	89.6312	89.4676	89.3041	.005452
45	90.0525	89.9073	89.7620	89.6168	89.4715	89.3263	89.1810	89.0358	88.8906	88.7453	88.6001	88.4548	.004841
44	88.9426	88.8132	88.6838	88.5544	88.4250	88.2956	88.1662	88.0369	87.9075	87.7781	87.6487	87.5193	.004313
43	87.7986	87.6824	87.5661	87.4499	87.3336	87.2174	87.1011	86.9849	86.8687	86.7524	86.6362	86.5199	.003875
42	86.6455	86.5397	86.4339	86.3280	86.2222	86.1164	86.0106	85.9048	85.7990	85.6931	85.5873	85.4815	.003527
41	85.4924	85.3956	85.2988	85.2020	85.1052	85.0084	84.9115	84.8147	84.7179	84.6211	84.5243	84.4275	.003227
40	84.3405	84.2520	84.1635	84.0750	83.9864	83.8979	83.8094	83.7209	83.6324	83.5438	83.4553	83.3668	.002950
39	83.1993	83.1177	83.0362	82.9546	82.8730	82.7915	82.7099	82.6283	82.5468	82.4652	82.3836	82.3021	.002719
38	82.0742	81.9986	81.9231	81.8475	81.7719	81.6964	81.6208	81.5452	81.4697	81.3941	81.3185	81.2430	.002519
37	80.9628	80.8930	80.8232	80.7533	80.6835	80.6137	80.5439	80.4741	80.4043	80.3344	80.2646	80.1948	.002327
36	79.8620	79.7977	79.7334	79.6691	79.6048	79.5405	79.4762	79.4120	79.3477	79.2834	79.2191	79.1548	.002143
35	78.7707	78.7117	78.6527	78.5936	78.5346	78.4756	78.4166	78.3576	78.2986	78.2395	78.1805	78.1215	.001967
34	77.6792	77.6259	77.5726	77.5192	77.4659	77.4126	77.3593	77.3060	77.2527	77.1993	77.1460	77.0927	.001777
33	76.5815	76.5341	76.4866	76.4392	76.3917	76.3443	76.2968	76.2494	76.2020	76.1545	76.1071	76.0596	.001581
32	75.4700	75.4288	75.3875	75.3463	75.3051	75.2639	75.2226	75.1814	75.1402	75.0990	75.0577	75.0165	.001374
31	74.3397	74.3048	74.2700	74.2351	74.2002	74.1654	74.1305	74.0956	74.0608	74.0259	73.9910	73.9562	.001162
30	73.1887	73.1601	73.1315	73.1029	73.0743	73.0457	73.0171	72.9885	72.9599	72.9313	72.9027	72.8741	.000953
29	72.0148	71.9924	71.9700	71.9476	71.9253	71.9029	71.8805	71.8581	71.8357	71.8133	71.7910	71.7686	.000746
28	70.8198	70.8033	70.7867	70.7702	70.7537	70.7371	70.7206	70.7041	70.6875	70.6710	70.6545	70.6379	.000551
27	69.6058	69.5947	69.5836	69.5726	69.5615	69.5504	69.5393	69.5283	69.5172	69.5061	69.4950	69.4840	.000369
26	68.3722	68.3664	68.3606	68.3549	68.3491	68.3433	68.3375	68.3318	68.3260	68.3202	68.3144	68.3087	.000192
25	67.1195	67.1188	67.1181	67.1174	67.1167	67.1160	67.1153	67.1146	67.1139	67.1132	67.1125	67.1118	.000023
24	65.8489	65.8530	65.8571	65.8612	65.8653	65.8694	65.8734	65.8775	65.8816	65.8857	65.8898	65.8939	.000136
23	64.5616	64.5702	64.5788	64.5875	64.5961	64.6047	64.6133	64.6220	64.6306	64.6392	64.6478	64.6565	.000287
22	63.2589	63.2718	63.2847	63.2975	63.3104	63.3233	63.3362	63.3491	63.3620	63.3748	63.3877	63.4006	.000429
21	61.9414	61.9583	61.9752	61.9922	62.0091	62.0260	62.0430	62.0599	62.0768	62.0937	62.1106	62.1276	.000564
20	60.6118	60.6324	60.6530	60.6736	60.6943	60.7149	60.7355	60.7561	60.7767	60.7973	60.8180	60.8386	.000637
19	59.2713	59.2954	59.3195	59.3436	59.3677	59.3918	59.4160	59.4401	59.4642	59.4883	59.5124	59.5365	.000803
18	57.9203	57.9476	57.9750	58.0023	58.0297	58.0570	58.0843	58.1117	58.1390	58.1664	58.1937	58.2211	.000911
17	56.5605	56.5909	56.6212	56.6516	56.6820	56.7123	56.7427	56.7731	56.8034	56.8338	56.8642	56.8945	.001012
16	55.1958	55.2287	55.2616	55.2945	55.3274	55.3603	55.3932	55.4261	55.4590	55.4919	55.5248	55.5577	.001097
15	53.8283	53.8635	53.8986	53.9338	53.9689	54.0041	54.0392	54.0744	54.1096	54.1447	54.1799	54.2150	.001172
14	52.4609	52.4979	52.5350	52.5720	52.6090	52.6461	52.6831	52.7201	52.7572	52.7942	52.8312	52.8683	.001234
13	51.0950	51.1337	51.1724	51.2110	51.2497	51.1884	51.3271	51.3658	51.4045	51.4431	51.4818	51.5205	.001289
12	49.7338	49.7738	49.8137	49.8537	49.8936	49.9336	49.9735	50.0135	50.0535	50.0934	50.1334	50.1733	.001332
11	48.3797	48.4206	48.4615	48.5025	48.5434	48.5843	48.6252	48.6662	48.7071	48.7480	48.7890	48.8299	.001364
10	47.0362	47.0776	47.1191	47.1605	47.2019	47.2434	47.2848	47.3262	47.3677	47.4091	47.4505	47.4920	.001381
Age.	0	1	2	3	4	5	6	7	8	9	10	11	Day.

Age.	0	1	2	3	4	5	6	7	8	9	10	11	Day.
10	38.0513	38.0861	38.1209	38.1557	38.1905	38.2253	38.2601	38.2949	38.3297	38.3645	38.3993	38.4341	.001160
11	39.2778	39.3128	39.3478	39.3827	39.4177	39.4527	39.4877	39.5227	39.5577	39.5926	39.6276	39.6626	.001166
12	40.5216	40.5567	40.5917	40.6268	40.6619	40.6969	40.7320	40.7671	40.8021	40.8372	40.8723	40.9073	.001169
13	41.7823	41.8173	41.8522	41.8872	41.9221	41.9571	41.9920	42.0270	42.0620	42.0969	42.1319	42.1668	.001165
14	43.0594	43.0940	43.1286	43.1632	43.1978	43.2324	43.2670	43.3015	43.3361	43.3707	43.4053	43.4399	.001153
15	44.3512	44.3854	44.4196	44.4539	44.4881	44.5223	44.5565	44.5908	44.6250	44.6592	44.6934	44.7277	.001141
16	45.6589	45.6930	45.7271	45.7612	45.7953	45.8294	45.8635	45.8976	45.9317	45.9658	45.9999	46.0340	.001137
17	46.9812	47.0139	47.0467	47.0794	47.1121	47.1449	47.1776	47.2103	47.2431	47.2758	47.3085	47.3413	.001091
18	48.3163	48.3477	48.3790	48.4104	48.4417	48.4731	48.5044	48.5358	48.5672	48.5985	48.6299	48.6612	.001045
19	49.6601	49.6898	49.7195	49.7492	49.7789	49.8086	49.8383	49.8681	49.8978	49.9275	49.9572	49.9869	.000990
20	51.0103	51.0380	51.0656	51.0933	51.1209	51.1486	51.1762	51.2039	51.2316	51.2592	51.2869	51.3145	.000922
21	52.3648	52.3901	52.4154	52.4407	52.4660	52.4913	52.5166	52.5419	52.5672	52.5925	52.6178	52.6431	.000843
22	53.7210	53.7435	53.7661	53.7886	53.8112	53.8337	53.8562	53.8788	53.9013	53.9239	53.9464	53.9690	.000751
23	55.0755	55.0950	55.1145	55.1340	55.1535	55.1730	55.1924	55.2119	55.2314	55.2509	55.2704	55.2899	.000650
24	56.4272	56.4431	56.4590	56.4749	56.4908	56.5067	56.5225	56.5384	56.5543	56.5702	56.5861	56.6020	.000530
25	57.7711	57.7832	57.7952	57.8073	57.8193	57.8314	57.8434	57.8555	57.8676	57.8796	57.8917	57.9037	.000402
26	59.1064	59.1143	59.1222	59.1301	59.1380	59.1459	59.1537	59.1616	59.1695	59.1774	59.1853	59.1932	.000263
27	60.4314	60.4349	60.4384	60.4420	60.4455	60.4490	60.4525	60.4561	60.4596	60.4631	60.4666	60.4702	.000117
28	61.7458	61.7445	61.7433	61.7420	61.7408	61.7395	61.7383	61.7370	61.7358	61.7345	61.7333	61.7320	.000042
29	63.0473	63.0410	63.0346	63.0283	63.0220	63.0157	63.0093	63.0030	62.9967	62.9904	62.9840	62.9777	.000211
30	64.3349	64.3232	64.3114	64.2997	64.2880	64.2763	64.2645	64.2528	64.2411	64.2294	64.2176	64.2059	.000391
31	65.6070	65.5896	65.5721	65.5547	65.5373	65.5198	65.5024	65.4850	65.4675	65.4501	65.4327	65.4152	.000581
32	66.8630	66.8395	66.8160	66.7925	66.7690	66.7455	66.7220	66.6986	66.6751	66.6516	66.6281	66.6046	.000783
33	68.1016	68.0717	68.0419	68.0120	67.9822	67.9523	67.9224	67.8926	67.8627	67.8329	67.8030	67.7732	.000995
34	69.3223	69.2858	69.2494	69.2129	69.1765	69.1400	69.1035	69.0671	69.0306	68.9942	68.9577	68.9213	.001215
35	70.5254	70.4818	70.4383	70.3947	70.3512	70.3076	70.2641	70.2205	70.1770	70.1334	70.0899	70.0463	.001452
36	71.7088	71.6577	71.6066	71.5555	71.5044	71.4533	71.4022	71.3512	71.3001	71.2490	71.1979	71.1468	.001703
37	72.8709	72.8121	72.7533	72.6945	72.6358	72.5770	72.5182	72.4594	72.4006	72.3418	72.2831	72.2243	.001959
38	74.0135	73.9468	73.8801	73.8134	73.7467	73.6800	73.6133	73.5467	73.4800	73.4133	73.3466	73.2799	.002223
39	75.1393	75.0647	74.9902	74.9156	74.8411	74.7665	74.6920	74.6174	74.5428	74.4683	74.3937	74.3192	.002485
40	76.2533	76.1711	76.0890	76.0068	75.9246	75.8425	75.7603	75.6781	75.5960	75.5138	75.4316	75.3495	.002739
41	77.3643	77.2746	77.1848	77.0951	77.0053	76.9156	76.8258	76.7361	76.6464	76.5566	76.4669	76.3771	.002991
42	78.4788	78.3818	78.2849	78.1879	78.0909	77.9940	77.8970	77.8000	77.7031	77.6061	77.5091	77.4122	.003232
43	79.6083	79.5037	79.3991	79.2944	79.1898	79.0852	78.9806	78.8760	78.7714	78.6667	78.5621	78.4575	.003487
44	80.7560	80.6433	80.5307	80.4180	80.3054	80.1927	80.0800	79.9674	79.8547	79.7421	79.6294	79.5168	.003755
45	81.9261	81.8050	81.6840	81.5629	81.4418	81.3207	81.1996	81.0786	80.9575	80.8364	80.7153	80.5943	.004036
46	83.1232	82.9925	82.8619	82.7312	82.6006	82.4699	82.3392	82.2086	82.0779	81.9473	81.8166	81.6860	.004355
47	84.3425	84.2007	84.0589	83.9171	83.7753	83.6335	83.4916	83.3498	83.2080	83.0662	82.9244	82.7826	.004727
48	85 5743	85.4204	85.2666	85.1127	84.9589	84.8050	84.6511	84.4973	84.3434	84.1896	84.0357	83.8819	.005125
49	86.8170	86.6494	86.4819	86.3143	86.1468	85.9792	85.8116	85.6441	85.4765	85.3090	85.1414	84.9738	.005585
50	88.0602	87.8758	87.6913	87.5069	87.3224	87.1380	86.9535	86.7691	86.5847	86.4002	86.2158	86.0313	.006148
51	89.2757	89.0711	88.8666	88.6620	88.4575	88.2530	88.0484	87.8438	87.6393	87.4347	87.2302	87.0256	.006818
52	90.4344	90.2068	89.9792	89.7515	89.5239	89.2963	89.0687	88.8411	88.6135	88.3858	88.1582	87.9306	.007587
53	91.5107	91.2502	90.9897	90.7292	90.4687	90.2082	89.9477	89.6873	89.4268	89.1663	88.9058	88.6453	.008683
54	92.3941	92.1005	91.8070	91.5134	91.2198	90.9263	90.6327	90.3391	90.0456	89.7520	89.4584	89.1649	.009785
55	93.0901	92.8030	92.5158	92.2287	91.9416	91.6544	91.3673	91.0802	90.7930	90.5059	90.2188	89.9316	.009571
56	94.0940	93.8721	93.6501	93.4282	93.2063	92.9844	92.7624	92.5405	92.3186	92.0967	91.8747	91.6528	.007397
57 or 52	**96.1538**	**96.4743**	**96.7948**	**97.1153**	**97.4359**	**97.7564**	**98.0769**	**98.3974**	**98.7179**	**99.0384**	**99.3590**	**99.6795**	**.010684**
51	94.3299	94.1701	94.0103	93.8505	93.6907	93.5309	93.3711	93.2113	93.0515	92.8917	92.7319	92.5721	.005327
50	93.4295	93.2097	92.9899	92.7700	92.5502	92.3304	92.1106	91.8908	91.6710	91.4511	91.2313	91.0115	.007327
49	92.7969	92.5691	92.3413	92.1136	91.8858	91.6580	91.4302	91.2025	90.9747	90.7469	90.5191	90.2914	.007592
48	91.9910	91.7913	91.5910	91.3906	91.1903	90.9900	90.7897	90.5894	90.3891	90.1887	89.9884	89.7881	.006677
47	91.0070	90.8342	90.6615	90.4887	90.3159	90.1432	89.9704	89.7976	89.6249	89.4521	89.2793	89.1066	.005759
46	89.9407	89.7869	89.6331	89.4793	89.3255	89.1717	89.0180	88.8642	88.7104	88.5566	88.4028	88.2490	.005126
45	88.8156	88.6783	88.5410	88.4037	88.2664	88.1291	87.9918	87.8545	87.7172	87.5799	87.4426	87.3053	.004577
44	87.6577	87.5341	87.4105	87.2869	87.1633	87.0397	86.9160	86.7924	86.6688	86.5452	86.4216	86.2980	.004120
43	86.4924	86.3797	86.2670	86.1543	86.0416	85.9289	85.8162	85.7036	85.5909	85.4782	85.3655	85.2528	.003756
42	85.3287	85.2255	85.1223	85.0191	84.9159	84.8127	84.7094	84.6062	84.5030	84.3998	84.2966	84.1934	.003440
41	84.1677	84.0732	83.9787	83.8842	83.7897	83.6952	83.6007	83.5063	83.4118	83.3173	83.2228	83.1283	.003150
40	83.0188	82.9316	82.8445	82.7573	82.6701	82.5830	82.4958	82.4086	82.3215	82.2343	82.1471	82.0600	.002905
39	81.8871	81.8063	81.7254	81.6446	81.5637	81.4829	81.4020	81.3212	81.2404	81.1595	81.0787	80.9978	.002695
38	80.7696	80.6948	80.6201	80.5453	80.4705	80.3958	80.3210	80.2462	80.1715	80.0967	80.0219	79.9472	.002492
37	79.6644	79.5954	79.5265	79.4575	79.3885	79.3196	79.2506	79.1816	79.1127	79.0437	78.9747	78.9058	.002299
36	78.5688	78.5054	78.4420	78.3785	78.3151	78.2517	78.1882	78.1248	78.0614	77.9980	77.9345	77.8711	.002114
35	77.4739	77.4164	77.3589	77.3014	77.2440	77.1865	77.1290	77.0715	77.0140	76.9565	76.8991	76.8416	.001916
34	76.3731	76.3217	76.2704	76.2190	76.1677	76.1163	76.0650	76.0136	75.9622	75.9109	75.8595	75.8082	.001712
33	75.2588	75.2139	75.1690	75.1241	75.0792	75.0343	74.9893	74.9444	74.8995	74.8546	74.8097	74.7648	.001497
32	74.1260	74.0877	74.0493	74.0110	73.9727	73.9343	73.8960	73.8577	73.8193	73.7810	73.7427	73.7043	.001278
31	72.9729	72.9410	72.9091	72.8773	72.8454	72.8135	72.7816	72.7498	72.7179	72.6860	72.6541	72.6223	.001062
30	71.7980	71.7725	71.7469	71.7214	71.6958	71.6703	71.6447	71.6192	71.5937	71.5681	71.5426	71.5170	.000851
29	70.6006	70.5811	70.5617	70.5422	70.5228	70.5033	70.4839	70.4644	70.4450	70.4255	70.4061	70.3866	.000648
28	69.3852	69.3714	69.3575	69.3437	69.3299	69.3161	69.3022	69.2884	69.2746	69.2608	69.2470	69.2331	.000461
27	68.1497	68.1414	68.1331	68.1248	68.1165	68.1082	68.0999	68.0916	68.0833	68.0750	68.0667	68.0584	.000277
26	66.8972	66.8940	66.8909	66.8877	66.8845	66.8814	66.8782	66.8750	66.8719	66.8687	66.8655	66.8624	.000105
25	65.6262	65.6280	65.6297	65.6315	65.6333	65.6350	65.6367	65.6385	65.6403	65.6420	65.6438	65.6455	.000058
24	64.3385	64.3449	64.3513	64.3578	64.3642	64.3706	64.3770	64.3835	64.3899	64.3963	64.4027	64.4092	.000214
23	63.0356	63.0464	63.0572	63.0680	63.0788	63.0896	63.1004	63.1112	63.1220	63.1328	63.1436	63.1544	.000360
22	61.7185	61.7334	61.7484	61.7633	61.7783	61.7932	61.8081	61.8231	61.8380	61.8530	61.8679	61.8829	.000498
21	60.3895	60.4082	60.4270	60.4457	60.4644	60.4831	60.5018	60.5206	60.5393	60.5580	60.5767	60.5955	.000624
20	59.0488	59.0711	59.0935	59.1158	59.1382	59.1605	59.1829	59.2052	59.2276	59.2500	59.2723	59.2946	.000745
19	57.6992	57.7248	57.7505	57.7761	57.8018	57.8274	57.8531	57.8787	57.9044	57.9300	57.9557	57.9813	.000855
18	56.3403	56.3691	56.3978	56.4266	56.4553	56.4841	56.5128	56.5416	56.5704	56.5991	56.6279	56.6566	.000958
17	54.9773	55.0087	55.0400	55.0714	55.1028	55.1341	55.1655	55.1969	55.2282	55.2596	55.2910	55.3223	.001045
16	53.6114	53.6451	53.6788	53.7125	53.7462	53.7799	53.8136	53.8473	53.8810	53.9147	53.9484	53.9821	.001123
15	52.2460	52.2817	52.3173	52.3530	52.3886	52.4243	52.4600	52.4956	52.5313	52.5669	52.6026	52.6382	.001188
14	50.8827	50.9200	50.9574	50.9947	51.0321	51.0694	51.1067	51.1441	51.1814	51.2188	51.2561	51.2935	.001245
13	49.5246	49.5632	49.6019	49.6405	49.6792	49.7178	49.7565	49.7951	49.8338	49.8724	49.9111	49.9497	.001288
12	48.1734	48.2131	48.2527	48.2924	48.3321	48.3718	48.4114	48.4511	48.4908	48.5305	48.5701	48.6098	.001322
11	46.8333	46.8736	46.9138	46.9541	46.9944	47.0347	47.0750	47.1152	47.1555	47.1958	47.2360	47.2763	.001342
10	45.5059	45.5465	45.5871	45.6277	45.6684	45.7090	45.7496	45.7902	45.8308	45.8714	45.9121	45.9527	.001354
Age.	0	1	2	3	4	5	6	7	8	9	10	11	Day.

Age.	0	1	2	3	4	5	6	7	8	9	10	11	Day.
10	39.5118	39.5480	39.5841	39.6203	39.6564	39.6926	39.7287	39.7649	39.8011	39.8372	39.8734	39.9095	.001205
11	40.7608	40.7971	40.8334	40.8697	40.9060	40.9423	40.9786	41.0149	41.0512	41.0875	41.1238	41.1601	.001210
12	42.0268	42.0630	42.0993	42.1355	42.1718	42.2080	42.2442	42.2805	42.3167	42.3530	42.3892	42.4255	.001208
13	43.3084	43.3443	43.3803	43.4162	43.4522	43.4881	43.5241	43.5600	43.5960	43.6320	43.6679	43.7038	.001198
14	44.6046	44.6402	44.6758	44.7114	44.7471	44.7827	44.8183	44.8539	44.8895	44.9251	44.9608	44.9964	.001187
15	45.9163	45.9514	45.9864	46.0215	46.0566	46.0916	46.1267	46.1618	46.1968	46.2319	46.2670	46.3020	.001168
16	47.2482	47.2820	47.3157	47.3495	47.3832	47.4170	47.4507	47.4845	47.5183	47.5520	47.5858	47.6195	.001125
17	48.5809	48.6138	48.6468	48.6797	48.7127	48.7457	48.7785	48.8115	48.8444	48.8774	48.9103	48.9433	.001098
18	49.9274	49.9588	49.9902	50.0215	50.0529	50.0843	50.1157	50.1471	50.1785	50.2098	50.2412	50.2726	.001046
19	51.2809	51.3103	51.3397	51.3691	51.3985	51.4279	51.4572	51.4866	51.5160	51.5454	51.5748	51.6042	.000980
20	52.6370	52.6642	52.6913	52.7185	52.7456	52.7728	52.8000	52.8271	52.8543	52.8814	52.9086	52.9357	.000905
21	53.9957	54.0202	54.0446	54.0691	54.0936	54.1181	54.1425	54.1670	54.1915	54.2160	54.2404	54.2649	.000816
22	55.3525	55.3740	55.3955	55.4170	55.4385	55.4600	55.4815	55.5031	55.5246	55.5461	55.5676	55.5891	.000717
23	56.7057	56.7237	56.7417	56.7598	56.7778	56.7958	56.8138	56.8319	56.8499	56.8679	56.8860	56.9040	.000601
24	58.0512	58.0656	58.0800	58.0944	58.1088	58.1232	58.1375	58.1519	58 1663	58.1807	58.1951	58.2095	.000480
25	59.3880	59.3983	59.4085	59.4188	59.4291	59.4393	59.4496	59.4599	59.4701	59.4804	59.4907	59.5009	.000342
26	60.7140	60.7200	60.7261	60.7321	60.7381	60.7442	60.7502	60.7562	60.7623	60.7683	60.7743	60.7804	.000201
27	62.0294	62.0308	62.0322	62.0336	62.0350	62.0364	62.0377	62.0391	62.0405	62.0419	62.0433	62.0447	.000046
28	63.3313	63.3278	63.3242	63.3207	63.3172	63.3137	63.3101	63.3066	63.3031	63.2996	63.2960	63.2925	.000117
29	64.6191	64.6103	64.6016	64.5928	64.5841	64.5753	64.5665	64.5578	64.5490	64.5403	64.5315	64.5228	.000292
30	65.8914	65.8771	65.8628	65.8485	65.8342	65.8199	65.8056	65.7914	65.7771	65.7628	65.7485	65.7342	.000476
31	67.1471	67.1269	67.1068	67.0866	67.0664	67.0463	67.0261	67.0059	66 9858	66.9656	66.9454	66.9253	.000672
32	68.3851	68.3588	68.3324	68.3061	68.2798	68.2535	68.2271	68.2008	68.1745	68.1482	68.1218	68.0955	.000877
33	69.6049	69.5722	69.5395	69.5068	69.4741	69.4414	69.4087	69.3761	69.3434	69.3107	69.2780	69.2453	.001090
34	70.8072	70.7677	70.7281	70.6886	70.6490	70.6095	70.5700	70.5304	70.4909	70.4513	70.4118	70.3722	.001318
35	71.9894	71.9426	71.8957	71.8489	71.8021	71.7553	71.7084	71.6616	71.6148	71.5680	71.5211	71.4743	.001561
36	73.1500	73.0958	73.0415	72.9873	72.9331	72.8788	72.8246	72.7704	72.7161	72.6619	72.6077	72.5534	.001808
37	74.2915	74.2297	74.1678	74.1060	74.0441	73.9823	73.9204	73.8586	73.7968	73.7349	73.6731	73.6112	.002061
38	75.4150	75.3456	75.2762	75.2069	75.1375	75.0681	74.9987	74.9294	74.8600	74.7906	74.7212	74.6519	.002312
39	76.5269	76.4503	76.3736	76.2970	76.2203	76.1437	76.0670	75.9904	75.9138	75.8371	75.7605	75.6838	.002555
40	77.6350	77.5512	77.4674	77.3835	77.2997	77.2159	77.1321	77.0483	76.9645	76.8806	76.7968	76.7130	.002794
41	78.7460	78.6553	78.5647	78.4740	78.3834	78.2927	78.2021	78.1114	78.0208	77.9301	77.8395	77.7488	.003022
42	79.8706	79.7727	79.6748	79.5770	79.4791	79.3812	79.2833	79.1855	79.0876	78.9897	78.8918	78.7940	.003262
43	81.0114	80.9059	80.8004	80.6950	80.5895	80.4840	80.3785	80.2731	80.1676	80.0621	79.9566	79.8512	.003516
44	82.1723	82.0589	81.9454	81.8320	81.7185	81.6051	81.4916	81.3782	81.2648	81.1513	81.0379	80.9244	.003781
45	83.3578	83.2353	83.1127	82.9902	82.8677	82.7451	82.6226	82.5001	82.3775	82.2550	82.1325	82.0099	.004084
46	84.5633	84.4301	84.2970	84.1638	84.0306	83.8974	83.7642	83.6311	83.4979	83.3647	83.2315	83.0984	.004439
47	85.7793	85.6346	85.4900	85.3453	85.2007	85.0560	84.9114	84.7667	84.6221	84.4774	84.3328	84.1881	.004822
48	87.0047	86.8469	86.6892	86.5314	86.3737	86.2159	86.0581	85.9004	85.7426	85.5849	85.4271	85.2694	.005258
49	88.2289	88.0550	87.8811	87.7072	87.5333	87.3594	87.1855	87.0116	86.8377	86.6638	86.4899	86.3160	.005797
50	89.4244	89.2312	89.0380	88.8448	88.6516	88.4584	88.2652	88.0720	87.8788	87.6856	87.4924	87.2992	.006440
51	90.5627	90.3473	90.1320	89.9166	89.7013	89.4859	89.2705	89.0552	88.8398	88.6245	88.4091	88.1938	.007178
52	91.6181	91.3711	91.1241	90.8771	90.6301	90.3831	90.1361	89.8891	89.6421	89.3951	89.1481	88.9011	.008233
53	92.4844	92.2056	91.9267	91.6479	91.3691	91.0902	90.8114	90.5326	90.2537	89.9749	89.6961	89.4172	.009294
54	93.1662	92.8942	92.6221	92.3501	92.0781	91.8060	91.5340	91.2620	90.9899	90.7179	90.4459	90.1738	.009068
55	94.1470	93.9390	93.7310	93.5231	93.3151	93.1071	92.8991	92.6912	92.4832	92.2752	92.0672	91.8593	.006932
56 or 53	**96.1538**	**96.4743**	**96.7948**	**97.1153**	**97.4359**	**97.7564**	**98.0769**	**98.3974**	**98.7179**	**99.0384**	**99.3590**	**99.6795**	**.010684**
52	94.2879	94.1171	93.9463	93.7755	93.6048	93.4340	93.2632	93.0924	92.9216	92.7508	92.5801	92.4093	.005693
51	93.3693	93.1375	92.9058	92.6740	92.4423	92.2105	91.9788	91.7470	91.5153	91.2835	91.0518	90.8200	.007725
50	92.7254	92.4860	92.2465	92.0070	91.7676	91.5281	91.2887	91.0492	90.8098	90.5703	90.3309	90.0914	.007982
49	91.9062	91.6952	91.4842	91.2732	91.0622	90.8512	90.6402	90.4292	90.2182	90.0072	89.7962	89.4852	.007033
48	90.9054	90.7229	90.5403	90.3578	90.1753	89.9927	89.8102	89.6277	89.4451	89.2626	89.0801	88.8975	.006084
47	89.8223	89.6595	89.4967	89.3338	89.1710	89.0082	88.8454	88.6826	88.5198	88.3570	88.1941	88 0313	.005427
46	88.6811	88.5354	88.3897	88.2440	88.0983	87.9526	87.8069	87.6612	87.5155	87.3698	87.2241	87.0784	.004857
45	87.5081	87.3767	87.2452	87.1138	86.9824	86.8510	86.7195	86.5881	86.4567	86.3253	86.1938	86.0624	.004381
44	86.3294	86.2094	86.0894	85.9694	85.8494	85.7294	85.6094	85.4895	85.3695	85.2495	85.1295	85.0095	.004000
43	85.1544	85.0444	84.9343	84.8243	84.7142	84.6042	84.4941	84.3841	84.2741	84.1640	84.0540	83.9439	.003668
42	83.9838	83.8829	83.7821	83.6812	83.5803	83.4795	83.3786	83.2777	83.1769	83.0760	82.9751	82.8743	.003362
41	82.8267	82.7336	82.6404	82.5473	82.4542	82.3611	82.2680	82.1748	82.0817	81.9886	81.8954	81.8023	.003104
40	81.6883	81.6019	81.5154	81.4290	81.3426	81.2561	81.1697	81.0833	80.9968	80.9104	80.8240	80.7375	.002881
39	80.5651	80.4851	80.4050	80.3250	80.2450	80.1650	80.0850	80.0049	79.9249	79.8449	79.7648	79.6848	.002667
38	79.4547	79.3808	79.3069	79.2330	79.1591	79.0852	79.0112	78.9373	78.8634	78.7895	78.7156	78.6417	.002463
37	78.3555	78.2874	78.2193	78.1512	78.0831	78.0150	77.9470	77.8789	77.8108	77.7427	77.6746	77.6065	.002270
36	77.2568	77.1949	77.1331	77.0712	77.0094	76.9475	76.8856	76.8238	76.7619	76.7001	76.6382	76.5764	.002062
35	76.1532	76.0977	76.0422	75.9867	75.9312	75.8757	75.8202	75.7647	75.7092	75.6537	75.5982	75.5427	.001850
34	75.0364	74.9876	74.9388	74.8900	74.8411	74.7923	74.7435	74.6947	74.6459	74.5970	74.5482	74.4994	.001627
33	73.9011	73.8591	73.8171	73.7751	73.7331	73.6911	73.6491	73.6072	73.5652	73.5232	73.4812	73.4392	.001400
32	72.7460	72.7107	72.6753	72.6400	72.6047	72.5693	72.5340	72.4987	72.4633	72.4280	72.3927	72.3573	.001177
31	71.5685	71.5398	71.5110	71.4823	71.4536	71.4248	71.3961	71.3674	71.3386	71.3099	71.2812	71.2524	.000958
30	70.3711	70.3486	70.3260	70.3035	70.2810	70.2585	70.2360	70.2134	70.1909	70.1684	70.1458	70.1233	.000751
29	69.1536	69.1369	69.1202	69.1034	69.0867	69.0700	69.0533	69.0366	69.0199	69.0031	68.9864	68.9697	.000557
28	67.9180	67.9069	67.8958	67.8847	67.8736	67.8625	67.8513	67.8402	67.8291	67.8180	67.8069	67.7958	.000370
27	66.6639	66.6581	66.6522	66.6464	66.6406	66.6348	66.6290	66.6231	66.6173	66.6115	66.6056	66.5998	.000194
26	65.3924	65.3917	65.3910	65.3904	65.3897	65.3890	65.3883	65.3877	65.3870	65.3863	65.3856	65.3850	.000022
25	64.1046	64.1087	64.1128	64.1170	64.1211	64.1252	64.1293	64.1334	64.1375	64.1416	64.1458	64.1499	.000137
24	62.8017	62.8103	62.8189	62.8275	62.8362	62.8448	62.8534	62.8620	62.8706	62.8792	62.8879	62.8965	.000287
23	61.4848	61.4977	61.5105	61.5234	61.5363	61.5491	61.5620	61.5749	61.5877	61.6006	61.6135	61.6263	.000429
22	60.1565	60.1732	60.1900	60.2067	60.2235	60.2402	60.2570	60.2737	60.2905	60.3072	60.3240	60.3407	.000558
21	58.8168	58.8373	58.8577	58.8782	58.8986	58.9191	58.9395	58.9600	58.9805	59.0009	59.0214	59.0418	.000682
20	57.4673	57.4912	57.5151	57.5390	57.5629	57.5868	57.6106	57.6345	57.6584	57.6823	57.7062	57.7301	.000796
19	56.1101	56.1372	56.1642	56.1913	56.2184	56.2454	56.2725	56.2996	56.3266	56.3537	56.3808	56.4078	.000902
18	54.7483	54.7781	54.8078	54.8376	54.8674	54.8971	54.9269	54.9567	54.9864	55.0162	55.0460	55.0757	.000992
17	53.3844	53.4166	53.4487	53.4809	53.5131	53.5453	53.5774	53.6096	53.6418	53.6740	53 7061	53.7383	.001072
16	52.0210	52.0552	52.0894	52.1236	52.1578	52.1920	52.2262	52.2604	52.2946	52.3288	52.3630	52.3972	.001140
15	50.6601	50.6961	50.7320	50.7680	50.8039	50.8399	50.8758	50.9118	50.9478	50.9837	51.0197	51.0556	.001198
14	49.3049	49.3422	49.3795	49.4168	49.4542	49.4915	49.5288	49.5661	49.6034	49.6407	49.6781	49.7154	.001244
13	47.9567	47.9951	48.0336	48.0720	48.1105	48.1489	48.1873	48.2258	48.2642	48.3027	48.3411	48.3796	.001281
12	46.6203	46.6594	46.6984	46.7375	46.7766	46.8156	46.8547	46.8938	46.9328	46.9719	47.0110	47.0500	.001302
11	45.2967	45.3362	45.3756	45.4151	45.4545	45.4940	45.5334	45.5729	45.6124	45.6518	45.6913	45.7307	.001315
10	43.9878	44.0274	44.0670	44.1066	44.1462	44.1858	44.2254	44.2650	44.3046	44.3442	44.3838	44.4234	.001320
Age.	0	1	2	3	4	5	6	7	8	9	10	11	Day.

Age.	0	1	2	3	4	5	6	7	8	9	10	11	Day.
10	40.9887	41.0262	41.0636	41.1011	41.1386	41.1760	41.2135	41.2510	41.2884	41.3259	41.3634	41.4008	.001249
11	42.2595	42.2970	42.3344	42.3719	42.4094	42.4468	42.4843	42.5218	42.5592	42.5967	42.6342	42.6716	.001249
12	43.5460	43.5832	43.6204	43.6577	43.6949	43.7321	43.7693	43.8066	43.8438	43.8810	43.9182	43.9555	.001241
13	44.8463	44.8833	44.9202	44.9572	44.9942	45.0312	45.0681	45.1051	45.1421	45.1791	45.2160	45.2530	.001232
14	46.1620	46.1985	46.2349	46.2714	46.3079	46.3443	46.3808	46.4173	46.4537	46.4902	46.5267	46.5631	.001215
15	47.4915	47.5272	47.5630	47.5987	47.6344	47.6701	47.7058	47.7416	47.7773	47.8130	47.8487	47.8845	.001191
16	48.8333	48.8678	48.9022	48.9367	48.9711	49.0056	49.0401	49.0746	49.1091	49.1436	49.1780	49.2125	.001149
17	50.1831	50.2161	50.2490	50.2820	50.3150	50.3480	50.3810	50.4139	50.4469	50.4799	50.5128	50.5458	.001099
18	51.5389	51.5700	51.6010	51.6321	51.6632	51.6942	51.7253	51.7564	51.7874	51.8185	51.8496	51.8806	.001035
19	52.8979	52.9268	52.9557	52.9846	53.0135	53.0424	53.0712	53.1001	53.1290	53.1579	53.1868	53.2157	.000963
20	54.2577	54.2840	54.3104	54.3367	54.3631	54.3894	54.4158	54.4421	54.4684	54.4948	54.5211	54.5475	.000878
21	55.6166	55.6401	55.6635	55.6870	55.7104	55.7339	55.7573	55.7808	55.8043	55.8277	55.8512	55.8746	.000782
22	56.9717	56.9918	57.0118	57.0319	57.0519	57.0720	57.0920	57.1121	57.1322	57.1522	57.1723	57.1923	.000668
23	58.3183	58.3348	58.3512	58.3677	58.3842	58.4006	58.4171	58.4336	58.4500	58.4665	58.4830	58.4994	.000549
24	59.6573	59.6697	59.6822	59.6946	59.7071	59.7195	59.7320	59.7444	59.7568	59.7693	59.7817	59.7942	.000416
25	60.9833	60.9917	61.0001	61.0086	61.0170	61.0254	61.0338	61.0423	61.0507	61.0591	61.0675	61.0760	.000281
26	62.2993	62.3032	62.3071	62.3110	62.3150	62.3189	62.3228	62.3267	62.3306	62.3345	62.3385	62.3424	.000130
27	63.6017	63.6008	63.6000	63.5991	63.5983	63.5974	63.5966	63.5957	63.5949	63.5940	63.5932	63.5923	.000028
28	64.8895	64.8836	64.8776	64.8717	64.8658	64.8599	64.8540	64.8480	64.8421	64.8362	64.8302	64.8243	.000197
29	66.1616	66.1503	66.1390	66.1277	66.1164	66.1051	66.0938	66.0826	66.0713	66.0600	66.0487	66.0374	.000376
30	67.4171	67.4001	67.3831	67.3661	67.3491	67.3321	67.3151	67.2982	67.2812	67.2642	67.2472	67.2302	.000566
31	68.6544	68.6314	68.6085	68.5855	68.5626	68.5396	68.5166	68.4937	68.4707	68.4478	68.4248	68.4019	.000765
32	69.8733	69.8442	69.8150	69.7859	69.7568	69.7276	69.6985	69.6694	69.6402	69.6111	69.5820	69.5528	.000971
33	71.0742	71.0385	71.0027	70.9670	70.9312	70.8955	70.8597	70.8240	70.7883	70.7525	70.7168	70.6810	.001191
34	72.2552	72.2124	72.1696	72.1268	72.0841	72.0413	71.9985	71.9557	71.9129	71.8701	71.8274	71.7846	.001426
35	73.4141	73.3642	73.3142	73.2643	73.2144	73.1644	73.1145	73.0646	73.0146	72.9647	72.9148	72.8648	.001664
36	74.5536	74.4963	74.4391	74.3818	74.3246	74.2673	74.2100	74.1528	74.0955	74.0383	73.9810	73.9238	.001908
37	75.6754	75.6109	75.5464	75.4819	75.4174	75.3529	75.2884	75.2240	75.1595	75.0950	75.0305	74.9660	.002150
38	76.7843	76.7129	76.6415	76.5700	76.4986	76.4272	76.3558	76.2844	76.2130	76.1415	76.0701	75.9987	.002380
39	77.8895	77.8112	77.7330	77.6547	77.5765	77.4982	77.4200	77.3417	77.2634	77.1852	77.1069	77.0287	.002608
40	78.9969	78.9122	78.8274	78.7427	78.6580	78.5733	78.4885	78.4038	78.3191	78.2344	78.1496	78.0649	.002824
41	80.1167	80.0252	79.9336	79.8421	79.7505	79.6590	79.5674	79.4759	79.3844	79.2928	79.2013	79.1097	.003051
42	81.2514	81.1527	81.0540	80.9552	80.8565	80.7578	80.6591	80.5604	80.4617	80.3630	80.2642	80.1655	.003290
43	82.4042	82.2980	82.1917	82.0854	81.9792	81.8730	81.7667	81.6604	81.5542	81.4480	81.3417	81.2354	.003542
44	83.5792	83.4643	83.3494	83.2346	83.1197	83.0048	82.8900	82.7751	82.6602	82.5453	82.4304	82.3156	.003829
45	84.7719	84.6469	84.5219	84.3969	84.2719	84.1469	84.0219	83.8969	83.7719	83.6469	83.5219	83.3969	.004167
46	85.9732	85.8372	85.7013	85.5653	85.4293	85.2934	85.1574	85.0214	84.8855	84.7495	84.6135	84.4776	.004532
47	87.1829	87.0343	86.8858	86.7372	86.5887	86.4401	86.2916	86.1430	85.9945	85.8460	85.6974	85.5488	.004952
48	88.3883	88.2243	88.0603	87.8964	87.7324	87.5684	87.4044	87.2405	87.0765	86.9125	86.7485	86.5846	.005466
49	89.5648	89.3823	89.1998	89.0173	88.8348	88.6523	88.4698	88.2874	88.1049	87.9224	87.7399	87.5574	.006083
50	90.6835	90.4797	90.2760	90.0722	89.8684	89.6646	89.4608	89.2571	89.0533	88.8495	88.6457	88.4420	.006792
51	91.7199	91.4856	91.2513	91.0170	90.7827	90.5484	90.3140	90.0797	89.8454	89.6111	89.3768	89.1425	.007810
52	92.5692	92.3043	92.0394	91.7744	91.5095	91.2446	90.9797	90.7148	90.4499	90.1850	89.9200	89.6551	.008830
53	93.2379	92.9801	92.7223	92.4645	92.2067	91.9489	91.6910	91.4332	91.1754	90.9176	90.6598	90.4020	.008593
54	94.1968	94.0020	93.8071	93.6123	93.4175	93.2226	93.0278	92.8330	92.6381	92.4433	92.2485	92.0536	.006494
55 or 54	**96.1538**	**96.4743**	**96.7948**	**97.1153**	**97.4359**	**97.7564**	**98.0769**	**98.3974**	**98.7179**	**99.0384**	**99.3590**	**99.6795**	**.010684**
53	94.2438	94.0613	93.8789	93.6964	93.5139	93.3315	93.1490	92.9665	92.7841	92.6016	92.4191	92.3367	.006082
52	93.3053	93.0609	92.8165	92.5721	92.3278	92.0834	91.8390	91.5946	91.3502	91.1058	90.8615	90.6171	.008146
51	92.6497	92.3979	92.1460	91.8942	91.6424	91.3906	91.1387	90.8869	90.6351	90.3833	90.1314	89.8796	.008394
50	91.8157	91.5934	91.3711	91.1487	90.9264	90.7041	90.4818	90.2595	90.0372	89.8148	89.5925	89.3702	.007410
49	90.7976	90.6048	90.4119	90.2191	90.0262	89.8334	89.6405	89.4477	89.2549	89.0620	88.8692	88.6763	.006428
48	89.6973	89.5249	89.3525	89.1801	89.0078	88.8354	88.6630	88.4906	88.3182	88.1458	87.9735	87.8011	.005746
47	88.5387	88.3841	88.2295	88.0750	87.9204	87.7658	87.6112	87.4567	87.3021	87.1475	86.9930	86.8384	.005152
46	87.3496	87.2099	87.0702	86.9305	86.7908	86.6511	86.5113	86.3716	86.2319	86.0922	85.9525	85.8128	.004657
45	86.1565	86.0288	85.9010	85.7733	85.6455	85.5178	85.3900	85.2623	85.1346	85.0068	84.8791	84.7513	.004258
44	84.9689	84.8516	84.7343	84.6170	84.4997	84.3824	84.2650	84.1477	84.0304	83.9131	83.7958	83.6785	.003910
43	83.7877	83.6800	83.5724	83.4647	83.3571	83.2494	83.1418	83.0341	82.9265	82.8188	82.7112	82.6055	.003588
42	82.6221	82.5226	82.4231	82.3237	82.2242	82.1247	82.0252	81.9258	81.8263	81.7268	81.6273	81.5279	.003316
41	81.4767	81.3843	81.2919	81.1995	81.1072	81.0148	80.9224	80.8300	80.7376	80.6452	80.5529	80.4605	.003079
40	80.3479	80.2623	80.1767	80.0910	80.0054	79.9198	79.8342	79.7486	79.6630	79.5773	79.4917	79.4061	.002854
39	79.2327	79.1535	79.0744	78.9952	78.9161	-8.8369	78.7577	78.6786	78.5994	78.5203	78.4411	78.3620	.002638
38	78.1292	78.0562	77.9831	77.9101	77.8371	77.7641	77.6910	77.6180	77.5450	77.4720	77.3990	77.3259	.002434
37	77.0276	76.9611	76.8946	76.8281	76.7616	76.6951	76.6285	76.5620	76.4955	76.4290	76.3625	76.2960	.002217
36	75.9209	75.8610	75.8012	75.7413	75.6814	75.6216	75.5617	75.5018	75.4420	75.3821	75.3222	75.2624	.001995
35	74.8015	74.7486	74.6957	74.6428	74.5899	74.5370	74.4840	74.4311	74.3782	74.3253	74.2724	74.2195	.001763
34	73.6642	73.6183	73.5725	73.5266	73.4808	73.4349	73.3890	73.3432	73.2973	73.2515	73.2056	73.1598	.001528
33	7[illegible].5069	72.4680	72.4290	72.3900	72.3511	72.3121	72.2732	72.2342	72.1953	72.1563	72.1174	72.0784	.001298
32	7[illegible]3278	71.2956	71.2635	71.2313	71.1992	71.1670	71.1348	71.1027	71.0705	71.0384	71.0062	70.9741	.001072
31	70[illegible]281	70.1024	70.0766	70.0509	70.0251	69.9994	69.9736	69.9479	69.9222	69.8964	69.8707	69.8449	.000858
30	68.9103	68.8906	68.8709	68.8512	68.8315	68.8118	68.7921	68.7724	68.7527	68.7330	68.7133	68.6936	.000657
29	67.6737	67.6597	67.6457	67.6318	67.6178	67.6038	67.5898	67.5759	67.5619	67.5479	67.5340	67.5200	.000466
28	66.4189	66.4104	66.4020	66.3935	66.3851	66.3766	66.3682	66.3597	66.3513	66.3428	66.3344	66.3260	.000282
27	65.1471	65.1439	65.1406	65.1374	65.1342	65.1309	65.1277	65.1245	65.1212	65.1180	65.1148	65.1115	.000108
26	63.8592	63.8609	63.8626	63.8643	63.8660	63.8677	63.8693	63.8710	63.8727	63.8744	63.8761	63.8778	.000056
25	62.5566	62.5629	62.5692	62.5756	62.5819	62.5882	62.5945	62.6009	62.6072	62.6135	62.6198	62.6262	.000211
24	61.2400	61.2507	61.2614	61.2721	61.2828	61.2935	61.3042	61.3149	61.3256	61.3363	61.3470	61.3577	.000357
23	59.9122	59.9269	59.9416	59.9562	59.9709	59.9856	60.0003	60.0150	60.0297	60.0443	60.0590	60.0737	.000489
22	58.5735	58.5920	58.6105	58.6290	58.6475	58.6660	58.6845	58.7030	58.7215	58.7400	58.7585	58.7770	.000617
21	57.2253	57.2473	57.2693	57.2913	57.3134	57.3354	57.3574	57.3794	57.4014	57.4234	57.4455	57.4675	.000734
20	55.8686	55.8939	55.9192	55.9445	55.9699	55.9952	56.0205	56.0458	56.0711	56.0964	56.1218	56.1471	.000844
19	54.5089	54.5370	54.5650	54.5931	54.6212	54.6493	54.6773	54.7054	54.7335	54.7616	54.7896	54.8177	.000936
18	53.1466	53.1772	53.2077	53.2383	53.2689	53.2994	53.3300	53.3606	53.3911	53.4217	53.4523	53.4828	.001019
17	51.7856	51.8183	51.8509	51.8836	51.9163	51.9489	51.9816	52.0143	52.0469	52.0796	52.1123	52.1449	.001087
16	50.4270	50.4615	50.4960	50.5305	50.5650	50.5995	50.6340	50.6685	50.7030	50.7375	50.7720	50.8065	.001150
15	49.0746	49.1105	49.1465	49.1824	49.2183	49.2543	49.2902	49.3261	49.3621	49.3980	49.4339	49.4699	.001198
14	47.7296	47.7667	47.8038	47.8409	47.8780	47.9151	47.9522	47.9894	48.0265	48.0636	48.1007	48.1378	.001237
13	46.3966	46.4344	46.4722	46.5100	46.5478	46.5856	46.6233	46.6611	46.6989	46.7367	46.7745	46.8123	.001260
12	45.0771	45.1153	45.1536	45.1918	45.2301	45.2683	45.3065	45.3448	45.3830	45.4213	45.4595	45.4978	.001275
11	43.7723	43.8107	43.8492	43.8876	43.9261	43.9645	44.0030	44.0414	44.0798	44.1183	44.1567	44.1952	.001281
10	42.4813	42.5199	42.5585	42.5972	42.6358	42.6744	42.7130	42.7517	42.7903	42.8289	42.8675	42.9062	.001287
Age.	0	1	2	3	4	5	6	7	8	9	10	11	Day.

LIFE POLICIES. **TABLE III.** **SYNOPSIS.**

	1st Year.		2nd Year.		3rd Year.		4th Year.		5th Year.		6th Year.		
Age.	3 per cent.	4 per cent.	3 per cent.	4 per cent.	3 per cent.	4 per cent.	3 per cent.	4 per cent.	3 per cent.	4 per cent.	3 per cent.	4 per cent.	Age.
10	.5569	.4115	1.1297	.8397	1.7250	1.2856	2.3368	1.7487	2.9667	2.2292	3.6155	2.7276	10
11	.5759	.4300	1.1745	.8777	1.7898	1.3428	2.4232	1.8253	3.0756	2.3258	3.7465	2.8441	11
12	.6020	.4496	1.2209	.9167	1.8580	1.4013	2.5142	1.9039	3.1890	2.4245	3.8831	2.9640	12
13	.6294	.4692	1.2635	.9560	1.9237	1.4609	2.6025	1.9838	3.3009	2.5257	4.0183	3.0863	13
14	.6450	.4890	1.3092	.9963	1.9923	1.5217	2.6951	2.0662	3.4171	2.6294	4.1590	3.2125	14
15	.6686	.5098	1.3562	1.0378	2.0634	1.5849	2.7901	2.1509	3.5369	2.7368	4.3036	3.3420	15
16	.6922	.5307	1.4042	1.0804	2.1358	1.6495	2.8876	2.2385	3.6595	2.8467	4.4519	3.4757	16
17	.7170	.5529	1.4537	1.1248	2.2107	1.7169	2.9880	2.3284	3.7860	2.9608	4.6057	3.6150	17
18	.7420	.5751	1.5045	1.1705	2.2874	1.7853	3.0911	2.4213	3.9168	3.0791	4.7640	3.7586	18
19	.7681	.5988	1.5569	1.2173	2.3666	1.8569	3.1985	2.5185	4.0520	3.2020	4.9282	3.9083	19
20	.7949	.6222	1.6109	1.2656	2.4493	1.9312	3.3093	2.6188	4.1922	3.3295	5.0986	4.0641	20
21	.8225	.6475	1.6676	1.3172	2.5345	2.0091	3.4246	2.7242	4.3382	3.4635	5.2756	4.2272	21
22	.8521	.6741	1.7262	1.3705	2.6236	2.0903	3.5448	2.8344	4.4900	3.6030	5.4598	4.3972	22
23	.8815	.7011	1.7866	1.4258	2.7158	2.1749	3.6692	2.9488	4.6474	3.7484	5.6504	4.5739	23
24	.9132	.7297	1.8506	1.4842	2.8123	2.2635	3.7992	3.0688	4.8111	3 9001	5.8470	4.7585	24
25	.9460	.7600	1.9166	1.5450	2.9126	2.3562	3.9339	3.1937	4.9793	4.0584	6.0553	4.9513	25
26	.9798	.7910	1.9853	1.6084	3.0163	2.4523	4.0718	3.3236	5.1580	4.2234	6.2693	5.1522	26
27	1.0154	.8239	2.0566	1.6746	3.1225	2.5528	4.2195	3.4598	5.3418	4.3959	6.4923	5.3620	27
28	1.0519	.8577	2.1287	1.7433	3.2369	2.6578	4.3708	3.6017	5.5330	4.5757	6.7241	5 5812	28
29	1.0883	.8932	2.2083	1.8158	3.3542	2.7677	4.5288	3.7502	5.7325	4.7643	6.9660	5.8118	29
30	1.1322	.9307	2.2908	1.8914	3.4784	2.8828	4.6954	3.9060	5.9424	4.9629	7.2230	6.0540	30
31	1.1718	.9697	2.3730	1.9704	3.6039	3.0033	4.8652	4.0700	6.1605	5.1714	7.4875	6.3084	31
32	1.2154	1.0104	2.4610	2.0535	3.7372	3.1307	5.0478	4.2428	6.3906	5.3909	7.7682	6.5783	32
33	1.2608	1.0536	2.5528	2.1419	3.8796	3.2653	5.2389	4.4252	6.6334	5.6247	8.0634	6.8632	33
34	1.3085	1.0998	2.6522	2.2353	4.0289	3.4075	5.4412	4.6197	6.8894	5.8714	8.3752	7.1652	34
35	1.3616	1.1481	2.7565	2.3338	4.1875	3.5590	5.6549	4.8247	7.1604	6.1338	8.7057	7.4856	35
36	1.4142	1.1990	2.8650	2.4390	4.3526	3.7193	5.8788	5.0426	7.4455	6.4112	9.0530	7.8260	36
37	1.4716	1.2551	2.9806	2.5509	4.5287	3.8903	6.1178	5.2754	7.7484	6.7075	9.4185	8.1866	37
38	1.5316	1.3123	3.1028	2.6687	4.7156	4.0715	6.3705	5.5217	8.0656	7.0196	9.8013	8.5617	38
39	1.5957	1.3744	3.2336	2.7959	4.9142	4.2654	6.6357	5.7832	8.3984	7.3457	10.1925	8.9482	39
40	1.6644	1.4412	3.3723	2.9313	5.1217	4.4702	6.9130	6.0545	8.7362	7.6793	10.5898	9.3417	40
41	1.7368	1.5118	3.5157	3.0733	5.3374	4.6808	7.1915	6.3293	9.0764	8.0160	10.9854	9.7348	41
42	1.8104	1.5855	3.6643	3.2176	5.5511	4.8915	7.4693	6.6041	9.4121	8.3492	11.3802	10.1260	42
43	1.8880	1.6584	3.8096	3.3593	5.7632	5.0995	7.7418	6.8727	9.7463	8.6781	11.7687	10.5135	43
44	1.9586	1.7296	3.9498	3.4991	5.9664	5.3022	8.0095	7.1381	10.0708	9.0044	12.1553	10.9023	44
45	2.0310	1.8007	4.0879	3.6356	6.1718	5.5037	8.2743	7.4029	10.4004	9.3342	12.5462	11.2940	45
46	2.0996	1.8685	4.2266	3.7710	6.3727	5.7050	8.5430	7.6716	10.7332	9.6674	12.9402	11.6901	46
47	2.1727	1.9386	4.3648	3.9095	6.5816	5.9136	8.8188	7.9473	11.0732	10.0086	13.3449	12.0951	47
48	2.2408	2.0098	4.5068	4.0536	6.7937	6.1275	9.0982	8.2295	11.4203	10.3573	13.7513	12.5089	48
49	2.3179	2.0857	4.6572	4.2021	7.0145	6.3473	9.3899	8.5187	11.7743	10.7144	14.1733	12.9335	49
50	2.3949	2.1616	4.8081	4.3524	7.2398	6.5701	9.6808	8.8125	12.1367	11.0789	14.6009	13.3664	50
51	2.4725	2.2392	4.9638	4.5059	7.4647	6.7979	9.9809	9.1143	12.5055	11.4524	15.0367	13.8086	51
52	2.5546	2.3186	5.1188	4.6631	7.6988	7.0326	10.2874	9.4242	12.8827	11.8343	15.4848	14.2637	52
53	2.6315	2.4002	5.2791	4.8259	7.9356	7.2743	10.5989	9.7416	13.2692	12.2286	15.9418	14.7315	53
54	2.7192	2.4854	5.4475	4.9940	8.1828	7.5220	10.9253	10.0702	13.6707	12.6346	16.4146	15.2119	54
55	2.8046	2.5724	5.6164	5.1650	8.4354	7.7781	11.2570	10.4079	14.0783	13.0509	16.8897	15.6981	55
56	2.8929	2.6609	5.7933	5.3430	8.6963	8.0423	11.5990	10.7550	14.4915	13.4721	17.3701	16.1897	56
57	2.9868	2.7555	5.9763	5.5285	8.9655	8.3154	11.9442	11.1068	14.9085	13.8987	17.8517	16.6841	57
58	3.0816	2.8516	6.1628	5.7175	9.2332	8.5879	12.2888	11.4590	15.3226	14.3233	18.3310	17.1771	58
59	3.1792	2.9500	6.3472	5.9047	9.5000	8.8600	12.6303	11.8084	15.7343	14.7459	18.8049	17.6656	59
60	3.2720	3.0445	6.5283	6.0896	9.7614	9.1277	12.9674	12.1545	16.1388	15.1629	19.2710	18.1486	60
61	3.3665	3.1408	6.7089	6.2742	10.0233	9.3961	13.3021	12.4990	16.5402	15.5784	19.7323	18.6247	61
62	3.4589	3.2350	6.8888	6.4582	10.2818	9.6617	13.6327	12.8409	16.9360	15.9861	20 1852	19.0944	62
63	3.5528	3.3308	7.0673	6.6415	10.5383	9.9270	13.9600	13.1773	17.3256	16.3895	20.6324	19.5591	63
64	3.6440	3.4247	7.2428	6.8235	10.7906	10.1857	14.2802	13.5086	17.7088	16.7874	21.0759	20.0207	64
65	3.7349	3.5193	7.4169	7.0007	11.0384	10.4415	14.5967	13.8366	18.0911	17.1845	21.5158	20.4790	65
66	3.8248	3.6085	7.5868	7.1748	11.2832	10.6937	14.9132	14.1637	18.4707	17.5783	21.9533	20.9344	66
67	3.9116	3.6998	7.7550	7.3504	11.5294	10.9504	15.2284	14.4928	18.8495	17.9744	22.3894	21.3916	67
68	3.9998	3.7909	7.9279	7.5292	11.7775	11.2077	15.5459	14.8153	19.2300	18.3716	22.8281	21.8498	68
69	4.0917	3.8856	8.1017	7.7091	12.0272	11.4669	15.8647	15.1552	19.6127	18.7705	23.2673	22.3089	69
70	4.1810	3.9780	8.2740	7.8878	12.2752	11.7253	16.1831	15.4866	19.9936	19.1681	23.7058	22.7676	70
71	4.2716	4.0718	8.4474	8.0682	12.5258	11.9854	16.5026	15.8194	20.3767	19.5680	24.1494	23.2317	71
72	4.3621	4.1660	8.6226	8.2495	12.7768	12.2462	16.8238	16.1539	20.7648	19.9732	24.5941	23.6972	72
73	4.4548	4.2610	8.7984	8.4315	13.0300	12.5091	17.1508	16.4944	21.1548	20.3803	25.0392	24.1618	73
74	4.5462	4.3561	8.9751	8.6151	13.2880	12.7778	17.4787	16.8367	21.5442	20.7865	25.4902	24.6329	74
75	4.6398	4.4530	9.1591	8.8053	13.5484	13.0490	17.8075	17.1788	21.9415	21.2003	25.9557	25.1181	75
76	4.7381	4.5551	9.3420	8.9966	13.8084	13.3188	18.1435	17.5278	22.3530	21.5741	26.4535	25.6347	76
77	4.8329	4.6535	9.5214	9.1820	14.0721	13.5918	18.4910	17.8879	22.7954	22.0856	27.0087	26.2079	77
78	4.9266	4.7495	9.7084	9.3746	14.3517	13.8804	18.8747	18.2829	23.3020	22.6064	27.6517	26.8681	78
79	5.0296	4.8557	9.9135	9.5862	14.6709	14.2082	19.3275	18.7473	23.9027	23.2215	28.4255	27.6597	79
80	5.1426	4.9719	10.1519	9.8298	15.0552	14.6006	19.8726	19.3031	24.6349	23.9678	29.3370	28.5960	80
81	5.2809	5.1121	10.4500	10.1325	15.5286	15.0810	20.5491	19.9898	25.5061	24.8602	30.4242	29.6947	81
82	5.4573	5.2908	10.8191	10.5059	16.1195	15.6792	21.3529	20.8120	26.5452	25.9070	31.6777	30.9682	82
83	5.6713	5.5065	11.2776	10.9687	16.8131	16.3883	22.3051	21.7679	27.7339	27.1118	33.0784	32.3904	83
84	5.9434	5.7806	11.8116	11.5159	17.6339	17.2090	23.3890	22.8644	29.0549	28.4506	34.5836	33.9198	84
85	6.2391	6.0870	12.4293	12.1296	18.5481	18.1319	24.5720	24.0608	30.4499	29.8656	36.1701	35.5327	85
86	6.6021	6.4340	13.1280	12.8254	19.5528	19.1386	25.8219	25.3197	31.9227	31.3540	37.8053	37.1910	06
87	6.9873	6.8308	13.8661	13.5782	20.5784	20.1843	27.1105	26.6336	33.4089	32.8720	39.3572	38.7737	87
88	7.3956	7.2421	14.6121	14.3325	21.6349	21.2546	28.4064	27.9504	34.8016	34.2848	40.6748	40.1312	88
89	7.7928	7.6440	15.3765	15.1066	22.6888	22.3251	29.5947	29.1541	35.9369	35.4213	41.6326	41.1243	89
90	8.2246	8.0803	16.1549	15.8962	23.6444	23.2905	30.5226	30.1150	36.6997	36.2514	41.6552	41.1820	90
91	8.6410	8.5030	16.8017	16.5472	24.2963	23.9717	31.0269	30.6476	36.4265	36.0115	40.6070	40.1630	91
92	8.9326	8.7918	17.1361	16.9062	24.5033	24.2025	30.4136	30.0650	34.9895	34.6023	41.0826	40.6585	92
93	9.0081	8.8965	17.0980	16.8961	23.5880	23.3237	28.6126	28.2984	35.3035	34.9384	47.9395	47.5470	93
94	8.8907	8.7808	16.0232	15.8361	21.5454	21.2965	28.8986	28.5849	42.7855	42.4248	**100.000**	**100.000**	**94** or **15**
95	7.8285	7.7344	13.8896	13.7205	21.9603	21.7105	37.2024	36.8826	**100.000**	**100.000**	95.7960	95.0239	14
96	6.5758	6.4879	15.3320	15.1477	31.8687	31.5917	**100.000**	**100.000**	95.8221	95.0472	94.8081	93.8567	13
97	9.3725	9.2606	27.0731	26.8454	**100.000**	**100.000**	95.8473	95.0695	94.8394	93.8843	94.3057	93.2601	12
98	19.5312	19.3799	**100.000**	**100.000**	95.8712	95.0907	94.8691	93.9106	94.3385	93.2891	93.9400	92.8235	11
99 or **10**	**100.000**	**100.000**	95.8942	95.1109	94.8977	93.9356	94.3700	93.3167	93.9737	92.8529	93.4619	92.2539	10
	90th Year.		**89th Year.**		**88th Year.**		**87th Year.**		**86th Year.**		**85th Year.**		**95**

LIFE POLICIES.					TABLE III.							SYNOPSIS.		
	7th Year.		8th Year.		9th Year.		10th Year.		11th Year.		12th Year.		
Age.	3 per cent.	4 per cent.	3 per cent.	4 per cent.	3 per cent.	4 per cent.	3 per cent-	4 per cent.	3 per cent.	4 per cent.	3 per cent.	4 per cent.	Age.
10	4.2826	3.2440	4.9689	3.7788	5.6740	4.3321	6.3987	4.9050	7.1426	5.4967	7.9064	6.1086	10
11	4.4367	3.3812	5.1457	3.9369	5.8744	4.5121	6.6226	5.1062	7.3907	5.7207	8.1797	6.3561	11
12	4.5963	3.5220	5.3292	4.0998	6.0817	4.6964	6.8542	5.3135	7.6478	5.9518	8.4620	6.6112	12
13	4.7557	3.6666	5.5128	4.2660	6.2900	4.8858	7.0884	5.5270	7.9076	6.1894	8.7486	6.8740	13
14	4.9208	3.8147	5.7029	4.4374	6.5063	5.0817	7.3307	5.7472	8.1769	6.4350	9.0456	7.1460	14
15	5.0908	3.9678	5.8994	4.6152	6.7291	5.2840	7.5808	5.9752	8.4552	6.6897	9.3522	7.4278	15
16	5.2660	4.1267	6.1013	4.7986	6.9587	5.4934	7.8390	6.2116	8.7420	6.9535	9.6687	7.7201	16
17	5.4468	4.2907	6.3102	4.9892	7.1966	5.7112	8.1060	6.4571	9.0391	7.2278	9.9959	8.0235	17
18	5.6336	4.4609	6.5264	5.1870	7.4423	5.9370	8.3822	6.7120	9.3458	7.5121	10.3324	8.3382	18
19	5.8276	4.6386	6.7504	5.3930	7.6973	6.1725	8.6682	6.9772	9.6621	7.8081	10.6850	8.6661	19
20	6.0285	4.8230	6.9827	5.6072	7.9612	6.4168	8.9628	7.2527	9.9936	8.1159	11.0483	9.0069	20
21	6.2375	5.0162	7.2237	5.8309	8.2334	6.6720	9.2725	7.5407	10.3356	8.4372	11.4254	9.3624	21
22	6.4543	5.2172	7.4723	6.0638	8.5200	6.9380	9.5920	7.8405	10.6908	8.7718	11.8168	9.7330	22
23	6.6772	5.4263	7.7339	6.3065	8.8150	7.2150	9.9233	8.1526	11.0590	9.1203	12.2228	10.1199	23
24	6.9131	5.6449	8.0039	6.5598	9.1220	7.5041	10.2678	8.4782	11.4419	9.4852	12.6477	10.5244	24
25	7.1561	5.8730	8.2845	6.8241	9.4409	7.8059	10.6258	8.8199	11.8427	9.8666	13.0894	10.9473	25
26	7.4085	6.1106	8.5759	7.0998	9.7722	8.1216	11.0007	9.1764	12.2593	10.2653	13.5505	11.3916	26
27	7.6713	6.3591	8.8794	7.3890	10.1200	8.4522	11.3911	9.5499	12.6951	10.6851	14.0322	11.8571	27
28	7.9446	6.6196	9.1980	7.6917	10.4821	8.7984	11.7994	9.9431	13.1502	11.1249	14.5361	12.3464	28
29	8.2327	6.8931	9.5304	8.0094	10.8618	9.1640	12.2270	10.3560	13.6276	11.5881	15.0652	12.8623	29
30	8.5351	7.1804	9.8811	8.3453	11.2613	9.5481	12.6773	10.7913	14.1307	12.0770	15.6221	13.4062	30
31	8.8489	7.4842	10.2450	8.6983	11.6772	9.9532	13.1473	11.2510	14.6577	12.5927	16.2008	13.9785	31
32	9.1807	7.8043	10.6300	9.0715	12.1175	10.3820	13.6438	11.7368	15.2072	13.1362	16.8081	14.5769	32
33	9.5304	8.1433	11.0362	9.4672	12.5814	10.8358	14.1640	12.2495	15.7846	13.7048	17.4340	15.1973	33
34	9.9002	8.5031	11.4651	9.8864	13.0679	11.3151	14.7092	12.7859	16.3797	14.2943	18.0780	15.8375	34
35	10.2913	8.8843	11.9154	10.3289	13.5784	11.8160	15.2711	13.3412	16.9919	14.9016	18.7347	16.4917	35
36	10.6995	9.2874	12.3855	10.7918	14.1015	12.3347	15.8461	13.9133	17.6129	15.5218	19.4030	17.1596	36
37	11.1287	9.7093	12.8693	11.2709	14.6389	12.8686	16.4311	14.4967	18.2468	16.1543	20.0788	17.8394	37
38	11.5680	10.1431	13.3640	11.7611	15.1830	13.4099	17.0258	15.0886	18.8851	16.7951	20.7653	18.5505	38
39	12.0165	10.5878	13.8637	12.2585	15.7352	13.9595	17.6235	15.6887	19.5329	17.4472	21.4599	19.2316	39
40	12.4670	11.0357	14.3688	12.7604	16.2876	14.5138	18.2280	16.2967	20.1863	18.1060	22.1597	19.9398	40
41	12.9194	11.4847	14.8707	13.2637	16.8439	15.0727	18.8354	16.9085	20.8422	18.7691	22.8643	20.6525	41
42	13.3661	11.9323	15.3742	13.7691	17.4008	15.6330	19.4431	17.5222	21.5009	19.4345	23.5666	21.3682	42
43	13.8138	12.3799	15.8779	14.2739	17.9577	16.1935	20.0535	18.1366	22.1573	20.1015	24.2740	22.0872	43
44	14.2590	12.8282	16.3790	14.7801	18.5151	16.7561	20.6594	18.7541	22.8168	20.7731	24.9814	22.8114	44
45	14.7084	13.2803	16.8873	15.2910	19.0744	17.3242	21.2742	19.3789	23.4827	21.4530	25.6963	23.5430	45
46	15.1838	13.7377	17.3967	15.8081	19.6428	17.9116	21.8965	20.0126	24.1560	22.1410	26.4213	24.2864	46
47	15.6252	14.2050	17.9195	16.3373	20.2215	18.4896	22.5294	20.6585	24.8433	22.8447	27.1593	25.0449	47
48	16.0965	14.6834	18.4496	16.8782	20.8088	19.0899	23.1741	21.3194	25.5415	23.5630	27.9087	25.8179	48
49	16.5804	15.1733	18.9936	17.4304	21.4131	19.7056	23.8348	21.9953	26.2562	24.2964	28.6691	26.6012	49
50	17.0714	15.6716	19.5483	17.9952	22.0275	20.3337	24.5064	22.6839	26.9765	25.0378	29.4348	27.3921	50
51	17.5744	16.1835	20.1144	18.5736	22.6541	20.9757	25.1848	23.3816	27.7034	25.7880	30.2040	28.1888	51
52	18.0891	16.7086	20.6932	19.1657	23.2881	21.6267	25.8706	24.0882	28.4346	26.5440	30.9772	28.9907	52
53	18.6142	17.2469	21.2771	19.7664	23.9273	22 2863	26.5586	24.8004	29.1678	27.3051	31.7489	29.7947	53
54	19.1496	17.7933	21.8714	20.3752	24.5737	22.9511	27.2535	25.5175	29.9044	28.0682	32.5224	30.5997	54
55	19.6875	18.3458	22.4655	20.9874	25.2201	23.6191	27.9451	26.2349	30.6363	28.8309	33.2893	31.3991	55
56	20.2282	18.9010	23.0623	21.6023	25.8659	24.2872	28.6348	26.9517	31.3644	29.5877	34.0491	32.1928	56
57	20.7703	19.4592	23.6574	22.2175	26.5087	24.9549	29.3196	27.6629	32.0844	30.3392	34.8009	32.9799	57
58	21.3070	20.0135	24.2461	22.8285	27.1435	25.6132	29.9934	28.3653	32.7936	31.0809	35.5435	33.7588	58
59	21.8733	20.5632	24.8271	23.4297	27.7676	26.2626	30.6567	29.0579	33.4940	31.8144	36.2747	34.5268	59
60	22.3587	21.1022	25.3958	24.0213	28.3798	26.9015	31.3103	29.7418	34.1823	32.5367	36.9937	35.2837	60
61	22.8721	21.6354	25.9571	24.6061	28.9867	27.5356	31.9558	30 4182	34.8624	33.2515	37.7038	36.0322	61
62	23.3776	22.1614	26.5128	25.1859	29.5854	28.1620	32.5932	31.0871	35.5335	33.9580	38.4054	36.7721	62
63	23.8799	22.6847	27.0625	25.7603	30.1781	28.7832	33.2238	31.7501	36.1986	34.6582	39.0991	37.5046	63
64	24.3758	23.2023	27.6061	26.3294	30.7640	29.3985	33.8483	32 4068	36.8557	35.3512	39.7855	38.2301	64
65	24.8683	23.7169	28.1457	26.8949	31.3466	30.0099	34.4677	33.0587	37.5083	36.0396	40.4692	38.9531	65
66	25.3578	24.2282	28.6830	27.4569	31.9252	30.6169	35.0837	33.7066	38.1595	36.7263	41.1482	39.6707	66
67	25.8467	24.7412	29.2179	28.0195	32.5021	31.2248	35.7002	34.3576	38.8077	37.4122	41.8224	40.3848	67
68	26.3364	25.2541	29.7543	28.5825	33.0828	31.8357	36.3167	35.0077	39.4544	38.0945	42.4993	41.1005	68
69	26.8275	25.7685	30.2945	29.1498	33.6633	32.4468	36.9315	35.6553	40.1036	38.7797	43.1838	41.8235	69
70	27.3207	26.2856	30.8332	29.7159	34.2408	33.0540	37.5482	36.3047	40.7598	39.4716	43.8882	42.5659	70
71	27.8151	26.8041	31.3714	30.2806	34.8231	33.6658	38.1749	36 9640	41.4398	40.1865	44.6356	43.3511	71
72	28.3091	27.3212	31.9148	30.8506	35.4162	34.2884	38.8268	37.6476	42.1652	40.9466	45.4453	44.1983	72
73	28.8094	27.8510	32.4704	31.4318	36.0366	34.9371	39.5273	38.3794	42.9569	41.7726	46.3471	45.1384	73
74	29.3219	28.3801	33.0543	32.0414	36.7077	35.6369	40.3247	39.1810	43.8456	42.6967	47.3490	46.1849	74
75	29.8659	28.9462	33.6933	32.7055	37.4538	36.4111	41.1711	40.0869	44.8415	43.7339	48.4831	47.3541	75
76	30.4671	29.5692	34.4105	33.4475	38.3088	37.2946	42.1577	41.1116	45.9765	44.9005	49.7513	48.6643	76
77	31.1483	30.2712	35.2404	34.3020	39.2808	38.3012	43.2895	42.2709	47.2520	46.2143	51.1530	50.1095	77
78	31.9516	31.0955	36.1973	35.2899	40.4096	39.4534	44.5733	43.5892	48.6724	47.6745	52.6723	51.6743	78
79	32.8911	32.0632	37.3216	36.4343	41.7012	40.7764	46.0127	45.0654	50.2199	49.2646	54.3141	53.3641	79
80	34.0022	33.1902	38.6137	37.7539	43.1536	42.2618	47.5835	46.6753	51.8946	50.9841	56.0513	55.1519	80
81	35.2857	34.4972	40.0717	39.2409	44.7418	43.8853	49.2866	48.4195	53.6687	52.8054	57.8073	56.9547	81
82	36.7305	35.9675	41.6610	40.8623	46.4592	45.6406	51.0856	50.2628	55.4550	54.6356	59.4676	58.6715	82
83	38.2935	37.5585	43.3686	42.6039	48.2621	47.4843	52.8836	52.1014	57.1280	56.3627	60.9396	60.1944	83
84	39.9638	39.2592	45.1515	44.4240	50.0508	49.3102	54.5504	53.8198	58.5912	57.8748	61.8329	61.1329	84
85	41.6856	41.0143	46.8947	46.2002	51.2313	50.9866	55.9746	55.2903	59.4211	58.7483	62.0895	61.4247	85
86	43.3609	42.7131	48.4630	47.8096	53.0450	52.3923	56.7209	56.0745	59 5669	58.9243	63.3564	62.7282	06
87	44.8200	44.2207	49.7259	49.1186	53.6616	53.0540	56.7087	56.0998	60.7662	60.1652	68.4290	67.8850	87
88	45.9492	45.3882	50.1806	49.6120	53.4566	52.8812	57.8189	57.2447	66.0574	65.5304	**100.000**	**100.000**	**88** or **21**
89	46.2019	45.6780	49.7396	49.2024	54.4503	53.9065	63 3466	62.8392	**100.000**	**100.000**	95.6135	94.8587	20
90	45.4918	45.9980	50.6006	50.0961	60.2489	59.7635	**100.000**	**100.000**	95.6472	94.8895	94.5907	93.6610	19
91	46.1736	45.7043	56.6866	56.2266	**100.000**	**100.000**	95.6795	94.9189	94.6309	93.6975	94.0756	93.0543	18
92	52.5899	52.1586	**100.000**	**100.000**	95.7105	94.9470	94.6694	93.7323	94.1181	93.0927	93.7041	92.6134	17
93 or **16**	**100.000**	**100.000**	95.7402	94.9738	94.7063	93.7656	94.1588	93.1293	93.7477	92.6526	93.2166	92.0367	16
15	95.7687	94.9994	94.7417	93.7974	94.1979	93.1643	93.7895	92.6901	93.2620	92.0773	92.6045	91.3147	15
14	94.7756	93.8277	94.2353	93.1978	93.8295	92.7258	93.3054	92.1160	92.6522	91.3571	91.9247	90.5131	14
13	94.2712	93.2297	93.8679	92.7600	93.3471	92.1530	92.6979	91.3977	91.9750	90.5577	91.1878	89.6475	13
12	93.9049	92.7925	93.3872	92.1883	92.7419	91.4364	92.0233	90.6001	91.2409	89.6940	90.4124	88.7363	12
11	93.4253	92.2219	92.7837	91.4732	92.0693	90.6405	91.2914	89.7384	90.4677	88.7847	89.6134	87.7988	11
10	92.8239	91.5083	92.1134	90.6790	91.3399	89.7806	90.5208	88.8309	89.6713	87.8490	88.7984	86.8433	10
96	**84th Year.**		**83rd Year.**		**82nd Year.**		**81st Year.**		**80th Year.**		**79th Year.**		

	13th Year.		14th Year.		15th Year.		16th Year.		17th Year.		18th Year.		
Age.	3 per cent.	4 per cent.	3 per cent.	4 per cent.	3 per cent.	4 per cent.	3 per cent.	4 per cent.	3 per cent.	4 per cent.	3 per cent.	4 per cent.	Age.
10	8.6911	6.7415	9.4960	7.3954	10.3226	8.0711	11.1710	8.7698	12.0414	9.4915	12.9346	10.2372	10
11	8.9893	7.0127	9.8203	7.6913	10.6735	8.3929	11.5488	9.1175	12.4470	9.8663	13.3679	10.6394	11
12	9.2980	7.2927	10.1561	7.9973	11.0364	8.7250	11.9398	9.4770	12.8661	10.2535	13.8143	11.0551	12
13	9.6119	7.5817	10.4975	8.3128	11.4064	9.0682	12.3383	9.8481	13.2923	10.6534	14.2741	11.4850	13
14	9.9368	7.8805	10.8514	8.6395	11.7891	9.4231	12.7491	10.2322	13.7370	11.0677	14.7478	11.9300	14
15	10.2727	8.1906	11.2165	8.9780	12.1827	9.7910	13.1771	10.6306	14.1944	11.4972	15.2373	12.3915	15
16	10.6189	8.5116	11.5916	9.3288	12.5926	10.1727	13.6169	11.0437	14.6667	11.9426	15.7427	12.8704	16
17	10.9754	8.8451	11.9834	9.6935	13.0148	10.5692	14.0720	11.4728	15.1554	12.4056	16.2655	13.3690	17
18	11.3478	9.1914	12.3866	10.0719	13.4514	10.9806	14.5426	11.9186	15.6608	12.8873	16.8092	13.8874	18
19	11.7316	9.5518	12.8044	10.4658	13.9038	11.4091	15.0303	12.3836	16.1873	13.3893	17.3725	14.4278	19
20	12.1294	9.9263	13.2373	10.8754	14.3725	11.8556	15.5384	12.8676	16.7329	13.9123	17.9582	14.9927	20
21	12.5421	10.3174	13.6865	11.3038	14.8617	12.3221	16.0657	13.3733	17.3009	14.4625	18.5675	15.5831	21
22	12.9706	10.7258	14.1556	11.7507	15.3696	12.8088	16.6150	13.9032	17.8921	15.0329	19.2023	16.2007	22
23	13.4179	11.1517	14.6423	12.2170	15.8984	13.3187	17.1865	14.4563	18.5080	15.6320	19.8644	16.8479	23
24	13.8830	11.5972	15.1503	12.7067	16.4498	13.8523	17.7830	15.0363	19.1515	16.2608	20.5557	17.5268	24
25	14.3684	12.0650	15.6799	13.2190	17.0254	14.4117	18.4064	15.6452	19.8236	16.9205	21.2751	18.2377	25
26	14.8745	12.5544	16.2329	13.7563	17.6271	14.9992	19.0578	16.2843	20.5232	17.6116	22.0237	18.9779	26
27	15.4039	13.0686	16.8120	14.3215	18.2568	15.6168	19.7367	16.9546	21.2521	18.3319	22.7945	19.7444	27
28	15.9586	13.6097	17.4182	14.9158	18.9133	16.2647	20.4442	17.6534	22.0024	19.0776	23.5865	20.5348	28
29	16.5403	14.1797	18.0513	15.5403	19.5985	16.9410	21.1732	18.3776	22.7742	19.8473	24.3904	21.3450	29
30	17.1497	14.7791	18.7139	16.1925	20.3060	17.6419	21.9245	19.1250	23.5638	20.6361	25.2245	22.1747	30
31	17.7830	15.4051	19.3933	16.8682	21.0304	18.3651	22.6884	19.8905	24.3681	21.4436	26.0629	23.0224	31
32	18.4375	16.0542	20.0940	17.5658	21.7717	19.1061	23.4714	20.6743	25.1862	22.2686	26.9204	23.8897	32
33	19.1109	16.7243	20.8092	18.2803	22.5298	19.8646	24.2658	21.4750	26.0212	23.1129	27.7929	24.7749	33
34	19.7980	17.4101	21.5406	19.0113	23.2987	20.6390	25.0766	22.2942	26.8710	23.9738	28.6790	25.6762	34
35	20.5003	18.1106	22.2818	19.7565	24.0832	21.4300	25.9013	23.1284	27.7334	24.8497	29.5795	26.5922	35
36	21.2090	18.8245	23.0353	20.5176	24.8785	22.2356	26.7358	23.9770	28.6074	25.7396	30.4861	27.5220	36
37	21.9313	19.5530	23.8009	21.2919	25.6849	23.0544	27.5833	24.8384	29.4889	26.6424	31.4064	28.4656	37
38	22.6628	20.2915	24.5750	22.0764	26.5017	23.8831	28.4358	25.7100	30.3817	27.5564	32.3342	29.4201	38
39	23.4018	21.0402	25.3585	22.8709	27.3227	24.7222	29.2989	26.5931	31.2818	28.4815	33.2697	30.3845	39
40	24.1482	21.7961	26.1442	23.6731	28.1525	25.5701	30.1675	27.4848	32.1877	29.4144	34.2131	31.3593	40
41	24.8941	22.5570	26.9363	24.4817	28.9855	26.4245	31.0399	28.3822	33.0995	30.3556	35.1611	32.3416	41
42	25.6451	23.3225	27.7303	25.2950	29.8210	27.2829	31.9171	29.2866	34.0160	31.3030	36.1129	33.3296	42
43	26.3978	24.0916	28.5270	26.1114	30.6618	28.1474	32.7985	30.1963	34.9349	32.2555	37.0638	34.3180	43
44	27.1516	24.8653	29.3275	26.9356	31.5053	29.0192	33.6828	31.1131	35.8528	33.2103	38.0122	35.3080	44
45	27.9156	25.6497	30.1359	27.7699	32.3580	29.9007	34.5713	32.0349	36.7739	34.1695	38.9608	36.2992	45
46	28.6886	26.4454	30.9557	28.6153	33.2149	30.7886	35.4632	32.9624	37.6954	35.1311	39.9090	37.2917	46
47	29.4750	27.2560	31.7826	29.4707	34.0791	31.6859	36.3592	33.8959	38.6203	36.0977	40.8570	38.2862	47
48	30.2675	28.0764	32 6150	30.3353	34.9458	32 5890	37.2570	34.8344	39.5434	37.0661	41.8014	39.2809	48
49	31.0705	28.9065	33.4546	31.2064	35.8189	33.4978	38.1576	35.7753	40.4674	38.0356	42.7444	40.2716	49
50	31.8756	29.7411	34.2959	32.0813	36.6902	34.4073	39.0547	36.7157	41.3858	38.9993	43.6785	41.2562	50
51	32.6838	30.5807	35.1368	32.9581	37.5594	35.3175	39.9476	37.6516	42.2966	39.9583	44.6047	42.2344	51
52	33.4924	31.4225	35.9764	33.8360	38.4252	36.2235	40.8338	38.5830	43.2003	40.9113	45.5244	43.2072	52
53	34.2980	32.2654	36.8110	34.7097	39.2827	37.1252	41.7113	39.5088	44.0963	41.8592	46.4337	44.1720	53
54	35.1032	33.1041	37.6418	35.5790	40.1360	38.0212	42.5855	40.4294	44.9850	42.7991	47.3360	45.1282	54
55	35.8988	33.9371	38.4627	36.4415	40.9806	38.9111	43.4483	41.3412	45.8639	43.7297	48.2254	46.0739	55
56	36.6871	34.7633	39.2776	37.2981	41.8165	39.7924	44.3018	42.2439	46.7315	44.6500	49.1044	47.0085	56
57	37.4687	35.5840	40.0831	38.1465	42.6425	40.6651	45.1445	43.1370	47.5882	45.5599	49.9709	47.9314	57
58	38.2384	36.3939	40.8766	38.9838	43.4557	41.5258	45.9746	44.0174	48.4308	46.4560	50.8234	48.8403	58
59	38.9968	37.1928	41.6578	39.8993	44.2568	42.3741	46.7910	44.8843	49.2598	47.3386	51.6640	49.7374	59
60	39.7421	37.9798	42.4265	40.6224	45.0439	43.2090	47.5937	45.7379	50.0768	48.2096	52.4895	50.6196	60
61	40.4789	38.7579	43.1849	41.4257	45.8210	44.0340	48.3881	46.5833	50.8824	49.0690	53.3022	51.4880	61
62	41.2056	39.5264	43.9335	42.2193	46.5900	44.8512	49.1713	47.4176	51.6754	49.9150	54.1059	52.3470	62
63	41.9248	40.2875	44.6765	43.0075	47.3502	45.6596	49.9441	48.2405	52.4616	50.7538	54.9063	53.2023	63
64	42.6385	41.0438	45.4108	43.7873	48.1002	46.4571	50.7105	49.0570	53.2453	51.5898	55.7143	54.0646	64
65	43.3463	41.7939	46.1374	44.5584	48.8465	47.2505	51.4771	49.8731	54.0395	52.4357	56.5477	54.9522	65
66	44.0476	42.5360	46.8618	45.3263	49.5945	48.0447	52.2563	50.7007	54.8618	53.3090	57.4218	55.8800	66
67	44.7485	43.2796	47.5899	46.0997	50.3576	48.8551	53.0667	51.5611	55.7285	54.2284	58.3597	56.8742	67
68	45.4563	44.0289	48.3367	46.8902	51.1561	49.7001	53.9262	52.4699	56.6646	55.2174	59.3683	57.9434	68
69	46.1842	44.7975	49.1211	47.7182	52.0066	50.5971	54.8590	53.4528	57.6754	56.2863	60.4697	59.0988	69
70	46.9504	45.6046	49.9590	48.5999	52.9331	51.5711	55.8697	54.5191	58.7832	57.4453	61.6631	60.3522	70
71	47.7755	46.4704	50.8794	49.5648	53.9441	52.6349	56.9847	55.6824	59.9903	58.7096	62.9493	61.6999	71
72	48.6875	47.4240	51.8890	50.6244	55.0653	53.8012	58.2050	56.9570	61.2960	60.0742	64.3122	63.1261	72
73	49.6946	48.4780	53.0158	51.7929	56.2987	55.0859	59.5307	58.3386	62.6844	61.5232	65.7534	64.6322	73
74	50.8252	49.6474	54.2612	53.0869	57.6438	56.4844	60.9446	59.8107	64.1567	63.0581	67.2539	66.1993	74
75	52.0827	50.9503	55.6265	54.5025	59.0845	57.9803	62.4496	61.3756	65.6943	64.6598	68.7587	67.7669	75
76	53.4675	52.3820	57.0937	56.0220	60.6226	59.5755	64 0252	63.0128	67.2386	66.2646	70.1898	69.2659	76
77	54.9596	53.9231	58.6640	57.6462	62.2358	61.2476	65.6092	64.6546	68.7071	67.7991	71.4893	70.6266	77
78	56.5648	55.5791	60.3180	59.3562	63.8627	62.9296	67.1180	66.2275	70.0414	69.1930	72.3867	71.5758	78
79	58.2618	57.3296	61.9901	61.0811	65.4141	64.5435	68.4890	67.6569	70.9559	70.1584	72.8657	72.0945	79
80	59.9771	59.0949	63.5824	62.7340	66.8202	66.0062	69.4177	68.6355	71.4287	70.6703	74.1066	73.3865	80
81	61.6081	60.7842	65.0214	64.2277	67.7597	66.9945	69.8798	69.1358	72.7028	71.9940	78.0343	77.4215	81
82	63.0712	62.3004	65.9622	65.2163	68.2005	67.4730	71.1809	70.4852	76.8096	76.2050	**100.000**	**100.000**	**82 or 27**
83	63.9974	63.2731	66.3689	65.6559	69.5174	68.8364	75.4710	74.8758	**100.000**	**100.000**	95.3779	94.6409	26
84	64.3427	63.6546	67.6847	67.0204	73.9962	73.4117	**100.000**	**100.000**	95.4216	94.6816	94.3103	93.4032	25
85	65.6427	64.9970	72.3531	71.7804	**100.000**	**100.000**	95.4634	94.7204	94.3623	93.4513	93.7793	92.7830	24
86	70.5134	69.9513	**100.000**	**100.000**	95.5034	94.7575	94.4120	93.4972	93.8341	92.8336	93.4001	92.3362	23
87 or 22	**100.000**	**100.000**	95.5417	94.7928	94.4596	93.5411	93.8866	92.8192	93.4563	92.3880	92.9006	91.7500	22
21	95.5784	94.8265	94.5052	93.5829	93.9369	92.9280	93.5102	92.4373	92.9590	91.8034	92.2719	91.0144	21
20	94.5489	93.6228	93.9851	92.9720	93.5617	92.4844	93.0149	91.8544	92.3333	91.0703	91.5743	90.1983	20
19	94.0313	93.0141	93.6112	92.5294	93.0686	91.9032	92.3922	91.1237	91.6390	90.2570	90.8189	89.3178	19
18	73.6586	92.5724	93.1200	91.9497	92.4486	91.1748	91.7011	90.3130	90.8870	89.3792	90.0251	88.3922	18
17	93.1693	91.9942	92.5028	91.2236	91.7606	90.3665	90.9524	89.4380	90.0966	88.4564	89.2091	87.4416	17
16	92.5547	91.2702	91.8176	90.4177	91.0150	89.4940	90.1652	88.5176	89.2838	87.5083	88.3781	86.4744	16
15	91.8723	90.4665	91.0751	89.5476	90.2309	88.5762	89.3555	87.5720	88.4558	86.5434	87.5339	85.4927	15
14	91.1326	89.5987	90.2939	88.6321	89.4241	87.6327	88.5303	86.6092	87.6143	85.5637	86.6839	84.5052	14
13	90.3544	88.6854	89.4900	87.6908	88.6017	86.6720	87.6914	85.6314	86.7668	84.5780	85.8313	83.5175	13
12	89.5532	87.7461	88.6703	86.7319	87.7655	85.6960	86.8464	84.6473	85.9167	83.5916	84.9795	82.5280	12
11	88.7358	86.7890	87.8360	85.7575	86.9222	84.7133	85.9978	83.6621	85.0660	82.6032	84.1224	81.5358	11
10	87.9037	85.8161	86.9950	84.7762	86.0758	83.7293	85.1492	82.6747	84.2108	81.6118	83.2615	80.5402	10
	78th Year.		77th Year.		76th Year.		75th Year.		74th Year.		73rd Year.		

Age.	19th Year.		20th Year.		21st Year.		22nd Year.		23rd Year.		24th Year.		Age.
	3 per cent.	4 per cent.	3 per cent.	4 per cent.	3 per cent.	4 per cent.	3 per cent.	4 per cent.	3 per cent.	4 per cent.	3 per cent.	4 per cent.	
10	13.8504	11.0071	14.7880	11.8020	15.7528	12.6228	16.7400	13.4701	17.7519	14.3445	18.7890	15.2470	10
11	14.3107	11.4376	15.2810	12.2618	16.2737	13.1126	17.2913	13.9906	18.3341	14.8968	19.4027	15.8328	11
12	14.7902	11.8829	15.7887	12.7374	16.8122	13.6192	17.8610	14.5293	18.9358	15.4693	20.0396	16.4398	12
13	15.2786	12.3433	16.3083	13.2290	17.3635	14.1433	18.4448	15.0875	19.5552	16.0624	20.6928	17.0688	13
14	15.7840	12.8200	16.8458	13.7385	17.9340	14.6872	19.0512	15.6667	20.1960	16.6778	21.3704	17.7236	14
15	16.3060	13.3146	17.4011	14.2680	18.5258	15.2522	19.6780	16.2684	20.8600	17.3192	22.0720	18.4043	15
16	16.8451	13.8287	17.9773	14.8180	19.1373	15.8393	20.3272	16.8956	21.5475	17.9862	22.7993	19.1134	16
17	17.4057	14.3635	18.5737	15.3903	19.7719	16.4522	21.0007	17.5486	22.2613	18.6819	23.5552	19.8538	17
18	17.9856	14.9199	19.1925	15.9877	20.4302	17.0902	21.6998	18.2297	23.0031	19.4082	24.3404	20.6266	18
19	18.5885	15.5018	19.8353	16.6107	21.1145	17.7568	22.4275	18.9421	23.7748	20.1675	25.1548	21.4334	19
20	19.2147	16.1083	20.5038	17.2613	21.8270	18.4538	23.1847	19.6866	24.5754	20.9599	25.9994	22.2708	20
21	19.8670	16.7433	21.2007	17.9432	22.5691	19.1838	23.9711	20.4651	25.4065	21.7841	26.8675	23.1369	21
22	20.5471	17.4085	21.9271	18.6571	23.3405	19.9468	24.7877	21.2744	26.2610	22.6360	27.7586	24.0290	22
23	21.2562	18.1050	22.6817	19.4034	24.1415	20.7401	25.6273	22.1109	27.1378	23.5134	28.6676	24.9426	23
24	21.9940	18.8344	23.4667	20.1804	24.9657	21.5610	26.4896	22.9734	28.0330	24.4127	29.5967	25.8780	24
25	22.7614	19.5937	24.2742	20.9844	25.8122	22.4071	27.3698	23.8570	28.9478	25.3331	30.5400	26.8338	25
26	23.5510	20.3792	25.1036	21.8129	26.6761	23.2739	28.2692	24.7613	29.8766	26.2735	31.5020	27.8112	26
27	24.3625	21.1895	25.9505	22.6621	27.5594	24.1614	29.1827	25.6856	30.8242	27.2356	32.4808	28.8084	27
28	25.1909	22.0196	26.8162	23.5314	28.4562	25.0683	30.1145	26.6310	31.7881	28.2170	33.4747	29.8244	28
29	26.0383	22.8698	27.6956	24.4200	29.3716	25.9963	31.0630	27.5960	32.7674	29.2173	34.4849	30.8584	29
30	26.9001	23.7388	28.5945	25.3294	30.3061	26.9434	32.0277	28.5793	33.7641	30.2353	35.5071	31.9098	30
31	27.7767	24.6279	29.5063	26.2571	31.2493	27.9084	33.0055	29.5799	34.7685	31.2701	36.5422	32.9783	31
32	28.6705	25.5350	30.4341	27.2024	32.2112	28.8903	33.9950	30.5971	35.7898	32.3220	37.5906	34.0630	32
33	29.5782	26.4593	31.3772	28.1645	33.1830	29.8886	34.9998	31.6312	36.8228	33.3900	38.6504	35.1624	33
34	30.5009	27.3995	32.3297	29.1420	34.1698	30.9031	36.0161	32.6807	37.8671	34.4720	39.7228	36.2775	34
35	31.4326	28.3541	33.2970	30.1347	35.1677	31.9320	37.0433	33.7433	38.9237	35.5689	40.8058	37.4063	35
36	32.3763	29.3233	34.2728	31.1415	36.1742	32.9738	38.0806	34.8206	39.9887	36.6793	41.8965	38.5472	36
37	33.3300	30.3059	35.2587	32.1604	37.1924	34.0296	39.1278	35.9109	41.0631	37.8015	42.9915	39.6951	37
38	34.2918	31.2981	36.2543	33.1911	38.2187	35.0963	40.1828	37.0109	42.1400	38.9286	44.0879	40.8467	38
39	35.2628	32.3027	37.2577	34.2332	39.2524	36.1733	41.2401	38.1166	43.2182	40.0601	45.1822	41.9992	39
40	36.2403	33.3167	38.2674	35.2839	40.2873	37.2541	42.2975	39.2248	44.2933	41.1910	46.2725	43.1498	40
41	37.2225	34.3375	39.2765	36.3366	41.3208	38.3361	43.3504	40.3310	45.3630	42.3185	47.3540	44.2939	41
42	38.2033	35.3594	40.2836	37.3896	42.3491	39.4151	44.3973	41.4330	46.4235	43.4388	48.4245	45.4293	42
43	39.1826	36.3809	41.2862	38.4390	43.3721	40.4895	45.4357	42.5276	47.4735	44.5502	49.4826	46.5511	43
44	40.1563	37.4009	42.2824	39.4860	44.3857	41.5574	46.4628	43.6151	48.5105	45.6497	50.5246	47.6606	44
45	41.1294	38.4209	43.2746	40.5298	45.3933	42.6227	47.4819	44.6932	49.5362	46.7394	51.5547	48.7585	45
46	42.0987	39.4393	44.2613	41.5706	46.3931	43.6790	48.4900	45.7628	50.5504	47.8189	52.5737	49.8464	46
47	43.0659	40.4580	45.2435	42.6066	47.3854	44.7300	49.4899	46.8253	51.5566	48.8914	53.5820	50.9245	47
48	44.0274	41.4720	46.2168	43.6374	48.3681	45.7740	50.4807	47.8810	52.5511	49.9543	54.5779	51.9921	48
49	44.9940	42.4814	47.1846	44.6618	49.3456	46.8120	51.4635	48.9279	53.5368	51.0074	55.5636	53.0484	49
50	45.9314	43.4831	48.1436	45.6790	50.3118	47.8400	52.4342	49.9638	54.5091	52.0483	56.5356	54.0916	50
51	46.8713	44.4790	49.0926	46.6876	51.2672	48.8584	53.3930	50.9889	55.4692	53.0773	57.4936	55.1213	51
52	47.8021	45.4665	50.0317	47.6870	52.2114	49.8663	54.3403	52.0025	56.4160	54.0934	58.4383	56.1376	52
53	48.7218	46.4452	50.9586	48.6763	53.1433	50.8632	55.2739	53.0037	57.3487	55.0964	59.3696	57.1418	53
54	49.6332	47.4142	51.8770	49.6549	54.0647	51.8480	56.1960	53.9922	58.2715	56.0879	60.2882	58.1313	54
55	50.5318	48.3717	52.7807	50.6207	54.9716	52.8196	57.1051	54.9687	59.1782	57.0642	61.1893	59.1035	55
56	51.4182	49.3169	53.6724	51.5794	55.8674	53.7797	58.0003	55.9305	60.0695	58.0236	62.0778	60.0618	56
57	52.2922	50.2500	54.5527	52.5162	56.7491	54.7258	58.8799	56.8761	60.9481	58.9701	62.9563	61.0100	57
58	53.1534	51.1707	55.4175	53.4430	57.6139	55.6542	59.7457	57.8075	61.8158	59.9053	63.8323	61.9550	58
59	54.0000	52.0764	56.2662	54.3525	58.4659	56.5690	60.6018	58.7283	62.6823	60.8382	64.7189	62.9102	59
60	54.8302	52.9650	57.1020	55.2488	59.3081	57.4738	61.4570	59.6478	63.5604	61.7838	65.6270	63.8872	60
61	55.6509	53.8436	57.9316	56.1385	60.1532	58.3807	62.3278	60.5827	64.4643	62.7532	66.5763	64.9063	61
62	56.4661	54.7162	58.7650	57.0312	61.0154	59.3046	63.2263	61.5454	65.4119	63.7683	67.5699	65.9738	62
63	57.2877	55.5947	59.6186	57.9440	61.9088	60.2598	64.1727	62.5570	66.4080	64.8363	68.6979	67.0987	63
64	58.1311	56.4950	60.5056	58.8905	62.8529	61.2669	65.1706	63.6247	67.4700	65.9651	69.7430	68.2900	64
65	59.0120	57.4327	61.4481	59.8934	63.8534	62.3348	66.2398	64.7582	68.5987	67.1655	70.9210	69.5434	65
66	59.9523	58.4304	62.4510	60.9609	64.9300	63.4726	67.3804	65.9678	69.7928	68.4324	72.1469	70.8454	66
67	60.9577	59.4994	63.5353	62.1052	66.0832	64.6938	68.5915	67.2506	71.0391	69.7540	73.4210	72.1980	67
68	62.0508	60.6493	64.7024	63.3373	67.3129	65.9925	69.8602	68.5920	72.3390	71.1298	74.7292	73.5847	68
69	63.2318	61.8927	65.9510	64.6525	68.6044	67.3544	71.1866	69.9923	73.6763	72.5438	76.0277	74.9577	69
70	64.4984	63.2235	67.2650	66.0347	69.9573	68.7792	72.5533	71.4339	75.0050	73.9454	77.2566	76.2683	70
71	65.8366	64.6276	68.6464	67.4857	71.3556	70.2504	73.9143	72.8660	76.2642	75.2800	78.3744	77.4506	71
72	67.2473	66.1056	70.0775	68.9877	72.7503	71.7142	75.2050	74.2307	77.4095	76.4934	79.1780	78.3115	72
73	68.7127	67.6395	71.5075	70.4846	74.0741	73.1105	76.3791	75.4716	78.2283	77.3687	79.6599	78.8370	73
74	70.1790	69.1710	72.8653	71.9137	75.2778	74.3799	77.2132	76.3615	78.7116	77.8951	80.7069	79.9420	74
75	71.5730	70.6345	74.1003	73.2130	76.1279	75.2848	77.6977	76.8883	79.7880	79.0286	83.7356	83.0928	75
76	72.8402	71.9646	74.9664	74.1330	76.6126	75.8112	78.8045	78.0512	82.9443	82.3048	**100.000**	**100.000**	**76 or 33**
77	73.7213	72.8985	75.4493	74.6568	77.7503	77.0037	82.0960	81.4603	**100.000**	**100.000**	95.0687	94.3498	32
78	74.2025	73.4199	76.6204	75.8814	81.1867	80.5554	**100.000**	**100.000**	95.1265	94.4046	93.9436	93.0595	31
79	75.4089	74.6787	80.2118	79.5859	**100.000**	**100.000**	95.1817	94.4566	94.0122	93.1241	93.3929	92.4224	30
80	79.1639	78.5440	**100.000**	**100.000**	95.2341	94.5062	94.0773	93.1855	93.4648	92.4901	93.0049	91.9691	29
81 or 28	**100.000**	**100.000**	95.2842	94.5533	94.1396	93.2440	93.5336	92.5545	93.0784	92.0380	92.4906	91.3705	28
27	95.3321	94.5982	94.1992	93.2997	93.5992	92.6158	93.1487	92.1035	92.5668	91.4416	91.8415	90.6178	27
26	94.2560	93.3527	93.6620	92.6743	93.2159	92.1660	92.6397	91.5093	91.9214	90.6920	91.1216	89.7830	26
25	93.7219	92.7299	93.2800	92.2255	92.7093	91.5738	91.9978	90.7627	91.2056	89.8607	90.3430	88.8833	25
24	93.3414	92.2823	92.7759	91.6353	92.0709	90.8301	91.2859	89.9347	90.4305	88.9645	89.5261	87.9389	24
23	92.8395	91.6940	92.1408	90.8944	91.3628	90.0052	90.5155	89.0418	89.6185	88.0235	88.6881	86.9706	23
22	92.2078	90.9558	91.4363	90.0726	90.5964	89.1157	89.7069	88.1042	88.7845	87.0585	87.7366	85.9874	22
21	91.5068	90.1369	90.6737	89.1862	89.7916	88.1812	88.8768	87.1423	87.9367	86.0781	86.9733	84.9911	21
20	90.7478	89.2534	89.8727	88.2547	88.9652	87.2223	88.0326	86.1647	87.0768	85.0845	86.1060	83.9910	20
19	89.9505	88.3251	89.0500	87.2988	88.1245	86.2475	87.1761	85.1738	86.2128	84.0868	85.2382	82.9926	19
18	89.1312	87.3719	88.2126	86.3266	87.2713	85.2590	86.3151	84.1783	85.3477	83.0904	84.3727	81.9943	18
17	88.2971	86.4022	87.3625	85.3271	86.4132	84.2658	84.4527	83.1839	84.4847	82.0939	83.5043	80.9953	17
16	87.4500	85.4184	86.5072	84.3493	85.5534	83.2731	84.5921	82.1889	83.6183	81.0961	82.6336	79.9945	16
15	86.5974	84.4291	85.6500	83.3584	84.6952	82.2797	83.7280	81.1925	82.7498	80.0965	81.7540	78.9847	15
14	85.7426	83.4397	84.7939	82.3663	83.8330	81.2845	82.8610	80.1939	81.8717	79.0874	80.8610	77.9608	14
13	84.8885	82.4491	83.9336	81.3723	82.9677	80.2868	81.9845	79.1855	80.9801	78.0642	79.9490	76.9165	13
12	84.0304	81.4561	83.0702	80.3754	82.0930	79.2791	81.0946	78.1628	80.0697	77.0203	79.0142	75.8475	12
11	83.1677	80.4598	82.1961	79.3682	81.2035	78.2567	80.1845	77.1191	79.1351	75.9513	78.0539	74.7522	11
10	82.2953	79.4531	81.3082	78.3462	80.2494	77.2132	79.2513	76.0503	78.1761	74.8561	77.0678	73.6289	10
	72nd Year.		71st Year.		70th Year.		69th Year.		68th Year.		67th Year.		

	25th Year.		26th Year.		27th Year.		28th Year.		29th Year.		30th Year.		
Age.	3 per cent.	4 per cent.	3 per cent.	4 per cent.	3 per cent.	4 per cent.	3 per cent.	4 per cent.	3 per cent.	4 per cent.	3 per cent.	4 per cent.	Age.
10	19.8516	16.1791	20.9428	17.1414	22.0609	18.1349	23.2078	19.1624	24.3839	20.2232	25.5906	21.3197	10
11	20.5001	16.7991	21.6243	17.7967	22.7777	18.8284	23.9604	19.8936	25.1738	20.9946	26.4192	22.1332	11
12	21.1703	17.4419	22.3304	18.4778	23.5199	19.5476	24.7403	20.6534	25.9930	21.7970	27.2783	22.9793	12
13	21.8599	18.1096	23.0567	19.1843	24.2844	20.2950	25.5447	21.4438	26.8378	22.6314	28.1624	23.8580	13
14	22.5746	18.8033	23.8101	19.9193	25.0783	21.0734	26.3795	22.2666	27.7123	23.4991	29.0771	24.7678	14
15	23.3155	19.5258	24.5919	20.6856	25.9016	21.8846	27.2431	23.1231	28.6167	24.3981	30.0149	25.7056	15
16	24.0843	20.2791	25.4028	21.4844	26.7534	22.7292	28.1362	24.0107	29.5438	25.3250	30.9747	26.6696	16
17	24.8829	21.0655	26.2428	22.3170	27.6354	23.6053	29.0527	24.9266	30.4936	26.2784	31.9529	27.6559	17
18	25.7102	21.8850	27.1128	23.1805	28.5403	24.5092	29.9917	25.8685	31.4615	27.2537	32.9507	28.6640	18
19	26.5679	22.7362	28.0061	24.0725	29.4683	25.4397	30.9492	26.8329	32.4494	28.2514	33.9631	29.6934	19
20	27.4488	23.6151	28.9223	24.9906	30.4146	26.3921	31.9265	27.8191	33.4519	29.2698	34.9944	30.7450	20
21	28.3528	24.5210	29.8571	25.9313	31.3811	27.3674	32.9187	28.8270	34.4736	30.3114	36.0428	31.8178	21
22	29.2753	25.4486	30.8120	26.8939	32.3623	28.3632	33.9301	29.8573	35.5124	31.3735	37.1068	32.9101	22
23	30.2174	26.3977	31.7811	27.8770	33.3624	29.3812	34.9582	30.9077	36.5664	32.4548	38.1868	34.0209	23
24	31.1743	27.3677	32.7696	28.8826	34.3796	30.4198	36.0021	31.9779	37.6369	33.5551	39.2780	35.1498	24
25	32.1500	28.3598	33.7749	29.9083	35.4123	31.4778	37.0622	33.0666	38.7184	34.6731	40.3847	36.2967	25
26	33.1424	29.3716	34.7954	30.9531	36.4611	32.5540	38 1331	34.1728	39.8154	35.8089	41.5033	37.4602	26
27	34.1503	30.4026	35.8323	32.0162	37.5209	33.6480	39.2198	35.2971	40.9244	36.9616	42.6334	38.6389	27
28	35.1741	31.4515	36.8800	33.0967	38.5963	34.7595	40.3184	36.4379	42.0449	38.1292	43.7759	39.8340	28
29	36.2089	32.5180	37.9435	34.1952	39.6839	35.8880	41.4288	37.5939	43.1782	39.3135	44.9292	41.0440	29
30	37.2608	33.6021	39.0203	35.3102	40.7844	37.0315	42.5531	38.7665	44.3233	40.5127	46.1058	42.2676	30
31	38.3219	34.7024	40.1062	36.4399	41.8951	38.1913	43.6857	39.9538	45.4760	41.7252	47.2600	43.4994	31
32	39.3961	35.8175	41.2062	37.5861	43.0180	39.3659	44.8295	41.1546	46.6347	42.9461	48.4312	44.7380	32
33	40.4828	36.9490	42.3169	38.7469	44.1507	40.5539	45.9781	42.3637	47.7968	44.1740	49.6024	45.9800	33
34	41.5803	38.0947	43.4376	39.9209	45.2883	41.7500	47.1302	43.5795	48.9589	45.4047	50.7722	47.2232	34
35	42.6877	39.2528	44.5629	41.1022	46.4292	42.9520	48.2821	44.7976	50.1196	46.6363	51.9372	48.4638	35
36	43.7977	40.4182	456.897	42.2895	47.5682	44.1565	49.4310	46.0165	51.2738	47.8653	53.0937	49.7001	36
37	44.9107	41.5892	46.8161	43.4788	48.7056	45.3614	50.5748	47.2326	52.4208	49.0897	54.2466	50.9268	37
38	46.0218	42.7604	47.9395	44.6670	49.8366	46.5619	51.7102	48.4426	53.5572	50.3030	55.3739	52.1417	38
39	47.1298	43 9311	49.0564	45.8513	50.9591	47.7570	52.8348	49.6423	54.6797	51.5053	56.4925	53.3437	39
40	48.2303	45.0967	50.1639	47.0289	52.0700	48.9404	53.9448	50.8295	55.7870	52.6735	57.5960	54.5316	40
41	49.3203	46.2543	51.2587	48.1938	53.1653	50.1105	55.0386	52.0017	56.8783	53.8667	58.6812	55.7019	41
42	50.3972	47.3985	52.3375	49.3446	54.2439	51.2649	56.1161	53 1586	57.9509	55.0219	59.7471	56.8534	42
43	51.4588	48.5286	53.4003	50.4798	55.3070	52.4040	57.1756	54.2973	59.0049	56.1583	60.7932	57.9847	43
44	52.5035	49.6447	54.4470	51.6013	56.3515	53.5266	58.2160	55.4189	60.0387	57.2762	61.8197	59.0966	44
45	53.5369	50.7495	55.4796	52.7087	57.3813	54.6447	59.2404	56.5242	61.0561	58.3767	62.8266	60.1899	45
46	54.5566	51.8415	56.4978	53.8024	58.3954	55.7270	60.2488	57.6135	62.0559	59.4599	63.8165	61.2652	46
47	55.5648	52.9228	57.5032	54.8840	59.3963	56.8064	61.2422	58.6880	63.0405	60.5276	64.7917	62.3256	47
48	56.5593	53.9921	58.4945	55.9525	60.3814	57.8712	62.2196	59.7472	64.0097	61.5808	65.7491	63.3686	48
49	57.5431	55.0491	59.4733	57.0072	61.3536	58.9216	63.1848	60.7928	64.9640	62.6173	66.6901	64.3928	49
50	58.5116	56.0914	60.4366	58.0466	62.3112	59.9577	64.1326	61.8210	65.8997	63.6343	67.6148	65.4001	50
51	59.4659	57.1198	61 3864	59.0730	63.2526	60.9775	65.0630	62.8309	66 8202	64.6357	68.5265	66.3940	51
52	60.4075	58.1356	62.3210	60.0837	64.1773	61.9795	65.9790	63.8264	67.7286	65.6242	69.4328	67.3816	52
53	61.3332	59.1362	63.2382	61.0771	65.0871	62.9670	66.8826	64.8083	68.6315	66.6073	70.3433	68.3741	53
54	62.2447	60.1199	64.1436	62.0563	65.9875	63.9429	67.7837	65.7861	69.5418	67.5963	71.2692	69.3806	54
55	63.1413	61.0893	65.0368	63.0239	66.8832	64.9141	68.6905	66.7705	70.4661	68.6002	72.2214	70.4153	55
56	64.0280	62.0475	65.9276	63.9877	67.7871	65.8930	69.6139	67.7711	71.4199	69.6342	73.2030	71.4826	56
57	64.9126	63.0033	66.8274	64.9607	68.7087	66.8901	70.5685	68.8041	72.4047	70.7030	74.2266	72.5880	57
58	65.8061	63.9678	67.7453	65.9520	69.6623	67.9201	71.5551	69.8729	73.4331	71.8113	75.2894	73.7368	58
59	66.7198	64.9525	68.6977	66.9785	70.6507	68.9886	72.5884	70.9838	74.5037	72.9659	76.3893	74.9237	59
60	67.6699	65.9747	69.6870	68.0459	71.6883	70.1019	73.6665	72.1442	75.6141	74.1615	77.5144	76.1421	60
61	68.6616	67.0425	70.7306	69.1630	72.7757	71.2695	74.7891	73.3501	76.7538	75.3872	78.6657	77.3760	61
62	69.7109	68.1631	71.8273	70.3378	73.9109	72.4860	75.9440	74.5892	77.9225	76.6425	79.8302	78.6285	62
63	70.8180	69.3462	72.9761	71.5661	75.0821	73.7896	77.1315	75.8615	79.1075	77.9140	80.9738	79.8558	63
64	71.9807	70.5864	74.1642	72.8348	76.2891	75.0290	78.3379	77.1530	80.2729	79.1617	82.0500	81.0156	64
65	73.1871	71.8715	75.3924	74.1443	77.5187	76.3428	79.5269	78.4227	81.3711	80.3424	83.0274	82.0685	65
66	74.4376	73.2012	76.6465	75.4799	78.7325	77.6357	80.6483	79.6253	82.3688	81.4144	83.7491	82.8519	66
67	75.7177	74.5620	77.8868	76.7985	79.8787	78.8626	81.6677	80.7181	83.1028	82.2089	84.2140	83.3641	67
68	76.9866	75.9076	79.0596	78.0505	80.9214	79.9778	82.4150	81.5264	83.5713	82.7250	85.1111	84.3247	68
69	78.1872	77.1856	80.1265	79.1889	81.6823	80.7985	82.8869	82.0443	84.4908	83.7071	87.5199	86.8646	69
70	79.2787	78.3974	80.9008	80.0223	82.1567	81.3184	83.8291	83.0484	86.9875	86.3336	**100.000**	**100.000**	70 or 39
71	80.0674	79.1946	81.3781	80.5444	83.1235	82.3462	86.4197	85.7674	**100.000**	**100.000**	94.6534	93.9519	38
72	80.5472	79.7186	82.3704	81.5968	85.8137	85.1633	**100.000**	**100.000**	94.7321	94.0278	93.4534	92.5922	37
73	81.5663	80.7968	85.1666	84.5183	**100.000**	**100.000**	94.8066	94.0994	93.5460	92.6811	92.8786	91.9341	36
74	84.4750	83.8293	**100.000**	**100.000**	94.8773	94.1672	93.6339	92.7651	92.9755	92.0267	92.4811	91.4735	35
75 or 34	**100.000**	**100.000**	94.9443	94.2313	93.7172	92.8447	93.0674	92.1144	92.5795	91.5673	91.9492	90.8604	34
33	95.0080	94.2921	93.7964	92.9200	93.1548	92.1975	92.6730	91.6561	92.0507	90.9567	91.2750	90.0862	33
32	93.8718	92.9916	93.2380	92.2763	92.7621	91.7405	92.1473	92.0481	91.3810	90.1864	90.5278	89.2280	32
31	93.3173	92.3512	92.8469	91.8206	92.2393	91.1349	91.4820	90.2815	90.6388	89.3325	89.7206	88.3045	31
30	92.9279	91.8967	92.3272	91.2174	91.5785	90.3720	90.7448	89.4318	89.8370	88.4131	88.8757	87.3363	30
29	92.4108	91.2958	91.6701	90.4580	90.8455	89.5262	89.9475	88.5166	88.9968	87.4494	88.0107	86.3461	29
28	91.7578	90.5398	90.9418	89.6160	90.0533	88.6151	89.1125	87.5570	88.1368	86.4632	87.1342	85.3428	28
27	91.0338	89.7016	90.1543	88.7089	89.2231	87.6596	88.2573	86.5748	87.2648	85.4636	86.2478	84.3287	27
26	90.2508	88.7982	89.3287	87.7572	88.3723	86.6810	87.3896	85.5786	86.3511	85.4529	85.3596	83.3128	26
25	89.4296	87.8502	88.4823	86.7822	87.5089	85.6882	86.5114	84.5708	85.4981	83.4396	84.4730	82.3008	25
24	88.5875	86.8786	87.6230	85.7926	86.6345	84.6834	85.6305	83.5601	84.6147	82.4300	83.5910	81.2911	24
23	87.7321	85.8922	86.7523	84.7908	85.7572	83.6757	84.7504	82.5532	83.7356	81.4223	82.7079	80.2825	23
22	86.8652	84.8933	84.8785	83.7857	84.8803	82.6708	83.8742	81.5475	82.8552	80.4154	81.8245	79.2742	22
21	84.9947	83.8907	85.0047	82.7830	84.0069	81.6670	82.9963	80.5422	81.9740	79.4087	80.9334	78.2580	21
20	85.1239	82.8901	84.1340	81.7811	83.1314	80.6633	82.1172	79.5365	81.0850	78.3933	80.0304	77.2292	20
19	84.2558	81.8902	83.2610	80.7791	82.2546	79.6590	81.2303	78.5227	80.1838	77.3756	79.1095	76.1814	19
18	83.3852	80.8896	82.3863	79.7760	81.3696	78.6462	80.3309	77.4958	79.2645	76.3184	78.1664	75.1097	18
17	82.5126	79.8878	81.5031	78.7643	80.4719	77.6202	79.4132	76.4493	78.3229	75.2474	77.1996	74.0132	17
16	81.6312	78.8770	80.6071	77.7390	79.5557	76.5743	78.4730	75.3787	77.3575	74.1510	76.2076	72.8894	16
15	80.7367	77.8524	79.6924	76.6937	78.6169	75.5042	77.5089	74.2828	76.3667	73.0277	75.1912	71.7404	15
14	79.8234	76.8077	78.7548	75.6240	77.6539	74.4086	76.5191	73.1595	75.3512	71.8786	74.1519	70.5680	14
13	78.8871	75.7384	77.7930	74.5286	76.6653	73.2855	75.5047	72.0105	74.3128	70.7061	73.0894	69.3719	13
12	77.9267	74.6432	76.8056	73.4056	75.6522	72.1364	74.4675	70.8378	73.2515	69.5096	72.0043	68.1526	12
11	76.9394	73.5200	75.7924	72.2562	74.6145	70.9632	73.4056	69.6407	72.1656	68.2895	70.8960	66.9110	11
10	75.9272	72.3704	74 7559	71.0827	73.5536	69.7656	72.3206	68.4200	70.9914	67.0472	69.7667	65.6484	10
	66th Year.		65th Year.		64th Year.		63rd Year.		62nd Year.		61st Year.		99

	31st Year.		32nd Year.		33rd Year.		34th Year.		35th Year.		36th Year.		
Age.	3 per cent.	4 per cent.	3 per cent.	4 per cent.	3 per cent.	4 per cent.	3 per cent.	4 per cent.	3 per cent.	4 per cent.	3 per cent.	4 per cent.	Age.
10	26.8290	22.4519	28.0999	23.6260	29.4016	24.8369	30.7345	26.0834	32.0911	27.3618	33.4703	28.6698	10
11	27.6972	23.3104	29.0061	24.5263	30.3465	25.7780	31.7108	27.0617	33.0977	28.3751	34.5023	29.7134	11
12	28.5949	24.2004	29.9430	25.4575	31.3152	26.7467	32.7101	28.0658	34.1229	29.4099	35.5542	30.7784	12
13	29.5187	25.1208	30.8991	26.4159	32.3025	27.7409	33.7239	29.0910	35.1639	30.4657	36.6167	31.8632	13
14	30.4662	26.0690	31.8784	27.4002	33.3087	28.7568	34.7577	30.1379	36.2196	31.5420	37.6980	32.9698	14
15	31.4362	27.0434	32.8758	28.4067	34.3382	29.7946	35.8056	31.2056	37.2936	32.6404	38.7953	34.0964	15
16	32.4239	28.0398	33.8922	29.4349	35.3735	30.8531	36.8715	32.2952	38.3833	33.7587	39.9068	35.2420	16
17	33.4314	29.0584	34.9231	30.4842	36.4315	31.9340	37.9539	33.4053	39.4879	34.8965	41.0337	36.4060	17
18	34.4531	30.0977	35.9724	31.5556	37.5058	33.0351	39.0509	34.5346	40.6079	36.0525	42.1708	37.5873	18
19	35.4938	31.1597	37.0360	32.6478	38.5953	34.1559	40.1639	35.6826	41.7385	37.2263	43.3227	38.7865	19
20	36.5512	32.2420	38.1199	33.7593	39.7007	35.2951	41.2875	36.8481	42.8840	38.4177	44.4858	40.0019	20
21	37.6242	33.3445	39.2176	34.8900	40.8170	36.4528	42.4263	38.0322	44.0410	39.6263	45.6599	41.2328	21
22	38.7135	34.4657	40.3262	36.0386	41.9488	37.6283	43.5769	39.2328	45.2092	40.8498	46.8457	42.4796	22
23	39.8134	35.6047	41.4500	37.2050	43.0920	38.8204	44.7383	40.4485	46.3889	42.0892	48.0409	43.7406	23
24	40.9291	36.7616	42.5858	38.3884	44.2468	40.0278	45.9120	41.6803	47.5787	43.3434	49.2453	45.0148	24
25	42.0567	37.9355	43.7330	39.5870	45.4135	41.2516	47.0956	42.9269	48.7776	44.6106	50.4536	46.2969	25
26	43.1955	39.1243	44.8922	40.8017	46.5903	42.4898	48.2883	44.1864	49.9804	45.8856	51.6642	47.5852	26
27	44.3469	40.3297	46.0618	42.0313	47.7766	43.7414	49.4854	45.4542	51.1859	47.1673	52.8744	48.8765	27
28	45.5085	41.5497	47.2409	43.2740	48.9672	45.0010	50.6852	46.7284	52.3909	48.4518	54.0824	50.1688	28
29	46.6800	42.7832	48.4247	44.5252	50.1609	46.2675	51.8848	48.0058	53.5942	49.7377	55.2853	51.4590	29
30	47.8572	44.0252	49.6126	45.7833	51.3554	47.5372	53.0836	49.2827	54.7933	51.0215	56.4817	52.7452	30
31	49.0355	45.2739	50.7983	47.0443	52.5463	48.8082	54.2755	50.5614	55.9833	52.3012	57.6669	54.0225	31
32	50.2149	46.5258	51.9837	48.3069	53.7334	50.0773	55.4614	51.8346	57.1649	53.5723	58.8405	55.2900	32
33	51.3929	47.7793	53.1642	49.5677	54.9134	51.3425	56.6379	53.0983	58.3341	54.8336	60.0006	56.5458	33
34	52.5661	49.0306	54.3377	50.8244	56.0842	52.5989	57.8020	54.3526	59.4899	56.0831	61.1474	57.7895	34
35	53.7323	50.2775	55.5020	52.0718	57.2426	53.8450	58.9528	55.5947	60.6323	57.3201	62.2783	59.0179	35
36	54.8877	51.5151	56.6524	53.3090	58.3862	55.0790	60.0889	56.8244	61.7840	58.5419	63.3912	60.2300	36
37	56.0306	52.7423	57.7893	54.5338	59.5164	56.3004	61.2090	58.0388	62.8660	59.7474	64.4859	61.4243	37
38	57.1588	53.9560	58.9118	55.7450	60.6297	57.5055	62.3114	59.2358	63.9554	60.9340	65.5611	62.5986	38
39	58.2727	55.1565	60.0173	56.9404	61.7252	58.6937	63.3948	60.4145	65.0255	62.1013	66.6155	63.7522	39
40	59.3690	56.3403	61.1045	58.1181	62.8012	59.8629	64.4583	61.5731	66.0741	63.2470	67.6482	64.8837	40
41	60.4462	57.5056	62.1716	59.2853	63.8567	61.0112	65.4999	62.7010	67.1006	64.4111	68.6594	65.9931	41
42	61.5030	58.6508	63.2179	60.4127	64.8901	62.1372	66.5191	63.8232	68.1055	65.4711	69.6469	67.0779	42
43	62.5397	59.7750	64.2427	61.5272	65.9018	63.2404	67.5174	64.9149	69.0873	66.5475	70.6102	68.1364	43
44	63.5546	60.8784	65.2457	62.6205	66.8924	64.3232	68.4924	65.9834	70.0447	67.5990	71.5513	69.1723	44
45	64.5514	61.9626	66.2310	63.6953	67.8630	65.3847	69.4462	67.0288	70.9830	68.6298	72.4752	70.1895	45
46	65.5309	63.0296	67.1968	64.7500	68.8128	66.4242	70.3814	68.0545	71.9046	69.6428	73.3883	71.1947	46
47	66.4933	64.0788	68.1440	65.7849	69.7462	67.4463	71.3021	69.0648	72.8176	70.6462	74.3010	72.1993	47
48	67.4365	65.1084	69.0743	66.8027	70.6647	68.4532	72.2138	70.0659	73.7302	71.6497	75.2201	73.2108	48
49	68.3654	66.1218	69.9923	67.8062	71.5769	69.4520	73.1281	71.0682	74.6521	72.6613	76.1586	74.2416	49
50	69.2802	67.1204	70.9025	68.8013	72.4904	70.4519	74.0506	72.0790	75.5928	73.6930	77.1156	75.2943	50
51	70.1885	68.1120	71.8154	69.7991	73.4139	71.4621	75.0515	73.1118	76.5541	74.7485	78.1021	76.3732	51
52	71.1009	69.1074	72.7399	70.8085	74.3601	72.4959	75.9598	74.1701	77.5469	75.8320	79.1158	77.4829	52
53	72.0253	70.1155	73.6879	71.8430	75.3295	73.5570	76.9583	75.2584	78.5683	76.9484	80.1533	78.6178	53
54	72.9768	71.1506	74.6628	72.9067	76.3356	74.6499	77.9891	76.3816	79.6169	78.0920	81.2053	79.7666	54
55	73.9546	72.2162	75.6741	74.0038	77.3738	75.7796	79.0472	77.5337	80.6800	79.2510	82.2690	80.9275	55
56	74.9728	73.3174	76.7210	75.1401	78.4426	76.9404	80.1225	78.7031	81.7574	80.4240	83.3337	82.0885	56
57	76.0274	74.4605	77.8004	76.3101	79.5303	78.1209	81.2139	79.8888	82.8372	81.5989	84.3703	83.2167	57
58	77.1169	75.6388	78.9001	77.5010	80.6355	79.3189	82.3495	81.0775	83.8891	82.7411	85.3404	84.2765	58
59	78.2293	76.8405	80.0198	78.7119	81.7463	80.5220	83.3768	82.2345	84.8743	83.8150	86.2190	85.2362	59
60	79.3638	78.0648	81.1469	79.9300	82.8310	81.6945	84.3776	83.3230	85.7665	84.7874	86.8808	85.9640	60
61	80.5092	79.2997	82.2502	81.1197	83.8491	82.7994	85.2851	84.3097	86.4370	85.5233	87.3289	86.4625	61
62	81.6319	80.5074	83.2865	82.2416	84.7724	83.8009	85.9645	85.0538	86.8875	86.0235	88.1165	87.3178	62
63	82.6877	81.6479	84.2269	83.2594	85.4617	84.5542	86.4177	85.5563	87.6907	86.3938	90.0948	89.4338	63
64	83.6458	82.6826	84.9261	84.0220	85.9174	85.0586	87.2373	86.4423	89.7300	89.0697	**100.000**	**100.000**	64 or 45
65	84.3561	83.4554	85.3848	84.5287	86.7546	85.9615	89.3416	88.6821	**100.000**	**100.000**	94.0724	93.3856	44
66	84.8177	83.9644	86.2407	85.4494	88.9280	88.2692	**100.000**	**100.000**	94.1843	93.4953	92.7727	91.9317	43
67	85.6935	84.9047	88.4877	87.8301	**100.000**	**100.000**	94.2896	93.5984	92.9036	92.0596	92.1697	91.2492	42
68	88.0191	87.3625	**100.000**	**100.000**	94.3888	93.6952	93.0268	92.1797	92.3057	91.3816	91.7641	90.7836	41
69 or 40	**100.000**	**100.000**	94.4822	93.7861	93.1429	92.2924	92.4337	91.5058	91.9012	90.9164	91.2133	90.1550	40
39	94.5702	93.8715	93.2523	92.3983	92.5545	91.6225	92.0304	91.0413	91.3535	90.2903	90.5098	89.3557	39
38	93.3557	92.4981	92.6685	91.7325	92.1525	91.1589	91.4860	90.4177	90.6551	89.4953	89.7300	88.4695	38
37	92.7764	91.8362	92.2680	91.2698	91.6112	90.5380	90.7926	89.6272	89.8810	88.6142	88.8886	87.5167	37
36	92.3773	91.3745	91.7299	90.6514	90.9228	89.7515	90.0242	88.7508	89.0457	87.6664	88.0096	86.5202	36
35	91.8425	90.7588	91.0464	89.8692	90.1600	88.8799	89.1949	87.8080	88.1729	86.6750	87.1130	85.5036	35
34	91.1636	89.9806	90.2888	89.0022	89.3362	87.9424	88.3276	86.8215	87.2816	85.6631	86.2064	84.4764	34
33	90.4112	89.1181	89.4707	88.0691	88.4748	86.9604	87.4420	85.8141	86.3806	84.6400	85.2930	83.4408	33
32	89.5984	88.1897	88.6149	87.0921	87.5946	85.9575	86.5462	84.7952	85.4717	83.6081	84.3803	82.4063	32
31	88.7483	87.2173	87.7400	86.0936	86.7038	84.9426	85.6419	83.7671	84.5633	82.5769	83.4722	81.3788	31
30	87.8788	86.2231	86.8544	85.0828	85.8045	83.9181	84.7381	82.7391	83.6593	81.5521	82.5720	80.3564	30
29	86.9974	85.2160	85.9590	84.0618	84.9042	82.8933	83.8371	81.7169	82.7616	80.5318	81.6733	79.3374	29
28	86.1067	84.1985	85.0630	83.0400	84.0071	81.8737	82.9429	80.6988	81.8651	79.5146	80.7748	78.3209	28
27	85.2147	83.1797	84.1695	82.0231	83.1161	80.8578	82.0493	79.6834	80.9700	78.4995	79.8715	77.2984	27
26	84.3247	82.1653	83.2816	81.0093	82.2252	79.8441	81.1565	78.6696	80.0688	77.4780	78.9575	76.2646	26
25	83.4397	81.1536	82.3933	79.9973	81.3348	78.8317	80.2573	77.6492	79.1566	76.4450	78.0266	75.2126	25
24	82.5541	80.1440	81.5052	78.9862	80.4376	77.8123	79.3470	76.6169	78.2273	75.3935	77.0742	74.1377	24
23	81.6683	79.1335	80.6101	77.9678	79.5291	76.7808	78.4192	75.5560	77.2763	74.3190	76.0988	73.0385	23
22	80.7757	78.1163	79.7035	76.9374	78.6031	75.7307	77.4700	74.4921	76.3026	73.2202	75.0990	71.9132	22
21	79.8704	77.0867	78.7791	75.8879	77.6553	74.6573	76.4974	73.3935	75.3039	72.0951	74.0755	70.7633	21
20	78.9478	76.0379	77.8329	74.8150	76.6842	73.5592	75.5001	72.2687	74.2816	70.9452	73.0302	69.5911	20
19	78.0032	74.9658	76.8633	73.7175	75.6884	72.4347	74.4791	71.1192	73.2374	69.7732	71.9628	68.3965	19
18	77.0350	73.8686	75.8687	72.5933	74.6685	71.2853	73.4360	69.9470	72.1708	68.5783	70.8733	67.1798	18
17	76.0418	72.7447	74.8501	71.4440	73.6265	70.1132	72.3704	68.7520	71.0821	67.3612	69.7632	65.9424	17
16	75.0242	71.5956	73.8090	70.2718	72.5616	68.9178	71.2823	67.5344	69.9725	66.1231	68.6326	64.6852	16
15	73.9841	70.4233	72.7451	69.0763	71.4743	67.7000	70.1732	66.2958	68.8423	64.8652	67.4827	63.4096	15
14	72.9308	69.2275	71.6583	67.8579	70.3656	66.4607	69.0433	65.0370	67.6925	63.5886	66.3141	62.1166	14
13	71.8347	68.0087	70.5501	66.6180	69.2360	65.2011	67.8936	63.7594	66.5239	62.2944	65.1291	60.8087	13
12	70.7274	66.7681	69.4212	65.3558	68.0869	63.9224	66.7254	62.4639	65.3390	60.9849	63.9280	59.4860	12
11	69.5973	65.5065	68.2707	64.0775	66.9170	62.6253	65.5387	61.1526	64.1358	59.6602	62.7095	58.1500	11
10	68.4474	64.2253	67.1013	62.7791	65.7306	61.3135	64.3355	59.8260	62.9172	58.3222	61.4784	56.8019	10
100	60th Year.		59th Year.		58th Year.		57th Year.		56th Year.		55th Year.		

	37th Year.		38th Year.		39th Year.		40th Year.		41st Year.		42nd Year.		
Age.	3 per cent.	4 per cent.	3 per cent.	4 per cent.	3 per cent.	4 per cent.	3 per cent.	4 per cent.	3 per cent.	4 per cent.	3 per cent.	4 per cent.	Age.
10	34.8671	30.0026	36.2823	31.3596	37.7101	32.7392	39.1539	34.1420	40.6111	35.5655	42.0794	37.0084	10
11	35.9254	31.0760	37.3612	32.4613	38.8131	33.8699	40.2784	35.2993	41.7550	36.7481	43.2429	38.2147	11
12	36.9983	32.1696	38.4587	33.5843	39.9325	35.0199	41.4166	36.4750	42.9142	37.9479	44.4164	39.4372	12
13	38.0859	33.2843	39.5686	34.7264	41.0628	36.1881	42.5684	37.6676	44.0797	39.1637	45.6002	40.6757	13
14	39.1900	34.4187	40.6936	35.8872	42.2086	37.3737	43.7293	38.8769	45.2597	40.3960	46.7947	41.9293	14
15	40.3086	35.5722	41.8334	37.0660	43.3641	38.5765	44.9041	40.1031	46.4498	41.6440	47.9985	43.1968	15
16	41.4419	36.7435	42.9828	38.2618	44.5332	39.7962	46.0888	41.3450	47.6484	42.9057	49.2121	44.4789	16
17	42.5854	37.9324	44.1466	39.4750	45.7131	41.0320	47.2835	42.6012	48.8581	44.1827	50.4340	45.7744	17
18	43.7433	39.1385	45.3210	40.7042	46.9028	42.2820	48.4887	43.8724	50.0751	45.4729	51.6633	47.0814	18
19	44.9123	40.3612	46.5059	41.9481	48.1037	43.5477	49.7029	45.1575	51.3019	46.7754	52.8953	48.3958	19
20	46.0918	41.5984	47.7019	43.2076	49.3135	44.8271	50.9249	46.4547	52.5307	48.0849	54.1287	49.7154	20
21	47.2829	42.8521	48.9074	44.4828	50.5317	46.1195	52.1503	47.7599	53.7612	49.4006	55.3605	51.0375	21
22	48.4836	44.1199	50.1214	45.7684	51.7535	47.4194	53.3777	49.0709	54.9903	50.7185	56.5894	52.3600	22
23	49.6928	45.4003	41.3389	47.0626	52.9770	48.7252	54.6035	50.3840	56.2163	52.0366	57.8118	53.6792	23
24	50.9060	46.6888	52.5587	48.3632	54.1997	50.0337	55.8268	51.6980	57.4365	53.3521	59.0262	54.9938	24
25	52.1215	47.9836	53.7776	49.6663	55.4198	51.3429	57.0443	53.0092	58.6486	54.6630	60.2302	56.2990	25
26	53.3361	49.2809	54.9940	50.9703	56.6340	52.6494	58.2537	54.3158	59.8504	55.9643	61.4209	57.5935	26
27	54.5486	50.5793	56.2049	52.2718	57.8406	53.9515	59.4531	55.6132	61.0393	57.2554	62.5975	58.8758	27
28	55.7556	51.8753	57.4081	53.5690	59.0371	55.2444	60.6395	56.9005	62.2138	58.5341	63.7599	60.1453	28
29	56.9553	53.1673	58.6017	54.8572	60.2210	56.5274	61.8121	58.1754	63.3747	59.8005	64.9060	61.3997	29
30	58.1462	54.4504	59.7834	56.1356	61.3920	57.7985	62.9726	59.4382	64.5199	61.0518	66.0354	62.6377	30
31	59.3228	55.7235	60.9498	57.4020	62.5476	59.0572	64.1135	60.6859	65.6464	62.2867	67.1450	63 8578	31
32	60.4868	56.9849	62.1036	58.6563	63.6880	60.3009	65.2391	61.9174	66.7554	63.5039	68.2364	65.0590	32
33	61.6373	58.2342	63.2413	59.8957	64.8114	61.5287	66.3464	63.1314	67.8456	64.7024	69.3074	66.2400	33
34	62.7719	59.4686	64.3621	61.1190	65.9167	62.7388	67.4350	64.3265	68.9155	65.8805	70.3577	67.3998	34
35	63.8896	60.6866	65.4648	62.3244	67.0033	63.9298	68.5033	65.5010	69.9647	67.0373	71.3879	68.5388	35
36	64.9881	61.8868	66.5478	63.5109	68.0686	65.1004	69.5501	66.6543	70.9929	68.1734	72.3948	69.6544	36
37	66.0679	63.0680	67.6106	64.6785	69.1134	66.2498	70.5768	67.7871	71.9988	69.2862	73.3783	70.7449	37
38	67.1268	64.2279	68.6520	65.8208	70.1373	67.3777	71.5807	68.8958	72.9807	70.3731	74.3397	71.8117	38
39	68.1645	65.3663	69.6729	66.9439	71.1386	68.4822	72.5604	69.9791	73.9405	71.4368	75.2807	72.8570	39
40	69.1811	66.4832	70.6705	68.0429	72.1155	69.5607	73.5180	71.0388	74.8798	72.4787	76.2064	73.8856	40
41	70.1741	67.5756	71.6435	69.1156	73.0697	70.6153	74.4546	72.0763	75.8036	73.5038	77.1241	74.9057	41
42	71.1423	68.6416	72.5937	70.1642	74.0031	71.6476	75.3760	73.0970	76.7198	74.5204	78.0401	75.9234	42
43	72.0884	69.6836	73.5238	71.1909	74.9220	72.6636	76.2926	74.1100	77.6352	75.5356	78.9644	76.9498	43
44	73.0143	70.7050	74.4394	72.2026	75.8343	73.6733	77.2048	75.1230	78.5596	76.5610	79.8973	77.9878	44
45	73.9287	71.7134	75.3515	73.2200	76.7494	74.6852	78.1313	76.1485	79.4957	77.6004	80.8494	79.0416	45
46	74.8406	72.7187	76.2674	74.2210	77.6779	75.7112	79.0706	77.1897	80.4524	78.6573	81.8182	80.1152	46
47	75.7585	73.7301	77.1992	75.2487	78.6218	76.7553	80.0332	78.2509	81.4283	79.6898	82.8018	81.2040	47
48	76.6928	74.7593	78.1470	76.2958	79.5898	77.8219	81.0159	79.3360	82.4198	80.8325	83.7898	82.2976	48
49	77.6461	75.8096	79.1219	77.3660	80.5807	78.9122	82.0169	80.4393	83.4183	81.9345	84.7821	83.3943	49
50	78.6265	76.8839	80.1199	78.4629	81.5902	80.0227	83.0248	81.5497	84.4210	83.0406	85.7671	84.4826	50
51	79.6321	77.9871	81.1385	79.5813	82.6083	81.1821	84.0387	82.6659	85.4179	84.1398	86.7205	85.5342	51
52	80.6603	79.1136	82.1674	80.7102	83.6341	82.2688	85.0482	83.7765	86.3838	85.2029	87.6104	86.5193	52
53	81.6999	80.2523	83.2050	81.8480	84.6563	83.3914	86.0269	84.8516	87.2856	86.1993	88.4160	87.4111	53
54	82.7511	81.4016	84.2416	82.9830	85.6492	84.4791	86.9420	85.8600	88.1029	87.1015	89.0343	88.0991	54
55	83.8011	82.5493	85.2481	84.0835	86.5770	85.4995	87.7704	86.7728	88.7278	87.7958	89.4690	88.5876	55
56	84.8224	83.6632	86.1897	85.1166	87.4175	86.4235	88.4025	87.4736	89.1651	88.2863	90.1806	89.3710	56
57	85.7782	84.7098	87.0426	86.0527	88.0570	87.1312	88.8424	87.9661	89.8881	89.0805	91.8631	91.1966	57
58	86.6437	85.6572	87.6893	86.7665	88.4988	87.6251	89.5768	88.7711	91.6126	90.9471	**100.000**	**100.000**	**58 or 51**
59	87.2979	86.3781	88.1332	87.2618	89.2454	88.4415	91.3459	90.6815	100.000	**100.000**	93.2522	92.5763	50
60	87.7435	86.8746	88.8922	88.0901	91.0617	90.3982	**100.000**	**100.000**	93.4086	92.7311	91.8087	90.9838	49
61	88.5165	87.7161	90.7594	90.0967	**100.000**	**100.000**	93.5563	92.8772	91.9923	91.1650	91.1641	90.2633	48
62	90.4375	89.7756	**100.000**	**100.000**	93.6963	93.0152	92.1663	91.3363	91.3561	90.4521	90.7477	89.7897	47
63 or 46	**100.000**	**100.000**	93.8286	93.1458	92.3307	91.4982	91.5376	90.6305	90.9420	89.9804	90.1726	89.1405	46
45	93.9538	93.2692	92.4865	91.6513	91.7095	90.7992	91.1259	90.1609	90.3722	89.3361	89.4327	88.3096	45
44	92.6337	91.7957	91.8718	90.9583	91.2997	90.3310	90.5608	89.5205	89.6397	88.5118	88.6140	87.3899	44
43	92.0253	91.1083	91.4640	90.4914	90.7390	89.6943	89.8353	88.7023	88.8290	87.5990	87.7332	86.4037	43
42	91.6185	90.6421	90.9066	89.8577	90.0193	88.8814	89.0312	87.7956	87.9553	86.6192	86.8161	85.3757	42
41	91.0646	90.0110	90.1926	89.0495	89.2217	87.9801	88.1645	86.8215	87.0451	85.5968	85.8841	84.3307	41
40	90.3559	89.2073	89.4014	88.1534	88.3615	87.0114	87.2607	85.8044	86.1191	84.5565	84.9459	83.2783	40
39	89.5702	88.3162	88.5472	87.1900	87.4640	85.9995	86.3405	84.7688	85.1861	83.5081	84.0030	82.2205	39
38	88.7226	87.3581	87.6558	86.1832	86.5498	84.9687	85.4130	83.7246	84.2480	82.4539	83.0644	81.1674	38
37	87.8376	86.3566	86.7477	85.1573	85.6277	83.9288	84.4799	82.6741	83.3140	81.4038	82.1345	80.1250	37
36	86.9351	85.5353	85.8309	84.1215	84.6993	82.8818	83.5499	81.6268	82.3871	80.3633	81.2151	79.0905	36
35	86.0254	84.3038	84.9077	83.0783	83.7739	81.8377	82.6269	80.5888	81.4709	79.3306	80.3001	78.0625	35
34	85.1052	83.2644	83.9862	82.0375	82.8542	80.8023	81.7133	79.5579	80.5578	78.3037	79.3889	77.0394	34
33	84.1881	82.2267	83.0704	81.0045	81.9439	79.7733	80.8029	78.5323	79.6488	77.2813	78.4740	76.0122	33
32	83.2762	81.1965	82.1633	79.9777	81.0363	78.7493	79.8961	77.5109	78.7356	76.2546	77.5501	74.9753	32
31	82.3723	80.1718	81.2585	78.9553	80.1317	77.7281	78.9848	76.4848	77.8132	75.2180	76.6103	73.9213	31
30	81.4707	79.1512	80.3566	77.9363	79.2228	76.7037	78.0644	75.4486	76.8752	74.1641	75.6505	72.8455	30
29	80.5704	78.1333	79.4015	76.9118	78.3031	75.6679	77.1268	74.3948	75.9155	73.0881	74.6674	71.7462	29
28	79.6650	77.1098	78.5313	75.8766	77.3674	74.6145	76.1688	73.3189	74.9339	71.9885	73.6610	70.6214	28
27	78.7493	76.0754	77.5973	74.8236	76.4108	73.5387	75.1884	72.2193	73.9284	70.8634	72.6317	69.4729	27
26	77.8168	75.0228	76.6420	73.7480	75.4316	72.4390	74.1839	71.0939	72.8998	69.7144	71.5813	68.3029	26
25	76.8629	73.9476	75.6640	72.6485	74.4281	71.3136	73.1562	69.9445	71.8501	68.5438	70.5094	67.1111	25
24	75.8862	72.8481	74.6616	71.5229	73.4014	70.1639	72.1072	68.7733	70.7787	67.3511	69.4163	65.8980	24
23	74.8850	71.7226	73.6359	70.3730	72.3531	68.9923	71.0364	67.5800	69.6860	66.1371	68.3033	64.6651	23
22	73.8605	70.5728	72.5887	69.2013	71.2831	67.7986	69.9442	66.3654	68.5734	64.9033	67.1710	63.4135	22
21	72.8141	69.4007	71.5194	68.0071	70.1915	66.5832	68.8319	65.1305	67.4411	63.6504	66.0204	62.1445	21
20	71.7457	68.2061	70.4284	66.7911	69.0796	65.3475	67.6999	63.8766	66.2905	62.3801	64.8523	60.8592	20
19	70.6556	66.9900	69.3171	65.5550	67.9480	64.0929	66.5494	62.6053	65.1223	61.0936	63.6692	59.5606	19
18	69.5448	65.7531	68.1858	64.2994	66.7976	62.8204	65.3811	61.3173	63.9387	59.7931	62.4707	58.2484	18
17	68.4140	64.4968	67.0357	63.0260	65.6293	61.5312	64.1973	60.0154	62.7398	58.4793	61.2580	56.9249	17
16	67.2639	63.2222	65.8672	61.7354	64.4451	60.2271	62.9977	58.6996	61.5262	57.1535	60.0335	55.5906	16
15	66.0955	61.9304	64.6828	60.4304	63.2451	58.9102	61.7834	57.3719	60.3007	55.8170	58.7993	54.2502	15
14	64.9106	60.6239	63.4822	59.1111	62.0299	57.5804	60.5567	56.0331	59.0650	54.4740	57.5571	52.9053	14
13	63.7095	59.3030	62.2663	57.7794	60.8023	56.2394	59.3199	54.6876	57.8214	53.1263	56.3102	51.5592	13
12	62.4935	57.9694	61.0383	56.4361	59.5648	54.8913	58.0753	53.3370	56.5733	51.7770	55.0604	50.2133	12
11	61.2627	56.6235	59.7977	55.0853	58.3168	53.5377	56.8232	51.9883	55.3192	50.4274	53.8078	48.8708	11
10	60.0216	55.2701	58.5490	53.7289	57.0638	52.1819	55.5681	50.6314	54.0651	49.0811	52.5568	47.5334	10
	54th Year.		53rd Year.		52nd Year.		51st Year.		50th Year.		49th Year.		

LIFE POL.		TAB. III.		SYN.			TERM POL.		TAB. IV.		AN. PREM.	
	43rd Year.		44th Year.		45th Year.		3 Per Cent.		4 Per Cent.				
Age.	3 per cent.	4 per cent	3 per cent.	4 per cent.	3 per cent.	4 per cent.	1 Year.	7 Years.	1 Year.	3 Years.	7 Years.	10 Years.	Age.
10	43.5590	38.4689	45.0443	39.9457	46.5386	41.4383	.6563	.6659	.6500	.6526	.6593	.6660	10
11	44.7365	39.6976	46.2392	41.1964	47.7469	42.7091	.6588	.6696	.6527	.6550	.6633	.6709	11
12	45.9278	40.9424	47.4442	42.4617	48.9646	43.9927	.6614	.6750	.6547	.6587	.6680	.6753	12
13	47.1259	42.2018	48.6556	43.7398	50.1891	45.2900	.6649	.6801	.6585	.6630	.6733	.6823	13
14	48.3338	43.4745	49.8770	45.0320	51.4216	46.5996	.6695	.6859	.6631	.6678	.6792	.6890	14
15	49.5517	44.7619	51.1062	46.3371	52.6607	47.9202	.6741	.6926	.6676	.6732	.6858	.6962	15
16	50.7771	46.0681	52.3420	47.6533	53.9014	49.2470	.6798	.6999	.6733	.6792	.6928	.7040	16
17	52.0098	47.3740	53.5801	58.9762	55.1428	50.5788	.6857	.7069	.6793	.6857	.7004	.7122	17
18	53.2448	48.6926	54.8188	50.3040	56.3817	51.9117	.6926	.7155	.6857	.6960	.7086	.7211	18
19	54.4811	50.0166	56.0555	51.6336	57.6168	53.2446	.6996	.7245	.6929	.6979	.7173	.7305	19
20	55.7153	51.3422	57.2887	52.9629	58.8451	54.5738	.7078	.7341	.7011	.7091	.7265	.7407	20
21	56.9465	52.6684	58.5153	54.2894	60.0647	55.8981	.7162	.7436	.7093	.7178	.7362	.7511	21
22	58.1713	53.9915	59.7335	55.6106	61.2736	57.2124	.7247	.7541	.7178	.7271	.7466	.7625	22
23	59.3875	55.3094	60.9409	56.9220	62.4687	58.5159	.7344	.7653	.7272	.7369	.7577	.7745	23
24	60.5934	56.6179	62.1348	58.2239	63.6494	59.8066	.7443	.7770	.7371	.7471	.7691	.7872	24
25	61.7859	57.9158	63.3144	59.5112	64.8155	61.0844	.7544	.7896	.7471	.7581	.7816	.8006	25
26	62.9640	59.2011	64.4794	60.7864	65.9642	62.3463	.7657	.8028	.7583	.7698	.7948	.8149	26
27	64.1279	60.4737	65.6278	62.0461	67.0960	63.5915	.7773	.8174	.7698	.7827	.8089	.8299	27
28	65.2751	61.7308	66.7584	63.2890	68.2085	64.8184	.7902	.8326	.7825	.7953	.8237	.8458	28
29	66.4050	62.9714	67.8705	64.5140	69.3218	66.0261	.8034	.8486	.7970	.8097	.8393	.8624	29
30	67.5170	64.1942	68.9640	65.7199	70.3750	67.2132	.8180	.8644	.8101	.8242	.8555	.8798	30
31	68.6086	65.3978	70.0357	66.9051	71.4260	68.3789	.8328	.8820	.8248	.8412	.8731	.8983	31
32	69.6804	66.5811	71.0872	68.0692	72.4578	69.5237	.8492	.9001	.8410	.8572	.8910	.9173	32
33	70.7315	67.7433	72.1183	69.2126	73.4658	70.6453	.8659	.9197	.8576	.8745	.9101	.9376	33
34	71.7622	68.8848	73.1269	70.3327	74.4509	71.7418	.8830	.9385	.8745	.8926	.9295	.9593	34
35	72.7706	70.0028	74.1121	71.4275	75.4142	72.8149	.9017	.9597	.8931	.9115	.9501	.9834	35
36	73.7548	71.0957	75.0748	72.4992	76.3566	73.8665	.9209	.9824	.9120	.9313	.9720	1.0102	36
37	74.7173	72.1655	76.0174	73.5494	77.2839	74.9015	.9405	1.0059	.9314	.9520	.9957	1.0407	37
38	75.6593	73.2132	76.9447	74.5825	78.2029	75.9273	.9618	1.0338	.9525	.9736	1.0227	1.0752	38
39	76.5861	74.2446	77.8638	75.6072	79.1192	76.9504	.9836	1.0650	.9741	.9962	1.0533	1.1145	39
40	77.5049	75.2673	78.7806	76.6292	80.0418	77.9802	1.0060	1.1014	.9963	1.0206	1.0892	1.1582	40
41	78.4215	76.2874	79.7040	77.6582	80.9703	79.0182	1.0302	1.1437	1.0207	1.0489	1.1310	1.2097	41
42	79.3452	77.3152	80.6339	78.6961	81.9125	80.0668	1.0571	1.1927	1.0476	1.0834	1.1795	1.2668	42
43	80.2768	78.3529	81.5790	79.7457	82.8661	81.1292	1.0923	1.2494	1.0819	1.1253	1.2351	1.3308	43
44	81.2245	79.4041	82.5364	80.8110	83.8279	82.2007	1.1356	1.3130	1.1246	1.1758	1.2974	1.4026	44
45	82.1875	80.4732	83.5049	81.8874	84.7903	83.2719	1.1866	1.3833	1.1743	1.2339	1.3681	1.4823	45
46	83.1629	81.5553	84.4750	82.9652	85.7519	84.3416	1.2465	1.4617	1.2323	1.2994	1.4448	1.5680	46
47	84.1420	82.6408	85.4463	84.0435	86.7039	85.4003	1.3122	1.5469	1.3017	1.3703	1.5288	1.6629	47
48	85.1231	83.7280	86.4086	85.1116	87.6226	86.4206	1.3844	1.6393	1.3712	1.4466	1.6209	1.7634	48
49	86.0970	84.8063	87.3389	86.1421	88.4795	87.3749	1.4622	1.7404	1.4481	1.5331	1.7186	1.8780	49
50	87.0385	85.8469	88.2061	87.1060	89.2546	88.2382	1.5474	1.8494	1.5290	1.6241	1.8276	1.9967	50
51	87.9167	86.8211	88.9910	87.9784	89.8528	88.9082	1.6406	1.9688	1.6322	1.7262	1.9427	2.1285	51
52	88.7119	87.7030	89.5956	88.6541	90.2798	89.3902	1.7424	2.0968	1.7218	1.8347	2.0742	2.2704	52
53	89.3228	88.3848	90.0250	89.1384	90.9599	90.1442	1.8536	2.2368	1.8360	1.9504	2.2100	2.4265	53
54	89.7554	88.8713	90.7155	89.9018	92.5289	91.8588	1.9721	2.3896	1.9601	2.0812	2.3602	2.5953	54
55	90.4560	89.6445	92.3201	91.6513	**100.000**	**100.000**	2.1033	2.5554	2.0688	2.2073	2.5230	2.7799	55
56	92.0985	91.4309	**100.000**	**100.000**	92.7255	92.0542	2.2422	2.7363	2.2310	2.3846	2.7045	2.9824	56
57 or 52	**100.000**	**100.000**	92.9113	92.2385	91.1918	90.3727	2.3960	2.9344	2.3787	2.5346	2.8986	3.2002	57
51	93.0866	92.4123	91.4086	90.5883	90.5201	89.6278	2.5617	3.1508	2.5964	2.7238	3.1192	3.4439	58
50	91.6144	90.7917	90.7471	89.8520	90.0958	89.1479	2.7423	3.3895	2.7160	2.9044	3.3408	3.6940	59
49	90.9616	90.0636	90.3254	89.3742	89.5037	88.4835	2.9452	3.6476	2.9169	3.1323	3.6035	3.9812	60
48	90.5422	89.5878	89.7389	88.7150	88.7376	87.6287	3.1662	3.9311	3.1357	3.3714	3.8827	4.2869	61
47	89.9619	88.9338	88.9823	87.8685	87.8916	86.6838	3.4097	4.2399	3.3770	3.6330	4.1863	4.6175	62
46	89.2139	88.0952	88.1458	86.9327	86.9830	85.6731	3.6738	4.5720	3.6383	3.9183	4.5152	4.9743	63
45	88.3865	87.1680	87.2474	85.9310	86.0412	84.6236	3.9609	4.9335	3.9257	4.2295	4.8715	5.3589	64
44	87.4972	86.1744	86.3146	84.8895	85.0882	83.5612	4.2798	5.3225	4.2384	4.5683	5.2565	5.7728	65
43	86.5730	85.1401	85.3697	83.8339	84.1333	82.4959	4.6256	5.7444	4.5784	4.9358	5.6719	6.2175	66
42	85.6346	84.0902	84.4205	82.7734	83.1763	81.4284	4.9975	6.1971	4.9492	5.3327	6.1194	6.6947	67
41	84.6911	83.0338	83.4685	81.7092	82.2266	80.3681	5.4009	6.6844	5.3491	5.7608	6.5941	7.2062	68
40	83.7437	81.9728	82.5224	80.6511	81.2870	79.3205	5.7337	7.2090	5.7776	6.2223	7.1181	7.7542	69
39	82 8013	80.9170	81.5856	79.6048	80.3603	78.2828	6.3042	7.7731	6.2436	6.7216	7.6835	8.8412	70
38	81.8676	79.8724	80.6611	78.5678	79.4390	77.2529	6.8114	8.3797	6.7458	7.2596	8.2751	8.9695	71
37	80.9456	78.8368	79.7416	77.5384	78.5236	76.2295	7.3597	9.0320	7.2892	7.8405	8.9195	9.6391	72
36	80.0281	77.8077	78.8273	76.5145	77.6052	75.2025	7.9499	9.7326	7.8729	8.4668	9.6114	10.3555	73
35	79.1156	76.7841	77.9101	75.4872	76.6785	74.1666	8.5891	10.4847	8.5068	9.1417	10.3545	11.3125	74
34	78.1991	75.7568	76.9837	74.4506	75.7359	73.1139	9.2777	11.2902	9.1885	9.8696	11.1500	11.7347	75
33	77.2739	74.7199	76.0418	73.3972	74.7730	72.0395	10.0173	12.1516	9.9210	10.6561	12.0013	12.7955	76
32	76.3330	73.6660	75.0796	72.3220	73.7883	70.9419	10.8223	13.0736	10.7182	11.5058	12.9124	13.7218	77
31	75.3716	72.5904	74.0954	71.2237	72.7799	69.8192	11.6937	14.0584	11.5812	12.4194	13.8856	14.7128	78
30	74.3887	71.4915	73.0881	70.1008	71.7496	68.6739	12.6274	15.1125	12.5058	13.3970	14.9272	15.7735	79
29	73.3810	70.3672	72.0570	68.9530	70.6974	67.5060	13.6317	16.2454	13.5010	14.4426	16.0467	16.9135	80
28	72.3509	69.2193	71.0056	67.7847	69.6247	66.3175	14.7024	17.4684	14.5608	15.5587	17.2542	18.1374	81
27	71.3000	68.0501	69.9332	66.5940	68.5313	65.1083	15.8440	18.7998	15.6940	16.7600	18.5696	19.4664	82
26	70.2278	66.8592	68.8396	65.3843	67.4184	63.8795	17.0899	20.2642	16.9126	18.0683	20.0143	20.9031	83
25	69.1345	65.6473	67.7266	64.1540	66.2865	62.6325	18.4045	21.8853	18.2385	19.5156	21.6144	22.4738	84
24	68.0213	64.4156	66.5944	62.9051	65.1368	61.3684	19.9121	23.6964	19.7205	21.1414	23.4021	24.1993	85
23	66.8890	63.1652	65.4441	61.6392	63.9699	60.0884	21.6000	25.7278	21.3923	22.9895	25.4075	26.1045	86
22	65.7386	61.8978	64.2769	60.3575	62.7885	58.7955	23.5178	28.0100	23.2918	25.1178	27.6617	28.2215	87
21	64.5707	60.6142	63.0946	59.0623	61.5922	57.4895	25.7547	30.5781	25.5070	27.5862	30.2002	30.6026	88
20	63.3879	59.3170	61.8975	57.7540	60.3621	56.1724	28.3866	33.4649	28.1138	30.4555	33.0564	33.3059	89
19	62.1902	58.0070	60.6865	56.4349	59.1612	54.8458	31.4392	36.6929	31.1369	33.7941	36.2541	36.3903	90
18	60.9782	56.6854	59.4642	55.1055	57.9313	53.5134	35.0386	40.3277	34.7017	37.6909	39.8589	39.9271	91
17	59.7549	55.3537	58.2329	53.7705	56.6943	52.1776	39.3459	44.4629	38.9677	42.1991	43.9620	43.9954	92
16	58.5220	54.0158	56.9941	52.4314	55.4533	50.8410	44.3910	49.1479	43.9698	47.3244	48.6070	48.6070	93
15	57.2816	52.6739	55.7511	51.0916	54.2096	49.5058	50.1266	54.3018	49.6396	52.9187	53.7286	53.7286	94
14	56.0365	51.3308	54.5049	49.7527	52.9660	48.1749	56.7252	59.8850	56.1798	58.7061	59.2714	59.2714	95
13	54.7882	49.9884	53.2588	48.4180	51.7240	46.8501	62.9756	65.2187	62.3701	64.0339	64.5617	64.5617	96
12	53.5402	48.6495	52.0147	47.0891	50.4890	45.5360	67.2143	70.0142	66.5679	69.3077	69.3077	69.3077	97
11	52.2910	47.3166	50.7741	45.7702	49.2586	44.2336	72.8155	77.5562	72.1155	76.7739	76.7739	76.7739	98
10	51.0483	45.9933	49.5412	44.4630	48.0380	42.9448	97.0874	97.0874	96.1538	96.1538	96.1538	96.1538	99
102	48th Year.		47th Year.		46th Year.								

Age.	0	1	2	3	4	5	6	7	8	9	10	11	12
10	2.6021	2.5555	2.5090	2.4625	2.4160	2.3695	2.3230	2.2765	2.2300	2.1835	2.1370	2.0905	2.0439
11	2.6420	2.5951	2.5483	2.5015	2.4546	2.4078	2.3610	2.3141	2.2673	2.2205	2.1736	2.1268	2.0800
12	2.6832	2.6369	2.5906	2.5442	2.4979	2.4516	2.4052	2.3589	2.3106	2.2662	2.2199	2.1736	2.1272
13	2.7270	2.6802	2.6335	2.5867	2.5400	2.4932	2.4465	2.3997	2.3530	2.3062	2.2595	2.2127	2.1660
14	2.7722	2.7251	2.6781	2.6311	2.5841	2.5371	2.4901	2.4431	2.3961	2.3491	2.3021	2.2551	2.2080
15	2.8190	2.7719	2.7248	2.6777	2.6306	2.5835	2.5364	2.4893	2.4422	2.3951	2.3480	2.3009	2.2538
16	2.8678	2.8204	2.7729	2.7255	2.6780	2.6306	2.5831	2.5357	2.4882	2.4408	2.3933	2.3459	2.2984
17	2.9184	2.8707	2.8229	2.7752	2.7274	2.6797	2.6319	2.5842	2.5364	2.4887	2.4409	2.3932	2.3454
18	2.9708	2.9227	2.8745	2.8263	2.7781	2.7299	2.6817	2.6335	2.5853	2.5371	2.4889	2.4407	2.3926
19	3.0250	2.9765	2.9281	2.8797	2.8313	2.7829	2.7345	2.6861	2.6377	2.5893	2.5409	2.4925	2.4441
20	3.0814	3.0324	2.9834	2.9344	2.8854	2.8364	2.7875	2.7386	2.6897	2.6408	2.5919	2.5430	2.4941
21	3.1397	3.0902	3.0407	2.9912	2.9417	2.8922	2.8428	2.7934	2.7440	2.6946	2.6452	2.5958	2.5464
22	3.2000	3.1500	3.1001	3.0502	3.0003	2.9504	2.9005	2.8506	2.8007	2.7508	2.7009	2.6510	2.6010
23	3.2625	3.2121	3.1616	3.1111	3.0606	3.0101	2.9596	2.9091	2.8586	2.8081	2.7576	2.7071	2.6566
24	3.3272	3.2762	3.2251	3.1740	3.1230	3.0719	3.0208	2.9698	2.9187	2.8676	2.8166	2.7655	2.7144
25	3.3941	3.3424	3.2907	3.2390	3.1873	3.1356	3.0840	3.0324	2.9808	2.9292	2.8776	2.8260	2.7744
26	3.4635	3.4112	3.3588	3.3064	3.2541	3.2017	3.1493	3.0970	3.0449	2.9922	2.9399	2.8875	2.8351
27	3.5352	3.4821	3.4290	3.3760	3.3230	3.2700	3.2170	3.1640	3.1110	3.0580	3.0050	2.9520	2.8990
28	3.6094	3.5557	3.5019	3.4481	3.3944	3.3406	3.2868	3.2331	3.1793	3.1255	3.0718	3.0180	2.9642
29	3.6863	3.6318	3.5772	3.5226	3.4680	3.4134	3.3588	3.3042	3.2496	3.1950	3.1404	3.0858	3.0312
30	3.7658	3.7103	3.6548	3.5993	3.5438	3.4883	3.4328	3.3773	3.3218	3.2664	3.2110	3.1556	3.1002
31	3.8480	3.7916	3.7352	3.6788	3.6224	3.5660	3.5096	3.4532	3.3968	3.3404	3.2840	3.2276	3.1713
32	3.9331	3.8756	3.8182	3.7608	3.7034	3.6460	3.5886	3.5312	3.4738	3.4164	3.3590	3.3016	3.2441
33	4.0210	3.9626	3.9042	3.8458	3.7874	3.7290	3.6706	3.6122	3.5537	3.4952	3.4367	3.3782	3.3197
34	4.1120	4.0525	3.9930	3.9335	3.8740	3.8145	3.7550	3.6955	3.6360	3.5765	3.5170	3.4574	3.3978
35	4.2062	4.1455	4.0848	4.0241	3.9634	3.9027	3.8420	3.7813	3.7206	3.6599	3.5992	3.5386	3.4780
36	4.3038	4.2419	4.1800	4.1181	4.0563	3.9944	3.9325	3.8706	3.8088	3.7469	3.6850	3.6231	3.5613
37	4.4050	4.3419	4.2788	4.2157	4.1526	4.0895	4.0264	3.9633	3.9002	3.8371	3.7740	3.7109	3.6477
38	4.5101	4.4457	4.3813	4.3169	4.2525	4.1881	4.1237	4.0593	3.9949	3.9305	3.8661	3.8017	3.7374
39	4.6195	4.5537	4.4879	4.4221	4.3564	4.2906	4.2248	4.1590	4.0933	4.0275	3.9617	3.8959	3.8302
40	4.7335	4.6663	4.5991	4.5319	4.4647	4.3975	4.3303	4.2631	4.1959	4.1287	4.0615	3.9943	3.9272
41	4.8526	4.7839	4.7152	4.6465	4.5778	4.5091	4.4404	4.3717	4.3030	4.2343	4.1656	4.0969	4.0282
42	4.9772	4.9068	4.8364	4.7660	4.6956	4.6252	4.5548	4.4844	4.4140	4.3436	4.2732	4.2028	4.1324
43	5.1078	5.0342	4.9606	4.8870	4.8134	4.7398	4.6662	4.5926	4.5190	4.4454	4.3718	4.2982	4.2246
44	5.2440	5.1682	5.0924	5.0167	4.9409	4.8651	4.7894	4.7136	4.6378	4.5621	4.4863	4.4105	4.3348
45	5.3858	5.3065	5.2272	5.1479	5.0686	4.9893	4.9100	4.8307	4.7514	4.6721	4.5928	4.5136	4.4343
46	5.5331	5.4494	5.3657	5.2820	5.1983	5.1146	5.0309	4.9472	4.8635	4.7798	4.6961	4.6124	4.5286
47	5.6851	5.5967	5.5083	5.4199	5.3315	5.2431	5.1547	5.0663	4.9779	4.8895	4.8012	4.7129	4.6246
48	5.8426	5.7489	5.6552	5.5615	5.4678	5.3741	5.2804	5.1867	5.0930	4.9993	4.9056	4.8119	4.7182
49	6.0054	5.9059	5.8064	5.7069	5.6074	5.5079	5.4084	5.3089	5.2094	5.1099	5.0104	4.9108	4.8112
50	6.1742	6.0685	5.9628	5.8571	5.7514	5.6457	5.5400	5.4343	5.3286	5.2229	5.1172	5.0115	4.9059
51	6.3488	6.2363	6.1237	6.0111	5.8985	5.7859	5.6733	5.5607	5.4480	5.3353	5.2226	5.1099	4.9972
52	6.5297	6.4095	6.2893	6.1691	6.0489	5.9287	5.8085	5.6883	5.5681	5.4479	5.3277	5.2075	5.0873
53	6.7172	6.5887	6.4602	6.3317	6.2032	6.0747	5.9462	5.8177	5.6892	5.5607	5.4322	5.3038	5.1754
54	6.9117	6.7743	6.6369	6.4995	6.3621	6.2247	6.0873	5.9499	5.8125	5.6751	5.5378	5.4005	5.2632
55	7.1140	6.9668	6.8197	6.6726	6.5255	6.3784	6.2312	6.0841	5.9370	5.7899	5.6428	5.4957	5.3485
56	7.3248	7.1670	7.0092	6.8513	6.6935	6.5357	6.3778	6.2200	6.0621	5.9043	5.7464	5.5885	5.4307
57	7.5443	7.3752	7.2061	7.0371	6.8681	6.6991	6.5301	6.3611	6.1921	6.0231	5.8541	5.6851	5.5161
58	7.7745	7.5926	7.4107	7.2288	7.0469	6.8650	6.6831	6.5012	6.3193	6.1374	5.9555	5.7736	5.5916
59	8.0151	7.8198	7.6245	7.4292	7.2339	7.0386	6.8433	6.6480	6.4527	6.2574	6.0621	5.8668	5.6714
60	8.2683	8.0576	7.8469	7.6362	7.4255	7.2148	7.0041	6.7934	6.5826	6.3718	6.1610	5.9502	5.7394
61	8.5339	8.3064	8.0789	7.8514	7.6239	7.3964	7.1689	6.9414	6.7138	6.4862	6.2586	6.0310	5.8034
62	8.8132	8.5672	8.3211	8.0750	7.8289	7.5828	7.3367	7.0905	6.8443	6.5981	6.3519	6.1057	5.8595
63	9.1068	8.8405	8.5742	8.3079	8.0416	7.7753	7.5090	7.2427	6.9764	6.7101	6.4438	6.1774	5.9110
64	9.4164	9.1278	8.8392	8.5507	8.2621	7.9735	7.6850	7.3964	7.1078	6.8193	6.5307	6.2421	5.9536
65	9.7429	9.4300	9.1172	8.8043	8.4915	8.1786	7.8658	7.5529	7.2401	6.9272	6.6144	6.3015	5.9887
66	10.0877	9.7485	9.4093	9.0701	8.7309	8.3917	8.0525	7.7133	7.3741	7.0349	6.6957	6.3564	6.0171
67	10.4526	10.0841	9.7159	9.3476	8.9794	8.6111	8.2429	7.8746	7.5064	7.1381	6.7699	6.4016	6.0334
68	10.8386	10.4392	10.0398	9.6404	9.2410	8.8416	8.4422	8.0428	7.6434	7.2440	6.8446	6.4451	6.0456
69	11.2484	10.8155	10.3829	9.9497	9.5168	9.0839	8.6510	8.2181	7.7852	7.3523	6.9194	6.4865	6.0536
70	11.6849	11.2155	10.7461	10.2767	9.8073	9.3379	8.8685	8.3991	7.9296	7.4601	6.9906	6.5211	6.0516
71	12.1504	11.6416	11.1328	10.6240	10.1152	9.6064	9.0976	8.5888	8.0800	7.5712	7.0624	6.5536	6.0448
72	12.6481	12.0967	11.5453	10.9939	11.4425	9.8911	9.3397	8.7883	8.2368	7.6853	7.1338	6.5823	6.0308
73	13.1811	12.5837	11.9863	11.3889	10.7915	10.1941	9.5967	8.9993	8.4020	7.8047	7.2074	6.6101	6.0128
74	13.7534	13.1061	12.4588	11.8116	11.1643	10.5170	9.8698	9.2225	8.5752	7.9280	7.2807	6.6334	5.9862
Age.	0	1	2	3	4	5	6	7	8	9	10	11	12

Age.	0	1	2	3	4	5	6	7	8	9	10	11	12
10	4.6460	4.6071	4.5681	4.5291	4.4902	4.4512	4.4122	4.3733	4.3343	4.2953	4.2564	4.2174	4.1784
11	4.7220	4.6837	4.6454	4.6071	4.5688	4.5305	4.4922	4.4539	4.4156	4.3773	4.3389	4.3005	4.262[illegible]
12	4.8104	4.7718	4.7332	4.6946	4.6560	4.6174	4.5788	4.5402	4.5017	4.4632	4.4247	4.3862	4.3477
13	4.8930	4.8543	4.8156	4.7769	4.7382	4.6995	4.6608	4.6221	4.5835	4.5449	4.5063	4.4677	4.4291
14	4.9802	4.9416	4.9030	4.8644	4.8258	4.7872	4.7486	4.7100	4.6714	4.6328	4.5942	4.5556	4.5171
15	5.0728	5.0340	4.9952	4.9564	4.9176	4.8788	4.8400	4.8012	4.7625	4.7238	4.6851	4.6464	4.6077
16	5.1662	5.1273	5.0884	5.0495	5.0106	4.9717	4.9328	4.8939	4.8550	4.8162	4.7774	4.7386	4.6998
17	5.2638	5.2247	5.1856	5.1465	5.1074	5.0683	5.0292	4.9901	4.9510	4.9119	4.8727	4.8335	4.7943
18	5.3634	5.3242	5.2850	5.2458	5.2066	5.1674	5.1282	5.0890	5.0498	5.0106	4.9715	4.9324	4.8933
19	5.4691	5.4296	5.3901	5.3506	5.3111	5.2716	5.2321	5.1926	5.1531	5.1136	5.0741	5.0347	4.9953
20	5.5755	5.5357	5.4959	5.4561	5.4163	5.3765	5.3367	5.2969	5.2572	5.2175	5.1778	5.1381	5.0984
21	5.6861	5.6460	5.6060	5.5660	5.5260	5.4860	5.4460	5.4060	5.3660	5.3260	5.2860	5.2460	5.2060
22	5.8010	5.7606	5.7203	5.6799	5.6396	5.5992	5.5589	5.5185	5.4782	5.4378	5.3975	5.3571	5.3168
23	5.9191	5.8784	5.8377	5.7970	5.7563	5.7156	5.6749	5.6342	5.5935	5.5528	5.5121	5.4715	5.4309
24	6.0416	6.0005	5.9594	5.9184	5.8774	5.8364	5.7954	5.7544	5.7134	5.6724	5.6314	5.5904	5.5494
25	6.1685	6.1271	6.0857	6.0443	6.0029	5.9615	5.9201	5.8787	5.8373	5.7958	5.7543	5.7128	5.6713
26	6.2986	6.2567	6.2148	6.1729	6.1310	6.0891	6.0472	6.0053	5.9635	5.9217	5.8799	5.8381	5.7963
27	6.4342	6.3919	6.3496	6.3073	6.2650	6.2227	6.1804	6.1381	6.0957	6.0533	6.0109	5.9685	5.9261
28	6.5736	6.5309	6.4882	6.4454	6.4026	6.3597	6.3168	6.2740	6.2312	6.1883	6.1453	6.1024	6.0591
29	6.7175	6.6741	6.6306	6.5871	6.5436	6.5001	6.4566	6.4131	6.3696	6.3262	6.2828	6.2394	6.1960
30	6.8660	6.8219	6.7778	6.7337	6.6896	6.6455	6.6014	6.5573	6.5132	6.4691	6.4251	6.3811	6.3371
31	7.0193	6.9745	6.9297	6.8849	6.8401	6.7953	6.7505	6.7057	6.6609	6.6162	6.5715	6.5268	6.4821
32	7.1772	7.1317	7.0862	7.0407	6.9952	6.9497	6.9042	6.8587	6.8132	6.7677	6.7223	6.6769	6.6315
33	7.3407	7.2945	7.2483	7.2022	7.1560	7.1099	7.0638	7.0176	6.9715	6.9253	6.8792	6.8330	6.7869
34	7.5098	7.4628	7.4158	7.3688	7.3218	7.2748	7.2278	7.1808	7.1338	7.0868	7.0399	6.9930	6.9461
35	7.6842	7.6364	7.5886	7.5408	7.4930	7.4452	7.3974	7.3496	7.3018	7.2540	7.2062	7.1584	7.1107
36	7.8651	7.8165	7.7678	7.7191	7.6705	7.6218	7.5732	7.5245	7.4759	7.4272	7.3786	7.3299	7.2813
37	8.0527	8.0032	7.9537	7.9042	7.8547	7.8052	7.7557	7.7062	7.6566	7.6070	7.5574	7.5078	7.4582
38	8.2475	8.1971	8.1467	8.0962	8.0457	7.9952	7.9447	7.8942	7.8437	7.7932	7.7427	7.6922	7.6417
39	8.4497	8.3983	8.3469	8.2955	8.2441	8.1927	8.1413	8.0899	8.0384	7.9869	7.9354	7.8839	7.8324
40	8.6607	8.6082	8.5557	8.5032	8.4507	8.3982	8.3457	8.2932	8.2408	8.1884	8.1360	8.0836	8.0312
41	8.8808	8.8271	8.7734	8.7197	8.6660	8.6123	8.5586	8.5049	8.4512	8.3975	8.3438	8.2901	8.2364
42	9.1096	9.0533	8.9970	8.9407	8.8844	8.8281	8.7718	8.7155	8.6592	8.6029	8.5466	8.4902	8.4338
43	9.3324	9.2753	9.2182	9.1611	9.1040	9.0469	8.9898	8.9327	8.8756	8.8185	8.7615	8.7045	8.6475
44	9.5788	9.5180	9.4572	9.3964	9.3356	9.2748	9.2140	9.1532	9.0924	9.0316	8.9707	8.9098	8.8489
45	9.8201	9.7555	9.6909	9.6263	9.5617	9.4971	9.4325	9.3679	9.3033	9.2387	9.1741	9.1095	9.0450
46	10.0617	9.9930	9.9243	9.8556	9.7869	9.7182	9.6495	9.5808	9.5121	9.4434	9.3747	9.3060	9.2374
47	10.3097	10.2365	10.1632	10.0899	10.0166	9.9433	9.8700	9.7967	9.7234	9.6502	9.5770	9.5038	9.4306
48	10.5608	10.4825	10.4042	10.3259	10.2476	10.1693	10.0910	10.0127	9.9344	9.8562	9.7780	9.6998	9.6216
49	10.8166	10.7329	10.6492	10.5655	10.4818	10.3981	10.3144	10.2307	10.1470	10.0633	9.9796	9.8960	9.8124
50	11.0801	10.9903	10.9005	10.8107	10.7209	10.6311	10.5413	10.4515	10.3617	10.2719	10.1821	10.0922	10.0023
51	11.3460	11.2495	11.1530	11.0565	10.9600	10.8635	10.7670	10.6705	10.5740	10.4775	10.3810	10.2845	10.1879
52	11.6170	11.5131	11.4092	11.3053	11.2014	11.0975	10.9936	10.8897	10.7858	10.6819	10.5780	10.4742	10.3704
53	11.8926	11.7808	11.6690	11.5572	11.4454	11.3336	11.2218	11.1100	10.9982	10.8864	10.7745	10.6626	10.5507
54	12.1749	12.0544	11.9338	11.8132	11.6927	11.5721	11.4515	11.3310	11.2104	11.0898	10.9693	10.8487	10.7281
55	12.4625	12.3323	12.2022	12.0721	11.9419	11.8118	11.6817	11.5515	11.4214	11.2913	11.1611	11.0310	10.9009
56	12.7555	12.6152	12.4750	12.3348	12.1945	12.0543	11.9141	11.7738	11.6336	11.4934	11.3531	11.2129	11.0727
57	13.0604	12.9086	12.7568	12.6050	12.4532	12.3014	12.1496	11.9978	11.8460	11.6942	11.5424	11.3906	11.2388
58	13.3661	13.2021	13.0381	12.8741	12.7101	12.5461	12.3821	12.2181	12.0541	11.8901	11.7261	11.5621	11.3981
59	13.6865	13.5085	13.3305	13.1525	12.9745	12.7965	12.6185	12.4405	12.2625	12.0845	11.9065	11.7285	11.5505
60	14.0077	13.8144	13.6211	13.4278	13.2345	13.0412	12.8479	12.6546	12.4613	12.2680	12.0747	11.8814	11.6882
61	14.3373	14.1270	13.9167	13.7064	13.4961	13.2858	13.0755	12.8652	12.6549	12.4446	12.2343	12.0240	11.8137
62	14.6727	14.4439	14.2151	13.9863	13.7575	13.5287	13.2999	13.0711	12.8423	12.6135	12.3846	12.1557	11.9268
63	15.0178	14.7685	14.5192	14.2699	14.0206	13.7713	13.5220	13.2727	13.0235	12.7743	12.5251	12.2759	12.0267
64	15.3700	15.0984	14.8268	14.5552	14.2836	14.0120	13.7404	13.4688	13.1972	12.9256	12.6539	12.3822	12.1105
65	15.7316	15.4356	15.1396	14.8436	14.5476	14.2516	13.9556	13.6596	13.3636	13.0677	12.7718	12.4759	12.1800
66	16.1048	15.7819	15.4590	15.1361	14.8132	14.4903	14.1674	13.8445	13.5216	13.1987	12.8759	12.5531	12.2303
67	16.4860	16.1342	15.7824	15.4306	15.0788	14.7270	14.3752	14.0234	13.6716	13.3198	12.9681	12.6164	12.2647
68	16.8842	16.5013	16.1184	15.7355	15.3526	14.9697	14.5868	14.2039	13.8210	13.4381	13.0552	12.6722	12.2892
69	17 3020	16.8851	16.4682	16.0513	15.6344	15.2175	14.8006	14.3837	13.9668	13.5499	13.1330	12.7161	12.2991
70	17.7365	17.2827	16.8290	16.3753	15.9216	15.4679	15.0143	14.5606	14.1070	13.6534	13.1998	12.7462	12.2926
71	18.1952	17.7017	17.2082	16.7147	16.2212	15.7277	15.2342	14.7407	14.2472	13.7536	13.2600	12.7664	12.2728
72	18.6789	18.1423	17.6057	17.0691	16.5325	15.9959	15.4593	14.9227	14.3862	13.8497	13.3132	12.7767	12.2402
73	19.1939	18.6105	18.0271	17.4437	16.8603	16.2769	15.6935	15.1101	14.5267	13.9433	13.3600	12.7767	12.1934
74	19.7396	19.1057	18.4718	17.8379	17.2040	16.5701	15.9362	15.3023	14.6684	14.0345	13.4006	12.7666	12.1326
Age.	0	1	2	3	4	5	6	7	8	9	10	11	12

Age.	0	1	2	3	4	5	6	7	8	9	10	11	12
10	6.7805	6.7502	6.7200	6.6897	6.6595	6.6292	6.5990	6.5687	6.5385	6.5082	6.4780	6.4478	6.4176
11	6.9041	6.8738	6.8435	6.8132	6.7829	6.7526	6.7223	6.6920	6.6617	6.6313	6.6009	6.5705	6.5401
12	7.0309	7.0006	6.9704	6.9401	6.9099	6.8796	6.8494	6.8191	6.7889	6.7587	6.7284	6.6982	6.6679
13	7.1561	7.1260	7.0959	7.0659	7.0359	7.0059	6.9759	6.9459	6.9159	6.8859	6.8559	6.8259	6.7959
14	7.2893	7.2592	7.2292	7.1992	7.1692	7.1392	7.1092	7.0792	7.0492	7.0192	6.9892	6.9592	6.9292
15	7.4267	7.3968	7.3669	7.3370	7.3071	7.2772	7.2473	7.2174	7.1875	7.1575	7.1275	7.0975	7.0675
16	7.5676	7.5376	7.5076	7.4776	7.4476	7.4176	7.3876	7.3576	7.3276	7.2976	7.2676	7.2376	7.2076
17	7.7127	7.6828	7.6529	7.6230	7.5931	7.5632	7.5333	7.5034	7.4736	7.4438	7.4140	7.3842	7.3544
18	7.8641	7.8341	7.8041	7.7741	7.7441	7.7141	7.6841	7.6541	7.6241	7.5941	7.5642	7.5343	7.5044
19	8.0203	7.9902	7.9601	7.9300	7.8999	7.8699	7.8399	7.8099	7.7799	7.7499	7.7199	7.6899	7.6599
20	8.1798	8.1498	8.1198	8.0898	8.0598	8.0297	7.9996	7.9695	7.9394	7.9093	7.8792	7.8491	7.8190
21	8.3457	8.3156	8.2855	8.2553	8.2251	8.1949	8.1647	8.1345	8.1043	8.0741	8.0439	8.0137	7.9835
22	8.5168	8.4865	8.4562	8.4259	8.3956	8.3653	8.3350	8.3047	8.2744	8.2441	8.2139	8.1837	8.1535
23	8.6934	8.6630	8.6326	8.6022	8.5718	8.5414	8.5110	8.4806	8.4502	8.4198	8.3895	8.3592	8.3289
24	8.8766	8.8461	8.8156	8.7851	8.7546	8.7241	8.6936	8.6631	8.6325	8.6019	8.5713	8.5407	8.5101
25	9.0654	9.0347	9.0040	8.9733	8.9426	8.9119	8.8812	8.8505	8.8198	8.7891	8.7584	8.7277	8.6970
26	9.2598	9.2289	9.1980	9.1671	9.1362	9.1053	9.0744	9.0435	9.0126	8.9817	8.9508	8.9198	8.8888
27	9.4613	9.4301	9.3989	9.3677	9.3365	9.3053	9.2741	9.2429	9.2117	9.1806	9.1495	9.1184	9.0873
28	9.6685	9.6371	9.6057	9.5743	9.5429	9.5115	9.4801	9.4487	9.4172	9.3857	9.3542	9.3227	9.2912
29	9.8823	9.8505	9.8187	9.7869	9.7551	9.7233	9.6915	9.6597	9.6280	9.5963	9.5646	9.5329	9.5012
30	10.1029	10.0708	10.0387	10.0066	9.9745	9.9424	9.9103	9.8782	9.8461	9.8139	9.7817	9.7495	9.7173
31	10.3301	10.2976	10.2651	10.2326	10.2001	10.1676	10.1351	10.1026	10.0701	10.0376	10.0051	9.9726	9.9400
32	10.5646	10.5317	10.4988	10.4659	10.4330	10.4001	10.3672	10.3343	10.3014	10.2685	10.2356	10.2028	10.1700
33	10.8079	10.7745	10.7412	10.7078	10.6745	10.6411	10.6078	10.5744	10.5411	10.5077	10.4744	10.4410	10.4077
34	11.0581	11.0241	10.9903	10.9565	10.9227	10.8889	10.8551	10.8213	10.7876	10.7541	10.7204	10.6867	10.6530
35	11.3169	11.2827	11.2485	11.2143	11.1801	11.1459	11.1117	11.0775	11.0433	11.0091	10.9748	10.9405	10.9062
36	11.5851	11.5504	11.5157	11.4810	11.4463	11.4116	11.3769	11.3422	11.3075	11.2728	11.2381	11.2034	11.1688
37	11.8632	11.8280	11.7928	11.7576	11.7224	11.6872	11.6520	11.6168	11.5816	11.5464	11.5112	11.4759	11.4406
38	12.1518	12.1161	12.0804	12.0447	12.0090	11.9733	11.9376	11.9019	11.8662	11.8305	11.7947	11.7589	11.7231
39	12.4519	12.4156	12.3793	12.3430	12.3067	12.2704	12.2341	12.1978	12.1615	12.1252	12.0889	12.0526	12.0163
40	12.7647	12.7276	12.6906	12.6535	12.6165	12.5794	12.5424	12.5053	12.4683	12.4312	12.3942	12.3571	12.3201
41	13.0890	13.0499	13.0108	12.9717	12.9326	12.8935	12.8544	12.8153	12.7762	12.7371	12.6979	12.6587	12.6195
42	13.4110	13.3717	13.3324	13.2931	13.2538	13.2145	13.1752	13.1359	13.0966	13.0573	13.0180	12.9787	12.9394
43	13.7553	13.7129	13.6705	13.6281	13.5857	13.5433	13.5009	13.4585	13.4161	13.3736	13.3311	13.2886	13.2461
44	14.0929	14.0474	14.0019	13.9564	13.9109	13.8654	13.8199	13.7744	13.7289	13.6834	13.6378	13.5922	13.5466
45	14.4308	14.3819	14.3330	14.2841	14.2352	14.1863	14.1374	14.0885	14.0396	13.9906	13.9416	13.8926	13.8436
46	14.7705	14.7177	14.6649	14.6121	14.5593	14.5065	14.4537	14.4009	14.3481	14.2953	14.2425	14.1897	14.1370
47	15.1157	15.0587	15.0017	14.9447	14.8877	14.8307	14.7737	14.7167	14.6596	14.6025	14.5454	14.4883	14.4312
48	15.4642	15.4025	15.3408	15.2791	15.2174	15.1557	15.0940	15.0323	14.9706	14.9090	14.8474	14.7858	14.7242
49	15.8178	15.7509	15.6840	15.6171	15.5502	15.4833	15.4164	15.3495	15.2826	15.2156	15.1486	15.0816	15.0146
50	16.1765	16.1037	16.0309	15.9581	15.8853	15.8125	15.7397	15.6669	15.5941	15.5214	15.4487	15.3760	15.3033
51	16.5367	16.4575	16.3783	16.2991	16.2199	16.1407	16.0615	15.9823	15.9031	15.8239	15.7447	15.6655	15.5864
52	16.9001	16.8140	16.7279	16.6418	16.5557	16.4696	16.3835	16.2974	16.2113	16.1251	16.0389	15.9527	15.8665
53	17.2679	17.1741	17.0803	16.9865	16.8927	16.7989	16.7051	16.6113	16.5175	16.4237	16.3299	16.2360	16.1421
54	17.6398	17.5375	17.4353	17.3330	17.2308	17.1285	17.0263	16.9240	16.8218	16.7195	16.6173	16.5150	16.4128
55	18.0149	17.9037	17.7925	17.6813	17.5701	17.4589	17.3477	17.2365	17.1253	17.0142	16.9031	16.7920	16.6809
56	18.3975	18.2760	18.1545	18.0330	17.9115	17.7900	17.6685	17.5470	17.4255	17.3040	17.1826	17.0612	16.9398
57	18.7831	18.6508	18.5185	18.3862	18.2539	18.1216	17.9893	17.8570	17.7247	17.5924	17.4601	17.3278	17.1955
58	19.1726	19.0278	18.8830	18.7382	18.5944	18.4486	18.3037	18.1590	18.0142	17.8694	17.7246	17.5796	17.4346
59	19.5656	19.4071	19.2486	19.0901	18.9316	18.7731	18 6146	18.4561	18.2976	18.1391	17.9806	17.8220	17.6634
60	19.9565	19.7826	19.6087	19.4348	19.2609	19.0870	18.9131	18.7392	18.5653	18.3915	18.2177	18.0439	17.8701
61	20.3476	20.1570	19.9664	19.7758	19.5852	19.3946	19.2040	19.0134	18.8229	18.6324	18.4419	18.2514	18.0609
62	20.7400	20.5309	20.3218	20.1127	19.9036	19.6945	19.4854	19.2763	19.0673	18.8583	18.6493	18.4403	18.2313
63	21.1335	20.9041	20.6748	20.4454	20.2161	19.9867	19.7574	19.5280	19.2987	19.0693	18.8400	18.6106	18.3813
64	21.5269	21.2754	21.0239	20.7724	20.5209	20.2694	20.0179	19.7664	19.5149	19.2633	19.0117	18.7601	18.5085
65	21.9229	21.5468	21.3707	21.0946	20.8185	20.5424	20.2663	19.9902	19.7141	19.4380	19.1619	18.8857	18.6095
66	22.3180	22.0154	21.7128	21.4102	21.1076	20.8050	20.5024	20.1998	19.8973	19.5948	19.2923	18.9898	18.6873
67	22.7173	22.3861	22.0549	21.7237	21.3925	21.0613	20.7301	20.3989	20.0677	19.7366	19.4055	19.0744	18.7433
68	23.1278	22.7654	22.4030	22.0406	21.6782	21.3158	20.9534	20.5910	20.2286	19.8662	19.5038	19.1413	18.7788
69	23.5475	23.1512	22.7549	22.3586	21.9623	21.5660	21.1697	20.7734	20.3771	19.9808	19.5845	19.1882	18.7920
70	23.9775	23.5443	23.1111	22.6779	22.2447	21.8115	21.3783	20.9451	20.5119	20.0788	19.6457	19.2126	18.7795
71	24.4232	23.9502	23.4772	23.0042	22.5312	22.0582	21.5852	21.1122	20.6392	20.1662	19.6932	19.2202	18.7472
72	24.8883	24.3718	23.8553	23.3388	22.8223	22.3058	21.7893	21.2728	20.7563	20.2398	19.7233	19.2068	18.6903
73	25.3745	24.8110	24.2475	23.6840	23.1205	22.5570	21.9935	21.4300	20.8664	20.3028	19.7392	19.1756	18.6120
74	25.8860	25.2716	24.6573	24.0429	23.4286	22.8142	22.1999	21.5855	20.9712	20.3568	19.7425	19.1281	18.5138
Age.	0	1	2	3	4	5	6	7	8	9	10	11	12

Age.	0	1	2	3	4	5	6	7	8	9	10	11	12
10	9.019,	8.9976	8.9755	8.9535	8.9315	8.9095	8.8875	8.8655	8.8435	8.8215	8.7995	8.7775	8.7555
11	9.1821	9.1604	9.1387	9.1169	9.0951	9.0733	9.0515	9.0297	9.0079	8.9861	8.9643	8.9425	8.9207
12	9.3511	9.3298	9.3085	9.2872	9.2659	9.2445	9.2231	9.2017	9.1803	9.1589	9.1375	9.1161	9.0947
13	9.5229	9.5018	9.4807	9.4596	9.4385	9.4174	9.3962	9.3750	9.3538	9.3326	9.3114	9.2902	9.2690
14	9.7014	9.6805	9.6596	9.6387	9.6178	9.5969	9.5759	9.5549	9.5339	9.5129	9.4919	9.4709	9.4499
15	9.8865	9.8656	9.8447	9.8238	9.8029	9.7821	9.7613	9.7405	9.7197	9.6989	9.6781	9.6573	9.6365
16	10.0754	10.0549	10.0344	10.0139	9.9934	9.9729	9.9524	9.9319	9.9114	9.8909	9.8704	9.8499	9.8284
17	10.2728	10.2523	10.2318	10.2113	10.1909	10.1705	10.1501	10.1297	10.1093	10.0889	10.0685	10.0481	10.0277
18	10.4752	10.4550	10.4348	10.4146	10.3944	10.3741	10.3538	10.3335	10.3132	10.2929	10.2726	10.2523	10.2320
19	10.6849	10.6649	10.6449	10.6248	10.6047	10.5846	10.5645	10.5444	10.5243	10.5042	10.4841	10.4640	10.4439
20	10.9004	10.8805	10.8606	10.8406	10.8206	10.8006	10.7806	10.7606	10.7406	10.7206	10.7006	10.6806	10.6606
21	11.1232	11.1033	11.0835	11.0636	11.0438	11.0239	11.0041	10.9843	10.9645	10.9447	10.9249	10.9050	10.8850
22	11.3535	11.3337	11.3140	11.2943	11.2746	11.2549	11.2352	11.2155	11.1958	11.1761	11.1564	11.1367	11.1170
23	11.5914	11.5717	11.5520	11.5324	11.5128	11.4932	11.4736	11.4540	11.4344	11.4148	11.3952	11.3756	11.3560
24	11.8373	11.8177	11.7981	11.7785	11.7589	11.7394	11.7199	11.7004	11.6809	11.6614	11.6419	11.6224	11.6029
25	12.0911	12.0717	12.0523	12.0329	12.0134	11.9939	11.9744	11.9549	11.9354	11.9159	11.8964	11.8769	11.8574
26	12.3523	12.3328	12.3133	12.2938	12.2743	12.2549	12.2355	12.2161	12.1967	12.1773	12.1579	12.1385	12.1191
27	12.6225	12.6032	12.5839	12.5646	12.5453	12.5260	12.5066	12.4872	12.4678	12.4484	12.4290	12.4096	12.3902
28	12.9006	12.8811	12.8616	12.8421	12.8227	12.8033	12.7839	12.7645	12.7451	12.7257	12.7063	12.6869	12.6675
29	13.1875	13.1681	13.1486	13.1291	13.1096	13.0901	13.0706	13.0511	13.0316	13.0121	12.9926	12.9731	12.9536
30	13.4831	13.4635	13.4439	13.4243	13.4047	13.3852	13.3657	13.3462	13.3267	13.3072	13.2877	13.2682	13.2487
31	13.7880	13.7685	13.7489	13.7294	13.7098	13.6903	13.6707	13.6512	13.6316	13.6121	13.5925	13.5730	13.5534
32	14.1031	14.0834	14.0637	14.0440	14.0243	14.0047	13.9851	13.9655	13.9459	13.9263	13.9067	13.8871	13.8675
33	14.4287	14.4089	14.3891	14.3693	14.3496	14.3299	14.3102	14.2905	14.2708	14.2511	14.2314	14.2117	14.1920
34	14.7650	14.7451	14.7253	14.7055	14.6857	14.6659	14.6461	14.6263	14.6065	14.5867	14.5669	14.5471	14.5273
35	15.1124	15.0926	15.0728	15.0530	15.0332	15.0133	14.9934	14.9735	14.9536	14.9337	14.9138	14.8939	14.8740
36	15.4726	15.4525	15.4325	15.4125	15.3925	15.3725	15.3525	15.3325	15.3125	15.2925	15.2725	15.2525	15.2327
37	15.8456	15.8256	15.8056	15.7856	15.7656	15.7456	15.7255	15.7054	15.6853	15.6652	15.6451	15.6250	15.6049
38	16.2332	16.2131	16.1930	16.1729	16.1527	16.1325	16.1123	16.0921	16.0719	16.0517	16.0315	16.0113	15.9911
39	16.6358	16.6154	16.5949	16 5745	16.5541	16.5336	16.5132	16.4928	16.4723	16.4518	16.4314	16.4109	16.3904
40	17.0536	17.0316	17.0096	16.9876	16.9656	16.9436	16.9216	16.8996	16.8776	16.8556	16.8336	16.8116	16.7896
41	17.4721	17.4505	17.4289	17.4073	17.3857	17.3641	17.3425	17.3209	17.2993	17.2777	17.2561	17.2345	17.2129
42	17.9166	17.8924	17.8683	17.8442	17.8201	17.7960	17.7719	17.7478	17.7237	17.6996	17.6755	17.6514	17.6273
43	18.3539	18.3273	18.3007	18.2741	18.2476	18.2211	18.1946	18.1681	18.1416	18.1151	18.0886	18.0621	18.0356
44	18.7906	18.7613	18.7320	18.7028	18.6736	18.6444	18.6152	18.5860	18.5568	18.5276	18.4984	18.4692	18.4400
45	19.2294	19.1970	19.1646	19.1322	19.0998	19.0675	19.0352	19.0029	18.9706	18.9383	18.9060	18.8737	18.8414
46	19.6701	19.6342	19.5983	19.5624	19.5265	19.4907	19.4549	19.4191	19.3833	19.3475	19.3117	19.2759	19.2401
47	20.1163	20.0766	20.0369	19.9972	19.9575	19.9179	19.8783	19.8387	19.7991	19.7595	19.7199	19.6803	19.6407
48	20.5668	20.5224	20.4780	20.4336	20.3893	20.3450	20.3007	20.2564	20.2121	20.1678	20.1235	20.0792	20.0349
49	21.0200	20.9711	20.9221	20.8731	20.8241	20.7751	20.7261	20.6771	20.6281	20.5792	20.5303	20.4814	20.4325
50	21.4775	21.4231	21.3687	21.3143	21.2599	21.2055	21.1511	21.0967	21.0423	20.9879	20.9335	20.8791	20.8248
51	21.9352	21.8749	21.8146	21.7543	21.6940	21.6337	21.5734	21.5131	21.4528	21.3925	21.3322	21.2719	21.2116
52	22.3962	22.3293	22.2624	22.1955	22.1286	22.0617	21.9948	21.9279	21.8610	21.7941	21.7272	21.6604	21.5936
53	22.8593	22.7851	22.7110	22.6368	22.5627	22.4885	22.4144	22.3402	22.2661	22.1919	22.1178	22.0436	21.9695
54	23.3245	23.2427	23.1609	23.0791	22.9973	22.9155	22.8337	22.7519	22.6701	22.5883	22.5064	22.4245	22.3426
55	23.7949	23.7041	23.6133	23.5225	23.4317	23.3409	23.2501	23.1593	23.0685	22.9777	22.8869	22.7961	22.7054
56	24.2646	24.1643	24.0640	23.9638	23.8636	23.7634	23.6632	23.5630	23.4628	23.3626	23.2624	23.1622	23.0618
57	24.7398	24.6287	24.5176	24.4064	24.2952	24.1840	24.0728	23.9616	23.8504	23.7392	23.6280	23.5168	23.4056
58	25.2091	25.0858	24.9626	24.8394	24.7162	24.5930	24.4698	24.3466	24.2234	24.1002	23.9769	23.8536	23.7303
59	25.6785	25.5418	25.4051	25.2684	25.1317	24.9950	24.8583	24.7216	24.5849	24.4481	24.3113	24.1745	24.0377
60	26.1384	25.9869	25.8354	25.6839	25.5324	25.3809	25.2294	25.0779	24.9264	24.7749	24.6234	24.4719	24.3204
61	26.5948	26.4268	26.2588	26.0909	25.9229	25.7550	25.5871	25.4191	25.[illegible]12	25.0832	24.9153	24.7473	24.5794
62	27.0445	26.8584	26.6723	26.4862	26.3001	26.1140	25.9279	25.7418	25.5558	25.3698	25.1838	24.9978	24.8118
63	27.4881	27.2823	27.0765	26.8707	26.6649	26.4591	26.2533	26.0475	25.8417	25.6358	25.4299	25.2240	25.0181
64	27.9249	27.6971	27.4692	27.2413	27.0134	26.7855	26.5576	26.3297	26.1018	25.8740	25.6462	25.4184	25.1906
65	28.3524	28.1007	27.8490	27.5973	27.3456	27.0939	26.8422	26.5905	26.3388	26.0872	25.8356	25.5840	25.3327
66	28.7750	28.4976	28.2202	27.9428	27.6654	27.3880	27.1106	26.8332	26.5558	26.2784	26.0010	25.7236	25.4463
67	29.1959	28.8902	28.5845	28.2788	27.9731	27.6674	27.3617	27.0560	26.7503	26.4447	26.1391	25.8335	25.5279
68	29.6174	29.2810	28.9446	28.6082	28.2718	27.9354	27.5990	27.2626	26.9263	26.5900	26.2537	25.9174	25.5811
69	30.0404	29.6706	29.3008	28.9310	28.5612	28.1914	27.8216	27.4518	27.0819	26.7120	26.3421	25.9722	25.6023
70	30.4644	30.0582	29.6520	29.2458	28.8396	28.4334	28.0272	27.6210	27.2148	26.8087	26.4026	25.9965	25.5904
71	30.8976	30.4517	30.0058	29.5599	29.1140	28.6681	28.2222	27.7763	27.3304	26.8845	26.4386	25.9926	25.5466
72	31.3384	30.8494	30.3604	29.8714	29.3824	28.8934	28.4044	27.9154	27.4263	26.9372	26.4481	25.9590	25.4699
73	31.7931	31.2573	30.7215	30.1857	29.6499	29.1141	28.5783	28.0425	27.5068	26.9711	26.4354	25.8997	25.3640
74	32.2672	31.6801	31.0930	30.5059	29.9188	29.3317	28.7446	28.1575	27.5704	26.9834	26.3964	25.8094	25.2224
Age.	0	1	2	3	4	5	6	7	8	9	10	11	12

Age.	0	1	2	3	4	5	6	7	8	9	10	11	12
10	11.3576	11.3443	11.3310	11.3177	11.3045	11.2913	11.2781	11.2649	11.2517	11.2385	11.2253	11.2121	11.1989
11	11.5627	11.5501	11.5375	11.5249	11.5123	11.4997	11.4870	11.4743	11.4616	11.4489	11.4362	11.4235	11.4108
12	11.7779	11.7656	11.7533	11.7410	11.7287	11.7164	11.7041	11.6918	11.6795	11.6672	11.6549	11.6426	11.6303
13	11.9960	11.9840	11.9720	11.9601	11.9482	11.9363	11.9244	11.9125	11.9006	11.8887	11.8768	11.8649	11.8530
14	12.2221	12.2106	12.1990	12.1874	12.1758	12.1642	12.1526	12.1410	12.1294	12.1178	12.1062	12.0946	12.0830
15	12.4555	12.4445	12.4335	12.4225	12.4115	12.4001	12.3890	12.3779	12.3668	12.3557	12.3446	12.3335	12.3227
16	12.6972	12.6865	12.6757	12.6649	12.6541	12.6433	12.6325	12.6217	12.6109	12.6001	12.5893	12.5785	12.5677
17	12.9461	12.9356	12.9251	12.9146	12.9041	12.8937	12.8833	12.8729	12.8625	12.8521	12.8417	12.8313	12.8209
18	13.2028	13.1927	13.1826	13.1725	13.1624	13.1524	13.1424	13.1324	13.1224	13.1124	13.1024	13.0924	13.0824
19	13.4689	13.4591	13.4493	13.4395	13.4298	13.4201	13.4104	13.4007	13.3910	13.3813	13.3716	13.3619	13.3522
20	13.7420	13.7326	13.7232	13.7138	13.7044	13.6950	13.6857	13.6764	13.6671	13.6578	13.6485	13.6392	13.6299
21	14.0247	14.0158	14.0068	13.9978	13.9888	13.9798	13.9708	13.9618	13.9528	13.9438	13.9348	13.9258	13.9168
22	14.3170	14.3084	14.2997	14.2911	14.2824	14.2738	14.2651	14.2565	14.2478	14.2392	14.2305	14.2219	14.2132
23	14.6185	14.6102	14.6019	14.5936	14.5853	14.5770	14.5687	14.5604	14.5521	14.5438	14.5355	14.5272	14.5189
24	14.9301	14.9222	14.9142	14.9062	14.8982	14.8902	14.8822	14.8742	14.8662	14.8582	14.8502	14.8422	14.8342
25	15.2515	15.2439	15.2363	15.2287	15.2210	15.2133	15.2056	15.1979	15.1902	15.1825	15.1748	15.1671	15.1594
26	15.5826	15.5753	15.5679	15.5605	15.5531	15.5457	15.5383	15.5309	15.5235	15.5161	15.5087	15.5013	15.4939
27	15.9254	15.9183	15.9112	15.9041	15.8970	15.8899	15.8827	15.8755	15.8683	15.8611	15.8539	15.8467	15.8395
28	16.2769	16.2700	16.2631	16.2562	16.2493	16.2425	16.2357	16.2289	16.2221	16.2153	16.2085	16.2017	16.1949
29	16.6399	16.6333	16.6267	16.6201	16.6135	16.6069	16.6004	16.5939	16.5874	16.5809	16.5744	16.5679	16.5614
30	17.0145	17.0082	17.0019	16.9956	16.9893	16.9830	16.9768	16.9706	16.9644	16.9582	16.9520	16.9458	16.9396
31	17.4014	17.3955	17.3896	17.3836	17.3776	17.3716	17.3656	17.3596	17.3536	17.3476	17.3416	17.3356	17.3296
32	17.8006	17.7950	17.7893	17.7836	17.7779	17.7722	17.7665	17.7608	17.7551	17.7494	17.7437	17.7380	17.7323
33	18.2130	18.2077	18.2024	18.1970	18.1916	18.1862	18.1808	18.1754	18.1700	18.1646	18.1592	18.1538	18.1484
34	18.6393	18.6343	18.6293	18.6243	18.6193	18.6143	18.6092	18.6041	18.5990	18.5939	18.5888	18.5837	18.5786
35	19.0802	19.0755	19.0708	19.0661	19.0614	19.0567	19.0519	19.0471	19.0423	19.0375	19.0327	19.0279	19.0231
36	19.5365	19.5321	19.5277	19.5233	19.5189	19.5145	19.5101	19.5057	19.5013	19.4969	19.4925	19.4881	19.4837
37	20.0099	20.0059	20.0019	19.9978	19.9937	19.9896	19.9855	19.9814	19.9773	19.9732	19.9691	19.9650	19.9609
38	20.5012	20.4974	20.4936	20.4898	20.4859	20.4820	20.4781	20.4742	20.4703	20.4664	20.4625	20.4586	20.4547
39	21.0099	21.0049	21.0000	20.9951	20.9902	20.9853	20.9804	20.9755	20.9706	20.9657	20.9608	20.9559	20.9510
40	21.5231	21.5191	21.5151	21.5111	21.5071	21.5032	21.4993	21.4954	21.4915	21.4876	21.4837	21.4798	21.4759
41	22.0655	22.0596	22.0538	22.0480	22.0422	22.0364	22.0306	22.0248	22.0190	22.0132	22.0074	22.0016	21.9958
42	22.6045	22.5970	22.5895	22.5820	22.5745	22.5669	22.5593	22.5517	22.5441	22.5365	22.5289	22.5213	22.5137
43	23.1434	23.1339	23.1243	23.1148	23.1052	23.0957	23.0861	23.0766	23.0670	23.0575	23.0479	23.0384	23.0288
44	23.6840	23.6721	23.6602	23.6483	23.6364	23.6245	23.6126	23.6007	23.5888	23.5769	23.5650	23.5531	23.5412
45	24.2272	24.2126	24.1980	24.1834	24.1688	24.1542	24.1396	24.1250	24.1104	24.0958	24.0812	24.0666	24.0520
46	24.7732	24.7557	24.7382	24.7207	24.7032	24.6856	24.6680	24.6504	24.6328	24.6152	24.5976	24.5800	24.5624
47	25.3258	25.3048	25.2837	25.2626	25.2415	25.2204	25.1993	25.1782	25.1571	25.1360	25.1149	25.0938	25.0727
48	25.8775	25.8528	25.8281	25.8034	25.7787	25.7540	25.7292	25.7044	25.6796	25.6548	25.6300	25.6052	25.5804
49	26.4379	26.4084	26.3789	26.3494	26.3199	26.2904	26.2609	26.2314	26.2019	26.1724	26.1430	26.1136	26.0842
50	26.9990	26.9647	26.9304	26.8961	26.8618	26.8275	26.7932	26.7589	26.7246	26.6903	26.6559	26.6215	26.5871
51	27.5604	27.5206	27.4808	27.4410	27.4012	27.3614	27.3216	27.2818	27.2421	27.2024	27.1627	27.1230	27.0833
52	28.1233	28.0775	28.0317	27.9859	27.9401	27.8943	27.8485	27.8027	27.7569	27.7111	27.6653	27.6195	27.5736
53	28.6867	28.6345	28.5823	28.5301	28.4779	28.4257	28.3735	28.3213	28.2691	28.2169	28.1647	28.1125	28.0604
54	29.2543	29.1945	29.1347	29.0749	29.0151	28.9553	28.8955	28.8357	28.7760	28.7163	28.6566	28.5969	28.5372
55	29.8194	29.7517	29.6840	29.6163	29.5486	29.4809	29.4132	29.3455	29.2778	29.2101	29.1424	29.0747	29.0069
56	30.3866	30.3095	30.2325	30.1554	30.0784	30.0013	29.9243	29.8472	29.7702	29.6931	29.6161	29.5390	29.4620
57	30.9499	30.8626	30.7753	30.6880	30.6007	30.5134	30.4261	30.3388	30.2515	30.1641	30.0767	29.9893	29.9019
58	31.5048	31.4059	31.3070	31.2081	31.1092	31.0103	30.9114	30.8125	30.7136	30.6147	30.5158	30.4168	30.3178
59	32.0528	31.9413	31.8297	31.7181	31.6065	31.4949	31.3833	31.2717	31.1600	31.0483	30.9366	30.8249	30.7132
60	32.5887	32.4628	32.3369	32.2110	32.0851	31.9592	31.8333	31.7074	31.5815	31.4556	31.3298	31.2040	31.0782
61	33.1133	32.9717	32.8301	32.6885	32.5469	32.4053	32.2637	32.1221	31.9805	31.8390	31.6975	31.5560	31.4145
62	33.6250	33.4662	33.3074	33.1486	32.9898	32.8310	32.6722	32.5134	32.3546	32.1958	32.0370	31.8782	31.7194
63	34.1249	33.9468	33.7687	33.5906	33.4125	33.2344	33.0563	32.8782	32.7002	32.5222	32.3442	32.1662	31.9882
64	34.6070	34.4081	34.2092	34.0103	33.8114	33.6125	33.4136	33.2147	33.0158	32.8170	32.6182	32.4194	32.2206
65	35.0756	34.8541	34.6326	34.4111	34.1896	33.9681	33.7466	33.5251	33.3036	33.0821	32.8607	32.6393	32.4179
66	35.5340	35.2876	35.0412	34.7948	34.5484	34.3020	34.0556	33.8092	33.5628	33.3164	33.0700	32.8237	32.5774
67	35.9805	35.7070	35.4335	35.1600	34.8865	34.6130	34.3395	34.0660	33.7924	33.5188	33.2452	32.9716	32.6980
68	36.4197	36.1165	35.8133	35.5101	35.2069	34.9037	34.6005	34.2973	33.9940	33.6907	33.3874	33.0841	32.7808
69	36.8507	36.5152	36.1797	35.8442	35.5087	35.1732	34.8377	34.5022	34.1667	33.8311	33.4955	33.1599	32.8243
70	37.2753	36.9043	36.5333	36.1623	35.7913	35.4203	35.0493	34.6783	34.3073	33.9363	33.5653	33.1943	32.8232
71	37.6970	37.2874	36.8778	36.4682	36.0586	35.6490	35.2394	34.8298	34.4202	34.0105	33.6008	33.1911	32.7814
72	38.1180	37.6664	37.2148	36.7632	36.3116	35.8600	35.4084	34.9568	34.5052	34.0536	33.6020	33.1503	32.6986
73	38.5451	38.0472	37.5493	37.0514	36.5535	36.0556	35.5577	35.0598	34.5619	34.0640	33.5662	33.0684	32.5706
74	38.9758	38.4272	37.8786	37.3300	36.7814	36.2328	35.6842	35.1356	34.5870	34.0385	33.4900	32.9415	32.3930
Age.	0	1	2	3	4	5	6	7	8	9	10	11	12

Age.	0	1	2	3	4	5	6	7	8	9	10	11	12
10	13.8010	13.7972	13.7934	13.7896	13.7858	13.7820	13.7782	13.7744	13.7706	13.7668	13.7630	13.7592	13.7554
11	14.0528	14.0494	14.0460	14.0426	14.0392	14.0359	14.0326	14.0293	14.0260	14.0227	14.0194	14.0161	14.0128
12	14.3135	14.3107	14.3079	14.3051	14.3023	14.2995	14.2968	14.2941	14.2914	14.2887	14.2860	14.2833	14.2806
13	14.5800	14.5778	14.5756	14.5734	14.5711	14.5688	14.5665	14.5642	14.5619	14.5596	14.5573	14.5550	14.5527
14	14.8552	14.8537	14.8522	14.8507	14.8492	14.8477	14.8461	14.8445	14.8429	14.8413	14.8397	14.8381	14.8365
15	15.1417	15.1407	15.1396	15.1385	15.1374	15.1363	15.1352	15.1341	15.1330	15.1319	15.1308	15.1297	15.1286
16	15.4355	15.4349	15.4343	15.4337	15.4332	15.4327	15.4322	15.4317	15.4312	15.4307	15.4302	15.4297	15.4292
17	15.7393	15.7393	15.7394	15.7394	15.7395	15.7395	15.7396	15.7396	15.7397	15.7397	15.7398	15.7398	15.7399
18	16.0532	16.0541	16.0550	16.0559	16.0568	16.0576	16.0584	16.0592	16.0600	16.0608	16.0616	16.0624	16.0632
19	16.3772	16.3783	16.3794	16.3805	16.3817	16.3829	16.3841	16.3853	16.3865	16.3877	16.3889	16.3901	16.3913
20	16.7113	16.7130	16.7147	16.7164	16.7181	16.7199	16.7217	16.7235	16.7253	16.7271	16.7289	16.7307	16.7325
21	17.0565	17.0589	17.0613	17.0636	17.0660	17.0683	17.0707	17.0730	17.0754	17.0777	17.0801	17.0824	17.0848
22	17.4132	17.4161	17.4190	17.4219	17.4248	17.4278	17.4308	17.4338	17.4368	17.4398	17.4428	17.4458	17.4488
23	17.7814	17.7850	17.7886	17.7922	17.7958	17.7994	17.8029	17.8064	17.8099	17.8134	17.8169	17.8204	17.8239
24	18.1614	18.1656	18.1698	18.1740	18.1782	18.1823	18.1864	18.1905	18.1946	18.1987	18.2028	18.2069	18.2110
25	18.5535	18.5583	18.5630	18.5677	18.5724	18.5771	18.5818	18.5865	18.5912	18.5959	18.6006	18.6053	18.6100
26	18.9574	18.9627	18.9680	18.9733	18.9786	18.9839	18.9892	18.9945	18.9998	19.0051	19.0104	19.0157	19.0210
27	19.3747	19.3805	19.3863	19.3921	19.3979	19.4038	19.4097	19.4156	19.4215	19.4274	19.4333	19.4392	19.4451
28	19.8043	19.8107	19.8171	19.8235	19.8300	19.8365	19.8430	19.8495	19.8560	19.8625	19.8690	19.8755	19.8820
29	20.2477	20.2548	20.2619	20.2690	20.2761	20.2832	20.2903	20.2974	20.3045	20.3116	20.3187	20.3258	20.3329
30	20.7054	20.7132	20.7210	20.7287	20.7364	20.7441	20.7518	20.7595	20.7672	20.7749	20.7826	20.7903	20.7980
31	21.1776	21.1859	21.1942	21.2025	21.2109	21.2193	21.2277	21.2361	21.2445	21.2529	21.2613	21.2697	21.2781
32	21.6654	21.6745	21.6836	21.6927	21.7018	21.7109	21.7199	21.7289	21.7379	21.7469	21.7559	21.7649	21.7739
33	22.1694	22.1791	22.1888	22.1985	22.2082	22.2180	22.2278	22.2376	22.2474	22.2572	22.2670	22.2768	22.2866
34	22.6906	22.7010	22.7114	22.7218	22.7323	22.7428	22.7533	22.7638	22.7743	22.7848	22.7953	22.8058	22.8163
35	23.2293	23.2405	23.2517	23.2629	23.2741	23.2853	23.2966	23.3079	23.3192	23.3305	23.3418	23.3531	23.3644
36	23.7875	23.7996	23.8117	23.8238	23.8358	23.8478	23.8598	23.8718	23.8838	23.8958	23.9078	23.9198	23.9318
37	24.3659	24.3786	24.3913	24.4040	24.4167	24.4294	24.4421	24.4548	24.4675	24.4802	24.4929	24.5056	24.5183
38	24.9648	24.9769	24.9890	25.0011	25.0133	25.0255	25.0377	25.0499	25.0621	25.0743	25.0865	25.0987	25.1109
39	25.5705	25.5843	25.5980	25.6117	25.6254	25.6391	25.6528	25.6665	25.6802	25.6939	25.7076	25.7213	25.7350
40	26.2094	26.2219	26.2344	26.2469	26.2593	26.2717	26.2841	26.2965	26.3089	26.3213	26.3337	26.3461	26.3585
41	26.8484	26.8598	26.8711	26.8825	26.8938	26.9052	26.9165	26.9279	26.9392	26.9506	26.9619	26.9733	26.9846
42	27.4909	27.5011	27.5112	27.5213	27.5314	27.5415	27.5516	27.5617	27.5718	27.5819	27.5920	27.6021	27.6122
43	28.1366	28.1452	28.1538	28.1623	28.1708	28.1793	28.1878	28.1963	28.2048	28.2133	28.2218	28.2303	28.2388
44	28.7852	28.7918	28.7984	28.8051	28.8117	28.8184	28.8250	28.8317	28.8383	28.8450	28.8516	28.8583	28.8649
45	29.4378	29.4424	29.4470	29.4516	29.4561	29.4606	29.4651	29.4696	29.4741	29.4786	29.4831	29.4876	29.4921
46	30.0955	30.0974	30.0993	30.1012	30.1031	30.1050	30.1069	30.1088	30.1107	30.1126	30.1145	30.1164	30.1183
47	30.7578	30.7567	30.7556	30.7546	30.7535	30.7525	30.7514	30.7504	30.7493	30.7483	30.7472	30.7462	30.7451
48	31.4230	31.4186	31.4141	31.4097	31.4052	31.4008	31.3963	31.3919	31.3874	31.3830	31.3785	31.3741	31.3696
49	32.0896	32.0815	32.0734	32.0653	32.0571	32.0489	32.0407	32.0325	32.0243	32.0161	32.0079	31.9997	31.9915
50	32.7613	32.7489	32.7364	32.7240	32.7115	32.6991	32.6866	32.6742	32.6617	32.6493	32.6368	32.6244	32.6119
51	33.4321	33.4148	33.3975	33.3803	33.3631	33.3459	33.3287	33.3115	33.2943	33.2771	33.2599	33.2427	33.2255
52	34.1033	34.0811	34.0589	34.0367	34.0145	33.9923	33.9700	33.9477	33.9254	33.9031	33.8808	33.8585	33.8362
53	34.7776	34.7493	34.7210	34.6926	34.6642	34.6358	34.6074	34.5790	34.5506	34.5222	34.4938	34.4654	34.4370
54	35.4489	35.4142	35.3794	35.3446	35.3097	35.2749	35.2401	35.2053	35.1705	35.1358	35.1011	35.0664	35.0317
55	36.1209	36.0785	36.0361	35.9937	35.9513	35.9089	35.8665	35.8241	35.7817	35.7393	35.6969	35.6546	35.6123
56	36.7868	36.7360	36.6852	36.6344	36.5836	36.5328	36.4820	36.4312	36.3804	36.3296	36.2787	36.2278	36.1769
57	37.4462	37.3858	37.3254	37.2650	37.2046	37.1442	37.0838	37.0234	36.9630	36.9026	36.8423	36.7820	36.7217
58	38.0923	38.0214	37.9505	37.8796	37.8087	37.7378	37.6669	37.5960	37.5251	37.4542	37.3832	37.3122	37.2412
59	38.7283	38.6455	38.5628	38.4800	38.3973	38.3145	38.2318	38.1490	38.0663	37.9835	37.9008	37.8180	37.7353
60	39.3465	39.2506	39.1547	39.0588	38.9629	38.8670	38.7711	38.6752	38.5793	38.4834	38.3875	38.2917	38.1959
61	39.9484	39.8381	39.7278	39.6175	39.5072	39.3969	39.2866	39.1763	39.0660	38.9557	38.8454	38.7350	38.6246
62	40.5326	40.4060	40.2795	40.1529	40.0264	39.8998	39.7733	39.6467	39.5202	39.3936	39.2671	39.1405	39.0140
63	41.0950	40.9509	40.8068	40.6627	40.5186	40.3745	40.2304	40.0863	39.9422	39.7981	39.6540	39.5099	39.3657
64	41.6370	41.4737	41.3104	41.1471	40.9838	40.8205	40.6572	40.4939	40.3307	40.1675	40.0043	39.8411	39.6779
65	42.1608	41.9764	41.7920	41.6076	41.4232	41.2388	41.0544	40.8700	40.6856	40.5012	40.3168	40.1323	39.9478
66	42.6651	42.4575	42.2500	42.0424	41.8349	41.6273	41.4198	41.2122	41.0047	40.7971	40.5896	40.3820	40.1745
67	43.1506	42.9176	42.6847	42.4517	42.2188	41.9858	41.7529	41.5199	41.2870	41.0540	40.8211	40.5881	40.3552
68	43.6194	43.3588	43.0981	42.8374	42.5768	42.3161	42.0555	41.7948	41.5342	41.2735	41.0129	40.7522	40.4916
69	44.0727	43.7815	43.4903	43.1991	42.9079	42.6167	42.3255	42.0343	41.7431	41.4519	41.1607	40.8696	40.5785
70	44.5081	44.1835	43.8589	43.5343	43.2097	42.8851	42.5605	42.2359	41.9114	41.5869	41.2624	40.9379	40.6134
71	44.9318	44.5708	44.2098	43.8488	43.4878	43.1268	42.7658	42.4048	42.0439	41.6830	41.3221	40.9612	40.6003
72	45.3467	44.9454	44.5442	44.1429	43.7417	43.3404	42.9392	42.5379	42.1367	41.7354	41.3342	40.9329	40.5317
73	45.7517	45.3061	44.8605	44.4149	43.9693	43.5237	43.0781	42.6325	42.1870	41.7415	41.2960	40.8505	40.4050
74	46.1464	45.6521	45.1578	44.6635	44.1692	43.6749	43.1806	42.6863	42.1920	41.6978	41.2036	40.7094	40.2152
Age.	0	1	2	3	4	5	6	7	8	9	10	11	12

Age.	0	1	2	3	4	5	6	7	8	9	10	11	12
10	16.3575	16.3633	16 3690	16.3747	16.3804	16.3861	16.3918	16.3975	16.4032	16.4089	16.4146	16.4203	16.4260
11	16.6548	16.6614	16.6679	16.6744	16.6809	16.6874	16.6939	16.7004	16.7069	16.7134	16.7199	16.7264	16.7329
12	16.9638	16.9709	16.9780	16.9851	16.9923	16.9995	17.0067	17.0139	17.0211	17.0283	17.0355	17.0427	17.0499
13	17.2797	17.2877	17.2958	17.3038	17.3119	17.3199	17.3280	17.3360	17.3441	17.3521	17.3602	17.3682	17.3763
14	17.6087	17.6174	17.6261	17.6348	17.6435	17.6522	17.6609	17.6696	17.6783	17.6870	17.6957	17.7044	17.7131
15	17.9476	17.9570	17.9664	17.9758	17.9852	17.9946	18.0041	18.0136	18.0231	18.0326	18.0421	18.0516	18.0611
16	18.2970	18.3073	18.3176	18.3279	18.3382	18.3485	18.3587	18.3689	18.3791	18.3893	18.3995	18.4097	18.4199
17	18.6583	18.6693	18.6803	18.6913	18.7023	18.7133	18.7243	18.7353	18.7463	18.7573	18.7683	18.7793	18.7903
18	19.0340	19.0455	19.0571	19.0686	19.0802	19.0917	19.1033	19.1148	19.1264	19.1379	19.1495	19.1610	19.1726
19	19.4163	19.4289	19.4416	19.4542	19.4669	19.4795	19.4922	19.5048	19.5175	19.5301	19.5428	19.5554	19.5681
20	19.8139	19.8273	19.8408	19.8542	19.8677	19.8811	19.8946	19.9080	19.9215	19.9349	19.9484	19.9618	19.9753
21	20.2245	20.2389	20.2532	20.2675	20.2818	20.2961	20.3104	20.3247	20.3390	20.3533	20.3676	20.3819	20.3962
22	20.6488	20.6640	20.6792	20.6944	20.7096	20.7247	20.7398	20.7549	20.7700	20.7851	20.8002	20.8153	20.8304
23	21.0864	21.1023	21.1182	21.1341	21.1502	21.1662	21.1822	21.1982	21.2142	21.2302	21.2462	21.2622	21.2782
24	21.5382	21.5550	21.5719	21.5887	21.6056	21.6224	21.6393	21.6561	21.6730	21.6898	21.7067	21.7235	21.7404
25	22.0041	22.0219	22.0397	22.0575	22.0753	22.0931	22.1108	22.1285	22.1462	22.1639	22.1816	22.1993	22.2170
26	22.4845	22.5032	22.5218	22.5404	22.5590	22.5776	22.5962	22.6148	22.6334	22.6520	22.6706	22.6892	22.7078
27	22.9803	22.9999	23.0195	23.0390	23.0585	23.0780	23.0975	23.1170	23.1365	23.1560	23.1755	23.1950	23.2145
28	23.4914	23.5119	23.5324	23.5529	23.5734	23.5939	23.6144	23.6349	23.6554	23.6759	23.6964	23.7169	23.7374
29	24.0192	24.0406	24.0620	24.0834	24.1048	24.1262	24.1476	24.1692	24.1907	24.2122	24.2337	24.2552	24.2767
30	24.5638	24.5862	24.6086	24.6310	24.6534	24.6759	24.6984	24.7209	24.7434	24.7659	24.7884	24.8109	24.8334
31	25.1261	25.1497	25.1733	25.1969	25.2204	25.2439	25.2674	25.2909	25.3144	25.3379	25.3614	25.3849	25.4084
32	25.7070	25.7317	25.7564	25.7811	25.8058	25.8304	25.8550	25.8796	25.9042	25.9288	25.9534	25.9780	26.0026
33	26.3076	26.3333	26.3591	26.3848	26.4106	26.4363	26.4621	26.4878	26.5136	26.5393	26.5651	26.5908	26.6166
34	26.9283	26.9553	26.9823	27.0093	27.0363	27.0633	27.0902	27.1171	27.1440	27.1709	27.1978	27.2247	27.2516
35	27.5706	27.5987	27.6269	27.6550	27.6832	27.7114	27.7395	27.7677	27.7959	27.8240	27.8522	27.8803	27.9084
36	28.2356	28.2648	28.2940	28.3233	28.3526	28.3819	28.4112	28.4405	28.4698	28.4991	28.5284	28 5577	28.5870
37	28.9233	28.9525	28.9817	29.0109	29.0402	29.0695	29.0988	29.1281	29.1574	29.1867	29.2160	29.2453	29.2746
38	29.6210	29.6523	29.6836	29.7149	29.7462	29.7775	29.8089	29.8403	29.8717	29.9031	29.9345	29.9659	29.9973
39	30.3545	30.3851	30.4157	30.4464	30.4771	30.5078	30.5385	30.5692	30.5999	30.6306	30.6613	30.6920	30.7227
40	31.0920	31.1222	31.1525	31.1828	31.2131	31.2434	31.2737	31.3040	31.3343	31.3646	31.3949	31.4252	31.4555
41	31.8372	31.8669	31.8966	31.9263	31.9560	31.9857	32.0155	32.0453	32.0751	32.1049	32.1347	32.1645	32.1943
42	32.5894	32.6183	32.6472	32.6761	32.7050	32.7339	32.7629	32.7919	32.8209	32.8499	32.8789	32.9079	32.9369
43	33.3466	33.3744	33.4022	33.4300	33.4579	33.4858	33.5137	33.5416	33.5695	33.5974	33.6253	33.6532	33.6811
44	34.1089	34.1355	34.1621	34.1887	34.2153	34.2419	34.2686	34.2953	34.3220	34.3487	34.3754	34.4021	34.4288
45	34.8779	34.9028	34.9277	34.9527	34.9777	35.0027	35.0277	35.0527	35.0777	35.1027	35.1277	35.1527	35.1777
46	35.6514	35.6745	35.6975	35.7205	35.7435	35.7665	35.7895	35.8125	35.8355	35.8585	35.8815	35.9045	35.9275
47	36.4302	36.4508	36.4714	36.4921	36.5128	36.5335	36.5542	36.5749	36.5956	36.6163	36.6370	36.6577	36.6784
48	37.2122	37.2302	37.2483	37.2664	37.2845	37.3026	37.3207	37.3388	37.3569	37.3750	37.3931	37.4112	37.4293
49	37.9969	38.0119	38.0269	38.0419	38.0569	38.0720	38.0871	38.1022	38.1173	38.1324	38.1475	38.1626	38.1777
50	38.7861	38.7978	38.8094	38.8210	38.8326	38.8442	38.8558	38.8674	38.8790	38.8906	38.9022	38.9138	38.9254
51	39.5743	39.5824	39.5905	39.5986	39.6067	39.6147	39.6227	39.6307	39.6387	39.6467	39.6547	39.6627	39.6707
52	40.3659	40.3693	40.3727	40.3761	40.3795	40.3830	40.3865	40.3900	40.3935	40.3970	40.4005	40.4040	40.4075
53	41.1542	41.1529	41.1516	41.1503	41.1489	41.1475	41.1461	41.1447	41.1433	41.1419	41.1405	41.1391	41.1377
54	41.9434	41.9363	41.9292	41.9220	41.9148	41.9076	41.9004	41.8932	41.8860	41.8788	41.8716	41.8644	41.8572
55	42.7263	42.7127	42.6991	42.6855	42.6719	42.6582	42.6445	42.6308	42.6171	42.6034	42.5897	42.5760	42.5623
56	43.5017	43.4806	43.4595	43.4384	43.4173	43.3962	43.3751	43.3540	43.3329	43.3118	43.2907	43.2696	43.2485
57	44.2660	44.2366	44.2073	44.1780	44.1487	44.1194	44.0901	44.0608	44.0315	44.0022	43.9729	43.9436	43.9143
58	45.0157	44.9772	44.9387	44.9001	44.8615	44.8229	44.7843	44.7457	44.7071	44.6685	44.6299	44.5913	44.5527
59	45.7504	45.7014	45.6524	45.6034	45.5544	45.5054	45.4565	45.4076	45.3587	45.3098	45.2609	45.2120	45.1631
60	46.4642	46.4039	46.3436	46.2833	46.2230	46.1627	46.1023	46.0419	45.9815	45.9211	45.8607	45.8003	45.7399
61	47.1585	47.0852	47.0119	46.9386	46.8653	46.7920	46.7187	46.6454	46.5721	46.4988	46.4255	46.3522	46.2789
62	47.8272	47.7399	47.6526	47.5653	47.4780	47.3907	47.3034	47.2161	47.1288	47.0415	46.9542	46.8669	46.7796
63	48.4725	48.3700	48.2674	48.1648	48.0622	47.9596	47.8570	47.7544	47.6518	47.5492	47.4466	47.3440	47.2414
64	49.0943	48.9748	48.8553	48.7358	48.6162	48.4966	48.3770	48.2574	48.1378	48.0182	47.8986	47.7790	47.6594
65	49.6907	49.5526	49.4145	49.2763	49.1381	48.9999	48.8617	48.7235	48.5853	48.4471	48.3089	48.1707	48.0325
66	50.2622	50.1036	49.9450	49.7863	49.6276	49.4689	49.3102	49.1515	48.9928	48.8341	48.6754	48.5167	48.3580
67	50.8078	50.6266	50.4454	50.2642	50.0831	49.9020	49.7209	49.5398	49.3587	49.1776	48.9965	48.8154	48.6343
68	51.3302	51.1242	50.9182	50.7122	50.5062	50.3002	50.0943	49.8884	49.6825	49.4766	49.2707	49.0648	48.8589
69	51.8269	51.5937	51.3605	51.1273	50.8941	50.6609	50.4278	50.1947	49.9616	49.7285	49.4954	49.2623	49.0292
70	52.2983	52.0354	51.7724	51.5095	51.2465	50.9836	50.7206	50.4577	50.1947	49.9318	49.6688	49.4059	49.1429
71	52.7507	52.4547	52.1587	51.8627	51.5667	51.2706	50.9745	50.6784	50.3823	50.0862	49.7901	49.4940	49.1979
72	53.1798	52.8472	52.5145	52.1819	51.8492	51.5166	51.1839	50.8513	50.5186	50.1859	49.8533	49.5206	49.1880
73	53.5861	53.2131	52.8401	52.4671	52.0941	51.7210	51.3479	50.9748	50.6017	50.2286	49.8555	49.4824	49.1093
74	53.9686	53.5513	53.1340	52.7167	52.2994	51.8821	51.4648	51.0475	50.6302	50.2129	49.7956	49.3783	48.9610
Age.	0	1	2	3	4	5	6	7	8	9	10	11	12

Age.	0	1	2	3	4	5	6	7	8	9	10	11	12
10	19.0281	19.0439	19.0597	19.0756	19.0915	19.1074	19.1233	19.1392	19.1551	19.1710	19.1869	19.2028	19.2187
11	19.3749	19.3917	19.4084	19.4251	19.4418	19.4585	19.4752	19.4919	19.5086	19.5253	19.5420	19.5587	19.5754
12	19.7331	19.7508	19.7685	19.7862	19.8039	19.8217	19.8395	19.8573	19.8751	19.8929	19.9107	19.9285	19.9463
13	20.1033	20.1220	20.1406	20.1592	20.1778	20.1964	20.2150	20.2336	20.2522	20.2708	20.2894	20.3080	20.3266
14	20.4853	20.5049	20.5245	20.5441	20.5636	20.5831	20.6026	20.6221	20.6416	20.6611	20.6806	20.7001	20.7196
15	20.8801	20.9007	20.9213	20.9419	20.9625	20.9831	21.0036	21.0241	21.0446	21.0651	21.0856	21.1061	21.1266
16	21.2877	21.3093	21.3308	21.3523	21.3738	21.3953	21.4168	21.4383	21.4598	21.4813	21.5028	21.5243	21.5458
17	21.7087	21.7313	21.7539	21.7764	21.7989	21.8214	21.8439	21.8664	21.8889	21.9114	21.9339	21.9564	21.9789
18	22.1434	22.1669	22.1905	22.2141	22.2377	22.2613	22.2849	22.3085	22.3321	22.3557	22.3793	22.4029	22.4265
19	22.5931	22.6178	22.6425	22.6672	22.6918	22.7164	22.7410	22.7656	22.7902	22.8148	22.8394	22.8640	22.8886
20	23.0567	23.0825	23.1083	23.1341	23.1598	23.1855	23.2112	23.2369	23.2626	23.2883	23.3140	23.3397	23.3654
21	23.5359	23.5628	23.5897	23.6165	23.6433	23.6701	23.6969	23.7237	23.7505	23.7773	23.8041	23.8309	23.8577
22	24.0304	24.0584	24.0864	24.1144	24.1424	24.1704	24.1983	24.2262	24.2541	24.2820	24.3099	24.3378	24.3657
23	24.5407	24.5697	24.5988	24.6279	24.6570	24.6861	24.7152	24.7443	24.7734	24.8025	24.8316	24.8607	24.8898
24	25.0676	25.0979	25.1282	25.1585	25.1888	25.2191	25.2493	25.2795	25.3097	25.3399	25.3701	25.4003	25.4305
25	25.6111	25.6426	25.6741	25.7056	25.7370	25.7684	25.7998	25.8312	25.8626	25.8940	25.9254	25.9568	25.9882
26	26.1713	26.2039	26.2365	26.2691	26.3017	26.3343	26.3670	26.3997	26.4324	26.4651	26.4978	26.5305	26.5632
27	26.7497	26.7836	26.8175	26.8514	26.8853	26.9192	26.9532	26.9872	27.0212	27.0552	27.0892	27.1232	27.1572
28	27.3468	27.3820	27.4172	27.4514	27.4876	27.5228	27.5581	27.5934	27.6287	27.6640	27.6993	27.7346	27.7699
29	27.9630	27.9997	28.0364	28.0730	28.1096	28.1462	28.1828	28.2194	28.2560	28.2926	28.3292	28.3658	28.4024
30	28.5992	28.6373	28.6754	28.7135	28.7516	28.7897	28.8277	28.8657	28.9037	28.9417	28.9797	29.0177	29.0557
31	29.2564	29.2960	29.3356	29.3752	29.4148	29.4544	29.4939	29.5334	29.5729	29.6124	29.6519	29.6914	29.7309
32	29.9357	29.9767	30.0178	30.0588	30.0999	30.1409	30.1820	30.2230	30.2641	30.3051	30.3462	30.3872	30.4283
33	30.6376	30.6802	30.7228	30.7654	30.8080	30.8507	30.8934	30.9361	30.9788	31.0215	31.0642	31.1069	31.1496
34	31.3636	31.4080	31.4524	31.4968	31.5411	31.5854	31.6297	31.6740	31.7183	31.7626	31.8069	31.8512	31,8955
35	32.1146	32.1606	32.2066	32.2526	32.2985	32.3444	32.3903	32.4362	32.4821	32.5280	32.5739	32.6198	32.6657
36	32.8908	32.9373	32.9838	33.0302	33.0766	33.1230	33.1694	33.2158	33.2622	33.3086	33 3550	33.4014	33.4478
37	33.6796	33.7286	33.7776	33.8266	33.8756	33.9246	33.9737	34.0228	34.0719	34.1210	34.1701	34.2192	34.2683
38	34.5074	34.5563	34.6052	34.6541	34.7031	34.7521	34.8011	34.8501	34.8991	34.9481	34.9971	35.0461	35.0951
39	35.3422	35.3914	35.4406	35.4898	35.5390	35.5882	35.6375	35.6868	35.7361	35.7854	35.8347	35.8840	35.9333
40	36.1890	36.2385	36.2880	36.3375	36.3869	36.4363	36.4857	36.5351	36.5845	36.6339	36.6833	36.7327	36.7821
41	37.0469	37.0962	37.1455	37.1949	37.2443	37.2937	37.3431	37.3925	37.4419	37.4913	37.5407	37.5901	37.6395
42	37.9141	37.9633	38.0125	38.0617	38.1109	38.1601	38.2092	38.2583	38.3074	38.3565	38.4056	38.4547	38.5038
43	38.7889	38.8378	38.8867	38.9356	38.9844	39.0332	39.0820	39.1308	39.1796	39.2284	39.2772	39.3260	39.3748
44	39.6728	39.7210	39.7691	39.8172	39.8653	39.9134	39.9615	40.0096	40.0577	40.1058	40.1539	40.2020	40.2501
45	40.5635	40.6106	40.6578	40.7049	40.7521	40.7992	40.8464	40.8935	40.9407	40.9878	41.0350	41.0821	41.1293
46	41.4606	41.5066	41.5526	41.5986	41.6446	41.6905	41.7364	41.7823	41.8282	41.8741	41.9200	41.9659	42.0118
47	42.3635	42.4081	42.4526	42.4971	42.5416	42.5861	42.6306	42.6751	42.7196	42.7641	42.8086	42.8531	42.8976
48	43.2719	43.3146	43.3573	43.4000	43.4427	43.4855	43.5283	43.5711	43.6139	43.6567	43.6995	43.7423	43.7851
49	44.1831	44.2237	44.2644	44.3050	44.3457	44.3863	44.4270	44.4676	44.5083	44.5489	44.5896	44.6302	44.6709
50	45.0996	45.1380	45.1765	45.2150	45.2535	45.2920	45.3305	45.3690	45.4075	45.4460	45.4845	45.5230	45.5615
51	46.0195	46.0549	46.0902	46.1256	46.1610	46.1963	46.2318	46.2673	46.3027	46.3382	46.3736	46.409[illegible]	46.4446
52	46.9372	46.9695	47.0018	47.0341	47.0664	47.0987	47.1311	47.1635	47.1959	47.2283	47.2607	47.2931	47.3255
53	47.8549	47.8835	47.9121	47.9407	47.9693	47.9979	48.0264	48.0549	48.0834	48.1119	48.1404	48.1689	48.1974
54	48.7689	48.7931	48.8173	48.8415	48.8656	48.8897	48.9138	48.9379	48.9620	48.9861	49.0102	49.0343	49.0584
55	49.6763	49.6952	49.7141	49.7330	49.7519	49.7709	49.7899	49.8089	49.8279	49.8469	49.8659	49.8849	49.9039
56	50.5733	50.5866	50.5998	50.6130	50.6262	50.6394	50.6526	50.6658	50.6790	50.6922	50.7054	50.7186	50.7318
57	51.4586	51.4652	51.4718	51.4784	51.4850	51.4916	51.4983	51.5050	51.5117	51.5184	51.5251	51.5318	51.5385
58	52.3272	52.3264	52.3256	52.3248	52.3240	52.3233	52.3226	52.3219	52.3212	52.3205	52.3198	52.3191	52.3184
59	53.1782	53.1694	53.1606	53.1517	53.1428	53.1339	53.1250	53.1161	53.1072	53.0983	53.0894	53.0805	53.0716
60	54.0082	53.9900	53.9718	53.9536	53.9354	53.9172	53.8989	53.8806	53.8623	53.8440	53.8257	53.8074	53.7891
61	54.8128	54.7845	54.7561	54.7278	54.6994	54.6711	54.6427	54.6144	54.5860	54.5577	54.5293	54.5010	54.4726
62	55.5928	55.5533	55.5140	55.4746	55.4352	55.3958	55.3564	55.3170	55.2776	55.2382	55.1988	55.1594	55.1198
63	56.3482	56.2964	56.2446	56.1928	56.1410	56.0893	56.0376	55.9859	55.9342	55.8825	55.8308	55.7791	55.7274
64	57.0758	57.0106	56.9454	56,8802	56 8149	56.7496	56.6843	56.6190	56.5537	56.4884	56.4231	56.3578	56,2925
65	57.7754	57.6951	57.6148	57.5345	57.4542	57.3740	57.2938	57.2136	57.1334	57.0532	56.9730	56.8928	56.8126
66	58.4457	58.3491	58.2525	58.1559	58.0593	57.9627	57.8661	57.7695	57.6729	57.5762	57.4795	57.3828	57.2861
67	59.0869	58.9721	58.8572	58.7424	58.6275	58.5127	58.3978	58.2830	58.1681	58.0533	57.9384	57.8236	57.7087
68	59.6975	59.5626	59.4277	59.2928	59.1579	59.0230	58.8882	58.7534	58.6186	58.4838	58.3490	58.2142	58.0794
69	60.2776	60.1207	59.9639	59.8071	59.6503	59.4935	59.3367	59.1799	59.0231	58.8663	58.7095	58.5527	58.3959
70	60.8278	60.6464	60.4650	60.2836	60.1022	59.9209	59.7396	59.5583	59.3770	59.1957	59.0144	58.8331	58.6518
71	61.3483	61.1399	60.9314	60.7229	60.5144	60.3059	60.0974	59.8889	59.6804	59.4719	59.2634	59.0549	58.8464
72	61.8361	61.5975	61.3589	61.1203	60.8816	60.6429	60.4042	60.1655	59.9268	59.6881	59.4494	59.2107	58.9720
73	62.2904	62.0186	61.7468	61.4750	61.2032	60.9314	60.6597	60.3880	60.1163	59.8446	59.5729	59.3012	59.0295
74	62.7144	62.4063	62.0982	61.7901	61.4820	61.1739	60.8657	60.5575	60.2493	59.9411	59.6329	59.3247	59.0165
Age.	0	1	2	3	4	5	6	7	8	9	10	11	12

Age.	0	1	2	3	4	5	6	7	8	9	10	11	12
10	21.8208	21.8471	21.8734	21.8997	21.9261	21.9525	21.9789	22.0053	22.0317	22.0581	22.0845	22.1109	22.1373
11	22.2174	22.2451	22.2727	22.3003	22.3279	22.3555	22.3831	22.4107	22.4383	22.4659	22.4935	22.5211	22.5487
12	22.6295	22.6582	22.6869	22.7156	22.7443	22.7729	22.8015	22.8301	22.8587	22.8873	22.9159	22.9445	22.9731
13	23.0536	23.0833	23.1130	23.1427	23.1724	23.2022	23.2320	23.2618	23.2916	23.3214	23.3512	23.3810	23.4107
14	23.4918	23.5227	23.5536	23.5845	23.6154	23.6464	23.6774	23.7084	23.7394	23.7704	23.8014	23.8324	23.8634
15	23.9456	23.9778	24.0100	24.0421	24.0742	24.1063	24.1384	24.1705	24.2026	24.2347	24.2668	24.2989	24.3310
16	24.4136	24.4469	24.4803	24.5136	24.5470	24.5803	24.6137	24.6470	24.6804	24.7137	24.7471	24.7804	24.8138
17	24.8973	24.9320	24.9667	25.0014	25.0361	25.0707	25.1053	25.1399	25.1745	25.2091	25.2437	25.2783	25.3129
18	25.3973	25.4333	25.4692	25.5051	25.5410	25.5769	25.6128	25.6487	25.6846	25.7205	25.7564	25.7923	25.8282
19	25.9136	25.9508	25.9881	26.0253	26.0626	26.0998	26.1371	26.1743	26.2116	26.2488	26.2861	26.3233	26.3606
20	26.4468	26.4853	26.5239	26.5625	26.6011	26.6397	26.6783	26.7169	26.7555	26.7941	26.8327	26.8713	26.9099
21	26.9974	27.0373	27.0772	27.1171	27.1571	27.1971	27.2371	27.2771	27.3171	27.3571	27.3971	27.4371	27.4771
22	27.5657	27.6070	27.6484	27.6898	27.7312	27.7726	27.8140	27.8554	27.8968	27.9382	27.9796	28.0210	28.0624
23	28.1523	28.1952	28.2381	28.2810	28.3239	28.3668	28.4096	28.4524	28.4952	28.5380	28.5808	28.6236	28.6664
24	28.7577	28.8021	28.8465	28.8908	28.9351	28.9794	29.0237	29.0680	29.1123	29.1566	29.2009	29.2452	29.2895
25	29.3823	29.4281	29.4739	29.5197	29.5655	29.6113	29.6572	29.7031	29.7490	29.7949	29.8408	29.8867	29.9326
26	30.0267	30.0741	30.1215	30.1689	30.2165	30.2640	30.3115	30.3590	30.4065	30.4540	30.5015	30.5490	30.5965
27	30.6924	30.7416	30.7908	30.8399	30.8890	30.9381	30.9872	31.0363	31.0854	31.1345	31.1836	31.2327	31.2818
28	31.3793	31.4301	31.4810	31.5318	31.5827	31.6335	31.6844	31.7352	31.7861	31.8369	31.8877	31.9386	31.9895
29	32.0887	32.1414	32.1941	32.2468	32.2994	32.3522	32.4048	32.4574	32.5100	32.5626	32.6152	32.6678	32.7202
30	32.8215	32.8761	32.9306	32.9851	33.0396	33.0941	33.1486	33.2031	33.2576	33.3121	33.3666	33.4211	33.4756
31	33.5789	33.6354	33.6919	33.7484	33.8048	33.8612	33.9176	33.9740	34.0304	34.0868	34.1432	34.1996	34.2560
32	34.3614	34.4198	34.4782	34.5366	34.5950	34.6534	34.7119	34.7704	34.8289	34.8874	34.9459	35.0044	35.0629
33	35.1706	35.2311	35.2916	35.3521	35.4126	35.4731	35.5337	35.5943	35.6549	35.7155	35.7761	35.8367	35.8973
34	36.0075	36.0702	36.1329	36.1955	36.2581	36.3207	36.3833	36.4459	36.5085	36.5711	36.6337	36.6963	36.7589
35	36.8719	36.9356	36.9993	37.0629	37.1265	37.1901	37.2537	37.3173	37.3809	37.4445	37.5081	37.5717	37.6353
36	37.7516	37.8185	37.8853	37.9521	38.0189	38.0857	38.1525	38.2193	38.2861	38.3529	38.4197	38.4865	38.5533
37	38.6733	38.7407	38.8081	38.8755	38.9428	39.0101	39.0774	39.1447	39.2120	39.2793	39.3466	39.4139	39.4812
38	39.6052	39.6734	39.7416	39.8098	39.8781	39.9464	40.0147	40.0830	40.1513	40.2196	40.2879	40.3562	40.4245
39	40.5528	40.6219	40.6910	40.7601	40.8292	40.8983	40.9675	41.0367	41.1059	41.1751	41.2443	41.3135	41.3827
40	41.5156	41.5854	41.6553	41.7252	41.7951	41.8650	41.9349	42.0048	42.0747	42.1446	42.2145	42.2844	42.3543
41	42.4921	42.5625	42.6330	42.7035	42.7740	42.8445	42.9150	42.9855	43.0560	43.1265	43.1970	43.2675	43.3380
42	43.4810	43.5521	43.6232	43.6943	43.7654	43.8365	43.9075	43.9785	44.0495	44.1205	44.1915	44.2625	44.3335
43	44.4826	44.5538	44.6251	44.6964	44.7677	44.8390	44.9103	44.9816	45.0529	45.1242	45.1955	45.2668	45.3381
44	45.4941	45.5655	45.6369	45.7083	45.7797	45.8511	45.9225	45.9939	46.0653	46.1367	46.2081	46.2795	46.3509
45	46.5151	46.5865	46.6579	46.7292	46.8005	46.8718	46.9431	47.0144	47.0857	47.1570	47.2283	47.2996	47.3709
46	47.5449	47.6159	47.6870	47.7581	47.8292	47.9003	47.9714	48.0425	48.1136	48.1847	48.2558	48.3269	48.3980
47	48.5827	48.6535	48.7241	48.7947	48.8653	48.9359	49.0066	49.0773	49.1480	49.2187	49.2894	49.3601	49.4306
48	49.6277	49.6977	49.7677	49.8377	49.9077	49.9777	50.0477	50.1177	50.1877	50.2577	50.3277	50.3977	50.4677
49	50.6763	50.7456	50.8149	50.8842	50.9536	51.0230	51.0924	51.1618	51.2312	51.3006	51.3700	51.4394	51.5088
50	51.7357	51.8036	51.8715	51.9395	52.0075	52.0755	52.1435	52.2115	52.2795	52.3475	52.4155	52.4835	52.5515
51	52.7934	52.8601	52.9268	52.9935	53.0602	53.1269	53.1937	53.2605	53.3273	53.3941	53.4609	53.5277	53.5945
52	53.8552	53.9201	53.9850	54.0499	54.1147	54.1795	54.2443	54.3091	54.3739	54.4387	54.5035	54.5683	54.6331
53	54.9146	54.9771	55.0396	55.1021	55.1646	55.2272	55.2898	55.3524	55.4150	55.4776	55.5402	55.6028	55.6654
54	55.9701	56.0300	56.0898	56.1496	56.2094	56.2692	56.3290	56.3888	56.4486	56.5084	56.5682	56.6280	56.6878
55	57.0179	57.0745	57.1311	57.1877	57.2444	57.3011	57.3578	57.4145	57.4712	57.5279	57.5846	57.6413	57.6980
56	58.0566	58.1095	58.1624	58.2153	58.2683	58.3213	58.3743	58.4273	58.4803	58.5333	58.5863	58.6393	58.6923
57	59.0828	59.1315	59.1802	59.2289	59.2777	59.3265	59.3753	59.4241	59.4729	59.5217	59.5705	59.6193	59.6681
58	60.0929	60.1371	60.1813	60.2254	60.2695	60.3136	60.3577	60.4018	60.4459	60.4900	60.5341	60.5782	60.6223
59	61.0867	61.1254	61.1641	61.2028	61.2415	61.2801	61.3187	61.3573	61.3959	61.4345	61.4731	61.5117	61.5503
60	62.0574	62.0901	62.1228	62.1556	62.1884	62.2212	62.2540	62.2868	62.3196	62.3524	62.3852	62.4180	62.4508
61	63.0065	63.0328	63.0591	63.0854	63.1118	63.1382	63.1646	63.1910	63.2174	63.2438	63.2702	63.2966	63.3230
62	63.9330	63.9521	63.9712	63.9904	64.0096	64.0288	64.0480	64.0672	64.0864	64.1056	64.1248	64.1440	64.1632
63	64.8342	64.8456	64.8570	64.8683	64.8796	64.8909	64.9022	64.9135	64.9248	64.9361	64.9474	64.9587	64.9700
64	65.7089	65.7116	65.7142	65.7168	65.7194	65.7220	65.7246	65.7272	65.7298	65.7324	65.7350	65.7376	65.7402
65	66.5555	66.5485	66.5416	66.5347	66.5278	66.5209	66.5140	66.5071	66.5002	66.4933	66.4864	66.4795	66.4726
66	67.3738	67.3562	67.3387	67.3212	67.3037	67.2862	67.2687	67.2512	67.2337	67.2162	67.1987	67.1812	67.1637
67	68.1613	68.1321	68.1029	68.0737	68.0446	68.0155	67.9864	67.9573	67.9282	67.8991	67.8700	67.8409	67.8118
68	68.9180	68.8761	68.8342	68.7923	68.7504	68.7085	68.6667	68.6249	68.5831	68.5413	68.4995	68.4577	68.4159
69	69.6443	69.5883	69.5323	69.4763	69.4202	69.3641	69.3080	69.2519	69.1958	69.1397	69.0836	69.0275	68.9714
70	70.3367	70.2649	70.1931	70.1213	70.0495	69.9777	69.9058	69.8339	69.7620	69.6901	69.6182	69.5463	69.4744
71	70.9968	70.9073	70.8178	70.7284	70.6390	70.5496	70.4602	70.3708	70.2814	70.1920	70.1026	70.0132	69.9238
72	71.6201	71.5116	71.4031	71.2946	71.1861	71.0775	70.9689	70.8603	70.7517	70.6431	70.5345	70.4259	70.3173
73	72.2106	72.0809	71.9512	71.8215	71.6919	71.5623	71.4327	71.3031	71.1735	71.0439	70.9143	70.7847	70.6551
74	72.7699	72.6173	72.4647	72.3121	72.1595	72.0069	71.8542	71.7015	71.5488	71.3961	71.2434	71.0907	70.9380
Age.	0	1	2	3	4	5	6	7	8	9	10	11	12

Age.	1	2	3	4	5	6	7	8	9	10	11	Age.
10	.9550	1.8671	2.7381	3.5699	4.3641	5.1226	5.8468	6.5382	7.1982	7.8283	8.4297	10
11	.9550	1.8670	2.7380	3.5697	4.3638	5.1220	5.8460	6.5371	7.1968	7.8266	8.4276	11
12	.9550	1.8670	2.7378	3.5694	4.3633	5.1213	5.8450	6.5358	7.1953	7.8246	8.4253	12
13	.9550	1.8669	2.7375	3.5690	4.3627	5.1205	5.8439	6.5344	7.1934	7.8224	8.4226	13
14	.9549	1.8667	2.7372	3.5685	4.3620	5.1195	5 8426	6.5327	7.1914	7.8199	8.4196	14
15	.9549	1.8666	2.7370	3.5680	4.3613	5.1185	5.8412	6.5310	7.1891	7.8172	8.4163	15
16	.9548	1.8664	2.7365	3.5675	4.3605	5.1174	5.8397	6.5290	7.1867	7.8142	8.4128	16
17	.9548	1.8662	2.7363	3.5669	4.3596	5.1161	5.8380	6.5269	7.1841	7.8110	8.4090	17
18	.9547	1.8660	2.7359	3.5661	4.3586	5.1147	5.8362	6.5246	7.1812	7.8075	8.4049	18
19	.9546	1.8658	2.7355	3.5655	4.3575	5.1133	5.8343	6.5221	7.1782	7.8039	8.4006	19
20	.9545	1.8655	2.7350	3.5648	4.3564	5.1117	5.8323	6.5195	7.1750	7.8000	8.3960	20
21	.9544	1.8653	2.7346	3.5639	4.3552	5.1101	5.8301	6.5168	7.1716	7.7959	8.3911	21
22	.9544	1.8651	2.7341	3.5631	4.3540	5.1084	5 8278	6.5139	7.1680	7.7916	8.3859	22
23	.9543	1.8648	2.7335	3.5621	4.3526	5.1065	5.8254	6.5108	7.1642	7.7869	8.3804	23
24	.9542	1.8645	2.7329	3.5613	4.3513	5.1046	5.8228	6.5075	7.1604	7.7821	8.3746	24
25	.9541	1.8642	2.7323	3.5602	4.3498	5.1025	5.8201	6.5041	7.1558	7.7769	8.3684	25
26	.9540	1.8639	2.7317	3.5592	4.3482	5.1004	5.8172	6.5004	7.1513	7.7714	8.3619	26
27	.9538	1.8635	2.7310	3.5581	4.3465	5.0980	5.8141	6.4964	7.1464	7.7655	8.3550	27
28	.9537	1.8631	2.7302	3.5568	4.3447	5.0955	5.8108	6.4923	7.1413	7.7594	8.3477	28
29	.9536	1.8628	2.7295	3.5556	4.3428	5.0928	5.8074	6.4879	7.1359	7.7528	8.3400	29
30	.9535	1.8624	2.7287	3.5542	4.3408	5.0901	5.8037	6.4833	7.1302	7.7460	8.3320	30
31	.9533	1.8619	2.7278	3.5528	4.3387	5.0872	5.7999	6.4784	7.1243	7.7388	8.3235	31
32	.9531	1.8614	2.7268	3.5512	4.3364	5.0841	5.7959	6.4734	7.1180	7.7312	8.3146	32
33	.9530	1.8609	2.7259	3.5497	4.3341	5.0809	5.7917	6.4681	7.1115	7.7235	8.3053	33
34	.9528	1.8604	2.7249	3.5480	4.3317	5.0776	5.7873	6.4625	7.1047	7.7153	8.2954	34
35	.9526	1.8599	2.7238	3.5463	4.3291	5.0741	5.7826	6.4567	7.0975	7.7064	8.2848	35
36	.9524	1.8593	2.7227	3.5445	4.3265	5.0704	5.7779	6.4506	7.0898	7.6969	8.2732	36
37	.9522	1.8588	2.7216	3.5426	4.3237	5.0666	5.7729	6.4440	7.0814	7.6865	8.2605	37
38	.9520	1.8581	2.7204	3.5407	4.3208	5.0625	5.7673	6.4367	7.0722	7.6749	8.2462	38
39	9518	1.8575	2.7191	3.5386	4.3177	5.0580	5.7612	6.4287	7.0618	7.6619	8.2302	39
40	.9516	1.8568	2.7178	3.5363	4.3142	5.0530	5.7543	6.4194	7.0499	7.6470	8.2120	40
41	.9513	1.8561	2.7163	3.5337	4.3101	5.0471	5.7461	6.4087	7.0361	7.6299	8.1911	41
42	.9511	1.8552	2.7145	3.5306	4.3053	5.0401	5.7365	6.3961	7.0202	7.6102	8.1673	42
43	.9507	1.8542	2.7123	3.5268	4.2994	5.0317	5.7252	6.3814	7.0017	7.5875	8.1399	43
44	.9503	1.8529	2.7096	3.5222	4.2925	5.0220	5.7122	6.3646	6.9808	7.5618	8.1092	44
45	.9498	1.8513	2.7065	3.5170	4.2846	5.0110	5.6976	6.3459	6.9574	7.5334	8.0753	45
46	.9492	1.8495	2.7029	3.5111	4.2759	4.9987	5.6813	6.3251	6.9316	7.5022	8.0381	46
47	.9485	1.8476	2.6991	3.5047	4.2663	4.9854	5.6637	6.3026	6.9037	7.4683	7.9980	47
48	.9478	1.8454	2.6949	3.4977	4.2559	4.9710	5.6445	6.2783	6.8733	7.4318	7.9542	48
49	.9471	1.8432	2.6903	3.4902	4.2446	4.9552	5.6238	6.2518	6.8409	7.3921	7.9072	49
50	.9463	1.8407	2.6853	3.4819	4.2323	4.9382	5.6013	6.2234	6.8052	7.3492	7.8569	50
51	.9453	1.8379	2.6798	3.4728	4.2189	4.9197	5.5771	6.1921	6.7670	7.3029	7.8015	51
52	.9443	1.8349	2.6738	3.4631	4.2045	4.8999	5.5505	6.1586	6.7256	7.2531	7.7424	52
53	.9432	1.8316	2.6675	3.4525	4.1890	4.8780	5.5220	6.1225	6.6810	7.1992	7.6786	53
54	.9419	1.8282	2.6605	3.4414	4.1719	4.8547	5.4913	6.0835	6.6329	7.1412	7.6100	54
55	.9408	1.8244	2.6534	3.4288	4.1537	4.8295	5.4581	6.0414	6.5810	7.0786	7.5360	55
56	.9393	1.8205	2.6449	3.4154	4.1338	4.8021	5.4221	5.9957	6.5247	7.0109	7.4562	56
57	.9382	1.8158	2.6361	3.4009	4.1124	4.7725	5.3831	5.9463	6.4640	6.9380	7.3704	57
58	.9359	1.8105	2.6262	3.3849	4.0887	4.7398	5.3404	5.8924	6.3979	6.8588	7.2776	58
59	.9344	1.8054	2 6159	3.3677	4.0633	4.7048	5.2944	5.8344	6.3269	6.7741	7.1782	59
60	.9324	1.7996	2.6043	3.3487	4.0352	4.6663	5.2441	5.7712	6.2498	6.6823	7.0712	60
61	.9302	1.7932	2.5916	3.3279	4.0048	4.6245	5.1898	5.7031	6.1671	6.5932	6.9571	61
62	.9278	1.7861	2.5777	3.3053	3.9717	4.5794	5.1312	5.6299	6.0783	6.4793	6.8355	62
63	.9252	1.7784	2.5627	3.2809	3.9359	4.5308	5.0683	5.5516	5.9837	6.3677	6.7067	63
64	.9223	1.7700	2.5463	3.2543	3.8972	4.4783	5.0007	5.4678	5.8829	6.2493	6.5705	64
65	.9192	1.7609	2.5286	3.2257	3.8557	4.4221	4.9286	5.3786	5.7759	6.1241	6.4270	65
66	.9158	1.7510	2.5094	3.1948	3.8111	4.3620	4.8517	5.2839	5.6628	5.9923	6.2764	66
67	.9120	1.7402	2.4887	3.1617	3.7633	4.2980	4.7700	5.1837	5.5435	5.8538	6.1188	67
68	.9081	1.7287	2.4666	3.1263	3.7125	4.2301	4.6837	5.0781	5.4183	5.7089	5.9548	68
69	.9038	1.7163	2.4428	3.0885	3.6584	4.1579	4.5923	4.9670	5.2870	5.5578	5.7841	69
70	.8991	1.7030	2.4173	3.0480	3.6007	4.0814	4.4959	4.8500	5.1496	5.4001	5.6071	70
71	.8941	1.6886	2.3900	3.0048	3.5394	4.0004	4.3943	4.7275	5.0060	5.2364	5.4243	71
72	.8887	1.6732	2.3608	2.9587	3.4744	3.9149	4.2875	4.5991	4.8567	5.0669	5.2360	72
73	.8828	1.6566	2.3295	2.9097	3.4055	3.8248	4.1754	4.4653	4.7018	4.8921	5.0429	73
74	.8765	1.6387	2.2960	2.8576	3.3325	3.7297	4.0581	4.3260	4.5416	4.7124	4.8455	74
75	.8697	1.6196	2.2603	2.8022	3.2554	3.6300	3.9357	4.1816	4.3765	4.5284	4.6444	75
76	.8623	1.5991	2.2222	2.7433	3.1741	3.5256	3.8084	4.0325	4.2071	4.3406	4.4403	76
77	.8544	1.5770	2.1813	2.6809	3.0885	3.4164	3.6763	3.8788	4.0335	4.1492	4.2336	77
78	.8458	1.5532	2.1379	2.6150	2.9988	3.3030	3.5400	3.7212	3.8566	3.9553	4.0250	78
79	.8364	1.5278	2.0919	2.5458	2.9054	3.1857	3.3999	3.5600	3.6767	3.7591	3.8152	79
80	.8265	1.5009	2.0435	2.4735	2.8085	3.0646	3.2560	3.3955	3.4941	3.5611	3.6047	80
81	.8159	1.4724	1.9927	2.3980	2.7078	2.9394	3.1082	3.2274	3.3085	3.3612	3.3937	81
82	.8046	1.4422	1.9390	2.3187	2.6025	2.8093	2.9555	3.0549	3.1195	3.1593	3.1820	82
83	.7924	1.4098	1.8817	2.2345	2.4915	2.6731	2.7967	2.8770	2.9296	2.9546	2.9694	83
84	.7792	1.3747	1.8199	2.1443	2.3735	2.5294	2.6308	2.6931	2.7288	2.7473	2.7560	84
85	.7643	1.3358	1.7521	2.0463	2.2464	2.3765	2.4565	2.5022	2.5261	2.5372	2.5416	85
86	.7476	1.2923	1.6772	1.9390	2.1093	2.2139	2.2737	2.3049	2.3194	2.3253	2.3272	86
87	.7286	1.2434	1.5936	1.8213	1.9612	2.0413	2.0830	2.1025	2.1102	2.1129	2.1136	87
88	.7065	1.1872	1.4997	1.6917	1.8016	1.8589	1.8855	1.8962	1.8998	1.9009	1.9011	88
89	.6804	1.1228	1.3946	1.5501	1.6312	1.6690	1.6840	1.6891	1.6907	1.6910		
90	.6502	1.0497	1.2782	1.3974	1.4529	1.4751	1.4826	1.4848	1.4853		18.5675	19
91	.6145	.9659	1.1494	1.2347	1.2687	1.2803	1.2837	1.2845		18.6807	18.6807	18
92	.5719	.8703	1.0091	1.0646	1.0834	1.0889	1.0902		18.7901	18.7901	18.7901	17
93	.5219	.7646	.8617	.8944	.9041	.9065		18.8957	18.8957	18.8957	18.8957	16
94	.4651	.6510	.7138	.7324	.7369		18.9975	18.9975	18.9975	18.9975	18.9975	15
95	.3997	.5348	.5747	.5843		19.0958	19.0958	19.0958	19.0958	19.0958	19.0958	14
96	.3378	.4378	.4618		19.1905	19.1905	19.1905	19.1905	19.1905	19.1905	19.1904	13
97	.2959	.3670		19.2817	19.2817	19.2817	19.2817	19.2817	19.2817	19.2817	19.2815	12
98	.2404		19.3693	19.3693	19.3693	19.3693	19.3693	19.3693	19.3692	19.3690	19.3689	11
		19.4535	19.4535	19.4535	19.4535	19.4535	19.4535	19.4534	19.4532	19.4531	19.4526	10
		89	88	87	86	85	84	83	82	81	80	

Age.	12	13	14	15	16	17	18	19	20	21	22	Age.
10	9.0038	9.5516	10.0744	10.5732	11.0491	11.5031	11.9361	12.3491	12.7429	13.1184	13.4764	10
11	9.0013	9.5487	10.0710	10.5693	11.0446	11.4981	11.9305	12.3429	12.7360	13.1108	13.4681	11
12	8.9985	9.5454	10.0672	10.5649	11.0397	11.4925	11.9245	12.3359	12.7284	13.1025	13.4589	12
13	8.9953	9.5416	10.0628	10.5600	11.0342	11.4863	11.9174	12.3283	12.7201	13.0933	13.4489	13
14	8.9917	9.5375	10.0582	10.5547	11.0282	11.4796	11.9099	12.3201	12.7109	13.0834	13.4382	14
15	8.9879	9.5331	10.0531	10.5489	11.0217	11.4723	11.9019	12.3112	12.7012	13.0727	13.4265	15
16	8.9838	9.5283	10.0476	10.5427	11.0146	11.4645	11.8931	12.3016	12.6907	13.0612	13.4142	16
17	8.9793	9.5232	10.0417	10.5360	11.0072	11.4561	11.8839	12.2914	12.6795	13.0490	13.4009	17
18	8.9745	9.5176	10.0354	10.5288	10.9991	11.4471	11.8739	12.2804	12.6675	13.0361	13.3868	18
19	8.9695	9.5118	10.0286	10.5212	10.9905	11.4376	11.8634	12.2689	12.6549	13.0223	13.3719	19
20	8.9641	9.5055	10.0215	10.5132	10.9815	11.4278	11.8523	12.2567	12.6415	13.0078	13.3562	20
21	8.9583	9.4989	10.0140	10.5046	10.9719	11.4169	11.8405	12.2437	12.6274	12.9924	13.3394	21
22	8.9523	9.4919	10.0060	10.4956	10.9618	11.4057	11.8281	12.2301	12.6125	12.9763	13.3220	22
23	8.9458	9.4845	9.9975	10.4860	10.9511	11.3938	11.8149	12.2157	12.5968	12.9591	13.3034	23
24	8.9391	9.4767	9.9885	10.4760	10.9398	11.3812	11.8011	12.2006	12.5802	12.9411	13.2837	24
25	8.9319	9.4684	9.9792	10.4650	10.9279	11.3680	11.7867	12.1845	12.5626	12.9218	13.2627	25
26	8.9243	9.4596	9.9692	10.4541	10.9153	11.3540	11.7711	12.1675	12.5439	12.9013	13.2402	26
27	8.9162	9.4504	9.9586	10.4422	10.9021	11.3393	11.7548	12.1494	12.5239	12.8793	13.2160	27
28	8.9077	9.4406	9.9475	10.4297	10.8881	11.3236	11.7374	12.1300	12.5026	12.8556	13.1899	28
29	8.8988	9.4303	9.9358	10.4165	10.8732	11.3069	11.7185	12.1093	12.4795	12.8301	13.1619	29
30	8.8894	9.4195	9.9235	10.4025	10.8574	11.2892	11.6989	12.0870	12.4547	12.8026	13.1315	30
31	8.8795	9.4082	9.9105	10.3876	10.8405	11.2701	11.6773	12.0629	12.4278	12.7727	13.0984	31
32	8.8691	9.3961	9.8966	10.3717	10.8223	11.2494	11.6539	12.0368	12.3986	12.7402	13.0625	32
33	8.8582	9.3833	9.8818	10.3546	10.8027	11.2271	11.6287	12.0083	12.3668	12.7048	13.0233	33
34	8.8465	9.3695	9.8657	10.3359	10.7813	11.2027	11.6011	11.9772	12.3319	12.6661	12.9806	34
35	8.8338	9.3545	9.8480	10.3155	10.7578	11.1758	11.5706	11.9429	12.2937	12.6237	12.9336	35
36	8.8199	9.3379	9.8286	10.2929	10.7318	11.1463	11.5371	11.9053	12.2517	12.5771	12.8823	36
37	8.8045	9.3197	9.8072	10.2680	10.7031	11.1135	11.5001	11.8638	12.2054	12.5258	12.8256	37
38	8.7873	9.2992	9.7831	10.2401	10.6711	11.0770	11.4591	11.8177	12.1543	12.4691	12.7635	38
39	8.7680	9.2763	9.7563	10.2090	10.6354	11.0366	11.4135	11.7669	12.0977	12.4068	12.6950	39
40	8.7460	9.2503	9.7257	10.1740	10.5956	10.9915	11.3629	11.7104	12.0352	12.3379	12.6197	40
41	8.7211	9.2209	9.6917	10.1347	10.5515	10.9411	11.3062	11.6476	11.9658	12.2619	12.5365	41
42	8.6927	9.1876	9.6532	10.0906	10.5008	10.8847	11.2434	11.5779	11.8892	12.1778	12.4449	42
43	8.6603	9.1499	9.6098	10.0412	10.4448	10.8219	11.1737	11.5009	11.8044	12.0852	12.3442	43
44	8.6242	9.1079	9.5616	9.9862	10.3829	10.7529	11.0970	11.4163	11.7116	11.9841	12.2344	44
45	8.5843	9.0618	9.5086	9.9260	10.3153	10.6775	11.0135	11.3249	11.6109	11.8745	12.1157	45
46	8.5407	9.0112	9.4507	9.8606	10.2419	10.5956	10.9229	11.2247	11.5021	11.7561	11.9879	46
47	8.4935	8.9566	9.3884	9.7901	10.1627	10.5075	10.8257	11.1179	11.3853	11.6295	11.8511	47
48	8.4425	8.8978	9.3214	9.7141	10.0775	10.4128	10.7209	11.0030	11.2609	11.4940	11.7052	48
49	8.3875	8.8343	9.2487	9.6322	9.9859	10.3109	10.6089	10.8802	11.1267	11.3495	11.5499	49
50	8.3281	8.7658	9.1707	9.5443	9.8873	10.2017	10.4882	10.7487	10.9839	11.1956	11.3847	50
51	8.2641	8.6920	9.0867	9.4494	9.7816	10.0846	10.3596	10.6083	10.8319	11.0318	11.2094	51
52	8.1951	8.6126	8.9964	9.3478	9.6683	9.9594	10.2224	10.4589	10.6703	10.8583	11.0243	52
53	8.1208	8.5272	8.8994	9.2388	9.5470	9.8254	10.0761	10.3000	10.4989	10.6746	10.8285	53
54	8.0409	8.4355	8.7954	9.1222	9.4174	9.6830	9.9204	10.1315	10.3177	10.4802	10.6229	54
55	7.9549	8.3365	8.6838	8.9974	9.2791	9.5311	9.7551	9.9528	10.1261	10.2769	10.4069	55
56	7.8623	8.2311	8.5644	8.8641	9.1320	9.3700	9.5803	9.7644	9.9247	10.0629	10.1809	56
57	7.7630	8.1178	8.4369	8.7221	8.9760	9.1992	9.3954	9.5661	9.7132	9.8388	9.9450	57
58	7.6559	7.9960	8.3001	8.5704	8.8090	9.0180	9.2001	9.3569	9.4909	9.6042	9.6989	58
59	7.5416	7.8665	8.1552	8.4100	8.6334	8.8276	8.9952	9.1383	9.2593	9.3604	9.4443	59
60	7.4189	7.7279	8.0007	8.2398	8.4476	8.6270	8.7801	8.9097	9.0180	9.1076	9.1807	60
61	7.2885	7.5810	7.8374	8.0604	8.2528	8.4171	8.5560	8.6721	8.7682	8.8467	8.9098	61
62	7.1500	7.4257	7.6654	7.8722	8.0488	8.1982	8.3231	8.4264	8.5106	8.5784	8.6322	62
63	7.0038	7.2622	7.4850	7.6754	7.8364	7.9711	8.0824	8.1732	8.2463	8.3042	8.3493	63
64	6.8498	7.0906	7.2964	7.4704	7.6160	7.7363	7.8345	7.9134	7.9760	8.0248	8.0621	64
65	6.6881	6.9112	7.0999	7.2577	7.3882	7.4946	7.5803	7.6482	7.7010	7.7414	7.7717	65
66	6.5191	6.7244	6.8961	7.0380	7.1539	7.2470	7.3209	7.3784	7.4224	7.4552	7.4792	66
67	6.3431	6.5305	6.6855	6.8120	6.9137	6.9943	7.0572	7.1052	7.1411	7.1673	7.1857	67
68	6.1603	6.3303	6.4689	6.5805	6.6689	6.7377	6.7904	6.8298	6.8584	6.8787	6.8925	68
69	5.9713	6.1240	6.2468	6.3442	6.4200	6.4780	6.5214	6.5530	6.5753	6.5905	6.6003	69
70	5.7761	5.9120	6.0197	6.1037	6.1679	6.2158	6.2508	6.2754	6.2922	6.3032	6.3099	70
71	5.5755	5.6953	5.7886	5.8600	5.9134	5.9522	5.9797	5.9983	6.0105	6.0180	6.0223	71
72	5.3700	5.4744	5.5542	5.6139	5.6574	5.6881	5.7090	5.7225	5.7309	5.7357	5.7382	72
73	5.1604	5.2502	5.3174	5.3663	5.4008	5.4243	5.4396	5.4490	5.4544	5.4572	5.4585	73
74	4.9472	5.0233	5.0787	5.1178	5.1444	5.1618	5.1736	5.1785	5.1817	5.1831	5.1837	74
75	4.7312	4.7944	4.8391	4.8695	4.8892	4.9014	4.9083	4.9119	4.9136	4.9143	4.9145	75
76	4.5130	4.5644	4.5993	4.6221	4.6360	4.6440	4.6482	4.6501	4.6509	4.6511	4.6512	76
77	4.2931	4.3336	4.3600	4.3762	4.3854	4.3903	4.3925	4.3934	4.3937	4.3938	4.3938	77
78	4.0724	4.1032	4.1222	4.1330	4.1387	4.1413	4.1424	4.1427	4.1428	4.1428		
79	3.8516	3.8741	3.8869	3.8935	3.8966	3.8979	3.8983	3.8984	3.8985		17.0396	30
80	3.6315	3.6468	3.6548	3.6585	3.6600	3.6605	3.6607	3.6607		17.2022	17.2022	29
81	3.4122	3.4219	3.4263	3.4281	3.4288	3.4289	3.4290		17.3597	17.3597	17.3597	28
82	3.1938	3.1994	3.2015	3.2023	3.2025	3.2026		17.5122	17.5122	17.5122	17.5122	27
83	2.9762	2.9790	2.9799	2.9802	2.9802		17.6598	17.6598	17.6598	17.6598	17.6598	26
84	2.7595	2.7606	2.7610	2.7610		17.8027	17.8027	17.8027	17.8027	17.8027	17.8026	25
85	2.5431	2.5435	2.5436		17.9409	17.9409	17.9409	17.9409	17.9409	17.9409	17.9407	24
86	2.3278	2.3279		18.0747	18.0747	18.0747	18.0747	18.0747	18.0746	18.0745	18.0742	23
87	2.1138		18.2041	18.2041	18.2041	18.2041	18.2041	18.2041	18.2039	18.2037	18.2033	22
		18.3293	18.3293	18.3293	18.3293	18.3293	18.3292	18.3291	18.3289	18.3285	18.3279	21
20	18.4504	18.4504	18.4504	18.4504	18.4503	18.4503	18.4502	18.4499	18.4496	18.4490	18.4481	20
19	18.5675	18.5675	18.5675	18.5675	18.5674	18.5673	18.5671	18.5668	18.5662	18.5653	18.5641	19
18	18.6807	18.6807	18.6807	18.6806	18.6805	18.6803	18.6799	18.6795	18.6786	18.6774	18.6757	18
17	18.7901	18.7901	18.7900	18.7899	18.7897	18.7894	18.7889	18.7881	18.7869	18.7856	18.7831	17
16	18.8956	18.8956	18.8955	18.8953	18.8950	18.8946	18.8938	18.8927	18.8911	18.8889	18.8861	16
15	18.9975	18.9974	18.9972	18.9969	18.9964	18.9957	18.9947	18.9933	18.9912	18.9884	18.9849	15
14	19.0957	19.0955	19.0953	19.0948	19.0940	19.0932	19.0917	19.0898	19.0871	19.0837	19.0793	14
13	19.1902	19.1900	19.1895	19.1890	19.1879	19.1866	19.1849	19.1822	19.1789	19.1747	19.1695	13
12	19.2812	19.2809	19.2802	19.2793	19.2779	19.2762	19.2737	19.2706	19.2666	19.2616	19.2552	12
11	19.3684	19.3679	19.3670	19.3658	19.3641	19.3617	19.3588	19.3549	19.3501	19.3441	19.3366	11
10	19.4520	19.4513	19.4501	19.4485	19.4463	19.4435	19.4398	19.4352	19.4294	19.4223	19.4137	10
	79	78	77	76	75	74	73	72	71	70	69	

Age.	23	24	25	26	27	28	29	30	31	32	33	Age.
10	13.8176	14.1427	14.4525	14.7476	15.0286	15.2961	15.5507	15.7930	16.0242	16.2438	16.4525	10
11	13.8085	14.1329	14.4418	14.7361	15.0164	15.2832	15.5369	15.7786	16.0084	16.2272	16.4348	11
12	13.7986	14.1221	14.4303	14.7237	15.0031	15.2689	15.5219	15.7626	15.9915	16.2092	16.4159	12
13	13.7878	14.1104	14.4179	14.7102	14.9886	15.2535	15.5056	15.7453	15.9732	16.1897	16.3954	13
14	13.7760	14.0979	14.4047	14.6967	14.9731	15.2369	15.4880	15.7266	15.9537	16.1688	16.3732	14
15	13.7635	14.0843	14.3896	14.6801	14.9565	15.2194	15.4693	15.7068	15.9323	16.1464	16.3495	15
16	13.7501	14.0698	14.3741	14.6635	14.9388	15.2005	15.4492	15.6855	15.9097	16.1224	16.3239	16
17	13.7358	14.0545	14.3576	14.6459	14.9200	15.1805	15.4279	15.6628	15.8855	16.0966	16.2966	17
18	13.7206	14.0381	14.3401	14.6272	14.9000	15.1592	15.4051	15.6384	15.8596	16.0689	16.2672	18
19	13.7045	14.0209	14.3216	14.6074	14.8788	15.1364	15.3808	15.6125	15.8318	16.0394	16.2356	19
20	13.6875	14.0026	14.3019	14.5863	14.8562	15.1122	15.3548	15.5846	15.8021	16.0076	16.2017	20
21	13.6696	13.9833	14.2811	14.5639	14.8321	15.0863	15.3270	15.5549	15.7701	15.9735	16.1653	21
22	13.6507	13.9628	14.2591	14.5400	14.8064	15.0586	15.2973	15.5229	15.7359	15.9369	16.1262	22
23	13.6305	13.9409	14.2353	14.5144	14.7787	15.0288	15.2656	15.4884	15.6989	15.8973	16.0839	23
24	13.6090	13.9176	14.2101	14.4870	14.7491	14.9968	15.2308	15.4514	15.6592	15.8548	16.0384	24
25	13.5861	13.8926	14.1829	14.4576	14.7172	14.9624	15.1936	15.4114	15.6163	15.8088	15.9893	25
26	13.5615	13.8657	14.1536	14.4268	14.6826	14.9251	15.1534	15.3682	15.5699	15.7592	15.9362	26
27	13.5349	13.8368	14.1221	14.3914	14.6458	14.8848	15.1099	15.3214	15.5198	15.7054	15.8789	27
28	13.5064	13.8055	14.0879	14.3541	14.6051	14.8412	15.0629	15.2709	15.4655	15.6474	15.8169	28
29	13.4755	13.7716	14.0509	14.3139	14.5615	14.7939	15.0120	15.2160	15.4068	15.5846	15.7499	29
30	13.4421	13.7349	14.0115	14.2703	14.5141	14.7428	14.9568	15.1567	15.3432	15.5167	15.6776	30
31	13.4056	13.6951	13.9673	14.2229	14.4628	14.6872	14.8969	15.0925	15.2744	15.4432	15.5994	31
32	13.3659	13.6516	13.9198	14.1714	14.4068	14.6269	14.8320	15.0228	15.1999	15.3637	15.5148	32
33	13.3229	13.6043	13.8683	14.1153	14.3462	14.5614	14.7617	14.9474	15.1193	15.2778	15.4234	33
34	13.2758	13.5529	13.8121	14.0549	14.2802	14.4903	14.6852	14.8655	15.0318	15.1847	15.3252	34
35	13.2244	13.4964	13.7514	13.9877	14.2082	14.4128	14.6021	14.7766	14.9370	15.0839	15.2180	35
36	13.1678	13.4347	13.6836	13.9151	14.1298	14.3285	14.5118	14.6801	14.8344	14.9751	15.1028	36
37	13.1059	13.3672	13.6102	13.8357	14.0444	14.2367	14.4135	14.5755	14.7232	14.8573	14.9782	37
38	13.0379	13.2934	13.5299	13.7489	13.9510	14.1367	14.3067	14.4619	14.6027	14.7300	14.8445	38
39	12.9632	13.2119	13.4420	13.6542	13.8496	14.0279	14.1909	14.3371	14.4725	14.5928	14.7002	39
40	12.8810	13.1228	13.3458	13.5507	13.7384	13.9096	14.0650	14.2055	14.3318	14.4447	14.5451	40
41	12.7903	13.0249	13.2402	13.4375	13.6174	13.7807	13 9283	14.0611	14.1798	14.2852	14.3783	41
42	12.6912	12.9176	13.1249	13.3140	13.4857	13.6409	13.7804	13.9052	14.0160	14.1139	14.1997	42
43	12.5822	12.8002	12.9991	13.1796	13.3428	13.4895	13.6207	13.7372	13.8401	13.9303	14.0088	43
44	12.4637	12.6729	12.8627	13.0343	13.1887	13.3267	13.4492	13.5575	13.6523	13.7349	13.8066	44
45	12.3358	12.5356	12.7162	12.8786	13.0238	13.1528	13.2667	13.3665	13.4533	13.5282	13.5921	45
46	12.1982	12.3883	12.5594	12.7122	12.8480	12.9679	13.0730	13.1645	13.2433	13.3106	13.3676	46
47	12.0514	12.2316	12.3925	12.5357	12.6620	12.7727	12.8691	12.9521	13 0231	13.0830	13.1332	47
48	11.8952	12.0649	12.2158	12.3489	12.4656	12.5672	12.6548	12.7296	12.7928	12.8457	12.8894	48
49	11.7289	11.8882	12.0287	12.1518	12.2589	12.3504	12.4303	12.4969	12.5527	12.5989	12.6366	49
50	11.5528	11.7011	11.8312	11.9443	12.0418	12.1249	12.1956	12.2544	12.3032	12.3429	12.3749	50
51	11.3662	11.5036	11.6232	11.7263	11.8143	11.8888	11.9510	12.0025	12.0446	12.0789	12.1052	51
52	11.1694	11.2959	11.4051	11.4982	11.5769	11.6428	11.6973	11.7417	11.7775	11.8058	11.8279	52
53	10.9625	11.0779	11.1766	11.2600	11.3297	11.3875	11.4345	11.4724	11.5025	11.5258	11.5432	53
54	10.7454	10.8499	10.9384	11.0123	11.0735	11.1235	11.1636	11.1954	11.2202	11.2391	11.2533	54
55	10.5179	10.6118	10.6904	10.7552	10.8082	10.8508	10.8846	10.9109	10.9309	10.9461	10.9569	55
56	10.2806	10.3641	10.4331	10.4897	10.5348	10.5707	10.5987	10.6199	10.6360	10.6476	10.6556	56
57	10.0338	10.1074	10.1673	10.2156	10.2538	10.2836	10.3063	10.3234	10.3357	10.3445	10.3505	57
58	9.7773	9.8412	9.8926	9.9335	9.9652	9.9893	10.0076	10.0208	10.0302	10.0365	10.0407	58
59	9.5125	9.5675	9.6110	9.6449	9.6707	9.6902	9.7043	9.7143	9.7211	9.7255	9.7282	59
60	9.2391	9.2862	9.3224	9.3501	9.3709	9.3860	9.3967	9.4040	9.4087	9.4115	9.4132	60
61	8.9597	8.9986	9.0286	9.0507	9.0668	9.0783	9.0861	9.0912	9.0942	9.0960	9.0970	61
62	8.6740	8.7060	8.7299	8.7474	8.7597	8.7680	8.7735	8.7768	8.7788	8.7798	8.7802	62
63	8.3838	8.4096	8.4284	8.4417	8.4507	8.4566	8.4602	8.4622	8.4633	8.4638	8.4640	63
64	8.0899	8.1103	8.1246	8.1344	8.1407	8.1446	8.1468	8.1480	8.1485	8.1488	8.1488	64
65	7.7937	7.8092	7.8198	7.8267	7.8309	7.8334	7.8346	7.8352	7.8354	7.8355	7.8355	65
66	7.4961	7.5076	7.5151	7.5197	7.5224	7.5237	7.5244	7.5246	7.5247	7.5247	7.5247	66
67	7.1983	7.2065	7.2115	7.2143	7.2159	7.2166	7.2169	7.2169	7.2169	7.2170		
68	6.9014	6.9069	6.9101	6.9118	6.9125	6.9128	6.9129	6.9130	6.9130		14.8609	41
69	6.6064	6.6099	6.6117	6.6125	6.6128	6.6130	6.6130	6.6130		15.0929	15.0929	40
70	6.3137	6.3157	6.3166	6.3170	6.3171	6.3172	6.3172		15.3172	15.3172	15.3172	39
71	6.0244	6.0255	6.0259	6.0261	6.0261	6.0261		15.5342	15.5342	15.5342	15.5342	38
72	5.7393	5.7398	5.7400	5.7400	5.7400		15.7442	15.7442	15.7442	15.7442	15.7441	37
73	5.4590	5.4592	5.4593	5.4593		15.9475	15.9475	15.9475	15.9475	15.9475	15.9474	36
74	5.1839	5.1840	5.1840		16.1444	16.1444	16.1444	16.1444	16.1443	16.1442	16.1439	35
75	4.9146	4.9146		16.3350	16.3350	16.3350	16.3350	16.3349	16.3349	16.3347	16.3342	34
76	4.6512		16.5196	16.5196	16.5196	16.5196	16.5196	16.5195	16.5193	16.5189	16.5182	33
		16.6984	16.6984	16.6984	16.6984	16.6984	16.6983	16.6981	16.6977	16.6971	16.6961	32
31	16.8717	16.8717	16.8717	16.8717	16.8717	16.8716	16.8714	16.8711	16.8705	16.8695	16.8679	31
30	17.0396	17.0396	17.0396	17.0396	17.0395	17.0393	17.0389	17.0384	17.0375	17.0359	17.0339	30
29	17.2022	17.2022	17.2022	17.2021	17.2019	17.2016	17.2011	17.2002	17.1988	17.1967	17.1939	29
28	17.3597	17.3597	17.3596	17.3594	17.3591	17.3586	17.3577	17.3564	17.3545	17.3517	17.3479	28
27	17.5122	17.5121	17.5119	17.5117	17.5112	17.5103	17.5091	17.5072	17.5046	17.5009	17.4962	27
26	17.6597	17.6596	17.6593	17.6588	17.6581	17.6568	17.6551	17.6526	17.6491	17.6446	17.6386	26
25	17.8025	17.8022	17.8018	17.8010	17.7999	17.7982	17.7958	17.7925	17.7881	17.7824	17.7751	25
24	17.9405	17.9400	17.9393	17.9382	17.9367	17.9343	17.9312	17.9270	17.9216	17.9146	17.9057	24
23	18.0738	18.0731	18.0719	18.0705	18.0684	18.0654	18.0614	18.0562	18.0495	18.0410	18.0305	23
22	18.2027	18.2017	18.2002	18.1981	18.1953	18.1915	18.1865	18.1801	18.1720	18.1620	18.1497	22
21	18.3269	18.3255	18.3236	18.3208	18.3172	18.3125	18.3064	18.2987	18.2891	18.2773	18.2632	21
20	18.4468	18.4449	18.4423	18.4388	18.4343	18.4285	18.4211	18.4119	18.4008	18.3872	18.3711	20
19	18.5623	18.5598	18.5565	18.5522	18.5466	18.5396	18.5308	18.5201	18.5072	18.4918	18.4735	19
18	18.6733	18.6702	18.6660	18.6607	18.6540	18.6457	18.6355	18.6232	18.6084	18.5909	18.5705	18
17	18.7801	18.7761	18.7710	18.7647	18.7567	18.7469	18.7352	18.7211	18.7044	18.6849	18.6619	17
16	18.8823	18.8775	18.8714	18.8638	18.8545	18.8432	18.8298	18.8139	18.7953	18.7737	18.7488	16
15	18.9802	18.9744	18.9672	18.9577	18.9474	18.9345	18.9194	18.9019	18.8810	18.8574	18.8304	15
14	19.0739	19.0666	19.0583	19.0479	19.0357	19.0213	19.0042	18.9846	18.9620	18.9360	18.9068	14
13	19.1628	19.1546	19.1448	19.1333	19.1193	19.1032	19.0843	19.0627	19.0381	19.0100	18.9786	13
12	19.2474	19.2382	19.2269	19.2137	19.1983	19.1803	19.1596	19.1361	19.1095	19.0795	19.0459	12
11	19.3277	19.3171	19.3045	19.2897	19.2725	19.2528	19.2303	19.2047	19.1761	19.1439	19.1083	11
10	19.4035	19.3915	19.3773	19.3609	19.3422	19.3207	19.2963	19.2689	19.2383	19.2042	19.1665	10
	68	67	66	65	64	63	62	61	60	59	58	

Age.	34	35	36	37	38	39	40	41	42	43	44	45	Age.
10	16.6509	16.8397	17.0188	17.1889	17.3502	17.5029	17.6479	17.7848	17.9144	18.0366	18.1521	18.2607	10
11	16.6325	16.8200	16.9981	17.1670	17.3271	17.4787	17.6221	17.7577	17.8859	18.0066	18.1204	18.2273	11
12	16.6123	16.7987	16.9756	17.1433	17.3020	17.4523	17.5943	17.7283	17.8548	17.9739	18.0861	18.1912	12
13	16.5907	16.7759	16.9514	17.1176	17.2748	17.4234	17.5640	17.6964	17.8211	17.9384	18.0487	18.1520	13
14	16.5672	16.7509	16.9251	17.0898	17.2455	17.3925	17.5312	17.6618	17.7847	17.9001	18.0083	18.1096	14
15	16.5419	16.7243	16.8969	17.0599	17.2138	17.3590	17.4958	17.6245	17.7454	17.8588	17.9649	18.0641	15
16	16.5149	16.6955	16.8663	17.0276	17.1796	17.3229	17.4577	17.5843	17.7030	17.8141	17.9179	18.0148	16
17	16.4858	16.6647	16.8336	16.9928	17.1429	17.2840	17.4166	17.5409	17.6575	17.7661	17.8675	17.9619	17
18	16.4545	16.6314	16.7982	16.9554	17.1032	17.2421	17.3724	17.4942	17.6082	17.7144	17.8132	17.9049	18
19	16.4209	16.5957	16.7603	16.9152	17.0606	17.1971	17.3247	17.4441	17.5553	17.6584	17.7548	17.8437	19
20	16.3848	16.5572	16.7195	16.8718	17.0148	17.1485	17.2735	17.3901	17.4985	17.5991	17.6921	17.7779	20
21	16.3459	16.5159	16.6756	16.8253	16.9654	17.0964	17.2185	17.3321	17.4374	17.5349	17.6248	17.7075	21
22	16.3042	16.4715	16.6284	16.7752	16.9124	17.0403	17.1593	17.2697	17.3718	17.4661	17.5526	17.6319	22
23	16.2592	16.4236	16.5774	16.7212	16.8552	16.9799	17.0956	17.2026	17.3013	17.3919	17.4751	17.5509	23
24	16.2107	16.3719	16.5225	16.6622	16.7937	16.9149	17.0271	17.1305	17.2255	17.3126	17.3920	17.4641	24
25	16.1583	16.3162	16.4634	16.6004	16.7274	16.8449	16.9533	17.0529	17.1442	17.2274	17.3029	17.3713	25
26	16.1017	16.2560	16.3996	16.5327	16.6559	16.7696	16.8740	16.9696	17.0569	17.1360	17.2076	17.2720	26
27	16.0407	16.1912	16.3307	16.4599	16.5789	16.6884	16.7887	16.8801	16.9631	17.0382	17.1057	17.1659	27
28	15.9747	16.1210	16.2564	16.3813	16.4961	16.6011	16.6970	16.7841	16.8627	16.9339	16.9967	17.0529	28
29	15.9034	16.0454	16.1763	16.2966	16.4069	16.5074	16.5986	16.6811	16.7553	16.8216	16.8805	16.9325	29
30	15.8265	15.9638	16.0899	16.2055	16.3109	16.4067	16.4935	16.5702	16.6405	16.7023	16.7568	16.8046	30
31	15.7434	15.8757	15.9966	16.1075	16.2078	16.2986	16.3802	16.4531	16.5179	16.5751	16.6253	16.6689	31
32	15.6536	15.7807	15.8967	16.0020	16.0972	16.1828	16.2593	16.3273	16.3873	16.4399	16.4857	16.5251	32
33	15.5568	15.6785	15.7889	15.8888	15.9786	16.0589	16.1302	16.1932	16.2484	16.2964	16.3378	16.3731	33
34	15.4524	15.5683	15.6731	15.7673	15.8515	15.9264	15.9925	16.0504	16.1008	16.1442	16.1813	16.2127	34
35	15.3397	15.4496	15.5486	15.6369	15.7155	15.7848	15.8456	15.8985	15.9441	15.9830	16.0159	16.0435	35
36	15.2182	15.3220	15.4149	15.4973	15.5701	15.6339	15.6894	15.7373	15.7782	15.8127	15.8416	15.8656	36
37	15.0875	15.1849	15.2715	15.3479	15.4149	15.4733	15.5235	15.5664	15.6027	15.6331	15.6582	15.6787	37
38	14.9468	15.0377	15.1180	15.1884	15.2496	15.3024	15.3474	15.3855	15.4174	15.4438	15.4653	15.4826	38
39	14.7957	14.8801	14.9539	15.0183	15.0737	15.1210	15.1611	15.1945	15.2223	15.2449	15.2630	15.2774	39
40	14.6337	14.7113	14.7789	14.8371	14.8869	14.9289	14.9641	14.9932	15.0169	15.0361	15.0515	15.0629	40
41	14.4599	14.5309	14.5921	14.6444	14.6886	14.7256	14.7562	14.7811	14.8012	14.8171	14.8295	14.8389	41
42	14.2743	14.3386	14.3936	14.4400	14.4789	14.5110	14.5372	14.5584	14.5751	14.5881	14.5980	14.6055	42
43	14.0764	14.1342	14.1830	14.2239	14.2577	14.2852	14.3074	14.3250	14.3387	14.3492	14.3570	14.3627	43
44	13.8668	13.9182	13.9611	13.9967	14.0257	14.0490	14.0675	14.0819	14.0929	14.1012	14.1071	14.1114	44
45	13.6462	13.6914	13.7289	13.7594	13.7839	13.8034	13.8186	13.8301	13.8388	13.8451	13.8496	13.8526	45
46	13.4152	13.4546	13.4867	13.5126	13.5331	13.5490	13.5611	13.5703	13.5769	13.5816	13.5849	13.5869	46
47	13.1747	13.2086	13.2359	13.2574	13.2742	13.2869	13.2967	13.3036	13.3086	13.3119	13.3141	13.3154	47
48	12.9251	12.9539	12.9766	12.9943	13.0078	13.0179	13.0253	13.0306	13.0341	13.0365	13.0378	13.0386	48
49	12.6669	12.6909	12.7096	12.7238	12.7345	12.7423	12.7478	12.7516	12.7540	12.7555	12.7563	12.7568	49
50	12.4003	12.4201	12.4351	12.4464	12.4546	12.4604	12.4644	12.4669	12.4686	12.4694	12.4699	12.4701	50
51	12.1261	12.1419	12.1539	12.1626	12.1687	12.1729	12.1756	12.1773	12.1782	12.1788	12.1789	12.1791	51
52	11.8447	11.8574	11.8665	11.8730	11.8775	11.8804	11.8821	11.8831	11.8837	11.8839	11.8840	11.8840	52
53	11.5570	11.5667	11.5736	11.5783	11.5814	11.5832	11.5843	11.5849	12.5851	11.5852	11.5853	11.5853	53
54	11.2636	11.2709	11.2759	11.2791	11.2810	11.2822	11.2828	11.2831	11.2832	11.2832	11.2832	11.2832	54
55	10.9647	10.9701	10.9734	10.9755	10.9767	10.9774	10.9777	10.9778	10.9778	10.9778	10.9778	11.5853	53
56	10.6615	10.6651	10.6673	10.6686	10.6693	10.6696	10.6698	10.6698	10.6698	10.6698	11.8840	11.8840	52
57	10.3544	10.3567	10.3581	10.3588	10.3591	10.3593	10.3593	10.3593	10.3593	12.1791	12.1791	12.1791	51
58	10.0431	10.0446	10.0454	10.0457	10.0459	10.0459	10.0459	10.0459	12.4705	12.4705	12.4704	12.4703	50
59	9.7297	9.7306	9.7310	9.7311	9.7311	9.7311	9.7311						
60	9.4142	9.4146	9.4147	9.4147	9.4147	9.4147		12.7571	12.7571	12.7571	12.7571	12.7570	49
61	9.0974	9.0976	9.0976	9.0976	9.0976		13.0394	13.0394	13.0394	13.0394	13.0393	13.0391	48
62	8.7804	8.7805	8.7805	8.7805		13.3169	13.3169	13.3169	13.3169	13.3168	13.3167	13.3162	47
63	8.4641	8.4641	8.4641		13.5896	13.5896	13.5896	13.5896	13.5895	13.5893	13.5889	13.5882	46
64	8.1488	8.1489		13.8571	13.8571	13.8571	13.8571	13.8570	13.8568	13.8565	13.8557	13.8546	45
65	7.8355		14.1185	14.1185	14.1185	14.1185	14.1185	14.1183	14.1178	14.1173	14.1162	14.1143	44
		14.3735	14.3735	14.3735	14.3735	14.3735	14.3733	14.3729	14.3723	14.3712	14.3695	14.3667	43
42	14.6212	14.6212	14.6212	14.6212	14.6211	14.6210	14.6207	14.6201	14.6191	14.6174	14.6147	14.6109	42
41	14.8609	14.8609	14.8609	14.8609	14.8608	14.8604	14.8599	14.8589	14.8573	14.8545	14.8512	14.8460	41
40	15.0929	15.0929	15.0929	15.0928	15.0925	15.0919	15.0909	15.0895	15.0871	15.0836	15.0787	15.0719	40
39	15.3172	15.3171	15.3170	15.3167	15.3162	15.3153	15.3139	15.3116	15.3083	15.3036	15.2972	15.2886	39
38	15.5341	15.5339	15.5337	15.5332	15.5324	15.5311	15.5289	15.5257	15.5213	15.5151	15.5070	15.4963	38
37	15.7441	15.7438	15.7433	15.7426	15.7413	15.7392	15.7362	15.7319	15.7261	15.7184	15.7082	15.6952	37
36	15.9471	15.9467	15.9459	15.9447	15.9427	15.9399	15.9359	15.9303	15.9229	15.9132	15.9008	15.8851	36
35	16.1435	16.1428	16.1416	16.1398	16.1371	16.1332	16.1279	16.1209	16.1117	16.0998	16.0849	16.0663	35
34	16.3336	16.3324	16.3306	16.3280	16.3244	16.3194	16.3127	16.3039	16.2926	16.2783	16.2606	16.2389	34
33	16.5171	16.5154	16.5129	16.5095	16.5047	16.4983	16.4899	16.4792	16.4656	16.4487	16.4280	16.4030	33
32	16.6944	16.6921	16.6888	16.6842	16.6781	16.6701	16.6599	16.6469	16.6309	16.6111	16.5873	16.5588	32
31	16.8657	16.8626	16.8582	16.8524	16.8448	16.8349	16.8227	16.8073	16.7885	16.7658	16.7386	16.7065	31
30	17.0308	17.0267	17.0211	17.0139	17.0046	16.9928	16.9782	16.9603	16.9386	16.9127	16.8821	16.8462	30
29	17.1899	17.1846	17.1777	17.1688	17.1576	17.1436	17.1266	17.1059	17.0812	17.0520	17.0178	16.9762	29
28	17.3429	17.3363	17.3278	17.3171	17.3038	17.2876	17.2679	17.2443	17.2164	17.1838	17.1459	17.1025	28
27	17.4899	17.4818	17.4716	17.4589	17.4434	17.4246	17.4021	17.3756	17.3445	17.3084	17.2669	17.2196	27
26	17.6308	17.6211	17.6090	17.5942	17.5763	17.5548	17.5295	17.4998	17.4654	17.4258	17.3807	17.3295	26
25	17.7657	17.7542	17.7401	17.7229	17.7025	17.6784	17.6500	17.6172	17.5794	17.5364	17.4876	17.4327	25
24	17.8947	17.8812	17.8649	17.8454	17.8223	17.7953	17.7639	17.7279	17.6868	17.6403	17.5879	17.5293	24
23	18.0177	18.0021	17.9835	17.9614	17.9357	17.9058	17.8714	17.8322	17.7878	17.7374	17.6819	17.6197	23
22	18.1349	18.1171	18.0961	18.0715	18.0429	18.0101	17.9727	17.9303	17.8826	17.8292	17.7699	17.7042	22
21	18.2462	18.2262	18.2029	18.1754	18.1441	18.1084	18.0679	18.0224	17.9715	17.9148	17.8522	17.7831	21
20	18.3519	18.3295	18.3035	18.2736	18.2395	18.2009	18.1574	18.1088	18.0548	17.9949	17.9290	17.8568	20
19	18.4521	18.4273	18.3979	18.3662	18.3293	18.2879	18.2414	18.1898	18.1327	18.0698	18.0009	17.9256	19
18	18.5468	18.5196	18.4885	18.4533	18.4137	18.3694	18.3201	18.2656	18.2056	18.1397	18.0678	17.9896	18
17	18.6363	18.6066	18.5730	18.5352	18.4929	18.4459	18.3938	18.3365	18.2736	18.2050	18.1303	18.0494	17
16	18.7205	18.6884	18.6523	18.6119	18.5669	18.5173	18.4626	18.4025	18.3370	18.2657	18.1884	18.1049	16
15	18.7996	18.7651	18.7266	18.6837	18.6364	18.5841	18.5268	18.4642	18.3961	18.3223	18.2425	18.1565	15
14	18.8739	18.8371	18.7962	18.7508	18.7009	18.6461	18.5865	18.5214	18.4509	18.3747	18.2927	18.2044	14
13	18.9434	18.9043	18.8612	18.8134	18.7613	18.7041	18.6421	18.5747	18.5019	18.4236	18.3393	18.2489	13
12	19.0084	18.9672	18.9216	18.8717	18.8172	18.7579	18.6937	18.6234	18.5493	18.4687	18.3824	18.2901	12
11	19.0689	19.0254	18.9778	18.9258	18.8692	18.8079	18.7413	18.6698	18.5929	18.5105	18.4222	18.3279	11
10	19.1250	19.0795	19.0299	18.9757	18.9171	18.8537	18.7855	18.7121	18.6333	18.5489	18.4589	18.3629	10
	57	56	55	54	53	52	51	50	49	48	47	46	

ENDOWMENT POLICIES.—4 PER CENT.

1st YEAR—D. or 35.

Age.	Value.	M. Diff.
10	2.7576	—.0458
11	2.9067	.0455
12	3.0700	.0452
13	3.2493	.0447
14	3.4472	.0441
15	3.6663	.0438
16	3.9099	.0433
17	4.1820	.0427
18	4.4878	.0421
19	4.8334	.0413
20	5.2270	.0404
21	5.6786	.0393
22	6.2017	.0379
23	6.8143	.0362
24	7.5407	.0341
25	8.4149	.0314
26	9.4865	.0281
27	10.8292	.0236
28	12.5594	.0176
29	14.8706	.0092
30	18.1113	+.0030
31	22.9797	.0217
32	31.1015	.0539
33	47.3580	.1198
34	96.1538	.3205

1st Year—D. or 40.

Age.	Value.	M. Diff.
10	2.1957	—.0480
11	2.2951	.0478
12	2.4026	.0477
13	2.5191	.0477
14	2.6455	.0472
15	2.7834	.0475
16	2.9333	.0470
17	3.0978	.0470
18	3.2783	.0469
19	3.4771	.0466
20	3.6973	.0466
21	3.9415	.0461
22	4.2147	.0459
23	4.5213	.0455
24	4.8676	.0448
25	5.2621	.0442
26	5.7145	.0433
27	6.2382	.0420
28	6.8518	.0408
29	7.5785	.0386
30	8.4534	.0362
31	9.5258	.0333
32	10.8688	.0291
33	12.5986	.0231
34	14.9096	.0149
35	18.1497	.0028
36	23.0158	+.0158
37	31.1340	.0487
38	47.3828	.1157
39	96.1538	.3205

1st Year—D. or 45.

Age.	Value.	M. Diff.
10	1.8191	—.0494
11	1.8895	.0496
12	1.9647	.0497
13	2.0455	.0495
14	2.1323	.0493
15	2.2258	.0495
16	2.3263	.0493
17	2.4352	.0496
18	2.5529	.0498
19	2.6806	.0499
20	2.8193	.0499
21	2.9706	.0501
22	3.1360	.0501
23	3.3176	.0502
24	3.5175	.0503
25	3.7384	.0501
26	3.9840	.0501
27	4.2578	.0498
28	4.5659	.0502
29	4.9131	.0496
30	5.3083	.0491
31	5.7618	.0487
32	6.2864	.0477
33	6.9004	.0466
34	7.6280	.0450
35	8.5033	.0428
36	9.5756	.0398
37	10.9186	.0359
38	12.6486	.0302
39	14.9590	.0221
40	18.1979	.0100
41	23.0623	+.0090
42	31.1768	+.0419
43	47.4171	.1100
44	96.1538	.3205

1st Year—D. or 50.

Age.	Value.	M. Diff.
10	1.5583	—.0505
11	1.6101	.0504
12	1.6655	.0507
13	1.7244	.0507
14	1.7872	.0505
15	1.8545	.0510
16	1.9261	.0510
17	2.0029	.0513
18	2.0852	.0517
19	2.1733	.0517
20	2.2682	.0521
21	2.3703	.0525
22	2.4803	.0526
23	2.5994	.0530
24	2.7284	.0534
25	2.8685	.0536
26	3.0212	.0539
27	3.1881	.0543
28	3.3711	.0547
29	3.5724	.0549
30	3.7949	.0552
31	4.0420	.0556
32	4.3174	.0558
33	4.6264	.0559
34	4.9754	.0560
35	5.3721	.0558
36	5.8269	.0553
37	6.3532	.0550
38	6.9690	.0541
39	7.6987	.0528
40	8.5763	.0508
41	9.6515	.0482
42	10.9983	.0448
43	12.7332	.0399
44	15.0485	.0330
45	18.2922	.0224
46	23.1595	.0051
47	31.2712	+.0272
48	47.4932	.0973
49	96.1538	.3205

1st Year—D. or 55.

Age.	Value.	M. Diff.
10	1.3751	—.0511
11	1.4151	.0512
12	1.4575	.0517
13	1.5024	.0515
14	1.5501	.0516
15	1.6008	.0520
16	1.6544	.0521
17	1.7116	.0525
18	1.7723	.0528
19	1.8370	.0531
20	1.9059	.0535
21	1.9795	.0541
22	2.0581	.0544
23	2.1422	.0549
24	2.2323	.0553
25	2.3291	.0559
26	2.4332	.0564
27	2.5455	.0570
28	2.6666	.0574
29	2.7979	.0581
30	2.9403	.0586
31	3.0956	.0595
32	3.2649	.0601
33	3.4505	.0607
34	3.6546	.0617
35	3.8800	.0619
36	4.1301	.0624
37	4.4091	.0631
38	4.7219	.0634
39	5.0753	.0638
40	5.4769	.0640
41	5.9377	.0641
42	6.4708	.0640
43	7.0949	.0642
44	7.8335	.0647
45	8.7207	.0646
46	9.8054	.0646
47	11.1605	.0637
48	12.9015	.0614
49	15.2209	.0564
50	18.4658	.0474
51	23.3291	.0311
52	31.4272	+.0025
53	47.6160	.0768
54	96.1538	.3205

1st Year—D. or 60.

Age.	Value.	M. Diff.
10	1.2471	—.0516
11	1.2793	.0519
12	1.3131	.0521
13	1.3489	.0522
14	1.3867	.0521
15	1.4267	.0526
16	1.4689	.0528
17	1.5136	.0531
18	1.5609	.0537
19	1.6109	.0540
20	1.6639	.0545
21	1.7200	.0551
22	1.7797	.0556
23	1.8429	.0560
24	1.9102	.0566
25	1.9819	.0572
26	2.0583	.0578
27	2.1399	.0586
28	2.2271	.0593
29	2.3205	.0599
30	2.4207	.0608
31	2.5285	.0618
32	2.6444	.0626
33	2.7696	.0635
34	2.9050	.0644
35	3.0520	.0653
36	3.2120	.0661
37	3.3867	.0673
38	3.5781	.0682
39	3.7888	.0693
40	4.0213	.0703
41	4.2798	.0712
42	4.5679	.0721
43	4.8915	.0738
44	5.2561	.0759
45	5.6699	.0781
46	6.1427	.0810
47	6.6874	.0839
48	7.3217	.0869
49	8.0698	.0897
50	8.9656	.0924
51	10.0585	.0955
52	11.4192	.0958
53	13.1663	.0961
54	15.4891	.0934
55	18.7336	.0861
56	23.5898	.0702
57	31.6683	.0359
58	47.8022	+.0458
59	96.1538	.3205

1st Year—D. or 65.

Age.	Value.	M. Diff.
10	1.1598	—.0523
11	1.1867	.0521
12	1.2148	.0519
13	1.2449	.0531
14	1.2763	.0529
15	1.3095	.0531
16	1.3443	.0533
17	1.3811	.0537
18	1.4198	.0542
19	1.4606	.0546
20	1.5037	.0552
21	1.5490	.0558
22	1.5969	.0562
23	1.6475	.0568
24	1.7010	.0579
25	1.7577	.0582
26	1.8176	.0587
27	1.8812	.0596
28	1.9488	.0605
29	2.0205	.0612
30	2.0967	.0620
31	2.1782	.0633
32	2.2649	.0642
33	2.3575	.0651
34	2.4568	.0663
35	2.5632	.0674
36	2.6776	.0684
37	2.8008	.0697
38	2.9339	.0710
39	3.0781	.0723
40	3.2345	.0733
41	3.4052	.0749
42	3.5915	.0763
43	3.7961	.0785
44	4.0205	.0814
45	4.2678	.0842
46	4.5411	.0881
47	4.8438	.0923
48	5.1811	.0968
49	5.5591	.1014
50	5.9859	.1065
51	6.4720	—.1128
52	7.0287	.1173
53	7.6764	.1237
54	8.4369	.1295
55	9.3449	.1354
56	10.4484	.1410
57	11.8201	.1455
58	13.5751	.1487
59	15.9038	.1491
60	19.1493	.1449
61	23.9967	.1308
62	32.0463	.0954
63	48.0977	.0035
64	96.1538	+.3205

1st Year—D. or 70.

Age.	Value.	M. Diff.
10	1.1032	—.0522
11	1.1268	.0524
12	1.1517	.0529
13	1.1779	.0535
14	1.2051	.0525
15	1.2342	.0534
16	1.2644	.0536
17	1.2963	.0541
18	1.3298	.0546
19	1.3649	.0550
20	1.4019	.0556
21	1.4407	.0563
22	1.4815	.0567
23	1.5245	.0574
24	1.5697	.0580
25	1.6174	.0587
26	1.6677	.0594
27	1.7208	.0603
28	1.7768	.0611
29	1.8360	.0618
30	1.8987	.0629
31	1.9652	.0646
32	2.0355	.0652
33	2.1101	.0663
34	2.1894	.0673
35	2.2739	.0687
36	2.3639	.0697
37	2.4600	.0711
38	2.5629	.0721
39	2.6733	.0742
40	2.7917	.0754
41	2.9194	.0769
42	3.0571	.0786
43	3.2063	.0811
44	3.3673	.0841
45	3.5417	.0874
46	3.7306	.0917
47	3.9352	.0963
48	4.1576	.1014
49	4.4000	.1068
50	4.6653	.1127
51	4.9572	.1201
52	5.2780	.1259
53	5.6352	.1340
54	6.0331	.1418
55	6.4804	.1505
56	6.9867	.1597
57	7.5654	.1691
58	8.2343	.1790
59	9.0171	.1894
60	9.9472	.2003
61	11.0722	.2116
62	12.4638	.2225
63	14.2347	.2318
64	16.5734	.2383
65	19.8187	.2390
66	24.6489	.2276
67	32.6471	.1899
68	48.5634	.0811
69	96.1538	+.3205

1st Year—D. or 75.

Age.	Value.	M. Diff.
10	1.0697	—.0524
11	1.0914	.0526
12	1.1143	.0530
13	1.1381	.0529
14	1.1632	.0528
15	1.1898	.0536
16	1.2173	.0537
17	1.2464	.0542
18	1.2769	.0548
19	1.3088	.0553
20	1.3422	.0558
21	1.3774	.0566
22	1.4142	.0572
23	1.4529	.0578
24	1.4934	—.0582
25	1.5361	.0590
26	1.5810	.0598
27	1.6282	.0606
28	1.6779	.0615
29	1.7302	.0622
30	1.7854	.0634
31	1.8437	.0646
32	1.9052	.0658
33	1.9700	.0667
34	2.0388	.0680
35	2.1116	.0692
36	2.1887	.0703
37	2.2708	.0720
38	2.3580	.0733
39	2.4510	.0750
40	2.5503	.0765
41	2.6565	.0785
42	2.7702	.0798
43	2.8923	.0823
44	3.0231	.0857
45	3.1631	.0889
46	3.3130	.0934
47	3.4734	.0984
48	3.6450	.1038
49	3.8291	.1094
50	4.0270	.1157
51	4.2407	.1237
52	4.4700	.1298
53	4.7194	.1385
54	4.9896	.1472
55	5.2838	.1568
56	5.6054	.1670
57	5.9584	.1779
58	6.3481	.1897
59	6.7808	.2026
60	7.2640	.2167
61	7.8074	.2320
62	8.4236	.2485
63	9.1295	.2662
64	9.9483	.2849
65	10.9120	.3043
66	12.0674	.3240
67	13.4847	.3438
68	15.2741	.3620
69	17.6204	.3764
70	20.8575	.3836
71	25.6523	.3755
72	33.5628	.3330
73	49.2660	.1982
74	96.1538	+.3205

2d YEAR—D. or 35.

Age.	Value.	M. Diff.
10	4.9660	—.0374
11	5.2678	.0366
12	5.5971	.0355
13	5.9624	.0342
14	6.3651	.0333
15	6.8072	.0319
16	7.2998	.0304
17	7.8516	.0288
18	8.4704	.0269
19	9.1716	.0248
20	9.9689	.0223
21	10.8852	.0193
22	11.9487	.0158
23	13.1938	.0115
24	14.6717	.0064
25	16.4525	.0001
26	18.6363	+.0079
27	21.3755	.0181
28	24.9080	.0315
29	29.6306	.0498
30	36.2591	.0760
31	46.2196	.1159
32	62.8501	.1835
33	96.1538	.3205

2d Year—D. or 40.

Age.	Value.	M. Diff.
10	3.8153	—.0420
11	4.0163	.0414
12	4.2330	.0410
13	4.4650	.0399
14	4.7246	.0397
15	4.9971	.0391
16	5.3031	.0383
17	5.6320	.0376
18	5.9942	.0367
19	6.3952	.0358
20	6.8357	.0348
21	7.3299	.0334
22	7.8785	.0320

ENDOWMENT POLICIES.—4 PER CENT.

2d Year—D. or 40.

Age	Value.	M. Diff.
23	8.4970	—.0304
24	9.1981	.0284
25	9.9934	.0261
26	10.9093	.0233
27	11.9728	.0200
28	13.2145	.0160
29	14.6933	.0110
30	16.4721	.0049
31	18.6518	+.0029
32	21.3888	.0130
33	24.9206	.0264
34	29.6404	.0448
35	36.2654	.0712
36	46.2210	.1120
37	62.8523	.1806
38	96.1538	.3205

2d Year—D. or 45.

Age	Value.	M. Diff.
10	3.0459	—.0450
11	3.1838	.0449
12	3.3333	.0442
13	3.4965	.0439
14	3.6727	.0439
15	3.8571	.0435
16	4.0610	.0433
17	4.2755	.0430
18	4.5085	.0426
19	4.7625	.0423
20	5.0399	.0419
21	5.3404	.0414
22	5.6712	.0409
23	6.0323	.0402
24	6.4318	.0395
25	6.8754	.0386
26	7.3663	.0376
27	7.9176	.0364
28	8.5298	.0349
29	9.2313	.0332
30	10.0274	.0312
31	10.9397	.0287
32	12.0000	.0256
33	13.2416	.0218
34	14.7159	.0171
35	16.4928	.0111
36	18.6731	.0036
37	21.4063	+.0066
38	24.9347	.0199
39	29.6525	.0385
40	36.2756	.0653
41	46.2330	.1063
42	62.8568	.1767
43	96.1538	.3205

2d Year—D. or 50.

Age	Value.	M. Diff.
10	2.5102	—.0471
11	2.6158	.0470
12	2.7225	.0467
13	2.8408	.0465
14	2.9683	.0467
15	3.0968	.0466
16	3.2401	.0465
17	3.3905	.0465
18	3.5504	.0464
19	3.7262	.0464
20	3.9111	.0464
21	4.1103	.0463
22	4.3289	.0462
23	4.5622	.0461
24	4.8166	.0460
25	5.0935	.0457
26	5.3957	.0456
27	5.7244	.0452
28	6.0861	.0449
29	6.4856	.0444
30	6.9270	.0438
31	7.4166	.0432
32	7.9655	.0422
33	8.5825	.0411
34	9.2791	.0396
35	10.0748	.0377
36	10.9900	.0359
37	12.0467	.0327
38	13.2894	.0292
39	14.7641	.0247
40	16.5425	.0189
41	18.7248	.0117
42	21.4590	.0019
43	24.9873	+.0103
44	29.7008	.0278
45	36.3157	.0536
46	46.2583	.0949
47	62.8685	.1678
48	96.1538	.3205

2d Year—D. or 55.

Age	Value.	M. Diff.
10	2.1366	—.0485
11	2.2156	.0488
12	2.2950	.0483
13	2.3863	.0483
14	2.4816	.0486
15	2.5774	.0486
16	2.6840	.0486
17	2.7934	.0488
18	2.9115	.0489
19	3.0365	.0491
20	3.1703	.0495
21	3.3096	.0493
22	3.4631	.0497
23	3.6255	.0498
24	3.8008	.0500
25	3.9879	.0502
26	4.1899	.0503
27	4.4070	.0506
28	4.6439	.0508
29	4.8986	.0509
30	5.1773	.0509
31	5.4772	.0511
32	5.8092	.0511
33	6.1722	.0510
34	6.5729	.0509
35	7.0169	.0505
36	7.5120	.0503
37	8.0611	.0495
38	8.6826	.0485
39	9.3853	.0476
40	10.1863	.0459
41	11.1063	.0442
42	12.1742	.0422
43	13.4195	.0408
44	14.8911	.0373
45	16.6667	.0341
46	18.8351	.0290
47	21.5561	.0217
48	25.0666	.0106
49	29.7646	+.0061
50	36.3625	.0316
51	46.2853	.0766
52	62.8848	.1535
53	96.1538	.3205

2d Year—D. or 60.

Age	Value.	M. Diff.
10	1.8752	—.0495
11	1.9361	.0498
12	2.0010	.0495
13	2.0720	.0495
14	2.1484	.0500
15	2.2227	.0500
16	2.3041	.0501
17	2.3895	.0505
18	2.4780	.0507
19	2.5736	.0510
20	2.6736	.0514
21	2.7792	.0515
22	2.8919	.0520
23	3.0134	.0523
24	3.1416	.0527
25	3.2770	.0530
26	3.4231	.0536
27	3.5767	.0539
28	3.7432	.0543
29	3.9224	.0550
30	4.1114	.0553
31	4.3152	.0558
32	4.5376	.0563
33	4.7767	.0568
34	5.0376	.0572
35	5.3204	.0575
36	5.6307	.0582
37	5.9661	.0583
38	6.3373	.0585
39	6.7455	.0589
40	7.1993	.0585
41	7.7055	.0588
42	8.2708	.0591
43	8.8980	.0601
44	9.6015	.0605
45	10.4032	.0619
46	11.3140	.0630
47	12.3677	.0638
48	13.6003	.0640
49	15.0630	.0637
50	16.8219	.0625
51	18.9709	.0586
52	21.6891	.0533
53	25.1795	.0437
54	29.8572	.0276
55	36.4340	.0011
56	46.3367	+.0452

2d Year—D. or 60.

Age	Value.	M. Diff.
57	62.9053	+.1317
58	96.1538	.3205

2d Year—D. or 65.

Age	Value.	M. Diff.
10	1.6921	—.0499
11	1.7483	.0504
12	1.8068	.0510
13	1.8526	.0502
14	1.9176	.0504
15	1.9823	.0509
16	2.0494	.0512
17	2.1179	.0515
18	2.1898	.0518
19	2.2662	.0522
20	2.3448	.0527
21	2.4287	.0528
22	2.5194	.0535
23	2.6131	.0543
24	2.7071	.0539
25	2.8169	.0549
26	2.9304	.0555
27	3.0478	.0561
28	3.1717	.0566
29	3.3069	.0575
30	3.4493	.0581
31	3.5971	.0588
32	3.7591	.0595
33	3.9336	.0603
34	4.1178	.0610
35	4.3176	.0617
36	4.5340	.0627
37	4.7649	.0633
38	5.0163	.0641
39	5.2884	.0648
40	5.5890	.0656
41	5.9113	.0664
42	6.2677	.0677
43	6.6506	.0701
44	7.0642	.0715
45	7.5250	.0747
46	8.0250	.0778
47	8.5805	.0812
48	9.2010	.0845
49	9.9011	.0881
50	10.6934	.0921
51	11.5900	.0948
52	12.6497	.0987
53	13.8685	.1017
54	15.3198	.1040
55	17.0647	.1054
56	19.2047	.1047
57	21.8942	.1014
58	25.3660	.0938
59	30.0180	.0776
60	36.5596	.0523
61	46.4238	.0021
62	62.9479	+.0966
63	96.1538	.3205

2d Year—D. or 70.

Age	Value.	M. Diff.
10	1.5799	—.0508
11	1.6250	.0510
12	1.6689	.0512
13	1.7142	.0503
14	1.7797	.0514
15	1.8272	.0516
16	1.8853	.0518
17	1.9439	.0522
18	2.0048	.0526
19	2.0695	.0528
20	2.1361	.0536
21	2.2056	.0538
22	2.2824	.0544
23	2.3602	.0549
24	2.4440	.0555
25	2.5306	.0560
26	2.6227	.0568
27	2.7179	.0573
28	2.8207	.0580
29	2.9301	.0590
30	3.0424	.0602
31	3.1549	.0601
32	3.2885	.0615
33	3.4252	.0623
34	3.5715	.0634
35	3.7240	.0641
36	3.8913	.0655
37	4.0664	.0669
38	4.2602	.0679
39	4.4563	.0683
40	4.6789	.0694
41	4.9146	.0707

2d Year—D. or 70.

Age	Value.	M. Diff.
42	5.1712	—.0724
43	5.4390	.0751
44	5.7256	.0775
45	6.0352	.0814
46	6.3610	.0855
47	6.7145	.0898
48	7.0980	.0943
49	7.5184	.0993
50	7.9779	.1061
51	8.4732	.1102
52	9.0454	.1167
53	9.6630	.1232
54	10.3644	.1301
55	11.1548	.1373
56	12.0573	.1442
57	13.1020	.1513
58	14.3201	.1584
59	15.7611	.1654
60	17.4909	.1717
61	19.6048	.1762
62	22.2571	.1776
63	25.6884	.1744
64	30.2869	.1622
65	36.7698	.1347
66	46.5662	.0780
67	63.0160	+.0409
68	96.1538	.3205

2d Year—D. or 75.

Age	Value.	M. Diff.
10	1.5101	—.0511
11	1.5514	.0512
12	1.5922	.0512
13	1.6411	.0511
14	1.6927	.0518
15	1.7359	.0520
16	1.7899	.0522
17	1.8423	.0526
18	1.8964	.0530
19	1.9542	.0535
20	2.0152	.0540
21	2.0757	.0544
22	2.1424	.0548
23	2.2128	.0555
24	2.2881	.0561
25	2.3641	.0567
26	2.4447	.0575
27	2.5290	.0582
28	2.6178	.0588
29	2.7135	.0598
30	2.8104	.0607
31	2.9121	.0617
32	3.0210	.0625
33	3.1393	.0634
34	3.2620	.0646
35	3.3924	.0656
36	3.5334	.0670
37	3.6773	.0679
38	3.8359	.0692
39	4.0020	.0702
40	4.1832	.0619
41	4.3712	.0726
42	4.5824	.0750
43	4.7974	.0780
44	5.0183	.0805
45	5.2594	.0850
46	5.5047	.0893
47	5.7658	.0942
48	6.0444	.0992
49	6.3449	.1049
50	6.6655	.1116
51	6.9970	.1174
52	7.3821	.1252
53	7.7769	.1328
54	8.2128	.1415
55	8.6864	.1504
56	9.2065	.1600
57	9.7823	.1703
58	10.4200	.1813
59	11.1309	.1934
60	11.9275	.2063
61	12.8305	.2200
62	13.8652	.2344
63	15.0650	.2489
64	16.4783	.2635
65	18.1728	.2772
66	20.2472	.2897
67	22.8435	.2981
68	26.2045	.3002
69	30.7244	.2913
70	37.1119	.2624
71	46.7985	.1948
72	63.1292	.0448
73	96.1538	+.3205

3d YEAR—D. or 35.

Age	Value.	M. Diff.
10	7.2745	—.0287
11	7.7352	.0271
12	8.2415	.0252
13	8.8015	.0237
14	9.4130	.0216
15	10.0905	.0194
16	10.8444	.0170
17	11.6877	.0142
18	12.6350	.0110
19	13.7076	.0074
20	14.9280	.0032
21	16.3325	+.0017
22	17.9611	.0076
23	19.8698	.0144
24	22.1352	.0228
25	24.8666	.0330
26	28.2172	.0458
27	32.4219	.0620
28	37.8451	.0832
29	45.0989	.1121
30	55.2818	.1530
31	70.5899	.2153
32	96.1538	.3205

3d Year—D. or 40.

Age	Value.	M. Diff.
10	5.5076	—.0356
11	5.8143	.0348
12	6.1433	.0334
13	6.5048	.0327
14	6.8932	.0316
15	7.3119	.0304
16	7.7764	.0291
17	8.2784	.0277
18	8.8318	.0261
19	9.4430	.0244
20	10.1151	.0223
21	10.8704	.0201
22	11.7089	.0175
23	12.6539	.0145
24	13.7253	.0110
25	14.9429	.0070
26	16.3445	.0023
27	17.9716	+.0033
28	19.8748	.0101
29	22.1400	.0183
30	24.8673	.0283
31	28.2124	.0411
32	32.4136	.0573
33	37.8359	.0788
34	45.0873	.1079
35	55.2689	.1496
36	70.5809	.2131
37	96.1538	.3205

3d Year—D. or 45.

Age	Value.	M. Diff.
10	4.3250	—.0404
11	4.5351	.0396
12	4.7672	.0389
13	5.0154	.0386
14	5.2784	.0380
15	5.5604	.0373
16	5.8683	.0367
17	6.1946	.0359
18	6.5507	.0352
19	6.9359	.0344
20	7.3560	.0333
21	7.8146	.0323
22	8.3170	.0311
23	8.8676	.0297
24	9.4751	.0280
25	10.1512	.0264
26	10.8907	.0236
27	11.7391	.0219
28	12.6767	.0192
29	13.7455	.0160
30	14.9618	.0122
31	16.3569	.0077
32	17.9787	.0023
33	19.8801	+.0043
34	22.1390	.0124
35	24.8633	.0223
36	28.2052	.0352
37	32.4043	.0515
38	37.8224	.0732
39	45.0735	.1045
40	55.2575	.1451
41	70.5713	.2100
42	96.1538	.3205

ENDOWMENT POLICIES.—4 PER CENT.

3d Year–D. or 50.

Age.	Value.	M. Diff.
10	3.5038	−.0435
11	3.6616	.0430
12	3.8274	.0426
13	4.0071	.0426
14	4.1954	.0422
15	4.3927	.0419
16	4.6085	.0417
17	4.8353	.0413
18	5.0790	.0410
19	5.3427	.0407
20	5.6220	.0402
21	5.9255	.0398
22	6.2546	.0393
23	6.6088	.0386
24	6.9934	.0380
25	7.4138	.0374
26	7.8699	.0365
27	8.3698	.0356
28	8.9187	.0345
29	9.5252	.0332
30	10.1964	.0318
31	10.9405	.0300
32	11.7763	.0279
33	12.7160	.0254
34	13.7792	.0223
35	14.9943	.0191
36	16.3867	.0145
37	18.0076	.0093
38	19.9084	.0028
39	22.1668	+.0051
40	24.8926	.0147
41	28.2357	.0274
42	32.4343	.0427
43	37.8438	.0637
44	45.0831	.0927
45	55.2511	.1356
46	70.5570	.2031
47	96.1538	.3205

3d Year–D. or 55.

Age.	Value.	M. Diff.
10	2.9298	−.0460
11	3.0453	.0453
12	3.1734	.0451
13	3.3099	.0454
14	3.4484	.0452
15	3.5948	.0450
16	3.7547	.0451
17	3.9189	.0449
18	4.0966	.0449
19	4.2840	.0450
20	4.4826	.0447
21	4.6970	.0448
22	4.9250	.0446
23	5.1697	.0445
24	5.4326	.0444
25	5.7146	.0442
26	6.0190	.0441
27	6.3455	.0438
28	6.7013	.0435
29	7.0863	.0432
30	7.5067	.0428
31	7.9602	.0422
32	8.4611	.0417
33	9.0104	.0407
34	9.6173	.0396
35	10.2915	.0387
36	11.0385	.0370
37	11.8760	.0351
38	12.8224	.0330
39	13.8895	.0302
40	15.1119	.0270
41	16.5136	.0234
42	18.1388	.0197
43	20.0245	.0141
44	22.2770	.0089
45	24.9786	.0013
46	28.2923	+.0092
47	32.4565	.0238
48	37.8405	.0443
49	45.0582	.0737
50	55.2078	.1197
51	70.5332	.1909
52	96.1538	.3205

3d Year–D. or 60.

Age.	Value.	M. Diff.
10	2.5280	−.0475
11	2.6178	.0471
12	2.7203	.0469
13	2.8274	.0473
14	2.9353	.0472
15	3.0492	.0472
16	3.1715	−.0474
17	3.2974	.0474
18	3.4310	.0476
19	3.5727	.0479
20	3.7202	.0477
21	3.8816	.0480
22	4.0481	.0481
23	4.2291	.0483
24	4.4196	.0484
25	4.6230	.0487
26	4.8387	.0488
27	5.0700	.0489
28	5.3193	.0493
29	5.5831	.0493
30	5.8683	.0495
31	6.1736	.0496
32	6.5060	.0496
33	6.8650	.0496
34	7.2560	.0494
35	7.6828	.0496
36	8.1445	.0492
37	8.6528	.0488
38	9.2129	.0484
39	9.8280	.0472
40	10.5192	.0467
41	11.2799	.0461
42	12.1295	.0460
43	13.0684	.0452
44	14.1321	.0453
45	15.3297	.0449
46	16.7003	.0440
47	18.2891	.0422
48	20.1540	.0395
49	22.3688	.0358
50	25.0370	.0287
51	28.3267	.0200
52	32.4682	.0063
53	37.8217	+.0142
54	45.0151	.0451
55	55.1544	.0939
56	70.4684	.1746
57	96.1538	.3205

3d Year–D. or 65.

Age.	Value.	M. Diff.
10	2.2529	−.0484
11	2.3306	.0489
12	2.4101	.0480
13	2.4952	.0482
14	2.5887	.0486
15	2.6804	.0487
16	2.7799	.0489
17	2.8804	.0491
18	2.9881	.0493
19	3.1005	.0497
20	3.2156	.0497
21	3.3434	.0502
22	3.4747	.0509
23	3.6084	.0503
24	3.7613	.0511
25	3.9163	.0516
26	4.0817	.0519
27	4.2564	.0522
28	4.4416	.0528
29	4.6379	.0532
30	4.8492	.0536
31	5.0699	.0541
32	5.3101	.0546
33	5.5678	.0550
34	5.8421	.0553
35	6.1407	.0552
36	6.4588	.0562
37	6.8055	.0566
38	7.1807	.0567
39	7.5894	.0571
40	8.0361	.0574
41	8.5192	.0580
42	9.0468	.0597
43	9.6055	.0603
44	10.2263	.0626
45	10.8967	.0649
46	11.6310	.0672
47	12.4500	.0694
48	13.3677	.0717
49	14.4032	.0743
50	15.5736	.0752
51	16.9244	.0773
52	18.4938	.0778
53	20.3246	.0777
54	22.5087	.0761
55	25.1450	.0719
56	28.3961	.0645
57	32.4971	.0520
58	37.8160	.0321
59	44.9705	+.0003
60	55.0818	.0540
61	70.3950	.1468
62	96.1538	.3205

3d Year–D. or 70.

Age.	Value.	M. Diff.
10	2.0736	−.0493
11	2.1396	.0493
12	2.2066	.0484
13	2.2880	.0494
14	2.3675	.0494
15	2.4424	.0496
16	2.5284	.0499
17	2.6142	.0502
18	2.7032	.0504
19	2.7989	.0509
20	2.8950	.0510
21	3.0013	.0515
22	3.1111	.0518
23	3.2261	.0523
24	3.3480	.0527
25	3.4760	.0533
26	3.6092	.0538
27	3.7510	.0543
28	3.9014	.0550
29	4.0586	.0560
30	4.2191	.0559
31	4.3984	.0569
32	4.5866	.0574
33	4.7879	.0583
34	5.0002	.0589
35	5.2283	.0599
36	5.4697	.0600
37	5.7354	.0616
38	6.0083	.0616
39	6.3106	.0625
40	6.6377	.0634
41	6.9860	.0646
42	7.3591	.0668
43	7.7439	.0687
44	8.1626	.0719
45	8.5997	.0753
46	9.0662	.0790
47	9.5726	.0828
48	10.1238	.0870
49	10.7273	.0921
50	11.3705	.0951
51	12.1079	.1012
52	12.9215	.1065
53	13.8196	.1119
54	14.8366	.1175
55	15.9877	.1225
56	17.3137	.1274
57	18.8518	.1319
58	20.6535	.1358
59	22.7830	.1375
60	25.3773	.1388
61	28.5622	.1351
62	32.5901	.1259
63	37.8307	.1069
64	44.9134	.0723
65	54.9718	.0105
66	70.2787	+.1022
67	96.1538	.3205

3d Year–D. or 75.

Age.	Value.	M. Diff.
10	1.9672	−.0495
11	2.0287	.0495
12	2.0925	.0493
13	2.1660	.0499
14	2.2346	.0499
15	2.3024	.0501
16	2.3812	.0505
17	2.4576	.0508
18	2.5371	.0512
19	2.6212	.0516
20	2.7096	.0519
21	2.8001	.0522
22	2.8989	.0527
23	3.0001	.0533
24	3.1082	.0537
25	3.2200	.0543
26	3.3362	.0549
27	3.4593	.0554
28	3.5899	.0563
29	3.7254	.0570
30	3.8675	.0577
31	4.0169	.0585
32	4.1756	.0592
33	4.3480	.0601
34	4.5259	.0609
35	4.7167	−.0620
36	4.9185	.0627
37	5.1335	.0638
38	5.3630	.0644
39	5.6110	.0659
40	5.8701	.0662
41	6.1560	.0682
42	6.4527	.0708
43	6.7536	.0729
44	7.0749	.0769
45	7.4027	.0808
46	7.7466	.0851
47	8.1085	.0896
48	8.4991	.0947
49	8.9149	.1008
50	9.3529	.1058
51	9.8297	.1129
52	10.3501	.1197
53	10.9021	.1273
54	11.5049	.1353
55	12.1650	.1437
56	12.8919	.1526
57	13.6974	.1621
58	14.5928	.1725
59	15.5907	.1834
60	16.7158	.1948
61	17.9978	.2065
62	19.4764	.2179
63	21.2076	.2288
64	23.2650	.2382
65	25.7585	.2454
66	28.8387	.2475
67	32.7508	.2421
68	37.8758	.2245
69	44.8486	.1860
70	54.8209	.1111
71	70.1125	+.0325
72	96.1538	.3205

4th Year–D. or 35.

Age.	Value.	M. Diff.
10	9.6874	−.0194
11	10.3172	.0171
12	11.0089	.0150
13	11.7667	.0124
14	12.6005	.0095
15	13.5238	.0064
16	14.5506	.0028
17	15.6996	+.0011
18	16.9904	.0056
19	18.4517	.0109
20	20.1170	.0169
21	22.0319	.0238
22	24.2534	.0320
23	26.8571	.0418
24	29.9493	.0535
25	33.6776	.0678
26	38.2529	.0856
27	43.9946	.1083
28	51.4034	.1378
29	61.3141	.1777
30	75.2293	.2344
31	96.1538	.3205

4th Year–D. or 40.

Age.	Value.	M. Diff.
10	7.2765	−.0291
11	7.6917	.0273
12	8.1457	.0263
13	8.6312	.0247
14	9.1598	.0231
15	9.7305	.0214
16	10.3602	.0194
17	11.0441	.0173
18	11.7969	.0151
19	12.6266	.0123
20	13.5446	.0094
21	14.5710	.0061
22	15.7135	.0022
23	17.0011	+.0021
24	18.4604	.0072
25	20.1210	.0130
26	22.0318	.0198
27	24.2499	.0278
28	26.8479	.0375
29	29.9381	.0492
30	33.6611	.0635
31	38.2310	.0813
32	43.9703	.1042
33	51.3795	.1341
34	61.2914	.1748
35	75.2135	.2325
36	96.1538	.3205

4th Year–D. or 45.

Age.	Value.	M. Diff.
10	5.6595	−.0352
11	5.9498	.0342
12	6.2653	.0337
13	6.5978	.0327
14	6.9553	.0318
15	7.3383	.0309
16	7.7542	.0297
17	8.1988	.0286
18	8.6815	.0275
19	9.2037	.0260
20	9.7753	.0245
21	10.3978	.0227
22	11.0802	.0208
23	11.8287	.0185
24	12.6561	.0163
25	13.5732	.0135
26	14.5912	.0103
27	15.7341	.0068
28	17.0121	.0026
29	18.4669	+.0021
30	20.1234	.0078
31	22.0362	.0136
32	24.2379	.0224
33	26.8325	.0320
34	29.9163	.0434
35	33.6337	.0580
36	38.2029	.0759
37	43.9386	.0993
38	51.3492	.1296
39	61.2663	.1708
40	75.1961	.2300
41	96.1538	.3205

4th Year–D. or 50.

Age.	Value.	M. Diff.
10	4.5396	−.0396
11	4.7554	.0390
12	4.9815	.0387
13	5.2206	.0382
14	5.4760	.0377
15	5.7441	.0372
16	6.0344	.0366
17	6.3427	.0360
18	6.6718	.0355
19	7.0272	.0346
20	7.4074	.0339
21	7.8177	.0330
22	8.2634	.0321
23	8.7429	.0310
24	9.2654	.0300
25	9.8330	.0286
26	10.4526	.0272
27	11.1306	.0255
28	11.8759	.0236
29	12.6993	.0215
30	13.6099	.0190
31	14.6228	.0161
32	15.7590	.0127
33	17.0381	.0087
34	18.4871	.0045
35	20.1371	+.0013
36	22.0400	.0078
37	24.2497	.0156
38	26.8432	.0251
39	29.9270	.0363
40	33.6457	.0507
41	38.2154	.0679
42	43.9455	.0906
43	51.3412	.1206
44	61.2442	.1627
45	75.1704	.2243
46	96.1538	.3205

4th Year–D. or 55.

Age.	Value.	M. Diff.
10	3.7532	−.0425
11	3.9168	.0422
12	4.0891	.0423
13	4.2679	.0420
14	4.4564	.0416
15	4.6551	.0415
16	4.8682	.0412
17	5.0912	.0410
18	5.3300	.0409
19	5.5806	.0403
20	5.8525	.0401
21	6.1394	.0398
22	6.4476	.0394
23	6.7774	.0390
24	7.1323	.0385
25	7.5133	.0380
26	7.9234	.0373
27	8.3653	.0368

ENDOWMENT POLICIES.—4 PER CENT.

4th Year—D. or 55.

Age.	Value.	M. Diff.
28	8.8464	—.0360
29	9.3659	.0351
30	9.9332	.0349
31	10.5493	.0330
32	11.2261	.0315
33	11.9721	.0298
34	12.7965	.0282
35	13.7071	.0258
36	14.7243	.0230
37	15.8645	.0201
38	17.1482	.0163
39	18.6039	.0122
40	20.2645	.0072
41	22.1700	.0022
42	24.3718	+.0046
43	26.9500	.0118
44	30.0034	.0214
45	33.6843	.0339
46	38.2083	.0506
47	43.9025	.0730
48	51.2737	.1037
49	61.1631	.1488
50	75.1097	.2149
51	96.1538	.3205

4th Year—D. or 60.

Age.	Value.	M. Diff.
10	3.2054	—.0448
11	3.3324	.0445
12	3.4706	.0448
13	3.6087	.0445
14	3.7555	.0448
15	3.9097	.0445
16	4.0719	.0443
17	4.2421	.0443
18	4.4210	.0445
19	4.6093	.0442
20	4.8116	.0443
21	5.0255	.0442
22	5.2503	.0442
23	5.4921	.0441
24	5.7491	.0442
25	6.0202	.0440
26	6.3116	.0438
27	6.6236	.0440
28	6.9548	.0437
29	7.3118	.0436
30	7.6952	.0433
31	8.1068	.0430
32	8.5547	.0426
33	9.0390	.0420
34	9.5681	.0417
35	10.1395	.0408
36	10.7663	.0398
37	11.4543	.0389
38	12.2102	.0371
39	13.0499	.0359
40	13.9799	.0344
41	15.0066	.0335
42	16.1454	.0317
43	17.4175	.0307
44	18.8443	.0290
45	20.4608	.0267
46	22.3155	.0234
47	24.4706	.0191
48	27.0011	.0134
49	30.0092	.0043
50	33.6578	+.0068
51	38.1450	.0228
52	43.8121	.0457
53	51.1586	.0782
54	61.0456	.1265
55	75.0148	.2005
56	96.1538	.3205

4th Year—D. or 65.

Age.	Value.	M. Diff.
10	2.8321	—.0469
11	2.9306	.0460
12	3.0489	.0460
13	3.1622	.0463
14	3.2823	.0463
15	3.4059	.0465
16	3.5370	.0465
17	3.6727	.0466
18	3.8159	.0469
19	3.9644	.0467
20	4.1227	.0471
21	4.2903	.0476
22	4.4607	.0469
23	4.6524	.0475
24	4.8495	.0478
25	5.0554	.0479
26	5.2769	.0480
27	5.5115	—.0485
28	5.7564	.0486
29	6.0200	.0489
30	6.3022	.0490
31	6.5990	.0493
32	6.9199	.0494
33	7.2650	.0494
34	7.6350	.0498
35	8.0316	.0496
36	8.4615	.0496
37	8.9274	.0493
38	9.4337	.0492
39	9.9825	.0490
40	10.5821	.0491
41	11.2287	.0501
42	11.9225	.0501
43	12.6774	.0517
44	13.4952	.0532
45	14.3851	.0546
46	15.3656	.0558
47	16.4610	.0570
48	17.6887	.0584
49	19.0712	.0580
50	20.6570	.0585
51	22.4694	.0576
52	24.5871	.0553
53	27.0684	.0515
54	30.0328	.0449
55	33.6268	.0348
56	38.0707	.0194
57	43.6929	+.0034
58	51.0055	.0381
59	60.8785	.0917
60	74.8795	.1771
61	96.1538	.3205

4th Year—D. or 70.

Age.	Value.	M. Diff.
10	2.5858	—.0476
11	2.6747	.0466
12	2.7775	.0475
13	2.8726	.0475
14	2.9792	.0475
15	3.0816	.0477
16	3.1944	.0479
17	3.3081	.0480
18	3.4277	.0484
19	3.5525	.0484
20	3.6850	.0488
21	3.8237	.0490
22	3.9708	.0494
23	4.1226	.0496
24	4.2851	.0501
25	4.4534	.0503
26	4.6316	.0506
27	4.8201	.0513
28	5.0181	.0513
29	5.2224	.0517
30	5.4486	.0526
31	5.6811	.0530
32	5.9323	.0536
33	6.1979	.0538
34	6.4834	.0546
35	6.7839	.0545
36	7.1132	.0557
37	7.4564	.0555
38	7.8319	.0560
39	8.2344	.0565
40	8.6690	.0573
41	9.1302	.0591
42	9.6142	.0604
43	10.1261	.0632
44	10.6665	.0660
45	11.2374	.0690
46	11.8490	.0722
47	12.5143	.0757
48	13.2374	.0799
49	14.0226	.0829
50	14.8946	.0874
51	15.8478	.0915
52	16.9215	.0956
53	18.1117	.0998
54	19.4601	.1033
55	20.9985	.1065
56	22.7715	.1090
57	24.8339	.1106
58	27.2574	.1104
59	30.1498	.1078
60	33.6593	.1007
61	38.0134	.0879
62	43.5430	.0651
63	50.7820	.0190
64	60.6193	+.0349
65	74.6648	.1392
66	96.1538	.3205

4th Year—D. or 75.

Age.	Value.	M. Diff.
10	2.4423	—.0478
11	2.5267	.0476
12	2.6148	.0481
13	2.7052	.0481
14	2.7982	.0482
15	2.8905	.0485
16	2.9929	.0487
17	3.0945	.0490
18	3.2000	.0493
19	3.3112	.0495
20	3.4292	.0498
21	3.5513	.0501
22	3.6804	.0505
23	3.8140	.0509
24	3.9573	.0513
25	4.1041	.0518
26	4.2585	.0522
27	4.4227	.0529
28	4.5922	.0534
29	4.7721	.0540
30	4.9609	.0546
31	5.1591	.0551
32	5.3708	.0558
33	5.5971	.0564
34	5.8340	.0573
35	6.0841	.0578
36	6.3551	.0586
37	6.6390	.0590
38	6.9482	.0602
39	7.2716	.0602
40	7.6258	.0618
41	7.9942	.0641
42	8.3735	.0658
43	8.7711	.0693
44	9.1754	.0727
45	9.5977	.0766
46	10.0379	.0806
47	10.5070	.0852
48	11.0074	.0907
49	11.5346	.0950
50	12.1109	.1014
51	12.7159	.1075
52	13.3843	.1143
53	14.0935	.1213
54	14.8714	.1287
55	15.7250	.1365
56	16.6661	.1447
57	17.7107	.1537
58	18.8710	.1629
59	20.1707	.1724
60	21.6423	.1820
61	23.3272	.1909
62	25.2848	.1989
63	27.5914	.2050
64	30.3554	.2084
65	33.7261	.2063
66	37.9359	.1961
67	43.3299	.1735
68	50.4563	.1306
69	60.2370	.0545
70	74.3454	+.0792
71	96.1538	.3205

5th YEAR—D. or 35.

Age.	Value.	M. Diff.
10	12.2124	—.0096
11	13.0193	.0071
12	13.8991	.0039
13	14.8677	.0005
14	15.9337	+.0032
15	17.1135	.0073
16	18.4265	.0120
17	19.8952	.0172
18	21.5456	.0232
19	23.4156	.0300
20	25.5462	.0379
21	27.9966	.0470
22	30.8392	.0578
23	34.1727	.0705
24	38.1321	.0859
25	42.9066	.1045
26	48.7668	.1277
27	56.1229	.1571
28	65.6162	.1954
29	78.3175	.2471
30	96.1538	.3205

5th Year—D. or 40.

Age.	Value.	M. Diff.
10	9.1235	—.0216
11	9.6597	.0203
12	10.2331	.0184
13	10.8537	.0164
14	11.5282	—.0143
15	12.2571	.0120
16	13.0603	.0093
17	13.9341	.0066
18	14.8941	.0033
19	15.9560	+.0002
20	17.1292	.0042
21	18.4398	.0087
22	19.9014	.0138
23	21.5480	.0176
24	23.4141	.0263
25	25.5391	.0341
26	27.9841	.0431
27	30.8231	.0538
28	34.1499	.0664
29	38.1064	.0818
30	42.8763	.1005
31	48.7330	.1239
32	56.0893	.1537
33	65.5870	.1927
34	78.2981	.2455
35	96.1538	.3205

5th Year—D. or 45.

Age.	Value.	M. Diff.
10	7.0566	—.0298
11	7.4285	.0291
12	7.8260	.0279
13	8.2505	.0267
14	8.7059	.0255
15	9.1935	.0240
16	9.7237	.0226
17	10.2904	.0211
18	10.9048	.0192
19	11.5728	.0173
20	12.3011	.0151
21	13.0955	.0127
22	13.9663	.0100
23	14.9228	.0072
24	15.9780	.0038
25	17.1495	+.0000
26	18.4513	.0043
27	19.9107	.0092
28	21.5462	.0148
29	23.4056	.0213
30	25.5249	.0289
31	27.9613	.0378
32	30.7931	.0485
33	34.1166	.0602
34	38.0649	.0766
35	42.8328	.0955
36	48.6899	.1199
37	56.0484	.1496
38	65.5526	.1892
39	78.2755	.2433
40	96.1538	.3205

5th Year—D. or 50.

Age.	Value.	M. Diff.
10	5.6231	—.0356
11	5.8979	.0351
12	6.1821	.0344
13	6.4868	.0337
14	6.8114	.0330
15	7.1522	.0321
16	7.5219	.0313
17	7.9134	.0305
18	8.3316	.0294
19	8.7849	.0284
20	9.2686	.0272
21	9.7916	.0260
22	10.3580	.0245
23	10.9702	.0231
24	11.6341	.0213
25	12.3582	.0194
26	13.1480	.0173
27	14.0128	.0149
28	14.9639	.0123
29	16.0135	.0091
30	17.1768	.0056
31	18.4712	.0015
32	19.9235	+.0033
33	21.5598	.0083
34	23.4084	.0150
35	25.5247	.0225
36	27.9600	.0313
37	30.7897	.0419
38	34.1129	.0543
39	38.0615	.0698
40	42.8307	.0881
41	48.6822	.1114
42	56.0305	.1415
43	65.5219	.1820
44	78.2449	+.2384
45	96.1538	.3205

5th Year—D. or 55.

Age.	Value.	M. Diff.
10	4.6181	—.0395
11	4.8253	.0394
12	5.0392	.0389
13	5.2669	.0384
14	5.5067	.0381
15	5.7577	.0377
16	6.0284	.0372
17	6.3112	.0370
18	6.6118	.0362
19	6.9344	.0358
20	7.2768	.0352
21	7.6418	.0346
22	8.0326	.0339
23	8.4519	.0332
24	8.9028	.0324
25	9.3862	.0315
26	9.9086	.0305
27	10.4694	.0293
28	11.0811	.0281
29	11.7423	.0267
30	12.4548	.0243
31	13.2490	.0232
32	14.1133	.0209
33	15.0648	.0187
34	16.1124	.0157
35	17.2775	.0123
36	18.5780	.0086
37	20.0325	.0040
38	21.6749	+.0011
39	23.5334	.0069
40	25.6546	.0129
41	28.0815	.0209
42	30.8976	.0294
43	34.1866	.0404
44	38.0942	.0542
45	42.8124	.0720
46	48.6207	.0954
47	55.9392	.1262
48	65.4190	.1698
49	78.1702	.2302
50	96.1538	.3205

5th Year—D. or 60.

Age.	Value.	M. Diff.
10	3.9155	—.0422
11	4.0778	.0424
12	4.2464	.0420
13	4.4230	.0418
14	4.6095	.0417
15	4.8029	.0414
16	5.0087	.0413
17	5.2235	.0413
18	5.4482	.0408
19	5.6902	.0408
20	5.9440	.0405
21	6.2149	.0404
22	6.4992	.0400
23	6.8060	.0399
24	7.1291	.0395
25	7.4741	.0391
26	7.8440	.0390
27	8.2356	.0385
28	8.6574	.0381
29	9.1095	.0375
30	9.5957	.0369
31	10.1190	.0361
32	10.6876	.0351
33	11.3047	.0345
34	11.9725	.0331
35	12.7019	.0317
36	13.5001	.0302
37	14.3742	.0279
38	15.3433	.0260
39	16.4083	.0239
40	17.5880	.0222
41	18.8848	.0196
42	20.3335	.0177
43	21.9410	.0150
44	23.7525	.0116
45	25.8105	.0071
46	28.1774	.0015
47	30.9288	+.0055
48	34.1615	.0161
49	38.0276	.0287
50	42.7044	.0463
51	48.4777	.0702
52	55.7794	.1031
53	65.2633	.1498
54	78.0523	.2177
55	96.1538	.3205

ENDOWMENT POLICIES.—4 PER CENT.

5th Year—D. or 65.

Age.	Value.	M. Diff.
10	3.4288	—.0440
11	3.5658	.0439
12	3.7120	.0441
13	3.8516	.0440
14	4.0032	.0441
15	4.1580	.0440
16	4.3238	.0440
17	4.4945	.0442
18	4.6731	.0439
19	4.8641	.0441
20	5.0617	.0446
21	5.2676	.0436
22	5.4952	.0441
23	5.7302	.0442
24	5.9772	.0442
25	6.2380	.0441
26	6.5181	.0444
27	6.8109	.0443
28	7.1215	.0443
29	7.4543	.0443
30	7.8105	.0443
31	8.1859	.0442
32	8.5918	.0439
33	9.0296	.0439
34	9.4945	.0435
35	9.9993	.0431
36	10.5441	.0425
37	11.1361	.0420
38	11.7770	.0413
39	12.4723	.0409
40	13.2278	.0414
41	14.0324	.0409
42	14.9122	.0417
43	15.8531	.0425
44	16.8773	.0431
45	17.9981	.0436
46	19.2369	.0439
47	20.6205	.0443
48	22.1690	.0427
49	23.9343	.0421
50	25.9407	.0397
51	28.2507	.0361
52	30.9518	.0306
53	34.1267	.0223
54	37.9308	.0103
55	42.5546	+.0068
56	48.2863	.0312
57	55.5537	.0666
58	65.0378	.1186
59	77.8821	.1973
60	96.1538	.3205

5th Year—D. or 70.

Age.	Value.	M. Diff.
10	3.1182	—.0448
11	3.2427	.0457
12	3.3590	.0455
13	3.4809	.0455
14	3.6148	.0456
15	3.7437	.0457
16	3.8840	.0458
17	4.0279	.0461
18	4.1762	.0459
19	4.3369	.0462
20	4.5013	.0463
21	4.6761	.0465
22	4.8594	.0466
23	5.0519	.0470
24	5.2540	.0473
25	5.4665	.0473
26	5.6913	.0477
27	5.9257	.0484
28	6.1697	.0479
29	6.4384	.0485
30	6.7064	.0479
31	7.0108	.0491
32	7.3245	.0491
33	7.6620	.0497
34	8.0179	.0491
35	8.4036	.0503
36	8.8081	.0498
37	9.2500	.0499
38	9.7232	.0501
39	10.2295	.0506
40	10.7728	.0519
41	11.3404	.0528
42	11.9465	.0551
43	12.5745	.0574
44	13.2420	.0606
45	13.9509	.0624
46	14.7135	.0653
47	15.5414	.0687
48	16.4368	.0711
49	17.4275	.0747

5th Year—D. or 70.

Age.	Value.	M. Diff.
50	18.5106	—.0778
51	19.7073	.0810
52	21.0519	.0840
53	22.5489	.0862
54	24.2539	.0880
55	26.2012	.0889
56	28.4507	.0887
57	31.0724	.0866
58	34.1666	.0817
59	37.8734	.0723
60	42.3978	.0570
61	48.0308	.0321
62	55.2260	+.0068
63	64.6892	.0676
64	77.6117	.1641
65	96.1538	.3205

5th Year—D. or 75.

Age.	Value.	M. Diff.
10	2.9382	—.0460
11	3.0466	.0463
12	3.1514	.0464
13	3.2659	.0463
14	3.3831	.0465
15	3.4989	.0467
16	3.6262	.0468
17	3.7534	.0471
18	3.8857	.0472
19	4.0260	.0473
20	4.1753	.0476
21	4.3273	.0479
22	4.4883	.0481
23	4.6566	.0485
24	4.8344	.0488
25	5.0188	.0491
26	5.2136	.0497
27	5.4160	.0501
28	5.6291	.0504
29	5.8548	.0509
30	6.0915	.0513
31	6.3416	.0518
32	6.6060	.0522
33	6.8899	.0529
34	7.1847	.0532
35	7.5024	.0538
36	7.8404	.0539
37	8.2020	.0548
38	8.5842	.0546
39	9.0001	.0559
40	9.4340	.0578
41	9.8819	.0591
42	10.3545	.0623
43	10.8316	.0652
44	11.3266	.0687
45	11.8411	.0722
46	12.3839	.0763
47	12.9578	.0813
48	13.5641	.0850
49	14.2234	.0908
50	14.9208	.0962
51	15.6665	.1023
52	16.4828	.1085
53	17.3570	.1150
54	18.3167	.1218
55	19.3707	.1289
56	20.5350	.1365
57	21.8253	.1444
58	23.2645	.1523
59	24.8829	.1601
60	26.7230	.1670
61	28.8440	.1728
62	31.3214	.1764
63	34.2610	.1770
64	37.8026	.1719
65	42.1628	.1586
66	47.6497	.1331
67	54.7330	.0884
68	64.1628	.0135
69	77.2031	+.1109
70	96.1538	.3205

6th YEAR—D. or 35.

Age.	Value.	M. Diff.
10	14.8549	+.0002
11	15.8412	.0037
12	16.9218	.0076
13	18.1104	.0118
14	19.4187	.0165
15	20.8677	.0217
16	22.4799	.0274
17	24.2832	.0341
18	26.3118	.0416
19	28.6093	.0502

6th Year—D. or 35.

Age.	Value.	M. Diff.
20	31.2282	+.0600
21	34.2395	.0715
22	37.7344	.0849
23	41.8334	.1008
24	46.7031	.1199
25	52.5755	.1432
26	59.7855	.1720
27	68.8368	.2086
28	80.5200	.2562
29	96.1535	.3205

6th Year—D. or 40.

Age.	Value.	M. Diff.
10	11.0597	—.0148
11	11.7112	.0126
12	12.4149	.0102
13	13.1760	.0078
14	14.0023	.0050
15	14.8976	.0020
16	15.8819	+.0012
17	16.9528	.0049
18	18.1331	.0089
19	19.4360	.0134
20	20.8767	.0185
21	22.4858	.0242
22	24.2817	.0306
23	26.3049	.0380
24	28.5976	.0465
25	31.2098	.0562
26	34.2158	.0676
27	37.7063	.0810
28	41.7987	.0970
29	46.6661	.1162
30	52.5360	.1397
31	59.7459	.1689
32	68.8023	.2062
33	80.4982	.2548
34	96.1538	.3205

6th Year—D. or 45.

Age.	Value.	M. Diff.
10	8.5176	—.0248
11	8.9690	.0234
12	9.4558	.0219
13	9.9756	.0205
14	10.5325	.0187
15	11.1309	.0170
16	11.7790	.0151
17	12.4729	.0129
18	13.2276	.0107
19	14.0460	.0081
20	14.9390	.0053
21	15.9133	.0022
22	16.9821	+.0011
23	18.1545	.0051
24	19.4505	.0094
25	20.8884	.0142
26	22.4866	.0197
27	24.2788	.0260
28	26.2892	.0331
29	28.5741	.0415
30	31.1800	.0512
31	34.1771	.0626
32	37.6612	.0758
33	41.7388	.0929
34	46.6121	.1114
35	52.4821	.1353
36	59.7046	.1645
37	68.7621	.2030
38	80.4719	.2528
39	96.1538	.3205

6th Year—D. or 50.

Age.	Value.	M. Diff.
10	6.7548	—.0318
11	7.0864	.0308
12	7.4349	.0299
13	7.8074	.0290
14	8.2029	.0280
15	8.6213	.0270
16	9.0721	.0259
17	9.5502	.0246
18	10.0636	.0233
19	10.6171	.0218
20	11.2100	.0203
21	11.8498	.0185
22	12.5443	.0168
23	13.2925	.0146
24	14.1066	.0123
25	14.9936	.0098
26	15.9617	.0069
27	17.0225	.0038

6th Year—D. or 50.

Age.	Value.	M. Diff.
28	18.1880	—.0002
29	19.4765	+.0039
30	20.9046	.0086
31	22.4952	.0140
32	24.2804	.0197
33	26.2863	.0271
34	28.5641	.0353
35	31.1663	.0449
36	34.1625	.0563
37	37.6455	.0694
38	41.7331	.0857
39	46.5978	.1045
40	52.4637	.1281
41	59.6708	.1578
42	68.7273	.1965
43	80.4394	.2484
44	96.1538	.3205

6th Year—D. or 55.

Age.	Value.	M. Diff.
10	5.5195	—.0367
11	5.7676	.0360
12	6.0299	.0354
13	6.3080	.0350
14	6.5991	.0343
15	6.9066	.0338
16	7.2359	.0333
17	7.5791	.0323
18	7.9498	.0318
19	8.3413	.0310
20	8.7600	.0302
21	9.2056	.0292
22	9.6836	.0282
23	10.1961	.0272
24	10.7463	.0260
25	11.3376	.0247
26	11.9753	.0232
27	12.6629	.0216
28	13.4106	.0198
29	14.2200	.0178
30	15.1037	.0155
31	16.0666	.0128
32	17.1275	.0101
33	18.2904	.0065
34	19.5787	.0026
35	21.0104	+.0017
36	22.6052	.0070
37	24.3939	.0128
38	26.4101	.0193
39	28.6913	.0262
40	31.2868	.0350
41	34.2695	.0445
42	37.7214	.0564
43	41.7661	.0708
44	46.5782	.0880
45	52.3976	.1133
46	59.5706	.1436
47	68.6136	.1855
48	80.3578	.2412
49	96.1538	.3205

6th Year—D. or 60.

Age.	Value.	M. Diff.
10	4.6563	—.0401
11	4.8485	.0397
12	5.0551	.0393
13	5.2708	.0391
14	5.4959	.0387
15	5.7323	.0384
16	5.9818	.0383
17	6.2416	.0377
18	6.5190	.0375
19	6.8117	.0371
20	7.1214	.0367
21	7.4506	.0362
22	7.7986	.0359
23	8.1699	.0353
24	8.5651	.0347
25	8.9867	.0344
26	9.4340	.0336
27	9.9137	.0329
28	10.4279	.0321
29	10.9797	.0312
30	11.5739	.0301
31	12.2137	.0288
32	12.9105	.0278
33	13.6608	.0260
34	14.4803	.0242
35	15.3738	.0223
36	16.3494	.0194
37	17.4266	.0171
38	18.6091	.0144
39	19.9098	.0121
40	21.3428	.0088

6th Year—D. or 60.

Age.	Value.	M. Diff.
41	22.9296	—.0061
42	24.6895	.0026
43	26.6526	+.0017
44	28.8693	.0071
45	31.3949	.0137
46	34.3016	.0218
47	37.6822	.0334
48	41.6768	.0470
49	46.4416	.0654
50	52.2251	.0898
51	59.3783	.1225
52	68.4356	.1673
53	80.2269	.2301
54	96.1538	.3205

6th Year—D. or 65.

Age.	Value.	M. Diff.
10	4.0607	—.0420
11	4.2253	.0421
12	4.3973	.0419
13	4.5680	.0419
14	4.7504	.0417
15	4.9395	.0416
16	5.1398	.0416
17	5.3454	.0412
18	5.5660	.0413
19	5.7955	.0416
20	6.0306	.0406
21	6.2930	.0409
22	6.5631	.0409
23	6.8469	.0407
24	7.1478	.0405
25	7.4661	.0405
26	7.8030	.0403
27	8.1601	.0401
28	8.5383	.0398
29	8.9433	.0396
30	9.3760	.0392
31	9.8341	.0387
32	10.3301	.0385
33	10.8598	.0378
34	11.4295	.0371
35	12.0454	.0361
36	12.7119	.0352
37	13.4334	.0342
38	14.2149	.0334
39	15.0595	.0334
40	15.9655	.0324
41	16.9471	.0327
42	18.0029	.0328
43	19.1387	.0328
44	20.3802	.0325
45	21.7433	.0320
46	23.2516	.0316
47	24.9332	.0292
48	26.8368	.0275
49	28.9886	.0241
50	31.4497	.0193
51	34.2896	.0126
52	37.6133	.0030
53	41.5357	+.0102
54	46.2440	.0284
55	51.9815	.0535
56	59.1085	.0888
57	68.1724	.1390
58	80.0365	.2118
59	96.1538	.3205

6th Year—D. or 70.

Age.	Value.	M. Diff.
10	3.6836	—.0439
11	3.8214	.0437
12	3.9641	.0436
13	4.1131	.0436
14	4.2731	.0436
15	4.4293	.0436
16	4.5994	.0438
17	4.7715	.0435
18	4.9553	.0437
19	5.1479	.0438
20	5.3475	.0438
21	5.5586	.0438
22	5.7814	.0440
23	6.0127	.0441
24	6.2583	.0441
25	6.5166	.0444
26	6.7864	.0449
27	7.0659	.0441
28	7.3731	.0447
29	7.6925	.0446
30	8.0307	.0449
31	8.3863	.0447
32	8.7703	.0450
33	9.1758	.0445

ENDOWMENT POLICIES.—4 PER CENT.

6th Year—D. or 70.

Age.	Value.	M. Diff.
34	9.6182	−.0454
35	10.0739	.0453
36	10.5743	.0443
37	11.1109	.0442
38	11.6845	.0443
39	12.2960	.0453
40	12.9411	.0458
41	13.6262	.0476
42	14.3427	.0494
43	15.0924	.0513
44	15.8814	.0525
45	16.7440	.0557
46	17.6610	.0585
47	18.6518	.0602
48	19.7417	.0631
49	20.9307	.0654
50	22.2424	.0677
51	23.6925	.0706
52	25.3219	.0709
53	27.1498	.0715
54	29.2311	.0711
55	31.6150	.0696
56	34.3727	.0659
57	37.5991	.0595
58	41.4201	.0492
59	46.0226	.0315
60	51.6607	.0056
61	58.7181	+.0498
62	67.7708	.0743
63	79.7355	.1570
64	96.1538	.3205

6th Year—D. or 75.

Age.	Value.	M. Diff.
10	3.4558	−.0448
11	3.5808	.0447
12	3.7095	.0446
13	3.8479	.0447
14	3.9883	.0447
15	4.1288	.0449
16	4.2814	.0450
17	4.4350	.0450
18	4.5961	.0450
19	4.7674	.0452
20	4.9461	.0454
21	5.1296	.0456
22	5.3248	.0458
23	5.5271	.0460
24	5.7418	.0461
25	5.9660	.0466
26	6.1984	.0469
27	6.4436	.0471
28	6.7017	.0474
29	6.9743	.0475
30	7.2618	.0482
31	7.5636	.0482
32	7.8845	.0488
33	8.2248	.0488
34	8.5857	.0492
35	8.9687	.0491
36	9.3824	.0498
37	9.8149	.0493
38	10.2873	.0503
39	10.7803	.0519
40	11.2908	.0529
41	11.8290	.0557
42	12.3776	.0582
43	12.9418	.0613
44	13.5251	.0644
45	14.1378	.0680
46	14.7810	.0724
47	15.4559	.0758
48	16.1886	.0810
49	16.9627	.0857
50	17.7934	.0911
51	18.6796	.0966
52	19.6513	.1023
53	20.6970	.1083
54	21.8450	.1144
55	23.1080	.1210
56	24.5014	.1278
57	26.0509	.1342
58	27.7849	.1405
59	29.7427	.1458
60	31.9826	.1498
61	34.5773	.1514
62	37.6282	.1500
63	41.2662	.1427
64	45.6883	.1273
65	51.1714	.1001
66	58.1203	.0550
67	67.1567	+.0177
68	79.2744	.1338
69	96.1538	.3205

7th YEAR—D. or 35.

Age.	Value.	M. Diff.
10	17.6145	+.0107
11	18.7926	.0149
12	20.0826	.0196
13	21.5009	.0247
14	23.0634	.0304
15	24.7938	.0367
16	26.7191	.0438
17	28.8746	.0518
18	31.2987	.0609
19	34.0448	.0713
20	37.1751	.0833
21	40.7758	.0972
22	44.9549	.1135
23	49.8577	.1327
24	55.6826	.1558
25	62.7086	.1839
26	71.3361	.2188
27	82.1688	.2630
28	96.1538	.3205

7th Year—D. or 40.

Age.	Value.	M. Diff.
10	13.0780	−.0072
11	13.8555	.0045
12	14.6947	.0018
13	15.6018	+.0013
14	16.5878	.0047
15	17.6568	.0082
16	18.8291	.0124
17	20.1098	.0168
18	21.5186	.0218
19	23.0741	.0273
20	24.7958	.0335
21	26.7176	.0405
22	28.8643	.0484
23	31.2824	.0574
24	34.0226	.0677
25	37.1467	.0796
26	40.7416	.0934
27	44.9163	.1098
28	49.8139	.1292
29	55.6387	.1526
30	62.6658	.1811
31	71.2986	.2166
32	82.1450	.2617
33	96.1538	.3205

7th Year—D. or 45.

Age.	Value.	M. Diff.
10	10.0391	−.0192
11	10.5778	.0175
12	11.1574	.0158
13	11.7757	.0138
14	12.4402	.0118
15	13.1528	.0097
16	13.9237	.0072
17	14.7529	.0046
18	15.6525	.0017
19	16.6290	+.0014
20	17.6942	.0050
21	18.8576	.0087
22	20.1318	.0131
23	21.5327	.0178
24	23.0705	.0240
25	24.7973	.0292
26	26.7072	.0359
27	28.8481	.0437
28	31.2528	.0525
29	33.9850	.0628
30	37.1025	.0747
31	40.6996	.0876
32	44.8568	.1051
33	49.7544	.1246
34	55.5773	.1486
35	62.6091	.1776
36	71.2537	.2137
37	82.1167	.2599
38	96.1538	.3205

7th Year—D. or 50.

Age.	Value.	M. Diff.
10	7.9320	−.0275
11	8.3267	.0264
12	8.7415	.0253
13	9.1834	.0241
14	9.6547	.0229
15	10.1523	.0216
16	10.6873	.0201
17	11.2581	.0185
18	11.8690	.0168
19	12.5284	.0150
20	13.2344	.0129
21	13.9980	−.0109
22	14.8236	.0084
23	15.7165	.0058
24	16.6870	.0029
25	17.7449	+.0004
26	18.9000	.0039
27	20.1649	.0080
28	21.5572	.0125
29	23.0958	.0177
30	24.8026	.0236
31	26.7051	.0299
32	28.8344	.0378
33	31.2381	.0467
34	33.9630	.0568
35	37.0772	.0687
36	40.6646	.0823
37	44.8316	.0990
38	49.7300	.1181
39	55.5502	.1417
40	62.5769	.1708
41	71.2157	.2078
42	82.0838	.2560
43	96.1538	.3205

7th Year—D. or 55.

Age.	Value.	M. Diff.
10	6.4548	−.0333
11	6.7504	.0326
12	7.0623	.0320
13	7.3907	.0312
14	7.7373	.0305
15	8.1023	.0298
16	8.4907	.0287
17	8.9028	.0280
18	9.3410	.0270
19	9.8069	.0260
20	10.3041	.0248
21	10.8347	.0236
22	11.4033	.0223
23	12.0123	.0208
24	12.6671	.0192
25	13.3709	.0175
26	14.1298	.0156
27	14.9490	.0135
28	15.8395	.0111
29	16.8044	.0084
30	17.8583	.0053
31	19.0089	.0023
32	20.2709	+.0018
33	21.6623	.0062
34	23.2026	.0111
35	24.9113	.0168
36	26.8192	.0232
37	28.9562	.0303
38	31.3637	.0378
39	34.0809	.0473
40	37.1842	.0575
41	40.7407	.0700
42	44.8685	.0853
43	49.7107	.1044
44	55.4872	.1278
45	62.4774	.1577
46	71.0994	.1978
47	82.0000	.2494
48	96.1538	.3205

7th Year—D. or 60.

Age.	Value.	M. Diff.
10	5.4221	−.0374
11	5.6520	.0369
12	5.8972	.0366
13	6.1508	.0361
14	6.4183	.0357
15	6.6978	.0354
16	6.9914	.0347
17	7.3031	.0343
18	7.6303	.0338
19	7.9778	.0333
20	8.3447	.0326
21	8.7362	.0321
22	9.1474	.0314
23	9.5891	.0305
24	10.0591	.0300
25	10.5561	.0290
26	11.0893	.0281
27	11.6588	.0270
28	12.2698	.0258
29	12.9262	.0245
30	13.6332	.0229
31	14.3970	.0215
32	15.2219	.0194
33	16.1183	.0173
34	17.0952	.0150
35	18.1584	−.0117
36	19.3282	.0089
37	20.6082	.0058
38	22.0139	.0029
39	23.5535	+.0010
40	25.2599	.0043
41	27.1365	.0085
42	29.2266	.0135
43	31.5645	.0197
44	34.2109	.0270
45	37.2292	.0359
46	40.7055	.0483
47	44.7709	.0626
48	49.5626	.0815
49	55.2966	.1060
50	62.2688	.1380
51	70.9063	.1810
52	81.8625	.2393
53	96.1538	.3205

7th Year—D. or 65.

Age.	Value.	M. Diff.
10	4.7166	−.0402
11	4.9068	.0399
12	5.1095	.0397
13	5.3107	.0394
14	5.5269	.0393
15	5.7500	.0392
16	5.9847	.0387
17	6.2317	.0386
18	6.4902	.0388
19	6.7567	.0377
20	7.0475	.0378
21	7.3515	.0377
22	7.6695	.0374
23	8.0062	.0370
24	8.3634	.0369
25	8.7374	.0364
26	9.1372	.0361
27	9.5604	.0356
28	10.0091	.0352
29	10.4887	.0346
30	11.0018	.0338
31	11.5478	.0334
32	12.1329	.0324
33	12.7643	.0314
34	13.4416	.0302
35	14.1751	.0290
36	14.9667	.0277
37	15.8235	.0264
38	16.7483	.0260
39	17.7367	.0246
40	18.8117	.0243
41	19.9605	.0240
42	21.2006	.0233
43	22.5416	.0224
44	24.0112	.0213
45	25.6271	.0201
46	27.4138	.0170
47	29.4268	.0145
48	31.6880	.0103
49	34.2584	.0045
50	37.2041	+.0031
51	40.6101	.0136
52	44.6059	.0276
53	49.3342	.0465
54	55.0221	.0719
55	61.9683	.1067
56	70.6223	.1549
57	81.6601	.2228
58	96.1538	.3205

7th Year—D. or 70.

Age.	Value.	M. Diff.
10	4.2695	−.0428
11	4.4235	.0417
12	4.5931	.0417
13	4.7679	.0417
14	4.9552	.0416
15	5.1404	.0416
16	5.3383	.0413
17	5.5456	.0414
18	5.7604	.0413
19	5.9876	.0413
20	6.2234	.0412
21	6.4734	.0412
22	6.7344	.0411
23	7.0085	.0410
24	7.2992	.0412
25	7.6016	.0415
26	7.9156	.0406
27	8.2573	.0410
28	8.6139	.0408
29	8.9935	.0410
30	9.3906	.0405
31	9.8148	−.0407
32	10.2652	.0399
33	10.7520	.0404
34	11.2625	.0393
35	11.8046	.0382
36	12.4068	.0386
37	13.0407	.0384
38	13.7158	.0391
39	14.4254	.0392
40	15.1835	.0406
41	15.9746	.0420
42	16.8074	.0435
43	17.6827	.0450
44	18.6185	.0468
45	19.6179	.0491
46	20.6894	.0502
47	21.8650	.0525
48	23.1420	.0541
49	24.5459	.0556
50	26.0951	.0568
51	27.8022	.0563
52	29.7495	.0568
53	31.9265	.0554
54	34.4105	.0527
55	37.2602	.0478
56	40.5682	.0402
57	44.4508	.0280
58	49.0641	.0055
59	54.6619	+.0163
60	61.5411	.0552
61	70.1926	.1110
62	81.3434	.1955
63	96.1538	.3205

7th Year—D. or 75.

Age.	Value.	M. Diff.
10	3.9876	−.0431
11	4.1362	.0429
12	4.2887	.0429
13	4.4501	.0429
14	4.6148	.0429
15	4.7803	.0430
16	4.9591	.0429
17	5.1412	.0428
18	5.3329	.0430
19	5.5333	.0431
20	5.7430	.0431
21	5.9603	.0433
22	6.1890	.0434
23	6.4276	.0434
24	6.6815	.0437
25	6.9426	.0438
26	7.2171	.0439
27	7.5065	.0441
28	7.8107	.0442
29	8.1341	.0445
30	8.4707	.0444
31	8.8284	.0448
32	9.2045	.0447
33	9.6094	.0449
34	10.0340	.0446
35	10.4910	.0451
36	10.9737	.0443
37	11.4941	.0451
38	12.0411	.0464
39	12.6082	.0471
40	13.2062	.0495
41	13.8173	.0517
42	14.4696	.0561
43	15.0984	.0570
44	15.7760	.0603
45	16.4848	.0659
46	17.2242	.0671
47	18.0201	.0717
48	18.8622	.0760
49	19.7631	.0808
50	20.7269	.0856
51	21.7607	.0906
52	22.8940	.0958
53	24.1173	.1011
54	25.4618	.1068
55	26.9394	.1124
56	28.5748	.1178
57	30.3985	.1229
58	32.4467	.1268
59	34.7735	.1294
60	37.4486	.1294
61	40.5674	.1264
62	44.2521	.1175
63	48.6838	.1007
64	54.1087	.0727
65	60.8817	.0277
66	69.5281	+.0425
67	80.8541	.1513
68	96.1538	.3205

8th YEAR—D. or 35.

AGE.	Value.	M. Diff.
10	20.5007	+.0217
11	21.8787	.0267
12	23.3873	.0322
13	25.0467	.0382
14	26.8750	.0449
15	28.8999	.0525
16	31.1549	.0609
17	33.6785	.0705
18	36.5178	.0812
19	39.7337	.0936
20	43.4014	.1078
21	47.6204	.1242
22	52.5181	.1435
23	58.2644	.1663
24	65.0932	.1937
25	73.3308	.2270
26	83.4483	.2683
27	96.1538	.3205

8th Year—D. or 40.

AGE.	Value.	M. Diff.
10	15.1876	+.0007
11	16.0961	.0038
12	17.0761	.0072
13	18.1371	.0108
14	19.2896	.0147
15	20.5388	.0192
16	21.9112	.0240
17	23.4096	.0293
18	25.0580	.0353
19	26.8789	.0419
20	28.8950	.0493
21	31.1449	.0576
22	33.6594	.0670
23	36.4919	.0777
24	39.7024	.0900
25	43.3636	.1042
26	47.5772	.1207
27	52.4718	.1402
28	58.2158	.1632
29	65.0479	.1910
30	73.2920	.2249
31	83.4235	.2670
32	96.1538	.3205

8th Year—D. or 45.

AGE.	Value.	M. Diff.
10	11.6282	—.0133
11	12.2574	.0114
12	12.9329	.0092
13	13.6556	.0070
14	14.4309	.0046
15	15.2626	.0019
16	16.1641	+.0011
17	17.1332	.0042
18	18.1850	.0077
19	19.3269	.0115
20	20.5732	.0156
21	21.9327	.0203
22	23.4244	.0255
23	25.0642	.0312
24	26.8756	.0376
25	28.8855	.0448
26	31.1221	.0530
27	33.6299	.0624
28	36.4492	.0739
29	39.6518	.0854
30	43.3076	.0994
31	47.5126	.1163
32	52.4046	.1359
33	58.1504	.1594
34	64.9867	.1877
35	73.2430	.2222
36	83.3935	.2654
37	96.1538	.3205

8th Year—D. or 50.

AGE.	Value.	M. Diff.
10	9.1605	—.0231
11	9.6202	.0219
12	10.1030	.0204
13	10.6190	.0190
14	11.1676	.0176
15	11.7474	.0158
16	12.3728	.0141
17	13.0385	.0121
18	13.7524	.0101
19	14.5214	.0078
20	15.3474	.0055
21	16.2377	.0027
22	17.2028	+.0002
23	18.2463	.0035
24	19.3809	.0071
25	20.6178	.0109
26	21.9679	.0154
27	23.4486	.0203
28	25.0782	.0259
29	26.8802	.0323
30	28.8807	.0389
31	31.1054	.0474
32	33.6056	.0566
33	36.4234	.0672
34	39.6195	.0795
35	43.2736	.0935
36	47.4798	.1105
37	52.3733	.1297
38	58.1166	.1530
39	64.9490	.1813
40	73.2022	.2167
41	83.3603	.2617
42	96.1538	.3205

8th Year—D. or 55.

AGE.	Value.	M. Diff.
10	7.4301	—.0299
11	7.7745	.0292
12	8.1358	.0282
13	8.5189	.0275
14	8.9218	.0265
15	9.3449	.0253
16	9.8007	.0245
17	10.2789	.0232
18	10.7899	.0220
19	11.3325	.0206
20	11.9127	.0192
21	12.5315	.0177
22	13.1940	.0160
23	13.9045	.0142
24	14.6685	.0122
25	15.4896	.0100
26	16.3758	.0076
27	17.3326	.0049
28	18.3725	.0019
29	19.5012	+.0015
30	20.7349	.0050
31	22.0775	.0094
32	23.5571	.0142
33	25.1876	.0195
34	26.9907	.0248
35	28.9932	.0325
36	31.2273	.0401
37	33.7289	.0482
38	36.5396	.0582
39	39.7243	.0696
40	43.3506	.0818
41	47.5185	.0975
42	52.3623	.1165
43	58.0585	.1401
44	64.8549	.1692
45	73.0903	.2075
46	83.2781	.2557
47	96.1538	.3205

8th Year—D. or 60.

AGE.	Value.	M. Diff.
10	6.2205	—.0347
11	6.4884	.0343
12	6.7710	.0336
13	7.0665	.0331
14	7.3764	.0327
15	7.6993	.0319
16	8.0442	.0314
17	8.4047	.0307
18	8.7857	.0300
19	9.1893	.0292
20	9.6173	.0286
21	10.0706	.0276
22	10.5508	.0266
23	11.0657	.0259
24	11.6092	.0247
25	12.1900	.0236
26	12.8106	.0223
27	13.4742	.0209
28	14.1868	.0193
29	14.9526	.0174
30	15.7796	.0158
31	16.6671	.0134
32	17.6330	.0109
33	18.6808	.0083
34	19.8204	.0046
35	21.0697	.0015
36	22.4329	+.0021
37	23.9252	.0054
38	25.5570	.0098
39	27.3541	.0137
40	29.3321	.0184
41	31.5182	.0240
42	33.9565	.0308
43	36.6921	.0388
44	39.7915	.0483
45	43.3298	.0612
46	47.4280	.0759
47	52.2088	.0950
48	57.8617	.1194
49	64.6381	.1508
50	72.8907	.1919
51	83.1364	.2467
52	96.1538	.3205

8th Year—D. or 65.

AGE.	Value.	M. Diff.
10	5.3945	—.0379
11	5.6151	.0377
12	5.8478	.0373
13	6.0824	.0370
14	6.3322	.0369
15	6.5892	.0363
16	6.8648	.0361
17	7.1491	.0362
18	7.4439	.0349
19	7.7654	.0350
20	8.0971	.0347
21	8.4481	.0342
22	8.8181	.0337
23	9.2101	.0334
24	9.6219	.0328
25	10.0575	.0323
26	10.5220	.0317
27	11.0140	.0310
28	11.5356	.0303
29	12.0937	.0293
30	12.6924	.0286
31	13.3250	.0274
32	14.0090	.0262
33	14.7447	.0247
34	15.5360	.0232
35	16.3903	.0215
36	17.3124	.0200
37	18.3072	.0192
38	19.3698	.0174
39	20.5200	.0167
40	21.7541	.0159
41	23.0780	.0147
42	24.5124	.0132
43	26.0691	.0115
44	27.7766	.0097
45	29.6535	.0060
46	31.7511	.0028
47	34.0967	+.0021
48	36.7460	.0085
49	39.7631	.0168
50	43.2268	.0280
51	47.2447	.0426
52	51.9660	.0619
53	57.5688	.0873
54	64.3215	.1214
55	72.5933	.1677
56	82.9292	.2313
57	96.1538	.3205

8th Year—D. or 70.

AGE.	Value.	M. Diff.
10	4.8587	—.0400
11	5.0497	.0399
12	5.2444	.0398
13	5.4458	.0396
14	5.6597	.0394
15	5.8755	.0391
16	6.1076	.0391
17	6.3455	.0389
18	6.5950	.0388
19	6.8575	.0386
20	7.1315	.0386
21	7.4192	.0384
22	7.7223	.0381
23	8.0408	.0382
24	8.3747	.0384
25	8.7205	.0373
26	9.0964	.0376
27	9.4858	.0373
28	9.9006	.0371
29	10.3376	.0366
30	10.8029	—.0366
31	11.2918	.0356
32	11.8215	.0358
33	12.3778	.0347
34	12.9798	.0341
35	13.6206	.0334
36	14.3073	.0330
37	15.0394	.0317
38	15.8094	.0331
39	16.6282	.0342
40	17.4880	.0352
41	18.3901	.0362
42	19.3420	.0372
43	20.3491	.0386
44	21.4246	.0404
45	22.5708	.0409
46	23.8182	.0426
47	25.1707	.0436
48	26.6508	.0445
49	28.2788	.0451
50	30.0783	.0446
51	32.0842	.0435
52	34.3462	.0412
53	36.8974	.0376
54	39.8112	.0319
55	43.1670	.0234
56	47.0727	.0103
57	51.6802	+.0082
58	57.2319	.0311
59	63.8750	.0731
60	72.1504	.1277
61	82.5971	.2070
62	96.1538	.3205

8th Year—D. or 75.

AGE.	Value.	M. Diff.
10	4.5407	—.0413
11	4.7128	.0413
12	4.8879	.0412
13	5.0735	.0411
14	5.2630	.0411
15	5.4544	.0410
16	5.6612	.0408
17	5.8736	.0408
18	6.0941	.0408
19	6.3250	.0408
20	6.5681	.0408
21	6.8183	.0408
22	7.0829	.0407
23	7.3602	.0409
24	7.6503	.0409
25	7.9529	.0409
26	8.2709	.0409
27	8.6055	.0409
28	8.9587	.0409
29	9.3308	.0409
30	9.7232	.0411
31	10.1342	.0408
32	10.5736	.0408
33	11.0408	.0403
34	11.5377	.0406
35	12.0619	.0397
36	12.6304	.0402
37	13.2233	.0413
38	13.8420	.0417
39	14.4939	.0438
40	15.1620	.0456
41	15.8537	.0479
42	16.5671	.0502
43	17.3065	.0530
44	18.0761	.0566
45	18.8767	.0589
46	19.7326	.0632
47	20.6327	.0669
48	21.5954	.0712
49	22.6229	.0754
50	23.7265	.0797
51	24.9140	.0843
52	26.2148	.0888
53	27.6236	.0937
54	29.1698	.0985
55	30.8743	.1029
56	32.7660	.1069
57	34.8821	.1097
58	37.2728	.1111
59	40.0018	.1098
60	43.1595	.1055
61	46.8587	.0955
62	51.2663	.0778
63	56.6044	.0493
64	63.1850	.0050
65	71.4612	+.0627
66	82.1053	.1651
67	96.1538	.3205

9th YEAR—D. or 35.

AGE.	Value.	M. Diff.
10	23.5187	+.0332
11	25.1054	.0390
12	26.8435	.0454
13	28.7549	.0524
14	30.8613	.0603
15	33.1963	.0691
16	35.7960	.0789
17	38.7061	.0900
18	41.9802	.1026
19	45.6899	.1170
20	49.9215	.1335
21	54.7898	.1527
22	60.4417	.1752
23	67.0747	.2018
24	74.9581	.2337
25	84.4695	.2725
26	96.1538	.3205

9th Year—D. or 40.

AGE.	Value.	M. Diff.
10	17.3918	+.0089
11	18.4365	.0126
12	19.5650	.0165
13	20.7862	.0207
14	22.1116	.0255
15	23.5528	.0306
16	25.1328	.0362
17	26.8592	.0425
18	28.7594	.0493
19	30.8583	.0573
20	33.1835	.0658
21	35.7775	.0756
22	38.6780	.0866
23	41.9459	.0992
24	45.6501	.1135
25	49.8758	.1302
26	54.7403	.1495
27	60.3918	.1723
28	67.0265	.1992
29	74.9182	.2317
30	84.4445	.2713
31	96.1538	.3205

9th Year—D. or 45.

AGE.	Value.	M. Diff.
10	13.2872	—.0073
11	14.0097	.0050
12	14.7870	.0025
13	15.6174	+.0001
14	16.5082	.0031
15	17.4664	.0063
16	18.5032	.0097
17	19.6192	.0134
18	20.8300	.0176
19	22.1458	.0220
20	23.5801	.0270
21	25.1472	.0325
22	26.8663	.0385
23	28.7562	.0453
24	30.8446	.0528
25	33.1618	.0614
26	35.7423	.0711
27	38.6363	.0821
28	41.9014	.0938
29	45.5891	.1089
30	49.8085	.1259
31	54.6697	.1454
32	60.3217	.1686
33	66.9630	.1961
34	74.8668	.2292
35	84.4129	.2698
36	96.1538	.3205

9th Year—D. or 50.

AGE.	Value.	M. Diff.
10	10.4417	—.0186
11	10.9679	.0170
12	11.5234	.0154
13	12.1150	.0138
14	12.7439	.0118
15	13.4121	.0099
16	14.1298	.0078
17	14.8957	.0055
18	15.7162	.0030
19	16.6016	.0004
20	17.5502	+.0026
21	18.5755	.0058
22	19.6858	.0093
23	20.8872	.0132
24	22.1939	.0174
25	23.6175	.0222
26	25.1737	.0274

ENDOWMENT POLICIES.—4 PER CENT.

9th Year—D. or 50.

Age.	Value.	M. Diff.
27	26.8804	+.0334
28	28.7600	.0401
29	30.8397	.0471
30	33.1430	.0559
31	35.7157	.0655
32	38.6018	.0764
33	41.8561	.0891
34	45.5492	.1033
35	49.7682	.1204
36	54.6324	.1395
37	60.2824	.1625
38	66.9213	.1901
39	74.8237	.2241
40	84.3794	.2666
41	96.1538	.3205

9th Year—D. or 55.

Age.	Value.	M. Diff.
10	8.4464	—.0265
11	8.8395	.0254
12	9.2545	.0244
13	9.6930	.0235
14	10.1535	.0221
15	10.6422	.0210
16	11.1607	.0195
17	11.7121	.0183
18	12.2981	.0168
19	12.9218	.0152
20	13.5879	.0134
21	14.2984	.0115
22	15.0597	.0095
23	15.8763	.0073
24	16.7541	.0047
25	17.6984	.0022
26	18.7174	+.0008
27	19.8188	.0041
28	21.0160	.0078
29	22.3075	.0125
30	23.7348	.0163
31	25.2855	.0215
32	26.9927	.0271
33	28.8717	.0337
34	30.9526	.0409
35	33.2631	.0489
36	35.8387	.0574
37	38.7159	.0678
38	41.9596	.0788
39	45.6251	.0921
40	49.8091	.1079
41	54.6258	.1270
42	60.2314	.1504
43	66.8341	.1787
44	74.7182	.2155
45	84.3012	.2610
46	96.1538	.3205

9th Year—D. or 60.

Age.	Value.	M. Diff.
10	7.0517	—.0320
11	7.3566	.0313
12	7.6804	.0307
13	8.0177	.0302
14	8.3703	.0292
15	8.7437	.0286
16	9.1365	.0278
17	9.5500	.0270
18	9.9861	.0260
19	10.4497	.0252
20	10.9383	.0241
21	11.4592	.0229
22	12.0110	.0221
23	12.5977	.0207
24	13.2229	.0193
25	13.8890	.0179
26	14.6013	.0162
27	15.3637	.0144
28	16.1825	.0123
29	17.0647	.0104
30	18.0112	.0077
31	19.0351	.0050
32	20.1469	.0020
33	21.3513	+.0019
34	22.6698	.0054
35	24.1041	.0093
36	25.6698	.0130
37	27.3769	.0178
38	29.2528	.0221
39	31.3068	.0273
40	33.5744	.0334
41	36.0862	.0407
42	38.8942	.0492
43	42.0491	.0591
44	45.6267	.0725

9th Year—D. or 60.

Age.	Value.	M. Diff.
45	49.7343	+.0875
46	54.4813	.1067
47	60.0366	.1309
48	66.6167	.1614
49	74.5173	.2009
50	84.1596	.2524
51	96.1538	.3205

9th Year—D. or 65.

Age.	Value.	M. Diff.
10	6.0990	—.0358
11	6.3492	.0353
12	6.6149	.0349
13	6.8828	.0347
14	7.1660	.0340
15	7.4634	.0337
16	7.7758	.0337
17	8.0958	.0323
18	8.4450	.0322
19	8.8066	.0319
20	9.1846	.0312
21	9.5867	.0306
22	10.0110	.0302
23	10.4565	.0295
24	10.9286	.0287
25	11.4276	.0280
26	11.9595	.0271
27	12.5227	.0262
28	13.1210	.0250
29	13.7626	.0242
30	14.4455	.0227
31	15.1744	.0213
32	15.9599	.0195
33	16.8061	.0178
34	17.7145	.0159
35	18.6949	.0140
36	19.7500	.0129
37	20.8771	.0108
38	22.0951	.0097
39	23.3975	.0084
40	24.7982	.0068
41	26.3068	.0048
42	27.9454	.0026
43	29.7272	.0003
44	31.6802	+.0038
45	33.8497	.0077
46	36.2584	.0132
47	38.9658	.0202
48	42.0294	.0291
49	45.5243	.0407
50	49.5488	.0557
51	54.2280	.0752
52	59.7377	.1004
53	66.2924	.1337
54	74.2150	.1782
55	83.9501	.2382
56	96.1538	.3205

9th Year—D. or 70.

Age.	Value.	M. Diff.
10	5.4820	—.0382
11	5.6973	.0380
12	5.9188	.0377
13	6.1489	.0376
14	6.3921	.0371
15	6.6398	.0370
16	6.9026	.0367
17	7.1747	.0365
18	7.4589	.0362
19	7.7592	.0352
20	8.0704	.0357
21	8.3995	.0354
22	8.7464	.0353
23	9.1073	.0354
24	9.4840	.0342
25	9.8898	.0343
26	10.3127	.0338
27	10.7596	.0336
28	11.2317	.0329
29	11.7344	.0327
30	12.2627	.0316
31	12.8295	.0316
32	13.4270	.0302
33	14.0718	.0294
34	14.7601	.0285
35	15.4934	.0278
36	16.2755	.0280
37	17.1192	.0291
38	17.9747	.0282
39	18.8912	.0288
40	19.8579	.0295
41	20.8749	.0301
42	21.9528	.0310

9th Year—D. or 70.

Age.	Value.	M. Diff.
43	23.0925	—.0323
44	24.3077	.0324
45	25.6217	.0336
46	27.0371	.0341
47	28.5821	.0344
48	30.2741	.0343
49	32.1378	.0332
50	34.2086	.0314
51	36.5193	.0285
52	39.1298	.0242
53	42.0809	.0178
54	45.4613	.0084
55	49.3668	+.0051
56	53.9355	.0240
57	59.3436	.0508
58	65.8394	.0881
59	73.7690	.1406
60	83.6296	.2148
61	96.1538	.3205

9th Year—D. or 75.

Age.	Value.	M. Diff.
10	5.1147	—.0397
11	5.3092	.0395
12	5.5084	.0394
13	5.7184	.0393
14	5.9335	.0391
15	6.1527	.0388
16	6.3895	.0388
17	6.6302	.0387
18	6.8809	.0385
19	7.1448	.0385
20	7.4203	.0384
21	7.7060	.0382
22	8.0086	.0383
23	8.3216	.0382
24	8.6526	.0381
25	8.9979	.0380
26	9.3604	.0378
27	9.7432	.0377
28	10.1451	.0375
29	10.5704	.0375
30	11.0156	.0371
31	11.4887	.0370
32	11.9891	.0363
33	12.5270	.0364
34	13.0894	.0353
35	13.6974	.0356
36	14.3364	.0364
37	14.9989	.0366
38	15.6999	.0384
39	16.4193	.0399
40	17.1650	.0419
41	17.9348	.0438
42	18.7352	.0462
43	19.5628	.0494
44	20.4201	.0513
45	21.3327	.0551
46	22.2877	.0584
47	23.3033	.0622
48	24.3866	.0659
49	25.5470	.0698
50	26.7966	.0736
51	28.1432	.0775
52	29.6190	.0817
53	31.2182	.0856
54	32.9778	.0893
55	34.9229	.0924
56	37.0881	.0943
57	39.5236	.0945
58	42.2881	.0923
59	45.4643	.0870
60	49.1573	.0761
61	53.5206	.0570
62	58.7559	.0292
63	65.1419	+.0144
64	73.0736	.0795
65	83.1253	.1764
66	96.1538	.3205

10th YEAR—D. or 35.

Age.	Value.	M. Diff.
10	26.6741	+.0452
11	28.4800	.0519
12	30.4580	.0592
13	32.6330	.0674
14	35.0325	.0764
15	37.6917	.0865
16	40.6532	.0978
17	43.9680	.1106
18	47.6992	.1251
19	51.9271	.1416
20	56.7510	.1607

10th Year—D. or 35.

Age.	Value.	M. Diff.
21	62.3009	+.1828
22	68.7457	.2086
23	76.3102	.2392
24	85.3026	.2759
25	96.1538	.3205

10th Year—D. or 40.

Age.	Value.	M. Diff.
10	19.6944	+.0176
11	20.8826	.0217
12	22.1656	.0262
13	23.5533	.0312
14	25.0630	.0366
15	26.7032	.0425
16	28.5008	.0491
17	30.4669	.0563
18	32.6299	.0644
19	35.0226	.0732
20	37.6708	.0833
21	40.6260	.0946
22	43.9322	.1073
23	47.6572	.1218
24	51.8802	.1384
25	56.7000	.1576
26	62.2490	.1800
27	68.6972	.2062
28	76.2689	.2374
29	85.2774	.2748
30	96.1538	.3205

10th Year—D. or 45.

Age.	Value.	M. Diff.
10	15.0181	—.0010
11	15.8390	+.0018
12	16.7220	.0045
13	17.6645	.0078
14	18.6782	.0111
15	19.7675	.0148
16	20.9460	.0187
17	22.2155	.0232
18	23.5940	.0278
19	25.0903	.0331
20	26.7233	.0389
21	28.5077	.0452
22	30.4648	.0523
23	32.6176	.0601
24	34.9959	.0690
25	37.6372	.0789
26	40.5793	.0901
27	43.8788	.1029
28	47.5934	.1173
29	51.8088	.1344
30	56.6278	.1537
31	62.1768	.1764
32	68.6308	.2032
33	76.2167	.2350
34	85.2451	.2734
35	96.1538	.3205

10th Year—D. or 50.

Age.	Value.	M. Diff.
10	11.7766	— 0138
11	12.3740	.0121
12	13.0036	.0103
13	13.6738	.0081
14	14.3889	.0060
15	15.1473	.0037
16	15.9627	.0013
17	16.8323	+.0015
18	17.7659	.0043
19	18.7702	.0075
20	19.8497	.0110
21	21.0154	.0147
22	22.2780	.0189
23	23.6450	.0233
24	25.1309	.0284
25	26.7520	.0339
26	28.5240	.0402
27	30.4688	.0472
28	32.6121	.0545
29	34.9778	.0636
30	37.6090	.0734
31	40.5433	.0847
32	43.8364	.0975
33	47.5513	.1119
34	51.7642	.1290
35	56.5847	.1480
36	62.1334	.1707
37	68.5858	.1976
38	76.1719	.2302
39	85.2112	.2703
40	96.1538	.3205

10th Year—D. or 55.

Age.	Value.	M. Diff.
10	9.5039	—.0229
11	9.9493	.0217
12	10.4188	.0206
13	10.9131	.0190
14	11.4382	.0170
15	11.9909	.0163
16	12.5812	.0148
17	13.2041	.0132
18	13.8694	.0113
19	14.5769	.0094
20	15.3325	.0074
21	16.1393	.0051
22	17.0037	.0027
23	17.9310	.0000
24	18.9302	+.0028
25	20.0012	.0061
26	21.1599	.0096
27	22.4131	.0137
28	23.7766	.0177
29	25.2553	.0226
30	26.8710	.0282
31	28.6392	.0341
32	30.5831	.0410
33	32.7267	.0484
34	35.0978	.0568
35	37.7299	.0656
36	40.6570	.0763
37	43.9381	.0876
38	47.6266	.1011
39	51.8056	.1171
40	56.5811	.1366
41	62.0876	.1592
42	68.5066	.1868
43	76.0735	.2222
44	85.1379	.2652
45	96.1538	.3205

10th Year—D. or 60.

Age.	Value.	M. Diff.
10	7.9145	—.0291
11	8.2600	.0284
12	8.6250	.0278
13	9.0044	.0267
14	9.4068	.0259
15	9.8274	.0250
16	10.2723	.0241
17	10.7399	.0230
18	11.2350	.0221
19	11.7579	.0208
20	12.3128	.0195
21	12.9039	.0184
22	13.5259	.0169
23	14.1925	.0154
24	14.9011	.0137
25	15.6565	.0119
26	16.4650	.0098
27	17.3307	.0075
28	18.2626	.0054
29	19.2606	.0025
30	20.3392	+.0015
31	21.5041	.0037
32	22.7668	.0079
33	24.1435	.0117
34	25.6395	.0159
35	27.2676	.0200
36	29.0381	.0251
37	30.9775	.0298
38	33.0964	.0354
39	35.4237	.0419
40	37.9970	.0496
41	40.8548	.0585
42	44.0529	.0688
43	47.6503	.0825
44	51.7528	.0976
45	56.4537	.1168
46	61.9043	.1407
47	68.2943	.1705
48	75.8756	.2084
49	84.9983	.2571
50	96.1538	.3205

10th Year—D. or 65.

Age.	Value.	M. Diff.
10	6.8292	—.0334
11	7.1121	.0330
12	7.4106	.0326
13	7.7115	.0318
14	8.0345	.0314
15	8.3683	.0313
16	8.7157	.0298
17	9.0895	.0296
18	9.4781	.0291
19	9.8852	.0284
20	10.3135	.0276
21	10.7691	.0271

ENDOWMENT POLICIES.—4 PER CENT.

10th Year—D. or 65.

Age.	Value.	M. Diff.
22	11.2458	—.0262
23	11.7506	.0254
24	12.2849	.0244
25	12.8499	.0235
26	13.4514	.0223
27	14.0896	.0210
28	14.7696	.0199
29	15.4932	.0183
30	16.2700	.0166
31	17.0976	.0147
32	17.9905	.0127
33	18.9503	.0106
34	19.9808	.0085
35	21.0898	.0071
36	22.2724	.0046
37	23.5489	.0032
38	24.9127	.0016
39	26.3744	+.0004
40	27.9511	.0028
41	29.6539	.0055
42	31.5055	.0082
43	33.5192	.0130
44	35.7486	.0173
45	38.2101	.0232
46	40.9578	.0306
47	44.0518	.0399
48	47.5591	.0520
49	51.5719	.0672
50	56.2032	.0867
51	61.6019	.1116
52	67.9709	.1442
53	75.5734	.1870
54	84.7901	.2439
55	96.1538	.3205

10th Year—D. or 70.

Age.	Value.	M. Diff.
10	6.1266	—.0363
11	6.3686	.0359
12	6.6183	.0358
13	6.8754	.0351
14	7.1525	.0350
15	7.4200	.0339
16	7.7266	.0343
17	8.0330	.0339
18	8.3546	.0337
19	8.7014	.0341
20	9.0435	.0328
21	9.4157	.0326
22	9.8042	.0326
23	10.2071	.0313
24	10.6430	.0312
25	11.0957	.0306
26	11.5742	.0302
27	12.0774	.0293
28	12.6140	.0291
29	13.1785	.0277
30	13.7828	.0275
31	14.4157	.0260
32	15.0999	.0250
33	15.8296	.0240
34	16.6071	.0230
35	17.4331	.0229
36	18.3039	.0221
37	19.2300	.0226
38	20.1995	.0229
39	21.2188	.0232
40	22.2959	.0235
41	23.4329	.0240
42	24.6382	.0244
43	25.9112	.0245
44	27.2867	.0252
45	28.7603	.0252
46	30.3588	.0251
47	32.1046	.0245
48	34.0195	.0228
49	36.1394	.0205
50	38.4967	.0169
51	41.1347	.0114
52	44.1176	.0050
53	47.5030	+.0048
54	51.3933	.0188
55	55.9087	.0379
56	61.2103	.0644
57	67.5180	.1010
58	75.1312	.1515
59	84.4732	.2219
60	96.1538	.3205

10th Year—D. or 75.

Age.	Value.	M. Diff.
10	5.7085	—.0379
11	5.9269	.0377
12	6.1502	.0375
13	6.3855	—.0372
14	6.6281	.0369
15	6.8770	.0367
16	7.1418	.0366
17	7.4124	.0364
18	7.6956	.0363
19	7.9915	.0361
20	8.3020	.0358
21	8.6253	.0358
22	8.9631	.0356
23	9.3163	.0353
24	9.6894	.0351
25	10.0784	.0350
26	10.4882	.0346
27	10.9190	.0343
28	11.3731	.0342
29	11.8501	.0336
30	12.3563	.0333
31	12.8891	.0325
32	13.4587	.0325
33	14.0604	.0311
34	14.7050	.0313
35	15.3817	.0319
36	16.0881	.0318
37	16.8307	.0337
38	17.5969	.0346
39	18.3913	.0363
40	19.2122	.0378
41	20.0656	.0399
42	20.9506	.0427
43	21.8621	.0443
44	22.8271	.0476
45	23.8343	.0505
46	24.8997	.0538
47	26.0306	.0571
48	27.2406	.0603
49	28.5390	.0636
50	29.9460	.0670
51	31.4535	.0706
52	33.1089	.0738
53	34.9098	.0768
54	36.8960	.0791
55	39.0979	.0801
56	41.5625	.0796
57	44.3473	.0765
58	47.5283	.0704
59	51.2013	.0588
60	55.5086	.0402
61	60.6341	.0117
62	66.8290	+.0310
63	74.4436	.0938
64	83.9760	.1858
65	96.1538	.3205

11th YEAR—D. or 35.

Age.	Value.	M. Diff.
10	29.9742	+.0578
11	32.0092	.0653
12	34.2381	.0738
13	36.6910	.0830
14	39.3967	.0934
15	42.3963	.1048
16	45.7368	.1177
17	49.4772	.1323
18	53.6881	.1488
19	58.4603	.1676
20	63.9059	.1893
21	70.1726	.2144
22	77.4505	.2439
23	85.9949	.2787
24	96.1538	.3205

11th Year—D. or 40.

Age.	Value.	M. Diff.
10	22.1009	+.0266
11	23.4385	.0312
12	24.8821	.0365
13	26.4472	.0421
14	28.1478	.0483
15	29.9967	.0551
16	32.0230	.0626
17	34.2402	.0708
18	36.6811	.0800
19	39.3779	.0902
20	42.3672	.1016
21	45.7021	.1145
22	49.4342	.1291
23	53.6397	.1457
24	58.4088	.1647
25	63.8533	.1866
26	70.1231	.2121
27	77.4095	.2421
28	85.9692	.2777
29	96.1538	.3205

11th Year—D. or 45.

Age.	Value.	M. Diff.
10	16.8257	+.0056
11	17.7499	.0086
12	18.7410	.0120
13	19.8031	.0156
14	20.9437	.0195
15	22.1705	.0237
16	23.4972	.0283
17	24.9296	.0331
18	26.4806	.0387
19	28.1680	.0447
20	30.0091	.0513
21	32.0209	.0586
22	34.2282	.0667
23	36.6568	.0758
24	39.3415	.0859
25	42.3224	.0974
26	45.6450	.1103
27	49.3720	.1248
28	53.5668	.1417
29	58.3341	.1609
30	63.7805	.1832
31	70.0558	.2093
32	77.3558	.2399
33	85.9368	.2764
34	96.1538	.3205

11th Year—D. or 50.

Age.	Value.	M. Diff.
10	13.1694	—.0089
11	13.8393	.0069
12	14.5458	.0047
13	15.3004	.0024
14	16.1036	+.0001
15	16.9574	.0027
16	17.8738	.0057
17	18.8536	.0087
18	19.9028	.0121
19	21.0340	.0158
20	22.2495	.0198
21	23.5625	.0241
22	24.9848	.0288
23	26.5245	.0341
24	28.2000	.0399
25	30.0278	.0464
26	32.0273	.0537
27	34.2233	.0613
28	36.6377	.0706
29	39.3137	.0806
30	42.2853	.0921
31	45.6014	.1050
32	49.3238	.1195
33	53.5203	.1366
34	58.2875	.1554
35	63.7329	.1777
36	70.0084	.2039
37	77.3096	.2353
38	85.9029	.2735
39	96.1538	.3205

11th Year—D. or 55.

Age.	Value.	M. Diff.
10	10.6047	—.0191
11	11.1042	.0179
12	11.6287	.0162
13	12.1870	.0148
14	12.7743	.0132
15	13.3962	.0116
16	14.0578	.0097
17	14.7578	.0077
18	15.5056	.0057
19	16.3006	.0034
20	17.1502	.0010
21	18.0574	+.0016
22	19.0296	.0045
23	20.0729	.0076
24	21.1956	.0110
25	22.4032	.0148
26	23.7088	.0190
27	25.1225	.0233
28	26.6554	.0286
29	28.3247	.0343
30	30.1496	.0405
31	32.1442	.0477
32	34.3401	.0554
33	36.7581	.0642
34	39.4344	.0730
35	42.3971	.0840
36	45.7028	.0955
37	49.3983	.1091
38	53.5617	.1252
39	58.2856	.1442
40	63.6978	.1663
41	69.9352	.1937
42	77.2188	+.2278
43	85.8348	.2687
44	96.1538	.3205

11th Year—D. or 60.

Age.	Value.	M. Diff.
10	8.8122	—.0262
11	9.1985	.0255
12	9.6050	.0243
13	10.0334	.0234
14	10.4823	.0224
15	10.9542	.0214
16	11.4522	.0201
17	11.9778	.0191
18	12.5312	.0177
19	13.1192	.0162
20	13.7430	.0150
21	14.4027	.0133
22	15.1030	.0116
23	15.8510	.0098
24	16.6468	.0078
25	17.4961	.0056
26	18.4052	.0030
27	19.3810	.0007
28	20.4253	+.0024
29	21.5514	.0057
30	22.7665	.0091
31	24.0772	.0135
32	25.5063	.0176
33	27.0537	.0220
34	28.7356	.0264
35	30.5595	.0318
36	32.5518	.0368
37	34.7220	.0428
38	37.0997	.0496
39	39.7157	.0576
40	42.6140	.0669
41	45.8368	.0774
42	49.4465	.0913
43	53.5314	.1065
44	58.1801	.1257
45	63.5254	.1492
46	69.7350	.1782
47	77.0274	.2148
48	85.6986	.2611
49	96.1538	.3205

11th Year—D. or 65.

Age.	Value.	M. Diff.
10	7.5880	—.0311
11	7.9033	.0306
12	8.2343	.0297
13	8.5747	.0293
14	8.9336	.0291
15	9.3019	.0274
16	9.7025	.0272
17	10.1151	.0265
18	10.5485	.0257
19	11.0051	.0248
20	11.4860	.0242
21	11.9930	.0232
22	12.5280	.0222
23	13.0938	.0211
24	13.6928	.0200
25	14.3261	.0187
26	15.0009	.0172
27	15.7190	.0160
28	16.4790	.0141
29	17.2942	.0123
30	18.1671	.0102
31	19.0994	.0080
32	20.1027	.0056
33	21.1808	.0033
34	22.3360	.0017
35	23.5679	+.0011
36	24.8946	.0028
37	26.3112	.0047
38	27.8275	.0071
39	29.4575	.0098
40	31.2194	.0129
41	33.1248	.0161
42	35.1959	.0213
43	37.4717	.0259
44	39.9761	.0323
45	42.7564	.0401
46	45.8667	.0497
47	49.3748	.0620
48	53.3637	.0774
49	57.9374	.0969
50	63.2297	.1215
51	69.4137	.1532
52	76.7302	.1945
53	85.4937	.2486
54	96.1538	.3205

11th Year—D. or 70.

Age.	Value.	M. Diff.
10	6.7945	—.0342
11	7.0644	.0340
12	7.3405	.0326
13	7.6418	.0338
14	7.9382	.0326
15	8.2492	.0322
16	8.5796	.0317
17	8.9228	.0314
18	9.2805	.0308
19	9.6577	.0303
20	10.0522	.0300
21	10.4655	.0297
22	10.8951	.0284
23	11.3566	.0283
24	11.8383	.0275
25	12.3459	.0270
26	12.8794	.0260
27	13.4460	.0255
28	14.0420	.0240
29	14.6818	.0237
30	15.3511	.0221
31	16.0687	.0209
32	16.8356	.0196
33	17.6522	.0185
34	18.5200	.0182
35	19.4324	.0172
36	20.4023	.0174
37	21.4190	.0174
38	22.4877	.0174
39	23.6133	.0174
40	24.8055	.0175
41	26.0647	.0180
42	27.3971	.0172
43	28.8237	.0175
44	30.3512	.0171
45	31.9992	.0164
46	33.7887	.0154
47	35.7460	.0141
48	37.9036	.0104
49	40.2938	.0064
50	42.9587	.0010
51	45.9472	+.0065
52	49.3359	.0167
53	53.1961	.0309
54	57.6519	.0501
55	62.8434	.0764
56	68.9701	.1121
57	76.2957	.1609
58	85.1840	.2280
59	96.1538	.3205

11th Year—D. or 75.

Age.	Value.	M. Diff.
10	6.3234	—.0361
11	6.5657	.0359
12	6.8142	.0355
13	7.0767	.0351
14	7.3486	.0349
15	7.6252	.0347
16	7.9195	.0343
17	8.2222	.0341
18	8.5371	.0339
19	8.8675	.0335
20	9.2151	.0334
21	9.5731	.0331
22	9.9505	.0327
23	10.3452	.0324
24	10.7613	.0320
25	11.1970	.0317
26	11.6539	.0312
27	12.1358	.0310
28	12.6408	.0302
29	13.1777	.0298
30	13.7422	.0289
31	14.3429	.0286
32	14.9750	.0272
33	15.6572	.0271
34	16.3687	.0276
35	17.1109	.0273
36	17.8953	.0286
37	18.7010	.0296
38	19.5398	.0310
39	20.4067	.0323
40	21.3083	.0341
41	22.2429	.0365
42	23.2082	.0376
43	24.2234	.0406
44	25.2788	.0431
45	26.3916	.0459
46	27.5673	.0488
47	28.8192	.0516
48	30.1617	.0545
49	31.6048	.0573
50	33.1653	.0603

ENDOWMENT POLICIES.—4 PER CENT.

11th Year—D. or 75.

Age.	Value.	M. Diff.
51	34.8472	—.0630
52	36.6930	.0652
53	38.7081	.0669
54	40.9364	.0672
55	43.4201	.0660
56	46.2125	.0622
57	49.3872	.0555
58	53.0316	.0434
59	57.2763	.0245
60	62.2904	+.0038
61	68.3017	.0455
62	75.6247	.1061
63	84.6989	.1938
64	96.1538	.3205

12th YEAR—D. or 35.

Age.	Value.	M. Diff.
10	33.4255	+.0710
11	35.7000	.0788
12	38.1936	.0890
13	40.9368	.0995
14	43.9642	.1111
15	47.3203	.1241
16	51.0592	.1386
17	55.2463	.1551
18	59.9612	.1737
19	65.3049	.1950
20	71.4044	.2195
21	78.4242	.2479
22	86.5786	.2811
23	96.1538	.3205

12th Year—D. or 40.

Age.	Value.	M. Diff.
10	24.6154	+.0359
11	26.1082	.0414
12	27.7230	.0472
13	29.4720	.0536
14	31.3728	.0606
15	33.4410	.0683
16	35.7069	.0767
17	38.1879	.0861
18	40.9192	.0964
19	43.9372	.1080
20	47.2841	.1210
21	51.0176	.1355
22	55.1975	.1521
23	59.9089	.1708
24	65.2523	.1924
25	71.3548	.2172
26	78.3829	.2462
27	86.5534	.2802
28	96.1538	.3205

12th Year—D. or 45.

Age.	Value.	M. Diff.
10	18.7122	+.0124
11	19.7428	.0160
12	20.8501	.0198
13	22.0357	.0239
14	23.3098	.0282
15	24.6804	.0331
16	26.1635	.0382
17	27.7622	.0439
18	29.4982	.0502
19	31.3855	.0569
20	33.4443	.0645
21	35.6951	.0728
22	38.1650	.0820
23	40.8838	.0923
24	43.8903	.1039
25	47.2293	.1169
26	50.9546	.1312
27	55.1272	.1482
28	59.8332	.1672
29	65.1781	.1900
30	71.2877	.2145
31	78.3292	.2440
32	86.5206	.2789
33	96.1538	.3205

12th Year—D. or 50.

Age.	Value.	M. Diff.
10	14.6208	—.0038
11	15.3661	.0014
12	16.1553	+.0010
13	16.9960	.0037
14	17.8923	.0065
15	18.8448	.0096
16	19.8686	.0128
17	20.9608	.0164

12th Year—D. or 50.

Age.	Value.	M. Diff.
18	22.1334	+.0202
19	23.3965	.0244
20	24.7548	.0290
21	26.2223	.0339
22	27.8111	.0394
23	29.5334	.0454
24	31.4075	.0521
25	33.4532	.0596
26	35.6927	.0674
27	38.1468	.0769
28	40.8561	.0872
29	43.8539	.0987
30	47.1850	.1118
31	50.9037	.1263
32	55.0751	.1432
33	59.7856	.1619
34	65.1281	.1838
35	71.2376	.2094
36	78.2820	.2397
37	86.4865	.2762
38	96.1538	.3205

12th Year—D. or 55.

Age.	Value.	M. Diff.
10	11.7508	—.0153
11	12.3044	.0135
12	12.8919	.0120
13	13.5113	.0103
14	14.1659	.0085
15	14.8578	.0065
16	15.5961	.0044
17	16.3769	.0022
18	17.2097	+.0003
19	18.0965	.0028
20	19.0440	.0056
21	20.0563	.0087
22	21.1413	.0120
23	22.3061	.0156
24	23.5593	.0196
25	24.9098	.0240
26	26.3705	.0285
27	27.9477	.0340
28	29.6652	.0400
29	31.5346	.0464
30	33.5762	.0538
31	35.8117	.0617
32	38.2699	.0705
33	40.9787	.0797
34	43.9653	.0909
35	47.2848	.1025
36	50.9785	.1163
37	55.1171	.1323
38	59.7857	.1510
39	65.0910	.1733
40	71.1705	.1996
41	78.1968	.2326
42	86.4232	.2716
43	96.1538	.3205

12th Year—D. or 60.

Age.	Value.	M. Diff.
10	9.7448	—.0233
11	10.1720	.0220
12	10.6269	.0211
13	11.1011	.0199
14	11.6005	.0188
15	12.1247	.0174
16	12.6798	.0162
17	13.2627	.0147
18	13.8800	.0131
19	14.5357	.0118
20	15.2267	.0099
21	15.9631	.0081
22	16.7431	.0061
23	17.5764	.0039
24	18.4638	.0015
25	19.4112	+.0012
26	20.4276	.0035
27	21.5126	.0070
28	22.6813	.0104
29	23.9399	.0140
30	25.2960	.0187
31	26.7678	.0230
32	28.3614	.0277
33	30.0877	.0323
34	31.9572	.0380
35	33.9936	.0433
36	36.2059	.0495
37	38.6221	.0566
38	41.2732	.0649
39	44.1962	.0744
40	47.4375	.0851
41	51.0456	.0992

12th Year—D. or 60.

Age.	Value.	M. Diff.
42	55.1099	+.1144
43	59.7011	.1335
44	64.9442	.1566
45	70.9855	.1850
46	78.0164	.2203
47	86.2925	.2645
48	96.1538	.3205

12th Year—D. or 65.

Age.	Value.	M. Diff.
10	8.3750	—.0287
11	8.7225	.0278
12	9.0925	.0272
13	9.4683	.0269
14	7.8612	.0252
15	10.2821	.0248
16	10.7208	.0241
17	11.1776	.0232
18	11.6597	.0221
19	12.1681	.0214
20	12.6997	.0203
21	13.2639	.0192
22	13.8588	.0180
23	14.4881	.0167
24	15.1540	.0153
25	15.8592	.0136
26	16.6122	.0123
27	17.4084	.0102
28	18.2580	.0082
29	19.1671	.0059
30	20.1418	.0035
31	21.1816	.0010
32	22.2999	+.0016
33	23.4989	.0034
34	24.7729	.0064
35	26.1442	.0084
36	27.6057	.0106
37	29.1688	.0132
38	30.8465	.0163
39	32.6537	.0197
40	34.6086	.0232
41	36.7226	.0288
42	39.0428	.0338
43	41.5786	.0405
44	44.3839	.0486
45	47.5053	.0585
46	51.0043	.0710
47	54.9625	.0865
48	59.4733	.1059
49	64.6589	.1301
50	70.6734	.1611
51	77.7245	.2009
52	86.0929	.2527
53	96.1538	.3205

12th Year—D. or 70.

Age.	Value.	M. Diff.
10	7.4877	—.0323
11	7.7835	.0315
12	8.0934	.0312
13	8.4137	.0307
14	8.7532	.0302
15	9.0972	.0296
16	9.4640	.0292
17	9.8428	.0286
18	10.2403	.0279
19	10.6593	.0275
20	11.0944	.0273
21	11.5480	.0257
22	12.0356	.0255
23	12.5420	.0246
24	13.0775	.0240
25	13.6390	.0229
26	14.2349	.0222
27	14.8607	.0207
28	15.5312	.0202
29	16.2330	.0183
30	16.9851	.0169
31	17.7836	.0156
32	18.6354	.0143
33	19.5400	.0137
34	20.4913	.0125
35	21.5001	.0125
36	22.5578	.0122
37	23.6705	.0120
38	24.8417	.0117
39	26.0781	.0114
40	27.3876	.0115
41	28.7686	.0104
42	30.2482	.0104
43	31.8199	.0095
44	33.5137	.0085
45	35.3436	.0070

12th Year—D. or 70.

Age.	Value.	M. Diff.
46	37.3343	—.0045
47	39.5122	.0004
48	41.9359	+.0031
49	44.6171	.0090
50	47.6120	.0169
51	50.9820	.0274
52	54.8145	.0418
53	59.2027	.0610
54	64.2863	.0870
55	70.2406	.1219
56	77.3023	.1690
57	85.7915	.2331
58	96.1538	.3205

12th Year—D. or 75.

Age.	Value.	M. Diff.
10	6.9595	—.0343
11	7.2266	.0339
12	7.5020	.0334
13	7.7936	.0331
14	8.0928	.0328
15	8.3987	.0324
16	8.7247	.0321
17	9.0588	.0318
18	9.4077	.0313
19	9.7748	.0311
20	10.1565	.0307
21	10.5535	.0303
22	10.9719	.0298
23	11.4090	.0293
24	11.8710	.0289
25	12.3530	.0283
26	12.8603	.0280
27	13.3922	.0271
28	13.9559	.0265
29	14.5500	.0254
30	15.1812	.0251
31	15.8430	.0235
32	16.5541	.0233
33	17.3014	.0235
34	18.0767	.0230
35	18.8952	.0242
36	19.7406	.0249
37	20.6166	.0261
38	21.5253	.0271
39	22.4702	.0286
40	23.4500	.0306
41	24.4617	.0315
42	25.5267	.0341
43	26.6283	.0362
44	27.7850	.0386
45	29.0033	.0411
46	30.2948	.0435
47	31.6734	.0459
48	33.1531	.0482
49	34.7466	.0507
50	36.4673	.0528
51	38.3325	.0546
52	40.3808	.0556
53	42.6250	.0554
54	45.1193	.0535
55	47.9118	.0492
56	51.0710	.0419
57	54.6801	.0295
58	58.8593	.0105
59	63.7631	+.0176
60	69.6005	.0584
61	76.6556	.1169
62	85.3220	.2007
63	96.1538	.3205

13th YEAR—D. or 35.

Age.	Value.	M. Diff.
10	37.0348	+.0849
11	39.5621	.0945
12	42.3321	.1051
13	45.3803	.1168
14	48.7445	.1298
15	52.4755	.1444
16	56.6328	.1607
17	61.2892	.1791
18	66.5332	.2000
19	72.4781	.2238
20	79.2649	.2513
21	87.0771	.2832
22	96.1538	.3205

13th Year—D. or 40.

Age.	Value.	M. Diff.
10	27.2419	+.0459
11	28.9003	.0519
12	30.6925	.0585

13th Year—D. or 40.

Age.	Value.	M. Diff.
13	32.6342	+.0657
14	34.7455	.0735
15	37.0435	.0821
16	39.5611	.0916
17	42.3186	.1021
18	45.3547	.1138
19	48.7107	.1268
20	52.4330	.1414
21	56.5856	.1578
22	61.2370	.1763
23	66.4804	.1975
24	72.4289	.2217
25	79.2238	.2497
26	87.0519	.2823
27	96.1538	.3205

13th Year—D. or 45.

Age.	Value.	M. Diff.
10	20.6806	+.0198
11	21.8247	.0235
12	23.0522	.0279
13	24.3674	.0325
14	25.7810	.0375
15	27.3031	.0428
16	28.9479	.0487
17	30.7242	.0551
18	32.6530	.0621
19	34.7492	.0698
20	37.0370	.0783
21	39.5387	.0876
22	42.2849	.0981
23	45.3091	.1098
24	48.6542	.1211
25	52.3704	.1373
26	56.5127	.1541
27	61.1635	.1728
28	66.4059	.1944
29	72.3712	.2183
30	79.1704	.2460
31	87.0194	.2811
32	96.1538	.3205

13th Year—D. or 50.

Age.	Value.	M. Diff.
10	16.1331	+.0016
11	16.9594	.0042
12	17.8330	.0071
13	18.7648	.0100
14	19.7575	.0133
15	20.8148	.0166
16	21.9481	.0204
17	23.1605	.0244
18	24.4614	.0288
19	25.8629	.0335
20	27.3708	.0386
21	28.9994	.0443
22	30.7644	.0505
23	32.6779	.0574
24	34.7614	.0651
25	37.0372	.0731
26	39.5231	.0827
27	42.2582	.0931
28	45.2731	.1047
29	48.6109	.1178
30	52.5212	.1323
31	56.4608	.1493
32	61.1119	.1678
33	66.3556	.1893
34	72.3099	.2133
35	79.1223	.2435
36	86.9854	.2785
37	96.1538	.3205

13th Year—D. or 55.

Age.	Value.	M. Diff.
10	12.9419	—.0109
11	13.5575	.0094
12	14.2051	.0075
13	14.8907	.0056
14	15.6145	.0034
15	16.3811	.0012
16	17.1980	+.0012
17	18.0626	.0037
18	18.9952	.0056
19	19.9677	.0094
20	21.0177	.0127
21	22.1400	.0161
22	23.3432	.0199
23	24.6353	.0240
24	26.0266	.0287
25	27.5274	.0334
26	29.1461	.0391

ENDOWMENT POLICIES.—4 PER CENT.

13th Year—D. or 55.

Age.	Value.	M. Diff.
27	30.9015	+.0452
28	32.8116	.0517
29	34.8893	.0594
30	37.1617	.0675
31	39.6480	.0765
32	42.3812	.0859
33	45.3853	.0971
34	48.7105	.1088
35	52.3949	.1227
36	56.5039	.1387
37	61.1135	.1573
38	66.3199	.1793
39	72.2463	.2048
40	79.0427	.2368
41	86.9260	.2742
42	96.1538	.3205

13th Year—D. or 60.

Age.	Value.	M. Diff.
10	10.7122	−.0198
11	11.1872	.0188
12	11.6873	.0176
13	12.2113	.0163
14	12.7622	.0148
15	13.3426	.0135
16	13.9540	.0119
17	14.5998	.0102
18	15.2835	.0088
19	16.0051	.0068
20	16.7713	.0048
21	17.5858	.0027
22	18.4493	.0003
23	19.3721	+.0022
24	20.3554	.0051
25	21.4074	.0078
26	22.5300	.0113
27	23.7363	.0149
28	25.0337	.0187
29	26.4289	.0235
30	27.9412	.0280
31	29.5719	.0329
32	31.3380	.0377
33	33.2447	.0437
34	35.3182	.0492
35	37.5648	.0556
36	40.0118	.0630
37	42.6880	.0715
38	45.6301	.0811
39	48.8772	.0921
40	52.4804	.1062
41	56.5153	.1215
42	61.0512	.1404
43	66.1944	.1632
44	72.0799	.1908
45	78.8749	.2250
46	86.8024	.2674
47	96.1538	.3205

13th Year—D. or 65.

Age.	Value.	M. Diff.
10	9.1898	−.0259
11	9.5759	.0253
12	9.9808	.0249
13	10.3901	.0231
14	10.8351	.0226
15	11.2937	.0220
16	11.7758	.0207
17	12.2807	.0196
18	12.8138	.0188
19	13.3720	.0175
20	13.9599	.0163
21	14.5830	.0150
22	15.2403	.0136
23	15.9352	.0120
24	16.6716	.0102
25	17.4535	.0087
26	18.2828	.0066
27	19.1667	.0044
28	20.1080	.0020
29	21.1164	+.0006
30	22.1959	.0033
31	23.3477	.0061
32	24.5834	.0082
33	25.8975	.0113
34	27.3064	.0135
35	28.8078	.0160
36	30.4104	.0189
37	32.1285	.0223
38	33.9761	.0260
39	35.9680	.0298
40	38.1215	.0357
41	40.4733	.0410
42	43.0397	.0480
43	45.8607	+.0564
44	48.9880	.0665
45	52.4755	.0791
46	56.3973	.0946
47	60.8439	.1139
48	65.9247	.1378
49	71.7795	.1680
50	78.5927	.2066
51	86.6079	.2562
52	96.1538	.3205

13th Year—D. or 70.

Age.	Value.	M. Diff.
10	8.2034	−.0299
11	8.5321	.0294
12	8.8708	.0288
13	9.2233	.0283
14	9.5958	.0276
15	9.9762	.0271
16	10.3782	.0264
17	10.7963	.0257
18	11.2352	.0252
19	11.6943	.0251
20	12.1689	.0232
21	12.6798	.0228
22	13.2115	.0219
23	13.7708	.0211
24	14.3594	.0198
25	14.9819	.0191
26	15.6361	.0174
27	16.3334	.0164
28	17.0656	.0148
29	17.8491	.0133
30	18.6804	.0117
31	19.5620	.0103
32	20.4996	.0095
33	21.4854	.0081
34	22.5309	.0078
35	23.6245	.0074
36	24.7750	.0069
37	25.9865	.0063
38	27.2648	.0058
39	28.6142	.0057
40	30.0404	.0042
41	31.5628	.0038
42	33.1800	.0025
43	34.9117	.0011
44	36.7791	+.0007
45	38.8008	.0036
46	41.0113	.0072
47	43.4424	.0120
48	46.1310	.0182
49	49.1250	.0264
50	52.4799	.0371
51	56.2680	.0516
52	60.5947	.0708
53	65.5698	.0964
54	71.3630	.1305
55	78.1834	.1761
56	86.3169	.2375
57	96.1538	.3205

13th Year—D. or 75.

Age.	Value.	M. Diff.
10	7.6174	−.0323
11	7.9113	.0318
12	8.2155	.0314
13	8.5341	.0311
14	8.8622	.0306
15	9.1995	.0302
16	9.5564	.0297
17	9.9241	.0292
18	10.3093	.0289
19	10.7101	.0284
20	11.1304	.0279
21	11.5678	.0274
22	12.0279	.0268
23	12.5103	.0262
24	13.0178	.0255
25	13.5494	.0251
26	14.1057	.0241
27	14.6954	.0234
28	15.3153	.0222
29	15.9749	.0217
30	16.6658	.0199
31	17.4052	.0196
32	18.1800	.0197
33	18.9895	.0190
34	19.8392	.0200
35	20.7168	.0205
36	21.6305	.0215
37	22.5742	.0222
38	23.5584	.0234
39	24.5786	−.0252
40	25.6324	.0257
41	26.7404	.0263
42	27.8881	.0297
43	29.0868	.0317
44	30.3446	.0338
45	31.6737	.0358
46	33.0864	.0379
47	34.5962	.0398
48	36.2195	.0418
49	37.9676	.0434
50	39.8604	.0446
51	41.9186	.0452
52	44.1835	.0444
53	46.6800	.0421
54	49.4664	.0373
55	52.6050	.0296
56	56.1733	.0169
57	60.2850	+.0022
58	65.0820	.0300
59	70.7553	.0698
60	77.5648	.1264
61	85.8660	.2067
62	96.1538	.3205

14th YEAR—D. or 35.

Age.	Value.	M. Diff.
10	40.8116	+.0995
11	43.6029	.1102
12	46.6634	.1219
13	50.0309	.1350
14	53.7494	.1495
15	57.8741	.1657
16	62.4709	.1839
17	67.6201	.2044
18	73.4208	.2277
19	79.9975	.2543
20	87.5075	.2849
21	96.1538	.3205

14th Year—D. or 40.

Age.	Value.	M. Diff.
10	29.9888	+.0563
11	31.8186	.0630
12	33.7968	.0703
13	35.9412	.0783
14	38.2730	.0871
15	40.8123	.0967
16	43.5939	.1073
17	46.6417	.1190
18	49.9986	.1320
19	53.7092	.1466
20	57.8268	.1628
21	62.4204	.1812
22	67.5677	.2020
23	73.3718	.2256
24	79.9571	.2528
25	87.4826	.2841
26	96.1538	.3205

14th Year—D. or 45.

Age.	Value.	M. Diff.
10	22.7370	+.0273
11	23.9958	.0319
12	25.3519	.0364
13	26.8028	.0416
14	28.3633	.0471
15	30.0422	.0532
16	31.8586	.0597
17	33.8209	.0668
18	35.9506	.0747
19	38.2672	.0833
20	40.7953	.0929
21	43.5610	.1034
22	46.5980	.1151
23	49.9437	.1282
24	53.6453	.1426
25	57.7560	.1593
26	62.3462	.1778
27	67.4954	.1990
28	73.3042	.2232
29	79.9036	.2508
30	87.4505	.2829
31	96.1538	.3205

14th Year—D. or 50.

Age.	Value.	M. Diff.
10	17.7112	+.0072
11	18.6202	.0102
12	19.5831	.0133
13	20.6092	.0167
14	21.7043	+.0202
15	22.8686	.0241
16	24.1189	.0283
17	25.4562	.0328
18	26.8917	.0377
19	28.4384	.0430
20	30.1023	.0488
21	31.9013	.0552
22	33.8508	.0623
23	35.9660	.0701
24	38.2707	.0782
25	40.7823	.0880
26	43.5369	.0985
27	46.5632	.1102
28	49.9009	.1234
29	53.5975	.1378
30	57.7041	.1547
31	62.2941	.1729
32	67.4423	.1940
33	73.2532	.2184
34	79.8553	.2468
35	87.4165	.2804
36	96.1538	.3205

14th Year—D. or 55.

Age.	Value.	M. Diff.
10	14.1859	−.0069
11	14.8603	.0049
12	15.5728	.0028
13	16.3265	.0006
14	17.1238	+.0018
15	17.9679	.0042
16	18.8663	.0070
17	19.8189	.0099
18	20.8351	.0130
19	21.9173	.0163
20	23.0756	.0199
21	24.3124	.0239
22	25.6397	.0282
23	27.0660	.0330
24	28.6032	.0379
25	30.2569	.0437
26	32.0480	.0500
27	33.9893	.0568
28	36.0991	.0646
29	38.3995	.0728
30	40.9121	.0820
31	43.6615	.0915
32	46.6766	.1028
33	50.0014	.1146
34	53.6715	.1285
35	57.7473	.1443
36	62.2982	.1628
37	67.4100	.1844
38	73.1933	.2094
39	79.7793	.2404
40	87.3606	.2764
41	96.1538	.3205

14th Year—D. or 60.

Age.	Value.	M. Diff.
10	11.7210	−.0167
11	12.2406	.0153
12	12.7897	.0140
13	13.3646	.0124
14	13.9708	.0110
15	14.6067	.0093
16	15.2799	.0074
17	15.9910	.0059
18	16.7394	.0038
19	17.5349	.0017
20	18.3777	+.0006
21	19.2739	.0031
22	20.2251	.0058
23	21.2416	.0088
24	22.3270	.0116
25	23.4827	.0153
26	24.7234	.0191
27	26.0548	.0230
28	27.4849	.0280
29	29.0319	.0327
30	30.6979	.0378
31	32.4954	.0428
32	34.4352	.0489
33	36.5383	.0546
34	38.8133	.0613
35	41.2844	.0688
36	43.9794	.0775
37	46.9326	.0873
38	50.1818	.0984
39	53.7709	.1126
40	57.7762	.1278
41	62.2531	.1466
42	67.3039	+.1690
43	73.0442	.1961
44	79.6263	.2275
45	87.2450	.2699
46	96.1538	.3205

14th Year—D. or 65.

Age.	Value.	M. Diff.
10	10.0386	−.0235
11	10.4592	.0230
12	10.8971	.0210
13	11.3581	.0205
14	11.8401	.0196
15	12.3415	.0185
16	12.8712	.0172
17	13.4263	.0163
18	14.0085	.0150
19	14.6221	.0136
20	15.2679	.0122
21	15.9524	.0106
22	16.6741	.0090
23	17.4382	.0070
24	18.2498	.0054
25	19.1064	.0031
26	20.0216	.0008
27	20.9951	+.0018
28	22.0335	.0045
29	23.1442	.0074
30	24.3327	.0103
31	25.5988	.0126
32	26.9461	.0160
33	28.3911	.0184
34	29.9258	.0211
35	31.5633	.0242
36	33.3152	.0278
37	35.1967	.0317
38	37.2214	.0358
39	39.4032	.0420
40	41.7840	.0476
41	44.3701	.0548
42	47.2071	.0635
43	50.3334	.0738
44	53.8068	.0865
45	57.6928	.1020
46	62.0738	.1211
47	67.0542	.1446
48	72.7591	.1742
49	79.3550	.2115
50	87.0576	.2592
51	96.1538	.3205

14th Year—D. or 70.

Age.	Value.	M. Diff.
10	8.9480	−.0278
11	9.3057	.0271
12	9.6766	.0265
13	10.0619	.0257
14	10.4699	.0251
15	10.8851	.0243
16	11.3263	.0235
17	11.7848	.0229
18	12.2629	.0225
19	12.7578	.0205
20	13.2923	.0203
21	13.8466	.0193
22	14.4305	.0186
23	15.0421	.0170
24	15.6909	.0161
25	16.3706	.0143
26	17.0947	.0134
27	17.8580	.0118
28	18.6650	.0098
29	19.5259	.0081
30	20.4384	.0065
31	21.4038	.0056
32	22.4206	.0040
33	23.4982	.0035
34	24.6260	.0029
35	25.8095	.0022
36	27.0559	.0013
37	28.3708	.0006
38	29.7579	.0001
39	31.2195	+.0016
40	32.7819	.0024
41	34.4371	.0039
42	36.2074	.0056
43	38.1043	.0078
44	40.1546	.0117
45	42.3860	.0150
46	44.8284	.0201
47	47.5220	.0266
48	50.5074	.0350
49	53.8411	.0459

ENDOWMENT POLICIES.—4 PER CENT.

14th Year—D. or 70.

Age.	Value.	M. Diff.
50	57.5805	+.0614
51	61.8449	.0796
52	66.7220	.1048
53	72.3615	.1382
54	78.9618	.1823
55	86.7767	.2414
56	96.1538	.3205

14th Year—D. or 75.

Age.	Value.	M. Diff.
10	8.2991	—.0302
11	8.6215	.0298
12	8.9525	.0294
13	9.2996	.0288
14	9.6588	.0284
15	10.0267	.0278
16	10.4169	.0272
17	10.8204	.0269
18	11.2389	.0263
19	11.6777	.0256
20	12.1378	.0251
21	12.6164	.0243
22	13.1211	.0237
23	13.6484	.0229
24	14.2048	.0223
25	14.7845	.0212
26	15.3978	.0205
27	16.0426	.0191
28	16.7268	.0185
29	17.4449	.0166
30	18.2121	.0161
31	19.0137	.0160
32	19.8492	.0152
33	20.7314	.0160
34	21.6386	.0163
35	22.5826	.0171
36	23.5618	.0176
37	24.5787	.0186
38	25.6357	.0201
39	26.7272	.0203
40	27.8741	.0223
41	29.0612	.0237
42	30.3021	.0254
43	31.5977	.0271
44	32.9616	.0287
45	34.4069	.0303
46	35.9452	.0319
47	37.5925	.0335
48	39.3633	.0347
49	41.2754	.0355
50	43.3519	.0356
51	45.6165	.0344
52	48.1205	.0316
53	50.8941	.0264
54	54.0084	.0183
55	57.5337	.0054
56	61.5764	+.0136
57	66.2698	.0411
58	71.7895	.0800
59	78.3733	.1348
60	86.3457	.2120
61	96.1538	.3205

15th YEAR—D. or 35.

Age.	Value.	M. Diff.
10	44.7632	+.1148
11	47.8319	.1266
12	51.1964	.1397
13	54.9000	.1541
14	58.9905	.1702
15	63.5288	.1882
16	68.5872	.2083
17	74.2550	.2311
18	80.6408	.2569
19	87.8826	.2865
20	96.1538	.3205

15th Year—D. or 40.

Age.	Value.	M. Diff.
10	32.8599	+.0672
11	34.8695	.0746
12	37.0432	.0828
13	39.4000	.0916
14	41.9636	.1013
15	44.7561	.1120
16	47.8147	.1238
17	51.1679	.1368
18	54.8614	.1513
19	58.9451	.1675
20	63.4782	.1848
21	68.5366	.2060
22	74.2066	.2275

15th Year—D. or 40.

Age.	Value.	M. Diff.
23	80.6008	+.2555
24	87.8582	.2857
25	96.1538	.3205

15th Year—D. or 45.

Age.	Value.	M. Diff.
10	24.8838	+.0353
11	26.2682	.0401
12	27.7539	.0454
13	29.3475	.0510
14	31.0608	.0572
15	32.9061	.0639
16	34.9014	.0712
17	37.0580	.0792
18	39.3999	.0879
19	41.9472	.0976
20	44.7289	.1073
21	47.7720	.1199
22	51.1151	.1331
23	54.7996	.1474
24	58.8742	.1640
25	63.4061	.1823
26	68.4639	.2031
27	74.1411	.2267
28	80.5477	.2536
29	87.8262	.2845
30	96.1538	.3205

15th Year—D. or 50.

Age.	Value.	M. Diff.
10	19.3563	+.0132
11	20.3527	.0164
12	21.4079	.0199
13	22.5342	.0235
14	23.7338	.0276
15	25.0125	.0319
16	26.3844	.0366
17	27.8527	.0416
18	29.4294	.0471
19	31.1275	.0531
20	32.9566	.0596
21	34.9341	.0667
22	37.0781	.0747
23	39.4065	.0829
24	41.9376	.0929
25	44.7069	.1034
26	47.7398	.1152
27	51.0737	.1284
28	54.7523	.1428
29	58.8237	.1595
30	63.3548	.1775
31	68.4109	.1983
32	74.0880	.2221
33	80.5001	.2497
34	87.7925	.2822
35	96.1538	.3205

15th Year—D. or 55.

Age.	Value.	M. Diff.
10	15.4783	—.0023
11	16.2170	.0002
12	16.9971	+.0021
13	17.8223	.0046
14	18.6951	.0072
15	19.6195	.0100
16	20.6045	.0131
17	21.6488	.0163
18	22.7629	.0198
19	23.9504	.0235
20	25.2201	.0276
21	26.5785	.0321
22	28.0363	.0371
23	29.6046	.0421
24	31.2899	.0481
25	33.1107	.0545
26	35.0816	.0614
27	37.2166	.0693
28	39.5409	.0777
29	42.0713	.0870
30	44.8358	.0966
31	47.8545	.1080
32	51.1754	.1199
33	54.8275	.1337
34	58.8677	.1495
35	63.3593	.1677
36	68.3815	.1890
37	74.0315	.2134
38	80.4277	.2436
39	87.7394	.2783
40	96.1538	.3205

15th Year—D. or 60.

Age.	Value.	M. Diff.
10	12.7678	—.0132
11	13.3359	.0118
12	13.9351	.0101
13	14.5645	.0086
14	15.2253	.0068
15	15.9220	.0048
16	16.6596	.0031
17	17.4342	.0009
18	18.2552	+.0013
19	19.1258	.0037
20	20.0487	.0063
21	21.0308	.0091
22	22.0738	.0123
23	23.1902	.0152
24	24.3767	.0190
25	25.6477	.0230
26	27.0104	.0271
27	28.4708	.0322
28	30.0485	.0370
29	31.7444	.0423
30	33.5719	.0475
31	35.5372	.0538
32	37.6665	.0596
33	39.9634	.0665
34	42.4537	.0742
35	45.1622	.0830
36	48.1214	.0930
37	51.3670	.1041
38	54.9404	.1183
39	58.9104	.1335
40	63.3315	.1521
41	68.2918	.1742
42	73.9001	.2006
43	80.2883	.2328
44	87.6324	.2721
45	96.1538	.3205

15th Year—D. or 65.

Age.	Value.	M. Diff.
10	10.9168	—.0211
11	11.3705	.0191
12	11.8594	.0188
13	12.3570	.0175
14	12.8813	.0163
15	13.4296	.0150
16	14.0087	.0139
17	14.6122	.0125
18	15.2489	.0110
19	15.9196	.0095
20	16.6258	.0079
21	17.3736	.0061
22	18.1632	.0040
23	19.0012	.0023
24	19.8859	+.0002
25	20.8268	.0026
26	21.8297	.0054
27	22.8981	.0082
28	24.0365	.0112
29	25.2536	.0143
30	26.5533	.0168
31	27.9280	.0203
32	29.4025	.0229
33	30.9692	.0250
34	32.6355	.0291
35	34.4172	.0329
36	36.3265	.0371
37	38.3783	.0414
38	40.5850	.0478
39	42.9850	.0536
40	45.5891	.0611
41	48.4331	.0699
42	51.5602	.0804
43	55.0147	.0932
44	58.8650	.1086
45	63.1843	.1275
46	68.0678	.1507
47	73.6333	.1796
48	80.0302	.2159
49	87.4525	.2619
50	96.1538	.3205

15th Year—D. or 70.

Age.	Value.	M. Diff.
10	9.7178	—.0254
11	10.1075	.0247
12	10.5109	.0244
13	10.9313	.0233
14	11.3735	.0224
15	11.8271	.0215
16	12.3082	.0208
17	12.8059	.0202
18	13.3227	.0185
19	13.8765	.0187
20	14.4507	.0167

15th Year—D. or 70.

Age.	Value.	M. Diff.
21	15.0563	—.0158
22	15.6882	.0140
23	16.3625	.0133
24	17.0672	.0114
25	17.8159	.0105
26	18.6001	.0083
27	19.4367	.0065
28	20.3243	.0047
29	21.2648	.0029
30	22.2592	.0019
31	23.3018	.0001
32	24.4082	+.0005
33	25.5657	.0013
34	26.7808	.0023
35	28.0573	.0033
36	29.4037	.0043
37	30.8239	.0050
38	32.3191	.0071
39	33.9123	.0081
40	35.6020	.0099
41	37.4031	.0124
42	39.3324	.0144
43	41.4045	.0180
44	43.6618	.0217
45	46.1080	.0276
46	48.8007	.0343
47	51.7758	.0429
48	55.0849	.0540
49	58.7925	.0687
50	62.9826	.0875
51	67.7568	.1124
52	73.2579	.1451
53	79.6546	.1879
54	87.1829	.2450
55	96.1538	.3205

15th Year—D. or 75.

Age.	Value.	M. Diff.
10	9.0062	—.0283
11	9.3550	.0278
12	9.7143	.0271
13	10.0922	.0266
14	10.4817	.0260
15	10.8825	.0253
16	11.3081	.0249
17	11.7444	.0242
18	12.2005	.0235
19	12.6786	.0228
20	13.1794	.0220
21	13.7020	.0213
22	14.2510	.0204
23	14.8263	.0197
24	15.4301	.0185
25	16.0659	.0176
26	16.7333	.0162
27	17.4415	.0154
28	18.1831	.0134
29	18.9761	.0128
30	19.8042	.0126
31	20.6651	.0116
32	21.5717	.0122
33	22.5098	.0124
34	23.4816	.0130
35	24.4892	.0133
36	25.5394	.0140
37	26.6268	.0153
38	27.7524	.0153
39	28.9341	.0170
40	30.1569	.0180
41	31.4337	.0195
42	32.7675	.0208
43	34.1649	.0221
44	35.6402	.0233
45	37.2058	.0245
46	38.8758	.0257
47	40.6642	.0267
48	42.5917	.0269
49	44.6791	.0266
50	46.9519	.0250
51	49.4449	.0218
52	52.2119	.0163
53	55.2972	.0080
54	58.7781	+.0051
55	62.7529	.0241
56	67.3457	.0511
57	72.7209	.0892
58	79.0973	.1424
59	86.7723	.2167
60	96.1538	.3205

16th YEAR—D. or 35.

Age.	Value.	M. Diff.
10	48.8988	+.1309
11	52.2579	.1439

16th Year—D. or 35.

Age.	Value.	M. Diff.
12	55.9425	+.1583
13	59.9989	.1743
14	64.4803	.1920
15	69.4530	.2119
16	74.9972	.2341
17	81.2100	.2593
18	88.2119	.2878
19	96.1538	.3205

16th Year—D. or 40.

Age.	Value.	M. Diff.
10	35.8615	+.0786
11	38.0601	.0868
12	40.4388	.0958
13	43.0187	.1056
14	45.8252	.1163
15	48.8835	.1281
16	52.2336	.1412
17	55.9076	.1556
18	59.9552	.1716
19	64.4320	.1895
20	69.4026	.2096
21	74.9505	.2322
22	81.1707	.2579
23	88.1879	.2871
24	96.1538	.3205

16th Year—D. or 45.

Age.	Value.	M. Diff.
10	27.1265	+.0435
11	28.6390	.0490
12	30.2638	.0547
13	32.0053	.0611
14	33.8794	.0679
15	35.8987	.0753
16	38.0825	.0834
17	40.4437	.0922
18	43.0078	.1019
19	45.7984	.1126
20	48.8358	.1252
21	52.1820	.1375
22	55.8481	.1518
23	59.8863	.1683
24	64.3599	.1863
25	69.3323	.2068
26	74.8849	.2299
27	81.1196	.2560
28	88.1563	.2860
29	96.1538	.3205

16th Year—D. or 50.

Age.	Value.	M. Diff.
10	21.0724	+.0193
11	22.1592	.0230
12	23.3127	.0267
13	24.5411	.0309
14	25.8523	.0353
15	27.2499	.0401
16	28.7496	.0463
17	30.3553	.0508
18	32.0792	.0570
19	33.9375	.0636
20	35.9396	.0709
21	38.1053	.0790
22	40.4551	.0873
23	43.0013	.0973
24	45.7804	.1079
25	48.8163	.1198
26	52.1433	.1321
27	55.8021	.1473
28	59.8365	.1639
29	64.3099	.1817
30	69.2800	.2022
31	74.8328	.2254
32	81.0710	.2523
33	88.1233	.2837
34	96.1538	.3205

16th Year—D. or 55.

Age.	Value.	M. Diff.
10	16.8253	+.0022
11	17.6295	.0047
12	18.4797	.0073
13	19.3798	.0100
14	20.3318	.0129
15	21.3407	.0161
16	22.4156	.0194
17	23.5558	.0230
18	24.7724	.0269
19	26.0694	.0312
20	27.4576	.0357

ENDOWMENT POLICIES.—4 PER CENT.

16th Year—D. or 55.

Age.	Value.	M. Diff.
21	28.9431	+.0408
22	30.5392	.0459
23	32.2520	.0521
24	34.0990	.0587
25	36.0938	.0658
26	38.2521	.0737
27	40.5936	.0822
28	43.1400	.0916
29	45.9126	.1013
30	48.9350	.1128
31	52.2462	.1246
32	55.8787	.1385
33	59.8823	.1541
34	64.3160	.1723
35	69.2521	.1931
36	74.7791	.2170
37	81.0016	.2464
38	88.0727	.2799
39	96.1538	.3205

16th Year—D. or 60.

Age.	Value.	M. Diff.
10	13.8562	—.0097
11	14.4737	.0080
12	15.1267	.0063
13	15.8099	.0044
14	16.5307	.0024
15	17.2907	.0006
16	18.0907	+.0018
17	18.9367	.0041
18	19.8315	.0066
19	20.7808	.0093
20	21.7879	.0122
21	22.8599	.0155
22	24.0008	.0186
23	25.2159	.0225
24	26.5151	.0266
25	27.9051	.0308
26	29.3933	.0362
27	30.9976	.0411
28	32.7200	.0465
29	34.5725	.0518
30	36.5622	.0583
31	38.7109	.0643
32	41.0267	.0713
33	43.5307	.0791
34	46.2488	.0881
35	49.2103	.0981
36	52.4488	.1093
37	56.0027	.1235
38	59.9382	.1387
39	64.3015	.1571
40	69.1781	.1789
41	74.6621	.2048
42	80.8759	.2361
43	87.9738	.2740
44	96.1538	.3205

16th Year—D. or 65.

Age.	Value.	M. Diff.
10	11.8236	—.0173
11	12.3275	.0166
12	12.8480	.0151
13	13.3917	.0142
14	13.9623	.0128
15	14.5595	.0117
16	15.1862	.0101
17	15.8435	.0086
18	16.5364	.0069
19	17.2665	.0052
20	18.0350	.0033
21	18.8496	.0012
22	19.7118	+.0007
23	20.6215	.0033
24	21.5890	.0058
25	22.6158	.0087
26	23.7116	.0117
27	24.8778	.0148
28	26.1201	.0180
29	27.4457	.0206
30	28.8510	.0243
31	30.3495	.0271
32	31.9422	.0302
33	33.6362	.0337
34	35.4420	.0377
35	37.3757	.0421
36	39.4491	.0466
37	41.6757	.0531
38	44.0922	.0591
39	46.7060	.0668
40	49.5565	.0758
41	52.6772	.0864
42	56.1161	.0992
43	59.9287	+.1147
44	64.1892	.1334
45	68.9830	.1563
46	74.4177	.1845
47	80.6326	.2198
48	87.8022	.2642
49	96.1538	.3205

16th Year—D. or 70.

Age.	Value.	M. Diff.
10	10.5158	—.0231
11	10.9581	.0222
12	11.3757	.0215
13	11.8201	.0197
14	12.3101	.0195
15	12.8037	.0192
16	13.3230	.0182
17	13.8587	.0163
18	14.4310	.0156
19	15.0167	.0135
20	15.6520	.0133
21	16.3077	.0117
22	17.0013	.0106
23	17.7272	.0087
24	18.4998	.0076
25	19.3076	.0053
26	20.1684	.0034
27	21.0796	.0014
28	22.0450	+.0004
29	23.0663	.0016
30	24.1355	.0027
31	25.2657	.0043
32	26.4498	.0054
33	27.6919	.0065
34	29.0975	.0077
35	30.3712	.0089
36	31.8194	.0098
37	33.3439	.0121
38	34.9672	.0133
39	36.6827	.0153
40	38.5123	.0177
41	40.4714	.0201
42	42.5628	.0244
43	44.8271	.0270
44	47.2904	.0345
45	49.9813	.0414
46	52.9427	.0502
47	56.2261	.0614
48	59.8908	.0761
49	64.0165	.0948
50	68.6983	.1193
51	74.0633	.1511
52	80.2765	.1928
53	87.5442	.2480
54	96.1538	.3205

16th Year—D. or 75.

Age.	Value.	M. Diff.
10	9.7365	—.0262
11	10.1134	.0255
12	10.5032	.0250
13	10.9109	.0243
14	11.3329	.0235
15	11.7689	.0230
16	12.2267	.0231
17	12.7003	.0215
18	13.1952	.0207
19	13.7135	.0198
20	14.2576	.0190
21	14.8239	.0180
22	15.4203	.0173
23	16.0424	.0159
24	16.7013	.0150
25	17.3904	.0134
26	18.1201	.0125
27	18.8845	.0104
28	19.6999	.0097
29	20.5525	.0093
30	21.4385	.0082
31	22.3693	.0087
32	23.3303	.0087
33	24.3312	.0091
34	25.3649	.0092
35	26.4415	.0097
36	27.5600	.0108
37	28.7137	.0106
38	29.9268	.0120
39	31.1815	.0128
40	32.4907	.0139
41	33.8567	.0149
42	35.2881	.0159
43	36.7925	.0167
44	38.3832	.0176
45	40.0751	—.0185
46	41.8802	.0190
47	43.8187	.0189
48	45.9139	.0183
49	48.1887	.0163
50	50.6792	.0128
51	53.4235	.0070
52	56.4869	+.0016
53	59.9211	.0148
54	63.8292	.0336
55	68.3259	.0603
56	73.5645	.0975
57	79.7493	.1492
58	87.1543	.2209
59	96.1538	.3205

17th YEAR—D. or 35.

Age.	Value.	M. Diff.
10	53.2271	+.1478
11	56.8919	.1622
12	60.9125	.1780
13	65.3397	.1955
14	70.2317	.2150
15	75.6617	.2368
16	81.7165	.2614
17	88.5033	.2890
18	96.1538	.3205

17th Year—D. or 40.

Age.	Value.	M. Diff.
10	39.0004	+.0906
11	41.3972	.0997
12	43.9912	.1095
13	46.8051	.1203
14	49.8668	.1321
15	53.2047	.1451
16	56.8610	.1595
17	60.8723	.1754
18	65.2931	.1931
19	70.1835	.2129
20	75.6154	.2349
21	81.6785	.2600
22	88.4798	.2883
23	96.1538	.3205

17th Year—D. or 45.

Age.	Value.	M. Diff.
10	29.4677	+.0523
11	31.1165	.0581
12	32.8851	.0642
13	34.7836	.0716
14	36.8265	.0791
15	39.0281	.0873
16	41.4096	.0962
17	43.9853	.1059
18	46.7836	.1167
19	49.8297	.1285
20	53.1580	.1416
21	56.8028	.1558
22	60.8057	.1721
23	65.2230	.1900
24	70.1135	.2101
25	75.5520	.2327
26	81.6273	.2582
27	88.4492	.2872
28	96.1538	.3205

17th Year—D. or 50.

Age.	Value.	M. Diff.
10	22.8617	+.0258
11	24.0448	.0296
12	25.2983	.0339
13	26.6361	.0385
14	28.0633	.0434
15	29.5857	.0487
16	31.2192	.0544
17	32.9683	.0606
18	34.8481	.0674
19	36.8741	.0748
20	39.0587	.0830
21	41.4236	.0914
22	43.9835	.1015
23	46.7687	.1121
24	49.8040	.1240
25	53.1219	.1371
26	56.7595	.1514
27	60.7573	.1678
28	65.1739	.1855
29	70.0625	.2056
30	75.5007	.2284
31	81.5798	.2546
32	88.4161	.2850
33	96.1538	.3205

17th Year—D. or 55.

Age.	Value.	M. Diff.
10	18.2269	+.0071
11	19.1008	.0097
12	20.0243	.0126
13	21.0020	.0157
14	22.0371	.0189
15	23.1341	.0223
16	24.3029	.0261
17	25.5436	.0301
18	26.8676	.0344
19	28.2803	.0391
20	29.7923	.0444
21	31.4127	.0496
22	33.1488	.0559
23	35.0188	.0626
24	37.0354	.0697
25	39.2120	.0778
26	41.5698	.0864
27	44.1252	.0959
28	46.9054	.1056
29	49.9257	.1171
30	53.2285	.1290
31	56.8376	.1428
32	60.8050	.1584
33	65.1823	.1762
34	70.0381	.1967
35	75.4497	.2202
36	81.5136	.2489
37	88.3677	.2814
38	96.1538	.3205

17th Year—D. or 60.

Age.	Value.	M. Diff.
10	14.9869	—.0059
11	15.6576	.0042
12	16.3636	.0022
13	17.1058	.0000
14	17.8890	+.0019
15	18.7105	.0043
16	19.5806	.0067
17	20.4992	.0093
18	21.4714	.0121
19	22.5033	.0152
20	23.5986	.0186
21	24.7665	.0218
22	26.0039	.0258
23	27.3293	.0301
24	28.7447	.0344
25	30.2572	.0382
26	31.8858	.0449
27	33.6308	.0504
28	35.5052	.0559
29	37.5150	.0625
30	39.6823	.0686
31	42.0111	.0757
32	44.5266	.0837
33	47.2497	.0927
34	50.2106	.1028
35	53.4395	.1141
36	56.9724	.1283
37	60.8718	.1434
38	65.1805	.1616
39	69.9753	.1831
40	75.3458	.2084
41	81.3990	.2390
42	88.2767	.2758
43	96.1538	.3205

17th Year—D. or 65.

Age.	Value.	M. Diff.
10	12.7755	—.0148
11	13.3149	.0136
12	13.8810	.0122
13	14.4661	.0108
14	15.0849	.0095
15	15.7291	.0079
16	16.4089	.0063
17	17.1215	.0045
18	17.8730	.0027
19	18.6644	.0007
20	19.4986	+.0015
21	20.3845	.0035
22	21.3172	.0062
23	22.3081	.0088
24	23.3598	.0118
25	24.4777	.0149
26	25.6693	.0182
27	26.9370	.0216
28	28.2854	.0243
29	29.7139	.0281
30	31.2398	.0311
31	32.8532	.0343
32	34.5694	.0380
33	36.3985	.0422
34	38.3514	+.0467
35	40.4435	.0514
36	42.6854	.0581
37	45.1143	.0643
38	47.7358	.0721
39	50.5858	.0812
40	53.7006	.0919
41	57.1190	.1048
42	60.8985	.1202
43	65.1010	.1388
44	69.8111	.1613
45	75.1260	.1890
46	81.1733	.2233
47	88.1143	.2663
48	96.1538	.3205

17th Year—D. or 70.

Age.	Value.	M. Diff.
10	11.3420	—.0206
11	11.7981	.0198
12	12.2697	.0187
13	12.7616	.0177
14	13.2816	.0169
15	13.8173	.0166
16	14.3692	.0142
17	14.9597	.0134
18	15.5731	.0121
19	16.2191	.0110
20	16.8937	.0093
21	17.6075	.0081
22	18.3551	.0060
23	19.1478	.0048
24	19.9785	.0024
25	20.8616	.0004
26	21.7956	+.0016
27	22.7831	.0036
28	23.8271	.0050
29	24.9214	.0071
30	26.0770	.0079
31	27.2829	.0091
32	28.5497	.0104
33	29.8799	.0120
34	31.2794	.0132
35	32.7518	.0143
36	34.3011	.0168
37	35.9487	.0183
38	37.6891	.0206
39	39.5402	.0232
40	41.5169	.0263
41	43.6318	.0303
42	45.9129	.0351
43	48.3577	.0428
44	51.0712	.0480
45	54.0200	.0570
46	57.2759	.0683
47	60.8984	.0829
48	64.9617	.1014
49	69.5541	.1256
50	74.7954	.1568
51	80.8340	.1974
52	87.8685	.2506
53	96.1538	.3205

17th Year—D. or 75.

Age.	Value.	M. Diff.
10	10.4915	—.0240
11	10.8986	.0234
12	11.3180	.0226
13	11.7579	.0217
14	12.2146	.0212
15	12.6825	.0204
16	13.1771	.0195
17	13.6891	.0187
18	14.2237	.0177
19	14.7849	.0168
20	15.3720	.0157
21	15.9851	.0149
22	16.6274	.0135
23	17.3039	.0124
24	18.0152	.0107
25	18.7657	.0098
26	19.5507	.0076
27	20.3878	.0067
28	21.2616	.0062
29	22.1709	.0050
30	23.1253	.0053
31	24.1090	.0052
32	25.1314	.0054
33	26.1925	.0053
34	27.2934	.0057
35	28.4363	.0066
36	29.6188	.0061
37	30.8576	.0073

ENDOWMENT POLICIES.—4 PER CENT.

17th Year—D. or 75.

AGE.	Value.	M. Diff.
38	32.1411	−.0079
39	33.4790	.0087
40	34.8742	.0095
41	36.3340	.0101
42	37.8681	.0107
43	39.4839	.0112
44	41.1952	.0117
45	43.0165	.0119
46	44.9656	.0115
47	47.0647	.0105
48	49.3392	.0082
49	51.8223	.0044
50	54.5526	+.0017
51	57.5806	.0104
52	60.9761	.0237
53	64.8177	.0424
54	69.2227	.0687
55	74.3332	.1051
56	80.3399	.1554
57	87.4983	.2248
58	96.1538	.3205

18th YEAR—D. or 35.

AGE.	Value.	M. Diff.
10	57.7588	+.1656
11	61.7446	.1814
12	66.1184	.1987
13	70.9351	.2179
14	76.2593	.2393
15	82.1700	.2632
16	88.7626	.2901
17	96.1538	.3205

18th Year—D. or 40.

AGE.	Value.	M. Diff.
10	42.2835	+.1033
11	44.8886	.1132
12	47.7083	.1240
13	50.7680	.1358
14	54.0981	.1488
15	57.7298	.1631
16	61.7081	.1789
17	66.0750	.1963
18	70.8885	.2149
19	76.2149	.2375
20	82.1324	.2619
21	88.7399	.2894
22	96.1538	.3205

18th Year—D. or 45.

AGE.	Value.	M. Diff.
10	31.9148	+.0614
11	33.7038	.0679
12	35.6200	.0754
13	37.6879	.0826
14	39.9077	.0908
15	42.3009	.0998
16	44.8900	.1096
17	47.6918	.1204
18	50.7364	.1322
19	54.0527	.1453
20	57.6763	.1594
21	61.6430	.1756
22	66.0071	.1933
23	70.8203	.2131
24	76.1520	.2353
25	82.0829	.2601
26	88.7095	.2884
27	96.1538	.3205

18th Year—D. or 50.

AGE.	Value.	M. Diff.
10	24.7294	+.0324
11	26.0105	.0368
12	27.3711	.0415
13	28.8224	.0465
14	30.3715	.0519
15	32.0247	.0577
16	33.7979	.0640
17	35.6987	.0709
18	37.7418	.0784
19	39.9449	.0867
20	42.3225	.0951
21	44.8905	.1053
22	47.6813	.1160
23	50.7134	.1278
24	54.0198	.1409
25	57.6354	.1551
26	61.5971	.1715
27	65.9594	.1889
28	70.7705	.2087
29	76.1021	+.2311
30	82.0363	.2567
31	88.6772	.2862
32	96.1538	.3205

18th Year—D. or 55.

AGE.	Value.	M. Diff.
10	19.6867	+.0121
11	20.6326	.0151
12	21.6329	.0182
13	22.6927	.0215
14	23.8138	.0251
15	25.0031	.0289
16	26.2703	.0331
17	27.6167	.0375
18	29.0530	.0424
19	30.5871	.0477
20	32.2307	.0531
21	33.9876	.0594
22	35.8774	.0662
23	37.9117	.0735
24	40.1046	.0816
25	42.4746	.0903
26	45.0399	.0998
27	47.8212	.1096
28	50.8392	.1212
29	54.1292	.1330
30	57.7171	.1468
31	61.6465	.1622
32	65.9701	.1799
33	70.7477	.2002
34	76.0534	.2232
35	81.9725	.2512
36	88.6309	.2827
37	96.1538	.3205

18th Year—D. or 60.

AGE.	Value.	M. Diff.
10	16.1633	−.0022
11	16.8863	.0001
12	17.6506	+.0022
13	18.4544	.0041
14	19.2980	.0067
15	20.1886	.0092
16	21.1301	.0119
17	22.1247	.0148
18	23.1781	.0180
19	24.2965	.0215
20	25.4860	.0248
21	26.7483	.0290
22	28.0938	.0333
23	29.5328	.0378
24	31.0678	.0433
25	32.7174	.0485
26	34.4831	.0541
27	36.3760	.0597
28	38.4031	.0664
29	40.5852	.0727
30	42.9267	.0799
31	45.4485	.0879
32	48.1752	.0970
33	51.1321	.1072
34	54.3498	.1185
35	57.8605	.1327
36	61.7240	.1477
37	65.9790	.1657
38	70.6978	.1868
39	75.9607	.2118
40	81.8684	.2416
41	88.5465	.2773
42	96.1538	.3205

18th Year—D. or 65.

AGE.	Value.	M. Diff.
10	13.7577	−.0119
11	14.3378	.0104
12	14.9490	.0088
13	15.5819	.0075
14	16.2470	.0058
15	16.9435	.0041
16	17.6779	.0022
17	18.4483	.0003
18	19.2601	+.0017
19	20.1162	.0041
20	21.0207	.0062
21	21.9758	.0089
22	22.9883	.0117
23	24.0619	.0148
24	25.2029	.0180
25	26.4147	.0214
26	27.7056	.0249
27	29.0771	.0278
28	30.5259	+.0317
29	32.0721	.0348
30	33.7095	.0382
31	35.4431	.0420
32	37.2904	.0464
33	39.2621	.0510
34	41.3683	.0558
35	43.6229	.0627
36	46.0603	.0690
37	48.6862	.0770
38	51.5348	.0862
39	54.6383	.0969
40	58.0379	.1098
41	61.7816	.1252
42	65.9324	.1436
43	70.5625	.1658
44	75.7669	.1930
45	81.6614	.2265
46	88.3943	.2682
47	96.1538	.3205

18th Year—D. or 70.

AGE.	Value.	M. Diff.
10	12.1983	−.0181
11	12.6877	.0171
12	13.1965	.0159
13	13.7274	.0150
14	14.2841	.0143
15	14.8526	.0122
16	15.4633	.0114
17	16.0947	.0100
18	16.7575	.0087
19	17.4522	.0079
20	18.1840	.0057
21	18.9509	.0035
22	19.7643	.0022
23	20.6142	.0011
24	21.5189	+.0024
25	22.4739	.0045
26	23.4829	.0067
27	24.5475	.0081
28	25.6636	.0103
29	26.8425	.0113
30	28.0711	.0127
31	29.3577	.0141
32	30.7099	.0157
33	32.1318	.0172
34	33.6272	.0185
35	35.1973	.0212
36	36.8662	.0256
37	38.6278	.0254
38	40.4989	.0282
39	42.4915	.0315
40	45.6236	.0358
41	46.9151	.0408
42	49.3907	.0468
43	52.0775	.0541
44	55.0146	.0632
45	58.2457	.0745
46	61.8255	.0891
47	65.8280	.1075
48	70.3360	.1313
49	75.4611	.1619
50	81.3421	.2015
51	88.1598	.2531
52	96.1538	.3205

18th Year—D. or 75.

AGE.	Value.	M. Diff.
10	11.2733	−.0218
11	11.7096	.0210
12	12.1609	.0201
13	12.6352	.0195
14	13.1234	.0186
15	13.6278	.0177
16	14.1603	.0167
17	14.7115	.0157
18	15.2884	.0147
19	15.8921	.0136
20	16.5254	.0126
21	17.1838	.0116
22	17.8798	.0100
23	18.6079	.0082
24	19.3797	.0072
25	20.1844	.0048
26	21.0410	.0039
27	21.9354	.0033
28	22.8647	.0019
29	23.8411	.0021
30	24.8472	.0018
31	25.8908	.0019
32	26.9719	.0017
33	28.0984	.0019
34	29.2638	−.0026
35	30.4688	.0020
36	31.7340	.0029
37	33.0408	.0033
38	34.4046	.0039
39	35.8255	.0043
40	37.3110	.0047
41	38.8697	.0050
42	40.5101	.0051
43	42.2417	.0054
44	44.0779	.0052
45	46.0373	.0046
46	48.1405	.0033
47	50.4116	.0007
48	52.8856	+.0034
49	55.5983	.0097
50	58.6000	.0186
51	61.9460	.0318
52	65.7301	.0505
53	70.0462	.0764
54	75.0363	.1120
55	80.8780	.1610
56	87.8099	.2282
57	96.1538	.3205

19th YEAR—D. or 35.

AGE.	Value.	M. Diff.
10	62.5043	+.1844
11	66.8275	.2015
12	71.5724	.2205
13	76.7992	.2415
14	82.5778	.2649
15	88.9948	.2911
16	96.1538	.3205

19th Year—D. or 40.

AGE.	Value.	M. Diff.
10	45.7183	+.1165
11	48.5418	.1274
12	51.5987	.1392
13	54.9170	.1521
14	58.5291	.1663
15	62.4698	.1820
16	66.7876	.1993
17	71.5286	.2184
18	76.7562	.2397
19	82.5417	.2636
20	88.9723	.2904
21	96.1538	.3205

19th Year—D. or 45.

AGE.	Value.	M. Diff.
10	34.4704	+.0710
11	36.4085	.0782
12	38.4897	.0858
13	40.7244	.0942
14	43.1302	.1032
15	45.7245	.1130
16	48.5369	.1235
17	51.5719	.1357
18	54.8760	.1488
19	58.4774	.1628
20	62.4088	.1789
21	66.7214	.1963
22	71.4625	.2158
23	76.6948	.2376
24	82.4927	.2619
25	88.9430	.2894
26	96.1538	.3205

19th Year—D. or 50.

AGE.	Value.	M. Diff.
10	26.6764	+.0395
11	28.0625	.0443
12	29.5343	.0494
13	31.1049	.0549
14	32.7818	.0608
15	34.5714	.0672
16	36.4925	.0742
17	38.5522	.0817
18	40.7676	.0901
19	43.1581	.0986
20	45.7325	.1088
21	48.5241	.1195
22	51.5531	.1314
23	54.8465	.1444
24	58.4391	.1586
25	62.3655	.1748
26	66.6759	.1920
27	71.4141	.2115
28	76.6462	.2335
29	82.4474	+.2585
30	88.9114	.2873
31	96.1538	.3205

19th Year—D. or 55.

AGE.	Value.	M. Diff.
10	21.2071	+.0174
11	22.2288	.0206
12	23.3089	.0241
13	24.4534	.0277
14	25.6653	.0317
15	26.9513	.0359
16	28.3215	.0404
17	29.7779	.0454
18	31.3336	.0508
19	32.9964	.0562
20	34.7739	.0626
21	36.6798	.0696
22	38.7296	.0769
23	40.9354	.0851
24	43.3161	.0939
25	45.8872	.1034
26	48.6704	.1133
27	51.6817	.1249
28	54.9597	.1368
29	58.5232	.1505
30	62.4185	.1658
31	66.6887	.1833
32	71.3940	.2032
33	76.6003	.2258
34	82.3861	.2532
35	88.8668	.2839
36	96.1538	.3205

19th Year—D. or 60.

AGE.	Value.	M. Diff.
10	17.3843	+.0020
11	18.1649	.0043
12	18.9898	.0063
13	19.8531	.0090
14	20.7649	.0116
15	21.7258	.0144
16	22.7421	.0174
17	23.8164	.0206
18	24.9549	.0243
19	26.1657	.0277
20	27.4479	.0319
21	28.8161	.0363
22	30.2729	.0409
23	31.8287	.0466
24	33.4979	.0518
25	35.2810	.0576
26	37.1909	.0632
27	39.2322	.0700
28	41.4269	.0764
29	43.7778	.0837
30	46.3059	.0918
31	49.0319	.1010
32	51.9841	.1112
33	55.1882	.1225
34	58.6764	.1367
35	62.5045	.1516
36	66.7079	.1694
37	71.3541	.1903
38	76.5180	.2148
39	82.2905	.2439
40	88.7885	.2787
41	96.1538	.3205

19th Year—D. or 65.

AGE.	Value.	M. Diff.
10	14.7751	−.0086
11	15.3999	.0070
12	16.0583	.0056
13	16.7368	.0038
14	17.4536	.0020
15	18.2041	.0001
16	18.9953	+.0019
17	19.8252	.0041
18	20.7008	.0065
19	21.6261	.0087
20	22.5986	.0116
21	23.6321	.0145
22	24.7259	.0176
23	25.8872	.0209
24	27.1203	.0245
25	28.4295	.0280
26	29.8220	.0310
27	31.2915	.0351
28	32.8553	.0383
29	34.5102	.0418
30	36.2644	.0458

ENDOWMENT POLICIES.—4 PER CENT.

19th Year—D. or 65.

AGE.	Value.	M. Diff.
31	38.1255	+.0502
32	40.1113	.0550
33	42.2314	.0600
34	44.4948	.0670
35	46.9387	.0734
36	49.5660	.0815
37	52.4107	.0908
38	55.5029	.1016
39	58.8798	.1145
40	62.5907	.1298
41	66.6894	.1481
42	71.2477	.1699
43	76.3484	.1966
44	82.1031	.2294
45	88.6471	.2699
46	96.1538	.3205

19th Year—D. or 70.

AGE.	Value.	M. Diff.
10	13.0838	—.0150
11	13.6098	.0143
12	14.1572	.0124
13	14.7249	.0133
14	15.3181	.0103
15	15.9402	.0094
16	16.5913	.0079
17	17.2714	.0066
18	17.9826	.0048
19	18.7337	.0034
20	19.5175	.0012
21	20.3492	+.0002
22	21.2190	.0028
23	22.1518	.0042
24	23.1172	.0073
25	24.1458	.0095
26	25.2315	.0110
27	26.3656	.0134
28	27.5638	.0147
29	28.8141	.0161
30	30.1221	.0176
31	31.4921	.0193
32	32.9337	.0210
33	34.4487	.0225
34	36.0390	.0253
35	37.7254	.0272
36	39.5372	.0271
37	41.3925	.0329
38	43.4002	.0363
39	45.5422	.0409
40	47.8445	.0460
41	50.3235	.0523
42	53.0099	.0597
43	55.9329	.0689
44	59.1401	.0803
45	62.6813	.0957
46	66.6253	.1131
47	71.0534	.1366
48	76.0694	.1655
49	81.8040	.2052
50	88.4049	.2570
51	96.1538	.3205

19th Year—D. or 75.

AGE.	Value.	M. Diff.
10	12.0808	—.0195
11	12.5487	.0185
12	13.0340	.0179
13	13.5395	.0169
14	14.0637	.0159
15	14.6056	.0149
16	15.1773	.0138
17	15.7698	.0127
18	16.3887	.0115
19	17.0380	.0105
20	17.7159	.0089
21	18.4274	.0077
22	19.1742	.0058
23	19.9620	.0047
24	20.7871	.0023
25	21.6624	.0012
26	22.5753	.0005
27	23.5241	+.0010
28	24.5194	.0009
29	25.5461	.0013
30	26.6108	.0014
31	27.7117	.0017
32	28.8567	.0017
33	30.0458	.0012
34	31.2714	.0020
35	32.5570	.0012
36	33.8879	.0011
37	35.2725	.0007
38	36.7164	.0005
39	38.2245	+.0004
40	39.8052	.0003
41	41.4663	.0005
42	43.2186	.0005
43	45.0695	.0010
44	47.0384	.0019
45	49.1458	.0035
46	51.4139	.0064
47	53.8768	.0106
48	56.5711	.0172
49	59.5440	.0261
50	62.8500	.0395
51	66.5690	.0580
52	70.8064	.0835
53	75.6821	.1184
54	81.3703	.1661
55	88.0939	.2314
56	96.1538	.3205

20th YEAR—D. or 35.

AGE.	Value.	M. Diff.
10	67.4750	+.2042
11	72.1528	.2228
12	77.2882	.2435
13	82.9462	.2664
14	89.2036	.2919
15	96.1538	.3205

20th Year—D. or 40.

AGE.	Value.	M. Diff.
10	49.3124	+.1305
11	52.3652	.1423
12	55.6717	.1552
13	59.2616	.1693
14	63.1704	.1849
15	67.4369	.2019
16	72.1119	.2209
17	77.2476	.2418
18	82.9112	.2652
19	89.1820	.2912
20	96.1538	.3205

20th Year—D. or 45.

AGE.	Value.	M. Diff.
10	37.1418	+.0811
11	39.2360	.0889
12	41.4845	.0973
13	43.9000	.1064
14	46.5010	.1163
15	49.3064	.1272
16	52.3448	.1389
17	55.6357	.1519
18	59.2142	.1659
19	63.1112	.1818
20	67.3744	.1991
21	72.0474	.2191
22	77.1883	.2397
23	82.8636	.2635
24	89.1531	.2903
25	96.1538	.3205

20th Year—D. or 50.

AGE.	Value.	M. Diff.
10	28.7089	+.0469
11	30.2039	.0521
12	31.7927	.0577
13	33.4882	.0637
14	35.2984	.0702
15	37.2326	.0772
16	39.3086	.0849
17	41.5360	.0933
18	43.9337	.1019
19	46.5150	.1121
20	49.3063	.1228
21	52.3285	.1346
22	55.6098	.1477
23	59.1791	.1617
24	63.0704	.1778
25	67.3313	.1949
26	72.0011	.2141
27	77.1408	.2357
28	82.8194	.2602
29	89.1223	.2883
30	96.1538	.3205

20th Year—D. or 55.

AGE.	Value.	M. Diff.
10	22.7907	+.0229
11	23.8913	.0264
12	25.0552	.0302
13	26.2884	+.0342
14	27.5959	.0385
15	28.9826	.0431
16	30.4611	.0482
17	32.0339	.0539
18	33.7155	.0592
19	35.5082	.0658
20	37.4312	.0727
21	39.4941	.0802
22	41.7109	.0884
23	44.0993	.0973
24	46.6752	.1068
25	49.4576	.1167
26	52.4631	.1283
27	55.7257	.1401
28	59.2673	.1537
29	63.1264	.1691
30	67.3483	.1863
31	71.9835	.2060
32	77.0977	.2282
33	82.7606	.2551
34	89.0794	.2850
35	96.1538	.3205

20th Year—D. or 60.

AGE.	Value.	M. Diff.
10	18.6548	+.0063
11	19.4954	.0084
12	20.3789	.0111
13	21.3095	.0138
14	22.2904	.0167
15	23.3250	.0198
16	24.4197	.0231
17	25.5777	.0269
18	26.8070	.0304
19	28.1087	.0347
20	29.4947	.0392
21	30.9720	.0438
22	32.5433	.0496
23	34.2304	.0550
24	36.0299	.0608
25	37.9539	.0666
26	40.0081	.0735
27	42.2126	.0799
28	44.5711	.0873
29	47.1029	.0955
30	49.8287	.1048
31	52.7728	.1150
32	55.9634	.1263
33	59.4279	.1404
34	63.2216	.1552
35	67.3754	.1728
36	71.9531	.1934
37	77.0242	.2175
38	82.6731	.2460
39	89.0061	.2799
40	96.1538	.3205

20th Year—D. or 65.

AGE.	Value.	M. Diff.
10	15.8316	—.0052
11	16.5030	.0038
12	17.2063	.0019
13	17.9360	.0000
14	18.7060	+.0020
15	19.5126	.0041
16	20.3626	.0063
17	21.2553	.0088
18	22.1991	.0111
19	23.1912	.0141
20	24.2411	.0170
21	25.3545	.0203
22	26.5344	.0237
23	27.7861	.0273
24	29.1148	.0310
25	30.5235	.0341
26	32.0118	.0382
27	33.5936	.0416
28	35.2636	.0452
29	37.0323	.0493
30	38.9106	.0539
31	40.9064	.0588
32	43.0363	.0638
33	45.3086	.0710
34	47.7557	.0775
35	50.3830	.0857
36	53.2214	.0951
37	56.3009	.1059
38	59.6560	.1188
39	63.3321	.1340
40	67.3830	.1521
41	71.8715	.1737
42	76.8787	.1999
43	82.5039	+.2320
44	88.8759	.2715
45	96.1538	.3205

20th Year—D. or 70.

AGE.	Value.	M. Diff.
10	14.0066	—.0131
11	14.5656	.0116
12	15.1496	.0107
13	15.7533	.0085
14	16.3996	.0075
15	17.0615	.0060
16	17.7610	.0046
17	18.4885	.0027
18	19.2552	.0012
19	20.0578	+.0011
20	20.9055	.0026
21	21.7929	.0053
22	22.7344	.0076
23	23.7268	.0099
24	24.7745	.0122
25	25.8775	.0139
26	27.0312	.0163
27	28.2470	.0176
28	29.5158	.0192
29	30.8427	.0209
30	32.2321	.0226
31	33.6892	.0246
32	35.2216	.0262
33	36.8287	.0292
34	38.5321	.0312
35	40.3254	.0341
36	42.2269	.0373
37	44.2471	.0409
38	46.3992	.0456
39	48.6962	.0518
40	51.1886	.0575
41	53.8705	.0649
42	56.7838	.0742
43	59.9662	.0857
44	63.4715	.1002
45	67.3715	.1175
46	71.7134	.1414
47	76.6275	.1708
48	82.2256	.2085
49	88.6662	.2573
50	96.1538	.3205

20th Year—D. or 75.

AGE.	Value.	M. Diff.
10	12.9161	—.0170
11	13.4177	.0163
12	13.9340	.0153
13	14.4750	.0142
14	15.0364	.0131
15	15.6166	.0119
16	16.2292	.0108
17	16.8636	.0095
18	17.5276	.0085
19	18.2209	.0068
20	18.9511	.0055
21	19.7127	.0036
22	20.5184	.0023
23	21.3587	+.0013
24	22.2534	.0022
25	23.1840	.0037
26	24.1502	.0038
27	25.1639	.0043
28	26.2083	.0045
29	27.2924	.0045
30	28.4130	.0050
31	29.5763	.0051
32	30.7823	.0047
33	32.0298	.0051
34	33.3341	.0051
35	34.6833	.0052
36	36.0896	.0050
37	37.5519	.0050
38	39.0800	.0051
39	40.6800	.0053
40	42.3595	.0057
41	44.1282	.0060
42	45.9951	.0068
43	47.9736	.0080
44	50.0847	.0098
45	52.3507	.0129
46	54.8032	.0174
47	57.4778	.0241
48	60.4221	.0332
49	63.6871	.0465
50	67.3508	.0649
51	71.5053	.0900
52	76.2782	.1243
53	81.8223	+.1709
54	88.3536	.2342
55	96.1538	.3205

21st YEAR—D. or 35.

AGE.	Value.	M. Diff.
10	72.6827	+.2250
11	77.7337	.2453
12	83.2799	.2678
13	89.3922	.2927
14	96.1538	.3205

21st Year—D. or 40.

AGE.	Value.	M. Diff.
10	53.0739	+.1452
11	56.3682	.1581
12	59.9369	.1721
13	63.8126	.1875
14	68.0342	.2044
15	72.6435	.2231
16	77.6955	.2436
17	83.2467	.2665
18	89.3712	.2920
19	96.1538	.3205

21st Year—D. or 45.

AGE.	Value.	M. Diff.
10	39.9346	+.0917
11	42.1920	.1002
12	44.6168	.1093
13	47.2220	.1192
14	50.0287	.1301
15	53.0582	.1419
16	56.3382	.1548
17	59.8936	.1687
18	63.7577	.1845
19	67.9735	.2016
20	72.5825	.2206
21	77.6476	.2408
22	83.2005	.2649
23	89.3431	.2911
24	96.1538	.3205

21st Year—D. or 50.

AGE.	Value.	M. Diff.
10	30.8300	+.0547
11	32.4396	.0604
12	34.1508	.0664
13	35.9768	.0730
14	37.9282	.0801
15	40.0137	.0878
16	42.2532	.0963
17	44.6583	.1049
18	47.2415	.1151
19	50.0335	.1259
20	53.0483	.1377
21	56.3147	.1507
22	59.8624	.1647
23	63.7195	.1806
24	67.9327	.1975
25	72.5382	.2165
26	77.5919	.2377
27	83.1575	.2617
28	89.3131	.2891
29	96.1538	.3205

21st Year—D. or 55.

AGE.	Value.	M. Diff.
10	24.4406	+.0287
11	25.6236	.0325
12	26.8749	.0367
13	28.2014	.0410
14	29.6082	.0457
15	31.1012	.0508
16	32.6939	.0565
17	34.3901	.0621
18	36.1986	.0687
19	38.1345	.0757
20	40.2099	.0832
21	42.4356	.0915
22	44.8304	.1004
23	47.4086	.1100
24	50.1895	.1199
25	53.1873	.1315
26	56.4360	.1433
27	59.9529	.1569
28	63.7784	.1721
29	67.9530	.1891
30	72.5242	.2086
31	77.5514	.2304

ENDOWMENT POLICIES.—4 PER CENT.

21st Year—D. or 55.

Age.	Value.	M. Diff.
32	83.1012	+.2567
33	89.2719	.2860
34	96.1538	.3205

21st Year—D. or 60.

Age.	Value.	M. Diff.
10	19.9770	+.0103
11	20.8754	.0131
12	21.8252	.0159
13	22.8240	.0189
14	23.8775	.0221
15	24.9893	.0255
16	26.1663	.0293
17	27.4137	.0329
18	28.7322	.0373
19	30.1359	.0419
20	31.6290	.0466
21	33.2182	.0525
22	34.9183	.0579
23	36.7329	.0638
24	38.6699	.0697
25	40.7346	.0767
26	42.9479	.0832
27	45.3117	.0906
28	47.8459	.0989
29	50.5694	.1082
30	53.5064	.1185
31	56.6811	.1297
32	60.1229	.1438
33	63.8820	.1585
34	67.9886	.1760
35	72.5017	.1963
36	77.4862	.2200
37	83.0207	.2479
38	89.2034	.2810
39	96.1538	.3205

21st Year—D. or 65.

Age.	Value.	M. Diff.
10	16.9287	−.0020
11	17.6447	.0001
12	18.3985	+.0019
13	19.1808	.0039
14	20.0062	.0061
15	20.8708	.0084
16	21.7826	.0110
17	21.7426	.0134
18	23.7521	.0164
19	24.8204	.0195
20	25.9489	.0228
21	27.1470	.0263
22	28.4158	.0300
23	29.7614	.0338
24	31.1876	.0370
25	32.6901	.0412
26	34.2883	.0447
27	35.9739	.0484
28	37.7549	.0526
29	39.6445	.0573
30	41.6538	.0623
31	43.7899	.0675
32	46.0675	.0747
33	48.5182	.0813
34	51.1428	.0896
35	53.9743	.0990
36	57.0396	.1099
37	60.3725	.1228
38	64.0156	.1379
39	68.0185	.1559
40	72.4432	.1772
41	77.3615	.2029
42	82.8694	.2343
43	89.0835	.2728
44	96.1538	.3205

21st Year—D. or 70.

Age.	Value.	M. Diff.
10	14.9529	−.0100
11	15.5531	.0091
12	16.1726	.0068
13	16.8291	.0058
14	17.5146	.0041
15	18.2240	.0026
16	18.9705	.0007
17	19.7528	+.0009
18	20.5704	.0033
19	21.4360	.0048
20	22.3386	.0076
21	23.2967	.0100
22	24.3067	.0124
23	25.3702	.0148
24	26.4911	.0166
25	27.6617	.0191
26	28.8946	.0205
27	30.1792	.0222
28	31.5232	.0240
29	32.9297	.0260
30	34.4041	.0280
31	35.9498	.0297
32	37.5717	.0329
33	39.2892	.0350
34	41.0962	.0381
35	43.0085	.0414
36	45.0383	.0460
37	47.1980	.0501
38	49.5097	.0555
39	51.9906	.0621
40	54.6697	.0696
41	57.5691	.0774
42	60.7317	.0907
43	64.2009	.1052
44	68.0412	.1231
45	72.3227	.1459
46	77.1409	.1748
47	82.6126	.2117
48	88.8859	.2691
49	96.1538	.3205

21st Year—D. or 75.

Age.	Value.	M. Diff.
10	13.7814	−.0148
11	14.3135	.0137
12	14.8650	.0126
13	15.4425	.0114
14	16.0420	.0102
15	16.6632	.0090
16	17.3167	.0076
17	17.9957	.0065
18	18.7031	.0048
19	19.4481	.0034
20	20.2279	.0014
21	21.0475	.0001
22	21.9049	+.0025
23	22.8139	.0038
24	23.7629	.0047
25	24.7459	.0064
26	25.7759	.0065
27	26.8376	.0072
28	27.9383	.0075
29	29.0770	.0081
30	30.2585	.0083
31	31.4813	.0081
32	32.7442	.0092
33	34.0685	.0088
34	35.4345	.0090
35	36.8570	.0090
36	38.3384	.0092
37	39.8822	.0095
38	41.4993	.0099
39	43.1946	.0106
40	44.9779	.0112
41	46.8571	.0122
42	48.8466	.0137
43	50.9620	.0157
44	53.2256	.0191
45	55.6690	.0238
46	58.3254	.0306
47	61.2407	.0398
48	64.4659	.0531
49	68.0748	.0713
50	72.1566	.0971
51	76.8262	.1297
52	82.2396	.1752
53	88.5921	.2369
54	96.1538	.3205

22d YEAR—D. or 35.

Age.	Value.	M. Diff.
10	78.1404	+.2470
11	83.5839	.2690
12	89.5630	.2934
13	96.1538	.3205

22d Year—D. or 40.

Age.	Value.	M. Diff.
10	57.0121	+.1607
11	60.5599	.1747
12	64.4046	.1899
13	68.5818	.2067
14	73.1326	.2251
15	78.1037	.2453
16	83.5525	.2678
17	89.5431	.2927
18	96.1538	.3205

22d Year—D. or 45.

Age.	Value.	M. Diff.
10	42.8543	+.1029
11	45.2836	.1120
12	47.8930	.1223
13	50.6984	.1328
14	53.7217	.1446
15	56.9865	.1567
16	60.5223	.1714
17	64.3535	.1870
18	68.5247	.2039
19	73.0730	.2226
20	78.0485	.2433
21	83.5073	.2663
22	89.5157	.2918
23	96.1538	.3205

22d Year—D. or 50.

Age.	Value.	M. Diff.
10	33.0445	+.0628
11	34.7740	.0690
12	36.6131	.0756
13	38.5773	.0828
14	40.6764	.0905
15	42.9218	.0990
16	45.3345	.1077
17	47.9202	.1180
18	50.7085	.1287
19	53.7174	.1405
20	56.9691	.1535
21	60.4934	.1674
22	64.3188	.1832
23	68.4864	.1999
24	73.0309	.2187
25	78.0047	.2396
26	83.4658	.2631
27	89.4865	.2899
28	96.1538	.3205

22d Year—D. or 55.

Age.	Value.	M. Diff.
10	26.1598	+.0347
11	27.4288	.0389
12	28.7723	.0433
13	30.1960	.0482
14	31.7068	.0534
15	33.3122	.0590
16	35.0262	.0647
17	36.8463	.0714
18	38.7956	.0785
19	40.8800	.0864
20	43.1143	.0944
21	45.5136	.1033
22	48.0936	.1129
23	50.8709	.1229
24	53.8608	.1345
25	57.0944	.1463
26	60.5892	.1597
27	64.3811	.1748
28	68.5097	.1918
29	73.0201	.2109
30	77.9676	.2324
31	83.4118	.2583
32	89.4469	.2868
33	96.1538	.3205

22d Year—D. or 60.

Age.	Value.	M. Diff.
10	21.3483	+.0151
11	22.3122	.0179
12	23.3293	.0210
13	24.3996	.0242
14	25.5291	.0277
15	26.7220	.0316
16	27.9870	.0353
17	29.3220	.0398
18	30.7408	.0445
19	32.2496	.0493
20	33.8525	.0552
21	35.5681	.0607
22	37.3930	.0667
23	39.3419	.0726
24	41.4164	.0797
25	43.6364	.0863
26	46.0048	.0938
27	48.5395	.1021
28	51.2599	.1114
29	54.1883	.1217
30	57.3486	.1329
31	60.7662	.1469
32	64.4928	.1615
33	68.5535	.1789
34	73.0057	.1989
35	77.9094	.2223
36	83.3379	+.2497
37	89.3826	.2820
38	96.1538	.3205

22d Year—D. or 65.

Age.	Value.	M. Diff.
10	18.0643	+.0016
11	18.8302	.0036
12	19.6359	.0058
13	20.4729	.0080
14	21.3555	.0104
15	22.2812	.0131
16	23.2594	.0155
17	24.2842	.0186
18	25.3688	.0218
19	26.5145	.0252
20	27.7264	.0288
21	29.0120	.0326
22	30.3729	.0364
23	31.8141	.0397
24	33.3323	.0441
25	34.9426	.0476
26	36.6422	.0514
27	38.4361	.0557
28	40.3352	.0605
29	42.3526	.0656
30	44.4983	.0709
31	46.7780	.0782
32	49.2292	.0849
33	51.8519	.0932
34	54.6745	.1027
35	57.7255	.1136
36	61.0357	.1264
37	64.6465	.1415
38	68.6044	.1593
39	72.9669	.1803
40	77.8038	.2057
41	83.2021	.2365
42	89.2728	.2741
43	96.1538	.3205

22d Year—D. or 70.

Age.	Value.	M. Diff.
10	15.9357	−.0075
11	16.5710	.0052
12	17.2427	.0040
13	17.9380	.0024
14	18.6703	.0008
15	19.4264	+.0012
16	20.2268	.0028
17	21.0595	.0053
18	21.9393	.0070
19	22.8590	.0098
20	23.8313	.0122
21	24.8569	.0148
22	25.9369	.0173
23	27.0724	.0191
24	28.2604	.0217
25	29.5083	.0233
26	30.8087	.0251
27	32.1669	.0270
28	33.5884	.0291
29	35.0780	.0312
30	36.6387	.0331
31	38.2718	.0355
32	40.0014	.0386
33	41.8197	.0418
34	43.7423	.0452
35	45.7790	.0501
36	47.9441	.0542
37	50.2586	.0597
38	52.7385	.0664
39	55.4088	.0742
40	58.2969	.0841
41	61.4383	.0953
42	64.8769	.1097
43	68.6694	.1274
44	72.8852	.1508
45	77.6149	.1784
46	82.9686	.2145
47	89.0880	.2617
48	96.1538	.3205

22d Year—D. or 75.

Age.	Value.	M. Diff.
10	14.6732	−.0123
11	15.2403	.0111
12	15.8282	.0099
13	16.4434	.0085
14	17.0831	.0073
15	17.7449	.0059
16	18.4423	.0046
17	19.1642	−.0028
18	19.9228	.0014
19	20.7166	+.0007
20	21.5536	.0021
21	22.4243	.0048
22	23.3495	.0061
23	24.3120	.0071
24	25.3124	.0088
25	26.3582	.0091
26	27.4353	.0099
27	28.5520	.0103
28	29.7061	.0110
29	30.9044	.0114
30	32.1440	.0113
31	33.4222	.0126
32	34.7603	.0123
33	36.1443	.0127
34	37.5815	.0128
35	39.0770	.0132
36	40.6374	.0137
37	42.2674	.0143
38	43.9767	.0151
39	45.7724	.0160
40	47.6622	.0172
41	49.6596	.0190
42	51.7809	.0212
43	54.0430	.0248
44	56.4776	.0297
45	59.1174	.0367
46	62.0058	.0459
47	65.1917	.0593
48	68.7483	.0773
49	72.7598	.1018
50	77.3370	.1347
51	82.6233	.1792
52	88.8123	.2393
53	96.1538	.3205

23d YEAR—D. or 35.

Age.	Value.	M. Diff.
10	83.8615	+.2701
11	89.7186	.2940
12	96.1538	.3205

23d Year—D. or 40.

Age.	Value.	M. Diff.
10	61.1360	+.1770
11	64.9508	.1922
12	69.0864	.2088
13	73.5808	.2269
14	78.4791	.2469
15	83.8311	.2690
16	89.6997	.2934
17	96.1538	.3205

23d Year—D. or 45.

Age.	Value.	M. Diff.
10	45.9080	+.1146
11	48.5175	.1246
12	51.3257	.1351
13	54.3378	.1472
14	57.5896	.1600
15	61.1025	.1738
16	64.9048	.1893
17	69.0329	.2061
18	73.5246	.2246
19	78.4253	.2449
20	83.7880	.2675
21	89.6730	.2925
22	96.1538	.3205

23d Year—D. or 50.

Age.	Value.	M. Diff.
10	35.3568	+.0713
11	37.2116	.0781
12	39.1861	.0853
13	41.2949	.0931
14	43.5502	.1017
15	45.9649	.1104
16	48.5535	.1207
17	51.3390	.1314
18	54.3385	.1432
19	57.5772	.1561
20	61.0791	.1699
21	64.8722	.1856
22	68.9977	.2021
23	73.4846	.2207
24	78.3834	.2413
25	83.7480	.2644
26	89.6447	.2907
27	96.1538	.3205

ENDOWMENT POLICIES.—4 PER CENT.

23d Year—D. or 55.

AGE.	Value.	M. Diff.
10	27.9513	+.0410
11	29.3106	.0456
12	30.7497	.0505
13	32.2764	.0557
14	33.8972	.0615
15	35.6214	.0672
16	37.4572	.0739
17	39.4148	.0811
18	41.5093	.0887
19	43.7541	.0968
20	46.1534	.1061
21	48.7329	.1155
22	51.5068	.1256
23	54.4877	.1373
24	57.7067	.1490
25	61.1788	.1624
26	64.9393	.1773
27	69.0237	.1941
28	73.4773	.2131
29	78.3492	.2343
30	83.6968	.2597
31	89.6066	.2876
32	96.1538	.3205

23d Year—D. or 60.

AGE.	Value.	M. Diff.
10	22.7761	+.0198
11	23.8064	.0229
12	24.8940	.0263
13	26.0393	.0299
14	27.2487	.0338
15	28.5282	.0375
16	29.8793	.0421
17	31.3130	.0469
18	32.8351	.0518
19	34.4517	.0578
20	36.1787	.0633
21	38.0165	.0694
22	39.9731	.0754
23	42.0563	.0825
24	44.2825	.0892
25	46.6537	.0967
26	49.1885	.1051
27	51.9045	.1144
28	54.8239	.1247
29	57.9690	.1359
30	61.3645	.1499
31	65.0581	.1644
32	69.0758	.1816
33	73.4700	.2014
34	78.2982	.2243
35	83.6284	.2513
36	89.5461	.2830
37	96.1538	.3205

23d Year—D. or 65.

AGE.	Value.	M. Diff.
10	19.2435	+.0053
11	20.0608	.0075
12	20.9204	.0099
13	21.8140	.0123
14	22.7569	.0151
15	23.7482	.0176
16	24.7902	.0208
17	25.8891	.0240
18	27.0500	.0275
19	28.2777	.0312
20	29.5757	.0350
21	30.9517	.0389
22	32.4067	.0423
23	33.9381	.0467
24	35.5619	.0504
25	37.2716	.0543
26	39.0770	.0587
27	40.9863	.0635
28	43.0101	.0687
29	45.1606	.0741
30	47.4459	.0815
31	49.8950	.0883
32	52.5132	.0966
33	55.3280	.1061
34	58.3634	.1170
35	61.6515	.1298
36	65.2305	.1448
37	69.1452	.1625
38	73.4498	.1833
39	78.2092	.2083
40	83.5070	.2385
41	89.4452	.2753
42	96.1538	.3205

23d Year—D. or 70.

AGE.	Value.	M. Diff.
10	16.9487	—.0036
11	17.6358	.0024
12	18.3459	.0007
13	19.0876	+.0009
14	19.8659	.0031
15	20.6755	.0047
16	21.5253	.0073
17	22.4195	.0090
18	23.3527	.0119
19	24.3412	.0144
20	25.3801	.0170
21	26.4747	.0196
22	27.6255	.0215
23	28.8263	.0242
24	30.0901	.0259
25	31.4048	.0278
26	32.7772	.0299
27	34.2115	.0320
28	35.7143	.0342
29	37.2883	.0362
30	38.9341	.0395
31	40.6625	.0428
32	42.5002	.0453
33	44.4309	.0489
34	46.4745	.0530
35	48.6537	.0571
36	50.9580	.0637
37	53.4355	.0705
38	56.0985	.0784
39	58.9726	.0879
40	62.0975	.0992
41	65.5009	.1139
42	69.2501	.1316
43	73.4046	.1538
44	78.0626	.1809
45	83.2975	.2171
46	89.2736	.2625
47	96.1538	.3205

23d Year—D. or 75.

AGE.	Value.	M. Diff.
10	15.5959	—.0096
11	16.1990	.0083
12	16.8241	.0079
13	17.4793	.0056
14	18.1591	.0041
15	18.8644	.0029
16	19.6042	.0010
17	20.3766	+.0006
18	21.1834	.0027
19	22.0339	.0041
20	22.9211	.0069
21	23.8588	.0083
22	24.8367	.0093
23	25.8497	.0112
24	26.9119	.0116
25	28.0038	.0125
26	29.1349	.0130
27	30.3039	.0138
28	31.5163	.0143
29	32.7714	.0143
30	34.0649	.0157
31	35.4167	.0156
32	36.8129	.0161
33	38.2663	.0164
34	39.7745	.0169
35	41.3467	.0176
36	42.9907	.0184
37	44.7101	.0194
38	46.5165	.0205
39	48.4150	.0219
40	50.4189	.0239
41	52.5434	.0264
42	54.8060	.0302
43	57.2331	.0352
44	59.8572	.0422
45	62.7208	.0517
46	65.8702	.0650
47	69.3761	.0829
48	73.3209	.1070
49	77.8099	.1394
50	82.9808	.1830
51	89.0147	.2415
52	96.1538	.3205

24th YEAR—D. or 35.

AGE.	Value.	M. Diff.
10	89.8607	+.2946
11	96.1538	.3205

24th Year—D. or 40.

AGE.	Value.	M. Diff.
10	65.4558	+.1943
11	69.5521	.2107
12	73.9940	.2287
13	78.8233	.2483
14	84.0875	.2701
15	89.8424	.2940
16	96.1538	.3205

24th Year—D. or 45.

AGE.	Value.	M. Diff.
10	49.1022	+.1270
11	51.9019	.1378
12	54.9113	.1496
13	58.1495	.1625
14	61.6422	.1760
15	65.4136	.1915
16	69.5031	.2080
17	73.9408	.2263
18	78.7722	.2464
19	84.0453	.2686
20	89.8168	.2931
21	96.1538	.3205

24th Year—D. or 50.

AGE.	Value.	M. Diff.
10	37.7712	+.0804
11	39.7587	.0876
12	41.8750	.0955
13	44.1366	.1041
14	46.5575	.1128
15	49.1439	.1231
16	51.9275	.1339
17	54.9187	.1456
18	58.1418	.1585
19	61.6235	.1722
20	65.3860	.1878
21	69.4698	.2042
22	73.9034	.2225
23	78.7320	.2428
24	84.0068	.2656
25	89.7895	.2913
26	96.1538	.3205

24th Year—D. or 55.

AGE.	Value.	M. Diff.
10	29.8187	+.0477
11	31.2725	.0526
12	32.8126	.0579
13	34.4475	.0646
14	36.1849	.0696
15	38.0287	.0764
16	39.9987	.0835
17	42.0996	.0912
18	44.3462	.0997
19	46.7523	.1086
20	49.3321	.1183
21	52.1012	.1282
22	55.0728	.1398
23	58.2771	.1515
24	61.7271	.1649
25	65.4568	.1797
26	69.5003	.1964
27	73.8989	.2151
28	78.7010	.2359
29	83.9581	.2609
30	89.7531	.2884
31	96.1538	.3205

24th Year—D. or 60.

AGE.	Value.	M. Diff.
10	24.2609	+.0248
11	25.3609	.0282
12	26.5225	.0319
13	27.7465	.0359
14	29.0412	.0397
15	30.4055	.0443
16	31.8538	.0491
17	33.3890	.0541
18	35.0170	.0602
19	36.7556	.0658
20	38.6025	.0719
21	40.5692	.0780
22	42.6572	.0851
23	44.8889	.0919
24	47.2627	.0995
25	49.7962	.1079
26	52.5076	.1172
27	55.4173	.1275
28	58.5474	.1387
29	61.9207	.1526
30	65.5846	.1670

24th Year—D. or 60.

AGE.	Value.	M. Diff.
31	69.5593	+.1841
32	73.8993	.2037
33	78.6563	.2263
34	83.8953	.2528
35	89.6959	.2838
36	96.1538	.3205

24th Year—D. or 65.

AGE.	Value.	M. Diff.
10	20.4674	+.0092
11	21.3381	.0116
12	22.2536	.0141
13	23.2068	.0170
14	24.2144	.0195
15	25.2686	.0227
16	26.3837	.0261
17	27.5578	.0296
18	28.7995	.0334
19	30.1121	.0373
20	31.4992	.0413
21	32.9677	.0447
22	34.5112	.0492
23	36.1463	.0530
24	37.8673	.0570
25	39.6807	.0615
26	41.5989	.0664
27	43.6301	.0717
28	45.7838	.0771
29	48.0703	.0846
30	50.5208	.0914
31	53.1324	.0998
32	55.9374	.1093
33	58.9588	.1202
34	62.2243	.1330
35	65.7728	.1479
36	69.6458	.1654
37	73.8955	.1859
38	78.5829	.2106
39	83.7863	.2403
40	89.6031	.2774
41	96.1538	.3205

24th Year—D. or 70.

AGE.	Value.	M. Diff.
10	18.0085	—.0009
11	18.7336	+.0009
12	19.4895	.0026
13	20.2763	.0048
14	21.1079	.0065
15	21.9664	.0091
16	22.8769	.0109
17	23.8243	.0138
18	24.8250	.0165
19	25.8791	.0183
20	26.9860	.0219
21	28.1503	.0238
22	29.3653	.0266
23	30.6415	.0283
24	31.9701	.0303
25	33.3553	.0324
26	34.8022	.0348
27	36.3163	.0371
28	37.9013	.0392
29	39.5586	.0426
30	41.3074	.0452
31	43.1415	.0485
32	45.0787	.0523
33	47.1272	.0564
34	49.2987	.0617
35	51.6130	.0674
36	54.0865	.0743
37	56.7417	.0823
38	59.6017	.0911
39	62.7011	.1035
40	66.0794	.1178
41	69.7867	.1353
42	73.8859	.1573
43	78.4565	.1850
44	83.6009	.2196
45	89.4451	.2639
46	96.1538	.3205

24th Year—D. or 75.

AGE.	Value.	M. Diff.
10	16.5504	—.0069
11	17.1903	.0054
12	17.8550	.0041
13	18.5499	.0025
14	19.2726	.0011
15	20.0199	+.0008
16	20.8096	.0024
17	21.6298	.0046

24th Year—D. or 75.

AGE.	Value.	M. Diff.
18	22.4925	+.0061
19	23.3925	.0089
20	24.3460	.0104
21	25.3356	.0115
22	26.3631	.0135
23	27.4371	.0139
24	28.5445	.0149
25	29.6894	.0155
26	30.8716	.0165
27	32.0979	.0171
28	33.3659	.0172
29	34.6735	.0187
30	36.0391	.0187
31	37.4475	.0193
32	38.9112	.0198
33	40.4336	.0205
34	42.0164	.0213
35	43.6699	.0223
36	45.4005	.0235
37	47.2141	.0247
38	49.1200	.0263
39	51.1289	.0285
40	53.2557	.0312
41	55.5166	.0352
42	57.9384	.0404
43	60.5483	.0477
44	63.3872	.0572
45	66.5043	.0703
46	69.9629	.0881
47	73.8440	.1119
48	78.2499	.1438
49	83.3119	.1864
50	89.2034	.2436
51	96.1538	.3205

25th YEAR—D. or 35.

AGE.	Value.	M. Diff.
10	96.1538	+.3205

25th Year—D. or 40.

AGE.	Value.	M. Diff.
10	69.9826	+.2125
11	74.3752	.2302
12	79.1405	.2496
13	84.3224	.2710
14	89.9737	.2945
15	96.1538	.3205

25th Year—D. or 45.

AGE.	Value.	M. Diff.
10	52.4451	+.1400
11	55.4450	.1519
12	58.6707	.1645
13	62.1433	.1781
14	65.8869	.1935
15	69.9370	.2099
16	74.3259	.2280
17	79.0919	.2478
18	84.2822	.2696
19	89.9487	.2937
20	96.1538	.3205

25th Year—D. or 50.

AGE.	Value.	M. Diff.
10	40.2941	+.0899
11	42.4205	.0978
12	44.6867	.1064
13	47.1104	.1152
14	49.6989	.1255
15	52.4761	.1362
16	55.4601	.1479
17	58.6693	.1607
18	62.1289	.1744
19	65.8635	.1899
20	69.9081	.2061
21	74.2903	.2242
22	79.0540	.2442
23	84.2452	.2667
24	89.9222	.2919
25	96.1538	.3205

25th Year—D. or 55.

AGE.	Value.	M. Diff.
10	31.7658	+.0546
11	33.3190	.0600
12	34.9655	.0659
13	36.7250	.0709
14	38.5698	.0786
15	40.5460	.0859
16	42.6559	.0936

ENDOWMENT POLICIES.—4 PER CENT.

25th Year—D. or 55.

AGE.	Value.	M. Diff.
17	44.9059	+.1021
18	47.3147	.1111
19	49.8929	.1207
20	52.6577	.1307
21	55.6194	.1422
22	58.8085	.1539
23	62.2374	.1672
24	65.9380	.1819
25	69.9422	.1984
26	74.2899	.2169
27	79.0255	.2373
28	84.1990	.2621
29	89.8874	.2891
30	96.1538	.3205

25th Year—D. or 60.

AGE.	Value.	M. Diff.
10	25.8056	+.0300
11	26.9787	.0337
12	28.2179	.0378
13	29.5260	.0417
14	30.9043	.0464
15	32.3643	.0513
16	33.9125	.0563
17	35.5518	.0624
18	37.2999	.0681
19	39.1561	.0743
20	41.1295	.0804
21	43.2249	.0876
22	45.4584	.0944
23	47.8343	.1021
24	50.3666	.1105
25	53.0724	.1198
26	55.9726	.1301
27	59.0873	.1413
28	62.4391	.1552
29	66.0728	.1695
30	70.0091	.1864
31	74.2967	.2057
32	78.9875	.2281
33	84.1412	.2541
34	89.8335	.2846
35	96.1538	.3205

25th Year—D. or 65.

AGE.	Value.	M. Diff.
10	21.7380	+.0132
11	22.6639	.0158
12	23.6381	.0188
13	24.6554	.0214
14	25.7251	.0247
15	26.8515	.0280
16	28.0407	.0317
17	29.2945	.0355
18	30.6198	.0395
19	32.0201	.0485
20	33.4983	.0471
21	35.0536	.0516
22	36.6990	.0554
23	38.4295	.0595
24	40.2521	.0641
25	42.1759	.0691
26	44.2133	.0744
27	46.3714	.0799
28	48.6579	.0875
29	51.1059	.0943
30	53.7144	.1028
31	56.5080	.1123
32	59.5140	.1232
33	62.7588	.1359
34	66.2771	.1508
35	70.1106	.1681
36	74.3080	.1885
37	78.9278	.2128
38	84.0439	.2419
39	89.7478	.2773
40	96.1538	.3205

25th Year—D. or 70.

AGE.	Value.	M. Diff.
10	19.1010	+.0024
11	19.8714	.0042
12	20.6764	.0061
13	21.5120	.0074
14	22.3913	.0101
15	23.3099	.0128
16	24.2725	.0158
17	25.2866	.0184
18	26.3524	.0212
19	27.4737	.0239
20	28.6494	.0260
21	29.8772	.0288

25th Year—D. or 70.

AGE.	Value.	M. Diff.
22	31.1660	+.0306
23	32.5057	.0320
24	33.9035	.0350
25	35.3620	.0373
26	36.8870	.0398
27	38.4817	.0419
28	40.1481	.0455
29	41.9053	.0482
30	43.7481	.0517
31	45.6892	.0555
32	47.7413	.0597
33	49.9143	.0651
34	52.2280	.0709
35	54.6962	.0771
36	57.3423	.0859
37	60.1891	.0955
38	63.2576	.1080
39	66.6158	.1214
40	70.2845	.1388
41	74.3300	.1606
42	78.8310	.1877
43	83.8831	.2217
44	89.6035	.2652
45	96.1538	.3205

25th Year—D. or 75.

AGE.	Value.	M. Diff.
10	17.5373	—.0040
11	18.2165	.0022
12	18.9204	.0010
13	19.6579	+.0005
14	20.4220	.0025
15	21.2189	.0041
16	22.0556	.0064
17	22.9311	.0080
18	23.8427	.0108
19	24.8083	.0124
20	25.8128	.0136
21	26.8513	.0156
22	27.9390	.0162
23	29.0573	.0172
24	30.2167	.0179
25	31.4117	.0190
26	32.6502	.0197
27	33.9308	.0199
28	35.2500	.0216
29	36.6283	.0217
30	38.0490	.0224
31	39.5233	.0231
32	41.0544	.0238
33	42.6493	.0248
34	44.3112	.0259
35	46.0489	.0273
36	47.8710	.0286
37	49.7811	.0305
38	51.7938	.0328
39	53.9217	.0357
40	56.1803	.0398
41	58.5951	.0452
42	61.1935	.0526
43	64.0125	.0621
44	67.0965	.0753
45	70.5112	.0930
46	74.3329	.1165
47	78.6600	.1478
48	83.6200	.1896
49	89.3781	.2455
50	96.1538	.3205

26th YEAR—D. or 40.

AGE.	Value.	M. Diff.
10	74.7277	+.2317
11	79.4332	.2509
12	84.5389	.2720
13	90.0940	.2951
14	96.1538	.3205

26th Year—D. or 45.

AGE.	Value.	M. Diff.
10	55.9447	+.1538
11	59.1558	.1665
12	62.6098	.1801
13	66.3264	.1953
14	70.3407	.2116
15	74.6813	.2295
16	79.3877	.2491
17	84.5006	.2704
18	90.0701	.2942
19	96.1538	.3205

26th Year—D. or 50.

AGE.	Value.	M. Diff.
10	42.9307	+.0999
11	45.2040	.1086
12	47.6290	.1173
13	50.2168	.1276
14	52.9917	.1384
15	55.9649	.1501
16	59.1615	.1628
17	62.6010	.1764
18	66.3068	.1918
19	70.3155	.2079
20	74.6494	.2258
21	79.3513	.2456
22	84.4652	.2677
23	90.0445	.2925
24	96.1538	.3205

26th Year—D. or 55.

AGE.	Value.	M. Diff.
10	33.7967	+.0620
11	35.4546	.0680
12	37.2139	.0739
13	39.0788	.0808
14	41.0635	.0881
15	43.1772	.0958
16	45.4337	.1043
17	47.8424	.1133
18	50.4196	.1230
19	53.1787	.1329
20	56.1317	.1445
21	59.3057	.1561
22	62.7138	.1693
23	66.3859	.1840
24	70.3532	.2003
25	74.6524	.2187
26	79.3265	.2390
27	84.4192	.2634
28	90.0112	.2897
29	96.1538	.3205

26th Year—D. or 60.

AGE.	Value.	M. Diff.
10	27.4132	+.0355
11	28.6629	.0397
12	29.9852	.0436
13	31.3756	.0484
14	32.8482	.0533
15	34.4067	.0584
16	36.0572	.0646
17	37.8147	.0703
18	39.6783	.0766
19	41.6587	.0827
20	43.7583	.0900
21	45.9964	.0968
22	48.3710	.1045
23	50.9019	.1129
24	53.6024	.1223
25	56.4925	.1326
26	59.5926	.1438
27	62.9231	.1567
28	66.5284	.1719
29	70.4271	.1885
30	74.6663	.2077
31	79.2940	.2297
32	84.3685	.2554
33	89.9603	.2853
34	96.1538	.3205

26th Year—D. or 65.

AGE.	Value.	M. Diff.
10	23.0567	+.0175
11	24.0408	.0204
12	25.0782	.0231
13	26.1568	.0265
14	27.2978	.0299
15	28.4974	.0336
16	29.7652	.0375
17	31.1015	.0415
18	32.5131	.0457
19	34.0030	.0493
20	35.5667	.0539
21	37.2222	.0579
22	38.9612	.0619
23	40.7912	.0666
24	42.7220	.0716
25	44.7627	.0770
26	46.9242	.0826
27	49.2119	.0902
28	51.6565	.0971
29	54.2585	.1056
30	57.0443	.1151
31	60.0338	.1260
32	63.2573	.1387

26th Year—D. or 65.

AGE.	Value.	M. Diff.
33	66.7478	+.1534
34	70.5430	.1706
35	74.6911	.1908
36	79.2471	.2148
37	84.2816	.2435
38	89.8812	.2782
39	96.1538	.3205

26th Year—D. or 70.

AGE.	Value.	M. Diff.
10	20.2334	+.0057
11	21.0485	.0080
12	21.9012	.0098
13	22.7885	.0126
14	23.7271	.0145
15	24.6973	.0176
16	25.7266	.0203
17	26.8042	.0231
18	27.9363	.0259
19	29.1253	.0281
20	30.3631	.0310
21	31.6636	.0329
22	33.0153	.0350
23	34.4187	.0373
24	35.8931	.0398
25	37.4272	.0424
26	39.0320	.0446
27	40.7058	.0483
28	42.4712	.0510
29	44.3201	.0538
30	46.2667	.0577
31	48.3199	.0628
32	50.4934	.0683
33	52.8052	.0742
34	55.2685	.0813
35	57.9048	.0893
36	60.7368	.0990
37	63.7956	.1031
38	67.1160	.1248
39	70.7462	.1420
40	74.7420	.1636
41	79.1765	.1987
42	84.1407	.2240
43	89.7497	.2665
44	96.1538	.3205

26th Year—D. or 75.

AGE.	Value.	M. Diff.
10	18.5590	—.0011
11	19.2812	+.0002
12	20.0231	.0020
13	20.8015	.0041
14	21.6147	.0058
15	22.4580	.0081
16	23.3495	.0098
17	24.2732	.0127
18	25.2498	.0143
19	26.2656	.0156
20	27.3183	.0177
21	28.4162	.0183
22	29.5473	.0194
23	30.7168	.0202
24	31.9254	.0214
25	33.1755	.0222
26	34.4672	.0225
27	35.7979	.0243
28	37.1866	.0245
29	38.6185	.0254
30	40.1036	.0261
31	41.6436	.0270
32	43.2454	.0281
33	44.9173	.0294
34	46.6612	.0309
35	48.4878	.0324
36	50.4035	.0343
37	52.4173	.0368
38	54.5454	.0399
39	56.8008	.0442
40	59.2085	.0497
41	61.7943	.0572
42	64.5949	.0668
43	67.6498	.0800
44	71.0234	.0975
45	74.7898	.1207
46	79.0434	.1516
47	83.9071	.1926
48	89.5406	.2473
49	96.1538	.3205

27th YEAR—D. or 40.

AGE.	Value.	M. Diff.
10	79.7038	+.2520
11	84.7388	.2728

27th Year—D. or 40.

AGE.	Value.	M. Diff.
12	90.2049	+.2955
13	96.1538	.3205

27th Year—D. or 45.

AGE.	Value.	M. Diff.
10	59.6099	+.1684
11	63.0439	.1819
12	66.7354	.1970
13	70.7155	.2132
14	75.0120	.2309
15	79.6607	.2502
16	84.7026	.2714
17	90.1809	.2948
18	96.1538	.3205

27th Year—D. or 50.

AGE.	Value.	M. Diff.
10	45.6877	+.1106
11	48.1167	.1194
12	50.7025	.1297
13	53.4729	.1404
14	56.4393	.1521
15	59.6203	.1648
16	63.0415	.1783
17	66.7209	.1936
18	70.6936	.2095
19	74.9832	.2273
20	79.6272	.2468
21	84.6684	.2686
22	90.1574	.2930
23	96.1538	.3205

27th Year—D. or 55.

AGE.	Value.	M. Diff.
10	35.9163	+.0699
11	37.6852	.0759
12	39.5579	.0828
13	41.5505	.0901
14	43.6704	.0979
15	45.9276	.1064
16	48.3396	.1154
17	50.9137	.1251
18	53.6680	.1351
19	56.6110	.1466
20	59.7712	.1582
21	63.1589	.1713
22	66.8039	.1859
23	70.7355	.2021
24	74.9896	.2202
25	79.6054	.2403
26	84.6272	.2643
27	90.1254	.2902
28	96.1538	.3205

27th Year—D. or 60.

AGE.	Value.	M. Diff.
10	29.0869	+.0415
11	30.4187	.0455
12	31.8220	.0503
13	33.3055	.0553
14	34.8751	.0604
15	36.5343	.0666
16	38.3013	.0724
17	40.1723	.0787
18	42.1580	.0849
19	44.2623	.0922
20	46.5019	.0991
21	48.8781	.1068
22	51.4046	.1152
23	54.0999	.1246
24	56.9805	.1349
25	60.0657	.1461
26	63.3760	.1598
27	66.9537	.1739
28	70.8168	.1905
29	75.0098	.2095
30	79.5791	.2312
31	84.5789	.2565
32	90.0775	.2860
33	96.1538	.3205

27th Year—D. or 65.

AGE.	Value.	M. Diff.
10	24.4262	+.0221
11	25.4728	.0248
12	26.5706	.0283
13	27.7199	.0317
14	28.9331	.0355
15	30.2103	.0394
16	31.5594	.0435

ENDOWMENT POLICIES.—4 PER CENT.

27th Year—D. or 65.

Age.	Value.	M. Diff.
17	32.9808	+.0478
18	34.4809	.0513
19	36.0548	.0560
20	37.7170	.0600
21	39.4645	.0642
22	41.3011	.0689
23	43.2374	.0740
24	45.2826	.0795
25	47.4449	.0851
26	49.7331	.0928
27	52.1755	.0997
28	54.7706	.1082
29	57.5458	.1178
30	60.5225	.1286
31	63.7240	.1413
32	67.1867	.1559
33	70.9465	.1729
34	75.0474	.1929
35	79.5436	.2166
36	84.5017	.2449
37	90.0043	.2791
38	96.1538	.3205

27th Year—D. or 70.

Age.	Value.	M. Diff.
10	21.4046	+.0095
11	22.2712	.0114
12	23.1711	.0142
13	24.1171	.0154
14	25.1066	.0193
15	26.1424	.0221
16	27.2344	.0249
17	28.3778	.0278
18	29.5768	.0301
19	30.8270	.0330
20	32.1374	.0349
21	33.4989	.0372
22	34.9173	.0396
23	37.3914	.0425
24	37.9404	.0447
25	39.5529	.0471
26	41.2347	.0517
27	43.0058	.0528
28	44.8601	.0574
29	46.8111	.0614
30	48.8573	.0666
31	51.0392	.0713
32	53.3490	.0772
33	55.8057	.0843
34	58.4329	.0917
35	61.2504	.1021
36	64.2887	.1138
37	67.5822	.1196
38	71.1761	.1451
39	75.1236	.1664
40	79.4970	.1928
41	84.3803	.2259
42	89.8852	.2676
43	96.1538	.3205

27th Year—D. or 75.

Age.	Value.	M. Diff.
10	19.6149	+.0019
11	20.3746	.0035
12	21.1613	.0056
13	21.9882	.0074
14	22.8473	.0097
15	23.7449	.0115
16	24.6839	.0145
17	25.6719	.0161
18	26.6981	.0175
19	27.7614	.0196
20	28.8727	.0203
21	30.0133	.0215
22	31.1947	.0224
23	32.4125	.0236
24	33.6752	.0245
25	34.9776	.0250
26	36.3183	.0268
27	37.7171	.0271
28	39.1581	.0281
29	40.6530	.0290
30	42.2021	.0300
31	43.8111	.0313
32	45.4881	.0326
33	47.2398	.0342
34	49.0703	.0359
35	50.9880	.0380
36	53.0043	.0406
37	55.1302	.0438
38	57.3820	.0483
39	59.7820	.0539
40	62.3554	.0615

27th Year—D. or 75.

Age.	Value.	M. Diff.
41	65.1373	+.0711
42	68.1663	.0843
43	71.5019	.1018
44	75.2165	.1247
45	79.4017	.1551
46	84.1754	.1954
47	89.6921	.2490
48	96.1538	.3205

28th YEAR—D. or 40.

Age.	Value.	M. Diff.
10	84.9235	+.2736
11	90.3072	.2960
12	96.1538	.3205

28th Year—D. or 45.

Age.	Value.	M. Diff.
10	63.4503	+.1836
11	67.1161	.1986
12	71.0644	.2146
13	75.3189	.2322
14	79.9146	.2513
15	84.8891	.2722
16	90.2855	.2952
17	96.1538	.3205

28th Year—D. or 50.

Age.	Value.	M. Diff.
10	48.5728	+.1213
11	51.1593	.1316
12	53.9242	.1423
13	56.8820	.1540
14	60.0516	.1666
15	63.4523	.1801
16	67.1073	.1953
17	71.0469	.2111
18	75.2930	.2286
19	79.8838	.2479
20	84.8571	.2694
21	90.2617	.2935
22	96.1538	.3205

28th Year—D. or 55.

Age.	Value.	M. Diff.
10	38.1297	+.0777
11	40.0107	.0847
12	42.0088	.0921
13	44.1343	.1001
14	46.3951	.1084
15	48.8055	.1174
16	51.3792	.1272
17	54.1270	.1371
18	57.0612	.1486
19	60.2070	.1602
20	63.5756	.1733
21	67.1946	.1877
22	71.0925	.2037
23	75.3031	.2218
24	79.8649	.2415
25	84.8182	.2652
26	90.2314	.2908
27	96.1538	.3205

28th Year—D. or 60.

Age.	Value.	M. Diff.
10	30.8317	+.0472
11	32.2435	.0521
12	33.7386	.0571
13	35.3177	.0623
14	36.9866	.0686
15	38.7606	.0744
16	40.6392	.0807
17	42.6304	.0870
18	44.7377	.0943
19	46.9795	.1012
20	49.3546	.1089
21	51.8794	.1174
22	54.5671	.1268
23	57.4385	.1371
24	60.5096	.1482
25	63.8001	.1619
26	67.3518	.1759
27	71.1806	.1924
28	75.3301	.2112
29	79.8441	.2327
30	84.9566	.2586
31	90.2869	.2872
32	96.1538	.3205

28th Year—D. or 65.

Age.	Value.	M. Diff.
10	25.8506	+.0264
11	26.9570	.0299
12	28.1245	.0334
13	29.3451	.0372
14	30.6350	.0412
15	31.9925	.0453
16	33.4256	.0496
17	34.9341	.0533
18	36.5168	.0581
19	38.1878	.0621
20	39.9405	.0664
21	41.7839	.0711
22	43.7247	.0763
23	45.7733	.0818
24	47.9377	.0875
25	50.2240	.0952
26	52.6639	.1022
27	55.2533	.1108
28	58.0176	.1202
29	60.9793	.1311
30	64.1628	.1437
31	67.5977	.1583
32	71.3227	.1752
33	75.3799	.1949
34	79.8193	.2183
35	84.7060	.2463
36	90.1183	.2798
37	96.1538	.3205

28th Year—D. or 70.

Age.	Value.	M. Diff.
10	22.6218	+.0129
11	23.5347	.0157
12	24.4927	.0177
13	25.4801	.0217
14	26.5434	.0238
15	27.6417	.0267
16	28.7982	.0288
17	30.0077	.0318
18	31.2770	.0341
19	32.5883	.0370
20	33.9587	.0393
21	35.3863	.0418
22	36.8741	.0444
23	38.4262	.0471
24	40.0470	.0495
25	41.7357	.0533
26	43.5228	.0554
27	45.3603	.0600
28	47.3252	.0641
29	49.3834	.0686
30	51.5554	.0741
31	53.8601	.0802
32	56.3111	.0874
33	58.9275	.0955
34	61.7224	.1060
35	64.7495	.1168
36	68.0177	.1308
37	71.5771	.1479
38	75.4800	.1690
39	79.7941	.1950
40	84.6025	.2277
41	90.0102	.2687
42	96.1538	.3205

28th Year—D. or 75.

Age.	Value.	M. Diff.
10	20.7077	+.0049
11	21.5075	.0070
12	22.3423	.0089
13	23.2146	.0112
14	24.1274	.0131
15	25.0721	.0161
16	26.0746	.0179
17	27.1116	.0193
18	28.1847	.0215
19	29.3058	.0223
20	30.4590	.0235
21	31.6491	.0245
22	32.8780	.0258
23	34.1491	.0268
24	35.4629	.0273
25	36.8133	.0292
26	38.2210	.0297
27	39.6709	.0308
28	41.1735	.0317
29	42.7310	.0328
30	44.3475	.0342
31	46.0299	.0357
32	47.7848	.0374
33	49.6207	.0392
34	51.5399	.0415
35	53.5556	.0442

28th Year—D. or 75.

Age.	Value.	M. Diff.
36	55.6808	+.0475
37	57.9269	.0521
38	60.3192	.0579
39	62.8801	.0655
40	65.6438	.0752
41	68.6473	.0884
42	71.9486	.1057
43	75.6152	.1285
44	79.7363	.1584
45	84.4263	.1981
46	89.8337	.2506
47	96.1538	.3205

29th YEAR—D. or 40.

Age.	Value.	M. Diff.
10	90.4019	+.2963
11	96.1538	.3205

29th Year—D. or 45.

Age.	Value.	M. Diff.
10	67.4725	+.2001
11	71.3886	.2160
12	75.6047	.2334
13	80.1504	.2523
14	85.0626	.2729
15	90.3811	.2956
16	96.1538	.3205

29th Year—D. or 50.

Age.	Value.	M. Diff.
10	51.5864	+.1334
11	54.3486	.1441
12	57.2973	.1557
13	60.4541	.1683
14	63.8383	.1817
15	67.4681	.1968
16	71.3765	.2125
17	75.5825	.2299
18	80.1219	.2490
19	85.0324	.2702
20	90.3584	.2939
21	96.1538	.3205

29th Year—D. or 55.

Age.	Value.	M. Diff.
10	40.4372	+.0865
11	42.4421	.0938
12	44.5709	.1017
13	46.8385	.1100
14	49.2462	.1193
15	51.8155	.1290
16	54.5595	.1390
17	57.4835	.1504
18	60.6163	.1620
19	63.9660	.1750
20	67.5605	.1893
21	71.4261	.2053
22	75.5952	.2232
23	80.1063	.2427
24	84.9958	.2661
25	90.3295	.2913
26	96.1538	.3205

29th Year—D. or 60.

Age.	Value.	M. Diff.
10	32.6450	+.0538
11	34.1475	.0588
12	35.7370	.0641
13	37.4140	.0704
14	39.1960	.0763
15	41.0800	.0826
16	43.0768	.0889
17	45.1875	.0963
18	47.4301	.1032
19	49.8048	.1110
20	52.3257	.1194
21	55.0084	.1289
22	57.8685	.1391
23	60.9264	.1502
24	64.1980	.1638
25	67.7244	.1778
26	71.5210	.1941
27	75.6291	.2127
28	80.0912	.2340
29	84.9566	.2586
30	90.2869	.2872
31	96.1538	.3205

29th Year—D. or 65.

Age.	Value.	M. Diff.
10	27.3268	+.0314
11	28.5022	.0350
12	29.7401	.0387
13	31.0366	.0429
14	32.4057	.0471
15	33.8461	.0514
16	35.3651	.0552
17	36.9551	.0600
18	38.6335	.0641
19	40.3933	.0684
20	42.2404	.0732
21	44.1861	.0785
22	46.2373	.0840
23	48.4027	.0897
24	50.6887	.0975
25	53.1239	.1045
26	55.7075	.1130
27	58.4625	.1226
28	61.4092	.1334
29	64.5726	.1460
30	67.9840	.1605
31	71.6750	.1773
32	75.6900	.1968
33	80.0767	.2199
34	84.8960	.2475
35	90.2242	.2805
36	96.1538	.3205

29th Year—D. or 70.

Age.	Value.	M. Diff.
10	23.8803	+.0171
11	24.8496	.0193
12	25.8573	.0234
13	26.9182	.0254
14	28.0341	.0284
15	29.1962	.0322
16	30.4179	.0337
17	31.6869	.0368
18	33.0164	.0389
19	34.3971	.0413
20	35.8323	.0430
21	37.3281	.0465
22	38.8884	.0492
23	40.5153	.0518
24	42.2107	.0557
25	43.9930	.0586
26	45.8553	.0625
27	47.8015	.0674
28	49.8706	.0712
29	42.0421	.0768
30	54.3437	.0830
31	56.7874	.0899
32	59.3948	.0983
33	62.1840	.1081
34	65.1840	.1196
35	68.4254	.1336
36	71.9516	.1505
37	75.8119	.1715
38	80.0711	.1964
39	84.8069	.2295
40	90.1162	.2705
41	96.1538	.3205

29th Year—D. or 75.

Age.	Value.	M. Diff.
10	21.8356	+.0084
11	22.6831	.0103
12	23.5629	.0128
13	24.4873	.0147
14	25.4475	.0177
15	26.4552	.0195
16	27.5062	.0210
17	28.5893	.0233
18	29.7195	.0241
19	30.8819	.0255
20	32.0838	.0265
21	33.3207	.0279
22	34.6019	.0289
23	35.9232	.0295
24	37.2840	.0316
25	38.7002	.0321
26	40.1579	.0333
27	41.6682	.0343
28	43.2320	.0355
29	44.8552	.0370
30	46.5435	.0386
31	48.3020	.0405
32	50.1392	.0424
33	52.0615	.0447
34	54.0761	.0478
35	56.1979	.0510
36	58.4400	.0557
37	60.8229	.0615

ENDOWMENT POLICIES.—4 PER CENT.

29th Year—D. or 75.

Age.	Value.	M. Diff.
38	63.3715	+.0693
39	66.1175	.0790
40	69.0965	.0922
41	72.3646	.1094
42	75.9873	.1319
43	80.0489	.1615
44	84.6605	.2005
45	89.9660	.2521
46	96.1538	.3205

30th YEAR—D. or 40.

Age.	Value.	M. Diff.
10	96.1538	+.3205

30th Year—D. or 45.

Age.	Value.	M. Diff.
10	71.6930	+.2173
11	75.8706	.2345
12	80.3699	.2532
13	85.2236	.2736
14	90.4700	.2960
15	96.1538	.3205

30th Year—D. or 50.

Age.	Value.	M. Diff.
10	54.7455	+.1458
11	57.6878	.1574
12	60.8316	.1699
13	64.1986	.1833
14	67.8062	.1983
15	71.6839	.2138
16	75.8526	.2311
17	80.3443	.2500
18	85.1952	.2710
19	90.4484	.2943
20	96.1538	.3205

30th Year—D. or 55.

Age.	Value.	M. Diff.
10	42.8501	+.0956
11	44.9833	.1035
12	47.2489	.1121
13	49.6609	.1211
14	52.2282	.1308
15	54.9658	.1406
16	57.8815	.1522
17	61.0002	.1637
18	64.3324	.1767
19	67.9030	.1909
20	71.7385	.2068
21	75.8696	.2244
22	80.3316	.2438
23	85.1612	.2668
24	90.4208	.2917
25	96.1538	.3205

30th Year—D. or 60.

Age.	Value.	M. Diff.
10	34.5371	+.0605
11	36.1328	.0657
12	37.8187	.0721
13	39.6074	.0780
14	41.4978	.0844
15	43.4982	.0907
16	45.6125	.0981
17	47.8563	.1051
18	50.2294	.1130
19	52.7472	.1214
20	55.4231	.1308
21	58.2748	.1411
22	61.3177	.1521
23	64.5716	.1657
24	68.0742	.1795
25	71.8397	.1958
26	75.9089	.2142
27	80.3218	.2352
28	85.1262	.2596
29	90.3807	.2877
30	96.1538	.3205

30th Year—D. or 65.

Age.	Value.	M. Diff.
10	28.8638	+.0365
11	30.1089	.0404
12	31.4215	.0446
13	32.7964	.0488
14	34.2474	.0531
15	35.7727	.0570
16	37.3718	.0618
17	39.0562	+.0660
18	40.8220	.0703
19	42.6747	.0752
20	44.6225	.0805
21	46.6766	.0861
22	48.8426	.0919
23	51.1271	.0996
24	53.5592	.1067
25	56.1353	.1152
26	58.8811	.1248
27	61.8145	.1356
28	64.9589	.1481
29	68.3452	.1625
30	72.0062	.1792
31	75.9804	.1986
32	80.3167	.2214
33	85.0734	.2486
34	90.3226	.2812
35	96.1538	.3205

30th Year—D. or 70.

Age.	Value.	M. Diff.
10	25.1881	+.0207
11	26.2079	.0240
12	27.2793	.0269
13	28.4009	.0300
14	29.5797	.0330
15	30.8065	.0354
16	32.0868	.0386
17	33.4251	.0406
18	34.8131	.0432
19	36.2575	.0458
20	37.7498	.0493
21	39.3270	.0513
22	40.9608	.0539
23	42.6608	.0579
24	44.4484	.0610
25	46.3142	.0648
26	48.2726	.0690
27	50.3313	.0737
28	52.5017	.0794
29	54.8000	.0855
30	57.2378	.0928
31	59.8309	.1012
32	62.6101	.1107
33	65.5910	.1222
34	68.8083	.1362
35	72.3024	.1530
36	76.1219	.1737
37	80.3295	.1992
38	85.0007	.2309
39	90.2337	.2706
40	96.1538	.3205

30th Year—D. or 75.

Age.	Value.	M. Diff.
10	23.0060	+.0117
11	23.8980	.0142
12	24.8305	.0161
13	25.8018	.0192
14	26.8234	.0211
15	27.8790	.0226
16	28.9753	.0250
17	30.1150	.0259
18	31.2858	.0273
19	32.4963	.0284
20	33.7441	.0298
21	35.0325	.0310
22	36.3631	.0317
23	37.7305	.0338
24	39.1561	.0344
25	40.6212	.0356
26	42.1379	.0368
27	43.7081	.0381
28	45.3364	.0397
29	47.0297	.0414
30	48.7923	.0433
31	50.6312	.0453
32	52.5527	.0478
33	54.5680	.0508
34	56.6862	.0543
35	58.9218	.0591
36	61.2971	.0650
37	63.8323	.0728
38	66.5611	.0826
39	69.5165	.0957
40	72.7531	.1128
41	76.3339	.1352
42	80.3407	.1644
43	84.8793	.2028
44	90.0896	.2534
45	96.1538	.3205

31st YEAR—D. or 45.

Age.	Value.	M. Diff.
10	76.1195	+.2356
11	80.5742	.2541
12	85.3735	.2743
13	90.5525	.2963
14	96.1538	.3205

31st Year—D. or 50.

Age.	Value.	M. Diff.
10	58.0530	+.1589
11	61.1866	.1715
12	64.5365	.1847
13	68.1222	.1996
14	71.9728	.2151
15	76.1044	.2320
16	80.5519	.2509
17	85.3472	.2717
18	90.5319	.2947
19	96.1538	.3205

31st Year—D. or 55.

Age.	Value.	M. Diff.
10	45.3723	+.1051
11	47.6399	.1137
12	50.0512	.1226
13	52.6165	.1325
14	55.3482	.1425
15	58.2544	.1538
16	61.3620	.1652
17	64.6761	.1782
18	68.2246	.1924
19	72.0319	.2081
20	76.1259	.2255
21	80.5423	.2448
22	85.3155	.2676
23	90.5058	.2921
24	96.1538	.3205

31st Year—D. or 60.

Age.	Value.	M. Diff.
10	36.5099	+.0673
11	38.2009	.0737
12	39.9971	.0797
13	41.8926	.0861
14	43.8976	.0925
15	46.0138	.0999
16	48.2591	.1069
17	50.6312	.1147
18	53.1450	.1232
19	55.8148	.1326
20	58.6566	.1429
21	61.6874	.1539
22	64.9224	.1674
23	68.4025	.1812
24	72.1388	.1973
25	76.1708	.2156
26	80.5376	.2364
27	85.2846	.2605
28	90.4682	.2882
29	96.1538	.3205

31st Year—D. or 65.

Age.	Value.	M. Diff.
10	30.4619	+.0419
11	31.7809	.0461
12	33.1710	.0504
13	34.6268	.0548
14	36.1615	.0587
15	37.7659	.0636
16	39.4581	.0678
17	41.2287	.0722
18	43.0859	.0779
19	45.0376	.0824
20	47.0920	.0881
21	49.2589	.0939
22	51.5418	.1017
23	53.9700	.1087
24	56.5402	.1173
25	59.2753	.1268
26	62.1959	.1377
27	65.3228	.1501
28	68.6851	.1644
29	72.3158	.1810
30	76.2533	.2002
31	80.5414	.2228
32	85.2388	.2497
33	90.4145	.2818
34	96.1538	.3205

31st Year—D. or 70.

Age.	Value.	M. Diff.
10	26.5398	+.0204
11	27.6225	.0284
12	28.7542	.0315
13	29.9383	.0345
14	31.1807	.0370
15	32.4654	.0402
16	33.8142	.0421
17	35.2101	.0450
18	36.6610	.0476
19	38.1715	.0504
20	39.7328	.0542
21	41.3834	.0560
22	43.0892	.0600
23	44.8800	.0631
24	46.7496	.0671
25	48.7094	.0713
26	50.7686	.0760
27	52.9364	.0818
28	55.2308	.0880
29	57.6625	.0953
30	60.2497	.1035
31	63.0110	.1132
32	65.9738	.1247
33	69.1676	.1386
34	72.6317	.1553
35	76.4122	.1758
36	80.5705	.2011
37	85.1797	.2324
38	90.3339	.2714
39	96.1538	.3205

31st Year—D. or 75.

Age.	Value.	M. Diff.
10	24.2155	+.0155
11	25.1597	.0175
12	26.1377	.0207
13	27.1708	.0226
14	28.2396	.0242
15	29.3402	.0266
16	30.4924	.0276
17	31.6720	.0290
18	32.8902	.0302
19	34.1458	.0317
20	35.4444	.0329
21	36.7814	.0337
22	38.1571	.0356
23	39.5884	.0365
24	41.0618	.0379
25	42.5848	.0391
26	44.1604	.0405
27	45.7936	.0422
28	47.4905	.0440
29	49.2565	.0461
30	51.0977	.0482
31	53.0189	.0507
32	55.0314	.0538
33	57.1476	.0574
34	59.3768	.0623
35	61.7424	.0683
36	64.2661	.0762
37	66.9771	.0859
38	69.9099	.0991
39	73.1164	.1161
40	76.6576	.1382
41	80.6124	.1671
42	85.0836	.2049
43	90.2051	.2547
44	96.1538	.3205

32d YEAR—D. or 45.

Age.	Value.	M. Diff.
10	80.7654	+.2549
11	85.5130	.2749
12	90.6293	.2967
13	96.1538	.3205

32d Year—D. or 50.

Age.	Value.	M. Diff.
10	61.5186	+.1729
11	64.8543	.1861
12	68.4186	.2009
13	72.2424	.2163
14	76.3411	.2333
15	80.7454	.2518
16	85.4891	.2723
17	90.6099	.2951
18	96.1538	.3205

32d Year—D. or 55.

Age.	Value.	M. Diff.
10	48.0087	+.1152
11	50.4197	.1244
12	52.9820	+.1341
13	55.7090	.1440
14	58.6081	.1553
15	61.7010	.1668
16	64.9991	.1798
17	68.5264	.1938
18	72.3056	.2094
19	76.3658	.2268
20	80.7379	.2459
21	85.4597	.2683
22	90.5852	.2925
23	96.1538	.3205

32d Year—D. or 60.

Age.	Value.	M. Diff.
10	38.5649	+.0753
11	40.3650	.0813
12	42.2665	.0878
13	44.2751	.0941
14	46.3941	.1016
15	48.6394	.1086
16	51.0108	.1164
17	53.5212	.1249
18	56.1844	.1344
19	59.0173	.1445
20	62.0348	.1555
21	65.2537	.1690
22	68.7108	.1827
23	72.4196	.1988
24	76.4167	.2169
25	80.7397	.2375
26	85.4327	.2613
27	90.5498	.2887
28	96.1538	.3205

32d Year—D. or 65.

Age.	Value.	M. Diff.
10	32.1250	+.0476
11	33.5207	.0519
12	34.9906	.0564
13	36.5292	.0603
14	38.1419	.0652
15	39.8383	.0694
16	41.6154	.0739
17	43.4759	.0789
18	45.4306	.0843
19	47.4873	.0900
20	49.6526	.0958
21	51.9343	.1036
22	54.3586	.1107
23	56.9222	.1192
24	59.6484	.1288
25	62.5550	.1396
26	65.6652	.1520
27	69.0055	.1663
28	72.6071	.1827
29	76.5084	.2018
30	80.7526	.2242
31	85.3936	.2507
32	90.5001	.2824
33	96.1538	.3205

32d Year—D. or 70.

Age.	Value.	M. Diff.
10	27.9476	+.0298
11	29.0900	.0329
12	30.2833	.0361
13	31.5306	.0386
14	32.8302	.0419
15	34.1823	.0441
16	35.5881	.0467
17	36.0460	.0495
18	38.5620	.0523
19	40.1457	.0548
20	41.7854	.0579
21	43.4955	.0620
22	45.2940	.0652
23	47.1616	.0693
24	49.1240	.0735
25	51.1827	.0783
26	53.3486	.0840
27	55.6385	.0903
28	58.0636	.0976
29	60.6416	.1058
30	63.3903	.1155
31	66.3345	.1270
32	69.5057	.1428
33	72.9418	.1574
34	76.6848	.1770
35	80.7963	.2028
36	85.3470	.2337
37	90.4284	.2720
38	96.1538	.3205

ENDOWMENT POLICIES.—4 PER CENT.

32d Year—D. or 75.

Age.	Value.	M. Diff.
10	25.4717	+.0188
11	26.4609	.0221
12	27.5002	.0240
13	28.5799	.0257
14	29.6931	.0281
15	30.8490	.0291
16	32.0404	.0307
17	33.2668	.0319
18	34.5296	.0335
19	35.8352	.0348
20	37.1815	.0356
21	38.5628	.0378
22	40.0015	.0386
23	41.4796	.0400
24	43.0098	.0414
25	44.5905	.0428
26	46.2278	.0446
27	47.9283	.0466
28	49.6964	.0486
29	51.5393	.0508
30	53.4609	.0535
31	55.4711	.0567
32	57.5822	.0604
33	59.8067	.0653
34	62.1629	.0714
35	64.6735	.0793
36	67.3687	.0891
37	70.2788	.1022
38	73.4566	.1191
39	76.9602	.1410
40	80.8663	.1696
41	85.2739	.2069
42	90.3129	.2559
43	96.1538	.3205

33d YEAR—D. or 45.

Age.	Value.	M. Diff.
10	85.6436	+.2754
11	90.7008	.2970
12	96.1538	.3205

33d Year—D. or 50.

Age.	Value.	M. Diff.
10	65.1514	+.1874
11	68.6973	.2021
12	72.4952	.2174
13	76.5620	.2342
14	80.9273	.2526
15	85.6214	.2729
16	90.6827	.2954
17	96.1538	.3205

33d Year—D. or 55.

Age.	Value.	M. Diff.
10	50.7674	+.1259
11	53.3281	.1355
12	56.0485	.1455
13	58.9390	.1568
14	62.0217	.1683
15	65.3037	.1811
16	68.8107	.1951
17	72.5632	.2106
18	76.5911	.2278
19	80.9241	.2467
20	85.5948	.2689
21	90.6593	.2929
22	96.1538	.3205

33d Year—D. or 60.

Age.	Value.	M. Diff.
10	40.7155	+.0828
11	42.6196	.0893
12	44.6326	.0957
13	46.7535	.1032
14	48.9998	.1102
15	51.3692	.1180
16	53.8767	.1266
17	56.5341	.1360
18	59.3575	.1462
19	62.3629	.1571
20	65.5651	.1706
21	69.0020	.1842
22	72.6833	.2001
23	76.6475	.2181
24	80.9293	.2385
25	85.5714	.2620
26	90.6262	.2891
27	96.1538	.3205

33d Year—D. or 65.

Age.	Value.	M. Diff.
10	33.8555	+.0533
11	35.3302	.0578
12	36.8817	.0618
13	38.4975	.0669
14	40.2009	.0711
15	41.9810	.0756
16	43.8467	.0806
17	45.8034	.0860
18	47.8614	.0917
19	50.0273	.0976
20	52.3056	.1054
21	54.7264	.1125
22	57.2836	.1211
23	60.0005	.1306
24	62.8950	.1414
25	65.9876	.1540
26	69.3070	.1680
27	72.8818	.1843
28	76.7485	.2032
29	80.9500	.2254
30	85.5392	.2517
31	90.5803	.2829
32	96.1538	.3205

33d Year—D. or 70.

Age.	Value.	M. Diff.
10	29.4083	+.0343
11	30.6117	.0374
12	31.8676	.0400
13	33.1712	.0434
14	34.5376	.0457
15	35.9461	.0491
16	37.4127	.0511
17	38.9358	.0540
18	40.5190	.0570
19	42.1686	.0597
20	43.8819	.0639
21	45.6799	.0671
22	47.5539	.0712
23	49.5172	.0755
24	51.5753	.0804
25	53.7391	.0862
26	56.0248	.0917
27	58.4429	.0998
28	61.0116	.1081
29	63.7478	.1178
30	66.6751	.1293
31	69.8241	.1430
32	73.2544	.1576
33	76.9404	.1797
34	81.0084	.2044
35	85.5036	.2349
36	90.5147	.2729
37	96.1538	.3205

33d Year—D. or 75.

Age.	Value.	M. Diff.
10	26.7672	+.0234
11	27.8171	.0254
12	28.9026	.0271
13	30.0261	.0296
14	31.1939	.0307
15	32.3886	.0323
16	33.6262	.0336
17	34.8964	.0352
18	36.2085	.0365
19	37.5611	.0374
20	38.9509	.0398
21	40.3943	.0406
22	41.8789	.0421
23	43.4129	.0435
24	44.9996	.0459
25	46.6408	.0469
26	48.3441	.0488
27	50.1143	.0511
28	51.9577	.0534
29	53.8794	.0561
30	55.8879	.0594
31	57.9946	.0631
32	60.2117	.0681
33	62.5603	.0743
34	65.0581	.0822
35	67.7365	.0920
36	70.6261	.1051
37	73.7756	.1219
38	77.2437	.1437
39	81.1036	.1719
40	85.4516	.2088
41	90.4132	.2570
42	96.1538	.3205

34th YEAR—D. or 45.

Age.	Value.	M. Diff.
10	90.7677	+.2973
11	96.1538	.3205

34th Year—D. or 50.

Age.	Value.	M. Diff.
10	68.9580	+.2033
11	72.7330	.2184
12	76.7691	.2351
13	81.0971	.2534
14	85.7458	.2734
15	90.7506	.2957
16	96.1538	.3205

34th Year—D. or 55.

Age.	Value.	M. Diff.
10	53.6528	+.1370
11	56.3691	.1468
12	59.2514	.1582
13	62.3234	.1696
14	65.5909	.1823
15	69.0762	.1964
16	72.8061	.2118
17	76.8020	.2288
18	81.0976	.2475
19	85.7212	.2696
20	90.7277	.2933
21	96.1538	.3205

34th Year—D. or 60.

Age.	Value.	M. Diff.
10	42.9559	+.0907
11	44.9702	.0971
12	47.0940	.1047
13	49.3404	.1117
14	51.7090	.1196
15	54.2124	.1281
16	56.8645	.1375
17	59.6794	.1477
18	62.6726	.1586
19	65.8593	.1720
20	69.2757	.1856
21	72.9323	.2014
22	76.8642	.2192
23	81.1073	.2395
24	85.7016	.2628
25	90.6977	.2895
26	96.1538	.3205

34th Year—D. or 65.

Age.	Value.	M. Diff.
10	35.6553	+.0592
11	37.2109	.0633
12	38.8384	.0683
13	40.5439	.0726
14	42.3299	.0771
15	44.1974	.0822
16	46.1578	.0876
17	48.2163	.0934
18	50.3819	.0993
19	52.6588	.1071
20	55.0742	.1143
21	57.6256	.1228
22	60.3335	.1324
23	63.2157	.1431
24	66.2928	.1555
25	69.5909	.1696
26	73.1402	.1858
27	76.9749	.2046
28	81.1359	.2266
29	85.6753	.2525
30	90.6557	.2835
31	96.1538	.3205

34th Year—D. or 70.

Age.	Value.	M. Diff.
10	30.9228	+.0388
11	32.1879	.0414
12	33.4996	.0448
13	34.8696	.0472
14	36.2911	.0498
15	37.7598	.0526
16	39.2897	.0556
17	40.8801	.0586
18	42.5323	.0615
19	44.2504	.0657
20	46.0504	.0690
21	47.9260	.0731
22	49.8896	.0775
23	51.9474	.0824
24	54.1095	.0882

34th Year—D. or 70.

Age.	Value.	M. Diff.
25	56.3910	+.0946
26	58.8032	.1019
27	61.3616	.1102
28	64.0855	.1199
29	66.9974	.1313
30	70.1254	.1450
31	73.5055	.1614
32	77.1812	.1816
33	81.2074	.2059
34	85.6506	.2361
35	90.5963	.2736
36	96.1538	.3205

34th Year—D. or 75.

Age.	Value.	M. Diff.
10	28.1174	+.0267
11	29.2130	.0284
12	30.3418	.0310
13	31.5194	.0321
14	32.7255	.0338
15	33.9658	.0351
16	35.2465	.0368
17	36.5654	.0382
18	37.9237	.0392
19	39.3191	.0416
20	40.7701	.0425
21	42.2586	.0440
22	43.7981	.0455
23	45.3876	.0471
24	47.0336	.0491
25	48.7396	.0511
26	50.5113	.0534
27	52.3554	.0558
28	54.2759	.0586
29	56.2826	.0619
30	58.3857	.0658
31	60.5960	.0708
32	62.9345	.0770
33	65.4217	.0850
34	68.0837	.0948
35	70.9522	.1078
36	74.0760	.1246
37	77.5095	.1462
38	81.3259	.1741
39	85.6177	.2105
40	90.5070	.2580
41	96.1538	.3205

35th YEAR—D. or 45.

Age.	Value.	M. Diff.
10	96.1538	+.3205

35th Year—D. or 50.

Age.	Value.	M. Diff.
10	72.9553	+.2194
11	76.9639	.2360
12	81.2563	.2541
13	85.8618	.2740
14	90.8143	.2960
15	96.1538	.3205

35th Year—D. or 55.

Age.	Value.	M. Diff.
10	56.6715	+.1482
11	59.5464	.1595
12	62.6074	.1709
13	65.8610	.1836
14	69.3292	.1975
15	73.0336	.2128
16	77.0016	.2298
17	81.2602	.2483
18	85.8399	.2702
19	90.7937	.2936
20	96.1532	.3205

35th Year—D. or 60.

Age.	Value.	M. Diff.
10	45.2917	+.0986
11	47.4153	.1061
12	49.6630	.1132
13	52.0300	.1210
14	54.5306	.1296
15	57.1765	.1390
16	59.9836	.1491
17	62.9654	.1600
18	66.1368	.1734
19	69.5342	.1869
20	73.1664	.2026
21	77.0689	.2203
22	81.2745	.2404
23	85.8238	+.2634
24	90.7649	.2899
25	96.1538	.3205

35th Year—D. or 65.

Age.	Value.	M. Diff.
10	37.5259	+.0646
11	39.1566	.0697
12	40.8727	.0741
13	42.6598	.0786
14	44.5320	.0837
15	46.4930	.0892
16	48.5538	.0950
17	50.7183	.1009
18	52.9931	.1088
19	55.4052	.1159
20	57.9491	.1245
21	60.6487	.1341
22	63.5191	.1449
23	66.5808	.1571
24	69.8597	.1711
25	73.3836	.1873
26	77.1879	.2059
27	81.3110	.2277
28	85.8034	.2534
29	90.7262	.2839
30	96.1538	.3205

35th Year—D. or 70.

Age.	Value.	M. Diff.
10	32.4912	+.0429
11	33.8117	.0462
12	35.1889	.0486
13	36.6134	.0513
14	38.0943	.0542
15	39.6257	.0572
16	41.2212	.0604
17	42.8793	.0632
18	44.5998	.0674
19	46.4036	.0708
20	48.2800	.0749
21	50.2438	.0794
22	52.3013	.0843
23	54.4603	.0902
24	56.7381	.0966
25	59.1434	.1039
26	61.6935	.1122
27	64.4047	.1219
28	67.3012	.1333
29	70.4095	.1469
30	73.7646	.1633
31	77.4079	.1832
32	81.3945	.2074
33	85.7887	.2370
34	90.6731	.2743
35	96.1538	.3205

35th Year—D. or 75.

Age.	Value.	M. Diff.
10	29.5072	+.0297
11	30.6456	.0323
12	31.8281	.0335
13	33.0433	.0352
14	34.2943	.0367
15	35.5773	.0384
16	36.9058	.0398
17	38.2704	.0408
18	39.6708	.0433
19	41.1266	.0443
20	42.6218	.0459
21	44.1643	.0474
22	45.7583	.0491
23	47.4062	.0511
24	49.1158	.0532
25	50.8889	.0556
26	52.7330	.0580
27	54.6527	.0609
28	56.6566	.0643
29	58.7559	.0683
30	60.9603	.0734
31	63.2898	.0796
32	65.7641	.0877
33	68.4119	.0974
34	71.2602	.1105
35	74.3580	.1271
36	77.7597	.1485
37	81.5343	.1762
38	85.7733	.2121
39	90.5947	.2590
40	96.1538	.3205

ENDOWMENT POLICIES.—4 PER CENT.

36th YEAR—D. or 50.

AGE.	Value.	M. Diff.
10	77.1461	+.2368
11	81.4060	.2547
12	85.9706	.2745
13	90.8739	.2963
14	96.1538	.3205

36th Year—D. or 55.

AGE.	Value.	M. Diff.
10	59.8247	+.1607
11	62.8756	.1721
12	66.1153	.1844
13	69.5663	.1985
14	73.2487	.2138
15	77.1882	.2307
16	81.4135	.2490
17	85.9513	.2708
18	90.8547	.2939
19	96.1538	.3205

36th Year—D. or 60.

AGE.	Value.	M. Diff.
10	47.7215	+.1074
11	49.9676	.1145
12	52.3341	.1224
13	54.8313	.1309
14	57.4721	.1404
15	60.2708	.1505
16	63.2422	.1614
17	66.3994	.1746
18	69.7781	.1881
19	73.3875	.2037
20	77.2612	.2213
21	81.4324	.2412
22	85.9386	.2641
23	90.8279	.2902
24	96.1538	.3205

36th Year—D. or 65.

AGE.	Value.	M. Diff.
10	39.4613	+.0710
11	41.1796	.0754
12	42.9761	.0801
13	44.8484	.0852
14	46.8128	.0907
15	48.8730	.0965
16	51.0382	.1024
17	53.3103	.1103
18	55.7185	.1175
19	58.2569	.1261
20	60.9468	.1356
21	63.8063	.1463
22	66.8532	.1586
23	70.1133	.1725
24	73.6140	.1886
25	77.3885	.2071
26	81.4759	.2287
27	85.9241	.2541
28	90.7926	.2844
29	96.1538	.3205

36th Year—D. or 70.

AGE.	Value.	M. Diff.
10	34.1075	+.0475
11	35.4927	.0499
12	36.9238	.0527
13	38.4069	.0556
14	39.9495	.0587
15	41.5466	.0618
16	43.2098	.0648
17	44.9336	.0691
18	46.7387	.0723
19	48.6175	.0766
20	50.5808	.0812
21	52.6372	.0861
22	54.7942	.0921
23	57.0669	.0984
24	59.4671	.1058
25	62.0081	.1141
26	64.7077	.1236
27	67.5885	.1352
28	70.6777	.1491
29	74.0090	.1650
30	77.6224	.1848
31	81.5710	.2088
32	85.9185	.2382
33	90.7423	.2751
34	96.1538	.3205

36th Year—D. or 75.

AGE.	Value.	M. Diff.
10	30.9335	+.0336
11	32.1250	.0349
12	33.3446	.0366
13	34.6042	.0381
14	35.8972	.0399
15	37.2276	.0414
16	38.6011	.0425
17	40.0070	.0449
18	41.4671	.0460
19	42.9664	.0477
20	44.5147	.0493
21	46.1109	.0510
22	47.7622	.0531
23	49.4726	.0553
24	51.2480	.0577
25	53.0922	.0602
26	55.0105	.0632
27	57.0119	.0667
28	59.1066	.0706
29	61.3053	.0758
30	63.6265	.0821
31	66.0890	.0901
32	68.7210	.0999
33	71.5512	.1130
34	74.6244	.1295
35	77.9947	.1507
36	81.7305	.1781
37	85.9192	.2136
38	90.6768	.2599
39	96.1538	.3205

37th YEAR—D. or 50.

AGE.	Value.	M. Diff.
10	81.5460	+.2554
11	86.0730	.2749
12	90.9297	.2965
13	96.1538	.3205

37th Year—D. or 55.

AGE.	Value.	M. Diff.
10	63.1286	+.1732
11	66.3555	.1858
12	69.7855	.1999
13	73.4513	.2148
14	77.3648	.2315
15	81.5571	.2497
16	86.0563	.2713
17	90.9120	.2942
18	96.1538	.3205

37th Year—D. or 60.

AGE.	Value.	M. Diff.
10	50.2578	+.1158
11	52.6212	.1237
12	55.1160	.1323
13	57.7516	.1416
14	60.5430	.1518
15	63.5035	.1626
16	66.6475	.1759
17	70.0088	.1893
18	73.5961	.2048
19	77.4429	.2223
20	81.5807	.2420
21	86.0470	.2646
22	90.8871	.2906
23	96.1538	.3205

37th Year—D. or 65.

AGE.	Value.	M. Diff.
10	41.4734	+.0767
11	43.2713	.0814
12	45.1518	.0865
13	47.1153	.0921
14	49.1774	.0979
15	51.3406	.1039
16	53.6118	.1118
17	56.0156	.1190
18	58.5483	.1276
19	61.2305	.1371
20	64.0779	.1479
21	67.1111	.1600
22	70.3531	.1739
23	73.8314	.1899
24	77.5783	.2082
25	81.6311	.2296
26	86.0377	.2549
27	90.8551	.2848
28	96.1538	.3205

37th Year—D. or 70.

AGE.	Value.	M. Diff.
10	35.7806	+.0504
11	37.2189	.0541
12	38.7080	.0570
13	40.2522	.0601
14	41.8593	.0633
15	43.5227	.0665
16	45.2514	.0706
17	47.0585	.0742
18	48.9377	.0793
19	50.9015	.0829
20	52.9565	.0878
21	55.1116	.0929
22	57.3803	.1002
23	59.7726	.1078
24	62.3059	.1159
25	64.9946	.1255
26	67.8587	.1371
27	70.9314	.1505
28	74.2397	.1666
29	77.8245	.1863
30	81.7378	.2100
31	86.0408	.2392
32	90.8129	.2755
33	96.1538	.3205

37th Year—D. or 75.

AGE.	Value.	M. Diff.
10	32.4064	+.0361
11	33.6346	.0379
12	34.8981	.0394
13	36.1991	.0413
14	37.5389	.0428
15	38.9137	.0440
16	40.3278	.0465
17	41.7927	.0476
18	43.2955	.0493
19	44.8471	.0510
20	46.4481	.0528
21	48.1007	.0550
22	49.8135	.0572
23	51.5886	.0597
24	53.4339	.0623
25	55.3509	.0653
26	57.3494	.0688
27	59.4399	.0729
28	61.6321	.0781
29	63.9453	.0844
30	66.3971	.0925
31	69.0143	.1023
32	71.8253	.1152
33	74.8761	.1317
34	78.2166	.1528
35	81.9148	.1799
36	86.0566	.2151
37	90.7537	.2608
38	96.1538	.3205

38th YEAR—D. or 50.

AGE.	Value.	M. Diff.
10	86.1687	+.2754
11	90.9822	.2968
12	96.1538	.3205

38th Year—D. or 55.

AGE.	Value.	M. Diff.
10	66.5820	+.1868
11	70.0003	.2005
12	73.6418	.2156
13	77.5309	.2323
14	81.6930	.2504
15	86.1546	.2718
16	90.9659	.2945
17	96.1538	.3205

38th Year—D. or 60.

AGE.	Value.	M. Diff.
10	52.8947	+.1249
11	55.3849	.1335
12	58.0162	.1429
13	60.8002	.1530
14	63.7512	.1638
15	66.8817	.1770
16	70.2269	.1903
17	73.7934	.2058
18	77.6144	.2232
19	81.7209	.2428
20	86.1488	.2652
21	90.9429	.2909
22	96.1538	.3205

38th Year—D. or 65.

AGE.	Value.	M. Diff.
10	43.5540	+.0827
11	45.4349	.0879
12	47.4052	.0935
13	49.4654	.0993
14	51.6292	.1053
15	53.8971	.1132
16	56.2982	.1204
17	58.8247	.1290
18	61.4990	.1385
19	64.3363	.1492
20	67.3549	.1614
21	70.5802	.1752
22	74.0370	.1911
23	77.7575	.2093
24	81.7730	.2310
25	86.1447	.2556
26	90.9140	.2852
27	96.1538	.3205

38th Year—D. or 70.

AGE.	Value.	M. Diff.
10	37.4985	+.0553
11	38.9943	.0583
12	40.5437	.0615
13	51.1517	.0647
14	43.8242	.0677
15	45.5528	.0720
16	47.3628	.0756
17	49.2436	.0798
18	51.2069	.0844
19	53.2612	.0894
20	55.4120	.0955
21	57.6669	.1027
22	60.0639	.1093
23	62.5910	.1174
24	65.2666	.1273
25	68.1191	.1386
26	71.1720	.1521
27	74.4579	.1681
28	78.0166	.1884
29	81.8952	.2112
30	86.1565	.2402
31	90.8767	.2760
32	96.1538	.3205

38th Year—D. or 75.

AGE.	Value.	M. Diff.
10	33.9094	+.0392
11	35.1809	.0407
12	36.4854	.0426
13	37.8326	.0442
14	39.2160	.0454
15	40.6310	.0480
16	42.1033	.0503
17	43.6102	.0510
18	45.1646	.0527
19	46.7681	.0546
20	48.4245	.0568
21	50.1377	.0590
22	51.9141	.0616
23	53.7579	.0642
24	55.6746	.0673
25	57.6704	.0709
26	59.7565	.0750
27	61.9427	.0803
28	64.2474	.0867
29	66.6888	.0947
30	69.2924	.1045
31	72.0855	.1174
32	75.1131	.1338
33	78.4263	.1547
34	82.0887	.1817
35	86.1856	.2164
36	90.8262	.2616
37	96.1538	.3205

39th YEAR—D. or 50.

AGE.	Value.	M. Diff.
10	91.0313	+.2970
11	96.1538	.3205

39th Year—D. or 55.

AGE.	Value.	M. Diff.
10	70.1992	+.2014
11	73.8219	.2165
12	77.6872	.2330
13	81.8208	.2510
14	86.2476	.2722
15	91.0165	.2947
16	96.1538	.3205

39th Year—D. or 60.

AGE.	Value.	M. Diff.
10	55.6410	+.1347
11	58.2660	.1441
12	61.0439	.1542
13	63.9853	.1649
14	67.1037	.1781
15	70.4328	.1914
16	73.9799	.2068
17	77.7766	.2240
18	81.8532	.2435
19	86.2451	.2658
20	90.9955	.2912
21	96.1538	.3205

39th Year—D. or 65.

AGE.	Value.	M. Diff.
10	45.7060	+.0891
11	47.6759	.0947
12	49.7414	.1006
13	51.9021	.1066
14	54.1691	.1146
15	56.5654	.1218
16	59.0874	.1303
17	61.7537	.1398
18	64.5810	.1505
19	67.5870	.1626
20	70.7949	.1764
21	74.2317	.1922
22	77.9269	.2103
23	81.9167	.2314
24	86.2460	.2562
25	90.9694	.2856
26	96.1538	.3205

39th Year—D. or 70.

AGE.	Value.	M. Diff.
10	39.2655	+.0596
11	40.8207	.0628
12	42.4333	.0661
13	44.1059	.0691
14	45.8419	.0735
15	47.6514	.0770
16	49.5343	.0813
17	51.4978	.0860
18	53.5500	.0910
19	55.6993	.0962
20	57.9593	.1036
21	60.3403	.1109
22	62.8571	.1192
23	65.5244	.1289
24	68.3639	.1402
25	71.3979	.1538
26	74.6649	.1696
27	78.1963	.1889
28	82.0538	.2115
29	86.2657	.2410
30	90.9371	.2765
31	96.1538	.3205

39th Year—D. or 75.

AGE.	Value.	M. Diff.
10	35.4491	+.0419
11	36.7609	.0439
12	38.1111	.0455
13	39.5013	.0468
14	40.9242	.0495
15	42.3969	.0506
16	43.9245	.0513
17	45.4681	.0543
18	47.0737	.0562
19	48.7318	.0585
20	50.4478	.0608
21	52.2236	.0634
22	54.0675	.0661
23	55.9816	.0692
24	57.9758	.0729
25	60.0576	.0771
26	62.2377	.0824
27	64.5345	.0887
28	66.9651	.0968
29	69.5557	.1066
30	72.3321	.1195
31	75.3381	.1358
32	78.6238	.1566
33	82.2532	.1833
34	86.3074	.2178
35	90.8943	.2623
36	96.1538	.3205

40th YEAR—D. or 50.

AGE.	Value.	M. Diff.
10	96.1538	+.3205

ENDOWMENT POLICIES.—4 PER CENT.

40th Year—D. or 55.

AGE.	Value.	M. Diff.
10	73.9916	+.2173
11	77.8348	.2337
12	81.9411	.2516
13	86.3352	.2726
14	91.0643	.2950
15	96.1538	.3205

40th Year—D. or 60.

AGE.	Value.	M. Diff.
10	58.5041	+.1452
11	61.2739	.1553
12	64.2070	.1660
13	67.3135	.1792
14	70.6279	.1924
15	74.1560	.2076
16	77.9298	.2248
17	81.9783	.2442
18	86.3359	.2663
19	91.0451	.2916
20	96.1538	.3205

40th Year—D. or 65.

AGE.	Value.	M. Diff.
10	47.9350	+.0959
11	49.9991	.1018
12	52.1638	.1079
13	54.4264	.1158
14	56.8203	.1230
15	59.3360	.1316
16	61.9958	.1411
17	64.8130	.1517
18	67.8066	.1637
19	70.9992	.1776
20	74.4157	.1933
21	78.0873	.2113
22	82.0478	.2323
23	86.3415	.2569
24	91.0218	.2859
25	96.1538	.3205

40th Year—D. or 70.

AGE.	Value.	M. Diff.
10	41.0833	+.0640
11	42.7009	.0673
12	44.3777	.0704
13	46.1128	.0748
14	47.9292	.0784
15	49.8098	.0828
16	51.7748	.0874
17	53.8257	.0925
18	55.9718	.0985
19	58.2286	.1050
20	60.6042	.1124
21	63.1121	.1208
22	65.7695	.1305
23	68.5958	.1417
24	71.6070	.1558
25	74.8609	.1710
26	78.3676	.1902
27	82.1842	.2134
28	86.3687	.2419
29	90.9940	.2777
30	96.1538	.3205

40th Year—D. or 75.

AGE.	Value.	M. Diff.
10	37.0219	+.0451
11	38.3790	.0468
12	39.7718	.0481
13	41.2009	.0508
14	42.6808	.0521
15	44.1942	.0540
16	45.7578	.0558
17	47.3659	.0578
18	49.0252	.0601
19	50.7420	.0625
20	52.5196	.0652
21	54.3619	.0679
22	56.2750	.0711
23	58.2653	.0748
24	60.3440	.0790
25	62.5183	.0843
26	64.8071	.0908
27	67.2277	.0989
28	69.8052	.1086
29	72.5656	.1215
30	75.5514	.1377
31	78.8113	.1583
32	82.4081	.1848
33	86.4225	.2189
34	90.9586	.2630
35	96.1538	.3205

41st YEAR—D. or 55.

AGE.	Value.	M. Diff.
10	77.9741	+.2344
11	82.0548	.2519
12	86.4175	.2731
13	91.1093	.2952
14	96.1538	.3205

41st Year—D. or 60.

AGE.	Value.	M. Diff.
10	61.4930	+.1563
11	64.4163	.1670
12	67.5122	.1801
13	70.8122	.1933
14	74.3228	.2085
15	78.0745	.2256
16	82.0965	.2448
17	86.4218	.2667
18	91.0919	.2918
19	96.1538	.3205

41st Year—D. or 65.

AGE.	Value.	M. Diff.
10	50.2458	+.1030
11	52.4080	.1091
12	54.6731	.1171
13	57.0615	.1242
14	59.5730	.1328
15	62.2249	.1423
16	65.0336	.1529
17	68.0149	.1650
18	71.1926	.1787
19	74.5908	.1943
20	78.2390	.2123
21	82.1720	.2330
22	86.4319	.2574
23	91.0713	.2863
24	96.1538	.3205

41st Year—D. or 70.

AGE.	Value.	M. Diff.
10	42.9547	+.0685
11	44.6354	.0716
12	46.3738	.0761
13	48.1889	.0797
14	50.0753	.0841
15	52.0372	.0888
16	54.0883	.0938
17	56.2319	.1000
18	58.4841	.1065
19	60.8538	.1139
20	63.3546	.1223
21	66.0023	.1319
22	68.8164	.1432
23	71.8208	.1566
24	75.0468	.1725
25	78.5300	.1914
26	82.3175	.2144
27	86.4661	.2426
28	91.0478	.2774
29	96.1538	.3205

41st Year—D. or 75.

AGE.	Value.	M. Diff.
10	38.6329	+.0480
11	40.0321	.0494
12	41.4633	.0521
13	42.9487	.0534
14	44.4687	.0554
15	46.0315	.0572
16	47.6447	.0593
17	49.3058	.0617
18	51.0230	.0641
19	52.8005	.0668
20	54.6436	.0696
21	56.5540	.0728
22	58.5420	.0766
23	60.6156	.0808
24	62.7851	.0862
25	65.0664	.0927
26	67.4771	.1008
27	70.0423	.1105
28	72.7868	.1233
29	75.7534	.1395
30	78.9890	.1600
31	82.5550	.1863
32	86.5309	.2200
33	91.0193	.2637
34	96.1538	.3205

42d YEAR—D. or 55.

AGE.	Value.	M. Diff.
10	82.1620	+.2526
11	86.4926	.2737
12	91.1516	.2954
13	96.1538	.3205

42d Year—D. or 60.

AGE.	Value.	M. Diff.
10	64.6156	+.1680
11	67.6999	.1811
12	70.9869	.1942
13	74.4805	.2093
14	78.2117	.2263
15	82.2081	.2454
16	86.5029	.2672
17	91.1362	.2920
18	96.1538	.3205

42d Year—D. or 65.

AGE.	Value.	M. Diff.
10	52.6418	+.1102
11	54.9034	.1182
12	57.2926	.1254
13	59.7973	.1340
14	62.4433	.1435
15	65.2423	.1540
16	68.2130	.1661
17	71.3761	.1797
18	74.7566	.1953
19	78.3834	.2131
20	82.2894	.2338
21	86.5175	.2580
22	91.1181	.2866
23	96.1538	.3205

42d Year—D. or 70.

AGE.	Value.	M. Diff.
10	44.8798	+.0728
11	46.6217	.0774
12	48.4390	.0810
13	50.3233	.0854
14	52.2898	.0901
15	54.3369	.0952
16	56.4795	.1013
17	58.7279	.1079
18	61.0908	.1145
19	63.5859	.1236
20	66.2236	.1333
21	69.0258	.1445
22	72.0157	.1578
23	75.2230	.1735
24	78.6866	.1923
25	82.4438	.2154
26	86.5585	.2434
27	91.0986	.2779
28	96.1538	.3205

42d Year—D. or 75.

AGE.	Value.	M. Diff.
10	40.2788	+.0505
11	41.7158	.0533
12	43.2028	.0547
13	44.7276	.0567
14	46.2962	.0586
15	47.9082	.0607
16	49.5735	.0631
17	51.2917	.0656
18	53.0688	.0684
19	54.9108	.0712
20	56.8208	.0745
21	58.8052	.0783
22	60.8752	.0826
23	63.0382	.0880
24	65.3131	.0945
25	67.7144	.1026
26	70.2674	.1124
27	72.9970	.1251
28	75.9447	.1412
29	79.1572	.1616
30	82.6944	.1876
31	86.6338	.2211
32	91.0765	.2643
33	96.1538	.3205

43d YEAR—D. or 55.

AGE.	Value.	M. Diff.
10	86.5687	+.2739
11	91.1919	.2956
12	96.1538	.3205

43d Year—D. or 60.

AGE.	Value.	M. Diff.
10	67.8786	+.1819
11	71.1518	.1950
12	74.6299	.2101
13	78.3413	.2270
14	82.3139	.2460
15	86.5796	.2676
16	91.1780	.2922
17	96.1538	.3205

43d Year—D. or 65.

AGE.	Value.	M. Diff.
10	55.1238	+.1193
11	57.5083	.1265
12	60.0122	.1351
13	62.6500	.1446
14	65.4413	.1551
15	68.4003	.1671
16	71.5505	.1807
17	74.9139	.1962
18	78.5200	.2139
19	82.4011	.2345
20	86.5984	.2585
21	91.1624	.2869
22	96.1538	.3205

43d Year—D. or 70.

AGE.	Value.	M. Diff.
10	46.8568	+.0785
11	48.6767	.0822
12	50.5622	.0866
13	52.5260	.0914
14	54.5764	.0965
15	56.7129	.1027
16	58.9600	.1092
17	61.3185	.1166
18	63.7952	.1258
19	66.4346	.1346
20	69.2249	.1458
21	72.2005	.1590
22	75.3905	.1747
23	78.8295	.1936
24	82.5634	.2163
25	86.6461	.2441
26	91.1468	.2783
27	96.1538	.3205

43d Year—D. or 75.

AGE.	Value.	M. Diff.
10	41.9550	+.0545
11	43.4472	.0559
12	44.9732	.0579
13	46.5460	.0600
14	48.1630	.0621
15	49.8265	.0645
16	51.5480	.0671
17	53.3253	.0698
18	55.1660	.0728
19	57.0741	.0761
20	59.0568	.0799
21	61.1220	.0842
22	63.2801	.0897
23	65.5470	.0962
24	67.9400	.1043
25	70.4816	.1141
26	73.1967	.1268
27	76.1265	.1428
28	79.3166	.1631
29	82.8263	.1889
30	86.7314	.2221
31	91.1308	.2649
32	96.1538	.3205

44th YEAR—D. or 55.

AGE.	Value.	M. Diff.
10	91.2294	+.2958
11	96.1538	.3205

44th Year—D. or 60.

AGE.	Value.	M. Diff.
10	71.3088	+.1958
11	74.7709	.2108
12	78.4640	.2276
13	82.4139	.2465
14	86.6522	.2680
15	91.2175	.2925
16	96.1538	.3205

44th Year—D. or 65.

AGE.	Value.	M. Diff.
10	57.7149	+.1275
11	60.2129	.1361
12	62.8481	.1456
13	65.6296	.1561
14	68.5791	.1681
15	71.7154	.1817
16	75.0634	.1971
17	78.6496	.2147
18	82.5068	.2351
19	86.6753	.2590
20	91.2044	.2871
21	96.1538	.3205

44th Year—D. or 70.

AGE.	Value.	M. Diff.
10	48.9020	+.0833
11	50.7895	.0878
12	52.7534	.0925
13	54.8003	.0977
14	56.9398	.1039
15	59.1798	.1104
16	61.5346	.1179
17	64.0146	.1262
18	66.6348	.1358
19	69.4148	.1470
20	72.3763	.1602
21	75.5496	.1758
22	78.9682	.1946
23	82.6769	.2172
24	86.7290	.2448
25	91.1925	.2787
26	96.1538	.3205

44th Year—D. or 75.

AGE.	Value.	M. Diff.
10	43.6789	+.0571
11	45.2095	.0592
12	46.7829	.0612
13	48.4035	.0634
14	50.0712	.0658
15	51.7903	.0684
16	53.5700	.0713
17	55.4100	.0742
18	57.3159	.0776
19	59.2956	.0815
20	61.3581	.0858
21	63.5100	.0913
22	65.7705	.0978
23	68.1540	.1060
24	70.6853	.1157
25	73.3866	.1284
26	76.2992	.1443
27	79.4681	.1645
28	82.9513	.1902
29	86.8237	.2231
30	91.1822	.2655
31	96.1538	.3205

45th YEAR—D. or 55.

AGE.	Value.	M. Diff.
10	96.1538	+.3205

45th Year—D. or 60.

AGE.	Value.	M. Diff.
10	74.9052	+.2115
11	78.5799	.2282
12	82.5086	.2470
13	86.7208	.2684
14	91.2550	.2927
15	96.1538	.3205

45th Year—D. or 65.

AGE.	Value.	M. Diff.
10	60.4050	+.1371
11	63.0330	.1466
12	65.8101	.1571
13	68.7481	.1691
14	71.8728	.1825
15	75.2048	.1979
16	78.7728	.2155
17	82.6071	.2358
18	86.7482	.2595
19	91.2442	.2874
20	96.1538	.3205

45th Year—D. or 70.

AGE.	Value.	M. Diff.
10	51.0048	+.0889
11	52.9697	.0937

45th Year—D. or 70.

Age.	Value.	M. Diff.
12	55.0151	+.0990
13	57.1509	.1051
14	59.3916	.1116
15	61.7392	.1191
16	64.2139	.1275
17	66.8258	.1371
18	69.5949	.1482
19	72.5439	.1613
20	75.7018	.1768
21	79.0998	.1955
22	82.7848	.2180
23	86.8077	.2454
24	91.2358	.2790
25	96.1538	.3205

45th Year—D. or 75.

Age.	Value.	M. Diff.
10	45.4334	+.0603
11	47.0108	.0624
12	48.6315	.0646
13	50.3021	.0671
14	52.0246	.0698
15	53.8013	.0726
16	55.6428	.0756
17	57.5471	.0790
18	59.5237	.0829
19	61.5821	.0873
20	63.7300	.0928
21	65.9831	.0994
22	68.3585	.1075
23	70.8785	.1173
24	73.5672	.1299
25	76.4635	.1458
26	79.6120	.1658
27	83.0701	.1913
28	86.9112	.2240
29	91.2310	.2661
30	96.1538	.3205

46th YEAR—D. or 60.

Age.	Value.	M. Diff.
10	78.6903	+.2288
11	82.5979	.2475
12	86.7858	.2688
13	91.2904	.2929
14	96.1538	.3205

46th Year—D. or 65.

Age.	Value.	M. Diff.
10	63.2100	+.1475
11	65.9785	.1580
12	68.9101	.1700
13	72.0217	.1834
14	75.3397	.1987
15	78.8893	.2161
16	82.7025	.2363
17	86.8173	.2600
18	91.2820	.2877
19	96.1538	.3205

46th Year—D. or 70.

Age.	Value.	M. Diff.
10	53.1746	+.0948
11	55.2209	.1000
12	57.3544	.1062
13	59.5896	.1128
14	61.9363	.1203
15	64.4027	.1286
16	67.0078	.1382
17	69.7667	.1493
18	72.7030	.1624
19	75.8449	.1779
20	79.2249	.1966
21	82.8871	.2188
22	86.8826	.2460
23	91.2769	.2793
24	96.1538	.3205

46th Year—D. or 75.

Age.	Value.	M. Diff.
10	47.2268	+.0635
11	48.8509	.0658
12	50.5210	.0683
13	52.2457	.0710
14	54.0250	.0740
15	55.8629	.0770
16	57.7677	.0804
17	59.7418	.0844
18	61.7960	.0888
19	63.9387	.0943

46th Year—D. or 75.

Age.	Value.	M. Diff.
20	66.1864	+.1009
21	68.5529	.1090
22	71.0631	.1188
23	73.7386	.1313
24	76.6197	.1472
25	79.7488	.1671
26	83.1829	.1925
27	86.9944	.2249
28	91.2772	.2666
29	96.1538	.3205

47th YEAR—D. or 60.

Age.	Value.	M. Diff.
10	82.6831	+.2480
11	86.8472	.2691
12	91.3239	.2931
13	96.1538	.3205

47th Year—D. or 65.

Age.	Value.	M. Diff.
10	66.1398	+.1589
11	69.0614	.1708
12	72.1643	.1842
13	75.4673	.1995
14	79.0005	.2168
15	82.7926	.2369
16	86.8831	.2604
17	91.3178	.2879
18	96.1538	.3205

47th Year—D. or 70.

Age.	Value.	M. Diff.
10	55.4151	+.1011
11	57.5477	.1073
12	59.7805	.1138
13	62.1206	.1213
14	64.5846	.1297
15	67.1800	.1393
16	69.9305	.1505
17	72.8547	.1635
18	75.9813	.1789
19	79.3443	.1973
20	82.9845	.2196
21	86.9536	.2466
22	91.3159	.2780
23	96.1538	.3205

47th Year—D. or 75.

Age.	Value.	M. Diff.
10	49.0588	+.0669
11	50.7317	.0695
12	52.4554	.0722
13	54.2361	.0752
14	56.0757	.0783
15	57.9762	.0817
16	59.9499	.0857
17	62.0006	.0901
18	64.1381	.0957
19	66.3793	.1023
20	68.7389	.1105
21	71.2386	.1202
22	73.9023	.1327
23	76.7678	.1485
24	79.8790	.1683
25	83.2902	.1935
26	87.0734	.2257
27	91.3210	.2671
28	96.1538	.3205

48th YEAR—D. or 60.

Age.	Value.	M. Diff.
10	86.9057	+.2694
11	91.3555	.2933
12	96.1538	.3205

48th Year—D. or 65.

Age.	Value.	M. Diff.
10	69.2062	+.1716
11	72.2975	.1850
12	75.5896	.2002
13	79.1057	.2175
14	82.8787	.2375
15	86.9452	.2608
16	91.3518	.2881
17	96.1538	.3205

48th Year—D. or 70.

Age.	Value.	M. Diff.
10	57.7309	+.1083
11	59.9616	.1148
12	62.2981	.1224
13	64.7547	.1307
14	67.3459	.1403
15	70.0854	.1513
16	72.9992	.1644
17	76.1124	.1797
18	79.4576	.1982
19	83.0774	.2203
20	87.0211	.2471
21	91.3530	.2800
22	96.1538	.3205

48th Year—D. or 75.

Age.	Value.	M. Diff.
10	50.9313	+.0706
11	52.6571	.0734
12	54.4362	.0764
13	56.2765	.0795
14	58.1779	.0830
15	60.1465	.0870
16	62.1957	.0915
17	64.3287	.0971
18	66.5635	.1036
19	68.9154	.1118
20	71.4065	.1215
21	74.0579	.1341
22	76.9094	.1497
23	80.0024	.1695
24	83.3923	.1945
25	87.1485	.2265
26	91.3627	.2675
27	96.1538	.3205

49th YEAR—D. or 60.

Age.	Value.	M. Diff.
10	91.3857	+.2934
11	96.1538	.3205

49th Year—D. or 65.

Age.	Value.	M. Diff.
10	72.4250	+.1857
11	75.7038	.2008
12	79.2064	.2181
13	82.9601	.2380
14	87.0045	.2612
15	91.3840	.2884
16	96.1538	.3205

49th Year—D. or 70.

Age.	Value.	M. Diff.
10	60.1332	+.1158
11	62.4667	.1234
12	64.9184	.1317
13	67.5011	.1413
14	70.2348	.1523
15	73.1351	.1654
16	76.2366	.1806
17	79.5655	.1981
18	83.1654	.2209
19	87.0855	.2476
20	91.3882	.2803
21	96.1538	.3205

49th Year—D. or 75.

Age.	Value.	M. Diff.
10	52.8483	+.0744
11	54.6288	.0775
12	56.4669	.0806
13	58.3681	.0842
14	60.3367	.0882
15	62.3802	.0927
16	64.5106	.0983
17	66.7397	.1049
18	69.0840	.1131
19	71.5658	.1228
20	74.2068	.1353
21	77.0440	.1509
22	80.1204	.1706
23	83.4891	.1955
24	87.2199	.2272
25	91.4023	.2678
26	96.1538	.3205

50th YEAR—D. or 60.

Age.	Value.	M. Diff.
10	96.1538	+.3205

50th Year—D. or 65.

Age.	Value.	M. Diff.
10	75.8131	+.2015
11	79.3006	.2186
12	83.0381	.2385
13	87.0606	.2615
14	91.4147	.2886
15	96.1538	.3205

50th Year—D. or 70.

Age.	Value.	M. Diff.
10	62.6266	+.1243
11	65.0739	.1327
12	67.6505	.1422
13	70.3743	.1533
14	73.2679	.1662
15	76.3544	.1814
16	79.6685	.1997
17	83.2495	.2209
18	87.1465	.2481
19	91.4218	.2806
20	96.1538	.3205

50th Year—D. or 75.

Age.	Value.	M. Diff.
10	54.8113	+.0786
11	56.6501	.0817
12	58.5486	.0853
13	60.5162	.0894
14	62.5586	.0939
15	64.6824	.0995
16	66.9078	.1061
17	69.2451	.1143
18	71.7180	.1240
19	74.3481	.1365
20	77.1728	.1521
21	80.2325	.1716
22	83.5816	.1964
23	87.2877	.2279
24	91.4400	.2684
25	96.1538	.3205

51st YEAR—D. or 65.

Age.	Value.	M. Diff.
10	79.3906	+.2192
11	83.1109	.2389
12	87.1144	.2619
13	91.4438	.2888
14	96.1538	.3205

51st Year—D. or 70.

Age.	Value.	M. Diff.
10	65.2214	+.1335
11	67.7925	.1431
12	70.5087	.1541
13	73.3911	.1671
14	76.4677	.1823
15	79.7658	.2004
16	83.3295	.2222
17	87.1967	.2493
18	91.4537	.2809
19	96.1538	.3205

51st Year—D. or 75.

Age.	Value.	M. Diff.
10	56.8238	+.0828
11	58.7222	.0864
12	60.6863	.0905
13	62.7269	.0950
14	64.8486	.1007
15	67.0666	.1073
16	69.3989	.1155
17	71.8635	.1252
18	74.4831	.1376
19	77.2950	.1531
20	80.3398	.1726
21	83.6695	.1973
22	87.3524	.2286
23	91.4758	.2688
24	96.1538	.3205

52d YEAR—D. or 65.

Age.	Value.	M. Diff.
10	83.1806	+.2393
11	87.1645	.2622
12	91.4716	.2890
13	96.1538	.3205

52d Yehr—D. or 70.

Age.	Value.	M. Diff.
10	67.9271	+.1440
11	70.6365	.1550
12	73.5099	.1679
13	76.5738	.1830
14	79.8598	.2011
15	83.4053	.2228
16	87.2604	.2490
17	91.4841	.2811
18	96.1538	.3205

52d Year—D. or 75.

Age.	Value.	M. Diff.
10	58.8867	+.0872
11	60.8501	.0915
12	62.8865	.0961
13	65.0055	.1018
14	67.2203	.1084
15	69.5442	.1166
16	72.0023	.1263
17	74.6121	.1387
18	77.4117	.1542
19	80.4416	.1736
20	83.7536	.1981
21	87.4140	.2293
22	91.5099	.2691
23	96.1538	.3205

53d YEAR—D. or 65.

Age.	Value.	M. Diff.
10	87.2126	+.2625
11	91.4976	.2891
12	96.1538	.3205

53d Year—D. or 70.

Age.	Value.	M. Diff.
10	70.7577	+.1557
11	73.6227	.1686
12	76.6759	.1837
13	79.9475	.2018
14	83.4783	.2233
15	87.3129	.2495
16	91.5131	.2814
17	96.1538	.3205

53d Year—D. or 75.

Age.	Value.	M. Diff.
10	61.0052	+.0926
11	63.0401	.0971
12	65.1542	.1028
13	67.3652	.1095
14	69.6847	.1177
15	72.1334	.1274
16	74.7352	.1398
17	77.5233	.1552
18	80.5389	.1745
19	83.8335	.1989
20	87.4729	.2299
21	91.5424	.2695
22	96.1538	.3205

54th YEAR—D. or 65.

Age.	Value.	M. Diff.
10	91.5225	+.2893
11	96.1538	.3205

54th Year—D. or 70.

Age.	Value.	M. Diff.
10	73.7293	+.1694
11	76.7729	.1844
12	80.0320	.2024
13	83.5466	.2239
14	87.3636	.2505
15	91.5405	.2816
16	96.1538	.3205

54th Year—D. or 75.

Age.	Value.	M. Diff.
10	63.1856	+.0981
11	65.2973	.1039
12	67.5027	.1105
13	69.8174	.1189
14	72.2603	.1284
15	74.8515	.1408
16	77.6297	.1561
17	80.6318	.1754
18	83.9097	.1996
19	87.5288	.2305
20	91.5735	.2698
21	96.1538	.3205

ENDOWMENT POLICIES.—4 PER CENT.

55th YEAR—D. or 65.

Age.	Value.	M. Diff.
10	96.1538	+.3205

55th Year—D. or 70.

Age.	Value.	M. Diff.
10	76.8649	+.1850
11	80.1123	.2030
12	83.6124	.2244
13	87.4109	.2502
14	91.5749	.2812
15	96.1538	.3205

55th Year—D. or 75.

Age.	Value.	M. Diff.
10	65.4329	+.1048
11	67.6350	.1115
12	69.9431	.1197
13	72.3801	.1293
14	74.9640	.1417
15	77.7303	.1570
16	80.7205	.1762
17	83.9826	.2003
18	87.5822	.2310
19	91.6030	.2702
20	96.1538	.3205

56th YEAR—D. or 70.

Age.	Value.	M. Diff.
10	80.1885	+.2035
11	83.6749	.2248
12	87.4565	+.2506
13	91.5916	.2820
14	96.1538	.3205

56th Year—D. or 75.

Age.	Value.	M. Diff.
10	67.7603	+.1124
11	70.0641	.1206
12	72.4936	.1303
13	75.0702	.1426
14	77.8277	.1579
15	80.8043	.1770
16	84.0521	.2010
17	87.6332	.2315
18	91.6312	.2705
19	96.1538	.3205

57th YEAR—D. or 70.

Age.	Value.	M. Diff.
10	83.7341	+.2253
11	87.4998	.2510
12	91.6154	.2822
13	96.1538	.3205

57th Year—D. or 75.

Age.	Value.	M. Diff.
10	70.1788	+.1215
11	72.6028	.1311
12	75.1709	.1435
13	77.9195	+.1587
14	80.8854	.1777
15	84.1179	.2017
16	87.6819	.2321
17	91.6581	.2708
18	96.1538	.3205

58th YEAR—D. or 70.

Age.	Value.	M. Diff.
10	87.5409	+.2513
11	91.6380	.2824
12	96.1538	.3205

58th Year—D. or 75.

Age.	Value.	M. Diff.
10	72.7063	+.1320
11	75.2677	.1443
12	78.0066	.1595
13	80.9619	.1785
14	84.1814	.2023
15	87.7279	.2325
16	91.6838	.2711
17	96.1538	.3205

59th YEAR—D. or 70.

Age.	Value.	M. Diff.
10	91.6595	+.2826
11	96.1538	.3205

59th Year—D. or 75.

Age.	Value.	M. Diff.
10	75.3595	+.1450
11	78.0903	.1602
12	81.0344	.1791
13	84.2414	.2029
14	87.7724	.2330
15	91.7080	.2713
16	96.1538	.3205

60th YEAR—D. or 70.

Age.	Value.	M. Diff.
10	96.1538	+.3205

60th Year—D. or 75.

Age.	Value.	M. Diff.
10	78.1697	+.1609
11	81.1043	.1798
12	84.2983	.2035
13	87.8144	.2334
14	91.7315	.2716
15	96.1538	.3205

61st YEAR—D. or 75.

Age.	Value.	M. Diff.
10	81.1704	+.1804
11	84.3530	.2040
12	87.8542	.2338
13	91.7537	+.2718
14	96.1538	.3205

62d YEAR—D. or 75.

Age.	Value.	M. Diff.
10	84.4049	+.2045
11	87.8925	.2343
12	91.7747	.2721
13	96.1538	.3205

63d YEAR—D. or 75.

Age.	Value.	M. Diff.
10	87.9288	+.2346
11	91.7949	.2723
12	96.1538	.3205

64th YEAR—D. or 75.

Age.	Value.	M. Diff.
10	91.8141	+.2725
11	96.1538	.3205

65th YEAR—D. or 75.

Age.	Value.	M. Diff.
10	96.1538	+.3205

TABLE VII.

SINGLE PREMIUMS OF ENDOWMENT POLICIES—4 PER CENT.

D. or 35.

Age.	Value.
10	41.7573
11	43.0443
12	44.3888
13	45.7935
14	47.2640
15	48.8043
16	50.4109
17	52.0920
18	53.8498
19	55.6874
20	57.6095
21	59.6197
22	61.7217
23	63.9214
24	66.2230
25	68.6318
26	71.1526
27	73.7918
28	76.5557
29	79.4507
30	82.4838
31	85.6625
32	88.9945
33	92.4886
34	96.1538

D. or 40.

Age.	Value.
10	36.3408
11	37.3726
12	38.4499
13	39.5757
14	40.7519
15	41.9846
16	43.2691
17	44.6119
18	46.0152
19	47.4808
20	49.0129
21	50.6136
22	52.2854
23	54.0341
24	55.8621
25	57.7728
26	59.7709
27	61.8608
28	64.0474
29	66.3353
30	68.7298
31	71.2368
32	73.8620
33	76.6119
34	79.4937
35	82.5143
36	85.6821
37	89.0048
38	92.4922
39	96.1538

D. or 45.

Age.	Value.
10	32.1089
11	32.9424
12	33.8111
13	34.7164
14	35.6652
15	36.6578
16	37.6904
17	38.7692
18	39.8955
19	41.0705
20	42.2979
21	43.5786
22	44.9147
23	46.3109
24	47.7685
25	49.2908
26	50.8805
27	52.5421
28	54.2769
29	56.0905
30	57.9864
31	59.9687
32	62.0418
33	64.2104
34	66.4799
35	68.8558
36	71.3442
37	73.9517
38	76.6817
39	79.5473
40	82.5525
41	85.7066
42	89.0184
43	92.4972
44	96.1538

D. or 50.

Age.	Value.
10	28.8316
11	29.5110
12	30.2182
13	30.9550
14	31.7260
15	32.5321
16	33.3695
17	34.2438
18	35.1557
19	36.1056
20	37.0968
21	38.1298
22	39.2059
23	40.3290
24	41.4999
25	42.7212
26	43.9946
27	45.3239
28	46.7093
29	48.1557
30	49.6652
31	51.2412
32	52.8867
33	54.6050
34	56.4005
35	58.2768
36	60.2389
37	62.2928
38	64.4365
39	66.6850
40	69.0388
41	71.5052
42	74.0906
43	76.7988
44	79.6443
45	82.6267
46	85.7580
47	89.0478
48	92.5083
49	96.1538

D. or 55.

Age.	Value.
10	26.3352
11	26.8975
12	27.4819
13	28.0875
14	28.7252
15	29.3898
16	30.0785
17	30.7969
18	31.5456
19	32.3241
20	33.1354
21	33.9797
22	34.8567
23	35.7730
24	36.7255
25	37.7175
26	38.7499
27	39.8261
28	40.9454
29	42.1121
30	43.3275
31	44.5938
32	45.9135
33	47.2891
34	48.7234
35	50.2194
36	51.7808
37	53.4119
38	55.1110
39	56.8885
40	58.7461
41	60.6884
42	62.7207
43	64.8459
44	67.0698
45	69.3918
46	71.8263
47	74.3702
48	77.0347
49	79.8283
50	82.7620
51	85.8469
52	89.0919
53	92.5263
54	96.1538

D. or 60.

Age.	Value.
10	24.4846
11	24.9596
12	25.4527
13	25.9636
14	26.5000
15	27.0603
16	27.6381
17	28.2412
18	28.8687
19	29.5201
20	30.1981
21	30.9023
22	31.6325
23	32.3947
24	33.1852
25	34.0072
26	34.8609
27	35.7495
28	36.6713
29	37.6307
30	38.6296
31	39.6647
32	40.7428
33	41.8641
34	43.0307
35	44.2446
36	45.5085
37	46.8265
38	48.1952
39	49.6241
40	51.1139
41	52.6649
42	54.2898
43	55.9816
44	57.7455
45	59.5797
46	61.4956
47	63.4869
48	65.5607
49	67.7227
50	69.9798
51	72.3417
52	74.8006
53	77.3922
54	80.1080
55	82.9664
56	85.9815
57	89.1701
58	92.5532
59	96.1538

D. or 65.

Age.	Value.
10	23.1664
11	23.5766
12	24.0083
13	24.4532
14	24.9099
15	25.3965
16	25.9012
17	26.4220
18	26.9633
19	27.5243
20	28.1073
21	28.7120
22	29.3376
23	29.9902
24	30.6653
25	31.3603
26	32.0930
27	32.8479
28	33.6293
29	34.4410
30	35.2843
31	36.1565
32	37.00[illegible]
33	38.0028
34	38.9790
35	39.9922
36	41.0444
37	42.1393
38	43.2728
39	44.4538
40	45.6817
41	46.9592
42	48.2891
43	49.6717
44	51.1090
45	52.5959
46	54.1428
47	55.7406
48	57.3939
49	59.1064
50	60.8820
51	62.7228
52	64.6285
53	66.6206
54	68.6874
55	70.8426
56	73.0936
57	75.4495
58	77.9226
59	80.5257
60	83.2744
61	86.1863
62	89.2841
63	92.5955
64	96.1538

D. or 70.

Age.	Value.
10	22.2880
11	22.6602
12	23.0437
13	23.4410
14	23.8542
15	24.2955
16	24.7425
17	25.2083
18	25.6923
19	26.1936
20	26.7125
21	27.2508
22	27.8066
23	28.3860
24	28.9842
25	29.6044
26	30.2464
27	30.9121
28	31.6000
29	32.3131
30	33.0528
31	33.8161
32	34.6021
33	35.4268
34	36.2759
35	37.1562
36	38.0663
37	39.0124
38	39.9890
39	41.0047
40	42.0563
41	43.1505
42	44.2857
43	45.4625
44	46.6816
45	47.9368
46	49.2376
47	50.5727
48	51.9457
49	53.3583
50	54.8126
51	56.3085
52	57.8491
53	59.4343
54	61.0684
55	62.7546
56	64.4957
57	66.3020
58	68.1622
59	70.0997
60	72.1162
61	74.2188
62	76.4183
63	78.7280
64	81.1643
65	83.7470
66	86.5024
67	89.4607
68	92.6612
69	96.1538

D. or 75.

Age.	Value.
10	21.7580
11	22.1048
12	22.4622
13	22.8337
14	23.2218
15	23.6276
16	24.0432
17	24.4759
18	24.9251
19	25.3887
20	25.8707
21	26.3682
22	26.8828
23	27.4161
24	27.9697
25	28.5412
26	29.1319
27	29.7437
28	30.3753
29	31.0288
30	31.7061
31	32.4036
32	33.1204
33	33.8723
34	34.6445
35	35.4440
36	36.2702
37	37.1253
38	38.0073
39	38.9232
40	39.8662
41	40.8522
42	41.8700
43	42.9222
44	44.0097
45	45.1249
46	46.2782
47	47.4539
48	48.6585
49	49.8890
50	51.1496
51	52.4372
52	53.7613
53	55.0975
54	56.4702
55	57.8733
56	59.3068
57	60.7717
58	62.2716
59	63.8075
60	65.3821
61	66.9961
62	68.6536
63	70.3574
64	72.1178
65	73.9388
66	75.8310
67	77.8088
68	79.8844
69	82.0831
70	84.4308
71	86.9615
72	89.7186
73	92.7584
74	96.1538

TABLE VIII.

TEN PREMIUM ENDOWMENT POLICIES.—4 PER CENT.

1st YEAR—D. or 35.

Age.	Value.	M. Diff.
10	5.0935	—.0367
11	5.2513	.0363
12	5.4164	.0359
13	5.5891	.0355
14	5.7700	.0351
15	5.9596	.0348
16	6.1577	.0345
17	6.3651	.0341
18	6.5821	.0338
19	6.8092	.0335
20	7.0470	.0332
21	7.2960	.0329
22	7.5565	.0326
23	7.8295	.0322
24	8.1151	.0319
25	8.4150	.0315

1st Year—D. or 40.

Age.	Value.	M. Diff.
10	4.4328	—.0393
11	4.5594	.0390
12	4.6917	.0387
13	4.8302	.0385
14	4.9750	.0383
15	5.1269	.0381
16	5.2853	.0379
17	5.4511	.0377
18	5.6245	.0376
19	5.8058	.0375
20	5.9955	.0374
21	6.1938	.0373
22	6.4012	.0372
23	6.6184	.0371
24	6.8455	.0370
25	7.0836	.0368
26	7.3327	.0367
27	7.5936	.0366
28	7.8669	.0366
29	8.1534	.0365
30	8.4536	.0364

1st Year—D. or 45.

Age.	Value.	M. Diff.
10	3.9166	—.0414
11	4.0189	.0412
12	4.1257	.0410
13	4.2371	.0408
14	4.3540	.0407
15	4.4764	.0406
16	4.6039	.0406
17	4.7372	.0406
18	4.8765	.0406
19	5.0219	.0406
20	5.1741	.0406
21	5.3329	.0407
22	5.4989	.0408
23	5.6724	.0409
24	5.8537	.0409
25	6.0436	.0410
26	6.2420	.0411
27	6.4497	.0412
28	6.6668	.0414
29	6.8942	.0415
30	7.1322	.0417
31	7.3814	.0420
32	7.6425	.0422
33	7.9160	.0424
34	8.2026	.0426
35	8.5033	.0429

1st Year—D. or 50.

Age.	Value.	M. Diff.
10	3.5168	—.0429
11	3.6003	.0428
12	3.6873	.0427
13	3.7780	.0426
14	3.8731	.0426
15	3.9726	.0426
16	4.0761	.0427
17	4.1842	.0428
18	4.2971	.0429
19	4.4149	.0430
20	4.5378	.0432
21	4.6661	.0434
22	4.7999	.0435
23	4.9397	.0438
24	5.0855	.0440
25	5.2381	.0442
26	5.3973	.0445
27	5.5636	.0448
28	5.7373	.0452
29	5.9189	.0455
30	6.1087	—.0459
31	6.3072	.0463
32	6.5147	.0468
33	6.7318	.0473
34	6.9590	.0478
35	7.1969	.0483
36	7.4462	.0488
37	7.7081	.0493
38	7.9825	.0498
39	8.2717	.0504
40	8.5764	.0509

1st Year—D. or 55.

Age.	Value.	M. Diff.
10	3.2123	—.0441
11	3.2815	.0441
12	3.3534	.0440
13	3.4281	.0440
14	3.5068	.0441
15	3.5889	.0441
16	3.6741	.0443
17	3.7630	.0444
18	3.8558	.0446
19	3.9525	.0448
20	4.0533	.0451
21	4.1583	.0454
22	4.2675	.0457
23	4.3817	.0460
24	4.5004	.0464
25	4.6246	.0467
26	4.7538	.0471
27	4.8888	.0475
28	5.0293	.0480
29	5.1761	.0485
30	5.3292	.0491
31	5.4889	.0497
32	5.6558	.0503
33	5.8299	.0510
34	6.0118	.0517
35	6.2018	.0524
36	6.4008	.0532
37	6.6092	.0539
38	6.8273	.0547
39	7.0566	.0555
40	7.2978	.0563
41	7.5519	.0572
42	7.8203	.0583
43	8.1040	.0598
44	8.4040	.0621
45	8.7204	.0646

1st Year—D. or 60.

Age.	Value.	M. Diff.
10	2.9866	—.0450
11	3.0450	.0449
12	3.1058	.0450
13	3.1688	.0450
14	3.2351	.0451
15	3.3044	.0453
16	3.3760	.0455
17	3.4508	.0457
18	3.5287	.0459
19	3.6096	.0462
20	3.6940	.0465
21	3.7817	.0469
22	3.8727	.0472
23	3.9679	.0477
24	4.0666	.0481
25	4.1697	.0485
26	4.2767	.0490
27	4.3883	.0496
28	4.5043	.0502
29	4.6252	.0508
30	4.7513	.0515
31	4.8822	.0522
32	5.0188	.0530
33	5.1611	.0538
34	5.3094	.0545
35	5.4640	.0555
36	5.6254	.0564
37	5.7943	.0573
38	5.9705	.0583
39	6.1555	.0593
40	6.3496	.0603
41	6.5535	.0615
42	6.7691	.0627
43	6.9962	.0646
44	7.2356	.0671
45	7.4873	.0700
46	7.7533	.0738
47	8.0325	.0779
48	8.3270	.0823
49	8.6371	.0872
50	8.9658	.0925

1st Year—D. or 65.

Age.	Value.	M. Diff.
10	2.8258	—.0456
11	2.8763	.0456
12	2.9295	.0456
13	2.9845	.0457
14	3.0410	.0459
15	3.1012	.0461
16	3.1638	.0463
17	3.2285	.0465
18	3.2958	.0468
19	3.3656	.0471
20	3.4382	.0475
21	3.5136	.0480
22	3.5918	.0484
23	3.6734	.0488
24	3.7578	.0493
25	3.8451	.0498
26	3.9372	.0504
27	4.0322	.0510
28	4.1307	.0517
29	4.2332	.0524
30	4.3399	.0531
31	4.4504	.0539
32	4.5654	.0548
33	4.6851	.0557
34	4.8094	.0566
35	4.9388	.0576
36	5.0736	.0587
37	5.2143	.0597
38	5.3607	.0609
39	5.5141	.0620
40	5.6748	.0632
41	5.8435	.0645
42	6.0209	.0660
43	6.2076	.0680
44	6.4040	.0708
45	6.6097	.0739
46	6.8261	.0779
47	7.0524	.0823
48	7.2897	.0871
49	7.5382	.0923
50	7.8002	.0980
51	8.0756	.1043
52	8.3654	.1117
53	8.6734	.1187
54	8.9988	.1266
55	9.3448	.1355

1st Year—D. or 70.

Age.	Value.	M. Diff.
10	2.7186	—.0461
11	2.7645	.0461
12	2.8118	.0461
13	2.8610	.0462
14	2.9121	.0464
15	2.9668	.0466
16	3.0223	.0468
17	3.0802	.0471
18	3.1404	.0475
19	3.2028	.0478
20	3.2676	.0482
21	3.3348	.0487
22	3.4043	.0491
23	3.4769	.0496
24	3.5518	.0502
25	3.6298	.0507
26	3.7106	.0513
27	3.7945	.0519
28	3.8814	.0527
29	3.9717	.0534
30	4.0654	.0543
31	4.1623	.0551
32	4.2624	.0561
33	4.3675	.0570
34	4.4759	.0580
35	4.5886	.0591
36	4.7055	.0602
37	4.8274	.0613
38	4.9539	.0626
39	5.0863	.0638
40	5.2245	.0651
41	5.3696	.0665
42	5.5217	.0681
43	5.6816	.0703
44	5.8493	.0732
45	6.0241	.0765
46	6.2078	.0807
47	6.3986	.0853
48	6.5977	.0903
49	6.8051	.0957
50	7.0226	.1017
51	7.2497	.1083
52	7.4873	.1160
53	7.7378	.1234
54	8.0006	.1317
55	8.2779	—.1411
56	8.5712	.1511
57	8.8820	.1618
58	9.2133	.1735
59	9.5675	.1862
60	9.9473	.2006

1st Year—D. or 75.

Age.	Value.	M. Diff.
10	2.6540	—.0463
11	2.6968	.0463
12	2.7409	.0464
13	2.7868	.0465
14	2.8349	.0467
15	2.8852	.0469
16	2.9369	.0472
17	2.9907	.0475
18	3.0466	.0478
19	3.1044	.0482
20	3.1646	.0486
21	3.2268	.0491
22	3.2912	.0495
23	3.3581	.0501
24	3.4275	.0507
25	3.4995	.0512
26	3.5739	.0519
27	3.6511	.0525
28	3.7310	.0533
29	3.8138	.0541
30	3.8998	.0549
31	3.9885	.0558
32	4.0805	.0568
33	4.1758	.0578
34	4.2746	.0588
35	4.3771	.0600
36	4.4834	.0612
37	4.5939	.0623
38	4.7084	.0636
39	4.8281	.0649
40	4.9528	.0663
41	5.0836	.0677
42	5.2199	.0694
43	5.3641	.0717
44	5.5145	.0746
45	5.6708	.0780
46	5.8346	.0824
47	6.0040	.0870
48	6.1802	.0922
49	6.3626	.0978
50	6.5533	.1039
51	6.7513	.1107
52	6.9570	.1181
53	7.1732	.1262
54	7.3982	.1348
55	7.6340	.1444
56	7.8816	.1548
57	8.1420	.1659
58	8.4171	.1780
59	8.7087	.1913
60	9.0185	.2062
61	9.3478	.2224
62	9.6991	.2404
63	10.0749	.2598
64	10.4779	.2811
65	10.9120	.3043

2d YEAR—D. or 35.

Age.	Value.	M. Diff.
10	9.7462	—.0185
11	10.0667	.0177
12	10.4022	.0167
13	10.7523	.0154
14	11.1182	.0143
15	11.5017	.0135
16	11.9017	.0123
17	12.3206	.0112
18	12.7581	.0099
19	13.2163	.0087
20	13.6953	.0074
21	14.1971	.0061
22	14.7223	.0047
23	15.2721	.0029
24	15.8475	.0014
25	16.4520	.0001

2d Year—D. or 40.

Age.	Value.	M. Diff.
10	8.3937	—.0239
11	8.6503	.0232
12	8.9187	.0225
13	9.1987	.0215
14	9.4906	.0208
15	9.7969	—.0202
16	10.1156	.0193
17	10.4493	.0186
18	10.7974	.0177
19	11.1618	.0169
20	11.5422	.0161
21	11.9401	.0151
22	12.3565	.0141
23	12.7918	.0131
24	13.2473	.0120
25	13.7252	.0111
26	14.2244	.0099
27	14.7476	.0087
28	15.2950	.0075
29	15.8694	.0062
30	16.4704	.0048

2d Year—D. or 45.

Age.	Value.	M. Diff.
10	7.3370	—.0279
11	7.5438	.0277
12	7.7600	.0271
13	7.9845	.0261
14	8.2193	.0257
15	8.4652	.0255
16	8.7205	.0249
17	8.9876	.0244
18	9.2659	.0238
19	9.5567	.0232
20	9.8603	.0228
21	10.1772	.0221
22	10.5087	.0215
23	10.8545	.0208
24	11.2161	.0201
25	11.5951	.0196
26	11.9904	.0189
27	12.4045	.0183
28	12.8366	.0175
29	13.2897	.0167
30	13.7630	.0159
31	14.2593	.0151
32	14.7785	.0142
33	15.3228	.0132
34	15.8937	.0122
35	16.4921	.0110

2d Year—D. or 50.

Age.	Value.	M. Diff.
10	6.5186	—.0311
11	6.6869	.0310
12	6.8625	.0306
13	7.0446	.0299
14	7.2348	.0297
15	7.4337	.0296
16	7.6400	.0291
17	7.8554	.0288
18	8.0796	.0285
19	8.3139	.0282
20	8.5574	.0279
21	8.8118	.0276
22	9.0773	.0272
23	9.3540	.0268
24	9.6428	.0264
25	9.9453	.0262
26	10.2602	.0259
27	10.5894	.0256
28	10.9325	.0252
29	11.2916	.0249
30	11.6661	.0244
31	12.0582	.0241
32	12.4674	.0237
33	12.8960	.0232
34	13.3449	.0228
35	13.8143	.0221
36	14.3066	.0217
37	14.8247	.0213
38	15.3669	.0203
39	15.9389	.0196
40	16.5422	.0189

2d Year—D. or 55.

Age.	Value.	M. Diff.
10	5.8952	—.0335
11	6.0343	.0338
12	6.1790	.0333
13	6.3283	.0326
14	6.4849	.0326
15	6.6482	.0327
16	6.8169	.0323
17	6.9931	.0322
18	7.1761	.0321
19	7.3671	.0320

TEN PREMIUM ENDOWMENT POLICIES.—4 PER CENT.

2d Year—D. or 55.

Age.	Value.	M. Diff.
20	7.5653	—.0320
21	7.7719	.0317
22	7.9871	.0315
23	8.2112	.0314
24	8.4445	.0312
25	8.6888	.0313
26	8.9431	.0313
27	9.2071	.0313
28	9.4821	.0311
29	9.7698	.0311
30	10.0690	.0310
31	10.3815	.0309
32	10.7074	.0310
33	11.0476	.0308
34	11.4035	.0309
35	11.7746	.0306
36	12.1636	.0307
37	12.5718	.0308
38	12.9982	.0305
39	13.4471	.0303
40	13.9200	.0301
41	14.4175	.0300
42	14.9415	.0303
43	15.4902	.0313
44	16.0634	.0323
45	16.6655	.0340

2d Year—D. or 60.

Age.	Value.	M. Diff.
10	5.4332	—.0353
11	5.5512	.0356
12	5.6721	.0353
13	5.7975	.0346
14	5.9287	.0348
15	6.0657	.0350
16	6.2066	.0348
17	6.3539	.0348
18	6.5064	.0348
19	6.6650	.0347
20	6.8296	.0349
21	7.0007	.0348
22	7.1786	.0347
23	7.3638	.0348
24	7.5560	.0348
25	7.7571	.0350
26	7.9649	.0351
27	8.1819	.0353
28	8.4066	.0353
29	8.6412	.0356
30	8.8850	.0360
31	9.1384	.0361
32	9.4020	.0363
33	9.6770	.0365
34	9.9650	.0369
35	10.2623	.0369
36	10.5741	.0373
37	10.9012	.0378
38	11.2414	.0378
39	11.5993	.0383
40	11.9753	.0383
41	12.3696	.0385
42	12.7850	.0396
43	13.2172	.0413
44	13.6655	.0430
45	14.1341	.0450
46	14.6210	.0481
47	15.1306	.0512
48	15.6658	.0546
49	16.2280	.0581
50	16.8215	.0626

2d Year—D. or 65.

Age.	Value.	M. Diff.
10	5.1041	—.0366
11	5.2048	.0364
12	5.3112	.0372
13	5.4202	.0370
14	5.5313	.0358
15	5.6497	.0362
16	5.7722	.0364
17	5.8987	.0366
18	6.0295	.0367
19	6.1654	.0367
20	6.3058	.0370
21	6.4517	.0369
22	6.6033	.0370
23	6.7607	.0378
24	6.9236	.0374
25	7.0922	.0371
26	7.2695	.0380
7	7.4525	.0383
28	7.6413	.0384
29	7.8381	.0389

2d Year—D. or 65.

Age.	Value.	M. Diff.
30	8.0421	—.0394
31	8.2536	.0397
32	8.4729	.0401
33	8.7015	.0405
34	8.9392	.0411
35	9.1858	.0414
36	9.4429	.0421
37	9.7121	.0428
38	9.9911	.0431
39	10.2840	.0436
40	10.5914	.0442
41	10.9133	.0450
42	11.2501	.0462
43	11.5991	.0483
44	11.9589	.0504
45	12.3325	.0531
46	12.7170	.0566
47	13.1173	.0604
48	13.5341	.0645
49	13.9687	.0688
50	14.4241	.0742
51	14.8997	.0790
52	15.3900	.0838
53	15.9228	.0912
54	16.4781	.0980
55	17.0642	.1053

2d Year—D. or 70.

Age.	Value.	M. Diff.
10	4.8846	—.0375
11	4.9760	.0379
12	5.0703	.0380
13	5.1674	.0371
14	5.2674	.0369
15	5.3746	.0378
16	5.4825	.0376
17	5.5951	.0377
18	5.7113	.0379
19	5.8320	.0381
20	5.9565	.0384
21	6.0856	.0384
22	6.2194	.0385
23	6.3583	.0389
24	6.5017	.0391
25	6.6613	.0403
26	6.8054	.0398
27	6.9656	.0403
28	7.1306	.0405
29	7.3024	.0411
30	7.4797	.0421
31	7.6633	.0421
32	7.8520	.0422
33	8.0506	.0431
34	8.2556	.0439
35	8.4680	.0445
36	8.6883	.0452
37	8.9189	.0461
38	9.1570	.0467
39	9.4067	.0474
40	9.6679	.0481
41	9.9413	.0492
42	10.2260	.0506
43	10.5198	.0530
44	10.8206	.0553
45	11.1303	.0584
46	11.4473	.0625
47	11.7742	.0666
48	12.1120	.0711
49	12.4616	.0759
50	12.8247	.0818
51	13.2001	.0874
52	13.5829	.0931
53	13.9952	.1010
54	14.4203	.1088
55	14.8631	.1172
56	15.3288	.1262
57	15.8219	.1358
58	16.3447	.1465
59	16.9001	.1586
60	17.4877	.1715

2d Year—D. or 75.

Age.	Value.	M. Diff.
10	4.7523	—.0381
11	4.8374	.0383
12	4.9251	.0382
13	5.0155	.0378
14	5.1094	.0378
15	5.2075	.0384
16	5.3076	.0383
17	5.4119	.0385
18	5.5193	.0386
19	5.6306	.0388

2d Year—D. or 75.

Age.	Value.	M. Diff.
20	5.7456	—.0392
21	5.8645	.0394
22	5.9878	.0395
23	6.1150	.0397
24	6.2471	.0401
25	6.3844	.0406
26	6.5254	.0410
27	6.6718	.0415
28	6.8225	.0418
29	6.9789	.0424
30	7.1404	.0431
31	7.3072	.0436
32	7.4793	.0442
33	7.6578	.0447
34	7.8431	.0455
35	8.0344	.0462
36	8.2330	.0472
37	8.4401	.0481
38	8.6536	.0488
39	8.8773	.0497
40	9.1106	.0509
41	9.3547	.0517
42	9.6069	.0528
43	9.8684	.0558
44	10.1339	.0583
45	10.4051	.0617
46	10.6809	.0659
47	10.9636	.0703
48	11.2540	.0751
49	11.5517	.0802
50	11.8594	.0866
51	12.1745	.0924
52	12.4970	.0989
53	12.8320	.1070
54	13.1784	.1153
55	13.5348	.1243
56	13.9051	.1340
57	14.2936	.1446
58	14.6980	.1561
59	15.1223	.1693
60	15.5627	.1836
61	16.0262	.1994
62	16.5134	.2164
63	17.0321	.2351
64	17.5824	.2554
65	18.1724	.2773

3d YEAR—D. or 35.

Age.	Value.	M. Diff.
10	14.6172	+.0001
11	15.1055	.0019
12	15.6181	.0038
13	16.1571	.0053
14	16.7159	.0072
15	17.2997	.0091
16	17.9121	.0110
17	18.5515	.0130
18	19.2209	.0151
19	19.9214	.0173
20	20.6532	.0196
21	21.4194	.0221
22	22.2227	.0246
23	23.0632	.0272
24	23.9453	.0301
25	24.8661	.0330

3d Year—D. or 40.

Age.	Value.	M. Diff.
10	12.5401	—.0079
11	12.9311	.0068
12	13.3401	.0051
13	13.7703	.0041
14	14.2166	.0027
15	14.6809	.0013
16	15.1690	+.0001
17	15.6775	.0017
18	16.2093	.0032
19	16.7652	.0047
20	17.3448	.0065
21	17.9529	.0082
22	18.5890	.0100
23	19.2529	.0120
24	19.9491	.0140
25	20.6760	.0161
26	21.4383	.0183
27	22.2364	.0206
28	23.0724	.0231
29	23.9479	.0257
30	24.8661	.0284

3d Year—D. or 45.

Age.	Value.	M. Diff.
10	10.9185	—.0145
11	11.2304	.0133
12	11.5603	—.0121
13	11.9079	.0114
14	12.2644	.0104
15	12.6359	.0094
16	13.0261	.0084
17	13.4323	.0072
18	13.8568	.0062
19	14.3004	.0051
20	14.7611	.0038
21	15.2447	.0026
22	15.7493	.0013
23	16.2768	+.0000
24	16.8282	.0015
25	17.4039	.0028
26	18.0056	.0044
27	18.6346	.0061
28	19.2940	.0077
29	19.9830	.0095
30	20.7046	.0113
31	21.4596	.0133
32	22.2502	.0154
33	23.0807	.0175
34	23.9501	.0200
35	24.8633	.0223

3d Year—D. or 50.

Age.	Value.	M. Diff.
10	9.6625	—.0193
11	9.9152	.0185
12	10.1825	.0176
13	10.4638	.0171
14	10.7518	.0163
15	11.0517	.0156
16	11.3667	.0150
17	11.6937	.0141
18	12.0349	.0134
19	12.3905	.0127
20	12.7605	.0118
21	13.1472	.0110
22	13.5509	.0101
23	13.9716	.0092
24	14.4111	.0082
25	14.8690	.0074
26	15.3465	.0063
27	15.8458	.0053
28	16.3674	.0042
29	16.9122	.0030
30	17.4815	.0019
31	18.0756	.0007
32	18.6978	+.0007
33	19.3495	.0021
34	20.0303	.0038
35	20.7461	.0049
36	21.4920	.0070
37	22.2769	.0087
38	23.1055	.0107
39	23.9752	.0128
40	24.8921	.0147

3d Year—D. or 55.

Age.	Value.	M. Diff.
10	8.7060	—.0233
11	8.9108	.0222
12	9.1326	.0217
13	9.3655	.0216
14	9.5999	.0209
15	9.8448	.0204
16	10.1027	.0200
17	10.3696	.0194
18	10.6473	.0189
19	10.9362	.0186
20	11.2349	.0178
21	11.5493	.0174
22	11.8765	.0168
23	12.2155	.0163
24	12.5701	.0156
25	12.9382	.0152
26	13.3218	.0145
27	13.7207	.0139
28	14.1388	.0133
29	15.5729	.0126
30	15.0262	.0120
31	15.4991	.0113
32	15.9914	.0105
33	16.5074	.0097
34	17.0450	.0087
35	17.6097	.0081
36	18.1956	.0070
37	18.8114	.0059
38	19.4601	.0047
39	20.1405	.0035
40	20.8569	.0024
41	21.6099	.0014

3d Year—D. or 55.

Age.	Value.	M. Diff.
42	22.3987	—.0012
43	23.2187	.0005
44	24.0803	.0010
45	24.9802	.0012

3d Year—D. or 60.

Age.	Value.	M. Diff.
10	7.9960	—.0260
11	8.1690	.0253
12	8.3540	.0249
13	8.5506	.0248
14	8.7461	.0243
15	8.9500	.0239
16	9.1656	.0237
17	9.3871	.0233
18	9.6178	.0230
19	9.8580	.0228
20	10.1046	.0223
21	10.3649	.0221
22	10.6351	.0218
23	10.9136	.0215
24	11.2046	.0211
25	11.5064	.0210
26	11.8201	.0205
27	12.1462	.0201
28	12.4878	.0201
29	12.8390	.0197
30	13.2049	.0194
31	13.5879	.0191
32	13.9853	.0188
33	14.4000	.0185
34	14.8312	.0179
35	15.2836	.0178
36	15.7518	.0172
37	16.2419	.0167
38	16.7581	.0164
39	17.2948	.0154
40	17.8653	.0152
41	18.4616	.0151
42	19.0790	.0157
43	19.7184	.0159
44	20.3877	.0174
45	21.0809	.0189
46	21.7969	.0206
47	22.5493	.0223
48	23.3378	.0244
49	24.1678	.0271
50	25.0359	.0287

3d Year—D. or 65.

Age.	Value.	M. Diff.
10	7.4915	—.0278
11	7.6444	.0280
12	7.7940	.0268
13	7.9633	.0266
14	8.1427	.0266
15	8.3171	.0264
16	8.4987	.0263
17	8.6883	.0261
18	8.8853	.0259
19	9.0902	.0259
20	9.3005	.0255
21	9.5221	.0255
22	9.7508	.0258
23	9.9807	.0247
24	10.2331	.0250
25	10.4921	.0251
26	10.7509	.0249
27	11.0245	.0247
28	11.3108	.0249
29	11.6044	.0248
30	11.9089	.0247
31	12.2274	.0247
32	12.5575	.0247
33	12.9001	.0247
34	13.2560	.0244
35	13.6283	.0248
36	14.0118	.0245
37	14.4131	.0245
38	14.8349	.0244
39	15.2746	.0242
40	15.7356	.0243
41	16.2166	.0247
42	16.7164	.0260
43	17.2277	.0270
44	17.7585	.0291
45	18.3050	.0315
46	18.8637	.0340
47	19.4449	.0368
48	20.0502	.0400
49	20.6815	.0440
50	21.3335	.0469
51	22.0268	.0517

TEN PREMIUM ENDOWMENT POLICIES.—4 PER CENT.

3d Year—D. or 65.

Age.	Value.	M. Diff.
52	22.7501	—.0561
53	23.5020	.0610
54	24.3014	.0664
55	25.1455	.0719

3d Year—D. or 70.

Age.	Value.	M. Diff.
10	7.1535	—.0293
11	7.2856	.0291
12	7.4260	.0279
13	7.5837	.0286
14	7.7367	.0283
15	7.8881	.0281
16	8.0535	.0280
17	8.2228	.0280
18	8.3968	.0278
19	8.5782	.0280
20	8.7637	.0276
21	8.9595	.0277
22	9.1615	.0277
23	9.3684	.0277
24	9.5848	.0276
25	9.8080	.0278
26	10.0383	.0278
27	10.2770	.0278
28	10.5262	.0281
29	10.7806	.0285
30	10.0396	.0278
31	11.3200	.0284
32	11.6080	.0285
33	11.9007	.0289
34	12.2049	.0288
35	12.5230	.0294
36	12.8509	.0294
37	13.1930	.0297
38	13.5503	.0297
39	13.9241	.0300
40	14.3153	.0304
41	14.7206	.0312
42	15.1406	.0330
43	15.5655	.0342
44	16.0057	.0370
45	16.4538	.0398
46	16.9055	.0430
47	17.3737	.0464
48	17.8569	.0504
49	18.3558	.0551
50	18.8651	.0591
51	19.4012	.0648
52	19.9531	.0705
53	20.5207	.0767
54	21.1158	.0837
55	21.7342	.0907
56	22.3860	.0986
57	23.0746	.1072
58	23.8004	.1168
59	24.5650	.1273
60	25.3768	.1388

3d Year—D. or 75.

Age.	Value.	M. Diff.
10	6.9495	—.0299
11	7.0739	.0296
12	7.2078	.0292
13	7.3493	.0296
14	7.4903	.0294
15	7.6321	.0291
16	7.7847	.0292
17	7.9401	.0290
18	8.1021	.0291
19	8.2692	.0291
20	8.4401	.0291
21	8.6188	.0290
22	8.8056	.0291
23	8.9967	.0292
24	9.1934	.0292
25	9.3972	.0294
26	9.6079	.0295
27	9.8255	.0296
28	10.0523	.0300
29	10.2839	.0302
30	10.5227	.0304
31	10.7721	.0307
32	11.0293	.0309
33	11.2970	.0313
34	11.5719	.0316
35	11.8569	.0321
36	12.1501	.0323
37	12.4567	.0328
38	12.7759	.0330
39	13.1095	.0339
40	13.4531	.0337
41	13.8177	.0351
42	14.1926	—.0370
43	14.5626	.0380
44	14.9485	.0418
45	15.3360	.0448
46	15.7249	.0485
47	16.1235	.0523
48	16.5324	.0567
49	16.9523	.0619
50	17.3736	.0664
51	17.8165	.0728
52	18.2669	.0791
53	18.7210	.0861
54	19.1932	.0939
55	19.6771	.1021
56	20.1783	.1115
57	20.7003	.1211
58	21.2417	.1323
59	21.7994	.1446
60	22.3780	.1581
61	22.9818	.1728
62	23.6157	.1889
63	24.2859	.2063
64	24.9954	.2250
65	25.7568	.2452

4th YEAR—D. or 35.

Age.	Value.	M. Diff.
10	19.7122	+.0200
11	20.3798	.0226
12	21.0804	.0247
13	21.8095	.0274
14	22.5722	.0299
15	23.3681	.0325
16	24.2012	.0354
17	25.0729	.0384
18	25.9845	.0414
19	26.9379	.0447
20	27.9357	.0481
21	28.9800	.0517
22	30.0746	.0554
23	31.2194	.0593
24	32.4212	.0635
25	33.6771	.0678

4th Year—D. or 40.

Age.	Value.	M. Diff.
10	16.8776	+.0088
11	17.4099	.0109
12	17.9701	.0125
13	18.5513	.0145
14	19.1594	.0164
15	19.7925	.0184
16	20.4555	.0206
17	21.1484	.0228
18	21.8718	.0250
19	22.6273	.0275
20	23.4180	.0301
21	24.2454	.0327
22	25.1105	.0355
23	26.0148	.0384
24	26.9626	.0415
25	27.9529	.0447
26	28.9910	.0480
27	30.0777	.0516
28	31.2167	.0554
29	32.4095	.0593
30	33.6601	.0635

4th Year—D. or 45.

Age.	Value.	M. Diff.
10	14.6615	+.0002
11	15.0903	.0018
12	15.5404	.0029
13	16.0077	.0044
14	16.4938	.0059
15	16.9999	.0073
16	17.5294	.0090
17	18.0827	.0106
18	18.6592	.0122
19	19.2611	.0141
20	19.8892	.0159
21	20.5463	.0179
22	21.2326	.0199
23	21.9493	.0221
24	22.7001	.0242
25	23.4817	.0266
26	24.3010	.0290
27	25.1569	.0316
28	26.0537	.0343
29	26.9911	.0371
30	27.9725	.0401
31	29.0002	.0433
32	30.0771	+.0466
33	31.2069	.0502
34	32.3924	.0537
35	33.6337	.0580

4th Year—D. or 50.

Age.	Value.	M. Diff.
10	12.9472	—.0065
11	13.2941	.0054
12	13.6585	.0046
13	14.0361	.0033
14	14.4287	.0023
15	14.8369	.0012
16	15.2633	+.0000
17	15.7083	.0012
18	16.1712	.0023
19	16.6530	.0037
20	17.1566	.0050
21	17.6814	.0064
22	18.2296	.0079
23	18.8004	.0095
24	19.3981	.0109
25	20.0186	.0126
26	20.6681	.0143
27	21.3460	.0161
28	22.0547	.0180
29	22.7946	.0199
30	23.5674	.0220
31	24.3751	.0241
32	25.2206	.0265
33	26.1060	.0290
34	27.0343	.0312
35	28.0022	.0343
36	29.0218	.0372
37	30.0899	.0404
38	31.2169	.0437
39	32.4008	.0469
40	33.6452	.0507

4th Year—D. or 55.

Age.	Value.	M. Diff.
10	11.6389	—.0115
11	11.9254	.0107
12	12.2254	.0102
13	12.5357	.0093
14	12.8558	.0085
15	13.1893	.0077
16	13.5373	.0068
17	13.9000	.0060
18	14.2762	.0053
19	14.6659	.0041
20	15.0747	.0033
21	15.4991	.0023
22	15.9425	.0013
23	16.4017	.0002
24	16.8832	+.0007
25	17.3808	.0019
26	17.9018	.0031
27	18.4431	.0042
28	19.0090	.0055
29	19.5978	.0068
30	20.2120	.0081
31	20.8530	.0096
32	21.5214	.0112
33	22.2209	.0128
34	22.9525	.0142
35	23.7145	.0162
36	24.5130	.0182
37	25.3499	.0202
38	26.2305	.0225
39	27.1551	.0246
40	28.1258	.0267
41	29.1445	.0282
42	30.2043	.0303
43	31.3166	.0313
44	32.4726	.0326
45	33.6858	.0340

4th Year—D. or 60.

Age.	Value.	M. Diff.
10	10.6717	—.0155
11	10.9110	.0146
12	11.1632	.0145
13	11.4222	.0136
14	11.6901	.0131
15	11.9676	.0126
16	12.2576	.0119
17	12.5586	.0113
18	12.8703	.0109
19	13.1934	.0100
20	13.5312	.0095
21	13.8812	.0088
22	14.2467	—.0082
23	14.6232	.0073
24	15.0181	.0068
25	15.4246	.0060
26	15.8502	.0051
27	16.2928	.0047
28	16.7507	.0037
29	17.2279	.0029
30	17.7233	.0021
31	18.2409	.0012
32	18.7788	.0002
33	19.3397	+.0009
34	19.9259	.0016
35	20.5337	.0029
36	21.1706	.0041
37	21.8354	.0051
38	22.5313	.0070
39	23.2658	.0080
40	24.0325	.0090
41	24.8342	.0094
42	25.6597	.0103
43	26.5235	.0099
44	27.4142	.0097
45	28.3415	.0094
46	29.3033	.0091
47	30.3136	.0086
48	31.3717	.0076
49	32.4799	.0078
50	33.6569	.0067

4th Year—D. or 65.

Age.	Value.	M. Diff.
10	9.9837	—.0188
11	10.1846	.0174
12	10.4018	.0170
13	10.6285	.0168
14	10.8640	.0164
15	11.1015	.0160
16	11.3468	.0155
17	11.6041	.0151
18	11.8701	.0148
19	12.1449	.0141
20	12.4330	.0139
21	12.7299	.0139
22	13.0331	.0125
23	13.3574	.0124
24	13.6907	.0121
25	14.0366	.0116
26	14.3895	.0111
27	14.7600	.0108
28	15.1430	.0103
29	15.5404	.0098
30	15.9523	.0094
31	16.3817	.0089
32	16.8269	.0083
33	17.2891	.0077
34	17.7720	.0074
35	18.2701	.0066
36	18.7913	.0060
37	19.3339	.0053
38	19.9033	.0045
39	20.4978	.0040
40	21.1181	.0036
41	21.7632	.0040
42	22.4252	.0041
43	23.1117	.0052
44	23.8138	.0066
45	24.5372	.0080
46	25.2815	.0096
47	26.0557	.0116
48	26.8599	.0142
49	27.6922	.0156
50	28.5711	.0188
51	29.4827	.0217
52	30.4421	.0246
53	31.4432	.0280
54	32.5032	.0313
55	33.6273	.0348

4th Year—D. or 70.

Age.	Value.	M. Diff.
10	9.5204	—.0203
11	9.7012	.0189
12	9.9033	.0194
13	10.1018	.0189
14	10.3097	.0185
15	10.5179	.0183
16	10.7397	.0180
17	10.9674	.0176
18	11.2030	.0175
19	11.4456	.0169
20	11.6999	.0168
21	11.9614	.0165
22	12.2339	—.0162
23	12.5130	.0158
24	12.8051	.0157
25	13.1044	.0154
26	13.4156	.0150
27	13.7385	.0150
28	14.0708	.0151
29	14.4097	.0157
30	14.7710	.0142
31	15.1415	.0139
32	15.5284	.0138
33	15.9213	.0134
34	16.3348	.0134
35	16.7592	.0129
36	17.2041	.0128
37	17.6635	.0123
38	18.1478	.0120
39	18.6505	.0118
40	19.1746	.0120
41	19.7157	.0129
42	20.2676	.0135
43	20.8368	.0154
44	21.4114	.0174
45	22.0002	.0197
46	22.5972	.0221
47	23.2149	.0250
48	23.8500	.0286
49	24.4998	.0315
50	25.1779	.0358
51	25.8732	.0401
52	26.5948	.0448
53	27.3382	.0502
54	28.1125	.0555
55	28.9241	.0615
56	29.7738	.0680
57	30.6705	.0753
58	31.6115	.0832
59	32.6053	.0918
60	33.6589	.1007

4th Year—D. or 75.

Age.	Value.	M. Diff.
10	9.2443	—.0211
11	9.4154	.0205
12	9.5983	.0206
13	9.7814	.0201
14	9.9723	.0199
15	10.1681	.0198
16	10.3714	.0193
17	10.5831	.0192
18	10.7998	.0190
19	11.0244	.0188
20	11.2560	.0184
21	11.4982	.0183
22	11.7478	.0182
23	12.0044	.0179
24	12.2704	.0178
25	12.5436	.0177
26	12.8275	.0174
27	13.1217	.0175
28	13.4235	.0173
29	13.7357	.0172
30	14.0579	.0172
31	14.3925	.0170
32	14.7392	.0170
33	15.0972	.0169
34	15.4676	.0171
35	15.8482	.0168
36	16.2460	.0169
37	16.6563	.0174
38	17.0885	.0169
39	17.5309	.0162
40	18.0014	.0170
41	18.4801	.0183
42	18.9680	.0191
43	19.4705	.0221
44	19.9617	.0239
45	20.4691	.0268
46	20.9772	.0296
47	21.5005	.0331
48	22.0327	.0375
49	22.5717	.0408
50	23.1304	.0461
51	23.6946	.0513
52	24.2746	.0570
53	24.8605	0634
54	25.4642	.0702
55	26.0856	.0776
56	26.7261	.0858
57	27.3894	.0952
58	28.0709	.1054
59	28.7733	.1167
60	29.4989	.1289
61	30.2561	.1422

TEN PREMIUM ENDOWMENT POLICIES.—4 PER CENT.

4th Year—D. or 75.

Age.	Value.	M. Diff.
62	31.0485	—.1567
63	31.8855	.1722
64	32.7734	.1888
65	33.7260	.2063

5th YEAR—D. or 35.

Age.	Value.	M. Diff.
10	25.0459	+.0409
11	25.9018	.0437
12	26.7930	.0469
13	27.7270	.0502
14	28.7007	.0536
15	29.7182	.0572
16	30.7839	.0610
17	31.8982	.0649
18	33.0633	.0691
19	34.2834	.0734
20	35.5596	.0781
21	36.8960	.0827
22	38.2954	.0878
23	39.7609	.0931
24	41.2979	.0987
25	42.9062	.1045

5th Year—D. or 40.

Age.	Value.	M. Diff.
10	21.4159	+.0266
11	22.0997	.0287
12	22.8112	.0312
13	23.5553	.0337
14	24.3312	.0363
15	25.1401	.0391
16	25.9879	.0420
17	26.8728	.0449
18	27.7964	.0482
19	28.7636	.0514
20	29.7741	.0548
21	30.8312	.0584
22	31.9372	.0622
23	33.0939	.0662
24	34.3057	.0704
25	35.5728	.0747
26	36.9002	.0794
27	38.2905	.0843
28	39.7479	.0893
29	41.2742	.0948
30	42.8754	.1005

5th Year—D. or 45.

Age.	Value.	M. Diff.
10	18.5809	+.0155
11	19.1302	.0170
12	19.7005	.0189
13	20.2981	.0209
14	20.9182	.0228
15	21.5644	.0250
16	22.2413	.0271
17	22.9470	.0293
18	23.6825	.0318
19	24.4524	.0342
20	25.2546	.0368
21	26.0940	.0394
22	26.9702	.0423
23	27.8870	.0451
24	28.8443	.0483
25	29.8445	.0515
26	30.8913	.0549
27	31.9854	.0585
28	33.1318	.0622
29	34.3302	.0662
30	35.5855	.0704
31	36.9008	.0749
32	38.2792	.0796
33	39.7250	.0844
34	41.2399	.0899
35	42.8328	.0955

5th Year—D. or 50.

Age.	Value.	M. Diff.
10	16.3856	+.0068
11	16.8300	.0079
12	17.2912	.0094
13	17.7741	.0109
14	18.2744	.0124
15	18.7948	.0140
16	19.3396	.0156
17	19.9066	.0172
18	20.4964	.0191
19	21.1125	.0208
20	21.7547	.0228
21	22.4248	.0247
22	23.1237	+.0268
23	23.8535	.0289
24	24.6143	.0312
25	25.4078	.0335
26	26.2368	.0360
27	27.1024	.0386
28	28.0074	.0412
29	28.9518	.0441
30	29.9396	.0471
31	30.9721	.0503
32	32.0533	.0540
33	33.1863	.0570
34	34.3681	.0611
35	35.6111	.0650
36	36.9145	.0693
37	38.2822	.0740
38	39.7243	.0783
39	41.2356	.0835
40	42.8303	.0881

5th Year—D. or 55.

Age.	Value.	M. Diff.
10	14.7131	+.0002
11	15.0782	.0010
12	15.4562	.0022
13	15.8526	.0033
14	16.2609	.0044
15	16.6853	.0056
16	17.1294	.0070
17	17.5910	.0079
18	18.0686	.0095
19	18.5692	.0107
20	19.0885	.0121
21	19.6299	.0135
22	20.1940	.0151
23	20.7810	.0165
24	21.3925	.0181
25	22.0285	.0198
26	22.6923	.0215
27	23.3828	.0234
28	24.1044	.0252
29	24.8553	.0273
30	25.6390	.0293
31	26.4572	.0316
32	27.3112	.0340
33	28.2050	.0362
34	29.1352	.0390
35	30.1111	.0418
36	31.1318	.0448
37	32.2018	.0479
38	33.3278	.0510
39	34.5069	.0543
40	35.7441	.0569
41	37.0346	.0604
42	38.3877	.0628
43	39.7961	.0657
44	41.2681	.0687
45	42.8137	.0720

5th Year—D. or 60.

Age.	Value.	M. Diff.
10	13.4724	—.0046
11	13.7801	.0042
12	14.0954	.0032
13	14.4272	.0023
14	14.7682	.0015
15	15.1210	.0006
16	15.4908	+.0003
17	15.8733	.0011
18	16.2686	.0023
19	16.6834	.0031
20	17.1116	.0042
21	17.5577	.0051
22	18.0216	.0063
23	18.5030	.0073
24	19.0031	.0085
25	19.5226	.0098
26	20.0654	.0107
27	20.6252	.0121
28	21.2103	.0134
29	21.8180	.0148
30	22.4496	.0162
31	23.1089	.0177
32	23.7949	.0194
33	24.5113	.0208
34	25.2544	.0227
35	26.0323	.0246
36	26.8449	.0263
37	27.6907	.0289
38	28.5856	.0307
39	29.5168	.0327
40	30.4900	.0340
41	31.5003	.0360
42	32.5518	+.0368
43	33.6390	.0379
44	34.7667	.0389
45	35.9421	.0400
46	37.1659	.0411
47	38.4495	.0418
48	39.7897	.0438
49	41.2111	.0447
50	42.7036	.0463

5th Year—D. or 65.

Age.	Value.	M. Diff.
10	12.5837	—.0080
11	12.8521	.0074
12	13.1273	.0070
13	13.4115	.0063
14	13.7088	.0057
15	14.0107	.0050
16	14.3244	.0043
17	14.6511	.0040
18	14.9877	.0028
19	15.3409	.0023
20	15.7048	.0019
21	16.0770	.0003
22	16.4751	+.0001
23	16.8815	.0007
24	17.3027	.0016
25	17.7426	.0025
26	18.1938	.0031
27	18.6620	.0041
28	19.1499	.0050
29	19.6556	.0059
30	20.1799	.0070
31	20.7258	.0080
32	21.2924	.0090
33	21.8822	.0098
34	22.4923	.0111
35	23.1296	.0123
36	23.7932	.0136
37	24.4848	.0150
38	25.2102	.0162
39	25.9645	.0174
40	26.7500	.0177
41	27.5586	.0186
42	28.3972	.0184
43	29.2571	.0181
44	30.1391	.0177
45	31.0509	.0173
46	31.9922	.0167
47	32.9694	.0153
48	33.9790	.0153
49	35.0428	.0137
50	36.1458	.0126
51	37.2993	.0115
52	38.5126	.0101
53	39.7811	.0089
54	41.1265	.0079
55	42.5550	.0068

5th Year—D. or 70.

Age.	Value.	M. Diff.
10	11.9956	—.0099
11	12.2387	.0102
12	12.4818	.0096
13	12.7361	.0090
14	12.9997	.0084
15	13.2657	.0080
16	13.5461	.0074
17	13.8358	.0070
18	14.1333	.0062
19	14.4454	.0058
20	14.7660	.0052
21	15.0988	.0047
22	15.4438	.0041
23	15.7997	.0036
24	16.1685	.0030
25	16.5497	.0023
26	16.9459	.0019
27	17.3529	.0017
28	17.7708	.0003
29	18.2130	.0000
30	18.6659	+.0007
31	19.1371	.0011
32	19.6252	.0021
33	20.1285	.0024
34	20.6495	.0034
35	21.1926	.0040
36	21.7559	.0051
37	22.3437	.0059
38	22.9582	.0066
39	23.5946	.0071
40	24.2555	.0068
41	24.9300	.0071
42	25.6275	+.0060
43	26.3333	.0048
44	27.0517	.0035
45	27.7884	.0021
46	28.5396	.0002
47	29.3134	—.0023
48	30.1040	.0038
49	30.9275	.0070
50	31.7708	.0098
51	32.6418	.0130
52	33.5446	.0167
53	34.4741	.0203
54	35.4477	.0244
55	36.4641	.0288
56	37.5295	.0338
57	38.6486	.0392
58	39.8262	.0449
59	41.0713	.0508
60	42.3974	.0570

5th Year—D. or 75.

Age.	Value.	M. Diff.
10	11.6450	—.0118
11	11.8660	.0117
12	12.0916	.0111
13	12.3272	.0106
14	12.5689	.0103
15	12.8163	.0097
16	13.0763	.0093
17	13.3430	.0089
18	13.6179	.0084
19	13.9038	.0078
20	14.1997	.0075
21	14.5054	.0071
22	14.8211	.0067
23	15.1477	.0062
24	15.4838	.0058
25	15.8312	.0052
26	16.1926	.0050
27	16.5626	.0045
28	16.9463	.0041
29	17.3429	.0036
30	17.7518	.0031
31	18.1773	.0027
32	18.6161	.0023
33	19.0703	.0020
34	19.5376	.0013
35	20.0243	.0009
36	20.5270	.0001
37	21.0419	+.0008
38	21.5942	.0012
39	22.1644	.0010
40	22.7499	.0003
41	23.3435	.0002
42	23.9586	—.0016
43	24.5690	.0031
44	25.1893	.0051
45	25.8187	.0071
46	26.4561	.0095
47	27.1069	.0130
48	27.7631	.0153
49	28.4443	.0194
50	29.1305	.0234
51	29.8307	.0278
52	30.5479	.0328
53	31.2727	.0381
54	32.0204	.0438
55	32.7883	.0503
56	33.5781	.0578
57	34.3894	.0658
58	35.2237	.0747
59	36.0832	.0846
60	36.9706	.0951
61	37.8971	.1065
62	38.8672	.1186
63	39.8943	.1316
64	40.9852	.1450
65	42.1625	.1586

6th YEAR—D. or 35.

Age.	Value.	M. Diff.
10	30.6305	+.0624
11	31.6771	.0662
12	32.7725	.0702
13	33.9184	.0743
14	35.1144	.0786
15	36.3647	.0832
16	37.6740	.0879
17	39.0423	.0929
18	40.4752	.0981
19	41.9737	.1036
20	43.5432	.1094
21	45.1847	.1155
22	46.9053	+.1219
23	48.7074	.1286
24	50.5970	.1357
25	52.5751	.1432

6th Year—D. or 40.

Age.	Value.	M. Diff.
10	26.1682	+.0448
11	27.0036	.0478
12	27.8773	.0508
13	28.7901	.0540
14	29.7424	.0574
15	30.7365	.0608
16	31.7771	.0645
17	32.8626	.0683
18	33.9990	.0723
19	35.1861	.0765
20	36.4277	.0809
21	37.7259	.0855
22	39.0849	.0904
23	40.5068	.0955
24	41.9957	.1008
25	43.5532	.1065
26	45.1855	.1124
27	46.8953	.1186
28	48.6869	.1253
29	50.5652	.1323
30	52.5353	.1397

6th Year—D. or 45.

Age.	Value.	M. Diff.
10	22.6833	+.0311
11	23.3531	.0333
12	24.0534	.0357
13	24.7855	.0382
14	25.5463	.0407
15	26.3404	.0434
16	27.1706	.0461
17	28.0356	.0491
18	28.9402	.0521
19	29.8842	.0552
20	30.8701	.0586
21	31.8996	.0621
22	32.9767	.0657
23	34.1011	.0695
24	35.2773	.0736
25	36.5062	.0778
26	37.7924	.0822
27	39.1374	.0868
28	40.5454	.0918
29	42.0191	.0970
30	43.5629	.1025
31	45.1808	.1082
32	46.8771	.1145
33	48.6538	.1210
34	50.5216	.1279
35	52.4819	.1353

6th Year—D. or 50.

Age.	Value.	M. Diff.
10	19.9840	+.0205
11	20.5256	.0222
12	21.0917	.0240
13	21.6829	.0259
14	22.2960	.0279
15	22.9353	.0298
16	23.6028	.0320
17	24.2972	.0342
18	25.0222	.0364
19	25.7773	.0388
20	26.5658	.0413
21	27.3870	.0439
22	28.2456	.0466
23	29.1396	.0495
24	30.0739	.0525
25	31.0479	.0555
26	32.0659	.0588
27	33.1290	.0622
28	34.2394	.0658
29	35.4001	.0697
30	36.6135	.0737
31	37.8830	.0779
32	39.2136	.0824
33	40.6015	.0872
34	42.0599	.0922
35	43.5881	.0976
36	45.1923	.1033
37	46.8762	.1092
38	48.6462	.1153
39	50.5094	.1215
40	52.4633	.1280

6th Year—D. or 55.

Age.	Value.	M. Diff.
10	17.9282	+.0123
11	18.3719	.0137
12	18.8358	.0151
13	19.3206	.0166
14	19.8206	.0181
15	20.3417	.0195
16	20.8854	.0211
17	21.4488	.0228
18	22.0382	.0245
19	22.6496	.0263
20	23.2870	.0282
21	23.9497	.0301
22	24.6421	.0321
23	25.3604	.0342
24	26.1106	.0364
25	26.8907	.0386
26	27.7047	.0410
27	28.5522	.0435
28	29.4367	.0461
29	30.3584	.0488
30	31.3205	.0517
31	32.3253	.0548
32	33.3754	.0580
33	34.4693	.0614
34	35.6152	.0650
35	36.8144	.0689
36	38.0696	.0729
37	39.3861	.0771
38	40.7674	.0813
39	42.2148	.0854
40	43.7253	.0896
41	45.3110	.0937
42	46.9621	.0981
43	48.6890	.1030
44	50.4970	.1078
45	52.3986	.1132

6th Year—D. or 60.

Age.	Value.	M. Diff.
10	16.4040	+.0064
11	16.7752	.0074
12	17.1632	.0085
13	17.5684	.0096
14	17.9853	.0108
15	18.4186	.0119
16	18.8704	.0131
17	19.3370	.0144
18	19.8251	.0157
19	20.3305	.0170
20	20.8559	.0184
21	21.4011	.0198
22	21.9702	.0213
23	22.5581	.0229
24	23.1717	.0245
25	23.8096	.0261
26	24.4706	.0278
27	25.1589	.0296
28	25.8753	.0314
29	26.6204	.0334
30	27.3951	.0355
31	28.2035	.0376
32	29.0467	.0399
33	29.9215	.0423
34	30.8363	.0448
35	31.7913	.0476
36	32.7862	.0504
37	33.8323	0533
38	34.9249	.0560
39	36.0643	.0586
40	37.2480	.0611
41	38.4857	.0633
42	39.7630	.0656
43	41.0898	.0679
44	42.4693	.0704
45	43.9099	.0730
46	45.4122	.0758
47	46.9832	.0787
48	48.6430	.0820
49	50.3842	.0857
50	52.2244	.0898

6th Year—D. or 65.

Age.	Value.	M. Diff.
10	15.3140	+.0021
11	15.6401	.0029
12	15.9729	.0038
13	16.3202	.0047
14	16.6816	.0056
15	17.0521	.0065
16	17.4364	.0074
17	17 8342	.0084
18	18.2502	+.0094
19	18.6795	.0104
20	19.1197	.0115
21	19.5874	.0125
22	20.0681	.0137
23	20.5636	.0148
24	21.0799	.0159
25	21.6180	.0172
26	22.1686	.0184
27	22.7430	.0197
28	23.3401	.0210
29	23.9595	.0224
30	24.6016	.0239
31	25.2699	.0254
32	25.9657	.0270
33	26.6845	.0287
34	27.4353	.0305
35	28.2160	.0324
36	29.0300	.0344
37	29.8794	.0363
38	30.7656	.0381
39	31.6870	.0395
40	32.6375	.0407
41	33.6248	.0416
42	34.6389	.0424
43	35.6813	.0431
44	36.7554	.0438
45	37.8678	.0444
46	39.0172	.0449
47	40.2053	.0454
48	41.4527	.0459
49	42.7454	.0465
50	44.0972	.0471
51	45.5123	.0478
52	46.9994	.0489
53	48.5614	.0501
54	50.2202	.0517
55	51.9818	.0535

6th Year—D. or 70.

Age.	Value.	M. Diff.
10	14.5955	—.0008
11	14.8803	.0001
12	15.1790	+.0007
13	15.4896	.0014
14	15.8105	.0021
15	16.1364	.0029
16	16.4795	.0036
17	16.8316	.0044
18	17.1995	.0052
19	17.5782	.0060
20	17.9712	.0068
21	18.3772	.0077
22	18.7994	.0086
23	19.2332	.0094
24	19.6845	.0103
25	20.1517	.0112
26	20.6332	.0121
27	21.1269	.0131
28	21.6491	.0141
29	22.1842	.0151
30	22.7391	.0161
31	23.3130	.0172
32	23.9122	.0185
33	24.5252	.0196
34	25.1663	.0209
35	25.8295	.0223
36	26.5225	.0238
37	27.2420	.0250
38	27.9911	.0261
39	28.7664	.0268
40	29.5621	.0272
41	30.3845	.0271
42	31.2206	.0270
43	32.0729	.0266
44	32.9433	.0260
45	33.8374	.0253
46	34.7501	.0244
47	35.6849	.0232
48	36.6556	.0218
49	37.6492	.0204
50	38.6754	.0186
51	39.7352	.0167
52	40.8312	.0148
53	41.9682	.0126
54	43.1558	.0104
55	44.3963	.0076
56	45.6944	.0049
57	47.0603	.0020
58	48.5004	—.0008
59	50.0287	.0034
60	51.6604	.0056

6th Year—D. or 75.

Age.	Value.	M. Diff.
10	14.1580	—.0025
11	14.4225	.0019
12	14.6995	.0012
13	14.9870	.0006
14	15.2808	+.0001
15	15.5855	.0007
16	15.9013	.0013
17	16.2267	.0020
18	16.5637	.0026
19	16.9141	.0033
20	17.2747	.0041
21	17.6471	.0047
22	18.0334	.0055
23	18.4311	.0062
24	18.8421	.0069
25	19.2681	.0076
26	19.7064	.0084
27	20.1595	.0091
28	20.6284	.0098
29	21.1131	.0107
30	21.6141	.0115
31	22.1329	.0123
32	22.6696	.0133
33	23.2222	.0142
34	23.7971	.0151
35	24.3903	.0162
36	25.0090	.0172
37	25.6455	.0182
38	26.3167	.0188
39	27.0040	.0191
40	27.7058	.0190
41	28.4293	.0184
42	29.1595	.0176
43	29.8963	.0166
44	30.6425	.0153
45	31.4046	.0138
46	32.1769	.0119
47	32.9552	.0098
48	33.7602	.0073
49	34.5739	.0046
50	35.4033	.0014
51	36.2485	—.0021
52	37.1114	.0058
53	37.9889	.0100
54	38.8924	.0145
55	39.8184	.0200
56	40.7666	.0259
57	41.7415	.0325
58	42.7444	.0396
59	43.7770	.0473
60	44.8482	.0555
61	45.9669	.0642
62	47.1425	.0734
63	48.3898	.0825
64	49.7227	.0915
65	51.1714	.1002

7th YEAR—D. or 35.

Age.	Value.	M. Diff.
10	36.4727	+.0851
11	37.7226	.0897
12	39.0310	.0945
13	40.3992	.0996
14	41.8282	.1048
15	43.3222	.1104
16	44.8867	.1162
17	46.5225	.1223
18	48.2350	.1287
19	50.0265	.1355
20	51.9035	.1425
21	53.8667	.1499
22	55.9246	.1578
23	58.0803	.1661
24	60.3407	.1748
25	62.7080	.1839

7th Year—D. or 40.

Age.	Value.	M. Diff.
10	31.1387	+.0641
11	32.1360	.0676
12	33.1790	.0714
13	34.2685	.0753
14	35.4057	.0793
15	36.5932	.0836
16	37.8359	.0881
17	39.1332	.0928
18	40.4908	.0977
19	41.9095	.1029
20	43.3939	.1083
21	44.9457	.1140
22	46.5705	.1199
23	48.2706	.1263
24	50.0511	.1330
25	51.9141	+.1399
26	53.8669	.1472
27	55.9126	.1550
28	58.0571	.1632
29	60.3060	.1719
30	62.6651	.1811

7th Year—D. or 45.

Age.	Value.	M. Diff.
10	26.9729	+.0476
11	27.7722	.0504
12	28.6079	.0533
13	29.4807	.0563
14	30.3891	.0594
15	31.3372	.0627
16	32.3282	.0662
17	33.3616	.0697
18	34.4416	.0735
19	35.5690	.0783
20	36.7473	.0816
21	37.9773	.0859
22	39.2644	.0904
23	40.6080	.0952
24	42.0139	.1002
25	43.4830	.1054
26	45.0209	.1110
27	46.6293	.1168
28	48.3136	.1230
29	50.0773	.1295
30	51.9249	.1364
31	53.8605	.1428
32	55.8931	.1514
33	58.0216	.1595
34	60.2593	.1683
35	62.6090	.1775

7th Year—D. or 50.

Age.	Value.	M. Diff.
10	23.7462	+.0349
11	24.3923	.0371
12	25.0674	.0393
13	25.7717	.0416
14	26.5034	.0440
15	27.2661	.0465
16	28.0623	.0492
17	28.8913	.0519
18	29.7564	.0547
19	30.6579	.0577
20	31.5995	.0609
21	32.5801	.0641
22	33.6053	.0675
23	34.6730	.0711
24	35.7890	.0748
25	36.9526	.0788
26	38.1691	.0829
27	39.4394	.0872
28	40.7668	.0918
29	42.1550	.0966
30	43.6062	.1017
31	45.1250	.1071
32	46.7174	.1128
33	48.3793	.1189
34	50.1255	.1253
35	51.9562	.1321
36	53.8777	.1392
37	55.8948	.1466
38	58.0124	.1543
39	60.2397	.1623
40	62.5765	.1707

7th Year—D. or 55.

Age.	Value.	M. Diff.
10	21.2887	+.0252
11	21.8179	.0269
12	22.3707	.0286
13	22.9474	.0304
14	23.5440	.0323
15	24.1652	.0342
16	24.8132	.0362
17	25.4855	.0383
18	26.1881	.0405
19	26.9175	.0427
20	27.6783	.0451
21	28.4691	.0475
22	29.2950	.0501
23	30.1524	.0528
24	31.0477	.0555
25	31.9789	.0585
26	32.9507	.0615
27	33.9627	.0647
28	35.0191	.0681
29	36.1207	.0716
30	37.2704	+.0754
31	38.4713	.0793
32	39.7274	.0835
33	41.0361	.0879
34	42.4072	.0926
35	43.8426	.0975
36	45.3452	.1026
37	46.9204	.1078
38	48.5699	.1131
39	50.2961	.1185
40	52.0980	.1240
41	53.9877	.1299
42	55.9599	.1361
43	58.0265	.1429
44	60.1948	.1502
45	62.4779	.1583

7th Year—D. or 60.

Age.	Value.	M. Diff.
10	19.4668	+.0180
11	19.9091	.0194
12	20.3712	.0207
13	20.8527	.0221
14	21.3497	.0235
15	21.8660	.0250
16	22.4039	.0266
17	22.9605	.0282
18	23.5418	.0299
19	24.1441	.0316
20	24.7709	.0334
21	25.4209	.0353
22	26.0990	.0372
23	26.8003	.0392
24	27.5319	.0412
25	28.2924	.0434
26	29.0811	.0456
27	29.9020	.0480
28	30.7569	.0505
29	31.6466	.0531
30	32.5718	.0558
31	33.5369	.0587
32	34.5445	.0617
33	35.5903	.0649
34	36.6839	.0683
35	37.8262	.0719
36	39.0162	.0755
37	40.2659	.0791
38	41.5678	.0826
39	42.9228	.0860
40	44.3302	.0893
41	45.7986	.0929
42	47.3191	.0965
43	48.9012	.1004
44	50.5499	.1046
45	52.2735	.1089
46	54.0750	.1136
47	55.9605	.1187
48	57.9539	.1245
49	60.0497	.1309
50	62.2675	.1380

7th Year—D. or 65.

Age.	Value.	M. Diff.
10	18.1645	+.0129
11	18.5515	.0140
12	18.9478	.0151
13	19.3609	.0162
14	19.7899	.0174
15	20.2312	.0185
16	20.6893	.0198
17	21.1636	.0210
18	21.6585	.0223
19	22.1698	.0237
20	22.6953	.0250
21	23.2515	.0265
22	23.8240	.0280
23	24.4145	.0295
24	25.0290	.0311
25	25.6692	.0327
26	26.3268	.0344
27	27.0112	.0361
28	27.7229	.0380
29	28.4619	.0399
30	29.2279	.0419
31	30.0250	.0440
32	30.8556	.0462
33	31.7141	.0486
34	32.6107	.0510
35	33.5437	.0536
36	34.5160	.0562
37	35.5296	.0586
38	36.5831	.0608
39	37.6751	.0629

TEN PREMIUM ENDOWMENT POLICIES.—4 PER CENT.

7th Year—D. or 65.

Age.	Value.	M. Diff.
40	38.8012	+.0647
41	39.9675	.0665
42	41.1688	.0683
43	42.4064	.0701
44	43.6850	.0720
45	45.0104	.0738
46	46.3826	.0758
47	47.8025	.0778
48	49.2931	.0801
49	50.8417	.0825
50	52.4624	.0852
51	54.1615	.0884
52	55.9512	.0921
53	57.8359	.0960
54	59.8394	.1010
55	61.9687	.1067

7th Year—D. or 70.

Age.	Value.	M. Diff.
10	17.3048	+.0098
11	17.6440	.0104
12	17.9990	.0113
13	18.3670	.0123
14	18.7485	.0132
15	19.1375	.0142
16	19.5452	.0152
17	19.9647	.0162
18	20.4021	.0173
19	20.8528	.0184
20	21.3209	.0195
21	21.8041	.0207
22	22.3064	.0219
23	22.8230	.0231
24	23.3602	.0243
25	23.9160	.0256
26	24.4896	.0268
27	25.0780	.0282
28	25.6992	.0296
29	26.3371	.0311
30	26.9983	.0326
31	27.6822	.0342
32	28.3961	.0359
33	29.1284	.0376
34	29.8933	.0395
35	30.6855	.0414
36	31.5121	.0433
37	32.3696	.0450
38	33.2580	.0464
39	34.1739	.0475
40	35.1129	.0482
41	36.0799	.0489
42	37.0659	.0495
43	38.0734	.0499
44	39.1051	.0503
45	40.1653	.0505
46	41.2503	.0505
47	42.3616	.0505
48	43.5150	.0505
49	44.6987	.0502
50	45.9213	.0500
51	47.1852	.0499
52	48.4959	.0497
53	49.8575	.0496
54	51.2806	.0493
55	52.7661	.0491
56	54.3243	.0491
57	55.9663	.0496
58	57.7047	.0505
59	59.5556	.0523
60	61.5403	.0552

7th Year—D. or 75.

Age.	Value.	M. Diff.
10	16.7820	+.0074
11	17.0968	.0083
12	17.4258	.0091
13	17.7667	.0099
14	18.1164	.0107
15	18.4788	.0116
16	18.8540	.0125
17	19.2414	.0133
18	19.6420	.0143
19	20.0584	.0152
20	20.4879	.0162
21	20.9307	.0171
22	21.3902	.0181
23	21.8632	.0192
24	22.3525	.0202
25	22.8589	.0212
26	23.3806	.0223
27	23.9196	.0234
28	24.4777	.0246
29	25.0550	.0258
30	25.6517	+.0270
31	26.2694	.0283
32	26.9092	.0296
33	27.5680	.0311
34	28.2534	.0326
35	28.9616	.0341
36	29.6991	.0356
37	30.4575	.0367
38	31.2513	.0376
39	32.0611	.0382
40	32.8868	.0383
41	33.7340	.0383
42	34.5912	.0381
43	35.4595	.0378
44	36.3409	.0372
45	37.2409	.0364
46	38.1549	.0353
47	39.0762	.0338
48	40.0277	.0326
49	40.9915	.0308
50	41.9737	.0288
51	42.9748	.0266
52	43.9991	.0242
53	45.0423	.0214
54	46.1154	.0181
55	47.2122	.0144
56	48.3370	.0103
57	49.4933	.0059
58	50.6868	.0012
59	51.9183	—.0037
60	53.2001	.0088
61	54.5440	.0139
62	55.9612	.0187
63	57.4742	.0227
64	59.1025	.0260
65	60.8816	.0277

8th YEAR—D. or 35.

Age.	Value.	M. Diff.
10	42.5874	+.1089
11	44.0506	.1144
12	45.5818	.1201
13	47.1833	.1261
14	48.8564	.1324
15	50.6064	.1390
16	52.4390	.1459
17	54.3552	.1532
18	56.3615	.1609
19	58.4611	.1689
20	60.6608	.1774
21	62.9624	.1863
22	65.3748	.1957
23	67.9027	.2055
24	70.5530	.2159
25	73.3303	.2270

8th Year—D. or 40.

Age.	Value.	M. Diff.
10	36.3403	+.0843
11	37.5073	.0885
12	38.7273	.0930
13	40.0022	.0976
14	41.3329	.1025
15	42.7235	.1076
16	44.1786	.1129
17	45.6977	.1185
18	47.2877	.1245
19	48.9499	.1306
20	50.6890	.1372
21	52.5075	.1440
22	54.4114	.1512
23	56.4044	.1587
24	58.4913	.1667
25	60.6761	.1751
26	62.9661	.1840
27	65.3661	.1934
28	67.8826	.2033
29	70.5220	.2138
30	73.2916	.2249

8th Year—D. or 45.

Age.	Value.	M. Diff.
10	31.4611	+.0650
11	32.3962	.0683
12	33.3732	.0718
13	34.3937	.0753
14	35.4563	.0791
15	36.5662	.0831
16	37.7261	.0872
17	38.9356	.0915
18	40.1999	.0960
19	41.5202	.1008
20	42.9002	+.1058
21	44.3410	.1110
22	45.8484	.1165
23	47.4228	.1222
24	49.0697	.1283
25	50.7919	.1346
26	52.5944	.1413
27	54.4807	.1485
28	56.4562	.1559
29	58.5254	.1638
30	60.6934	.1731
31	62.9658	.1811
32	65.3523	.1905
33	67.8525	.2005
34	70.4814	.2111
35	73.2424	.2223

8th Year—D. or 50.

Age.	Value.	M. Diff.
10	27.6818	+.0501
11	28.4375	.0526
12	29.2262	.0553
13	30.0492	.0581
14	30.9047	.0610
15	31.7969	.0641
16	32.7284	.0672
17	33.6980	.0705
18	34.7103	.0740
19	35.7657	.0776
20	36.8676	.0814
21	38.0158	.0854
22	39.2156	.0895
23	40.4662	.0939
24	41.7726	.0985
25	43.1361	.1041
26	44.5610	.1083
27	46.0498	.1136
28	47.6060	.1192
29	49.2336	.1252
30	50.9357	.1315
31	52.7178	.1381
32	54.5863	.1451
33	56.5377	.1525
34	58.5883	.1604
35	60.7383	.1686
36	62.9947	.1773
37	65.3623	.1863
38	67.8459	.1958
39	70.4593	.2059
40	73.2018	.2167

8th Year—D. or 55.

Age.	Value.	M. Diff.
10	24.8035	+.0387
11	25.4222	.0407
12	26.0676	.0428
13	26.7408	.0450
14	27.4380	.0472
15	28.1643	.0496
16	28.9219	.0520
17	29.7078	.0545
18	30.5293	.0572
19	31.3828	.0600
20	32.2726	.0629
21	33.1980	.0659
22	34.1637	.0691
23	35.1675	.0723
24	36.2147	.0758
25	37.3052	.0793
26	38.4425	.0831
27	39.6280	.0871
28	40.8656	.0913
29	42.1563	.0957
30	43.5038	.1004
31	44.9120	.1053
32	46.3851	.1105
33	47.9208	.1160
34	49.5300	.1218
35	51.2145	.1278
36	52.9777	.1340
37	54.8238	.1404
38	56.7543	.1470
39	58.7750	.1538
40	60.8838	.1611
41	63.0983	.1689
42	65.4139	.1773
43	67.8452	.1864
44	70.4008	.1963
45	73.0955	.2071

8th Year—D. or 60.

Age.	Value.	M. Diff.
10	22.6697	+.0303
11	23.1865	.0318
12	23.7255	+.0335
13	24.2872	.0352
14	24.8674	.0370
15	25.4709	.0388
16	26.0993	.0407
17	26.7496	.0427
18	27.4288	.0448
19	28.1330	.0469
20	28.8656	.0491
21	29.6257	.0514
22	30.4178	.0539
23	31.2384	.0563
24	32.0934	.0589
25	32.9831	.0616
26	33.9055	.0645
27	34.8663	.0675
28	35.8672	.0706
29	36.9087	.0738
30	37.9926	.0773
31	39.1234	.0810
32	40.3040	.0848
33	41.5304	.0889
34	42.8131	.0931
35	44.1526	.0975
36	45.5477	.1019
37	47.0095	.1063
38	48.5291	.1107
39	50.1108	.1151
40	51.7520	.1198
41	53.4665	.1247
42	55.2463	.1299
43	57.1020	.1355
44	59.0393	.1415
45	61.0674	.1480
46	63.1915	.1550
47	65.4177	.1628
48	67.7753	.1715
49	70.2573	.1811
50	72.8897	.1919

8th Year—D. or 65.

Age.	Value.	M. Diff.
10	21.1449	+.0242
11	21.5958	.0256
12	22.0583	.0273
13	22.5401	.0283
14	23.0393	.0297
15	23.5549	.0312
16	24.0905	.0327
17	24.6443	.0343
18	25.2221	.0359
19	25.8197	.0376
20	26.4340	.0394
21	27.0832	.0412
22	27.7515	.0430
23	28.4421	.0449
24	29.1595	.0469
25	29.9068	.0490
26	30.6763	.0512
27	31.4767	.0535
28	32.3092	.0558
29	33.1736	.0583
30	34.0702	.0609
31	35.0035	.0636
32	35.9757	.0665
33	36.9819	.0696
34	38.0326	.0727
35	39.1258	.0760
36	40.2641	.0791
37	41.4477	.0820
38	42.6739	.0849
39	43.9444	.0876
40	45.2523	.0904
41	46.6091	.0933
42	48.0092	.0962
43	49.4555	.0993
44	50.9526	.1025
45	52.5063	.1059
46	54.1180	.1095
47	55.7882	.1134
48	57.5440	.1177
49	59.3700	.1224
50	61.2853	.1278
51	63.2985	.1338
52	65.4215	.1407
53	67.6613	.1483
54	70.0503	.1572
55	72.5937	.1677

8th Year—D. or 70.

Age.	Value.	M. Diff.
10	20.1373	+.0203
11	20.5335	.0213
12	20.9467	+.0225
13	21.3755	.0236
14	21.8193	.0249
15	22.2746	.0243
16	22.7502	.0274
17	23.2396	.0286
18	23.7500	.0300
19	24.2765	.0314
20	24.8227	.0328
21	25.3870	.0343
22	25.9727	.0358
23	26.5765	.0374
24	27.2032	.0389
25	27.8524	.0406
26	28.5221	.0423
27	29.2104	.0441
28	29.9360	.0460
29	30.6816	.0479
30	31.4547	.0499
31	32.2551	.0521
32	33.0893	.0544
33	33.9476	.0567
34	34.8435	.0591
35	35.7712	.0616
36	36.7375	.0639
37	37.7370	.0659
38	38.7681	.0677
39	39.8303	.0693
40	40.9163	.0708
41	42.0367	.0723
42	43.1813	.0737
43	44.3543	.0751
44	45.5576	.0765
45	46.7952	.0778
46	48.0646	.0791
47	49.3657	.0805
48	50.7182	.0819
49	52.1067	.0833
50	53.5440	.0850
51	55.0337	.0869
52	56.5798	.0889
53	58.1902	.0910
54	59.8724	.0936
55	61.6335	.0965
56	63.4850	.1003
57	65.4433	.1049
58	67.5243	.1106
59	69.7501	.1181
60	72.1496	.1276

8th Year—D. or 75.

Age.	Value.	M. Diff.
10	19.5252	+.0178
11	19.8927	.0188
12	20.2754	.0198
13	20.6724	.0209
14	21.0799	.0219
15	21.5028	.0230
16	21.9405	.0241
17	22.3921	.0253
18	22.8596	.0265
19	23.3454	.0277
20	23.8464	.0289
21	24.3633	.0302
22	24.8990	.0315
23	25.4512	.0328
24	26.0220	.0341
25	26.6132	.0355
26	27.2219	.0370
27	27.8514	.0385
28	28.5036	.0401
29	29.1778	.0417
30	29.8752	.0434
31	30.5976	.0451
32	31.3455	.0470
33	32.1165	.0489
34	32.9188	.0509
35	33.7476	.0529
36	34.6092	.0547
37	35.4923	.0561
38	36.4109	.0574
39	37.3476	.0582
40	38.2993	.0590
41	39.2775	.0596
42	40.2685	.0602
43	41.2767	.0605
44	42.3015	.0608
45	43.3482	.0609
46	44.4134	.0608
47	45.4869	.0606
48	46.5987	.0602
49	47.7234	.0597
50	48.8720	.0592
51	50.0456	.0585

TEN PREMIUM ENDOWMENT POLICIES.—4 PER CENT.

8th Year—D. or 75.

Age.	Value.	M. Diff.
52	51.2461	+.0577
53	52.4722	.0565
54	53.7302	.0552
55	55.0188	.0536
56	56.3419	.0521
57	57.7066	.0505
58	59.1188	.0491
59	60.5823	.0478
60	62.1133	.0469
61	63.7252	.0469
62	65.4364	.0479
63	67.2764	.0505
64	69.2686	.0551
65	71.4610	.0627

9th YEAR—D. or 35.

Age.	Value.	M. Diff.
10	48.9882	+.1339
11	50.6746	.1403
12	52.4397	.1470
13	54.2857	.1540
14	56.2151	.1614
15	58.2341	.1691
16	60.3478	.1772
17	62.5587	.1857
18	64.8740	.1947
19	67.2971	.2041
20	69.8363	.2141
21	72.4937	.2245
22	75.2793	.2356
23	78.1987	.2472
24	81.2598	.2595
25	84.4690	.2725

9th Year—D. or 40.

Age.	Value.	M. Diff.
10	41.7843	+.1054
11	43.1287	.1104
12	44.5346	.1156
13	46.0036	.1211
14	47.5375	.1268
15	49.1415	.1328
16	50.8191	.1390
17	52.5713	.1456
18	54.4057	.1526
19	56.3234	.1599
20	58.3304	.1675
21	60.4292	.1756
22	62.6269	.1841
23	64.9277	.1930
24	67.3375	.2024
25	69.8611	.2124
26	72.5069	.2229
27	75.2804	.2339
28	78.1892	.2457
29	81.2408	.2581
30	84.4439	.2713

9th Year—D. or 45.

Age.	Value.	M. Diff.
10	36.1576	+.0832
11	37.2345	.0871
12	38.3599	.0911
13	39.5348	.0953
14	40.7594	.0998
15	42.0393	.1044
16	43.3760	.1093
17	44.7705	.1135
18	46.2287	.1197
19	47.7512	.1253
20	49.3433	.1312
21	51.0054	.1374
22	52.7448	+.1438
23	54.5615	.1507
24	56.4625	.1578
25	58.4508	.1671
26	60.5325	.1734
27	62.7118	.1819
28	64.9942	.1908
29	67.3857	.2002
30	69.8923	.2102
31	72.5204	.2208
32	75.2810	.2320
33	78.1744	.2439
34	81.2168	.2565
35	84.4129	.2698

9th Year—D. or 50.

Age.	Value.	M. Diff.
10	31.7994	+.0659
11	32.6693	.0689
12	33.5773	.0721
13	34.5243	.0754
14	35.5097	.0788
15	36.5381	.0824
16	37.6109	.0862
17	38.7283	.0901
18	39.8954	.0942
19	41.1120	.0985
20	42.3825	.1030
21	43.7064	.1078
22	45.0901	.1127
23	46.5324	.1179
24	48.0396	.1233
25	49.6131	.1291
26	51.2579	.1351
27	52.9771	.1415
28	54.7742	.1482
29	56.6544	.1553
30	58.6218	.1629
31	60.6817	.1709
32	62.8420	.1793
33	65.0997	.1881
34	67.4717	.1975
35	69.9590	.2074
36	72.5683	.2177
37	75.3059	.2287
38	78.1783	.2403
39	81.2019	.2529
40	84.3790	.2665

9th Year—D. or 55.

Age.	Value.	M. Diff.
10	28.4801	+.0528
11	29.1920	.0552
12	29.9346	.0576
13	30.7084	.0602
14	31.5112	.0629
15	32.3481	.0657
16	33.2200	.0686
17	34.1253	.0716
18	35.0718	.0748
19	36.0551	.0781
20	37.0806	.0816
21	38.1470	.0852
22	39.2599	.0890
23	40.4170	.0929
24	41.6243	.0870
25	42.8819	.1014
26	44.1939	.1060
27	45.5623	.1108
28	46.9905	.1158
29	48.4807	.1212
30	50.0373	.1268
31	51.6641	.1328
32	53.3665	+.1391
33	55.1423	.1457
34	57.0029	.1526
35	58.9500	.1598
36	60.9866	.1672
37	63.1173	.1750
38	65.3452	.1831
39	67.6770	.1918
40	70.1144	.2011
41	72.6768	.2111
42	75.3619	.2220
43	78.1861	.2339
44	81.1605	.2468
45	84.3015	.2610

9th Year—D. or 60.

Age.	Value.	M. Diff.
10	26.0195	+.0431
11	26.6137	.0450
12	27.2335	.0469
13	27.8786	.0489
14	28.5463	.0511
15	29.2413	.0533
16	29.9640	.0556
17	30.7128	.0580
18	31.4950	.0604
19	32.3056	.0630
20	33.1494	.0657
21	34.0247	.0685
22	34.9368	.0714
23	35.8822	.0744
24	36.8673	.0775
25	37.8924	.0809
26	38.9558	.0844
27	40.0642	.0880
28	41.2184	.0918
29	42.4200	.0958
30	43.6717	.1001
31	44.9771	.1045
32	46.3405	.1093
33	47.7579	.1142
34	49.2400	.1193
35	50.7870	.1245
36	52.3961	.1298
37	54.0793	.1352
38	55.8285	.1406
39	57.6479	.1464
40	59.5390	.1526
41	61.5165	.1592
42	63.5747	.1662
43	65.7244	.1738
44	67.9731	.1819
45	70.3305	.1909
46	72.8052	.2007
47	75.4041	.2115
48	78.1598	.2236
49	81.0671	.2371
50	84.1589	.2524

9th Year—D. or 65.

Age.	Value.	M. Diff.
10	24.2616	+.0361
11	24.7788	.0378
12	25.3159	.0393
13	25.8639	.0409
14	26.4368	.0427
15	27.0305	.0444
16	27.6467	.0463
17	28.2840	.0482
18	28.9491	.0502
19	29.6366	.0523
20	30.3444	.0543
21	31.0907	.0566
22	31.8598	+.0588
23	32.6548	.0612
24	33.4808	.0637
25	34.3402	.0663
26	35.2278	.0689
27	36.1505	.0718
28	37.1098	.0747
29	38.1063	.0778
30	39.1412	.0810
31	40.2177	.0844
32	41.3396	.0881
33	42.5020	.0918
34	43.7149	.0956
35	44.9763	.0995
36	46.2869	.1031
37	47.6466	.1068
38	49.0540	.1104
39	50.5101	.1142
40	52.0119	.1180
41	53.5716	.1221
42	55.1848	.1264
43	56.8547	.1310
44	58.5866	.1358
45	60.3867	.1409
46	62.2578	.1466
47	64.2017	.1527
48	66.2463	.1595
49	68.3773	.1670
50	70.6193	.1754
51	72.9800	.1849
52	75.4749	.1955
53	78.1141	.2077
54	80.9360	.2218
55	83.9504	.2382

9th Year—D. or 70.

Age.	Value.	M. Diff.
10	23.0991	+.0315
11	23.5542	.0328
12	24.0286	.0342
13	24.5204	.0356
14	25.0297	.0371
15	25.5546	.0385
16	26.1007	.0401
17	26.6636	.0417
18	27.2507	.0434
19	27.8561	.0451
20	28.4845	.0468
21	29.1334	.0487
22	29.8070	.0505
23	30.5016	.0524
24	31.2227	.0544
25	31.9695	.0565
26	32.7406	.0587
27	33.5342	.0609
28	34.3692	.0633
29	35.2283	.0658
30	36.1199	.0683
31	37.0427	.0710
32	38.0040	.0739
33	38.9957	.0768
34	40.0292	.0798
35	41.0989	.0827
36	42.2094	.0854
37	43.3549	.0879
38	44.5349	.0903
39	45.7480	.0926
40	46.9904	.0950
41	48.2736	.0975
42	49.5878	.0999
43	50.9375	.1024
44	52.3248	.1050
45	53.7530	.1076
46	55.2214	.1105
47	56.7300	+.1134
48	58.2982	.1167
49	59.9116	.1203
50	61.5870	.1241
51	63.3258	.1284
52	65.1341	.1330
53	67.0204	.1383
54	68.9959	.1443
55	71.0699	.1514
56	73.2594	.1598
57	75.5836	.1697
58	78.0655	.1818
59	80.7348	.1966
60	83.6282	.2148

9th Year—D. or 75.

Age.	Value.	M. Diff.
10	22.3934	+.0287
11	22.8153	.0299
12	23.2545	.0311
13	23.7096	.0324
14	24.1778	.0337
15	24.6643	.0350
16	25.1668	.0364
17	25.6859	.0378
18	26.2237	.0392
19	26.7817	.0408
20	27.3579	.0423
21	27.9520	.0439
22	28.5679	.0455
23	29.2026	.0471
24	29.8593	.0488
25	30.5390	.0506
26	31.2396	.0525
27	31.9645	.0544
28	32.7152	.0564
29	33.4915	.0585
30	34.2956	.0607
31	35.1278	.0630
32	35.9900	.0654
33	36.8797	.0678
34	37.8048	.0703
35	38.7597	.0726
36	39.7487	.0746
37	40.7592	.0765
38	41.8076	.0781
39	42.8742	.0796
40	43.9597	.0812
41	45.0765	.0826
42	46.2104	.0839
43	47.3674	.0852
44	48.5454	.0864
45	49.7493	.0875
46	50.9771	.0887
47	52.2178	.0897
48	53.5016	.0908
49	54.8025	.0920
50	56.1359	.0931
51	57.4992	.0943
52	58.8955	.0953
53	60.3231	.0964
54	61.7903	.0976
55	63.2963	.0990
56	64.8489	.1007
57	66.4550	.1028
58	68.1245	.1056
59	69.8648	.1092
60	71.6952	.1141
61	73.6353	.1207
62	75.7107	.1293
63	77.9567	.1409
64	80.4075	.1561
65	83.1251	.1764

FIVE PREMIUM POLICIES—1st YEAR—4 PER CENT.

AGE.	0.	1.	2.	3.	4.	5.	6.	7.	8.	9.	10.	11.	12.
10	4.6680	4.6296	4.5912	4.5528	4.5144	4.4760	4.4376	4.3992	4.3608	4.3224	4.2840	4.2456	4.2072
11	4.7391	4.7007	4.6623	4.6239	4.5856	8.5473	4.5090	4.4707	4.4324	4.3941	4.3558	4.3175	4.2791
12	4.8124	4.7741	4.7358	4.6975	4.6592	4.6209	4.5826	4.5443	4.5061	4.4679	4.4297	4.3915	4.3533
13	4.8903	4.8520	4.8137	4.7754	4.7371	4.6988	4.6606	4.6224	4.5842	4.5460	4.5078	4.4696	4.4314
14	4.9705	4.9322	4.8939	4.8556	4.8173	4.7790	4.7407	4.7024	4.6641	4.6258	4.5875	4.5492	4.5109
15	5.0536	5.0152	4.9768	4.9384	4.9001	4.8618	4.8235	4.7852	4.7469	4.7086	4.6702	4.6320	4.5932
16	5.1403	5.1018	5.0633	5.0248	4.9863	4.9478	4.9093	4.8708	4.8323	4.7938	4.7553	4.7168	4.6784
17	5.2299	5.1912	5.1525	5.1138	5.0751	5.0364	4.9977	4.9591	4.9205	4.8819	4.8433	4.8047	4.7665
18	5.3229	5.2840	5.2451	5.2062	5.1674	5.1286	5.0898	5.0510	5.0122	4.9734	4.9346	4.8958	4.8570
19	5.4188	5.3797	5.3406	5.3015	5.2624	5.2233	5.1842	5.1452	5.1062	5.0672	5.0282	4.9892	4.9506
20	5.5184	5.4791	5.4398	5.4005	5.3613	5.3220	5.2827	5.2434	5.2041	5.1648	5.1255	5.0862	5.0469
21	5.6211	5.5816	5.5421	5.5026	5.4630	5.4234	5.3838	5.3442	5.3046	5.2650	5.2254	5.1858	5.1462
22	5.7280	5.6881	5.6482	5.6083	5.5684	5.5285	5.4887	5.4489	5.4091	5.3693	5.3295	5.2897	5.2499
23	5.8384	5.7983	5.7581	5.7179	5.6777	5.6375	5.5973	5.5571	5.5169	5.4767	5.4365	5.3963	5.3561
24	5.9523	5.9118	5.8713	5.8308	5.7903	5.7498	5.7093	5.6687	5.6281	5.5875	5.5467	5.5061	5.4657
25	6.0703	6.0294	5.9885	5.9476	5.9067	5.8658	5.8249	5.7840	5.7431	5.7022	5.6613	5.6204	5.5795
26	6.1923	6.1509	6.1095	6.0681	6.0267	5.9854	5.9441	5.9028	5.8615	5.8202	5.7789	5.7376	5.6963
27	6.3183	6.2766	6.2349	6.1932	6.1514	6.1096	6.0678	6.0260	5.9842	5.9424	5.9006	5.8588	5.8170
28	6.4487	6.4064	6.3641	6.3218	6.2795	6.2372	6.1949	6.1526	6.1103	6.0680	6.0257	5.9834	5.9411
29	6.5834	6.5405	6.4976	6.4547	6.4119	6.3691	6.3263	6.2835	6.2407	6.1979	6.1551	6.1123	6.0695
30	6.7227	6.6792	6.6357	6.5922	6.5487	6.5052	6.4617	6.4183	6.3749	6.3315	6.2881	6.2447	6.2013
31	6.8667	6.8227	6.7787	6.7347	6.6907	6.6466	6.6025	6.5584	6.5143	6.4702	6.4261	6.3820	6.3379
32	7.0154	6.9707	6.9260	6.8812	6.8364	6.7916	6.7468	6.7020	6.6572	6.6124	6.5676	6.5228	6.4780
33	7.1690	7.1234	7.0779	7.0324	6.9869	6.9414	6.8959	6.8504	6.8049	6.7594	6.7139	6.6684	6.6229
34	7.3277	7.2814	7.2351	7.1888	7.1425	7.0962	7.0500	7.0038	6.9576	6.9114	6.8652	6.8190	6.7728
35	7.4918	7.4448	7.3978	7.3508	7.3038	7.2567	7.2096	7.1625	7.1154	7.0683	7.0212	6.9741	6.9270
36	7.6613	7.6134	7.5655	7.5176	7.4697	7.4218	7.3739	7.3259	7.2779	7.2299	7.1819	7.1339	7.0863
37	7.8366	7.7878	7.7390	7.6902	7.6414	7.5926	7.5438	7.4951	7.4464	7.3977	7.3490	7.3003	7.2516
38	8.0179	7.9682	7.9185	7.8688	7.8191	7.7694	7.7197	7.7700	7.6203	7.6706	7.5209	7.5712	7.4215
39	8.2054	8.1547	8.1040	8.0533	8.0026	7.9519	7.9012	7.8505	7.7999	7.7493	7.6987	7.6481	7.5975
40	8.3997	8.3480	8.2963	8.2446	8.1929	8.1413	8.0897	8.0381	7.9865	7.9349	7.8833	7.8317	7.7801
41	8.6014	8.5486	8.4958	8.4431	8.3904	8.3377	8.2850	8.2323	8.1796	8.1269	8.0742	8.0215	7.9688
42	8.8108	8.7567	8.7026	8.6486	8.5946	8.5406	8.4866	8.4326	8.3786	8.3246	8.2706	8.2166	8.1626
43	9.0286	8.9727	8.9168	8.8609	8.8051	8.7493	8.6935	8.6377	8.5819	8.5261	8.4703	8.4145	8.3587
44	9.2546	9.1964	9.1382	9.0799	9.0216	8.9633	8.9050	8.8467	8.7884	8.7301	8.6718	8.6135	8.5552
45	9.4879	9.4266	9.3653	9.3040	9.2427	9.1815	9.1203	9.0591	8.9979	8.9367	8.8755	8.8143	8.7531
46	9.7285	9.6635	9.5985	9.5336	9.4687	9.4038	9.3389	9.2740	9.2091	9.1442	9.0793	9.0144	8.9487
47	9.9747	9.9056	9.8365	9.7675	9.6985	9.6295	9.5605	9.4915	9.4225	9.3535	9.2845	9.2155	9.1457
48	10.2278	10.1541	10.0804	10.0067	9.9330	9.8594	9.7858	9.7122	9.6386	9.5650	9.4914	9.4178	9.3442
49	10.4869	10.4082	10.3295	10.2508	10.1722	10.0936	10.0150	9.9364	9.8578	9.7792	9.7006	9.6220	9.5434
50	10.7523	10.6682	10.5841	10.5000	10.4159	10.3318	10.2478	10.1638	10.0798	9.9958	9.9118	9.8278	9.7438
51	11.0246	10.9346	10.8446	10.7546	10.6646	10.5745	10.4844	10.3943	10.3042	10.2141	10.1240	10.0339	9.9438
52	11.3029	11.2061	11.1093	11.0126	10.9159	10.8192	10.7225	10.6258	10.5291	10.4324	10.3357	10.2390	10.1423
53	11.5878	11.4837	11.3796	11.2755	11.1714	11.0674	10.9634	10.8594	10.7554	10.6514	10.5474	10.4434	10.3394
54	11.8784	11.7665	11.6546	11.5427	11.4308	11.3189	11.2070	11.0952	10.9834	10.8716	10.7598	10.6480	10.5362
55	12.1773	12.0567	11.9361	11.8155	11.6950	11.5745	11.4540	11.3335	11.2130	11.0925	10.9720	10.8515	10.7304
56	12.4826	12.3526	12.2226	12.0926	11.9626	11.8325	11.7024	11.5723	11.4422	11.3121	11.1820	11.0519	10.9218
57	12.7951	12.6550	12.5149	12.3748	12.2347	12.0946	11.9544	11.8142	11.6740	11.5338	11.3936	11.2534	11.1132
58	13.1166	12.9652	12.8139	12.6626	12.5113	12.3600	12.2087	12.0574	11.9061	11.7548	11.6035	11.4522	11.3009
59	13.4454	13.2818	13.1182	12.9546	12.7910	12.6274	12.4639	12.3004	12.1369	11.9734	11.8099	11.6464	11.4829
60	13.7843	13.6070	13.4297	13.2523	13.0749	12.8975	12.7201	12.5427	12.3653	12.1879	12.0105	11.8331	11.6557
61	14.1321	13.9395	13.7469	13.5543	13.3618	13.1693	12.9768	12.7843	12.5918	12.3993	12.2068	12.0143	11.8218
62	14.4896	14.2802	14.0708	13.8615	13.6522	13.4429	13.2336	13.0243	12.8150	12.6057	12.3964	12.1871	11.9778
63	14.8567	14.6292	14.4017	14.1742	13.9467	13.7191	13.4915	13.2639	13.0363	12.8087	12.5811	12.3535	12.1259
64	15.2344	14.9867	14.7390	14.4913	14.2436	13.9959	13.7482	13.5005	13.2527	13.0049	12.7571	12.5093	12.2619
65	15.6229	15.3532	15.0835	14.8138	14.5440	14.2742	14.0044	13.7346	13.4648	13.1950	12.9252	12.6554	12.3856
66	16.0228	15.7291	15.4354	15.1416	14.8478	14.5540	14.2602	13.9664	13.6726	13.3788	13.0850	12.7912	12.4974
67	16.4350	16.1148	15.7946	15.4744	15.1542	14.8340	14.5139	14.1938	13.8737	13.5536	13.2335	12.9134	12.5933
68	16.8591	16.5104	16.1617	15.8130	15.4644	15.1158	14.7672	14.4186	14.0700	13.7214	13.3728	13.0242	12.6756
69	17.2973	16.9183	16.5389	16.1597	15.7805	15.4013	15.0221	14.6429	14.2637	13.8845	13.5053	13.1261	12.7464
70	17.7513	17.3386	16.9259	16.5133	16.1007	15.6881	15.2755	14.8629	14.4503	14.0377	13.6251	13.2125	12.7991
71	18.2223	17.7734	17.3245	16.8756	16.4267	15.9778	15.5289	15.0800	14.6311	14.1823	13.7335	13.2847	12.8359
72	18.7123	18.2241	17.7359	17.2477	16.7596	16.2715	15.7834	15.2953	14.8072	14.3191	13.8310	13.3429	12.8548
73	19.2230	18.6924	18.1618	17.6312	17.1006	16.5690	16.0384	15.5079	14.9774	14.4469	13.9164	13.3859	12.8563
74	19.7575	19.1807	18.6039	18.0271	17.4504	16.8737	16.2970	15.7203	15.1436	14.5669	13.9902	13.4135	12.8367
AGE.	0.	1.	2.	3.	4.	5.	6.	7.	8.	9.	10.	11.	12.

FIVE PREMIUM POLICIES—2d YEAR—4 PER CENT.

AGE.	0.	1.	2.	3.	4.	5.	6.	7.	8.	9.	10.	11.	12.
10	8.8752	8.8529	8.8306	8.8082	8.7858	8.7634	8.7410	8.7186	8.6962	8.6738	8.6514	8.6290	8.6066
11	9.0182	8.9964	8.9746	8.9528	8.9310	8.9092	8.8875	8.8658	8.8441	8.8224	8.8007	8.7790	8.7573
12	9.1657	9.1447	9.1236	9.1025	9.0814	9.0603	9.0392	9.0181	8.9970	8.9759	8.9548	8.9337	8.9126
13	9.3217	9.3004	9.2791	9.2578	9.2365	9.2153	9.1941	9.1729	9.1517	9.1305	9.1093	9.0881	9.0669
14	9.4814	9.4605	9.4396	9.4187	9.3978	9.3769	9.3560	9.3351	9.3142	9.2933	9.2724	9.2515	9.2306
15	9.6468	9.6261	9.6054	9.5847	9.5641	9.5435	9.5229	9.5023	9.4817	9.4611	9.4405	9.4199	9.3993
16	9.8187	9.7982	9.7777	9.7572	9.7367	9.7162	9.6957	9.6752	9.6547	9.6342	9.6137	9.5932	9.5727
17	9.9964	9.9759	9.9555	9.9351	9.9147	9.8943	9.8739	9.8535	9.8331	9.8127	9.7923	9.7719	9.7515
18	10.1799	10.1598	10.1397	10.1195	10.0993	10.0791	10.0589	10.0387	10.0185	9.9983	9.9781	9.9579	9.9377
19	10.3694	10.3495	10.3296	10.3096	10.2896	10.2696	10.2496	10.2296	10.2096	10.1896	10.1696	10.1496	10.1296
20	10.5653	10.5455	10.5257	10.5059	10.4861	10.4663	10.4464	10.4265	10.4066	10.3867	10.3668	10.3469	10.3270
21	10.7673	10.7478	10.7283	10.7087	10.6891	10.6695	10.6499	10.6303	10.6107	10.5911	10.5715	10.5619	10.5323
22	10.9779	10.9583	10.9387	10.9191	10.8995	10.8799	10.8603	10.8406	10.8209	10.8012	10.7815	10.7618	10.7421
23	11.1945	11.1749	11.1553	11.1357	11.1161	11.0965	11.0769	11.0573	11.0377	11.0181	10.9985	10.9789	10.9593
24	11.4180	11.3985	11.3790	11.3595	11.3400	11.3205	11.3011	11.2817	11.2623	11.2429	11.2235	11.2041	11.1847
25	11.6498	11.6303	11.6108	11.5913	11.5718	11.5523	11.5329	11.5135	11.4941	11.4747	11.4553	11.4359	11.4165
26	11.8886	11.8693	11.8500	11.8307	11.8114	11.7920	11.7726	11.7532	11.7338	11.7144	11.6950	11.6756	11.6562
27	12.1353	12.1159	12.0965	12.0772	12.0579	12.0386	12.0193	12.0000	11.9807	11.9614	11.9421	11.9228	11.9035
28	12.3898	12.3704	12.3511	12.3318	12.3125	12.2932	12.2739	12.2546	12.2353	12.2160	12.1967	12.1774	12.1581
29	12.6529	12.6336	12.6144	12.5952	12.5760	12.5568	12.5376	12.5184	12.4992	12.4800	12.4608	12.4416	12.4214
30	12.9240	12.9047	12.8854	12.8662	12.8470	12.8278	12.8086	12.7894	12.7702	12.7510	12.7318	12.7126	12.6924
31	13.2046	13.1851	13.1656	13.1461	13.1267	13.1073	13.0879	13.0685	13.0491	13.0297	13.0103	12.9909	12.9715
32	13.4934	13.4740	13.4546	13.4351	13.4156	13.3961	13.3766	13.3571	[illegible]	13.3181	13.2986	13.2791	13.2596
33	13.7919	13.7723	13.7527	13.7331	13.7136	13.6940	73.6745	13.6550	13.6355	13.6160	13.5965	13.5770	13.5574
34	14.1005	14.0809	14.0613	14.0417	14.0221	14.0025	13.9828	13.9631	13.9434	13.9237	13.9040	13.8843	13.8646
35	14.4188	14.3991	14.3794	14.3597	14.3400	14.3202	14.3004	14.2806	14.2608	14.2410	14.2212	14.2014	14.1816
36	14.7476	14.7278	14.7080	14.6882	14.6684	14.6486	14.6288	14.6089	14.5890	14.5691	14.5492	14.5293	14.5094
37	15.0882	15.0683	15.0483	15.0283	15.0083	14.9883	14.9683	14.9483	14.9283	14.9083	14.8883	14.8683	14.8483
38	15.4394	15.4193	15.3992	15.3791	15.3590	15.3389	15.3188	15.2987	15.2786	15.2585	15.2384	15.2183	15.1982
39	15.8029	15.7827	15.7625	15.7423	15.7221	15.7019	15.6817	15.6615	15.6413	15.6211	15.6009	15.5807	15.5605
40	16.1798	16.1595	16.1392	16.1189	16.0986	16.0782	16.0578	16.0374	16.0170	15.9966	15.9762	15.9558	15.9354
41	16.5702	16.5495	16.5288	16.5081	16.4874	16.4666	16.4458	16.4250	16.4042	16.3834	16.3626	16.3418	16.3210
42	16.9734	16.9510	16.9286	16.9062	16.8838	16.8615	16.8392	16.8169	16.7946	16.7723	16.7500	16.7277	16.7054
43	17.3873	17.3644	17.3416	17.3188	17.2960	17.2732	17.2504	17.2276	17.2048	17.1820	17.1592	17.1364	17.1136
44	17.8098	17.7853	17.7608	17.7362	17.7116	17.6870	17.6624	17.6378	17.6132	17.5886	17.5640	17.5394	17.5148
45	18.2410	18.2139	18.1869	18.1599	18.1329	18.1059	18.0789	18.0519	18.0249	17.9979	17.9709	17.9439	17.9169
46	18.6772	18.6474	18.6176	18.5878	18.5580	18.5283	18.4986	18.4689	18.4392	18.4095	18.3798	18.3501	18.3204
47	19.1204	19.0876	19.0548	19.0220	18.9893	18.9566	18.9239	18.8912	18.8585	18.8258	18.7931	18.7604	18.7277
48	19.5720	19.5358	19.4996	19.4634	19.4272	19.3910	19.3547	19.3184	19.2821	19.2458	19.2095	19.1732	19.1369
49	20.0303	19.9902	19.9501	19.9101	19.8701	19.8301	19.7901	19.7501	19.7101	19.6701	19.6301	19.5901	19.5501
50	20.4961	20.4517	20.4073	20.3629	20.3186	20.2743	20.2300	20.1857	20.1414	20.0971	20.0528	20.0085	19.9642
51	20.9684	20.9191	20.8698	20.8206	20.7714	20.7222	20.6730	20.6238	20.5746	20.5254	20.4762	20.4270	20.3778
52	21.4452	21.3907	21.3362	21.2817	21.2272	21.1726	21.1180	21.0634	21.0088	20.9542	20.8996	20.8450	20.7904
53	21.9272	21.8669	21.8066	21.7462	21.6858	21.6254	21.5650	21.5046	21.4442	21.3838	21.3234	21.2630	21.2026
54	22.4146	22.3479	22.2811	22.2143	22.1475	22.0807	22.0139	21.9471	21.8803	21.8135	21.7467	21.6799	21.6131
55	22.9077	22.8338	22.7600	22.6862	22.6124	22.5386	22.4648	22.3910	22.3172	22.2434	22.1696	22.0958	22.0220
56	23.4044	23.3231	23.2418	23.1605	23.0792	22.9979	22.9165	22.8351	22.7537	22.6723	22.5909	22.5095	22.4281
57	23.9083	23.8185	23.7287	23.6389	23.5491	23.4593	23.3695	23.2797	23.1899	23.1001	23.0103	22.9205	22.8307
58	24.4175	24.3179	24.2183	24.1187	24.0191	23.9195	23.8199	23.7202	23.6205	23.5208	23.4211	23.3214	23.2217
59	24.9283	24.8183	24.7083	24.5983	24.4882	24.3781	24.2680	24.1579	24.0478	23.9377	23.8276	23.7175	23.6074
60	25.4400	25.3181	25.1963	25.0745	24.9527	24.8309	24.7091	24.5873	24.4655	24.3437	24.2219	24.1001	23.9783
61	25.9539	25.8189	25.6839	25.5489	25.4139	25.2790	25.1441	25.0092	24.8743	24.7394	24.6045	24.4696	24.3347
62	26.4674	26.3181	26.1688	26.0194	25.8700	25.7206	25.5712	25.4218	25.2724	25.1230	24.9736	24.8242	24.6758
63	26.9826	26.8173	26.6520	26.4867	26.3214	26.1561	25.9909	25.8257	25.6605	25.4953	25.3301	25.1649	24.9997
64	27.4963	27.3136	27.1309	26.9482	26.7654	26.5826	26.3998	26.2170	26.0342	25.8514	25.6686	25.4858	25.3030
65	28.0085	27.8066	27.6047	27.4028	27.2010	26.9992	26.7974	26.5956	26.3938	26.1920	25.9902	25.7884	25.5866
66	28.5202	28.2971	28.0740	27.8509	27.6278	27.4048	27.1818	26.9588	26.7358	26.5128	26.2898	26.0668	25.8438
67	29.0283	28.7822	28.5361	28.2901	28.0441	27.7981	27.5521	27.3061	27.0601	26.8141	26.5681	26.3221	26.0761
68	29.5347	29.2640	28.9933	28.7226	28.4520	28.1814	27.9108	27.6402	27.3696	27.0990	26.8284	26.5578	26.2872
69	30.0437	29.7459	29.4481	29.1503	28.8526	28.5549	28.2572	27.9595	27.6618	27.3641	27.0664	26.7687	26.4710
70	30.5504	30.2232	29.8960	29.5688	29.2417	28.9146	28.5875	28.2604	27.9333	27.6062	27.2791	26.9520	26.6249
71	31.0582	30.6991	30.3400	29.9808	29.6216	29.2624	28.9032	28.5440	28.1848	27.8256	27.4664	27.1072	26.7480
72	31.5671	31.1732	30.7793	30.3854	29.9910	29.5970	29.2030	28.8090	28.4150	28.0210	27.6270	27.2330	26.8394
73	32.0793	31.6472	31.2152	30.7832	30.3512	29.9192	29.4872	29.0552	28.6232	28.1912	27.7592	27.3272	26.8952
74	32.5942	32.1209	31.6475	31.1741	30.7007	30.2273	29.7539	29.2805	28.8071	28.3337	27.8603	27.3869	26.9135
AGE.	0.	1.	2.	3.	4.	5.	6.	7.	8.	9.	10.	11.	12.

FIVE PREMIUM POLICIES—3d YEAR—4 PER CENT.

Age.	0.	1.	2.	3.	4.	5.	6.	7.	8.	9.	10.	11.	12.
10	13.2746	13.2698	13.2650	13.2602	13.2555	13.2508	13.2461	13.2414	13.2367	13.2320	13.2273	13.2226	13.2179
11	13.4964	13.4919	13.4874	13.4830	13.4786	13.4742	13.4698	13.4654	13.4610	13.4566	13.4522	13.4478	13.4434
12	13.7250	13.7211	13.7172	13.7133	13.7094	13.7055	13.7016	13.6976	13.6936	13.6896	13.6856	13.6816	13.6776
13	13.9572	13.9539	13.9506	13.9473	13.9441	13.9409	13.9377	13.9345	13.9313	13.9281	13.9249	13.9217	13.9184
14	14.2011	14.1983	14.1955	14.1927	14.1899	14.1871	14.1844	14.1817	14.1790	14.1763	14.1736	14.1709	14.1680
15	14.4529	14.4508	14.4487	14.4466	14.4444	14.4422	14.4400	14.4378	14.4356	14.4334	14.4312	14.4290	14.4268
16	14.7130	14.7112	14.7094	14.7076	14.7058	14.7040	14.7023	14.7006	14.6989	14.6972	14.6955	14.6938	14.6921
17	14.9814	14.9804	14.9794	14.9784	14.9774	14.9764	14.9753	14.9742	14.9731	14.9720	14.9709	14.9698	14.9687
18	15.2606	15.2599	15.2592	15.2585	15.2578	15.2572	15.2566	15.2560	15.2554	15.2548	15.2542	15.2536	15.2530
19	15.5484	15.5484	15.5484	15.5483	15.5482	15.5481	15.5480	15.5479	15.5478	15.5477	15.5476	15.5475	15.5474
20	15.8454	15.8458	15.8462	15.8467	15.8472	15.8477	15.8482	15.8487	15.8492	15.8497	15.8502	15.8507	15.8512
21	16.1534	16.1544	16.1554	16.1564	16.1574	16.1584	16.1594	16.1604	16.1614	16.1624	16.1634	16.1644	16.1654
22	16.4701	16.4716	16.4731	16.4746	16.4761	16.4776	16.4791	16.4807	16.4823	16.4839	16.4855	16.4871	16.4887
23	16.7977	16.7999	16.8021	16.8043	16.8065	16.8086	16.8107	16.8128	16.8149	16.8170	16.8191	16.8212	16.8233
24	17.1370	17.1396	17.1422	17.1449	17.1476	17.1503	17.1530	17.1557	17.1584	17.1611	17.1638	17.1665	17.1692
25	17.4868	17.4900	17.4932	17.4964	17.4996	17.5028	17.5061	17.5094	17.5127	17.5160	17.5193	17.5226	17.5259
26	17.8485	17.8524	17.8562	17.8600	17.8638	17.8676	17.8714	17.8752	17.8790	17.8828	17.8866	17.8904	17.8942
27	18.2218	18.2261	18.2304	18.2347	18.2391	18.2435	18.2479	18.2523	18.2567	18.2611	18.2655	18.2699	18.2743
28	18.6068	18.6117	18.6166	18.6215	18.6264	18.6313	18.6362	18.6412	18.6462	18.6512	18.6562	18.6612	18.6662
29	19.0048	19.0103	19.0159	19.0215	19.0271	19.0327	19.0383	19.0439	19.0495	19.0551	19.0607	19.0663	19.0707
30	19.4151	19.4212	19.4273	19.4334	19.4395	19.4455	19.4515	19.4575	19.4635	19.4695	19.4755	19.4815	19.4875
31	19.8382	19.8449	19.8515	19.8581	19.8647	19.8713	19.8779	19.8845	19.8911	19.8977	19.9043	19.9109	19.9175
32	20.2750	20.2823	20.2896	20.2969	20.3041	20.3113	20.3185	20.3257	20.3329	20.3399	20.3471	20.3543	20.3617
33	20.7264	20.7343	20.7421	20.7499	20.7577	20.7655	20.7733	20.7811	20.7889	20.7967	20.8045	20.8123	20.8201
34	21.1923	21.2007	21.2091	21.2175	21.2259	21.2343	21.2427	21.2512	21.2597	21.2682	21.2767	21.2852	21.2937
35	21.6734	21.6824	21.6914	21.7005	21.7096	21.7187	21.7278	21.7369	21.7460	21.7551	21.7642	21.7733	21.7824
36	22.1707	22.1804	22.1901	22.1999	22.2097	22.2195	22.2293	22.2391	22.2489	22.2587	22.2685	22.2783	22.2881
37	22.6849	22.6953	22.7057	22.7161	22.7265	22.7369	22.7473	22.7578	22.7683	22.7788	22.7893	22.7998	22.8103
38	23.2161	23.2273	23.2384	23.2495	23.2606	23.2717	23.2829	23.2940	23.3051	23.3162	23.3273	23.3384	23.3504
39	23.7659	23.7779	23.7899	23.8019	23.8139	23.8258	23.8377	23.8496	23.8615	23.8734	23.8853	23.8972	23.9091
40	24.3351	24.3477	24.3603	24 3729	24.3854	24.3979	24.4104	24.4229	24.4354	24.4479	24.4604	24.4729	24.4854
41	24.9224	24.9343	24.9463	24.9583	24.9703	24.9823	24.9943	25.0063	25.0183	25.0303	25.0423	25.0543	25.0663
42	25.5162	25.5296	25.5430	25.5564	25.5698	25.5833	25.5968	25.6103	25.6238	25.6373	25.6508	25.6643	25.6778
43	26.1422	26.1544	26.1665	26.1786	26.1907	26.2028	26.2149	26.2270	26.2391	26.2512	26.2633	26.2754	26.2876
44	26.7694	26.7805	26.7916	26.8026	26.8136	26.8246	26.8356	26.8466	26.8576	26.8686	26.8796	26.8906	26.9016
45	27.4048	27.4146	27.4244	27.4341	27.4438	27.4535	27.4632	27.4729	27.4826	27.4923	27.5020	27.5117	27.5214
46	28.0489	28.0569	28.0649	28.0730	28.0811	28.0892	28.0973	28.1054	28.1135	28.1216	28.1297	28.1378	28.1459
47	28.7024	28.7087	28.7150	28.7213	28.7276	28.7339	28.7401	28.7463	28.7525	28.7587	28.7649	28.7711	28.7773
48	29.3647	29.3689	29.3731	29.3773	29.3815	29.3857	29.3899	29.3941	29.3983	29.4025	29.4067	29.4109	29.4151
49	30.0370	30.0387	30.0404	30.0420	30.0436	30.0452	30.0468	30.0484	30.0500	30.0516	30.0532	30.0548	30.0564
50	30.7165	30.7153	30.7141	30.7129	30.7117	30.7104	30.7091	30.7078	30.7065	30.7052	30.7039	30.7026	30.7013
51	31.4024	31.3979	31.3934	31.3889	31.3844	31.3798	31.3752	31.3706	31.3660	31.3614	31.3568	31.3522	31.3476
52	32.0933	32.0850	32.0768	32.0686	32.0604	32.0522	32.0440	32.0352	32.0270	32.0188	32.0106	32.0024	31.9948
53	32.7904	32.7781	32.7658	32.7535	32.7412	32.7289	32.7167	32.7045	32.6923	32.6801	32.6679	32.6557	32.6435
54	33.4915	33.4750	33.4584	33.4418	33.4252	33.4086	33.3920	33.3754	33.3588	33.3422	33.3256	33.3090	33.2924
55	34.1993	34.1774	34.1555	34.1336	34.1117	34.0898	34.0679	34.0460	34.0241	34.0022	33.9803	33.9584	33.9365
56	34.9107	34.8831	34.8555	34.8279	34.8003	34.7727	34.7451	34.7175	34.6899	34.6623	34.6347	34.6071	34.5795
57	35.6258	35.5919	35.5580	35.5241	35.4902	35.4563	35.4224	35.3884	35.3544	35.3204	35.2864	35.2524	35.2184
58	36.3383	36.2973	36.2563	36.2153	36.1742	36.1331	36.0920	36.0509	36.0098	35.9687	35.9276	35.8865	35.8454
59	37.0528	37.0037	36.9546	36.9055	36.8564	36.8073	36.7582	36.7090	36.6598	36.6106	36.5614	36.5122	36.4630
60	37.7626	37.7042	37.6458	37.5874	37.5291	37.4708	37.4125	37.3542	37.2959	37.2376	37.1793	37.1210	37.0627
61	38.4668	38.3985	38.3302	38.2618	38.1934	38.1250	38.0566	37.9882	37.9198	37.8514	37.7830	37.7146	37.6472
62	39.1654	39.0858	39.0062	38.9266	38.8470	38.7673	38.6876	38.6079	38.5282	38.4485	38.3688	38.2891	38.2094
63	39.8564	39.7642	39.6720	39.5798	39.4876	39.3954	39.3033	39.2112	39.1191	39.0270	38.9349	38.8428	38.7507
64	40.5374	40.4317	40.3260	40.2202	40.1144	40.0086	39.9028	39.7970	39.6912	39.5854	39.4796	39.3738	39.2680
65	41.2095	41.0883	40.9671	40.8460	40.7249	40.6038	40.4827	40.3616	40.2405	40.1194	39.9983	39.8772	39.7561
66	41.8666	41.7291	41.5915	41.4539	41.3163	41.1787	41.0411	40.9035	40.7659	40.6283	40.4907	40.3531	40.2155
67	42.5111	42.3557	42.2002	42.0447	41.8892	41.7337	41.5782	41.4227	41.2672	41.1117	40.9562	40.8007	40.6452
68	43.1464	42.9711	42.7959	42.6207	42.4455	42.2703	42.0951	41.9199	41.7447	41.5695	41.3943	41.2191	41.0439
69	43.7683	43.5717	43.3751	43.1785	42.9818	42.7851	42.5884	42.3917	42.1950	41.9983	41.8016	41.6050	41.4082
70	44.3762	44.1558	43.9353	43.7148	43.4943	43.2738	43.0533	42.8328	42.6123	42.3918	42.1713	41.9508	41.7305
71	44.9703	44.7246	44.4789	44.2332	43.9875	43.7418	43.4961	43.2504	43.0047	42.7590	42.5133	42.2676	42.0219
72	45.5517	45.2778	45.0040	44.7302	44.4564	44.1826	43.9088	43.6350	43.3612	43.0874	42.8136	42.5398	42.2660
73	46.1182	45.8138	45.5094	45.2050	44.9006	44.5962	44.2918	43.9873	43.6828	43.3783	43.0738	42.7693	42.4648
74	46.6710	46.3331	45.9952	45.6573	45.3194	44.9816	44.6438	44.3060	43.9682	43.6304	43.2926	42.9548	42.6170
Age.	0.	1.	2.	3.	4.	5.	6.	7.	8.	9.	10.	11.	12.

FIVE PREMIUM POLICIES—4th YEAR—4 PER CENT.

AGE.	0.	1.	2.	3.	4.	5.	6.	7.	8.	9.	10.	11.	12.
10	17.8859	17.8988	17.9117	17.9246	17.9375	17.9503	17.9631	17.9759	17.9887	18.0015	18.0143	18.0271	18.0399
11	18.1825	18.1962	18.2099	18.2236	18.2373	18.2509	18.2645	18.2781	18.2917	18.3053	18.3189	18.3325	18.3461
12	18.4900	18.5047	18.5194	18.5341	18.5488	18.5634	18.5780	18.5926	18.6072	18.6218	18.6364	18.6510	18.6656
13	18.8087	18.8242	18.8397	18.8552	18.8706	18.8860	18.9014	18.9168	18.9322	18.9476	18.9630	18.9784	18.9938
14	19.1385	19.1549	19.1713	19.1877	19.2040	19.2203	19.2366	19.2529	19.2692	19.2855	19.3018	19.3181	19.3344
15	19.4804	19.4976	19.5148	17.5319	19.5490	19.5661	19.5832	19.6003	19.6174	19.6345	19.6516	19.6687	19.6858
16	19.8324	19.8505	19.8686	19.8867	19.9048	19.9230	19.9412	19.9594	19.9776	19.9958	20.0140	20.0322	20.0504
17	20.1986	20.2175	20.2364	20.2554	20.2744	20.2934	20.3124	20.3314	20.3504	20.3694	20.3884	20.4074	20.4264
18	20.5759	20.5959	20.6158	20.6357	20.6556	20.6755	20.6954	20.7153	20.7352	20.7551	20.7750	20.7949	20.8148
19	20.9662	20.9870	21.0078	21.0287	21.0496	21.0705	21.0914	21.1123	21.1332	21.1541	21.1750	21.1959	21.2168
20	21.3696	21.3916	21.4136	21.4355	21.4574	21.4793	21.5012	21.5231	21.5450	21.5669	21.5888	21.6107	21.6316
21	21.7865	21.8094	21.8323	21.8552	21.8781	21.9009	21.9237	21.9465	21.9693	21.9921	22.0149	22.0377	22.0605
22	22.2167	22.2405	22.2644	22.2883	22.3122	22.3361	22.3600	22.3839	22.4078	22.4317	22.4556	22.4795	22.5033
23	22.6617	22.6867	22.7116	22.7365	22.7614	22.7863	22.8112	22.8361	22.8610	22.8859	22.9108	22.9357	22.9606
24	23.1215	23.1474	23.1733	23.1993	23.2253	23.2513	23.2773	23.3033	23.3293	23.3553	23.3813	23.4073	23.4333
25	23.5962	23.6232	23.6502	23.6772	23.7042	23.7313	23.7584	23.7855	23.8126	23.8397	23.8668	23.8939	23.9210
26	24.0865	24.1146	24.1427	24.1708	24.1989	24.2271	24.2553	24.2835	24.3117	24.3399	24.3681	24.3963	24.4245
27	24.5926	24.6218	24.6511	24.6804	24.7097	24.7390	24.7683	24.7976	24.8269	24.8562	24.8855	24.9148	24.9441
28	25.1149	25.1454	25.1759	25.2064	25.2369	25.2674	25.2978	25.3282	25.3586	25.3890	25.4194	25.4498	25.4802
29	25.6541	25.6857	25.7173	25.7489	25.7805	25.8121	25.8437	25.8753	25.9069	25.9385	25.9701	26.0017	26.0333
30	26.2102	26.2431	26.2760	26.3088	26.3416	26.3744	26.4072	26.4400	26.4728	26.5056	26.5384	26.5712	26.6040
31	26.7842	26.8182	26.8523	26.8864	26.9205	26.9546	26.9887	27.0228	27.0569	27.0910	27.1251	27.1592	27.1933
32	27.3771	27.4124	27.4477	27.4830	27.5184	27.5538	27.5892	27.6246	27.6600	27.6954	27.7308	27.7662	27.8016
33	27.9891	28.0259	28.0627	28.0995	28.1363	28.1730	28.2097	28.2464	28.2831	28.3198	28.3565	28.3932	28.4299
34	28.6214	28.6596	28.6978	28.7359	28.7740	28.8121	28.8502	28.8883	28.9264	28.9645	29.0026	29.0407	29.0788
35	29.2742	29.3139	29.3536	29.3932	29.4328	29.4724	29.5120	29.5516	29.5912	29.6308	29.6704	29.7100	29.7496
36	29.9494	29.9906	30.0317	30.0728	30.1139	30.1550	30.1961	30.2372	30.2783	30.3194	30.3605	30.4016	30.4427
37	30.6469	30.6897	30.7324	30.7751	30.8178	30.8605	30.9032	30.9459	30.9886	31.0313	31.0740	31.1167	31.1594
38	31.3683	31.4127	31.4571	31.5015	31.5459	31.5903	31.6346	31.6789	31.7232	31.7675	31.8118	31.8561	31.9004
39	32.1145	32.1605	32.2065	32.2524	32.2983	32.3442	32.3901	32.4360	32.4819	32.5278	32.5737	32.6196	32.6655
40	32.8851	32.9314	32.9778	33.0242	33.0706	33.1170	33.1634	33.2098	33.2562	33.3026	33.3490	33.3954	33.4418
41	33.6677	33.7167	33.7657	33.8147	33.8637	33.9127	33.9617	34.0107	34.0597	34.1087	34.1577	34.2067	34.2557
42	34.4886	34.5375	34.5864	34.6353	34.6842	34.7331	34.7820	34.8309	34.8798	34.9287	34.9776	35.0265	35.0754
43	35.3162	35.3653	35.4144	35.4635	35.5126	35.5617	35.6108	35.6600	35.7092	35.7584	35.8076	35.8568	35.9060
44	36.1562	36.2054	36.2546	36.3039	36.3532	36.4025	36.4518	36.5011	36.5504	36.5997	36.6490	36.6983	36.7476
45	37.0093	37.0586	37.1079	37.1571	37.2063	37.2555	37.3047	37.3539	37.4031	37.4523	37.5015	37.5507	37.5999
46	37.8744	37.9233	37.9722	38.0211	38.0701	38.1191	38.1681	38.2171	38.2661	38.3151	38.3641	38.4131	38.4621
47	38.7520	38.8006	38.8492	38.8978	38.9464	38.9951	39.0438	39.0925	39.1412	39.1899	39.2386	39.2873	39.3360
48	39.6429	39.6909	39.7389	39.7869	39.8349	39.8828	39.9307	39.9786	40.0265	40.0744	40.1223	40.1702	40.2181
49	40.5433	40.5904	40.6375	40.6846	40.7317	40.7788	40.8258	40.8728	40.9198	40.9668	41.0138	41.0608	41.1080
50	41.4536	41.4995	41.5454	41.5913	41.6372	41.6831	41.7290	41.7749	41.8208	41.8667	41.9126	41.9585	42.0044
51	42.3722	42.4168	42.4614	42.5060	42.5505	42.5950	42.6395	42.6840	42.7285	42.7730	42.8175	42.8620	42.9065
52	43.2977	43.3407	43.3837	43.4267	43.4696	43.5125	43.5554	43.5983	43.6412	43.6841	43.7270	43.7699	43.8128
53	44.2313	44.2723	44.3133	44.3543	44.3953	44.4362	44.4771	44.5180	44.5589	44.5998	44.6407	44.6816	44.7225
54	45.1708	45.2096	45.2484	45.2872	45.3260	45.3648	45.4036	45.4423	45.4810	45.5197	45.5584	45.5971	45.6358
55	46.1138	46.1501	46.1864	46.2226	46.2589	46.2952	46.3315	46.3678	46.4041	46.4404	46.4767	46.5130	46.5484
56	47.0621	47.0954	47.1287	47.1619	47.1951	47.2283	47.2615	47.2947	47.3279	47.3611	47.3943	47.4275	47.4607
57	48.0135	48.0431	48.0727	48.1022	48.1317	48.1612	48.1907	48.2202	48.2497	48.2792	48.3087	48.3382	48.3677
58	48.9620	48.9874	49.0128	49.0382	49.0636	49.0889	49.1142	49.1395	49.1648	49.1901	49.2154	49.2407	49.2660
59	49.9084	49.9288	49.9493	49.9698	49.9903	50.0108	50.0313	50.0518	50.0723	50.0928	50.1133	50.1338	50.1541
60	50.8470	50.8620	50.8770	50.8920	50.9070	50.9220	50.9371	50.9522	50.9673	50.9824	50.9975	51.0126	51.0277
61	51.7783	51.7871	51.7960	51.8049	51.8138	51.8227	51.8316	51.8405	51.8494	51.8583	51.8672	51.8761	51.8850
62	52.6990	52.7009	52.7028	52.7048	52.7068	52.7088	52.7108	52.7128	52.7148	52.7168	52.7188	52.7208	52.7228
63	53.6074	53.6017	53.5961	53.5905	53.5849	53.5793	53.5737	53.5681	53.5625	53.5569	53.5513	53.5457	53.5401
64	54.5024	54.4882	54.4740	54.4597	54.4454	54.4311	54.4168	54.4025	54.3882	54.3739	54.3596	54.3453	54.3310
65	55.3790	55.3555	55.3320	55.3085	55.2850	55.2614	55.2378	55.2142	55.1906	55.1670	55.1434	55.1198	55.0962
66	56.2383	56.2047	56.1711	56.1374	56.1037	56.0700	56.0363	56.0026	55.9689	55.9352	55.9015	55.8678	55.8341
67	57.0802	57.0353	56.9904	56.9455	56.9006	56.8557	56.8108	56.7659	56.7210	56.6761	56.6312	56.5863	56.5414
68	57.9030	57.8459	57.7888	57.7317	57.6746	57.6175	57.5604	57.5033	57.4462	57.3891	57.3320	57.2749	57.2177
69	58.7055	58.6349	58.5643	58.4938	58.4233	58.3528	58.2823	58.2118	58.1413	58.0708	58.0003	57.9298	57.8593
70	59.4858	59.4006	59.3154	59.2302	59.1450	59.0599	58.9748	58.8897	58.8046	58.7195	58.6344	58.5493	58.4642
71	60.2442	60.1429	60.0416	59.9403	59.8390	59.7377	59.6365	59.5353	59.4341	59.3329	59.2317	59.1305	59.0291
72	60.9783	60.8594	60.7405	60.6216	60.5027	60.3838	60.2649	60.1461	60.0273	59.9085	59.7897	59.6709	59.5521
73	61.6878	61.5497	61.4116	61.2735	61.1355	60.9975	60.8595	60.7215	60.5835	60.4455	60.3075	60.1695	60.0315
74	62.3745	62.2151	62.0557	61.8963	61.7369	61.5775	61.4181	61.2568	61.0995	60.9402	60.7809	60.6216	60.4623
AGE.	0.	1.	2.	3.	4.	5.	6.	7.	8.	9.	10.	11.	12.

TEMPORARY INSURANCE—ANNUAL PREMIUMS—4 PER CENT.

AGE.	1.	2.	3.	4.	5.	6.	7.	8.	9.	10.	11.	AGE.
10	.6500	.6505	.6522	.6538	.6552	.6573	.6591	.6613	.6636	.6659	.6683	10
11	.6525	.6537	.6554	.6569	.6591	.6610	.6633	.6658	.6683	.6708	.6735	11
12	.6550	.6574	.6587	.6612	.6632	.6656	.6682	.6708	.6734	.6764	.6793	12
13	.6585	.6602	.6631	.6652	.6678	.6706	.6733	.6761	.6792	.6823	.6856	13
14	.6630	.6653	.6675	.6703	.6732	.6761	.6790	.6822	.6855	.6890	.6923	14
15	.6677	.6708	.6735	.6765	.6790	.6825	.6858	.6892	.6929	.6962	.7001	15
16	.6733	.6758	.6790	.6823	.6859	.6890	.6926	.6964	.7001	.7037	.7075	16
17	.6791	.6823	.6860	.6892	.6929	.6966	.7005	.7042	.7082	.7123	.7165	17
18	.6860	.6893	.6927	.6966	.7006	.7046	.7084	.7125	.7166	.7209	.7253	18
19	.6929	.6968	.7013	.7051	.7089	.7131	.7174	.7219	.7261	.7306	.7351	19
20	.7010	.7051	.7087	.7133	.7178	.7217	.7265	.7309	.7358	.7409	.7456	20
21	.7093	.7135	.7175	.7222	.7268	.7318	.7362	.7413	.7460	.7512	.7564	21
22	.7177	.7223	.7277	.7310	.7363	.7409	.7464	.7516	.7569	.7625	.7679	22
23	.7273	.7320	.7367	.7421	.7467	.7524	.7577	.7629	.7686	.7743	.7804	23
24	.7371	.7419	.7464	.7526	.7586	.7635	.7694	.7753	.7811	.7872	.7934	24
25	.7471	.7525	.7580	.7637	.7694	.7755	.7812	.7877	.7944	.8005	.8071	25
26	.7583	.7640	.7699	.7764	.7819	.7883	.7951	.8016	.8079	.8151	.8218	26
27	.7698	.7761	.7827	.7881	.7955	.8020	.8087	.8153	.8229	.8297	.8372	27
28	.7826	.7894	.7953	.8025	.8092	.8169	.8235	.8313	.8384	.8459	.8531	28
29	.7956	.8021	.8096	.8166	.8241	.8309	.8393	.8466	.8547	.8623	.8699	29
30	.8101	.8165	.8243	.8320	.8399	.8479	.8560	.8639	.8711	.8799	.8884	30
31	.8248	.8332	.8409	.8488	.8565	.8649	.8731	.8811	.8896	.8985	.9067	31
32	.8410	.8491	.8572	.8659	.8740	.8824	.8906	.8996	.9087	.9167	.9265	32
33	.8576	.8659	.8745	.8833	.8917	.9008	.9100	.9194	.9282	.9379	.9479	33
34	.8746	.8837	.8927	.9016	.9108	.9204	.9295	.9386	.9486	.9596	.9709	34
35	.8931	.9024	.9116	.9209	.9307	.9402	.9503	.9606	.9715	.9833	.9968	35
36	.9122	.9215	.9312	.9413	.9511	.9614	.9713	.9835	.9959	1.0101	1.0259	36
37	.9314	.9414	.9520	.9621	.9728	.9833	.9956	1.0086	1.0244	1.0404	1.0583	37
38	.9525	.9631	.9734	.9845	.9957	1.0084	1.0229	1.0381	1.0558	1.0755	1.0957	38
39	.9741	.9849	.9964	1.0080	1.0214	1.0366	1.0531	1.0732	1.0927	1.1149	1.1380	39
40	.9963	1.0081	1.0202	1.0347	1.0509	1.0689	1.0891	1.1109	1.1345	1.1584	1.1842	40
41	1.0204	1.0335	1.0490	1.0666	1.0859	1.1076	1.1310	1.1553	1.1818	1.2090	1.2380	41
42	1.0476	1.0641	1.0833	1.1042	1.1277	1.1528	1.1794	1.2071	1.2364	1.2671	1.2982	42
43	1.0818	1.1032	1.1255	1.1506	1.1775	1.2058	1.2352	1.2654	1.2974	1.3310	1.3650	43
44	1.1247	1.1487	1.1757	1.2044	1.2344	1.2655	1.2973	1.3319	1.3663	1.4023	1.4399	44
45	1.1742	1.2032	1.2338	1.2655	1.2982	1.3316	1.3681	1.4043	1.4424	1.4812	1.5224	45
46	1.2345	1.2662	1.2995	1.3336	1.3685	1.4069	1.4448	1.4848	1.5258	1.5685	1.6123	46
47	1.2996	1.3349	1.3704	1.4068	1.4473	1.4869	1.5289	1.5719	1.6167	1.6629	1.7086	47
48	1.3711	1.4087	1.4463	1.4893	1.5307	1.5749	1.6200	1.6690	1.7156	1.7634	1.8179	48
49	1.4481	1.4869	1.5290	1.5762	1.6226	1.6699	1.7193	1.7703	1.8204	1.8779	1.9314	49
50	1.5326	1.5792	1.6240	1.6727	1.7223	1.7742	1.8277	1.8800	1.9407	1.9967	2.0566	50
51	1.6248	1.6761	1.7266	1.7781	1.8323	1.8884	1.9429	2.0070	2.0656	2.1285	2.1937	51
52	1.7257	1.7772	1.8320	1.8896	1.9488	2.0057	2.0740	2.1354	2.2017	2.2704	2.3410	52
53	1.8359	1.8924	1.9525	2.0145	2.0734	2.1460	2.2100	2.2797	2.3519	2.4264	2.5030	53
54	1.9532	2.0165	2.0812	2.1420	2.2202	2.2868	2.3601	2.4363	2.5149	2.5957	2.6789	54
55	2.0831	2.1514	2.2136	2.2978	2.3665	2.4438	2.5243	2.6073	2.6926	2.7803	2.8703	55
56	2.2237	2.2846	2.3785	2.4493	2.5308	2.6158	2.7032	2.7934	2.8863	2.9815	3.0781	56
57	2.3730	2.4639	2.5349	2.6209	2.7104	2.8029	2.8986	2.9969	3.0976	3.2001	3.3047	57
58	2.5371	2.6367	2.7236	2.8164	2.9133	3.0138	3.1171	3.2232	3.3319	3.4423	3.5542	58
59	2.7160	2.7991	2.9039	3.0103	3.1183	3.2294	3.3425	3.4586	3.5763	3.6955	3.8151	59
60	2.9169	3.0227	3.1327	3.2449	3.3621	3.4811	3.6034	3.7279	3.8541	3.9809	4.1088	60
61	3.1358	3.2520	3.3712	3.4949	3.6212	3.7504	3.8830	4.0167	4.1513	4.2870	4.4221	61
62	3.3770	3.5027	3.6331	3.7667	3.9037	4.0445	4.1863	4.3293	4.4736	4.6176	4.7605	62
63	3.6384	3.7763	3.9184	4.0639	4.2121	4.3627	4.5150	4.6684	4.8214	4.9741	5.1253	63
64	3.9255	4.0757	4.2293	4.3873	4.5475	4.7067	4.8714	5.0347	5.1975	5.3590	5.5181	64
65	4.2386	4.4012	4.5682	4.7373	4.9091	5.0827	5.2561	5.4298	5.6023	5.7723	5.9396	65
66	4.5782	4.7556	4.9358	5.1181	5.3020	5.4871	5.6722	5.8565	6.0389	6.2179	6.3920	66
67	4.9494	5.1399	5.3326	5.5280	5.7253	5.9221	6.1198	6.3146	6.5068	6.6945	6.8769	67
68	5.3490	5.5530	5.7607	5.9704	6.1811	6.3917	6.6005	6.8076	7.0095	7.2065	7.3952	68
69	5.7776	5.9989	6.2222	6.4474	6.6721	6.8968	7.1194	7.3364	7.5491	7.7535	7.9507	69
70	6.2436	6.4813	6.7216	6.9623	7.2029	7.4415	7.6755	7.9055	8.1270	8.3415	8.5434	70
71	6.7460	7.0022	7.2596	7.5175	7.7741	8.0270	8.2750	8.5156	8.7498	8.9693	9.1757	71
72	7.2889	7.5639	7.8404	8.1164	8.3890	8.6574	8.9187	9.1728	9.4123	9.6390	9.8485	72
73	7.8734	8.1700	8.4668	8.7606	9.0512	9.3349	9.6121	9.8749	10.1234	10.3545	10.5663	73
74	8.5065	8.8252	9.1417	9.4560	9.7642	10.0668	10.3543	10.6274	10.8821	11.1169	11.3298	74
75	9.1885	9.5294	9.8697	10.2044	10.5350	10.8499	11.1501	11.4313	11.6917	11.9289	12.1429	75
76	9.9211	10.2900	10.6536	11.0158	11.3600	11.6903	12.0010	12.2902	12.5550	12.7954	13.0102	76
77	10.7182	11.1125	11.5079	11.8846	12.2478	12.5914	12.9123	13.2083	13.4785	13.7219	13.9369	77
78	11.5812	12.0082	12.4194	12.8184	13.1979	13.5543	13.8856	14.1902	14.4665	14.7127	14.9275	78
79	12.5066	12.9644	13.4010	13.8189	14.2150	14.5855	14.9292	15.2438	15.5265	15.7753	15.9891	79
80	13.5006	13.9752	14.4386	14.8804	15.2956	15.6851	16.0446	16.3708	16.6604	16.9116	17.1210	80
81	14.5611	15.0690	15.5588	16.0245	16.4658	16.8773	17.2547	17.5934	17.8901	18.1398	18.3397	81
82	15.6917	16.2370	16.7593	17.2597	17.7329	18.1713	18.5691	18.9217	19.2216	19.4640	19.6507	82
83	16.9146	17.4997	18.0689	18.6131	19.1230	19.5928	20.0142	20.3764	20.6729	20.9032	21.0696	83
84	18.2383	18.8874	19.5157	20.1117	20.6684	21.1742	21.6144	21.9799	22.2664	22.4737	22.6086	84
85	19.7207	20.4449	21.1411	21.8017	22.4112	22.9490	23.4021	23.7621	24.0259	24.1993	24.2996	85
86	21.3923	22.2046	22.9895	23.7262	24.3863	24.9513	25.4074	25.7465	25.9723	26.1045	26.1677	86
87	23.2918	24.2257	25.1183	25.9304	26.6387	27.2211	27.6616	27.9595	28.1362	28.2215	28.2541	87
88	25.5071	26.5860	27.5860	28.4762	29.2244	29.8023	30.2001	30.4402	30.5579	30.6026	30.6174	88
89	28.1137	29.3379	30.4556	31.4216	32.1862	32.7246	33.0563	33.2211	33.2840	33.3059	33.3146	89
90	31.1279	32.5414	33.7940	34.8140	35.5517	36.0180	36.2541	36.3455	36.3774	36.3903		
91	34.7103	36.3254	37.6909	38.7109	39.3777	39.7233	39.8589	39.9071	39.9271		1.2349	18
92	38.9676	40.7855	42.1991	43.1651	43.6810	43.8873	43.9621	43.9954		1.2068	1.2069	17
93	43.9642	45.9120	47.8243	48.1084	48.4280	48.5485	48.6070		1.1800	1.1794	1.1794	16
94	49.6446	51.7192	52.9186	53.4189	53.6194	53.7286		1.1544	1.1546	1.1546	1.1546	15
95	56.1798	57.9476	58.7147	59.0464	59.2714		1.1300	1.1298	1.1298	1.1298	1.1298	14
96	62.3701	63.4301	64.0265	64.5617		1.1066	1.1063	1.1071	1.1071	1.1071	1.1063	13
97	66.5680	67.8345	69.3079		1.0843	1.0839	1.0839	1.0839	1.0839	1.0839	1.0839	12
98	72.1154	76.7740		1.0632	1.0632	1.0632	1.0632	1.0632	1.0632	1.0632	1.0624	11
99	96.1538		1.0429	1.0432	1.0432	1.0432	1.0425	1.0425	1.0425	1.0425	1.0417	10
AGE.			90.	89.	88.	87.	86.	85.	84.	83.	82.	AGE.

TEMPORARY INSURANCE — ANNUAL PREMIUMS — 4 PER CENT.

AGE.	12.	13.	14.	15.	16.	17.	18.	19.	20.	21.	22.	AGE.
10	.6709	.6736	.6765	.6793	.6823	.6852	.6884	.6914	.6947	.6980	.7013	10
11	.6764	.6793	.6823	.6854	.6884	.6918	.6949	.6984	.7018	.7053	.7089	11
12	.6824	.6854	.6888	.6919	.6954	.6987	.7023	.7058	.7095	.7134	.7172	12
13	.6889	.6923	.6955	.6991	.7026	.7064	.7100	.7139	.7179	.7218	.7257	13
14	.6960	.6993	.7031	.7067	.7106	.7145	.7185	.7226	.7268	.7309	.7353	14
15	.7035	.7075	.7112	.7153	.7193	.7234	.7278	.7321	.7363	.7409	.7454	15
16	.7115	.7156	.7199	.7240	.7283	.7329	.7373	.7418	.7466	.7512	.7559	16
17	.7206	.7249	.7291	.7336	.7384	.7430	.7476	.7526	.7574	.7623	.7674	17
18	.7300	.7344	.7391	.7440	.7486	.7536	.7588	.7638	.7689	.7742	.7793	18
19	.7397	.7448	.7497	.7547	.7599	.7651	.7703	.7758	.7811	.7864	.7922	19
20	.7506	.7557	.7609	.7663	.7719	.7773	.7828	.7883	.7940	.7999	.8053	20
21	.7617	.7671	.7729	.7783	.7841	.7899	.7955	.8015	.8076	.8134	.8196	21
22	.7738	.7793	.7852	.7912	.7971	.8031	.8093	.8154	.8217	.8280	.8347	22
23	.7862	.7925	.7985	.8047	.8109	.8173	.8238	.8301	.8368	.8436	.8510	23
24	.7997	.8062	.8126	.8190	.8256	.8324	.8390	.8459	.8530	.8605	.8686	24
25	.8139	.8202	.8271	.8340	.8408	.8476	.8548	.8625	.8702	.8788	.8880	25
26	.8287	.8359	.8427	.8500	.8573	.8647	.8724	.8805	.8892	.8990	.9093	26
27	.8443	.8514	.8590	.8666	.8741	.8821	.8908	.8998	.9101	.9209	.9322	27
28	.8609	.8687	.8766	.8843	.8926	.9016	.9111	.9219	.9331	.9451	.9579	28
29	.8785	.8862	.8942	.9029	.9123	.9224	.9335	.9453	.9578	.9716	.9855	29
30	.8960	.9047	.9140	.9235	.9341	.9457	.9580	.9715	.9857	1.0000	1.0162	30
31	.9157	.9250	.9349	.9464	.9581	.9711	.9852	1.0002	1.0156	1.0326	1.0498	31
32	.9362	.9470	.9582	.9709	.9849	.9994	1.0151	1.0313	1.0492	1.0674	1.0864	32
33	.9586	.9709	.9846	.9986	1.0142	1.0308	1.0479	1.0664	1.0858	1.1058	1.1270	33
34	.9837	.9978	1.0125	1.0295	1.0465	1.0649	1.0847	1.1049	1.1255	1.1479	1.1704	34
35	1.0116	1.0276	1.0451	1.0630	1.0824	1.1030	1.1243	1.1468	1.1700	1.1940	1.2192	35
36	1.0428	1.0613	1.0808	1.1007	1.1225	1.1453	1.1686	1.1932	1.2184	1.2447	1.2712	36
37	1.0779	1.0986	1.1196	1.1432	1.1668	1.1915	1.2173	1.2440	1.2720	1.3000	1.3303	37
38	1.1176	1.1399	1.1649	1.1897	1.2159	1.2431	1.2717	1.3004	1.3303	1.3622	1.3928	38
39	1.1616	1.1875	1.2144	1.2419	1.2712	1.3003	1.3310	1.3624	1.3957	1.4284	1.4631	39
40	1.2122	1.2400	1.2691	1.2995	1.3308	1.3637	1.3959	1.4314	1.4663	1.5025	1.5394	40
41	1.2675	1.2989	1.3302	1.3639	1.3980	1.4323	1.4704	1.5060	1.5437	1.5831	1.6234	41
42	1.3305	1.3643	1.3998	1.4350	1.4712	1.5108	1.5488	1.5895	1.6309	1.6729	1.7158	42
43	1.4014	1.4372	1.4751	1.5137	1.5554	1.5953	1.6376	1.6812	1.7249	1.7706	1.8169	43
44	1.4783	1.5189	1.5587	1.6026	1.6445	1.6890	1.7343	1.7808	1.8289	1.8771	1.9271	44
45	1.5642	1.6060	1.6523	1.6963	1.7430	1.7914	1.8403	1.8904	1.9418	1.9944	2.0468	45
46	1.6561	1.7048	1.7509	1.8002	1.8510	1.9026	1.9559	2.0101	2.0649	2.1201	2.1768	46
47	1.7601	1.8091	1.8609	1.9135	1.9678	2.0232	2.0803	2.1388	2.1977	2.2569	2.3168	47
48	1.8688	1.9225	1.9790	2.0361	2.0954	2.1555	2.2165	2.2779	2.3411	2.4043	2.4673	48
49	1.9882	2.0471	2.1067	2.1693	2.2321	2.2973	2.3622	2.4289	2.4958	2.5624	2.6287	49
50	2.1185	2.1820	2.2473	2.3142	2.3821	2.4507	2.5212	2.5919	2.6624	2.7333	2.8029	50
51	2.2606	2.3293	2.3999	2.4719	2.5451	2.6191	2.6935	2.7686	2.8429	2.9164	2.9890	51
52	2.4135	2.4880	2.5642	2.6413	2.7199	2.7988	2.8779	2.9568	3.0349	3.1119	3.1874	52
53	2.5817	2.6622	2.7436	2.8266	2.9101	2.9939	3.0777	3.1605	3.2423	3.3225	3.4004	53
54	2.7637	2.8499	2.9379	3.0266	3.1155	3.2041	3.2920	3.3790	3.4642	3.5472	3.6275	54
55	2.9616	3.0547	3.1486	3.2427	3.3369	3.4304	3.5227	3.6133	3.7016	3.7871	3.8689	55
56	3.1770	3.2764	3.3762	3.4762	3.5756	3.6736	3.7702	3.8642	3.9553	4.0428	4.1262	56
57	3.4101	3.5163	3.6226	3.7280	3.8325	3.9352	4.0354	4.1327	4.2261	4.3154	4.3994	57
58	3.6663	3.7793	3.8913	4.0026	4.1119	4.2187	4.3226	4.4223	4.5177	4.6077	4.6923	58
59	3.9357	4.0548	4.1735	4.2900	4.4042	4.5151	4.6220	4.7241	4.8207	4.9119	4.9956	59
60	4.2355	4.3618	4.4859	4.6078	4.7263	4.8409	4.9500	5.0538	5.1517	5.2417	5.3244	60
61	4.5564	4.6891	4.8193	4.9460	5.0655	5.1858	5.2973	5.4024	5.4996	5.5886	5.6691	61
62	4.9024	5.0413	5.1769	5.3081	5.4343	5.5540	5.6673	5.7723	5.8683	5.9556	6.0329	62
63	5.2738	5.4200	5.5602	5.6958	5.8246	5.9467	6.0599	6.1640	6.2584	6.3425	6.4166	63
64	5.6738	5.8246	5.9704	6.1092	6.2412	6.3638	6.4766	6.5791	6.6705	6.7513	6.8213	64
65	6.1019	6.2589	6.4085	6.5512	6.6836	6.8061	6.9175	7.0171	7.1057	7.1823	7.2478	65
66	6.5611	6.7227	6.8770	7.0210	7.1541	7.2754	7.3842	7.4807	7.5643	7.6366	7.6976	66
67	7.0515	7.2188	7.3752	7.5195	7.6524	7.7713	7.8770	8.9689	8.0489	8.1156	8.1715	67
68	7.5767	7.7463	7.9042	8.0489	8.1791	8.2953	8.3969	8.4849	8.5591	8.6214	8.6712	68
69	8.1353	8.3082	8.4661	8.6096	8.7375	8.8492	8.9466	9.0294	9.0983	9.1541	9.1984	69
70	8.7318	8.9056	9.0627	9.2039	9.3274	9.4361	9.5279	9.6049	9.6680	9.7173	9.7547	70
71	9.3657	9.5390	9.6956	9.8334	9.9532	10.0564	10.1427	10.2129	10.2688	10.3118	10.3415	71
72	10.0411	10.2142	10.3666	10.5003	10.6168	10.7132	10.7934	10.8573	10.9056	10.9396	10.9636	72
73	10.7577	10.9279	11.0787	11.2088	11.3184	11.4090	11.4813	11.5363	11.5760	11.6034	11.6199	73
74	11.5209	11.6898	11.8362	11.9609	12.0642	12.1469	12.2103	12.2565	12.2877	12.3068	12.3172	74
75	12.3330	12.4990	12.6409	12.7592	12.8544	12.9277	12.9813	13.0177	13.0401	13.0525	13.0581	75
76	13.1987	13.3611	13.4973	13.6073	13.6926	13.7553	13.7980	13.8243	13.8387	13.8456	13.8479	76
77	14.1234	14.2806	14.4089	14.5086	14.5822	14.6327	14.6640	14.6815	14.6895	14.6921	14.6932	77
78	15.1105	15.2605	15.3778	15.4652	15.5253	15.5627	15.5838	15.5932	15.5966	15.5979	15.5980	78
79	16.1657	16.3047	16.4091	16.4813	16.5268	16.5520	16.5634	16.5679	16.5691	16.5679		
80	17.2871	17.4127	17.5002	17.5555	17.5862	17.6005	17.6056	17.6072	17.6099		1.6477	29
81	18.4922	18.5991	18.6672	18.7050	18.7229	18.7292	18.7316	18.7321		1.6005	1.6006	28
82	19.7826	19.8666	19.9146	19.9370	19.9450	19.9480	19.9487		1.5557	1.5556	1.5556	27
83	21.1737	21.2344	21.2623	21.2729	21.2766	21.2779		1.5129	1.5129	1.5129	1.5128	26
84	22.6859	22.7224	22.7360	22.7405	22.7422		1.4722	1.4721	1.4721	1.4721	1.4721	25
85	24.3474	24.3652	24.3711	24.3733		1.4334	1.4335	1.4335	1.4333	1.4332	1.4331	24
86	26.1915	26.1995	26.2025		1.3963	1.3963	1.3962	1.3962	1.3962	1.3961	1.3959	23
87	28.2647	28.2688		1.3610	1.3609	1.3609	1.3610	1.3609	1.3608	1.3604	1.3598	22
88	30.6234		1.3273	1.3273	1.3273	1.3272	1.3272	1.3270	1.3267	1.3263	1.3255	21
		1.2948	1.2951	1.2951	1.2951	1.2951	1.2949	1.2946	1.2940	1.2934	1.2924	20
19	1.2643	1.2643	1.2643	1.2643	1.2643	1.2641	1.2639	1.2634	1.2629	1.2618	1.2605	19
18	1.2348	1.2348	1.2348	1.2349	1.2346	1.2345	1.2340	1.2333	1.2324	1.2312	1.2295	18
17	1.2070	1.2069	1.2068	1.2066	1.2065	1.2059	1.2054	1.2046	1.2034	1.2018	1.1997	17
16	1.1794	1.1795	1.1796	1.1789	1.1784	1.1784	1.1771	1.1759	1.1749	1.1731	1.1708	16
15	1.1546	1.1546	1.1537	1.1537	1.1538	1.1520	1.1512	1.1506	1.1482	1.1459	1.1429	15
14	1.1298	1.1289	1.1290	1.1290	1.1274	1.1267	1.1260	1.1237	1.1215	1.1186	1.1160	14
13	1.1063	1.1064	1.1064	1.1049	1.1042	1.1036	1.1006	1.0985	1.0965	1.0932	1.0899	13
12	1.0831	1.0832	1.0817	1.0810	1.0804	1.0783	1.0772	1.0746	1.0713	1.0683	1.0639	12
11	1.0625	1.0611	1.0605	1.0599	1.0579	1.0556	1.0536	1.0513	1.0476	1.0434	1.0395	11
10	1.0413	1.0407	1.0394	1.0376	1.0358	1.0334	1.0312	1.0277	1.0245	1.0208	1.0159	10
AGE.	81.	80.	79.	78.	77.	76.	75.	74.	73.	72.	71.	AGE.

TEMPORARY INSURANCE—ANNUAL PREMIUMS—4 PER CENT.

AGE.	23.	24.	25.	26.	27.	28.	29.	30.	31,	32.	33.	34.	AGE.
10	.7049	.7083	.7113	.7153	.7194	.7233	.7264	.7300	.7347	.7378	.7421	.7466	10
11	.7126	.7162	.7202	.7239	.7269	.7309	.7361	.7390	.7439	.7484	.7522	.7561	11
12	.7209	.7250	.7289	.7330	.7371	.7412	.7449	.7493	.7531	.7575	.7626	.7675	12
13	.7301	.7341	.7383	.7426	.7469	.7513	.7557	.7601	.7647	.7695	.7741	.7802	13
14	.7395	.7439	.7484	.7529	.7575	.7621	.7666	.7714	.7765	.7819	.7875	.7935	14
15	.7499	.7546	.7592	.7640	.7688	.7735	.7785	.7838	.7894	.7952	.8016	.8082	15
16	.7608	.7655	.7705	.7754	.7805	.7856	.7912	.7969	.8031	.8098	.8167	.8240	16
17	.7724	.7776	.7827	.7880	.7933	.7990	.8051	.8116	.8184	.8256	.8333	.8414	17
18	.7847	.7899	.7953	.8010	.8070	.8132	.8200	.8272	.8349	.8429	.8514	.8603	18
19	.7976	.8033	.8092	.8153	.8219	.8290	.8365	.8445	.8529	.8616	.8710	.8806	19
20	.8112	.8175	.8239	.8307	.8381	.8457	.8543	.8632	.8723	.8822	.8924	.9030	20
21	.8261	.8325	.8398	.8476	.8557	.8646	.8737	.8832	.8935	.9043	.9154	.9271	21
22	.8415	.8490	.8571	.8656	.8749	.8844	.8946	.9055	.9166	.9283	.9404	.9530	22
23	.8586	.8673	.8762	.8856	.8958	.9064	.9178	.9294	.9416	.9544	.9678	.9813	23
24	.8776	.8868	.8969	.9075	.9185	.9304	.9428	.9555	.9692	.9828	.9972	1.0119	24
25	.8975	.9083	.9193	.9310	.9436	.9564	.9696	.9839	.9982	1.0135	1.0289	1.0453	25
26	.9204	.9319	.9441	.9572	.9706	.9849	.9997	1.0149	1.0310	1.0469	1.0642	1.0811	26
27	.9445	.9574	.9711	.9852	1.0002	1.0155	1.0317	1.0484	1.0653	1.0836	1.1013	1.1200	27
28	.9714	.9858	1.0006	1.0164	1.0324	1.0495	1.0670	1.0844	1.1036	1.1223	1.1422	1.1624	28
29	1.0000	1.0162	1.0328	1.0497	1.0676	1.0859	1.1046	1.1249	1.1446	1.1652	1.1862	1.2079	29
30	1.0329	1.0500	1.0680	1.0866	1.1057	1.1255	1.1466	1.1673	1.1890	1.2113	1.2340	1.2570	30
31	1.0679	1.0867	1.1063	1.1269	1.1474	1.1696	1.1914	1.2142	1.2374	1.2613	1.2858	1.3107	31
32	1.1062	1.1271	1.1482	1.1700	1.1934	1.2160	1.2400	1.2648	1.2901	1.3156	1.3418	1.3682	32
33	1.1483	1.1708	1.1939	1.2182	1.2422	1.2677	1.2937	1.3198	1.3467	1.3742	1.4023	1.4305	33
34	1.1943	1.2182	1.2442	1.2694	1.2960	1.3234	1.3509	1.3797	1.4087	1.4380	1.4674	1.4975	34
35	1.2441	1.2714	1.2983	1.3263	1.3548	1.3840	1.4141	1.4443	1.4752	1.5065	1.5380	1.5695	35
36	1.3003	1.3283	1.3574	1.3877	1.4185	1.4499	1.4820	1.5148	1.5477	1.5810	1.6140	1.6470	36
37	1.3598	1.3907	1.4224	1.4548	1.4881	1.5220	1.5565	1.5909	1.6257	1.6607	1.6955	1.7299	37
38	1.4255	1.4591	1.4936	1.5284	1.5641	1.6001	1.6367	1.6733	1.7110	1.7469	1.7836	1.8194	38
39	1.4986	1.5342	1.5709	1.6084	1.6467	1.6853	1.7240	1.7629	1.8013	1.8399	1.8776	1.9147	39
40	1.5772	1.6163	1.6559	1.6959	1.7361	1.7773	1.8183	1.8592	1.8996	1.9399	1.9789	2.0167	40
41	1.6641	1.7059	1.7480	1.7913	1.8343	1.8771	1.9202	1.9633	2.0054	2.0467	2.0871	2.1262	41
42	1.7598	1.8042	1.8494	1.8947	1.9404	1.9863	2.0313	2.0757	2.1194	2.1615	2.2025	2.2420	42
43	1.8637	1.9113	1.9596	2.0073	2.0558	2.1033	2.1502	2.1959	2.2409	2.2847	2.3265	2.3660	43
44	1.9773	2.0277	2.0785	2.1292	2.1794	2.2290	2.2777	2.3259	2.3717	2.4154	2.4573	2.4970	44
45	2.1005	2.1541	2.2076	2.2606	2.3130	2.3645	2.4149	2.4634	2.5103	2.5551	2.5972	2.6362	45
46	2.2329	2.2899	2.3459	2.4019	2.4564	2.5091	2.5605	2.6101	2.6571	2.7017	2.7437	2.7825	46
47	2.3764	2.4356	2.4942	2.5519	2.6083	2.6633	2.7152	2.7651	2.8124	2.8569	2.8982	2.9359	47
48	2.5307	2.5927	2.6530	2.7128	2.7704	2.8262	2.8797	2.9300	2.9766	3.0205	3.0599	3.0963	48
49	2.6943	2.7589	2.8230	2.8841	2.9426	2.9987	3.0522	3.1025	3.1499	3.1919	3.2305	3.2650	49
50	2.8713	2.9385	3.0034	3.0654	3.1259	3.1827	3.2362	3.2851	3.3306	3.3719	3.4086	3.4409	50
51	3.0604	3.1292	3.1960	3.2602	3.3207	3.3768	3.4299	3.4782	3.5215	3.5608	3.5961	3.6254	51
52	3.2604	3.3312	3.3986	3.4639	3.5237	3.5811	3.6319	3.6790	3.7210	3.7588	3.7893	3.8180	52
53	3.4759	3.5480	3.6166	3.6801	3.7409	3.7956	3.8462	3.8911	3.9308	3.9644	3.9946	4.0187	53
54	3.7042	3.7774	3.8461	3.9105	3.9694	4.0232	4.0711	4.1135	4.1504	4.1819	4.2085	4.2307	54
55	3.9471	4.0205	4.0893	4.1525	4.2100	4.2616	4.3071	4.3467	4.3806	4.4093	4.4330	4.4523	55
56	4.2048	4.2785	4.3462	4.4077	4.4632	4.5120	4.5545	4.5911	4.6221	4.6476	4.6686	4.6852	56
57	4.4784	4.5509	4.6171	4.6766	4.7291	4.7749	4.8145	4.8479	4.8756	4.8983	4.9161	4.9299	57
58	4.7702	4.8415	4.9054	4.9622	5.0116	5.0543	5.0905	5.1204	5.1449	5.1642	5.1792	5.1902	58
59	5.0724	5.1412	5.2024	5.2559	5.3022	5.3411	5.3737	5.4003	5.4214	5.4378	5.4497	5.4581	59
60	5.3987	5.4649	5.5228	5.5727	5.6150	5.6505	5.6794	5.7023	5.7202	5.7332	5.7426	5.7489	60
61	5.7408	5.8034	5.8575	5.9037	5.9421	5.9735	5.9988	6.0182	6.0326	6.0429	6.0494	6.0535	61
62	6.1011	6.1599	6.2104	6.2521	6.2867	6.3144	6.3354	6.3514	6.3623	6.3697	6.3743	6.3765	62
63	6.4808	6.5357	6.5815	6.6194	6.6494	6.6728	6.6902	6.7025	6.7108	6.7158	6.7182	6.7195	63
64	6.8814	6.9315	6.9729	7.0063	7.0320	7.0512	7.0651	7.0737	7.0792	7.0819	7.0836	7.0838	64
65	7.3032	7.3487	7.3852	7.4137	7.4352	7.4500	7.4602	7.4664	7.4697	7.4709	7.4711	7.4717	65
66	7.7476	7.7886	7.8201	7.8438	7.8602	7.8716	7.8782	7.8819	7.8832	7.8845	7.8844	7.8846	66
67	8.2168	8.2514	8.2782	8.2969	8.3093	8.3170	8.3207	8.3230	8.3237	8.3233	8.3237		
68	8.7104	8.7404	8.7609	8.7749	8.7839	8.7881	8.7903	8.7906	8.7910	8.7913		2.4586	41
69	9.2316	9.2547	9.2709	9.2807	9.2855	9.2880	9.2888	9.2892	9.2892		2.3677	2.3675	40
70	9.7815	9.7993	9.8103	9.8158	9.8192	9.8202	9.8201	9.8202		2.2823	2.2826	2.2826	39
71	10.3625	10.3751	10.3820	10.3846	10.3858	10.3864	10.3865		2.2018	2.2016	2.2016	2.2016	38
72	10.9774	10.9853	10.9883	10.9903	10.9903	10.9906		2.1260	2.1257	2.1260	2.1260	2.1257	37
73	11.6286	11.6330	11.6345	11.6351	11.6356		2.0544	2.0542	2.0542	2.0542	2.0539	2.0537	36
74	12.3221	12.3237	12.3243	12.3247		1.9866	1.9866	1.9869	1.9866	1.9866	1.9861	1.9856	35
75	13.0601	13.0609	13.0611		1.9225	1.9224	1.9224	1.9224	1.9225	1.9220	1.9215	1.9203	34
76	13.8485	13.8491		1.8616	1.8619	1.8619	1.8616	1.8614	1.8612	1.8605	1.8596	1.8584	33
77	14.6936		1.8040	1.8039	1.8039	1.8039	1.8039	1.8036	1.8030	1.8022	1.8010	1.7990	32
		1.7492	1.7491	1.7493	1.7493	1.7491	1.7489	1.7483	1.7475	1.7464	1.7445	1.7419	31
30	1.6972	1.6971	1.6971	1.6971	1.6969	1.6967	1.6961	1.6954	1.6943	1.6925	1.6900	1.6870	30
29	1.6475	1.6477	1.6475	1.6474	1.6472	1.6469	1.6461	1.6449	1.6432	1.6411	1.6381	1.6343	29
28	1.6004	1.6004	1.6004	1.6002	1.5999	1.5989	1.5979	1.5965	1.5945	1.5913	1.5879	1.5836	28
27	1.5556	1.5554	1.5552	1.5549	1.5541	1.5532	1.5517	1.5498	1.5470	1.5437	1.5395	1.5342	27
26	1.5130	1.5126	1.5124	1.5116	1.5107	1.5093	1.5075	1.5048	1.5015	1.4977	1.4927	1.4869	26
25	1.4718	1.4715	1.4709	1.4700	1.4686	1.4669	1.4644	1.4614	1.4576	1.4530	1.4473	1.4409	25
24	1.4328	1.4321	1.4313	1.4300	1.4284	1.4260	1.4232	1.4196	1.4152	1.4099	1.4037	1.3963	24
23	1.3951	1.3945	1.3933	1.3917	1.3893	1.3867	1.3833	1.3790	1.3741	1.3681	1.3612	1.3533	23
22	1.3592	1.3581	1.3565	1.3543	1.3519	1.3485	1.3446	1.3398	1.3342	1.3277	1.3201	1.3116	22
21	1.3244	1.3230	1.3211	1.3185	1.3155	1.3117	1.3071	1.3019	1.2956	1.2885	1.2803	1.2715	21
20	1.2911	1.2891	1.2869	1.2839	1.2803	1.2761	1.2710	1.2650	1.2581	1.2504	1.2420	1.2325	20
19	1.2587	1.2565	1.2537	1.2503	1.2461	1.2413	1.2358	1.2293	1.2220	1.2140	1.2049	1.1951	19
18	1.2274	1.2249	1.2215	1.2177	1.2131	1.2077	1.2014	1.1946	1.1869	1.1783	1.1691	1.1591	18
17	1.1972	1.1941	1.1905	1.1861	1.1810	1.1753	1.1686	1.1612	1.1531	1.1443	1.1348	1.1246	17
16	1.1675	1.1644	1.1600	1.1545	1.1498	1.1431	1.1359	1.1280	1.1201	1.1105	1.1015	1.0916	16
15	1.1392	1.1356	1.1305	1.1259	1.1196	1.1129	1.1059	1.0984	1.0888	1.0807	1.0707	1.0595	15
14	1.1126	1.1078	1.1033	1.0973	1.0902	1.0834	1.0763	1.0680	1.0595	1.0499	1.0401	1.0304	14
13	1.0854	1.0803	1.0755	1.0695	1.0630	1.0562	1.0476	1.0394	1.0303	1.0211	1.0109	1.0016	13
12	1.0599	1.0545	1.0480	1.0419	1.0354	1.0279	1.0202	1.0114	1.0034	.9937	.9848	.9750	12
11	1.0345	1.0290	1.0232	1.0171	1.0092	1.0018	.9942	.9851	.9766	.9681	.9589	.9496	11
10	1.0107	1.0051	.9986	.9918	.9848	.9769	.9689	.9614	.9527	.9438	.9350	.9256	10
AGE.	70.	69.	68.	67.	66.	65.	64.	63.	62.	61.	60.	59.	AGE.

TEMPORARY INSURANCE—ANNUAL PREMIUMS—4 PER CENT.

AGE.	35.	36.	37.	38.	39.	40.	41.	42.	43.	44.	45.	46.	AGE.
10	.7502	.7548	.7599	.7641	.7704	.7754	.7816	.7881	.7946	.8006	.8074	.8149	10
11	.7616	.7662	.7713	.7770	.7823	.7896	.7955	.8025	.8087	.8166	.8246	.8316	11
12	.7723	.7786	.7845	.7910	.7969	.8030	.8104	.8177	.8260	.8334	.8409	.8498	12
13	.7861	.7916	.7983	.8053	.8128	.8204	.8271	.8349	.8437	.8523	.8616	.8700	13
14	.7999	.8066	.8133	.8203	.8280	.8360	.8450	.8537	.8623	.8721	.8817	.8920	14
15	.8152	.8226	.8304	.8385	.8469	.8555	.8647	.8741	.8834	.8932	.9031	.9135	15
16	.8317	.8399	.8483	.8571	.8663	.8759	.8856	.8957	.9065	.9169	.9278	.9391	16
17	.8500	.8588	.8681	.8777	.8876	.8980	.9084	.9195	.9307	.9423	.9540	.9661	17
18	.8695	.8792	.8893	.8997	.9105	.9215	.9333	.9449	.9579	.9693	.9819	.9949	18
19	.8909	.9015	.9124	.9239	.9353	.9476	.9598	.9725	.9854	.9986	1.0122	1.0259	19
20	.9140	.9255	.9373	.9494	.9624	.9751	.9884	1.0020	1.0159	1.0302	1.0440	1.0591	20
21	.9390	.9516	.9642	.9778	.9911	1.0051	1.0194	1.0339	1.0489	1.0639	1.0793	1.0947	21
22	.9662	.9795	.9938	1.0076	1.0222	1.0373	1.0526	1.0683	1.0842	1.1004	1.1165	1.1328	22
23	.9954	1.0103	1.0248	1.0404	1.0562	1.0722	1.0886	1.1052	1.1221	1.1392	1.1563	1.1734	23
24	1.0275	1.0429	1.0592	1.0758	1.0925	1.1096	1.1272	1.1450	1.1630	1.1809	1.1989	1.2169	24
25	1.0615	1.0784	1.0959	1.1134	1.1319	1.1502	1.1688	1.1875	1.2065	1.2253	1.2442	1.2628	25
26	1.0989	1.1172	1.1359	1.1549	1.1741	1.1937	1.2135	1.2334	1.2532	1.2731	1.2926	1.3118	26
27	1.1392	1.1588	1.1786	1.1990	1.2197	1.2405	1.2613	1.2821	1.3030	1.3235	1.3437	1.3635	27
28	1.1829	1.2039	1.2252	1.2468	1.2685	1.2906	1.3126	1.3346	1.3562	1.3774	1.3982	1.4182	28
29	1.2298	1.2523	1.2751	1.2981	1.3212	1.3443	1.3673	1.3900	1.4124	1.4342	1.4575	1.4761	29
30	1.2807	1.3049	1.3289	1.3532	1.3776	1.4018	1.4257	1.4492	1.4722	1.4946	1.5161	1.5370	30
31	1.3360	1.3613	1.3867	1.4124	1.4378	1.4630	1.4877	1.5122	1.5358	1.5584	1.5800	1.6005	31
32	1.3950	1.4218	1.4488	1.4756	1.5023	1.5284	1.5539	1.5788	1.6027	1.6254	1.6472	1.6676	32
33	1.4587	1.4871	1.5156	1.5433	1.5707	1.5977	1.6239	1.6490	1.6732	1.6962	1.7178	1.7377	33
34	1.5271	1.5571	1.5865	1.6157	1.6438	1.6714	1.6979	1.7234	1.7475	1.7702	1.7912	1.8111	34
35	1.6009	1.6319	1.6624	1.6923	1.7214	1.7494	1.7763	1.8016	1.8256	1.8481	1.8689	1.8876	35
36	1.6796	1.7118	1.7433	1.7741	1.8039	1.8329	1.8591	1.8844	1.9079	1.9297	1.9495	1.9672	36
37	1.7641	1.7974	1.8299	1.8610	1.8906	1.9189	1.9457	1.9708	1.9942	2.0149	2.0339	2.0507	37
38	1.8545	1.8888	1.9217	1.9529	1.9832	2.0114	2.0376	2.0620	2.0839	2.1043	2.1221	2.1377	38
39	1.9509	1.9855	2.0190	2.0510	2.0809	2.1085	2.1347	2.1579	2.1791	2.1976	2.2144	2.2283	39
40	2.0534	2.0888	2.1222	2.1538	2.1834	2.2108	2.2356	2.2582	2.2781	2.2955	2.3103	2.3232	40
41	2.1631	2.1984	2.2319	2.2632	2.2919	2.3186	2.3421	2.3632	2.3817	2.3977	2.4111	2.4227	41
42	2.2799	2.3152	2.3480	2.3787	2.4066	2.4319	2.4543	2.4739	2.4910	2.5052	2.5175	2.5270	42
43	2.4036	2.4382	2.4712	2.5004	2.5272	2.5510	2.5718	2.5899	2.6049	2.6181	2.6282	2.6369	43
44	2.5342	2.5692	2.6002	2.6286	2.6539	2.6755	2.6947	2.7112	2.7247	2.7359	2.7452	2.7522	44
45	2.6728	2.7056	2.7359	2.7626	2.7867	2.8066	2.8242	2.8380	2.8505	2.8599	2.8673	2.8733	45
46	2.8179	2.8500	2.8785	2.9035	2.9247	2.9435	2.9588	2.9715	2.9814	2.9900	2.9964	3.0005	46
47	2.9695	2.9999	3.0264	3.0496	3.0695	3.0859	3.0994	3.1106	3.1192	3.1255	3.1305	3.1341	47
48	3.1293	3.1577	3.1824	3.2030	3.2204	3.2350	3.2463	3.2561	3.2628	3.2682	3.2714	3.2742	48
49	3.2946	3.3210	3.3437	3.3623	3.3779	3.3906	3.4004	3.4076	3.4140	3.4175	3.4199	3.4210	49
50	3.4691	3.4926	3.5126	3.5299	3.5422	3.5534	3.5619	3.5680	3.5710	3.5742	3.5763	3.5769	50
51	3.6514	3.6727	3.6906	3.7045	3.7164	3.7248	3.7314	3.7354	3.7389	3.7403	3.7410	3.7417	51
52	3.8400	3.8600	3.8750	3.8870	3.8968	3.9039	3.9082	3.9112	3.9135	3.9142	3.9151	3.9151	52
53	4.0399	4.0560	4.0693	4.0797	4.0871	4.0918	4.0954	4.0977	4.0987	4.0992	4.0991	4.0991	53
54	4.2485	4.2627	4.2737	4.2816	4.2872	4.2909	4.2930	4.2942	4.2946	4.2949	4.2950	4.2950	54
55	4.4677	4.4794	4.4880	4.4942	4.4980	4.5004	4.5016	4.5023	4.5025	4.5025	4.5025		
56	4.6977	4.7072	4.7138	4.7179	4.7207	4.7219	4.7227	4.7229	4.7228	4.7230		4.0996	53
57	4.9400	4.9471	4.9518	4.9548	4.9562	4.9569	4.9569	4.9571	4.9571		3.9151	3.9150	52
58	5.1981	5.2031	5.2062	5.2077	5.2085	5.2088	5.2089	5.2067		3.7415	3.7425	3.7418	51
59	5.4638	5.4670	5.4689	5.4696	5.4700	5.4700	5.4724		3.5775	3.5769	3.5769	3.5776	50
60	5.7522	5.7543	5.7551	5.7556	5.7554	5.7556		3.4227	3.4222	3.4229	3.4223	3.4223	49
61	6.0556	6.0567	6.0570	6.0570	6.0572		3.2767	3.2764	3.2764	3.2764	3.2765	3.2753	48
62	6.3777	6.3781	6.3780	6.3782		3.1385	3.1382	3.1389	3.1383	3.1377	3.1372	3.1361	47
63	6.7199	6.7199	6.7199		3.0080	3.0078	3.0078	3.0078	3.0079	3.0074	3.0059	3.0034	46
64	7.0840	7.0841		2.8845	2.8845	2.8845	2.8845	2.8840	2.8836	2.8821	2.8803	2.8777	45
65	7.4718		2.7682	2.7679	2.7683	2.7679	2.7679	2.7670	2.7661	2.7644	2.7619	2.7574	44
		2.6585	2.6586	2.6586	2.6582	2.6582	2.6573	2.6570	2.6549	2.6522	2.6483	2.6439	43
42	2.5554	2.5555	2.5551	2.5551	2.5552	2.5548	2.5540	2.5517	2.5495	2.5463	2.5418	2.5347	42
41	2.4581	2.4581	2.4585	2.4581	2.4578	2.4567	2.4553	2.4533	2.4499	2.4452	2.4393	2.4321	41
40	2.3679	2.3679	2.3675	2.3672	2.3661	2.3649	2.3626	2.3598	2.3553	2.3499	2.3427	2.3339	40
39	2.2822	2.2819	2.2816	2.2810	2.2794	2.2776	2.2746	2.2708	2.2653	2.2589	2.2505	2.2405	39
38	2.2016	2.2013	2.2005	2.1989	2.1975	2.1947	2.1909	2.1856	2.1799	2.1717	2.1623	2.1511	38
37	2.1255	2.1246	2.1235	2.1219	2.1192	2.1156	2.1110	2.1052	2.0975	2.0889	2.0778	2.0654	37
36	2.0529	2.0521	2.0504	2.0478	2.0444	2.0403	2.0346	2.0276	2.0192	2.0089	1.9972	1.9831	36
35	1.9846	1.9829	1.9805	1.9775	1.9734	1.9678	1.9615	1.9533	1.9439	1.9325	1.9196	1.9046	35
34	1.9190	1.9167	1.9139	1.9098	1.9049	1.8987	1.8912	1.8821	1.8716	1.8592	1.8447	1.8286	34
33	1.8563	1.8535	1.8497	1.8451	1.8392	1.8321	1.8234	1.8135	1.8015	1.7883	1.7731	1.7565	33
32	1.7962	1.7926	1.7885	1.7827	1.7760	1.7680	1.7583	1.7472	1.7345	1.7220	1.7041	1.6869	32
31	1.7386	1.7345	1.7290	1.7229	1.7149	1.7060	1.6955	1.6834	1.6698	1.6549	1.6380	1.6199	31
30	1.6831	1.6779	1.6721	1.6647	1.6563	1.6461	1.6347	1.6217	1.6076	1.5917	1.5748	1.5565	30
29	1.6296	1.6239	1.6169	1.6087	1.5993	1.5884	1.5763	1.5627	1.5477	1.5315	1.5140	1.4955	29
28	1.5780	1.5716	1.5638	1.5549	1.5446	1.5331	1.5200	1.5060	1.4905	1.4739	1.4562	1.4376	28
27	1.5280	1.5207	1.5122	1.5025	1.4916	1.4791	1.4658	1.4511	1.4354	1.4187	1.4013	1.3827	27
26	1.4799	1.4720	1.4627	1.4525	1.4406	1.4279	1.4139	1.3989	1.3831	1.3661	1.3488	1.3305	26
25	1.4332	1.4243	1.4143	1.4035	1.3911	1.3780	1.3639	1.3488	1.3328	1.3164	1.2989	1.2812	25
24	1.3881	1.3786	1.3683	1.3566	1.3441	1.3307	1.3162	1.3011	1.2852	1.2688	1.2518	1.2344	24
23	1.3443	1.3344	1.3234	1.3115	1.2987	1.2850	1.2707	1.2557	1.2400	1.2239	1.2074	1.1906	23
22	1.3021	1.2917	1.2803	1.2681	1.2552	1.2416	1.2274	1.2124	1.1970	1.1812	1.1652	1.1489	22
21	1.2614	1.2508	1.2392	1.2269	1.2139	1.2002	1.1859	1.1713	1.1564	1.1413	1.1258	1.1103	21
20	1.2224	1.2114	1.1996	1.1871	1.1742	1.1607	1.1469	1.1327	1.1181	1.1034	1.0886	1.0738	20
19	1.1846	1.1735	1.1617	1.1495	1.1365	1.1233	1.1097	1.0960	1.0820	1.0679	1.0539	1.0398	19
18	1.1486	1.1373	1.1256	1.1132	1.1008	1.0879	1.0746	1.0613	1.0480	1.0345	1.0212	1.0080	18
17	1.1139	1.1027	1.0912	1.0792	1.0669	1.0544	1.0418	1.0289	1.0161	1.0034	.9908	.9783	17
16	1.0802	1.0694	1.0580	1.0462	1.0344	1.0227	1.0106	.9985	.9863	.9742	.9623	.9507	16
15	1.0502	1.0389	1.0277	1.0166	1.0046	.9929	.9808	.9700	.9579	.9466	.9356	.9250	15
14	1.0196	1.0089	.9983	.9869	.9765	.9655	.9548	.9425	.9324	.9218	.9117	.9011	14
13	.9922	.9820	.9711	.9613	.9500	.9389	.9289	.9193	.9091	.8986	.8885	.8790	13
12	.9646	.9543	.9449	.9347	.9250	.9147	.9047	.8951	.8858	.8771	.8679	.8586	12
11	.9398	.9308	.9205	.9112	.9013	.8926	.8834	.8746	.8654	.8567	.8478	.8402	11
10	.9170	.9072	.8983	.8889	.8806	.8718	.8627	.8539	.8456	.8378	.8299	.8224	10
AGE.	58.	57.	56.	55.	54.	53.	52.	51.	50.	49.	48.	47.	AGE.

Net Amt at Risk

COMPLEMENTS—LIFE POLICIES—4 PER CENT.

on basis Ter Reserve

Age.	1.	2.	3.	4.	5.	6.	7.	8.	9.	10.	11.	12.	13.	14.	15.	16.	17.	18.	19.	Age.
15	.994902	.989622	.984151	.978491	.972632	.966580	.960322	.953848	.947150	.940248	.933103	.925722	.918094	.910220	.902090	.893694	.885028	.876085	.866854	15
16	.994693	.989196	.983505	.977615	.971533	.965243	.958733	.952014	.945066	.937884	.930465	.922799	.914884	.906712	.898273	.889563	.880574	.871296	.861713	16
17	.994471	.988752	.982831	.976716	.970392	.963850	.957093	.950108	.942888	.935429	.927722	.919765	.911549	.903065	.894308	.885272	.875944	.866310	.856365	17
18	.994249	.988295	.982147	.975787	.969209	.962414	.955391	.948130	.940630	.932880	.924879	.916829	.908086	.899281	.890194	.880814	.871127	.861126	.850801	18
19	.994012	.987827	.981431	.974815	.967980	.960917	.953614	.946070	.938275	.930228	.921919	.913339	.904482	.895342	.885909	.876164	.866107	.855722	.844982	19
20	.993778	.987344	.980688	.973812	.966705	.959359	.951770	.943928	.935832	.927473	.918841	.909931	.900737	.891246	.881444	.871324	.860877	.850073	.838917	20
21	.993525	.986828	.979909	.972758	.965365	.957728	.949838	.941691	.933280	.924593	.915628	.906376	.896826	.886962	.876779	.866267	.855375	.844169	.832567	21
22	.993259	.986295	.979097	.971656	.963970	.956028	.947828	.939362	.930620	.921595	.912282	.902670	.892742	.882493	.871912	.860968	.849671	.837993	.825915	22
23	.992989	.985742	.978251	.970512	.962516	.954261	.945737	.936935	.927850	.918474	.908797	.898801	.888483	.877830	.866813	.855437	.843680	.831521	.818950	23
24	.992703	.985158	.977365	.969312	.960999	.952415	.943551	.934402	.924959	.915218	.905148	.894756	.884028	.872933	.861477	.849637	.837392	.824732	.811656	24
25	.992400	.984550	.976438	.968063	.959416	.950487	.941270	.931759	.921941	.911801	.901334	.890527	.879350	.867810	.855883	.843548	.830795	.817623	.804063	25
26	.992090	.983916	.975477	.966764	.957766	.948478	.938894	.929002	.918784	.908236	.897347	.886084	.874456	.862437	.850008	.837157	.823884	.810221	.796208	26
27	.991761	.983254	.974472	.965402	.956041	.946380	.936409	.926110	.915478	.904501	.893149	.881429	.869314	.856785	.843832	.830454	.816681	.802556	.788105	27
28	.991423	.982567	.973422	.963983	.954243	.944188	.933804	.923083	.912016	.900569	.888751	.876536	.863903	.850842	.837353	.823466	.809224	.794652	.779804	28
29	.991068	.981842	.972323	.962498	.952357	.941882	.931069	.919906	.908360	.896440	.884119	.871377	.858203	.844597	.830090	.816224	.801527	.786550	.771302	29
30	.990693	.981086	.971172	.960940	.950371	.939460	.928196	.916547	.904519	.892087	.879230	.865938	.852209	.838075	.823581	.808750	.793639	.778253	.762612	30
31	.990303	.980296	.969967	.959300	.948286	.936916	.925158	.913017	.900468	.887490	.874073	.860215	.845949	.831318	.816349	.801095	.785564	.769776	.753721	31
32	.989896	.979465	.968693	.957572	.946091	.934217	.921957	.909285	.896180	.882632	.868638	.854231	.839458	.824342	.808939	.793257	.777314	.761103	.744650	32
33	.989464	.978581	.967347	.955748	.943753	.931368	.918567	.905328	.891642	.877505	.862952	.848027	.832757	.817197	.801354	.785250	.768871	.752251	.735407	33
34	.989002	.977647	.965925	.953803	.941286	.928348	.914969	.901136	.886849	.872141	.857057	.841625	.825899	.809887	.793610	.777058	.760262	.743238	.726005	34
35	.988519	.976667	.964409	.951753	.938662	.925144	.911157	.896711	.881840	.866588	.850984	.835083	.818894	.802435	.785700	.768716	.751503	.734078	.716459	35
36	.988010	.975610	.962807	.949574	.935868	.921740	.907126	.892082	.876653	.860867	.844782	.828404	.811755	.794824	.777644	.760230	.742604	.724780	.706767	36
37	.987449	.974491	.961097	.947246	.932925	.918134	.902907	.887291	.871314	.855033	.838457	.821606	.804470	.787081	.769456	.751616	.733576	.715344	.696941	37
38	.986877	.973313	.959285	.944783	.929804	.914383	.898569	.882389	.865901	.849114	.832049	.814495	.797085	.779236	.761169	.742900	.724436	.705799	.687019	38
39	.986256	.972041	.957346	.942168	.926543	.910518	.894122	.877415	.860405	.843113	.825528	.807684	.789598	.771291	.752778	.734069	.715185	.696155	.676973	39
40	.985588	.970687	.955298	.939455	.923207	.906583	.889643	.872396	.854862	.837033	.818940	.800602	.782039	.763269	.744299	.725152	.705856	.686407	.666833	40
41	.984882	.969267	.953192	.936707	.919840	.902652	.885153	.867363	.849273	.830915	.812309	.793475	.774430	.755183	.735755	.716178	.696444	.676584	.656625	41
42	.984145	.967824	.951085	.933959	.916508	.898740	.880677	.862309	.843670	.824778	.805655	.786318	.766775	.747050	.727171	.707134	.686970	.666704	.646406	42
43	.983416	.966407	.949005	.931273	.913219	.894865	.876201	.857261	.838065	.818634	.798985	.779128	.759084	.738886	.718526	.698037	.677445	.656820	.636191	43
44	.982704	.965009	.946978	.928619	.909956	.890977	.871718	.852199	.832439	.812459	.792269	.771886	.751347	.730644	.709808	.688869	.667897	.646920	.625991	44
45	.981993	.963644	.944963	.925971	.906658	.887060	.867197	.847090	.826758	.806211	.785470	.764570	.743503	.722301	.700993	.679651	.658305	.637008	.615791	45
46	.981315	.962290	.942950	.923284	.903326	.883099	.862623	.841919	.820884	.799874	.778590	.757136	.735546	.713847	.692114	.670376	.648689	.627083	.605607	46
47	.980614	.960905	.940864	.920527	.899914	.879249	.857950	.836627	.815104	.793415	.771553	.749551	.727440	.705293	.683141	.661041	.639023	.617138	.595420	47
48	.979902	.959464	.938725	.917705	.896427	.874911	.853166	.831218	.809101	.786866	.764370	.741821	.719236	.696647	.674110	.651656	.629339	.607191	.585280	48
49	.979143	.957979	.936527	.914813	.892856	.870665	.848267	.825696	.802944	.780047	.757036	.733988	.710935	.687936	.665022	.642247	.619644	.597284	.575186	49
50	.978384	.956476	.934299	.911875	.889211	.866336	.843284	.820048	.796663	.773161	.749622	.726079	.702589	.679187	.655927	.632843	.610007	.587438	.565169	50
51	.977608	.954941	.932021	.908857	.885476	.861914	.838165	.814264	.790243	.766184	.742120	.718112	.694193	.670419	.646825	.623484	.600417	.577656	.555210	51
52	.976814	.953369	.929674	.905758	.881657	.857363	.832914	.808343	.783733	.759118	.734560	.710093	.685775	.661640	.637765	.614170	.590887	.567928	.545335	52
53	.975998	.951741	.927257	.902584	.877714	.852685	.827531	.802336	.777137	.751996	.726949	.702053	.677346	.652903	.628748	.604912	.581408	.558280	.535548	53
54	.975146	.950860	.924780	.899298	.873654	.847881	.822067	.796248	.770489	.744825	.719318	.694003	.668959	.644210	.619788	.595706	.572009	.548718	.525458	54
55	.974276	.948350	.922219	.895921	.869491	.843019	.816542	.790126	.763809	.737651	.711691	.686009	.660629	.635585	.610889	.586588	.562703	.539261	.516283	55
56	.973391	.946570	.919577	.892450	.865279	.838103	.810990	.783977	.757128	.730483	.704123	.678072	.652367	.627019	.602076	.577561	.553500	.529915	.506831	56
57	.972445	.944715	.916846	.888932	.861013	.833159	.805408	.777825	.750451	.723371	.696608	.670201	.644160	.618535	.593349	.568630	.544401	.520686	.497500	57
58	.971484	.942825	.914121	.885410	.856767	.828229	.799865	.771715	.743868	.716347	.689191	.662412	.636061	.610162	.584742	.559826	.535440	.511597	.488293	58
59	.970500	.940953	.911400	.881916	.852541	.823344	.794368	.765703	.737374	.709421	.681856	.654732	.628072	.601907	.576259	.551157	.526614	.502626	.479236	59
60	.969555	.939104	.908723	.878455	.848371	.818514	.788978	.759787	.730985	.702582	.674633	.647163	.620202	.593776	.567910	.542621	.517904	.493804	.470350	60
61	.968592	.937258	.906039	.875010	.844216	.813753	.783646	.753939	.724644	.695818	.667485	.639678	.612421	.585743	.559660	.534167	.509310	.485120	.461564	61
62	.967650	.935418	.903383	.871591	.840139	.809056	.778386	.748141	.718380	.689129	.660420	.632279	.604736	.577807	.551488	.525824	.500850	.476530	.452838	62
63	.966692	.933585	.900730	.868227	.836105	.804409	.773153	.742397	.712168	.682499	.653418	.624954	.597125	.569925	.543404	.517595	.492462	.467977	.444053	63
64	.965753	.931765	.898143	.864914	.832126	.799793	.767977	.736706	.706015	.675932	.646488	.617699	.589562	.562127	.535429	.509430	.484102	.459354	.435050	64
65	.964807	.929993	.895585	.861634	.828155	.795210	.762831	.731051	.699901	.669413	.639604	.610469	.582061	.554416	.527495	.501269	.475643	.450478	.425673	65
66	.963915	.928252	.893063	.858363	.824217	.790056	.757718	.725431	.693831	.662934	.632737	.603293	.574640	.746737	.519553	.492993	.466910	.441200	.415696	66
67	.963002	.926496	.890496	.855072	.820256	.786084	.752588	.719805	.687752	.656424	.625878	.596152	.567204	.539003	.511449	.484389	.457716	.431258	.405006	67
68	.962091	.924708	.887923	.851847	.816284	.781502	.747459	.714175	.681643	.649923	.619055	.588995	.559711	.531098	.502999	.475301	.447826	.420566	.393507	68
69	.961144	.922909	.885331	.848448	.812295	.776911	.742315	.708502	.675532	.643447	.612203	.581765	.552025	.522818	.494029	.465472	.437137	.409012	.381073	69
Age.	1.	2.	3.	4.	5.	6.	7.	8.	9.	10.	11.	12.	13.	14.	15.	16.	17.	18.	19.	Age.

TABLE XII.

Age.	20.	21.	22.	23.	24.	25.	26.	27.	28.	29.	30.	31.	32.	33.	34.	35.	36.	37.	38.	Age.
15	.857320	.847478	.837316	.826808	.815957	.804742	.793144	.781154	.768769	.756019	.742944	.729566	.715933	.702054	.687944	.673596	.659036	.644278	.629340	15
16	.851820	.841607	.831044	.820138	.808866	.797209	.785156	.772708	.759893	.746750	.733304	.719602	.705651	.691469	.677048	.662413	.647580	.632565	.617382	16
17	.846097	.835478	.824514	.813181	.801462	.789345	.776830	.763947	.750734	.737216	.723441	.709416	.695158	.680660	.665947	.651035	.635940	.620676	.605250	17
18	.840123	.829098	.817703	.805918	.793734	.781150	.768195	.754908	.741315	.727463	.713360	.699023	.684444	.669649	.654654	.639475	.624127	.608615	.592958	18
19	.833893	.822432	.810579	.798325	.785666	.772638	.759275	.745603	.731671	.717486	.703066	.688403	.673522	.658441	.643174	.627737	.612135	.596388	.580519	19
20	.827387	.815462	.803134	.790401	.777292	.763849	.750094	.736079	.721809	.707302	.692550	.677580	.662407	.647049	.631519	.615823	.599981	.584016	.567924	20
21	.820568	.808162	.795349	.782159	.768631	.754790	.740687	.726326	.711730	.696886	.681822	.666555	.651100	.635472	.619678	.603737	.587672	.571479	.555172	21
22	.813429	.800532	.787256	.773640	.759710	.745514	.731061	.716368	.701427	.686265	.670899	.655343	.639614	.623717	.607672	.591502	.575204	.558801	.542316	22
23	.805966	.792599	.778891	.764866	.750574	.736023	.721230	.706188	.690923	.675452	.659791	.643953	.627950	.611796	.595515	.579108	.562594	.545997	.529374	23
24	.798196	.784390	.770266	.755873	.741220	.726323	.711174	.695802	.680221	.664449	.648502	.632384	.616116	.599722	.583197	.566566	.549852	.533112	.516368	24
25	.790156	.775929	.761430	.746669	.731662	.716402	.700917	.685222	.669334	.653269	.637033	.620645	.704130	.587484	.570731	.553894	.537031	.520164	.503337	25
26	.781871	.767261	.752387	.737265	.721888	.706284	.690469	.674460	.658272	.641911	.625398	.608757	.591983	.575102	.558136	.541144	.524148	.507191	.490297	26
27	.773379	.758386	.743144	.727644	.711916	.605974	.679838	.663520	.647029	.630384	.613611	.596703	.579687	.562586	.545458	.528327	.511235	.494207	.477282	27
28	.764686	.749317	.733690	.717830	.701756	.685485	.669033	.652405	.635621	.618708	.601660	.584503	.567260	.549990	.532716	.515482	.498312	.481247	.464310	28
29	.755700	.740037	.724040	.707827	.691416	.674820	.658048	.641120	.624061	.606865	.589560	.572168	.554748	.537325	.519942	.502623	.485410	.468327	.451428	29
30	.746706	.730566	.714207	.697647	.680902	.663979	.646898	.629685	.612335	.594873	.577324	.559748	.542167	.524628	.507173	.489785	.472548	.455496	.438644	30
31	.737429	.720916	.704201	.687299	.670217	.652976	.635601	.618087	.600462	.582748	.565006	.547261	.529557	.511918	.494386	.476988	.459775	.442765	.425980	31
32	.727976	.711097	.694029	.676780	.659370	.641825	.624139	.606341	.588454	.570539	.552620	.534742	.516931	.499227	.481654	.464277	.447100	.430151	.413437	32
33	.718355	.701114	.683688	.666100	.648376	.630510	.612531	.594461	.576363	.558260	.540200	.522207	.504323	.486575	.469017	.451664	.434542	.417658	.401043	33
34	.708580	.690969	.673193	.655280	.637225	.619053	.600791	.582500	.564205	.545953	.527768	.509694	.491756	.474011	.456474	.439169	.422105	.405314	.388810	34
35	.698653	.680680	.662567	.644311	.625937	.607472	.588978	.570480	.552024	.533637	.515362	.497225	.479282	.461550	.444053	.426799	.409821	.393134	.376756	35
36	.688585	.670262	.651794	.633207	.614528	.595818	.577105	.558435	.539835	.521347	.502999	.484849	.466910	.449210	.431756	.414581	.397700	.381132	.364891	36
37	.678396	.659704	.640891	.621985	.603049	.584108	.565212	.546386	.527674	.509103	.490732	.472577	.454662	.436996	.419612	.402525	.385757	.369320	.353215	37
38	.668089	.649037	.629891	.610714	.591533	.572396	.553330	.534381	.515574	.496970	.478583	.460440	.442550	.424945	.407642	.390660	.374014	.357721	.341792	38
39	.657668	.638267	.618834	.599399	.580008	.560689	.541487	.522430	.503577	.484947	.466563	.448435	.430596	.413063	.395855	.378987	.362478	.346337	.330561	39
40	.647161	.627459	.607752	.588090	.568502	.549033	.529711	.510596	.491705	.473265	.454684	.436597	.418819	.401371	.384269	.367530	.351163	.335168	.319571	40
41	.636634	.616639	.596690	.576815	.557061	.537457	.518062	.498895	.479983	.461333	.442981	.424944	.407147	.389888	.372990	.355889	.340069	.324244	.308844	41
42	.626104	.605849	.585670	.565612	.545707	.526015	.506554	.487351	.468414	.449781	.431466	.413492	.395873	.378628	.361768	.345289	.329221	.313584	.298358	42
43	.615610	.595105	.574724	.554498	.534489	.514714	.495202	.475960	.457027	.438417	.420153	.402250	.384728	.367596	.350851	.334525	.318636	.303164	.288091	43
44	.605140	.584426	.563849	.543503	.523394	.503553	.483987	.464734	.445811	.427238	.409034	.391216	.373795	.356768	.340166	.324010	.308277	.292950	.277974	44
45	.594702	.573773	.553068	.532606	.512415	.492505	.472913	.453553	.434758	.416233	.398101	.380374	.363047	.346153	.329712	.313702	.298105	.282866	.267800	45
46	.584294	.563210	.542372	.521811	.501536	.481585	.461976	.442730	.423865	.405401	.387348	.369704	.352500	.335758	.319455	.303572	.288053	.272813	.257790	46
47	.573934	.552700	.531747	.511086	.490755	.470772	.451160	.431936	.413120	.394724	.376744	.359212	.342151	.325537	.309352	.293538	.278007	.262699	.247513	47
48	.563626	.542260	.521190	.500457	.480079	.460079	.440475	.421288	.402528	.384192	.366314	.348916	.331973	.315468	.299341	.283503	.267892	.252407	.237042	48
49	.553382	.531880	.510721	.489926	.469516	.449509	.429928	.410784	.392072	.373827	.356072	.338782	.321938	.305480	.289338	.273387	.257584	.241904	.226340	49
50	.543210	.521600	.500362	.479517	.459084	.439086	.419534	.400423	.381790	.363657	.345999	.328796	.311987	.295481	.279210	.263070	.247057	.231161	.215371	50
51	.533124	.511416	.490111	.469227	.448787	.428802	.409270	.390225	.371691	.353643	.336060	.318880	.302009	.285379	.268882	.252515	.236268	.220129	.204187	51
52	.523130	.501337	.479975	.459066	.438624	.418644	.399163	.380205	.361736	.343758	.326184	.308926	.291915	.275041	.258299	.241680	.225171	.208864	.192898	52
53	.513237	.491368	.469963	.449036	.428582	.408638	.389229	.370330	.351917	.333927	.316259	.298845	.281570	.264430	.247416	.230516	.213822	.197477	.181520	53
54	.503451	.481520	.460078	.439121	.418687	.398801	.379437	.360571	.342139	.324037	.306194	.288494	.270933	.253501	.236184	.219080	.202334	.185984	.170170	54
55	.493793	.471804	.450313	.429358	.408965	.389107	.369761	.350859	.332295	.313998	.295847	.277838	.259962	.242204	.224663	.207490	.190725	.174507	.159165	55
56	.484206	.462203	.440695	.419764	.399382	.379525	.360123	.341070	.322289	.303658	.285174	.266826	.248599	.230596	.212969	.195760	.179115	.163368	.148834	56
57	.474838	.452742	.431239	.410299	.389900	.369967	.350393	.331099	.311959	.292970	.274120	.255395	.236899	.218791	.201112	.184011	.167833	.152902	.139473	57
58	.465570	.443458	.421925	.400947	.380450	.360322	.340480	.320799	.301271	.281887	.262632	.243612	.224990	.206811	.189225	.172589	.157235	.143428	.132335	58
59	.456475	.434310	.412717	.391618	.370898	.350475	.330215	.310114	.290162	.270341	.250763	.231595	.212881	.194780	.177655	.161850	.147638	.136219	.127382	59
60	.447512	.425262	.403522	.382162	.361128	.340253	.319541	.298981	.278558	.258385	.238579	.219352	.200700	.183055	.166770	.152126	.140360	.131254	.119099	60
61	.438615	.416193	.394173	.372468	.350937	.329575	.308370	.287305	.266499	.246128	.226240	.207003	.188803	.172006	.156903	.144767	.135375	.122839	.099033	61
62	.429688	.406954	.384546	.362317	.340262	.319369	.296622	.275140	.254108	.233575	.213715	.194926	.177584	.161991	.149462	.139765	.126822	.102244		
63	.420560	.397402	.374430	.351637	.329013	.306538	.284339	.262104	.241385	.220860	.201442	.183521	.167406	.154458	.144437	.136062	.105662		.052072	22
64	.411095	.387331	.363753	.340349	.317100	.294136	.271652	.249710	.228470	.208383	.189844	.173174	.159780	.149414	.135577	.109303		.051735	.064171	21
65	.401066	.376652	.352418	.328345	.304566	.281285	.258557	.236572	.215773	.196576	.179315	.165446	.154713	.140385	.113179		.051413	.063772	.070280	20
66	.390391	.365274	.340322	.315676	.291546	.267988	.245201	.223643	.203747	.185856	.171481	.160356	.145506	.117308		.051105	.063390	.069859	.074706	19
67	.378948	.353062	.327494	.302460	.278020	.254380	.232015	.211374	.192819	.177911	.166359	.150953	.121699		.050811	.063025	.069457	.074276	.080503	18
68	.366627	.340075	.314080	.288702	.264153	.240924	.219495	.200222	.184736	.172750	.156753	.126375		.050530	.062677	.069073	.073866	.080058	.087764	17
69	.353475	.326456	.300077	.274562	.250423	.228144	.208111	.192015	.179557	.162929	.131354		.050262	.062344	.068707	.073474	.079633	.087298	.095823	16
												.050006	.062026	.068357	.073099	.079227	.086853	.095335	.104524	15
Age.	20.	21.	22.	23.	24.	25.	26.	27.	28.	29.	30.	84.	83.	82.	81.	80.	79.	78.	77.	Age.

TABLE XII.

COMPLEMENTS—LIFE POLICIES—4 PER CENT.

Age.	39.	40.	41.	42.	43.	44.	45.	46.	47.	48.	49.	50.	51.	52.	53.	54.	55.	56.	57.	Age.
15	.614235	.598969	.583560	.568032	.552381	.536629	.520798	.504942	.489084	.473261	.457498	.441830	.426281	.410898	.395696	.380696	.365904	.351348	.337042	15
16	.602038	.586550	.570943	.555211	.539319	.523467	.507530	.491590	.475686	.459842	.444094	.428465	.413004	.397729	.382646	.367778	.353148	.338769	.324656	16
17	.589680	.573988	.558173	.542256	.526260	.510238	.494212	.478224	.462295	.446463	.430751	.415207	.399846	.384688	.369740	.355032	.340576	.326388	.312480	17
18	.577180	.561276	.545271	.529186	.513074	.496960	.480883	.464866	.448945	.433146	.417516	.402069	.386827	.371796	.357006	.342469	.328202	.314217	.300530	18
19	.564523	.548425	.532246	.516042	.499834	.483664	.467554	.451542	.435651	.419930	.404394	.389064	.373947	.359071	.344450	.330100	.316035	.302268	.288808	19
20	.551729	.535453	.519151	.502846	.486578	.470371	.454262	.438276	.422460	.406830	.391408	.376199	.361234	.346525	.332089	.317939	.304089	.290548	.277313	20
21	.538805	.522401	.505994	.489625	.473316	.457106	.441019	.425105	.409377	.393858	.378555	.363496	.348695	.334168	.319929	.305993	.292367	.279049	.266065	21
22	.525806	.509291	.492815	.476400	.460085	.443894	.427876	.412045	.396425	.381022	.365865	.350967	.336346	.322014	.307987	.294272	.280868	.267798	.255079	22
23	.512748	.496160	.479634	.463208	.446906	.430780	.414841	.399116	.383608	.368348	.353349	.338629	.324200	.310077	.296270	.282774	.269615	.256810	.244440	23
24	.499663	.483020	.466479	.450062	.433821	.417761	.401934	.386316	.370949	.355844	.341020	.326489	.312267	.298361	.284771	.271519	.258623	.246065	.233831	24
25	.486571	.469908	.453370	.437010	.420842	.404888	.389156	.373675	.358460	.343527	.328889	.314562	.300555	.286864	.273515	.260524	.247874	.235550	.223508	25
26	.473506	.456842	.440357	.424065	.407989	.392136	.376537	.361205	.346157	.331408	.316971	.302856	.289061	.275610	.262520	.249772	.237354	.225220	.213304	26
27	.460485	.443868	.427446	.411242	.395263	.379539	.364085	.348917	.334060	.319499	.305271	.291366	.277807	.264613	.251764	.239246	.227016	.215005	.203166	27
28	.447556	.430995	.414659	.398547	.382692	.367110	.351816	.336825	.322153	.307807	.293786	.280115	.266811	.253855	.241234	.228902	.216791	.204854	.193012	28
29	.434726	.418246	.401995	.386003	.370286	.354860	.339739	.324940	.310470	.296328	.282538	.269119	.256052	.243321	.230882	.218667	.206626	.194682	.182831	29
30	.422015	.405618	.389482	.373623	.358058	.342801	.327868	.313261	.298992	.285085	.271545	.258359	.245514	.232963	.220637	.208488	.196436	.184479	.172609	30
31	.409428	.393141	.377133	.361422	.346022	.330949	.316211	.301808	.287763	.274096	.260787	.247820	.235152	.222719	.210447	.198282	.186212	.174231	.162329	31
32	.396991	.380826	.364961	.349410	.334189	.319308	.304763	.290581	.276780	.263340	.250247	.237454	.224891	.212507	.200223	.188035	.175937	.163919	.152048	32
33	.384713	.368686	.352976	.337660	.322567	.307874	.293547	.279605	.266028	.252801	.239878	.227187	.214677	.202267	.189955	.177733	.165592	.153600	.141859	33
34	.372612	.356735	.341195	.326002	.311152	.296673	.282582	.268861	.255494	.242432	.229606	.216963	.204421	.191977	.179625	.167356	.155236	.143369	.131785	34
35	.360702	.344990	.329627	.314612	.299972	.285725	.271851	.258334	.245128	.232159	.219375	.206694	.194112	.181623	.169217	.156962	.144964	.133250	.121920	35
36	.348996	.333457	.318266	.303456	.289043	.275008	.261335	.247975	.234855	.221923	.209095	.196367	.183732	.171182	.158785	.144647	.134798	.123336	.112492	36
37	.337502	.322129	.307138	.292551	.278345	.264506	.250985	.237705	.224616	.211632	.198750	.185962	.173259	.160712	.148427	.136434	.124833	.113858	.103728	37
38	.326223	.311042	.296269	.281883	.267868	.254175	.240727	.227471	.214322	.201276	.188326	.175461	.162754	.150313	.138168	.126419	.115305	.105047	.095823	38
39	.315178	.300209	.285632	.271430	.257554	.243928	.230496	.217172	.203952	.190830	.177795	.164919	.152312	.140005	.128100	.116838	.106443	.097097	.089587	39
40	.304393	.289612	.275213	.261144	.247327	.233708	.220198	.206795	.193489	.180272	.167217	.154435	.141956	.129886	.118466	.107927	.098450	.090836	.084942	40
41	.293847	.279237	.264962	.250943	.237126	.223418	.209818	.196319	.182908	.169662	.156693	.144032	.131785	.120199	.109505	.099890	.092164	.086184	.078203	41
42	.283524	.269030	.254796	.240766	.226848	.213039	.199332	.185716	.172266	.159098	.146243	.133808	.122044	.111186	.101423	.093579	.087508	.079404	.064016	42
43	.273364	.258900	.244644	.230502	.216471	.202543	.188708	.175041	.161661	.148599	.135963	.124010	.112977	.103057	095086	.088917	.080683	.065047		
44	.263267	.248770	.234390	.220122	.205959	.191890	.177993	.164388	.151105	.138256	.126101	.114882	.104795	.096690	.090417	.082043	.066144		.063048	41
45	.253148	.238515	.223996	.209584	.195268	.181126	.167281	.153764	.140690	.128320	.116904	.106639	.098391	.092008	.083487	.067308		.062139	.077076	40
46	.242888	.228103	.213427	.198848	.184447	.170348	.156584	.143269	.130673	.119048	.108595	.100196	.093695	.085018	.068542		.061285	.076017	.083775	39
47	.232447	.217491	.203102	.187960	.173592	.159565	.145997	.133162	.121315	.110662	.102103	.095479	.086637	.069848		.060481	.075019	.082675	.088411	38
48	.221781	.206640	.191675	.177024	.162720	.148884	.135794	.123723	.112850	.104122	.097367	.088350	.071228		.059722	.074078	.081638	.087302	.094620	37
49	.210878	.195607	.180655	.166057	.151937	.138579	.126251	.115165	.106258	.099364	.090162	.072689		.059006	.073189	.080659	.086255	.093486	.102485	36
													.058328	.072349	.079733	.085265	.092412	.101308	.111201	35
50	.199773	.184503	.169594	.155174	.141531	.128940	.117618	.108521	.101480	.092083	.074237									
51	.188179	.173341	.158602	.144658	.131789	.120216	.110918	.103722	.094117	.075877		.057687	.071553	.078856	.084327	.091396	.100194	.109978	.120576	34
52	.177312	.162235	.147971	.134807	.122970	.113459	.106098	.096273	.077615		.057079	.070800	.078025	.083439	.090433	.099138	.108819	.119309	.130396	33
53	.166086	.151484	.138007	.125889	.116152	.108616	.098558	.079458		.056502	.070084	.077237	.082595	.079519	.098136	.107720	.118103	.129079	.140425	32
54	.155209	.141400	.128985	.119009	.111287	.100982	.081412		.055954	.069405	.076488	.081794	.088651	.097185	.106675	.116955	.127827	.139064	.150574	31
55	.145005	.132272	.122042	.114124	.103555	.083487		.055434	.068759	.075776	.081033	.087826	.096280	.105682	.115869	.126637	.137769	.149172	.160819	30
56	.135765	.125264	.117137	.106290	.085691		.054938	.068145	.075099	.080309	.087042	.095420	.104738	.114834	.125506	.136539	.147840	.159382	.171067	29
57	.128688	.120339	.109195	.088034		.054467	.067560	.074455	.079620	.086295	.094602	.103840	.113849	.124430	.135368	.146572	.158015	.169600	.181263	28
58	.123749	.112289	.090529		.054018	.067003	.073842	.078965	.085584	.093822	.102984	.112911	.123404	.134252	.145364	.156713	.168203	.179769	.191422	27
59	.115585	.093185		.053591	.066473	.073257	.078340	.084907	.093080	.102170	.112018	.122428	.133190	.144214	.155471	.166872	.178347	.189907	.201559	26
			.053184	.065968	.072701	.077745	.084262	.092373	.101393	.111167	.121498	.132178	.143118	.154292	.165604	.176992	.188464	.200027	.211683	25
60	.096018																			
		.052796	.065487	.072170	.077177	.083647	.091699	.100653	.110355	.120611	.131214	.142074	.153166	.164399	.175700	.187089	.198560	.210138	.221877	24
23	.052425	.065028	.071664	.076638	.083060	.091056	.099948	.109582	.119765	.130294	.141078	.152092	.163243	.174468	.185777	.197175	.208665	.200232	.232192	23
22	.064589	.071808	.076120	.082500	.090442	.099274	.108843	.118958	.129415	.140126	.151067	.162143	.173292	.184525	.195846	.207258	.218837	.230626	.242693	22
21	.070720	.075627	.081966	.089856	.098631	.108138	.118188	.128577	.139219	.150089	.161093	.172170	.183330	.194578	.205913	.217420	.229133	.241121	.253427	21
20	.075156	.081456	.089297	.098017	.107466	.117453	.127777	.138353	.149155	.160090	.171099	.182189	.193367	.204635	.216067	.227708	.239621	.251850	.264408	20
19	.080968	.088763	.097430	.106822	.116749	.127012	.137525	.148262	.159132	.170074	.181098	.192209	.203410	.214773	.226244	.238186	.250342	.262825	.275653	19
18	.088252	.096870	.106208	.116078	.126281	.136734	.147410	.158217	.169096	.180057	.191104	.202240	.213538	.225042	.236816	.248903	.261314	.274067	.287147	18
17	.096335	.105620	.115436	.125584	.135978	.146729	.157342	.168161	.179061	.190047	.201122	.212357	.223798	.235507	.247526	.259868	.272553	.285560	.298868	17
16	.105060	.114824	.124917	.135256	.145816	.156507	.167269	.178111	.189039	.200055	.211230	.222610	.234257	.246213	.258490	.271106	.284044	.297282	.310822	16
15	.114238	.124280	.134566	.145073	.155709	.166416	.177203	.188075	.199035	.210153	.221476	.233063	.244958	.257172	.269723	.282596	.295767	.309237	.323000	15
Age.	**76.**	**75.**	**74.**	**73.**	**72.**	**71.**	**70.**	**69.**	**68.**	**67.**	**66.**	**65.**	**64.**	**63.**	**62.**	**61.**	**60.**	**59.**	**58.**	**Age.**

TABLE XII.

TABLE XIII.

Age.	1.	2.	3.	4.	5.	6.	7.	8.	9.
15	.977462	.953923	.929325	.903635	.876773	.848714	.819389	.788734	.756690
16	.977016	.953002	.927924	.901716	.874323	.845708	.815801	.784542	.751862
17	.976546	.952057	.926456	.899723	.871791	.842601	.812097	.780211	.746871
18	.976074	.951067	.924956	.897680	.869176	.839368	.808274	.775735	.741718
19	.975559	.950047	.923401	.895561	.866478	.836087	.804319	.771114	.736394
20	.975059	.949016	.921810	.893394	.863701	.832675	.800247	.766346	.730901
21	.974534	.947940	.920165	.891150	.860832	.829152	.796038	.761423	.725229
22	.973990	.946832	.918465	.888830	.857868	.825512	.791696	.756343	.719376
23	.973434	.945691	.916711	.886440	.854811	.821761	.787218	.751102	.713336
24	.972856	.944506	.914899	.883971	.851658	.817890	.782596	.745695	.707105
25	.972256	.943287	.913030	.881426	.848406	.813900	.777830	.740118	.700674
26	.971649	.942037	.911112	.878809	.845061	.809790	.772922	.734368	.694035
27	.971010	.940739	.909127	.876098	.841605	.805549	.767855	.728428	.687182
28	.970358	.939409	.907088	.873325	.838051	.801180	.762626	.722301	.680105
29	.969688	.938040	.904988	.870464	.834386	.796671	.757233	.715976	.672798
30	.968998	.936629	.902827	.867513	.830604	.792020	.751666	.709443	.665244
31	.968287	.935179	.900600	.864466	.826704	.787219	.745916	.702691	.657440
32	.967559	.933685	.898300	.861325	.822677	.782261	.739974	.695717	.649371
33	.966803	.932131	.895923	.858080	.818516	.777134	.733834	.688504	.641027
34	.966022	.930539	.893470	.854727	.814214	.771837	.727484	.681045	.632411
35	.965220	.928893	.890938	.851260	.809769	.766356	.720916	.673343	.623647
36	.964387	.927187	.888312	.847673	.805163	.760682	.714130	.665522	.614467
37	.963523	.925418	.885594	.843951	.800391	.754817	.707254	.657317	.605188
38	.962626	.923583	.882769	.840089	.795453	.748891	.700027	.649049	.595755
39	.961698	.921676	.879837	.836096	.790490	.742650	.692773	.640667	.586173
40	.960728	.919688	.876799	.832104	.785241	.736415	.685995	.632179	.576457
41	.959718	.917636	.873805	.827871	.780042	.730154	.678057	.623605	.566620
42	.958676	.915662	.870606	.823726	.774863	.723878	.670631	.614962	.556665
43	.957754	.913525	.867539	.819644	.769712	.717612	.663189	.606252	.546619
44	.956652	.911511	.864534	.815600	.764588	.711351	.655712	.597499	.536491
45	.955657	.909550	.861564	.811586	.759480	.705079	.648223	.588707	.526291
46	.954714	.907626	.858630	.807599	.754376	.698817	.640725	.579882	.516020
47	.953754	.905694	.855688	.803593	.749273	.692549	.633216	.571024	.505694
48	.952818	.903784	.852758	.799651	.744196	.686304	.625707	.562149	.495323
49	.951888	.901876	.849854	.795675	.739158	.680185	.618223	.553291	.484912
50	.950941	.899977	.846967	.791752	.734129	.673881	.610746	.544385	.474485
51	.950028	.898121	.844136	.787884	.729167	.667745	.603293	.535554	.464055
52	.949127	.896296	.841335	.784064	.724264	.661638	.595925	.526745	.453669
53	.948246	.894493	.838579	.780305	.719396	.655630	.588623	.518026	.443346
54	.947368	.892719	.835872	.776574	.714628	.649683	.581428	.509416	.433122
55	.946515	.890991	.833191	.772946	.709931	.643877	.574377	.500961	.423020
56	.945693	.889273	.830602	.769382	.705380	.638231	.567515	.492682	.413077
57	.944839	.887612	.828045	.765944	.700981	.632783	.560857	.484615	.403319
58	.944084	.886019	.825654	.762697	.696822	.627588	.554473	.476816	.393777
59	.943286	.884495	.823366	.759623	.692868	.622647	.548369	.469284	.384497
60	.942606	.883118	.821299	.756796	.689218	.618041	.542601	.462109	.375492
61	.941966	.881863	.819391	.754206	.685855	.613754	.537211	.455274	.366770
62	.941405	.880732	.817687	.751882	.682806	.609860	.532204	.448802	.358368
63	.940890	.879733	.816187	.749819	.690118	.606343	.527586	.442726	.350300
64	.940464	.878895	.814915	.748094	.677794	.603221	.523406	.437075	.342598
65	.940113	.878200	.813905	.746673	.675821	.600522	.519675	.431874	.335274
66	.939829	.877697	.813127	.745537	.674226	.598255	.516420	.427139	.328363
67	.939666	.877353	.812567	.744721	.673020	.596448	.513657	.422913	.321882
68	.939544	.877108	.812212	.744189	.672192	.595084	.511411	.419206	.315841
69	.939464	.877009	.812080	.743977	.671757	.594215	.509708	.416041	.310286
Age.	1.	2.	3.	4.	5.	6.	7.	8.	9.

TABLE XIV.

Age.	1.	2.	3.	4.	Age.
15	.954068	.906007	.855732	.803142	15
16	.953216	.904273	.853079	.799496	16
17	.952335	.902485	.850313	.795736	17
18	.951430	.900623	.847470	.791852	18
19	.950494	.898704	.844526	.787832	19
20	.949531	.896730	.841488	.783384	20
21	.948538	.894677	.838345	.779395	21
22	.947501	.892579	.835113	.774967	22
23	.946439	.890407	.831767	.770394	23
24	.945343	.888153	.828308	.765667	24
25	.944205	.885835	.824741	.760790	25
26	.943037	.883438	.821058	.755755	26
27	.941830	.880965	.817257	.750559	27
28	.940589	.878419	.813338	.745198	28
29	.939305	.875786	.809293	.739667	29
30	.937987	.873076	.805125	.733960	30
31	.936621	.870285	.800825	.728067	31
32	.935220	.867404	.796383	.721984	32
33	.933771	.864426	.791799	.715701	33
34	.932272	.861354	.787063	.709212	34
35	.930730	.858184	.782176	.702504	35
36	.929137	.854906	.777119	.695573	36
37	.927484	.851517	.771897	.688406	37
38	.925785	.848018	.766496	.680996	38
39	.924025	.844395	.760909	.673345	39
40	.922199	.840646	.755146	.665582	40
41	.920312	.836790	.749337	.657443	41
42	.918374	.832946	.743222	.649246	42
43	.916413	.828864	.737124	.640940	43
44	.914448	.824852	.730984	.632524	44
45	.912469	.820831	.724786	.624001	45
46	.910513	.816796	.718541	.615379	46
47	.908543	.812723	.712227	.606640	47
48	.906558	.808631	.705849	.597819	48
49	.903566	.804499	.699436	.588920	49
50	.902562	.800357	.692987	.579956	50
51	.900562	.796222	.686524	.570935	51
52	.898577	.792096	.680052	.561872	52
53	.896606	.787974	.673565	.552775	53
54	.894638	.783869	.667076	.543642	54
55	.892396	.779780	.660635	.534516	55
56	.890782	.775719	.654205	.525393	56
57	.888868	.771693	.647816	.516323	57
58	.886991	.767783	.641546	.507340	58
59	.885971	.763926	.635370	.498459	59
60	.883443	.760217	.629373	.489723	60
61	.881782	.756653	.623528	.481150	61
62	.880222	.753242	.617906	.472772	62
63	.878741	.750003	.612493	.464599	63
64	.877381	.746970	.607320	.456690	64
65	.876144	.744134	.602439	.449038	65
66	.875026	.741562	.597895	.441659	66
67	.874067	.739239	.593548	.434586	67
68	.873244	.737128	.589561	.427823	68
69	.872536	.735290	.585518	.421407	69
Age.	1.	2.	3.	4.	Age.

TABLE XV.

Age.	Com.	Age.	Age.	Com.	Age.
15	.769148	15	68	.304346	68
16	.765220	16	69	.292808	69
17	.761158	17			
18	.756951	18	70	.281431	70
19	.752605	19	71	.270235	71
			72	.259232	72
20	.748093	20	73	.248434	73
21	.743436	21	74	.237845	74
22	.738623	22	75	.227486	75
23	.733643	23	76	.217356	76
24	.728500	24	77	.207455	77
25	.723184	25	78	.197802	78
26	.717687	26	79	.188407	79
27	.712010	27			
28	.706144	28	80	.179258	80
29	.700087	29	81	.170346	81
			82	.161638	82
30	.693832	30	83	.153086	83
31	.687376	31	84	.144656	84
32	.680711	32	85	.136294	85
33	.673833	33	86	.127998	86
34	.666733	34	87	.119763	87
35	.659400	35	88	.111583	88
36	.651830	36	89	.103503	89
37	.644011	37			
38	.635935	38	90	.095592	90
39	.627586	39	91	.087859	91
			92	.080394	92
40	.618960	40	93	.073325	93
41	.610040	41	94	.066803	94
42	.600817	42	95	.060938	95
43	.591291	43	96	.056225	96
44	.581485	44	97	.052576	97
45	.571429	45	98	.047710	98
46	.561138	46	99	.038452	99
47	.550654	47			
48	.539978	48	100	.000000	100
49	.529122	49			
50	.518094	50			
51	.506893	51			
52	.495540	52			
53	.484051	53			
54	.472433	54			
55	.460688	55			
56	.448843	56			
57	.436897	57			
58	.424858	58			
59	.412743	59			
60	.400567	60			
61	.388372	61			
62	.376174	62			
63	.364005	63			
64	.351880	64			
65	.339829	65			
66	.327876	66			
67	.316032	67			
Age.	Com.	Age.	Age.	Com.	Age.

FIRST YEAR.—ENDOWMENT POLICIES.—4 PER CENT.—(Arranged by Terms.)

In 5 Years.

Age.	Initial Value.	Annual Diff.
10	180.358	+1.685
11	180.374	1.662
12	180.389	1.644
13	180.407	1.614
14	180.428	1.577
15	180.449	1.537
16	180.479	1.491
17	180.506	1.442
18	180.538	1.385
19	180.573	1.327
20	180.610	1.260
21	180.647	1.191
22	180.685	1.120
23	180.728	1.030
24	180.782	.959
25	180.823	.875
26	180.873	.781
27	180.933	.685
28	180.986	.578
29	181.047	.470
30	181.114	.348
31	181.184	.225
32	181.273	.091
33	181.332	—.047
34	181.414	.170
35	181.498	.346
36	181.583	.505
37	181.675	.667
38	181.769	.743
39	181.871	1.023
40	181.979	1.209
41	182.107	1.409
42	182.258	1.637
43	182.446	1.922
44	182.668	2.280
45	182.922	2.694
46	183.213	3.199
47	183.535	3.744
48	183.872	4.344
49	184.248	4.992
50	184.657	5.700
51	185.108	6.475
52	185.597	7.324
53	186.129	8.252
54	186.705	9.240
55	187.336	10.336
56	188.019	11.524
57	188.763	12.785
58	189.582	14.174
59	190.493	15.689
60	191.497	17.395
61	192.596	19.255
62	193.804	21.311
63	195.134	23.542
64	196.596	25.996
65	198.182	28.682

In 10 Years.

Age.	Initial Value.	Annual Diff.
10	83.516	—2.877
11	83.536	2.898
12	83.561	2.922
13	83.587	2.953
14	83.618	2.997
15	83.651	3.037
16	83.685	3.089
17	83.728	3.146
18	83.768	—3.209
19	83.815	3.275
20	83.866	3.352
21	83.913	3.427
22	83.968	3.506
23	84.022	3.593
24	84.085	3.684
25	84.148	3.779
26	84.221	3.887
27	84.289	3.990
28	84.370	4.113
29	84.449	4.232
30	84.536	4.368
31	84.630	4.510
32	84.714	4.651
33	84.823	4.816
34	84.926	4.975
35	85.032	5.144
36	85.149	5.323
37	85.276	5.501
38	85.423	5.703
39	85.584	5.905
40	85.759	6.102
41	85.972	6.324
42	86.229	6.585
43	86.513	6.896
44	86.837	7.291
45	87.202	7.749
46	87.615	8.316
47	88.061	8.827
48	88.547	9.592
49	89.073	10.308
50	89.656	11.101
51	90.293	11.968
52	90.973	12.903
53	91.728	13.939
54	92.549	15.037
55	93.448	16.253
56	94.435	17.573
57	95.514	18.969
58	96.741	20.541
59	97.991	22.153
60	99.470	24.068
2	102.81	28.40
3	104.73	30.86

In 15 Years.

Age.	Initial Value.	Annual Diff.
10	51.838	—4.368
11	51.865	4.391
12	51.896	4.412
13	51.931	4.446
14	51.968	4.491
15	52.012	4.534
16	52.055	4.588
17	52.103	4.643
18	52.157	4.711
19	52.210	4.776
20	52.270	4.864
21	52.331	4.938
22	52.398	5.015
23	52.467	5.106
24	52.541	5.201
25	52.619	5.297
26	52.704	5.400
27	52.791	5.5[illegible]7
28	52.884	5.641
29	52.979	5.764
30	53.082	—5.904
31	53.196	6.050
32	53.308	6.200
33	53.435	6.362
34	53.574	6.529
35	53.718	6.701
36	53.883	6.883
37	54.071	7.071
38	54.275	7.270
39	54.509	7.475
40	54.769	7.683
41	55.068	7.909
42	55.403	8.162
43	55.784	8.480
44	56.233	8.907
45	56.697	9.365
46	57.222	9.940
47	57.800	10.567
48	58.426	11.259
49	59.110	11.879
50	59.860	12.796
51	60.684	13.683
52	61.569	14.537
53	62.554	15.696
54	63.628	16.819
55	64.803	18.059
7	67.51	20.83

In 20 Years.

Age.	Initial Value.	Annual Diff.
10	36.449	—5.097
11	36.484	5.110
12	36.523	5.137
13	36.567	5.172
14	36.613	5.213
15	36.662	5.259
16	36.717	5.314
17	36.774	5.370
18	36.836	5.436
19	36.902	5.504
20	36.972	5.583
21	37.047	5.666
22	37.123	5.745
23	37.206	5.840
24	37.293	5.934
25	37.383	6.030
26	37.482	6.144
27	37.587	6.252
28	37.701	6.378
29	37.817	6.501
30	37.951	6.645
31	38.088	6.784
32	38.246	6.945
33	38.414	7.106
34	38.594	7.264
35	38.801	7.447
36	39.024	7.626
37	39.276	7.812
38	39.551	8.009
39	39.871	8.148
40	40.216	8.427
41	40.598	8.642
42	41.047	8.909
43	41.530	9.223
44	42.078	9.636
45	42.678	10.107
46	43.342	10.688
47	44.064	11.314
48	44.851	—11.998
49	45.710	12.736
50	46.649	13.541

In 25 Years.

Age.	Initial Value.	Annual Diff.
10	27.576	—5.508
11	27.620	5.535
12	27.666	5.555
13	27.717	5.588
14	27.772	5.632
15	27.832	5.677
16	27.895	5.732
17	27.964	5.788
18	28.034	5.855
19	28.113	5.922
20	28.194	6.001
21	28.279	6.082
22	28.370	6.164
23	28.469	6.257
24	28.574	6.353
25	28.684	6.450
26	28.807	6.559
27	28.938	6.670
28	29.081	6.794
29	29.235	6.920
30	29.404	7.061
31	29.588	7.202
32	29.789	7.359
33	30.040	7.518
34	30.257	7.680
35	30.522	7.857
36	30.814	8.038
37	31.140	8.219
38	31.503	8.418
39	31.901	8.619
40	32.348	8.824
41	32.837	9.046
42	33.379	9.297
43	34.003	9.617
44	34.674	10.022
45	35.419	10.491

In 30 Years.

Age.	Initial Value.	Annual Diff.
10	21.957	—5.774
11	22.001	5.796
12	22.061	5.819
13	22.123	5.842
14	22.187	5.895
15	22.258	5.941
16	22.330	5.995
17	22.411	6.051
18	22.494	6.118
19	22.586	6.184
20	22.683	6.263
21	22.794	6.344
22	22.899	6.425
23	23.091	6.518
24	23.149	6.613
25	23.290	6.709
26	23.445	6.817
27	23.611	6.928
28	23.788	7.051
29	23.996	7.175
30	24.206	—7.315
31	24.444	7.454
32	24.701	7.609
33	24.983	7.766
34	25.294	7.926
35	25.631	8.100
36	26.006	8.279
37	26.415	8.456
38	26.866	8.651
39	27.368	8.848
40	27.917	9.049

In 35 Years.

Age.	Initial Value.	Annual Diff.
10	18.189	—5.950
11	18.255	5.973
12	18.319	5.996
13	18.389	6.029
14	18.462	6.071
15	18.544	6.116
16	18.631	6.168
17	18.728	6.224
18	18.829	6.291
19	18.940	6.368
20	19.060	6.436
21	19.188	6.516
22	19.328	6.596
23	19.477	6.688
24	19.643	6.782
25	19.817	6.877
26	20.012	6.983
27	20.221	7.092
28	20.450	7.214
29	20.696	7.336
30	20.967	7.473
31	21.266	7.611
32	21.585	7.763
33	21.936	7.916
34	22.318	8.074
35	22.739	8.244
36	23.197	8.397

In 40 Years.

Age.	Initial Value.	Annual Diff.
10	15.579	—6.073
11	15.659	6.095
12	15.740	6.117
13	15.825	6.149
14	15.900	6.192
15	16.006	6.236
16	16.114	6.289
17	16.231	6.344
18	16.354	6.409
19	16.494	6.474
20	16.639	6.552
21	16.798	6.630
22	16.969	6.709
23	17.156	6.799
24	17.356	6.892
25	17.577	6.985
26	17.814	7.089
27	18.073	7.196
28	18.352	7.315
29	18.656	7.435
30	18.987	7.569

THIRTY-NINTH YEAR.

In 40 Years.			In 40 Yeags.			In 40 Years.			In 40 Years.			In 40 Years.		
10	910.313	+35.640	15	910.165	+35.364	19	909.990	+35.054	23	909.820	+34.562	27	909.561	+33.894
11	910.300	35.578	16	910.122	35.288	20	909.955	34.944	24	909.788	34.450	28	909.482	33.704
12	910.259	35.539	17	910.080	35.219	21	909.951	34.840	25	909.694	34.272	29	909.420	33.462
13	910.227	35.472	18	910.041	35.143	22	909.823	34.711	26	909.630	34.085	30	909.371	33.180
14	910.191	35.444												

THIRTY-EIGHTH YEAR.

In 40 Years.			In 40 Years.			In 40 Years.			In 40 Years.			In 40 Years.		
10	861.687	+33.050	15	861.546	+32.616	19	861.497	+32.013	23	861.465	+30.199	27	801.463	+30.035
11	861.725	32.939	16	861.568	32.431	20	861.488	31.824	24	861.489	30.943	28	861.490	29.804
12	861.657	32.848	17	861.541	32.298	21	861.514	31.639	25	861.447	30.672	29	861.520	29.398
13	861.643	32.755	18	861.534	32.139	22	861.423	31.430	26	861.442	30.366	30	861.565	28.824
14	861.601	32.682												

SECOND YEAR.—ENDOWMENT POLICIES.—4 PER CENT.—(Arranged by Terms.)

In 5 Years.

Age.	Initial Value.	Annual Diff.
10	362.401	+10.235
11	362.410	10.223
12	362.422	10.200
13	362.428	10.171
14	362.433	10.141
15	362.435	10.115
16	362.449	10.066
17	362.454	10.021
18	362.461	9.975
19	362.473	9.923
20	362.480	9.870
21	362.485	9.815
22	362.490	9.751
23	362.496	9.687
24	362.513	9.622
25	362.521	9.549
26	362.527	9.473
27	362.541	9.390
28	362.556	9.305
29	362.564	9.210
30	362.576	9.113
31	362.593	9.007
32	362.607	8.899
33	362.615	8.787
34	362.638	8.665
35	362.650	8.540
36	362.661	8.412
37	362.683	8.276
38	362.695	8.134
39	362.719	7.989
40	362.749	7.830
41	362.805	7.653
42	362.879	7.431
43	362.970	7.151
44	363.056	6.828
45	363.150	6.432
46	363.227	6.004
47	363.326	5.533
48	363.400	5.032
49	363.504	4.466
50	363.614	3.856
51	363.741	3.188
52	363.870	2.456
53	364.006	1.675
54	364.170	.810
55	364.336	—.136
56	364.514	1.131
57	364.741	2.231
58	364.990	3.443
59	365.297	4.787
60	365.599	6.269
61	365.937	7.909
62	366.297	9.694
63	366.726	11.661
64	367.196	13.816
65	367.682	16.169

In 10 Years.

Age.	Initial Value.	Annual Diff.
10	164.154	+.899
11	164.176	.879
12	164.200	.850
13	164.221	.811
14	164.237	.771
15	164.266	.724
16	164.284	.673
17	164.310	.615
18	164.327	+.555
19	164.355	.486
20	164.377	.414
21	164.399	.342
22	164.429	.259
23	164.454	.174
24	164.488	.089
25	164.519	—.012
26	164.552	.108
27	164.590	.218
28	164.625	.330
29	164.667	.445
30	164.705	.582
31	164.746	.684
32	164.785	.865
33	164.827	1.013
34	164.874	1.173
35	164.921	1.338
36	164.976	1.505
37	165.053	1.689
38	165.140	1.871
39	165.260	2.060
40	165.420	2.264
41	165.624	2.493
42	165.867	2.784
43	166.130	3.145
44	166.385	3.568
45	166.659	4.084
46	166.914	4.646
47	167.192	5.263
48	167.502	5.924
49	167.852	6.656
50	168.211	7.453
51	168.613	8.326
52	169.047	9.281
53	169.517	10.298
54	170.061	11.425
55	170.644	12.607
56	171.296	13.944
57	172.060	15.379
58	172.907	16.924
59	173.861	18.674
60	174.874	20.585
2	177.22	24.08
3	178.60	27.52

In 15 Years.

Age.	Initial Value.	Annual Diff.
10	99.306	—2.156
11	99.338	2.177
12	99.381	2.208
13	99.416	2.249
14	99.445	2.292
15	99.490	2.343
16	99.522	2.396
17	99.565	2.459
18	99.602	2.523
19	99.644	2.598
20	99.686	2.674
21	99.730	2.751
22	99.782	2.839
23	99.829	2.930
24	99.883	3.023
25	99.942	3.125
26	100.007	3.224
27	100.064	3.350
28	100.127	3.470
29	100.196	3.604
30	100.262	—3.740
31	100.338	3.890
32	100.418	4.043
33	100.508	4.200
34	100.617	4.370
35	100.737	4.545
36	100.886	4.721
37	101.069	4.948
38	101.281	5.106
39	101.542	5.303
40	101.855	5.516
41	102.227	5.755
42	102.648	6.058
43	103.095	6.443
44	103.548	6.890
45	104.030	7.438
46	104.507	8.032
47	105.032	8.685
48	105.586	9.389
49	106.231	10.159
50	106.923	11.000
51	107.679	11.922
52	108.506	12.929
53	109.413	13.999
54	110.437	15.184
55	111.549	16.466
5	114.19	19.32

In 20 Years.

Age.	Initial Value.	Annual Diff.
10	67.806	—3.538
11	67.854	3.660
12	67.911	3.692
13	67.961	3.734
14	68.013	3.778
15	68.066	3.830
16	68.120	3.884
17	68.178	3.949
18	68.237	4.014
19	68.300	4.090
20	68.361	4.170
21	68.426	4.248
22	68.501	4.339
23	68.572	4.431
24	68.652	4.526
25	68.737	4.632
26	68.826	4.740
27	68.924	4.861
28	69.022	4.983
29	69.136	5.120
30	69.257	5.258
31	69.394	5.411
32	69.545	5.567
33	69.721	5.725
34	69.927	5.897
35	70.153	6.073
36	70.424	6.248
37	70.739	6.440
38	71.096	6.634
39	71.589	6.827
40	72.002	7.043
41	72.561	7.282
42	73.180	7.585
43	73.840	7.973
44	74.518	8.423
45	75.249	8.978
46	75.994	9.578
47	76.811	10.238
48	77.704	—10.947
49	78.686	11.724
50	79.761	12.572
2	82.25	14.54

In 25 Years.

Age.	Initial Value.	Annual Diff.
10	49.660	—4.495
11	49.709	4.516
12	49.777	4.548
13	49.846	4.588
14	49.912	4.634
15	49.987	4.686
16	50.058	4.740
17	50.140	4.805
18	50.213	4.871
19	50.304	4.948
20	50.387	5.027
21	50.476	5.107
22	50.576	5.198
23	50.681	5.291
24	50.795	5.385
25	50.918	5.491
26	51.055	5.600
27	51.206	5.721
28	51.368	5.843
29	51.550	5.979
30	51.747	6.117
31	51.974	6.267
32	52.219	6.422
33	52.542	6.578
34	52.834	6.747
35	53.187	6.921
36	53.590	7.093
37	54.061	7.280
38	54.588	7.470
39	55.183	7.662
40	55.872	7.868
41	56.628	8.101
42	57.465	8.399
43	58.389	8.781
44	59.326	9.227
45	60.347	9.775

In 30 Years.

Age.	Initial Value.	Annual Diff.
10	38.130	—5.037
11	38.206	5.058
12	38.303	5.089
13	38.394	5.130
14	38.479	5.174
15	38.575	5.226
16	38.665	5.280
17	38.771	5.345
18	38.870	5.410
19	38.988	5.486
20	39.103	5.565
21	39.244	5.643
22	39.373	5.735
23	39.520	5.827
24	39.685	5.920
25	39.871	6.024
26	40.073	6.131
27	40.294	6.250
28	40.525	6.371
29	40.817	6.504
30	41.097	—6.638
31	41.434	6.786
32	41.793	6.937
33	42.200	7.089
34	42.662	7.253
35	43.162	7.422
36	43.733	7.587
37	44.374	7.769
38	45.081	7.952
39	45.888	8.135
40	46.785	8.333

In 35 Years.

Age.	Initial Value.	Annual Diff.
10	30.428	—5.400
11	30.537	5.420
12	30.632	5.451
13	30.749	5.491
14	30.853	5.534
15	30.972	5.584
16	31.093	5.637
17	31.232	5.703
18	31.367	5.767
19	31.522	5.843
20	31.684	5.919
21	31.860	5.997
22	32.060	6.085
23	32.266	6.175
24	32.504	6.266
25	32.757	6.368
26	33.041	6.472
27	33.350	6.587
28	33.686	6.703
29	34.056	6.834
30	34.461	6.964
31	34.921	7.106
32	35.407	7.252
33	35.956	7.398
34	36.562	7.556
35	37.234	7.718

In 40 Years.

Age.	Initial Value.	Annual Diff.
10	25.085	—5.651
11	25.223	5.670
12	25.363	5.700
13	25.501	5.739
14	25.608	5.782
15	25.776	5.832
16	25.939	5.884
17	26.118	5.946
18	26.299	6.008
19	26.514	6.081
20	26.726	6.156
21	26.966	6.231
22	27.229	6.317
23	27.513	6.404
24	27.820	6.492
25	28.169	6.589
26	28.539	6.689
27	28.950	6.801
28	29.389	6.912
29	29.877	7.038
30	30.405	7.152

THIRTY-SEVENTH YEAR.

In 40 Years.

Age.	Initial Value.	Annual Diff.
10	815.460	+30.650
11	815.530	30.524
12	815.611	30.394
13	815.523	30.279
14	815.529	30.164
15	815.571	+29.964
16	815.602	29.845
17	815.709	29.591
18	815.686	29.468
19	815.738	+29.289
20	815.807	29.040
21	815.906	28.810
22	815.914	28.539
23	816.059	+28.250
24	816.001	27.911
25	816.311	27.552
26	816.449	27.170
27	816.654	+26.746
28	816.890	26.395
29	817.130	25.874
30	817.378	25.200

THIRTY-SIXTH YEAR.

In 40 Years.

Age.	Initial Value.	Annual Diff.
10	771.461	+28.417
11	771.568	28.275
12	771.607	28.142
13	771.703	27.994
14	771.773	27.848
15	771.745	27.674
16	771.999	27.482
17	772.185	27.293
18	772.290	27.031
19	772.416	+26.828
20	772.612	26.556
21	772.835	26.273
22	772.984	25.960
23	773.274	+25.629
24	773.395	25.250
25	773.885	24.852
26	774.223	24.403
27	774.671	+23.920
28	775.180	23.506
29	775.690	22.905
30	776.224	22.136

THIRD YEAR.—ENDOWMENT POLICIES.—4 PER CENT.—(Arranged by Terms.)

In 5 Years.

AGE.	Initial Value.	Diff.
10	553.009	+19.216
11	553.007	19.190
12	553.011	19.170
13	553.006	19.150
14	553.002	19.124
15	552.989	19.100
16	552.984	19.070
17	552.981	19.034
18	552.975	19.000
19	552.969	18.970
20	552.960	18.924
21	552.947	18.880
22	552.926	18.834
23	552.911	18.790
24	552.917	18.739
25	552.893	18.665
26	552.873	18.628
27	552.864	18.569
28	552.841	18.502
29	552.821	18.434
30	552.803	18.351
31	552.784	18.286
32	552.779	18.211
33	552.734	18.124
34	552.717	18.035
35	552.688	17.945
36	552.656	17.851
37	552.634	17.754
38	552.598	17.652
39	552.579	17.541
40	552.558	17.416
41	552.565	17.263
42	552.568	17.069
43	552.567	16.845
44	552.552	16.571
45	552.504	16.272
46	552.444	15.943
47	552.394	15.576
48	552.304	15.198
49	552.218	14.772
50	552.127	14.304
51	552.037	13.791
52	551.923	13.244
53	551.810	12.637
54	551.685	11.976
55	551.542	11.272
56	551.402	10.496
57	551.273	9.550
58	551.139	8.693
59	551.003	7.647
60	550.827	6.485
61	550.624	5.219
62	550.407	3.818
63	550.199	2.281
64	549.976	.601
65	549.695	—1.255

In 10 Years.

AGE.	Initial Value.	Diff.
10	248.567	+4.857
11	248.592	4.831
12	248.610	4.791
13	248.619	4.760
14	248.624	4.717
15	248.642	4.678
16	248.646	4.618
17	248.652	4.564
18	248.650	+4.501
19	248.655	4.437
20	248.654	4.372
21	248.654	4.296
22	248.655	4.219
23	248.656	4.140
24	248.656	4.043
25	248.656	3962 [illegible]
26	248.662	3.863
27	248.663	3.761
28	248.663	3.647
29	248.662	3.531
30	248.658	3.406
31	248.654	3.246
32	248.641	3.140
33	248.634	2.994
34	248.624	2.843
35	248.616	2.691
36	248.621	2.427
37	248.642	2.358
38	248.689	2.186
39	248.780	1.999
40	248.919	1.793
41	249.107	1.538
42	249.306	1.205
43	249.497	.825
44	249.656	.357
45	249.780	—.150
46	249.883	.691
47	249.987	1.316
48	250.125	1.979
49	250.263	2.704
50	250.414	3.499
51	250.575	4.370
52	250.743	5.298
53	250.947	6.327
54	251.185	7.442
55	251.486	8.626
56	251.786	9.933
57	252.206	11.355
58	252.690	12.966
59	253.209	14.705
60	253.761	16.643
2	255.09	21.08

In 15 Years.

AGE.	Initial Value.	Diff.
10	148.986	+.157
11	149.025	.134
12	149.070	.096
13	149.098	.055
14	149.124	.003
15	149.160	—.043
16	149.181	.104
17	149.210	.164
18	149.236	.235
19	149.257	.307
20	149.282	.381
21	149.311	.465
22	149.340	.652
23	149.367	.660
24	149.403	.738
25	149.437	.838
26	149.479	.951
27	149.505	1.066
28	149.541	1.193
29	149.573	1.323
30	149.605	—1.467
31	149.641	1.614
32	149.685	1.762
33	149.743	1.925
34	149.818	2.093
35	149.912	2.261
36	150.052	2.442
37	150.227	2.626
38	150.451	2.814
39	150.747	3.011
40	151.108	3.243
41	151.540	3.524
42	151.996	3.884
43	152.443	4.305
44	152.880	4.823
45	153.291	5.385
46	153.700	6.005
47	154.147	6.674
48	154.615	7.408
49	155.181	8.207
50	155.782	9.083
51	156.435	10.041
52	157.152	11.060
53	157.969	12.187
54	158.881	13.407
55	159.887	14.701
6	161.06	16.12

In 20 Years.

AGE.	Initial Value.	Diff.
10	100.615	—2.116
11	100.677	2.147
12	100.742	2.186
13	100.794	2.228
14	100.849	2.278
15	100.900	2.330
16	100.953	2.393
17	101.003	2.456
18	101.060	2.530
19	101.112	2.605
20	101.163	2.683
21	101.224	2.770
22	101.285	2.860
23	101.345	2.952
24	101.420	3.054
25	101.490	3.159
26	101.569	3.276
27	101.649	3.395
28	101.737	3.528
29	101.834	3.663
30	101.948	3.811
31	102.073	3.961
32	102.222	4.114
33	102.408	4.280
34	102.627	4.450
35	102.879	4.621
36	103.194	4.796
37	103.574	4.989
38	104.017	5.177
39	104.629	5.374
40	105.173	5.603
41	105.885	5.990
42	106.637	6.257
43	107.400	6.686
44	108.173	7.216
45	108.949	7.791
46	109.756	8.424
47	110.634	9.107
48	111.606	—9.853
49	112.672	10.667
50	113.842	11.558
2	116.52	13.57

In 25 Years.

AGE.	Initial Value.	Diff.
10	72.745	—3.432
11	72.813	3.462
12	72.895	3.501
13	72.975	3.543
14	73.050	3.595
15	73.133	3.646
16	73.213	3.710
17	73.299	3.773
18	73.376	3.848
19	73.469	3.925
20	73.554	4.003
21	73.648	4.092
22	73.748	4.183
23	73.859	4.275
24	73.984	4.378
25	74.111	4.484
26	74.262	4.602
27	74.423	4.720
28	74.606	4.853
29	74.806	4.987
30	75.034	5.133
31	75.295	5.283
32	75.586	5.434
33	75.984	5.597
34	76.344	5.764
35	76.788	5.929
36	77.311	6.109
37	77.921	6.288
38	78.621	6.468
39	79.422	6.663
40	80.352	6.880
41	81.364	7.161
42	82.457	7.521
43	83.611	7.943
44	84.773	8.467
45	85.991	9.036

In 30 Years.

AGE.	Initial Value.	Diff.
10	55.075	—4.265
11	55.149	4.295
12	55.275	4.333
13	55.387	4.376
14	55.492	4.425
15	55.607	4.478
16	55.715	4.541
17	55.837	4.603
18	55.954	4.679
19	56.088	4.754
20	56.221	4.832
21	56.395	4.918
22	56.537	5.009
23	56.712	5.101
24	56.914	5.202
25	57.137	5.306
26	57.387	5.420
27	57.655	5.537
28	57.942	5.667
29	58.309	5.795
30	58.665	—5.939
31	59.092	6.083
32	59.557	6.228
33	60.094	6.386
34	60.703	6.545
35	61.371	6.702
36	62.152	6.873
37	63.020	7.044
38	63.995	7.213
39	65.121	7.395
40	66.369	7.601

In 35 Years.

AGE.	Initial Value.	Diff.
10	43.217	—4.822
11	43.372	4.850
12	43.490	4.890
13	43.647	4.930
14	43.781	4.977
15	43.932	5.026
16	44.087	5.092
17	44.257	5.154
18	44.429	5.228
19	44.619	5.302
20	44.825	5.377
21	45.051	5.463
22	45.303	5.549
23	45.568	5.638
24	45.881	5.734
25	46.206	5.834
26	46.581	5.945
27	46.984	6.056
28	47.433	6.180
29	47.918	6.304
30	48.464	6.440
31	49.081	6.577
32	49.740	6.715
33	50.494	6.863
34	51.324	7.014
35	52.255	7.160

In 40 Years.

AGE.	Initial Value.	Diff.
10	35.013	—5.209
11	35.212	5.235
12	35.403	5.272
13	35.587	5.311
14	35.726	5.361
15	35.950	5.409
16	36.160	5.470
17	36.403	5.528
18	36.645	5.599
19	36.927	5.669
20	37.209	5.741
21	37.533	5.823
22	37.881	5.906
23	38.265	5.989
24	38.684	6.082
25	39.157	6.176
26	39.664	6.281
27	40.222	6.386
28	40.829	6.502
29	41.495	6.619
30	42.240	6.746

THIRTY-FIFTH YEAR.

In 40 Years.

AGE.	Initial Value.	Diff.
10	729.553	+26.333
11	729.713	26.188
12	729.827	26.035
13	729.982	25.885
14	730.141	25.724
15	730.210	+25.529
16	730.575	25.304
17	730.838	25.116
18	731.062	24.753
19	731.334	+24.601
20	731.664	24.312
21	732.038	23.999
22	732.361	23.653
23	732.818	+23.300
24	733.140	22.899
25	733.836	22.476
26	734.409	21.991
27	735.125	+21.483
28	735.960	21.010
29	736.800	20.376
30	737.646	19.596

FOURTH YEAR.—ENDOWMENT POLICIES.—4 PER CENT.—(Arranged by Terms.)

In 5 Years.

AGE.	Initial Value.	Diff.
10	752.578	+28.603
11	752.571	28.594
12	752.570	28.583
13	752.562	28.570
14	752.554	28.557
15	752.536	28.540
16	752.530	28.523
17	752.521	28.504
18	752.511	28.485
19	752.503	28.466
20	752.494	28.444
21	752.474	28.419
22	752.445	28.395
23	752.429	28.368
24	752.418	28.342
25	752.401	28.312
26	752.374	28.281
27	752.366	28.247
28	752.329	28.210
29	752.302	28.171
30	752.278	28.133
31	752.254	28.092
32	752.263	28.051
33	752.190	28.000
34	752.166	27.953
35	752.131	27.905
36	752.090	27.854
37	752.063	27.802
38	752.019	27.743
39	751.991	27.679
40	751.953	27.598
41	751.935	27.498
42	751.895	27.381
43	751.858	27.242
44	751.791	27.083
45	751.698	26.911
46	751.600	26.725
47	751.505	26.522
48	751.374	26.299
49	751.238	26.052
50	751.088	25.783
51	750.936	25.496
52	750.764	25.176
53	750.576	24.830
54	750.366	24.457
55	750.150	24.048
56	749.917	23.602
57	749.686	23.095
58	749.414	22.540
59	749.143	21.925
60	748.809	21.252
61	748.439	20.505
62	748.029	19.682
63	747.614	18.782
64	747.173	17.789
65	746.622	16.699

In 10 Years.

AGE.	Initial Value.	Diff.
10	336.958	+8.998
11	336.960	8.968
12	336.963	8.936
13	336.966	8.898
14	336.969	8.858
15	336.970	8.812
16	336.949	8.763
17	336.943	8.707
18	336.919	+8.649
19	336.906	8.591
20	336.889	8.525
21	336.863	8.455
22	336.841	8.386
23	336.816	8.308
24	336.804	8.228
25	336.826	8.135
26	336.743	8.049
27	336.715	7.947
28	336.678	7.844
29	336.643	7.731
30	336.600	7.615
31	336.590	7.498
32	336.502	7.366
33	336.448	7.231
34	336.390	7.094
35	336.340	6.948
36	336.298	6.797
37	336.278	6.643
38	336.295	6.477
39	336.359	6.292
40	336.475	6.062
41	336.617	5.773
42	336.734	5.435
43	336.834	5.024
44	336.852	4.573
45	336.836	4.075
46	336.787	3.536
47	336.729	2.944
48	336.693	2.298
49	336.636	1.588
50	336.571	.811
51	336.493	—.019
52	336.422	.939
53	336.348	1.939
54	336.292	3.002
55	336.309	4.169
56	336.287	5.449
57	336.366	6.886
58	336.431	8.468
59	336.526	10.199
60	336.590	12.097

In 15 Years.

AGE.	Initial Value.	Diff.
10	200.979	+2.585
11	201.023	2.549
12	201.063	2.512
13	201.084	2.466
14	201.099	2.414
15	201.129	2.363
16	201.132	2.305
17	201.150	2.238
18	201.157	2.170
19	201.163	2.100
20	201.171	2.023
21	201.178	1.938
22	201.186	1.835
23	201.195	1.762
24	201.207	1.667
25	201.219	1.561
26	201.231	1.452
27	201.231	1.331
28	201.231	1.207
29	201.230	1.072
30	201.230	+.933
31	201.231	.791
32	201.233	.636
33	201.253	.476
34	201.296	.317
35	201.371	.144
36	201.496	—.030
37	201.670	.207
38	201.912	.497
39	202.244	.609
40	202.634	.875
41	203.084	1.212
42	203.518	1.605
43	203.929	2.095
44	204.278	2.619
45	204.604	3.203
46	204.920	3.836
47	205.272	4.528
48	205.625	5.288
49	206.083	6.115
50	206.558	7.021
51	207.072	7.986
52	207.666	9.055
53	208.337	10.211
54	209.101	11.437
55	209.990	12.783

In 20 Years.

AGE.	Initial Value.	Diff.
10	134.946	—.529
11	135.015	.567
12	135.081	.607
13	135.131	.655
14	135.184	.705
15	135.232	.769
16	135.277	.826
17	135.321	.897
18	135.367	.970
19	135.408	1.044
20	135.453	1.129
21	135.499	1.216
22	135.548	1.304
23	135.599	1.403
24	135.659	1.505
25	135.715	1.621
26	135.776	1.734
27	135.840	1.862
28	135.908	1.990
29	135.991	2.121
30	136.088	2.262
31	136.202	2.431
32	136.352	2.692
33	136.539	2.756
34	136.774	2.920
35	137.058	3.096
36	137.415	3.265
37	137.860	3.454
38	138.384	3.656
39	139.121	3.856
40	139.782	4.133
41	140.599	4.480
42	141.422	4.888
43	142.248	5.391
44	143.034	5.941
45	143.837	5.548
46	144.671	6.203
47	145.589	7.922
48	146.603	—8.703
49	147.716	9.559
50	148.937	10.492

In 25 Years.

AGE.	Initial Value.	Diff.
10	96.875	—2.327
11	96.971	2.364
12	97.060	2.405
13	97.149	2.457
14	97.227	2.505
15	97.319	2.565
16	97.398	2.627
17	97.490	2.706
18	97.562	2.765
19	97.657	2.851
20	97.745	2.937
21	97.835	3.026
22	97.935	3.117
23	98.053	3.216
24	98.180	3.319
25	98.311	3.433
26	98.467	3.550
27	98.641	3.679
28	98.834	3.808
29	99.054	3.952
30	99.305	4.097
31	99.600	4.243
32	99.941	4.403
33	100.407	4.564
34	100.837	4.722
35	101.381	4.895
36	102.016	5.068
37	102.773	5.240
38	103.656	5.423
39	104.660	5.629
40	105.820	5.896
41	107.040	6.236
42	108.307	6.636
43	109.671	7.134
44	110.980	7.680
45	112.374	8.281

In 30 Years.

AGE.	Initial Value.	Diff.
10	72.765	—3.465
11	72.855	3.503
12	73.003	3.541
13	73.134	3.591
14	73.254	3.641
15	73.387	3.702
16	73.504	3.763
17	73.645	3.836
18	73.769	3.911
19	73.920	3.985
20	74.072	4.071
21	74.271	4.157
22	74.427	4.249
23	74.630	4.346
24	74.861	4.448
25	75.121	4.560
26	75.412	4.672
27	75.729	4.798
28	76.063	4.926
29	76.510	5.060
30	76.932	—5.202
31	77.453	5.341
32	78.030	5.495
33	78.691	5.645
34	79.452	5.795
35	80.300	5.959
36	81.285	6.118
37	82.391	6.277
38	83.648	6.446
39	85.094	6.637
40	86.685	6.886

In 35 Years.

AGE.	Initial Value.	Diff.
10	56.584	—4.227
11	56.777	4.262
12	56.909	4.303
13	57.106	4.345
14	57.266	4.394
15	57.450	4.459
16	57.626	4.519
17	57.831	4.589
18	58.030	4.662
19	58.257	4.735
20	58.508	4.818
21	58.776	4.903
22	59.082	4.986
23	59.407	5.081
24	59.790	5.177
25	60.189	5.285
26	60.648	5.391
27	61.149	5.510
28	61.703	5.629
29	62.310	5.759
30	62.991	5.891
31	63.770	6.020
32	64.610	6.161
33	65.567	6.303
34	66.628	6.439
35	67.834	6.587

In 40 Years.

AGE.	Initial Value.	Diff.
10	45.385	—4.755
11	45.636	4.789
12	45.871	4.824
13	46.101	4.870
14	46.265	4.920
15	46.547	4.976
16	46.804	5.033
17	47.106	5.100
18	47.400	5.169
19	47.752	5.237
20	48.107	5.316
21	48.508	5.395
22	48.944	5.475
23	49.432	5.563
24	49.958	5.653
25	50.558	5.752
26	51.197	5.851
27	51.909	5.971
28	52.679	6.071
29	53.532	6.191
30	54.481	6.311

THIRTY-FOURTH YEAR.

In 35 Years.

AGE.	Initial Value.	Diff.
10	907.670	+35.662
11	907.614	35.683
12	907.600	35.628
13	907.573	35.585
14	907.537	35.544
15	907.517	35.489
16	907.457	35.438
17	907.429	35.384
18	907.366	35.332
19	907.303	35.271
20	907.289	35.183
21	907.218	+35.118
22	907.184	35.038
23	907.123	34.952
24	907.049	34.865
25	906.977	34.729
26	906.904	34.590
27	906.820	34.461
28	906.739	34.363
29	906.664	34.170
30	906.557	33.996
31	906.434	33.845
32	906.336	+33.614
33	906.217	33.368
34	906.121	33.086
35	905.960	32.831

In 40 Years.

AGE.	Initial Value.	Diff.
10	689.580	+24.396
11	689.786	+24.228
12	689.962	24.088
13	690.234	23.920
14	690.479	23.754
15	690.660	23.543
16	691.121	23.338
17	691.498	23.109
18	691.853	22.842
19	692.263	22.583
20	692.757	22.372
21	693.292	21.948
22	693.792	+21.599
23	694.458	21.204
24	694.994	20.790
25	695.909	20.152
26	696.726	19.860
27	697.721	19.341
28	698.890	18.833
29	700.059	18.180
30	701.254	17.400

FIFTH YEAR.—ENDOWMENT POLICIES.—4 PER CENT.—(Arranged by Terms.)

In 10 Years.

Age.	Initial Value.	Diff.
10	429.450	+13.336
11	429.465	13.309
12	429.457	13.276
13	429.451	13.242
14	429.431	13.201
15	429.436	13.159
16	429.399	13.111
17	429.377	13.062
18	429.336	13.012
19	429.311	12.954
20	429.277	12.895
21	429.231	12.834
22	429.194	12.767
23	429.148	12.698
24	429.119	12.621
25	429.110	12.545
26	429.010	12.454
27	428.953	12.365
28	428.890	12.267
29	428.824	12.167
30	428.751	12.064
31	428.714	11.954
32	428.589	11.834
33	428.499	11.715
34	428.407	11.588
35	428.321	11.457
36	428.245	11.323
37	428.199	11.178
38	428.192	11.017
39	428.231	10.818
40	428.301	10.569
41	428.366	10.280
42	428.392	9.925
43	428.370	9.537
44	428.264	9.107
45	428.117	8.642
46	427.938	8.129
47	427.731	7.567
48	427.538	6.952
49	427.301	6.277
50	427.038	5.556
51	426.762	4.754
52	426.460	3.884
53	426.137	2.956
54	425.839	1.935
55	425.589	.823
56	425.272	—.437
57	424.995	1.811
58	424.680	3.336
59	424.349	+5.997
60	423.965	6.837

In 15 Years.

Age.	Initial Value.	Diff.
10	255.400	+5.117
11	255.436	+5.082
12	255.472	5.047
13	255.481	4.997
14	255.487	4.936
15	255.504	4.890
16	255.492	4.827
17	255.492	4.763
18	255.483	4.697
19	255.470	4.623
20	255.464	4.545
21	255.448	4.467
22	255.439	4.380
23	255.425	4.290
24	255.416	4.191
25	255.400	4.089
26	255.386	3.974
27	255.350	3.859
28	255.321	3.732
29	255.282	3.601
30	255.237	3.467
31	255.202	3.321
32	255.179	3.171
33	255.164	3.020
34	255.184	2.857
35	255.235	2.691
36	255.352	2.524
37	255.532	2.346
38	255.790	2.147
39	256.143	1.898
40	256.528	1.584
41	256.940	1.219
42	257.319	.767
43	257.625	.275
44	257.880	—.270
45	258.099	.863
46	258.309	1.514
47	258.543	2.231
48	258.755	3.013
49	259.077	3.857
50	259.396	4.765
51	259.764	5.770
52	260.185	6.861
53	260.681	8.016
54	261.291	9.285
55	262.011	10.666

In 20 Years.

Age.	Initial Value.	Diff.
10	170.865	+1.125
11	170.931	1.084
12	170.997	1.042
13	171.042	.993
14	171.091	.937
15	171.126	.878
16	171.168	+.810
17	171.198	.740
18	171.234	.669
19	171.266	.587
20	171.295	.499
21	171.327	.418
22	171.367	.323
23	171.400	.224
24	171.447	.115
25	171.477	.004
26	171.525	—.120
27	171.565	.250
28	171.617	.384
29	171.689	.525
30	171.755	.669
31	171.861	.825
32	172.004	.985
33	172.195	1.143
34	172.451	1.313
35	172.760	1.485
36	173.165	1.643
37	173.681	1.841
38	174.291	2.048
39	175.130	2.301
40	175.862	2.636
41	176.724	3.022
42	177.576	3.501
43	178.389	4.023
44	179.170	4.603
45	179.966	5.231
46	180.808	5.919
47	181.728	6.671
48	182.750	7.462
49	183.868	8.388
50	185.097	9.339
1	186.45	10.31
2	187.99	11.53

In 25 Years.

Age.	Initial Value.	Diff.
10	122.124	—1.178
11	122.227	1.215
12	122.321	1.261
13	122.409	1.311
14	122.494	1.370
15	122.586	1.429
16	122.666	1.499
17	122.754	1.573
18	122.831	1.647
19	122.919	1.731
20	123.002	1.817
21	123.088	1.905
22	123.188	1.993
23	123.306	2.103
24	123.435	2.214
25	123.562	2.328
26	123.724	—2.454
27	123.900	2.580
28	124.107	2.720
29	124.337	2.862
30	124.612	3.006
31	124.945	3.159
32	125.327	3.317
33	125.863	3.470
34	126.372	3.636
35	127.008	3.802
36	127.762	3.968
37	128.673	4.143
38	129.736	4.339
39	130.932	4.590
40	132.274	4.915
41	133.641	5.298
42	135.082	5.773
43	136.540	6.294
44	137.974	6.871
45	139.512	7.493

In 30 Years.

Age.	Initial Value.	Diff.
10	91.235	—2.636
11	91.353	2.675
12	91.583	2.722
13	91.666	2.769
14	91.800	2.828
15	91.943	2.887
16	92.071	2.958
17	92.220	3.029
18	92.352	3.105
19	92.521	3.187
20	92.684	3.273
21	92.908	3.359
22	93.077	3.456
23	93.303	3.556
24	93.562	3.664
25	93.851	3.774
26	94.185	3.897
27	94.542	4.019
28	94.925	4.155
29	95.446	4.289
30	95.936	4.426
31	96.556	4.572
32	97.236	4.720
33	98.029	4.863
34	98.951	5.018
35	99.972	5.172
36	101.173	5.321
37	102.529	5.480
38	104.068	5.660
39	105.825	5.894
40	107.716	6.201
3	113.93	7.51

In 35 Years.

Age.	Initial Value.	Diff.
10	70.566	—3.612
11	70.760	3.648
12	70.925	3.696
13	71.150	3.739
14	71.334	3.799
15	71.535	3.857
16	71.738	3.927
17	71.970	3.996
18	72.197	4.065
19	72.462	4.148
20	72.750	4.230
21	73.061	4.314
22	73.424	4.405
23	73.803	4.500
24	74.256	4.601
25	74.721	4.697
26	75.269	4.820
27	75.860	4.930
28	76.524	5.060
29	77.247	5.186
30	78.067	5.311
31	79.016	5.443
32	80.034	5.579
33	81.200	5.707
34	82.507	5.847
35	83.986	5.980

In 40 Years.

Age.	Initial Value.	Diff.
10	56.231	—4.288
11	56.471	4.323
12	56.724	4.367
13	57.036	4.411
14	57.298	4.468
15	57.577	4.520
16	57.885	4.586
17	58.237	4.652
18	58.625	4.719
19	59.009	4.793
20	59.430	4.871
21	59.911	4.967
22	60.438	5.031
23	61.025	5.117
24	61.661	5.213
25	62.383	5.306
26	63.160	5.412
27	64.011	5.516
28	64.960	5.629
29	65.997	5.742
30	67.157	5.851

THIRTY-THIRD YEAR.

In 35 Years.

Age.	Initial Value.	Diff.
10	856.436	+33.054
11	856.366	33.022
12	856.324	32.973
13	856.292	32.908
14	856.250	32.835
15	856.229	32.754
16	856.167	32.649
17	856.143	32.568
18	856.073	32.454
19	856.009	32.354
20	855.996	32.233
21	855.933	+32.087
22	855.916	31.950
23	855.857	31.799
24	855.769	31.637
25	855.714	31.435
26	855.659	31.229
27	855.569	31.020
28	855.523	30.776
29	855.472	30.484
30	855.392	30.190
31	855.303	29.894
32	855.246	+29.515
33	855.175	29.096
34	855.133	28.658
35	855.033	28.188

In 40 Years.

Age.	Initial Value.	Diff.
10	651.814	+22.494
11	651.755	+22.397
12	651.987	22.253
13	652.281	22.108
14	652.636	21.935
15	652.929	21.724
16	653.500	21.499
17	653.999	21.208
18	654.478	20.981
19	655.038	20.742
20	655.651	20.472
21	656.413	20.081
22	657.104	+19.718
23	657.973	19.329
24	658.735	18.903
25	659.876	18.480
26	660.934	17.969
27	662.210	17.442
28	663.720	16.936
29	665.210	16.293
30	666.751	15.316

THIRTY-SECOND YEAR.

In 35 Years.

Age.	Initial Value.	Diff.
10	807.654	—30.586
11	807.581	30.554
12	807.522	30.492
13	807.497	30.423
14	807.440	30.338
15	807.470	30.225
16	807.432	30.094
17	807.446	29.979
18	807.386	29.848
19	807.370	29.699
20	807.394	29.542
21	807.364	+29.371
22	807.437	29.171
23	807.416	28.974
24	807.379	28.759
25	807.397	28.493
26	807.407	28.231
27	807.409	27.929
28	807.443	27.640
29	807.491	27.273
30	807.526	26.903
31	807.544	26.497
32	807.655	+26.026
33	807.723	25.506
34	807.879	24.924
35	807.971	24.323

In 40 Years.

Age.	Initial Value.	Diff.
10	615.186	+20.726
11	615.445	+20.636
12	615.723	20.512
13	616.068	20.363
14	616.500	20.228
15	616.907	20.015
16	617.582	19.794
17	618.199	19.569
18	618.813	19.285
19	619.529	19.024
20	620.348	18.660
21	621.232	18.383
22	622.128	+18.006
23	623.179	17.638
24	624.180	17.189
25	625.550	16.557
26	626.841	16.270
27	628.398	15.749
28	630.207	15.260
29	632.833	14.621
30	633.903	13.850

SIXTH YEAR.—ENDOWMENT POLICIES.—4 PER CENT.—(Arranged by Terms.)

In 10 Years.

Age.	Initial Value.	Diff.
10	526.300	+17.887
11	526.311	17.861
12	526.293	17.832
13	526.280	17.799
14	526.248	17.764
15	526.247	17.725
16	526.197	17.683
17	526.166	17.642
18	526.116	17.594
19	526.079	17.544
20	526.035	17.484
21	525.978	17.438
22	525.928	17.380
23	525.870	17.317
24	525.827	17.253
25	525.804	17.182
26	525.682	17.104
27	525.609	17.023
28	525.525	16.941
29	525.441	16.854
30	525.351	16.762
31	525.294	16.665
32	525.144	16.564
33	525.034	16.459
34	524.918	16.349
35	524.811	16.237
36	524.718	16.116
37	524.655	15.981
38	524.629	15.815
39	524.629	15.607
40	524.632	15.368
41	524.622	15.078
42	524.540	14.755
43	524.419	14.409
44	524.210	14.014
45	523.965	13.588
46	523.682	13.120
47	523.356	12.606
48	523.037	12.044
49	522.655	11.442
50	522.250	10.773
51	521.804	10.045
52	521.321	9.268
53	520.821	8.411
54	520.323	7.477
55	519.861	6.424
56	519.269	5.265
57	518.699	3.984
58	518.051	2.583
59	517.394	1.034
60	516.600	—.679

In 15 Years.

Age.	Initial Value.	Diff.
10	312.353	+7.773
11	312.382	+7.735
12	312.416	7.695
13	312.409	7.641
14	312.398	7.587
15	312.406	7.539
16	312.374	7.478
17	312.359	7.418
18	312.336	7.348
19	312.303	7.276
20	312.279	7.204
21	312.247	7.122
22	312.217	7.039
23	312.183	6.946
24	312.149	6.851
25	312.109	6.747
26	312.063	6.638
27	311.999	6.519
28	311.936	6.398
29	311.863	6.273
30	311.787	6.137
31	311.715	5.995
32	311.660	5.854
33	311.619	5.702
34	311.612	5.547
35	311.646	5.389
36	311.762	5.222
37	311.947	5.036
38	312.212	4.805
39	312.549	4.514
40	312.881	4.176
41	313.227	3.760
42	313.492	3.306
43	313.691	2.801
44	313.831	2.253
45	313.934	1.648
46	314.020	.986
47	314.111	.259
48	314.160	—.539
49	314.329	1.383
50	314.490	2.322
51	314.672	3.340
52	314.898	4.421
53	315.220	5.608
54	315.633	6.900
55	316.149	8.352

In 20 Years.

Age.	Initial Value.	Diff.
10	208.438	+2.861
11	208.499	2.817
12	208.563	2.771
13	208.601	2.717
14	208.641	2.662
15	208.667	2.596
16	208.695	+2.529
17	208.712	2.461
18	208.740	2.383
19	208.755	2.302
20	208.766	2.220
21	208.790	2.128
22	208.813	2.034
23	208.829	1.930
24	208.855	1.823
25	208.865	1.703
26	208.888	1.583
27	208.902	1.449
28	208.932	1.309
29	208.983	1.175
30	209.036	1.024
31	209.126	.870
32	209.263	.717
33	209.464	.553
34	209.735	.387
35	210.074	.220
36	210.530	.057
37	211.115	—.147
38	211.797	.401
39	212.695	.709
40	213.439	1.080
41	214.307	1.535
42	215.117	2.031
43	215.899	2.582
44	216.644	3.180
45	217.413	3.838
46	218.229	4.558
47	219.118	5.346
48	220.108	6.205
49	221.191	7.117
50	222.411	8.125
1	223.76	9.21
2	225.27	10.37

In 25 Years.

Age.	Initial Value.	Diff.
10	148.549	+.025
11	148.632	—.017
12	148.726	.063
13	148.815	.120
14	148.896	.178
15	148.989	.246
16	149.062	.317
17	149.145	.389
18	149.218	.469
19	149.301	.555
20	149.379	.639
21	149.462	.735
22	149.555	.833
23	149.672	.940
24	149.795	1.052
25	149.918	1.175
26	150.077	—1.296
27	150.258	1.434
28	150.468	1.572
29	150.710	1.712
30	151.010	1.863
31	151.374	2.015
32	151.799	2.166
33	152.413	2.329
34	152.993	2.486
35	153.728	2.645
36	154.608	2.816
37	155.670	3.006
38	156.900	3.246
39	158.243	3.557
40	159.707	3.921
41	161.180	4.377
42	162.610	4.873
43	164.149	5.426
44	165.777	6.028
45	167.438	6.680

In 30 Years.

Age.	Initial Value.	Diff.
10	110.597	—1.767
11	110.825	1.805
12	110.932	1.862
13	111.020	1.916
14	111.159	1.973
15	111.314	2.041
16	111.443	2.112
17	111.602	2.184
18	111.741	2.267
19	111.920	2.349
20	112.094	2.435
21	112.343	2.526
22	112.520	2.636
23	112.766	2.732
24	113.047	2.841
25	113.367	2.959
26	113.733	3.079
27	114.134	3.210
28	114.558	3.344
29	115.133	3.472
30	115.716	3.619
31	116.428	3.761
32	117.217	3.900
33	118.149	4.051
34	119.227	4.197
35	120.431	4.341
36	121.858	4.492
37	123.464	4.662
38	125.354	4.886
39	127.239	5.175
40	129.432	5.522
1 2	136.35	6.97

In 35 Years.

Age.	Initial Value.	Diff.
10	85.176	—2.968
11	85.357	3.011
12	85.538	3.058
13	85.800	3.112
14	85.997	3.169
15	86.222	3.236
16	86.443	3.306
17	86.702	3.374
18	86.957	3.454
19	87.254	3.534
20	87.580	3.615
21	87.935	3.704
22	88.347	3.796
23	88.780	3.896
24	89.298	3.996
25	89.841	4.108
26	90.461	4.220
27	91.146	4.342
28	91.914	4.462
29	92.757	4.583
30	93.760	4.712
31	94.819	4.840
32	96.040	4.962
33	97.429	5.095
34	98.978	5.222
35	100.745	5.342

In 40 Years.

Age.	Initial Value.	Diff.
10	67.548	—3.801
11	67.802	3.843
12	68.089	3.885
13	68.451	3.938
14	68.740	3.993
15	69.063	3.954
16	69.413	4.118
17	69.816	4.182
18	70.270	4.256
19	70.710	4.328
20	71.198	4.403
21	71.762	4.485
22	72.376	4.568
23	73.064	4.659
24	73.804	4.751
25	74.654	4.851
26	76.562	4.950
27	76.568	5.058
28	77.683	5.165
29	78.911	5.269
30	80.293	5.380

THIRTY-FIRST YEAR.

In 35 Years.

Age.	Initial Value.	Diff.
10	761.195	+28.267
11	761.077	28.226
12	761.061	28.154
13	761.033	28.033
14	761.005	27.983
15	761.068	27.868
16	761.056	27.735
17	761.134	27.594
18	761.128	27.419
19	761.172	27.258
20	761.259	27.075
21	761.293	+26.873
22	761.448	26.661
23	761.538	26.411
24	761.580	26.168
25	761.708	25.859
26	761.843	25.545
27	761.948	25.230
28	762.134	24.869
29	762.327	24.460
30	762.533	24.021
31	762.730	23.565
32	763.050	+23.020
33	763.341	22.436
34	763.768	21.785
35	764.128	21.104

In 40 Years.

Age.	Initial Value.	Diff.
10	580.530	+19.062
11	580.803	+18.976
12	581.105	18.874
13	581.523	18.752
14	581.979	18.613
15	582.477	18.423
16	583.251	18.207
17	583.985	17.983
18	584.777	17.704
19	585.587	17.457
20	586.568	17.144
21	587.612	16.822
22	588.687	+16.471
23	589.952	16.071
24	591.166	15.658
25	592.753	15.216
26	594.295	14.733
27	596.105	14.230
28	598.235	13.749
29	600.327	13.150
30	602.497	12.420

THIRTIETH YEAR.

In 35 Years.

Age.	Initial Value.	Diff.
10	716.930	+26.069
11	716.831	26.027
12	716.798	25.956
13	716.770	25.886
14	716.771	25.782
15	716.861	25.673
16	716.887	25.528
17	717.031	25.385
18	717.083	25.206
19	717.222	25.010
20	717.389	24.810
21	717.511	+24.584
22	717.767	24.353
23	717.978	24.093
24	718.142	23.803
25	718.397	23.488
26	718.675	23.149
27	718.934	22.783
28	719.294	22.400
29	719.661	21.959
30	720.062	21.490
31	720.487	20.993
32	721.041	+20.424
33	721.615	19.790
34	722.343	19.096
35	723.024	18.365

In 40 Years.

Age.	Initial Value.	Diff.
10	547.455	+17.464
11	547.728	+17.392
12	548.048	17.296
13	548.477	17.194
14	548.997	17.074
15	549.557	16.913
16	550.404	16.723
17	551.249	16.505
18	552.143	16.243
19	553.117	15.984
20	554.242	15.688
21	555.440	15.374
22	556.683	+15.034
23	558.133	14.663
24	559.569	14.241
25	561.353	13.824
26	563.132	13.350
27	565.189	12.853
28	567.532	12.320
29	569.902	11.649
30	572.378	11.136

SEVENTH YEAR.—ENDOWMENT POLICIES.—4 PER CENT.—(Arranged by Terms.)

In 10 Years.

Age.	Initial Value.	Diff.
10	627.701	+22.666
11	627.709	22.639
12	627.685	22.613
13	627.666	22.587
14	627.628	22.554
15	627.624	22.525
16	627.567	22.492
17	627.535	22.455
18	627.478	22.415
19	627.437	22.377
20	627.382	22.333
21	627.329	22.287
22	627.275	22.239
23	627.231	22.189
24	627.167	22.132
25	627.135	22.076
26	627.104	22.009
27	626.923	21.946
28	626.834	21.878
29	626.745	21.806
30	626.649	21.729
31	626.585	21.652
32	626.429	21.569
33	626.313	21.484
34	626.190	21.396
35	626.081	21.302
36	625.984	21.195
37	625.914	21.066
38	625.864	20.903
39	625.816	20.717
40	625.763	20.479
41	625.676	20.241
42	625.518	19.966
43	625.310	19.665
44	625.063	19.334
45	624.759	18.971
46	624.417	18.569
47	624.020	18.128
48	623.628	17.658
49	623.174	17.134
50	622.679	16.549
51	622.137	15.945
52	621.566	15.281
53	620.960	14.544
54	620.349	13.713
55	619.734	12.806
56	618.968	11.791
57	618.198	10.685
58	617.341	9.459
59	616.430	8.106
60	615.397	6.619

In 15 Years.

Age.	Initial Value.	Diff.
10	371.962	+10.555
11	371.981	+10.519
12	372.008	10.474
13	371.981	10.428
14	371.961	10.366
15	371.957	10.322
16	371.907	10.265
17	371.881	10.202
18	371.840	10.135
19	371.789	10.058
20	371.753	9.994
21	371.701	9.916
22	371.654	9.834
23	371.597	9.745
24	371.542	9.647
25	371.476	9.549
26	371.404	9.440
27	371.308	9.329
28	371.217	9.213
29	371.116	9.188
30	371.007	8.957
31	370.902	8.846
32	370.824	8.686
33	370.756	8.542
34	370.730	8.396
35	370.755	8.240
36	370.870	8.070
37	371.052	7.855
38	371.292	7.587
39	371.571	7.278
40	371.826	6.897
41	372.055	6.483
42	372.204	6.022
43	372.283	5.520
44	372.305	4.966
45	372.280	4.358
46	372.231	3.689
47	372.169	2.956
48	372.039	2.170
49	372.055	1.307
50	372.027	.367
51	372.010	—.634
52	372.051	1.732
53	372.167	2.929
54	372.360	4.285
55	372.601	5.743

In 20 Years.

Age.	Initial Value.	Diff.
10	247.747	+4.675
11	247.800	4.632
12	247.858	4.575
13	247.884	4.526
14	247.916	4.466
15	247.926	4.405
16	247.941	+4.337
17	247.947	4.262
18	247.960	4.185
19	247.959	4.107
20	247.958	4.019
21	247.963	3.929
22	247.970	3.829
23	247.964	3.726
24	247.971	3.613
25	247.952	3.497
26	247.954	3.370
27	247.938	3.239
28	247.940	3.105
29	247.977	2.962
30	248.010	2.812
31	248.086	2.664
32	248.224	2.506
33	248.429	2.347
34	248.719	2.181
35	249.093	2.017
36	249.595	1.905
37	250.253	1.592
38	250.950	1.292
39	251.852	.950
40	252.572	.514
41	253.377	.045
42	254.128	—.477
43	254.850	1.045
44	255.541	1.671
45	256.253	2.357
46	257.011	3.110
47	257.833	3.932
48	258.753	4.805
49	259.785	5.770
50	260.939	6.812
1	262.23	7.91
2	263.71	9.12

In 25 Years.

Age.	Initial Value.	Diff.
10	176.145	+1.280
11	176.235	1.240
12	176.329	1.184
13	176.412	1.127
14	176.490	1.062
15	176.595	.995
16	176.640	.927
17	176.720	.847
18	176.783	.765
19	176.859	.681
20	176.934	.591
21	177.006	.494
22	177.092	.390
23	177.201	.280
24	177.317	.163
25	177.427	.041
26	177.588	—.090
27	177.762	.227
28	177.977	.362
29	178.233	.508
30	178.551	.658
31	178.947	.802
32	179.422	.962
33	180.104	1.119
34	180.764	1.270
35	181.605	1.435
36	182.606	1.618
37	183.804	1.852
38	185.157	2.149
39	186.587	2.501
40	188.134	2.935
41	189.640	3.413
42	191.118	3.939
43	192.816	4.514
44	194.423	5.146
45	196.177	5.835

In 30 Years.

Age.	Initial Value.	Diff.
10	130.780	—.865
11	131.018	.911
12	131.139	.967
13	131.227	1.021
14	131.373	1.085
15	131.531	1.153
16	131.661	1.224
17	131.829	1.303
18	131.968	1.387
19	132.157	1.469
20	132.342	1.563
21	132.611	1.654
22	132.793	1.761
23	133.053	1.866
24	133.355	1.983
25	133.698	2.100
26	134.099	2.230
27	134.535	2.359
28	135.002	2.490
29	135.647	2.617
30	136.303	2.768
31	137.111	2.902
32	138.018	3.051
33	139.081	3.191
34	140.324	3.329
35	141.721	3.476
36	143.372	3.538
37	145.217	3.852
38	147.344	4.133
39	149.422	4.460
40	151.827	4.877
1/3	159.32	6.39

In 35 Years.

Age.	Initial Value.	Diff.
10	100.391	—2.303
11	100.591	2.341
12	100.789	2.402
13	101.077	2.453
14	101.290	2.519
15	101.530	2.586
16	101.768	2.654
17	102.056	2.731
18	102.332	2.810
19	102.660	2.888
20	103.025	2.976
21	103.419	3.068
22	104.079	3.164
23	104.361	3.263
24	104.945	3.370
25	105.550	3.480
26	106.253	3.598
27	107.023	3.716
28	107.902	3.833
29	108.870	3.959
30	110.018	4.083
31	111.235	4.199
32	112.663	4.327
33	114.270	4.448
34	116.074	4.563
35	118.142	4.682

In 40 Years.

Age.	Initial Value.	Diff.
10	79.320	—3.298
11	79.613	3.339
12	79.936	3.391
13	80.267	3.444
14	80.659	3.505
15	81.015	3.565
16	81.409	3.628
17	81.865	3.699
18	82.388	3.771
19	82.870	3.841
20	83.434	3.921
21	84.075	4.002
22	84.777	4.091
23	85.561	4.179
24	86.409	4.276
25	87.380	4.371
26	88.426	4.475
27	89.583	4.578
28	90.870	4.676
29	92.298	4.783
30	93.900	4.887

TWENTY-NINTH YEAR.

In 30 Years.

Age.	Initial Value.	Diff.
10	904.019	+35.537
11	903.999	35.523
12	903.934	35.507
13	903.894	35.506
14	903.843	35.494
15	903.823	35.464
16	903.751	35.443
17	903.722	35.418
18	903.663	35.375
19	903.635	35.324
20	903.599	35.269
21	903.529	35.208
22	903.494	35.144
23	903.414	35.092
24	903.330	35.044
25	903.288	34.846
26	903.222	34.858
27	903.142	+34.777
28	903.080	34.673
29	902.963	34.590
30	902.869	34.489
31	902.781	34.322
32	902.638	34.191
33	902.520	34.023
34	902.379	33.870
35	902.242	33.646
36	902.068	33.475
37	901.879	33.234
38	901.721	32.948
39	901.509	32.676
40	901.162	32.350

In 35 Years.

Age.	Initial Value.	Diff.
10	674.720	+23.997
11	674.654	23.939
12	674.610	23.877
13	674.598	23.795
14	674.613	23.706
15	674.725	23.592
16	674.783	23.463
17	674.985	23.328
18	675.109	23.135
19	675.346	22.936
20	675.610	22.719
21	675.835	22.488
22	676.200	22.239
23	676.544	21.967
24	676.837	21.673
25	677.244	21.321
26	677.679	20.978
27	678.099	+20.604
28	678.669	20.185
29	679.231	19.730
30	679.840	19.249
31	680.498	18.740
32	681.315	18.141
33	682.176	17.503
34	683.231	16.810
35	684.248	16.017

In 40 Years.

Age.	Initial Value.	Diff.
10	515.864	+15.985
11	516.160	15.890
12	516.485	15.807
13	516.933	15.711
14	517.473	+15.616
15	518.074	15.477
16	518.972	15.308
17	519.900	15.118
18	520.901	14.870
19	521.998	14.629
20	523.270	14.334
21	524.604	14.038
22	526.008	13.705
23	527.625	13.352
24	529.261	12.952
25	531.239	12.540
26	533.221	12.098
27	535.507	11.619
28	538.140	11.084
29	540.790	10.540
30	543.437	9.840

EIGHTH YEAR.—ENDOWMENT POLICIES.—4 PER CENT.—(Arranged by Terms.)

In 10 Years.

Age.	Initial Value.	Diff.
10	733.875	+27.671
11	733.885	27.655
12	733.858	27.635
13	733.838	27.613
14	733.798	27.592
15	733.801	27.572
16	733.746	27.545
17	733.717	27.518
18	733.661	27.490
19	733.628	27.461
20	733.578	27.429
21	733.529	27.396
22	733.481	27.361
23	733.444	27.322
24	733.386	27.282
25	733.370	27.240
26	733.231	27.193
27	733.158	27.146
28	733.080	27.096
29	733.001	27.042
30	732.914	26.987
31	732.863	26.934
32	732.719	26.873
33	732.617	26.813
34	732.509	26.745
35	732.415	26.671
36	732.329	26.581
37	732.258	26.468
38	732.187	26.339
39	732.113	26.183
40	732.005	26.010
41	731.893	25.821
42	731.707	25.613
43	731.487	25.384
44	731.236	25.134
45	730.936	24.856
46	730.601	24.549
47	730.206	24.220
48	729.833	23.857
49	729.385	23.459
50	728.884	23.033
51	728.379	22.564
52	727.824	22.050
53	727.232	21.467
54	726.611	20.828
55	725.989	20.122
56	725.193	19.341
57	724.398	18.481
58	723.507	17.524
59	722.558	16.477
60	721.488	15.312

In 15 Years.

Age.	Initial Value.	Diff.
10	434.353	+13.475
11	434.364	+13.436
12	434.379	13.395
13	434.340	13.347
14	434.304	13.287
15	434.291	13.249
16	434.227	13.191
17	434.187	13.131
18	434.131	13.070
19	434.057	13.002
20	434.017	12.933
21	433.949	12.856
22	433.884	12.777
23	433.810	12.689
24	433.731	12.600
25	433.645	12.501
26	433.547	12.400
27	433.427	12.296
28	433.313	12.185
29	433.184	12.064
30	433.047	11.943
31	432.920	11.816
32	432.820	11.685
33	432.733	11.551
34	432.697	11.408
35	432.715	11.249
36	432.826	11.058
37	432.976	10.814
38	433.154	10.533
39	433.357	10.189
40	433.492	9.816
41	433.606	9.402
42	433.632	8.950
43	433.594	8.450
44	433.492	7.900
45	433.336	7.294
46	433.145	6.629
47	432.924	5.918
48	432.627	5.124
49	432.471	4.272
50	432.253	3.362
51	432.054	2.359
52	431.893	1.266
53	431.793	.036
54	431.712	—1.307
55	431.662	2.792

In 20 Years.

Age.	Initial Value.	Diff.
10	288.870	+6.579
11	288.916	6.531
12	288.957	6.481
13	288.976	6.422
14	288.995	6.362
15	288.994	6.300
16	288.995	+6.230
17	288.983	6.156
18	288.982	6.082
19	288.968	5.998
20	288.949	5.912
21	288.937	5.816
22	288.922	5.722
23	288.895	5.612
24	288.879	5.502
25	288.833	5.380
26	288.807	5.256
27	288.764	5.128
28	288.744	4.990
29	288.758	4.848
30	288.772	4.705
31	288.840	4.554
32	288.974	4.400
33	289.188	4.247
34	289.497	4.083
35	289.909	3.902
36	290.506	3.701
37	291.110	3.392
38	291.796	3.061
39	292.668	2.659
40	293.299	2.210
41	294.027	1.719
42	294.693	1.183
43	295.338	.590
44	295.947	—.060
45	296.574	.782
46	297.241	1.558
47	297.962	2.391
48	298.798	3.311
49	299.726	4.306
50	300.780	5.357
1 (handwritten)	302.00	6.81
2 (handwritten)	303.40	7.72

In 25 Years.

Age.	Initial Value.	Diff.
10	204.915	+2.601
11	205.095	2.550
12	205.179	2.498
13	205.256	2.434
14	205.324	2.369
15	205.422	2.255
16	205.462	2.224
17	205.531	2.147
18	205.582	2.065
19	205.653	1.977
20	205.719	1.886
21	205.779	1.782
22	205.852	1.676
23	205.950	1.562
24	206.054	1.444
25	206.152	1.314
26	206.305	+1.184
27	206.473	1.051
28	206.696	.908
29	206.960	.761
30	207.297	.618
31	207.733	.464
32	208.249	.312
33	209.005	.159
34	209.751	.006
35	210.692	—.173
36	211.812	.403
37	213.092	.687
38	214.511	1.022
39	215.997	1.444
40	217.547	1.901
41	219.064	2.407
42	220.560	2.957
43	222.295	3.561
44	223.951	4.228
45	225.761	4.955

In 30 Years.

Age.	Initial Value.	Diff.
10	151.876	+.083
11	152.115	.018
12	152.235	—.027
13	152.329	.086
14	152.475	.153
15	152.636	.222
16	152.767	.300
17	152.937	.379
18	153.075	.463
19	153.274	.551
20	153.462	.656
21	153.751	.742
22	153.931	.850
23	154.206	.965
24	154.521	1.080
25	154.888	1.206
26	155.314	1.332
27	155.787	1.460
28	156.300	1.599
29	157.006	1.732
30	157.741	1.866
31	158.653	2.009
32	159.668	2.149
33	160.873	2.283
34	162.289	2.424
35	163.876	2.582
36	165.740	2.788
37	167.780	3.058
38	170.087	3.376
39	172.320	3.777
40	174.867	4.215
3 (handwritten)	182.87	5.80

In 35 Years.

Age.	Initial Value.	Diff.
10	116.282	—1.593
11	116.495	1.654
12	116.696	1.710
13	117.003	1.770
14	117.233	1.836
15	117.488	1.902
16	117.745	1.977
17	118.053	2.055
18	118.351	2.133
19	118.712	2.218
20	119.109	2.308
21	119.539	2.403
22	120.043	2.499
23	120.575	2.608
24	121.218	2.712
25	121.887	2.830
26	122.667	2.945
27	123.528	3.058
28	124.519	3.180
29	125.607	3.302
30	126.924	3.416
31	128.292	3.538
32	129.921	3.655
33	131.758	3.765
34	133.829	3.880
35	136.200	4.006

In 40 Years.

Age.	Initial Value.	Diff.
10	91.605	—2.772
11	91.928	2.822
12	92.205	2.874
13	92.649	2.933
14	93.060	2.994
15	93.456	3.052
16	93.895	3.122
17	94.397	3.191
18	94.981	3.261
19	95.529	3.337
20	96.152	3.417
21	96.871	3.504
22	97.655	3.589
23	98.538	3.684
24	99.489	3.777
25	100.586	3.877
26	101.765	3.976
27	103.078	4.071
28	104.546	4.174
29	106.161	4.274
30	107.990	4.353

TWENTY-EIGHTH YEAR.

In 30 Years.

Age.	Initial Value.	Diff.
10	849.235	+32.808
11	849.174	32.765
12	849.111	32.749
13	849.024	32.737
14	848.940	32.706
15	848.901	32.674
16	848.807	32.604
17	848.758	32.563
18	848.660	32.499
19	848.643	32.416
20	848.592	32.334
21	848.496	32.229
22	848.465	32.130
23	848.366	32.019
24	848.270	31.902
25	848.195	31.793
26	848.259	31.611
27	848.053	+31.468
28	847.993	31.279
29	847.850	31.125
30	847.556	30.910
31	847.618	30.729
32	847.487	30.440
33	847.351	30.176
34	847.211	29.884
35	847.051	29.550
36	846.886	29.196
37	846.669	28.785
38	846.499	28.344
39	846.267	27.878
40	846.025	27.326

In 35 Years.

Age.	Initial Value.	Diff.
10	634.503	+22.048
11	634.424	21.983
12	634.403	21.899
13	634.390	21.827
14	634.425	21.736
15	634.537	21.644
16	634.630	21.512
17	634.884	21.383
18	635.072	21.208
19	635.396	21.010
20	635.756	20.794
21	636.108	20.539
22	636.584	20.288
23	637.053	19.914
24	637.476	19.722
25	638.001	19.372
26	638.663	19.002

In 35 Years.

Age.	Initial Value.	Diff.
27	639.260	+18.618
28	640.020	18.199
29	640.802	17.724
30	641.513	17.235
31	642.509	16.731
32	643.590	16.220
33	644.759	15.481
34	646.221	14.783
35	647.491	14.018

In 40 Years.

Age.	Initial Value.	Diff.
10	485.728	+14.577
11	486.049	14.480
12	486.395	14.380
13	486.812	14.297
14	487.357	+14.208
15	487.974	14.094
16	488.892	13.956
17	489.867	13.802
18	490.960	13.578
19	492.168	13.346
20	493.558	13.074
21	495.026	12.780
22	496.570	12.468
23	498.340	12.129
24	500.143	11.762
25	502.240	11.424
26	504.482	10.926
27	506.956	10.478
28	509.821	9.971
29	512.697	9.433
30	515.554	8.892

NINTH YEAR.—ENDOWMENT POLICIES.—4 PER CENT.—(Arranged by Terms.)

In 10 Years.

Age.	Initial Value.	Diff.
10	845.060	+32.932
11	845.077	32.923
12	845.053	32.912
13	845.038	32.902
14	845.006	32.890
15	845.025	32.878
16	844.978	32.862
17	844.962	32.849
18	844.919	32.833
19	844.903	32.817
20	844.870	32.800
21	844.838	32.782
22	844.809	32.761
23	844.790	32.740
24	844.755	32.717
25	844.759	32.698
26	844.642	32.669
27	844.595	32.645
28	844.544	32.615
29	844.493	32.584
30	844.437	32.558
31	844.423	32.520
32	844.313	32.498
33	844.250	32.459
34	844.177	32.422
35	844.119	32.375
36	844.060	32.317
37	844.004	32.250
38	843.946	32.168
39	843.876	32.078
40	843.778	31.980
41	843.690	31.874
42	843.543	31.754
43	843.383	31.624
44	843.209	31.479
45	842.998	31.320
46	842.765	31.150
47	842.484	30.958
48	842.237	30.752
49	841.921	30.529
50	841.573	30.282
51	841.231	30.015
52	840.851	29.708
53	840.427	29.371
54	839.988	28.998
55	839.560	28.594
56	838.968	28.134
57	838.394	27.630
58	837.738	27.073
59	837.057	26.457
60	836.272	25.776

In 15 Years.

Age.	Initial Value.	Diff.
10	499.664	+16.536
11	499.664	+16.500
12	499.671	16.459
13	499.618	16.415
14	499.570	16.358
15	499.552	16.321
16	499.473	16.267
17	499.422	16.213
18	499.359	16.156
19	499.269	16.091
20	499.220	16.024
21	499.137	15.953
22	499.059	15.876
23	498.967	15.796
24	498.873	15.709
25	498.766	15.620
26	498.650	15.527
27	498.513	15.427
28	498.379	15.321
29	498.228	15.213
30	498.073	15.100
31	497.928	14.982
32	497.815	14.863
33	497.719	14.735
34	497.676	14.593
35	497.684	14.418
36	497.770	14.203
37	497.859	13.953
38	497.962	13.648
39	498.054	13.318
40	498.077	12.951
41	498.076	12.553
42	497.988	12.111
43	497.835	11.624
44	497.613	10.087
45	497.328	10.496
46	496.999	9.863
47	496.641	9.159
48	496.169	8.388
49	495.852	7.579
50	495.474	6.683
51	495.091	5.704
52	494.733	4.601
53	494.384	3.398
54	494.032	2.063
55	493.674	.611

In 20 Years.

Age.	Initial Value.	Diff.
10	331.897	+8.571
11	331.931	8.524
12	331.962	8.470
13	331.964	8.413
14	331.970	8.355
15	331.957	8.288
16	331.942	+8.219
17	331.913	8.149
18	331.901	8.071
19	331.868	7.989
20	331.833	7.899
21	331.798	7.808
22	331.767	7.706
23	331.712	7.601
24	331.672	7.487
25	331.597	7.368
26	331.546	7.247
27	331.479	7.116
28	331.433	6.980
29	331.425	6.845
30	331.427	6.700
31	331.484	6.555
32	331.618	6.406
33	331.847	6.250
34	332.177	6.077
35	332.610	5.861
36	333.210	5.619
37	333.777	5.289
38	334.411	4.894
39	335.193	4.484
40	335.722	4.014
41	336.351	3.512
42	336.918	2.955
43	337.461	2.343
44	337.964	1.667
45	338.470	.926
46	339.023	.137
47	339.632	—.736
48	340.337	1.681
49	341.131	2.681
50	342.076	3.776

In 25 Years.

Age.	Initial Value.	Diff.
10	235.187	+3.977
11	235.265	3.928
12	235.343	3.867
13	235.407	3.802
14	235.465	3.738
15	235.558	3.668
16	235.581	3.590
17	235.642	3.512
18	235.681	3.427
19	235.743	3.347
20	235.799	3.240
21	235.840	3.135
22	235.898	3.021
23	235.981	2.912
24	236.072	2.785
25	236.150	2.658
26	236.296	+2.527
27	236.462	2.389
28	236.685	2.246
29	236.956	2.107
30	237.319	1.955
31	237.785	1.807
32	238.350	1.659
33	239.184	1.504
34	240.014	1.337
35	241.041	1.114
36	242.233	.835
37	243.545	.509
38	244.992	.108
39	246.464	—.334
40	247.984	.818
41	249.494	1.347
42	250.986	1.924
43	252.727	2.559
44	254.407	3.266
45	256.225	4.032

In 30 Years.

Age.	Initial Value.	Diff.
10	173.918	+1.066
11	174.153	1.012
12	174.275	.951
13	174.366	.881
14	174.509	.823
15	174.672	.750
16	174.797	.671
17	174.969	.591
18	175.106	.501
19	175.309	.410
20	175.499	.312
21	175.803	.216
22	175.980	.098
23	176.260	—.016
24	176.590	.140
25	176.972	.265
26	177.427	.386
27	177.938	.523
28	178.489	.661
29	179.260	.786
30	180.081	.931
31	181.088	1.065
32	182.220	1.195
33	183.573	1.335
34	185.159	1.488
35	186.925	1.689
36	188.958	1.951
37	191.137	2.256
38	193.487	2.647
39	195.901	3.070
40	198.569	3.537

In 35 Years.

Age.	Initial Value.	Diff.
10	132.872	—.880
11	133.086	.928
12	133.295	.995
13	133.612	1.065
14	133.859	1.119
15	134.130	1.192
16	134.399	1.269
17	124.726	1.345
18	135.047	1.430
19	135.434	1.519
20	135.861	1.615
21	136.324	1.706
22	136.872	1.811
23	137.444	1.918
24	138.149	2.030
25	138.874	2.144
26	139.734	2.255
27	140.691	2.375
28	141.789	2.493
29	143.001	2.607
30	144.455	2.727
31	146.010	2.837
32	147.851	2.946
33	149.929	3.054
34	152.267	3.180
35	154.933	3.349

In 40 Years.

Age.	Initial Value.	Diff.
10	104.417	—2.230
11	104.688	2.281
12	105.063	2.339
13	105.542	2.397
14	105.985	2.457
15	106.410	2.522
16	106.887	2.591
17	107.437	2.658
18	108.084	2.735
19	108.686	2.811
20	109.374	2.896
21	110.165	2.980
22	111.035	3.074
23	112.010	3.163
24	113.068	3.263
25	114.286	3.358
26	115.603	3.450
27	117.080	3.550
28	118.724	3.646
29	120.543	3.733
30	122.624	3.825

TWENTY-SEVENTH YEAR.

In 30 Years.

Age.	Initial Value.	Diff.
10	797.038	+30.218
11	796.965	30.186
12	796.887	30.138
13	796.782	30.109
14	796.666	30.077
15	796.617	30.036
16	796.501	29.966
17	796.455	29.902
18	796.341	29.815
19	796.329	29.728
20	796.294	29.625
21	796.201	29.491
22	796.207	29.359
23	796.129	29.208
24	796.067	29.044
25	796.013	28.882
26	796.115	28.693
27	795.961	+28.371
28	795.947	28.238
29	795.737	28.029
30	795.791	27.743
31	795.724	27.460
32	795.597	27.179
33	795.558	26.800
34	795.516	26.411
35	795.427	25.983
36	795.360	25.530
37	795.228	25.016
38	795.179	24.425
39	795.062	23.854
40	794.970	23.118

In 35 Years.

Age.	Initial Value.	Diff.
10	596.099	+20.198
11	596.055	20.126
12	596.043	20.045
13	596.051	19.961
14	596.104	19.869
15	596.216	19.787
16	596.307	19.672
17	596.613	19.543
18	596.850	19.393
19	597.248	19.208
20	597.711	18.985
21	598.171	18.749
22	598.767	18.489
23	599.368	18.208
24	599.929	17.913
25	600.657	17.573
26	601.425	17.218
27	602.228	+16.811
28	603.172	16.398
29	604.170	15.929
30	605.225	15.428
31	606.333	14.922
32	607.670	14.335
33	609.113	13.710
34	610.787	13.009
35	612.489	12.263

In 40 Years.

Age.	Initial Value.	Diff.
10	456.877	+13.233
11	457.208	13.151
12	457.582	13.046
13	458.030	12.964
14	458.580	+12.869
15	459.201	13.767
16	460.109	12.659
17	461.114	12.522
18	462.359	12.234
19	463.657	12.149
20	465.030	11.890
21	466.613	11.615
22	468.290	11.310
23	470.191	10.993
24	472.143	10.644
25	474.449	10.212
26	476.806	9.863
27	479.467	9.416
28	482.495	8.953
29	485.527	8.444
30	488.573	7.882

TENTH YEAR.—ENDOWMENT POLICIES.—4 PER CENT.—(Arranged by Terms.)

In 15 Years.

Age.	Initial Value.	Diff.
10	568.036	+19.751
11	568.028	19.715
12	568.027	19.680
13	567.964	19.641
14	567.908	19.583
15	567.885	19.552
16	567.795	19.505
17	567.739	19.454
18	567.661	19.400
19	567.570	19.341
20	567.514	19.282
21	567.422	19.214
22	567.333	19.146
23	567.231	19.070
24	567.124	18.994
25	567.006	18.914
26	566.880	18.828
27	566.730	18.735
28	566.583	18.642
29	566.421	18.545
30	566.256	18.443
31	566.102	18.338
32	565.988	18.227
33	565.889	18.103
34	565.840	17.951
35	565.822	17.762
36	565.859	17.547
37	565.881	17.284
38	565.885	16.998
39	565.880	16.683
40	565.797	16.438
41	565.697	15.960
42	565.505	15.541
43	565.250	15.078
44	564.921	14.567
45	564.522	14.020
46	564.087	13.410
47	563.599	12.746
48	562.975	12.031
49	562.540	11.256
50	562.016	10.405
51	561.473	9.442
52	560.908	8.391
53	560.339	7.224
54	559.722	+5.955
55	559.089	4.650

In 20 Years.

Age.	Initial Value.	Diff.
10	376.916	+10.663
11	376.939	10.612
12	376.956	10.569
13	376.943	10.506
14	376.938	10.444
15	376.908	10.379
16	376.878	10.314
17	376.836	10.240
18	376.809	10.164
19	376.759	10.080
20	376.704	10.002
21	376.651	9.898
22	376.596	9.800
23	376.518	9.692
24	376.452	9.582
25	376.349	9.468
26	376.276	9.345
27	376.182	9.216
28	376.112	9.087
29	376.089	8.952
30	376.097	8.791
31	376.127	8.634
32	376.268	8.522
33	376.509	8.358
34	376.851	8.155
35	377.270	7.899
36	377.830	7.635
37	378.331	7.245
38	378.859	6.860
39	379.543	6.424
40	379.949	5.949
41	380.468	5.430
42	380.915	4.857
43	381.337	4.226
44	381.708	3.530
45	382.074	2.787
46	382.500	1.965
47	382.957	+1.073
48	383.406	.129
49	384.141	—.912
50	384.953	2.031

In 25 Years.

Age.	Initial Value.	Diff.
10	265.741	+5.416
11	266.813	5.364
12	266.876	5.305
13	266.926	5.243
14	266.971	5.170
15	267.058	5.101
16	267.066	5.026
17	267.118	4.945
18	267.142	4.867
19	267.193	4.764
20	267.233	4.665
21	267.254	4.555
22	267.289	4.444
23	267.362	4.323
24	267.421	4.200
25	267.492	4.074
26	267.630	3.939
27	267.789	3.799
28	268.012	3.666
29	268.298	3.513
30	268.678	3.371
31	269.180	3.230
32	269.798	3.073
33	270.708	2.909
34	271.608	2.697
35	272.677	2.428
36	273.892	2.113
37	275.204	1.725
38	276.603	1.304
39	278.041	.834
40	279.504	.332
41	280.984	—.226
42	282.451	.833
43	284.161	1.507
44	285.825	2.249
45	287.612	3.030

In 30 Years.

Age.	Initial Value.	Diff.
10	196.944	+2.099
11	197.170	2.038
12	197.294	1.979
13	197.380	1.917
14	197.519	1.844
15	197.680	1.769
16	197.798	1.692
17	197.971	1.605
18	198.101	1.514
19	198.305	1.414
20	198.494	1.320
21	198.813	1.215
22	198.977	1.097
23	199.263	.976
24	199.599	.853
25	199.997	.732
26	200.486	.597
27	201.026	.464
28	201.616	.334
29	202.460	.199
30	203.356	.063
31	204.467	—.065
32	205.726	.202
33	207.221	.351
34	208.965	.548
35	210.867	.806
36	213.013	1.102
37	215.294	1.480
38	217.816	1.891
39	220.189	2.341
40	222.949	2.827

In 35 Years.

Age.	Initial Value.	Diff.
10	150.182	—.120
11	150.403	.176
12	150.589	.244
13	150.936	.301
14	151.202	.375
15	151.482	.448
16	151.761	.525
17	152.109	.605
18	152.246	—.692
19	152.855	.785
20	153.309	.880
21	153.806	.985
22	154.389	1.086
23	155.003	1.201
24	155.752	1.310
25	156.547	1.422
26	157.491	1.543
27	158.537	1.657
28	159.746	1.766
29	161.100	1.887
30	162.700	1.996
31	164.429	2.099
32	166.490	2.210
33	168.811	2.328
34	171.405	2.496
35	174.323	2.716

In 40 Years.

Age.	Initial Value.	Diff.
10	117.766	—1.663
11	118.653	1.719
12	118.548	1.778
13	118.971	1.834
14	119.439	1.903
15	119.894	1.965
16	120.410	2.035
17	121.010	2.106
18	121.623	2.185
19	122.369	2.266
20	123.117	2.350
21	123.983	2.441
22	124.930	2.531
23	126.003	2.627
24	127.161	2.723
25	128.505	2.811
26	129.957	2.909
27	131.603	3.003
28	133.430	3.087
29	135.466	3.183
30	137.786	3.257

TWENTY-SIXTH YEAR.

In 30 Years.

Age.	Initial Value.	Diff.
10	747.277	+27.791
11	747.211	27.733
12	747.130	27.686
13	747.012	27.637
14	746.880	27.589
15	746.822	27.547
16	746.685	27.476
17	746.668	27.386
18	746.505	27.332
19	746.520	27.223
20	746.513	27.098
21	746.432	26.965
22	746.509	26.799
23	746.481	26.619
24	746.480	26.428
25	746.484	26.229
26	746.646	26.022
27	746.559	+25.681
28	746.649	25.490
29	746.615	25.238
30	746.663	24.917
31	746.697	24.593
32	746.671	24.195
33	746.716	23.849
34	746.842	23.390
35	746.885	22.901
36	747.001	22.363
37	747.023	21.780
38	747.213	21.096
39	747.295	20.415
40	747.413	19.634

In 35 Years.

Age.	Initial Value.	Diff.
10	559.447	+18.453
11	559.429	18.383
12	559.437	18.296
13	559.466	18.200
14	559.568	18.104
15	559.660	18.012
16	559.765	17.911
17	560.081	17.805
18	560.354	17.667
19	560.806	17.502
20	561.343	17.308
21	561.909	17.074
22	562.613	16.824
23	563.352	16.549
24	564.045	16.258
25	564.925	15.909
26	565.850	15.533
27	566.834	+15.173
28	567.971	14.751
29	569.169	14.298
30	570.443	13.809
31	571.795	13.284
32	573.365	12.720
33	575.068	12.009
34	577.012	11.450
35	579.034	10.616

In 40 Years.

Age.	Initial Value.	Diff.
10	429.307	+11.971
11	429.662	11.875
12	430.047	11.786
13	430.520	11.682
14	431.077	+11.595
15	431.694	11.501
16	432.584	11.401
17	433.585	11.298
18	434.841	11.152
19	436.067	10.978
20	437.623	10.669
21	439.305	10.510
22	441.091	10.229
23	443.114	9.921
24	445.189	9.598
25	447.646	9.249
26	450.126	8.867
27	452.940	8.454
28	456.181	8.001
29	459.423	7.528
30	462.667	6.924

TWENTY-FIFTH YEAR.

In 30 Years.

Age.	Initial Value.	Diff.
10	699.826	+25.482
11	699.761	25.419
12	699.689	25.360
13	699.571	25.308
14	679.438	25.245
15	699.385	25.189
16	699.228	25.117
17	699.213	25.044
18	699.052	24.949
19	699.082	24.852
20	699.096	24.734
21	699.650	24.588
22	699.185	24.425
23	699.228	24.234
24	699.302	24.019
25	699.385	23.799
26	699.639	23.554
27	699.636	+23.302
28	699.836	23.005
29	699.926	22.701
30	700.091	22.348
31	700.264	21.989
32	700.387	21.583
33	700.537	21.150
34	700.871	20.687
35	701.084	20.160
36	701.413	19.592
37	701.655	18.953
38	702.080	18.250
39	702.428	17.516
40	702.841	16.655

In 35 Years.

Age.	Initial Value.	Diff.
10	524.451	+16.809
11	524.458	16.724
12	524.492	16.633
13	524.540	16.546
14	524.656	16.440
15	524.772	16.344
16	524.889	16.245
17	525.206	16.146
18	525.496	16.029
19	525.984	15.882
20	526.569	15.714
21	527.213	15.508
22	528.025	15.260
23	528.881	14.994
24	529.715	14.694
25	530.724	14.470
26	531.896	13.932
27	532.951	+13.662
28	534.268	13.253
29	535.676	12.791
30	537.144	12.328
31	538.713	11.824
32	540.527	11.253
33	542.460	10.672
34	544.659	10.029
35	546.950	9.345

In 40 Years.

Age.	Initial Value.	Diff.
10	402.941	+10.776
11	403.321	10.679
12	403.728	10.579
13	404.205	10.491
14	404.770	+10.399
15	405.392	10.276
16	406.254	10.216
17	407.244	10.110
18	408.483	9.996
19	409.720	9.863
20	411.287	9.698
21	413.034	9.473
22	414.916	9.205
23	417.034	8.924
24	419.223	8.610
25	421.781	8.288
26	424.381	7.932
27	427.320	7.547
28	430.703	7.125
29	434.086	6.661
30	437.480	6.204

ELEVENTH YEAR.—ENDOWMENT POLICIES.—4 PER CENT.—(Arranged by Terms.)

In 15 Years.

Age.	Initial Value.	Diff.
10	639.623	+23.127
11	639.607	23.096
12	639.604	23.067
13	639.536	23.030
14	639.473	22.976
15	639.449	22.955
16	639.355	22.911
17	639.297	22.861
18	639.217	22.818
19	639.121	22.769
20	639.066	22.714
21	638.968	22.656
22	638.877	22.593
23	638.769	22.531
24	638.660	22.464
25	638.540	22.393
26	638.411	22.316
27	638.255	22.238
28	638.108	22.158
29	637.946	22.073
30	637.782	21.986
31	637.632	21.892
32	637.525	21.789
33	637.427	21.662
34	637.362	21.506
35	637.304	21.324
36	637.292	21.106
37	637.234	20.868
38	637.158	20.606
39	637.071	20.324
40	636.904	20.007
41	636.725	19.663
42	636.452	19.279
43	636.119	18.857
44	635.709	18.402
45	635.240	17.895
46	634.722	17.342
47	634.144	16.750
48	633.424	16.089
49	632.905	15.383
50	632.280	14.578
51	631.593	13.697
52	630.873	12.717
53	630.118	11.649
54	629.304	+10.466
55	628.443	9.163

In 20 Years.

Age.	Initial Value.	Diff.
10	424.027	+12.855
11	424.035	12.808
12	424.049	12.759
13	424.015	12.710
14	423.995	12.641
15	423.950	12.580
16	423.909	12.510
17	423.850	12.441
18	423.810	12.364
19	423.741	12.283
20	423.678	12.194
21	423.594	12.103
22	423.519	12.003
23	423.415	11.902
24	423.329	11.794
25	423.201	11.679
26	423.104	11.559
27	422.985	11.438
28	422.898	11.311
29	422.860	11.180
30	422.878	11.008
31	422.888	10.907
32	423.034	10.752
33	423.279	10.562
34	423.603	10.323
35	423.968	10.047
36	424.461	9.747
37	424.851	9.347
38	425.273	8.943
39	425.735	8.605
40	426.111	8.025
41	426.503	7.498
42	426.814	6.910
43	427.096	6.265
44	427.315	5.573
45	427.539	4.804
46	427.805	3.971
47	428.091	+3.086
48	428.485	2.115
49	428.960	1.060
50	429.575	—.125

In 25 Years.

Age.	Initial Value.	Diff.
10	299.742	+6.930
11	299.797	6.896
12	299.847	6.817
13	299.886	6.750
14	299.911	6.680
15	299.991	6.610
16	299.987	6.521
17	300.027	6.449
18	300.043	6.358
19	300.070	6.264
20	300.092	6.159
21	300.088	6.052
22	300.103	5.932
23	300.154	5.816
24	300.185	5.696
25	300.278	5.561
26	300.376	5.428
27	300.526	5.296
28	300.759	5.151
29	301.050	5.011
30	301.453	4.870
31	301.998	4.721
32	302.664	4.558
33	303.637	4.352
34	304.562	4.097
35	305.627	3.794
36	306.789	3.417
37	308.059	3.009
38	309.410	2.564
39	310.746	2.078
40	312.204	1.547
41	313.595	.962
42	315.003	.318
43	316.647	—.389
44	318.260	1.147
45	319.981	1.976

In 30 Years.

Age.	Initial Value.	Diff.
10	221.009	+3.180
11	221.210	3.117
12	221.341	3.053
13	221.420	2.989
14	221.550	2.914
15	221.707	2.842
16	221.820	2.757
17	221.987	2.672
18	222.109	2.574
19	222.304	2.478
20	222.497	2.369
21	222.822	2.264
22	222.973	2.141
23	223.258	2.017
24	223.601	1.899
25	224.019	1.779
26	224.528	1.638
27	225.101	1.508
28	225.738	1.370
29	226.645	1.249
30	227.625	1.112
31	228.846	.981
32	230.225	.832
33	231.853	.637
34	233.711	.388
35	235.692	.098
36	237.917	—.270
37	240.229	.669
38	242.801	1.111
39	245.206	1.577
40	248.039	2.099

In 35 Years.

Age.	Initial Value.	Diff.
10	168.257	+.667
11	168.472	.612
12	168.774	.555
13	168.994	.481
14	169.289	.405
15	169.578	.333
16	169.867	.249
17	170.232	.168
18	170.583	+.074
19	171.010	—.018
20	171.489	.122
21	172.009	.222
22	172.631	.334
23	173.279	.446
24	174.075	.550
25	174.942	.671
26	175.964	.786
27	177.101	.896
28	178.430	1.013
29	179.919	1.123
30	181.671	1.227
31	183.586	1.328
32	185.865	1.450
33	188.419	1.613
34	191.237	1.831
35	194.346	2.099

In 40 Years.

Age.	Initial Value.	Diff.
10	131.694	—1.076
11	132.097	1.131
12	132.511	1.188
13	132.963	1.253
14	133.448	1.321
15	133.935	1.383
16	134.489	1.458
17	135.135	1.532
18	135.884	1.614
19	136.597	1.695
20	137.406	1.785
21	138.340	1.874
22	139.368	1.969
23	140.532	2.062
24	141.794	2.152
25	143.271	2.247
26	144.862	2.341
27	146.673	2.422
28	148.695	2.510
29	150.939	2.593
30	153.516	2.657

TWENTY-FOURTH YEAR.

In 25 Years.

Age.	Initial Value.	Diff.
10	898.607	+35.352
11	898.585	35.344
12	898.543	35.329
13	898.500	35.300
14	898.465	35.188
15	898.436	35.276
16	898.376	35.259
17	898.321	35.239
18	898.272	35.218
19	898.225	35.204
20	898.184	35.164
21	898.101	35.143
22	898.043	35.110
23	898.017	35.065
24	897.946	35.034
25	897.895	34.949
26	897.838	34.898
27	897.765	34.834
28	897.682	34.762
29	897.600	34.688
30	897.526	34.601
31	897.429	34.510
32	897.318	34.419
33	897.216	34.293
34	897.096	34.190
35	896.959	+34.069
36	896.814	33.895
37	896.622	33.761
38	896.470	33.573
39	896.236	33.390
40	896.040	33.166
41	895.688	32.905
42	895.505	32.674
43	895.185	32.358
44	894.849	32.006
45	894.414	31.710

In 30 Years.

Age.	Initial Value.	Diff.
10	654.558	+23.304
11	654.511	23.236
12	654.445	23.171
13	654.330	23.108
14	654.191	23.050
15	654.162	22.965
16	654.003	+22.885
17	653.985	22.817
18	653.822	22.726
19	653.870	22.626
20	653.901	22.512
21	653.882	22.374
22	654.083	22.203
23	654.194	22.015
24	654.349	21.804
25	654.521	21.564
26	654.876	21.308
27	654.981	21.034
28	655.301	20.727
29	655.518	20.423
30	655.846	20.031
31	656.162	19.658
32	656.449	19.237
33	656.826	18.764
34	657.297	18.290
35	657.694	17.749
36	658.247	17.160
37	658.739	16.501
38	659.425	15.773
39	660.048	15.020
40	660.788	14.136

In 35 Years.

Age.	Initial Value.	Diff.
10	491.022	+15.234
11	491.050	15.164
12	491.116	15.064
13	491.185	14.969
14	491.333	14.871
15	491.463	14.765
16	491.598	14.660
17	491.916	14.562
18	492.211	14.456
19	492.705	14.339
20	493.322	14.187
21	494.020	14.005
22	494.904	13.793
23	495.867	13.537
24	496.822	13.256
25	497.962	12.934
26	499.263	12.611
27	500.581	12.247
28	501.955	11.863
29	503.546	11.432
30	505.208	10.962
31	506.971	10.487
32	509.003	9.939
33	511.171	9.353
34	513.591	8.748
35	516.117	+8.094

In 40 Years.

Age.	Initial Value.	Diff.
10	377.712	+9.635
11	378.109	9.546
12	378.536	9.448
13	379.030	9.348
14	379.596	9.266
15	380.226	9.160
16	381.070	9.060
17	382.040	8.973
18	383.246	8.872
19	384.462	8.774
20	386.020	8.628
21	387.784	8.452
22	389.713	8.233
23	391.906	7.972
24	394.183	7.684
25	396.828	7.376
26	399.525	7.043
27	402.562	6.685
28	405.781	6.299
29	409.207	5.873
30	413.074	5.424

TWELFTH YEAR.—ENDOWMENT POLICIES.—4 PER CENT.—(Arranged by Terms.)

In 15 Years.

Age.	Initial Value.	Diff.
10	714.586	+26.675
11	714.567	26.652
12	714.568	26.626
13	714.497	26.595
14	714.432	26.548
15	714.416	26.534
16	714.321	26.497
17	714.268	26.462
18	714.191	26.422
19	714.100	26.378
20	714.050	26.338
21	713.956	26.285
22	713.868	26.237
23	713.768	26.185
24	713.666	26.130
25	713.553	26.070
26	713.430	26.010
27	713.283	25.947
28	713.149	25.882
29	712.999	25.799
30	712.851	25.740
31	712.716	25.658
32	712.624	25.560
33	712.524	25.436
34	712.439	25.295
35	712.348	25.125
36	712.284	24.940
37	712.171	24.735
38	712.039	24.514
39	711.903	24.271
40	711.680	24.001
41	711.456	23.705
42	711.137	23.376
43	710.767	23.023
44	710.332	22.628
45	709.833	22.196
46	709.289	21.734
47	708.693	21.221
48	707.931	20.653
49	707.397	20.027
50	706.717	19.335
51	705.968	18.565
52	705.164	17.721
53	704.322	16.788
54	703.397	+15.756
55	702.410	14.624

In 20 Years.

Age.	Initial Value.	Diff.
10	473.330	+15.160
11	473.327	15.115
12	473.332	15.064
13	473.291	15.009
14	473.249	14.953
15	473.193	14.890
16	473.136	14.826
17	473.065	14.756
18	473.011	14.682
19	472.926	14.600
20	472.844	14.516
21	472.742	14.424
22	472.645	14.330
23	472.522	14.232
24	472.416	14.128
25	472.264	14.016
26	472.146	13.905
27	472.010	13.786
28	471.908	13.665
29	471.859	13.543
30	471.836	13.306
31	471.885	13.266
32	472.030	13.089
33	472.253	12.868
34	472.523	12.614
35	472.814	12.302
36	473.230	11.974
37	473.473	11.591
38	473.770	11.197
39	474.106	10.859
40	474.349	10.266
41	474.606	9.729
42	474.766	9.136
43	474.894	8.502
44	474.965	7.791
45	475.021	7.022
46	475.116	6.204
47	475.238	+5.304
48	475.450	4.325
49	475.731	3.223
50	476.103	2.025

In 25 Years.

Age.	Initial Value.	Diff.
10	334.255	+8.517
11	334.313	8.465
12	334.330	8.405
13	334.353	8.334
14	334.369	8.267
15	334.433	8.198
16	334.411	8.113
17	334.440	8.029
18	334.435	7.937
19	334.447	7.835
20	334.445	7.734
21	334.419	7.621
22	334.465	7.509
23	334.439	7.394
24	334.445	7.265
25	334.532	7.132
26	334.611	7.007
27	334.760	6.870
28	334.991	6.722
29	335.296	6.593
30	335.727	6.451
31	336.307	6.295
32	337.011	6.087
33	338.007	5.841
34	338.916	5.553
35	339.942	5.187
36	341.020	4.799
37	342.208	4.369
38	343.477	3.908
39	344.725	3.396
40	346.099	2.844
41	347.394	2.223
42	348.705	1.551
43	350.251	.833
44	351.797	.027
45	353.414	—.832

In 30 Years.

Age.	Initial Value.	Diff.
10	246.154	+4.309
11	246.346	4.248
12	246.464	4.182
13	246.532	4.114
14	246.651	4.042
15	246.807	3.962
16	246.907	3.876
17	247.070	3.786
18	247.177	3.686
19	247.369	3.584
20	247.549	3.477
21	247.880	3.365
22	248.013	3.242
23	248.294	3.124
24	248.649	2.994
25	249.078	2.863
26	249.621	2.742
27	250.220	2.603
28	250.896	2.472
29	251.880	2.347
30	252.943	2.216
31	254.271	2.066
32	255.758	1.877
33	257.473	1.633
34	259.393	1.350
35	261.421	.990
36	263.653	.604
37	265.975	.174
38	268.564	—.287
39	270.987	.786
40	273.857	1.338

In 35 Years.

Age.	Initial Value.	Diff.
10	187.122	+1.495
11	187.329	1.439
12	187.617	1.373
13	187.874	1.301
14	188.158	1.226
15	188.455	1.149
16	188.747	1.064
17	189.128	.974
18	189.486	+.880
19	189.932	.779
20	190.427	.679
21	190.975	.568
22	191.625	.460
23	192.310	.340
24	193.158	.237
25	194.088	.118
26	195.190	.012
27	196.426	—.105
28	197.867	.213
29	199.502	.318
30	201.418	.424
31	203.514	.538
32	206.000	.704
33	208.742	.916
34	211.734	1.172
35	214.996	1.497

In 40 Years.

Age.	Initial Value.	Diff.
10	146.208	—.459
11	146.628	.514
12	147.063	.577
13	147.536	.643
14	148.039	.705
15	148.558	.777
16	149.145	.852
17	149.834	.933
18	150.633	1.014
19	151.396	1.106
20	152.260	1.191
21	153.264	1.288
22	154.368	1.380
23	155.626	1.468
24	156.998	1.564
25	158.601	1.654
26	160.335	1.738
27	162.324	1.823
28	164.237	1.903
29	167.002	1.971
30	169.846	2.037

TWENTY-THIRD YEAR.

In 25 Years.

Age.	Initial Value.	Diff.
10	838.615	+32.420
11	838.581	32.394
12	838.506	32.371
13	838.442	32.339
14	838.380	32.303
15	838.312	32.302
16	838.213	32.258
17	838.148	32.209
18	838.041	32.187
19	837.974	32.138
20	837.886	32.104
21	837.780	32.032
22	837.680	31.983
23	837.635	31.913
24	837.539	31.835
25	837.480	31.734
26	837.404	31.627
27	837.309	31.513
28	837.207	31.384
29	837.093	31.262
30	836.999	31.113
31	836.861	30.950
32	836.750	30.769
33	836.618	30.571
34	836.465	30.374
35	836.287	+30.160
36	836.079	29.911
37	835.847	29.625
38	835.666	29.341
39	835.342	28.983
40	835.072	28.630
41	834.645	28.196
42	834.353	27.765
43	833.925	27.264
44	833.509	26.660
45	832.931	26.066

In 30 Years.

Age.	Initial Value.	Diff.
10	611.366	+21.235
11	611.326	21.159
12	611.258	21.097
13	611.168	21.029
14	611.046	20.948
15	611.029	20.875
16	610.560	+20.784
17	610.875	20.699
18	610.726	20.602
19	610.768	20.516
20	610.804	20.414
21	610.806	20.282
22	611.059	20.125
23	611.232	19.943
24	611.465	19.725
25	611.746	19.485
26	612.207	19.214
27	612.422	18.938
28	612.804	18.619
29	613.224	18.302
30	613.645	17.928
31	614.187	17.531
32	614.650	17.098
33	615.214	16.629
34	615.890	16.123
35	616.473	15.580
36	617.252	14.989
37	617.994	14.320
38	618.950	13.592
39	620.859	12.833
40	620.921	11.950

In 35 Years.

Age.	Initial Value.	Diff.
10	459.080	+13.750
11	459.125	13.674
12	459.217	13.586
13	459.323	13.484
14	459.493	13.378
15	459.638	13.281
16	459.794	13.173
17	460.124	13.064
18	460.413	12.969
19	460.914	12.851
20	461.526	12.736
21	462.250	12.582
22	463.182	12.394
23	464.211	12.179
24	465.271	11.910
25	466.537	11.609
26	467.957	11.284
27	469.317	10.943
28	470.932	10.573
29	472.678	10.164
30	474.459	9.723
31	476.463	9.246
32	478.681	8.737
33	481.056	8.179
34	483.691	7.574
35	486.423	+6.955

In 40 Years.

Age.	Initial Value.	Diff.
10	353.568	+8.550
11	353.979	8.464
12	354.418	8.374
13	354.936	8.274
14	355.509	8.179
15	356.134	8.086
16	356.961	7.985
17	357.920	7.889
18	359.096	7.792
19	360.267	7.711
20	361.778	7.603
21	363.523	7.463
22	365.460	7.282
23	367.677	7.073
24	370.022	6.805
25	372.730	6.521
26	375.508	6.204
27	378.616	5.873
28	381.917	5.511
29	385.429	5.122
30	389.341	4.750

THIRTEENTH YEAR.—ENDOWMENT POLICIES,—4 PER CENT.—(Arranged by Terms.)

In 15 Years.

Age.	Initial Value.	Diff.
10	793.097	+30.407
11	793.083	30.389
12	793.091	30.370
13	793.023	30.348
14	792.965	30.306
15	792.962	30.303
16	792.873	30.277
17	792.834	30.250
18	792.769	30.220
19	792.688	30.181
20	792.658	30.156
21	792.573	30.122
22	792.503	30.087
23	792.421	30.049
24	792.338	30.007
25	792.243	29.945
26	792.143	29.922
27	792.020	29.876
28	791.914	29.830
29	791.793	29.797
30	791.674	29.720
31	791.566	29.651
32	791.494	29.567
33	791.395	29.469
34	791.305	29.350
35	791.193	29.222
36	791.110	29.080
37	790.975	28.927
38	790.828	28.757
39	790.682	28.573
40	790.450	28.366
41	790.229	28.141
42	789.918	27.896
43	789.581	27.723
44	789.181	27.323
45	788.727	27.001
46	788.248	26.646
47	787.713	26.256
48	787.002	25.801
49	786.533	25.345
50	785.911	24.788
51	785.211	24.197
52	784.459	23.541
53	783.665	22.816
54	782.780	+22.017
55	781.838	21.132

In 20 Years.

Age.	Initial Value.	Diff.
10	524.938	+17.583
11	524.926	17.538
12	524.920	17.489
13	524.866	17.438
14	524.815	17.382
15	524.746	17.323
16	524.679	17.259
17	524.595	17.193
18	524.530	17.120
19	524.428	17.043
20	524.332	16.961
21	524.211	16.877
22	524.098	16.788
23	523.959	16.692
24	523.837	16.593
25	523.664	16.489
26	523.534	16.383
27	523.383	16.271
28	523.272	16.158
29	523.221	16.039
30	523.192	15.801
31	523.241	15.743
32	523.363	15.541
33	523.533	15.310
34	523.734	15.028
35	523.915	14.721
36	524.200	14.420
37	524.345	14.021
38	524.521	13.619
39	524.731	13.287
40	524.828	12.693
41	524.940	12.159
42	524.944	11.583
43	524.929	10.942
44	524.833	10.241
45	524.721	9.484
46	524.660	8.673
47	524.603	+7.777
48	524.625	6.770
49	524.665	5.670
50	524.781	4.457

In 25 Years.

Age.	Initial Value.	Diff.
10	370.348	+10.183
11	370.398	10.127
12	370.401	10.064
13	370.404	10.001
14	370.408	9.932
15	370.463	9.858
16	370.419	9.774
17	370.433	9.694
18	370.406	9.591
19	370.395	9.497
20	370.373	9.390
21	370.319	9.280
22	370.284	9.169
23	370.302	9.047
24	370.274	8.958
25	370.372	8.798
26	370.425	8.670
27	370.568	8.534
28	370.804	8.405
29	371.124	8.261
30	371.582	8.106
31	372.190	7.912
32	372.887	7.674
33	373.860	7.391
34	374.726	7.050
35	375.651	6.677
36	376.633	6.264
37	377.717	5.823
38	378.888	5.339
39	380.022	4.804
40	381.291	4.225
41	382.454	3.576
42	383.730	2.898
43	385.077	2.131
44	386.510	1.304
45	387.991	.432

In 30 Years.

Age.	Initial Value.	Diff.
10	272.419	+5.498
11	272.607	5.432
12	272.711	5.363
13	272.769	5.299
14	272.880	5.220
15	273.027	5.142
16	273.113	5.049
17	273.267	4.957
18	273.357	4.854
19	273.539	4.750
20	273.709	4.635
21	274.639	4.525
22	274.154	4.405
23	274.437	4.279
24	274.792	4.149
25	275.231	4.026
26	275.818	3.890
27	276.434	3.764
28	277.156	3.632
29	278.213	3.511
30	279.365	3.359
31	280.781	3.172
32	282.336	2.933
33	284.089	2.653
34	286.037	2.305
35	288.042	1.925
36	290.263	1.514
37	292.564	1.063
38	295.145	.569
39	297.559	.042
40	300.436	—.547

In 35 Years.

Age.	Initial Value.	Diff.
10	206.806	+2.365
11	207.013	2.305
12	207.299	2.235
13	207.554	2.163
14	207.846	2.083
15	208.148	2.004
16	208.442	1.912
17	208.830	1.822
18	209.195	+1.719
19	209.651	1.620
20	210.166	1.512
21	210.731	1.402
22	211.413	1.298
23	212.137	1.180
24	213.028	1.068
25	214.023	.956
26	215.214	.840
27	216.542	.733
28	218.104	.630
29	219.890	.519
30	221.959	.404
31	224.232	.247
32	226.881	.033
33	229.762	—.218
34	232.890	.541
35	236.238	.884

In 40 Years.

Age.	Initial Value.	Diff.
10	161.331	+.188
11	161.768	.127
12	162.218	.061
13	162.719	—.003
14	163.242	.064
15	163.787	.145
16	164.407	.226
17	165.132	.304
18	165.872	.395
19	166.787	.480
20	167.708	.576
21	168.774	.670
22	169.957	.757
23	171.314	.853
24	172.790	.945
25	174.524	1.026
26	176.411	1.114
27	178.574	1.191
28	180.986	1.259
29	183.687	1.328
30	186.796	1.402

TWENTY-SECOND YEAR.

In 25 Years.

Age.	Initial Value.	Diff.
10	781.404	+29.622
11	781.361	29.610
12	781.276	29.564
13	781.189	29.536
14	781.117	29.481
15	781.052	29.438
16	780.920	29.388
17	780.839	29.345
18	780.698	29.299
19	780.603	29.258
20	780.493	29.199
21	780.357	29.134
22	780.248	29.052
23	780.191	28.975
24	780.085	28.888
25	780.047	28.751
26	779.983	28.614
27	779.912	28.359
28	779.817	28.299
29	779.733	28.115
30	779.651	27.934
31	779.560	27.723
32	779.469	27.482
33	779.371	27.229
34	779.248	26.970
35	779.092	+26.683
36	778.905	26.350
37	778.698	25.999
38	778.541	25.602
39	778.260	25.171
40	778.049	24.685
41	777.648	24.152
42	777.383	23.596
43	777.004	22.925
44	776.649	22.184
45	776.101	21.419

In 30 Years.

Age.	Initial Value.	Diff.
10	570.121	+19.272
11	570.118	19.197
12	570.074	19.129
13	569.976	19.059
14	569.880	18.979
15	569.878	18.893
16	569.733	+18.806
17	569.749	18.715
18	569.617	18.615
19	569.665	18.517
20	569.703	18.418
21	569.807	18.305
22	569.997	18.163
23	570.220	17.993
24	570.521	17.795
25	570.906	17.550
26	571.458	17.294
27	571.792	17.009
28	572.378	16.678
29	572.863	16.374
30	573.486	15.992
31	574.140	15.603
32	574.788	15.161
33	575.538	14.693
34	576.407	14.189
35	577.209	13.623
36	578.206	13.040
37	579.180	12.399
38	580.180	11.680
39	581.582	10.921
40	582.961	10.043

In 35 Years.

Age.	Initial Value.	Diff.
10	428.543	+12.342
11	428.614	12.265
12	428.727	12.163
13	428.961	12.079
14	429.052	11.979
15	429.226	11.866
16	429.397	11.766
17	429.741	11.655
18	430.040	11.544
19	430.532	11.442
20	431.138	11.328
21	431.856	11.206
22	432.807	11.047
23	433.871	10.863
24	435.003	10.633
25	436.364	10.348
26	437.886	10.049
27	439.378	9.718
28	441.114	9.368
29	442.996	8.976
30	444.983	8.563
31	447.089	8.117
32	449.485	7.611
33	452.027	7.093
34	454.844	6.519
35	457.780	+5.904

In 40 Years.

Age.	Initial Value.	Diff.
10	330.445	+7.533
11	330.880	7.437
12	331.338	7.340
13	331.852	7.259
14	332.436	7.165
15	333.068	7.060
16	333.867	6.970
17	334.818	6.871
18	335.962	6.771
19	337.091	6.692
20	338.544	6.595
21	340.231	6.494
22	342.135	6.356
23	344.344	6.177
24	346.703	5.963
25	349.452	5.701
26	352.284	5.411
27	355.444	5.099
28	358.796	4.768
29	362.372	4.401
30	366.387	3.972

FOURTEENTH YEAR.—ENDOWMENT POLICIES.—4 PER CENT.—(Arranged by Terms.)

In 15 Years.

Age.	Initial Value.	Diff.
10	875.340	+34.331
11	875.336	34.319
12	875.358	34.312
13	875.302	34.299
14	875.257	34.265
15	875.277	34.276
16	875.205	34.260
17	875.188	34.245
18	875.145	34.228
19	875.085	34.209
20	875.084	34.196
21	875.027	34.176
22	874.988	34.157
23	874.938	34.133
24	874.887	34.109
25	874.808	34.089
26	874.768	34.066
27	874.686	34.042
28	874.629	34.015
29	874.570	33.926
30	874.477	33.949
31	874.409	33.904
32	874.371	33.855
33	874.299	33.791
34	874.226	33.725
35	874.135	33.650
36	874.076	33.573
37	873.971	33.484
38	873.860	33.387
39	873.763	33.283
40	873.585	33.162
41	873.438	33.038
42	873.221	32.895
43	872.995	32.740
44	872.725	32.572
45	872.426	32.385
46	872.119	32.180
47	871.768	31.950
48	871.221	31.682
49	870.987	31.411
50	870.558	31.102
51	870.086	30.756
52	869.574	30.373
53	869.036	29.952
54	868.426	+29.482
55	867.774	28.967

In 20 Years.

Age.	Initial Value.	Diff.
10	578.969	+20.127
11	578.948	20.084
12	578.933	20.041
13	578.870	19.991
14	578.810	19.940
15	578.732	19.883
16	578.645	19.825
17	578.562	19.758
18	578.487	19.693
19	578.373	19.618
20	578.265	19.544
21	578.133	19.465
22	578.009	19.382
23	577.856	19.291
24	577.723	19.201
25	577.537	19.105
26	577.400	19.007
27	577.241	18.904
28	577.129	18.797
29	577.079	18.678
30	577.043	18.427
31	577.074	18.351
32	577.148	18.144
33	577.255	17.893
34	577.359	17.620
35	577.435	17.319
36	577.606	17.041
37	577.641	16.640
38	577.694	16.247
39	577.714	15.994
40	577.734	15.340
41	577.704	14.831
42	577.569	14.258
43	577.404	13.648
44	577.151	12.971
45	576.893	12.235
46	576.673	11.434
47	576.441	+10.529
48	576.245	9.542
49	576.046	8.449
50	575.891	7.263

In 25 Years.

Age.	Initial Value.	Diff.
10	408.116	+11.937
11	408.145	11.877
12	408.131	11.815
13	408.122	11.752
14	408.112	11.681
15	408.153	11.607
16	408.088	11.524
17	408.091	11.434
18	408.031	11.351
19	408.005	11.240
20	407.957	11.136
21	407.878	11.036
22	407.823	10.919
23	407.818	10.810
24	407.796	10.683
25	407.823	10.550
26	407.902	10.421
27	408.040	10.298
28	408.290	10.166
29	408.620	10.014
30	409.092	9.825
31	409.690	9.598
32	410.350	9.330
33	411.267	9.000
34	412.033	8.654
35	412.850	8.254
36	413.711	7.833
37	414.680	7.374
38	415.730	6.873
39	416.727	6.314
40	417.864	5.706
41	418.867	5.053
42	420.010	4.340
43	421.201	3.554
44	422.498	2.712
45	423.832	1.809

In 30 Years.

Age.	Initial Value.	Diff.
10	299.888	+6.742
11	300.052	6.674
12	300.146	6.609
13	300.191	6.539
14	300.287	6.460
15	300.427	6.376
16	300.492	6.284
17	300.637	6.187
18	300.705	6.082
19	300.875	5.972
20	301.027	5.859
21	301.358	5.754
22	301.458	5.621
23	301.735	5.493
24	302.090	5.373
25	302.547	5.235
26	303.163	5.114
27	303.809	4.987
28	304.576	4.856
29	305.710	4.722
30	306.930	4.530
31	308.397	4.298
32	309.970	4.020
33	311.725	3.680
34	313.636	3.309
35	315.598	2.904
36	317.783	2.473
37	320.042	1.995
38	322.586	1.472
39	324.961	.909
40	327.806	.286

In 35 Years.

Age.	Initial Value.	Diff.
10	227.370	+3.282
11	227.503	3.210
12	227.843	3.140
13	228.096	3.065
14	228.391	2.983
15	228.690	2.895
16	228.985	2.815
17	229.380	2.706
18	229.743	+2.603
19	230.211	2.498
20	230.738	2.389
21	231.321	2.284
22	232.039	2.169
23	232.794	2.052
24	233.729	1.947
25	234.796	1.828
26	236.066	1.720
27	237.496	1.617
28	239.184	1.510
29	241.115	1.389
30	243.327	1.227
31	245.735	1.025
32	248.499	.773
33	251.480	.455
34	254.677	.014
35	258:093	—.261

In 40 Years.

Age.	Initial Value.	Diff.
10	177.112	+.863
11	177.560	.797
12	178.022	.733
13	178.542	.665
14	179.081	.592
15	179.648	.514
16	180.295	.434
17	181.059	.345
18	181.940	.258
19	182.801	.167
20	183.771	.072
21	184.902	—.016
22	186.169	.114
23	187.617	.205
24	189.201	.290
25	191.075	.374
26	193.111	.455
27	195.456	.523
28	198.079	.592
29	201.015	.672
30	204.381	.785

TWENTY-FIRST YEAR.

In 25 Years.

Age.	Initial Value.	Diff.
10	726.827	+27.000
11	726.789	26.962
12	726.697	26.913
13	726.604	26.868
14	726.519	26.816
15	726.460	26.770
16	726.311	26.694
17	726.219	26.656
18	726.073	26.591
19	725.961	26.529
20	725.832	26.467
21	725.671	26.397
22	725.544	26.324
23	725.499	26.223
24	725.405	26.116
25	725.382	25.978
26	725.351	25.825
27	725.328	25.646
28	725.287	25.349
29	725.240	25.248
30	725.213	25.024
31	725.180	24.792
32	725.157	24.513
33	725.143	24.206
34	725.093	23.898
35	725.021	+23.459
36	724.908	23.173
37	724.792	22.756
38	724.729	22.219
39	724.539	21.810
40	724.440	21.271
41	724.158	20.643
42	724.008	20.000
43	723.771	19.236
44	723.572	18.395
45	723.183	17.509

In 30 Years.

Age.	Initial Value.	Diff.
10	530.739	+17.410
11	530.760	17.337
12	530.731	17.265
13	530.649	17.194
14	530.579	17.114
15	530.596	17.024
16	530.480	+16.923
17	530.502	16.836
18	530.397	16.726
19	530.450	16.629
20	530.493	16.527
21	530.497	16.416
22	530.799	16.299
23	531.051	16.150
24	531.409	15.963
25	531.863	15.753
26	532.523	15.490
27	532.962	15.209
28	533.680	14.890
29	534.304	14.570
30	535.064	14.214
31	535.869	13.827
32	536.694	13.393
33	537.634	12.921
34	538.690	12.423
35	539.691	11.877
36	540.917	11.293
37	542.115	10.650
38	543.566	9.949
39	545.002	9.220
40	546.668	8.376

In 35 Years.

Age.	Initial Value.	Diff.
10	399.346	+11.004
11	399.437	10.929
12	399.581	10.835
13	399.735	10.739
14	399.951	10.639
15	400.148	10.534
16	400.343	10.423
17	400.692	10.321
18	401.006	10.205
19	401.494	10.098
20	402.086	9.992
21	402.792	9.876
22	403.715	9.754
23	404.697	9.697
24	405.917	9.453
25	407.346	9.168
26	408.912	8.882
27	410.582	8.575
28	412.430	8.234
29	414.421	7.869
30	416.536	7.475
31	418.768	7.062
32	421.312	6.588
33	424.015	6.076
34	426.968	5.548
35	430.075	+4.966

In 40 Years.

Age.	Initial Value.	Diff.
10	308.300	+6.552
11	308.746	6.468
12	309.220	6.375
13	309.748	6.281
14	310.330	6.199
15	310.967	6.095
16	311.745	5.998
17	312.681	5.906
18	313.803	5.804
19	314.891	5.716
20	316.280	5.625
21	317.893	5.540
22	319.727	5.439
23	321.883	5.305
24	324.223	5.124
25	326.953	4.922
26	329.821	4.650
27	333.006	4.365
28	336.393	4.050
29	339.999	3.717
30	344.022	3.259

FIFTEENTH YEAR.—ENDOWMENT POLICIES.—4 PER CENT.—(Arranged by Terms.)

In 20 Years.

Age.	Initial Value.	Diff.
10	635.544	+22.802
11	635.516	22.765
12	635.498	22.724
13	635.427	22.679
14	635.363	22.631
15	635.278	22.581
16	635.197	22.524
17	635.094	22.466
18	635.017	22.404
19	634.893	22.339
20	634.781	22.272
21	634.643	22.199
22	634.514	22.122
23	634.352	22.040
24	634.217	21.963
25	634.026	21.875
26	633.890	21.789
27	633.733	21.692
28	633.625	21.588
29	633.576	21.462
30	633.520	21.199
31	633.515	21.124
32	633.536	20.905
33	633.560	20.669
34	633.576	20.408
35	633.553	20.127
36	633.633	19.864
37	633.555	19.480
38	633.495	19.105
39	633.374	18.904
40	633.287	18.253
41	633.140	17.763
42	632.869	17.222
43	632.575	16.646
44	632.199	16.006

In 20 Years.

Age.	Initial Value.	Diff.
45	631.806	+15.305
46	631.447	14.518
47	631.031	13.654
48	630.637	12.699
49	630.206	11.657
50	629.807	10.508

In 25 Years.

Age.	Initial Value.	Diff.
10	447.632	+13.769
11	447.642	13.714
12	447.612	13.662
13	447.591	13.593
14	447.565	13.522
15	447.592	13.447
16	447.507	13.360
17	447.489	13.274
18	447.416	13.181
19	447.358	13.082
20	447.287	12.985
21	447.187	12.874
22	447.112	12.758
23	447.087	12.648
24	447.043	12.546
25	447.009	12.405
26	447.130	12.286
27	447.276	12.157
28	447.537	12.016
29	447.869	11.836
30	448.321	11.618
31	448.876	11.363
32	449.469	11.055
33	450.284	10.719

In 25 Years.

Age.	Initial Value.	Diff.
34	450.944	+10.354
35	451.626	9.955
36	452.358	9.518
37	453.194	9.044
38	454.106	8.521
39	454.942	7.941
40	455.918	7.330
41	456.757	6.648
42	457.747	5.925
43	458.748	5.130
44	459.894	4.259
45	461.050	3.310

In 30 Years.

Age.	Initial Value.	Diff.
10	328.579	+8.052
11	328.735	7.989
12	328.816	7.917
13	328.853	7.842
14	328.934	7.769
15	329.061	7.669
16	329.106	7.576
17	329.235	7.480
18	329.281	7.370
19	329.433	7.265
20	329.569	7.154
21	329.706	7.044
22	329.978	6.909
23	330.247	6.789
24	330.612	6.660
25	331.082	6.532
26	331.732	6.412
27	332.407	6.281

In 30 Years.

Age.	Initial Value.	Diff.
28	333.220	+6.132
29	334.418	5.962
30	335.666	5.726
31	337.139	5.456
32	338.691	5.125
33	340.388	4.764
34	342.239	4.374
35	344.133	3.948
36	346.262	3.484
37	348.452	2.977
38	350.931	2.424
39	353.236	1.823
40	356.007	1.183

In 35 Years.

Age.	Initial Value.	Diff.
10	248.838	+4.224
11	249.018	4.161
12	249.292	4.088
13	249.540	4.013
14	249.836	3.923
15	250.129	3.834
16	250.421	3.736
17	250.814	3.635
18	251.175	3.530
19	251.649	3.422
20	252.187	3.318
21	252.793	3.204
22	253.536	3.089
23	254.323	2.981
24	255.309	2.865
25	256.441	2.754
26	257.808	2.650

In 35 Years.

Age.	Initial Value.	Diff.
27	259.334	+2.542
28	261.144	2.424
29	263.210	2.258
30	265.533	2.054
31	268.016	1.808
32	270.857	1.494
33	273.871	1.156
34	277.119	.784
35	280.571	.390

In 40 Years.

Age.	Initial Value.	Diff.
10	193.563	+1.565
11	194.017	1.503
12	194.493	1.433
13	195.033	1.360
14	195.581	1.282
15	196.168	1.208
16	196.843	1.117
17	197.637	1.032
18	198.552	.936
19	199.462	.845
20	200.482	.754
21	201.684	.659
22	203.024	.566
23	204.568	.482
24	206.267	.391
25	208.278	.312
26	210.471	.241
27	213.006	.172
28	215.839	.093
29	218.999	—.028
30	222.573	.188

TWENTIETH YEAR.

In 25 Years.

Age.	Initial Value.	Diff.
10	674.750	+24.494
11	674.709	24.460
12	674.636	24.395
13	674.537	24.350
14	674.447	24.290
15	674.396	24.242
16	674.235	24.171
17	674.156	24.099
18	674.011	24.028
19	673.891	23.957
20	673.757	23.881
21	673.573	23.809
22	673.445	23.729
23	673.398	23.632
24	673.318	23.523
25	673.313	23.383
26	673.316	23.228
27	673.353	23.037
28	673.381	22.825
29	673.406	22.599
30	673.441	22.358
31	673.508	22.084
32	673.556	21.802
33	673.656	21.465
34	673.715	21.121

In 25 Years.

Age.	Initial Value.	Diff.
35	673.771	+20.738
36	673.725	20.329
37	673.760	19.872
38	673.846	19.390
39	673.769	18.839
40	673.872	18.250
41	673.720	17.591
42	673.751	16.883
43	673.690	16.080
44	673.712	15.176
45	673.567	14.207

In 30 Years.

Age.	Initial Value.	Diff.
10	493.124	+15.643
11	493.172	15.575
12	493.152	15.502
13	493.089	15.427
14	493.053	15.339
15	493.084	15.254

In 30 Years.

Age.	Initial Value.	Diff.
16	492.996	+15.154
17	493.035	15.056
18	492.949	14.954
19	493.019	14.854
20	493.079	14.731
21	493.081	14.622
22	493.389	14.511
23	493.648	14.384
24	494.030	14.230
25	494.538	14.035
26	495.259	13.809
27	495.815	13.536
28	496.646	13.226
29	497.396	12.919
30	498.218	12.558
31	499.241	12.184
32	500.231	11.762
33	501.343	11.308
34	502.585	10.811
35	503.772	10.278
36	505.212	9.699
37	506.637	9.063
38	508.301	8.390
39	509.856	7.789
40	511.871	6.880

In 35 Years.

Age.	Initial Value.	Diff.
10	371.418	+9.734
11	371.535	9.654
12	371.705	9.567
13	371.882	9.472
14	372.120	9.369
15	372.335	9.269
16	372.553	9.159
17	372.911	9.053
18	373.231	8.946
19	373.724	8.830
20	374.306	8.720
21	374.987	8.617
22	375.879	8.508
23	376.846	8.374
24	378.062	8.222
25	379.487	8.018
26	381.181	7.779
27	382.871	7.490
28	384.805	7.175
29	386.901	6.824
30	389.105	6.454
31	391.447	6.062
32	394.105	5.022
33	396.930	5.049
34	400.017	4.623

In 35 Years.

Age.	Initial Value.	Diff.
35	403.242	+4.094

In 40 Years.

Age.	Initial Value.	Diff.
10	287.089	+5.625
11	287.549	5.539
12	288.030	5.454
13	288.565	5.360
14	289.149	5.274
15	289.781	5.180
16	290.542	5.079
17	291.467	4.983
18	292.546	4.888
19	293.671	4.796
20	294.941	4.700
21	296.477	4.618
22	298.227	4.531
23	300.288	4.439
24	302.565	4.302
25	305.245	4.131
26	308.088	3.920
27	311.277	3.656
28	314.668	3.372
29	318.293	3.050
30	322.308	2.627

SIXTEENTH YEAR. ENDOWMENT POLICIES.—4 PER CENT.—(Arranged by Terms.)

In 20 Years.

Age.	Initial Value.	Diff.
10	694.794	+25.609
11	694.765	25.585
12	694.746	25.550
13	694.672	25.510
14	694.607	25.470
15	694.522	25.421
16	694.438	25.373
17	694.334	25.321
18	694.258	25.269
19	694.134	25.213
20	694.025	25.154
21	693.887	25.088
22	693.759	25.022
23	693.597	24.955
24	693.473	24.885
25	693.285	24.810
26	693.162	24.724
27	693.012	24.643
28	692.912	24.538
29	692.857	24.408
30	692.809	24.112
31	692.729	24.073
32	692.685	23.896
33	692.641	23.660
34	692.581	23.426
35	692.489	23.165
36	692.460	22.936
37	692.310	22.575
38	692.154	22.232
39	692.000	22.021
40	691.753	21.457
41	691.508	21.012
42	691.133	20.530
43	690.754	19.998
44	690.282	19.413

In 20 Years.

Age.	Initial Value.	Diff.
45	689.789	+18.750
46	689.305	18.023
47	688.746	17.223
48	688.186	16.347
49	687.574	15.376
50	686.968	14.312

In 25 Years.

Age.	Initial Value.	Diff.
10	488.988	+15.699
11	488.976	15.650
12	488.940	15.612
13	488.901	15.526
14	488.859	15.456
15	488.871	15.379
16	488.762	15.293
17	488.727	15.210
18	488.631	15.119
19	488.553	15.031
20	488.465	14.926
21	488.340	14.820
22	488.240	14.714
23	488.204	14.604
24	488.153	14.490
25	488.163	14.367
26	488.223	14.248
27	488.371	14.119
28	488.634	13.946
29	488.940	13.743
30	489.343	13.503
31	489.827	13.215
32	490.313	12.896
33	491.020	12.444

In 25 Years.

Age.	Initial Value.	Diff.
34	491.555	+12.198
35	492.103	11.774
36	492.690	11.332
37	493.378	10.834
38	494.130	10.299
39	494.784	9.729
40	495.596	9.091
41	496.242	8.393
42	497.042	7.670
43	497.871	6.951
44	498.837	5.945
45	499.709	4.973

In 30 Years.

Age.	Initial Value.	Diff.
10	358.615	+9.424
11	358.742	9.357
12	358.802	9.284
13	358.818	9.209
14	358.890	9.119
15	358.988	9.038
16	359.012	8.938
17	359.126	8.840
18	359.145	8.726
19	359.284	8.625
20	359.406	8.507
21	359.454	8.378
22	359.786	8.271
23	360.055	8.140
24	360.421	8.019
25	360.904	7.897
26	361.599	7.771
27	362.299	7.629

In 30 Years.

Age.	Initial Value.	Diff.
28	363.140	+7.442
29	364.366	7.235
30	365.598	6.958
31	367.039	6.645
32	368.517	6.294
33	370.135	5.909
34	371.907	5.498
35	373.712	5.044
36	375.752	4.657
37	377.844	4.021
38	380.228	3.380
39	382.421	2.813
40	385.107	2.129

In 35 Years.

Age.	Initial Value.	Diff.
10	271.265	+5.224
11	271.424	5.159
12	271.689	5.082
13	271.932	4.997
14	272.221	4.910
15	272.507	4.814
16	272.788	4.713
17	273.179	4.611
18	273.534	4.503
19	274.011	4.401
20	274.565	4.287
21	275.185	4.173
22	275.953	4.063
23	276.781	3.945
24	277.807	3.839
25	279.012	3.730
26	280.480	3.618

In 35 Years.

Age.	Initial Value.	Diff.
27	282.097	+3.500
28	284.018	3.339
29	286.174	3.127
30	288.510	2.883
31	291.080	2.581
32	293.936	2.246
33	296.963	1.879
34	300.231	1.487
35	303.700	1.065

In 40 Years.

Age.	Initial Value.	Diff.
10	210.724	+2.307
11	211.188	2.239
12	211.672	2.166
13	212.217	2.089
14	212.771	2.014
15	213.380	1.924
16	214.074	1.836
17	214.900	1.746
18	215.842	1.648
19	216.801	1.564
20	217.875	1.464
21	219.141	1.369
22	220.559	1.285
23	222.200	1.195
24	224.014	1.109
25	226.167	1.038
26	228.525	.965
27	231.251	.884
28	234.284	.765
29	237.627	.596
30	241.372	.397

NINETEENTH YEAR.

In 20 Years.

Age.	Initial Value.	Diff.
10	890.081	+34.992
11	890.061	34.982
12	890.058	34.972
13	890.011	34.956
14	889.985	34.942
15	889.934	34.949
16	889.897	34.913
17	889.840	34 895
18	889.829	34.877
19	889.760	34.856
20	889.716	34.841
21	889.643	34.818
22	889.596	34.801
23	889.516	34.777
24	889.489	34.753
25	889.387	34.723
26	889.349	34.685
27	889.275	34.642
28	889.221	34.591
29	889.182	34.536
30	889.036	34.467
31	889.005	34.407
32	888.932	34.334
33	888.853	34.259
34	888.760	34.167
35	888.653	34.092
36	888.550	34.027
37	888.389	33.851
38	888.217	33.723
39	888.051	33.601
40	887.848	33.458
41	887.676	33.276
42	887.392	33.083
43	887.139	32.877
44	886.792	32.642

In 20 Years.

Age.	Initial Value.	Diff.
45	886.423	+32.385
46	886.084	32.104
47	885.654	31.788
48	885.223	31.441
49	884.721	31.054
50	884.226	30.634

In 25 Years.

Age.	Initial Value.	Diff.
10	625.043	+22.125
11	625.015	22.084
12	624.947	22.023
13	624.838	21.982
14	624.767	22.898
15	624.734	21.840
16	624.566	21.774
17	624.501	21.691
18	624.358	21.619
19	624.240	21.538
20	624.113	21.450
21	623.934	21.360
22	623.798	21.277
23	623.751	21.178
24	623.669	21.085
25	623.655	20.942
26	623.713	20.796
27	623.797	20.618
28	623.920	20.380
29	624.017	20.154
30	624.148	19.889
31	624.310	19.610
32	624.463	19.294
33	624.685	18.953

In 25 Years.

Age.	Initial Value.	Diff.
34	624.865	+18.593
35	625.058	18.191
36	625.159	17.752
37	625.341	17.279
38	625.590	16.753
39	625.678	16.190
40	625.947	15.577
41	625.983	14.900
42	626.212	14.156
43	626.382	13.313
44	626.648	12.380
45	626.772	11.386

In 30 Years.

Age.	Initial Value.	Diff.
10	457.183	+13.976
11	457.247	13.895
12	457.250	13.824
13	457.204	13.752
14	457.204	13.662
15	457.254	13.572
16	457.188	13.478
17	457.235	13.371
18	457.189	13.266
19	457.276	13.157
20	457.349	13.047
21	457.358	12.929
22	447.668	12.822
23	457.928	12.701
24	458.315	12.566
25	458.841	12.407
26	459.601	12.203
27	460.230	11.968

In 30 Years.

Age.	Initial Value.	Diff.
28	461.168	+11.670
29	462.037	11.369
30	462.993	11.019
31	464.139	10.658
32	465.281	10.349
33	466.543	9.817
34	467.953	9.338
35	469.333	8.808
36	470.948	8.258
37	472.578	7.644
38	474.454	6.973
39	476.202	6.290
40	478.425	5.529

In 35 Years.

Age.	Initial Value.	Diff.
10	344.704	+8.522
11	344.832	8.454
12	345.034	8.362
13	345.231	8.272
14	345.487	8.171
15	345.725	8.066
16	345.956	7.966
17	346.329	7.854
18	346.659	7.743
19	347.148	7.636
20	347.726	7.520
21	348.389	7.410
22	349.246	7.305
23	350.183	7.186
24	351.359	7.070
25	352.768	6.902
26	354.450	6.704

In 35 Years.

Age.	Initial Value.	Diff.
27	356.186	+6.464
28	358.185	6.170
29	360.350	5.845
30	362.644	5.493
31	365.064	5.123
32	367.810	4.710
33	370.724	4.270
34	373.904	3.785
35	377.247	3.256

In 40 Years.

Age.	Initial Value.	Diff.
10	266.764	+4.734
11	267.229	4.657
12	267.718	4.571
13	268.258	4.485
14	268.844	4.398
15	269.474	4.301
16	270.217	4.211
17	271.124	4.122
18	272.175	4.013
19	273.250	3.927
20	274.473	3.829
21	275.940	3.739
22	277.601	3.657
23	279.556	8.576
24	281.727	3.482
25	284.311	3.357
26	287.094	3.161
27	290.226	2.978
28	293.613	2.712
29	297.213	2.424
30	301.209	2.112

SEVENTEENTH YEAR.—ENDOWMENT POLICIES.—4 PER CENT.—(Arranged by Terms.)

In 20 Years.

Age.	Initial Value.	Diff.
10	756.851	+28.582
11	756.834	28.555
12	756.820	28.526
13	756.748	28.494
14	756.690	28.457
15	756.606	28.419
16	756.528	28.379
17	756.429	28.338
18	756.364	28.296
19	756.249	28.249
20	756.151	28.199
21	756.020	28.146
22	755.904	28.096
23	755.757	28.039
24	755.651	27.984
25	755.479	27.921
26	755.369	27.852
27	755.242	27.769
28	755.149	27.666
29	755.084	27.550
30	754.971	27.300
31	754.892	27.250
32	754.805	27.082
33	754.713	26.899
34	754.604	26.698
35	754.465	26.476
36	754.370	26.284
37	754.160	25.968
38	753.940	25.681
39	753.687	25.574
40	753.423	25.013
41	753.125	24.641
42	752.705	24.222
43	752.285	23.768
44	751.772	23.246

In 20 Years.

Age.	Initial Value.	Diff.
45	751.217	+22.675
46	750.668	22.044
47	750.030	21.351
48	749.383	20.584
49	748.661	19.738
50	747.933	18.811

In 25 Years.

Age.	Initial Value.	Diff.
10	532.271	+17.737
11	532.236	17.732
12	532.218	17.626
13	532.144	17.559
14	532.087	17.499
15	532.082	17.420
16	531.950	17.334
17	531.901	17.256
18	531.784	17.175
19	531.697	17.074
20	531.585	16.982
21	531.439	16.881
22	531.324	16.775
23	531.277	16.679
24	531.287	16.568
25	531.219	16.446
26	531.278	16.324
27	531.428	16.170
28	531.661	15.974
29	531.918	15.753
30	532.250	15.485
31	532.630	15.194
32	532.998	14.869
33	533.483	14.523

In 25 Years.

Age.	Initial Value.	Diff.
34	534.000	+14.159
35	534.399	13.742
36	534.836	13.284
37	535.352	12.781
38	535.932	12.253
39	536.414	11.659
40	537.035	11.023
41	537.472	10.340
42	538.095	9.609
43	538.715	8.770
44	539.466	7.851
45	540.151	6.843

In 30 Years.

Age.	Initial Value.	Diff.
10	390.004	+10.862
11	390.116	10.794
12	390.159	10.724
13	390.150	10.639
14	390.196	10.561
15	390.284	10.474
16	390.280	10.372
17	390.377	10.269
18	390.365	10.166
19	390.495	10.050
20	390.596	9.946
21	390.626	9.816
22	390.956	9.700
23	391.214	9.589
24	391.589	9.437
25	392.091	9.331
26	392.825	9.199
27	393.539	9.017

In 30 Years.

Age.	Initial Value.	Diff.
28	394.370	+8.794
29	395.587	8.548
30	396.762	8.235
31	398.128	7.899
32	399.512	7.524
33	401.027	7.126
34	402.699	6.694
35	404.387	6.297
36	406.315	5.701
37	408.280	5.130
38	410.483	4.523
39	412.595	3.874
40	415.153	3.153

In 35 Years.

Age.	Initial Value.	Diff.
10	294.677	+6.271
11	294.828	6.205
12	295.080	6.119
13	295.308	6.039
14	295.593	5.940
15	295.865	5.843
16	296.132	5.740
17	296.518	5.636
18	296.860	5.531
19	297.352	5.420
20	297.912	5.307
21	298.546	5.196
22	299.344	5.082
23	300.203	4.969
24	301.279	4.867
25	302.559	4.751
26	304.120	4.634

In 35 Years.

Age.	Initial Value.	Diff.
27	305.118	+4.472
28	307.807	4.265
29	310.009	4.018
30	312.398	3.712
31	314.917	3.393
32	317.767	3.024
33	320.778	2.639
34	324.046	2.219
35	327.504	1.767

In 40 Years.

Age.	Initial Value.	Diff.
10	228.617	+3.080
11	229.085	3.007
12	229.574	2.930
13	230.122	2.854
14	230.693	2.770
15	231.310	2.682
16	232.024	2.589
17	232.877	2.496
18	233.855	2.404
19	234.859	2.309
20	235.978	2.211
21	237.308	2.126
22	238.813	2.030
23	240.551	1.949
24	242.479	1.872
25	244.782	1.787
26	247.304	1.710
27	250.208	1.589
28	253.401	1.418
29	256.879	1.215
30	260.756	.954

EIGHTEENTH YEAR.

In 20 Years.

Age.	Initial Value.	Diff.
10	821.881	+31.702
11	821.873	31.684
12	821.870	31.664
13	821.808	31.637
14	821.760	31.612
15	821.688	31.583
16	821.624	31.556
17	821.541	31.525
18	821.497	31.495
19	821.400	31.458
20	821.322	31.422
21	821.211	31.387
22	821.123	31.350
23	821.001	31.310
24	820.928	31.268
25	820.784	31.219
26	820.704	31.162
27	820.598	31.090
28	820.514	31.008
29	820.453	30.910
30	820.321	30.695
31	820.232	30.683
32	820.131	30.557
33	820.024	30.417
34	819.899	30.264
35	819.750	30.064
36	819.620	30.007
37	819.403	29.711
38	819.175	29.488
39	818.927	29.458
40	818.649	28.986
41	818.371	28.700
42	817.969	28.381
43	817.586	28.020
44	817.095	27.620

In 20 Years.

Age.	Initial Value.	Diff.
45	816.570	+27.175
46	816.052	26.692
47	815.442	26.151
48	814.817	25.556
49	814.110	24.900
50	813.397	24.176

In 25 Years.

Age.	Initial Value.	Diff.
10	577.588	+19.872
11	577.578	19.827
12	577.510	19.771
13	577.420	19.701
14	577.348	19.637
15	577.334	19.568
16	577.179	19.492
17	577.121	19.416
18	576.993	19.331
19	576.884	19.243
20	576.761	19.158
21	576.599	19.056
22	576.469	18.959
23	576.415	18.867
24	576.339	18.766
25	576.354	18.644
26	576.409	18.497
27	576.536	18.323
28	576.716	18.123
29	576.906	17.876
30	577.139	17.605
31	577.412	17.310
32	577.666	16.998
33	578.020	16.644

In 25 Years.

Age.	Initial Value.	Diff.
34	578.416	+16.192
35	578.663	15.873
36	578.934	15.411
37	579.273	14.928
38	579.688	14.399
39	579.974	13.805
40	580.406	13.193
41	580.649	12.497
42	581.083	11.750
43	581.478	10.911
44	582.001	9.963
45	582.403	8.960

In 30 Years.

Age.	Initial Value.	Diff.
10	422.835	+12.382
11	422.928	12.314
12	422.956	12.225
13	422.912	12.159
14	422.944	12.073
15	423.016	11.980
16	422.982	11.876
17	423.057	11.785
18	423.025	11.670
19	423.131	11.559
20	423.215	11.451
21	423.236	11.328
22	423.555	11.214
23	423.812	11.097
24	424.195	10.971
25	424.712	10.839
26	425.479	10.667
27	426.167	10.458

In 30 Years.

Age.	Initial Value.	Diff.
28	426.952	+10.208
29	428.123	9.920
30	429.203	9.584
31	430.471	9.224
32	431.737	8.843
33	433.136	8.424
34	434.687	7.972
35	436.235	7.467
36	438.022	6.920
37	439.825	6.338
38	441.878	5.699
39	443.830	5.013
40	446.223	4.285

In 35 Years.

Age.	Initial Value.	Diff.
10	319.148	+7.374
11	319.280	7.299
12	319.508	7.217
13	319.726	7.126
14	319.995	7.030
15	320.252	6.929
16	320.503	6.822
17	320.882	6.719
18	321.226	6.604
19	321.712	6.496
20	322.279	6.387
21	322.930	6.271
22	323.754	6.164
23	324.649	6.057
24	325.779	5.947
25	327.127	5.724
26	328.776	5.657

In 35 Years.

Age.	Initial Value.	Diff.
27	330.511	+5.454
28	332.522	5.213
29	334.733	4.911
30	337.095	4.586
31	339.568	4.232
32	342.376	3.849
33	345.353	3.435
34	348.593	2.983
35	352.010	2.498

In 40 Years.

Age.	Initial Value.	Diff.
10	247.294	+3.887
11	247.761	3.813
12	248.251	3.734
13	248.794	3.648
14	249.370	3.567
15	249.998	3.470
16	250.727	3.376
17	251.604	3.289
18	253.109	3.188
19	253.662	3.094
20	254.828	3.006
21	256.232	2.910
22	257.812	2.820
23	259.656	2.744
24	261.707	2.664
25	264.156	2.578
26	266.828	2.452
27	269.870	2.283
28	273.172	2.078
29	276.750	1.807
30	280.697	1.525

FIRST YEAR.—TEN PREM. ENDOWM'T POLICIES.—4 PER CENT.—(Arranged by Terms.)

In 15 Years.

Age.	Initial Value.	Difference.
10	70.024	—3.509
11	70.051	3.533
12	70.082	3.555
13	70.118	3.588
14	70.156	3.630
15	70.201	3.674
16	70.247	3.727
17	70.297	3.781
18	70.353	3.846
19	70.409	3.910
20	70.470	3.984
21	70.535	4.065
22	70.603	4.145
23	70.677	4.233
24	70.751	4.327
25	70.836	4.416
26	70.923	4.526
27	71.016	4.634
28	71.109	4.755
29	71.214	4.877
30	71.322	5.004
31	71.436	5.152
32	71.557	5.305
33	71.685	5.461
34	71.822	5.621
35	71.969	5.796
36	72.130	5.974
37	72.309	6.154
38	72.504	6.351
39	72.726	6.551
40	72.977	6.756
41	73.266	6.958
42	73.597	7.228
43	73.967	7.545
44	74.402	7.943
45	74.873	8.400
46	75.401	8.970
47	75.970	9.579
48	76.592	10.250
49	77.263	10.972
50	78.002	11.760
51	78.802	12.628
52	79.674	13.574
53	80.621	14.608

In 15 Years.

Age.	Initial Value.	Difference.
54	81.653	—15.708
55	82.779	16.932

In 20 Years.

Age.	Initial Value.	Difference.
10	59.350	—4.012
11	59.389	4.036
12	59.433	4.058
13	59.484	4.090
14	59.537	4.132
15	59.596	4.176
16	59.658	4.228
17	59.725	4.282
18	59.797	4.347
19	59.873	4.412
20	59.955	4.488
21	60.041	4.565
22	60.130	4.645
23	60.227	4.735
24	60.326	4.826
25	60.436	4.920
26	60.550	5.026
27	60.672	5.135
28	60.801	5.255
29	60.939	5.377
30	61.087	5.508
31	61.246	5.651
32	61.417	5.803
33	61.601	5.959
34	61.801	6.117
35	62.018	6.288
36	62.257	6.468
37	62.521	6.644
38	62.809	6.839
39	63.133	7.037
40	63.497	7.236
41	63.905	7.457
42	64.366	7.703
43	64.877	8.016
44	65.464	8.411
45	66.097	8.868
46	66.788	9.431

In 20 Years.

Age.	Initial Value.	Difference.
47	67.555	—10.036
48	68.376	10.702
49	69.260	11.420
50	70.226	12.204

In 25 Years.

Age.	Initial Value.	Difference.
10	50.937	—4.404
11	50.992	4.430
12	51.050	4.453
13	51.116	4.484
14	51.187	4.526
15	51.269	4.572
16	51.351	4.621
17	51.440	4.674
18	51.534	4.739
19	51.634	4.804
20	51.740	4.872
21	51.853	4.957
22	51.972	5.045
23	52.099	5.124
24	52.233	5.216
25	52.376	5.304
26	52.537	5.413
27	52.706	5.520
28	52.886	5.639
29	53.081	5.759
30	53.292	5.892
31	53.519	6.020
32	53.766	6.179
33	54.034	6.332
34	54.324	6.487
35	54.640	6.666
36	54.985	6.830
37	55.366	7.003
38	55.779	7.194
39	56.239	7.386
40	56.748	7.584
41	57.313	7.794
42	57.942	8.034
43	58.630	8.340
44	59.408	8.728
45	60.242	9.180

In 30 Years.

Age.	Initial Value.	Difference.
10	44.328	—4.716
11	44.380	4.742
12	44.476	4.763
13	44.566	4.793
14	44.659	4.834
15	44.764	4.872
16	44.870	4.928
17	44.985	4.981
18	45.108	5.044
19	45.238	5.107
20	45.378	5.184
21	45.528	5.259
22	45.686	5.335
23	45.861	5.423
24	46.044	5.513
25	46.246	5.604
26	46.461	5.706
27	46.695	5.831
28	46.945	5.927
29	47.217	6.045
30	47.513	6.180
31	47.829	6.309
32	48.173	6.454
33	48.546	6.603
34	48.950	6.754
35	49.388	6.912
36	49.865	7.086
37	50.386	7.253
38	50.949	7.437
39	51.569	7.623
40	52.245	7.812

In 35 Years.

Age.	Initial Value.	Difference.
10	39.166	—4.968
11	39.269	4.983
12	39.369	5.003
13	39.480	5.034
14	39.594	5.074
15	39.726	5.112
16	39.864	5.165
17	40.013	5.216

In 35 Years.

Age.	Initial Value.	Difference.
18	40.174	—5.278
19	40.347	5.340
20	40.533	5.412
21	40.732	5.487
22	40.945	5.563
23	41.178	5.648
24	41.426	5.735
25	41.697	5.820
26	41.986	5.922
27	42.301	6.024
28	42.638	6.126
29	43.003	6.249
30	43.399	6.372
31	43.822	6.505
32	44.281	6.646
33	44.776	6.789
34	45.309	6.934
35	45.886	7.092

In 40 Years.

Age.	Initial Value.	Difference.
10	35.168	—5.148
11	35.302	5.170
12	35.440	5.188
13	35.584	5.217
14	35.719	5.256
15	35.889	5.292
16	36.068	5.345
17	36.262	5.394
18	36.472	5.454
19	36.697	5.513
20	36.940	5.580
21	37.200	5.656
22	37.479	5.728
23	37.783	5.811
24	38.107	5.895
25	38.451	5.976
26	38.836	6.074
27	39.242	6.172
28	39.678	6.280
29	40.148	6.389
30	40.654	6.516

SECOND YEAR.

In 15 Years.

Age.	Initial Value.	Difference.
10	136.539	—.403
11	136.569	.422
12	136.609	.452
13	136.648	.492
14	136.682	.532
15	136.728	.581
16	136.767	.631
17	136.813	.692
18	136.858	.751
19	136.907	.822
20	136.953	.888
21	137.005	.969
22	137.061	1.053
23	137.121	1.139
24	137.175	1.227
25	137.252	1.332
26	137.320	1.424
27	137.397	1.537
28	137.463	1.658
29	137.551	1.779
30	137.630	1.908
31	137.720	2.051
32	137.809	2.208
33	137.909	2.347
34	138.023	2.508
35	138.143	2.652
36	138.286	2.844
37	138.464	3.026
38	138.657	3.213
39	138.901	3.401
40	139.200	3.612
41	139.554	3.834
42	139.966	4.123
43	140.389	4.490
44	140.861	4.916
45	141.341	5.400
46	141.832	6.006
47	142.361	6.629
48	142.934	7.302
49	143.554	8.038
50	144.241	8.904
51	144.976	9.721
52	145.774	10.683
53	146.634	11.708

In 15 Years.

Age.	Initial Value.	Difference.
54	147.598	—12.841
55	148.631	14.064

In 20 Years.

Age.	Initial Value.	Difference.
10	114.688	—1.431
11	114.742	1.451
12	114.808	1.480
13	114.878	1.518
14	114.942	1.559
15	115.017	1.620
16	115.088	1.658
17	115.168	1.718
18	115.247	1.778
19	115.334	1.850
20	115.422	1.932
21	115.517	1.997
22	115.615	2.079
23	115.719	2.166
24	115.826	2.255
25	115.951	2.357
26	116.074	2.454
27	116.209	2.565
28	116.347	2.680
29	116.501	2.806
30	116.661	2.928
31	116.841	3.076
32	117.031	3.222
33	117.243	3.369
34	117.485	3.529
35	117.746	3.672
36	118.046	3.858
37	118.398	4.037
38	118.779	4.219
39	119.229	4.401
40	119.753	4.596
41	120.353	4.822
42	121.029	5.107
43	121.736	5.467
44	122.517	5.886
45	123.325	6.372
46	124.135	6.967

In 20 Years.

Age.	Initial Value.	Difference.
47	125.074	—7.581
48	126.050	8.245
49	127.100	8.973
50	128.247	9.816

In 25 Years.

Age.	Initial Value.	Difference.
10	97.462	—2.220
11	97.554	2.260
12	97.647	2.289
13	97.748	2.327
14	97.848	2.367
15	97.969	2.424
16	98.081	2.463
17	98.206	2.523
18	98.329	2.583
19	98.464	2.653
20	98.603	2.736
21	98.749	2.798
22	98.909	2.881
23	99.074	2.966
24	99.250	3.052
25	99.453	3.144
26	99.681	3.246
27	99.892	3.357
28	100.133	3.469
29	100.403	3.593
30	100.690	3.732
31	101.008	3.856
32	101.353	3.996
33	101.736	4.148
34	102.161	4.291
35	102.623	4.428
36	103.140	4.607
37	103.729	4.777
38	104.364	4.949
39	105.092	5.121
40	105.914	5.304
41	106.832	5.518
42	107.850	5.788
43	108.920	6.137
44	110.088	6.543
45	111.303	7.008

In 30 Years.

Age.	Initial Value.	Difference.
10	83.937	—2.868
11	84.032	2.898
12	84.189	2.924
13	84.339	2.961
14	84.484	2.998
15	84.652	3.060
16	84.812	3.092
17	84.989	3.151
18	85.172	3.208
19	85.369	3.278
20	85.574	3.348
21	85.797	3.417
22	86.037	3.497
23	86.299	3.579
24	86.575	3.663
25	86.888	3.756
26	87.216	3.850
27	87.559	3.956
28	87.963	4.060
29	88.389	4.178
30	88.850	4.320
31	89.349	4.429
32	89.892	4.562
33	90.489	4.695
34	91.146	4.841
35	91.858	4.968
36	92.644	5.132
37	93.519	5.291
38	94.461	5.450
39	95.515	5.609
40	96.679	5.772

In 35 Years.

Age.	Initial Value.	Difference.
10	73.370	—3.348
11	73.555	3.392
12	73.735	3.417
13	73.926	3.452
14	74.114	3.489
15	74.337	3.552
16	74.555	3.578
17	74.810	3.634

In 35 Years.

Age.	Initial Value.	Difference.
18	75.070	—3.688
19	75.354	3.754
20	75.653	3.840
21	75.977	3.867
22	76.328	3.963
23	76.708	4.040
24	77.117	4.118
25	77.571	4.200
26	78.050	4.295
27	78.578	4.392
28	79.150	4.490
29	79.757	4.601
30	80.421	4.728
31	81.139	4.834
32	81.916	4.956
33	82.763	5.077
34	83.684	5.212
35	84.680	5.340

In 40 Years.

Age.	Initial Value.	Difference.
10	65.186	—3.732
11	65.434	3.775
12	65.692	3.797
13	65.951	3.827
14	66.182	3.864
15	66.482	3.924
16	66.791	3.947
17	67.130	3.999
18	67.490	4.052
19	67.881	4.110
20	68.296	4.188
21	68.744	4.232
22	69.230	4.303
23	69.755	4.374
24	70.319	4.445
25	70.922	4.512
26	71.598	4.606
27	72.312	4.696
28	73.076	4.786
29	73.907	4.886
30	74.797	5.052

THIRD YEAR.—TEN PREM. ENDOWM'T POLICIES.—4 PER CENT.—(Arranged by Terms.)

In 15 Years.

AGE.	Initial Value.	Difference.
10	206.160	+2.859
11	206.198	2.831
12	206.239	2.796
13	206.274	2.757
14	206.306	2.713
15	206.348	2.669
16	206.383	2.612
17	206.418	2.557
18	206.458	2.492
19	206.494	2.424
20	206.532	2.352
21	206.571	2.278
22	206.611	2.199
23	206.659	2.117
24	206.699	2.028
25	206.760	1.932
26	206.818	1.832
27	206.875	1.727
28	206.914	1.608
29	206.986	1.489
30	207.046	1.356
31	207.105	1.223
32	207.158	1.084
33	207.246	.936
34	207.336	.780
35	207.461	.588
36	207.572	.457
37	207.747	.287
38	207.948	.112
39	208.224	—.074
40	208.569	.288
41	208.986	.546
42	209.440	.881
43	209.866	1.269
44	210.347	1.745
45	210.809	2.268
46	211.227	2.858
47	211.702	3.459
48	212.224	4.135
49	212.779	4.874
50	213.335	5.628
51	214.057	6.571
52	214.765	7.515
53	215.547	8.557
54	216.410	—9.691
55	217.342	10.888

In 20 Years.

AGE.	Initial Value.	Difference.
10	172.607	+1.276
11	172.680	1.249
12	172.761	1.215
13	172.846	1.179
14	172.920	1.133
15	172.997	1.092
16	173.088	1.032
17	173.175	.977
18	173.266	.910
19	173.357	.843
20	173.448	.780
21	173.561	.697
22	173.666	.617
23	173.780	.535
24	173.897	.445
25	174.039	.336
26	174.170	.248
27	174.316	.142
28	174.568	.026
29	174.634	—.096
30	174.815	.228
31	175.011	.360
32	175.226	.496
33	175.475	.646
34	175.747	.797
35	176.097	.972
36	176.445	1.111
37	176.882	1.276
38	177.369	1.443
39	177.961	1.620
40	178.653	1.824
41	179.436	2.078
42	180.289	2.405
43	181.188	2.787
44	182.095	3.259
45	183.050	3.780
46	183.986	4.340
47	185.048	—4.948
48	186.181	5.612
49	187.387	6.342
50	188.651	7.092

In 25 Years.

AGE.	Initial Value.	Difference.
10	146.172	+.012
11	146.286	.005
12	146.408	—.030
13	146.537	.065
14	146.668	.109
15	146.809	.134
16	146.969	.208
17	147.123	.263
18	147.280	.327
19	147.445	.393
20	147.611	.456
21	147.804	.536
22	148.000	.615
23	148.207	.685
24	148.431	.783
25	148.690	.885
26	148.972	.974
27	149.241	1.078
28	149.550	1.191
29	149.891	1.307
30	150.262	1.440
31	150.671	1.562
32	151.123	1.690
33	151.632	1.831
34	152.194	1.974
35	152.836	2.136
36	153.518	2.268
37	154.318	2.418
38	155.194	2.570
39	156.210	2.734
40	157.356	2.916
41	158.627	3.156
42	160.004	3.463
43	161.413	3.830
44	162.953	4.282
45	164.538	4.776

In 30 Years.

AGE.	Initial Value.	Difference.
10	125.401	—.948
11	125.521	.975
12	125.741	1.006
13	125.944	1.039
14	126.145	1.081
15	126.359	1.128
16	126.590	1.176
17	126.823	1.228
18	127.072	1.290
19	127.329	1.354
20	127.605	1.416
21	127.908	1.490
22	128.226	1.565
23	128.581	1.640
24	128.956	1.723
25	129.382	1.824
26	129.827	1.904
27	130.298	1.999
28	130.848	2.104
29	131.428	2.212
30	132.049	2.328
31	132.749	2.446
32	133.503	2.563
33	134.340	2.691
34	135.255	2.819
35	136.283	2.976
36	137.377	3.079
37	138.614	3.213
38	139.960	3.347
39	141.475	3.488
40	143.153	3.648

In 35 Years.

AGE.	Initial Value.	Difference.
10	109.185	—1.710
11	109.432	1.733
12	109.687	1.764
13	109.954	1.795
14	110.219	1.835
15	110.517	1.872
16	110.841	1.923
17	111.189	1.971
18	111.556	—2.030
19	111.947	2.088
20	112.349	2.136
21	112.822	2.213
22	113.310	2.283
23	113.846	2.350
24	114.425	2.425
25	115.064	2.532
26	115.741	2.588
27	116.487	2.672
28	117.298	2.768
29	118.159	2.862
30	119.089	2.964
31	120.127	3.069
32	121.241	3.172
33	122.462	3.282
34	123.781	3.394
35	125.230	3.528

In 40 Years.

AGE.	Initial Value.	Difference.
10	96.625	—2.316
11	96.961	2.321
12	97.335	2.347
13	97.706	2.374
14	98.037	2.411
15	98.448	2.448
16	98.912	2.490
17	99.393	2.532
18	99.910	2.584
19	100.468	2.636
20	101.046	2.676
21	101.712	2.746
22	102.406	2.807
23	103.164	2.865
24	103.981	2.930
25	104.921	3.012
26	105.828	3.069
27	106.858	3.141
28	107.968	3.223
29	109.169	3.303
30	110.396	3.360

FOURTH YEAR.

In 15 Years.

AGE.	Initial Value.	Difference.
10	279.043	+6.267
11	279.080	6.234
12	279.117	6.199
13	279.149	6.159
14	279.175	6.119
15	279.218	6.069
16	279.242	6.020
17	279.272	5.960
18	279.301	5.899
19	279.327	5.838
20	279.357	5.772
21	279.384	5.693
22	279.513	5.619
23	279.453	5.539
24	279.478	5.454
25	279.529	5.364
26	279.573	5.266
27	279.617	5.159
28	279.631	5.049
29	279.689	4.941
30	279.725	4.812
31	279.764	4.676
32	279.799	4.545
33	279.867	4.404
34	279.937	4.262
35	280.022	4.116
36	280.159	3.954
37	280.348	3.797
38	280.564	3.626
39	280.875	3.437
40	281.258	3.204
41	281.706	2.900
42	282.156	2.552
43	282.564	2.120
44	283.004	1.650
45	283.415	1.128
46	283.790	.573
47	284.213	—.045
48	284.681	.712
49	285.168	1.451
50	285.711	2.256
51	286.288	3.112
52	286.924	4.060
53	287.611	5.090
54	288.372	—6.180
55	289.241	7.380

In 20 Years.

AGE.	Initial Value.	Difference.
10	233.233	+4.108
11	233.318	4.075
12	233.409	4.043
13	233.509	4.000
14	233.590	3.958
15	233.681	3.900
16	233.778	3.861
17	233.877	3.799
18	233.973	3.737
19	234.073	3.673
20	234.180	3.612
21	234.299	3.530
22	234.413	3.454
23	234.542	3.373
24	234.668	3.286
25	234.817	3.192
26	234.968	3.094
27	235.120	2.987
28	235.295	2.879
29	235.477	2.758
30	235.674	2.640
31	235.897	2.511
32	236.147	2.374
33	236.430	2.233
34	236.741	2.098
35	237.145	1.944
36	237.591	1.800
37	238.127	1.650
38	238.735	1.489
39	239.474	1.309
40	240.325	1.080
41	241.263	.786
42	242.250	.443
43	243.288	.015
44	244.300	—.448
45	245.372	.960
46	246.454	1.517
47	247.655	—2.120
48	248.945	2.780
49	250.305	3.502
50	251.779	4.296

In 25 Years.

AGE.	Initial Value.	Difference.
10	197.122	+2.400
11	197.283	2.374
12	197.428	2.341
13	197.588	2.300
14	197.746	2.261
15	197.925	2.208
16	198.112	2.161
17	198.300	2.102
18	198.487	2.041
19	198.686	1.981
20	198.892	1.908
21	199.121	1.840
22	199.357	1.767
23	199.611	1.689
24	199.881	1.602
25	200.186	1.512
26	200.545	1.420
27	200.869	1.315
28	201.245	1.208
29	201.665	1.096
30	202.120	.972
31	202.628	.862
32	203.199	.735
33	203.835	.606
34	204.524	.482
35	205.337	.348
36	206.235	.210
37	207.266	.077
38	208.403	—.064
39	209.715	.222
40	211.181	.432
41	212.784	.702
42	214.483	1.025
43	216.213	1.429
44	218.079	1.871
45	220.002	2.364

In 30 Years.

AGE.	Initial Value.	Difference.
10	168.776	+1.056
11	168.943	1.034
12	169.211	1.007
13	169.471	.970
14	169.723	.933
15	169.999	.876
16	170.284	.839
17	170.580	.783
18	170.890	.725
19	171.213	.667
20	171.566	.600
21	171.946	.535
22	172.347	.467
23	172.802	.393
24	173.277	.315
25	173.808	.228
26	174.384	.146
27	174.994	.051
28	175.689	—.044
29	176.433	.146
30	177.233	.252
31	178.112	.352
32	179.113	.463
33	180.195	.574
34	181.386	.680
35	182.701	.792
36	184.163	.907
37	185.787	1.013
38	187.562	1.129
39	189.556	1.260
40	191.746	1.440

In 35 Years.

AGE.	Initial Value.	Difference.
10	146.615	+.024
11	146.968	—.002
12	147.292	.029
13	147.639	.064
14	147.978	.097
15	148.369	.144
16	148.782	.182
17	149.231	.233
18	149.700	—.285
19	150.206	.337
20	150.747	.396
21	151.341	.454
22	151.972	.515
23	152.674	.579
24	153.426	.647
25	154.246	.720
26	155.139	.790
27	156.116	.871
28	157.168	.950
29	158.300	1.038
30	159.523	1.128
31	160.880	1.206
32	162.350	1.291
33	163.956	1.386
34	165.696	1.467
35	167.592	1.548

In 40 Years.

AGE.	Initial Value.	Difference.
10	129.472	—.780
11	129.942	.807
12	130.428	.827
13	130.916	.855
14	131.345	.886
15	131.893	.924
16	132.490	.958
17	133.123	1.002
18	133.798	1.045
19	134.529	1.087
20	135.312	1.140
21	136.166	1.185
22	137.078	1.231
23	138.082	1.284
24	139.158	1.336
25	140.366	1.392
26	141.595	1.451
27	142.959	1.514
28	144.423	1.576
29	146.014	1.642
30	147.710	1.704

FIFTH YEAR.—TEN PREM. ENDOWM'T POLICIES.—4 PER CENT.—(Arranged by Terms.)

In 15 Years.

Age.	Initial Value.	Difference.
10	355.334	+9.835
11	355.365	9.805
12	355.398	9.772
13	355.426	9.734
14	355.450	9.685
15	355.489	9.646
16	355.509	9.593
17	355.529	9.540
18	355.552	9.483
19	355.574	9.422
20	355.596	9.372
21	355.612	9.289
22	355.635	9.216
23	355.669	9.141
24	355.683	9.056
25	355.728	8.964
26	355.762	8.878
27	355.792	8.781
28	355.799	8.672
29	355.834	8.565
30	355.855	8.448
31	355.876	8.330
32	355.901	8.192
33	355.955	8.076
34	356.021	7.940
35	356.111	7.800
36	356.243	7.659
37	356.454	7.509
38	356.694	7.329
39	357.038	7.128
40	357.441	6.828
41	357.872	6.554
42	358.305	6.175
43	358.647	5.759
44	359.056	5.299
45	359.421	4.800
46	359.764	4.254
47	360.138	3.661
48	360.561	3.003
49	360.980	2.281
50	361.458	1.512
51	361.978	.670
52	362.538	—.246
53	363.142	1.220
54	363.885	—2.290
55	364.641	3.456

In 20 Years.

Age.	Initial Value.	Difference.
10	296.691	+7.067
11	296.782	7.058
12	296.885	7.002
13	296.994	6.964
14	297.076	6.919
15	297.182	6.864
16	297.297	6.819
17	297.401	6.765
18	297.501	6.706
19	297.619	6.644
20	297.741	6.576
21	297.870	6.509
22	297.997	6.437
23	298.142	6.357
24	298.280	6.274
25	298.445	6.180
26	298.612	6.089
27	298.779	5.989
28	298.975	5.882
29	299.174	5.766
30	299.396	5.652
31	299.654	5.534
32	299.938	5.408
33	300.264	5.285
34	300.630	5.150
35	301.111	5.016
36	301.648	4.882
37	302.298	4.741
38	303.033	4.580
39	303.916	4.372
40	304.900	4.080
41	305.954	3.808
42	307.059	3.430
43	308.190	3.016
44	309.316	2.559
45	210.509	2.076
46	311.745	1.519
47	313.090	+.934
48	314.541	.285
49	316.063	—.427
50	317.708	1.176

In 25 Years.

Age.	Initial Value.	Difference.
10	250.459	+4.908
11	250.649	4.856
12	250.819	4.820
13	251.004	4.785
14	251.194	4.740
15	251.401	4.692
16	251.624	4.643
17	251.842	4.588
18	252.062	4.533
19	252.301	4.472
20	252.546	4.416
21	252.814	4.340
22	253.096	4.270
23	253.399	4.192
24	253.716	4.109
25	254.078	4.020
26	254.512	3.934
27	254.890	3.837
28	255.339	3.735
29	255.842	3.629
30	256.390	3.516
31	257.009	3.412
32	257.700	3.298
33	258.475	3.189
34	259.320	3.067
35	260.323	2.952
36	261.430	2.837
37	262.709	2.716
38	264.118	2.577
39	265.732	2.397
40	267.500	2.124
41	269.395	1.878
42	271.400	1.525
43	273.414	1.134
44	275.616	.704
45	277.884	.252

In 30 Years.

Age.	Initial Value.	Difference.
10	214.159	+3.192
11	214.374	3.139
12	214.704	3.111
13	215.007	3.078
14	215.305	3.036
15	215.644	3.000
16	215.993	2.945
17	216.348	2.894
18	216.723	2.843
19	217.118	2.783
20	217.547	2.736
21	218.009	2.664
22	218.500	2.602
23	219.056	2.530
24	219.636	2.455
25	220.285	2.376
26	220.991	2.297
27	221.740	2.212
28	222.590	2.124
29	223.504	2.033
30	224.496	1.944
31	225.579	1.849
32	226.823	1.755
33	228.167	1.668
34	229.656	1.571
35	231.296	1.476
36	233.121	1.394
37	235.160	1.306
38	237.382	1.201
39	239.865	1.055
40	242.555	.816

In 35 Years.

Age.	Initial Value.	Difference.
10	185.809	+1.860
11	186.235	1.813
12	186.632	1.785
13	187.055	1.775
14	187.471	1.761
15	187.948	1.680
16	188.464	1.636
17	189.011	1.592
18	189.589	+1.547
19	190.216	1.496
20	190.885	1.452
21	191.619	1.395
22	192.402	1.341
23	193.273	1.280
24	194.205	1.221
25	195.226	1.176
26	196.335	1.091
27	197.546	1.028
28	198.856	.956
29	200.265	.886
30	201.799	.840
31	203.496	.749
32	205.334	.681
33	207.346	.624
34	209.538	.557
35	211.926	.480

In 40 Years.

Age.	Initial Value.	Difference.
10	163.856	+.816
11	164.437	.781
12	165.041	.760
13	165.645	.739
14	166.178	.704
15	166.853	.672
16	167.600	.640
17	168.383	.606
18	169.225	.573
19	170.139	.534
20	171.116	.504
21	172.181	.458
22	173.326	.417
23	174.581	.378
24	175.929	.334
25	177.426	.300
26	178.980	.245
27	180.687	.202
28	182.525	.154
29	184.520	.108
30	186.659	.072

SIXTH YEAR.

In 15 Years.

Age.	Initial Value.	Difference.
10	435.194	+13.578
11	435.221	13.549
12	435.252	13.519
13	435.278	13.480
14	435.291	13.439
15	435.336	13.395
16	435.349	13.349
17	435.366	13.298
18	435.387	13.249
19	435.405	13.189
20	435.432	13.128
21	435.436	13.068
22	435.454	13.002
23	435.487	12.934
24	435.490	12.859
25	435.532	12.780
26	435.563	12.689
27	435.580	12.597
28	435.588	12.504
29	435.613	12.404
30	435.629	12.300
31	435.642	12.186
32	435.650	12.084
33	435.716	11.957
34	435.782	11.835
35	435.881	11.712
36	436.031	11.579
37	436.272	11.433
38	436.528	11.148
39	436.891	11.019
40	437.253	10.752
41	437.692	10.422
42	438.077	10.065
43	438.377	9.557
44	438.757	9.233
45	439.099	8.760
46	439.419	8.242
47	439.769	7.674
48	440.156	7.044
49	440.524	6.378
50	440.972	5.652
51	441.450	4.853
52	441.966	4.010
53	442.543	3.074
54	443.258	+2.060
55	443.963	.912

In 20 Years.

Age.	Initial Value.	Difference.
10	363.108	+10.175
11	363.209	10.143
12	363.320	10.111
13	363.442	10.068
14	363.432	10.031
15	363.647	9.984
16	363.774	9.933
17	363.891	9.883
18	364.004	9.827
19	364.136	9.765
20	364.277	9.708
21	364.420	9.642
22	364.564	9.575
23	364.726	9.499
24	364.880	9.419
25	365.062	9.336
26	365.251	9.247
27	365.440	9.152
28	365.658	9.050
29	365.879	8.954
30	366.135	8.844
31	366.434	8.730
32	366.763	8.626
33	367.151	8.503
34	367.571	8.384
35	368.144	8.268
36	368.777	8.141
37	369.550	8.004
38	370.422	7.822
39	371.421	7.595
40	372.480	7.332
41	373.667	6.998
42	374.855	6.639
43	376.093	6.233
44	377.339	5.803
45	378.678	5.328
46	380.072	4.807
47	381.579	+4.244
48	383.202	3.621
49	384.896	2.963
50	386.754	2.232

In 25 Years.

Age.	Initial Value.	Difference.
10	306.305	+7.488
11	306.497	7.453
12	306.689	7.424
13	306.905	7.400
14	307.121	7.344
15	307.365	7.296
16	307.618	7.240
17	307.870	7.203
18	308.129	7.147
19	308.407	7.091
20	308.701	7.032
21	309.007	6.970
22	309.338	6.898
23	309.690	6.824
24	310.058	6.750
25	310.479	6.660
26	310.993	6.580
27	311.433	6.495
28	311.960	6.399
29	312.552	6.309
30	313.205	6.204
31	313.940	6.108
32	314.764	6.012
33	315.698	5.905
34	316.701	5.805
35	317.913	5.712
36	319.242	5.609
37	320.781	5.494
38	322.474	5.337
39	324.368	5.128
40	326.375	4.884
41	328.586	4.590
42	330.867	4.253
43	333.178	3.874
44	335.728	3.478
45	338.374	3.036

In 30 Years.

Age.	Initial Value.	Difference.
10	261.682	+5.376
11	261.910	5.346
12	262.301	5.319
13	262.651	5.283
14	262.990	5.248
15	263.404	5.208
16	263.808	5.162
17	264.227	5.115
18	264.674	5.067
19	265.139	5.010
20	265.658	4.956
21	266.201	4.903
22	266.788	4.840
23	267.447	4.775
24	268.135	4.709
25	268.907	4.632
26	269.749	4.565
27	270.647	4.488
28	271.659	4.411
29	272.755	4.339
30	273.951	4.267
31	275.247	4.177
32	276.751	4.106
33	278.381	4.026
34	280.177	3.954
35	282.160	3.888
36	284.380	3.823
37	286.852	3.746
38	289.532	3.631
39	292.489	3.468
40	295.621	3.264

In 35 Years.

Age.	Initial Value.	Difference.
10	226.853	+3.732
11	227.307	3.707
12	227.786	3.694
13	228.290	3.653
14	228.785	3.622
15	229.353	3.576
16	229.964	3.547
17	230.616	3.508
18	231.310	+3.467
19	232.059	3.422
20	232.870	3.384
21	233.746	3.337
22	234.688	3.283
23	235.731	3.236
24	236.852	3.187
25	238.096	3.132
26	239.412	3.080
27	240.875	3.023
28	242.450	2.969
29	244.154	2.920
30	246.016	2.868
31	248.067	2.813
32	250.296	2.778
33	252.746	2.734
34	255.404	2.703
35	258.295	2.676

In 40 Years.

Age.	Initial Value.	Difference.
10	199.840	+2.460
11	200.520	2.439
12	201.241	2.429
13	201.968	2.404
14	202.601	2.375
15	203.417	2.340
16	204.308	2.321
17	205.251	2.295
18	206.270	2.266
19	207.370	2.236
20	208.559	2.208
21	209.839	2.180
22	211.222	2.151
23	212.742	2.121
24	214.370	2.091
25	216.180	2.064
26	218.061	2.032
27	220.131	2.002
28	222.357	1.975
29	224.776	1.959
30	227.391	1.932

SEVENTH YEAR.—TEN PREM. ENDOWM'T POLICIES.—4 PER CENT.—(Arranged by Terms.)

In 15 Years.

Age.	Initial Value.	Difference.
10	518.796	+17.507
11	518.821	17.480
12	518.853	17.444
13	518.866	17.416
14	518.886	17.375
15	518.933	17.337
16	518.946	17.295
17	518.961	17.253
18	518.988	17.204
19	519.003	17.152
20	519.035	17.100
21	519.039	17.047
22	519.059	16.989
23	519.098	16.926
24	519.100	16.854
25	519.141	16.788
26	519.175	16.707
27	519.200	16.628
28	519.203	16.545
29	519.231	16.458
30	519.249	16.368
31	519.264	16.269
32	519.291	16.169
33	519.358	16.066
34	519.438	15.964
35	519.562	15.852
36	519.740	15.730
37	520.004	15.576
38	520.280	15.380
39	520.636	15.156
40	520.980	14.880
41	521.380	14.583
42	521.739	14.254
43	521.997	13.886
44	522.392	13.494
45	522.735	13.068
46	523.062	12.593
47	523.413	12.064
48	523.792	11.508
49	524.175	10.889
50	524.624	10.224
51	525.105	9.520
52	525.650	8.749
53	526.238	7.890
54	526.981	+6.937
55	527.661	5.892

In 20 Years.

Age.	Initial Value.	Difference.
10	432.633	+13.428
11	432.741	13.400
12	432.864	13.365
13	432.994	13.336
14	433.100	13.290
15	433.222	13.248
16	433.365	13.203
17	433.499	13.157
18	433.628	13.104
19	433.774	13.053
20	433.939	12.996
21	434.103	12.937
22	434.269	12.874
23	434.452	12.804
24	434.625	12.731
25	434.830	12.648
26	435.048	12.575
27	435.264	12.485
28	435.509	12.404
29	435.772	12.305
30	436.062	12.204
31	436.410	12.117
32	436.806	12.011
33	437.255	11.909
34	437.746	11.817
35	438.426	11.700
36	439.165	11.586
37	440.065	11.432
38	441.053	11.237
39	442.149	11.010
40	443.302	10.716
41	444.570	10.418
42	445.860	10.074
43	447.213	9.708
44	448.606	9.304
45	450.104	8.856
46	451.687	8.375
47	453.378	+7.846
48	455.199	7.293
49	457.119	6.674
50	459.213	6.000

In 25 Years.

Age.	Initial Value.	Difference.
10	364.727	+10.212
11	364.942	10.185
12	365.163	10.153
13	365.421	10.119
14	365.652	10.075
15	365.932	10.032
16	366.209	9.994
17	366.513	9.948
18	366.800	9.894
19	367.132	9.845
20	367.473	9.792
21	367.830	9.732
22	368.208	9.666
23	368.613	9.604
24	369.041	9.529
25	369.526	9.456
26	370.020	9.372
27	370.624	9.297
28	371.245	9.219
29	371.942	9.130
30	372.704	9.048
31	373.567	8.966
32	374.542	8.875
33	375.637	8.794
34	376.820	8.712
35	378.262	8.628
36	379.826	8.533
37	381.631	8.407
38	383.590	8.233
39	385.745	8.028
40	388.012	7.765
41	390.489	7.484
42	393.062	7.169
43	395.682	6.828
44	398.614	6.464
45	401.653	6.060

In 30 Years.

Age.	Initial Value.	Difference.
10	311.387	+7.692
11	311.653	7.664
12	312.106	7.630
13	312.500	7.601
14	312.887	7.562
15	313.372	7.524
16	313.840	7.488
17	314.327	7.447
18	314.849	7.400
19	315.387	7.354
20	315.995	7.308
21	316.632	7.254
22	317.314	7.199
23	318.083	7.144
24	318.888	7.079
25	319.789	7.020
26	320.775	6.951
27	321.830	6.888
28	323.015	6.829
29	324.311	6.759
30	325.718	6.696
31	327.343	6.650
32	329.030	6.581
33	330.953	6.529
34	333.081	6.487
35	335.437	6.431
36	338.068	6.381
37	340.984	6.294
38	344.112	6.168
39	347.526	6.008
40	351.129	5.784

In 35 Years.

Age.	Initial Value.	Difference.
10	269.729	+5.712
11	270.253	5.700
12	270.839	5.683
13	271.403	5.648
14	272.001	5.615
15	272.661	5.580
16	273.375	5.551
17	274.137	5.519
18	274.951	+5.481
19	275.828	5.446
20	276.783	5.412
21	277.815	5.370
22	278.916	5.331
23	280.145	5.294
24	281.465	5.249
25	282.924	5.208
26	284.478	5.169
27	286.199	5.139
28	288.057	5.095
29	290.077	5.059
30	292.279	5.028
31	294.702	5.006
32	297.355	4.983
33	300.256	4.974
34	303.406	4.972
35	306.855	4.968

In 40 Years.

Age.	Initial Value.	Difference.
10	237.462	+4.188
11	238.261	4.182
12	239.110	4.165
13	239.956	4.151
14	240.695	4.120
15	241.652	4.104
16	242.697	4.084
17	243.808	4.063
18	245.008	4.042
19	246.303	4.025
20	247.709	4.008
21	249.219	3.990
22	250.852	3.971
23	252.646	3.955
24	254.568	3.937
25	256.692	3.924
26	258.929	3.911
27	261.375	3.903
28	264.010	3.904
29	266.883	3.902
30	269.983	3.912

EIGHTH YEAR.

In 15 Years.

Age.	Initial Value.	Difference.
10	606.328	+21.624
11	606.351	21.595
12	606.369	21.571
13	606.400	21.541
14	606.422	21.512
15	606.471	21.482
16	606.489	21.447
17	606.511	21.404
18	606.544	21.369
19	606.564	21.326
20	606.608	21.288
21	606.621	21.234
22	606.651	21.189
23	606.701	21.134
24	606.705	21.075
25	606.761	21.012
26	606.805	20.949
27	606.843	20.887
28	606.867	20.816
29	606.903	20.751
30	606.934	20.672
31	606.969	20.589
32	607.017	20.507
33	607.109	20.425
34	607.223	20.322
35	607.383	20.232
36	607.600	20.117
37	607.879	19.963
38	608.164	19.783
39	608.518	19.566
40	608.838	19.332
41	609.229	19.069
42	609.590	18.788
43	609.860	18.462
44	610.288	18.132
45	610.674	17.760
46	611.056	17.341
47	611.447	16.898
48	611.892	16.419
49	612.343	15.893
50	612.853	15.336
51	613.427	14.729
52	614.063	14.060
53	614.749	13.311
54	615.581	+12.488
55	616.335	11.580

In 20 Years.

Age.	Initial Value.	Difference.
10	505.411	+16.847
11	505.530	16.817
12	505.662	16.791
13	505.814	16.755
14	505.927	16.722
15	506.064	16.680
16	506.226	16.647
17	506.381	16.601
18	506.529	16.559
19	506.700	16.512
20	506.890	16.464
21	507.081	16.409
22	507.273	16.354
23	507.483	16.289
24	507.682	16.227
25	507.919	16.152
26	508.173	16.074
27	508.421	16.017
28	508.714	15.934
29	509.016	15.854
30	509.357	15.780
31	509.773	15.690
32	510.234	15.607
33	510.765	15.527
34	511.354	15.441
35	512.145	15.346
36	512.998	15.213
37	514.008	15.055
38	515.099	14.868
39	516.292	14.630
40	517.520	14.376
41	518.893	14.094
42	520.300	13.798
43	521.808	13.456
44	523.374	13.107
45	525.063	12.708
46	526.860	12.261
47	528.779	+11.818
48	530.858	11.319
49	533.063	10.773
50	535.440	10.200

In 25 Years.

Age.	Initial Value.	Difference.
10	425.874	+13.068
11	426.119	13.045
12	426.366	13.015
13	426.656	12.980
14	426.924	12.947
15	427.235	12.912
16	427.554	12.872
17	427.901	12.829
18	428.228	12.783
19	428.611	12.742
20	429.002	12.696
21	429.415	12.635
22	429.846	12.584
23	430.316	12.519
24	430.803	12.457
25	431.361	12.392
26	431.9[illegible]9	12.321
27	432.617	12.264
28	433.350	12.189
29	434.153	12.115
30	435.038	12.048
31	436.05[illegible]	[illegible].975
32	437.183	11.909
33	438.465	11.847
34	439.846	11.781
35	441.526	11.700
36	443.334	11.604
37	445.394	11.468
38	447.602	11.299
39	450.012	11.078
40	452.523	10.850
41	455.286	10.594
42	458.173	10.323
43	461.250	10.019
44	464.486	9.697
45	467.952	9.336

In 30 Years.

Age.	Initial Value.	Difference.
10	363.403	+10.116
11	363.814	10.085
12	364.222	10.062
13	364.677	10.031
14	365.098	9.998
15	365.662	9.972
16	366.198	9.932
17	366.759	9.890
18	367.357	9.854
19	367.979	9.806
20	368.676	9.768
21	369.414	9.724
22	370.199	9.693
23	371.088	9.629
24	372.011	9.577
25	373.052	9.516
26	374.187	9.474
27	375.413	9.424
28	376.789	9.374
29	378.317	9.323
30	379.926	9.276
31	381.812	9.245
32	383.784	9.202
33	386.028	9.179
34	388.518	9.151
35	391.258	9.118
36	394.300	9.062
37	397.664	8.968
38	401.229	8.849
39	405.103	8.683
40	409.163	8.496

In 35 Years.

Age.	Initial Value.	Difference.
10	314.611	+7.800
11	315.201	7.781
12	315.861	7.764
13	316.511	7.737
14	317.210	7.712
15	317.969	7.693
16	318.790	7.662
17	319.669	7.634
18	320.606	+7.604
19	321.621	7.579
20	322.726	7.549
21	323.917	7.520
22	325.192	7.490
23	326.617	7.459
24	328.140	7.429
25	329.831	7.392
26	331.633	7.376
27	333.619	7.356
28	335.790	7.334
29	338.139	7.318
30	340.702	7.308
31	343.530	7.308
32	346.619	7.324
33	350.006	7.347
34	353.657	7.371
35	357.712	7.392

In 40 Years.

Age.	Initial Value.	Difference.
10	276.818	+6.012
11	277.745	6.000
12	278.715	5.993
13	279.691	5.980
14	280.534	5.958
15	281.643	5.953
16	282.849	5.937
17	284.133	5.923
18	285.522	5.914
19	287.025	5.908
20	288.656	5.893
21	290.409	5.891
22	292.302	5.885
23	294.384	5.880
24	296.612	5.882
25	299.068	5.883
26	301.676	5.891
27	304.520	5.910
28	307.592	5.924
29	310.933	5.958
30	314.547	5.988

In 15 Years.

Age.	Initial Value.	Difference.
10	697.976	+25.945
11	697.997	25.931
12	698.032	25.911
13	698.059	25.887
14	698.100	25.864
15	698.140	25.842
16	698.183	25.809
17	698.212	25.779
18	698.265	25.752
19	698.299	25.726
20	698.363	25.692
21	698.390	25.654
22	698.443	25.619
23	698.502	25.572
24	698.543	25.524
25	698.611	25.488
26	698.677	25.438
27	698.745	25.368
28	698.802	25.331
29	698.868	25.279
30	698.923	25.224
31	698.994	25.165
32	699.091	25.106
33	699.219	25.042
34	699.366	24.970
35	699.590	24.888
36	699.847	24.773
37	700.141	24.647
38	700.451	24.487
39	700.809	24.317
40	701.144	24.132
41	701.564	23.928
42	701.975	23.704
43	702.385	23.452
44	702.822	23.193
45	703.305	22.908
46	703.798	22.588
47	704.315	22.249
48	704.903	21.873
49	705.509	21.485
50	706.193	21.048
51	706.958	20.581
52	707.787	20.061
53	708.681	19.483

In 15 Years.

Age.	Initial Value.	Difference.
54	709.652	+18.760
55	710.699	18.168

In 20 Years.

Age.	Initial Value.	Difference.
10	581.608	+20.430
11	581.736	20.410
12	581.886	20.380
13	582.053	20.352
14	582.186	20.323
15	582.341	20.292
16	582.531	20.254
17	582.707	20.224
18	582.885	20.192
19	583.085	20.148
20	583.304	20.100
21	583.521	20.064
22	583.757	20.019
23	583.999	19.968
24	584.235	19.910
25	584.508	19.852
26	584.800	19.804
27	585.100	19.744
28	585.449	19.673
29	585.800	19.615
30	586.218	19.548
31	586.709	19.479
32	587.258	19.422
33	587.893	19.356
34	588.586	19.279
35	589.500	19.176
36	590.458	19.057
37	591.574	18.907
38	592.776	18.722
39	594.055	18.526
40	595.390	18.312
41	596.892	18.075
42	598.464	17.816
43	600.151	17.542
44	601.945	17.248
45	603.867	16.908
46	605.919	16.558

In 20 Years.

Age.	Initial Value.	Difference.
47	608.142	+16.199
48	610.543	15.783
49	613.106	15.350
50	615.870	14.892

In 25 Years.

Age.	Initial Value.	Difference.
10	489.882	+16.068
11	490.156	16.051
12	490.436	16.020
13	490.752	15.992
14	491.068	15.964
15	491.415	15.936
16	491.777	15.899
17	492.170	15.864
18	492.555	15.829
19	492.987	15.787
20	493.433	15.742
21	493.903	15.702
22	494.402	15.651
23	494.934	15.602
24	495.498	15.546
25	496.131	15.492
26	496.807	15.436
27	497.577	15.389
28	498.425	15.323
29	499.339	15.276
30	500.373	15.216
31	501.546	15.168
32	502.858	15.127
33	504.346	15.076
34	505.941	15.024
35	507.870	14.940
36	509.913	14.848
37	512.218	14.718
38	514.680	14.550
39	517.319	14.369
40	520.119	14.160
41	523.193	13.948
42	526.428	13.734
43	529.889	13.477
44	533.591	13.210
45	537.530	12.910

In 30 Years.

Age.	Initial Value.	Difference.
10	417.843	+12.648
11	418.296	12.631
12	418.770	12.605
13	419.284	12.582
14	419.745	12.555
15	420.393	12.528
16	421.000	12.499
17	421.634	12.466
18	422.319	12.442
19	423.023	12.402
20	423.825	12.360
21	424.666	12.332
22	425.568	12.290
23	426.568	12.252
24	427.632	12.210
25	428.819	12.168
26	430.122	12.134
27	431.532	12.098
28	433.108	12.058
29	434.827	12.037
30	436.717	12.012
31	438.866	11.996
32	441.159	11.982
33	443.753	11.976
34	446.549	11.969
35	449.763	11.940
36	453.211	11.873
37	457.018	11.798
38	461.027	11.680
39	465.355	11.549
40	469.904	11.400

In 35 Years.

Age.	Initial Value.	Difference.
10	361.576	+9.983
11	362.232	9.972
12	362.970	9.951
13	363.708	9.937
14	364.516	9.912
15	365.381	9.888
16	366.316	9.870
17	367.316	9.852

In 35 Years.

Age.	Initial Value.	Difference.
18	368.384	+9.[illegible]
19	369.547	9.808
20	370.806	9.792
21	372.169	9.776
22	373.627	9.753
23	375.254	9.737
24	376.994	9.717
25	378.924	9.708
26	380.990	9.703
27	383.266	9.694
28	385.762	9.697
29	388.450	9.711
30	391.412	9.720
31	394.660	9.751
32	398.224	9.800
33	402.119	9.850
34	406.307	9.899
35	410.989	9.925

In 40 Years.

Age.	Initial Value.	Difference.
10	317.994	+7.918
11	318.947	7.913
12	320.148	7.906
13	321.255	7.902
14	322.211	7.890
15	323.481	7.884
16	324.854	7.883
17	326.318	7.880
18	327.908	7.880
19	329.630	7.882
20	331.494	7.884
21	333.500	7.890
22	335.666	7.896
23	338.047	7.912
24	340.601	7.926
25	343.402	7.956
26	346.403	7.987
27	349.672	8.021
28	353.179	8.068
29	357.039	8.131
30	361.199	8.196

SINGLE PREMIUMS.

In 5 Years.

Age	Value
20	824.433
21	824.463
22	824.495
23	824.530
24	824.567
25	824.609
26	824.647
27	824.690
28	824.736
29	824.785
30	824.824
31	824.883
32	824.953
33	825.012
34	825.077
35	825.143
36	825.214
37	825.295
38	825.359
39	825.437
40	825.525
41	825.627
42	825.747
43	825.868
44	826.068
45	826.267
46	826.496
47	826.743
48	827.009
49	827.300
50	827.620
51	827.965
52	828.347
53	828.749
54	829.187
55	829.664
56	830.178
57	830.732
58	831.341
59	832.010
60	832.744
61	833.541
62	834.410
63	835.350

In 5 Years.

Age	Value
64	836.371
65	837.470

In 10 Years.

Age	Value
20	685.577
21	685.705
22	685.845
23	685.991
24	686.149
25	686.304
26	686.491
27	686.676
28	686.873
29	687.081
30	687.281
31	687.531
32	687.768
33	688.019
34	688.281
35	688.558
36	688.857
37	689.187
38	689.520
39	689.930
40	690.388
41	690.918
42	691.534
43	692.176
44	693.048
45	693.918
46	694.937
47	696.011
48	697.174
49	698.432
50	699.798
51	701.268
52	702.865
53	704.576
54	706.424
55	708.426
56	710.589

In 10 Years.

Age	Value
57	712.923
58	715.456
59	718.197
60	721.162

In 15 Years.

Age	Value
20	576.090
21	576.387
22	576.687
23	577.017
24	577.361
25	577.715
26	578.111
27	578.523
28	578.924
29	579.391
30	579.844
31	580.366
32	580.899
33	581.471
34	582.092
35	582.768
36	583.517
37	584.364
38	585.263
39	586.297
40	587.[illegible]
41	588.776
42	590.263
43	591.865
44	593.788
45	595.797
46	598.048
47	600.448
48	603.030
49	605.814
50	608.820
51	612.049
52	615.530
53	619.254
54	623.252

In 15 Years.

Age	Value
55	627.546

In 20 Years.

Age	Value
20	490.118
21	490.628
22	491.144
23	491.703
24	492.288
25	492.887
26	493.561
27	494.264
28	495.000
29	495.796
30	496.631
31	497.580
32	498.586
33	499.680
34	500.879
35	502.194
36	503.644
37	505.262
38	507.005
39	508.966
40	511.139
41	513.552
42	516.233
43	519.130
44	522.451
45	525.959
46	529.819
47	533.936
48	538.342
49	543.066
50	548.126

In 25 Years.

Age	Value
20	422.964
21	423.724

In 25 Years.

Age	Value
22	424.505
23	425.348
24	426.248
25	427.199
26	428.244
27	429.366
28	430.560
29	431.863
30	433.242
31	434.807
32	436.476
33	438.294
34	440.279
35	442.446
36	444.820
37	447.437
38	450.261
39	453.389
40	456.817
41	460.579
42	464.708
43	469.144
44	474.119
45	479.368

In 30 Years.

Age	Value
20	370.968
21	372.038
22	373.167
23	374.414
24	375.741
25	377.164
26	378.718
27	380.397
28	382.197
29	384.157
30	386.259
31	388.586
32	391.071
33	393.782
34	396.726

In 30 Years.

Age	Value
35	399.922
36	403.396
37	407.192
38	411.274
39	415.737
40	420.563

In 35 Years.

Age	Value
20	331.340
21	332.848
22	334.438
23	336.186
24	338.055
25	340.052
26	342.243
27	344.601
28	347.129
29	349.870
30	352.804
31	356.026
32	359.472
33	363.198
34	367.218
35	371.562

In 40 Years.

Age	Value
20	301.971
21	303.986
22	306.127
23	308.467
24	310.967
25	313.648
26	316.560
27	319.687
28	323.034
29	326.642
30	330.528

LIFE POLICIES.—FIFTEEN PREMIUMS.—4 PER CENT.

1st Year.

Age.	Initial Value.	Final Value.
13	20.197	14.254
14	20.536	14.561
15	20.886	14.881
16	21.252	15.206
17	21.634	15.547
18	22.027	15.887
19	22.432	16.340
20	22.856	16.601
21	23.294	16.974
22	23.749	17.365
23	24.220	17.759
24	24.708	18.170
25	25.213	18.596
26	25.737	19.030
27	26.280	19.481
28	26.842	19.939
29	27.425	20.417
30	28.028	20.900
31	28.653	21.405
32	29.302	21.919
33	29.974	22.454
34	30.671	23.011
35	31.397	23.584
36	32.153	24.182
37	32.940	24.811
38	33.763	25.460
39	34.622	26.141
40	35.526	26.864
41	36.473	27.613
42	37.470	28.383
43	38.522	29.140
44	39.626	29.863
45	40.783	30.576
46	41.994	31.236
47	43.254	31.899
48	44.569	32.556
49	45.945	33.222
50	47.382	33.878
51	48.887	34.528
52	50.464	35.166
53	52.119	35.794
54	53.859	36.440
55	55.692	37.058
56	57.626	37.676
57	59.670	38.323
58	61.842	38.958
59	64.145	39.583
60	66.598	40.144
	74.934	41.687

2d Year.

Age.	Initial Value.	Final Value.
13	34.451	29.126
14	35.096	29.764
15	35.767	30.413
16	36.458	31.070
17	37.181	31.715
18	37.914	32.429
19	38.672	33.178
20	39.457	33.907
21	40.268	34.678
22	41.114	35.457
23	41.979	36.266
24	42.878	37.104
25	43.809	37.973
26	44.767	38.861
27	45.761	39.774
28	46.781	40.718
29	47.842	41.679
30	48.928	42.677
31	50.058	43.701
32	51.221	44.746
33	52.428	45.843
34	53.682	46.985
35	54.981	48.158
36	56.335	49.376
37	57.751	50.658
38	59.223	51.986
39	60.763	53.397
40	62.390	54.842
41	64.086	56.369
42	65.853	57.887
43	67.662	59.365
44	69.489	60.802
45	71.359	62.173
46	73.230	63.494
47	75.153	64.831
48	77.125	66.161
49	79.167	67.470
50	81.260	68.778
51	83.415	70.060
52	85.630	71.327
53	87.913	72.591
54	90.299	73.840
55	92.750	75.074
56	95.302	76.320
57	97.993	77.580
58	100.800	78.790
59	103.728	79.963
60	106.742	81.050

3d Year.

Age.	Initial Value.	Final Value.
13	49.323	44.670
14	50.299	45.628
15	51.299	46.618
16	52.322	47.613
17	53.349	48.635
18	54.456	49.705
19	55.630	50.832
20	56.763	51.958
21	57.972	53.128
22	59.206	54.325
23	60.486	55.567
24	61.812	56.847
25	63.186	58.172
26	64.598	59.529
27	66.054	60.924
28	67.560	62.364
29	69.104	63.837
30	70.705	65.358
31	72.354	66.925
32	74.048	68.538
33	75.817	70.214
34	77.656	71.962
35	79.555	73.762
36	81.529	75.636
37	83.598	77.599
38	85.749	79.641
39	88.019	81.795
40	90.368	84.005
41	92.842	86.276
42	95.357	88.509
43	97.887	90.697
44	100.428	92.792
45	102.956	94.842
46	105.488	96.829
47	108.085	98.809
48	110.730	100.833
49	113.415	102.790
50	116.160	104.738
51	118.947	106.648
52	121.791	108.550
53	124.710	110.427
54	127.699	112.282
55	130.766	114.129
56	133.946	115.981
57	137.250	117.823
58	140.632	119.547
59	144.108	121.216
60	147.648	122.744

4th Year.

Age.	Initial Value.	Final Value.
13	64.867	60.885
14	66.163	62.186
15	67.504	63.515
16	68.865	64.889
17	70.269	66.272
18	71.732	67.725
19	73.264	69.248
20	74.814	70.777
21	76.422	72.368
22	78.074	74.002
23	79.787	75.689
24	81.555	77.430
25	83.385	79.228
26	85.266	81.072
27	87.204	82.967
28	89.206	84.925
29	91.262	86.926
30	93.386	88.996
31	95.578	91.135
32	97.840	93.333
33	100.188	95.619
34	102.633	97.997
35	105.159	100.457
36	107.789	103.014
37	110.539	105.692
38	113.404	108.479
39	116.417	111.393
40	119.531	114.348
41	122.749	117.332
42	125.979	120.276
43	129.219	123.129
44	132.418	125.904
45	135.625	128.625
46	138.823	131.289
47	142.063	133.972
48	145.402	136.628
49	148.735	139.235
50	152.120	141.819
51	155.535	144.372
52	159.014	146.893
53	162.546	149.382
54	166.141	151.859
55	169.821	154.304
56	173.607	156.731
57	177.493	158.544
58	181.389	161.294
59	185.361	163.394
60	189.342	165.332
2	197.51	168.74

5th Year.

Age.	Initial Value.	Final Value.
13	81.082	77.813
14	82.721	79.455
15	84.401	81.164
16	86.141	82.900
17	87.906	84.670
18	89.752	86.524
19	91.680	88.445
20	93.633	90.406
21	95.662	92.437
22	97.751	94.520
23	99.909	96.673
24	102.138	98.891
25	104.441	101.180
26	106.809	103.530
27	109.247	105.948
28	111.767	108.438
29	114.351	110.996
30	117.024	113.643
31	119.788	116.373
32	122.635	119.187
33	125.593	122.109
34	128.668	125.152
35	131.854	128.299
36	135.167	131.574
37	138.632	134.997
38	142.242	138.547
39	146.015	142.206
40	149.874	145.876
41	153.805	149.573
42	157.746	153.183
43	161.651	156.727
44	165.530	160.173
45	169.408	163.587
46	173.283	166.941
47	177.226	170.294
48	181.197	173.613
49	185.180	176.872
50	189.201	180.110
51	193.259	183.297
52	197.357	186.441
53	201.501	189.555
54	205.718	192.640
55	209.996	195.677
56	214.357	198.620
57	218.214	201.462
58	223.136	204.108
59	227.539	206.618
60	231.930	208.909
2	240.73	212.90

6th Year.

Age.	Initial Value.	Final Value.
13	98.010	95.477
14	99.990	97.486
15	102.050	99.567
16	104.152	101.692
17	106.304	103.867
18	108.551	106.132
19	110.877	108.478
20	113.262	110.884
21	115.731	113.368
22	118.269	115.922
23	120.893	118.555
24	123.599	121.272
25	126.393	124.069
26	129.267	126.949
27	132.228	129.907
28	135.280	132.958
29	138.421	136.100
30	141.671	139.344
31	145.026	142.694
32	148.489	146.157
33	152.083	149.744
34	155.823	153.480
35	159.696	157.353
36	163.727	161.376
37	167.937	165.563
38	172.310	169.863
39	176.828	174.242
40	181.402	178.628
41	186.046	182.999
42	190.853	187.295
43	195.249	191.531
44	199.799	195.677
45	204.370	199.790
46	208.935	203.839
47	213.548	207.873
48	218.182	211.861
49	222.817	215.800
50	227.492	219.687
51	232.184	223.514
52	236.905	227.312
53	241.674	231.052
54	246.499	234.744
55	251.369	238.318
56	256.246	241.769
57	261.132	245.063
58	265.950	248.138
59	270.763	251.016
60	275.507	253.626

7th Year.

Age.	Initial Value.	Final Value.
13	115.674	113.916
14	118.021	116.299
15	120.453	118.771
16	122.944	121.303
17	125.501	123.894
18	128.159	126.590
19	130.910	129.382
20	133.740	132.246
21	136.662	135.205
22	139.671	138.244
23	142.775	141.382
24	145.980	144.613
25	149.282	147.944
26	152.686	151.371
27	156.187	154.897
28	159.800	158.538
29	163.525	162.285
30	167.372	166.156
31	171.347	170.162
32	175.459	174.298
33	179.718	178.585
34	184.151	183.052
35	188.750	187.679
36	193.529	192.472
37	198.503	197.414
38	203.626	202.442
39	208.864	207.541
40	214.154	212.611
41	219.472	217.677
42	224.765	222.671
43	230.053	227.622
44	235.303	232.482
45	240.573	237.308
46	245.833	242.063
47	251.127	246.791
48	256.430	251.482
49	261.745	256.099
50	267.069	260.653
51	272.401	265.162
52	277.776	269.615
53	283.171	273.991
54	288.603	278.252
55	294.010	282.368
56	299.395	286.305
57	304.733	290.059
58	309.980	293.538
59	315.161	296.768
60	320.224	299.689

8th Year.

Age.	Initial Value.	Final Value.
13	134.113	133.158
14	136.834	135.933
15	139.657	138.815
16	142.555	141.766
17	145.528	144.793
18	148.617	147.941
19	151.814	151.193
20	155.102	154.537
21	158.499	157.986
22	161.993	161.535
23	165.602	165.193
24	169.321	168.965
25	173.157	172.848
26	177.118	176.861
27	181.177	180.974
28	185.380	185.228
29	189.710	189.610
30	194.184	194.144
31	198.815	198.831
32	203.600	203.677
33	208.559	208.702
34	213.723	213.930
35	219.076	219.333
36	224.625	224.890
37	230.354	230.568
38	236.203	236.328
39	242.163	242.119
40	248.137	247.897
41	254.150	253.674
42	260.141	259.394
43	266.144	265.076
44	272.108	270.668
45	278.091	276.225
46	284.057	281.705
47	290.045	287.167
48	296.051	292.567
49	302.044	297.888
50	308.035	303.159
51	314.049	308.362
52	320.079	313.492
53	326.110	318.480
54	332.111	323.328
55	338.060	327.980
56	343.931	332.428
57	349.729	336.636
58	355.380	340.525
59	360.913	344.121
60	366.287	347.344

9th Year.

Age.	Initial Value.	Final Value.
13	153.355	153.243
14	156.468	156.430
15	159.701	159.734
16	163.018	163.123
17	166.427	166.609
18	169.968	170.223
19	173.625	173.957
20	177.393	177.797
21	181.280	181.761
22	185.284	185.836
23	189.413	190.042
24	193.673	194.373
25	198.061	198.838
26	202.598	203.457
27	207.254	208.190
28	212.070	213.087
29	217.035	218.142
30	222.172	223.365
31	227.484	228.770
32	232.979	234.365
33	238.676	240.159
34	244.601	246.172
35	250.730	252.348
36	257.043	258.653
37	263.508	265.074
38	270.091	271.542
39	276.741	278.053
40	283.423	284.558
41	290.147	291.076
42	296.864	297.542
43	303.598	303.981
44	310.294	310.328
45	317.008	316.641
46	323.699	322.893
47	330.421	329.103
48	337.136	335.248
49	343.833	341.331
50	350.541	347.342
51	357.249	353.272

LIFE POLICIES.—FIFTEEN PREMIUMS.—4 PER CENT.

9th Year.

Age.	Initial Value.	Final Value.
52	363.956	359.071
53	370.599	364.705
54	377.187	370.153
55	383.672	375.384
56	390.054	380.360
57	396.306	385.051
58	402.367	389.389
59	408.266	393.371
60	413.942	396.953

10th Year.

Age.	Initial Value.	Final Value.
13	173.440	174.214
14	176.965	177.825
15	180.620	181.571
16	184.375	185.421
17	188.243	189.380
18	192.250	193.483
19	196.389	197.715
20	200.658	202.077
21	205.055	206.573
22	209.585	211.202
23	214.262	215.973
24	219.081	220.896
25	224.051	225.973
26	229.194	231.221
27	234.470	236.606
28	239.929	242.184
29	245.567	247.939
30	251.393	253.890
31	257.423	260.053
32	263.667	266.429
33	270.133	273.018
34	276.843	279.814
35	283.745	286.752
36	290.806	293.815
37	298.014	300.960
38	305.305	308.167
39	312.675	315.420
40	320.084	322.686
41	327.549	329.971
42	335.012	337.213
43	342.503	344.438
44	349.954	351.571
45	357.424	358.694
46	364.887	365.742
47	372.357	372.745
48	379.817	379.701
49	387.276	386.582
50	394.724	393.379
51	402.159	400.045
52	409.535	406.564
53	416.824	412.877
54	424.012	418.988
55	431.076	424.838
56	437.986	430.397
57	444.721	435.639
58	451.231	440.480
59	457.516	444.939
60	463.551	448.984

11th Year.

Age.	Initial Value.	Final Value.
13	194.411	196.107
14	198.360	200.163
15	202.457	204.373
16	206.673	208.699
17	211.014	213.155
18	215.510	217.764
19	220.147	222.520
20	224.933	227.421
21	229.867	232.478
22	234.951	237.681
23	240.193	243.050
24	245.604	248.594
25	251.186	254.307
26	256.958	260.217
27	262.886	266.293
28	269.026	272.581
29	275.364	279.075
30	281.918	285.795
31	288.706	292.749
32	295.731	299.933
33	302.992	307.319
34	310.485	314.891
35	318.149	322.603
36	325.968	330.410
37	333.900	338.313
38	341.930	346.286
39	350.042	354.319
40	358.212	362.377
41	366.444	370.464
42	374.683	378.517
43	382.960	386.566
44	391.197	394.546
45	399.477	402.512
46	407.736	410.410
47	415.999	418.283
48	424.270	426.098
49	432.527	433.837
50	440.761	441.447
51	448.932	448.918
52	457.028	456.211
53	464.996	463.287
54	472.847	470.129
55	480.530	476.683
56	488.023	482.924
57	495.309	488.809
58	502.322	494.282
59	509.084	499.366
60	515.582	503.998

12th Year.

Age.	Initial Value.	Final Value.
13	216.304	218.969
14	220.698	223.493
15	225.259	228.183
16	229.951	233.008
17	234.789	237.979
18	239.791	243.120
19	244.952	248.418
20	250.277	253.888
21	255.772	259.526
22	261.430	265.335
23	267.270	271.333
24	273.302	277.524
25	279.520	283.907
26	285.954	290.518
27	292.573	297.315
28	299.423	304.352
29	306.500	311.627
30	313.823	319.151
31	321.402	326.925
32	329.235	334.922
33	337.293	343.101
34	345.562	351.465
35	354.000	359.942
36	362.563	368.531
37	371.253	377.223
38	380.049	386.003
39	388.941	394.853
40	397.903	403.744
41	406.937	412.674
42	415.987	421.582
43	425.088	430.524
44	434.172	439.394
45	443.295	448.267
46	452.404	457.102
47	461.537	465.906
48	470.667	474.656
49	479.782	483.299
50	488.829	491.810
51	497.805	500.162
52	506.675	508.338
53	515.406	516.274
54	523.988	523.963
55	532.375	531.357
56	540.550	538.413
57	548.479	545.113
58	556.124	551.415
59	563.511	557.305
60	570.596	562.742

13th Year.

Age.	Initial Value.	Final Value.
13	239.166	242.850
14	244.028	247.858
15	249.069	253.052
16	254.260	258.395
17	259.613	263.907
18	265.147	269.599
19	270.850	275.469
20	276.744	281.529
21	282.820	287.781
22	289.084	294.228
23	295.553	300.882
24	302.232	307.753
25	309.120	314.846
26	316.255	322.190
27	323.595	329.749
28	331.194	337.578
29	339.052	345.670
30	347.179	354.028
31	355.578	362.630
32	364.224	371.441
33	373.075	380.432
34	382.136	389.585
35	391.339	398.868
36	400.684	408.274
37	410.163	417.801
38	419.766	427.430
39	429.475	437.143
40	439.270	446.914
41	449.147	456.740
42	459.052	466.579
43	469.046	476.466
44	479.020	486.301
45	489.050	496.178
46	499.096	506.026
47	509.160	515.852
48	519.225	525.603
49	529.244	535.258
50	539.192	544.771
51	549.049	554.140
52	558.802	563.327
53	568.393	572.274
54	577.822	580.985
55	587.049	589.396
56	596.039	597.489
57	604.783	605.255
58	613.257	612.634
59	621.450	619.621
60	629.340	626.176

14th Year.

Age.	Initial Value.	Final Value.
13	263.047	267.793
14	268.393	273.321
15	273.938	279.027
16	279.647	284.916
17	285.541	290.988
18	291.626	297.262
19	297.901	303.735
20	304.385	310.411
21	311.075	317.306
22	317.977	324.421
23	325.102	331.769
24	332.461	339.357
25	340.059	347.201
26	347.927	355.303
27	356.029	363.680
28	364.420	372.341
29	373.095	381.284
30	382.056	390.487
31	391.283	399.918
32	400.743	409.560
33	410.406	419.372
34	420.256	429.351
35	430.265	439.481
36	440.427	449.753
37	450.741	460.167
38	461.193	470.697
39	471.765	481.327
40	482.440	492.041
41	493.213	502.839
42	504.049	513.687
43	514.988	524.581
44	525.927	535.516
45	536.961	546.474
46	548.020	557.439
47	559.106	568.374
48	570.172	579.257
49	581.203	590.056
50	592.153	600.738
51	603.027	611.284
52	613.791	621.660
53	624.393	631.849
54	634.844	641.795
55	645.088	651.500
56	655.115	660.943
57	664.925	670.095
58	674.476	678.926
59	683.766	687.421
60	692.774	695.557

TABLE XVI.

LIFE POLICIES.—TWENTY PREMIUMS.—4 PER CENT.

1st Year.

Age.	Initial Value.	Final Value.
13	16.764	10.659
14	17.048	10.910
15	17.343	11.170
16	17.650	11.434
17	17.970	11.709
18	18.301	11.984
19	18.645	12.273
20	19.002	12.563
21	19.372	12.865
22	19.757	13.181
23	20.154	13.498
24	20.567	13.830
25	20.996	14.176
26	21.441	14.527
27	21.901	14.896
28	22.380	15.260
29	22.878	15.648
30	23.395	16.041
31	23.932	16.452
32	24.491	16.872
33	25.074	17.312
34	25.681	17.774
35	26.316	18.250
36	26.979	18.749
37	27.674	19.281
38	28.403	19.830
39	29.170	20.413
40	29.979	21.035
41	30.838	21.684
42	31.737	22.355
43	32.694	23.010
44	33.707	23.635
45	34.773	24.248
46	35.900	24.803
47	37.081	25.399
48	38.325	25.969
49	39.635	26.559
50	41.018	27.152
51	42.479	27.749
52	44.023	28.345
53	45.664	28.950
54	47.399	29.583
55	49.240	30.200
56	51.202	30.837
57	53.293	31.523
58	55.532	32.218
59	57.925	32.926
60	60.489	33.592

2d Year.

Age.	Initial Value.	Final Value.
13	27.423	21.766
14	27.958	22.285
15	28.513	22.815
16	29.084	23.358
17	29.679	23.890
18	30.285	24.466
19	30.918	25.050
20	31.565	25.644
21	32.237	26.263
22	32.938	26.885
23	33.652	27.551
24	34.397	28.228
25	35.172	28.914
26	35.968	29.626
27	36.797	30.380
28	37.640	31.136
29	38.526	31.909
30	39.436	32.714
31	40.384	33.548
32	41.363	34.411
33	42.386	35.304
34	43.455	36.241
35	44.556	37.210
36	45.728	38.240
37	46.955	39.313
38	48.233	40.445
39	49.583	41.638
40	51.014	42.892
41	52.517	44.196
42	54.092	45.513
43	55.704	46.787
44	57.342	48.009
45	59.021	49.196
46	60.703	50.303
47	62.480	51.458
48	64.294	52.601
49	66.194	53.769
50	68.170	54.926
51	70.228	56.097
52	72.368	57.269
53	74.614	58.419
54	76.982	59.629

LIFE POLICIES.—TWENTY PREMIUMS.—4 PER CENT.

2d Year.

Age.	Initial Value.	Final Value.
55	79.440	60.895
56	82.039	62.185
57	84.816	63.515
58	87.750	64.827
59	90.851	66.143
60	94.081	67.436
1	97.50	68.67

3d Year.

Age.	Initial Value.	Final Value.
13	38.530	33.367
14	39.333	34.142
15	40.158	34.949
16	41.008	35.762
17	41.860	36.599
18	42.767	37.465
19	43.695	38.349
20	44.646	39.261
21	45.635	40.202
22	46.642	41.157
23	47.705	42.172
24	48.795	43.200
25	49.910	44.253
26	51.067	45.334
27	52.281	46.479
28	53.516	47.634
29	54.787	48.818
30	56.109	50.043
31	57.480	51.317
32	58.902	52.640
33	60.378	54.007
34	61.922	55.442
35	63.526	56.928
36	65.219	58.503
37	66.987	60.143
38	68.848	61.863
39	70.808	63.705
40	72.871	65.605
41	75.029	67.546
42	77.250	69.457
43	79.481	71.319
44	81.716	73.085
45	83.969	74.824
46	86.203	76.484
47	88.539	78.194
48	90.926	79.902
49	93.404	81.621
50	95.944	83.332
51	98.576	85.046
52	101.292	86.794
53	104.083	88.489
54	107.028	90.251
55	110.135	92.132
56	113.387	94.008
57	116.808	95.942
58	120.359	97.802
59	124.068	99.674
60	127.925	101.490
1	131.91	103.24

4th Year.

Age.	Initial Value.	Final Value.
13	50.131	45.451
14	51.190	46.506
15	52.292	47.582
16	53.412	48.699
17	54.569	49.825
18	55.766	50.996
19	56.994	52.200
20	58.263	53.433
21	59.574	54.716
22	60.914	56.014
23	62.326	57.384
24	63.767	58.781
25	65.249	60.212
26	66.775	61.687
27	68.380	63.224
28	70.014	64.790
29	71.696	66.396
30	73.438	68.064
31	75.249	69.798
32	77.131	71.596
33	79.081	73.455
34	81.123	75.408
35	83.244	77.438
36	85.482	79.577
37	87.817	81.819
38	90.266	84.177
39	92.875	86.637
40	95.584	89.160
41	98.379	91.690
42	101.194	94.179
43	104.013	96.575
44	106.792	98.882
45	109.597	101.164
46	112.384	103.366
47	115.275	105.633
48	118.227	107.880
49	121.256	110.134
50	124.350	112.375
51	127.525	114.631
52	130.817	116.910
53	134.153	119.153
54	137.650	121.500
55	141.372	123.909
56	145.210	126.337
57	149.235	128.772
58	153.334	131.135
59	157.599	133.473
60	161.979	135.754
1	166.27	137.97

5th Year.

Age.	Initial Value.	Final Value.
13	62.215	58.052
14	63.554	59.378
15	64.925	60.761
16	66.349	62.166
17	67.795	63.599
18	69.297	65.091
19	70.845	66.619
20	72.435	68.189
21	74.088	69.818
22	75.771	71.481
23	77.538	73.220
24	79.348	74.997
25	81.208	76.818
26	83.128	78.692
27	85.125	80.643
28	87.170	82.633
29	89.274	84.682
30	91.459	86.811
31	93.730	89.020
32	96.087	91.310
33	98.529	93.690
34	101.089	96.181
35	103.754	98.783
36	106.556	101.509
37	109.493	104.366
38	112.580	107.359
39	115.807	110.433
40	119.139	113.534
41	122.523	116.636
42	125.916	119.650
43	129.269	122.574
44	132.589	125.425
45	135.937	128.240
46	139.266	130.995
47	142.714	133.783
48	146.205	136.554
49	149.769	139.326
50	153.393	142.101
51	157.110	144.871
52	160.933	147.669
53	164.817	150.449
54	168.899	153.310
55	173.149	156.239
56	177.539	159.135
57	182.065	162.021
58	186.667	164.806
59	191.398	167.551
60	196.243	170.216
1	201.21	172.76

6th Year.

Age.	Initial Value.	Final Value.
13	74.816	71.182
14	76.426	72.801
15	78.104	74.481
16	79.816	76.194
17	81.569	77.949
18	83.392	79.767
19	85.264	81.634
20	87.191	83.558
21	89.190	85.546
22	91.238	87.583
23	93.374	89.700
24	95.564	91.873
25	97.814	94.094
26	100.133	96.387
27	102.544	98.763
28	105.013	101.197
29	107.560	103.710
30	110.206	106.314
31	112.952	109.017
32	115.801	111.829
33	118.764	114.745
34	121.862	117.799
35	125.099	120.995
36	128.488	124.335
37	132.040	127.819
38	135.762	131.420
39	139.603	135.070
40	143.513	138.736
41	147.469	142.357
42	151.387	145.899
43	155.268	149.349
44	159.132	152.736
45	163.013	156.082
46	166.895	159.366
47	170.864	162.671
48	174.879	165.949
49	178.961	169.244
50	183.119	172.517
51	187.350	175.783
52	191.692	179.101
53	196.113	182.384
54	200.709	185.738
55	205.479	189.099
56	210.337	192.414
57	215.314	195.678
58	220.338	198.836
59	225.476	201.913
60	230.705	204.883
1	236.00	207.73

7th Year.

Age.	Initial Value.	Final Value.
13	87.946	84.869
14	89.849	86.785
15	91.824	88.775
16	93.844	90.812
17	95.919	92.895
18	98.068	95.053
19	100.279	97.276
20	102.560	99.561
21	104.918	101.925
22	107.340	104.344
23	109.854	106.858
24	112.440	109.435
25	115.090	112.077
26	117.828	114.799
27	120.664	117.621
28	123.577	120.521
29	126.588	123.511
30	129.709	126.611
31	132.949	129.837
32	136.320	133.186
33	139.819	136.666
34	143.480	140.312
35	147.311	144.121
36	151.314	148.085
37	155.493	152.174
38	159.823	156.348
39	164.240	160.559
40	168.715	164.740
41	173.190	168.884
42	177.636	172.948
43	182.043	176.928
44	186.443	180.844
45	190.855	184.713
46	195.266	188.504
47	199.752	192.321
48	204.274	196.116
49	208.879	199.901
50	213.535	203.660
51	218.262	207.433
52	223.124	211.237
53	228.048	214.997
54	233.137	218.763
55	238.339	222.518
56	243.616	226.183
57	248.971	229.786
58	254.368	233.240
59	259.838	236.579
60	265.372	239.791
1	270.97	241.84

8th Year.

Age.	Initial Value.	Final Value.
13	101.633	99.131
14	103.833	101.357
15	106.118	103.673
16	108.462	106.039
17	110.865	108.465
18	113.354	110.981
19	115.921	113.567
20	118.563	116.230
21	121.297	118.978
22	124.101	121.799
23	127.012	124.718
24	130.002	127.719
25	133.073	130.793
26	136.240	133.965
27	139.522	137.256
28	142.901	140.635
29	146.389	144.125
30	150.006	147.750
31	153.769	151.514
32	157.677	155.428
33	161.740	159.501
34	165.993	163.758
35	170.437	168.192
36	175.064	172.759
37	179.848	177.420
38	184.751	182.154
39	189.729	186.879
40	194.719	191.581
41	199.717	196.245
42	204.685	200.836
43	209.622	205.341
44	214.551	209.780
45	219.486	214.162
46	224.404	218.458
47	229.402	222.790
48	234.441	227.074
49	239.536	231.341
50	244.678	235.600
51	249.912	239.851
52	255.260	244.120
53	260.661	248.284
54	266.162	252.429
55	271.758	256.516
56	277.385	260.498
57	283.079	264.370
58	288.772	268.058
59	294.504	271.602
60	300.280	274.971

9th Year.

Age.	Initial Value.	Final Value.
13	115.895	113.995
14	118.405	116.547
15	121.016	119.194
16	123.689	121.904
17	126.435	124.691
18	129.282	127.573
19	132.212	130.539
20	135.232	133.590
21	138.351	136.741
22	141.556	139.972
23	144.872	143.318
24	148.286	146.754
25	151.789	150.282
26	155.406	153.927
27	159.157	157.700
28	163.015	161.581
29	167.003	165.600
30	171.145	169.766
31	175.446	174.097
32	179.919	178.605
33	184.575	183.291
34	189.439	188.172
35	194.508	193.211
36	199.738	198.351
37	205.094	203.572
38	210.557	208.822
39	216.049	214.068
40	221.560	219.290
41	227.078	224.481
42	232.573	229.596
43	238.035	234.623
44	243.487	239.579
45	248.935	244.467
46	254.358	249.283
47	259.871	254.107
48	265.399	258.875
49	270.976	263.642
50	276.618	268.378
51	282.330	273.091
52	288.143	277.759
53	293.948	282.301
54	299.828	286.772
55	305.756	291.164
56	311.700	295.403
57	317.663	299.490
58	323.590	303.365
59	329.527	307.039
60	335.460	310.523

10th Year.

Age.	Initial Value.	Final Value.
13	130.759	129.492
14	133.595	132.376
15	136.537	135.370
16	139.554	138.442
17	142.661	141.598
18	145.874	144.863
19	149.184	148.219
20	152.592	151.677
21	156.113	155.240
22	159.729	158.903
23	163.472	162.687
24	167.321	166.581
25	171.278	170.585
26	175.368	174.717
27	179.601	178.996
28	183.961	183.408
29	188.478	187.973
30	193.161	192.709
31	198.029	197.636
32	203.096	202.759
33	208.365	208.071
34	213.853	213.559
35	219.527	219.176
36	225.330	224.878
37	231.246	230.618
38	237.225	236.393
39	243.238	242.161
40	249.269	247.912
41	255.314	253.630
42	261.333	259.270
43	267.317	264.815
44	273.286	270.285
45	279.240	275.697
46	285.183	281.014
47	291.188	286.331
48	297.200	291.606
49	303.277	296.855
50	309.396	302.058
51	315.570	307.176
52	321.782	312.224
53	327.965	317.099
54	334.171	321.878
55	340.404	326.526
56	346.605	330.978
57	352.783	335.243
58	358.897	339.241
59	364.964	343.015
60	371.012	346.591

11th Year.

Age.	Initial Value.	Final Value.
13	146.256	145.644
14	149.424	148.876
15	152.713	152.234
16	156.092	155.677
17	159.568	159.219
18	163.164	162.877
19	166.864	166.643
20	170.679	170.518
21	174.612	174.515
22	178.660	178.622
23	182.841	182.867
24	187.148	187.241
25	191.581	191.737
26	196.158	196.380
27	200.897	201.194
28	205.788	206.155
29	210.851	211.295
30	216.104	216.631
31	221.568	222.176
32	227.250	227.928
33	233.145	233.851
34	239.240	239.919

LIFE POLICIES.—TWENTY PREMIUMS.—4 PER CENT.

11th Year.

Age.	Initial Value.	Final Value.
35	245.492	246.106
36	251.857	252.332
37	258.292	258.603
38	264.796	264.906
39	271.331	271.208
40	277.891	277.491
41	284.463	283.738
42	291.607	289.903
43	297.509	295.967
44	303.992	301.972
45	310.470	307.895
46	316.914	313.719
47	323.412	319.556
48	329.931	325.326
49	336.490	331.055
50	343.076	336.677
51	349.655	342.189
52	356.247	347.583
53	362.763	352.783
54	369.277	357.832
55	375.766	362.704
56	382.180	367.345
57	388.536	371.739
58	394.773	375.842
59	400.940	379.706
60	407.080	383.320

12th Year.

Age.	Initial Value.	Final Value.
13	162.408	162.484
14	165.924	166.082
15	169.577	169.813
16	173.327	173.644
17	177.189	177.583
18	181.178	181.654
19	185.288	185.840
20	189.520	190.154
21	193.887	194.598
22	198.379	199.172
23	203.021	203.901
24	207.808	208.771
25	212.733	213.783
26	217.821	218.967
27	223.095	224.334
28	228.535	229.874
29	234.173	235.620
30	240.026	241.578
31	246.108	247.756
32	252.419	254.124
33	258.925	260.634
34	265.600	267.276
35	272.422	273.998
36	279.311	280.962
37	286.277	287.569
38	293.309	294.414
39	300.378	301.256
40	307.470	308.077
41	314.571	314.857
42	321.640	321.552
43	328.661	328.160
44	335.679	334.693
45	342.668	341.137
46	349.619	347.501
47	356.637	353.853
48	363.651	360.124
49	370.690	366.294
50	377.695	372.334
51	384.668	378.217
52	391.606	383.959
53	398.447	389.459
54	405.231	394.761
55	411.944	399.847
56	418.547	404.644
57	425.032	409.166
58	431.374	413.381
59	437.631	417.209
60	443.809	420.935

13th Year.

Age.	Initial Value.	Final Value.
13	179.248	180.047
14	183.130	184.020
15	187.156	188.142
16	191.294	192.373
17	195.553	196.729
18	199.955	201.223
19	204.485	205.852
20	209.156	210.618
21	213.970	215.532
22	218.929	220.597
23	224.055	225.827
24	229.338	231.218
25	234.779	236.776
26	240.408	242.520
27	246.235	248.471
28	252.254	254.621
29	258.498	260.995
30	264.973	267.592
31	271.688	274.392
32	278.615	281.354
33	285.708	288.447
34	292.957	295.632
35	300.314	302.905
36	307.741	310.215
37	315.243	317.575
38	322.817	324.970
39	330.426	332.361
40	338.056	339.728
41	345.690	347.050
42	353.289	354.304
43	360.854	361.455
44	368.400	368.532
45	375.910	375.535
46	383.401	382.442
47	390.934	389.323
48	398.449	396.066
49	405.929	402.687
50	413.352	409.134
51	420.696	415.403
52	427.982	421.483
53	435.123	427.282
54	442.160	432.842
55	449.087	438.129
56	455.846	443.100
57	462.459	447.776
58	468.913	452.092
59	475.224	456.072
60	481.424	459.726

14th Year.

Age.	Initial Value.	Final Value.
13	196.811	198.361
14	201.068	202.728
15	205.485	207.252
16	210.023	211.903
17	214.699	216.688
18	219.524	221.628
19	224.497	226.713
20	229.620	231.955
21	234.904	237.363
22	240.354	242.937
23	245.981	248.692
24	251.785	254.635
25	257.772	260.760
26	263.961	267.094
27	270.372	273.661
28	277.001	280.445
29	283.873	287.465
30	290.987	294.691
31	298.324	302.094
32	305.845	309.649
33	313.521	317.297
34	321.313	325.043
35	329.221	332.877
36	337.194	340.753
37	345.249	348.677
38	353.373	356.637
39	361.531	364.588
40	369.707	372.514
41	377.883	380.413
42	386.041	388.229
43	394.149	395.945
44	402.239	403.610
45	410.308	411.184
46	418.342	418.656
47	426.404	426.049
48	434.391	433.286
49	442.322	440.360
50	450.152	447.242
51	457.882	453.903
52	465.506	460.337
53	472.946	466.461
54	480.241	472.287
55	487.369	477.815
56	494.302	483.010
57	501.069	487.856
58	507.624	492.310
59	513.997	496.380
60	520.215	500.089

15th Year.

Age.	Initial Value.	Final Value.
13	215.125	217.465
14	219.776	222.237
15	224.595	227.185
16	229.553	232.267
17	234.658	237.503
18	239.929	242.904
19	245.358	248.470
20	250.957	254.212
21	256.735	260.133
22	262.694	266.240
23	268.846	272.552
24	275.202	279.068
25	281.756	285.791
26	288.535	292.748
27	295.562	299.955
28	302.825	307.392
29	310.343	315.051
30	318.086	322.890
31	326.026	330.896
32	334.140	339.019
33	342.371	347.243
34	350.724	355.564
35	359.193	363.982
36	367.732	372.438
37	376.351	380.944
38	385.040	389.485
39	393.758	398.014
40	402.493	406.538
41	411.246	415.023
42	419.966	423.430
43	428.639	431.761
44	437.317	440.035
45	445.957	448.210
46	45[illegible].556	456.243
47	463.130	464.182
48	471.611	471.929
49	479.995	479.500
50	488.260	486.841
51	496.382	493.929
52	504.360	500.764
53	512.125	507.246
54	519.686	513.405
55	527.055	519.250
56	534.212	524.719
57	541.149	529.807
58	547.842	534.466
59	554.305	538.705
60	560.578	542.530

16th Year.

Age.	Initial Value.	Final Value.
13	234.229	237.391
14	239.285	242.590
15	244.528	247.973
16	249.917	253.510
17	255.473	259.212
18	261.205	265.099
19	267.115	271.170
20	273.214	277.431
21	279.505	283.891
22	285.997	290.563
23	292.706	297.454
24	299.635	304.575
25	306.787	311.929
26	314.189	319.535
27	321.856	327.402
28	329.772	335.487
29	337.929	343.770
30	346.285	352.226
31	354.828	360.815
32	363.510	369.529
33	372.317	378.345
34	381.245	387.266
35	390.298	396.287
36	399.417	405.346
37	408.618	414.454
38	417.888	423.598
39	427.184	432.749
40	436.517	441.887
41	445.856	450.993
42	455.167	460.048
43	464.455	469.023
44	473.742	477.947
45	482.983	486.732
46	492.143	495.372
47	501.263	503.890
48	510.254	512.206
49	519.135	520.318
50	527.859	528.175
51	536.408	535.760
52	544.787	543.058
53	552.910	549.993
54	560.804	556.593
55	568.490	562.843
56	575.921	568.698
57	583.100	574.142
58	589.998	579.136
59	596.630	583.659
60	603.019	587.744

17th Year.

Age.	Initial Value.	Final Value.
13	254.155	258.183
14	259.638	263.821
15	265.316	269.664
16	271.160	275.671
17	277.182	281.864
18	283.400	288.262
19	289.815	294.858
20	296.433	301.665
21	303.263	308.695
22	310.320	315.956
23	317.608	323.458
24	325.142	331.218
25	332.925	339.230
26	340.976	347.506
27	349.303	356.030
28	357.867	364.751
29	366.648	373.666
30	375.621	382.721
31	384.747	391.918
32	394.020	401.243
33	403.419	410.680
34	412.947	420.224
35	422.603	429.873
36	432.325	439.560
37	442.128	449.298
38	452.001	459.094
39	461.919	468.890
40	471.866	478.684
41	481.826	488.475
42	491.785	498.217
43	501.717	507.887
44	511.654	517.483
45	521.505	526.938
46	531.272	536.235
47	540.971	545.408
48	550.531	554.359
49	559.953	563.092
50	569.193	571.562
51	578.239	579.736
52	587.081	587.624
53	595.657	595.160
54	603.992	602.329
55	612.983	609.144
56	619.900	615.553
57	627.435	621.543
58	634.668	627.062
59	641.584	632.079
60	648.233	636.675

18th Year.

Age.	Initial Value.	Final Value.
13	274.947	279.878
14	280.869	285.979
15	287.007	292.297
16	293.321	298.800
17	299.834	305.511
18	306.563	312.440
19	313.503	319.588
20	320.667	326.993
21	328.067	334.598
22	335.713	342.480
23	343.612	350.628
24	351.785	359.053
25	360.226	367.746
26	368.947	376.692
27	377.931	385.865
28	387.131	395.231
29	396.544	404.764
30	406.116	414.446
31	415.850	424.275
32	425.734	434.237
33	435.754	444.327
34	445.905	454.524
35	456.189	464.832
36	466.539	475.180
37	476.972	485.602
38	487.497	496.080
39	498.060	506.571
40	508.663	517.092
41	519.308	527.616
42	529.954	538.107
43	540.581	548.508
44	551.190	558.851
45	561.711	569.044
46	572.135	579.094
47	582.489	589.010
48	592.684	598.702
49	602.727	608.181
50	612.580	617.389
51	622.215	626.316
52	631.647	634.980
53	640.824	643.294
54	649.728	651.249
55	658.384	658.860
56	666.755	666.083
57	674.836	672.891
58	682.594	679.246
59	690.004	685.114
60	697.164	690.557

19th Year.

Age.	Initial Value.	Final Value.
13	296.642	302.525
14	303.027	309.119
15	309.640	315.924
16	316.450	322.950
17	323.481	330.200
18	330.741	337.688
19	338.233	345.420
20	345.995	353.412
21	353.970	361.668
22	362.237	370.203
23	370.782	379.029
24	379.620	388.142
25	388.742	397.519
26	398.133	407.130
27	407.766	416.961
28	417.611	426.966
29	427.642	437.144
30	437.841	447.483
31	448.207	457.974
32	458.723	468.616
33	469.401	479.386
34	480.205	490.268
35	491.148	501.251
36	502.159	512.333
37	513.276	523.483
38	524.483	534.700
39	535.741	545.972
40	547.071	557.278
41	558.449	568.600
42	569.844	579.891
43	581.202	591.132
44	592.558	602.288
45	603.817	613.347
46	614.994	624.271
47	626.091	635.043
48	637.027	645.643
49	647.816	656.019
50	658.407	666.174
51	668.795	676.090
52	679.003	685.742
53	688.958	695.104
54	698.648	704.167
55	708.100	712.915
56	717.285	721.312
57	726.184	729.351
58	734.778	737.013
59	743.039	744.273
60	751.046	751.104

ACTUARIES' RATE OF MORTALITY AND COMMUTATION COLUMNS AT 4 PER CENT.[*]

Age.	l_x	d_x	v^x	D_x	$_\omega N_x$	$\frac{_\omega S_x}{1000}$	C_x	$_\omega M_x$	$_\omega R_x$	$_\omega \Pi_x$	Age.
10	100000	676	.675564	67556	1381771	24815	439.1	14411	427355	.21331	10
11	99324	674	.649581	64519	1314215	23433	421.0	13972	412944	.21658	11
12	98650	672	.624597	61616	1249696	22119	403.6	13551	398971	.21992	12
13	97978	671	.600574	58843	1188079	20869	387.5	13148	385420	.22341	13
14	97307	671	.577475	56192	1129236	19681	372.6	12760	372272	.22707	14
15	96636	671	.555265	53658	1073044	18552	358.2	12388	359512	.23084	15
16	95965	672	.533908	51236	1019385	17479	345.0	12029	347125	.23476	16
17	95293	673	.513373	48921	968149	16459	332.2	11684	335095	.23884	17
18	94620	675	.493628	46707	919228	15491	320.4	11352	323411	.24303	18
19	93945	677	.474642	44590	872521	14572	309.0	11032	312059	.24742	19
20	93268	680	.456387	42566	827931	13699	298.4	10723	301027	.25188	20
21	92588	683	.438834	40631	785364	12872	288.2	10424	290304	.25657	21
22	91905	686	.421955	38780	744733	12086	278.3	10136	279880	.26138	22
23	91219	690	.405726	37010	705954	11341	269.2	9857.9	269744	.26634	23
24	90529	694	.390121	35317	668944	10635	260.3	9588.7	259886	.27149	24
25	89835	698	.375117	33699	633626	9966.6	251.8	9328.4	250297	.27680	25
26	89137	703	.360689	32151	599928	9332.9	243.8	9076.6	240969	.28229	26
27	88434	708	.346817	30670	567777	8733.0	236.1	8832.8	231892	.28798	27
28	87726	714	.333477	29255	537107	8165.2	229.0	8596.7	223059	.29384	28
29	87012	720	.320651	27901	507852	7628.1	222.0	8367.7	214463	.29991	29
30	86292	727	.308319	26605	479952	7120.3	215.5	8145.8	206095	.30614	30
31	85565	734	.296460	25367	453346	6640.3	209.2	7930.2	197949	.31261	31
32	84831	742	.285058	24182	427980	6187.0	203.4	7721.0	190019	.31931	32
33	84089	750	.274094	23048	403798	5759.0	197.7	7517.6	182298	.32615	33
34	83339	758	.263552	21964	380750	5355.2	192.1	7319.9	174780	.33327	34
35	82581	767	.253415	20927	358785	4974.4	186.9	7127.9	167460	.34061	35
36	81814	776	.243669	19935	337858	4615.7	181.8	6941.0	160332	.34816	36
37	81038	785	.234297	18987	317922	4277.8	176.9	6759.2	153392	.35600	37
38	80253	795	.225285	18080	298936	3959.9	172.2	6582.3	146632	.36408	38
39	79458	805	.216621	17212	280856	3660.9	167.7	6410.1	140050	.37242	39
40	78653	815	.208289	16383	263643	3380.1	163.2	6242.4	133640	.38104	40
41	77838	826	.200278	15589	247261	3116.4	159.0	6079.2	127398	.38996	41
42	77012	839	.192575	14831	231671	2869.2	155.4	5920.1	121318	.39918	42
43	76173	857	.185168	14105	216841	2637.5	152.6	5764.8	115398	.40869	43
44	75316	881	.178046	13410	202736	2420.7	150.8	5612.2	109633	.41849	44
45	74435	909	.171198	12743	189327	2217.9	149.6	5461.4	104021	.42857	45
46	73526	944	.164614	12103	176884	2028.6	149.4	5311.7	98560	.43884	46
47	72582	981	.158283	11488	164480	1852.0	149.3	5162.3	93248	.44934	47
48	71601	1021	.152195	10897	152992	1687.5	149.4	5013.0	88086	.46004	48
49	70580	1063	.146341	10329	124094	1534.6	149.6	4863.6	83073	.47088	49
50	69517	1108	.140713	9781.9	131766	1392.5	149.9	4714.0	78209	.48192	50
51	68409	1156	.135301	9255.8	121984	1260.7	150.4	4564.1	73495	.49311	51
52	67253	1207	.130077	8749.4	112728	1138.7	151.0	4413.7	68931	.50446	52
53	66046	1261	.125093	8261.9	103978	1026.0	151.7	4262.7	64517	.51597	53
54	64785	1316	.120282	7792.5	95717	922.01	152.2	4111.0	60255	.52759	54
55	63469	1375	.115656	7340.5	87924	826.29	152.9	3958.8	56144	.53932	55
56	62094	1436	.111207	6905.3	80584	738.37	153.6	3805.9	52185	.55115	56
57	60658	1497	.106930	6486.2	73678	657.78	153.9	3652.4	48379	.56312	57
58	59161	1561	.102817	6082.8	67192	584.10	154.3	3498.5	44727	.57515	58
59	57600	1627	.098863	5694.5	61109	516.91	154.7	3344.1	41228	.58727	59
60	55973	1698	.095060	5320.8	55415	455.80	155.2	3189.5	37884	.59943	60
61	54275	1770	.091404	4961.0	50094	400.39	155.6	3034.3	34695	.61162	61
62	52505	1844	.087889	4614.6	45133	350.29	155.8	2878.7	31660	.62385	62
63	50661	1917	.084508	4281.3	40518	305.16	155.8	2722.9	28782	.63609	63
64	48744	1990	.081258	3960.8	36237	264.64	155.5	2567.1	26059	.64811	64
65	46754	2061	.078133	3653.0	32276	228.41	154.8	2411.6	23492	.66019	65
66	44693	2128	.075128	3357.7	28623	196.13	153.7	2256.8	21080	.67211	66
67	42565	2191	.072238	3074.8	25266	167.51	152.2	2103.1	18823	.68396	67
68	40374	2246	.069460	2804.4	22191	142.24	150.0	1950.9	16720	.69566	68
69	38128	2291	.066788	2546.5	19386	120.05	147.1	1800.9	14769	.70720	69
70	35837	2327	.064219	2301.4	16840	100.66	143.7	1653.7	12968	.71858	70
71	33510	2351	.061749	2069.2	14539	83.823	139.6	1510.0	11315	.72977	71
72	31159	2362	.059374	1850.0	12469	69.285	134.8	1370.5	9804.6	.74077	72
73	28797	2358	.057091	1644.0	10619	56.815	129.4	1235.6	8434.1	.75159	73
74	26439	2339	.054895	1451.4	8975.3	46.196	123.5	1106.2	7198.5	.76216	74
75	24100	2303	.052784	1272.1	7523.9	37.221	116.9	982.71	6092.4	.77251	75
76	21797	2249	.050754	1106.3	6251.8	29.697	109.8	865.82	5109.7	.78265	76
77	19548	2179	.048801	953.97	5145.6	23.445	102.3	756.07	4243.8	.79254	77
78	17369	2092	.046924	815.03	4191.6	18.299	94.39	653.82	3487.8	.80219	78
79	15277	1987	.045120	689.29	3376.6	14.108	86.20	559.41	2834.0	.81157	79
80	13290	1866	.043384	576.58	2687.3	10.731	77.84	473.22	2274.5	.82072	80
81	11424	1730	.041716	476.56	2110.7	8.0441	69.39	395.38	1801.3	.82965	81
82	9694	1582	.040111	388.84	1634.1	5.9334	61.01	325.99	1405.9	.83835	82
83	8112	1427	.038569	312.87	1245.3	4.2993	52.92	264.97	1079.9	.84693	83
84	6685	1268	.037085	247.91	932.42	3.0540	45.21	212.05	814.96	.85535	84
85	5417	1111	.035659	193.16	684.50	2.1216	38.09	166.84	662.91	.86369	85
86	4306	958	.034287	147.64	491.34	1.4371	31.58	128.74	436.07	.87200	86
87	3348	811	.032969	110.38	343.70	.94571	25.71	97.160	307.33	.88022	87
88	2537	673	.031701	80.424	233.32	.60202	20.52	71.450	210.17	.88843	88
89	1864	545	.030481	56.817	152.90	.36870	15.97	50.936	138.72	.89650	89
90	1319	427	.029309	38.658	96.078	.21580	12.03	34.963	87.788	.90444	90
91	892	322	.028182	25.134	57.420	.11972	8.726	22.930	52.820	.91216	91
92	570	231	.027098	15.446	32.285	.06230	6.019	14.204	29.890	.91962	92
93	339	155	.026056	8.8328	16.839	.03002	3.883	8.1852	15.686	.92670	93
94	184	95	.025053	4.6098	8.0064	.01318	2.288	4.3019	7.5008	.93320	94
95	89	52	.024090	2.1440	3.3968	.00517	1.204	2.0134	3.1989	.93908	95
96	37	24	.023163	.85704	1.2528	.001775	.5345	.80886	1.1846	.94378	96
97	13	9	.022272	.28954	.39579	.000523	.1927	.27432	.37570	.94743	97
98	4	3	.021416	.085663	.10625	.000127	.0618	.08158	.10138	.95231	98
99	1	1	.020592	.020592	.02059	.000021	.0198	.0198	.01980	.96154	99

CURTATE SUMMATIONS OF $v^x l_x = D_x$. ACTUARIES' MORTALITY, 4 per cent.

Age.	${}_{80}N_x$	${}_{79}N_x$	${}_{78}N_x$	${}_{77}N_x$	${}_{76}N_x$	${}_{75}N_x$	${}_{74}N_x$	${}_{73}N_x$	${}_{72}N_x$	${}_{71}N_x$	${}_{70}N_x$	${}_{69}N_x$	Age.
10	1379083	1378393	1377578	1376624	1375518	1374246	1372795	1371151	1369301	1367232	1364931	1362385	10
11	1311527	1310837	1310022	1309068	1307962	1306690	1305239	1303595	1301745	1299676	1297375	1294829	11
12	1247008	1246318	1245503	1244549	1243443	1242171	1240720	1239076	1237226	1235157	1232856	1230310	12
13	1185391	1184701	1183886	1182932	1181826	1180554	1179103	1177459	1175609	1173540	1171239	1168693	13
14	1126508	1125818	1125003	1124049	1122943	1121671	1120220	1118576	1116726	1114697	1112396	1109850	14
15	1070356	1069666	1068851	1067897	1066791	1065519	1064068	1062424	1060574	1058505	1056204	1053658	15
16	1016697	1016007	1015192	1014238	1013132	1011860	1010409	1008765	1006915	1004846	1002545	999999	16
17	965461	964771	963956	963002	961896	960624	959173	957529	955679	953610	951309	948763	17
18	916540	915850	915035	914081	912975	911703	910252	908608	906758	904689	902388	899842	18
19	869833	869143	868328	867374	866268	864996	863545	861901	860051	857982	855681	853135	19
20	825243	824553	823738	822784	821678	820406	818955	817311	815461	813392	811091	808545	20
21	782676	781986	781171	780217	779111	777839	776388	774744	772894	770826	768525	765979	21
22	742046	741356	740541	739587	738481	737209	735758	734114	732264	730195	727894	725348	22
23	703266	702576	701761	700807	699701	698429	696978	695334	693484	691415	689114	686568	23
24	666256	665566	664751	663797	662691	661419	659968	658324	656474	654405	652104	649558	24
25	630938	630248	629433	628479	627373	626101	624650	623006	621156	619088	616787	614241	25
26	597240	596550	595735	594781	593675	592403	590952	589308	587458	585389	583088	580542	26
27	565089	564399	563584	562630	561524	560252	558801	557157	555307	553238	550938	548392	27
28	534419	533729	532914	531960	530854	527582	528131	526487	524637	522568	520267	517721	28
29	505164	504474	503659	502705	501599	500327	498876	497232	495382	493313	491012	488466	29
30	477264	476574	475759	474805	473699	472427	470976	469332	467482	465413	463112	460566	30
31	450659	449969	449154	448200	447094	445822	444371	442727	440877	438808	436507	433961	31
32	425292	424602	423787	422833	421727	420455	419004	417360	415510	413441	411140	408594	32
33	401110	400420	399605	398651	397545	396273	394822	393178	391328	389259	386958	384412	33
34	378061	377371	376556	375602	374496	373224	371773	370129	368279	366210	363910	361364	34
35	356098	355408	354593	353639	352533	351261	349810	348166	346316	344247	341946	339400	35
36	335170	334480	333665	332711	331605	330333	328882	327238	325388	323319	321018	318472	36
37	315235	314545	313730	312776	311670	310398	308947	307303	305453	303384	301083	298537	37
38	296249	295559	294744	293790	292684	291412	289961	288317	286467	284398	282096	279550	38
39	278168	277478	276663	275709	274603	273331	271880	270236	268386	266317	264015	261469	39
40	260956	260266	259451	258497	257391	256119	254668	253024	251174	249105	246804	244258	40
41	244573	243883	243068	242114	241008	239736	238285	236641	234791	232722	230421	227875	41
42	228984	228294	227479	226525	225419	224147	222696	221052	219202	217133	214832	212286	42
43	214164	213474	212659	211705	210599	209327	207876	206232	204382	202303	200002	197456	43
44	200049	199359	198544	197590	196484	195212	193761	192117	190267	188198	185897	183351	44
45	186639	185949	185134	184180	183074	181802	180351	178707	176857	174788	172487	169941	45
46	173896	173206	172391	171437	170331	169059	167608	165964	164114	162045	159744	157198	46
47	161792	161102	160287	159333	158227	156955	155504	153860	152010	149941	147640	145094	47
48	150304	149614	148799	147845	146739	145467	144016	142372	140522	138453	136152	133606	48
49	139407	138717	137902	136948	135842	134570	133119	131475	129625	127555	125255	122709	49
50	129078	128388	127573	126619	125513	124241	122790	121146	119296	117227	114926	112380	50
51	119296	118606	117791	116837	115731	114459	113008	111364	109514	107445	105144	102598	51
52	110040	109350	108535	107581	106475	105203	103752	102108	100258	98189	95889	93343	52
53	101291	100601	99786	98832	97726	96454	95003	93359	91509	89440	87139	84593	53
54	93029	92339	91524	90570	89464	88192	86741	85097	83247	81178	78877	76331	54
55	85235	84545	83730	82776	81670	80398	78947	77303	75453	73384	71084	68538	55
56	77895	77205	76390	75436	74330	73058	71607	69963	68113	66044	63743	61197	56
57	70989	70300	69485	68531	67425	66153	64702	63058	61208	59139	56838	54292	57
58	64502	63813	62998	62044	60938	59666	58215	56571	54721	52652	50352	47806	58
59	58421	57732	56917	55963	54857	53585	52134	50490	48640	46571	44270	41724	59
60	52726	52037	51222	50268	49162	47890	46439	44795	42945	40876	38575	36029	60
61	47405	46716	45901	44947	43841	42569	41118	39474	37624	35555	33254	30708	61
62	42444	41755	40940	39986	38880	37608	36157	34513	32663	30594	28293	25747	62
63	37830	37141	36326	35372	34266	32994	31543	29899	28049	25980	23679	21133	63
64	33549	32860	32045	31091	29985	28713	27262	25618	23768	21699	19398	16852	64
65	29588	28899	28084	27130	26024	24752	23301	21657	19807	17738	15437	12891	65
66	25935	25246	24431	23477	22371	21099	19648	18004	16154	14085	11784	9238	66
67	22577	21888	21073	20119	19013	17741	16290	14646	12796	10727	8426	5880	67
68	19502	18813	17998	17044	15938	14666	13215	11571	9721	7652	5351	2804	68
69	16698	16009	15194	14240	13134	11862	10411	8767	6917	4848	2546		
70	14151	13462	12647	11693	10587	9315	7864	6220	4370	2301		40630	21
71	11850	11161	10346	9392	8286	7014	5563	3919	2069		42566	83196	20
72	9781	9092	8277	7323	6217	4945	3494	1850		44590	87156	127786	19
73	7931	7242	6427	5473	4367	3095	1644		46707	91297	133863	174493	18
74	6287	5598	4783	3829	2723	1451		48921	95628	140218	182784	223414	17
75	4836	4147	3332	2378	1272		51236	100157	146864	191454	234620	274650	16
76	3564	2875	2060	1106		53659	104895	153816	200523	245113	287679	328309	15
77	2458	1769	954		56192	109851	161087	210008	256715	301305	343871	384501	14
78	1504	815		58843	115035	168694	219930	268851	315558	360148	402714	443344	13
79	689		61616	120460	176652	230311	281547	330468	377175	421765	464331	504961	12
		64519	126136	184979	241171	294830	346066	394987	441694	486284	528850	569480	11
10	67556	132076	193692	252535	308727	362386	413622	462543	509250	553840	596406	637036	10
Age.	${}_{11}N_x$	${}_{12}N_x$	${}_{13}N_x$	${}_{14}N_x$	${}_{15}N_x$	${}_{16}N_x$	${}_{17}N_x$	${}_{18}N_x$	${}_{19}N_x$	${}_{20}N_x$	${}_{21}N_x$	${}_{22}N_x$	Age.

CURTATE SUMMATIONS OF $v^x l_x = D_x$. ACTUARIES' MORTALITY, 4 per cent.

Age.	${}_{68}N_x$	${}_{67}N_x$	${}_{66}N_x$	${}_{65}N_x$	${}_{64}N_x$	${}_{63}N_x$	${}_{62}N_x$	${}_{61}N_x$	${}_{60}N_x$	${}_{59}N_x$	${}_{58}N_x$	${}_{57}N_x$	Age.
10	1359581	1356506	1353147	1349494	1345533	1341252	1336637	1331676	1326355	1320661	1314578	1308092	10
11	1292025	1288950	1285591	1281938	1277977	1273696	1269081	1264120	1258799	1253105	1247022	1240536	11
12	1227506	1224431	1221072	1217419	1213458	1209177	1204562	1199601	1194280	1188586	1182503	1176017	12
13	1165889	1162814	1159455	1155802	1151841	1147560	1142945	1137984	1132663	1126969	1120886	1114400	13
14	1107046	1103971	1100612	1096959	1092998	1088717	1084102	1079141	1073820	1068126	1062043	1055557	14
15	1050854	1047779	1044420	1040767	1036806	1032525	1027910	1022949	1017628	1011934	1005851	999365	15
16	997195	994120	990761	987108	983147	978866	974251	969290	963969	958275	952192	945707	16
17	945959	942884	939525	935872	931911	927630	923015	918054	912733	907039	900956	894470	17
18	897038	893963	890604	886951	882990	878709	874094	869133	863812	858118	852035	845549	18
19	850331	847256	843897	840244	836283	832002	827387	822426	817105	811411	805328	798842	19
20	805741	802666	799307	795654	791693	787412	782797	777836	772515	766821	760738	754252	20
21	763175	760100	756741	753088	749127	744846	740231	735270	729949	724255	718172	711686	21
22	722544	719469	716110	712457	708496	704215	699600	694639	689318	683624	677541	671055	22
23	683764	680689	677330	673677	669716	665435	660820	655859	650538	644844	638761	632275	23
24	646754	643679	640320	636667	632716	628425	623810	618849	613528	607834	601751	595265	24
25	611437	608362	605003	601350	597389	593108	588493	583532	578211	572517	566434	559948	25
26	577738	574663	571304	567651	563690	559409	554794	549833	544512	538818	532735	526249	26
27	545588	542513	539154	535501	531540	527259	522644	517683	512362	506668	500585	494099	27
28	514917	511842	508483	504830	500869	496588	491973	487012	481691	475997	469914	463428	28
29	485662	482587	479228	475575	471614	467333	462718	457757	452436	446742	440659	434173	29
30	457762	454687	451328	447675	443714	439433	434818	429857	424536	418842	412759	406273	30
31	431157	428082	424723	421070	417109	412828	408213	403252	397931	392237	386154	379668	31
32	405790	402715	399356	395703	391742	387461	382846	377885	372564	366870	360787	354301	32
33	381608	378533	375174	371521	367560	363279	358664	353703	348382	342688	336605	330119	33
34	358560	355485	352126	348473	344512	340231	335616	330655	325334	319640	313557	307071	34
35	336596	333521	330162	326509	322548	318267	313652	308691	303370	297676	291593	285107	35
36	315668	312593	309234	305581	301620	297339	292724	287763	282442	276748	270665	264179	36
37	295733	292658	289299	285646	281681	277404	272789	267828	262507	256813	250730	244244	37
38	276746	273671	270312	266659	262698	258417	253802	248841	243520	237826	231743	225257	38
39	258665	255590	252231	248578	244617	240336	235721	230760	225439	219745	213662	207176	39
40	241454	238379	235020	231367	227406	223125	218510	213549	208228	202534	196451	189965	40
41	225071	221996	218637	214984	211023	206742	202127	197166	191845	186151	180068	173582	41
42	209482	206407	203048	199395	195434	191153	186538	181577	176256	170562	164479	157993	42
43	194652	191577	188218	184565	180604	176323	171708	166747	161426	155732	149649	143163	43
44	180547	177472	174113	170460	166499	162218	157603	152642	147321	141627	135544	129058	44
45	167137	164062	160703	157050	153089	148808	144193	139232	133911	128217	122134	115645	45
46	154394	151319	147960	144307	140346	136065	131450	126489	121168	115474	109391	102905	46
47	142290	139215	135856	132203	128242	123961	119346	114385	109064	103370	97287	90801	47
48	130802	127727	124368	120715	116754	112473	107858	102897	97576	91882	85799	79313	48
49	119905	116830	113471	109818	105857	101576	96961	92000	86679	80985	74902	68416	49
50	109576	106501	103142	99489	95528	91247	86632	81671	76350	70656	64573	58087	50
51	99794	96719	93360	89707	85746	81465	76850	71889	66568	60874	54791	48305	51
52	90539	87464	84105	80452	76491	72210	67595	62634	57313	51619	45536	39050	52
53	81789	78714	75355	71702	67741	63460	58845	53884	48563	42869	36786	30300	53
54	73527	70452	67093	63440	59479	55198	50583	45622	40301	34607	28524	22038	54
55	65734	62659	59300	55647	51686	47405	42790	37829	32508	26814	20731	14245	55
56	58393	55318	51959	48306	44345	40064	35449	30488	25167	19473	13390	6905	56
57	51488	48413	45054	41401	37440	33159	28544	23583	18262	12568	6486		
58	45002	41927	38568	34915	30954	26673	22058	17097	11776	6083		23048	33
59	38920	35845	32486	28833	24872	20591	15976	11015	5694		24182	47230	32
60	33225	30150	26791	23138	19177	14896	10281	5321		25367	49549	72597	31
61	27904	24829	21470	17817	13856	9575	4961		26605	51972	76154	99202	30
62	22943	19868	16509	12856	8895	4615		27901	54505	79872	104054	127102	29
63	18329	15254	11895	8242	4281		29255	57155	83760	109127	133309	156357	28
64	14048	10973	7614	3961		30670	59926	87827	114432	139799	163981	187029	27
65	10087	7012	3653		32151	62820	92075	119976	146581	171948	196130	219178	26
66	6434	3359		33699	65849	96519	125774	153675	180280	205647	229829	252877	25
67	3075		35317	69015	101166	131836	161091	189992	215577	240964	265146	288194	24
		37010	72326	106025	138176	168846	198101	226002	252607	277974	302156	325204	23
22	38780	75789	111106	144805	176956	207626	236881	264782	291387	316754	340936	363984	22
21	79410	116420	151737	185436	217587	248257	277512	305413	332018	357385	381567	404615	21
20	121976	158986	194303	228002	260153	290823	320078	347979	374584	399951	424133	447181	20
19	166566	203576	238893	272592	304743	335413	364668	392569	419174	444551	468723	491771	19
18	213273	250283	285600	319299	351450	382120	411375	439276	465881	491248	515430	538478	18
17	262194	299204	334521	368220	400371	431041	460296	488197	514802	540169	564351	587399	17
16	313430	350440	385757	419456	451607	482277	511532	539433	566038	591405	615587	638635	16
15	367089	404099	439416	473115	505266	535936	565191	593092	619697	645064	669246	692294	15
14	423281	460291	495608	529307	561458	592128	621383	649284	675889	701256	725438	748486	14
13	482124	519134	554451	588150	620301	650971	680226	708127	734732	760099	784281	807329	13
12	543741	580751	616068	649767	681918	712588	741843	769744	796349	821716	845898	868946	12
11	608260	645270	680587	714286	746437	777107	806362	834263	860868	886235	910417	933465	11
10	675816	712826	748143	781842	813993	844663	873918	901819	928424	953791	977973	1001021	10
Age.	${}_{23}N_x$	${}_{24}N_x$	${}_{25}N_x$	${}_{26}N_x$	${}_{27}N_x$	${}_{28}N_x$	${}_{29}N_x$	${}_{30}N_x$	${}_{31}N_x$	${}_{32}N_x$	${}_{33}N_x$	${}_{34}N_x$	Age.

CURTATE SUMMATIONS OF $v^x l_x = D_x$. ACTUARIES' MORTALITY, 4 per cent.

AGE.	$_{56}N_x$	$_{55}N_x$	$_{54}N_x$	$_{53}N_x$	$_{52}N_x$	$_{51}N_x$	$_{50}N_x$	$_{49}N_x$	$_{48}N_x$	$_{47}N_x$	$_{46}N_x$	AGE.
10	1301187	1293847	1286055	1277793	1269043	1259787	1250005	1239676	1228779	1217290	1205187	10
11	1233631	1226291	1218499	1210237	1201487	1192231	1182449	1172120	1161223	1149734	1137631	11
12	1169112	1161772	1153980	1145718	1136968	1127712	1117930	1107601	1096704	1085215	1073112	12
13	1107465	1100155	1092363	1084101	1075351	1066095	1056313	1045984	1035087	1023598	1011495	13
14	1048652	1041312	1033520	1025258	1016508	1007252	997470	987141	976244	964755	952652	14
15	992460	985120	977328	969066	960316	951060	941278	930949	920052	908563	896460	15
16	938801	931461	923669	915407	906657	897401	887619	877290	866393	854904	842801	16
17	887565	880225	872433	864171	855421	846165	836383	826054	815157	803668	791565	17
18	838644	831304	823512	815250	806500	797244	787462	777133	766236	754747	742644	18
19	791937	784597	776805	768543	759793	750537	740755	730426	719529	708040	695937	19
20	747347	740007	732215	723953	715203	705947	696165	685836	674939	663450	651347	20
21	704781	697441	689649	681387	672637	663381	653599	643270	632373	620884	608781	21
22	664150	656810	649018	640756	632006	622750	612968	602639	591742	580253	568150	22
23	625370	618030	610238	601976	593226	583970	574188	563859	552962	541473	529370	23
24	588360	581020	573228	564966	556216	546960	537178	526849	515952	504463	492360	24
25	553043	545703	537911	529649	520899	511643	501861	491532	480635	469146	457043	25
26	519344	512004	504212	495950	487200	477944	468162	457833	446936	435447	423344	26
27	487194	479854	472062	463800	455050	445794	436012	425683	414786	403297	391194	27
28	456523	449183	441391	433129	424379	415123	405341	395012	384115	372626	360523	28
29	427268	419928	412136	403874	395124	385868	376086	365757	354860	343371	331268	29
30	399368	392028	384236	375974	367224	357968	348186	337857	326960	315471	303368	30
31	372763	365423	357631	349369	340619	331363	321581	311252	300355	288866	276763	31
32	347396	340056	332264	324002	315252	305996	296214	285885	274988	263499	251396	32
33	323214	315874	308082	299820	291070	281814	272032	261703	250806	239317	227214	33
34	300166	292826	285033	276772	268022	258766	248984	238655	227758	216269	204166	34
35	278202	270862	263070	254808	246058	236802	227020	216691	205794	194305	182202	35
36	257274	249934	242142	233880	225130	215874	206092	195763	184866	173377	161274	36
37	237339	229999	222207	213945	205195	195939	186157	175828	164931	153442	141339	37
38	218352	211012	203220	194958	186208	176952	167170	156841	145944	134455	122352	38
39	200271	192931	185139	176877	168127	158871	149089	138760	127863	116374	104271	39
40	183060	175720	167928	159666	150916	141660	131878	121549	110652	99163	87060	40
41	166677	159337	151545	143283	134533	125277	115495	105166	94269	82780	70677	41
42	151088	143748	135956	127694	118944	109688	99906	89577	78680	67191	55088	42
43	136258	128918	121126	112864	104114	94858	85076	74747	63850	52361	40258	43
44	122153	114813	107021	98759	90009	80753	70971	60642	49745	38256	26153	44
45	108743	101403	93611	85349	76599	67343	57561	47232	36335	24846	12743	45
46	96000	88660	80868	72606	63856	54600	44818	34489	23592	12103		
47	83896	76556	68764	60502	51752	42496	32714	22385	11489		13410	44
48	72408	65068	57276	49014	40264	31008	21226	10897		14104	27515	43
49	61511	54171	46379	38117	29367	20111	10329		14831	28935	42345	42
50	51182	43842	36050	27788	19038	9782		15589	30420	44524	57934	41
51	41400	34060	26268	18006	9256		16383	31972	46803	60907	74317	40
52	32145	24805	17013	8750		17212	33594	49183	64014	78118	91528	39
53	23395	16055	8262		18080	35292	51675	67264	82095	96199	109609	38
54	15133	7792		18987	37067	54279	70662	86251	101082	115186	128596	37
55	7340		19936	38922	57002	74214	90597	106186	121017	135121	148531	36
		20927	40863	59850	77930	95142	111525	127114	141945	156049	169459	35
34	21964	42891	62827	81814	99894	117106	133489	149078	163909	178013	191423	34
33	45012	65939	85875	104862	122942	140154	156537	172126	186957	201061	214471	33
32	69194	90121	110057	129044	147124	164336	180719	196308	211139	225243	238653	32
31	94561	115488	135424	154411	172491	189703	206086	221675	236506	250610	264020	31
30	121166	142093	162029	181016	199096	216308	232691	248280	263111	277215	290625	30
29	149066	169993	189929	208916	226996	244208	260591	276180	291011	305115	318525	29
28	178321	199248	219184	238171	256251	273463	289846	305435	320266	334370	347780	28
27	208993	229920	249856	268843	286922	304134	320517	336106	350937	365041	378451	27
26	241142	262069	282005	300992	319072	336284	352667	368256	383087	397191	410601	26
25	274841	295768	315704	334691	352771	369983	386366	401955	416786	430890	444300	25
24	310158	331085	351021	370008	388088	405300	421683	437272	452103	466207	479617	24
23	347168	368095	388031	407018	425098	442310	458693	474282	489113	503217	516627	23
22	385948	406875	426811	445798	463878	481090	497473	513062	527893	541997	555407	22
21	426579	447506	467442	486429	504509	521721	538104	553693	568524	582628	596038	21
20	469145	490072	510008	528995	547075	564287	580670	596259	611090	625194	638604	20
19	513735	534662	554598	573585	591665	608877	625260	640849	655680	669784	683194	19
18	560442	581369	601305	620292	638372	655584	671967	687556	702387	716491	729901	18
17	609363	630290	650226	669213	687293	704505	720888	736477	751308	765412	778822	17
16	660599	681526	701462	720449	738529	755741	772124	787713	802544	816648	830058	16
15	714258	735185	755121	774108	792188	809400	825783	841372	856203	870307	883717	15
14	770450	791377	811313	830300	848380	865592	881975	897564	912395	926499	939909	14
13	829293	850220	870156	889143	907223	924435	940818	956407	971238	985342	998752	13
12	890910	911837	931773	950760	968840	986052	1002435	1018024	1032855	1046959	1060369	12
11	955429	976356	996292	1015279	1033359	1050571	1066954	1082543	1097374	1111478	1124888	11
10	1022985	1043912	1063848	1082835	1100915	1118127	1134510	1150099	1164930	1179034	1192444	10
AGE.	$_{35}N_x$	$_{36}N_x$	$_{37}N_x$	$_{38}N_x$	$_{39}N_x$	$_{40}N_x$	$_{41}N_x$	$_{42}N_x$	$_{43}N_x$	$_{44}N_x$	$_{45}N_x$	AGE.

TABLE XVIII.

INSURANCE VALUES, per $1,000.

WHOLE LIFE POLICIES.—PAID UP.

Age.	Value.	Age.	Value.	Age.	Value.	Age.	Value.	Age.	Value.	Age.	Value.	Age.	Value.	Age.	Value.
10	123.559	22	130.977	33	140.050	44	151.415	55	160.217	66	153.304	77	124.717	88	78.996
11	124.088	23	131.723	34	140.963	45	152.577	56	160.286	67	151.608	78	121.156	89	74.449
12	124.563	24	132.485	35	141.894	46	153.700	57	160.311	68	149.716	79	117.456	90	69.933
13	125.093	25	133.267	36	142.839	47	154.764	58	160.184	69	147.629	80	113.615	91	65.504
14	125.689	26	134.058	37	143.813	48	155.755	59	159.916	70	145.357	81	109.633	92	61.190
15	126.234	27	134.866	38	144.804	49	156.682	60	159.510	71	142.907	82	105.531	93	57.061
16	126.865	28	135.697	39	145.823	50	157.510	61	158.925	72	140.276	83	101.300	94	53.081
17	127.509	29	136.536	40	146.873	51	158.258	62	158.169	73	137.573	84	96.988	95	49.090
18	128.166	30	137.393	41	147.962	52	158.909	63	157.234	74	134.509	85	92.558	96	43.790
19	128.839	31	138.266	42	149.084	53	159.435	64	156.121	75	131.391	86	88.289	97	32.569
20	129.528	32	139.151	43	150.241	54	159.849	65	154.811	76	128.116	87	83.549	98	26.851
21	130.251														

LIFE POLICIES.—FIVE PREMIUMS. / LIFE POLICIES.—TEN PREMIUMS.

Age.	Five: 1st year.	Five: 2d year.	Five: 3d year.	Five: 4th year.	Ten: 1st year.	Ten: 2d year.	Ten: 3d year.	Ten: 4th year.	Ten: 5th year.	Ten: 6th year.	Ten: 7th year.	Ten: 8th year.	Ten: 9th year.	Age.
15	129.341	128.798	128.512	128.513	133.089	132.516	132.065	131.716	131.473	131.354	131.390	131.570	131.929	15
16	130.054	129.494	129.196	129.196	133.865	133.319	132.856	132.491	132.239	132.131	132.151	132.334	132.697	16
17	130.788	130.206	129.898	129.895	134.708	134.144	133.666	133.291	133.043	132.913	132.931	133.114	133.485	17
18	131.525	130.928	130.618	130.629	135.531	134.947	134.454	134.129	133.857	133.720	133.733	133.916	134.283	18
19	132.303	131.689	131.374	131.367	136.467	135.868	135.377	134.975	134.694	134.546	134.555	134.729	135.099	19
20	133.097	132.477	132.134	132.124	137.395	136.790	136.265	135.848	135.550	135.393	135.388	135.568	135.937	20
21	133.933	133.275	132.919	132.900	138.307	137.729	137.185	136.748	136.437	136.260	136.242	136.413	136.785	21
22	134.775	134.094	133.718	133.694	139.359	138.695	138.128	137.673	137.336	137.144	137.121	137.279	137.652	22
23	135.645	134.934	134.543	134.501	140.387	139.697	139.107	138.620	138.193	138.057	138.014	138.164	138.534	23
24	136.539	135.800	135.378	135.326	141.461	140.746	140.109	139.596	139.220	138.988	138.929	139.068	139.431	24
25	137.461	136.679	136.231	136.131	142.551	141.794	141.136	140.601	140.192	139.938	139.862	139.985	140.341	25
26	138.400	137.581	137.112	137.028	143.680	142.890	142.207	141.632	141.194	140.913	140.812	140.918	141.265	26
27	139.367	138.514	138.006	137.904	144.851	144.029	143.300	142.691	142.218	141.906	141.778	141.866	142.209	27
28	140.365	139.458	138.918	138.806	146.069	145.195	144.425	143.776	143.265	142.917	142.762	142.836	143.168	28
29	141.385	140.431	139.853	139.704	147.320	146.401	145.585	144.889	144 335	143.951	143.771	143.822	144.156	29
30	142.438	141.428	140.804	140.626	148.613	147.642	146.772	146.027	145.430	145.012	144.798	144.839	145.163	30
31	143.518	142.430	141.774	141.567	149.954	148.923	147.996	147.197	146.556	146.093	145.860	145.877	146.197	31
32	144.620	143.481	142.757	142.520	151.333	150.235	149.247	148.399	147.705	147.211	146.942	146.943	147.265	32
33	145.748	144.539	143.767	143.493	152.752	151.591	150.546	149.635	148.897	148.356	148.057	148.045	148.372	33
34	146.905	145.626	144.794	144.495	154.213	152.986	151.875	150.913	150.122	149.538	149.213	149.191	149.515	34
35	148.098	146.738	145.856	145.518	155.739	154.435	153.265	152.336	151.389	150.767	150.418	150.378	150.697	35
36	149.318	147.886	146.939	146.569	157.322	155.950	154.702	153.611	152.715	152.057	151.674	151.611	151.900	36
37	150.587	149.064	148.056	147.655	158.983	157.532	156.211	155.060	154.115	153.412	152.989	152.874	153.095	37
38	151.886	150.278	149.211	148.780	160.733	159.199	157.811	156.602	155.598	154.839	154.346	154.139	154.256	38
39	153.237	151.341	150.414	149.943	162.590	160.982	159.524	158.248	157.177	156.331	155.721	155.382	155.365	39
40	154.650	152.866	151.666	151.150	164.583	162.902	161.366	160.013	158.841	157.858	157.094	156.580	156.405	40
41	156.142	154.257	152.976	152.382	166.741	164.970	163.347	161.876	160.549	159.386	158.420	157.715	157.383	41
42	157.732	155.733	154.330	153.611	169.084	167.223	165.475	163.827	162.300	160.908	159.711	158.809	158.273	42
43	159.437	157.281	155.701	154.814	171.641	169.645	167.709	165.840	164.058	162.403	160.970	159.821	159.088	43
44	161.258	158.873	157.068	155.966	174.405	172.204	170.033	167.891	165.816	163.889	162.165	160.767	159.810	44
45	163.147	160.484	158.400	157.056	177.347	174.900	172.436	169.975	167.597	165.346	163.329	161.648	160.525	45
46	165.098	162.093	159.689	158.091	180.460	177.695	174.892	172.104	169.371	166.788	164.439	162.430	160.930	46
47	167.069	163.677	160.938	159.037	183.714	180.595	177.447	174.275	171.173	168.209	165.475	163.123	161.405	47
48	169.065	165.266	162.133	159.921	187.115	183.637	180.075	176.504	172.985	169.589	166.450	163.801	161.585	48
49	171.082	166.822	163.281	160.215	190.734	186.835	182.853	178.839	174.845	170.989	167.494	164.211	161.736	49
50	173.155	168.382	164.380	161.411	194.455	190.108	185.650	181.125	176.619	172.349	168.195	164.617	161.752	50
51	175.253	169.928	165.398	162.002	198.348	193.499	188.500	183.424	178.460	173.468	168.984	164.917	161.641	51
52	177.400	171.445	166.355	162.576	202.599	197.205	191.639	186.072	180.341	174.857	169.706	165.119	161.413	52
53	179.573	172.936	167.325	162.862	207.013	201.019	194.927	188.551	182.270	176.146	170.383	165.253	161.030	53
54	181.784	174.505	168.051	163.128	211.704	205.157	198.236	191.256	184.284	177.471	171.061	165.273	160.503	54
55	184.138	175.891	168.804	163.274	216.767	209.396	201.819	194.109	186.386	178.849	171.674	165.194	159.821	55
56	186.391	177.359	169.485	163.306	222.016	213.971	205.646	197.151	188.645	180.250	172.263	165.018	158.997	56
57	188.816	178.839	170.113	163.240	227.721	218.891	209.746	200.440	191.005	181.713	172.824	164.757	158.009	57
58	191.264	180.366	170.725	163.037	233.884	224.226	214.240	203.935	193.539	183.239	173.387	164.397	156.863	58
59	194.096	181.985	171.276	162.709	240.526	230.030	219.045	207.709	196.244	184.876	173.949	163.957	155.575	59
60	196.980	183.630	171.784	162.249	247.790	236.265	224.229	211.794	199.171	186.611	174.524	163.450	154.139	60
61	200.065	185.359	172.249	161.667	255.585	243.019	229.834	216.211	202.331	188.494	175.143	162.888	152.560	61
62	203.379	187.174	172.703	160.951	264.079	250.364	235.971	221.051	205.824	190.618	175.911	162.271	150.858	62
63	206.924	189.121	173.131	160.108	273.054	258.141	242.471	226.164	209.478	192.781	176.579	161.652	149.050	63
64	210.771	191.186	173.554	159.150	282.851	266.641	249.574	231.778	213.556	195.259	177.472	161.047	147.142	64
65	214.901	193.394	173.983	158.072	293.321	275.794	257.218	237.896	217.989	198.017	178.537	160.471	145.246	65

WHOLE LIFE POLICIES.—ANNUAL PREMIUMS.—FACTORS FOR INSURANCE VALUE.

Age.	$\frac{D_x}{_{100}N_x}$	$\frac{_{100}\Delta_x}{D_x}$	Age.	$\frac{D_x}{_{100}N_x}$	$\frac{_{100}\Delta_x}{D_x}$	Age.	$\frac{D_x}{_{100}N_x}$	$\frac{_{100}\Delta_x}{D_x}$	Age.	$\frac{D_x}{_{100}N_x}$	$\frac{_{100}\Delta_x}{D_x}$	Age.	$\frac{D_x}{_{100}N_x}$	$\frac{_{100}\Delta_x}{D_x}$
10	.048891	3.2122	28	.054467	3.5281	46	.068542	3.9962	64	.10930	4.0592	82	.23795	2.7443
11	.049093	3.2248	29	.054938	3.5500	47	.069847	4.0239	65	.11318	4.0256	83	.25124	2.6344
12	.049305	3.2382	30	.055433	3.5723	48	.071228	4.0498	66	.11731	3.9861	84	.26588	2.5218
13	.049528	3.2523	31	.055954	3.5949	49	.072690	4.0737	67	.12170	3.9420	85	.28220	2.4071
14	.049761	3.2671	32	.056502	3.6179	50	.074237	4.0954	68	.12637	3.8928	86	.30049	2.2907
15	.050006	3.2825	33	.057079	3.6412	51	.075877	4.1148	69	.13135	3.8386	87	.32115	2.1730
16	.050262	3.2985	34	.057687	3.6650	52	.077615	4.1315	70	.13666	3.7795	88	.34470	2.0549
17	.050530	3.3152	35	.058328	3.6892	53	.079458	4.1453	71	.14233	3.7157	89	.37161	1.9371
18	.050811	3.3323	36	.059006	3.7138	54	.081412	4.1560	72	.14837	3.6473	90	.40236	1.8201
19	.051105	3.3499	37	.059722	3.7390	55	.083487	4.1635	73	.15482	3.5745	91	.43773	1.7058
20	.051413	3.3680	38	.060480	3.7649	56	.085691	4.1675	74	.16171	3.4975	92	.47842	1.5951
21	.051735	3.3865	39	.061285	3.7914	57	.088034	4.1679	75	.16907	3.4164	93	.52453	1.4902
22	.052072	3.4054	40	.062139	3.8187	58	.090528	4.1648	76	.17695	3.3314	94	.57575	1.3923
23	.052425	3.4248	41	.063048	3.8470	59	.093185	4.1579	77	.18540	3.2427	95	.63117	1.3024
24	.052796	3.4446	42	.064016	3.8762	60	.096018	4.1472	78	.19444	3.1503	96	.68408	1.2036
25	.053184	3.4649	43	.065047	3.9063	61	.099033	4.1321	79	.20414	3.0542	97	.73154	1.0391
26	.053591	3.4855	44	.066144	3.9368	62	.102244	4.1125	80	.21456	2.9545	98	.80624	.7212
27	.054018	3.5066	45	.067308	3.9669	63	.105662	4.0882	81	.22578	2.8511			

ENDOWMENT POLICIES.—FACTORS FOR INSURANCE VALUE.

AGE.	$\frac{D_x}{_{80}N_x}$	$\frac{_{80}\Delta_x}{D_x}$	$\frac{D_x}{_{79}N_x}$	$\frac{_{79}\Delta_x}{D_x}$	$\frac{D_x}{_{78}N_x}$	$\frac{_{78}\Delta_x}{D_x}$	$\frac{D_x}{_{77}N_x}$	$\frac{_{77}\Delta_x}{D_x}$	$\frac{D_x}{_{76}N_x}$	$\frac{_{76}\Delta_x}{D_x}$	$\frac{D_x}{_{75}N_x}$	$\frac{_{75}\Delta_x}{D_x}$	AGE.
10	.04898	3.104	.049005	3.084	.04902	3.062	.04907	3.038	.04910	3.014	.04915	2.986	10
11	.04919	3.112	.04922	3.091	.04925	3.068	.04928	3.044	.04932	3.018	.04937	2.989	11
12	.04942	3.120	.04944	3.098	.04947	3.074	.04951	3.049	.04955	3.021	.04960	2.992	12
13	.04964	3.129	.04966	3.106	.04968	3.082	.04972	3.055	.04979	3.026	.04984	2.995	13
14	.04988	3.138	.04991	3.114	.04994	3.089	.04998	3.061	.05004	3.031	.05010	2.998	14
15	.05012	3.148	.05016	3.123	.05020	3.097	.05024	3.068	.05030	3.036	.05035	3.002	15
16	.05039	3.158	.05042	3.132	.05046	3.104	.05051	3.074	.05058	3.041	.05063	3.006	16
17	.05067	3.168	.05070	3.141	.05074	3.112	.05080	3.080	.05086	3.047	.05092	3.010	17
18	.05096	3.178	.05099	3.151	.05103	3.121	.05109	3.088	.05116	3.052	.05122	3.014	18
19	.05126	3.189	.05130	3.160	.05134	3.128	.05141	3.094	.05148	3.057	.05155	3.017	19
20	.05158	3.200	.05162	3.170	.05166	3.137	.05174	3.101	.05180	3.063	.05188	3.021	20
21	.05192	3.211	.05197	3.180	.05202	3.145	.05208	3.108	.05216	3.068	.05224	3.024	21
22	.05226	3.222	.05230	3.190	.05235	3.154	.05243	3.114	.05250	3.073	.05260	3.028	22
23	.05260	3.234	.05267	3.199	.05272	3.162	.05280	3.121	.05288	3.077	.05298	3.031	23
24	.05300	3.245	.05307	3.210	.05313	3.170	.05320	3.128	.05330	3.082	.05338	3.033	24
25	.05340	3.256	.05346	3.219	.05353	3.178	.05360	3.134	.05370	3.086	.05381	3.036	25
26	.05384	3.268	.05390	3.228	.05398	3.186	.05406	3.140	.05416	3.090	.05428	3.037	26
27	.05428	3.279	.05434	3.238	.05442	3.193	.05451	3.145	.05462	3.093	.05474	3.038	27
28	.05474	3.290	.05481	3.247	.05490	3.201	.05500	3.150	.05511	3.096	.05524	3.039	28
29	.05522	3.302	.05529	3.257	.05538	3.208	.05550	3.156	.05562	3.100	.05576	3.040	29
30	.05574	3.313	.05582	3.266	.05592	3.215	.05602	3.161	.05616	3.102	.05632	3.040	30
31	.05628	3.323	.05637	3.274	.05647	3.222	.05659	3.165	.05674	3.104	.05689	3.038	31
32	.05686	3.334	.05696	3.284	.05707	3.228	.05718	3.169	.05734	3.105	.05752	3.037	32
33	.05745	3.344	.05756	3.292	.05767	3.234	.05781	3.172	.05796	3.106	.05816	3.035	33
34	.05809	3.354	.05821	3.300	.05832	3.239	.05848	3.174	.05865	3.105	.05885	3.032	34
35	.05876	3.364	.05889	3.307	.05902	3.244	.05916	3.177	.05936	3.104	.05957	3.028	35
36	.05948	3.374	.05962	3.314	.05976	3.250	.05992	3.178	.06012	3.103	.06035	3.023	36
37	.06022	3.384	.06037	3.322	.06052	3.253	.06071	3.180	.06090	3.100	.06116	3.018	37
38	.06103	3.393	.06119	3.328	.06135	3.256	.06153	3.180	.06177	3.098	.06204	3.011	38
39	.06188	3.402	.06205	3.334	.06222	3.260	.06244	3.180	.06268	3.094	.06206	3.004	39
40	.06276	3.412	.06295	3.341	.06313	3.262	.06337	3.180	.06364	3.090	.06396	2.996	40
41	.06373	3.421	.06393	3.347	.06413	3.266	.06438	3.178	.06468	3.086	.06503	2.988	41
42	.06476	3.430	.06497	3.353	.06519	3.268	.06547	3.177	.06579	3.081	.06616	2.979	42
43	.06587	3.439	.06609	3.358	.06634	3.270	.06663	3.176	.06698	3.074	.06740	2.968	43
44	.06703	3.448	.06727	3.364	.06754	3.272	.06786	3.173	.06824	3.068	.06868	2.957	44
45	.06828	3.454	.06854	3.366	.06884	3.270	.06920	3.167	.06961	3.057	.07009	2.942	45
46	.06960	3.460	.06889	3.368	.06922	3.268	.07060	3.160	.07105	3.046	.07160	2.925	46
47	.07100	3.462	.07132	3.366	.07168	3.261	.07208	3.149	.07260	3.030	.07320	2.904	47
48	.07250	3.461	.07285	3.360	.07324	3.250	.07371	3.134	.07425	3.009	.07491	2.879	48
49	.07409	3.457	.07447	3.352	.07491	3.236	.07541	3.114	.07603	2.985	.07675	2.849	49
50	.07578	3.448	.07620	3.338	.07668	3.218	.07725	3.090	.07792	2.955	.07872	2.814	50
51	.07760	3.436	.07804	3.320	.07857	3.195	.07920	3.062	.07996	2.921	.08084	2.773	51
52	.07951	3.418	.08000	3.297	.08060	3.166	.08132	3.027	.08217	2.881	.08318	2.727	52
53	.08156	3.396	.08212	3.269	.08279	3.132	.08360	2.987	.08454	2.834	.08565	2.674	53
54	.08377	3.368	.08439	3.236	.08516	3.092	.08603	2.940	.08709	2.782	.08836	2.615	54
55	.08613	3.334	.08684	3.196	.08767	3.048	.08868	2.888	.08988	2.723	.09130	2.550	55
56	.08864	3.294	.08944	3.150	.09040	2.994	.09156	2.828	.09290	2.655	.09452	2.475	56
57	.09137	3.248	.09226	3.096	.09334	2.933	.09464	2.761	.09620	2.581	.09805	2.394	57
58	.09429	3.196	.09532	3.037	.09656	2.866	.09802	2.687	.09980	2.499	.10194	2.305	58
59	.09748	3.136	.09864	2.969	.10005	2.790	.10174	2.603	.10380	2.408	.10627	2.207	59
60	.10090	3.068	.10223	2.893	.10386	2.707	.10583	2.511	.10820	2.309	.11110	2.101	60
61	.10465	2.992	.10620	2.808	.10808	2.614	.11035	2.410	.11314	2.200	.11654	1.984	61
62	.10873	2.906	.11051	2.714	.11270	2.511	.11539	2.299	.11870	2.081	.12270	1.858	62
63	.11316	2.811	.11526	2.609	.11786	2.398	.12102	2.177	.12492	1.951	.12976	1.722	63
64	.11806	2.705	.12053	2.494	.12358	2.273	.12738	2.045	.13210	1.811	.13794	1.577	64
65	.12347	2.588	.12642	2.367	.13009	2.138	.13467	1.900	.14038	1.661	.14760	1.422	65
66	.12944	2.460	.13300	2.230	.13743	1.990	.14302	1.745	.15007	1.500	.15915	1.257	66
67	.13620	2.318	.14048	2.078	.14590	1.830	.15283	1.578	.16170	1.328	.17330	1.084	67
68	.14380	2.165	.14907	1.915	.15580	1.658	.16453	1.461	.17595	1.148	.19120	.905	68
69	.15252	1.998	.15905	1.738	.16762	1.475	.17882	1.213	.19388	.9604	.21650	.722	69
70	.16260	1.818	.17094	1.549	.18194	1.281	.19680	1.018	.21737	.7688	.24705	.5401	70
71	.17461	1.624	.18538	1.349	.20000	1.077	.22032	.8168	.24970	.5770	.29500	.3655	71
72	.18914	1.418	.20348	1.138	.22348	.8676	.25264	.6152	.29850	.3917	.37410	.2072	72
73	.20730	1.200	.22700	.9191	.25580	.6551	.30040	.4192	.37640	.2229	.53115	.07871	73
74	.23085	.9730	.25926	.6972	.27045	.4484	.37904	.2396	.53302	.08508			
75	.26306	.7408	.30670	.4791	.38180	.2574	.53500	.09188			.51153	.006630	14
76	.31040	.5115	.38480	.2763	.53705	.09916			.51152	.006586	.34881	.01921	13
77	.38801	.2968	.53920	.1071			.51151	.006553	.34880	.01910	.26755	.03713	12
78	.54195	.1158			.51150	.006526	.34879	.01902	.26754	.03695	.21885	.05985	11
10			.51149	.006502	.34878	.01895	.26752	.03680	.21882	.05964	.18641	.08688	10
AGE.			$\frac{D_x}{_{12}N_x}$	$\frac{_{12}\Delta_x}{D_x}$	$\frac{D_x}{_{13}N_x}$	$\frac{_{13}\Delta_x}{D_x}$	$\frac{D_x}{_{14}N_x}$	$\frac{_{14}\Delta_x}{D_x}$	$\frac{D_x}{_{15}N_x}$	$\frac{_{15}\Delta_x}{D_x}$	$\frac{D_x}{_{16}N_x}$	$\frac{_{16}\Delta_x}{D_x}$	AGE.

ENDOWMENT POLICIES.—FACTORS FOR INSURANCE VALUE.

Age.	$\frac{D_x}{_{74}N_x}$	$\frac{_{74}\Delta_x}{D_x}$	$\frac{D_x}{_{73}N_x}$	$\frac{_{73}\Delta_x}{D_x}$	$\frac{D_x}{_{72}N_x}$	$\frac{_{72}\Delta_x}{D_x}$	$\frac{D_x}{_{71}N_x}$	$\frac{_{71}\Delta_x}{D_x}$	$\frac{D_x}{_{70}N_x}$	$\frac{_{70}\Delta_x}{D_x}$	$\frac{D_x}{_{69}N_x}$	$\frac{_{69}\Delta_x}{D_x}$	Age.
10	.04921	2.957	.04927	2.926	.04931	2.894	.04940	2.858	.04949	2.824	.04959	2.787	10
11	.04942	2.958	.04948	2.926	.04956	2.892	.04964	2.855	.04973	2.820	.04983	2.782	11
12	.04966	2.960	.04973	2.927	.04979	2.891	.04988	2.853	.04998	2.816	.05008	2.776	12
13	.04990	2.962	.04996	2.927	.05005	2.890	.05013	2.851	.05024	2.812	.05035	2.771	13
14	.05016	2.964	.05022	2.928	.05032	2.890	.05041	2.848	.05051	2.809	.05063	2.765	14
15	.05042	2.967	.05050	2.929	.05058	2.889	.05068	2.846	.05080	2.805	.05092	2.760	15
16	.05070	2.969	.05079	2.930	.05088	2.888	.05099	2.845	.05111	2.800	.05124	2.754	16
17	.05100	2.972	.05110	2.931	.05119	2.887	.05130	2.843	.05142	2.795	.05157	2.748	17
18	.05130	2.974	.05140	2.931	.05150	2.886	.05162	2.839	.05176	2.791	.05190	2.741	18
19	.05164	2.975	.05174	2.931	.05184	2.884	.05198	2.836	.05212	2.785	.05227	2.733	19
20	.05197	2.978	.05208	2.931	.05220	2.882	.05232	2.832	.05248	2.779	.05265	2.725	20
21	.05234	2.979	.05245	2.931	.05257	2.880	.05272	2.827	.05287	2.773	.05305	2.717	21
22	.05270	2.980	.05282	2.930	.05295	2.878	.05310	2.823	.05328	2.766	.05346	2.707	22
23	.05310	2.981	.05322	2.929	.05335	2.874	.05352	2.817	.05371	2.758	.05391	2.697	23
24	.05351	2.981	.05364	2.927	.05379	2.870	.05396	2.811	.05416	2.750	.05437	2.686	24
25	.05393	2.982	.05408	2.925	.05425	2.865	.05442	2.804	.05464	2.741	.05486	2.675	25
26	.05441	2.981	.05456	2.922	.05474	2.860	.05493	2.796	.05514	2.730	.05539	2.662	26
27	.05488	2.980	.05504	2.919	.05523	2.854	.05544	2.788	.05567	2.719	.05593	2.648	27
28	.05539	2.978	.05556	2.915	.05576	2.847	.05598	2.779	.05623	2.707	.05651	2.634	28
29	.05592	2.976	.05610	2.910	.05632	2.840	.05655	2.769	.05682	2.694	.05712	2.618	29
30	.05648	2.974	.05668	2.905	.05691	2.832	.05716	2.758	.05745	2.681	.05777	2.601	30
31	.05708	2.970	.05730	2.898	.05753	2.823	.05781	2.745	.05812	2.664	.05845	2.582	31
32	.05771	2.966	.05794	2.891	.05819	2.812	.05848	2.730	.05882	2.648	.05918	2.562	32
33	.05836	2.964	.05863	2.883	.05890	2.801	.05920	2.717	.05957	2.631	.05995	2.542	33
34	.05908	2.954	.05934	2.873	.05964	2.788	.05998	2.701	.06036	2.611	.06078	2.519	34
35	.05980	2.947	.06011	2.863	.06043	2.775	.06079	2.684	.06120	2.591	.06165	2.495	35
36	.06061	2.939	.06091	2.851	.06127	2.759	.06165	2.665	.06210	2.568	.06257	2.470	36
37	.06144	2.930	.06177	2.839	.06215	2.743	.06258	2.646	.06305	2.545	.06359	2.443	37
38	.06233	2.920	.06270	2.825	.06311	2.726	.06356	2.624	.06409	2.520	.06467	2.414	38
39	.06331	2.909	.06368	2.811	.06413	2.707	.06463	2.602	.06519	2.494	.06583	2.383	39
40	.06432	2.897	.06475	2.795	.06522	2.687	.06576	2.578	.06638	2.466	.06707	2.352	40
41	.06543	2.885	.06588	2.778	.06640	2.667	.06699	2.553	.06766	2.437	.06841	2.318	41
42	.06660	2.871	.06708	2.761	.06765	2.644	.06830	2.527	.06904	2.406	.06987	2.283	42
43	.06785	2.857	.06840	2.742	.06901	2.621	.06972	2.498	.07052	2.373	.07143	2.246	43
44	.06920	2.841	.06980	2.721	.07047	2.596	.07125	2.469	.07214	2.339	.07314	2.207	44
45	.07065	2.821	.07131	2.697	.07205	2.567	.07292	2.435	.07388	2.301	.07499	2.164	45
46	.07221	2.790	.07292	2.670	.07375	2.535	.07468	2.399	.07577	2.260	.07700	2.119	46
47	.07388	2.773	.07467	2.639	.07558	2.499	.07660	2.357	.07782	2.213	.07918	2.068	47
48	.07567	2.742	.07655	2.603	.07755	2.457	.07870	2.311	.08004	2.161	.08156	2.011	48
49	.07760	2.707	.07856	2.562	.07968	2.411	.08096	2.259	.08246	2.106	.08417	1.951	49
50	.07967	2.667	.08020	2.514	.08200	2.359	.08344	2.203	.08512	2.043	.08704	1.884	50
51	.08190	2.620	.08307	2.463	.08450	2.302	.08613	2.140	.08803	1.976	.09021	1.812	51
52	.08432	2.568	.08570	2.405	.08727	2.238	.08911	2.071	.09120	1.902	.09373	1.733	52
53	.08696	2.510	.08851	2.340	.09028	2.168	.09268	1.994	.09481	1.821	.09767	1.648	53
54	.08984	2.444	.09156	2.268	.09360	2.091	.09597	1.912	.09879	1.733	.10209	1.557	54
55	.09300	2.372	.09497	2.190	.09728	2.006	.10000	1.822	.10327	1.639	.10710	1.459	55
56	.09644	2.291	.09868	2.104	.10138	1.914	.10456	1.725	.10833	1.528	.11284	1.355	56
57	.10022	2.203	.10285	2.009	.10598	1.814	.10970	1.621	.11412	1.430	.11947	1.245	57
58	.10450	2.107	.10752	1.907	.11124	1.707	.11553	1.510	.12081	1.316	.12724	1.128	58
59	.10923	2.003	.11278	1.797	.11710	1.592	.12230	1.391	.12863	1.195	.13648	1.006	59
60	.11457	1.890	.11878	1.679	.12389	1.469	.13015	1.265	.13793	1.068	.14768	.8798	60
61	.12066	1.767	.12568	1.551	.13187	1.339	.13953	1.133	.14911	.9337	.16155	.7488	61
62	.12764	1.636	.13371	1.416	.14128	1.201	.15084	.9943	.16310	.7989	.17923	.6182	62
63	.13571	1.495	.14320	1.271	.15262	1.056	.16479	.8508	.18081	.6603	.20259	.4867	63
64	.14530	1.346	.15460	1.120	.16667	.9052	.18255	.7040	.20419	.5206	.23504	.3587	64
65	.15678	1.187	.16870	.9624	.18444	.7508	.20595	.5568	.23664	.3846	.28338	.2388	65
66	.17088	1.022	.18652	.8000	.20782	.5951	.23834	.4122	.28494	.2567	.36346	.1329	66
67	.18882	.8612	.20995	.6352	.24030	.4415	.28670	.2757	.36492	.1432	.52293	.04949	67
68	.21220	.6778	.24234	.4728	.28850	.2962	.36644	.1543	.52408	.05348			
69	.24460	.5054	.29045	.3178	.36819	.1661	.52530	.05776			.51164	.007010	20
70	.29270	.3410	.37000	.1789	.52662	.06244			.51161	.006929	.34895	.02023	19
71	.37190	.1925	.52800	.06747			.51159	.006860	.34892	.02002	.26770	.03897	18
72	.52950	.07287			.51158	.006793	.34889	.01982	.26767	.03858	.21900	.06258	17
			.51156	.006736	.34887	.01965	.26764	.03823	.21897	.06201	.18656	.09052	16
15	.51155	.006678	.34885	.01949	.26762	.03791	.21894	.06148	.18654	.08970	.16342	.1222	15
14	.34883	.01934	.26760	.03762	.21891	.06098	.18651	.08898	.16340	.1212	.14615	.1573	14
13	.26756	.03735	.21889	.06053	.18647	.08832	.16338	.1203	.14612	.1561	.13273	.1953	13
12	.21886	.06014	.18644	.08772	.16337	.1195	.14610	.1550	.13270	.1939	.12201	.2358	12
11	.18642	.08726	.16334	.1188	.14607	.1541	.13267	.1927	.12200	.2343	.11329	.2787	11
10	.16331	.1182	.14606	.1532	.13265	.1916	.12197	.2330	.11328	.2771	.10603	.3236	10
Age.	$\frac{D_x}{_{17}N_x}$	$\frac{_{17}\Delta_x}{D_x}$	$\frac{D_x}{_{18}N_x}$	$\frac{_{18}\Delta_x}{D_x}$	$\frac{D_x}{_{19}N_x}$	$\frac{_{19}\Delta_x}{D_x}$	$\frac{D_x}{_{20}N_x}$	$\frac{_{20}\Delta_x}{D_x}$	$\frac{D_x}{_{21}N_x}$	$\frac{_{21}\Delta_x}{D_x}$	$\frac{D_x}{_{22}N_x}$	$\frac{_{22}\Delta_x}{D_x}$	Age.

TABLE XX.

ENDOWMENT POLICIES.—FACTORS FOR INSURANCE VALUE.

AGE.	$\frac{D_x}{_{68}N_x}$	$\frac{_{68}\Delta_x}{D_x}$	$\frac{D_x}{_{67}N_x}$	$\frac{_{67}\Delta_x}{D_x}$	$\frac{D_x}{_{66}N_x}$	$\frac{_{66}\Delta_x}{D_x}$	$\frac{D_x}{_{65}N_x}$	$\frac{_{65}\Delta_x}{D_x}$	$\frac{D_x}{_{64}N_x}$	$\frac{_{64}\Delta_x}{D_x}$	$\frac{D_x}{_{63}N_x}$	$\frac{_{63}\Delta_x}{D_x}$	AGE.
10	.04969	2.749	.04980	2.710	.04992	2.670	.05006	2.628	.05021	2.586	.05037	2.542	10
11	.04994	2.742	.05005	2.702	.05018	2.660	.05033	2.616	.05049	2.572	.05065	2.528	11
12	.05019	2.736	.05032	2.693	.05046	2.649	.05061	2.604	.05077	2.559	.05095	2.512	12
13	.05047	2.728	.05060	2.684	.05075	2.638	.05091	2.592	.05109	2.544	.05127	2.497	13
14	.05076	2.721	.05090	2.675	.05105	2.628	.05123	2.580	.05141	2.531	.05161	2.481	14
15	.05106	2.714	.05121	2.667	.05138	2.617	.05156	2.567	.05175	2.516	.05197	2.464	15
16	.05138	2.706	.05154	2.657	.05172	2.605	.05190	2.554	.05212	2.501	.05234	2.447	16
17	.05172	2.698	.05188	2.647	.05208	2.593	.05228	2.540	.05250	2.485	.05274	2.430	17
18	.05207	2.688	.05224	2.635	.05244	2.570	.05266	2.524	.05289	2.469	.05316	2.411	18
19	.05245	2.679	.05263	2.624	.05284	2.567	.05308	2.510	.05332	2.451	.05360	2.391	19
20	.05282	2.668	.05303	2.612	.05326	2.553	.05350	2.493	.05377	2.433	.05405	2.371	20
21	.05324	2.658	.05345	2.599	.05369	2.538	.05396	2.476	.05424	2.413	.05455	2.349	21
22	.05367	2.647	.05390	2.586	.05416	2.522	.05443	2.458	.05473	2.392	.05506	2.326	22
23	.05413	2.634	.05437	2.571	.05464	2.505	.05494	2.439	.05527	2.370	.05562	2.301	23
24	.05460	2.621	.05486	2.555	.05515	2.487	.05547	2.418	.05582	2.347	.05620	2.277	24
25	.05511	2.607	.05539	2.539	.05570	2.468	.05604	2.397	.05641	2.323	.05682	2.251	25
26	.05565	2.592	.05595	2.520	.05628	2.447	.05664	2.373	.05704	2.297	.05748	2.223	26
27	.05622	2.576	.05654	2.501	.05689	2.426	.05728	2.349	.05771	2.271	.05817	2.193	27
28	.05681	2.558	.05715	2.481	.05753	2.402	.05795	2.323	.05841	2.243	.05892	2.163	28
29	.05745	2.540	.05781	2.460	.05822	2.378	.05867	2.297	.05916	2.213	.05971	2.130	29
30	.05812	2.520	.05851	2.437	.05895	2.353	.05943	2.268	.05997	2.182	.06054	2.096	30
31	.05884	2.498	.05926	2.413	.05973	2.325	.06025	2.237	.06081	2.148	.06144	2.059	31
32	.05960	2.475	.06004	2.387	.06055	2.296	.06110	2.206	.06173	2.113	.06241	2.022	32
33	.06040	2.451	.06089	2.350	.06143	2.265	.06204	2.172	.06270	2.077	.06344	1.984	33
34	.06125	2.425	.06178	2.330	.06237	2.233	.06302	2.136	.06376	2.038	.06455	1.941	34
35	.06217	2.398	.06274	2.300	.06338	2.199	.06409	2.099	.06488	1.998	.06574	1.897	35
36	.06314	2.369	.06377	2.266	.06446	2.163	.06524	2.060	.06609	1.955	.06705	1.852	36
37	.06420	2.338	.06488	2.232	.06563	2.125	.06647	2.018	.06740	1.911	.06845	1.804	37
38	.06533	2.306	.06606	2.197	.06689	2.085	.06781	1.975	.06883	1.865	.06997	1.755	38
39	.06654	2.271	.06734	2.158	.06824	2.044	.06925	1.930	.07037	1.816	.07162	1.703	39
40	.06785	2.236	.06873	2.120	.06971	2.001	.07081	1.884	.07204	1.767	.07342	1.651	40
41	.06926	2.198	.07022	2.078	.07130	1.956	.07252	1.835	.07388	1.715	.07541	1.596	41
42	.07080	2.159	.07185	2.035	.07304	1.909	.07438	1.785	.07589	1.661	.07758	1.539	42
43	.07246	2.118	.07363	1.990	.07494	1.860	.07643	1.733	.07810	1.606	.08000	1.480	43
44	.07427	2.075	.07556	1.943	.07702	1.809	.07867	1.678	.08054	1.548	.08267	1.420	44
45	.07624	2.028	.07767	1.891	.07930	1.754	.08114	1.619	.08324	1.486	.08564	1.355	45
46	.07841	1.978	.07999	1.837	.08180	1.696	.08388	1.558	.08624	1.422	.08895	1.289	46
47	.08074	1.922	.08252	1.777	.08456	1.632	.08690	1.492	.08958	1.353	.09268	1.217	47
48	.08326	1.862	.08532	1.713	.08762	1.564	.09027	1.420	.09334	1.279	.09689	1.142	48
49	.08614	1.797	.08841	1.644	.09103	1.492	.09405	1.345	.09757	1.201	.10168	1.062	49
50	.08927	1.725	.09185	1.569	.09484	1.414	.09832	1.265	.10240	1.119	.10720	.9784	50
51	.09275	1.649	.09570	1.489	.09914	1.331	.10318	1.180	.10794	1.032	.11362	.8917	51
52	.09664	1.567	.10003	1.403	.10403	1.243	.10875	1.090	.11439	.9419	.12117	.8014	52
53	.10102	1.478	.10496	1.312	.10964	1.149	.11523	.9953	.12196	.8476	.13019	.7081	53
54	.10598	1.384	.11061	1.215	.11614	1.051	.12283	.8967	.13101	.7500	.14117	.6129	54
55	.11167	1.283	.11715	1.113	.12379	.9494	.13191	.7948	.14202	.6501	.15485	.5168	55
56	.11826	1.117	.12483	1.006	.13290	.8427	.14295	.6900	.15572	.5489	.17236	.4209	56
57	.12597	1.065	.13398	.8935	.14396	.7324	.15667	.5834	.17324	.4477	.19561	.3270	57
58	.13517	.9480	.14508	.7784	.15772	.6207	.17422	.4769	.19651	.3487	.22815	.2378	58
59	.14631	.8274	.15886	.6608	.17529	.5084	.19750	.3721	.22895	.2540	.27655	.1560	59
60	.16014	.7040	.17648	.5426	.19860	.3977	.22996	.2719	.27746	.1671	.35720	.08554	60
61	.17779	.5791	.19981	.4253	.23107	.2911	.27844	.1792	.35804	.09186	.51812	.03136	61
62	.20113	.4550	.23226	.3121	.27952	.1924	.35894	.09877	.51879	.03377			
63	.23358	.3346	.28067	.2068	.35992	.1063	.51945	.03639			.51178	.007584	26
64	.28195	.2222	.36096	.1145	.52020	.03926			.51175	.007473	.34916	.02184	25
65	.36215	.1233	.52097	.04240			.51172	.007372	.34911	.02154	.26790	.04195	24
66	.52186	.04578			.51170	.007275	.34905	.02125	.26786	.04138	.21919	.06718	23
			.51169	.007178	.34903	.02097	.26782	.04084	.21915	.06631	.18680	.09687	22
21	.51166	.007092	.34900	.02071	.26779	.04033	.21911	.06545	.18675	.09566	.16365	.1304	21
20	.34897	.02047	.26776	.03986	.21908	.06468	.18670	.09448	.16362	.1288	.14636	.1673	20
19	.26774	.03940	.21905	.06393	.18666	.09336	.16359	.1273	.14632	.1654	.13295	.2071	19
18	.21903	.06323	.18663	.09234	.16354	.1259	.14628	.1635	.13290	.2047	.12223	.2493	18
17	.18661	.09140	.16351	.1246	.14625	.1617	.13286	.2025	.12220	.2466	.11350	.2936	17
16	.16346	.1234	.14621	.1601	.13282	.2005	.12216	.2441	.11345	.2906	.10623	.3397	16
15	.14618	.1587	.13278	.1986	.12211	.2417	.11341	.2877	.10620	.3364	.10012	.3872	15
14	.13275	.1968	.12208	.2396	.11337	.2851	.10617	.3332	.10009	.3836	.09491	.4360	14
13	.12205	.2376	.11333	.2827	.10614	.3303	.10006	.3802	.09487	.4321	.09039	.4857	13
12	.11331	.2805	.10611	.3278	.10003	.3772	.09483	.4285	.09036	.4816	.08647	.5363	12
11	.10607	.3255	.09999	.3745	.09480	.4255	.09032	.4783	.08644	.5323	.08302	.5877	11
10	.09996	.3722	.09477	.4228	.09030	.4750	.08641	.5286	.08299	.5836	.07998	.6396	10
AGE.	$\frac{D_x}{_{23}N_x}$	$\frac{_{23}\Delta_x}{D_x}$	$\frac{D_x}{_{24}N_x}$	$\frac{_{24}\Delta_x}{D_x}$	$\frac{D_x}{_{25}N_x}$	$\frac{_{25}\Delta_x}{D_x}$	$\frac{D_x}{_{26}N_x}$	$\frac{_{26}\Delta_x}{D_x}$	$\frac{D_x}{_{27}N_x}$	$\frac{_{27}\Delta_x}{D_x}$	$\frac{D_x}{_{28}N_x}$	$\frac{_{28}\Delta_x}{D_x}$	AGE.

ENDOWMENT POLICIES.—FACTORS FOR INSURANCE VALUE.

Age.	$\frac{D_x}{{}_{62}N_x}$	$\frac{{}_{62}\Delta_x}{D_x}$	$\frac{D_x}{{}_{61}N_x}$	$\frac{{}_{61}\Delta_x}{D_x}$	$\frac{D_x}{{}_{60}N_x}$	$\frac{{}_{60}\Delta_x}{D_x}$	$\frac{D_x}{{}_{59}N_x}$	$\frac{{}_{59}\Delta_x}{D_x}$	$\frac{D_x}{{}_{58}N_x}$	$\frac{{}_{58}\Delta_x}{D_x}$	$\frac{D_x}{{}_{57}N_x}$	$\frac{{}_{57}\Delta_x}{D_x}$	Age.
10	.05054	2.498	.05073	2.453	.05093	2.407	.05115	2.360	.05138	2.312	.05164	2.264	10
11	.05084	2.481	.05104	2.435	.05125	2.387	.05148	2.338	.05174	2.289	.05201	2.240	11
12	.05115	2.464	.05136	2.416	.05159	2.367	.05184	2.316	.05211	2.266	.05240	2.214	12
13	.05148	2.447	.05171	2.397	.05195	2.346	.05222	2.294	.05250	2.242	.05281	2.189	13
14	.05183	2.429	.05208	2.378	.05234	2.324	.05261	2.272	.05292	2.217	.05324	2.163	14
15	.05220	2.412	.05246	2.358	.05273	2.302	.05303	2.248	.05335	2.192	.05369	2.136	15
16	.05259	2.392	.05286	2.337	.05316	2.280	.05347	2.224	.05381	2.166	.05418	2.107	16
17	.05300	2.373	.05328	2.315	.05360	2.257	.05393	2.198	.05430	2.139	.05469	2.078	17
18	.05344	2.353	.05374	2.293	.05407	2.232	.05443	2.172	.05482	2.109	.05524	2.047	18
19	.05389	2.330	.05422	2.269	.05458	2.206	.05495	2.144	.05537	2.080	.05582	2.016	19
20	.05438	2.308	.05473	2.244	.05510	2.180	.05551	2.115	.05595	2.049	.05644	1.983	20
21	.05489	2.284	.05526	2.218	.05566	2.152	.05610	2.085	.05657	2.017	.05709	1.949	21
22	.05543	2.259	.05582	2.191	.05626	2.123	.05673	2.053	.05724	1.983	.05779	1.914	22
23	.05601	2.233	.05643	2.163	.05689	2.091	.05740	2.021	.05795	1.949	.05853	1.876	23
24	.05661	2.205	.05706	2.132	.05757	2.060	.05810	1.986	.05869	1.912	.05933	1.838	24
25	.05726	2.175	.05775	2.101	.05828	2.026	.05886	1.950	.05949	1.874	.06018	1.798	25
26	.05796	2.145	.05847	2.068	.05905	1.991	.05968	1.913	.06036	1.834	.06110	1.756	26
27	.05868	2.114	.05925	2.034	.05987	1.954	.06054	1.874	.06128	1.794	.06207	1.713	27
28	.05947	2.081	.06007	1.998	.06073	1.916	.06146	1.833	.06225	1.751	.06313	1.668	28
29	.06030	2.045	.06094	1.960	.06166	1.876	.06245	1.791	.06332	1.706	.06426	1.621	29
30	.06118	2.009	.06189	1.920	.06267	1.834	.06352	1.747	.06446	1.660	.06548	1.573	30
31	.06214	1.969	.06290	1.880	.06374	1.790	.06466	1.700	.06569	1.611	.06681	1.522	31
32	.06317	1.929	.06400	1.837	.06491	1.744	.06591	1.653	.06702	1.561	.06825	1.471	32
33	.06425	1.887	.06516	1.792	.06616	1.697	.06725	1.603	.06848	1.509	.06981	1.417	33
34	.06544	1.842	.06643	1.744	.06751	1.647	.06874	1.551	.07005	1.456	.07152	1.360	34
35	.06672	1.796	.06779	1.696	.06898	1.596	.07030	1.498	.07177	1.399	.07340	1.303	35
36	.06811	1.748	.06928	1.645	.07058	1.543	.07203	1.441	.07366	1.342	.07546	1.244	36
37	.06960	1.698	.07089	1.592	.07233	1.487	.07393	1.384	.07572	1.282	.07773	1.183	37
38	.07124	1.645	.07265	1.537	.07424	1.430	.07602	1.325	.07801	1.222	.08026	1.120	38
39	.07302	1.591	.07459	1.480	.07636	1.371	.07834	1.264	.08056	1.159	.08309	1.056	39
40	.07497	1.536	.07672	1.422	.07868	1.311	.08089	1.201	.08339	1.095	.08625	.9906	40
41	.07713	1.478	.07906	1.362	.08126	1.248	.08374	1.127	.08658	1.029	.08981	.9246	41
42	.07951	1.418	.08168	1.300	.08414	1.185	.08695	1.072	.09017	.9628	.09387	.8576	42
43	.08216	1.357	.08459	1.237	.08738	1.119	.09057	1.006	.09426	.8954	.09853	.7900	43
44	.08509	1.294	.08785	1.172	.09102	1.053	.09468	.9376	.09893	.8270	.10391	.7212	44
45	.08838	1.228	.09152	1.103	.09516	.9831	.09939	.8673	.10434	.7566	.11019	.6515	45
46	.09208	1.159	.09569	1.033	.09990	.9114	.10479	.7953	.11065	.6850	.11762	.5810	46
47	.09626	1.085	.10044	.9581	.10534	.8365	.11114	.7208	.11809	.6115	.12652	.5091	47
48	.10103	1.008	.10590	.8806	.11168	.7592	.11860	.6444	.12701	.5367	.13740	.4371	48
49	.10651	.9282	.11227	.8004	.11916	.6797	.12754	.5664	.13790	.4614	.15097	.3653	49
50	.11291	.8446	.11977	.7174	.12812	.5982	.13844	.4876	.15149	.3862	.16840	.2949	50
51	.12044	.7580	.12875	.6322	.13904	.5157	.15205	.4088	.16893	.3123	.19161	.2272	51
52	.12944	.6690	.13969	.5459	.15266	.4330	.16950	.3310	.19214	.2409	.22406	.1636	52
53	.14040	.5782	.15333	.4589	.17013	.3510	.19272	.2556	.22459	.1737	.27267	.1062	53
54	.15405	.4867	.17080	.3726	.19336	.2715	.22517	.1846	.27319	.1129	.35359	.05754	54
55	.17155	.3958	.19405	.2886	.22581	.1964	.27376	.1202	.35408	.06131	.51531	.02083	55
56	.19475	.3071	.22649	.2091	.27438	.1281	.35461	.06538	.51571	.02224			
57	.22723	.2228	.27504	.1366	.35517	.06973	.51608	.02373			.51200	.008412	32
58	.27576	.1458	.35578	.07452	.51654	.02537			.51196	.008246	.34942	.02412	31
59	.35644	.07974	.51698	.02716			.51192	.008100	.34936	.02369	.26820	.04618	30
60	.51754	.02918			.51188	.007956	.34930	.02327	.26813	.04536	.21952	.07372	29
			.51185	.007823	.34925	.02288	.26808	.04427	.21945	.07244	.18711	.1060	28
27	.51181	.007698	.34921	.02250	.26805	.04387	.21940	.07095	.18706	.1042	.16399	.1422	27
26	.34918	.02216	.26800	.04319	.21935	.07014	.18700	.1022	.16394	.1399	.14670	.1819	26
25	.26795	.04255	.21928	.06910	.18693	.1010	.16388	.1375	.14663	.1791	.13326	.2245	25
24	.21923	.06810	.18689	.09954	.16384	.1358	.14658	.1762	.13321	.2212	.12257	.2696	24
23	.18685	.09818	.16378	.1339	.14652	.1740	.13316	.2178	.12250	.2656	.11381	.3166	23
22	.16372	.1321	.14646	.1716	.13310	.2150	.12244	.2619	.11375	.3121	.10655	.3652	22
21	.14641	.1694	.13305	.2122	.12239	.2585	.11370	.3077	.10649	.3602	.10042	.4151	21
20	.13300	.2096	.12233	.2553	.11365	.3040	.10644	.3554	.10036	.4097	.09520	.4661	20
19	.12228	.2522	.11360	.3003	.10639	.3512	.10031	.4044	.09514	.4601	.09067	.5176	19
18	.11355	.2969	.10633	.3471	.10024	.3997	.09508	.4545	.09062	.5114	.08674	.5698	18
17	.10628	.3432	.10020	.3953	.09503	.4493	.09058	.5052	.08669	.5632	.08329	.6224	17
16	.10015	.3912	.09499	.4447	.09052	.5000	.08665	.5568	.08324	.6155	.08022	.6752	16
15	.09495	.4401	.09048	.4949	.08660	.5512	.08318	.6089	.08017	.6679	.07751	.7279	15
14	.09044	.4901	.08655	.5458	.08314	.6030	.08013	.6610	.07746	.7205	.07508	.7806	14
13	.08651	.5409	.08310	.5974	.08009	.6550	.07742	.7134	.07503	.7731	.07288	.8332	13
12	.08306	.5922	.08006	.6493	.07737	.7072	.07499	.7658	.07284	.8256	.07092	.8855	12
11	.08001	.6442	.07734	.7014	.07495	.7599	.07280	.8185	.07087	.8781	.06912	.9379	11
10	.07730	.6965	.07490	.7540	.07277	.8121	.07082	.8711	.06908	.9304	.06749	.9897	10
Age.	$\frac{D_x}{{}_{29}N_x}$	$\frac{{}_{29}\Delta_x}{D_x}$	$\frac{D_x}{{}_{30}N_x}$	$\frac{{}_{30}\Delta_x}{D_x}$	$\frac{D_x}{{}_{31}N_x}$	$\frac{{}_{31}\Delta_x}{D_x}$	$\frac{D_x}{{}_{32}N_x}$	$\frac{{}_{32}\Delta_x}{D_x}$	$\frac{D_x}{{}_{33}N_x}$	$\frac{{}_{33}\Delta_x}{D_x}$	$\frac{D_x}{{}_{34}N_x}$	$\frac{{}_{34}\Delta_x}{D_x}$	Age.

ENDOWMENT POLICIES.—FACTORS FOR INSURANCE VALUE.

Age.	$\frac{D_x}{{}_{56}N_x}$	$\frac{{}_{56}\Delta_x}{D_x}$	$\frac{D_x}{{}_{55}N_x}$	$\frac{{}_{55}\Delta_x}{D_x}$	$\frac{D_x}{{}_{54}N_x}$	$\frac{{}_{54}\Delta_x}{D_x}$	$\frac{D_x}{{}_{53}N_x}$	$\frac{{}_{53}\Delta_x}{D_x}$	$\frac{D_x}{{}_{52}N_x}$	$\frac{{}_{52}\Delta_x}{D_x}$	$\frac{D_x}{{}_{51}N_x}$	$\frac{{}_{51}\Delta_x}{D_x}$	Age.
10	.05191	2.215	.05221	2.165	.05252	2.109	.05287	2.064	.05323	2.012	.05362	1.960	10
11	.05230	2.189	.05261	2.138	.05295	2.086	.05331	2.033	.05370	1.980	.05412	1.926	11
12	.05271	2.162	.05304	2.109	.05340	2.056	.05378	2.001	.05420	1.947	.05464	1.892	12
13	.05313	2.135	.05349	2.080	.05387	2.025	.05428	1.970	.05472	1.914	.05519	1.857	13
14	.05358	2.107	.05396	2.051	.05437	1.995	.05481	1.937	.05528	1.879	.05579	1.821	14
15	.05406	2.078	.05447	2.020	.05491	1.961	.05537	1.903	.05588	1.844	.05642	1.784	15
16	.05458	2.048	.05501	1.988	.05547	1.929	.05597	1.868	.05651	1.812	.05709	1.746	16
17	.05512	2.017	.05558	1.956	.05607	1.894	.05661	1.811	.05719	1.769	.05782	1.707	17
18	.05570	1.984	.05618	1.922	.05671	1.858	.05729	1.794	.05791	1.730	.05859	1.666	18
19	.05631	1.951	.05683	1.887	.05740	1.821	.05802	1.756	.05869	1.690	.05942	1.624	19
20	.05690	1.917	.05752	1.850	.05813	1.783	.05879	1.716	.05952	1.648	.06030	1.581	20
21	.05765	1.881	.05825	1.812	.05892	1.743	.05963	1.674	.06041	1.605	.06125	1.536	21
22	.05839	1.844	.05904	1.773	.05975	1.702	.06052	1.632	.06136	1.561	.06227	1.491	22
23	.05918	1.804	.05989	1.732	.06065	1.659	.06149	1.587	.06240	1.516	.06338	1.443	23
24	.06003	1.764	.06078	1.690	.06161	1.615	.06251	1.541	.06349	1.467	.06457	1.394	24
25	.06093	1.722	.06175	1.646	.06265	1.570	.06363	1.495	.06469	1.418	.06586	1.344	25
26	.06191	1.678	.06280	1.600	.06377	1.522	.06482	1.445	.06600	1.368	.06728	1.289	26
27	.06296	1.633	.06392	1.553	.06497	1.473	.06613	1.395	.06740	1.316	.06880	1.239	27
28	.06408	1.586	.06513	1.505	.06628	1.423	.06754	1.343	.06894	1.262	.07047	1.184	28
29	.06530	1.537	.06645	1.454	.06770	1.371	.06908	1.290	.07061	1.208	.07230	1.128	29
30	.06662	1.487	.06787	1.402	.06925	1.317	.07076	1.234	.07245	1.152	.07433	1.071	30
31	.06805	1.435	.06942	1.348	.07093	1.262	.07261	1.177	.07447	1.093	.07656	1.012	31
32	.06961	1.381	.07112	1.292	.07278	1.205	.07464	1.119	.07670	1.034	.07903	.9518	32
33	.07130	1.325	.07296	1.235	.07481	1.146	.07688	1.059	.07918	.9736	.08178	.8906	33
34	.07317	1.267	.07501	1.176	.07706	1.086	.07936	.9981	.08195	.9118	.08488	.8285	34
35	.07522	1.208	.07726	1.115	.07954	1.024	.08212	.9357	.08504	.8490	.08838	.7657	35
36	.07749	1.148	.07976	1.053	.08233	.9612	.08523	.8724	.08854	.7854	.09235	.7026	36
37	.08000	1.085	.08254	.9898	.08545	.8973	.08874	.8080	.09253	.7212	.09689	.6385	37
38	.08280	1.021	.08569	.9252	.08897	.8324	.09274	.7426	.09710	.6565	.10217	.5748	38
39	.08594	.9562	.08922	.8597	.09298	.7665	.09730	.6773	.10238	.5919	.10834	.5114	39
40	.08949	.8903	.09323	.7934	.09756	.7005	.10259	.6118	.10856	.5276	.11564	.4489	40
41	.09353	.8236	.09784	.7267	.10288	.6344	.10880	.5466	.11587	.4641	.12443	.3875	41
42	.09816	.7565	.10317	.6601	.10908	.5684	.11614	.4823	.12468	.4017	.13521	.3280	42
43	.10351	.6890	.10941	.5933	.11645	.5032	.12497	.4190	.13547	.3412	.14869	.2701	43
44	.10978	.6210	.11679	.5267	.12530	.4384	.13578	.3568	.14898	.2824	.16606	.2155	44
45	.11719	.5525	.12567	.4599	.13613	.3743	.14931	.2962	.16636	.2260	.18923	.1642	45
46	.12608	.4836	.13651	.3936	.14967	.3115	.16670	.2377	.18954	.1727	.22167	.1172	46
47	.13694	.4146	.15007	.3281	.16707	.2504	.18989	.1819	.22199	.1234	.27034	.07534	47
48	.15050	.3459	.16747	.2640	.09026	.1919	.22233	.1301	.27064	.07945	.35143	.04042	48
49	.16792	.2789	.19067	.2027	.22270	.1375	.27098	.08394	.35171	.04271	.51359	.01449	49
50	.19112	.2145	.22312	.1455	.27134	.0888	.35202	.04519	.51381	.01533			
51	.22357	.1542	.27175	.09420	.35236	.04793	.51404	.01625			.51229	.009524	38
52	.27219	.1000	.35273	.05089	.51428	.01727			.51223	.009316	.34980	.02725	37
53	.35315	.05407	.51460	.01836			.51219	.009120	.34972	.02668	.26862	.05202	36
54	.51493	.01953			.51213	.008932	.34966	.02613	.26854	.05096	.21996	.08280	35
			.51209	.008746	.34955	.02559	.26845	.04990	.21989	.08112	.18755	.1187	34
33	.51205	.008577	.34954	.02508	.26839	.04891	.21980	.07952	.18748	.1163	.16445	.1588	33
32	.34948	.02460	.26832	.04798	.21972	.07797	.18741	.1141	.16438	.1557	.14715	.2025	32
31	.26826	.04706	.21965	.07648	.18731	.1119	.16429	.1528	.14708	.1987	.13373	.2491	31
30	.21959	.07507	.18724	.1098	.16420	.1499	.14698	.1949	.13364	.2445	.12300	.2891	30
29	.18718	.1078	.16413	.1472	.14691	.1914	.13356	.2400	.12292	.2927	.11424	.3489	29
28	.16406	.1446	.14682	.1881	.13348	.2358	.12285	.2875	.11416	.3428	.10699	.4012	28
27	.14676	.1849	.13341	.2318	.12276	.2826	.11410	.3369	.10690	.3944	.10085	.4547	27
26	.13334	.2281	.12270	.2780	.11401	.3313	.10682	.3878	.10077	.4472	.09561	.5089	26
25	.12262	.2737	.11395	.3261	.10674	.3818	.10069	.4400	.09552	.5009	.09109	.5638	25
24	.11387	.3212	.10668	.3759	.10062	.4333	.09546	.4931	.09100	.5550	.08714	.6188	24
23	.10661	.3704	.10055	.4269	.09539	.4858	.09094	.5467	.08707	.6096	.08368	.6741	23
22	.10048	.4209	.09531	.4788	.09086	.5388	.08698	.6008	.08360	.6642	.08060	.7291	22
21	.09526	.4722	.09080	.5314	.08693	.5923	.08354	.6548	.08053	.7187	.07788	.7838	21
20	.09074	.5244	.08686	.5845	.08346	.6460	.08046	.7090	.07780	.7732	.07544	.8382	20
19	.08680	.5769	.08340	.6377	.08040	.6998	.07774	.7628	.07537	.8270	.07323	.8919	19
18	.08334	.6298	.08034	.6911	.07768	.7535	.07530	.8168	.07316	.8807	.07125	.9454	18
17	.08028	.6829	.07762	.7444	.07524	.8068	.07310	.8698	.07119	.9337	.06944	.9978	17
16	.07757	.7358	.07518	.7974	.07304	.8598	.07111	.9226	.06938	.9859	.06780	1.050	16
15	.07512	.7888	.07299	.8505	.07107	.9124	.06932	.9750	.06773	1.040	.06629	1.101	15
14	.07294	.8414	.07101	.9028	.06927	.9644	.06768	1.027	.06624	1.089	.06492	1.152	14
13	.07096	.8938	.06922	.9550	.06763	1.016	.06618	1.078	.06486	1.139	.06365	1.201	13
12	.06917	.9459	.06758	1.007	.06613	1.067	.06481	1.128	.66360	1.189	.06249	1.250	12
11	.06754	.9978	.06608	1.058	.06475	1.118	.06353	1.178	.06244	1.238	.06140	1.298	11
10	.06605	1.049	.06471	1.109	.06350	1.168	.06239	1.227	.06137	1.286	.06042	1.343	10
Age.	$\frac{D_x}{{}_{35}N_x}$	$\frac{{}_{35}\Delta_x}{D_x}$	$\frac{D_x}{{}_{36}N_x}$	$\frac{{}_{36}\Delta_x}{D_x}$	$\frac{D_x}{{}_{37}N_x}$	$\frac{{}_{37}\Delta_x}{D_x}$	$\frac{D_x}{{}_{38}N_x}$	$\frac{{}_{38}\Delta_x}{D_x}$	$\frac{D_x}{{}_{39}N_x}$	$\frac{{}_{39}\Delta_x}{D_x}$	$\frac{D_x}{{}_{40}N_x}$	$\frac{{}_{40}\Delta_x}{D_x}$	Age.

ENDOWMENT POLICIES.—FACTORS FOR INSURANCE VALUE.

Age.	$\frac{D_x}{{}_{50}N_x}$	$\frac{{}_{50}\Delta_x}{D_x}$	$\frac{D_x}{{}_{49}N_x}$	$\frac{{}_{49}\Delta_x}{D_x}$	$\frac{D_x}{{}_{48}N_x}$	$\frac{{}_{48}\Delta_x}{D_x}$	$\frac{D_x}{{}_{47}N_x}$	$\frac{{}_{47}\Delta_x}{D_x}$	$\frac{D_x}{{}_{46}N_x}$	$\frac{{}_{46}\Delta_x}{D_x}$	Age.
10	.05404	1.907	.05450	1.854	.05498	1.800	.05550	1.744	.05605	1.680	10
11	.05456	1.872	.05504	1.817	.05556	1.762	.05611	1.705	.05671	1.649	11
12	.05512	1.836	.05563	1.780	.05618	1.723	.05678	1.665	.05742	1.607	12
13	.05571	1.799	.05626	1.741	.05685	1.683	.05749	1.624	.05817	1.565	13
14	.05633	1.762	.05693	1.703	.05756	1.643	.05824	1.582	.05899	1.522	14
15	.05701	1.723	.05764	1.662	.05832	1.601	.05906	1.540	.05986	1.478	15
16	.05772	1.683	.05840	1.622	.05914	1.559	.05994	1.496	.06080	1.432	16
17	.05850	1.643	.05922	1.579	.06002	1.515	.06087	1.451	.06181	1.386	17
18	.05931	1.600	.06010	1.536	.06096	1.470	.06189	1.404	.06289	1.339	18
19	.06020	1.557	.06105	1.490	.06197	1.424	.06298	1.357	.06408	1.290	19
20	.06114	1.512	.06206	1.445	.06306	1.377	.06416	1.309	.06536	1.241	20
21	.06217	1.464	.06315	1.397	.06425	1.328	.06544	1.259	.06675	1.190	21
22	.06326	1.419	.06435	1.349	.06554	1.278	.06684	1.208	.06826	1.138	22
23	.06446	1.370	.06564	1.298	.06694	1.226	.06835	1.155	.06992	1.085	23
24	.06575	1.320	.06704	1.247	.06845	1.174	.07002	1.102	.07173	1.030	24
25	.06714	1.268	.06857	1.194	.07012	1.120	.07183	1.047	.07373	.9750	25
26	.06868	1.215	.07023	1.140	.07194	1.065	.07384	.9913	.07596	.9184	26
27	.07034	1.161	.07205	1.085	.07394	1.009	.07606	.9348	.07840	.8614	27
28	.07217	1.105	.07406	1.028	.07617	.9521	.07852	.8771	.08113	.8036	28
29	.07419	1.048	.07628	.9706	.07863	.8938	.08126	.8186	.08423	.7452	29
30	.07642	.9900	.07874	.9120	.08137	.8348	.08433	.7595	.08769	.6864	30
31	.07888	.9306	.08149	.8522	.08446	.7749	.08781	.6999	.09166	.6272	31
32	.08164	.8702	.08459	.7917	.08794	.7146	.09178	.6400	.09620	.5681	32
33	.08473	.8088	.08808	.7304	.09189	.6536	.09632	.5798	.10145	.5089	33
34	.08822	.7469	.09204	.6687	.09644	.5925	.10157	.5198	.10759	.4508	34
35	.09218	.6843	.09657	.6068	.10169	.5316	.10771	.4603	.11485	.3929	35
36	.09674	.6213	.10183	.5449	.10783	.4711	.11498	.4017	.12360	.3365	36
37	.10199	.5585	.10797	.4835	.11511	.4114	.12373	.3444	.13431	.2821	37
38	.10816	.4961	.11528	.4229	.12390	.3531	.13448	.2889	.14778	.2299	38
39	.11546	.4344	.12405	.3629	.13462	.2966	.14791	.2358	.16507	.1810	39
40	.12423	.3740	.13478	.3053	.14804	.2424	.16521	.1858	.18818	.1357	40
41	.13498	.3154	.14824	.2502	.16537	.1914	.18834	.1396	.22057	.09512	41
42	.14844	.2593	.16556	.1982	.18849	.1443	.22072	.09816	.26922	.06015	42
43	.16579	.2063	.18870	.1500	.22091	.1019	.26938	.06232	.35036	.03180	43
44	.18895	.1567	.22113	.1063	.26952	.06497	.35053	.03309	.51274	.01125	44
45	.22139	.1114	.26980	.06804	.35071	.03461	.51288	.01174			
46	.27006	.7153	.35093	.03640	.51303	.01234			.51262	.01082	43
47	.35118	.03833	.51322	.01300			.51255	.01048	.35023	.03073	42
48	.51339	.01371			.51247	.01021	.35013	.02988	.26909	.05837	41
			.51241	.009966	.35001	.02915	.26898	.05690	.22045	.09258	40
39	.51236	.009747	.34996	.02850	.26888	.05560	.22034	.09039	.18805	.1323	39
38	.34987	.02787	.26880	.05435	.22023	.08836	.18795	.1293	.16495	.1766	38
37	.26870	.05317	.22014	.08643	.18784	.1265	.16484	.1727	.14764	.2247	37
36	.22005	.08458	.18775	.1237	.16473	.1690	.14753	.2198	.13420	.2757	36
35	.18765	.1212	.16464	.1655	.14741	.2152	.13410	.2699	.12350	.3293	35
34	.16455	.1621	.14733	.2108	.13400	.2644	.12339	.3224	.11475	.3846	34
33	.14724	.2065	.13390	.2590	.12328	.3160	.11463	.3767	.10748	.4412	33
32	.13381	.2540	.12319	.3097	.11454	.3693	.10736	.4325	.10133	.4988	32
31	.12310	.3038	.11444	.3622	.10726	.4241	.10122	.4890	.09608	.5569	31
30	.11434	.3554	.10715	.4162	.10112	.4798	.09598	.5464	.09155	.6152	30
29	.10707	.4085	.10103	.4711	.09588	.5363	.09145	.6038	.08759	.6736	29
28	.10093	.4627	.09578	.5268	.09134	.5931	.08750	.6614	.08412	.7319	28
27	.09569	.5176	.09125	.5828	.08741	.6500	.08402	.7190	.08105	.7894	27
26	.09116	.5730	.08732	.6390	.08394	.7068	.08095	.7762	.07831	.8466	26
25	.08722	.6288	.08384	.6954	.08085	.7636	.07821	.8328	.07585	.9033	25
24	.08376	.6844	.08077	.7514	.07811	.8196	.07577	.8890	.07365	.9591	24
23	.08069	.7399	.07803	.8070	.07568	.8753	.07354	.9443	.07164	1.014	23
22	.07795	.7952	.07559	.8622	.07346	.9302	.07156	.9988	.06982	1.068	22
21	.07551	.8499	.07338	.9168	.07147	.9842	.06973	1.052	.06818	1.121	21
20	.07330	.9041	.07139	.9706	.06966	1.038	.06809	1.105	.06665	1.173	20
19	.07132	.9574	.06959	1.024	.06801	1.090	.06658	1.157	.06527	1.223	19
18	.06952	1.010	.06794	1.076	.06650	1.142	.06519	1.207	.06399	1.273	18
17	.06786	1.062	.06643	1.127	.06512	1.192	.06391	1.257	.06282	1.321	17
16	.06636	1.114	.06505	1.177	.06384	1.242	.06274	1.305	.06172	1.362	16
15	.06498	1.164	.06377	1.227	.06267	1.290	.06165	1.353	.06072	1.415	15
14	.06371	1.214	.06261	1.276	.06159	1.338	.06065	1.399	.05979	1.461	14
13	.06254	1.262	.06153	1.324	.06059	1.385	.05972	1.445	.05893	1.505	13
12	.06148	1.310	.06053	1.370	.05966	1.430	.05886	1.490	.05812	1.549	12
11	.06047	1.358	.05959	1.416	.05879	1.475	.05805	1.534	.05735	1.591	11
10	.05954	1.404	.05874	1.462	.05799	1.520	.05730	1.577	.05665	1.634	10
Age.	$\frac{D_x}{{}_{41}N_x}$	$\frac{{}_{41}\Delta_x}{D_x}$	$\frac{D_x}{{}_{42}N_x}$	$\frac{{}_{42}\Delta_x}{D_x}$	$\frac{D_x}{{}_{43}N_x}$	$\frac{{}_{43}\Delta_x}{D_x}$	$\frac{D_x}{{}_{44}N_x}$	$\frac{{}_{44}\Delta_x}{D_x}$	$\frac{D_x}{{}_{45}N_x}$	$\frac{{}_{45}\Delta_x}{D_x}$	Age.

ENDOWMENT POLICIES.—D. or 80.—4 PER CENT.

1st Year.

Age.	Value.	Diff.
10	10.525	—6.313
11	10.730	6.303
12	10.942	6.347
13	11.181	6.367
14	11.414	6.376
15	11.668	6.454
16	11.926	6.484
17	12.209	6.535
18	12.498	6.586
19	12.803	6.651
20	13.119	6.723
21	13.454	6.770
22	13.798	6.848
23	14.160	6.951
24	14.548	7.020
25	14.949	7.097
26	15.371	7.253
27	15.811	7.290
28	16.279	7.411
29	16.768	7.544
30	17.284	7.640
31	17.828	7.753
32	18.397	7.936
33	19.002	8.083
34	19.636	8.192
35	20.308	8.378
36	21.017	8.527
37	21.771	8.641
38	22.566	8.896
39	23.420	9.068
40	24.317	9.251
41	25.276	9.405
42	26.305	9.660
43	27.404	9.953
44	28.574	10.342
45	29.817	10.837
46	31.141	11.306
47	32.546	11.956
48	34.041	12.581
49	35.635	13.335
50	37.312	14.052
51	39.132	14.922
52	41.051	15.851
53	43.101	16.841
54	45.303	17.993
55	47.657	19.067
56	50.187	20.407
57	52.900	21.750
58	55.861	23.331
59	58.988	24.938
60	62.542	26.752
61	66.186	28.736
62	70.257	30.927
63	74.708	33.288
64	79.598	35.858
65	84.998	38.638

2d Year.

Age.	Value.	Diff.
10	14.737	—6.177
11	15.157	6.155
12	15.537	6.149
13	15.995	6.167
14	16.452	6.228
15	16.882	6.254
16	17.368	6.283
17	17.883	6.333
18	18.410	6.384
19	18.955	6.447
20	19.515	6.516
21	20.058	6.548
22	20.748	6.638
23	21.369	6.689
24	22.076	6.756
25	22.802	6.882
26	23.499	6.919
27	24.332	7.022
28	25.147	7.137
29	25.992	7.212
30	26.928	7.308
31	27.841	7.411
32	28.858	7.588
33	29.921	7.681
34	31.080	7.840
35	32.238	7.968
36	33.507	8.057
37	34.901	8.281
38	36.236	8.406
39	37.772	8.572
40	39.383	8.683
41	41.147	8.897
42	42.950	9.140
43	44.855	—9.495
44	46.806	9.936
45	48.797	10.357
46	50.976	10.956
47	53.136	11.526
48	55.501	12.221
49	57.935	12.895
50	60.572	13.662
51	63.342	14.532
52	66.251	15.441
53	69.361	16.501
54	72.613	17.573
55	76.247	18.807
56	79.967	19.967
57	84.050	21.390
58	88.391	22.921
59	93.038	24.508
60	98.152	26.332
61	103.636	28.316
62	109.607	30.477
63	116.128	32.788
64	123.338	35.268
65	131.358	37.918

3d Year.

Age.	Value.	Diff.
10	19.15	—5.98
11	19.73	5.96
12	20.33	5.95
13	21.01	6.02
14	21.64	6.03
15	22.30	6.06
16	23.01	6.08
17	23.76	6.13
18	24.53	6.19
19	25.31	6.24
20	26.12	6.26
21	27.00	6.34
22	27.91	6.38
23	28.84	6.42
24	29.87	6.55
25	30.87	6.57
26	31.95	6.65
27	33.12	6.74
28	34.29	6.81
29	35.55	6.89
30	36.90	7.02
31	38.26	7.14
32	39.67	7.20
33	41.24	7.34
34	42.88	7.38
35	44.58	7.49
36	46.47	7.69
37	48.39	7.80
38	50.40	7.93
39	52.62	8.01
40	55.02	8.19
41	57.53	8.38
42	60.12	8.70
43	62.76	9.07
44	65.44	9.47
45	68.26	10.02
46	71.16	10.55
47	74.16	11.18
48	77.32	11.78
49	80.67	12.51
50	84.22	13.30
51	87.94	14.16
52	91.86	15.13
53	95.96	16.10
54	100.34	17.14
55	105.10	18.30
56	110.19	19.61
57	115.56	20.96
58	121.33	22.49
59	127.52	24.12
60	134.27	25.97
61	141.51	27.90
62	149.39	30.01
63	158.05	32.21
64	167.67	34.58
65	178.44	37.06

4th Year.

Age.	Value.	Diff.
10	23.69	—5.77
11	24.50	5.76
12	25.32	5.80
13	26.17	5.82
14	27.02	5.82
15	27.91	—5.85
16	28.86	5.88
17	29.84	5.93
18	30.84	5.97
19	31.87	5.98
20	32.98	6.06
21	34.11	6.08
22	35.33	6.12
23	36.58	6.22
24	37.87	6.23
25	39.25	6.30
26	40.67	6.38
27	42.19	6.42
28	43.76	6.48
29	45.43	6.60
30	47.16	6.69
31	48.95	6.74
32	50.87	6.86
33	52.90	6.93
34	55.14	7.04
35	57.40	7.15
36	59.80	7.22
37	62.36	7.31
38	65.04	7.37
39	68.03	7.53
40	71.15	7.69
41	74.43	7.95
42	77.72	8.29
43	81.09	8.64
44	84.54	9.12
45	88.06	9.61
46	91.75	10.19
47	95.53	10.75
48	99.58	11.42
49	103.79	12.13
50	108.23	12.89
51	112.91	13.83
52	117.78	14.75
53	122.96	15.71
54	128.50	16.75
55	134.46	17.95
56	140.77	19.22
57	147.50	20.60
58	154.70	22.13
59	162.39	23.74
60	170.75	25.51
61	179.80	27.40
62	189.64	29.42
63	200.55	31.57
64	212.69	33.75
65	226.38	35.98

5th Year.

Age.	Value.	Diff.
10	28.44	—5.57
11	29.47	5.61
12	30.46	5.61
13	31.53	5.62
14	32.61	5.63
15	33.73	5.66
16	34.91	5.68
17	36.12	5.72
18	37.37	5.72
19	38.69	5.78
20	40.04	5.80
21	41.48	5.82
22	43.01	5.85
23	44.52	5.90
24	46.19	5.96
25	47.90	6.03
26	49.66	6.06
27	51.58	6.10
28	53.56	6.21
29	55.60	6.27
30	57.75	6.30
31	60.04	6.40
32	62.41	6.46
33	64.97	6.47
34	67.74	6.62
35	70.56	6.68
36	73.60	6.75
37	76.82	6.78
38	82.24	6.90
39	83.92	7.02
40	87.78	7.24
41	91.76	7.55
42	95.73	7.84
43	99.85	8.30
44	103.99	8.73
45	108.27	9.27
46	112.70	9.77
47	117.33	10.40
48	122.20	—11.06
49	127.29	11.79
50	132.65	12.62
51	138.21	13.45
52	144.08	14.33
53	150.35	15.28
54	157.05	16.41
55	164.17	17.59
56	171.74	18.84
57	179.80	20.21
58	188.43	21.73
59	197.64	23.29
60	207.69	25.05
61	218.59	26.90
62	230.48	28.81
63	243.69	30.74
64	258.54	32.74
65	275.40	34.60

6th Year.

Age.	Value.	Diff.
10	33.39	—5.42
11	34.59	5.42
12	35.79	5.39
13	37.09	5.42
14	38.39	5.42
15	39.74	5.45
16	41.16	5.48
17	42.61	5.47
18	44.15	5.43
19	45.71	5.52
20	47.36	5.52
21	49.19	5.61
22	50.96	5.66
23	52.78	5.62
24	54.78	5.70
25	56.82	5.71
26	58.97	5.73
27	61.29	5.82
28	63.63	5.88
29	66.10	5.90
30	68.73	5.96
31	71.47	6.01
32	74.35	6.01
33	77.50	6.13
34	80.76	6.16
35	84.19	6.21
36	87.87	6.21
37	91.81	6.29
38	95.91	6.38
39	100.32	6.59
40	104.86	6.86
41	109.49	7.13
42	114.19	7.53
43	118.95	7.92
44	123.83	8.40
45	128.82	8.87
46	134.07	9.43
47	139.47	10.02
48	145.18	10.68
49	151.13	11.48
50	157.34	12.24
51	163.89	13.06
52	170.80	13.94
53	178.17	14.96
54	185.94	16.00
55	194.24	17.19
56	203.09	18.48
57	212.49	19.84
58	222.56	21.36
59	233.34	22.89
60	245.59	25.06
61	257.88	26.30
62	271.93	28.03
63	287.66	29.80
64	305.40	31.40
65	325.80	32.90

7th Year.

Age.	Value.	Diff.
10	38.49	—5.23
11	39.90	5.22
12	41.34	5.22
13	42.85	5.23
14	44.38	5.22
15	45.96	5.25
16	47.61	5.23
17	49.35	5.27
18	51.12	5.26
19	52.99	5.26
20	54.96	—5.34
21	56.30	5.30
22	59.10	5.33
23	61.32	5.38
24	63.63	5.37
25	66.06	5.38
26	68.61	5.47
27	71.28	5.51
28	74.03	5.50
29	76.97	5.56
30	80.05	5.57
31	83.29	5.56
32	86.74	5.66
33	90.37	5.67
34	94.24	5.72
35	98.29	5.67
36	102.68	5.73
37	107.29	5.83
38	112.10	5.97
39	117.15	6.23
40	122.32	6.43
41	127.64	6.79
42	132.96	7.12
43	138.43	7.56
44	144.00	7.99
45	149.77	8.53
46	155.78	9.08
47	162.00	9.69
48	168.54	10.42
49	175.28	11.08
50	182.41	11.83
51	189.96	12.68
52	197.91	13.62
53	206.31	14.58
54	215.24	15.70
55	224.71	16.83
56	234.80	18.10
57	245.55	19.45
58	257.06	20.90
59	269.44	22.39
60	282.98	23.95
61	297.77	25.53
62	314.16	27.13
63	332.57	28.56
64	353.60	29.80
65	377.90	30.70

8th Year.

Age.	Value.	Diff.
10	43.79	—5.05
11	45.41	5.02
12	47.06	5.01
13	48.80	5.04
14	50.57	5.03
15	52.38	5.01
16	54.31	5.03
17	56.29	5.02
18	58.36	5.00
19	60.53	5.07
20	62.74	5.02
21	65.10	5.04
22	67.57	5.08
23	70.10	5.05
24	72.81	5.07
25	75.63	5.13
26	78.51	5.14
27	81.58	5.11
28	84.81	5.16
29	88.18	5.17
30	91.76	5.13
31	95.56	5.22
32	99.48	5.21
33	103.90	5.22
34	108.16	5.16
35	112.93	5.21
36	117.97	5.27
37	123.23	5.36
38	128.70	5.61
39	134.34	5.79
40	140.21	6.12
41	146.13	6.42
42	152.14	6.80
43	158.27	7.18
44	164.58	7.67
45	171.06	8.16
46	177.84	8.73
47	184.86	9.41
48	192.16	10.04
49	199.83	10.73
50	207.89	11.49
51	216.41	12.36
52	225.34	13.27

ENDOWMENT POLICIES.--D. or 80.—4 PER CENT.

8th Year.

AGE.	Value.	Diff.
53	234.83	—14.28
54	244.84	15.32
55	255.54	16.49
56	266.89	17.75
57	279.00	19.05
58	292.02	20.47
59	306.04	21.84
60	321.48	23.28
61	338.43	24.71
62	357.29	25.88
63	378.72	26.82
64	403.40	27.61
65	432.20	27.90

9th Year.

AGE.	Value.	Diff.
10	49.26	—4.83
11	51.12	4.83
12	52.99	4.81
13	54.94	4.80
14	56.95	4.78
15	59.04	4.80
16	61.21	4.77
17	63.48	4.76
18	65.86	4.81
19	68.26	4.74
20	70.84	4.76
21	73.51	4.79
22	76.29	4.76
23	79.21	4.74
24	82.29	4.79
25	85.45	4.80
26	88.74	4.76
27	92.28	4.79
28	95.93	4.79
29	99.78	4.73
30	103.91	4.79
31	108.17	4.77
32	112.67	4.76
33	117.48	4.68
34	122.64	4.70
35	128.03	4.74
36	133.72	4.84
37	139.64	5.04
38	145.66	5.18
39	151.97	5.49
40	158.41	5.72
41	164.99	6.08
42	171.64	6.43
43	178.49	6.84
44	185.48	7.30
45	192.72	7.85
46	200.25	8.45
47	208.00	9.02
48	216.16	9.66
49	224.73	10.37
50	233.71	11.16
51	243.18	12.03
52	253.12	12.92
53	263.65	13.90
54	274.82	14.97
55	286.71	16.15
56	299.33	17.32
57	312.85	18.55
58	327.41	19.92
59	343.19	21.05
60	360.65	22.45
61	379.91	23.41
62	401.67	24.39
63	426.61	24.91
64	455.40	25.00
65	489.30	24.19

10th Year.

AGE.	Value.	Diff.
10	54.95	—4.65
11	57.02	4.63
12	59.12	4.62
13	61.32	4.58
14	63.58	4.57
15	65.91	4.55
16	68.37	4.58
17	70.93	4.57
18	73.55	4.51
19	76.32	4.50
20	79.20	4.52
21	82.17	4.46
22	85.33	4.44
23	88.63	4.47
24	92.05	4.49
25	95.60	—4.44
26	99.35	4.45
27	103.30	4.42
28	107.42	4.36
29	111.82	4.40
30	116.40	4.36
31	121.23	4.32
32	126.31	4.25
33	131.80	4.24
34	137.58	4.25
35	143.59	4.32
36	149.90	4.49
37	156.37	4.60
38	163.05	4.88
39	169.90	5.09
40	177.01	5.45
41	184.19	5.72
42	191.51	6.08
43	199.05	6.54
44	206.75	7.00
45	214.69	7.55
46	222.94	8.05
47	231.53	8.69
48	240.54	9.29
49	249.99	10.08
50	259.86	10.86
51	270.28	11.68
52	281.25	12.60
53	292.85	13.60
54	305.15	14.65
55	318.22	15.73
56	332.20	16.91
57	347.20	18.10
58	363.35	19.22
59	381.13	20.40
60	400.65	21.18
61	422.69	22.04
62	447.54	22.38
63	476.41	22.51
64	510.00	21.49
65	550.11	19.59

11th Year.

AGE.	Value.	Diff.
10	60.82	—4.44
11	63.12	4.44
12	65.44	4.36
13	67.92	4.39
14	70.42	4.34
15	73.03	4.30
16	75.77	4.32
17	78.57	4.25
18	81.54	4.24
19	84.62	4.19
20	87.80	4.20
21	91.16	4.16
22	94.69	4.18
23	98.32	4.16
24	102.11	4.10
25	106.11	4.11
26	110.27	4.06
27	114.69	3.98
28	119.34	4.01
29	124.19	3.95
30	129.32	3.90
31	134.74	3.83
32	140.46	3.79
33	146.56	3.76
34	152.97	3.85
35	159.58	3.98
36	166.43	4.07
37	173.54	4.30
38	180.74	4.49
39	188.23	4.81
40	195.88	5.03
41	203.75	5.40
42	211.73	5.75
43	219.91	6.16
44	228.32	6.72
45	236.96	7.21
46	246.03	7.78
47	255.39	8.32
48	265.29	9.08
49	275.54	9.74
50	286.31	10.46
51	297.73	11.38
52	309.70	12.28
53	322.35	13.25
54	335.80	14.30
55	350.15	15.34
56	365.48	16.45
57	382.00	17.40
58	399.99	—18.39
59	419.72	19.20
60	441.92	19.82
61	466.84	20.04
62	495.42	20.02
63	528.61	18.91
64	568.11	17.00
65	615.52	13.34

12th Year.

AGE.	Value.	Diff.
10	66.90	—4.26
11	69.41	4.18
12	72.02	4.18
13	74.71	4.12
14	77.49	4.08
15	80.40	4.11
16	83.38	4.02
17	86.53	4.00
18	89.80	4.00
19	93.23	3.99
20	96.72	3.88
21	100.45	3.90
22	104.31	3.89
23	108.32	3.80
24	112.56	3.80
25	116.95	3.74
26	121.58	3.64
27	125.52	3.65
28	131.61	3.59
29	137.01	3.52
30	142.70	3.39
31	148.74	3.35
32	155.07	3.32
33	161.80	3.37
34	168.76	3.47
35	175.91	3.56
36	183.38	3.77
37	191.01	3.95
38	198.82	4.17
39	206.84	4.41
40	215.17	4.73
41	223.63	5.05
42	232.28	5.47
43	241.15	5.94
44	250.17	6.32
45	259.57	6.86
46	269.39	7.45
47	279.62	8.08
48	290.25	8.70
49	301.43	9.38
50	313.16	10.26
51	325.48	11.04
52	338.47	11.97
53	352.20	12.85
54	366.80	13.90
55	382.47	14.77
56	399.22	15.76
57	417.50	16.70
58	437.46	17.36
59	459.51	17.80
60	484.55	17.95
61	512.99	17.89
62	545.66	16.85
63	584.41	15.05
64	630.71	11.11
65	687.18	5.38

13th Year.

AGE.	Value.	Diff.
10	73.16	—4.00
11	75.96	4.00
12	78.78	3.93
13	81.77	3.89
14	84.82	3.85
15	87.96	3.80
16	91.29	3.77
17	94.74	3.74
18	98.30	3.66
19	102.04	3.63
20	105.96	3.63
21	110.00	3.60
22	114.22	3.50
23	118.68	3.48
24	123.31	3.41
25	128.16	3.31
26	133.31	3.31
27	138.68	3.22
28	144.30	3.15
29	150.26	3.01
30	156.59	—2.97
31	163.22	2.91
32	170.15	2.94
33	177.43	3.02
34	184.93	3.09
35	192.66	3.21
36	200.63	3.41
37	208.83	3.63
38	217.22	3.87
39	225.85	4.10
40	134.76	4.41
41	243.86	4.75
42	253.11	5.20
43	262.61	5.61
44	272.42	6.07
45	282.53	6.55
46	293.08	7.12
47	304.09	7.74
48	315.59	8.39
49	327.68	9.18
50	340.21	9.86
51	353.57	10.73
52	367.55	11.55
53	382.45	12.45
54	398.20	13.20
55	415.36	14.33
56	433.65	14.99
57	453.70	15.62
58	475.96	16.06
59	500.70	16.10
60	529.05	15.87
61	561.29	14.69
62	599.07	12.47
63	644.41	9.03
64	699.20	3.58
65	766.80	+5.40

14th Year.

AGE.	Value.	Diff.
10	79.68	—3.80
11	82.69	3.73
12	85.79	3.67
13	89.06	3.69
14	92.38	3.59
15	95.83	3.54
16	99.45	3.51
17	103.21	3.45
18	107.14	3.39
19	111.21	3.36
20	115.45	3.32
21	119.85	3.21
22	124.52	3.19
23	129.36	3.13
24	134.45	2.99
25	139.80	2.95
26	145.37	2.88
27	151.27	2.78
28	157.42	2.62
29	164.02	2.59
30	170.90	2.48
31	178.14	2.53
32	185.61	2.56
33	193.41	2.63
34	201.48	2.79
35	209.76	2.91
36	218.24	3.09
37	226.97	3.30
38	235.92	3.53
39	245.17	3.82
40	254.67	4.08
41	264.39	4.48
42	274.21	4.81
43	284.40	5.30
44	294.92	5.72
45	305.80	6.25
46	317.10	6.80
47	328.89	7.39
48	341.24	8.04
49	354.13	8.83
50	367.66	9.56
51	381.97	10.37
52	397.05	11.25
53	413.10	12.00
54	430.30	12.80
55	448.69	13.39
56	468.85	14.03
57	490.98	14.30
58	515.76	14.45
59	543.59	13.89
60	575.63	12.75
61	612.79	10.60
62	656.86	7.26
63	710.09	—1.71
64	775.22	+6.96
65	857.20	19.37

15th Year.

AGE.	Value.	Diff.
10	86.40	—3.57
11	89.69	3.51
12	93.06	3.48
13	96.55	3.39
14	100.20	3.33
15	103.96	3.30
16	107.87	3.21
17	111.97	3.15
18	116.25	3.12
19	120.65	3.05
20	125.25	2.95
21	130.09	2.91
22	135.13	2.83
23	140.39	2.67
24	146.01	2.69
25	151.80	2.58
26	157.86	2.45
27	164.30	2.30
28	171.08	2.22
29	178.20	2.11
30	185.70	2.14
31	193.44	2.19
32	201.45	2.24
33	209.78	2.33
34	218.33	2.45
35	227.16	2.66
36	236.17	2.77
37	245.44	2.95
38	254.96	3.21
39	264.77	3.52
40	274.91	3.88
41	285.19	4.24
42	295.70	4.55
43	306.50	4.80
44	317.77	5.47
45	329.37	5.97
46	341.44	6.54
47	354.05	7.17
48	367.24	7.84
49	380.93	8.53
50	395.41	9.21
51	410.73	10.03
52	426.85	10.75
53	444.22	11.50
54	462.80	12.10
55	482.96	12.51
56	505.01	12.74
57	529.58	12.69
58	557.17	12.17
59	588.69	11.08
60	625.33	9.03
61	668.38	5.57
62	719.86	.26
63	783.09	+8.10
64	861.78	20.22
65	961.54	38.46

16th Year.

AGE.	Value.	Diff.
10	93.35	—3.32
11	96.91	3.31
12	100.52	3.19
13	104.35	3.15
14	108.28	3.10
15	112.33	3.00
16	116.59	2.91
17	121.03	2.88
18	125.50	2.63
19	130.40	2.70
20	135.42	2.65
21	140.63	2.56
22	146.10	2.40
23	151.88	2.37
24	157.87	2.26
25	164.17	2.13
26	170.78	1.96
27	177.81	1.86
28	185.14	1.78
29	192.86	1.76
30	200.84	1.79
31	209.08	1.77
32	217.61	1.91
33	226.45	2.00
34	235.52	2.12

ENDOWMENT POLICIES.—D. or 80.—4 PER CENT.

16th Year.

Age.	Value.	Diff.
35	244.81	—2.21
36	254.52	2.47
37	269.26	2.66
38	274.32	2.91
39	284.67	3.22
40	295.35	3.54
41	306.23	3.84
42	317.45	4.25
43	329.02	4.72
44	340.87	5.17
45	353.22	5.72
46	366.04	6.24
47	379.43	6.83
48	393.44	7.54
49	408.03	8.13
50	428.51	8.91
51	439.83	9.53
52	457.15	10.14
53	475.80	10.60
54	496.00	11.10
55	518.11	11.31
56	542.46	11.23
57	569.79	10.59
58	600.86	9.46
59	636.60	7.30
60	678.75	3.85
61	729.00	+1.40
62	789.86	9.37
63	865.90	20.90
64	961.54	38.46

17th Year.

Age.	Value.	Diff.
10	100.55	—3.14
11	104.33	3.01
12	108.27	2.94
13	112.38	2.88
14	116.59	2.79
15	121.00	2.70
16	125.61	2.66
17	130.36	2.56
18	135.30	2.45
19	140.50	2.40
20	145.89	2.29
21	151.52	2.12
22	157.50	2.10
23	163.67	1.94
24	170.16	1.81
25	176.99	1.64
26	184.19	—1.54
27	191.70	1.41
28	199.64	1.38
29	207.87	1.42
30	216.33	1.38
31	225.14	1.49
32	234.10	1.55
33	243.45	1.70
34	253.04	1.84
35	262.91	2.01
36	272.97	2.12
37	283.37	2.42
38	293.98	2.68
39	304.87	2.97
40	316.12	3.22
41	327.67	3.52
42	339.50	3.90
43	351.70	4.40
44	364.27	4.87
45	377.32	5.42
46	390.94	5.94
47	405.15	6.55
48	419.94	7.14
49	435.53	7.78
50	451.91	8.41
51	469.43	9.03
52	488.06	9.46
53	508.30	9.80
54	530.20	9.90
55	554.46	9.76
56	581.42	9.12
57	612.10	8.06
58	647.26	5.94
59	688.29	2.48
60	737.35	+2.85
61	796.59	10.21
62	869.49	21.71
63	961.54	38.46

18th Year.

Age.	Value.	Diff.
10	107.93	—2.83
11	112.05	2.75
12	116.27	2.67
13	120.68	2.60
14	125.21	2.46
15	129.97	2.43
16	134.88	2.36
17	139.99	2.23
18	145.35	2.15
19	150.90	2.07
20	156.72	1.88
21	162.85	1.83
22	169.20	1.66
23	175.89	1.54
24	182.90	1.35
25	190.30	1.21
26	198.02	1.11
27	206.16	1.06
28	214.54	1.05
29	223.22	1.02
30	232.23	1.12
31	241.48	1.18
32	250.95	1.30
33	260.75	1.35
34	270.84	1.49
35	281.20	1.70
36	291.87	1.92
37	302.72	2.11
38	313.87	2.42
39	325.32	2.62
40	337.22	2.92
41	349.43	3.33
42	361.90	3.75
43	374.70	4.05
44	387.97	4.55
45	401.72	5.02
46	416.14	5.74
47	431.15	6.30
48	446.84	6.84
49	463.38	7.43
50	480.81	7.81
51	499.53	8.29
52	519.65	8.63
53	541.60	8.70
54	565.60	8.55
55	592.36	7.84
56	622.48	6.48
57	656.94	4.34
58	697.18	1.18
59	744.80	+4.00
60	802.65	17.15
61	872.99	21.89
62	961.54	38.46

19th Year.

Age.	Value.	Diff.
10	115.62	—2.58
11	120.03	—2.53
12	124.54	2.40
13	129.26	2.19
14	134.16	2.24
15	139.21	2.15
16	144.45	1.99
17	149.97	1.92
18	155.70	1.81
19	161.68	1.63
20	167.96	1.56
21	174.47	1.42
22	181.34	1.26
23	188.51	1.03
24	196.10	.95
25	204.04	.80
26	212.28	.73
27	220.91	.71
28	229.77	.67
29	238.97	.72
30	248.39	.78
31	258.13	.88
32	268.05	.94
33	278.40	1.10
34	288.99	1.24
35	299.81	1.36
36	310.97	1.62
37	322.38	1.88
38	334.02	2.02
39	346.12	2.31
40	358.62	2.67
41	371.38	2.98
42	384.45	3.35
43	398.05	3.85
44	411.99	4.37
45	426.52	4.87
46	441.54	5.24
47	457.40	5.85
48	474.04	6.37
49	491.58	6.78
50	510.31	7.31
51	530.37	7.53
52	552.07	7.47
53	576.00	7.20
54	602.35	6.45
55	632.18	5.44
56	666.19	3.37
57	705.50	.09
58	751.86	+5.14
59	807.79	12.21
60	876.25	22.55
61	961.54	38.46

20th Year.

Age.	Value.	Diff.
10	123.56	—2.34
11	128.23	2.21
12	133.08	2.08
13	138.15	2.05
14	143.33	1.93
15	148.73	1.81
16	154.39	1.71
17	160.26	1.57
18	166.39	1.39
19	172.85	1.35
20	179.52	1.16
21	186.50	.98
22	193.88	.78
23	201.64	.64
24	209.70	.45
25	218.19	.41
26	226.92	.42
27	236.01	.36
28	245.88	.42
29	255.02	.43
30	264.89	.49
31	275.08	.57
32	285.51	.66
33	296.30	.75
34	307.39	.94
35	318.76	1.17
36	330.37	1.36
37	342.27	1.49
38	354.57	1.77
39	367.23	2.13
40	380.27	2.37
41	393.68	2.78
42	407.40	3.10
43	421.60	3.50
44	436.19	3.97
45	451.47	4.47
46	467.44	5.09
47	484.10	5.50
48	501.74	5.94
49	520.43	6.33
50	540.31	6.31
51	561.97	6.35
52	585.65	6.05
53	611.90	5.40
54	641.20	4.20
55	674.40	1.86
56	713.01	+1.39
57	758.49	6.01
58	812.86	13.09
59	878.99	23.51
60	961.54	38.46

TABLE XXI.

ANNUAL INTEREST AND DISCOUNT FACTORS.

i=interest of a unit.

$r=1+i$=amount of a unit.

$v=\frac{1}{r}$=present value of a unit.

$d=1-v$=discount of a unit.

$p=\frac{v}{d}=\frac{1}{i}$=principal or perpetuity of a unit.

FOUR PER CENT.

$i=$ .04	$\lambda i=-2.6020600$
$r=$ 1.04	$\lambda r=$ 0.017033339299
$v=$ .96153846	$\lambda v=-1.9829666607$
$d=$ .0384615	$\lambda d=-2.5850268$
$p=$25	$\lambda p=$ 1.3979400

FOUR AND ONE-HALF PER CENT.

$i=$ .045	$\lambda i=-2.6532125$
$r=$ 1.045	$\lambda r=$ 0.01911629
$v=$ .9569378	$\lambda v=-1.98088371$
$d=$ .0430622	$\lambda d=-2.6340962$
$p=$22.22222	$\lambda p=$ 1.3467875

FIVE PER CENT.

$i=$ .05	$\lambda i=-2.6989700$
$r=$ 1.05	$\lambda r=$ 0.021189299
$v=$ .95238095	$\lambda v=-1.9788107$
$d=$ .047619	$\lambda d=-2.6777808$
$p=$20	$\lambda p=$ 1.3010300

SIX PER CENT.

$i=$ .06	$\lambda i=-2.7781513$
$r=$ 1.06	$\lambda r=$ 0.025305865
$v=$ .94339623	$\lambda v=-1.97469413$
$d=$ .05660377	$\lambda d=-2.7528453$
$p=$16.6667	$\lambda p=$ 1.2218496

SEVEN PER CENT.

$i=$ .07	$\lambda i=-2.8450980$
$r=$ 1.07	$\lambda r=$ 0.0293837777
$v=$ .934580	$\lambda v=-1.9706162223$
$d=$ .065420	$\lambda d=-2.8157105$
$p=$14.2857	$\lambda p=$ 1.1549020

r^n=amount of a unit at the end of n years at compound interest.

v^n=present value of a unit due at the end of n years.

$p-pv^n$=present value per unit of an annuity certain of n payments, the first due in one year.

pv^n=present value of the reversion of an estate p, to be enjoyed after n years, or the annuity certain of a unit deferred n years, first payment at the end of $n+1$ years.

CO-EFFICIENTS OF ACCUMULATION.

If Φ is the premium fund in hand per $1 insured, at the beginning of any policy year, to find H_{x+n} which, normally, should be in hand at the end of it, the policy being still in force. Formulas $H_{x+n}=u_{x+n-1}(\Phi-c_{x+n-1})$ or $H_{x+n}=u_{x+n-1}\Phi-k_{x+n-1}$

Age.	4 Per Cent.		4½ Per Cent.	5 Per Cent.	5½ Per Cent.	6 Per Cent.	6½ Per Cent.	7 Per Cent.	7½ Per Cent.	8 Per Cent.		4 Per Cent.	Age.
	$u_x=r\frac{l_x}{l_{x+1}}$	$c_x=v\frac{d_x}{l_x}$	u_x	u_x	u_x	u_x	u_x	u_x	u_x	u_x	$k_x=\frac{d_x}{l_{x+1}}$	$\delta_x=k_x D_x$	
10	1.04708	.006500	1.05211	1.05715	1.06218	1.06721	1.07225	1.07728	1.08231	1.08734	.006806	459.79	10
11	1.04710	.006525	1.05213	1.05717	1.06221	1.06724	1.07228	1.07731	1.08234	1.08738	.006832	440.81	11
12	1.04713	.006550	1.05216	1.05720	1.06223	1.06727	1.07230	1.07734	1.08237	1.08741	.006859	422.61	12
13	1.04717	.006585	1.05220	1.05724	1.06227	1.06731	1.07234	1.07738	1.08241	1.08744	.006896	405.76	13
14	1.04722	.006630	1.05225	1.05729	1.06232	1.06736	1.07239	1.07743	1.08247	1.08750	.006944	390.18	14
15	1.04727	.006677	1.05231	1.05734	1.06238	1.06741	1.07245	1.07748	1.08252	1.08755	.006992	375.18	15
16	1.04733	.006733	1.05237	1.05740	1.06244	1.06748	1.07251	1.07755	1.08258	1.08762	.007052	361.32	16
17	1.04740	.006791	1.05243	1.05747	1.06250	1.06754	1.07257	1.07761	1.08264	1.08768	.007113	347.96	17
18	1.04747	.006860	1.05251	1.05754	1.06258	1.06762	1.07265	1.07769	1.08272	1.08776	.007185	335.59	18
19	1.04755	.006929	1.05259	1.05762	1.06266	1.06770	1.07273	1.07777	1.08280	1.08784	.007259	323.66	19
20	1.04764	.007010	1.05267	1.05771	1.06275	1.06779	1.07282	1.07786	1.08289	1.08793	.007344	312.62	20
21	1.04773	.007093	1.05277	1.05780	1.06284	1.06788	1.07291	1.07795	1.08299	1.08803	.007432	301.95	21
22	1.04782	.007177	1.05286	1.05790	1.06293	1.06797	1.07301	1.07805	1.08308	1.08812	.007520	291.64	22
23	1.04793	.007273	1.05296	1.05800	1.06304	1.06808	1.07312	1.07816	1.08319	1.08823	.007622	282.08	23
24	1.04803	.007371	1.05307	1.05811	1.06315	1.06819	1.07323	1.07827	1.08330	1.08834	.007725	272.84	24
25	1.04814	.007471	1.05318	1.05822	1.06326	1.06830	1.07334	1.07838	1.08342	1.08846	.007831	263.88	25
26	1.04827	.007583	1.05331	1.05835	1.06339	1.06843	1.07346	1.07851	1.08354	1.08858	.007949	255.58	26
27	1.04839	.007698	1.05343	1.05847	1.06352	1.06856	1.07359	1.07864	1.08367	1.08871	.008071	247.53	27
28	1.04854	.007826	1.05357	1.05862	1.06365	1.06870	1.07373	1.07878	1.08381	1.08886	.008206	240.06	28
29	1.04868	.007956	1.05372	1.05876	1.06380	1.06885	1.07389	1.07893	1.08397	1.08901	.008344	232.80	29
30	1.04884	.008101	1.05388	1.05892	1.06396	1.06901	1.07405	1.07909	1.08413	1.08917	.008496	226.05	30
31	1.04900	.008248	1.05404	1.05909	1.06413	1.06917	1.07421	1.07926	1.08430	1.08934	.008653	219.48	31
32	1.04918	.008410	1.05422	1.05927	1.06431	1.06935	1.07440	1.07944	1.08448	1.08953	.008824	213.38	32
33	1.04936	.008576	1.05440	1.05945	1.06449	1.06954	1.07458	1.07963	1.08467	1.08972	.008999	207.42	33
34	1.04955	.008746	1.05459	1.05964	1.06468	1.06973	1.07477	1.07982	1.08487	1.08991	.009179	201.61	34
35	1.04975	.008931	1.05475	1.05984	1.06489	1.06994	1.07498	1.08003	1.08508	1.09012	.009375	196.20	35
36	1.04996	.009122	1.05501	1.06005	1.06510	1.07015	1.07521	1.08026	1.08529	1.09034	.009576	190.90	36
37	1.05017	.009314	1.05522	1.06027	1.06532	1.07037	1.07542	1.08047	1.08551	1.09056	.009782	185.72	37
38	1.05040	.009525	1.05545	1.06051	1.06555	1.07061	1.07565	1.08071	1.08575	1.09080	.010005	180.90	38
39	1.05064	.009741	1.05569	1.06075	1.06580	1.07085	1.07590	1.08095	1.08600	1.09105	.010235	176.16	39
40	1.05089	.009963	1.05594	1.06099	1.06605	1.07110	1.07615	1.08120	1.08625	1.09131	.010470	171.53	40
41	1.05116	.010204	1.05620	1.06126	1.06631	1.07137	1.07642	1.08148	1.08653	1.09158	.010726	167.20	41
42	1.05146	.010476	1.05651	1.06157	1.06662	1.07168	1.07673	1.08179	1.08684	1.09189	.011014	163.35	42
43	1.05183	.010818	1.05689	1.06195	1.06700	1.07206	1.07712	1.08218	1.08723	1.09229	.011379	160.50	43
44	1.05231	.011247	1.05737	1.06243	1.06749	1.07255	1.07760	1.08266	1.08775	1.09278	.011836	158.71	44
45	1.05286	.011742	1.05792	1.06298	1.06804	1.07311	1.07817	1.08323	1.08829	1.09335	.012363	157.54	45
46	1.05353	.012345	1.05859	1.06366	1.06872	1.07379	1.07885	1.08392	1.08898	1.09405	.013006	157.42	46
47	1.05425	.012996	1.05932	1.06439	1.06945	1.07452	1.07959	1.08466	1.08973	1.09479	.013701	157.40	47
48	1.05504	.013711	1.06011	1.06519	1.07026	1.07533	1.08041	1.08548	1.09055	1.09562	.014466	157.64	48
49	1.05590	.014482	1.06098	1.06606	1.07113	1.07621	1.08128	1.08636	1.09144	1.09651	.015291	157.94	49
50	1.05684	.015326	1.06193	1.06701	1.07209	1.07717	1.08225	1.08733	1.09241	1.09749	.016197	158.44	50
51	1.05788	.016248	1.06296	1.06805	1.07313	1.07822	1.08330	1.08839	1.09348	1.09856	.017189	159.09	51
52	1.05901	.017257	1.06410	1.06919	1.07428	1.07937	1.08446	1.08956	1.09464	1.09974	.018275	159.89	52
53	1.06024	.018359	1.06534	1.07044	1.07553	1.08063	1.08573	1.09083	1.09592	1.10102	.019464	160.81	53
54	1.06156	.019532	1.06667	1.07177	1.07688	1.08198	1.08808	1.09219	1.09729	1.10240	.020735	161.58	54
55	1.06303	.020831	1.06814	1.07325	1.07836	1.08347	1.08852	1.09369	1.09880	1.10391	.022144	162.55	55
56	1.06462	.022237	1.06974	1.07486	1.07997	1.08509	1.09021	1.09533	1.10045	1.10557	.023674	163.47	56
57	1.06632	.023730	1.07144	1.07657	1.08169	1.08682	1.09195	1.09708	1.10220	1.10732	.025304	164.13	57
58	1.06819	.025371	1.07332	1.07846	1.08359	1.08873	1.09386	1.09900	1.10413	1.10927	.027101	164.85	58
59	1.07023	.027160	1.07537	1.08052	1.08567	1.09081	1.09596	1.10110	1.10625	1.11139	.029068	165.53	59
60	1.07254	.029169	1.07770	1.08285	1.08802	1.09316	1.09831	1.10348	1.10863	1.11380	.031285	166.46	60
61	1.07506	.031357	1.08023	1.08540	1.09056	1.09573	1.10090	1.10607	1.11124	1.11641	.033711	167.24	61
62	1.07786	.033770	1.08304	1.08822	1.09340	1.09858	1.10377	1.10895	1.11413	1.11931	.036399	167.97	62
63	1.08090	.036384	1.08610	1.09130	1.09649	1.10169	1.10688	1.11208	1.11728	1.12247	.039328	168.37	63
64	1.08427	.039255	1.08948	1.09469	1.09993	1.10512	1.11033	1.11554	1.12075	1.12597	.042563	168.59	64
65	1.08796	.042386	1.09319	1.09842	1.10365	1.10888	1.11411	1.11934	1.12457	1.12980	.046115	168.46	65
66	1.09199	.045782	1.09724	1.10249	1.10774	1.11130	1.11824	1.12349	1.12874	1.13399	.049994	167.86	66
67	1.09644	.049494	1.10170	1.10698	1.11225	1.11752	1.12273	1.12807	1.13334	1.13861	.054268	166.86	67
68	1.10126	.053490	1.10656	1.11185	1.11714	1.12244	1.12773	1.13303	1.13833	1.14361	.058907	165.20	68
69	1.10648	.057776	1.11180	1.11713	1.12244	1.12776	1.13308	1.13840	1.14372	1.14904	.063928	162.79	69
70	1.11222	.062436	1.11757	1.12291	1.12826	1.13361	1.13895	1.14430	1.14965	1.15499	.069442	159.82	70
71	1.11847	.067460	1.12385	1.12922	1.13460	1.13998	1.14535	1.15073	1.15611	1.16149	.075452	156.13	71
72	1.12530	.072889	1.13071	1.13612	1.14153	1.14694	1.15235	1.15776	1.16317	1.16858	.082022	151.75	72
73	1.13275	.078734	1.13820	1.14365	1.14909	1.15454	1.15998	1.16543	1.17088	1.17632	.089180	146.62	73
74	1.14093	.085065	1.14642	1.15191	1.15739	1.16288	1.16835	1.17385	1.17933	1.18481	.097054	140.86	74
75	1.14988	.091885	1.15541	1.16094	1.16646	1.17200	1.17752	1.18305	1.18858	1.19410	.105657	134.40	75
76	1.15965	.099211	1.16523	1.17080	1.17638	1.18195	1.18752	1.19310	1.19867	1.20425	.115050	127.28	76
77	1.17047	.107182	1.17610	1.18173	1.18735	1.19258	2.19860	1.20424	1.20986	1.21548	.125453	119.68	77
78	1.18242	.115812	1.18810	1.19379	1.19947	1.20516	1.21083	1.21652	1.22220	1.22789	.136938	111.61	78
79	1.19549	.125062	1.20124	1.20699	1.21274	1.21848	1.22422	1.22998	1.23572	1.24147	.149511	103.06	79
80	1.20987	.135006	1.21569	1.22151	1.22733	1.23314	1.23895	1.24477	1.25059	1.25640	.163340	94.18	80
81	1.22560	.145611	1.23149	1.23738	1.24328	1.24917	1.25506	1.26095	1.26685	1.27273	.178461	85.05	81
82	1.24282	.156917	1.24880	1.25477	1.26074	1.26672	1.27269	1.27867	1.28464	1.29062	.195020	75.83	82
83	1.26200	.169146	1.26807	1.27414	1.28020	1.28627	1.29233	1.29840	1.30447	1.31053	.213463	66.79	83
84	1.28344	.182383	1.28961	1.29578	1.30195	1.30812	1.31429	1.32046	1.32662	1.33279	.234078	58.03	84
85	1.30833	.197207	1.31462	1.32091	1.32720	1.33349	1.33978	1.34607	1.35236	1.35864	.258012	49.84	85
86	1.33759	.213923	1.34402	1.35045	1.35688	1.36331	1.36973	1.37617	1.38260	1.38902	.286141	42.25	86
87	1.37246	.232917	1.37901	1.38565	1.39225	1.39885	1.40544	1.41201	1.41864	1.42524	.319669	35.28	87
88	1.41549	.255071	1.42231	1.42910	1.43591	1.44271	1.44951	1.45633	1.46313	1.46992	.361052	29.04	88
89	1.46972	.281137	1.47678	1.48385	1.49091	1.49798	1.50503	1.51212	1.51917	1.52623	.413192	23.48	89
90	1.53785	.311279	1.54525	1.55263	1.56002	1.56742	1.57479	1.58221	1.58959	1.69698	.478700	15.97	90
91	1.62751	.347103	1.63534	1.64316	1.65099	1.65881	1.66662	1.67446	1.68229	1.69010	.464912	12.03	91
92	1.74867	.389676	1.75709	1.76549	1.77389	1.78230	1.79069	1.79912	1.80752	1.81589	.681416	8.725	92
93	1.91609	.439641	1.92529	1.93451	1.94371	1.95294	1.96212	1.97136	1.98054	1.98974	.842391	6.019	93
94	2.15011	.496446	2.16046	2.17079	2.18115	2.19146	2.20177	2.21213	2.22246	2.23277	1.06742	3.883	94
95	2.50162	.561798	2.51363	2.52568	2.53771	2.54973	2.56171	2.57378	2.58576	2.69781	1.40541	2.288	95
96	2.95999	.623701	2.97425	2.98846	3.00275	3.01692	3.03115	3.04538	3.05960	3.07380	1.84826	1.204	96
97	3.37999	.665680	3.39600	3.41250	3.42875	3.44500	3.46120	3.47750	3.49370	3.50990	2.25000	.5345	97
98	4.16000	.721154	4.18000	4.20000	4.22000	4.24000	4.25990	4.28000	4.30000	4.32000	3.00000	.1927	98
99	∞	.961538	∞	∞	∞	∞	∞	∞	∞	∞	∞	∞	99

TABLE XXII.

	$\Sigma k_x N_{x+1}$	Σk_x	CURTATE SUMMATIONS OF $\frac{d_x}{l_{x+1}} = k_x$										
AGE.	${}_{\omega}\Delta_x$	${}_{\omega}\Theta_x$	${}_{79}\Theta_x$	${}_{78}\Theta_x$	${}_{77}\Theta_x$	${}_{76}\Theta_x$	${}_{75}\Theta_x$	${}_{74}\Theta_x$	${}_{73}\Theta_x$	${}_{72}\Theta_x$	${}_{71}\Theta_x$	${}_{70}\Theta_x$	AGE.
10	217008	16.7477	1.8003	1.6749	1.5598	1.4541	1.3571	1.2679	1.1859	1.1104	1.0410	.97708	10
11	208063	16.7409	1.7935	1.6681	1.5530	1.4473	1.3503	1.2611	1.1791	1.1036	1.0342	.97027	11
12	199525	16.7341	1.7867	1.6612	1.5462	1.4405	1.3435	1.2543	1.1723	1.0968	1.0274	.96344	12
13	191376	16.7272	1.7798	1.6544	1.5393	1.4337	1.3366	1.2474	1.1654	1.0900	1.0205	.95658	13
14	183589	16.7203	1.7729	1.6475	1.5324	1.4268	1.3297	1.2405	1.1585	1.0831	1.0136	.94969	14
15	176139	16.7134	1.7660	1.6405	1.5255	1.4198	1.3228	1.2336	1.1516	1.0761	1.0067	.94274	15
16	169011	16.7064	1.7590	1.6335	1.5185	1.4128	1.3158	1.2266	1.1446	1.0691	.99968	.93575	16
17	162184	16.6993	1.7519	1.6265	1.5114	1.4058	1.3087	1.2195	1.1375	1.0621	.99263	.92870	17
18	155645	16.6922	1.7448	1.6194	1.5043	1.3987	1.3016	1.2124	1.1304	1.0550	.98551	.92158	18
19	149376	16.6850	1.7376	1.6122	1.4971	1.3915	1.2944	1.2052	1.1232	1.0478	.97833	.91440	19
20	143367	16.6778	1.7304	1.6049	1.4899	1.3842	1.2872	1.1980	1.1160	1.0405	.97107	.90714	20
21	137599	16.6704	1.7230	1.5976	1.4825	1.3769	1.2798	1.1906	1.1086	1.0332	.96373	.89980	21
22	132064	16.6630	1.7156	1.5901	1.4751	1.3694	1.2724	1.1832	1.1012	1.0257	.95629	.89237	22
23	126755	16.6555	1.7081	1.5826	1.4676	1.3619	1.2649	1.1757	1.0937	1.0182	.94877	.88484	23
24	121656	16.6478	1.7005	1.5750	1.4600	1.3543	1.2572	1.1681	1.0860	1.0106	.94115	.87722	24
25	116761	16.6401	1.6927	1.5673	1.4522	1.3466	1.2495	1.1603	1.0783	1.0029	.93343	.86950	25
26	112064	16.6323	1.6849	1.5594	1.4444	1.3387	1.2417	1.1525	1.0705	.99504	.92560	.86167	26
27	107550	16.6243	1.6770	1.5515	1.4364	1.3308	1.2337	1.1446	1.0625	.98709	.91765	.85372	27
28	103215	16.6163	1.6689	1.5434	1.4284	1.3227	1.2257	1.1365	1.0545	.97902	.90958	.84565	28
29	99048	16.6081	1.6607	1.5352	1.4202	1.3145	1.2175	1.1283	1.0463	.97081	.90137	.83744	29
30	95043	16.5997	1.6523	1.5269	1.4118	1.3062	1.2091	1.1199	1.0379	.96247	.89303	.82910	30
31	91192	16.5912	1.6438	1.5184	1.4033	1.2977	1.2006	1.1114	1.0294	.95397	.88453	.82060	31
32	87489	16.5826	1.6352	1.5097	1.3947	1.2890	1.1920	1.1028	1.0208	.94532	.87588	.81195	32
33	83925	16.5737	1.6264	1.5009	1.3859	1.2802	1.1831	1.0940	1.0119	.93649	.86705	.80312	33
34	80499	16.5647	1.6174	1.4919	1.3769	1.2712	1.1742	1.0850	1.0029	.92750	.85805	.79412	34
35	77206	16.5556	1.6082	1.4827	1.3677	1.2620	1.1650	1.0758	.99377	.91832	.84887	.78495	35
36	74038	16.5462	1.5988	1.4733	1.3583	1.2526	1.1556	1.0664	.98439	.90894	.83950	.77557	36
37	70994	16.5366	1.5892	1.4638	1.3487	1.2431	1.1460	1.0568	.97482	.89937	.82992	.76600	37
38	68070	16.5268	1.5795	1.4540	1.3389	1.2333	1.1362	1.0471	.96504	.88958	.82014	.75621	38
39	65260	16.5168	1.5694	1.4440	1.3289	1.2233	1.1262	1.0371	.95503	.87958	.81014	.74621	39
40	62562	16.5066	1.5592	1.4338	1.3187	1.2131	1.1160	1.0268	.94480	.86934	.79990	.73597	40
41	59973	16.4961	1.5487	1.4233	1.3082	1.2026	1.1055	1.0163	.93433	.85887	.78943	.72550	41
42	57488	16.4854	1.5380	1.4126	1.2975	1.1919	1.0948	1.0056	.92360	.84815	.77871	.71478	42
43	55099	16.4744	1.5270	1.4015	1.2865	1.1808	1.0838	.99461	.91259	.83713	.76769	.70376	43
44	52793	16.4630	1.5156	1.3902	1.2751	1.1695	1.0724	.98323	.90121	.82575	.75631	.69238	44
45	50552	16.4512	1.5038	1.3783	1.2633	1.1576	1.0606	.97139	.88937	.81392	.74448	.68055	45
46	48369	16.4388	1.4914	1.3660	1.2509	1.1453	1.0482	.95903	.87701	.80156	.73211	.66818	46
47	46229	16.4258	1.4784	1.3530	1.2379	1.1322	1.0352	.94602	.86400	.78855	.71911	.65518	47
48	44133	16.4121	1.4647	1.3393	1.2242	1.1186	1.0215	.93232	.85030	.77485	.70541	.64148	48
49	42078	16.3976	1.4502	1.3248	1.2097	1.1041	1.0070	.91786	.83583	.76038	.69094	.62701	49
50	40063	16.3823	1.4350	1.3095	1.1944	1.0888	.99175	.90256	.82054	.74509	.67565	.61172	50
51	38087	16.3661	1.4188	1.2933	1.1782	1.0726	.97555	.88637	.80435	.72889	.65945	.59552	51
52	36149	16.3490	1.4016	1.2761	1.1611	1.0554	.95836	.86918	.78716	.71171	.64226	.57833	52
53	34248	16.3307	1.3833	1.2578	1.1428	1.0371	.94008	.85090	.76888	.69343	.62399	.56006	53
54	32385	16.3112	1.3638	1.2384	1.1233	1.0177	.92062	.83144	.74942	.67397	.60452	.54060	54
55	30562	16.2905	1.3431	1.2176	1.1026	.99694	.89989	.81071	.72868	.65323	.58379	.51986	55
56	28778	16.2683	1.3209	1.1955	1.0804	.97480	.87774	.78856	.70654	.63109	.56164	.49772	56
57	27034	16.2447	1.2973	1.1718	1.0568	.95112	.85407	.76489	.68287	.60741	.53797	.47404	57
58	25333	16.2194	1.2720	1.1465	1.0315	.92582	.82876	.73958	.65756	.58211	.51267	.44874	58
59	23677	16.1923	1.2449	1.1194	1.0044	.89872	.80166	.71248	.63046	.55501	.48557	.42164	59
60	22066	16.1632	1.2158	1.0904	.97530	.86965	.77259	.68341	.60139	.52594	.45650	.39257	60
61	20499	16.1319	1.1845	1.0591	.94402	.83836	.74131	.65213	.57011	.49466	.42521	.36129	61
62	18978	16.0982	1.1508	1.0254	.91031	.80465	.70760	.61842	.53640	.46094	.39150	.32757	62
63	17503	16.0618	1.1144	.98896	.87391	.76825	.67120	.58202	.50000	.42456	.35510	.29118	63
64	16078	16.0225	1.0751	.94963	.83458	.72892	.63187	.54269	.46067	.38522	.31578	.25185	64
65	14704	15.9799	1.0325	.90707	.79202	.68636	.58931	.50013	.41811	.34265	.27321	.20928	65
66	13384	15.9338	.98641	.86095	.74590	.64025	.54319	.45401	.37199	.29654	.22710	.16317	66
67	12121	15.8838	.93641	.81096	.69591	.59025	.49320	.40402	.32200	.24655	.17710	.11318	67
68	10917	15.8295	.88214	.75669	.64164	.53599	.43893	.34975	.26773	.19228	.12284	.058907	68
69	9775	15.7706	.82324	.69778	.58274	.47708	.38002	.29084	.20882	.13337	.063928		
70	8698	15.7067	.75931	.63386	.51881	.41315	.31610	.22692	.14489	.069442		.007259	19
71	7689	15.6373	.68987	.56441	.44937	.34371	.24665	.15747	.075452		.007185	.014444	18
72	6748	15.5618	.61442	.48896	.37391	.26826	.17120	.082022		.007113	.014298	.021557	17
73	5877	15.4798	.53239	.40694	.29189	.18623	.089180		.007052	.014165	.021350	.028609	16
74	5076	15.3906	.44321	.31776	.20271	.097054		.006992	.014044	.021157	.028342	.035601	15
75	4346	15.2935	.34616	.22071	.10566		.006944	.013936	.020988	.028101	.035286	.042545	14
76	3685	15.1879	.24050	.11505		.006896	.013840	.020832	.027884	.034997	.042182	.049441	13
77	3093	15.0728	.12545		.006859	.013755	.020699	.027691	.034743	.041856	.049041	.056300	12
78	2568	14.9474		.006832	.013691	.020587	.027531	.034523	.041575	.048688	.055873	.063132	11
			.006806	.013638	.020497	.027393	.034337	.041329	.048381	.055494	.062679	.069938	10
AGE.			${}_{12}\Theta_x$	${}_{13}\Theta_x$	${}_{14}\Theta_x$	${}_{15}\Theta_x$	${}_{16}\Theta_x$	${}_{17}\Theta_x$	${}_{18}\Theta_x$	${}_{19}\Theta_x$	${}_{20}\Theta_x$	${}_{21}\Theta_x$	AGE.

TABLE XXIII.

CURTATE SUMMATIONS OF $\frac{d_x}{l_{x+1}}=k_x$

AGE.	$_{69}\Theta_x$	$_{68}\Theta_x$	$_{67}\Theta_x$	$_{66}\Theta_x$	$_{65}\Theta_x$	$_{64}\Theta_x$	$_{63}\Theta_x$	$_{62}\Theta_x$	$_{61}\Theta_x$	$_{60}\Theta_x$	$_{59}\Theta_x$	$_{58}\Theta_x$	AGE.
10	.91817	.86390	.81391	.76780	.72523	.68590	.64951	.61579	.58451	.55544	.52834	.50304	10
11	.91137	.85710	.80710	.76099	.71843	.67910	.64270	.60899	.57770	.54864	.52153	.49623	11
12	.90453	.85027	.80027	.75416	.71159	.67227	.63587	.60216	.57087	.54180	.51470	.48940	12
13	.89768	.84341	.79341	.74730	.70456	.66541	.62901	.59530	.56401	.53494	.50784	.48254	13
14	.89078	.83651	.78652	.74040	.69784	.65851	.62211	.58840	.55712	.52805	.50095	.47564	14
15	.88384	.82957	.77957	.73346	.69090	.65157	.61517	.58146	.55017	.52110	.49400	.46870	15
16	.87684	.82258	.77258	.72647	.68390	.64458	.60818	.57447	.54318	.51411	.48701	.46171	16
17	.86979	.81552	.76553	.71941	.67685	.63752	.60112	.56741	.53613	.50706	.47996	.45466	17
18	.86268	.80841	.75842	.71230	.66974	.63041	.59401	.56030	.52902	.49995	.47285	.44754	18
19	.85549	.80123	.75123	.70512	.66255	.62323	.58683	.55311	.52183	.49276	.46566	.44036	19
20	.84823	.79397	.74397	.69786	.65529	.61597	.57957	.54586	.51457	.48550	.45840	.43310	20
21	.84089	.78662	.73663	.69051	.64795	.60862	.57222	.53851	.50723	.47816	.45106	.42575	21
22	.83346	.77919	.72920	.68308	.64052	.60119	.56479	.53108	.49980	.47073	.44363	.41832	22
23	.82594	.77167	.72168	.67556	.63300	.59367	.55727	.52356	.49228	.46321	.43611	.41080	23
24	.81832	.76405	.71405	.66794	.62538	.58605	.54965	.51594	.48465	.45559	.42848	.40318	24
25	.81059	.75632	.70633	.66021	.61765	.57832	.54192	.50821	.47693	.44786	.42076	.39545	25
26	.80276	.74849	.69850	.65238	.60982	.57049	.53409	.50038	.46910	.44003	.41293	.38762	26
27	.79481	.74054	.69055	.64443	.60187	.56254	.52614	.49243	.46115	.43208	.40498	.37968	27
28	.78674	.73247	.68248	.63636	.59380	.55447	.51807	.48436	.45308	.42401	.39691	.37161	28
29	.77853	.72427	.67427	.62816	.58559	.54627	.50987	.47616	.44487	.41580	.38870	.36340	29
30	.77019	.71592	.66593	.61981	.57725	.53792	.50152	.46781	.43653	.40746	.38036	.35505	30
31	.76169	.70743	.65743	.61132	.56875	.52943	.49303	.45932	.42803	.39896	.37186	.34656	31
32	.75304	.69877	.64878	.60266	.56010	.52077	.48437	.45066	.41938	.39031	.36321	.33791	32
33	.74422	.68995	.63996	.59384	.55128	.51195	.47555	.44184	.41055	.38149	.35439	.32908	33
34	.73522	.68095	.63096	.58484	.54228	.50295	.46655	.43284	.40155	.37249	.34539	.32008	34
35	.72604	.67177	.62178	.57566	.53310	.49377	.45737	.42366	.39238	.36331	.33621	.31090	35
36	.71666	.66240	.61240	.56629	.52372	.48440	.44800	.41429	.38300	.35393	.32683	.30153	36
37	.70709	.65282	.60283	.55671	.51415	.47482	.43842	.40471	.37343	.34436	.31726	.29195	37
38	.69731	.64304	.59304	.54693	.50437	.46504	.42864	.39493	.36364	.33458	.30747	.28217	38
39	.68730	.63303	.58304	.53692	.49436	.45503	.41863	.38492	.35364	.32457	.29747	.27217	39
40	.67707	.62280	.57280	.52669	.48413	.44480	.40840	.37469	.34340	.31434	.28723	.26193	40
41	.66660	.61233	.56233	.51622	.47366	.43433	.39793	.36422	.33293	.30387	.27676	.25146	41
42	.65587	.60160	.55161	.50549	.46293	.42360	.38720	.35349	.32221	.29314	.26604	.24073	42
43	.64486	.59059	.54059	.49448	.45192	.41259	.37619	.34248	.31119	.28213	.25502	.22972	43
44	.63348	.57921	.52922	.48310	.44054	.40121	.36481	.33110	.29981	.27075	.24365	.21834	44
45	.62164	.56737	.51738	.47126	.42870	.38937	.35297	.31926	.28798	.25891	.23181	.20651	45
46	.60928	.55501	.50502	.45890	.41634	.37701	.34061	.30690	.27562	.24655	.21945	.19414	46
47	.59627	.54200	.49201	.44590	.40333	.36400	.32761	.29389	.26261	.23354	.20644	.18114	47
48	.58257	.52830	.47831	.43219	.38963	.35030	.31390	.28019	.24891	.21984	.19274	.16744	48
49	.56811	.51384	.46384	.41773	.37517	.33584	.29944	.26573	.23444	.20537	.17827	.15297	49
50	.55281	.49855	.44855	.40244	.35987	.32055	.28415	.25044	.21915	.19008	.16298	.13768	50
51	.53662	.48235	.43236	.38624	.34368	.30435	.26795	.23424	.20295	.17389	.14679	.12148	51
52	.51943	.46516	.41517	.36905	.32649	.28716	.25076	.21705	.18577	.15670	.12960	.10429	52
53	.50115	.44689	.39689	.35078	.30821	.26889	.23249	.19878	.16749	.13842	.11132	.086017	53
54	.48169	.42742	.37743	.33131	.28875	.24942	.21302	.17931	.14803	.11896	.091857	.066553	54
55	.46095	.40669	.35669	.31058	.26801	.22869	.19229	.15858	.12729	.098223	.071122	.045818	55
56	.43881	.38454	.33455	.28843	.24587	.20654	.17014	.13643	.10515	.076079	.048978	.023674	56
57	.41514	.36087	.31087	.26476	.22220	.18287	.14647	.11276	.081473	.052405	.025304		
58	.38983	.33556	.28557	.23946	.19689	.15756	.12117	.087454	.056169	.027101		.008653	31
59	.36273	.30846	.25847	.21235	.16979	.13047	.094064	.060353	.029068				
											.008496	.017149	30
60	.33366	.27940	.22940	.18329	.14072	.10140	.064996	.031285					
61	.30238	.24811	.19812	.15200	.10944	.070110	.033711			.008344	.016840	.025493	29
62	.26867	.21440	.16441	.11829	.075727	.036399			.008206	.016550	.025046	.033699	28
63	.23227	.17800	.12801	.081891	.039328			.008071	.016277	.024621	.033117	.041770	27
64	.19294	.13867	.088678	.042563			.007949	.016020	.024226	.032570	.040066	.048719	26
65	.15038	.096109	.046115			.007831	.015780	.023851	.032057	.040401	.049897	.057550	25
66	.10426	.049994			.007725	.015556	.023505	.031576	.039782	.048126	.056622	.065275	24
67	.054268			.007622	.015347	.023178	.031127	.039198	.047404	.055748	.064244	.072897	23
			.007520	.015142	.022867	.030698	.038647	.046718	.054924	.063268	.071764	.080417	22
		.007432	.014952	.022574	.030299	.038130	.046079	.054150	.062356	.070700	.079196	.087849	21
20	.007344	.014776	.022296	.029918	.037643	.045474	.053423	.061494	.069700	.078044	.086540	.095193	20
19	.014603	.022035	.029555	.037177	.044902	.052733	.060682	.068753	.076959	.085303	.093799	.10245	19
18	.021788	.029220	.036740	.044362	.052087	.059918	.067867	.075938	.084144	.092488	.10098	.10964	18
17	.028901	.036333	.043853	.051475	.059200	.067031	.074980	.083051	.091257	.099601	.10810	.11675	17
16	.035953	.043385	.050905	.058527	.066252	.074083	.082032	.090103	.098309	.10665	.11515	.12380	16
15	.042945	.050377	.057897	.065519	.073244	.081075	.089024	.097095	.10530	.11365	.12214	.13079	15
14	.049889	.057321	.064841	.072463	.080188	.088019	.095968	.10404	.11225	.12059	.12909	.13774	14
13	.056785	.064217	.071737	.079359	.087084	.094915	.10286	.11094	.11914	.12749	.13598	.14463	13
12	.063644	.071076	.078596	.086218	.093943	.10177	.10972	.11779	.12600	.13434	.14284	.15149	12
11	.070476	.077908	.085428	.093050	.10078	.10861	.11656	.12463	.13283	.14118	.14967	.15833	11
10	.077282	.084714	.092234	.099856	.10758	.11541	.12336	.13143	.13964	.14798	.15648	.16513	10
AGE.	$_{22}\Theta_x$	$_{23}\Theta_x$	$_{24}\Theta_x$	$_{25}\Theta_x$	$_{26}\Theta_x$	$_{27}\Theta_x$	$_{28}\Theta_x$	$_{29}\Theta_x$	$_{30}\Theta_x$	$_{31}\Theta_x$	$_{32}\Theta_x$	$_{33}\Theta_x$	AGE.

TABLE XXIII.

CURTATE SUMMATIONS OF $\frac{d_x}{l_{x+1}}=k_x$

AGE.	${}_{57}\Theta_x$	${}_{56}\Theta_x$	${}_{55}\Theta_x$	${}_{54}\Theta_x$	${}_{53}\Theta_x$	${}_{52}\Theta_x$	${}_{51}\Theta_x$	${}_{50}\Theta_x$	${}_{49}\Theta_x$	${}_{48}\Theta_x$	${}_{47}\Theta_x$	${}_{46}\Theta_x$	AGE.
10	.47936	.45722	.43648	.41702	.39874	.38156	.36536	.35007	.33560	.32190	.30889	.29653	10
11	.47256	.45041	.42968	.41021	.39194	.37475	.35855	.34326	.32880	.31509	.30209	.28973	11
12	.46572	.44358	.42285	.40338	.38511	.36792	.35172	.33643	.32196	.30826	.29526	.28289	12
13	.45887	.43672	.41599	.39652	.37825	.36106	.34486	.32957	.31510	.30140	.28840	.27603	13
14	.45197	.42983	.40909	.38963	.37135	.35416	.33797	.32267	.30821	.29451	.28150	.26914	14
15	.44503	.42280	.40215	.38268	.36441	.34722	.33102	.31573	.30126	.28757	.27456	.26219	15
16	.43803	.41589	.39515	.37569	.35742	.34023	.32403	.30874	.29427	.28057	.26757	.25520	16
17	.43098	.40884	.38810	.36864	.35036	.33317	.31698	.30169	.28722	.27352	.26051	.24815	17
18	.42387	.40172	.38099	.36153	.34325	.32606	.30986	.29457	.28011	.26641	.25340	.24104	18
19	.41668	.39454	.37380	.35434	.33607	.31888	.30268	.28739	.27292	.25922	.24621	.23385	19
20	.40942	.38728	.36655	.34708	.32881	.31162	.29542	.28013	.26566	.25196	.23896	.22659	20
21	.40208	.37994	.35920	.33974	.32146	.30427	.28808	.27279	.25832	.24462	.23161	.21925	21
22	.39465	.37250	.35177	.33231	.31403	.29684	.28064	.26535	.25089	.23719	.22418	.21182	22
23	.38713	.36498	.34425	.32479	.30651	.28932	.27312	.25783	.24337	.22967	.21666	.20430	23
24	.37951	.35736	.33663	.31716	.29889	.28170	.26550	.25021	.23575	.22204	.20904	.19668	24
25	.37178	.34964	.32890	.30944	.29116	.27397	.25778	.24249	.22802	.21432	.20131	.18895	25
26	.36395	.34181	.32107	.30161	.28333	.26614	.24995	.23466	.22019	.20649	.19348	.18112	26
27	.35600	.33386	.31312	.29366	.27538	.25819	.24200	.22671	.21224	.19854	.18553	.17317	27
28	.34793	.32579	.30505	.28559	.26731	.25012	.23393	.21864	.20417	.19047	.17746	.16510	28
29	.33972	.31758	.29685	.27738	.25911	.24192	.22572	.21043	.19516	.18226	.16926	.15689	29
30	.33138	.30924	.28850	.26904	.25076	.23357	.21738	.20209	.18762	.17392	.16091	.14855	30
31	.32288	.30074	.28001	.26054	.24227	.22508	.20888	.19359	.17912	.16542	.15242	.14005	31
32	.31423	.29209	.27135	.25189	.23361	.21642	.20023	.18494	.17047	.15677	.14376	.13140	32
33	.30541	.28326	.26253	.24306	.22479	.20760	.19140	.17611	.16165	.14795	.13494	.12258	33
34	.29641	.27426	.25353	.23407	.21579	.19860	.18240	.16711	.15265	.13895	.12594	.11358	34
35	.28723	.26509	.24435	.22489	.20661	.18942	.17323	.15793	.14347	.12977	.11676	.10440	35
36	.27785	.25571	.23498	.21551	.19724	.18005	.16385	.14856	.13409	.12039	.10739	.095023	36
37	.26828	.24613	.22540	.20594	.18766	.17047	.15427	.13898	.12452	.11082	.097810	.085447	37
38	.25850	.23635	.21562	.19615	.17788	.16069	.14449	.12920	.11474	.10103	.088028	.075665	38
39	.24849	.22635	.20561	.18615	.16787	.15068	.13449	.11920	.10473	.091029	.078023	.065660	39
40	.23826	.21611	.19538	.17591	.15764	.14045	.12425	.10896	.094495	.080794	.067788	.055425	40
41	.22779	.20564	.18491	.16544	.14717	.12998	.11378	.098491	.084025	.070324	.057318	.044955	41
42	.21706	.19492	.17418	.15472	.13644	.11925	.10306	.087765	.073299	.059598	.046592	.034229	42
43	.20605	.18390	.16317	.14370	.12543	.10824	.092042	.076751	.062285	.048584	.035578	.023215	43
44	.19467	.17252	.15179	.13232	.11405	.096860	.080663	.065372	.050906	.037205	.024199	.011836	44
45	.18283	.16069	.13995	.12049	.10221	.085024	.068827	.053536	.039070	.025369	.012363		
46	.17047	.14832	.12759	.10813	.089850	.072661	.056464	.041173	.026707	.013006			
47	.15746	.13532	.11458	.095119	.076844	.059655	.043458	.028167	.013701			.011379	43
48	.14376	.12162	.10088	.081418	.063143	.045954	.029757	.014466			.011014	.022393	42
49	.12930	.10715	.086416	.066952	.048677	.031488	.015291			.010726	.021740	.033119	41
									.010470	.021196	.032210	.043589	40
50	.11400	.091860	.071125	.051661	.033386	.016197							
51	.097807	.075663	.054928	.035464	.017189			.010235	.020705	.031431	.042445	.053824	39
52	.080618	.058474	.037739	.018275			.010005	.020240	.030710	.041436	.052450	.063829	38
53	.062343	.040199	.019464			.009782	.019787	.030022	.040492	.051218	.062232	.073611	37
54	.042879	.020735			.009576	.019358	.029363	.039598	.050068	.060794	.071808	.083187	36
55	.022144			.009375	.018951	.028733	.038738	.048973	.059443	.070169	.081183	.092562	35
			.009179	.018554	.028130	.037912	.047917	.058152	.068622	.079348	.090362	.10174	34
		.008999	.018178	.027553	.037129	.046911	.056916	.067151	.077621	.088347	.099361	.11074	33
32	.008824	.017823	.027002	.036377	.045953	.055735	.065740	.075975	.086445	.097171	.10819	.11956	32
31	.017477	.026476	.035655	.045030	.054606	.064388	.074393	.084628	.095098	.10582	.11684	.12822	31
30	.025973	.034972	.044151	.053526	.063102	.072884	.082889	.093124	.10359	.11432	.12533	.13671	30
29	.034317	.043316	.052495	.061870	.071446	.081228	.091233	.10147	.11194	.12266	.13368	.14506	29
28	.042523	.051522	.060701	.070076	.079652	.089434	.099439	.10967	.12014	.13087	.14188	.15326	28
27	.050594	.059593	.068772	.078147	.087723	.097505	.10751	.11775	.12822	.13894	.14996	.16133	27
26	.058544	.067542	.076721	.086096	.095672	.10545	.11546	.12569	.13616	.14689	.15790	.16928	26
25	.066374	.075373	.084552	.093927	.10350	.11329	.12329	.13353	.14400	.15472	.16574	.17711	25
24	.074099	.083098	.092277	.10165	.11123	.12101	.13102	.14125	.15172	.16245	.17346	.18484	24
23	.081721	.090720	.099899	.10927	.11885	.12863	.13864	.14887	.15934	.17007	.18108	.19246	23
22	.089241	.098240	.10742	.11679	.12637	.13615	.14616	.15639	.16686	.17759	.18860	.19998	22
21	.096673	.10567	.11485	.12423	.13380	.14358	.15359	.16382	.17429	.18502	.19603	.20741	21
20	.10402	.11302	.12220	.13157	.14115	.15093	.16093	.17117	.18164	.19236	.20338	.21476	20
19	.11128	.12028	.12945	.13883	.14841	.15819	.16819	.17843	.18890	.19962	.21064	.22202	19
18	.11846	.12746	.13664	.14601	.15559	.16537	.17538	.18561	.19608	.20681	.21782	.22920	18
17	.12557	.13457	.14375	.15313	.16270	.17249	.18249	.19273	.20320	.21392	.22494	.23631	17
16	.13263	.14163	.15080	.16018	.16976	.17954	.18954	.19978	.21025	.22097	.23199	.24337	16
15	.13962	.14862	.15780	.16717	.17675	.18653	.19653	.20677	.21724	.22797	.23898	.25036	15
14	.14656	.15556	.16474	.17412	.18369	.19347	.20348	.21371	.22418	.23491	.24592	.25734	14
13	.15346	.16246	.17164	.18101	.19059	.20037	.21037	.22061	.23108	.24181	.25282	.26420	13
12	.16032	.16932	.17850	.18787	.19745	.20723	.21723	.22747	.23794	.24866	.25968	.27106	12
11	.16715	.17615	.18533	.19470	.20428	.21406	.22407	.23430	.24477	.25550	.26651	.27789	11
10	.17396	.18295	.19123	.20151	.21108	.22087	.23087	.24111	.25158	.26230	.27332	.28470	10
AGE.	${}_{34}\Theta_x$	${}_{35}\Theta_x$	${}_{36}\Theta_x$	${}_{37}\Theta_x$	${}_{38}\Theta_x$	${}_{39}\Theta_x$	${}_{40}\Theta_x$	${}_{41}\Theta_x$	${}_{42}\Theta_x$	${}_{43}\Theta_x$	${}_{44}\Theta_x$	${}_{45}\Theta_x$	AGE.

TABLE XXIII.

www.ingramcontent.com/pod-product-compliance
Lightning Source LLC
LaVergne TN
LVHW011213110826
845150LV00006B/1422